E[illegible]

OF

AMERICAN QUAKER GENEALOGY

BY

WILLIAM WADE HINSHAW

THOMAS WORTH MARSHALL

Editor and Compiler

VOLUME III

CONTAINING EVERY ITEM OF GENEALOGICAL VALUE FOUND IN ALL

RECORDS AND MINUTES

(KNOWN TO BE IN EXISTENCE)

OF

ALL MEETINGS OF ALL GRADES EVER ORGANIZED
IN NEW YORK CITY AND ON LONG ISLAND

(1657 to the Present Time)

Including Both

HICKSITE AND ORTHODOX GROUPS

OF THE

NEW YORK YEARLY MEETING OF THE SOCIETY OF FRIENDS

Note: The material in this book consists of data of genealogical interest recorded in the books of four Monthly Meetings covering the activities of the members of twenty-two Meetings for Worship and other meetings in New York City and on Long Island. These records are supplemented by vital records found in many Family Bibles of early Long Island Friends; also by Burial Registers and Tombstone data from several Burial Grounds, Quaker and non-Quaker, graciously furnished by the Long Island Historical Association, Brooklyn, N. Y.

Names of Monthly Meetings (in this book) and dates of organizations:

1. NEW YORK (ORIGINALLY FLUSHING) MONTHLY MEETING (N. Y.) . 1672
2. WESTBURY MONTHLY MEETING (L. I.) 1672
3. JERICHO MONTHLY MEETING (L. I.) 1789
4. FLUSHING MONTHLY MEETING (SECOND ORGANIZATION) (L. I.) . 1805

Special Compiler for this Book:

JOHN COX, JR.

Acknowledgment is hereby made of valuable aid in making identifications by references to the collection: "Sixty Long Island Families" (Cocks), and the published Family Genealogies of: Cocks, Cox, Frost, Underhill, Seaman, Jones, and the Oyster Bay "Town" Records 1653-1878.

Genealogical Publishing Co., Inc.

Originally published: Ann Arbor, Michigan, 1940
Reprinted: Genealogical Publishing Co., Inc.
Baltimore, 1969, 1991
Library of Congress Catalogue Card Number 68-31728
International Standard Book Number 0-8063-0180-5
Made in the United States of America

AFFECTIONATELY AND FILIALLY
DEDICATED TO
THE MEMORY OF ALL OUR QUAKER ANCESTORS
WHOSE METICULOUSLY KEPT RECORDS
FURNISH THE DATA FOR THIS
ENCYCLOPEDIA OF AMERICAN QUAKER GENEALOGY

F O R E W O R D

It is a great satisfaction to be able now to publish in book form, as Volume III of my Encyclopedia of American Quaker Genealogy, the complete genealogical data found in all records and minutes (known to be in existence) of all of the Friends' Meetings ever organized in New York City and on Long Island, these records dating from the time of the first arrival of Friends at New Amsterdam (called New York from 1664) in 1657.

While the earliest marriage actually recorded in these meetings was in 1663, on Long Island, many clues to marriages of much earlier dates and consummated in Europe will be found in this book. We have been very fortunate in being able to quote marriages, births, deaths, etc., from many Family Bibles of early Long Island Friends, which give us much information concerning these families prior to the first records found of the meetings, and even reaching back into Europe in some cases. We have quoted extensively, also, from a collection of data called "Sixty Long Island Families", compiled by George Cocks, though not published, for which priveledge I extend my thanks. The compiler has also "filled in" copious data from Burial Registers and Tombstone inscriptions from several Burial Grounds, Quaker and Non-Quaker, this important data being graciously furnished by the Long Island Historical Association, Brooklyn, N. Y., and copied out for us (without charge of any kind) by Miss Eda Huntington, Librarian.

He has been aided also, in making identifications of individuals, by references to the published Family Genealogies of:-Cocks, Cox, Frost, Underhill, Seaman, Jones, and the Oyster Bay "Town" records 1653-1878.

Although we name only the four Monthly Meetings:-New York, Westbury, Jericho and Flushing, the memberships of these four Monthly Meetings covered a wide territory and were members of established Meetings for Worship at many places, including:-New York, Purchase, Westchester, Flushing, Oyster Bay, Westbury, Hempstead, Gravesend, Maspeth Kills, Jericho, Cow Neck, Rockaway, Huntington, Secatogue, Half Hollow Hills, Jerusalem, Bethpage, Matinecock, Brooklyn, Manhattanville, Seamans and possibly others, the records of which were kept by the above named four Monthly Meetings.

It is to be remembered that a Monthly Meeting is a business meeting, its attendants consisting of delegates from several Meetings for Worship and Preparative Meetings, all belonging to the Monthly Meeting. Thus all Friends living in New York City and on Long Island belonged to and were controlled by one or another of the four named Monthly Meetings.

For the history and development of the Society of Friends in New York City and on Long Island, I refer readers to the Historical Narrative (found on another page) taken from the writings of John Cox, Jr., the eminent Quaker historian whose tireless work covering some thousands of hours of intensive labor in research and compiling has made this book possible.

Unusual importance is attached to this book in that every item in the entire volume was extracted from original books of Minutes and Records and compiled into alphabetical order by Mr. John Cox, Jr., who has long been known as custodian of all Quaker records stored in the fireproof vaults of the New York Yearly Meeting of Friends, and as the author of a splendid book entitled "Quakerism in the City of New York, 1657-1930", Printed by Quinn & Boden Company, Rahway, N. J., 1930.

On account of the danger of hastening the complete loss of their records from careless handling, the vault committee of the New York Yearly Meeting has for years allowed no one excepting John Cox Jr., to search the 1700 precious, frail books, for ancestral data. Now, in the realization that these wonderful records can be made accessible to all who may be interested, through being published in my Encyclopedia, the vault committee has authorized John Cox Jr., to make complete compilations for me, thus not only removing any need for allowing the books to be examined for genealogical data, but also making sure that the precious data shall forever be preserved.

Needless to say, I am especially and profoundly grateful to Mr. Cox for compiling the material for this book which will forever live as a memorial to his care and concern for the permanent preservation of the records of New York and Long Island Meetings.

I am especially happy thus to be able to make these records available to the millions of descendants of these early settlers of New York and Long Island who braved the dangers of ocean travel in coming to America from England, Holland, Ireland, Scotland, Wales, Germany and France in small sail-boats which took from two to four months to make the voyage. Descendants may well feel proud of such ancestors.

I wish again to express my appreciation of the aid given to this work by many men and women in high places in American History and Genealogy. No friends have been lost, and many new names have been added to the long list of individuals who have been constantly thinking and working for the success of this great venture, without which we could not have progressed thus far on the road to completion. Many librarians and individuals have written asking when they might subscribe for Volume III. The first actual subscription to this book was received last June from one of our most enthusiastic friends, Mr. J. Prescott Beach, President of the New Jersey Society of Sons of the American Revolution, who, on receipt of a friendly letter from me saying that I expected to publish Volume III some time the coming Fall, immediately sent me his check for two copies (one for himself and one for his wife), without even waiting for my formal announcement. His letter seemed a happy omen for the future.

I want to mention some names not mentioned heretofore, of prominent men and women who have more recently come to our support and whose efforts in our behalf are deeply appreciated: Dr. Gilbert H. Doane, Director of the University of Wisconsin Libraries, Madison, Wis., one of the most learned genealogist-historians in America, and author of a fine book:-"Searching For Your Ancestors."; Mrs. Alberta M. Trethewey, Litt. D., a prominent genealogist of the New England Historic Genealogical Society, of Boston; Dr. Charles C. Crittenden, Editor of the Quarterly Review of the North Carolina Historical Commission, of Raleigh; Mr. Henry James Young, Researcher for the Historical Society of York Co., York, Pa.; Dr. Wm. I. Utterback, Head of the Zoology Department of Marshall College, Huntington, West Virginia, who is himself author and publisher of a valuable book on the Genealogy of the Utterback and allied families; Dr. Alexander C. Flick, Historian of the New York State Historical Association, Albany; Mr. Meredith B. Colket, Jr., Assistant Editor of the American Genealogist, New Haven, Conn.; Miss Pearl Idol, Genealogist for the Hunt Family of North Carolina, High Point; Miss Jessica Ferguson, Genealogist of the Pennsylvania State Library and Historical Museum, Harrisburg; Mrs. Bertha Baker, Librarian of the Historical and Fine Arts Department of the State of Iowa, Des Moines; Mr. Mahlon H. Janney, Registrar of the District of Columbia Society of Colonial Wars, Washington, D. C.; Mr. William W. Badgley, Registrar of the District of Columbia Society of the Sons of the American Revolution, Washington, D.C.; Mrs. Morgan Bunting, Custodian of Darby Friends Meeting, Darby, Pa.; Miss Rebecca Smedley, Custodian of Chester Friends Meeting, Media, Pa.; Miss Harriett P. Marine, Custodian of the Hicksite Yearly Meeting Vaults, Baltimore, Md.; Miss Bertha E. King, Custodian of the Orthodox Yearly Meeting Vaults, Baltimore, Md.; Mrs. H. D. Brown, Jr. (known to genealogy as Douglas Summers Brown), Genealogist of Richmond, Va.; Mrs. Matilda W. Evans, Genealogist, West Chester, Pa.; and many others whose names will be mentioned in a later volume, all of whom deserve high credit from me.

But I cannot close this Foreword without again speaking of the wonderful assistance given me by Thomas W. Marshall, who has from the beginning superintended all work in compiling of data and who carefully edits every item published, working untiringly without any kind of remuneration excepting the satisfaction of doing a wonderful work for humanity; and of Dr. Walter C. Woodward, who has from the beginning directed personally the entire work of distribution and advertising for my entire project, also without remuneration other than the satisfaction of aiding in the creation of this greatest genealogical work of all times. Without the active aid of these two men, I could not have "carried on" thus far.

Washington, D. C.
February 1, 1940

WILLIAM WADE HINSHAW

E D I T O R ' S N O T E

All the records for this volume were compiled from the originals by John Cox, Jr. In preparing them for publication his arrangement has been generally followed, with only a few changes. This plan of arrangement differs from that used in volumes I and II in that the items from birth and death records and those from minutes, marriage registers, etc., are combined together, instead of being compiled separately, as has previously been done. It is believed that the new arrangement will be found to be a convenient and satisfactory one.

It is desired to call attention to one specific change made in preparing John Cox's material for the printer. In his previously published books, and in his compilation of material for this volume, Mr. Cox followed the old custom of writing dates - number of day first, followed by the month and year - for all dates prior to the adoption of the present or "New Style" Calender in 1752. Thus: 24/10 Mo (Dec) 1725,-the name of the month being inserted in parenthesis to avoid the confusion that frequently arises from the fact that March was the first month under the "Old Style" Calender. For dates subsequent to 1752, Mr. Cox has used the usual present day form in which the number of the month is written first, followed by the day and year. Thus: 7 Mo. 27, 1848. In order to have the same order for all dates and to conform to the plan used in volumes I and II, the Editor has transposed the "Old Style" dates to the same order as the later ones. Thus: 10 Mo (Dec) 24, 1725.

For the information of readers who may not be fully informed regarding the 1752 change in the calender, the account given in the Introduction to volume II is repeated here.

The "Old Style" calender was superseded in 1752 by the Gregorian (New Style) calender. By act of Parliament passed in 1750 the day following 2 September, 1752, was called 14 September. At the same time, the beginning of the legal year was changed from the 25th of March to the 1st of January. Many other European countries had adopted the Gregorian calender, with the year beginning 1 January, as early as 1700. Because of the resulting confusion, it had become the custom in England and her colonies to give two dates for the period intervening between 1 January and 25 March, as 13 January 1709/10. The day following 24 March 1709/10 was 25 March 1710. The manner of dating in use among Friends, in which months were designated by numbers instead of by names, added to the confusion. January was the 11th month, February was the 12th, and all of March was called the first month although the new year did not begin until the 25th day of the month. Thus, the last day of 12th month was followed by the first day of first month of the same year, and the 24th day of first month was followed by the 25th day of first month of the succeeding year. * * * * * It should be borne in mind that dates of births were often recorded many years after the events; that dates of births occurring before 1752 but recorded afterward were often translated into "New Style" before recording. Sometimes the letters NS or OS indicate whether this translation was or was not made; more often, perhaps, the designation has been omitted. Therefore, it will often be impossible to say definitely that a given date is according to the "Old Style" or the "New Style".

T.W.M.

C O N T E N T S

ABBREVIATIONS

ack mo	acknowledged marriage out
Ama.	Amawalk
b	born
Balt.	Baltimore
Beth.	Bethpage
bHS	buried Houston Street
Bkn.	Brooklyn
bPP	buried Prospect Park
bur	buried
Burl.	Burlington
c	circa (about)
cert	certificate
ch	child, children
Chap.	Chappaqua
Cincin.	Cincinnati
clear	clear with respect to marriage
Coeym.	Coeymans
com	complained, complained of
comm app	committee appointed
con	condemned
Corn.	Cornwall
d	died
dec	deceased
dis	disowned, disowned for
dmi	declared marriage intentions first time
dmist	declared marriage intentions second time
dt	daughter, daughters
Duanesby-Duanes.	Duanesbury
end	endorsed
fam	family
Farm.	Farmington
Flush.	Flushing
form	formerly
G.C.	Glen Cove
gc	granted certificate
gct	granted certificate to
gl	granted letter
h	husband
H. & R.	Hardwick & Randolph
Ham.	Hamburgh
Hemp.	Hempstead
Hudson & Chat.	Hudson & Chatham
jas	joined another society
Jer.	Jericho
L.I.	Long Island
ltm	liberated to marry or left at liberty to marry
m	marry, married, marrying, marriage
Man.	Manhasset
Marl.	Marlboro
mbr	member
mbrp	membership
M.C.	Musketa Cove (or Glen Cove)
mcd	married contrary to discip-line
MH	meeting house
Mk.	Matinecock
MM	monthly meeting
mou	married out of unity
Mtg	meeting
N.B.	New Bedford
NDMM	Philadelphia MM for the Northern District
N.E.	New England
N. Hemp.	North Hempstead
ni	not identified
nm	non member
N.P.	Nine Partners
O.B.	Oyster Bay
Plains.	Plainsfield
Po'keepsie	Poughkeepsie
prc	produced a certificate
prcf	produced a certificate from
Pur.	Purchase
QM	Quarterly Meeting
Queensby.	Queensbury
R. & P.	Rahway & Plainfield
rec	receive, received
recrq	received by request
relrq	released by request
rem	remove, removed
rem cert	removal certificate
Renss.	Rensselaer
rmt	reported married to
roc	received on certificate
rocf	received on certificate from
Roch.	Rochester
rol	received on letter
rolf	received on letter from
rpd	reported
rq	request, requests, requested
rqc	requested certificate
rqcuc	requested to come under care
rst	reinstate reinstated
s	son sons
Sara.	Saratoga
Scip.	Scipio
SDMM	Philadelphia MM for the Southern District
Shrews.	Shrewsbury
S.I.	Staten Island
uc	under care (of mtg)
unm	unmarried
w	wife
W. & Jericho	Westbury & Jericho
Wby	Westbury
WDMM	Philadelphia MM for the Western District
YM	Yearly Meeting

HISTORICAL NARRATIVE

(This Narrative is taken almost verbatim from the book "Quakerism in New York City" and other writings of John Cox, Jr.)

The genesis of Quakerism in this Province (New Netherland, now New York State) was the arrival of the ship "Woodhouse" at Nieuw Amsterdam, on the 1st day of the Sixth Month, called August, 1657.

A band of earnest Quakers, intent upon getting to New England, could get no passage from the mother country (England) owing to the high fines to which Captains of vessels were subject who carried Quakers. Robert Fowler (of Bridlington), himself a ministering Friend, having a small vessell (the Woodhouse) nearly finished for the coastwise trade, says in his True Relation, "This vessel was appointed for this service from the beginning, as I have often had it manifested to me; that it was said within me several times, 'Thou hast her not for nothing'; and also New England presented itself before me." So, Robert offered his little coasting vessel to his fellow-religionists. How they ever crossed the stormy Atlantic can never be told more graphically than in the brief account written by Robert Fowler himself and printed in Bowden's History of Friends, vol. 1, p. 65. The little boat was too small for ocean travel, but Fowler in his log states: "We saw the Lord leading our vessel as it were a man leading a horse by the hand." They were carried too far south for the Massachusetts colonies and so landed at New Amsterdam (New York), with its barely 1000 inhabitants of Dutch settlers governed by their last and strongest Director-General, Stuyvesant.

The voyage of the Woodhouse took two whole months; but instead of reaching Boston as intended, they reached New Amsterdam, entering through the Sound and Hell Gate. They anchored their little vessel at this little town on Saturday, the first day of the Sixth Month (August) 1657. The vessel looked harmless, but its cargo was destined to greatly disturb the quiet Dutch town and its energetic Governor. There were eleven preachers on the ship, every one an active center of contagion. Boston had deported six of these to London the year before, so, this was their second voyage. They were: Christopher Holder, John Copeland, William Brend, Sarah Gibbons, Mary Weatherhead and Dorothy Waugh. The five who were making their first voyage were: William Robinson, Humphrey Norton, Richard Doudney, Robert Hodgson and Mary Clark. Of these, Robert Hodgson, Richard Doudney, Sarah Gibbons, Mary Weatherhead and Dorothy Waugh landed at New Amsterdam, the rest remaining on the ship and sailing soon for Newport, Rhode Island. The next day, August 1st, while the ship was at anchor, which was the Sabbath, Robert Fowler and Robert Hodgson made a visit to Director-General Stuyvesant. "He was moderate," remarks Fowler, "both in words and actions." On Monday, Mary Weatherhead and Dorothy Waugh went into the streets and publicly exhorted the people. It is not easy for us to appreciate the scandalized feelings of the citizens. Their women scolded each other over the garden fence (or possibly their husbands over the breakfast table) but in the street they were silent. These two women were arrested, put in chains and thrown into separate noisome dungeons, where they were kept for eight days, when they were led out to a boat with their hands tied behind them, and shipped to Rhode Island, which the Dutch considered the Latrina of New England, on account of its tolerance for religious liberty. The other three Quakers who had landed went to the English settlements on Long Island,-to Gravesend, Jamaica and Hempstead, from whence two went on and across to Rhode Island, but Robert Hodgson called the inhabitants of Hempstead to a meeting in an orchard on the following First-Day. Hempstead men were largely of the theocratic type of mind; they had their publicly paid minister, and they had heard of the Quakers. A magistrate sent the constable to arrest Hodgson, who was found pacing the orchard in quiet meditation before the appointed time. Robert says that the magistrate "kept me a prisoner in his house, but while he went to his worship many staid and heard the truth declared." This meeting, at which an imprisoned minister spoke, perhaps from a window, was the earliest Quaker meeting in this Province. The date was the 9th of 6th month (August) 1657. The magistrate, returning from church to find his house a chapel, forthwith removed Hodgson to another house, but to little purpose. "In the latter part of the day many came to me, and those who had been my enemies, after they had heard the truth, confessed to it."

Stuyvesant, notified of the danger, sent the sheriff, the jailer and twelve musketeers to bring the prisoner and his entertainers to the city. Two hospitable women, one with a four months old child in her arms, who had entertained the stranger, were taken to New Amsterdam in a cart, to the tail of which the pinioned Hodgson was secured. Twenty miles they traveled, mostly at night. At the end of the journey the women were soon released, but Robert was led to a dungeon, "full of vermin", and "so odious, for wet and dirt, as I never saw." Robert was sentenced, without being allowed to plead, to two years work at a wheelbarrow or to pay a fine of 600 Guilders. He would do neither, so he was ordered back to the dungeon, and to see no Englishmen. Brought forth in a few days to hear a paper in Dutch (which he knew not) and at which the Dutch people shook their heads in disapproval, he was again put in the dungeon for a few days, then chained to a wheelbarrow, and commanded to work. Knowing that he had not transgressed the Dutch law (i.e., a law of Holland) he refused, was beaten by "a lusty crabbed negro slave" with a tarred rope, fainted and fell, was raised, refainted at about the hundredth blow, was taken to the fort and there left all day in the hot August sunshine, where, unfed, he again fainted. Back again to the dungeon, where his mind "was staid upon the Lord." A week later, stripped to the waist, he was hung up by the hands with a weight to his feet, and beaten with rods. Two more nights and a day in the dungeon, and without food. Again refusing to work or pay a fine, he was again suspended and beaten. A woman came, like a good Samaritan, to dress his wounds. Her husband vainly offered a fatted ox to be allowed to remove Hodgson to his own home. Citizens offered to raise money for the fine, but Robert felt not easy to accept their offer. When strength returned he willingly labored enough to pay for the coarse food he had eaten. After about five weeks he was set free, and went to Rhode Island.

It was by sufferings, in hunger, in cold, among vermin, among men cruel in their ignorance, that this meeting for worship of God and service of man was begun. But there must be further endurance of persecution before Quakerism was to be well established (in this Province). In the meantime it spread like fire in the stubble through the untheocratic English Townships of Flushing and Oyster Bay. The inhabitants of Flushing, could not accept Stuyvesant's order forbidding entertainment of a Quaker, and Edward Heart, the Town Clerk, drew up a manly protest, which was signed by him, and by the Schout (Sheriff), Tobias Feake and twenty six other citizens. It stated, courteously but firmly, that they could not find it in their hearts to condemn nor to persecute Quakers, desiring "in this case not to judge least we be judged; neither to condemn least we be condemned." Several of the signers afterwards became Quakers. Stuyvesant abolished the Township Government and set up a Dutch organization instead. Tobias Feake and Edward Heart were imprisoned, the former driven from the Colony, and the latter excused on his abject apology. The Town Meeting could be destroyed, but Quakerism could not be stamped out.

Again in 1662 came persecution. Hannah Bowne of Flushing having joined the Quakers, her husband, John, also heard the truth and embraced it. John was banished, and Hannah later died in London in the service of Truth.

After the English took the province in 1664 Stuyvesant retired to his estate, or bouwery, where he soon died, but not before personally apologizing to John Bowne.

Friends increased rapidly and probably had meetings for Worship with more or less regularity from 1657 in Flushing, Oysterbay, Gravesend and other places. After John Bowne's house was built, in 1661, a meeting was regularly held there until the Flushing meeting house was built, in 1694. Meetings for Discipline were organized early, probably before 1665, but no minutes were kept or written until the 2nd of 3rd Month, 1671, when at the Half Year's Meeting at Oysterbay, the earliest minute in America was written. Marriages, however, were recorded as early as 1663. (NB: The above paragraph is quoted from John Cox's "Catalogue of Records")

George Rofe, coming from England in 1661 by way of Maryland, "in a small boat with only two Friends," says of New Amsterdam: "I had service among both Dutch and English. I was in the chief city of the Dutch, and gave a good sound, but they forced me away; and so we had meeting through the Islands in good service."

John Burnyeat appears to have held the first Quaker meeting in this city, in 1671, on his return from New England. He states in his Truth Exalted, 1691, p 142, how he was at the Autumn Half Yearly Meeting at Oyster Bay, whence he "went to Flushing, and down to Gravesend; and when I had visited Friends there, I went to New York, and had a meeting; and then took shipping for Maryland there."

William Edmundson says in his Journal for 1672 (Dublin Edition, p 63) "I took Passage by Sea (from Maryland) and about Ten Days after landed safe at New-York where no Friends lived. John Evans of Jamaica being in my company at that time, we lodged at a Dutch Woman's House, who kept an Inn, and I was moved of the Lord to get a Meeting, in that town; for there had not been one there before; so I spoke to the Woman of the House to let us have a Meeting, who was very willing, and let us have a large Dining-Room; also furnished it with Seats, we gave notice thereof, and had a brave large Meeting, some of the Chief Officers, Magistrates and leading Men of the Town were at it, very attentive they were, the Lord's Power being over them all. Several of them appeared very loving after the Meeting." He evidently had not heard of Burnyeat's preaching there the year before.

This Dutch woman was the widow Matje Wessels, who for many years kept an inn by the waterside. She had seen John Bowne banished, and had kept his chest for him the night previous. She was a notable woman, and has had noted descendants. Edmundson says that she and her daughter wept when he left them. Many other earnest preachers of the word came to America, and most of these cheered the little Quaker band here, but George Fox, who came to America in 1672, did not enter this city then renamed New Yorke.

MEETING FOR WORSHIP:

The meeting for worship has always been the very core and center of all Quaker organization. Without this frequent gathering for Divine light and leading none of the other phases of Quaker activity would be possible. The Quaker meeting is begun with silence, and without a program. Not a mere physical stillness, but a living quiet out of which speech or prayer may develop, and surely spiritual strength and comfort, if sought.

John Greenleaf Whittier in his poem "The Meeting" says:

And so I find it well to come
For deeper rest to this still room,
For here the habit of the soul
Feels less the outer world's control;
The strength of mutual purpose pleads
More earnestly our common needs;
And from the silence multiplied
By these still forms on either side,
The world that time and sense have known,
Falls off and leaves us God alone.

THE MONTHLY MEETING:

The Monthly Meeting is the executive body of the Quaker organization. It is attended by delegates from the several Meetings for Worship which belong to and are governed by it. It is a business meeting which administers the affairs of its subordinate meetings. It keeps all records, such as births, deaths, marriages, disownments, certificates of removal, members received and released, etc., for all of the Meetings for Worship which it controls; and since these are the records which are of interest to genealogy, it is usually only necessary to search the Monthly Meeting books for genealogical purposes. However, to find the very earliest records in America it is necessary to search the books kept by the meetings for Worship prior to the dates when the Monthly Meeting to which they belonged was organized. After that, the complete records of interest to genealogy were always kept by the Monthly Meeting.

The records of the Monthly Meeting, its subordinate meetings and subsidiary organizations, are numerous and valuable; and, since they cover every activity of the members, they give an intimate picture of the social life, and somewhat of the special contribution of the Quakers to the religious life of the locality represented. But the most important of these to posterity are the Vital Statistics, all of which have been carefully preserved for almost 300 years.

THE YEARLY MEETING:

The Yearly Meeting is the legislative body governing all other bodies, and is attended by delegates appointed by all branches of the lower bodies; only the delegates sent by the Quarterly Meetings have the power to decide questions brought before the Meeting.

The first Yearly Meeting to be held in America was held in Rhode Island in 1660, and came to be known as the New England Yearly Meeting. Until the New York Yearly Meeting was organized in 1696, all subordinate meetings in New York and on Long Island were under the jurisdiction of the New England Yearly Meeting. There has been some question by historians as to the date of the first Yearly Meeting held in New England, some claiming it was held in 1659, others that it was held in 1660 and still others that it was held in 1661. But be that as it may, the New York Yearly Meeting was set off from the New England Yearly Meeting by the following minute:

"At a Generall Yearly meeting at ye house of Walter Newberrys in Rhoad Island ye: 14th:daye of ye:4th mo; 1695--------
It is also Agreed yt ye meeting at Longe Island shall Bee From this time a Yearely meeting and yt John Bowne & John Rodman Shall take Ceare to (sic.) Receive all Such papers as Shall Come to ye yearly meeting in Long Island (sic.) & Correspond with Friends Appoynted in London --------
------------------The Second Daye following:ye Epistle to Friends was Red & ordered to bee sent: Soe ye meeting Concluded Refering to ye next yearely meeting."

The first session was on 3rd Mo. (May) 29, 1696, and it has met every year since in the latter part of the same month (called 5th Mo. since the change from Old Style to New Style in 1752.)

By the following minute of the Yearly Meeting in 1746, Westbury Quarterly Meeting seems to have been held three times in the year, and the Yearly Meeting took the place of the fourth Quarter.

"Whereas this meeting is now concluded to be an Yearly Meeting & not a Quarterly One it is Thought proper that the order of the State of Meetings or anything Else from the Monthly Meetings of Flushing & Westbury be first Carryed into the Quarterly Meeting at Westbury in the Twelfth Month & from thence Recommended unto this meeting until Friends see cause to Order it Otherways & that the order shall always come in writing."

It was generally called the "Yearly Meeting held at Flushing" till 1777, the "Yearly

Meeting held at Westbury" 1778-1793, the "Yearly Meeting held in the City of New York" 1794 to 1893 when the name of the Fifteenth Street Yearly Meeting was changed to its present form. After the separation in 1827, two separate Yearly Meetings were organized, the one held at Fifteenth Street being called Hicksite, and the one held at Twentieth Street being called Orthodox. The Hicksite Branch, being the largest, retained most of the books of the meetings which had been kept prior to 1827, and continued in them the records of its own members. The Orthodox Branch, after reorganizing in 1828, started a new set of books beginning with that year. (It is to be remembered, however, that both branches were of the same origin and had the same ancestors and the same ancestral genealogical records. Genealogy does not recognize differences between religious beliefs; nor are ancestral genealogical records affected by family quarrels. The Hicksite Friends and the Orthodox Friends are fruits of the same ancestral tree, although they grew on separate branches after 1827. The genealogical records of both branches, therefore, are compiled together in this Volume, as if no differences had ever occurred.

The Quakers of New York City were in no sense withdrawn from the world. Many have gained high standing as Doctors, Educators, Scientists and leaders in Social Welfare in the civic life of the city. In business they were largely Merchants, Importers, Manufacturers, Bankers, etc. They were austere and severe with importers of slaves. Awakened by John Woolman, those who held slaves freed them, and the Meeting disowned the few who failed to do so. Living under a discipline too strict for the good of Society, they disowned for offences which to us appear trivial, especially that of "marrying out", thereby losing a member instead of gaining one. Quakers everywhere were required to live up to their agreements, pay their honest debts, deal fairly and honestly with all men and submit their differences with each other to arbitration by the Meetings.

On the whole, we of today have difficulty in our effort to live up to the principles to which they quietly bore a steadfast witness.

N E W   Y O R K   M O N T H L Y   M E E T I N G

The New York Monthly Meeting cannot be considered apart from Flushing Monthly Meeting, because it was generally called Flushing Monthly Meeting until 1795, when the name of Flushing Monthly Meeting was changed to Monthly Meeting of Friends of New York, as of the date 7th Mo. 1, 1795. During the next ten years there was no Flushing Monthly Meeting, and all Friends of Flushing, Newtown, Maspeth Kills and Brooklyn were attached to the Monthly Meeting of Friends of New York. By 1805, however, the meeting had become so large that a second Flushing Monthly Meeting, consisting of Friends of Flushing and Newtown, was set off from the Monthly Meeting of New York, as a separate Monthly Meeting.

But the changing of the name from Flushing Monthly Meeting to the Monthly Meeting of Friends of New York did not change the membership in the least; nor did it necessitate the starting of new books of minutes and records, since all that was needful was to go right on writing the minutes and records in the same books which had been in use by Flushing Monthly Meeting since its inception, the exact date of which cannot be determined, though it is thought to have been 1672.

While Quakerism had been increasing rapidly on Long Island since 1657, William Edmundson says in his Journal of 1672, "I took passage by Sea (from Maryland) and about ten days after landed safe at New York where no Friends lived." (See Historical Narrative). The earliest mention in the meeting records of the meeting in New York City is under the date of 12th of 8th Month (October) 1681, when the weekly Fifth day meeting in New York having been of late neglected, and they desiring the meeting to take care of the establishment thereof, it was agreed the "ye first day meeting shall remaine at Rob: Storys & ye fifth day meeting at Lew Morris house Untill a Publick Meeting House shall be provided."

Therefore it must be assumed that after the visit of William Edmundson (1672) persecution of Quakers in New York was lifted and Quakerism there began to flourish. But it was not until 1697 that a Quaker Meeting House was actually built in New York City; and it was not until a hundred years thereafter that Quakers in New York City became so numerous and so influential that the name of Flushing Monthly Meeting was changed to Monthly Meeting of Friends in New York. (See Historical Sketch of Flushing Monthly Meeting.)

In 1685 Isaac Horner, an Oyster Bay man, collected all available vital statistics of Friends on Long Island and copied them all in a single parchment bound book. This same book was used thereafter by Flushing Monthly Meeting for its own records. Thus the early records of Westbury Monthly Meeting were preserved in the books of Flushing Monthly Meeting. But Flushing Monthly Meeting finally (1795) became New York Monthly Meeting, and (1805) a new Flushing Monthly Meeting was organized. Thus all early records of Westbury and Flushing are found in the books of New York Monthly Meeting. This is to be remembered by the searcher, and is pointed out here to avoid confusion.

MEETING HOUSES:

The earliest meeting house in the province was built at Oyster Bay Village in 1672, but Flushing was the center of Quaker influence. The Flushing Meeting house, built 1694, and later enlarged, is the oldest house of worship in continuous use in the State of New York.

The first meeting house in New York City was built in 1697 on the north side of Green Street (now Liberty Place). This was succeeded by a larger house facing on Crown Street (now Liberty Street) in 1748. These two adjacent sites are now covered by the Chamber of Commerce of the State of New York. The ground was sold in 1825 and the meeting removed to Hester Street. From this third meeting house, after the Separation of 1828, the Orthodox group removed to Henry Street, thence to Orchard Street and in 1859 to the present meeting house on Twentieth Street, at Gramercy Park. The "liberal" or Hicksite group removed from Hester Street in 1861 to the present meeting house on Fifteenth Street at Stuyvesant Square. Other meeting houses have been built and torn down, but these two are the lineal successors of the little meeting house of 1697. A meeting at Newtown, L. I. was also a part of this Monthly Meeting. The two branches which separated in 1828 are in good unity, and joint meetings and activities are numerous.

VITAL RECORDS:

The following data has been extracted from the various and numerous records of both branches of Friends, all of which are collected together in Friends' Record Room, 15 Rutherford Place, New York City.

The record of marriages begins in 1663, preceded by an account of the celebrated case, in England, whereby the legality of Quaker marriages was indisputably established. Births as early as 1640 are recorded. The earliest extant minute of a Quaker meeting, 23/3d Mo. (May) 1671, is in our records. Burials in New York City from 1696 to 1819 were in the original ground on Green Street (now Liberty Place) corner of Liberty Street. In 1819 land for a burial ground was purchased on Houston Street. When the Liberty Street ground was sold in 1825 the bones of the early members were removed to a vault in the Houston Street ground. The present cemetery, of both branches, was begun in 1847 on the Coney Island Plank Road, outside of Brooklyn. When the Houston Street ground was sold in 1874, the bones of the pioneers were reenterred in Westbury Meeting ground. Prospect Park now entirely surrounds our cemetery.

RECORDS

ABBOTT
Agnes, dt Israel & Agnes DEAN, b 8-30-1824 dis mo 10m 1846
Alice rocf Queensbury 1m 1819; dis 11m 1829 (H)
George B. cf Chesterfield 12-8-1812; ct Chesterfield 9-5-1821 (clear)
Henry d 9-17-1895 bPP; m Isabella ----- d 11-15-1881 ae 55y bPP
Ch: Henry b 7-20-1856 d 9-19-1887 bPP
Mary " 12-30-1857
William " 5-28-1859 d 3-31-1879 bPP
James
Isabella d 2-26-1864 ae 1y 6m bPP
Annie " 7-26-1866 ae 11m bPP
Elizabeth " 10-22-1868 bPP
Isabella recrq 1859
Henry recrq 12-1864
ct Corn 2-1871 for all
cf Corn 4-5-1875
Isaac, s Robert cf Oswego 7-17-1816 (clear); dis mo 10m-1845
James, s Henry & Isabella, ct Corn with parents 2-1871; cf Corn with parents 4-5-1876; relrq 12-6-1893
Robert b Preston, Lancashire, d 8-9-1826 ae 72y 10m 12d; m Alice ----- d 6-4-1837 ae 82y 11m 18d bHS
Ch: Agnes 14
Robert 12
William 10
Joseph 8
Mary Ann 1
Alice cf Hardshaw, Eng., 8-19-1794 to Abington; endorsed to N. Y., 1-26-1801
Alice & ch, Agnes, Joseph & Mary, ct Oswego 3-4-1801 (Agnes clear)
Robert & Alice rocf Oswego, 1-15-1817
Robert & Alice ct Queensbury, 2-3-1817
Robert & Alice cf Queensbury, 12-31-1818
Robert (nm) d 2-17-1834 ae 52y bHS
Roy Twining, s Edw. H. A. & Lydia (Van Horn), b Lambertville, N. J., 8-5-1897; m 7-3-1926, Mary Isabella BRIGHT (nm) dt Grant & Emma
Roy recrq 5-14-1934 (parents mbr at Wrightstown, Pa.)
William ct Oswego 7-4-1810 (clear)

ABENDROTH
William Philip (nm), s Jno. W. & Cordelia (Young), N. Y.; m 6-5-1913 at Tacie P. Willets', Mabel Maria WILLETS, dt Robert R., dec, & Tacie (Parry), Harrison

ACKERMAN
Marietta rocf Ama. 9-4-1867; dis 11-7-1883 (H)

ACKLEY
Hiram, s Jonathan, d 7-7-1803 ae 3m bHS

ADAMS
Abel, s Samuel (dec) & Anna, Marlboro, m 2-8-1854 at N. Y., Hannah T. BRUFF, wd Charles, dt Harrison & Phebe PALMER; ct Marl. 1855
Anna C., dt James C. & Harriet C., b 1-3-1891
David Paul, s James C. & Harriet C., b 5-23-1893
Dorcas, dt Abel & Abigail, Marlborough; m 1777 Lodowick HOXSIE
Eliza (nm) d 6-27-1878 ae 75y bPP (H)
Elizabeth, active mbr 1676-1689
Emma Frances, dt David & Hannah C., rocf Balto. 1864 with parents; m 1865 John D. SHERMAN
Eunice (late Harned) dis mo 1-4-1781
Eustatia, w James, d 11-15-1860; cf Coeym. 2-1834; ct Marl. 4-1840; cf Cherry St., Phila., 12-1847 (H)
Hannah C., w David
Ch: Emma Frances
Henry Graham
Anna
cf Balto. 1864
ct Indianapolis 2-1872 for all but Emma
Henry m Abigail SHERMAN
Ch: Elizabeth S. b Albany 4-14-1834 d 12- 9-1921
Josephine Parker b Bethlehem 4-3-1838 d 10-20-1918
Elizabeth recrq of parents
Josephine P. birthright
Elizabeth & Josephine P. transferred to N. Y. 1-8-1916 when Albany laid down
Henry C., s Wm. & Helen (Coolidge); m 2-7-1891 Clara W. CORLIES, dt J. Edgar & Mary B., b N. Y. 5-8-1871 d 10-27-1909
James & Eustacia
Ch: Mary Susannah
cf Coeymans 7-26-1832 with infant named; J dis 6-1836 E dis 2-1837
James C. d 12-29-1919; m Harriet C. ----- d 12-29-1919
Ch: Walter J.
Anna C. b 1- 3-1891; name erased
David Paul b 5-23-1893; name erased
cf Indianapolis 12-1888 with 1 ch named
John, s John & Elizabeth, Flushing; m Joane -----
Ch: Mary b 5 Mo (May) 3, 1656
Martha " 1 Mo (Mar) 4, 1658/9
Rebecca " 12Mo (Feb) 13, 1661/2
John m 2nd Elizabeth -----
Ch: John b 6 Mo (Aug) 17, 1664 d 10-30-1688
Elizabeth b 1 Mo (Mar) 9, 1665
Sarah " 2 Mo (Apr)24, 1668
James " 8 Mo (Oct) 4, 1671
Susannah " 9 Mo (Nov) 6, 1674
Hannah "12 Mo (Feb)15, 1675/6
Deborah " 3 Mo (May) 7, 1678
John " 7 Mo (Sep)10, 1680
Abigail "11 Mo (Jan) 2, 1682
Thomas "11 Mo (Jan)12, 1684
Marcey "10 Mo (Dec)13, 1686

ADAMS, John & Elizabeth, continued
Ch: Phebe b 12 Mo (Feb) 9, 1690
John active mbr from 1676
John L. (nm) m Mary Jane CURRY (nm), dt John & Anna (Turner), d 12-31-1922 ae 88y 4m 13d
Lewis d 7-16-1901 bHS [(H)
Marian H., w Wm. Clark, dt James R. & Eliza H. TABER, b 4-6-1882
Rebekah, dt John & Joan, Flushing, m 1686 Henry CLIFTON, Flushing,
Walter J., s James C. & Harriet C.; cf Indianapolis 12-1888 with parents; relrq 11-6-1907
Sarah m 1690 John COWPERTHWAIT
William Clark (nm) m 5-7-1907 Marion H. TABER, dt Jas. R. & Eliza H., b 4-6-1882
----- & ----- (nm)
Ch: Mary Susan b Albany d 6-27-1836 bHS
William b New York d 12-30-1830 ae 16y 8m bHS

ADAMSON
William (nm) b Ireland d 10-31-1813 ae 50y bHS (unm)

AGNEW
Mary (nm) b Stamford, Conn d 9-24-1815 ae 33y bHS (unm)

AIMES
Sarah S. cf Phila. 7-24-1845; ct Salem, Mass. 3-1873
William, colored (nm), s Frances, d 11-4-1906 ae 20y 11m 28d bPP (H)

AITKEN
Elizabeth L. (nm), dt John & Lydia, New York; m 1-12-1848 Wm. H. LOINES (H)
Jessie, dt John & Jane (Stoddard), b Edinburgh, Scot., 7-28-1894; m Alexander KENNEDY; both recrq 9-14-1917

AKERLY
Benjamin (nm) b New York d 12-10-1815 ae 43y bHS (unm)
Jackamiah (nm) b Cow Neck, N. J., d 9-18-1816 ae 70y bHS
Jackamiah (nm) b New York d 8-7-1816 ae 27y bHS (m)
Susannah, wd ----- b New York d 2-25-1824 ae 71y bHS

AKIN
Abiel & Sylvia G.
Ch: Lucy E.
Henry Franklin b 8-30-1858
Carrie W.
cf Sandwich, Mass. 1856
all relrq 8-1870

ALBAUGH
Mary E., dt Henry C. & Sarah J. (Hull) b Balto. 11-27-1866; m 1886 Artis H. EHRMAN cf Balto. 10-9-1897; name rem 11-9-1925 as she had not been heard of for many years

ALBERTSON
Alice, dt Wm. & Mary W. (Gillam), b Phila. 2-8-1866; m 1896 Charles Coale PRICE; cf Race St. 1-5-1901 with him & his 3 ch; ct Race St. 6-7-1902 for all (H)
Edith Agnes (nm), dt Geo. Fitz R. & Agnes E. (Green); m 1923 Philip Ward FRANCIS (H)
William, s Wm., of Newtown, Gloster Co., N. J.; m 8 Mo (Oct) 9, 1695, Esther WILLIS, dt Henry & Mary, at her father's

ALDRICH
Catharine W., dt Eli S. & Margaret Ann, b Cornwall-on-Hudson, 6-30-1857; m 1884 Charles Henry RIDER recrq 1-2-1886 (H)

ALEXANDER
George (nm) m Rachel -----, d 10-24-1907 bPP
Ch: Rachel E. b 12-17-1854
Martha d 8-31-1859 ae 2y 5m bPP
Rachel, the mother, recrq 3-2-1892
Joseph F., Dublin rq care as to his failure 1-15-1868; care discontinued 1869
Franklin B. (nm) d about 1895 bPP
Rachel E. (nm), dt George & Rachel, b New York 12-17-1854 d 9-21-1924 bPP; m Edwin E. ANDERSON (nm)
Samuel cf Kingston, Eng., 6-7-1905
Sarah, w -----, b New Bedford d 1-4-1826 ae 51y bHS

ALIOTH
Ann Augusta, w Chas. B., dt Rich. H. & Emily BOWNE, d 8----1927; ret a mbr 3-1872 & gct MM at Junction City, Kansas, where she now lives

ALLAWAY
Hastings (nm), s John, d 4-6-1918 ae 72y bPP (unm) (H)

ALLEN
Alfred Benjamin cf Lewer & Chichester, Eng., 7-19-1839; cert ret to Chichester, Eng., 12-12-1840 (he having returned)
Ann H. cf Adrian, Mich. 10-1845; ct Cincinnati 10-7-1846, ret 8-1847; ct Cincinnati 4-5-1848 (H)
Anna W., dt Isaac H. & Susan W., letter to Flatbush Cong. Ch. Bkn 4-6-1904 [w Henry E.
Arthur L. (nm) & ----- (nm; sister Inez B.Peelle
Ch: ----- b 1-17-1924 d 1-19-1924 bPP
Barzillai (nm) & -----
Ch: ----- stillborn 3-2-1846 bHS
Caroline, dt Joseph W. & Harriet, b 4-10-1835; ct R & P 8-1852 (H)
Catharine A., dt Joseph W. & Harriet, b 4-27-1837; ct R & P 1852 (H)
David, Shrewsbury; m at Wby, 4 Mo (June) 24, 1724 Mary BIRDSALL, wd Stephen, of Little Egg Harbor
David (nm) b Nantucket d 4-12-1811 ae 28 y bHS

ALLEN, continued
Eliza, wd ----- b New York d 12-16-1835 ae 30y 5m bHS
Elizabeth dis 9-6-1815
Elizabeth L. rocf Winnescheik, Iowa, 7-1884; ct Winnescheik, Iowa, 10-1888
Elsie, w Jacob, rocf N.P. 7-19-1827; dis 6-1830 (O); ct Center, Ohio, 8-1830 (H)
Eunice Vandevoort (form Allen) dis mo 7-3-1811
Experience, Shrewsbury, m 1692 Benjamin FIELD, Flushing; brought cert of clear from Shrews. 6 Mo (Aug) 4, 1692
Florence, dt James M. H. & Rebecca, b 8-8-1867 m 1889 Robt. Cone CAWL; recrq 6-1889
Frederick Jerome, s James M. H. & Rebecca, Bkn.; m Bkn. 6-15-1901 Agnes Roberta BARRET, dt James E. & Mary J., N. Y.
Ch: Jerome Frederick b 10-19-1902; associate mbr 1912
    Frederick J. recrq 2-6-1901
    Agnes recrq 2-6-1901
George L. (nm) & -----
Ch: George C. d 9-8-1816 ae 11m 12d bHS
Gilbert rocf New Bedford 2-18-1812, apprentice; complaint from New Bedford for mo rec 4-2-1823; New Bedford informed he not a mbr here
Hannah, dt Isaac H. & Susan W., recrq of parents; dis 11-3-1858 after ref to Scipio for jas
Henry & -----
Ch: Amy d 6-14-1813 ae 1y 21d bHS (nm)
    mo before 7-3-1811; dis 8-7-1811
Isaac d Poughkeepsie 12----1828; cf Oswego 12-14-1825
Isaac H. d 5-12-1881 ae 74y 11m; m Susan H. ----- d 8-11-1890 ae 73y (mo c. 1833)
Ch: Infant stillborn 2-15-1834 bHS
    Sarah Jane b 2-8-1836 d 6-30-1917 bPP
    Edward S. d 4-22-1865 ae 23y bPP
    Infant stillborn 2-21-1845 bHS
    Hannah
    Susan H.
    Mary Louisa
    Anna Willis b 1-1-1848 d 7-19-1921 (nm) bPP
    cf Oswego 1-14-1835; ch recrq of parents 1859; Susan H. recrq 1859; having mo Oswego refers it to N. Y. 6-18-1834 with his ack. rpd favorably 5-11-1834
James M. H. (nm) m Rebecca MAGUIRE, dt John & Mary V. D., b Bkn. 9-27-1839 d 1-31-1926 bPP (nm)
Jane rocf Rockhill MM, Ire., 8-21-1828 (clear); m John HAYDOCK
John Carlin (nm), s Jesse E. & Minnie (Clark); m 7-14-1932 Beatrice Alice ROWE, dt Alfred T. & Elsie E. (Klingsmith), b Woodhaven, N. Y., 11-12-1913; Beatrice recrq 10-12-1931; divorced John (H)
Joseph Edward, s Joseph W. & Harriet, b 1-4-1824; ct R. & P. 5-1863 (H)
Joseph W. d 12-6-1857 ae 62y; m Harriet -----(H)
Ch: Joseph Edward b 1-4-1824
    Margaret Elizabeth b 8-7-1825 d 2-6-1832
    Mary Matilda b 4-10-1827
    Joseph Walker b 6-10-1831
    Mirriam Borden b 4- 2-1829
    George C. b 6-10-1833 d 1- 3-1835
    Caroline b 4-10-1835
    Catharine A. b 4-27-1837
    Julia " 5-28-1842
    cf Shrewsbury 11-6-1815; minor; cert of clear to R. & P. 11-6-1822; Harriet cf R. & P. 8-20-1823; all dis 1830-1849 (O); ct R. & P. 8-1852 for all but Joseph, Edward & Mirriam (H)
Joseph Walker, s Joseph W. & Harriet, b 6-10-1831; dis 8-6-1858 (H)
Julia, dt Joseph W. & Harriet, b 5-28-1842; ct R. & P. 8-1852 (H)
Maria rocf Dublin 11-15-1831 (clear); mo to ----- BOWNER; dis 6-1-1836
Marion (nm), dt Martin D. & Adelaide L.; m 1886 Wm. Bunting WEEKS (H)
Martin D. (nm), s Jas. W. & Diadema (Doane), d 7-13-1919 ae 76y bPP; m Adelaide NICKERSON (nm), dt Stephen & Sarah, d 11-13-1915 ae 74y 27d bPP (H)
Mary mo, Wby refers it to this MM 11-7-1798; rpd favorably 12-5-1798; cf Wby as w of Nehemiah 1-16-1799; d his wd 8-23-1833 (H)
Mary rocf R. & P. 6-18-1788 (clear); ct Upper Springfield 9-2-1789 (clear)
Mary Anna rocf Ireland 1852; mo to ----- PALMER before 1856; dis 10-1856
Mary Louisa, dt Isaac H. & Susan W., recrq of parents 1859; m John Hartley SEER
Mary Matilda, dt Joseph W. & Harriet, b 4-10-1827; dis 11-7-1849 (H)
Mary W., w Wm. B. (m 11-15-1859), dt Jacob H. & Ann L. SUTTON, d 5-1-1879; cf Scipio 3-1855 with parents (H)
Mirriam Borden, dt Joseph W. & Harriet, b 4-2-1829; ct R. & P. 4-2-1862 (H)
Nehemiah b Bridgeport d 10-24-1826 ae 69y bHS; m Mary ----- b L. I. d 8-23-1833 ae 79y 2m bHS (wd)
Nehemiah d 12-3-1801 ae 14d bHS
Pamela (late Keese) dis mo 3-4-1772
Pamela ack ref to Wby 4-3-1816; Wby rpd accepting her as a mbr 7-3-1816
Pauline (nm), dt Wm. Young & Robenia (Gratz); m 1923 Hallowell DAVIS (H)
Phebe gct Oswego 2-7-1821 (clear)
Richard recrq 9-1829; ct Paltz (Plains MM) 4-1838 (H)
Sarah, w -----, dt Liddeman & ----- HULL, N. Y. b Purchase d 4-28-1809 ae 49y 2m 14d bHS
Ch: (perhaps) Henry d 4-24-1809 ae 21d
Sarah, w Walter
Ch: Eunice
    Phebe d 11-30-1851
    Henry
    Elizabeth
    Sarah

ALLEN, Sarah & Walter, continued
Ch: Paulina
Walter
Jedediah
cf Creek for Sarah & 8 ch as named 7-17-1803
Stephen & Sarah
Ch: Charles
cf N P 6-20-1811; ct N P 9-1-1813 with 2 infant ch (one not named)
Tristram cf Nantucket 7-26-1827 (clear); mo before 6-1830; dis 10-1830; rec on ack 4-1834; ct Adrian 9-2-1835
Walter (nm), widower, b Dartmouth, Mass. d 11-23-1812 ae 57y 7m bHS
William (nm) d 4-21-1839 ae 62y 8m bHS; m Elizabeth ----- (nm) b N. J. d 3-26-1848 ae 65y 8m bHS
William A. (nm) & -----
Ch: George Tappan b N. Y. d 4- 4-1845 ae 2y 17d bHS
William active mbr from 1676
----- & ----- (nm)
Ch: Alfred d 12-12-1810 ae 3y 11m bHS
Elizabeth C. b N. Y. d 12-23-1823 ae 14y bHS

ALLEY
Alexander (nm) m Eleanor Graves MARINE, dt Arlando & Viola (Browne) b Bkn 8-25-1891 (m 7-13-1929)
Ch: Barbara Jane rec as associate 3-6-1935
Amos ct Fairfax, Va. 11-1-1798 (clear); cf Balto. 7-11-1808 (clear)
Enos & Rebecca
Ch: Lydia
cf N P 5-18-1772; took cert of clear to Creek 6-4-1794; took cert of clear to Jericho, 1-4-1804; Rebecca, cf Jericho 10-18-1804; cert to Wyanoke, Va. 3-7-1810 for Rebecca rem with h; cf Wyanoke,Va. for Rebecca 7-12-1811; cert to Jericho 2-1-1815 for Rebecca, w Enos
Louise, dt Saul & Mary; m 1860 Thomas A. WHITAKER (H)
Lydia, minor, dt Enos & Rebecca, ct Wby 2-1-1815
Lydia T., dt Rowland & Sarah TITUS, Bkn; m 1862 Samuel P. HOSIER; cf Wby 6-4-1862 (H)
Robert W. cf Jericho 3-21-1822, apprentice skipper; d at south (H)
Sarah Elizabeth, dt Sidney B. & Elizabeth (Titus), b 8-21-1839; m 1858 Nathaniel M. WEEKS; ct Wby 5-1-1850 (H)
Saul (nm) & -----
Ch: Caroline b N. Y. d 9-17-1838 ae 1y 9m bHS
Mary " " " 7-28-1841 ae 20y 5m bHS
Josephine" " "11-15-1841 ae 7y 9m bHS
Sidney B. d 9-3-1847; m Elizabeth ----- d 1-30-1844 (H)
Ch: William L. b 5- 8-1837
Sarah Elizabeth " 8-21-1839
cf Wby 8-1837

William L., s Sidney B. & Elizabeth W., b 5-8-1837 N. Y. d 3-2-1908; m Emily F. SMITH, dt Jonathan & Mary A. (nm), b Islip 3-17-1877 (m 1860) (H)
Ch: Emily T. b 3-25-1866
Edward T. " 3-28-1869
Sidney " 12-10-1875 d 4-17-1916
ct Wby 5-1-1850 for William; cf Wby 4-15-1868 for William; Emily recrq 3-17-1877; ch names entered by comm. 3-17-1877

ALLINSON
James m Phila. 1806 Bernice -----
Ch: Rebecca b 8-27-1807
Samuel " 12-24-1808
cf Burlington 11-5-1804 (clear); took cert of clear to Phila. 5-7-1806; Bernice brought cert from Phila. 7-22-1806; cert to Phila. 4-5-1809 for all
John C. cf Burlington 7-12-1807; ct Burlington 12-5-1810 (clear)
Samuel C. cf ND MM 6-24-1806 (clear); ct Burlington 5-6-1812

ALLIS
Caleb W. & Latitia W.
Ch: Frances J.
cf Scip. 1868 with ch; ct Scip. 8-1872 for parents
Frances J.,dt Caleb & Letitia W. d 7-1920; m Willis A. BARNES (nm); cf Scip. with parents 1868; ct Chicago 3-1877; cf Chicago 9-1887

ALSOP
Elizabeth Billings, dt Wm. K., b 11-24-1902; recrq of father 3-1920; name erased 3-1926
Esther, dt Samuel, Jr. & Esther K., Denver, Colo.; m 1901 Channing Page HARRIS, Bridgeport, Conn.
Esther K., w Samuel, Jr.
Ch: Susan K.
William K.
Esther
cf WD MM 5-2-1900 with 3 ch named; ct Lansdown, Pa., 6-8-1904 for Esther K.
Hannah, Newtown, d 1757 ae near 91y
John & Mary
Ch: Robert b 4-17-1783
Thomas Jenkins b 7- 4-1787
Sarah " 7-10-1792
John cf Wby 5-29-1771; ct Purchase, 10-2-1776; cf Creek 11-18-1790; ct Hudson 5-1-1794
Richard & Susanna [Alsopp] mo before 7 Mo (Sept) 1, 1748; his ack sent to Wby; Susanna dis 12 Mo 6, 1750/51
Robert cf Hudson 3-24-1801; mo before 8-7-1805; dis next month
Sarah rem with h to Pa. 7-5-1754
Susan Kite, dt Samuel, Jr. & Esther; m 1903 William Brown BELL
William K., s Samuel, Jr. & Esther K.; m -----

ALSOP, William K., continued
Ch: Elizabeth Billings b 11-24-1902
William K., Jr. " 1-12-1907
cf WD MM with mother 5-2-1900

ALWAY (H)
Hester (Esther) recrq 1807 d 1-5-1852 ae 85y bPP
John [Always] d 10-6-1798 bHS; m -----
Ch: Hester Ann b Woodbridge, N. J. d 6-22-1825 ae 5y 8m 14d bHS
Virginia b N. Y. d 1-11-1830 ae 5y 2m 20d bHS
Jerome b N. Y. d 3-14-1834 ae 2y 10m 14d bHS
Norman b N. Y. d 1-15-1836 ae 1m 14d bHS

AMESS
----- (nm) m Pearl B. STANLEY
cf Westfield, Ind. 12-6-1905 for Pearl; ct Los Angeles 1-4-1933

AMIES
Robert C. (nm) d 4-16-1858 ae 37y 9m bPP

AMMERMAN
Margaret recrq 5-2-1821 d 1850 (O); d 9-1847 (H)

AMOS
George Howard, s Godfrey & Sarah, d 1923 or before (nm); m 10-31-1900 Clara Louise WILLETS, dt Wm. U. & Clara (Hitt), b N. Y. 7-6-1878
Ch: Jeanne Louise C. b 9-29-1901 N. Y.
George Oliver " 6-30-1907 Floral Pk.
William Willets " 7-29-1911
Clara's name entered by comm. 1-10-1879; ch recrq of parents 4-5-1902, 3-13-1909 and 11-12-1923

ANDERSON
Edwin E. (nm) m Rachel E. ALEXANDER (nm), dt George & Rachel, b N. Y. 12-17-1854 d 9-12-1924 bPP
Esther, w -----
Ch: Mary
ct Flush. 9-2-1829 & accepted there (O); Flushing MM laid down and attached to N.Y. (O); dis 10-6-1830 by N. Y. (O); Flushing minutes give Mary's name
Israel & Rachel
Ch: Sarah
Phebe
Rachel
ct Pur. 4-4-1804 with their 3 ch
James gct Shrews. 1-5-1831
James Jr. b Scotland d 6-18-1824 ae 28y 7m bHS (m)
James gct Wby 11-1-1809 (clear); cf Wby 6-14-1815 (clear); ct Shrewsbury 1-1831 (H)
Ch: Infant stillborn 3-4-1822
Mary Jane
cf Flushing for Esther 4-4-1822; ct Flushing 8-1829 for Esther & Mary Jane
Jane, wd, b Tranins, Scotland, d 12-15-1826 ae 67y bHS
Jane, Jr. rocf Wby 6-14-1815 (clear)
Mary Jane, dt James & Esther, rocf Flushing with mother, 4-4-1822; ct Flushing 9-2-1829 (H)
Peter (nm) b Leith, Scotland, d 10-5-1822 bHS
Peter H. (nm) b N. Y. d 3-8-1823 ae 19y 10m bHS
Susan, w J. J. (m 1873) wd Theodore TOPPEN [unm dt Shadrach & Mary RICKETSON, b Clove, N. Y. 10-30-1841 d 10-30-1921; cf Oswego 8-1854 with parents (H)

ANDREWS
Eleanor (nm), dt Wm. Arthur & Eldenna (Bedle); m 1929 Valentine Kirk RAWSON (H)
Elizabeth H., dt Geo. R. & Emeline W., Rutherford, N. J., b Goshen 9-7-1895; m 1921 Barton L. JENKS, Rutherford (H)
George Rutt, s Geo. F. & Mary E. (Hulbert), b N. Y. 2-2-1865 d 6-1930; m 10-3-1894 Emelene W. HAWKINS, dt Lewis W. & Sarah, Goshen, b 3-25-1869 (H)
Ch: Elizabeth Holbert b 9- 7-1895 at Goshen
George Rutt, Jr. " 1-29-1897 " N. Y.
Sarah Louise " 8-21-1898 " Goshen
Cornelia Hawkins " 11-18-1901 " Rutherford, N. J.
cf Corn. for Emelene 10-3-1895; ch names entered by order of MM 1-7-1899; George (father) recrq 9-10-1917
George Rutt, Jr., s George R. & Emeline W. (Hawkins), b N. Y. 1-29-1897; m Helen BOOKER (nm); recrq of parents 1-7-1899; relrq 5-14-1924 to join Episcopal Church (H)
Joseph & Jane (H)
Ch: George T. b La Crosse, Wis. 8-15-1864
John H. " " " " 8-15-1864
Mary T. " " " " 7-1-1869
ch rocf Wilmington, Del. 2-1-1882
Philo (nm) b New Haven d 6-7-1848 ae 69y 11m 10d bHS (m)
Samuel m 8 Mo (Oct) 30, 1663 Mary WRIGHT at Anthony Wright's (earliest m cert recorded) rem to Mansfield, N. J. 1685
Ch: Mordica b 6 Mo (Aug) 11, 1664
Peter " 11 Mo (Jan) 12, 1668 d 3 Mo 1669
Hester " 10 Mo (Dec) 12, 1673
Hannah " 2 Mo (Apr) 23, 1675
Edward " 1 Mo (Mar) 16, 1677/78
Jacob " 7 Mo (Sep) 12, 1680
Mary " 5 Mo (July) 29, 1683
Samuel active mbr from 1672; Mary active mbr from 1672
Samuel (nm) b N. Y. d 7-26-1832 ae 30y bHS (m)
Sara Louise, dt Geo. R. & Emeline W., Rutherford, N. J., b 8-21-1898 Goshen; m 1920 James K. SINCLAIRE, of Rutherford; recrq of parents 1-7-1899 (H)

ANGELIS
Gideon recrq 9-7-1820; dis 12-1827

ANGELL
Charles H., s Augustus & Eliza (Smith), b 3-9-1853 at Ghent; m 12-25-1899 Maud M. -----; transferred to N. Y. 1-8-1916 (H)
Joseph Thorn, s Augustus & Eliza (Smith), b 4-25-1846 at Ghent d 3-21-1822; m 11-26-1872 Mary A. PARKER, dt Benj. A. & Eliza A.; transferred to N. Y. 1-8-1916 (H)
William H., s Augustus & Eliza (Smith), b 2-10-1851 at Ghent d 1920; m 5-18-1905 Margaret VAN SHAAK, dt Samuel & Eliza MERWIN; transferred to N. Y. 1-8-1916 (H)

ANGEVINE
Almira B., dt Frank & Bethia, b 2-1-1866 Bkn.; m 4-23-1890 Dr. Crawford D. BEASLEY
Bethia, dt Frank & Bethia, b 3-21-1876 Bkn.; m Irving BROWN; recrq of parents 11-27-1878
David (nm) b Scarsdale d 5-4-1821 ae 50y bHS (m)
Fannie mo Purchase refers it to this MM 5-2-1798; rpd favorable & cf Purchase 8-9-1798
Frances, w David, ct Pur. 6-4-1806
Frank (nm), s Henry & Caroline, N. Y.; m 2-19-1863 Bethia Y. COLEMAN, at Geo. Coleman's (not under care of N. Y.) dt Charles S., dec, & Sophia B., dec
Ch: Mary Louise b 8-18-1864
Almira " 2- 1-1866
Frank Jr. " 1- 4-1868 d 3- 6-1899
Henry " 10-11-1873
Bethia Coleman " 5-31-1876
Caroline " 7-19-1878 d 7-19-1880 bPP
cf Troy for Bethia 8-5-1863; ch recrq of parents 11-27-1878; ct Bkn for ch
Gilbert (nm) m Ann ----- (nm) b N. Y. d 9-27-1813 ae 68y bHS
Henry, s Frank & Bethia b 10-11-1873 Bkn; m Laura W. ----- (nm) (m 4-22-1900); recrq of parents 11-27-1878
Mary (nm), dt Henry, d 12-31-1915 ae 80y 6m bPP
Mary Louise, dt Frank & Bethia, b 8-18-1864 Bkn; m Theron LAWRENCE; recrq of parents 11-27-1878

ANTHONY
Anna R. mo Creek ref to N. Y. 2-1846; dis & rpd to Creek 3-1846
Lydia Ann (nm), w -----, b New Bedford d 11-1-1833 ae 25y bHS
Martha d 9-25-1854; cf Verona 11-1840

ANTRIM
Elizabeth L. (nm) d 1855 bPP in grave with E. C. Knight
Edna K. d 10-3-1866 ae 11y bPP
Hannah [Antram] cf Green St. Phila. 4-1845; ct R & P 8-1855; cf R & P 4-1860; ct Pur 7-4-1806
Hannah, w John (nm) d 2-28-1882 ae 64 bPP

ARCHER
Anna, wd, b Westchester d 10-7-1823 ae 86y bHS
Florence, dt Isaac H. & Eliz. M. (Olcott), b 3-21-1867 Bkn; m 6-21-1893 Stanley H. CHADWICK; recrq 4-9-1917; relrq 1-18-1934 (H)
Isaac H. rocf Pur. 3-4-1863; dis mo 4-3-1865 (H)
James B. (nm), s Richard & Jane, b N. Y. d 6-6-1847 ae 35y bHS (m)
Josiah (nm) & -----
Ch: Alfred b N. Y. d 1-17-1830 ae 2y 2m bHS
Abigail Jane b N. Y. d 8-24-1831 ae 1y 6m bHS
Phebe b West Co. d 10-29-1835 ae 55y bHS
Phebe, dt Thomas & Abigail THORN, N. Y.; m 1840 David P. SMITH; mo to Josiah Archer before 7-3-1822 & dis; rst 9-1828 (H)
Richard m Jane ----- d 6-23-1858
Ch: James B. b N. Y. d 6-6-1847 ae 35y
Jane recrq 12-6-1815; ct R & P 3-4-1818 for Jane, ret with reasons why not accepted; ct Amawalk 9-7-1820 for Jane, rem with h
Sarah b 6-14-1834; m John Hicks MACY (H)
Stephen recrq 8-1830; ct Chap. 1-1832 (H)
Thomas (nm) & -----
Ch: Jonah b Pur. d 10-8-1826 ae 4y 6m bHS
----- & ----- (nm)
Ch: Mary d 1-15-1811 ae 5m bHS

ARCHIBALD
Mary, w John, dt Geo. D. & Martha VAIL (sister of Addison), d 3-9-1864 ae 39y bPP
Ch: Martha E. d 1878
Araminta " 10- 9-1866 ae 8y
Mary mo; ch recrq of mother 6-1860

ARDING
Abigail, wd, b Newtown, L. I. d 8-31-1828 ae 84y 6m bHS

ARMITAGE
Sarah, dt Seth & Anna (Phillips), Yonge St., b 7-10-1835; m 3-22-1855 John A. CRONE (nm); cf Yonge St. 2-7-1894; ct East Hamburg 9-10-1910 (H)

ARMOUR
Mary L. (nm) d 4-2-1856 ae 18y 6m bPP

ARMSTRONG
Alice H. (form Gardner) recrq 6-1887
Mary mo before 7-6-1763, dealt with but rpd dec 1-4-1764
----- & ----- (nm)
Ch: Mary d 3-21-1811 ae 4y 4m bHS

ARNOLD
Amy d 5-26-1892; m John LOCKWOOD
Benjamin C., s Joseph & Dorcas, Arnoldtown, N. Y.; m 5-11-1854 Mary J. GRIFFEN,

ARNOLD, Benjamin C. & Mary J., continued
at Thos. T. Griffen's, dt Thos. T. & Mary M., N. Y.; ct Plains 12-6-1854 for Mary (H)
Elizabeth, dt Joseph, Jr. & Sarah (Griffen), b 11-16-1865 N. Y.; m 1892 John Hampton VALENTINE; m 2d 1924 Isaac B. DE VOL (H)
Jacob (nm) b Dutchess Co. d 10-21-1831 ae 17y bHS
John rocf Shrewsbury 2-1836 (minor); ct Shrewsbury 11-1855 (H)
John (nm) & -----
Ch: Amanda d 2-13-1842 ae 2m 10d bHS
John R. (nm), s Zenas S. & Alice M.; m 8-11-1917 Eugenia RIDGELEY, dt Daniel M. & Ellen (Madden), b 9-4-1884, Wyoming, Del.; cf Wilmington 12-12-1921 for Eugenia
Joseph, Jr., s Joseph & Dorcas, Arnoldton, b 4-2-1829 Arnoldtown, N. Y. d 2-8-1913 bPP; m 12-6-1855 Sarah Elizabeth GRIFFEN, at T. T. Griffen's, dt Thos. T. & Mary M., N. Y. (H)
Ch: Carrie b 9-23-1856 d 1-17-1910 bPP
Josephine b 9- 3-1858
Charles " 3- 1-1860 d 4- 8-1898
Elizabeth " 11-16-1865
Mabelle Thorne b 8-4-1877 d 3-20-1893 bPP
cf Oswego 3-4-1863
Josephine, dt Jos. Jr. & Sarah E., b 9-3-1858 Arnoldtown, N. Y.; m 10-12-1881 Edwin C. CLOYD (nm) (H)
Levi & Hannah rocf Chesterfield 4-2-1805; ct Chesterfield for both 2-3-1808
Richard (nm) b Dutch. Co. d 3-24-1835 ae 25y bHS
Sarah Eliz., w -----, dt Thos. T. & Mary GRIFFEN, b 5-10-1834
Ch: Carrie b 9-25-1856

ARRIET (or Arnett)
John Hartas rocf Brighouse, Eng. 2-5-1834 stating that he lives at Yonge St.; cert forwarded to Yonge St. & not recorded

ARSON
Dereck, Flushing; m 1 Mo (Mar) 28, 1700 Hannah HEDGER, at Flushing

ARTHUR
Phebe A. d 9-11-1899; m 1876 Charles D. ATKINS; recrq 3-1873; m proposals rec 10-1876 but mo before 12-1876; she retained; his cert ret to Smyrna

ARTOIS
Rebecca W. recrq 5-1871; d 1899

ASH
Edward (nm) drowned in ship Bristol 1-28-1837 ae 22y 5m bHS

ASHBY
William rocf Bugbrook, North Hants, 6-14-1811 (clear); ct Hudson 6-7-1815 (clear)

ASHTON
Lydia rocf Phila. 3-29-1765; ct Phila. 11-6-1766

ASKEW
James d 1902; m -----
Ch: William
recrq 12-1872; William recrq 10-1873

ATHERTON
Charles & Mary
Ch: Deborah P.
cf Burlington 1-1-1844 with ch named; ct Providence 11-6-1844 with ch named

ATKINS
Amelia Anne, dt William & Kathleen (Kingston) b 5-6-1845 Ireland d 11-27-1925 bPP; m William FERGUSON (nm)
Amelia Anne bur as a mbr but no record found
Charles D. m Phebe Ann ARTHUR d 9-11-1899; m proposals rec 10-1876 & comm. appeared as to Phebe's clearness. Did not appear 11th mo; cf Smyrna 12-6-1876 for Charles, but he had mcd, cert ret to Smyrna

ATKINSON
Francis Whitmer, s Chas. F. & Helen (Hopkins), Moorestown, N. J.; m 11-26-1913 at 281 Sterling Place, Bkn. Elsie HAVILAND, dt Edward & Jemima, Bkn., b 3-26-1889 Bkn. d 1932
Ch: Francis Whitmer Jr. b 4-15-1915
John Hopkins " 12-12-1918
Edward Haviland " 10- 2-1920
ch mbr of father's MM under discipline 1930; Moorestown notified
John m 10-5-1881 at 131 St. Felix St., Bkn. Anna H. WELDING, dt Watson J. & Sarah H.; cf ND MM with mother 3-1853; ct WD MM 1-1886
John M. (nm) d 1895; m Charlotte M. ----- (nm) d 5-8-1929 (both bPP)
Jonathan brought cf Lancaster, Eng., 8-6-1752; took cert to Lancaster, Eng. 9-6-1753
Louise, dt Amos & Isabella (Hutchinson), b 9-23-1870 at Newcastle-on-Tyne; m 1901 Robert MAITLAND (H)

ATTERBURY
Elizabeth recrq 3-7-1821; ct Hudson 6-5-1822 (clear); cf Hudson 2-2-1848; d 1-22-1859
----- & ----- (nm)
Ch: James b N. Y. d 10-31-1823 ae 2y 5m bHS

ATWATER
Jeremiah W. (nm), s Wm. C. & Harriet H., d 5-26-1922; m 10-25-1855 Jane Louise CARPENTER, dt Chas. M. & Charlotte U., b 7-20-1836 N. Y. rem to Chester; Jane Louise changed to Louisa C. (H)

AUDI
Badeah recrq 7-1915
Aneesie recrq 7-1915

AUGUSTINE
Louisa, w Joseph, dt Francis H. & Deborah MACY; mo before 11-1878 (H); rel 12-1878; attended Dr. Hall's Church

AUSTIN
Rachel G. (nm) d 6-12-1834 ae 42y bHS (of Nantucket)

BABBITT
Mary Rogers, dt Isaac N., Jr. & Eliz. G., b 9-1-1873 Fairhaven, Mass.; m 10-15-1906 David J. BURDICK (H)

BABCOCK
Elizabeth (or Badcock) d 1-20-1806; cf Hudson 9-1826 (clear); ct Scipio 11-5-1831 (clear) cf Scipio 11-7-1838; ct Troy 8-4-1847; cf Troy 4-1855
Elizabeth rocf Troy 4-1855 d 1-20-1866
Helena (nm) b N. Y. d 5-11-1845 ae 58y bHS (wd)

BABRIDGE
----- & -----
Ch: Mary b N. Y. d 11-21-1827 ae 2y 3m bHS
Emma b N. Y. d 9-20-1833 ae 1y 2m bHS

BACHMAN
Jessie H. rocf Ypsilanti, Mich. 11-4-1914; letter to First Cong. Ch., Montclair, 3-1917 (H)

BACKER
Jacob & Eliza
Ch: Jacob b 5-29-1816

BACKHOUSE
Thomas, s Wm. & Eliz. (dec), rocf Lancaster, Eng. 5-5-1777 (clear); ct Devenshire House 7-5-1780

BACKUS
Amanda N., w Frederick B., rocf Phila. Green St. 5-7-1873; relrq 6-1-1887

BACON
Fanny H., dt George B. & Lavinia, b 1-24-1872 Bkn.; m 1896 Wm. W. JACKSON; recrq 1-8-1922
----- & Matilda R. (H)
cf Thaxter, Eng. 4-5-1905 for Matilda; rel 2-1922 to jas

BADCOCK
Elizabeth (or Babcock) rocf Hudson 1826; ct Scipio 10-5-1831 (clear)

BADGLEY
Anthony, s Anthony Sr., Flushing, d 2 Mo (Apr) 3, 1732; m 9 Mo (Nov) 12, 1719 at Flushing Phebe HAIGHT, dt Samuel, dec, d 11 Mo (Jan) 20, 1731

BAGGOTT
Estelle M., dt Chas. E. (nm) & Eugenia L. (Valory) (nm) b 8-8-1894 N. Y.; recrq 11-14-1914; relrq 1-12-1920 (H)

BAHLER
Elsie Margarita, dt Martin & Annie L., b 3-28-1878 N. J.; m 1911 Barclay H. HUTCHINSON
Elsie Margarite recrq 4-13-1912; ct R. & P. 11-12-1917 for both (H)

BAILEY
Charles H. b 1-29-1864 Keesport, N. Y. d 7-25-1894 bPP; m Georgia RHODES, dt Hiram & Esther, b 9-21-1865
Ch: Harry Rhodes b 1- 1-1890
Arthur de Kamp b 9-24-1891
Donald b 5-28-1893
Charles recrq 12-4-1889; Georgia recrq of parents 4-1872; Georgia m 2nd ----- HALL
Daniel, s Daniel & Rosannah, rocf Cornwall 4-25-1811 (minor); dis 8-1846
George (or Bailes), s Daniel & Rosannah, rocf Cornwall 4-25-1811 (minor); dis 12-3-1823
Georgia, wd Charles H., dt Hiram & Esther RHODES; m ----- HALL; recrq of parents 4-1872
----- m Katharine McCONAUGHY, dt ----- & Eleanor; Katharine recrq 5-1915
Rosanna, w Daniel, d 1843
Ch: Rosanna
Mary dis 6-1831
cf Cornwall 3-28-1811 with two dt named

BAIN
William (nm) b Pa. d 3-31-1831 ae 29y bHS

BAINBRIDGE
Mary Phillips rocf Hardshaw West & Liverpool MM, Eng. 5-1921; name erased 10-1928

BAKER
Aaron gct Farm. 8-6-1806, rem with his fam
Aaron m 1800 by Methodist preacher, Sarah PANCOAST; cf Chap. 6-15-1792 (clear); dis mo 4-2-1800
Aaron, s Samuel & Mary Ann (both dec), Genoa, N. Y.; m N. Y. 9-12-1811 Elizabeth RIDGWAY, dt Thos. (dec) & Eliz.; ct Scipio 11-6-1811 for Elizabeth
Benjamin (nm) b White Plains d 2-15-1812 ae 40y 3m 20d bHS
Catharine rocf R. & P. 8-18-1819; ct R. & P. 7-11-1827
Daniel b 1844 d 4-21-1899 ae 55y bPP
Dobel d 4-1-1873 (or 1-15-1873 ae 83y); m Mary C. ----- d 8-11-1869 ae 82 (both bPP) (m Phila) (H)
Ch: George Corlies
Joseph
Hannah D. b 1-17-1826
William Dobel b 9-18-1829
Sarah Haydock d 2-12-1881 ae 58y

BAKER, Dobel & Mary C., continued
cf ND MM 11-22-1825 with ch
Elizabeth, dt Richard, d 7-10-1803 ae 21y bHS
George C., s Dobel & Mary, d 5-13-1863; m Phebe C. ----- (H)
Ch: Hannah M. b 2-17-1846
Mary C. " 4-20-1849
George Dobel " 3- 6-1851 d 8-26-1852
Sarah H. " 3- 2-1853
Robert Haydock b 7- 3-1855
cf Shrewsbury 3-1845 for Phebe; dis 1-1859 for jas; George C. dis 6-4-1862, joined a military Co. & neglected mtg
George Howard, s Geo. W. (dec) & Martha, Cambridge, Mass.; m 6-15-1894 at L. M. Stabler's, Louise M. STABLER, dt Edward (dec) & Louisa M., Bkn. (H)
Hannah D., dt Dobel & Mary C., N. Y., b 1-17-1826; m 1847 Robt. Cornell WHITE (H)
Hannah W., dt George C. & Phebe C., b 2-17-1846; dis 6-5-1878
Harriet (nm) b L. I. d 12-12-1832 ae 22y bHS
Isaac ct ND MM 2-20-1823 (clear)
Jacob & Elizabeth
Ch: Robert d 9-28-1803 ae 1y 3m
Jesse (nm) & -----
Ch: William b Bkn. d 8-8-1831 ae 1y 3m bHS
John mo before 6-3-1807 & rem to Farmington; ref to that MM
Joseph, s Dobel & Mary C., N. Y.; m 11-4-1847 at Robert White's, Rachel C. WHITE, dt Robert Jr. & Hannah G., N. Y. (H)
Ch: Margaret Corlies b 10-16-1848
Anna H. " 10- 8-1852 d 4-25-1921
Joseph dis 1-1855; Rachel dis 5-1855
Joseph C. (nm) & -----
Ch: Robert White d 12-31-1859 ae 4y 6m bPP
Margaret C., dt Joseph & Rachel C., N. Y., b N. Y. 10-16-1848; m 11-4-1867 Wharton BARKER; ct Phila. 11-4-1868 (H)
Martha (or Boker), w Aaron, cf Hard. & Randolph 6-7-1821; dis 12-1830
Mary C., dt Geo. C. & Phebe C. (White), b 4-20-1849 d 4-28-1904; m 7-7-1869 Thomas B. LONG (nm); lived Flushing (H)
Robert d 5-12-1790; cf Kennett MM, Del. 6-12-1766; m among Friends but appeared under arms; rem many years ago; rec 11-6-1766
Samuel cf Wby, young 11-24-1784; ct Chap. 12-5-1787 (clear)
Samuel Henry d 4-21-1899; cf Dublin 4-5-1893
Sally Ann, dt Gilbert, d 12-19-1802 ae 3m bHS
Sarah H., dt Geo. C. & Phebe C., b 3-2-1853; relrq 7-3-1878
Sharpless (nm) m 4-5-1899 Gertrude HAYES
Gertrude recrq 8-14-1909; m 2nd James J. BARRA, 4-26-1927 (H)
Tamar cf Wby 3-16-1803 (clear); ct Scipio 4-3-1811 (clear)
William (nm) & -----
Ch: Stephen d 2-13-1890 ae 9m bHS
William, s Dobel & Mary C., b 9-18-1829; dis 5-1856 (H)

BALDERSTON
Julia O., dt Wm. & Ann (Fogg), b 1-19-1878 Lower Makefield, Pa.; cf Makefield 1-8-1934

BALDWIN
Ann, dt Benjamin & Elizabeth, b 2-9-1788; ct Farmington 4-2-1806 with her mother (clear)
Anna W., w William S., recrq 6-7-1911
Benjamin & Elizabeth
Ch: Jemima b 12-21-1778
Joshua " 7- 7-1783
Hannah " 11- 9-1785
Anne " 2- 9-1788
Elizabeth " 9-16-1792
Elizabeth, w Jesse, cf Corn 8-25-1825 (clear); dis 1831; Jesse a seaman (H)
Elizabeth cf Wby 10-15-1794, she living in N. Y. & having form mo now rst; ct Farmington 4-2-1806 (clear)
Florence May (nm) m 1909 Harold Reginald WILLETS (H)
Hannah, dt Benj. & Eliz., N. Y.; m 1804 William RENOUF
James C. T. (nm) m 11-25-1902, Boston, Mass., Alice C. SMITH, dt Thos. T. & Sarah B., b 1-15-1808 in Bkn.; relrq 1-13-1917 (H)
Jamima, dt Benj. & Eliz., N. Y.; m 1800 Abraham BUNKER
Jesse m Elizabeth -----, b L. I. d 4-30-1830 (or 5-3-1830 ae 53y 7m)
Ch: Mary
Sarah d 4-25-1827 ae 18y
Esther dis 11-1827
cf Wby 9-14-1808 with 2 ch named; ct Jericho 1-5-1814 with 3 ch named, including Esther; cf Jericho 4-14-1825 for parents with ch, Sarah & Esther; Sarah clear; Esther a minor; both dis 1829-1830
Jesse, Jr., s Jesse & Mary; m N. Y. 7-12-1832, Elizabeth SEAMAN, dt Jonah & Martha
Ch: Elizabeth d 4-5-1834 ae 9d
ct R & P for both 7-1836
Joshua gct Farmington 2-4-1806
Phebe (form Underhill) dis 5-6-1835 for mo
Sarah rocf Wby & Jericho 1834
Thomas (nm) m Eliza C. (nm) b N. Y. d 7-17-1844 ae 48y bHS
Thomas C. recrq 5-3-1854; relrq 7-5-1871, absent over 5y (H)
William S. (nm) & Annie
Annie recrq 6-7-1911

BALLARD
Achilles & Penina
cf Richmond, Ind. 12-4-1872; ct Whitewater, Ind., 8-4-1875 (H)
Mary d 6-14-1892; cf Indianapolis 6-11-1890

BALLINGER
Edward, s Isaac (dec) & Esther, N. Y., b N. J. d 8-8-1837 ae 36y 8m; m N. Y. 5-15-1828, Eliza PEARSALL, dt Wm. & Elizabeth, N. Y., d 12-5-1888 ae 88y 9m 24d bPP (H)

BALLINGER, Edward & Eliza, continued
Ch: William Pearsall b 2-11-1829
Mary E. b ------1831 d 3-3-1832
James Elizabeth b 8-15-1834
Edward, Jr. b 4-14-1836
cf Woodbury 2-27-1826; dis 1-1830 (O)
Edward, Jr., s Edward & Eliza P., b 4-14-1836; killed in battle of Antietam 9-1862; relrq 5-7-1862 (H)
Esther rocf Burlington 6-4-1827; dis 6-1830 (O); ct Phila. 9-1829 (H)
Jacob rocf Burlington 4-6-1827, apprentice to brother, Joseph I.; ct Phila. 4-7-1830 (clear) (O); ct Phila. 9-1829 (H)
Jane Elizabeth, dt Edw. & Eliza P., N. Y.; m 1853 Jacob CAPRON (H)
Joseph I. rocf Burlington 8-1827; ct Woodbury 2-1831 (H); ct Woodbury 11-7-1832 (clear); cert returned by Woodbury as he had rem to Centreville, Ind.; ct West Grove, Ind. 6-5-1833 (clear)
Priscilla rocf Woodbury, N. J. 10-1828 (H); dis 6-1830 (O); ct Phila. 9-1829 (H)
Sarah, dt ----- & Esther, rocf Burlington 6-4-1827; dis 6-1830 (O); ct Phila. 9-1829 (H)
William Pearsall, dt Edward & Eliza, b 2-11-1829 (H)
Ch: Elizabeth d 12-30-1874 ae 12y bPP
mo before 7-6-1853; dis 8-1853

BANCKER
Mary E. (nm), w Frederick A., d 9-5-1876 ae 23y 4m 3d bPP (H)

BANER
Dr. William J. (nm), s Isaac & Sarah, b 6-9-1821 d 11-6-1885 bPP; m Martha FOWLER, dt Horace & Mary (T----) d 9-10-1894 ae 70y 10m 6d bPP (Wm. J. b Springborough)
Ch: Walter bPP) bur in
Charlotte Anna bPP) one grave
Oriella Eugenia d 11-11-1861 ae 4y 8m 3d bPP
Marinna d 11-24-1861 ae 12y 4m 24d bPP
cf Springborough, O. 7-1847 (H); Cincinnati (O) asks N. Y. (O) to deal with him as he had joined Hicksites 10-1865; dis by Cincinnati recorded 9-1860 (O)

BANK
Elsie m R. B. SLEEM; recrq 5-5-1909; ct Poughkeepsie 3-1928
Willis (Banks) rocf Oblong 10-1854; ct Oblong 8-6-1879 (H)

BANYON
Herbert (nm) m Helen Ware THOMPSON, dt William, d 2-3-1920 ae 40y bPP (nm) (H)
Ch: Arthur Ware d 4-16-1920 ae 19y bPP (nm)

BARBER
Ellen took rem cert 5 Mo (July) 4, 1689, destination not stated
Samuel rocf Green St., Phila. 7-1850; ct Salem, N. J., 3-7-1855 (H)
Samuel (nm) & Mary (nm)
Ch: Alonzo d 12-28-1851 ae 1y 11m 20d bPP

BARDIZBANIAN
Vartan & Elizabeth
Ch: Esther
Dorothy
cf Constantinople 10-3-1894 for Vartan; Elizabeth & Esther recrq 12-6-1911; Dorothey recrq 5-1915

BARIGHT
Augustin, s John & Eleanor, Pleasant Valley, N. Y.; m N. Y. 9-13-1815, Mary PEARSALL, dt William & Elizabeth, N. Y.
Ch: William P.
John
Martha Ann
Eliza P.
Edward R.
Augustin, Jr.
George P. b 5-28-1830
Walter
ct Oswego for Mary, to settle with h; cf Oswego for both with 5 ch named; parents dis 1830; ch rem to Roch. 1834 (O); ct Roch. for all 12-1833 (H)
Edward (nm) d 7-24-1866 bPP; m Sophia ----- (nm)
Ch: Sophia E. d 1862 ae 17m bPP
Sarah Eliza d 8-9-1864 ae 3m 11d bPP
Edward P., s Augustin & Mary, d 1-28-1898; m ----- (H)
Ch: Augusta Ellen d 7-17-1869 ae 6m bPP
cf Oswego 9-1827 with parents; ct Roch. 12-1833 with parents; cf Roch. 11-1854 (H)
George P. rocf Roch. 6-3-1868; ct Shrewsbury 4-2-1879 (H)

BARKER
Abraham m 1809 Priscilla -----
Ch: Sarah b 2-20-1810
Henry Hopkins
Ann Mifflin b 5-21-1813
cf New Bedford 1-17-1804 (clear); cf Balto. WD 1-10-1810 for Priscilla; ct SD MM 3-6-1816
Andrew Signourey, s Jacob & Elizabeth, b 11-11-1811 d 8-11-1846; rem from HS to PP, bur in grave with T. Hazan (H)
Anna Hazard, dt Jacob & Elizabeth, b 10-25-1813;

BARKER, Anna, continued
m ----- WARD; dis 12-1839 (O); dis 8-1-1860 for having joined the R. C. Church, as Anna H. B. Ward (H)
Annie (or Anna), w Wm. C., dt Shadrach & May RICKETSON, b 2-14-1837 (m 5-8-1859 at Hennepin, Ill.) (H)
Caleb (nm) m Emily NEWBOLD (nm), dt John & Susan, d 10-5-1909 ae 66y 2m 8d bPP (H)
David (nm) m Julia A. BARNES (nm) dt ----- & Alathea, d 11-27-1904 ae 84y 2d
Ch: Caroline Crook d 10- 4-1854 ae 1y 9m 10d bHS, rem to PP
Joseph Rudd d 1-18-1859 ae 5m 14d bPP
Caleb " 10- 5-1909 ae 66y 2m 8d bPP
David d 1-8-1890 ae 77y 11m 11d bPP; cf Oswego 5-1837 (H); cf Oswego 1-20-1836 (clear) (O); dis 12-1839 (O)
Eliza B., dt David & Mary (Harcourt), b Barkerville 5-22-1817 d 6-4-1903; m 1850 Thomas W. Griffen (H)
Elizabeth m ----- GOODRICH; cf Providence 5-3-1893 for Elizabeth Barker Goodrich; name erased 2-1926
Elizabeth rocf Burlington 6-6-1803 (clear) with her niece, Elizabeth Ellison; ct Goshen, Pa. for both 8-1-1810
Elizabeth d 9-18-1861 ae 77y 9m 16d bPP
Eliz. H., dt Abraham & Margaret B., b Lynn, Mass.; m 1866, Joseph P. HEWHALL, of Liverton, R. I.; cf R. I. 1859
Erastus B. (nm), s David D. & Julia (Barnes), d 6-26-1917 ae 76y 5m 14d bPP; m 11-28-1865, Maria Louisa HAVILAND, dt Rich. F. & Matilda H., b 11-28-1846 Bkn. d 10-7-1920 ae 73y 11m bPP
Ch: Richard H. d 1-1-1929 ae 62y bPP
cf Chap. for Maria with father 1-1851
Isaac rocf Nantucket 9-28-1814 to live with uncle Abraham Barker; ct SD MM 3-6-1816, rem with uncle Abraham; cf Nantucket 1823; dis 3-1830
Jacob m Eliza ----- d 9-18-1861
Ch: Robert b 6-11-1802; d 9-28-1803
Robert H. " 7-20-1804
Thomas H. " 6-21-1807
Wm. Hapgood b 8-21-1809
Andrew Signourey b 11-11-1811 d 8-11-1846
Anna Hazard b 10-25-1813
cf ND MM 3-28-1798 to live with Isaac Hicks; cert of clear to New Bedford 8-5-1801
Ch: (these nm owing to Jacob's dis)
Jacob b 5-23-1816
John W. " d 12-19-1825 ae 5h bHS
Mary " 1-10-1826 ae 2y 6m bHS
cf New Bedford for Eliza 12-22-1801; Jacob dis 1-4-1815 for war sentiments; Eliza dis 1830 (O)
John rocf Amawalk 12-13-1800 (lad)
Joshua, s John & Elizabeth (dec); m N. Y. 11-11-1801 Phebe COX, dt Samuel (dec) & Sarah; cf ND MM 9-23-1800 (clear); ct Chesterfield 3-7-1804 for Joshua & Phebe
Maria Louise, w Erastus B., dt Rich. F. & Matilda H. HAVILAND (m 11-28-1865); cf Chap. with father 1-1851 (H)
Myra T., dt Wm. C. & Beulah T.; m George MARSHALL (nm); relrq 6-4-1898
Capt. Peleg (nm) b Nantucket d 6-2-1816 ae 52y (m)
Rebecca T., dt Wm. C. & Beulah T., b Bkn. 1-13-1855; m 10-18-1876 Edward B. BELCHER (H)
Richard H. & Olivia (H)
Ch: Marie Louise d 12-4-1888 ae 2y 3m 7d bPP (all nm) (H)
Robert H., s Jacob & Elizabeth, b 6-11-1802; dis 8-1830 for administering oath, after a yr of dealing
Sarah, wd Peleg; d 2-14-1839 ae 64y; ct Balto. 8-31-1818 (clear); cf Balto. WD 7-9-1824; dis 7-1830 (H) (bHS)
Thomas Hazard, s Jacob & Elizabeth, b 6-21-1807 (or 6-1-1807); dis 9-2-1840 (O) for accepting position of U. S. Consul & Administering oaths
Wharton, s Abraham & Sarah W. (dec), Phila.; m at John Corlies White's, Woodside, (not under care of N. Y. MM) Margaret C. BARKER, dt Joseph & Rachel C., N. Y.
William, s James, rocf ND MM 12-31-1806, under care of his uncle, Abraham Barker
William C. b Nantucket d 1-25-1824 ae 34y bHS; mo before 1-3-1816; dis 2-7-1816
William C. m Beulah T. ----- d 5-28-1861 (H)
Ch: ----- b 4- 5-1851 d 5-19-1851
William C. b 2- 4-1853 d 1-10-1854
Rebecca T. " 1-13-1855
Mira T. " 3- 5-1857
cf Oswego 11-1845 for Wm.; cf Phila. 11-1852 for Beulah; Wm. C. dis 11-2-1864; Wm. agreed to arbitration and would not abide by result, 1862, so dis
William C. (nm) s S. G. & Edith (Castlebury); m 5- 8-1859 Annie RICKETSON, dt Shadrach & Mary
William Hapgood (or Hazard), s Jacob & Elizabeth, b 8-21-1809; mo before 2-6-1833; dis 12-1830 (O); dis 3-1833 for mo (H)
----- & -----
Ch: John Newbold d 7- 5-1871 ae 7m 6d bPP
Julia A. " 7-14-1877 ae 7m bPP

BARMORE
Philip & Hannah
Ch: Maria
Henry b 10-16-1856
cf Oswego 2-6-1856 with 1 ch; ct Clear Creek 10-7-1868 with 2 ch
----- & -----
Ch: Emeline b N. Y. d 7-28-1833 ae 5d bHS

BARNARD
Anna Sykes (form Barnard) dis mo 11-4-1801 & rpd to Hudson
Benjamin (nm) b Nantucket d 10-16-1830 ae 49y

BARNARD, Benjamin, continued
bHS
Charles having mo Hudson ref. to this MM 11-7-1804; rpd adversely 1-2-1805
Infant of Charles H. d 7-2-1811 ae 7d bHS
Edward (nm) & -----
Ch: George b N. Y. d 12-24-1834 ae 18d bHS
Mary (form Hawxhurst) dis mo 11-1836 (H)
Phebe, dt Valentine, mo to ----- PEASE before 9-7-1808; cf Hudson 12-23-1806 (clear); dis 11-2-1808
Valentine b Nantucket d 12-21-1823 ae 74y; m Anna ---- b Nantucket d 6-30-1814 ae 63y (nm)
Ch: Phebe
cf Hudson 7-25-1809
----- & -----
Ch: Thomas b N. Y. d 2-18-1825 ae 1y 7m bHS
Benjamin b N. Y. d 5-11-1825 ae 8d bHS
Charles b N. Y. d 3-29-1827 ae 7m bHS
Cornelius L. b N. Y. d 6-30-1829 ae 3y 10m bHS

BARNES
Aaron rocf Pur. 11-1842; d 7-18-1848 (H)
Ann (nm)d 6-16-1831 ae 54y bHS
Anna, dt David H. & Naomi (Haviland), b White Plains 8-10-1834 d 11-8-1925; m 1868 Henry B. HALLOCK (H)
Anna M. C. rec by ack. 1-1-1849; ct Roch. 1855
Ann Eliza, dt Henry & Emily (Wildey), b Clinton, N. Y., 10-16-1839 d 1-14-1913; m 1857 John STRINGHAM; cf Creek with h & ch 11-3-1891 (H)
Annie P., dt Joseph & Phebe Ann (McClintock), d 1-2-1908; m John WALLACE; cf Phila. 11-10-1906 with h & s (H)
Ellen d 5-27-1832 ae 32y bHS (sister of Joseph & bur same grave)
George, s Robert S. & Ann, b 1-16-1814 d 9-23-1859 ae 45y bPP; mo to Mary ----; dis 1841
George, s George & Mary, d 5-22-1923 ae 75y 9m 18d (unm) (probably s of above)
Hannah Weldon (form Barnes), dt Josiah & Phebe, b 8-22-1827; rpd mo
Henry W., s Robert S. & Ann, b 1-27-1805; dis mo 1-1832 (H); dis 1831(O); lived in Boston 1830
James, s Robert S. & Ann, b 11-20-1811; relrq 5-7-1862
James (nm) & -----
Ch: Infant stillborn 12-16-1842 bHS
Sarah M. d 8-21-1847 ae 8m bHS
Infant stillborn bPP
John, s Robert S. & Ann, b 11-20-1811; rel 7-5-1871 absent over 5y
John dis mo 8-1841; referred to Alum Creek, O., rpd unfavorable
John A. (nm)m Phebe C. MILLER, dt Benj. C.& Laura F., wd John C. SMITH
Joseph d 4-25-1832 ae 34y bHS; dis mo 2-7-1821
Ch: Eliza d 1-11-1846 ae 19y 3m 18d bHS (unm)
Susan Jane d 7-4-1846 ae 24y bHS (unm)

Josiah, s Stephen & Hannah, N. Y. (both dec); m N. Y. 11-9-1826 Phebe FIELD, dt Josiah & Hannah (dec), N. Y. (H)
Ch: Hannah G. b 8-22-1827
Mary F. " 8-14-1829
Sarah F. " 5-19-1833 d 12-17-1845
Josiah F. " 4-11-1835
Josiah F., s Josiah & Phebe, b 4-11-1835; rel 7-5-1871, absent over 5y (H)
Mary, dt Robert & Eliz.; m 1820 Wm. C. WHITE
Mary T., dt Josiah & Phebe, b 8-14-1829; dis 3-1855 (H)
Phebe rocf Pur. 10-6-1869; ct Pur. 10-4-1871 (H)
Phebe Ann, dt Robert & Ann, b 5-19-1807; ct Little Egg Harbor 4-1-1835 (clear)
Phebe F. gct Pur. 5-2-1827
Robert S. (nm) d 5-21-1835 ae 80y; m Ann WILLITS, d 6-16-1831 ae 51y
Ch: Susan Jane d 7- 1-1816 ae 21y 7m 9d
Joseph " 4-25-1832 ae 34y
Eliza " 1----1816 ae 19y 3m 28d
Eleanor b 7-20-1800 d 5-27-1832
William B. b 11-25-1802 d 7-10-1833
Henry W. " 1-27-1805
Phebe Ann " 5-19-1807
Robert S. " 8- 3-1809 d 4- 9-1872
John " 11-20-1811
James " 11-20-1811
George " 1-16-1814
Walter " 3-17-1817 " 2- 9-1897
Ann (late Willits) mo before 2-7-1798, ack. accepted 12-5-1798; all dis 1829-1841 (O); all withdrew (H) all bHS & rem to PP
Walter, s Geo. & Mary, d 5-11-1916 ae 65y 11m 25d
William B., s Robt. S. & Ann, d 7-16-1833 ae 30y bHS; dis 1-1832 (H)
Willis A. (nm) m Frances J. ALLIS, dt Caleb & Letitia, d 7-1920; Frances rocf Scip. with parents 1868; ct Chicago 3-1877; cf Chicago for Frances 9-1887

BARNETT
----- m Mary MURRAY, N. Y.; mo by priest before 5-2-1771

BARNEY
Albert C. d New Bedford 1840 (H); cf New Bedford, minor; ct WD MM 3-3-1830 (clear) (O)
Ann Eliza d 3-21-1828
Avis M., dt Wm. H. & Mary N.; m 1857 David N. WALKER
Benjamin (nm) b R. I. d 12-11-1834 ae 77y 6m bHS (unm)
Caroline, dt Wm. H. & Mary N., b 9-23-1847; ct Oswego 4-6-1859 (H)
Charles d New Orleans with yellow fever, 10-18-1841; m Avis ----- d 11-26-1859 ae 70y 6m
Ch: Charles Gorham
William Henry
Josiah Macy
Eliza Ann b 3-20-1827 d 3-24-1827
cf Nantucket ND 6-28-1826 with 3 ch named

BARNEY, Charles & Avis M., continued
parents dis 1830,1831; ch dis 1838,1839
Charles Gorham, s Charles & Avis rocf Nantucket with parents 6-2-1826; dis 3-5-1851 (H)
Eliza Ann, dt Charles & Avis, b 3-20-1827 d 9-11-1862; m 4-29-1857, Lewis EDWARDS; cf Nantucket 1-1857 (H)
Josiah Macy, s Charles & Avis, rocf Nantucket with parents 6-28-1826; dis mo 3-1846 (H)
Lydia d 9-19-1857 ae 91y 11m bPP; at Nantucket 11-3-1847 (H)
Susan Rebecca rocf Nantucket 5-1841; dis 9-7-1853 (H)
William H., s Charles & Avis, d at Mobile, 6-22-1865; m N. Y. 9-13-1837, Mary N. CORLIES dt Benjamin & Phebe, N. Y., d 7-30-1852 (or 8-30-1852 ae 33y 6m 22d
Ch: Avis M. b 7- 6-1838
Frances Augusta b 9-14-1840
Charles " 6- 6-1842 d 1-21-1843
William Henry " 8-24-1844
Caroline " 9-23-1847
Mary Powell " 8-26-1849
cf Nantucket 9-1826; ct Oswego for 4 ch 4-6-1859 (H)

BARNUM
Ida M., w David L., dt Ezekiel & Phebe C. MILLER (m 10-14-1899), b 4-2-1864 at Bkn. (H)

BARRA
James J. (nm), s Gesto & Filipino; m 4-26-1927, Gertrude HAYES, wd Sharpless BAKER, dt Henry N. & Marietta Hayes, b Unionville, Pa., 10-11-1876; Gertrude recrq 8-14-1909

BARRETT
Agnes Roberta, dt James C. & Mary J., N. Y.; m 1901 Frederick J. ALLEN; Agnes recrq 2-6-1901
Edward (nm) & -----
Ch: Eleanor F. b Dutch. Co. d 12-31-1847 ae 2y bHS
Fannie Ray, dt Lucy E., b Beverly, Mass. 1878 d Liberty, N. Y. 4-4-1907 bPP; m George F. EGBERT; Fannie recrq 5-5-1897
George, s Wyman R. & Phebe M., d 1893; cf Queensbury 7-1864 with parents; information of d rec from John H. Kemp, Central City, Colo. 11-22-1897
Isaac, s Wyman R. & Phebe M., rocf Queensbury with parents 7-1864; name erased 11-1886
James m Mary J. CROSBY, dt Robert & Ann (Root), b Dumfries, Scot. 6-19-1843 d 5-3-1909 bPP
Jeannette, dt James & Mary J., b Hoboken, N. J. 6-6-1878 d 12-2-1900 ae 22y 5m 6d; recrq 11-3-1897
Mary Jane recrq 2-6-1901
Wyman R. & Phebe M.
Ch: George
Isaac
cf Queensbury 7-1864 with 2 ch; ct Farm. 6-1880 for parents
----- m Bessie M. BECK, dt James T. & Lucy B.; Bessie recrq 5-5-1897; Bessie M. m 2d Camille DE VEZE

BARRINGTON
Benjamin d 3-20-1903; m Kate ----- d 10-12-1901
Ch: Sarah recrq 2-1875
Jane (or Jennie)
Benjamin d 10-23-1903
Robert Walker
William Thomas
Charles Burdick d 5-21-1875
Parents recrq 5-1874; ch recrq of parents 2-1875
Robert Walker, s Benjamin & Kate, recrq of parents 2-3-1875; relrq to join Mad. Square Presby. Ch. 6-3-1896
Sarah, dt Benjamin & Kate, d 2-27-1931; recrq of parents 2-3-1875; rel

BARRON
Edward F. (nm) m Margaret UNDERHILL
Ch: Elizabeth E. b 12-13-1919
Margaret recrq 6-2-1919
Elizabeth recrq of mother 2-1922; Elizabeth's name erased 5-1-1935 as Elizabeth Underhill Barron

BARROW
Edmund Prior, s John, Jr. & Elizabeth, b 11-22-1828; ct Scipio 6-1840
Elenor H., w Henry, b N. Y. d 2-13-1830 ae 31y
Elizabeth, dt John, Jr. & Elizabeth, b 3-11-1830, ct Scipio 6-1840
Elizabeth M., w Henry, cf Wby 10-1844; d 12-28-1885
Henry (nm), s Henry H. & Eleanor P. (dec) N.Y.; m at Caroline K. Jenkins' 1-15-1856, Mary K. JENKINS, dt Thomas W. (dec) & Caroline K., N. Y. (mo) (H)
Ch: Eleanor P.
Caroline J.
Elizabeth K.
Anna J.
ch recrq of mother 4-1872; ct Chap. 3-5-1873 for Mary & ch
Henry H., s John & Rebecca, b 8-12-1802 d 4-6-1863 ae 60y bPP; m Eleanor BARROW, b N. Y. d 2-13-1830 ae 31y bPP; dis mo to his first cousin 11-1828 (H); dis mo to his first cousin 4-1829 (O)
John, s John & Abigail (dec), Lancaster, Eng., b Eng. d 12-30-1838 ae 71y 11m 5d bPP, Merchant, N. Y.; m Shrewsbury 12-9-1790, Mary LAWRENCE, dt Richard & Alice, Shrewsbury, d 12-6-1798 bHS
Ch: Abigail b 3-29-1792 d 2-1-1832 bPP
Mary " 4- 6-1795
John " 4-22-1796
Lawrence " 10-19-1797
John m 2nd Rebecca HAYDOCK, dt Henry & Hannah

BARROW, John & Rebecca, continued
N. Y., b 12-14-1766, N. Y. d 1-30-1825
(m N. Y. 9-9-1801)
Ch: Henry H. b 8-12-1802 d 4-6-1863 bPF
Elizabeth b 11- 7-1805 d 12- 8-1825
cf Lancaster, Eng., 4-28-1784 (clear); ct Lancaster, Eng., 3-1-1787 (clear); cf Lancaster, Eng., 2-4-1788 (clear); cf Shrewsbury 1-3-1791 for Elizabeth
John, Jr., s John & Mary, b 4-22-1796 d 2-2-1874 (H); m Wby 11-22-1821 Elizabeth MOODE
Ch: Infant stillborn 9-19-1823
John D. b 9-24-1824
Rebecca H. b 12- 6-1826
Edmund Prior b 11-22-1828
Elizabeth b 3- 1-1830
William b 8-23-1832
Charles Henry b 11-26-1834
Thomas b 1-17-1836
George b 3-14-1839
Edward b 8-25-1841 at Skaneateles
Mary L. b 9-25-1846
cert of clear to Wby 11-7-1821; Elizabeth rocf Wby 6-19-1822; ct Scipio 6-1840 for Elizabeth
John Dodgson, s John Jr. & Elizabeth, b 9-24-1824; ct Lancaster, Eng. 8-3-1842, minor
Lawrence, s John & Mary, b 10-19-1797 d 5-29-1875; m Mary WING; cf Oblong 7-1837 for Mary; ct N. P. for both 1-1850 (H)
Mary, dt John & Mary; m 1819 Robert I. WALKER
Robert a mbr 1697

BARRY
William, s John & Rebecca (Demarest) (nm); m Esther ----- d 3-4-1880 ae 55y bPP (H)
Ch: William (nm)
(probably) Mary Esther d 10-25-1853 ae 5m 5d bPP
William recrq 8-1854; Esther recrq 5-1868
William, s John (dec) & Rebecca, N. Y., b N.Y. 10-19-1826 d 1-10-1906; m 2nd at William Barry's 7-6-1881, Phila A. BATTEY, dt Jesse B. & Esther (Bure), Manchester, N.J., b 1-11-1846 Blackstone, Mass. d 1917; Phila recrq 5-7-1884 (H)

BARTLETT
Elizabeth Louisa, w Edward, dt Josh. W. & Sarah BROWN, b 11-16-1844 d 9-4-1887 ae 42y bPP
Ch: Edith Louisa b 1-22-1869 d 8-23-1896
Ernest Russell b 6-20-1871 d 4-15-1901
cf Scip. with mother 6-4-1845; ch names entered by comm. 1873 (H)
John & Sarah
Ch: John Kemp b 5-5-1832
Sarah Elizabeth b 2-11-1836 d 3-12-1839
cf Third Haven 1-1829 for John; cf Third Haven 5-1832 for Sarah; ct Third Haven 7-1843 with ch (H)
Phebe M. rocf Pur. 10-1845; dis 12-5-1860 for jas (H)
Susan M., w William, rocf Third Haven 1832; ct Third Haven 8-1843 (H)
Thomas & Phebe M. (m at Pur)
Ch: Mary Elizabeth b 12-14-1845 d 3-14-1846
cf Third Haven 12-12-1833; dis 4-4-1849; Phebe M. rocf Pur. 10-1845; dis 12-5-1860; cf Wilmington 11-30-1833, minor (O); dis 12-1840 (O)
----- m Lizzie Louisa BROWN, dt Joshua W. & Sarah F., d 9-4-1887 ae 42y bPP (H)

BARTON
Anna, dt Richard, d 12-30-1900 ae 60y 5m 13d m ----- CROMWELL (nm) (H)
Anna Irene, dt Jessie & Anna M.; m ----- SPARKS; recrq 4-4-1906
Eleanor visited at rq of Corn.; dis jas 8-3-1859
James gct Corn. 1-1837 (H); recrq 9-7-1820; ct Pur. MM in Westchester Co. 10-1-1823 (clear); cert returned 1824; dis 7-1830 (O)
Jesse d 1-23-1929; m Anna (or Annie) M. ----- d 12-22-1928
Ch: Jessie Emma
Anna Irene
Jesse recrq 4-3-1895; Annie M. rocf Marl. 12-1888; first ch recrq of parents 12-2-1903 & full mbr 3-2-1904; Anna I. recrq 4-4-1906
Jessie Emma, dt Jesse & Anna M.; m 1915 Charles Walter PRATT; recrq of parents 12-2-1903; ct First Baptist Ch., Ossining for both 7-10-1929; ch still mbr N. Y.
Dr. Joshua L., s Daniel & Mary, b E. Farnham, Quebec 10-15-1849 d 9-10-1926 at Glens Falls Hospital bPP; m Pur. 8-17-1882 Maria COLLINS, dt Richard S. & Sarah (Willets), b N. Y. 11-19-1858; Maria gct Pur. with parents 8-1860; cf Yorktown 5-1885 for Joshua; cf Pur. 11-1885 for Maria
Lucy (nm), dt John (nm) & Eliz. (Fowler) (nm); m 7-16-1916 Howard CHAPMAN, b Glendale, O. 1-11-1875 (H)
Maria rocf N. P. 4-1845; ct Alexandria 11-4-1846 (H)
Mary, wd, b Staten Island d 10-25-1826 ae 54y bHS
Phebe Jane, dt Reuben & Phebe G. BIRDSALL, dis 2-1843 (H)

BASMAJIAN
Sarkis T., s David (dec) & Mary, Jersey City; m N. Y. 1-10-1887, at Sarkis', Vargin M. KAPHAELIAN, of Melkisetek Arden, Jersey City; cf Constantinople, Turkey 11-1884 as Kuirkjian & so recorded, but transferred correctly; Armenians; Sarkis T. m 2d at Sarkis Basmajian's, N. Y., 3-15-1890, Gadar SARAFIAN, dt George & Solomon

BASMAJIAN, Sarkis T. & Gadar, continued
both dec; Sarkis rel 9-9-1931

BASSETT
----- & -----
Ch: William W. d 7-14-1873 ae 3m 2d bPP

BATES (see Betts)
Charles E. (nm) & ----
Ch: Alice E. d 12-23-1864 ae 1y 8m 23d bPP
Charles E. d 11-8-1861 ae 28y 11m bPP (H)
Elizabeth, dt Joseph & Susan R. EVERNGHIM, b 11-8-1816; dis mo 5-3-1837 (O); dis mo 3-1837 (H)
Isaac having mo Creek refers it to N. Y., 3-19-1847; dis 12-1847; Creek notified
John Stebbins (nm), s Geo. Anson & Myra A.; m 9-28-1890, Jeannette PETTIT, dt John & Mary Frances, b Hempstead 11-14-1863; Jeannette recrq 4-14-1924
Joseph, Oblong MM informs 6-6-1781 he rem without consent of mtg & since transgressed good order; comm rpd mo 7-5-1781; ack. accepted 12-4-1782 & forwarded to Oblong; letter to Oblong re temporary affairs 6-9-1784

BATTELLE
Catharine B., dt Lindley & Eliza MURRAY; dis 3-1-1843

BATTEY
Anna K., dt Jonathan & Anna; m ----- NEWBURY; relrq 9-2-1898; attends Bapt. Ch. with h
Jesse d 6-25-1886; cf Roch. 7-5-1865
Jonathan d 1-20-1875 ae 62y bPP; m Anna G. -----, b Keesville, N. Y. d 2-10-1893 bPP
Ch: Mary K. b 4-24-1848 d 12-26-1927 bPP (unm)
Elizabeth K. d 8-25-1866 ae 15y bPP
Lydia K.
Anna K.
Lois C.
William J.
Ruth H.
cf Peru 10-1864 for all
Lydia K., dt Jonathan & Anna; m Dr. Charles H. REYNOLDS; ct Marl. 5-3-1905 for Lydia K. Reynolds
Lois C. (changed name to Caroline L.), dt Jonathan & Anna; m William C. TABER; cf Peru with parents 10-1864
Phila A., dt Jesse & Esther, Manchester, N. J.; m 1881 Wm. BARRY
Ruth H., dt Jonathan & Anna, b Bkn. 3-31-1862 d 1-12-1921 bPP; m Charles L. JOHNSTON, M.D.
William A. & Rhoda B.
Ch: Ruth Osborn b 4-26-1903
Janet " 12- 4-1906
William A. Jr. b ------1911
cf Providence 2-7-1900 for William; cf Marl. 4-2-1902 for Rhoda; ct Haverford 12-27-1917 for all; ch associate 1903,1906,1911
William J., s Jonathan & Anna, rocf Peru with parents 10-1864; relrq 8-4-1885

BAUER
Albert b Bkn. 5-15-1891; recrq 5-8-1917; name erased 10-1928

BAUWIS
Deborah, dt Geo. & Sarah FERGUSON, d 1-16-1908 ae 94y bPP

BAXLEY
Ellen, dt Ellwood & Sarah P. COOPER (m 12-4-1907); in Monticello, Calif. 1912

BAXTER
Philip & -----
Ch: Maria d 6- 8-1814 ae 6m 7d bHS (nm)
Philip Arestus d 11-9-1818 ae 1y 4m bHS (nm)
Robert d 9- 3-1820 ae 1y 6m 20d bHS (nm)
dis mo to his half sister's dt 7-3-1811

BAYLIS
Charles W., s Isaac W. & Celia M. (Remson) (nm), b Queens Co. 8-1-1864; m 11-2-1887, Elma C. WILLETS, dt Wm. U. & Clara (Hitt), b N. Y. 4-2-1866
Ch: Elma Willets b 8- 5-1889
Clifford W. d 2-17-1891 ae 7m 12d bPP
Clara Remsen " 9-11-1894
Charles William b 3-31-1897
Elma C., name entered by comm. 1-10-1879;
Elma W. name entered by comm. 3-26-1890;
other ch recrq of parents; Charles recrq 8-8-1903
Charles Wm., s Chas. W. & Elma C., b N. Y., 3-31-1897; m 12-29-1917 Helen KELLY; separated from w
Clara Remson, s Chas. W. & Elma C., b N. Y., 9-11-1894; m 7-16-1921, Henry Walker PRINDLE, s Wm. Porter & Mary W. (H)
Daniel (nm) b Oyster Bay d 2-9-1825 ae 73y bHS
Daniel S. & -----
Ch: Franklin d 9-9-1837 ae 11m 19d bHS
Infant stillborn 1-25-1830
dis 5-1829(H)
Elma Willets, dt Chas. W. & Elma C., b N. Y. 8-5-1889; m 4-27-1909, Sylvester Davis TUTHILL; recrq of parents 3-26-1890 (H)
Maria, dt Rosannah, d 6-1-1848; dis 4-6-1831 as Hicksite
Rosannah [Baylies], wd -----
Ch: Maria b N. Y. d 6-1-1848 ae 51y
Rosanna mo to James DODGE before 8-7-1813; con mo 12-1-1813; Maria recrq of mother
----- & -----
Ch: Elsie E. d 2-4-1873 ae 74y bPP

BEACH
Barbara (nm), dt Minta P.; m 6-20-1925 Lewis Griscom BENNETT
John Henry & Louisa Annie
both recrq 2-5-1890; both named erased 3-

BEACH, John Henry & Louisa Annie, continued
1928

BEAGLE
Mordecai, s William, d 4-28-1804 ae 57y bHS
Mordecai d 6-10-1800 bHS

BEAK
----- & -----
Ch: Alfred Latcham d 8-18-1831 ae 8y 8m bHS

BEALE
Abigail N., s Joseph H. & Mary, b 5-27-1824; relrq 1-6-1900
Joseph Hoare, s Caleb & Margaret, of Cork (both dec); m Manhattanville 9-9-1819, Mary NICHOLSON, dt Joseph & Abigail, of Belfast (both dec)
Ch: Caleb b 9-9-1821 d 3-5-1827
Abigail Nicholson b 5-27-1824
Margaret b 2-22-1826
Caleb b 10-30-1828
Elizabeth N. b 2-20-1831 d 6-10-1898
Limerick MM, Ire. rq care 5-7-1817; rpd favorably 6-14-1817; he established in business here; cf Limerick 1-13-1818; all dis 1830-1849 (0) ct Pur (not found); cf Pur. 3-1853 for Mary & 3 dt (H)
Margaret, dt Jos. H. & Mary N., b 2-22-1826 d 1-25-1897; m Alexander DAVIS; cf Pur. with mother 3-1853; ret a mbr (H)
William Henry rocf Cork, Ire., 2-1872; ct China, Me., 12-7-1874

BEAMAN
Ebenezer dis mo 12-1-1784
Hannah con mo 1-4-1762

BEASLEY
Dr. Crawford D. (nm), s Lester W. & Eliz. (both nm), d 3-13-1924 ae 66y; m 4-23-1890, Almira ANGEVINE, dt Frank & Bethia, b Bkn. 2-1-1866; Almira's name entered by comm. 11-27-1878

BEAT
John, Jr. recrq 3-1884

BEATTIE
Eunice (nm), dt James W. & Gertrude; m 1917 Herbert H. FINK; Herbert recrq 6-12-1915

BECK
Bessie M., dt James T. & Lucy E.; m ----- BARRETT; m 2nd Camille DE VEZE (rpd 1931); recrq 5-5-1897
James T., s James S. & Mary (Thomas), b Phila. 10-15-1858 d 4-6-1920 bPP; m Lucy E. ----- d 3-6-1931 ae 73y
Ch: Bessie M.
James recrq 4-5-1893; Lucy recrq 5-3-1893
Bessie recrq 5-5-1897
Walter S. (nm) m 9-8-1934 Helen D. Mc AFEE, adopted dt Jas. R. & Effie D., b N. Y. 5-19-1910; Helen recrq of foster parents 2-10-1917
Wally (nm), s Adam & Marie (Voxarx); m 1918 Austin Allen SCOTT

BECKER
Amelia Louise, s William & Fredericks (Whormann), d 10-10-1928 ae 78y; m John F. R. TROEGER (both nm, bPP)

BECKET
Mary m 1691 Samuel BOWNE

BECKWITH
----- m Abbie L. HUBBARD, dt Sylvester & Mary Ann, b 4-18-1880 ae 30y 2m 25d bPP

BEDELL
Caleb C. (nm) d 5-2-1890 ae 69y 1m bPP; m Martha R. ----- d 3-30-1875 ae 44y bPP
Ch: Clarence L. d 7-29-1879 ae 19y bPP
Howard R. " 5- 5-1880 ae 23y 2m 10d bPP (H) (all nm)
Ella May, dt Caleb C. & Martha, d 9-14-1923 ae 54y 8m 1d bPP; m Harry M. PARTRIDGE (both nm) (H)
Jennie Rhoda, dt Otis T. & Jane, recrq of parents 4-1869; relrq 1-1888
Jotham (nm) b L. I. d 7-23-1813 ae 26y bHS (unm)
Martha, dt Lewis & ----- RAYMOND, d 3-30-1875; cf Hudson 2-2-1859
Otis T. & Jane
Ch: Jennie Rhoda
cf Coey. 11-1864 for Otis; Jane recrq 4-1869; Rhoda recrq of parents 4-1869; Otis relrq 9-5-1877; Jane & Jennie relrq 1-1888
----- (nm) b Chap. d 12-28-1809 ae 2y 4m bHS

BELCHER
Edward B. (nm), s Edw. H. K. (nm) & Margaret (nm); m 10-18-1876, Rebecca T. BARKER, dt Wm. C. & Beulah T., b Bkn. 1-13-1855 d 3-21 (or 20) 1833 ae 79y bPP
Ch: Edward H. (nm) d 4-14-1823 ae 48y 7m 27d

BELDEN
Abigail, w Horace (form Sutton), b N. Y. d 4-4-1831 ae 40y; dis mo 2-3-1813; listed as a mbr in 1840, so perhaps rst (bHS)
Henry F. & Phebe
cf Corn. 12-26-1816 for both
Sarah m Hezekiah FITCH
Thomas W. (nm) b N. Y. d 1-28-1839 ae 27y 26d bHS (unm)

BELING
Aelian Arnold (nm) s Wm. Wright & Maria (Prince) m 2-11-1911 Mabel Asche JACKSON, dt Rev. C. L. & Martha (Pogue) (nm), b 12-23-1891 at Albany
Ch: John Kingsman
Mabel recrq 7-12-1926; John K. recrq 6-13-1932 (H)

BELING, continued
John Kingsman, s Aelian A. & Mabel A. J., recrq 6-13-1932

BELKNAP
Jessie, dt Augusta Julia, d 3-26-1930 ae 66y bPP; m John W. HUTCHISON (both nm)

BELL
Abraham & Mary
Ch: Eliza Greer b 6-22-1817
Mary " 9----1819
Abraham d 3-2-1856; m Mary C. CHRISTY, b Ireland d 9-17-1832 ae 47y
Ch: Elizabeth d 1818
Rebecca Harvey
Thomas Christy
James Christy
Infant stillborn 4-1-1823
Mary Christy b 10- 2-1819 d 11-24-1909
Ann Eliza d 3- 8-1891 ae 66y 11m 4d
Abraham Jr. b 10-20-1826 d 11-8-1831
William
cf Sadsbury, Pa. 2-20-1799; cert of clear to Ireland 3-4-1812; cf Lurgan, Ireland 5-18-1816 for Mary & 2 ch, Rebecca & Thomas
Arthur Hallock Bell rocf Marl. 11-1920; ct Marl. 5-1922
David gct Roch. 1-4-1826, apprentice
Elizabeth, dt Jacob & Mary, b 1803; ct Farm. 5-7-1823 (clear)
Francis Hilliard, ch Winslow M. & Bessie, rocf Marl. with parents 6-9-1897; jas; name rem 2-3-1904
Francis I. rocf Abington 2-1863; ct Frankford 6-1876
Frederick D. d 7-19-1931 m -----
Ch: Gilbert Easten
cf Frankford 2-5-1906; Gilbert recrq of parents 6-1921; Gilbert active mbr 5-1925
Hannah Christy Jr. rocf Lisburn 7-13-1843; ct Cincinnati 2-4-1846 (clear)
Henry Hilary & -----
Ch: Henry Hilary Jr.
George Thomas d 8-29-1868 ae 15y bPP
Winslow Manly
Arthur Ernest
cf Lisburn, Ireland 9-1868; ct Marl. 11-1882 with Winslow & Arthur
Henry Hilary, Jr., s Henry Hilary; m Elizabeth M. JOHNSON, dt William; cf Lisburn with father 9-1868; Elizabeth recrq of father 9-1867; Elizabeth relrq 1-1880; Henry relrq 1-1880
Herbert Hallock rocf Marl. 11-1920; ct Marl. 5-1922
Jacob & Mary
Ch: Charles, 17, d 4-29-1820 (or 4-29-1821) ae 18y 8m (b Liverpool)
Elizabeth, 15
David, 11
Jacob Dun, 7
John, 5
cf Hardshaw West 10-15-1818 with 5 ch named Mary dis 5-2-1821; ct Hardshaw West 4-3-1822 for Jacob & 2 s, Jacob & John
Jacob Harvey, s James C. & Harriet, b 10-11-1853; m 11-9-1882, Elizabeth COCK, dt Wm. & Mary E., Flushing; ct Pur. 1-13-1917 for Jacob (H)
James Christy, s Abraham & Mary C., d 5-19-1897; m 1845, Harriet THOMAS, dt Philip E. & Elizabeth (George), b Balto. 10-25-1820 d 11-12-1903
Ch: Philip Thomas b 2-28-1846 d 5-24-1914
John Wetherhead b 2- 8-1848 d 2-21-1919
James C., Jr. " 1-11-1850
Elizabeth " 8-22-1851
Jacob Harvey " 10-11-1853
cf Lurgan, Ireland 2-9-1837; dis 10-1840 (O); cf Balto. 1-1847 for Harriet T. (H)
James C., Jr., s James C. & Harriet, b 1-11-1850 d 12-31-1923; m Eliza DENNIS
Jemima rocf Corn. 8-27-1818 (clear); dis 9-7-1820 for neglecting mtg
John, s Wm. (dec) & Hannah C., Richmond, Ind., Santa Clara, Calif.; m N. Y. 6-5-1883, Hannah Booth COOPER, dt David S. & Eliza Ann BOOTH, Chester Co., Orange, N. Y.; ct San Jose 12-1883 for Hannah & her 2 ch; she m 1st John Lister Cooper
Margaret R., dt Jos. D. & Susan Evernghim, dis 10-1833 (H); dis 1-1832 (O)
Mary Lewin, dt Wm. & Nannie T., b 3-11-1855; m 6-19-1878 Charles Sexton LINDSAY (nm)
Nannie, dt Wm. & Ann (Thomas), b 6-10-1861; m 6-3-1885, Alex N. Spencer LE DUC (nm)(H)
Rebecca H., s Abraham & Mary C., N. Y.; m 1845 Saunders COATES, of Mobile (H)
Samuel rocf Cork, but as he lives in Phila., cert forwarded there 3-2-1831
Thomas Christy, s Abraham & Mary, d Yonkers, 9-12-1864; ct Flushing 11-1840 (H)
William & Hannah
Ch: Charlotte Wakefield
John
Isabella Wakefield
Wilhelmina
William Edmund
cf Lisburn, Ireland, 7-13-1843 with 5 ch named; ct Cincinnati 2-4-1846 with same ch, rem with h
William, s Abraham & Mary C.; m Balto. 12-5-1853 Nannie I. THOMAS, dt Wm. G. & Mary Lewin (Wethered), b Balto. 11-7-1835 d 12-19-1904
Ch: Mary Lewin b 3-11-1855
Rebecca " 8-20-1858 d 3- 3-1866
Nannie " 6-10-1861
Elizabeth " 4-13-1864 d 8- 3-1863
Tacey " 10-23-1871 " 7-13-1872
cf Lurgan, Ireland, 2-16-1805 (clear); ct Lurgan, Ireland, 7-1-1807 (not recorded); cf Lurgan, Ireland (not found); cf Balto. 11-1855 for Ann T. & Mary L. (Ann changed to Nannie at her rq; changed back to Ann 1900) (H)

BELL, continued
William, s Abraham & Melina R., Bayside; m at 15th St. 9-5-1905, Ella E. HOLLEY, dt Samuel P. & Ann Eliza (dec), Bkn., b Bkn. 11-17-1886; Ella recrq 4-8-1905; Ella gct Flush. 1-13-1906
Wm. Brown, s Thomas A. & Eliz. D., Winnipeg, Manitoba; m N. Y. 11-7-1903, Susan Kite ALSOP, dt Samuel Jr. (dec) & Esther; Susan gct Winnepeg
William Haydock rocf Lurgan, Ire., 3-1870; ct Queensbury 5-7-1873
Winslow m Bessie HILLIARD
Ch: Francis Hilliard
Winslow M. Jr.
Josephine Mary A.
Bessie Margaret
Olivia Horner
Henry Hilary
cf Marl. 6-9-1897 for all; parents rel by letter to Congregation Ch, Poughkeepsie 12-4-1901, including all ch except Francis H.
----- & -----
Ch: Deborah R. b N. Y. d 7-10-1825 ae 1y 6m bHS
Hannah d 5-4-1861 ae 84y bPP

BELSON
Frederick recrq 5-1863; d 1-25-1816

BENEDICT
----- (nm) m Sarah CROMWELL, wd Henry B., dt Wm. & Caroline H. SEAMAN, d 12-30-1913 ae 77y bPP (H)

BENEZET
Sarah rocf Plainfield 12-18-1765; she had come from Middletown, Pa. with cert; con mo

BENNETT
Grace A. (nm), dt Benjamin & Emma T.; m 1892 Joshua T. HICKS (H)
Harry (nm) m 4-30-1913, Ida MEAD, dt George V. & Mary (Birdsall), b N. Y. 4-19-1879 d 6-19-1934 (H)
Lewis Griscom, s R. Grant & Eliza H., b Newtown, Pa. 11-27-1902; m 6-20-1925 Barbara BEACH (nm), dt Minta P. (H)
Reuben Grant, s Leander W. & Ruthanna (Allen), b Freeport, O. 12-5-1868; m 8-26-1899 Eliza HOLMES, dt Thomas D. & Sarah L. (Griscom), b Moorestown, N. J. 8-26-1870 (H)
Ch: Lewis Griscom b 11-27-1902
Ruth Allen " 8-25-1904 d 8-13-1907
Ann Elizabeth " 9- 6-1909
Roliff (nm) & Isabella (nm)
Ch: Delilah d 1-4-1864 ae 1y 3m 8d bPP

BENSON
John rocf Kendall, Eng., 4-7-1797 (clear); ct Oblong 4-3-1799 (clear); cert to Oblong 4-3-1799 ret, not rec, sent again 5 Mo 1802, rec by Oblong
----- m Clara TRACE; Clara recrq 4-2-1902

BENTLEY
Bernice m Vernon LEE; rocf Greensboro, N. C. 1-4-1933
John (nm) m Mary WING
Ch: Infant stillborn 9-8-1832 bHS
Mary dis mo 9-5-1832

BENWELL
Thomas Riggs, having mo before leaving Eng. without knowledge of Friends or near relatives; Devenshire House refers it to N. Y. 4-9-1851; rpd favorably 10-1851

BERGEN
Sarah, dt Jacob BOWNE; dis mo 7-4-1832

BERGER
Timothy (nm) & -----
Ch: Hester b N. Y. d 1-17-1830 ae 9d bHS

BERKINGOFF
David (nm), s Alex. & Esther Reine, b Nibelsk, Russia, 10-15-1896; m 1-28-1931 Helen FRANKFURT (nm), dt Myron & Secunda; recrq 11-10-1924

BERNARD
Abijah (nm) b Nantucket d 3-31-1811 ae 31y bHS (m)

BERRY
Nicholas (nm) m Sarah Ann -----, b N. Y. d 11-5-1833 ae 25y bHS
Ch: Elizabeth b N. Y. d 6-22-1833 ae 3m bHS
Sally Ann (form Lundy) d 1834; recrq 12-1818; dis 1833 (H); dis 2-4-1829 (O)

BERTINE
Elizabeth b Wert Co. d 3-21-1829 ae 49y 6m 27d bHS

BERTSCHE
Carl Victor, s Auguste & Mathilde, b Weilburg, Germany, 1-31-1881; m 6-2-1912 Bertha WOELFLER, dt Ludwig & Clara (Muchlenthal), b N. Y. 6-16-1888 (H)
Ch: Edwin Carl b 4-18-1915
Wm. Irving " 10-18-1918
Edithe Claire b 10- 1-1924
Parents recrq 5-9-1927; ch recrq of parents 5-9-1927

BESSONET
John mo before 9-2-1778; con mo 2-4-1779
John P. (nm) d 12-8-1841 ae 74y 5m 14d bHS (concussion of brain)

BETBLY
----- & -----
Ch: Lorenzo b N. Y. d 9-14-1838 ae 1y 7m bHS

BETTS (see Bates)
Deborah, dt Benjamin FIELD, Flushing; m 7-4-

BETTS, Deborah, continued
1759; dis 8-7-1760
Jane m 1699 Richard OSBURN
Jane con mo 11-4-1773
Joseph, s Richard, Newton, con mo 10 Mo 5, 1745
Richard, Newtown, & -----
Ch: Joseph
William
Sarah, Newtown, con mo 10-4-1769; ct Wby 9-1-1784 (clear); cf Wby 4-28-1786 (Clear)
Sarah Ann, w John, rocf Upper Springfield 7-6-1836; omitted from list 5-1880
Thomas, Newtown, b 6 Mo (Aug.) 14, 1689; m Susannah STEVENSON, b 5 Mo (July) 22, 1684 d 1 Mo (Mar) 21, 1723/4
Ch: Anne b 10 Mo (Dec) 14, 1714
Thomas " 9 Mo (Nov) 1, 1716
John " 7 Mo (Sep) 15, 1718
Stephen " 1 Mo (Mar) 26, 1720/21
Thomas " 12 Mo (Feb) 18, 1722/3
Susannah " 12 Mo (Feb) 18, 1722/3
William, s Richard (Newton), con mo 10 Mo 6, 1744
----- & -----, Newtown; m Sarah -----, b 3 Mo (May) 8, 1727
Ch: (probably) Jane b 8-21-1752
----- & -----
Ch: William d 6- 1-1836 ae 1y 3m bHS
Elizabeth d 8-21-1836 ae 1y 6m bHS

BICKENSTAFF
Hannah, Flushing, 2nd w John BOWNE (m 1680); brought rem cert, clear, from Tupton, Derbyshire, 1679

BICKLEY (or Bigley)
William d 9 Mo (Nov) 2, 1707;m Susannah ----- d 1 Mo (Mar) 1707; William, active mbr from 1696

BIDDLE
William C., s Wm. W. & Mary B. (Taggart), b Camden, 9-11-1877; cf Phila. 6-13-1908
----- & -----
Ch: Emily d 8-16-1834 ae 1y 5m bHS
Frances " 12-15-1841 ae 5y 1m 28d bHS

BIELE
Alma, dt Charles F. & Friedericke (Prediger), b N. Y. 8-12-1884; m 1907 Robert Edward LEBER; both recrq 12-12-1921

BIGLAND
Cert for Amos from Hardshaw West. offered 12-4-1861, but as he does not attend, cert returned to Eng.

BIGONEY
Eva P., dt Jos. Warley & Phebe W. (Galloney), b Bucks Co., Pa., 3-25-1854; recrq 5-7-1904

BILES
Elizabeth rocf Falls MM, Pa. with sister, Sarah, 5-1-1782; dis mo 3-5-1783
Sarah rocf Falls MM, Pa., with sister, Elizabeth, 5-1-1782; ct R & P 8-3-1786 (clear), rem to Novia Scotia, within your limits

BILLIN
Charles W., s George & Virginia T., b Bkn. 9-2-1863; m Gertrude HEES, (nm) dt Albert F. & Amelia; name entered by comm. 4-31-1873; relrq 4-11-1908(H)
Eugene P., s George & Virginia T. (Stratton), b Bkn. 4-30-1868; m 10-15-1897, Jesse MARTIN (nm), dt Wm. Logan & Mary (Leet); name entered by comm. 1873
George (nm) m Virginia STRATTAN, dt Enock Jr. & Amy (Thorn), b Phila. 3-20-1838 d 3-9-1914 (m 6-8-1859)
Ch: Ida R. b 7- 2-1860
Charles W. " 9- 2-1863
Eugene Percival b 4-30-1868
Virginia rocf Phila. with parents, 10-1848; ch's names entered by comm. 1873 (H)

BILLINGS
Charles W. (nm), s Stephen & Maria F.; m 1-27-1890 Mary B. WHITE b Shrews 12-1-1869, dt Robert B. & Susan B. P. (Cook); cf Shrews. 4-4-1894 (H)
Daniel, s James & Sarah, d 3-8-1875 ae 52y bPP; cf Oswego 7-14-1824 with parents (H); dis 1842 (0) [rah -----
James b New Rochelle d 1-14-1830 ae 54y; m Sa-
Ch: Catharine B. d 7- 1-1825 ae 6m 23d
Daniel dis 1842 (0)
Jeremiah " 1848 (0)
Bathsheba d 8-10-1833 ae 10y 9m
Sarah b 7-17-1826 d 6-19-1827
Sarah " 3-14-1828 " 5- 2-1829
Hester M. " 1-15-1830 " 1-17-1832
cf Oswego 7-14-1824 with 3ch; James dis 11-1829; Sarah dis 1-1832 (0)
Jeremiah, s James & Sarah, dis 8-1848 (H) dis 1848 (0)
John [Billins], s Daniel, rocf Pur. 2-9-1797, a lad placed with a Friend
John (or Billins) dis 1801; rst 10-7-1812 & ct Oswego
Mary B., w Charles W., dt Robt. B. & Susan B. P. WHITE (m 1-27-1890) (H)

BILLS [bPP
Alanson m Clarissa ----- d 7-4-1858 ae 55y 5m both recrq 1-1851 & 5-1851
David rocf R & P 1-15-1807, apprentice; ct Farm. 8-3-1808 (clear) with brother, Thomas
Thomas rocf R & P 7-15-1802, apprentice, with a Friend; ct Farm. 8-3-1808 (clear) with brother, David

BINFORD
Micajah M. & Susannah R.
rocf Whitewater 11-3-1897 for both; ct Whitewater 7-11-1900

BINGHAM
Emeline M. (form Smith) dis mo 7-1848

BINNS
Alfred Watson d 1916; rocf Hardshaw East. 12-3-1890
William rocf Southwark, Eng. 3-13-1832 (clear); dis mo 8-1839
----- & -----
Ch: Mary b England d 8- 4-1827 ae 1y 5m bHS

BIRD (see Byrd)
Betsy Ann, dt Matthew & Sarah, rocf Chap. with parents 5-12-1825; ct Chap. 1-6-1830 (clear)
Daisy I., dt Wm. & Frances Emma (Hyatt), b Chap. 10-14-1885; m James Mc COUBREY (nm)
Lucilla K., dt Wm. & Frances Emma, b Chap. 3-19-1888; cf Chap. 2-4-1925
Matthew & Sarah
Ch: Betsy Ann
Catharine G.
Marrietta
cf Chap. 5-12-1825 with 3 ch named; ct Chap. 4-4-1827 with 2 minor ch, Catharine G. & Marietta
Dr. Orphens Brainard (nm), s Henry L. & Eliza (Martin), b E. Smithfield, Pa. 2-11-1844; m 1-1-1889 Sarah M. WALKER, dt Charles & Sarah C. (Murphy), b Lahaska, Pa. 12-17-1846; cf Green St., Phila. 1-4-1902; ct Orange Grove, Pasadena 8-13-1910 (H)
Sarah M. rocf Phila. Green St., 1-4-1902 (H)

BIRDSALL (see Burdsall)
Abraham d 11-18-1855 ae 63y bPP; m Nancy ----- (nm) b L. I. d 9-29-1829 ae 38y bHS
Ch: Zadock M. d 1-10-1822 ae 1y 5m bHS
James " 10-16-1827 ae 11m bHS
cf Chap. 11-10-1809, minor; dis mo 6-1-1814
Abraham Y. rocf Marl. 9-1-1869; ct Marl. 10-1880
Albert rocf Marl. 1855; mo 1-1859, referred to Marl. for dealing & retained a mbr by Marl. 6-1859
Alvin T. d 8-1875; m Mattie C. -----
cf Whitewater 5-27-1874 for Alvin; cf Chester, Ind. 2-3-1875 for Mattie; ct Whitewater 4-1880 for Mattie
Amos (nm) b N. Y. d 6-22-1843 ae 44y bHS; m -----
Ch: Deborah d 2-11-1831 ae 3m bHS
Amy Anna, dt Jos. C. & Martha DODGE; cf Chap. 5-1850; dis mo 3-1860 (H)
Ann cf Amawalk 9-12-1845 (clear); ct Corn.
Ann C., dt James & Jerusha, rocf Pur. 7-9-1845, rem with parents; dis 3-1857
Anna W. b 1833 d 1-5-1901 bur 2-6-1901 bPP
Anna Wood, dt Thos. W. & Margaret, b 2-4-1852; relrq 3-3-1875
Arthur Wood, s Wm. Jr. & Caroline, b 12-11-1860; mbrp relinquished 3-1880
Dr. Ashahel H. d 8-8-1897; cf Marl. 6-1884
Avis, w Thomas, cf Wby & Jericho, 11-20-1830; dis 12-1831 (O)
Benjamin rocf Pur. 7-10-1844; dis 10-1852
Caroline, dt Samuel & Susan H., b 8-30-1840 d 1-4-1884; m 4-6-1861 William VONDERSMITH (H) (mo)
Caroline, dt Wm. Jr. & Caroline, b 11-20-1855; mbrp relinquished 3-1880
Charles mo before 1-1847; ret. mbrp; mo before 7-1854; ret mbrp; cf Amawalk 7-11-1845 (clear); ct Corn. 5-1867
Charles G. rocf Stanfordville 3-1916
Charles Thomas, s Geo. H. & Phebe, ct Sandwich, Mass. 4-1880
Charlotte Mary, dt Geo. H. Jr. & Eleanor C., b 12-30-1876; letter to Westfield M. E. Church, N. J., 11-1923 [bPP
Daniel Thornton, s Thornton, d 9-4-1897 ae 57y; m Frances E. LINES (nm), dt Oliver Todd Lines, b Chicago d 8-22-1933 ae 89y bPP
Ch: a son d 4-17-1888 ae 1y 2m bPP
cf Frankford 8-30-1853; mbrp relinquished 5-1880
David d 4-25-1850; m Mary -----
Ch: Sarah
Solomon dis 3-1839
Phebe
Moses T. d 12-8-1831
Zepheniah
cf Chap. 2-11-1830 with 4 ch named (O)
Edgar rocf Glens Falls 3-6-1901; ct Glens Falls 6-1917
Edward S. dis mo 8-1850 & Ama. notified
Elias G. rocf Marl. 4-22-1846 (clear)
Elias G. rocf Marl. 1846; dis (O)
Eliza Ann m David BOOTH; cf Marl. 3-25-1846 (clear); retained a mbr 11-1847
Elizabeth, wd Samuel, d 8-1831; recrq 6-5-1816
Elizabeth H., w Reuben L., dt Josiah & Catharine (Mailor) CORNELL, b Monroe 10-16-1835 (m 11-15-1855); cf Chap. 12-3-1879 (H)
Elizabeth, dt Jacob & Amy (Dodge), b Chap. 3-18-1837 d 3-4-1920; m 1854 John FOSTER (nm) (H)
Elizabeth M., dt Geo. H. & Phebe ; m ----- BLANVELT; m 2nd ----- LAWSON; ret a mbr 2-1853
Ellwood rocf Chesterfield 4-1842; ct Pur. 6-6-1849 (H)
Ernest Wood, s Wm. Jr. & Caroline, b 1-29-1852; mbrp relinquished 3-1880
Esther, dt Geo. H. & Phebe, b 9-15-1840; m Hiram RHODES
Evelyn Westervelt, dt Thos. H. & Sarah F., b 9-5-1873; name erased
Florence, dt Geo. H., Jr. & Eleanor C.; m 1903 Warren VALENTINE
Frances d 3-28-1852; cf R & P 10-1841; ct Pur. 1-1845; cf Pur. 1-1851 (H)
Frank Chase, s Geo. H. & Eleanor; m 1894 Lindley Hoag LEGGETT; recrq 7-1886
George Henry, s George, d 8-28-1839
George H. d 5-11-1871 ae 66y bPP; m Phebe ---- d 5-19-1893

BIRDSALL, George H. & Phebe, continued
Ch: Elizabeth M.
    Charles Thomas
    Sarah Jane b 11-21-1834
    Phebe Anna " 7-14-1837
    George Henry " 3-26-1839
    Esther " 9-15-1840
    George R.
    Thomas H. " 8-15-1848
    cf Ama. 5-9-1834 with 2 ch; ct Ama. 10-5-1842 with 5 ch; cf Corn. 9-23-1847 with 6 ch
George H. Jr., s Geo. H. & Phebe, b 3-26-1835 d 5-15-1907; m Eleanor C. ----- d 11-1923
Ch: Frank Chase
    Wm. Edward Walling b 12-10-1874
    Charlotte M. " 12-30-1876
    Florence Eleanor " 8-22-1880
    cf Corn. 9-23-1847 for George; Eleanor C. recrq 3-1872
Hannah C., dt Jonathan & Philena, b 11-18-1836; dis mo 12-1854 to ----- SAMPSON
Henry & Angeline A.
Ch: William J. b 5- 3-1834
    Elizabeth " 4-29-1836
    John P. " 8- 2-1838
    Adelia " 3-23-1840
    Henry C. "
    cf Ama. 10-1833 for parents; ct Ama. 10-1844 for all(H)
Henry Young m Louise BLAND
Ch: Robert Bland
    letter from James M. E. Ch., Bkn. 4-3-1901 for Henry; Louise recrq 5-1909; Robert recrq of parents 5-1909
Isaac, s Jonathan & Philena, b 2-17-1839; mo before 7-1864; ret a mbr; mbrp relinquished 8 Mo 3, 1880
Jacob & Amy
Ch: Henry
    Andrew
    Elizabeth T.
    cf Chap. 2-1857 with 2 ch named; ct Chap. 11-2-1864 with first 2 ch
Jacob (nm) & -----
Ch: Mary d 5- 1-1832 ae 1d bHS
James, s William & Mary D., b 4-29-1835; mo before 12-1860, ret. mbrp
Ch: Son d 8- 3-1864 ae 3m bPP
    dt " 9-20-1866 ae 1y 2m bPP
    relrq 6-1871
James d 10-18-1783 ae 88y bPP; m Jerusha ----- d 10-18-1883 ae 82y bPP
Ch: Levinia
    James L.
    Anna C.
    William Edwin
    Parents dis at rq of Pur. 3-1845; cf Pur. 7-9-1845 for ch
James F. & Avis C.
Ch: Phebe S. b 4- 7-1830
    Sarah Jane " 7-31-1833
    Avis S. " 8-24-1839
    cf Ama. 6-12-1829 (clear); dis 1-1831 (0)
    cf Jericho 1-1831 for Avis; ct Pur. for parents & 2 ch 6-1858
James L., s James & Jerusha, cf Pur. 7-9-1845 rem with (dis) parents; dis mo 3-1856
Jesse, s Jonathan & Sarah, Corn. (both dec); m N. Y. 5-5-1869 Emmeline COLLINS, dt John & Eliz. (both dec), N. Y.; ct Corn. 4-1872 for Emeline
John rocf Marl. 4-22-1846 (clear); ct Marl. 10-6-1847 (clear)
John (nm) & -----
Ch: Infant stillborn 8-4-1828
Jonathan d 4-19-1849; m Philena ----- d 6-23-1895 bPP
Ch: Anna d 2- 3-1901
    Jonathan M. b 1-27-1833
    Mary Jane " 11- 9-1834 d 9-25-1882
    Hannah C. " 11-18-1836
    Isaac " 2-17-1839
    William N. " 6-17-1841 d 9-26-1842
    Albert
    John Wm. d 9-21-1863
    James A. " 3-13-1874 ae 22y bPP
    Martha
    cf Chap. 2-11-1830 with inf dt named (0); cf Chap. 8-1829 (H)
Jonathan M., s Jonathan & Philena, b 1-27-1833; dis mo 1-6-1858
Joseph m Edna ALLEN, b Bkn. d 10-2-1829 ae 37y
Ch: Infant stillborn 5-13-1822
    Nehemiah d 3-21-1827
    Mary A. b 9-12-1829 d 9-10-1833
    Joseph mo before 8-1-1821, case discontinued 11-7-1821
Joseph m 2nd Ann -----
Ch: Benjamin
    Jane
    Infant stillborn 10-22-1834
    cf Chap. 12-1832 for Ann; ct Chap. 11-1836 for all
Lavinia, dt James & Jerusha; rocf Pur. 7-9-1845 rem with parents; dis 8-1849
Lois B., w Charles; rocf Marl. 11-1854; ct Corn. 12-1866; cf Corn. 2-1867; ct Corn. 5-1867
Louisa W., dt Thos. W. & Margaret, b 12-23-1849; relrq 2-2-1876
Lydia gct Scipio 8-1-1821 (clear)
Lydia (form Spague) dis mo 1-2-1833; cf Chap. 2-11-1830 (clear), rem with parents
Martha, dt Jonathan & Philena; m ----- WHITLEY
Martha W., dt Wm. & Martha, N. Y.; m 1848 Edward CROMWELL
Mary, wd Stephen, of Little Egg Harbor, N. J.; m 1724 David ALLEN, of Shrewsbury
Mary, dt Reuben & Sarah, b 6-23-1840 d 8-9-1816; m 6-23-1868 George V. MEAD, b 6-23-1868 (nm) (H)
Mary Ann rocf Chap. 2-11-1830 (clear); dis 11-1831 (0)
Mary B. rocf Creek 10-18-1833
Mary P., dt Jonathan & Mary, N. Y.; m ----- HEALEY; m 2nd 1838 Nathan CLARK

BIRDSALL, continued
Nathan mo before 5-4-1814, dis
Nathan D. rocf Marl. 1847; dis
Phebe, dt David & Mary; m Capt. ROBINSON; cf Chap. with parents 2-11-1830; rel 3-1880
Phebe Ann, dt George H. & Phebe, b 7-14-1837 d 1-21-1903; m William BURNETT (nm)
Phebe Jane, dt Reuben & Phebe G., b 12-24-1823; dis mo 2-1843 to ---- BARTON (H)
Phebe S., dt James F. & Avis C., b 4-7-1830; m 1852 Robert EMBREE
Rachel Y., dt William & Mary D., b 2-24-1834 d 12- 5-1862; m Henry Q. MACK
Reuben d 3-6-1851 ae 57y 9m 15d; m Phebe G. ----- b Wert Co. d 3-11-1833 ae 32y
Ch: Edmund L. b 4- 6-1817
Susan Ann " 8-15-1820
Phebe Jane " 12-24-1823
Caroline " 8- 1-1829 (or 7-1-1828)
Reuben Jr. " 2-15-1833 d 7- 7-1859 ae 25 bPP
cf Ama. 1-1829 with 3 ch; cf Ama. 3-13-1829 (O) with 3 ch; all dis 1830-1843 (O)
Reuben m 2nd Sarah BIRDSALL, dt Henry & Jerusha, d 8-20-1882 (m N. Y. 3-13-1839)
Ch: Mary S. b 6-23-1840
Reuben L. (nm), s Daniel L. (nm) & Abigail (nm); m 11-15-1855, Elizabeth H. CORNELL, dt Josiah & Catharine (Mailler), b Monroe N. Y. 10-16-1835 d 10-3-1918; cf Chap. 12-3-1879 (H)
Richard & Mercy
cf Marl. 6-25-1834 for both; ct Marl. 10-7-1835 for both
Richard d 9-12-1855; cf R & P 9-1843 (H)
Samuel, s Henry & Jerusha (dec) N. Y., d 5-28-1882 ae 83y bPP; m Susan Ann BIRDSALL, dt Reuben & Phebe G., d 4-5-1866 ae 45y (m 8-8-1838) (H)
Ch: George F. d 9-17-1864 ae 22y 7d
Infant stillborn 9-4-1846
Henry b 7- 8-1839 d 8- 7-1839
Caroline " 8-30-1840
George " 9-10-1842 " 9-17-1864
Susan " 11-27-1844 " 8-13-1864
Phebe " 8-14-1849 " 9- 6-1849
Sarah d 11-16-1803 ae 75y bHS
Sarah, dt Henry & Jerusha, N. Y.; m 1839 Reuben BIRDSALL (H)
Sarah Jane, dt Geo. H. & Phebe, b 11-21-1834; m ----- EVANS (nm); ret a mbr
Sarah S., dt Reuben & Sarah, b 6-23-1840; m 1868 George V. MEAD (H)
Dr. Stephen T. & S. Josephine
Ch: Mabel b 7- 5-1872
Edgar " 8-21-1876
Agnes " 9-19-1878
Lilian Eloise b 2-28-1884
cf Marl. 7-11-1877 for Stephen; cf Queensbury 10-1869 for S. Josephine; ct Glens Falls 1-1886 for all
Solomon, s David & Mary, dis mo 4-1839
Susan, dt Samuel & Susan Ann, b 11-27-1844 d 8-13-1864; m 5-31-1862 Edward FISHER (nm)(H)
Susan Ann, dt Reuben & Phebe G., N. Y.; m 1838 Samuel BIRDSALL (H)
Sylvia rocf Ama. 10-12-1816 (clear)
Thomas H., s Geo. H. & Phebe, b 8-15-1848; m Sarah Frances -----
Ch: Evelyn Westervelt b 9- 5-1873
Sarah recrq 7-1872; Thomas relrq 3-2-1898; Sarah F.'s name erased 2-7-1900
Thomas W., s Wm. & Martha (dec), N. Y., d 5-18-1866 ae 42y bPP; m N. Y. 12-13-1848 Margaret WOOD, dt John & Sarah M., b 8-20-1823 d 3-22-1912 bPP
Ch: Louisa W. b 12-23-1849
Anna Wood " 2- 4-1852
Elizabeth " 1- 9-1854 d 2-25-1856 bPP
Infant dt d 9-12-1866 ae 1y 6m bPP
Thomas W. relrq 7-1858
William d 7-30-1859 ae 61y 21d bPP; m 1819 Martha ----- d 9-24-1831 ae 37y 4m bHS
Ch: Lydia Ann b 11-15-1819 d 5-16-1861 bPP
William " 10-30-1822
Thomas W. " 5-21-1824
Infant stillborn 6-30-1826
Martha W. b 6- 2-1828
Infant stillborn 9-12-1831
cf Pur. 9-10-1813, minor; dis mo 6-2-1819; rst 7-4-1821; Martha recrq 1829; ch recrq of parents 2-1830
Wm. & ch gct Frankford 5-1-1850
William m 2nd 1833 Mary D. -----
Ch: Rachel Thornton b 2-24-1834
James " 4-29-1835
Elizabeth Y. " 6-25-1838
Daniel Thornton " 1-25-1840
Mary " 12-19-1846
cf Creek 1833 for Mary D.
William m 3rd Martha S. ----- d 7-30-1859
cf Frankford 8-30-1853; Martha S. rocf Frankford 1856; ct Frankford 11-7-1860 for Martha S.
William, Jr., s Wm. & Martha (dec), N. Y., b 10-30-1822 d 12-3-1873 bPP; m N. Y. 9-12-1849 Caroline WOOD, dt John & Sarah, N. Y., d 11-1920
Ch: John W. b 6-27-1850 d 3-17-1856 bPP
Ernest Wood " 1-29-1852
Sarah W. " 6- 9-1853 " 9-27-1854
Caroline " 11-20-1855
Arthur Wood " 12-11-1860
William relrq 1-1867
Wm. Edward Walling, s Geo. H. Jr. & Eleanor H., b 12-10-1874; m Clara E. -----
Ch: Joseph Edgar b 4- 3-1898
cf Indianapolis 4-6-1898; letter to Eliot Congregational Ch., Newton, Mass., 4-1914 for all
William Edwin, s James & Jerusha, rocf Pur. 7-9-1845, rem with parents; relrq 8-1869
Zephaniah, s Zadoc & Eliz. (dec); m N. Y. 1-9-1893 Mary B. WHITE, dt Amos & Ann, Bkn.
Ch: Cornelia b 4-25-1834
Charles

BIRDSALL, Zephaniah & Mary B., continued
cf Chap. 2-11-1830 (clear); Z. dis 3-1835 (0); ct Livonia, Mich. 1-1843 for all (H)
----- & -----
Ch: James b N. Y. d 1-6-1821 ae 5y 4m bHS
Martha " " " 1-11-1837 ae 4m bHS
Andrew bPP
Thomas H. d 11-17-1861 ae 1y 1m bPP
Phebe " about 1891 bPP

BIRKELL (or Birkill)
John rocf Oblong 4-16-1798; dis mo 2-6-1805

BIRKET
Benjamin rocf Kendal MM, Eng., 4-6-1781 (clear) having brought cf Phila. after serving apprenticeship there

BISHOP
Edward rocf Mt. Holley 10-6-1825; ct Burlington 8-4-1830 (clear)
H., s Sam'l Perkins & Eliz. (Hunter) (Hoge), b Cincinnati 4-30-1852 d 2-27-1925 bPP; m Arete C. ----; Arete C. recrq 4-8-1913; H. nm
Joseph rocf Pur. 7-12-1826 (clear); dis 1-1830 (0); dis 1-1840 (H)

BISPHAM
Joseph Mutton (nm), d 8-21-1832 ae 58y 5m bHS

BLACK
Edward (nm) & -----
Ch: Sarah b N. Y. d 6-22-1833 ae 2y 4m bHS
Job (nm) & -----
Ch: William b N. Y. d 6-17-1831 ae 1y 3m 26d bHS
Thomas (nm) b N. J. d 10-17-1838 ae 63y 7m bHS
----- & -----
Ch: Alfred d 11-19-1834 ae 1y 3m bHS
Samuel L. b N. Y. d 8-25-1836 ae 1y 4m 29d bHS
John Jr. " " " 7-20-1838 ae 1y 2m bHS

BLACKBURN
Isabelle, dt Alexander & Margaret S. (Hail), b Chicago 3-9-1874; m 1898 Samuel Archibald SMITH (H)
Philip Conklin, s Isaiah P. & Anna B. (Conklin), b Chicago 8-30-1907; cf Dunning Creek 5-11-1925 (H)

BLACKFORD
Martha C. rocf Cincinnati 1854; ct Cincinnati 7-1860

BLACKWELL
Charles G. d 3-11-1852 ae 3y 7m (gr s of H. Matlock) bPP
Elizabeth S. (form Matlack) gct Roch. 4-1842; rocf Balt. 6-1852; ct Balt. 9-3-1862 (H)

BLADES
Elizabeth, wd, b N. Y. d 12-21-1826 ae 25y bHS
Henry b L. I. d 11-18-1825 ae 30y bHS; recrq 9-6-1815; dis mo 1-6-1819

BLADY
----- & ----- (nm)
Ch: John b N. Y. d 11-27-1823 ae 11m 9d bHS

BLAIN
Joseph (nm) b Liverpool d 7-23-1824 ae 32y bHS (m)

BLAKEY
Joshua (nm) b Bucks Co., Pa. d 3-26-1827 ae 26y bHS (m)

BLANCHARD
Lenore (nm) m Philip Van Everen STOUGHTON
Mary H., dt Chas. Henry & Caroline C. (Yale), b Charleston in Boston 6-23-1860; m 1882 Louis F. WADE; recrq 7-14-1924
Mary R., w Wm., dt Wm. & Hannah RENOUF, of Troy, b 2-23-1810 d 3-31-1901 ae 92 (wd); cf Troy 8-4-1847 (H)

BLAND
Louise m Henry Y. BIRDSALL; recrq 5-1909

BLANVELT
Elizabeth M., dt Geo. H. & Phebe BIRDSALL; m 2nd ----- LAWSON

BLASDELL
James (nm) m Martha (nm) b Me. d 3-8-1840 ae 40y 2m bHS
Ch: Martha d 12-3-1840 ae 1y 3m 27d bHS
James H. Jr. d 12-14-1844 ae 18y 6m bHS (H)

BLATCHLEY
Bayard P. d 12-5-1878; cf Cincinnati 12-2-1868; recrq 5-3-1820; ct Cincinnati 2-7-1849 (H)
Cornelius Camden b N. J. d 12-5-1831 ae 58y 11m 3d; ct Falls MM, Pa., 8-13-1806 (clear); cf Chesterfield 1-7-1812; dis 5-1829 (0); attended & preached in a mtg held by dis mbr 3-1831; dis 6-1831 (H)
Ebenezer D. (nm) b Essex Co., N. J. d 5-17-1827 ae 41y bHS (unm)

BLOODGOOD
Elizabeth (nm) d 12-19-1809 ae 5m 22d bHS
Francis with w gct Pur. 4 Mo (June) 5, 1740
Joseph m Rebecca ----- b Marl. d 2-22-1812 ae 31y bHS
Ch: George d 11-22-1811 ae 1y 8m 3d bHS
Sarah " 2- 4-1812 ae 2m 2d bHS
cf Oswego 9-8-1811; ct Oswego 7-1-1812
Samuel d 11-7-1892, Flushing; m Sarah M. ----- d 1848; cf Plains 12-26-1848; Sarah d before cert rec
Sarah con mo 1 Mo 3, 1736

BLOOMER
Nellie recrq 4-3-1912

BLUNT
Edmund (nm) d 1-24-1894 ae 51y bPP; m Eugene BUNTING, dt Wm. & Phebe L., d 4-7-1916 ae 74y bPP (H)

BOARDMAN
Phebe b Little Nine Partners in Dutchess Co. d 10-23-1827 ae 40y bES (unm)

BOCKUS
Ann (nm) b L. I. d 11-28-1819 ae 31y bHS

BODEN
James S. (nm), s Edward (nm) & Martha (nm); m 1-30-1882 Phebe C. HAWXHURST, dt James C. & Julia E., b Jericho 1-5-1844 d 1908; Phebe rocf Jericho with parents 10-1857

BOERAEM (or Booraem - Borem)
Timothy rocf Wby 6-1827; dis 6-5-1833 for non-attend. (O); d 1833 (H)

BOGARDUS
James F., s Joseph A. & Eliz. F., b N. Y. 3-26-1896; ct Swarthmore 6-11-1923 (H)
Joseph A., s James & Elizabeth (Arnold), b 9-27-1851 d 4-22-1896 bPP; m Anna C. ---- d 7-18-1878
Joseph A. m 2nd Elizabeth F. FURNAS, dt Davis & Jane (Satterthwait), Miami, O., b Waynesville, O. 8-10-1855 d 8-24-1933 bPP (m 1-24-1884)
Ch: Infant stillborn 10-11-1884 bPP
Elizabeth b 10-18-1884 d 11-22-1888 bPP
Joseph Lannin b 3-24-1891 d 6-10-1891 bPP
James Furnas " 3-26-1896
cf Miami, O. for Elizabeth 6-4-1884; ct Swarthmore 6-11-1923; Joseph recrq 4-2-1873

BOGERT
Charlotte R., dt Rudolphus R. & Elsie (Comstock), b Bkn. 9-22-1880; m Antonio Elias Borges DOS SANTOS (nm) (m 4-28-1926) name entered by comm. 11-18-1884 (H)
Helen, dt Rudolphus R. & Elsie C., Bkn., b Bkn. 10-10-1876; m 1910 Samuel B. WILLIAMS; name entered by comm. 11-18-1884 (H)
Henry & Rachel [Bogart]
Ch: Peter Titus b 4- 9-1858
Amy Avis " 7-21-1860
Keturah Seaman " 10-13-1862
Martha S. " 2-24-1865 d 8-22-1868
Hannah Ella " 12-14-1867
George Henry " 12-30-1869
cf Corn. 3-5-1851 for Rachel; Henry recrq 10-1863 with Amy Avis; ct R & P 3-15-1873 for all (H)
Mary [Bogart], wd, b N. Y. d 4-10-1824 ae 85y bHS
Rachel [Bogart] rocf Corn. 3-5-1851; ct R & P 3-5-1873 (H)
Rudolphus Ritzema, s Rudolphus & Wealtty Jane, b 2-17-1842 d 1-23-1907 bPP; m at Nathan Comstock's 11-24-1875 Elsie COMSTOCK, dt Nathan & Charlotte H., Bkn., b Bkn. 11-24-1854 d 1-26-1932, ashes bPP
Ch: Helen b 10-10-1876
Charlotte R. b 9-22-1880
Rudolphus recrq 7-9-1904; ch names entered by comm. 11-18-1884 (H)

BOKER
Martha rocf Hardwick & Rahway 9-1821; ct Phila. 1833 (H)
----- & ----- (nm)
Ch: Caroline b N. Y. d (apparently) 12-24-1825 ae 4y bHS

BOLTON
Abel James rocf Phila. 3-26-1802 (clear), having lived in N. Y. several yr.; ct Gwynned 2-3-1819 (clear)
Mary d 7-30-1851; m Nathan MARSHALL; cf Concord with h & 2 ch 6-1829 (H)

BOND
Phebe J., dt Samuel & Jane YEATES, d 5-29-1894; was in Memphis, Tenn. 1871 (H)
Thomas (nm) & -----
Ch: Henry d 11-30-1830 ae 6m bHS

BONES
Mary B., w William, d 11-3-1886; cf Scipio 6-1854 (H)

BONNER (H)
Deborah rocf Chap. 11-1850; ct Chap. 10-7-1868
Maria (form Allen) rocf Dublin 11-15-1831 (clear); dis mo 6-1-1836

BOOCOCK
Mary C., dt Elias & Jane UNDERHILL, b 10-3-1843; relrq 5-5-1869 (H)

BOODY
Margery Hill (nm), dt Alvino & Anna L. (Weeks); m 1919 Stephen VALENTINE, Jr. (H)

BOOK
Henry having mo ND MM refers it to N. Y. 10-24-1837; rpd adversely; dis rec from Phila. 3-7-1838

BOOKER
Aaron (nm) & -----
Ch: Mary C. b Phila. d 11-9-1826 ae 22y bHS (unm)

BOOTH
Ann d 10-5-1903 ae 89y 2m bPP; m William MOTT (both nm) (H)
Eliza Ann, w David (form Birdsall) rocf Marl. 3-25-1846 (clear); ret a mbr 11-1847
Hannah, dt David S. & Eliza Ann, Chester, Orange Co., N. Y.; m John Lister COOPER; m 2nd 1883 John BELL; cf Corn; ct San Jose Calif. 12-1883 for her & her 2 ch

BOOTH, continued
J. Franklin rocf East Branch, Ind. 12-3-1902; name erased 1-2-1929
Ruth rocf Coey. 5-1852; ct Creek 7-5-1865 (H)

BORDEN
Benjamin rocf H & R 4-1846; ct Chester, Pa. 1-1849 (H)
Sarah [Bordals] rocf Burlington 3-5-1761
Walter Henry, s Wm. L. & Jane, Shrewsbury; m at Hannah Hance's, Bkn., 3-2-1876 Jane E. HANCE, dt Anselm B. & Ellen (both dec), Bkn. (Hannah Hance not under care of N. Y. MM); ct Shrewsbury for Jane E. (H)

BOREM
Timothy T. rocf Wby 3-14-1827; dis 6-1833

BORGESON
Oscar m Adele VAN INGER, dt William & Mary, d 10-12-1917 ae 42y bPP; both nm (H)

BOSTWICK
Catharine M., dt John & Mary T., rocf Plains with parents; ct Burlington 2-5-1840 with sister, minor
David S. rocf Plains 5-23-1837 (clear); dis 1-1840
George T. rocf Plains 5-23-1837 (clear); dis 3-7-1838
Isaiah T., s John & Mary, b 10-11-1807; rocf Plains 5-12-1832; ct Plains 1833; cf Plains 4-10-1837; dis 9-1843 for separation from fam
James M., s John & Mary F.; dis mo 5-1-1839
John d 3-12-1850; m Mary -----
Ch: Isaiah (or Josiah) b 10-11-1807
Elizabeth
George F.
David S.
James M. dis 5-1839
John, Jr. dis 10-1842
Lemuel " 4-1843
Martha Willis b 10-22-1824
Maryanna F. " 10- 3-1826
William F. d 1846
Catharine M.
ct Marl. for John & Mary, 4-3-1811; cf Plains 12-23-1823 with 7ch named; ct Plains 3-4-1829 with 9 ch named; cf Plains 5-23-1837 for John & his 7 minor ch (last named) John & Mary dis 1829 (H)
Lemuel, s John & Mary T., dis mo 5-1843
Martha W., dt John & Mary T., b 10-22-1824; cf Plains with parents; ct Haddonfield 2-5-1840, minor
Mary Anna T., dt John & Mary T., b 10-3-1826; cf Plains with parents; ct Burlington 2-5-1840 with sister, minor
William, s John & Mary, d 3-6-1846
----- & -----
Ch: Caroline b N. Y. d 10-26-1828 ae 1y 3m bHS
Josiah d 5-10-1887 ae 77y 5m bHS

BOUTELLEAU
Gustave, s Edmund & Emma; m 1873 Emma HAVILAND, dt David & Mary C., b 7-24-1844 d Limoges, France 1932 (H)

BOUTON
----- & -----
Ch: Gertrude b N. Y.

BOWDEN
Charles rocf Tottenham 7-1868; ct Haddonfield 3-1871; cf Haddonfield 10-1871; relrq 5-1872

BOWERMAN
Dr. Albert C., s Gideon H. & Mary C. (Christy), West Lake, Canada; m 8-19-1895 Lilian THORNE (nm), dt James P. & Helen H. (Farrington); cf West Lake 7-4-1883 (H)
Arthur Lindley, s J. Philip & Edith M., b 11-4-1889; m Gertrude -----; Arthur recrq of parents 1-3-1894; ct Germantown 5-1920; Gertrude recrq 3-1927; Arthur granted letter to First Presbyterian Church, Charlestown, West Va., 11-4-1889
Benjamin d 11-10-1846 ae 58y; m Mary ----- d 5-7-1879; cf East Hoosac 11-3-1841
J. Philip & Edith M.
Ch: Mary Winifred b 7-28-1884
Philip Ivan " 3-23-1886
cf Toronto 10-4-1893 for parents; first four ch recrq of parents 1-3-1894
J. Philip m 2nd Mary Alice -----
Ch: Arthur Lindley b 11- 4-1889
Walter Gregory " 11-16-1893
Herbert Clyde " 2-27-1899
cf Poughkeepsie 6-10-1903 for Mary A. (not clear as to which w is mother of Arthur & Walter
Mary Winifred, dt J. Philip & Edith M., b 7-28-1884; m ----- BURGESS; recrq of parents 1-3-1894
Walter Gregory, s J. Philip & Edith M., b 11-16-1893; recrq of parents 1-3-1894; relrq 11-1928

BOWMAN
Martha rocf N. P. 12-21-1809 for her and Mary Bowman; ct Oswego 1-11-1815 with Mary, both clear
Mary rocf N. P. 12-21-1809 for her & Martha Bowman; ct Oswego 1-11-1815 with Martha, both clear

BOWNE
Abigail, s John, Flushing; m 1686 at Jericho, Richard WILLITS [rst 7-7-1773
Abigail Embree (form Bowne) dis mo 1-1-1772;
Abigail, dt Samuel, N. Y.; m 1778 Wm. Kenyon
Abigail gct Pur. 3-2-1814 (clear)
Abigail, dt Samuel & Hannah, N. Y.; m 1829 Franklin Haines; cf Flushing with mother (H); dis 10-1830 (O)

BOWNE, continued

Amelia C., dt Sidney R. & Jemima H., b 1-5-1834; relrq 3-4-1868 (H)

Amy, dt John & Mary, Flushing; m 1717 Richard HALLETT

Amy, dt Samuel, Flushing; m 1734 Stephen LAWRENCE

Amy, dt Robt. L. & Naomi, b 12-20-1804; cf Duanes 1838; ct Balto. 1857

Ann, dt Richard & Penelope, N. Y.; m 1828 Jas. Morton REDMOND

Ann d 1-30-1863 (probably dt John & Ann)

Ann Augusta, dt Richard H. & Emily L., b 11-24-1848; m ----- ALIOTH; ret mbrp 3-1872 & gct MM at Junction City, Kansas, where she now lives

Benjamin, Flushing; m at Pur.; cert of clear 11 Mo 4, 1738

Benjamin rocf Flushing 8-2-1810, apprentice; dis 2-3-1819 for failure

Caroline b 3-25-1779 d 2-6-1848; ct Flushing 6-1-1825 (clear); cf Flushing 11-5-1829 (clear)

Catharine d 11-5-1830 ae 40y bHS (not identified as a mbr)

Catharine, dt Jas. & Caroline, Flushing; m 1783, John MURRAY, Jr.

Daniel, s Thomas & Hannah, O. B. & N. Y.; m Flushing 10 Mo (Dec) 11, 1746 Sarah STRINGHAM, dt Samuel, Flushing, d 7-6-1780

Ch: Thomas b 1 Mo (Mar) 27, 1748/9 d 7 Mo (Sept) 12, 1751
Ann b 5 Mo (July) 31, 1751 d 11-11-1783
Mary " 1- 5-1754
Thomas " 2-19-1763
Sarah d 6-16-1788

Daniel, s Thomas & Mary, d 7-6-1809 ae 88y 5m bHS (widower)

Deborah rocf Pur. 6-14-1770

Dorothy, dt John; m 1689 Henry FRANKLIN; d 9 Mo (Nov) 26, 1690

Edward & Mary Anna
Ch: ----- stillborn 1-1856 bPP

Edward S., s Samuel & Elizabeth, Balto., d about 1895 bPP; m Sarah H. CARLE, dt John & Susan H., N. Y. (m at John Carle's 2-16-1860); cf Balto. 10-7-1868 for Sarah (H)

Eliza b 3-1814 d 1-29-1861; m 1813 Samuel UNDERHILL (H)

Eliza d 8-29-1830 (in childbirth) ae 38y (not identified)

Eliza, dt Richard & Penelope, N. Y.; m 1833 Neely LOCKWOOD (H)

Eliza H., dt Sidney R. & Jemima H.; m 1848 Ellwood Walter (H)

Elizabeth, dt Samuel, Flushing; m 1742 Thomas DOBSON

Elizabeth rocf Shrewsbury 3-7-1774

Elizabeth, dt James & Caroline, b 1772; m before 4-3-1796 George TOWNSEND (mo); dis 6-2-1796

Elizabeth Kearns (form Bowne), wd, dis mo 8-6-1800; cf Fairfax, Va. 3-28-1801 for her s, Wm. & Josiah Bowne

Elizabeth dis 8-1829 (H)

Elizabeth, dt John & Hannah, Flushing; m John PRIAR; m 2nd Samuel TITUS

Elizabeth F. dis mo 6-7-1837 to ----- WILLETS

Elizabeth H., dt Sidney B. & Jemima H., West-Chester; m 1848 Ellwood WALTER (H)

Elizabeth L., dt Robert & Sarah, Flushing; cf R & P 1-17-1838; ct R & P 1-6-1841

Elizabeth d 1-14-1852 (probably dt James & Caroline

George gct Butternuts 11-7-1810 (clear)

George, s George, d 10-23-1797; m Abigail -----

Ch: Robert b 6- 3-1771
Susannah Smith " 6-20-1772
Samuel
George
Joseph
Richard
George took cert to Phila. 8-27-1755 & brought cert from that mtg 10-5-1757 (clear) ct Burl. with 2 ch, Robert & Samuel, 6-1-1779; cf Phila. with 5 ch 4-29-1785

George F. d 3-11-1896; cf Flushing 3-1846 (H)

Gulielma, dt Robert L. & Naomi, N. Y.; m 1845 Daniel BREED, Jr.

Hannah, dt John, Flushing; m 1691 Benjamin FIELD

Hannah, dt Samuel, Flushing; m 1717 Richard LAWRENCE

Hannah rocf Oswego 12-15-1802

Hannah, dt Robert & Rachel, N. Y.; m 1810 Benjamin S. Collins

Hannah, w Samuel, b 1831

Ch: Abigail
Lindley
cf Flushing 9-1829 with dt named; cf Lindly 10-1829; ct Milton, Mich, 3-1841 for all

Hannah, dt Robt. L. & Naomi, d 4-11-1858 ae 41y 7m bPP; dis mo 12-1846 to Amos LAWRENCE

Hannah S., dt Moses & Ann SHIPLEY, d 6-12-1805 ae 23y

Henry & -----
Ch: Joshua 10-13-1817

Isaac (nm) b N. Y. d 3-9-1841 ae 45y bHS

Jacob & -----

Ch: Sarah
Abigail
cf Pur. 7-12-1810 with his dt, Sarah & Abigail; dis mo 10-7-1812; Abbie S. d 12-1857 ae 50y bPP (perhaps this Abigail)

James, s Samuel & Sarah, Flushing; m Flushing 11-11-1762 Caroline RODMAN, dt Thos. & Eliz., Flushing, b Flushing d 1-12-1818 ae 84y bHS

Ch: Elizabeth b 3-10-1772
John R. " 5-27-1774
Mary R. " 9- 8-1776
Caroline " 3-25-1779

James gc of rem to Phila. 7-5-1781 (clear); cf Cape May 5-31-1784 (clear); ct Great Egg Harber 4-5-1786 (clear)

Jane, dt Robert & Eliz.; m 1812 Reuben HAINES, of Phila.

BOWNE, continued
Jane, dt John L. & Elizabeth, N. Y., b 1818; m 1841 Wm. F. MOTT, Jr.
John, s Thos., b Matlock, Eng., 3 Mo (May)1627 d Flushing 10 Mo (Dec) 20, 1695; m Hannah FEAKE, b 6-1637 d London 11 Mo (Jan) 31, 1677/78 (m 3 Mo (May) 7, 1656)
Ch: John b 1 Mo (Mar) 13, 1656/7 d 6 Mo 30, 1673
Elizabeth b 8 Mo (Oct) 8, 1658
Mary " 11 Mo (Jan) 6, 1660/1
Abigail " 12 Mo (Feb) 5, 1662/3
Hannah " 2 Mo (Apr)10, 1665
Samuel " 7 Mo (Sep) 21, 1667
Dorothy " 1 Mo (Mar) 29, 1669
Martha Johanna b 6 Mo (Aug) 17, 1673
John m 2nd Hannah BICKERSTAFF, b Eng., d 4 Mo (June) 7, 1690 (m Flushing 12 Mo (Feb) 2, 1679/80
Ch: Sarah b 10 Mo (Dec) 14, 1680 d 3 Mo 18, 1681
Sarah " 12 Mo (Feb) 17, 1681/2
John " 7 Mo (Sept) 10, 1683 d 8 Mo 25, 1683
Thomas " 9 Mo (Nov) 26, 1684 d 10 Mo 17, 1684
John " 7 Mo (Sept) 9, 1686
Abigail " 5 Mo (July) 5, 1688 d 5 Mo 13, 1688
John m 3rd, 4 Mo (June) 26, 1693 Mary COCK
Ch: Amy b 2 Mo (Apr) 1, 1694
Ruth " 11 Mo (Jan) 30, 1695/6 d young
John most active mbr; treasurer for mtg 1691; his banishment brought religious liberty
John, s John & Hannah, Flushing, b 7 Mo (Sep) 9, 1686; m Flushing 5 Mo (July) 21, 1714 Elizabeth LAWRENCE, dt Joseph & Mary (Townley)
Ch: John b 3 Mo 16, 1716
John, s John, Flushing, rqct Sadsbury 1-6-1768; rem some yrs ago to Lancaster Co., Pa., 2-4-1768; he lived in or near Sadsbury 20 yrs; m an Episcopalian; no cert till he condemns this, 5-5-1768
John, s John & Dinah, Flushing; m Flushing 2-20-1783 Ann FIELD, dt Caleb (dec) & Ann, Flushing
Ch: Mary b 1- 7-1784
Anne " 9- 5-1785
Elizabeth " 8-30-1787
Catharine " 9-20-1789
John, s Samuel & Mary, Flushing, Rocky Hill, d 4 Mo (June) 14, 1757; m 2 Mo (Apr) 6, 1738 at Mk. Dinah UNDERHILL, dt Samuel & Hannah, Mk.
Ch: Thomas b 3 Mo (May) 11, 1739
Mary " 2 Mo (Apr) 14, 1741
John " 11 Mo (Jan) 31, 1742/43
Robert " 11 Mo (Jan) 31, 1744/45
John took cert of clear 1 Mo 2, 1737/38
John, Flushing; m Dinah ----- d 1-2-1770
John & Ann
Ch: Mary b 4-24-1802
John, s Robert H., rocf R & P 1838; dis 12-1852
John L. d 4-4-1847; m at New Bedford, Mass. 1801 Elizabeth ----- d 9-29-1830
Ch: John b 7-27-1810
Sarah H. " 6- 1-1812 d 3-24-1895
William H. b 3-13-1814; dis 10-1843
Elizabeth " 4-13-1816 d 1- 2-1909 bPP
Jane " ------1818
Mary " 9- 8-1820 " 3- 5-1897 bPP
Anna " 10-26-1822 " 12-28-1897 bPP
Robert " 5- 6-1825
Catharine " ------1830 " 6-1836
cf New Bedford 1-16-1810 for Elizabeth H.; John L. failed but ret. 8-2-1815; John L. & Eliza dis 1829 (H)
John R. dis mo 10-6-1813
Joseph, s Samuel, Flushing; m Flushing 9 Mo (Nov) 13, 1735 Sarah LAWRENCE, dt Obadiah (dec), Flushing
Joseph, Flushing; m 4 Mo (June) 13, 1745 Judith MORRELL, dt Jonathan, Newtown; Judith m 2nd 3-10-1757 Joseph RODMAN
Joseph having been placed with a Friend in N.Y. in his minority, cf Sara for him 12-3-1794
Josiah, s Elizabeth, rocf Fairfax, Va., 3-28-1801; ct Marl. 2-3-1813
Judith, Flushing; m 1757 Joseph RODMAN
Lindley M. rocf Flushing 8-4-1825 (clear); dis 5-1832
Margaret rocf Wby 2 Mo (Apr) 1, 1742
Margaret rocf Wby 10-26-1785 (clear)
Maria, dt Sidney B. & Jemima, b 4-9-1824; m ----- THOMAS (nm); relrq 6-2-1880
Martha Johanna, dt John; m 1695 Joseph THORN
Mary, Flushing; m 1719 John KEESE
Mary, dt Thomas & Hannah; m 1737, Henry COCK
Mary, dt Robert (dec) & Margaret, Flushing; m 1746 Henry HAYDOCK
Mary, dt Samuel (dec), Flushing; m 1749 John FARRINGTON
Mary, dt Daniel, Flushing; m 1774 Walter FRANKLIN, N. Y.
Mary Minturn (form Bowne) dis mo 6-4-1794
Mary A., dt Richard M. & Penelope, b 3-10-1815; dis mo 12-7-1836 to ----- REYNOLDS (0); dis 10-1836 (H)
Matilda, dt Robert & Naomi, dis mo 5-4-1842 to ----- FROST
Matthew & Elizabeth
Ch: Richard b 9-26-1779
Robert Martin b 12-29-1781
William " 7- 3-1784 d 3-25-1801
Sidney " 6-19-1788
Josiah " 8-27-1793
Matthew took cert of clear to Pur. 11-2-1775; Elizabeth brought cert from Pur. 3-8-1781; Elizabeth with 4 ch rocf N.P. 6-17-1789; Elizabeth with 4 ch gct Pur. 7-3-1793; ct N.P. with w & 3 ch 7-6-1785
Richard M. d 7-27-1818 ae 38y 10m 2d bHS; m

BOWNE, Richard M., continued
Stanford 1804 Penelope ----- d 1-13-1850
bHS, rem from HS
Ch: Mary b 5-17-1805 d 5-13-1814 bHS
Eliza. " 5-31-1807
Ann
Samuel " 6- 6-1812
Mary A. " 3-10-1815
cert of clear to Stanford 7-4-1804; Penelope rocf Stanford 2-23-1805; Richard dis 10-1-1817; all dis 1829-1839 (0)
Richard, s Matthew & Eliz., b 9-26-1779; cf Pur. 4-10-1794, a minor
Richard H., s Robert H. & Sarah, N. Y., d 5-1-1881; m N. Y., 5-10-1837 Emily L. COCK, dt Thos. & Eliz. T. (dec)
Ch: Robert S. b 5----1838 d 2-24-1844
Thomas C. " 3-14-1841
Sarah E. " 9- 1-1844
Eliza P. " 12- 8-1846
Ann Augusta " 11-24-1848
Robert, s Samuel, Flushing, d 6 Mo (Aug) 16, 1743; m Cow Neck (Manhasset) 9 Mo (Nov) 6, 1724 Margaret LATHAM, dt Joseph, Cow Neck
Ch: Margaret d 8-23-1804 ae 70y
Robert d 8- 2-1818 ae 74y bHS; m Elizabeth ----- d 4-19-1837 ae 86y 4m
Ch: Mary b 9- 7-1774
Robert H. " 10-27-1776
John S. " 2-11-1779
Sarah " 9- 7-1781
Hannah " 8-14-1784
Elizabeth " 10- 4-1789
Jane P. " 1-31-1792 [bHS
William H. " 3-10-1794 d 10-28-1815
Robert took cert of clear to Shrewsbury 11-4-1773; Robert & w, Eliz., & s, Robert, gct Shrewsbury 1-7-1778; cf Shrewsbury 12-1-1783
Robert, s John L. & Elizabeth, b 5- 6-1825; mbrp relinquished 10-1861 for mo
Robert H., s Robert & Elizabeth, b 10-27-1776; m -----
Ch: Robert S. b 11-27-1803 d 11-12-1830 bHS
Hannah S. " 10- 6-1805 " 4- 2-1812 bHS
Robert m 2nd Sarah HARTSHORNE, Jr., dt Richard & Jane (dec) (m Rahway 11-6-1807)
Ch: Elizabeth L.
Richard H. b 10-22-1810
Hugh H.
William " 11-10-1816
John L. " 2-20-1824 ae 10m
cert of clear to R. & P. 11-4-1807; Sarah rocf R. & P. 2-24-1808; ct R. & P. 8-6-1828 (0) with their 4 minor ch, Elizabeth L., Hugh H., William & John; cf R. & P. 1-17-1838 with s, John; ct R. & P. 1-6-1841 for Robert & Sarah
Robert L. m Amy ROBINSON, dt Thomas & Sarah, d 5-29-1802 (or 5-27-1802) ae 32y bHS
Ch: George b 12- 7-1794
Rowland R. " 9- 5-1796
Child d 12-12-1798 bHS
Robert took cert of clear to Sara. 11-2-1803; cf Newport 7-29-1794 for Amy, w Robt.
Robert m 2nd 1803 Naomi -----
Ch: Amy b 12-20-1804
Abigail " 1-28-1807 d 12-1857
Amelia
Matilda dis 5-1842
Hannah " 12-1846
Gulielma
cf Duanes. for the 6 ch 4-17-1838 (all clear) cf Duanes for Naomi 10-25-1839; ct Balto. for Naomi 1837; cf Sara. 5-14-1804 for Naomi
Robert L. gct Butternuts 3-3-1813
Robert M., s Matthew & Eliz., b 12-29-1781; cf Pur. 4-10-1794, a minor
Samuel, s John, Flushing; m at Falls of Del. 8 Mo (Oct) 4, 1691 Mary BECKIT
Ch: Samuel b 11 Mo (Jan) 29, 1692/93
Thomas " 2 Mo (Apr) 7, 1694
Esther " 2 Mo (Apr) 30, 1695
Hannah " 1 Mo (Mar) 31, 1697
John " 7 Mo (Sep) 11, 1698
Mary " 8 Mo (Oct) 21, 1699 d 6 Mo 21, 1707
Robert " 11 Mo (Jan) 17, 1700/01
William " 2 Mo (Apr) 1, 1702 d 2 Mo 15, 1702
Elizabeth " 8 Mo (Oct) 11, 1704
Benjamin " 1 Mo (Mar) 13, 1706/7 d 3 Mo 13,1707
Samuel m 2nd at Flushing 10 Mo (Dec) 8, 1709 Hannah SMITH, d 8 Mo (Oct) 11, 1733
Ch: Sarah b 7 Mo (Sep) 30, 1710
Joseph "12 Mo (Feb) 25, 1711/12
Emy " 8 Mo (Oct) 17, 1715
Benjamin " 6 Mo (Aug) 1, 1717
Elizabeth " 9 Mo (Nov) 26, 1720
Samuel m 3rd at Flushing 14 Nov. 1734 Grace COWPERTHWAIT, wd, d 11-22-1760 ae 84 (Samuel d 3 Mo (May) 30, 1745, treasurer of mtg)
Samuel, Jr., s Samuel & Mary, Flushing & O.B., b 11 Mo (Jan) 29, 1692/3 d 3 Mo (May) 31, 1769; m 1716 Sarah FRANKLIN, Jr., dt Henry
Ch: William b 1 Mo (Mar) 6, 1719/20 [& Sarah
Samuel " 3 Mo (May) 14, 1721
Mary " 1 Mo (Mar) 3, 1723/4
cf Samuel 2 Mo (Apr) 5, 1749, he intending shortly for ould Eng.; returned 8 Mo (Oct) 4, 1749 with cf London
Samuel, Flushing; m Sarah ----- d 6-7-1767
Samuel, s Samuel & Sarah, Flushing, b Flushing 3 Mo (May) 14, 1721 d 2-24-1784; m 9 Mo (Nov) 20, 1741 Abigail BURLING, dt James & Elizabeth, N. Y., b N. Y. 12 Mo (Feb) 25, 1723/4 d 12-6-1785
Ch: Edward b 7 Mo (Sep) 3, 1742 d 7 Mo 1742
James " 1 Mo (Mar) 20, 1743/44
Samuel " 6 Mo (Aug) 4, 1746 d 6 Mo (Aug) 2, 1746 (error in orig. record) [1752
Elizabeth b 9 Mo (Nov) 19, 1748 d 11-22-
Samuel, 2nd b 4 Mo (Jun) 25, 1750 d 7-23-1752

BOWNE, Samuel & Abigail, continued
Ch: Nathan b 7-19-1752
Abigail " 10-21-1754
Sarah " 1-14-1757 d 11-11-1759
Samuel 3rd " 9-15-1758 " 5-22-1760
Mary " 8- 8-1761 " 8-24-1761
William " 3- 9-1763
Samuel 4th " 4- 5-1767 " 4-25-1803 (or 4-26-1803)
(Samuel & Abigail mo, ack. accepted 12 Mo. (Feb) 3, 1742/3)
Samuel, s Samuel & Abigail, Merchant, N. Y.; m N. Y. 3-11-1789, Hannah PEARSALL, dt Thos. & Eliz., N. Y., b N. Y. d 12-3-1831 ae 62y 6m
Ch: Eliza b 1-15-1790
Thomas Pearsall b 11-30-1792
Hannah " 1-18-1795
Samuel " 6-18-1797 d 11-1-1798
Lindley " 8-21-1800
Abigail " 1-25-1803
cf Flush. 3-4-1825 for Hannah & dt, Abigail
Samuel, s Richard M. & Penelope, b 6-6-1812; dis mo 4-1836 to ----- AKERLY
Sarah, Flushing; m 1696 Thomas FORD, Jr.
Sarah, dt Samuel & Hannah, Flushing; m 1730 Wm. BURLING, Jr.
Sarah, dt Samuel, Flush.; m 1753 William TITUS
Sarah (nm), wd, b Flush. d 6-13-1812 ae 73y 1m 17d bHS
Sarah Minturn (form Bowne) dis mo 1-7-1800
Sarah Seaman (form Bowne) dis mo 7-3-1811
Sarah Bergen (form Bowne), dt Jacob (?); dis mo 7-1832 (if dt of Jacob cf Pur. with father 7-12-1810)
Sarah W. m 8-27-1845 Henry CROMWELL (H)
Scott H. rocf Flush. 2-1-1816, apprentice; dis mo 9-1829 (0); ct Flush. 4-1830 (H)
Sidney, s Elizabeth, rocf Fairfax, Va., to Pur. 5-26-1798, minor; cf Pur. 12-13-1798 (both cert recorded); ct Pur. 7-13-1808 (clear)
Sidney B. b 6-6-1788 d 10-5-1865; m Jemima H. ----- b 8-10-1790 d 1-25-1863
Ch: William H.
Josiah Q. b 3-25-1815 d 10-10-1859
Richard M. b 3-14-1817
Eliza H. " 7-27-1819
Sarah W. (or M.) b 8-14-1822 d 4-13-1875
Maria B. b 4- 9-1824
Sidney F. " 3- 6-1829 d 2- 4-1855
Thomas B. " 6-11-1831
Amelia C. " 1- 5-1834
cf Pur. 11-1836 for all
Thomas, Flush., b Matlock, Eng., 1595 d 4 Mo (June) 18, 1677 ----- MATLOCK
Ch: John b 3 Mo (May) 1627
Dorothy
Truth never came to America
Thomas, s Jacob, Flush., d 3-28-1762; m Wby 1 Mo (Mar) 7, 1716/17 Hannah UNDERHILL, dt John (dec) d 5-2-1761
Ch: Thomas d 11 Mo (Jan) 27, 1738/9
Thomas, Flushing, dis mo 1-7-1778
Thomas certified mbr 3-2-1758
Thomas, s Jacob, rocf Wby 7-28-1773 (orig) rec 12-1-1773
Thomas B., s Sidney R. & Jemima H., b 6-11-1831; relrq 1-1855 (H)
Thomas C., s Richard H. & Emily L., b 3-14-1841; relinquished mbrp 11-1886
Thomas P. rocf Chesterfield 2-8-1814; dis 1-1829 (0); dis 2-1829 (H)
Walter dis mo 11-2-1803
Willett, s William & Eliza (Willet), Flush., b 6 Mo (Aug) 8, 1745; mo 1769 Deborah CORNELL
Ch: William b 3-15-1771
Willett m 2nd Hannah UNDERHILL, b 3-26-1755
Ch: Philip b 8- 5-1785
James " 10-26-1787
Samuel " 1- 1-1789
John Willett b 10-17-1790
Hannah " 7-23-1792
Benjamin " 2- 9-1794
Scott " 9-30-1796
Willett con mo 10-6-1779
William, N. Y., d 8 Mo (Oct) 18, 1747; m bet. 7 Mo 6 & 8 Mo (Oct) 3, 1744, Elizabeth WILLETS, dt John & Mary, Flushing, d 1746 in N. Y.
William, s Willet & Deborah, Flush., d 1-11-1801 bHS; m Flush. 9-11-1794 Mary ROBBINS, dt Samuel & Eliz. (dec), Pur., b 5-15-1773
Ch: Isaac Willett b 8- 2-1795
William dis mo 2-3-1813
William, s Elizabeth, rocf Fairfax, Va., 3-28-[1801
William, s Robert H., b 11-10-1816 d 7-1872; cf R. & P. 1-17-1838
William H., s Sidney B. & Jemima H.; m ----- (mo)
dis 11 mo 1840; cf Pur. 11-1836 with parents
William H. m 2nd 9-13-1844 Mary A. CLEMENT, dt Jonathan & Deborah, d 10-29-1892; cf Westchester PM (Pur. MM) 11-1836 for Mary with parents
William N. rocf Upper Springfield 7-8-1812, apprentice with Collins & Murray; dis 11-1832 (H); dis 5-1837 (0)
William T. dis mo 4-7-1819
----- & -----
Ch: Alexander Murray d 4-17-1811 ae 10m 21d bHS
John L. (prob. mbr) stillborn 9-18-1830 bHS

BOWRON
Alice, dt Joshua & Agnes, N. Y.; m 1822 John D. RAKE; cf two weeks mtg at Glasgow 2-11-1819 (clear), she crossed the Atlantic to N. Y. last year
Ann Elizabeth, dt Wm. L. & Mary M., roc with parents 1-12-1826; ct Chap. 2-1833
Elizabeth M. (nm) dt Watson A. & Hannah; m 6-6-1885 Henry S. BOWRON
Freelove G., dt Wm. L. & Mary M. (Sands), Chap., b North Castle 3-18-1839 d 8-25-1929; recrq 1-4-1893 (unm)
Hannah C., dt Henry C. & Deborah C., b 1-29-1820 d 12-9-1902 ae 82y 10m 10d; cf Chap.

BOWRON, Hannah C., continued
1-1824 (unm)
Henry C. b 6-24-1797 d 1-20-1867; m Deborah
----- b 6-25-1795 d 9-1-1867 (H)
Ch: Joshua W. b 10-13-1817
Hannah C. " 1-29-1822 (or 1-29-1820)
Sarah B. " 5-27-1821
Job B. " 2-11-1826 d 10-1-1884
Watson B. " 2-10-1829 " 7-24-1829
Thomas C. " 2- 4-1834 " 3- 3-1838
cf Chap. 7-11-1817; ct Chap. 5-5-1819 with Deborah; cf Chap. 9-11-1823 with first 3 ch
Henry S., s Joshua W. & Anna M., b 4-25-1850 N. Y. d 6-11-1922; m 6-6-1885 Elizabeth M. BOWRON (nm), dt Watson A. & Hannah (Moore) (H)
Jacob, s Wm. L. & Mary M., rocf Chap. 1-12-1826 with parents; ct Chap. 6-3-1832
Dr. John S., s Wm. & Mary, Northcastle; m N. Y. 5-9-1821 Sarah S. FIELD, dt Josiah & Hannah G., N. Y., d 10-7-1850 ae 48y bPP (H)
Ch: John b 2-15-1822 d 4- 2-1887 bPP
George W. " 5-24-1824 " 9-30-1881 bPP
Josiah F. " 9- 9-1826
Maria Amelia b 2-23-1829
Ch: William Henry H. b 6-18-1836 d 3- 7-1837
Thomas Tom " 4-15-1838 " 12-9-1841 bPP
Joshua W. " 9-23-1831 " 12- 5-1841 bPP
William " 10-23-1834 d 5-16-1835
Mary Augusta " 10-16-1842
ct Pur. 4-7-1824 for Sarah S.; cf Pur. 6-9-1830 with 4 ch named; John S. dis 4-1843; parents dis 1832; ch dis 1848-1849
Joshua W., s Henry C. & Deborah, b 10-13-1817 d 10-1-1895; m before 10-3-1849 Anna Maria HOAG, dt John, d 5-11-1890 (mo; Joshua ret a mbr)
Ch: Henry Snowden b 4-25-1850
cf Chap. 2-1-1888 for Anna Maria Bowron
Josiah F., s John S. & Sarah (Field), b 9-9-1825 d 11-7-1895 bPP; m 10-5-1856 Eliza CHADWICK (nm), d 11-21-1892 ae 57y bPP (mo) Josiah dis mo 1-1857 (H)
Maria Amelia, dt Dr. John S. & Sarah, b 2-23-1829 d 3-21-1900 bPP; m Wm. LOLFREY (or TOLEFREE)
Maria Amelia m 2nd ----- KNOWLTON (all nm); dis 5-6-1868 for non-attendance (H)
Mary Augusta, s John S. & Sarah, b 10-16-1842 d 12-12-1893 bPP; m 1-2-1867 Sidney FIRTH (nm); dis mo 2-7-1867 (H)
Mary S., dt Wm. L. & Mary M., b 2-10-1829; dis joining Presbyterian Church, 7-1856 (H)
Sarah, dt Henry C. & Deborah, N. Y.; m 1859 William COCKS (H)
Watson d 7-3-1876 ae 69y 8m bPP rem to Greenwood 1-16-1900; m before 1832 Hannah MOOSE (mo before 4-1832) (all nm)
Ch: Elizabeth M.
cf Chap. 10-9-1828 (clear); dis 8-1829 (0); dis 8-1832 (H)
William L. m Mary M. ----- d 1-14-1890
Ch: Jacob d ------1890
Ann Elizabeth
Maria M. b 1----1827 d 1-14-1896
Mary S. " 2-10-1829
Almira
Mary M. rocf Chap. 6-1851 with Maria & Mary; cf Chap. 1-12-1826 with 2 ch named; ct Chap. for 2 ch named; rem with parents 6-3-1832 (0); Chap. informed that Jacob had dec before cert came; parents dis 1830 (0); John dis (H) 8-1832; ct Chap. 7-1833 for the others

BOYD
Elizabeth rocf Pur. 5-1861; mbrp relinquished 3-1880
Isaac (nm) & -----
Ch: Peter d 9- 6-1817 ae 1y 10m 11d bHS
Josephus b Westchester Co. d 7-25-1821 ae 31y 10m bHS; cf Pur. 7-11-1811 (clear); dis mo 2-4-1818
Peter (nm) & -----
Ch: Susan d 6-30-1818 ae 9m
James " 5-22-1837 ae 35y bHS
----- & -----
Ch: Sarah Esther b N. Y. d 12-2-1826 ae 2y
Christiana (dt Daniel) d 10-15-1834 ae 1y 27d bHS

BOYER
Jane (nm) d 6-7-1855 ae 92y 23d bPP

BOYLE
Merritt Alfred (nm), s Stephen S. & Sarah (nm); m 11-28-1917 Rebecca HOPKINS, dt Chas. F. & Georgina, b 2-2-1887 Norwood, O.; name dropped 1932 (H)

BRADBURY
Abraham rocf Coeymans 3-24-1803; ct Duanesburg 4-6-1806
Ann rocf Newton MM, Cheshire 6-25-1802 (clear)
Phebe, dt William & Phebe LAWTON, d 9-18-1806 ae 67y
Ch: Naomi
Martha
Hannah
Ruth
Ann
Abraham
cf Morley, Cheshire, to Coeymans 4-28-1802 with 4 dt named, all unm, endorsed to N. Y. 8-25-1803; ct Duanesburg 6-1-1808 for Naomi, Martha, Ann, Hannah & Ruth, having rem with their brother, Abraham (all clear)

BRADLEY
Albert (nm) m 6-27-1900 Fannie MOREY, dt Gardner P. & Lydia (Robinson), b Nassau 3-4-1823 Fanny transferred from Albany 1-8-1916 (H)
Floyd H., s Wm. J. & Anna R., Camden, N. J.; m N. Y. 4-15-1816 Hazel B. DILLISTIN, dt Howard P. & Jennie B., Bkn. (H)

BRADLEY, continued
Laura (nm) d 10-14-1854 ae 14y 7m 10d bPP
----- m 7-1840 Ann WRAY, dt Christopher & Eliz., d 5-1-1846 ae 30y bHS
Ch: Mary d 4-16-1846 ae 6m bHS
dis mo 7-10-1842

BRADY
Dorinda F., w John T. H., dt Gilbert FOWLER (m 1845); cf Creek 10-1833; ct Clear Creek, Ill. 6-7-1848 (H)
Edward rocf York, Eng. 3-16-1836 (clear); dis 9-1840
Emeline C., dt John & Lydia C.; m 1843 ----- UNDERHILL; recrq 1-1833; ct Clear Creek, Ill. 1845 (H)
Harriet A., dt John & Lydia C., recrq of mother 1-1833; ct Clear Creek with mother 10-7-1846 (H)
John (nm) & -----
Ch: Thomas d 4-20-1832 ae 1y 6m bHS
Lydia C., w John
Ch: Emeline C.
Harriet
Harriet recrq of mother 1-1833; Emeline recrq 1-1833; ct Clear Creek for Lydia 10-7-1846; cf Chap. 7-8-1824; dis 8-1830 (O)
Susan B. dis 4-1837 (H)

BRAGG
Henry rocf Lisburn, Ireland 6-1848; ct Lisburn, Ireland 1851
Isaac, Pardshaw MM in Cumberland, Eng. rq care 10-2-1816; mo here; correspondence & dis from Hardshaw, 5-17-1817

BRANDRETH
Mary, dt Timothy, West Jersey; m 1709 Jonathan HEWSTIS, of Westchester

BRANDT
Albertus, Merchant, N. Y.; m at John Delavall's N. Y., 12 Mo (Feb) 21, 1667/8 Susanna TELNER, Jr., dt Jacob, N. Y.
Ch: Maria b 10 Mo (Dec) 16, 1688
William gc 3 Mo (May) 3, 1705 to place not stated

BRANNING
William C. & Achsah
Ch: Mary D. b 1827
cf Chesterfield 1-3-1826 for Wm. C.; cf Chesterfield 6-5-1827 for Achsah; ct Chesterfield 10-1-1828 with infant ch, Mary (O)

BRANSON
Charles F., s Lindley M. & Anna M., Cadiz, O.; m N. Y. 4-30-1910 Anna M. JACKSON, dt Wm. M. & Anna M., N. Y., b N. Y. 12-27-1881
Ch: Anna Florence, b Pittsburgh 7-24-1913
Charles F., Jr." Cleveland, O., 12-15-1916 d 12-15-1916
Anna's name entered by comm 3-4-1882; ct Germantown
Joseph m Lydia ----- d 8-9-1830 ae 43y bHS
Ch: Lydia d 8-16-1811 ae 1y 1m bHS
cf Shrewsbury 2-7-1814 for Lydia, w Joseph; Lydia dis 6-1830
Joseph (nm) & -----
Ch: Robert b Shrewsbury d 5-5-1813 ae 10m bHS
George " N. Y. d 3-31-1815 ae 7m bHS
Henry W. " 6-30-1817 ae 6m 1d bHS

BRANTINGHAM
Hannah m 1-7-1795 ----- DAVENPORT; dis mo 3-2-1796; had left before this date
Jacob rocf Pur. 1-10-1811 (clear); dis mo 10-12-1814
Joseph (nm) b England d 11-5-1823 ae 51y bHS (m)
Sarah m 12-7-1803 ----- SINIONS; dis mo next month
Thomas b Iveston, Eng., Co. Durham; dis before coming here; d 8-11-1820 ae 78y; m Hannah ----- b Liverpool d 8-13-1824 ae 77y
Ch: Joseph
Hannah
Sarah
Jacob
cf New Castle MM to Horseley Down, Eng., 7-11-1791 for Hannah with 4 ch named, readdressed to N. Y. 11-2-1797; ct Pur. 3-2-1809 for Hannah & s, Jacob, rem with h; cf Pur. for Hannah 1-10-1811

BRAYNTON
Patience gct Swansea, Mass., 9-4-1771

BREAR
Abel d 2-1-1886; m Elizabeth P. ----- d 2-15-1897; cf Wilmington 6-3-1885 for both (H)

BREED
Daniel, Jr., s Daniel & Mary (dec), N. Y.; m N. Y. 8-7-1845 Gulielma BOWNE, dt Robert L. (dec) & Naomi, N. Y.
Ch: Ella Amelia b 7-11-1849 d 1-31-1853 [for both
cf Weare 8-10-1837 (clear); ct Balto. 1855
Preston Hamilton, s Benj. B. (dec) & Hannah, Lynn, Mass.; m 10-7-1898 at Walter H. Knight's, New Brighton, N. Y., Mary Estelle KNIGHT, dt Geo. Henry & Anna, N. Y. cf Cincinnati 3-1889 for Mary; ct Salem, Mass., 10-4-1893 for Mary

BREWSTER
E. Franklin (nm), s John H. & Emily (Smith); m Roch. 6-1-1880 Sarah R. MACY, dt Silvanus J. & Caroline (Ridgway), b N. Y. 11-10-1861
Sarah R. m 2nd 10-7-1915 James MARWICK; she took ct Alexandria 4-11-1921 (H)

BREWSTER, continued
Elizabeth, dt Samuel & Eliz. MOTT, d 2-1-1895 (H)
----- & -----
Ch: Matilda b Canandaigua d 1-10-1835 ae 5y bHS
Mary E. d 9-25-1860 ae 78y bPP

BRIEN
James (nm) d 9-25-1868 ae 40y bPP; m Sarah Jane HAYDOCK, dt John & Jane, b 11-22-1837
ct R. & P. 5-1870 for Sarah
Mary A. (nm) d 11-18-1873 ae 76y bPP

BRIGGS
Alanson C. d 7-1-1931 (or 6-28-1931 bPP) (unm) recrq 11-1923
Charity C. d 4-11-1875; cf Ama. 9-1851 (H)
Lydia C. rocf Duanes. 11-1840; ct Duanes. 1-1847 (H)
Mary d 9-26-1798 bHS (nm)
Wilmer A., s Theo. S. & Sarah (Leedom), Wrightstown, Pa.; m 9-2-1877 Frances J. JANNEY, dt Stephen T. & Harriet J., b Makefield, Pa. 2-26-1854 (H); cf Wrightstown 8-1-1888 for Wilmer; cf Makefield for Frances 5-2-1888; Frances resigned 10-9-1922
----- & ----- (nm)
Ch: Edward b N. Y. d 1-22-1827 ae 10m 11d bHS
George " " " 5-16-1827 ae 1y 2m bHS

BRIGHT
Mary Isabella (nm), dt Grant & Emma (nm); m 1926 Roy Twining ABBOTT

BRINKERHOFF
Emma H. , w Chas. C., b 4-23-1860; cf Phila. 9-5-1884; relrq 4-4-1896 (H)
George S., s Abm. & Jane E. (Wright), b Jamaica, L. I., 6-9-1833 d 6-22-1919; m 9-10-1878 Martha H. SEAMAN, dt John & Amy (Pearsall), Corn., b Monroe 8-13-1834 d 4-25-1931
George recrq 3-10-1900; Martha rocf Corn. 1-1-1879 (H)

BRINKMAN
----- (nm) m Cornelia DEAN, dt Israel & Agnes, d 9-23-1841 ae 25y 2m 28d bHS
Ch: Infant d 10-13-1841 ae 20d bHS
Cornelia dis mo by Episcopalian Minister 4-7-1841

BRINTON
Ruth Hoops (nm) m 1932 Charles A. PERERA

BRISON
Clifford Scarnell, s Alfred & Eliz. (Scarnell), b Bristol, Eng., 8-23-1886; cf Westminster & Longford 10-11-1920; ct Bristol 6-8-1925; came back to N. Y. but not connected with Friends; m a nm (H)

BRISTOW
George Clement rocf Kingston, Eng., 2-6-1907; name erased 8-1920; returned to England (H)

BRITT
Benjamin, s Stephen & Ann Louisa, b N. Y. 8-18-1843 d 3-3-1912; m 6-9-1870 Emma VALENTINE (nm), dt Townsend & Ann (H)
Stephen d 5-23-1890; m Ann Louisa ----- d 9-21-1894 (H)
Ch: Benjamin b 8-18-1843
cf Pur. for parents 9-1841
----- [Britts] m Hannah Maria NYHOLM, dt Fred H.
Hannah recrq 4-2-1919

BROADHEAD
Mary, dt Jeptha & Anna, b Eng. 3-13-1850; m 1870 Geo. Edward JENKINS (H)

BROADWAY
Catharine d 1-22-1854; rocf Verona 3-7-1849 (H)

BROCKELBANK
Lillian, dt Caleb & Marie (Outhouse) (dec), b Canandaigna 1-27-1876; recrq 5-14-1934 (H)

BROOKS
Abraham [Brooke] m Phebe ----- d 8-31-1929 (m at Wby) (H)
Ch: Sarah H. b 1-28-1822
Amy S.
Mary H. " 5-20-1819
Lydia d 3-29-1824 ae 1y
Elizabeth W. b 8-18-1825
Phebe H.
cf Wby 5-14-1806, apprentice with Richard Bowne; cert of clear to Wby 5-16-1816; Phebe rocf Wby 6-18-1817; Abraham dis 1-1831 (O)
Abraham m 2nd at N. P. Sarah HAIGHT
Ch: Infant stillborn 11-19-1831
cf N. P. 6-1831 for Sarah; ct Wby for all 9-1833 (H)
Catharine rocf Corn. 6-27-1839; ct Corn. 11-1872
Charles [Brook] rem (clear) from Shrewsbury 10-6-1777
Charles m 1-6- (or 2-4-1773) Mary CHILD
Charles brought cert of clear from Shrewsbury; Mary took cert there 3-3-1773; cf Shrewsbury for Charles 10-6-1777; ct Ratcliff 7-7-1879; cf 2 weeks mtg, London, 6-12-1780; ct Devonshire House 3-6-1782 (clear); cf there not found; ct South River Va. 6-7-1786 (clear); cf there 2-16-1788, endorsed to R. P. 6-4-1788
Charles m Phebe Jane ----- d 1-29-1891 ae 63y bPP (both nm) (H)
Charles T., s Morgan & Frona Maria, Urbana, Ill., b St. Paul, 5-2-1891; m Greenwich, Conn. 6-4-1914 Eleanor M. STABLER, dt Edw.

BROOKS, Charles T. & Eleanor M., continued
& Eliz. T., Bkn., b Bkn., 9-27-1892
Charles F. recrq 11-12-1917; ct Alexandria 10-13-1919 for both (H)
Elijah [Brooke] & -----
Ch: Mary b 5-20-1819
Elizabeth [Brook], dt Abraham & Phebe, b 8-18-1825; ct Wby & Jericho 3-1834
Erica May, dt Howard & Mary L. (Gilpin), b London, 7-9-1894; cf Kingston, Eng., 10-12-1925 (H)
Lawrence G. (nm), s John G. & Helen L., Cambridge, Mass.; m at N. P. Hallowell's 10-12-1912, Susan M. HALLOWELL, of Norwood P. & Sarah W., Medford, Mass., b W. Medford, Mass. 12-19-1883 (H)
Ch: John Graham 2nd b 10-8-1913
Ann " 4-10-1917
Charlotte Hallowell b 8- 9-1920
ch recrq of parents 12-14-1931
Mary [Brook], dt Abraham & Phebe, b 5-20-1819; ct Wby & Jericho 3-1834
Nell [Brooke], dt Orson H. & Lu (Smith), b Chicago 6-19-1887; m Walter LOUDENBACK; both recrq 6-6-1917
Phebe Jane, dt Stephen & Leah H. MILLER, b L. I. d 8-31-1829 ae 37y; m Isaac C. FROST (H)
Sally D. d 4-19-1889; recrq 2-4-1880 (H)
Stephen H. d 3-13-1911 ae 52y 1m 4d; m Carrie SUTTON (both nm) (H) (Stephen H. bPP)
Walter & Sarah
Ch: Mary d 10-13-1839 ae 2y 16d (all nm) bHS

BROOMELL
Geo. Lupton, s Seneca P. & Rebecca J. (Lupton), b Balto. 7-31-1885; cf Balto. 4-13-1912; ct Green St., Phila. 12-14-----
John Paul, s Seneca P. & Hannah P. (dec), Balto. b Brick Mtg, Pa., 11-28-1878; m 6 Riverview Terrace 3-29-1912 Ethel B. CLOSE, dt James & Charlotte, N. Y., b London, 9-13-1881 (H)
Ch: (two adopted)
both relrq 3-11-1935 to join Christian Science Church

BROTHERTON
Grace b N. J. d 6-14-1839 ae 44y bHS (unm)

BROUGHT
----- & ----- (nm)
Ch: Raymond d 7-25-1898 infant bur in Caleb Peele's lot, Prospect Park

BROUWER
Mary rocf Chap. 4-1849; ct Chap. 8-1853

BROWER
----- & -----
Ch: Anna Hazard b N. Orleans d 6-24-1838 ae 1y 1m 2d bHS

BROWN
Aaron L., s Thos. H. & Phebe Ann (Leggett), Chicago, b 10-21-1841; m 12-28-1865 by Mayor, Elizabeth HICKS, dt Robt. M. & Rose Anna (Leggett), b Manhasset 10-4-1839 d 10-6-1915; had joined U. S. Army during the late war 7-3-1867, also mo by the Mayor, dis 5-6-1868 (H)
Alexander & Phebe
cf N. P. 1-17-1805 for both
Alexander b Scotland 7-23-1849 d Port Washington, L. I. 7-23-1932 bPP; m Agnes ----- letters from M. E. Ch. Nostrand & De Kolb. Bkn., 5-1924
Alice Pennell, dt Edw. H. & Mary R., b 2-16-1857; relrq 7-3-1878
Allan H. recrq 5-1-1929
Alvin & -----
Ch: George H. b N. Y. d 6-16-1817 ae 4y 4m 7d bHS
Infant stillborn 7-21-1817 bHS
cf Hudson 5-26-1812; dis mo 12-4-1816
Anna d 1-29-1882; cf Hudson 5-1847; cf Hudson 5-1847 for Joseph M. (H)
Anna C. rocf WD MM 8-1880
Bertha rocf Phila. 9-6-1911; ct Phila. WD 7-1914
Carolina, dt Geo. E. & Lucia, b 5-10-1856 d 12-23-1886; Frederick HARRIS (NM)(H)
Caroline J., s Caleb & Phebe W., d 7-14-1846 ae 16y 2m 18d bPP; cf Ama. 9-1844 (H)
Catharine b 12-3-1767, wd Nathanial, d 6-13-1862 ae 94y 6m 10d; cf Corn. 11-23-1821; dis 5-1829
Charity d 6-29-1851 ae 78y 6m; cf Creek 3-1837 (H)
Daniel C., s Nathaniel & Rebecca, Corn.; m 4-10-1839 Mary UNDERHILL, dt Samuel & Phebe, (dec), N. Y. (H)
David S. d 5-10-1872; m Elizabeth ----- d 8-29-1855 ae 66y 5m 10d bPP
David S. m 2nd Sarah S. ----- d 8-27-1872 recrq 9-5-1818; cf Oblong 2-3-1858 for Sarah S. (H)
Dorothea W., dt Caleb & Phebe W., d 3-4-1852 ae 26y 1m 7d bPP; cf Ama. 1884, minor (H)
Edward T., s John & Mary T. (both dec) Phila., d 3-12-1889; m N. Y. 5-9-1855 Marianna WOOD, dt Walter R. (dec) & Mary Anna, N.Y., b 1-29-1827 d 1-2-1888
Ch: Thornton Edward b 7-24-1857 d 10-17-1876
Anna Wood " 2-28-1863
cf Phila. Green St. 1856 for Edward
Edward H., s Caleb & Phebe W. (both dec), Bkn.; m at John S. Roberts' 2-20-1856 Mary R. ROBERTS, dt John S. & Sarah Ann, N. Y.
Ch: Alice Pennell b 2-16-1857
Charles " 6-21-1861 d 11-23-1888
Mary Churchman " 11-26-1872
cf Ama. 9-1844; Edward relrq 4-1-1874; Mary & 2 dt relrq 7-3-1878 (H)
Effingham (nm) & -----
Ch: Infant stillborn 10-13-1827 bHS
Elijah rocf SD MM 10-27-1813; ct SD MM 7-2-1817
Elizabeth (late Biles) dis mo 3-5-1783

BROWN, continued
Elizabeth mo 1789 by a Priest, ack. referred to Bridgetown MM. Comm. to prepare cert to Bridgetown or Plainfield 7-1-1789; comm. rpd 8-6-1789 that she was dec
Elizabeth rocf WD MM 2-16-1825, minor, with sister, Mary Jane
Elizabeth, w Aaron L., dt Robt. & Rosanna HICKS (m by Mayor 12-28-1865); rocf Wby with mother 1-1853; ret mbrp (H)
Ellen d 10-4-1798 bHS
Esther m 1842 ----- SICKLES (or SICKLY) cf Creek 11-1840; dis mo 12-1842 (H)
Esther H., dt Thos. H. & Phebe, b 6-5-1857; relrq 6-4-1879
Florence, dt Geo. Evans & Mary E. (Taylor), b Bedford Village 12-5-1881; m 1908 Charles MAURICE; both recrq 9-8-1919 (H)
Franklin, s Isaac D., d 7-8-1915 ae 67y bPP; m Eva Jennie CROZIER, dt Hiram B. & Delia, d 4-20-1915 ae 62y 7m 9d bPP (H)
Ch: George Betts d 5-10-1925 ae 37y 8m 11d bPP (all nm)
George (nm) b N. Y. d 2-16-1827 ae 33y 3m bHS
George Edward, s George E. & Lucia C., b 5-4-1862 d 5-27-1901; m Lucia C. ----- d 3-24-1874 (H)
Ch: Joseph C. b 6-10-1853 d 12-25-1878
Caroline " 5-10-1856
George Edward b 5- 4-1862 d 5-27-1901
cf Ama. 9-1844 for George; cf Albany 5-1853 for Lucia; George relrq 5-1-1878
George W. d 1848; cf ND MM 4-25-1815 (H)
Gideon recrq 11-7-1821; dis 7-1830; d 11-16-1857 (or 10-17-1857) ae 63y 4m bPP
Gilbert b West Co. d 12-20-1843 ae 83y 9m 17d; m Lavinia ----- (H)
Ch: David S.
Samuel d 10-4-1818 ae 16y bHS
rq mbrp 8-7-1816, returned to him 3-5-1817; recrq 5-3-1820; ct Ama. 12-1-1824 for both; Lavinia recrq 6-1813; cf Ama. 5-1840 for Gilbert
Goold b 1-5-1779; cf Pembroke, Mass., 1-26-1815 (clear); ct Salem 4-4-1838 (clear) (O); dis 1-1832 (H) (The Grammarian)
Harry m Florence Edna WHITSON, dt Henry & Phebe, d 4-30-1901 ae 24y 11m bPP (both nm) (H)
Henry Franklin, s Frank O. & Kath. L. (nm); m 4-1-1932 Elsie WILLIAMS, dt Samuel B. & Helen, b Bkn., 1-24-1912; Henry recrq 12-11-1933 (H)
Henry T., WD MM asks N. Y. to visit him re non-attendance 1-1868; dis by Phila. & N. Y. notified 5-1868
Isaac (nm) & -----
Ch: David S. b N. Y. d 2-22-1821 ae 2y bHS
Joseph " " " 3-23-1834 " 3d bHS
William " " " 1-4-1844 ae 25y bHS (unm)
David S. Jr. d 2-14-1844 ae 23y 10d bHS (unm)
Irving (nm) m Bethia ANGEVINE, dt Frank & Bethia, b Bkn., 3-21-1876
Bethia recrq of parents 11-27-1878 (H)
Jacob taught in Friends' School here; cf Chesterfield, N. J. 2-6-1798, rem some time since; dis mo 4-4-1804 & accepting office of Commissioner for expenditure of proceeds thereof
John, Flushing, lately from Nevis & banished from Bermuda, gc 3 Mo (May) 23, 1682 (rem)
John (nm) b Pa. d 6-21-1831 ae 61y bHS
John & Ann (m Middletown, Pa. 1801)
Ch: Mary
cf Falls, Pa. 10-7-1795 (clear); took cert of clear to Middletown, Pa., 3-4-1801; Ann rocf Middletown, Pa., 7-9-1801; ct Middletown 6-26-1803 with their infant ch, Mary
John L. gct New Bedford 9-6-1809 (clear)
Joseph d before 1760; m -----
Ch: Sarah
Joseph M. d 8-4-1889; cf Hudson 5-1847 (H)
Joshua W., s Caleb & Phebe W., N. Y.; m at Jos. Willet's 4-9-1840 Rachel S. WILLETS, dt Joseph & Phebe, Bkn., d Peekskill 9-7-1840 (H)
cf Ama. 7-1829 for Joshua
Joshua W. m 2nd Sarah F. FROST d 9-28-1898 (H)
Ch: Louisa Elizabeth b 11-16-1844
Joshua Wm. (changed to Wm. Jay) b 11-15-1846 d 8-18-1878
Leslie Russell b 7-10-1851 d 9-20-1881 bPP
cf Scip. 6-4-1845 for Sarah with Louisa
Joshua W. (father) d 4-28-1887 (or 5-28-1887) ae 74y 6m 9d
Josiah rocf Buckingham, Pa. 5-6-1816, minor; ct Buckingham 11-3-1819 (clear)
Lavinia recrq 6-2-1813
Louisa Elizabeth (changed to Elizabeth Louisa) dt Josh. W. & Sarah, b 11-16-1844 d 10-4-1887 ae 42y bPP; m Edward BARTLETT (H)
cf Scip. with mother 6-4-1845
Mary, dt Edward H. & Mary, b Bkn., 11-26-1872; m 1896 Harry Carleton SLACK; relrq 2-14-1921 (H)
Mary (nm) m 1900 George H. COCKS (H)
George recrq 4-14-1924
Mary (nm), dt William & Mary B.; m 1909 Donald McKAY (H)
Mary C., dt Edward H. & Mary R., b 11-26-1872; m 10-16-1890 Harry Carleton SLACK (nm) (H)
Mary H. d 4-3-1851; cf Ama. 9-1844 (H)
Mary Jane rocf WD MM 2-16-1825 with minor sister, Elizabeth; dis joining M. E. Ch. 8-1829
Mary L., dt Thos. H. & Phebe Ann, b 4-14-1848 d Chicago 11-1-1871; m John J. P. ODELL (H)
Matthias M. rocf R. P. 8-10-1821, minor; dis mo by priest 9-1829 (O); dis mo by priest 9-1835 (H)
Merritt J., s Thos. H. & Phebe Ann, b 11-24-1852; ct Chicago 5-5-1880 (H)
Mordecai rocf R. P. 5-25-1820, apprentice with Wager Hull; dis 1-1828
Moses rocf Buckingham 4-5-1819

BROWN, continued
Nathan d 12-1-1810 ae 59y; cf Ama. 8-11-1810
Nathaniel b Crum Pond d 12-1-1810 ae 59y 7m 8d bHS (m elsewhere)
Nathaniel (nm) b Phila. d 4-29-1809 ae 44y bHS
Nathaniel (nm) b N. Y. d 5-15-1842 ae 72y bHS (m)
Nathaniel M. (nm) d 10-6-1843 ae 24y 4m 5d bPP; m Susan R. ----- d 4 (or 5) 2-1872 bPP (H)
Ch: Louisa F. b 5-12-1843 d 11-4 (or 3) 1857 bPP
cf Ama. 9-1840 for Nathaniel; cf Troy 9-1842 for Susan; Susan relrq 11-3-1869
Peace b Dutch. Co. d 10-1-1846 ae 82y bHS
Phebe gct Marl. 8-5-1807 (clear)
Phebe W., dt Thos. H. & Phebe Ann, b 9-2-1845; ct Central Ex. Mtg, Chicago, 3-5-1890 (H)
Priscilla gct Hitching in Herts, Eng., 6-4-1783 (clear) to accompany her sister. Attended when of ability of body. Her sister about to settle in your parts with her h
Ralph Wolcott (nm), s Joseph B. & Emma F.; m at Hallowell Davis' 8-7-1926 Esther F. DAVIS, dt Horace A. & Anna N., Hopkinton, Mass., b Dongon Hills, N. Y. 1-16-1906
Esther recrq of parents 10-13-1906 (H)
Rhoda (nm) b Dutchess Co., d 2-9-1815 ae 68y bHS
Reuben L., s Thos. H. & Phebe Ann, b 7-15-1850; relrq 9-2-1885 (H)
Richard T., s Caleb & Phebe W. (both dec), Bkn., m at John S. Roberts' 2-8-1859 Anna C. ROBERTS, dt John S. & Sarah Anna (Churchman) Bkn., b N. Y. 10-10-1837 d 1-3-1916 bPP (H)
Ch: Fannie R. b 11-16-1860
Frederick M. " 5- 7-1864
Pennell C. " 9- 2-1868
Samuel b N. Y. d 1-26-1846 ae 87y 3m 6d; m Amy ----- d 12-8-1840 ae 70y
Samuel recrq 8-1816; Samuel dis 12-1829 (O)
Amy dis 1840 (O)
Samuel, s Nathaniel & Charity, N. Y., d 11-15-1882 ae 88y 10m 19d bPP; m N. Y. 8-9-1832 Rachel HOPPER, dt Isaac T. & Sarah (dec) d 11-24-1887 ae 89y bPP (H)
Ch: Isaac H. b 5- 7-1833 d 5-28-1835
Isaac H. " 8-22-1835 " 12-30-1839
Ann Eliza " 5-26-1838 " 12-27-1838
Sarah H. " 4- 5-1840
Samuel H. " 5-17-1842 d 4- 5-1872
Samuel recrq 12-2-1812; ct Creek (not found) cf Creek 5-1832 for Samuel; cf Phila. 11-1829 for Rachel; ct N. P. 12-1869 for both; cf N. P. for both 1-7-1874
Samuel, s Samuel H. & Annie S. (Browse), b N.Y. 3-11-1866; m 5-1888 Frances E. MORGAN (nm) cf N. P. 1-7-1874
Samuel H., s Samuel & Rachel (Hopper), b 5-17-1842 d 4-5-1872; m Annie S. BROWSE, d 12-20-1866 ae 27y 9m 7d bPP (H)
Ch: Annie S. d 5-28-1871 ae 7y bPP
Samuel b N. Y. 3-11-1866
ct N. P. 3-1-1871
Samuel H. m 2nd Jane E. DRURY, dt Gardner P. & Abigail (Gore), b Boston 9-2-1844 d 4-29-1913 (m 10-20-1869) (H)
Ch: Gardner D. d 5-30-1872 ae 1y 6m 16d
Jane recrq 2-4-1905
Samuel W. rocf ND MM 12-22-1835; "said to be in Vicksburg 1841"
Dr. Sanger M., s Stewart & Catharine, b Bloomfield, Ont., 2-16-1852 d 4-1-1928; m 7-9-1885 Bella CHRISTY (nm) (H)
Ch: Christy b 5- 3-1886
cf West Lake, Ont. 7-7-1880 for Sanger; Christy's name entered by comm. 10-6-1886
Sarah, dt Joseph (dec); m 1760 ----- MITCHELL
Sarah b L. I. d 5-30-1840 ae 86y bHS (unm)
Sarah Degroot (form Brown) dis mo 1-6-1847; cf Creek 7-1841 (H)
Sarah C. d 2-27-1900; cf Oswego 3-1838; ct Phila., Cherry St. 12-1842; cf Phila., Green St., 2-1850; ct Oswego 8-1852; cf Norwich 3-4-1857 (H)
Sarah H., dt Samuel & Rachel, Bkn., b N. Y. 4-5-1840 d 5-24-1905; m 1861 Wilson M. POWELL (H)
Sarah W. rocf R. & P. 9-1835; ct R. P. 3-1840 (H)
Susannah gc 10-6-1756 (rem)
Stephen dis mo 2-5-1823
Stephen C. rocf Amawalk 1-12-1822 (clear); dis 1823
Thomas gct N. P. 10-2-1776, having rem; cf N. P. 3-18-1785; ct Corn. 2-8-1792
Thomas (nm) b Phila. d 12-11-1813 ae 52y bHS
Thomas, Jr. d 8-23-1801 bHS; ct Creek 10-7-1789 (clear); a mbr of Creek; dis mo 11-4-1790
Thomas H., s Caleb & Phebe W., b 6-19-1815; m at Mary M. Leggett's 9-3-1840 Phebe Ann LEGGETT, dt Reuben (dec) & Mary M., b 4-1-1815 d 12-16-1853 ae 38y 8m 15d bPP (H)
Ch: Aaron L. b 10-21-1841
Thomas H. Jr. b 11- 4-1843
Phebe W. " 9- 2-1845
Mary L. " 4-14-1848
Reuben L. " 7-15-1850
Merritt J. " 11-24-1852
Thomas H. m 2nd Phebe HOAG, dt Sanford (dec) & Esther (m at Deborah S. Underhill's, Bkn., 4-17-1856) (H)
Ch: Esther H. b 6- 5-1857
Sandford " 6-11-1859
Ellie Louisa " 3-24-1862
Hannah A. " 8-20-1864
cf Ama. 1-1840 for Thomas H.; Thomas & Phebe gct Chicago 5-5-1880; ct Central E. Mtg., Chicago 5-5-1880 for last 3 ch & for Merritt J. with parents
Thomas H., s Thos. H. & Phebe Ann, b 11-4-1843; relrq 9-2-1885
Vernon Lee m Bernice HENLEY
Vernon rocf Washington, D. C. 1-4-1933;
Bernice rocf Greensboro, N. C., 1-4-1933
William (nm) & -----

BROWN, William, continued
Ch: Harriet Clarissa b N. Y. d 5-17-1847 ae 1y 3m 14d
William A. rocf Salem, Mass., 5-1852; relrq 5-1865
Wm. Barker rocf Pembroke 9-24-1818; ct Falmouth Mass., 1-3-1827 (clear)
William M. d 1-6-1898 bPF; cf Ama. 9-1844
W. Brewer recrq 6-12-1918
----- m Sarah Clark GRIFFEN, dt Cornelia H., d 7-18-1904 ae 47y 9m 22d bPP (both nm)(H)
----- & ----- (bPP) (H)

Ch:				
Ch:	Caroline J.	d 7-14-1846	ae 16y 2m 18d
	Mary H.	" 4- 3-1851	" 40y 2m 17d
	Isaac D.	" 5-18-1851	" 36y 2m 11d
	Charity	" 6-29-1851	" 78y 6m
	Dorothea W.	" 3- 4-1852	" 26y 1m 7d
	Henry D.	" 9-26-1856	" 11y
	Jacob	" 2-28-1847	" 31y
	Helen		
	Elizabeth	" 11-30-1856	" 66y
	Edwin P.	" 6-27-1886	" 46y
	Catharine	" 6-13-1862	" 94y 6m

----- & ----- (bPP
Ch: J. W. d 10-18-1876 ae 20y
----- & -----
Ch: Emila b N. Y. d 1-25-1826 ae 1y bHS
Charles W. b N. Y. d 7-16-1837 ae 4m bHS

BROWNING
Clarence Perry, s Oscar F. & Mary (Foster), b Flush. 1-1-1867; m 10-2-1891 Eva Stanton BABCOCK, dt Joshua S. & Sarah (White), b Salem, Mass., 6-27-1866 (H)
Ch: Paul Babcock b 9- 7-1892
Robert Stanton " 3-15-1894
Eunice " 2-26-1897
All recrq 6-9-1906
Eunice, dt Clarence P. & Eva S., b 2-26-1897; m 1923 Edward Mitchell PULLWITZ (H) recrq 6-9-1906
Oscar F., s Perry M. & Julia Ann, Ghent, N. Y., d 5-4-1878; m Flushing 8-10-1865 Mary FOSTER, dt John B. & Mary E., Flushing
Ch: Clarence P. b 1- 1-1867
Martha F.
Marion E. " 2-22-1875
Oscar recrq 12-1864; ct Chap. 4-1880 for Mary & ch; ct Pokeepsie 7-2-1873, ret as they did not settle there
Paul Babcock, s Clarence P. & Eva S., b 9-7-1892; m 10-12-1819 Alma Eugenie JOHNSON (nm), dt Chas. E. & Gertrude (H) recrq 6-9-1906
Robert Stanton, s Clarence P. & Eva S., b 3-15-1894; m 1-1923 Eva B. BROWNING (nm) (H) recrq 6-9-1906

BROWNSON
Eunice, wd, b New Bedford d 1-19-1832 ae 52y bHS

BRUFF
Charles, s Christopher & Mary (both dec), Talbot Co., Md., d 11-8-1841 ae 40y 11m 16d bHS; m N. Y. 5-12-1825 Hannah PALMER, dt Harrison (dec) & Phebe, N. Y.
Ch: Phebe Ann b 3-26-1826 d 11- 8-1826
Richard P. b 4- 5-1827
Charles Jr. b 11- 6-1828
Harison P. " 5-14-1830 d 6-29-1834 bHS
Phebe P. " 8-20-1831
James Berry " 6- 8-1833
cf Phila 7-29-1824; Hannah m 2nd Abel ADAMS
Charles, Jr., s Charles & Hannah, b 11-6-1828; relrq 3-1861
Hannah F., wd Charles, dt Harrison & Phebe PALMER, N. Y.; m 1854 Abel ADAMS
James Berry, s Chas. & Hannah, b 6-8-1833; ct Upper Springfield, Ohio, 1856
Phebe P., dt Charles & Hannah, b 8-20-1831; relrq 3-1861
Richard P., s Charles & Hannah, b 4-5-1827; relrq 3-1861

BRUNCK
Loretta recrq 3-11-1916; relrq 7-8-1916

BRUNNER
Henry (nm) & ----- (H)
Ch: Annie d 12-20-1880 ae 1y 20d bPP

BRUSH
Cornelius (nm) m Mary ----- d 1-13-1846 ae 72y
Ch: Infant stillborn 12-5-1814 bHS

BRYAN
Darby, comm to rp their knowledge of her to Friends of Jamaica, W. I., 8 Mo (Oct) 6, 1687
Elijah rocf Devonshire House 7-9-1818 (clear); dis mo 11-7-1821 under name of Bryant
Sarah Jane, dt John & Jane HAYDOCK, b 11-22-1837 d 1-10-1906 bPP
William, Jr. rocf Devonshire House 2-4-1817 (clear); dis 11-1830

BRYANT
Adeline, dt Jas. & Lydia H. WEEKE, d 1-23-1881 ae 54y 3m 20d (H)
James (nm) & -----
Ch: Charles b N. Y. d 5-12-1848 ae 1y 9m bHS
Phebe M., dt Ezekiel & Sarah GRIFFEN, dis mo 6-1849

BRYSON
Margaret & -----
Ch: Rebecca Hardy d 7- 2-1836 ae 6y 2m 15d bHS
John " 10-18-1833 ae 1y 6m bHS
cf Edinburgh MM 12-12-1833; ct Edinburgh 5-5-1847

BUCHANNAN
Abigail d 7-5-1828; con mo 9-4-1822

BUCK
James gct Phila or elsewhere from Leeds MM, Eng., 6-21-1784 (clear); ct Brig House, Leeds, 11-1-1787 (clear)

BUCKHOUSE
Thomas rocf Lancaster, Eng., 9-3-1777

BUCKHOUT
Adaline, dt John J. & Jane H. (Hall) MACY, Hudson, b Greenport 11-13-1843 d 2-23-1913 (m Peter Buckhout (nm) 9-23-1874) (H)
cf Hudson & Chat. 12-5-1896
William B. rocf Chap. 3-1842; dis 2-1844 (H)

BUCKLEY
Ann, dt Phineas & Mary, gct Middletown 8-1-1804 with father & sister, Sarah (clear)
Elizabeth rocf Middletown 5-8-1794 (clear); ct Middletown 6-7-1798 (clear); cf Middleton 6-5-1800 (clear); cf Middletown 8-1-1804 (clear)
Elizabeth W., dt Phineas & Mary; m 1796 Samuel UNDERHILL
Jacob, s Peter & Phebe, rocf Chap. with parents 1827; ct Ama. 3-1852 (H)
Mary Anna, dt Thomas & Anna, N. Y.; m 1821 Walter R. WOOD
Jane L., dt Thos. & Anna, b 1-14-1817; ct Balt.
John dis mo 5-1-1822
Peter d 6-28-1840; m Phebe ----- (H)
Ch: William d 5- 5-1854
Jacob
cf Chap. 8-1827 with 2 ch; ct Paltz 4-1838 for parents
Phineas & Mary
Ch: Elizabeth Williams d 4-3-1841 ae 80y 11m 20d bHS
Sarah
Deborah
Ann
Phineas William
cf Middletown, Pa. 7-4-1793 with w & 5 ch; ct Middletown 6-7-1798 with ch, Sarah, Anne & Phineas; cf Middletown 6-5-1800 with 3 ch, Sarah, Ann & Phineas; ct Middletown 8-1-1804 with s, Phineas. The father clear
Phineas William, s Phineas & Mary, d at New Orleans; cf Middletown 11-9-1809
Sarah, dt Phineas & Mary, gct Middletown 8-1-1804 with father & sister, Ann (clear)
Thomas, s Phineas & Mary, Bristol, Pa., d 4-28-1846 ae 75y; m N. Y. 9-11-1793 Anna LAWRENCE, dt John & Ann, N. Y., d 7-11-1846 ae 74y
Ch: William L. b 10- 6-1794 d 9- 9-1812 ae 17y 11m 3d bHS
John Lawrence b 7-31-1797; dis 1822
Phineas Henry " 3- 1-1800; " 1824
Mary Anna " 7-22-1802
Elizabeth Williams b 7-31-1805 d 4-23-1841
Effingham Laurence b 5-10-1808 dis 12-
Jane Lawrence " 1-14-1812 [1833 (O)
cf Wilmington 10-10-1792 (clear); parents & Effingham dis 1829 (H)

BUCKMAN
Edna, dt Chas. H. & Mary B.; m 1904 Wilmer R. KEARNS (H)
cf Green St. 4-10-1909; ct Gwynedd with h & youngest dt
Thomas Smith, s Chas. H. & Mary P. (Begley), b Phila. abt 1887; m 6-3-1911 Ina F. STEINER (m by M. E. minister) (H)
Ch: Donald Albert b 12-24-1914 at Rockville Centre, L. I.

BUCKWELL
Carolyn C., dt Jas. F. & Carrie E. (Cook), b Westfield, N. J. 1-16-1907; m 12-15-1931 Myron GLASER (nm), s Sam'l Jerome & Henrietta (Herzog) (nm) (H)
recrq 2-10-1919
Donald, s Jas. F. & Carrie E., b Westfield, N. J., 7-17-1909; recrq 2-10-1919 (H)
Helen C., dt Jas. F. & Carrie (Cook), b Bkn., 6-8-1903; m Chas. E. KOESTING (nm); recrq 2-10-1919 (H)
James F. (nm) m Carrie E. COOK, dt Cornelius & Caroline (Olson), b Bkn. 12-30-1873 (H)
Ch: Helen Cook b 6- 8-1903
Ruth Elizabeth " 5-22-1905
Carolyn C. " 1-16-1907
Donald " 7-17-1909
Carolyn C. & Donald recrq 2-10-1919; Helen recrq 4-12-1926; Carrie E. & Ruth recrq 12-10-1928

BUEANNAN
Abigail (nm) b North Castle drowned 7-5-1828 ae 39y bHS

BUFFINGTON
Isabel gc 8 Mo (Oct) 2, 1740 (rem)

BUFFUM
Benjamin, s David & Susan Ann, Middletown, R. I.; m N. Y. 11-11-1846 Ellen KING, dt John & Mary R.
Ellen K. gct Uxbridge, Mass., 5-5-1847
David rocf Smithfield, R. I. 11-26-1835 (clear); dis mo 3-4-1840
Rebecca, w Arnold, rocf New Garden, Pa., 2-21-1846; rem to R. & P. with h

BUIK
James rocf Brighouse MM, Eng., 3-1-1769

BULKLEY
Caroline (nm) b Indiana 1844 d W. Nyack 1935 bPP; m 1867 Stephen R. POST
Peter & Phebe
Ch: William
Jacob

BULKLEY, Peter & Phebe, continued
cf Ama. 2-9-1827 with 2 ch; Peter dis 1-1832; Phebe dis 4-1830; ch dis 1839
----- m Ruth FENNYERE
recrq 4-3-1907

BULL
Anna, dt Ebenezer & Jane (Pearsall), b Hamptonburgh, N. Y. 9-15-1828 d there 5-26-1921; m 1853 Samuel C. WEEKS (H)

BULLOCK
Elizabeth, late of Barbados; m 1701 Elnathan FIELD, Flushing
Patience, late of Bermuda; m 1701 Nathaniel FIELD
cf Bermuda 5 Mo (July) 3, 1701 for Patience (clear)

BUNKER
Abel, a mbr of Hudson; dis mo 8-2-1797
Abigail rocf Hudson 6-24-1817; b N. J. d 3-25-1831 (or 3-26-1831) ae 70y (H)
Abishai (now 1795 called Robert), s William
Abraham, s Silas & Deborah (both dec), Hudson; m N. Y. 12-10-1800 Jamima BALDWIN, dt Benj. & Eliz., N. Y.
cf Hudson for Abraham (clear)
Alexander C., s Timothy W. & Eunice C., d 4-27-1907 ae 90y 5m 18d bPP; m Mary P. ----- d 8-19-1906 ae 86y 5m 21d
Ch: Edward H. (or S.)
Robert A. d 4-20-1859 (or 4-24-1859) ae 15y 1m 14d bPP
cf Hudson 4-4-1838 (clear); cf Jericho 6-1858 with w & 2 ch named; ct Jericho 4-5-1876 for parents
Anna S., dt Reuben & Abigail; rocf Hudson with parents 2-24-1824; relrq 3-3-1858 (H)
Barzillai d 1829; m Lydia ----- d 10-14-1826
Ch: George
Merab
Eunice
Reuben
cf N. P. 5-18-1792 with w & 4 ch; ct N. Y. for all, they living at Hudson 4-3-1793; cf Hudson 4-25-1815 for both, with gr dt, Maria Bunker; ct Nantucket 4-5-1820 for both with minor gr ch, Maria; cf Nantucket 5-3-1821 with gr dt, Maria; Barzilai dis 3-1830 (0)
Benjamin F. (nm) & -----
Ch: Julia b N. Y. d 12-21-1837 ae 10m 2d bHS
Bethuel, s Elihu & Mirriam, rocf Hudson with parents 11-26-1816; dis 1823
Cyrus E. (nm) & -----
Ch: Caroline b N. Y. d 12-22-1830 ae 2y 3m 28d bHS
Edward H. (or S.), s Alex. C. & Mary P., Bkn., d 6-7-1897 ae 56y 5m 22d bPP; m at Paul Bunker's, Bkn., 12-25-1860 Alice LOINES, dt John (dec) & Mary B., Bkn., b 9-5-1844 N. Y. d 12-4-1911 (H)
Ch: Lucy Howard b 11- 6-1861 d 1-17-1864 [bPP
Phebe Anna " 12-18-1863
Harold " 12-21-1869
Alice (changed to Elsie, later to Elise) b 6- 1-1879 d 11-10-1924
cf Jericho 6-1858 with his parents [bPP
Elihu S. m Mirriam ----- d 9-1833
Ch: William I.
Bethuel
Frederick E.
Robert S.
cf Hudson 11-26-1816 with 4 ch named; Elihu dis 1824
Elihu S. m 2nd Judith LEGGETT, d 6-7-1840 (mo before 12-10-1834); Judith's acknowledgment accepted by Pur. 3-11-1835; cf Pur. 11-1836 (H)
Frederick E., s Elihu & Mirriam, rocf Hudson with parents 11-26-1816; dis mo 5-1834 (H); dis mo 2-1833 (0)
Harold, s Edw. S. & Alice L., b Bkn. 12-21-1869; name removed (H)
Henry William rocf Hudson 9-23-1823 (clear); ct Hudson 8-1837 (H)
Hepzibah, dt William & Mariam, gct Nantucket 7-1-1795 (clear); she now living with her uncle there
Jemima gct N. P. 1-1-1806 (clear)
Lydia, dt Silas & Deborah; m Benjamin MACY; m 2nd 1849 Hezekiah WILLIAMS; m 3rd 1851 Nathaniel STARBUCK (H)
ct Troy 9-3-1851
Lydia C., dt Timothy W. & Eunice (Coffin) b Hudson 11-11-1818 d Hudson; m 1838 Robert COFFIN
cf Hudson 5-21-1822 with parents; ct Hudson 4-4-1838 (clear)
Maria gr dt Barzilla & Lydia, gct Nantucket with gr parents 4-5-1820, minor; cf Nantucket 5-3-1821 with gr parents; dis 2-1841
Mariam, w Wm., rocf Creek 12-17-1790 with dt, Hephzibah
Mary, dt Elizabeth, recrq 8-1824
Mary, dt Reuben & Abigail, N. Y.; m 1843 John LOINES
Mary C., dt Timothy W. & Eunice C., d 11-20-1885; ct Hudson 4-4-1838 (clear); cf Hudson 9-1858
Obed (nm) b Nantucket d 6-17-1812 ae 37y 4m bHS (m)
Paul, s Reuben & Abigail (both dec) Bkn., d 12-6-1876 ae 71y 5m 1d bPP; m at Abm. W. Leggett's 6-27-1869 Phebe G. LEGGETT, dt Isaac & Judith (both dec), d 3-14-1889 ae 67y 6m 13d (H)
Ch: Alice b 7----1863
Sarah "
cf Hudson 6-22-1824 (clear); Phebe G. rocf Pur. 11-1836
Paul m Almira S. ----- d 3-3-1867 ae 61y bPP (both nm) (H)
Phebe, dt Timothy & Eunice C., dis mo 5-6-1835 to ----- VAN SICKLIN

BUNKER, continued
Phebe A., dt Edw. S. & Alice L., b Bkn. 12-18-1863; m 1916 Wm. A. LOINES (H)
Phebe Anna, dt Paul & Almira (Starbuck), b Boston 1-8-1832 d 1-27-1922 ae 90y 19d; m 1857 Josiah T. TUBBY (H)
recrq 4-1878
Phebe J., dt Timothy W. & Eunice C.; m ----- VANSICKLER (mo) (H)
ct Hudson 4-1834
Prince, having mo Nantucket refers it to this MM 7-3-1801, referred to Hudson 10-7-1801 as he now lives there
Rebecca rocf Nantucket 1-31-1811 (clear); ct WD MM 6-3-1818 (clear)
Reuben d 5-25-1853 ae 80y 7m bPP; m Abigail ---
Ch: Anna S. dis 12-1839; d 8-31-1885 ae 72y
Mary " " "
Paul " 6-1830
cf Hudson 2-24-1824 with 2 ch named; Reuben dis 8-1-1829
Robert (form named Abishai), s William, Hudson, rocf Hudson, 11-4-1795, minor
Robert S., s Elihu & Mirriam, rocf Hudson with parents 11-26-1816; dis 11-1826
Robert T., s Timothy W. & Eunice C., d 3-18-1891 ae 75y bPP; m Rachel F. ----- (nm) d 12-25-1886 ae 70y bPP
Ch: Marie Louise (nm) d 4-18-1902 ae 58y bPP
ct Hudson 4-4-1838 (clear) (O); cf Hudson 12-1841 (H)
Timothy W. m Eunice C. COFFIN, d at Hudson
Ch: Mary C.
Phebe J. dis 5-1835
Alexander C.
Robert T.
Lydia C.
cf Hudson 5-21-1822; Timothy dis 10-1829 (O); Eunice dis 11-1829 (O); ct Hudson 6-1836 (H) for all but Phebe (H)
William dis mo 10-7-1818
William A., s William; m Mariam -----
Ch: Hephzibah
ct Oblong 11-4-1795, a minor; having mo Oblong refers it to N. Y. 3-1-1797, complaint returned 4-5-1797 as he was far away & his fam in Hudson; cf Creek 12-7-1790 for Mariam & dt
William Henry rocf Hudson 1823; dis 2-1830
----- & -----
Ch: Charles b N. Y. d 9-11-1827 ae 1y 11m bHS
Lewis " Hudson d 7-5-1828 ae 8m bHS
Charles " Albany " 9-15-1829 ae 3y bHS

BUNN
John McDowell (nm), s David M. & Jane (McDowell) (nm); m 5-26-1925 Anna B. WEEKS, dt Silas B. & Emma (Willets), b Bkn. 12-31-1879 (H)

BUNTING
Charles T. b 12-13-1804 d 12-3-1881; m at Crosswicks, N. J. 4-7-1830 Phebe M. BURDSALL, dt Richard (dec), d 1-21-1892 (H)
Ch: Elizabeth M. b 5- 9-1831 d 2- 4-1921 ae 89y 10m
Ella Frances " 9- 4-1837 " 11-24-1899
Sarah Louisa " 2-14-1841 " 11- 2-1856
bPP rem to Greenwood 4-19-1881
Jane R. b 1- 6-1847
cf Chesterfield 7-1831; builder of 15th St. Mtg & School houses
Eugene, dt Wm. & Phebe L., d 4-7-1916 ae 74y; m Edmund BLUNT (H)
Jane R., dt Chas. T. & Phebe M., b 1- 6-1847 d 7-10-1936; m 1887 Joseph F. MOORE (mbr Radnor, Pa.) (H)
Ch: Edwin Bunting b 11-16-1888
Elwood Burdsall " 11-23-1890
Joseph N., s Newbury & Elizabeth (Haines), b Crosswicks, N. J. 10-15-1857 d 5-21-1905; m 9-11-1900 Alice GRIFFIN, dt Stephen & Jane A., b 4-7-1863 d 9-27-1903 (H)
Ch: Alice Elizabeth b 9-27-1903
Joseph recrq 8-6-1884
Sarah, wd, recrq 3-1874; ct Lurgan, Ireland, 1-6-1875
William (nm) d 3-31-1907 ae 90y 3m 17d bPP; m Phebe L. ----- d 11-28-1893 ae 72y bPP
Ch: Leonora d 10- 3-1844 ae 21d bHS
Eugene m Edmund BLUNT

BURDEN
Samuel, of R. I., m Elizabeth CROSSE, Exon. Eng. (m at John Ferris', Westchester, 4 Mo (June) 1, 1679
He, a stranger, had declared his intention at Tapsham MM, Eng.

BURDETT
Joseph Henry (nm), s Joseph & Jennie (nm); m 12-26-1904 Edith P. ROBINS, dt Silas T. & Susan H., b 9-14-1879
Ch: Howard J. d 11-25-1916 ae 6y 10m 5d bPP

BURDGE
Franklin (nm), s Ira & Harriet; m 9-10-1891 Ella L. JACKSON, dt Samuel K. & Eliz. (Curtis), b N. Y. 5-20-1853 d 1-18-1933 (H)
Ella recrq 1-7-1892

BURDICK
David J., s David M. & Julia C. (Osborn), b Liverton, R. I. 11-19-1854 d 2-23-1923; m 10-15-1906 Mary Rogers BABBITT, dt Isaac N., Jr. & Eliz. G., b Fairhaven, Mass., 9-1-1873

BURDSALL (see BIRDSALL)
Ann rocf Burlington 1-7-1761 as Ann Burdall
Fanny d 3-31-1851 ae 68y 24d bPP
Jane C., dt Richard & Frances (Crowell), b Trenton, N. J., 8-24-1817 d 1-5-1902; m 1840 Isaac D. RUSSELL (H)
cf R. & P. 2-1842; ct Pur. 1-1845; cf Pur. 1851 with ch
Mary rocf R. & P. 8-22-1810; ct R. & P. 11-6-

BURDSALL, Mary, continued
1811 (clear)
Richard, Jr. rocf R. & P. 4-18-1810; ct R. & P. 10-2-1811

BURGER
Stephen D. & M. Antoinette
Stephen D. recrq 9-1883; M. Antoinette recrq 4-1882; lived Portchester, N. Y.
Timothy H., s Nicholas & Catharine, N. Y., b 4-8-1797 d 11-19-1872 bPP; m N. Y. 1-9-1822, Deborah SWART, dt John & Deborah, Middletown, N. J., b N. J. d 9-1-1842 ae 42y 10m
Ch: Hester Falconer b 1- 8-1830 d 1-17-1830
Rachel F. " 5- 7-1839 " 8-15-1839
both recrq 2-7-1821; both dis 1830

BURGESS
Mary J. rocf Grange, Ire., 1-10-1883; ct Mt. Mellick, Ire., 6-1888
Valeria, dt Israel & Agnes DEAN, b 3-29-1818; dis mo 11-1845
----- (nm) m Mary Winifred BOWERMAN, dt J. Philip & Edith M., b 7-28-1884
recrq of parents 1-3-1894

BURKE
Arthur, s Francis P. & Catharine (Greene) (nm) b N. Y. 11-11-1883; m 2-4-1922 Frances HURT, dt Hastings H. & Laura (Love) (nm), b St. Paul 11-14-1894
Ch: John b 11-27-1922
Elizabeth McDonald b 9-16-1924
Parents recrq 11-12-1923; John recrq of parents 2-9-1931; John b Englewood; Elizabeth b White Plains
Mary, dt Thomas & Elizabeth, m ----- HYATT
recrq of mother 1824; dis mo 11-1849
Mary Ann d 1-16-1879 m ----- VAN HOUTON
Ch: (adopted) Mary Ella
recrq 10-1809; Mary Ella recrq of Mary Ann 12-1870; relrq 12-1878
Thomas d 7-17-1851; m 2-4-1818 Elizabeth DOXY, d 11-14-1838 ae 56y 2m 14d
Ch: Mary
Elizabeth dis mo 3-4-1818, rst 5-1824; Thomas recrq 1-1829; Mary recrq of parents 1824; Elizabeth dis 1829 (H); Mary withdrew (H)
----- & -----
Ch: Elizabeth Ann d 3-18-1827 ae 4d

BURKHILL
John (nm) b Chester, Eng., d 4-3-1811 ae 45y bHS

BURKLE
Juliet (nm) b N. Y. d 4-25-1827 ae 16y bHS (unm)

BURLING
Abigail, dt James; m 1741 Samuel BOWNE
Alice G., dt Samuel & Phebe H., Bkn., b Bkn., 8-3-1870; m 1897 Edward T. ROBINSON (H)
Ch: Eleanor b 5-14-1901
Ann, dt John & Ann, N. Y.; m 1755 John LAWRENCE
Ann dis mo 1-5-1814
Ann, wd, cf Pur.
Ch: Phebe
Peter
William
James
Philip (invalid)
ct Pur. 5-1-1799 for Anne & dt, Phebe;
ct Pur. for 4 s same date (clear)
Benjamin d 7 Mo (Sept) 15, 1747
Benjamin gct N. P. 9-6-1781, having rem some time since
Benjamin F. & Hannah
Ch: Catharine H.
Mary F. b 2-17-1815
Ann Louisa " 9-26-1817
Susan Matilda" 2-15-1820
cf Pur. 7-9-1812 for Benj. & Hannah; ct Pur. 7-3-1822 with 4 ch named
Catharine, dt Thos. & Sarah, N. Y.; m 1791 Joseph HOPKINS
Ebenezer & Mary
Ch: Rebecca b 5 Mo (July) 16, 1737
Hannah " 2 Mo (Apr) 4, 1739
ack. for both accepted 9 Mo 3, 1737
Ebenezer (nm) b Eastchester d 12-13-1824 ae 59y 7m 12d bHS
Edward b Eng. & Grace
Ch: Edward b 9 Mo (Nov) 4, 1674 in Eng. d 10 Mo 6, 1687
Grace b 8 Mo (Oct) 29, 1676
William b 10 Mo (Dec) 26, 1678
Rebecca " 6 Mo (Aug) 1681
Jane " 5 Mo (July) 17, 1684
Sarah " 3 Mo (May) 12, 1687
Benjamin b 12 Mo (Feb) 6, 1689/90 d N. Y. 10 Mo (Dec) 21, 1709
Edward Carpenter, s Edward & Grace, d N. Y. 3 Mo (May) 1749; m at John Ferris' 4 Mo (June) 11, 1700 Phebe FERRIS, dt John & Mary, Westchester
Ch: James b 3 Mo (May) 9, 1701
John " 6 Mo (Aug) 9, 1703
Phebe " 8 Mo (Oct) 24, 1705
Sarah " 5 Mo (July) 25, 1712
Edward " 12 Mo (Feb) 3, 1713/14
Martha " 9 Mo (Nov) 29, 1715
Edward, N. Y. m bet. 1 Mo 7 & 2 Mo (Apr) 4, 1723 Mary ROGERS, late of Nantucket, d 8 Mo (Oct) 10, 1731
Edward gc 4 Mo 7, 1733 (clear)
Edward, N. Y. m Flushing 8 Mo 20, 1743 Anna FARRINGTON, Flushing
Edward, s Jas. (dec) & Eliz., d 11-20-1805 ae 79y; m Newtown 10-12-1757 Deborah VAN WYCK, dt William & Martha, Newtown
Edward gct Corn 1-4-1797 with w & dt; cert was not rec & was returned 2 or 3 yrs later
Edward F. rocf Pur. 3-1865; relrq 11-3-1875
Elias active mbr from 1681

BURLING, continued
Elizabeth con mo 7-6-1763
George dis mo 6-5-1771
Hannah, dt William, Flushing; m 1730 Anthony FIELD
James, N. Y., d 1-8-1754; m bet. 3 Mo 2 & 4 Mo (June) 6, 1723 Elizabeth GALE
James, s William, dis mo 10-3-1759, also for being treasurer of the militia
James & Hannah
Ch: John
cf Pur. 6-8-1820; ct Pur. 3-4-1829 for James & Hannah; parents dis 1829 (H)
Jane, Flushing; m 1717 James MOTT
Jane, dt John & Ann; m 1770 Ebenezer HAVILAND
John, s Edward, N. Y., d 7-20-1785; m Flushing 5 Mo (July) 5, 1733 Anne DOBSON, dt Thomas (dec), N. Y.
Ch: Phebe
Peter
William
James
Philip
ct Pur. 6-4-1777 for all; cf Pur. 3-8-1781 for all
John & w rocf Pur. 3-1-1753; John with w & ch rocf Pur. 6-7-1753; certified mbr 1755
John, s Thomas, d 8-10-1820
John active mbr from 1681
John gct Pur. 3-4-1829 (clear)
John m Pur. Hannah ----
Ch: Catharine
John gct Pur. 11-6-1766 (clear); Hannah, his wife, rocf Pur. 3-12-1767; ct Pur. not found; cf Pur. with w & dt 7-6-1785; certified mbr 1755
John C. & Elizabeth
cf Pur. 5-1856 for John C. (H); ct Pur. 3-4-1874 for John C. (H); cf Pur. 2-1861 for Elizabeth (O); ct Pur. 7-6-1873 for Elizabeth (O)
John T. rocf Pur. 1856; mo before 2-1861, ret mbrp; ct Pur. 8-1864; unable to attend regularly as he is in business as Apothecary
Joseph, s Thomas, rocf Pur. 6-13-1805, placed with a Friend
Joseph rocf Farm. 9-1837, minor; ct Scipio 6-1839 (H)
Lancaster con mo 11-6-1798
Martha gct Ama. 7-5-1815 (clear)
Mary, dt John; m 1765 James PARSONS
Mary (late Shepherd) dis mo 8-4-1813; appealed to QM 10-28-1813, which confirmed judgment of MM 4-21-1814
Mary d 1-24-1859; cf Pur. 5-1853 (H)
Phebe, dt Ann, gct Pur. 5-1-1799 (clear)
Rachel Helms (form Burling) dis mo before 6-5-1771
Rebeckah, dt William, Flushing; m 1729 Robert FIELD
Richard, s Samuel, rocf Pur. 3-13-1817, minor, placed with his uncle; ct Pur. 6-5-1822 (clear)
Samuel con mo bef 4 Mo (June) 7, 1744
Samuel d 11-12-1757, N. Y.; m Burlington, N. J., 1752 Jane -----
Samuel gct Burl. 3-25-1752 (clear); Jane rocf Burl. 11-2-1752; they rem to Burl. 12-16-1753; returned 7-7-1757; Jane rem to Burl. 2-2-1759
Samuel d 10- 2-1800 bHS
Samuel (nm) b N. Y. d 7-25-1843 ae 73y 5m bHS
Samuel, s Benj. F. & Hannah (Hosier), b New Rochelle 4-1-1826 d 1-26-1908; m 9-15-1857 Phebe H. HAVILAND, dt John & Ann (Cromwell), b Pur. 7-9-1833 d 5-25-1920 (H)
Ch: De Witt Livingston b 11-1-1859 d 7-25-1861
William Clinton " 3-21-1861
Anna H. " 11-15-1863 " 8- 9-1864
Alice Gertrude " 8- 3-1870
cf Pur. 6-4-1856 for Samuel; cf Pur. 3-2-1859 for Phebe
Sarah, Flushing; m 1716 John WAY
Sarah, dt Edward, Flushing; m 1737 Benjamin SMITH, of Trenton, N. J.
rem to Trenton 11 Mo (Jan) 5, 1737/8
Sarah, dt James (dec) & Eliz., Flushing; m 1754 Caleb LAWRENCE
Sarah rocf Rahway 9-4-1771
Sarah, dt Thomas, Pur., gct Pur. 1-4-1797 (clear)
Sarah W. d 9-21-1858 ae 82y bPP; m William R. LOWERRE (both nm)
Thomas m bet 5-7- & 6-4-1761 Phebe VAN WYCK
Thomas, N. Y., b West Co. d 12-24-1831 (or 12-25-1831) ae 85y 3m; m Susanna ----- d 9-23-1831 ae 82y
Ch: Anne b 5-30-1784
Anne 2nd " 11-19-1786
Maria " 3-15-1789
Maria 2nd " 9-26-1791
Thomas C. " 4-15-1795
cf Creek 1-16-1784 for Thos. & Susanna
Thomas gct N. P. 6-3-1778 having rem some time past
Thomas & -----
Ch: Sarah
Thos. gct Pur. with 2 minor ch, 6-4-1777
Thomas, s John & Anne, N. Y., m N. Y. 12-12-1781 Henrietta HULL, dt Oliver & Penelope
Ch: Joseph b 10-17-1782 d 11-15-1783
Mary " 12- 9-1783
Ann " 11-28-1785 " 5-30-1786
Joseph " 8-30-1787
Ann " 4-20-1789 " 9- 2-1816
Thomas " 8-19-1791
cf Pur. 3-8-1781 (clear); ct Pur. 1-6-1796 with Mary, Joseph, Ann & Thomas
Thomas H. d 4-13-1866; m Elizabeth ----- d 11-11-1866
Ch: Thomas H. d 12-14-1821
Thomas W.
Ann b 2- 9-1816
Henrietta b 12-14-1821

BURLING, Thomas H. & Elizabeth, continued
ct Pur. 8-6-1823 with 3 ch named; cf Marl. 12-1848 for parents (H)
Walter gct Tortola for commerce 1-6-1762
William d 8 Mo (Oct) 10, 174[4]; m Rebecca ---- d 2 Mo (Apr) 2, 1729
Ch: Mary b 7 Mo (Sept) 15, 1706 d 6 Mo 7, 1727
William " 7 Mo (Sept) 18, 1708
Benjamin " 9 Mo (Nov) 18, 1710
Rebekah " 12 Mo (Feb) 28, 1711/12
Hannah " 10 Mo (Dec) 10, 1713
Sarah " 6 Mo (Aug) 2, 1715
Ebenezer " 6 Mo (Aug) 2, 1717
Amy " 2 Mo (Apr) 20, 1724 d 5 Mo 12, 1741
William, Flushing, d before 1747; m Flushing between 3 Mo 7 & 4 Mo (June) 4, 1730 Mary DOUGHTY, dt Francis, d 8 Mo (Oct) 25, 1747
William (nm) & ----
Ch: Mary d 4-29-1816 ae 5m bHS
William, Jr., Flushing, d 4 Mo (June) 1745; m Flushing 1 Mo (Mar) 12, 1729/30 Sarah BOWNE, dt Samuel & Hannah
Ch: Hannah b 12 Mo (Feb) 6, 1730/1 d 3 Mo 23,1732
Joseph " 8 Mo (Oct) 8, 1732
Hannah " 2 Mo (Apr) 7, 1734
Sarah " 4 Mo (June) 19, 1736
Rebecca " 5 Mo (July) 30, 1738
William Clinton b Bkn. 3-21-1861 d 9-22-1923; m 2-22-1887 Lillie T. RAYMOND (nm) d 4-9-1932 (H)
Ch: Wm. Raymond
Lillie B. m ----- PEATMAN
Alice B. " ----- SINGLETON
Wm. Raymond, s Wm. C. & Lillie T., b Bkn., 12-29-1888 d 2-11-1929; m 6-8-1912 Lillie P. PEREIRA, dt Russell & Lillie (Swimney), b Bkn. 2-26-1890
William recrq 2-14-1914; Lillie recrq 3-13-1928
William S. m Portsmouth, R. I., Elizabeth -----
Ch: Mary b 2-15-1802
Caroline " 12-22-1803
John " 10-17-1805 d 12-5-1808 ae 3y
Thomas " 10- 8-1807
William
cf Portsmouth 12-26-1799 for Elizabeth; ct Scipio 4-3-1811 with their 4 ch, Mary, Caroline, Thomas & William
----- & -----
Ch: Wm. James d 2-16-1832 ae 1y 1m 8d
----- & -----
Ch: Walter b N. Y. d 2-16-1824 ae 6m
Mary " " " 4-17-1836 ae 2y 6m bHS
William James " 2-16-1932 ae 1y 1m 8d bHS

BURNETT
Henry m Mary HALLETT
Ch: Annabella b 6- 6-1784
Jane " 7-17-1794
Mary mo before 10-3-1783; con mo 4-7-1784
John [Burnet] rocf R. & P. 10-20-1790 (clear) ct Westland MM 8-1-1793 (clear)
Phebe A. [Burnet], dt Geo. H. & Phebe BIRDSALL, d 1-27-1903
Thomas [Burnet], Newtown, b 4-14-1766
Thomas rocf R. & P. 5-2-1790 (clear); ct R. & P. 5-2-1793 (clear)
William (nm) m Phebe Anna BIRDSALL, dt George H. & Phebe, b 7-14-1837 d 1-21-1903 bPP
----- & -----
Ch: Willie H. d 11-18-1888 ae 29y bPP
Alden M. " about 1893 bPP

BURNS
Wm. P. (nm), s Jas. Warren; m 10-27-1923 Ruth Ann Winifred MALONE, dt Jas. E. & Anne F. (Brown), b N. Y. 4-14-1904 (H)
Separated, she resumed maiden name; Ruth recrq 2-9-1931

BURR
Barzillai rocf Shrewsbury 5-11-1831
Elizabeth d in Phila 1-6-1858 ae 74y bPP
John, s Henry, Northampton, N. J.; m Wby 3 Mo (May) 29, 1712 Keziah WRIGHT, dt John (dec) & Rachel, O.B.

BURRELL
William (nm) b Eng. d 3-16-1824 ae 86y bHS (m)

BURROUGHS
Elizabeth gct New Castle, Pa. 9 Mo (Nov) 1, 1733
Anna, w Charles (H)
Ch: Penelope
ct Wby 1-3-1838, returned cert 7-1838; recrq 5-1821 with her ch; dis 2-1841 (O)

BURT
Margaret A. (nm), dt John & Mary J. (Martin); m 1888 Arthur HAVILAND (H)
Mary rst 10-3-1821 on rq of Chap. (living here)
Penelope, dt Charles & Anna, recrq of mother 1821; dis mo to first cousin ----- HAUX-HURST 11-1828 (O); dis mo 11-1829 (H)

BURTIS
Jesse & -----
Ch: William (nm) d 10-22-1814 ae 5d bHS
recrq 4-5-1815; ct Cincinnati 12-3-1817

BURTON
George John, s John & Jane (Payter), b Ashley-de-la-Zouch, Eng., 11-27-1874; m 7-6-1895 Martha R. WILSON (nm), dt Robert & Mary (Anderson) (nm)
George recrq 3-13-1928; relrq 9-9-1929
Mary Ann, w R. B., dt ----- JOHNSON, d 12-5-1886 N. Y. ae 70y 19d bPP (H)
cf Phila. Spruce St. 9-1842; in Vermont 1858

BUSH
Dorothea b N. J. d 3-24-1812 ae 17y 10m bHS (unm)
Jonas (nm) & -----
Ch: John Thomas d 11-5-1816 ae 6y bHS

BUSHONG
Dr. Charles H., s Gilbert & Edith K. (Paxson), Pa., b Lancaster Co., Pa. 10-1-1856 d 12-20-1903; m Anna KEENE, dt Samuel & Rebecca Jr., b Lancaster Co., Pa. 4-21-1868 d 7-8-1894 (H)
cf Sadsbury 2-5-1890 for Charles; Anna recrq 11-6-1889
Charles H. m 2nd at 15th St. 5-25-1899 Nora E. KEENE, dt Samuel (dec) & Rebecca, Jr., b Lancaster Co., Pa., 4-21-1868 d 3-14-1930
Nora K. recrq 7-8-1899

BUSSELLE
Alfred, s Samuel D. & Sarah E. (both dec), N.Y., b 5-25-1874; m at Phebe Anna Murray's 10-1-1903 Harriet C. MURRAY, dt Robt. I. & Phebe Ann, Chap.
Ch: Robert Murray b 9- 3-1904
Alfred Jr. " 8-28-1905
Ann " 5-18-1910
Harriet C. recrq of parents 2-17-1897; ch active mbr 12-1924
Anna Maria, dt George & Elizabeth, N. Y.; m 1844 Edward MARSHALL, Jr.
cf Bristol, Eng. with parents 6-13-1820
Francis, s George & Elizabeth, b 6-25-1828; dis mo 8-1854
George d 4-14-1851; m Elizabeth ----- d 11-13-1851
Ch: George
Alfred d 4-23-1877
Richard dis 12-1844
Charles " 9-1842
Ann Maria
Sophia Jane
Samuel Daw b 2-16-1825
Francis " 2-26-1828
John Hare " 9-16-1830
cf Bristol, Eng. to Phila. or elsewhere in America 6-13-1820 with first 4 ch named; George dis 3-1839; rst 5-1849
John Hare, s George & Elizabeth, b 9-16-1830; dis mo by a priest 2-1857
Richard, s George & Elizabeth, dis mo 1-1845
Robert Murray, s Alfred & Harriet (Murray), b Chap. 9-3-1904
associate 9-3-1904; active mbr 12-1924
Samuel Daw, s Geo. & Eliz. (dec), N. Y.; m 1-20-1864 at Edw. Marshall's, N. Y. Sarah Eliza MOSS, dt John (dec) & Eliza, N. Y. d 8-19-1897
Ch: Samuel Marshall b 7-25-1865 d 7-25-1865 bPP
Samuel Marshall " 6-26-1868
Alfred " 5-25-1874
cf Dublin 8-11-1863 for Sarah
S. Marshall, s Samuel D. & Sarah E., b 6-26-1868; m Agnes HARRIS
Ch: Samuel Marshall Jr. b 7-30-1900 d 2-13-1901
Samuel Marshall Jr. " 6-10-1903
Margaret " 10- 9-1904 " 2-19-1907
cf Toronto 2-7-1900 for Agnes; ct Toronto 9-1913 for both with s
Sophia Jane, dt Geo. & Elizabeth, N. Y.; m 1846 Christopher WRAY

BUTLER
John b Bristol, Eng. d 10-20-1830 ae 37y 11m bHS
Joseph M. b Pa. d 10-13-1815 ae 20y 9m bHS (d in a boarding house)
Lydia (form Mott) dis mo 1-5-1842
Phillipa, w John (nm)
Ch: Harriet
Philip John
cf Bristol, Eng. 2-5-1828 with 2 ch named; ct Bristol, Eng. 7-4-1832 with same ch

BUZBY
Mordecai, s Amos & Rebecca, N. Y.; m N. Y. b 6-13-1828 Eleanor EVANS, dt Joseph & Alice, N. Y. (H)
Ch: Alice E. b 1-23-1829
Joseph E. " 6-14-1830
Anna W. " 10- 5-1832
Edward P. " 10-30-1833
Henry C. " 5- 5-1838
Robert E. " 5- 2-1840
William M. " 12-18-1842
cf Burl. 5-7-1828; ct Phila. Cherry St. 4-1846 for all
Mordecai m at Alex. McDowell's 6-9-1853 Eliza. Ann MC DOWELL, dt Alex. & Sarah, N. Y.
cf Burl. 1827; dis 8-1829 (O); ct Phila. Cherry St. 5-1855 for Elizabeth Ann (H)
William J. rocf Evesham, N. J. 5-1-1912

BYERLY
David Davis (or David B.) d 6-21-1868 lost on Lake Erie; m Sarah Ann ----- (H)
Ch: Rebecca Frances b 6- 1-1848
David Homer " 2- 7-1850 d 6-3-1857 (or 5-31-1857) bPP
Elizabeth Wayne b 12-12-1854
cf Phila. 5-3-1854 for all; ct Phila. 11-5-1873 for Sarah
Ellwood d 1-8-1869; m Rebecca P. ----- (H)
Ch: William E. b 12-13-1849
Martha G. " 2-10-1853
cf Phila. 3-1852 with ch, Wm. E.; ct Phila. 7-4-1888 for Rebecca & Martha
Rebecca Frances, dt David D. & Sarah A., b 6-1-1848; mo to R. F. EELS; ct Phila. 3-4-1874 as Eels (H)

BYERLY, continued
Dr. Wm. Elwood, s Ellwood & Rebecca P., b 12-13-1849 d Swarthmore, Pa. 12-1935 ae 86y
cf Phila. with parents 3-1852; Prof. at Swarthmore; Prof. in Cornell 1875-1877; Prof. in Harvard College 1880-1893

BYRD (see BIRD)
Evelyn (nm), dt Geo. Radcliffe & Amy (Pierson); m 1915 Charles Harold VAN BUSKIRK (H)
James, s Thomas & Hannah, Merchant, N. Y.; m 1-9-1793 Elizabeth PEARSALL, dt Thomas & Elizabeth
Ch: James d 6-25-1801 bHS
Thomas & Hannah were from Uffulm, Eng.; cf Bridport & Sherborne, Dorset, 3-9-1790 (clear)
Joseph d 3-31-1799 bHS
Joseph b Eng. d 5-10-1838 ae 71y; m Elizabeth ----- d 5-30-1849 (m Shrewsbury 1791)
Ch: ----- d 8-13-1798
Richard b 7-14-1795 d 3-25-1837
Ann " 11- 3-1798 " 5- 9-1831
Dt d 3-13-1799
cf Nailsworth, Eng. 11-11-1784 (clear); similar cert from Falmouth, Corn. accompanied the other; ct Shrewsbury 10-5-1791 (clear); Elizabeth rocf Shrewsbury (not found); Joseph dis 12-1829 (O); Elizabeth dis 10-1829 (O); Ch dis 1829 (O)
Margaret, dt Philip G. & Ella R.; m 1923 Arthur Joy RAWSON (H)
Margaret mbr at Swarthmore

BYRON
Ada, wd, dt Seth & Sally PANCOAST; m 2nd 1874 Emil FINK (H)
cf Phila. 7-13-1912; ct Phila. 11-14-1932

BYRNES
John [Byrne] (nm) m Selena Grace WHITFIELD, d 8-1-1887 ae 34y bPP
Selena recrq 7-1872
Mary Longbotham, dt Eliz. W., d 12-7-1861; m ----- BYRNE (nm)
Caroline, dt Joseph & Rebecca, gct Le Ray 11-5-1823 (clear); this cert not sent & she dis 1825
Daniel & Esther
Ch: Jonathan
Eleanor
Jacob F.
cf Nottingham, Md. 9-17-1824; ct Wilmington 11-2-1825 with 3 ch named
Joseph, s Daniel & Dinah, Corn., N. Y., d 1-11-1841 ae 71y 26d bHS; m N. Y. 4-15-1795 Rebecca P. CLARKE, dt Nathaniel & Mary (dec), N. Y.
Ch: Elizabeth b 8-1801 d 8-1802 ae 1y
Robert Ralston dis 1825
Walter
Caroline dis 1824
cf Phila. 4-25-1792 (clear); ct Bush River, S. C. 4-6-1803 for Rebecca with 3 ch named; ct same for Joseph, conditional, he being bankrupt. If not accepted, to be dealt with. He settled in Charleston, S. C.
Thomas S. b Wilmington, Del. d 10-8-1825 ae 40y; m Lydia BYRNES (nm), b Maryland d 2-22-1816 ae 18y bHS
cf Corn. 8-25-1808 (clear); dis mo 8-2-1815
----- & ----- (nm)
Ch: Ann P. b N. Y. d 12-5-1822 ae 2y 9m 13d bHS
Thomas S. b N. Y. d 2-4-1825 ae 2y 10d
Walter F. d 3-10-1828 ae 2y bPP

CAHALEY
----- (nm) m Mabel M. HOYT, dt Geo. A. & Emeline, b 3-21-1883
Mabel was in Minneapolis 1912; ct Minneapolis 6-1920

CALDWELL
Jane (nm) bPP

CALEN
----- & ----- (nm)
Ch: Susan d 7-31-1828 ae 1h bHS

CALLIN
Eugene Walker (nm), s Albert C. & Mary (Walker) m 5-20-1926 Louise MERRITT, dt James H. & Adele O., b Bkn., 3-27-1924 (H)
Louise's name dropped 5-14-1934

CALLISTER
J. Henry & Jennie C.
Ch: Constance b 8-31-1912 d 8- 3-1932
Kenneth " 9-12-1915
cf Po'keepsie 12-6-1911 for parents; Constance active mbr 7-1925

CAMLIN
----- & -----
Ch: Louisa d 11-10-1863 ae 3y bPP

CAMP
Mary D. b N. J. d 4-12-1816 ae 64y bHS
mbr from Rahway

CAMPBELL
A. H. (nm) & ----- (H)
Ch: Ada M. d 8-19-1870 ae 7m bPP
Ann, w Jehoakim (nm), dt Thomas & Caty (Bedell) NELSON, b N. Balt., N. Y. 10-17-1816 d 10-1-1902 (m 11-15-1854)(H)
cf Wby 2-2-1848
Archibald b Scotland d 2-26-1832 ae 74y 9m bHS
cf Cornwall 2-26-1824 (clear); dis 4-1830 (O) (unm)
Allen R. (nm), s Walter L. & Helen (LaGorughe) (nm); m 8-6-1907 Gertrude DUBOIS, dt John Coert & Evaline P. (Kimball) (nm), b Hudson 4-29-1878
Gertrude recrq 5-9-1927; Gertrude gct Pur.

CAMPBELL, Allen R. & Gertrude, continued
5-14-1934
Patrick (nm) m 1781 Sarah PEARSALL, dt Thomas & Ann, N. Y., b 8 Mo (Oct) 18, 1746
Ch: Patrick (adopted as Patrick Campbell Pearsall, by Thomas Pearsall, the parents having d early
Sarah dis mo 3-7-1781
Susan W., w Alex. H., dt Jos. & Hannah WHITSON, d 4-2-1891 (m 5-1-1860) (H)
ret mbrp

CANBY
Sally rocf Phila. Green St. 9-1837; ct Phila. Cherry St. 12-1843; cf Phila. Cherry St. 7-1848; ct Phila. Cherry St. 8-7-1850 (H)

CANNON
Abigail (late Knowles) dis mo 3-6-1805
Matt d 8-16-1800 bHS; m -----
Ch: Sarah d 8-30-1803 ae 2y

CAPRON
George Truman, s Jacob & Jane, b 5-30-1858; relrq 4-4-1894
Grace A., dt Jacob & Jane E., b N. Y. 1-22-1878; m 1920 William C. HAVILAND; ct Pur. 1-10-1921 (H)
Jacob, s Orion & Rosalinda, d 4-7-1891 ae 63y 4m 24d; m at Benjamin Price's, Bkn. 5-7-1853 Jane Eliz. BALLINGER, dt Edward (dec) & Eliza P., N. Y., d 2-25-1899 ae 63y 6m 10 d (H)

Ch:			
Edward B.	b	4- 9-1856	d 2- 3-1857
George Truman	"	5-30-1858	
Wm. Orion	"	11- 1-1860	" 12-27-1862
Elizabeth B.	"	8- 5-1865	" 2- 5-1916
Jacob	"	7-17-1867	" 8-11-1867
Allen Newman	"	2- 2-1873	" 4-23-1873
Grace A.	"	1-25-1878	
----- stillborn 1857			
----- " 1868			

cf Galway 4-1850
Willet S. rocf Uxbridge, Mass. 5-27-1836, minor; dis 9-7-1842

CAPSTACK
Sarah b Lancashire d 7-25-1821 ae 75y bHS
cf Marsden, Eng. 7-17-1794 (clear); ct N. P. 3-1-1797 (clear); cf N. P. 2-18-1808 (clear) (unm)

CAREY (see CARY)
Ferris A. (nm), s John & Abigail (nm); m 7-30-1856 Maplet H. CARPENTER, dt Thos. & Sarah (Weeks), b New Castle, N. Y. 7-5-1833 d 2-15-1903 (H)
cf Chap. 7-4-1877 for Maplet
Howard L., s Chas. E. & Ellen H., Fairmont, Ind., b Fairmount, Ind. 11-28-1892; m 6-26-1920 at Florence A. Cawl's, Henrietta E. CAWL, dt Robert E. (dec) & Florence A., Bkn., b 9-25-1894

Ch:		
Robert Charles	b	4-30-1921
Melvin Donald	"	6-30-1922
Frances Ellen	"	6- 8-1926

cf Fairmount, Ind. 12-29-1917; Melvin D. active mbr 4-1935

CARHART
Benjamin I., s Edwin M. & Emily Jane (Gurney), b New Balt., N. Y. 11-17-1860 d 4-20-1934; m 10-22-1908 Elizabeth PARSONS, dt Stephen & Rosana (Croswell), b New Balt. 8-18-1862
cf Albany for Benjamin 3-13-1909; Elizabeth recrq 2-13-1909 (H)
Hendrick [Carhartt] rocf Jericho 5-15-1800 (clear)

CARLE
Edward, s Jacob & Phebe, dis 5-1833 (H)
Edward Hicks, s John Jr. & Cornelia, b N. Y. 12-28-1882; m 6-12-1912 Margaret Hayes THORNE (nm), dt Oakleigh (nm)(H)
Jacob d 8-1831; m Phebe ----- b 1-14-1770 d 2-8-1859 (H)

Ch:			
Ann			d 3- 7-1877
Mary			
John			
Elizabeth	b	9- 3-1807	d 8- 8-1808
Edward	"	12-25-1808	

cf Wby 5-14-1806 with Ann & John; parents dis 1829 (O); ch dis 1830-1832 (O)
John, Jr., s Jacob & Phebe, d 10-28-1888; m Susan H. HICKS, d 1-24-1872 (H)

Ch:			
Phebe Ann	b	12-27-1833	d 3- 9-1846
Sarah H.	"	10- 6-1836	
Silas J.	"	3- 2-1841	" 9-21-1843
Edward Hicks	"	6- 1-1844	" 3-14-1877
John Jr.	"	8-24-1847	

cf Wby 5-14-1806 with parents; cf Makefield 11-1833 for Susan H.
John, Jr., s John Jr. & Susan H. (dec), b 8-24-1847; m at R. R. Willets' 10-15-1874 Cornelia P. WILLETS, dt Robert R. & Lydia, N. Y., b 1-4-1850 d 7-28-1892 (H)

Ch:		
Robert W.	b	7-22-1875
Susan W.	"	3-27-1879
Edward Hicks	"	12-28-1882

Cornelia recrq of mother 4-1857 (O)
Mary, dt Jacob & Phebe, N. Y.; m 1823 Richard EVERIT
cf Wby 7-19-1809, minor, left with her gr parents
Sarah H., s John & Susan H., N. Y.; m 1860 Edward S. BOWNE, of Baltimore (H)
ct Balt. 10-7-1868
Silas & Mary Elizabeth (H)
cf Wby 1-4-1809 (clear); mo before 4-7-1819, care discontinued 6-2-1819; Mary Elizabeth recrq 10-3-1821; both dis 1829-1830 (O); ct Wby 4-1833 (H) for both
Susan W., s John J. & Cornelia, b N. Y. 3-27-1879; m 5-9-1906 Duncan EDWARDS (nm) (H)
Thomas, Flushing, m Flushing 2 Mo (Apr) 17, 1718 Mary GRIFFIN

CARLETON

Bukk Griffith, s Bukk G. & Clarice E., b N. Y. 5-3-1909; m 6-16-1934 Mary ZUCKER, dt Richard D. & Mary E. (Bannan), b Landsdowne, Pa., 6-15-1910 (H)
both recrq 1-14-1935

Edward Ash [Carlton] d 10-28-1837

CARMALT

William H., s Caleb & Sarah (Price), Scip., b Friendsville, Pa., 8-3-1836 d 7-17-1929; m 12-8-1863 Laura WOOLSEY, (nm) dt Wm. S. & Laura W. JOHNSON (H)

CARMAN

Anna d 2-14-1887 (H)
cf Creek 11-6-1867

David P. d 4-28-1898 (H)
cf Stanford 8-1852; ct Stanford 4-7-1858; cf Stanford 11-1859

Henrietta Simpson (form Carman) dis mo by a Bapt. minister 3-6-1861 (H)
cf Oswego 10-1856

James S. d 12-11-1907 ae 77y 6m 7d bPP; m Julia S. PURDY, dt Alex. & Alchie, d 12-30-1912 ae 74y 3m 8d bPP (both nm) (H)

Sarah F., s Samuel R. & Sarah A., N. Y.; m 1861 Edward B. WILLETS (H)

----- & -----
Ch: Edward Martindale d 5- 4-1859 ae 3y 2m bPP

CARMICHAEL

Alice, w D. F., dt Joshua D. & Rebecca G. EVANS
cf Phila. 2-21-1854 with mother; mbrp relinquished 5-1880

CARMODAY

Cornelius rocf Wby 6-26-1786 (clear)

CARNES

Elizabeth (late Bowne) dis mo 8-6-1800

CARPENTER

Aaron d 4-28-1868 (H)
cf Ama. 12-7-1859

Aaron, s Isaac & Lydia (both dec), d 8-18-1873 ae 61y 2m 8d bPP; m 5-11-1836 Jane S. WEEKS, dt Jesse K. & Eliza, b 2-14-1814 d 10-16-1881 (O-H)
Ch: George W. b 2-28-1838
Emily Eliza " 10-28-1844
Frederick J. " 11-29-1851
Augustus Henry " 6- 4-1856
cf Pur. 11-9-1833 (clear)

Abraham & Anna
cf Chap. for both 6-14-1822; ct Ama. 6-7-1826, Anna a minister; cf Ama. 10-1852 for Abm.; dis 12-7-1853

Abraham Clock, s Zeno, d 11-8-1869
recrq of his gr father, Zeno 3-1-1820; dis 12-1839

A. Lincoln, s Robert R. & Hannah W., N. Y., b N. Y. 1-21-1861 d 3-22-1934; m at Mary A. Hull's 1-15-1884 Anna E. HULL (nm), dt Samuel B. & Elizabeth, N. Y. (H)

Adaline, s John T. & Sarah; m 7-6-1864 Frank STICKNEY (H)
name erased 9-7-1864, had joined Congregational Ch in Milwaukee

Adelia Augusta (changed to Amelia Augusta), dt Townsend & Phebe, b 4-12-1829; m David L. UNDERHILL (nm) (H)

Alice, dt Frederick J. & Sarah, b N. Y. 1-11-1876 (H)
name entered by comm. 10-12-1880; relrq 11-11-1905

Alpheus d 11-19-1866 ae 37y (H)
cf Pur. 6-1-1853

Amanda M., w David L., dt Abm. C. & Eliza B. UNDERHILL, b 4-27-1825 (m 9-22-1857)(H)
At Seneca, Ill. 1859

Amos (nm) b Adams, Mass. d 6-5-1827 ae 29y bHS (m)

Ann Eliza, dt Enock & Sophia, N. Y.; m 2-4-1855 Ira M. DAVENPORT (H)

Ann L., dt Isaac & Patience (Halsted), b Somers 5-1-1824; m 8-2-1843 Thomas H. HARRIS; m 2nd 2-20-1856 Henry H. HALLOCK (nm)
cf Ama. 4-1-1844; in Kalamazoo 1900 & later

Anna Lily, dt Wm. H. & Sarah F., b N. Y. 11-3-1894; m 9-20-1916 Robert Russell HOLBROOK, b 11-3-1894 (H)

Artemus d Pur. 3-16-1836; m Rebecca C. -----(H)
Ch: William b 9-25-1830 d 10- 9-1830
Phebe Jane " 1----1834
cf Pur. 8-10-1825 (clear); dis 4-1830 (O); cf Pur. 10-1829 for Rebecca; ct Pur. 8-1838 for Rebecca

Arthur M. D., s Wm. H. & Sarah F., b N. Y. 1-3-1891; m 10-14-1915 Dora DOWNING (nm), dt James & Julia (H)
recrq of parents 10-6-1894

Asa rocf Oswego 8-17-1825 (clear); dis 2-1830 (O); ct Oswego 11-1-1838; cf Oswego 3-7-1849; dis 7-4-1849

Augustus Henry, s Chas. M. & Charlotte, b N. Y. 6-4-1856; relrq 2-14-1921 (H)

Azariah, s Joseph T. & Hannah, b 10-19-1828 d 6-30-1899 ae 70y; m Mary C. BAXTER (nm)
Ch: Charles B. b 4-16-1854
cf Chap. 3-5-1851; ct Chap. 6-4-1862; cf Chap. 1-5-1876

Beatrice J., dt Wm. H. & Sarah F., b N. Y. 2-28-1887; m 6-4-1925 John C. GRIFFIN (nm)
recrq of parents 10-6-1894 (H)

Benjamin, s John T. & Sarah, d Calif. 10-19-1871
cf Pur. 4-1837

Caleb Pierce d 4-14-1881; m Amelia LAWRENCE (nm) (H)
Ch: William Henry b 4-21-1860
cf Ama. 10-1847; Wm. Henry recrq 10-7-1894

Caroline, dt Henry M. & Abby Jane, N. Y.; m 1846 John Hicks MACY

CARPENTER, continued
Caroline, dt James & Mary (Haviland), b N. Y. 3-22-1837 d 4-20-1910; m 1856 Benjamin WILLIAMSON (H)
cf Pur. 9-1860; in Madison, Wis. 1879-1899
Catharine B., dt Isaac Jr. & Catharine, b 2-19-1865 (H)
name entered by comm 1873; relrq 4-6-1892
Charles B., s Azariah & Mary C, (Baxter), b 4-16-1854 Bkn d 11-29-1921; m 6-5-1878 Anna Therese REIMER, dt Carl H. G. & Ann (H)
Ch: Mary C. b 10-24-1885
Chas. recrq 12-6-1893; Mary C. recrq 6-13-1908
Charles M., s Josiah & Charlotte, N. Y., d 11-27-1889; m N. Y. 1-10-1833 Charlotte M. UNDERHILL, dt Israel & Zeruiah (both dec), N. Y., d 4-20-1871 ae 59y bPP (H)
Ch: Cornelia b 6-20-1834 d 9-16-1835
Jane Louisa " 7-20-1836
Phebe Anna (changed to Anna) b 9- 8-1838 d 6-16-1911
Sarah b 2- 9-1842 d 10-17-1896
Lucretia d 9-16-1835 ae 1y 2m 25d
cf Pur. 12-1830
Charles M., s Silas & Ada; m 12-1914 Katherine SPINK, dt Thomas H. & Eliza (Gillen), b N. Y. 7-31-1883 (H)
Clarissa rocf Pur. 1-14-1819, rem with h
Cynthia rocf Danby, Vt. 3-1845; ct Danby 9-[1851
Daniel (nm) & -----
Ch: Ezra b West. Co. d 10-24-1832 ae 28y bHS
Daniel F. & Hannah H.
Ch: John H. b 12-13-1827
Edmund " 5-23-1831
William Henry b 11-15-1836
cf Chap. 7-1833; ct Pur. 8-1837
Daniel H. rocf Oswego 8-17-1825 (clear); dis 4-1831 (O); dis 2-1837 (H)
Daniel J., s Edmund M. & Anna (Stringham), b White Plains 4-17-1854 d 12-8-1908; m 7-13-1881 Emma FASSETT (nm) (H)
cf Creek 9-1-1869
David rocf Pur. 12-10-1812 (clear)
David dis mo 1-1-1817
David gct Chap. 9-3-1817
David, s Zeno, gct Scipio 1-3-1827
David L., s Enoch & Sophia (Lane), b 6-21-1824 d 1----1903; m 2-12-1849 Emeline LAWRENCE, dt Isaac & Pauline (H)
cf Pur. 1-1842
David L. (nm), s Abraham & Ruth; m 9-22-1857 b N. Y. 4-27-1825 d 12-10-1910 (H)
cf Chap. 6-1825 with her mother
David R. rocf Chap. 8-9-1816 (clear)
Dorothy m 1818 ----- TREDWELL
cf Pur. 5-14-1807 (clear); ct Pur. 4-4-1810 (clear); cf Pur. 1-12-1815 (clear); dis mo 11-4-1818
Edith, dt Robert H. & Amy T. (Griffen), b 2-23-1864; m 1893 Fred Lincoln WEARE (H) (nm)
Edith, dt Miles B. & Josephine E.; m 1896 Valentine Everit MACY (H)

Edmund M. m Anna H. STRINGHAM
Ch: John E.
Daniel J. b 4-17-1854
George W.
Edith H.
Mary Emma
Walter T. d 12-19-1874 ae 5y 10m 5d bPP
cf Creek for all 7-16-1869; ct Rock 2-6-1878 for parents with Edith & Mary E. (H)
Edmund T. m Maria ----- d 4-8-1835 ae 33y 6m bHS (both nm)
Edward rocf Pur. 8-7-1844, minor; dis mo 1-1847
Edward H., s Isaac, Jr. & Abby S., b 5-20-1832
cf Pur. 6-1-1853; relrq 3-2-1892 (H)
Eliakim (nm) b Port Chester d 5-6-1827 ae 18y bHS (unm)
Elisha m Letitia ----- d 5-23-1846
cf Pur. for both 2-13-1833; Elisha dis mo by a priest 2-1847; Letitia dis mo by a priest 5-1846
Eliza, dt Benj. (H)
cf Ama. 8-1840 with sisters, Sarah W. & Mary; ct Chap. 7-1-1892
Elizabeth P., dt Wm. H. & Sarah F., b N. Y. 2-28-1887; m 2-21-1912 Wm. Jay GRIFFIN (nm)
recrq of parents 10-6-1894 (H)
Ellwood, s Robert R. & Hannah W., N. Y., b N. Y. 1-22-1863; m at 634 Greenwich St., 1-22-1884 Hattie A. CARPENTER (nm), dt Caleb P. & Amelia C., N. Y. (H)
Elnathan & Hannah F. (H)
Ch: Phebe F. b 11- 9-1834 (or 9-11-1834)
Jacob A "
cf Pur. 6-9-1830 (clear); dis 7-1831 (O); cf Pur. 1832 for Hannah; ct Plains 8-1837 for both; cf Plains 2-1844 with 2 ch named
Elsie, dt Geo. W. & Priscilla, b 4-20-1867; relrq 1-6-1900 (H)
Emily, dt Thos. & Phebe; m 1845 William WRIGHT (H)
Emily Eliza, dt Aaron & Jane S., b 10-28-1844; m 1867 Leonard J. CARPENTER (nm); relrq 12-9-1899 (H)
Emma Jane, dt Thos. & Sarah (Weeks), b New Castle 5-23-1839 d 2-21-1916; m 1861 James Edward WEEKS (H)
Esther d 7-22-1881 ae 94y 8m 29d bPP (H)
cf Roch. 3-1847
Esther T., wd Isaac, rocf Pur. 10-1863; ct Pokeepsie 7-1-1874
Ezra rocf Centre MM, Ohio 3-18-1826; ct Cincinnati 2-3-1830 (clear)
Francis W., s Wm. S. & Eliz. H., b 4-13-1845; ct Pur. 6-4-1873
Franklin T., s Isaac & Abby (Sutton), b N. Y. 2-16-1827 d 10-28-1908 bPP; m 1-15-1857 Jane W. WILLETTS, dt Jacob & Deborah, N. P., b Washington, N. Y., 7-25-1830 d 4-12-1919 bPP
Ch: Jacob Willetts b 3-24-1859
Frederick Walton b 5-12-1876
cf Pur. 6-1-1853 for Franklin

CARPENTER, Franklin T. & Jane W., continued
cf N. P. 6-1858 for Jane; ct N. P. for both 9-2-1868; cf N. P. for both 1-10-1897
Frederick J., s Aaron & Jane S., b 11-29-1851; m Sarah ----- (nm) (H)
Ch: Alice b 1-11-1876
Emily J. d 3-16-1878 ae 2m 15d
mbrp cancelled 6-9-1900; Alice's name entered by comm. 10-12-1880
Frederick Walton, s Franklin T. & Jane W., N. Y., b Millbrook 5-12-1876 d 3- 1-1925 ashes bPP; m at Emma W. Schachtil's 6-26-1906 Dorothy E. DRESLER, dt John H. & Sophia F. (both dec), b N. Y. 2-18-1876 (H) Prof. at Hartford
George W., s Aaron & Jane S. (Weeks), b 2-28-1838 d after 1900; m Priscilla H. ----- (m 4----1859) (H)
Ch: Howard Irving b 2- 1-1860
Albert Hinman " 4-14-1863
Elsie " 4-20-1867
Priscilla rocf Pur. 2-1861; relrq 1-6-1900
George W., s Edmund M. & Anna H., rocf Creek with parents 7-16-1869; ct Bristol, Pa., 7-7-1880 (H)
Hannah m Richard KEELER (H)
cf Pur. 6-10-1859; ct Pur. 5-6-1868 as Keeler
Harry S. m Mary DEAN (d rpd 7-1928)
Ch: Dean b 8-4-1902
Mary rolf Summerfield M. E. Church, Port Chester, 5-7-1913; Dean recrq of mother & consent of father 5-7-1913
Hattie A., dt Caleb P. & Amelia C., N. Y.; m 1884 Ellwood CARPENTER (H)
Henry & Lydia
Ch: Sarah
Mary E.
Phebe H.
cf Oswego 7-1829; ct Roch. 11-1835
Henry H., s Wright & Hannah (Hallock), b Ama. 5-13-1831 d 4-29-1916; m Laura KING (nm) cf Ama. 9-3-1873 (H)
Henry M. m Deborah ----- d 4-29-1891
Ch: William H.
Josephine b N. Y. d 2- 8-1834 ae 1y 6m bHS
Josiah d 2- 2-1832 ae 2y 4m bHS
Pur. rq action on his ack 5-7-1823; rpd adversely 8-6-1823; Deborah rocf Pur. 4-1849
Horace (nm), s James & Phebe; m 9-7-1847 Mary T. DAVENPORT, dt Wm. D. & Phebe C. (Marshall), b Duanes. 4-23-1829 d 9-28-1919
cf Chap. 7-1853 for Mary; in Ill. 1859 (H)
Howard Irving, s Geo. W. & Priscilla, b 2-1-1860; relrq 2-10-1900 (H)
Isaac, s Isaac, rocf Pur. 1-7-1835 with brother, Thomas, minors; dis 12-1840
Isaac rocf Pur. 4-1838; dis 3-1852
Isaac, Jr. d 6-11-1880; m Abby S. ----- d 7-22-1853
Ch: Franklin T. b 2-16-1827
Alpheus " 8- 2-1829
Edward H. " 5-20-1832
Ch: Isaac Warner d 10-22-1835
Ophelia
Walton
cf Pur. 5-12-1824 (clear); cf Chap. 6-9-1825 for Abby S.; Isaac, Jr. dis 1-1830; Abby S. dis 5-1843 (0); ct Pur. for all 11-1837
Isaac, Jr. m 2nd Pur. Catharine H. ----- d 3-30-1898 (H)
Ch: Catharine B. b 2-19-1865
cf Pur. 6-1-1853 for Isaac; cf Pur. 11-1857 for Catharine
Isaac, Jr. & Rebecca C. (H)
Ch: Phebe Jane
Mary Elizabeth d 12- 3-1841
Eliza H. b 5-22-1843
Charles M. " 11- 2-1849
cf Pur. 3-1841; ct Pur. 2-1851
Isaac W., s Isaac, Jr. & Abby S.; m ----- (H)
Ch: Isaac Burling d 4-13-1881 ae 3y 2m 22d
ct Pur. with parents 11-1837; cf Pur. 6-1-1853; relrq 3-2-1892
Israel & Amully (Emily)
Ch: Hannah Field
cf Pur. 1-10-1811 with their dt, Hannah; ct Pur. 2-12-1812 with minor dt, Hannah Field & an infant dt
Jacob & Hannah (H)
cf Ama. 11-1854; ct Ama. 2-7-1857
James, s Joseph T. & Hannah, rocf Chap. 1828 with parents; ct Chap. 2-3-1841, minor
James (nm) & -----
Ch: Infant d 7-27-1845 ae 14d bHS
James rocf Ama. 2-1853; ct Ama. 10-1859 (H)
James G. rocf Pur. 1-1842; dis 12-8-1859 (H)
James S., s ----- & Sophice, rocf Pur. with mother 1-1842; dis 12-8-1859 (H)
Jane, dt Wright & Hannah H., N. Y.; m 1884 Geo. A. McDOWELL (H)
Jane, dt Thos. & Phebe, N. Y.; m 1842 Elias UNDERHILL (H)
Jane Louisa, dt Charles M. & Charlotte, b N. Y. 7-20-1836; m 10-25-1855 Jeremiah W. ATWATER (nm), s Wm. C. & Harriet H. (H)
Jesse G. rocf Ama. 5-3-1848; ct Ama. 8-1859 (H)
John, O. B., m Wby 6 Mo (Aug) 12, 1713 Martha FEAKE, dt John & Elizabeth (dec)
John & Eleanor
Ch: Emily b 11-23-1845
Cecelia " 3-29-1850
Infant " 3- 4-1856
cf Marl. 5-23-1855; ct Marl. 11-1857
John rocf Ama. 11-1859; ct Ama. 1-1865 (H)
John T. d 4-17-1867 (or 4-15-1867); m Sarah ----- d 2-11-1838
Ch: Phebe Jane
Benjamin
Adeline
Sarah Ann
Maria Louisa b 1-22-1837
cf Pur. 12-8-1824 (clear); ct Pur. 1-3-1827 (clear); cf Pur. 4-1837; ct Pur. 2-1842; cf Pur. 4-1842, returned; John T. in

CARPENTER, continued
Milwaukee 1859
Joseph d 4-8-1859; m Phebe Jane ----- d 3-19-1847 (H)
Ch: Samuel b 1-31-1847 d 7-26-1847
Thomas " 1-31-1847 " 8- 7-1847
Joseph rocf Ama. 8-1845; Phebe Jr. rocf Chap. 10-1846
Joseph T. & Hannah
Ch: Phebe S.
James
Azariah b 10-19-1828
cf Chap. 3-13-1828 with 2 ch named; parents dis 1830 (O); ct Chap. 1-1835
Laura E., dt Jas. E. & Henrietta (Hawkes), b N. Y. 6-29-1873
recrq 12-5-1896 (unm) (H)
Maplet H., dt Thos. & Sarah (Weeks), b New Castle, N. Y. 7-5-1833 d 2-15-1903; m 1856 Ferris A. CAREY (H)
cf Chap. 7-4-1877
Maria & -----
Ch: Rebecca dis 2-2-1847
cf Pur. 8-13-1845 with dt
Maria Louisa, dt Wm. T. & Esther Jane, Bkn., b 3-2-1841; m 1866 Joshua W. SUTTON (H)
Mary, dt Benj.; m Joseph SMITH (H)
cf Ama. 8-1846 with sisters, Sarah W. & Eliza; ct Ama. 10-1859
Mary, dt Chas. B. & Anna T., b Bkn. 10-24-1885; m 1912 Frederick A. LYDECKER (H)
Mary E., dt Timothy & Jemima; m James L. LEWIS
cf Chap. with parents 7-1830; ct Chap. 12-1-1875 (H)
Mary Elizabeth, dt Aaron B. & Adelia A., N. Y.; m 1849 Richard A. LOINES (H)
Mary H., dt Wright & Hannah (Hallock), b Ama. 10-31-1836 d 4-17-1925 (H)
cf Ama. 10-31-1859 (unm)
Nathaniel, Jr., Northcastle, d 2 Mo (Apr) 25, 1730
Nathaniel rocf Pur. 1-8-1823 (clear)
Nathaniel & Zerviah
Ch: Catharine
Mary T. b 5-10-1823
Edward
cf Chap. 6-14-1822 with ch, Catharine; ct Ama. 6-7-1826 with 3 ch named
Ophelia, dt Isaac & Abby S., N. Y.; m 1856 Wm. H. THORN (H)
Peter J., s Thos. & Sarah (Weeks), b New Castle 12-23-1840 d 7-16-1908; m 8-19-1862 Phebe H. HUNT, dt Lewis P. & Charlotte (Weeks), b Chap. 1-30-1840 d 7-22-1915 (H)
cf Chap. 11-1-1871 for both
Phebe rocf Pur. 8-10-1809 (clear); ct Ama. 2-12-1812
Phebe, dt Zeno, gct Creek, 8-7-1816 (minor)
Phebe, dt Joseph T. & Hannah, rocf Chap. 1828 with parents; ct Chap. 4-7-1841
Phebe H., dt Timothy & Jemima; m ----- COX (H)
dis 4-1849 (O)
Phebe Jane (or Ann), dt John T. & Sarah; m before 7-6-1864 Willard B. JOHNSON (H)
name erased 9-7-1864; joined Congregational Church in Milwaukee
Phebe K. d 11-17-1850 (H)
cf Oswego 5-6-1846
Rachel, dt Zeno, gct Marl. 8-7-1816 (minor)
Rachel D., dt Isaac & Patience, N. Y.; m ----- HUNTER; m 2nd 1856 Elisha H. POWELL (H)
cf Ama. 3-2-1853 for Rachel D. Hunter
Rebecca rocf Pur. 8-13-1845 (clear)
Rebecca M. dis joining Baptists 2-1847
Rebecca W., w Henry M., d 7-7-1843; cf Pur. 11-1840 (H)
Rees & Sarah
Ch: Jacob B.
David
Phebe b 12-28-1817
cf Chap. 6-14-1816; ct Chap. 6-2-1819 for all named
Richard E. & Mary T.
ct Wby & Jericho 11-1864 (clear); cf Pur. 11-7-1860 for Richard; cf Wby & Jericho 5-1866 for Mary; ct N. P. 12-2-1874 for both
Robert, s Charles (dec) & Phebe Jane, Harrison; m at Joseph Hagan's 5-4-1848 Phebe C. HAGAN dt Joseph & Sarah Eliz., N. Y., b 8-18-1828
cf Troy 9-1843 for Phebe; ct Pur. 5-1849 for Phebe
Robert H., s Benj. & Martha (dec), d 11-7-1882 ae 55y 4m 6d bPP; m at T. T. Griffen's 5-11-1853 Amy T. GRIFFEN, dt Thos. T. & Mary M., N. Y., d 1-28-1895 ae 65y 11m 11d bPP (H)
Ch: Caroline b 4- 3-1854 d 7-14-1854
Eveline " 9- 2-1855
Stephen G. " 11-16-1856
Mary " 11-23-1861 " 4- 1-1931 bPP
Edith " 2-23-1864
Sarah " 1-31-1867
cf Ama. 7-1852
Robert R., s Wright & Hannah (Hallock), b Ama. 9-19-1829 d 10-24-1903; m 12-15-1853 Hannah W. POWELL, dt Rich'd S. & Sarah T. (Underhill), b Bethpage 11-22-1834 d 3-3-1904 (H)
Ch: Richard W. b 7-12-1857 d 10-11-1887
Abm. Lincoln " 1-21-1861
Ellwood " 1-22-1863
cf Ama. 9-1852 for Robert; Hannah rocf Jericho 2-18-1858 with infant s, Richard W.
Samuel & Rebecca
Ch: Lovinah
Israel
Rachel
Matt
cf Pur. 2-11-1796 with their 4 ch; ct Pur. 4-3-1799 with same 4 ch
Samuel rocf Pur. 8-7-1844 (minor); dis 1-1847
Sarah b L. I. d 7-6-1812 ae 68y bHS (unm)
Sarah dis mo 4-3-1810 & rpd to Pur.; cf Pur. 7-12-1810
Sarah gct Pur. 4-3-1816 (clear)
Sarah, dt Robert H. & Amy T. (Griffin), N. Y.,

CARPENTER, Sarah, continued
b N. Y. 1-31-1867; m 1897 Henry W. GILLINGHAM (H)
Sarah A., dt Joseph & Charlotte; m 1867 David S. HAVILAND (H)
Sarah Ann, dt Zeno, gct Marl. 8-7-1816 (minor)
Sarah Ann, dt John T. & Sarah; m before 7-6-1864 Charles HURVEY (H) (mo)
cf Pur. 4-1837; released 9-7-1864; joined Congregational Church in Milwaukee
Sarah Ann, dt Wright & Hannah (Hallock), b Ama. 5-8-1833 d 9-13-1915; cf Ama. 8-1859 (unm) (H)
Sarah W., dt Benj., d 3-6-1886; cf Ama. 8-1846 with sisters, Eliza & Mary (H)
Serena A., dt James & Mary A. (Jube), b N. Y. 3-1839 d Lobo. 4-4-1912; m 1856 John MINARD cf Lobo, Ontario 1-7-1899; ct Lobo 10-14-1911 (H)
Sidney H., s Wm. Henry & Sarah F., b N. Y. 3-12-1884; m Edna Wallace HACKETT, dt Wm. N. recrq of parents 10-6-1894 (Edna nm)
Silas rem to Greenwich, R. I. 9 Mo (Nov) 1, 1744
Silas S. d 10-17-1914; m Ada C. THOMPSON (H)
Ch: Charles M. d 7-28-1905 ae 35y bPP
Sophia & ----- (H)
Ch: Emma b 3-26-1823 d 3-7-1842
David L.
Ann Eliza
James S.
cf Pur. 1-1842; ct Oblong 9-4-1850
Stephen G., s Robt. H. & Amy T., b 11-16-1856 N. Y. d 5-2-1927; m Mae RAINSTEIN (nm) (H)
Thomas, Jr. rocf Pur. 5-8-1817 (clear)
Thomas (name changed to William T.), s Isaac & Lydia, rocf Pur. 1-7-1835 with brother, Isaac (minors)
Thomas, s Josiah & Charlotte, N. Y., d 8-11-1849; m N. Y. 10-10-1821 Phebe UNDERHILL, dt Israel & Zerriah, N. Y., d 7-16-1849
Ch: Jane b 10-14-1822
Emily " 3- 8-1827
Walter " 7-30-1829
Mary " 2- 3-1833 d 8-11-1835
Sarah " 6- 5-1836 " 10- 6-1837
Charlotte " 4-20-1839 " 12- 7-1842
Thomas brought cf Wby 3-26-1777; ct Wby 9-2-1778; cf Wby 1817; both dis 1829-1830 (0); Jane dis 1849 (0); cf Pur. 7-1817
Thomas & ----- (H)
Ch: William
Thomas m 2nd Jane -----
Ch: Elizabeth b 11-24-1844
Mary " 7-20-1848
cf Pur. 10-1844 for Thomas; cf Ama. 2-4-1846 for Jane; ct Pur. for all 1-4-1854
Timothy & Jemima (H)
Ch: Mary E.
Phebe H.
cf Chap. 7-1830 with 2 ch named; ct Chap. 3-5-1851 for parents; all dis (0)
Townsend d 6-29-1868 ae 68y 1m 28d m Phebe ----- b 6-5-1805 d 9-1-1884
Ch: Isaac T. b 1-10-1825 d 12-16-1902
David R. d 12-28-1849
Amelia Augusta (changed to Adelia Augusta) b 4-12-1829 d 11-19-1915
cf Pur. 10-11-1826 for both with ch, Isaac T.; both dis 6-1830 (0); Townsend dis (H) 1833
Uriah F. rocf Pur. 7-11-1816, minor, placed; dis mo 6-5-1822
Walter, s Thomas & Phebe (Underhill), b 7-30-1829 d 6-17-1875 ae 45y 10m 17d bPP; m Elizabeth ---- (nm) d 11-17-1880 ae 50y bPP (H)
Walton, s Isaac Jr. & Abby S., d 5-16-1885; ct Pur. 11-1837 with parents; cf Pur. 6-1-1853 (H)
Willets, s Franklin T. & Jane W. (both dec), N. Y., b Bkn. 3-24-1859 d 2-6-1925 bPP; m N. Y. 6-30-1920 Alice HOEKSTRA (nm), dt Jacob A. & Eliza A. (dec), N. Y. (H)
William, s Josiah, rocf Pur. 12-10-1834 (minor); dis 12-1839
William E. b Po'keepsie d 5-10-1826 ae 19y 2m bHS (unm)
William H. (nm) & -----
Ch: Infant stillborn 9-12-1837 bHS
William H., s Henry M. & Deborah, recrq 4-1868; ct Pur. 5-7-1884 (H)
Wm. Harold, s Wm. H. & Sarah F., b N. Y. 10-22-1885; m 6-1-1916 Myrtle L. WILLIAMS (nm), dt David & Laura (nm) (H)
recrq of parents 10-6-1894
Wm. Henry, s Caleb P. & Amelia (Lawrence), b N. Y. 4-21-1860 d 12-27-1925; m 6-6-1883 Sarah Frances HULL, dt Sam'l G. & Elizabeth (Weston), b 12-29-1855 (H)
Ch: Sidney H. b 3-12-1884
Wm. Harold " 10-22-1885
Elizabeth P. " 2-28-1887
Beatrice J. " 2-28-1887
Arthur McDowell" 1- 3-1891
Winola Dorothy " 11-25-1892
Anna Lily " 11- 3-1894
both recrq 10-6-1894 with 6 ch; ch recrq of parents 10-6-1894
William S., s Josiah & Charlotte, d 3-30-1888; m at Sarah Loines' 11-11-1840 Eliz. H. LOINES, dt Richard (dec) & Sarah, N. Y.(H)
Ch: Francis W. b 4-13-1845
cf Pur. 6-1835; ct Pur. 4-3-1872 for parents; ct Pur. 6-4-1873 for Francis
William T. (changed from Thomas), s Isaac & Lydia, d 5-8-1878 ae 69y 1m bPP; m Esther -----, d 1-7-1849 (H)
Ch: Maria Louisa
Sarah b 11- 8-1846 d 7-23-1847
cf Pur. 1-7-1835 as Thomas, with brother, Isaac; cf Pur. 1-1845
William T. m 2nd Phebe S. WEEKS, dt Jesse K. (dec) & Eliza (Sutton), b 9-26-1827 Chap. d 9-9-1906 (m at Eliza Weeks' 11-22-1859)
Ch: Caroline Esther b 10-2-1860 d 2- 7-1928

CARPENTER, William T. & Phebe S., continued
cf Chap. 10-1830 for Phebe with parents
Winola Dorothy, dt Wm. H. & Sarah E., b N. Y. 11-25-1892; m 11-6-1921 Raymond Rossiter GRACEY (nm) (H)
recrq of parents 10-6-1894
Zeno, Jr., s Daniel & Sarah (Tompkins); m Esther HALSTED, dt David & Naomi, d 4-19-1812 ae 24y 9m 6d bHS (Zeno, Jr. d 8-1832 (H))
Ch: Amos
Phebe
Rachel b 4-30-1810
Sarah Ann
Abraham Clock (?)
cf Oswego 11-15-1809 for both with 2 ch, Amos & Phebe
Zeno, Jr. m 2nd before 3-3-1813 Elizabeth ----- (nm), d 10-28-1813 ae 22y (mo)
Zeno, Jr. m 3rd at Middlesex, Conn, 11-19-1818 Clariss (or Claretta) WHITING, dt Samuel & Molly, Stratford, d 8-25-1819
Ch: Elizabeth d 8-20-1819 ae 5d
ct Pur. 11-4-1818 (clear)
Zeno m Ellen ---- b Fairfield, Conn. d 8-7-1814 ae 25y 4m
Zeno dis 7-1839
Zophen d 4-27-1812 ae 39y bHS; rocf Pur. 8-10-1809 (clear) (unm)
----- & -----
Ch: George b N. Y. d 6-25-1824 ae 8m 27d bHS
William " " " 5-26-1824 " 1y 3m 15d bHS
Ann Maria " " " 5- 3-1834 " 14d bHS
Ann Maria d 4- 8-1835 ae 33y 6m bHS (unm, perhaps mbr)
Merrill E. d 8-22-1866 ae 3y 9m bPP

CARR
Caroline M., w William, d 8-9-1898, rocf Hudson 7-6-1859; lived Amherst, Mass. (H)
Hannah, dt Richard WILLITS, Jericho, d 11 Mo. 27, 1727/8
John M. & Rachel T. (H)
Ch: Oliver K.
Ruth Anna
cf Milford, Ind. 6-1857; ct Prarie Grove, Iowa, 1-1865 for parents & Ruth Anna
Jurdenette (nm), dt Chauncey & Caroline; m 9-23-1885 Fannie HOAG, dt William & Amy H. (Gurney), b New Balt., N. Y. 12-2-1861(H)
Transfer from Albany for Fannie 1-8-1916; resigned to join Christian Science Church at Medway
Oliver K., s John M. & Rachel T., m ----- (nm)
Ch: John M., Jr.
Rachel, Jr.
cf Milford, Ind. with parents 6-1857; m out west; ct Prarie Grove, Iowa for all but w 5-1865

CARROLL
Daniel J., s Joseph & Mary (nm), Jamestown, Ind. m N. Y. 2-24-1929 Marcia B. GOODBODY, dt Marcus & Lydia M. (H); rem to Canada; Daniel joined Lobo MM; rem to Eng. with 2 ch
Joseph Fisher, s Isaac & Ann (both dec), N. Y.; m N. Y. 12-8-1819 Amy HAWXHURST, dt Daniel (dec) & Hannah, N. Y.
Ch: Edward b 9- 8-1820 d 5-31-1827
Ann " 5-28-1823
Mary T. " 8- 2-1829
cf Cork 7-8-1819 (clear); Amy dis 6-1830; Joseph gct Exeter, Pa. 4-1838 with ch, Ann; ct Exeter, Pa. 4-4-1838 with dt (0); ct Maiden Creek, Pa. 11-1841 (H); Joseph dis 1829 (H)
Samuel M. d 3-5-1804 ae 19y bHS (unm)

CARTER
Abraham rocf Chesterfield 6-7-1825 (minor); ct Green St., Phila. 11-14-1827 (clear)
Catharine, dt Wm. SMART, dis 4-1849 (H)
Elizabeth, dt Richard Lee & Mary E. (Knowlton) b Knowlton, Quebec, 2-10-1875; recrq 4-13-1925 (unm)
Kate (nm), dt Oliver S.; m 1-12-1880 George H. MACY

CARTLAND
Alfred Lindley & Jennie M.
Ch: Alice Farr b 10-23-1897
Edith Hulda " 12- 9-1898
George Lindley b 5- 1-1900
Melville Pierpont b 1- 5-1910
Ruth Eleanor " 1- 5-1910
cf Pokeepsie 12-6-1911 for Alfred; Jennie M. recrq 12-6-1911; 4 ch recrq of parents 12-6-1911; Jennie's name erased, jas; Ruth active mbr 1-1922
George L., s Alfred L. & Jennie M., b 6-1-1900; m Lena ----- (nm)
Ch: George Edward b 12-5-1934 d 12-6-1934 bPP
Ruth Eleanor, dt Alfred L. & Jennie M., b 1-5-1910; m 1932 Harold V. LINNEKIN (nm)
active mbr 1-1922

CARVER
D. Frederick, s David (dec) & Sarah M., Phila., b Phila. 5-4-1869 d 12-5-1932 bPP; m at E. D. Miller's 1-15-1896 Carolyn A. MILLER, dt Henry W. (dec) & Eliz. D.(avenport), b 11-5-1866 N. Y. (H)
cf Phila. for Frederick 5-13-1929
John Linton, s John & Phebe A. (Tomlinson), Media, Pa., b Byberry, Pa. 2-18-1873; m at Bkn. 6-23-1898 Cora HAVILAND, dt David S. & Sarah A., Bkn., b 1-29-1874 Newark (H)
ct Alton, Southampton & Poole 10-8-1928; John Linton principal of Friends' Seminary
Mabel, dt Wm. A. & Eliz. (Dye), b Troy, O., 1-6-1880 d 3-26-1934; m 1-22-1904 Alexander Wilson CROUCH (nm) (H)
recrq 6-9-1924

CARY
Alice L., dt Jervis & Sarah (Eddy), b Glens Falls 9-30-1866 d 12-1-1926 bPP; m Edward

CARY, Alice L., continued
S. SCALES
cf Glens Falls for both with ch 12-5-1906
Beulah (nm), dt Jesse Logan & Rose (Brock); m 1925 Wesley EASTMAN (H)
Eliza E., dt Joseph & Lydia (Chase), b Albany 6-10-1833 d 1-4-1918; transferred from Albany 1-8-1816 (unm) (H)
John Milton rocf Sara. 12-1831; dis 11-1832 (H)
Maria, dt Joseph & Lydia (Chase), b Albany 12-16-1837 d 7-12-1924; transferred from Albany 1-8-1916 (unm) (H)
Charles W. (nm) b L. I. d 12-6-1840 ae 27y bHS (unm) killed by falling of building

CASE
Elizabeth A., w James, rocf Providence 3-28-1838; ct Providence 11-3-1841
Frances W., w Robt. L., Jr., dt Wm. F. & Frances L. WARING, b 12-5-1847; relrq 10-1880

CASSON
Curtis rocf New Castle, Eng., 8-1-1832; forwarded to Oswego, returned from Oswego 9-5-1832 as he had left, forwarded to Roch. 1-2-1833

CASTLE
Arnold, about to rem to Phila., asks cert of clear 8 Mo (Oct) 8, 1722. No further mention

CATON
Jacomiah dealt with at rq of Corn. 1-5-1831 for military service & joining Bapt.; rpd favorably 2-2-1831

CAUSTIN
Martha rocf Pur. 10-9-1800 (clear)

CAVANAGH
----- & ----- (nm)
Ch: Infant d 1895 bPP

CAWL
Eliza (form Chapman) d 2-1867; cf Tipperary 5-1-1854
Franklin R., s Robert C. & Florence (Allen), b 8-27-1890; m 6-4-1914 Abbie PRETLOW
both gct Providence 5-7-1919
Henrietta E., dt Robt E. & Florence A., Bkn., b 9-25-1894; m 1920 Howard L. CAREY
Hugh d 12-12-1905; recrq 5-1882
Robert Cone, s Hugh & Mary E. (Hudson), b Troy 5-3-1868 d 6-29-1913 bPP; m 8-8-1889 Florence ALLEN, dt James M. H. & Rebecca, b 8-8-1867
Ch: Franklin R. b 8-27-1890
Ruth Florence " 9-20-1892
Henrietta Estelle b 9-25-1894
Melvin Allen " 1- 5-1898
Stephen " 8-28-1900 d 10-8-1900
Robert recrq 4-1888
Florence recrq 5-1889
Ruth Florence, s Robert C. & Florence (Allen), b 9-20-1892; m 1917 Ernest J. DWEES
ct WD MM 11-5-1919
----- m Elizabeth ----- d 2-9-1862 ae 32y bPP
Ch: Infant s d 5-10-1862 ae 1y 5m bPP

CECIL
Ella L., dt Alfred & Margaret, b Bkn. 12-8-1868; m 1890 George RIDER (H)
recrq 4-14-1924

CERNEA
William T. d 6-8-1895; cf Phila. 10-2-1878 (H)

CHACE
Marcia R., dt Wm. Henry & Marcia (Algar), b Jersey City 3-23-1845 d 7-27-1932; m 1868 George T. POWELL (H)
both transferred from Albany 1-8-1916

CHADWICK
Aaron d 2-5-1898; m Emma W. ----- (H)
Ch: Clarence W.
John L. d 10-23-1882 ae 7y 6m 23d bPP
cf Renss. 4-1-1863 for Aaron
Clarence W., s Aaron (H)
name entered by comm 3-10-1885; relrq 1-4-1893
Mary, dt Daniel & Phebe WILLIS, N. Y.; m 1818 David HARKNESS
Stanley H. (nm), s John R. & Annie H. (nm); m 6-21-1893 Florence ARCHER, dt Isaac H. & Eliz. M. (Olcott), b Bkn. 3-21-1867 (H)
Ch: Paul A. b 4-10-1901
Paul recrq 4-9-1818; Florence recrq 11-12-1917; relrq 1-18-1934

CHALMERS
Gordon Keith (nm), s Everett & Sarah (Hayward) (nm); m 9-3-1929 Roberta T. SWARTZ, dt Wm. King & Carrie (Teale), b Bkn. 6-9-1903 (H)
Roberta recrq 1-11-1926

CHAMBERLAIN
Catharine Ann, (nm), dt Gilbert & Eleanor (Howard); m 1874 David F. HALSTED (H)

CHAMBERS
Ann d 6-1857 ae 66y bPP (nm)
Charlotte H. d 2-14-1908; recrq 1864 (sister of Frances J.)
Frances Jane d 6-25-1889 ae 68y bPP; recrq 1864 (sister of Charlotte)
Miles d 3-20-1863 ae 73y bPP; m Ann -----
Ch: Infant stillborn 9-25-1824 bHS
Benjamin I. (or J.) (prob.) b N. Y. d 1-15-1827 ae 5y 4m bHS
Luceny (prob) d 9-13-1832 ae 2y 4m bHS
Charlotte H. " 2-1908 bPP
recrq 6-6-1860; had attended mtg of Jews for 10 yr

CHAMBERS, continued
----- & -----
Ch: Mary d 3- 1-1884 ae 61y bPP

CHAMPION
Mary, Wby; m 1698 Martin JERVIS
Rebecca L. rocf Mt. Holly 5-1857; d 4-8-1891 (H)

CHANDLER
George rocf Bybury 8-1826; ND MM requested to deal with him for non-attendance; dis 2-2-1831 (O); ct Phila. 8-1830 (H)

CHANG
Charles C. recrq 4-1928

CHANTLER
David rocf Dorking & Horsham MM, Eng., 11-9-1831 (clear); ct Pelham 8-7-1833 (clear)

CHAPIN
Ethel E., dt William C. & Lydia H., b Bkn. 2-12-1891 d 9-5-1929 bPP; recrq 5-6-1908
Lydia Underhill rocf Hartland 5-4-1898
----- & Carrie
Ch: Inez b 10-11-1897 d 12-5-1901 bPP (all nm)

CHAPMAN
A. Wright, s Noah & Mariana W., b Glendale, O. 1-13-1872; m 1-23-1909 Grace W. STEVENSON (nm), dt Morris & Lydia (Walton) (nm) (H)
cf Cincinnati with parents 2-2-1881
Baldwin (nm) d 9-28-1894 ae 75y; m Virginia W. ----- (nm) d 2-15-1854 ae 31y 2m 1d bPP
Ch: Albert d 7-10-1853 ae 6m 25d bPP
William E.
Charles H., s Noah H. & Mariana W., b Springboro, O., 9-16-1865; m 4-3-1903 Mary PINE, dt Wm. & Cath. Jane (Poponoe), b Cincinnati 1-8-1876 (H)
Ch: James Wright b 8-11-1905
Mariana " 7-12-1909
ch recrq of parents
Charlotte H., dt Noah H. & Marianna W., Bkn., b Glendale, O., 9-16-1877; m 1899 Henry C. TURNER (H)
David rocf Wrightstown, Pa. 9-3-1782 (clear); dis mo 9-5-1787
Eliza d 2-1867 m ----- CAWL
cf Tipperary, Ireland 5-1-1854
Esther F., w Isaac, rocf Pur. 10-1863
Howard, s Noah & Mariana W., b Glendale, O. 1-11-1875; m 7-16-1910 Lucy BARTON, dt John & Eliz. (Fowler), b Rome 3-7-1863 (H)
Ch: John Barton b 6-14-1913
Elizabeth Foulke b 5-15-1916
cf Cincinnati with parents 2-2-1881; Lucy recrq 5-10-1926; ch recrq of parents 5-10-1926; ct Pur. for all
Josephine A., w Edward, d 12-1923; rocf Ama. 2-1869
Josiah (nm), s Josiah & Anna, d 11-28-1846 ae 23y 8m 26d bPP
Mariana, dt Chas. H. & Mary P., Pleasantville; m 1834 Wm. L. GRANGER, of Pelham (H)
Martha P. d 7-10-1889; rocf Birmingham, Pa. 8-1873
Noah H., s Jos. B. & Charlotte (Haines), Miami, O., b Waynesville, O. 1-24-1836 d 5-25-1914; m 6-24-1864 Mariana W. WRIGHT, dt Aaron & Mary (Willets), b N. Y. 3-14-1843 d 11-9-1907 (H)
Ch: Charles H. b 9-16-1865
Mary W. " 11- 3-1869
A. Wright " 10-13-1872
Howard " 1-11-1875
Charlotte H. " 9-16-1877
cf Cincinnati 2-2-1881 for all
Robert (nm), d 7-26-1871 ae 26y bPP; m Laura TERRY, dt Zelah & Letty, b Newburgh, N. Y. 2-1850 d 7-2-1898 bPP
Samuel Baldwin m Virginia ----- d 2-15-1854 (H)
Ch: Mary Ellen b 2-14-1845 d 7-2-1868 bPP
Josiah " 1-28-1847 " 8-7-1849
William Edward b 4-11-1849
Edward Danforth b 1-15-1851 d 7-19-1874 bPP
Albert T. d 8-31-1853 ae 6m 25d bPP
cf Phila. Cherry St. 11-1840; Virginia recrq 3-1845; Samuel relrq 2-3-1809
William rocf WD MM 6-1868; ct Waterford, Ire., 9-5-1877
Wm. Edward, s Samuel B. & Virginia, b 11-11-1849 d 12-12-1883 bPP; relrq 12-7-1874 (H)

CHAPPEL (or CHAPPLE)
John, Flushing; m at Sarah Pedley's house 1 Mo (Mar) 6, 1704/5 Sarah PEDLEY, Great Neck

CHARLETON
Edward Ash (nm) d 1-28-1837 ae 22y 5m bHS; "of England"
James Hale (nm) d 12-13-1836 ae 24y drowned on board the ship Bristol bHS; from Bristol, England
Margery [Charlton], w Benjamin, rocf WD MM 2-7-1821; cert returned & addressed to Green St., Phila. 9-5-1821

CHARLICK
Henry, Flushing; m Flushing 1 Mo (Mar) 8, 1721/2 Mary SMITH, dt Edward & Ailse, Westchester
Henry about to rem, ct Eastchester (Pur.) 1 Mo (Mar) 2, 1726/7

CHASE
Borden b R. I. d 6-10-1829 ae 55y; m Ruth B. ----- d 12-30-1860 (H)
Ch: Eliza Brown
Sarah Folger b Nantucket d 12-1-1826 ae 18y
Caroline " 1- 5-1812
William B. " 9-26-1814
cf Nantucket 1-2-1811 for the 4 named; mother, Eliza & Caroline dis 1830-1836 (O)

CHASE, Borden & Ruth, continued
ct Mt. Holley 8-1838 for Ruth
Caroline, dt Borden & Ruth B.; m ----- STRATTON
dis 5-1836 (H)
Eliza B., dt Borden & Ruth; m before 10-1831
----- FOWLER; dis mo 10-5-1831
Harriet A., dt Jas. B. & Mary L., rocf Scip. 12-2-1891 with parents; ct Scipio 12-1-1897
James B. d 7-15-1895; m Mary L. -----
Ch: Harriet A.
cf Scip. 12-2-1891 with 1 ch named; ct Scip. 6-9-1897 for Mary; ct Scip. 12-1-1897 for Harriet
Joseph W. rocf Little Egg Harbor 1-13-1842
Josiah D. & Mary B.
Ch: Caroline
Phebe G. b 10-23-1849 d 3-5-1854
cf Oswego 1846 with 1 ch; ct N. P. 9-7-1859 for parents
Thomas, s Anthony & Lydia E. (dec), Worcester, Mass.; m N. Y. 2-8-1860 Alice U. CROMWELL, dt Wm. & Caroline (dec), N. Y., b 7-15-1836
Ch: William Cromwell b 9-29-1862
ct Radnor, Pa. 4-1863 for Alice & ch
Thomas H. d Chatham 4-28-1853; cf Chatham 7-1831 (H)
Thomas Herbert rocf WD MM 7-2-1890
Willard d 12-18-1891 ae 85y 9m 12d bPP; m Elizabeth A. ----- d 4-24-1891 ae 64y 6m bPP
Ch: Alice d 1-28-1872 ae 9m 4d bPP
Edward d 3-23-1911 ae 56y bPP
all nm (H)
William B., dt Borden & Ruth, b 9-26-1814; ct Phila. 8-2-1837 (clear) (O); dis 11-1835 (H)

CHATTEN
----- & ----- (nm)
Ch: Stephen J. b N. Y. d 11-16-1826 ae 11m 20d bHS

CHATTERTON
Joan, Flushing, d 9 Mo (Nov) 10, 1686 (or 1696)

CHAUNCEY
Arline, dt Daniel & Kate (Cunningham) (nm), b N. Y. 4-16-1916; recrq of parents 11-12-1928 (H)

CHEE
Loy Ding Chu & Cherry
both recrq 3-1928

CHEESEMAN
Ann, dt John C. & Martha, b 8-11-1815; dis 5-1837 (H); dis 1-1838 (O)
Benjamin F. dis visiting theater 11-7-1821
Edward (nm) b Cow Neck, L. I. d 9-25-1821 ae 42y bHS (unm)
Eliza, dt Forman & Ann, N. Y.; m 1813 Lindley MURRAY
Forman m Ann ----- b Phila. d 2-13-1820 ae 52y
Ch: Jacob
John
Eliza
Margaret
Benjamin
cf Phila. 3-25-1795 for Ann, having rem with her h; ct Pur. for Ann with 4 ch as named 5-7-1800; cf Pur. for both with 3 ch, Eliza, Margaret & Benjamin; Forman dealt with 6-3-1818 for building & launching a war vessel, case discontinued 9-2-1818
Jacob, s Forman & Ann, rocf Pur. 6-13-1805 (minor)
John C., s Forman & Ann, N. Y., d 10-11-1872; m N. Y. 12-15-1814 Martha M. (or H.) HICKS, dt Willet & Mary, d 7-2-1872
Ch: Ann b 8-11-1815
Alexander
Willet Hicks b 8-28-1817 d 8-26-1818
John C., Jr. d 8-15-1825 ae 6m 6d
Timothy Matlack b 10-27-1824
John C., Jr. " 6----1826 d 8-11-1827
John C., Jr. " ------1831 " 8-28-1832
cf Pur. 6-13-1805, minor; parents dis 1829, 1831 (O); parents dis 5-1837 (H)
Margaret m before 12-4-1822 ----- SWEET; dis mo 4-2-1823 after ref to Oswego
Timothy M., s John C. & Martha, b 10-27-1824; dis 10-1847 (H)
William (nm) & -----
Ch: Mary d 7- 9-1820 ae 3y 2d bHS
----- & -----
Ch: William d 4-17-1814 ae 6m bHS
Margaret b N. Y. d 3-24-1827 ae 4y
James " 4-20-1834 ae 2y 11m 13d bHS

CHENEY
Florence M. d 3-6-1876 ae 25y 4m 7d bPP (rem to Forest Hill Cem., Boston, Mass. 1929 or 1930) (she was dt of Mrs. Doane, w Mr. Cheney) (H)
Moses Edward (nm), s Edw. J. & Eliz. (Rice); m 5-3-1926 Florence DAHL, dt George W. & Anabel B. (Cox), b Bkn. 7-22-1901(H)
Florence recrq 4-13-1925

CHEVALIER
Olive E. recrq 5-4-1892; letter to Trinity M. E. Church, New Britain, Conn. 8-1-1894

CHICHESTER
Sarah E. (form Robinson) d 6-29-1841 (H)

CHILD
Hannah m 1755 Joseph DELAPLAINE
John Mason rocf Phila. 9-2-1885; disappeared 1886 & never heard of since. Recorded as dead 1906; principal of Friends Seminary (H)
Josephine F. (nm), dt Agnetus & Josephine; m 1906 Frederick E. MAINE (H)
Mary m 1773 Charles BROOKS, of Shrewsbury; took cert to Shrewsbury 3-3-1773

CHILD, continued
Sarah Louise, dt Wm. & Anna (Thomas), d 3-27-1931 ae 89y bPP; m George Haviland SHEFFIELD (H)

CHINSLEY
Elwood A. (nm), s Leonard & Ethel (Sewell); m 8-16-1935 Edith STUBBS, dt Horace R. & Lauretta (Williamson), b Bkn. 2-8-1915 (H)
Edith recrq of parents 12-13-1920

CHRISTY
Hannah m William BELL
John Luckey [Christie] rocf Warwickshire South 3-5-1850; ct Sugar River, Ind. 1856
Mary Margaret (nm) m 1896 Wm. B. COLEMAN (H)

CHURCH
Anna B. rocf Plains 1841
Austin Harris, s Isaac Monroe & Harriet L. (Carpenter), b Mauch Chunk, 1-20-1906; m 9-10-1932 Ruth PARRY, dt Charles C. & Minnie H., b Rushland, Pa. 7-16-1905
Austin recrq 7-10-1933; cf Wrightstown 5-13-1935 for Ruth (H)
Benjamin d 8-18-1799 bHS
Benjamin d 5-31-1801 bHS
Mary A., dt Stephen K. & Anna B., relrq 10-1872
Stephen H. d 3-12-1892; m Anna B. ----- d 12-5-1874
Ch: Mary A.
Stephen recrq 4-1842; cf Plains 11-24-1840 for Anna B.; ct Plains 11-1-1843 for both; cf Plains 1851 with 1 ch; ct Pickering 1855; cf Pickering 8-1871 for all

CHURCHILL
Ann Maria (nm), b N. Y. d 3-26-1836 ae 22y 8m 8d bHS

CHURCHMAN
Alfred, s Owen & Mary, of age 1-1-1843; cf Concord 1-9-1825 with mother; relrq 3-2-1870 (H)
Caroline, dt Micajah & Eliza; m ----- MUSSER; dis 8-4-1858, then at Dayton, Ohio (H)
Emily, dt Micajah & Eliza, rocf Darby with parents 1825; ct Center, Del. 6-1834 (H); ct Concord, Pa. 11-6-1839 (O) (minor); "joined the Baptists and rem we don't know where"
Hannah, dt Joseph & Hannah, rocf Green St., Phila. 1-20-1853; ct Chester 7-4-1855 (H)
Mary, w Owen, d 6-23-1839 ae 53y (H)
Ch: William M. d 10-28-1831 ae 29y 3m 9d
Pennell " 11-23-1856 ae 42y 10m 27d
Sarah Ann
Alfred of age 1-1-1843
Pennell d 11-28-1865
cf Concord 1-9-1825 with 4 ch named
Micajah & Eliza
Ch: Sinclair dis 12-1840 (O)
William H.
Emily
Caroline S. b 1-22-1826
cf Darby, Pa. 3-29-1825 with w (not named) & ch named; Micajah dis 9-1835; Eliza dis 9-1829; Micajah marked "off" in (O)
Owen (nm) d 3-4-1867 ae 81y 4m 20d bHS; m Mary ----- (nm) b Del. Co., Pa. d 6-23-1839 ae 53y 8m 2d bHS
Ch: Mary d 6-23-1839 ae 53y bPP
William M. " 10-28-1831 ae 23y bPP
Pennell, dt Owen & Mary, b 11-23 (or 24) 1856 ae 42y 10m 27d bPP rem to Phila. 4-3-1918 (H)
Phebe, dt Joseph & Hannah; m Caleb D. PIERCE, of Phila. (H)
cf Green St., Phila. 1-20-1853; ct Chester 7-4-1855
Rebecca C., dt Edw. & Reb., of Del. Co., Pa.; m ----- HEWES; m 2nd 1841 Bartholomew FUSSELL, of Phila. (H)
Samuel (nm) & Sarah
Ch: Isabel d ae 7y bPP
Sarah Ann, dt Owen & Mary; m 1834 John S. ROBERTS; dis 1-1835 (O)
Sinclair, s Micajah & Eliza, dis 12-1840 (O); dis 5-7-1845 (H)
William (nm), s Owen, b Phila. d 10-28-1831 ae 25y bHS
Wm. H., s Micajah & Eliza, gct Phila. Cherry St. 3-1838 (H)

CILLEY
Sherberne A. (nm) d 3-1-1863 ae 38y bPP

CLAPP
Allen rocf Pur. 5-16-1792 (clear); con mo 12-2-1795; ct Pur. 5-6-1801
Benjamin, Rye, d 12 Mo (Feb) 21, 1726
Benjamin dmi Sarah SMITH, dt Edward, Westchester, 3 Mo 3, 1722; comm. found him not clear; not passed
Elizabeth, Jr. rocf Pur. 6-11-1807 (clear); dis 9-1829 (O); ct Pur. 8-1833 (H)
Henry Frost, s Samuel H. & Anna W. (Frost), b 7-4-1852 d 7-27-1914; m 9-14-1880 Belle S. REEVE (nm) (H)
cf Creek 1-5-1881
Herbert W., s Sam'l & Anna W. (Frost), b Pleasant Valley 11-11-1855; m 11-11-1897 Mary M. EARL (nm), dt Thomas (H)
cf Creek 2-4-1880
John, Rye, d 3 Mo (Mary) 10, 1730
John d 7-16-1857 ae 70y bPP; m Phebe H. ----- d 8-12-1851
Ch: Samuel H.
Phoebe b 6-30-1818
Isaac H. " 2-29-1820 d 11-21-1852
John " 4-25-1824 " 3-29-1826
Margaret " 2- 2-1826
John " 9-1831 d 9-30-1885
cf Pur. 5-9-1805 (clear); ct Wby 12-6-1815 (clear); Phebe H. rocf Wby 8-2-1817
John, s John & Phebe H., b 9----1831 d 9-30-

CLAPP, John, continued
1885, mo before 3-1875; his acknowledgement ret. to overseer 4-1875, ret a mbr
John A. gct Scipio 10-6-1824 (minor)
Margaret, dt John & Phebe, N. Y.; m 1851 Geo. T. HUSSEY
Phebe, b Westchester Co., d 7-23-1816 ae 74y bHS; "bur from Samuel Robins'"
Phebe, dt John & Phebe H., N. Y.; m 1842 Richard H. THOMAS, of Baltimore
Samuel H., s John & Phebe H., d 11-11-1848; m Phebe M. KIMBER
Ch: Samuel H., Jr. b 11-13-1846
ct WD MM 4-1845 (clear); Phebe M. rocf WD MM 7-16-1845, rem to live with h; ct Phila. for Phebe with Samuel H. 11-6-1850
Silas rocf Uxbridge, Mass. 5-26-1837 (clear); ct Uxbridge 1849
William, Jr. m before 4-6-1803 Elizabeth A. ----- d 12-20-1862 (or 12-20-1861) (H)
Ch: John
Arthur
Anna
Maria A. d 8-8-1879
John A.
Ann Eliza
Infant stillborn 9-16-1815
cf Pur. 2-14-1799 (clear); con mo 12-7-1803; 5 ch recrq of parents 6-7-1815; he failed & dis 11-5-1817; ct Scipio 10-6-1824 for Elizabeth & 2 dt, Maria & Ann Eliza; cf Scipio 9-1855 for Elizabeth & Maria A.
William R. rocf Pur. 5-12-1824 (clear); ct Pur. 2-5-1840 (clear) (O); dis 1-1832 (H)

CLARK
Abigail (form Langdon) dis mo 9-5-1810
Alfred Clark rocf Hardshaw West. 12-28-1854; mo before 12-1860, ret a mbr; relrq 1-1866
Alfred d 4- 4-1859; m Isabella BLISSING
cf Pool & Southampton 8-6-1857 for both; ct Waterford, Ire. 7-5-1876 for Isabella
Amanda K., dt Rufus & Sarah G., d 5-13-1895 ae 73y 5m 8d; m Dr. Charles MILLER (H)
Amy m before 7-5-1809 ----- DUDLEY; dis mo 2-7-1810
Andrew H. m Martha ----- d 4-19-1880 ae 70y bPP (both nm) (H)
Ann Louise (nm), dt Henry T.; m 1896 John Wm. Hutchinson, Jr. (H)
John's name removed 3-13-1933
Annie M. [Clarke] rocf Hardshaw West 7-1861; cert ret to Eng. (probably dt Sarah, who had same date)
Benjamin, s Norman & Sarah (dec), N. Y.; m N.Y. 7-18-1810 Deborah M. FRANKLIN, dt Thos. & Sarah P. (dec), N. Y., d 1869
Ch: Maria T. b 1-31-1812
Sarah Hammond " 1-25-1815 d 12-27-1826
Mary Anna " 12-22-1819
Benjamin Franklin
Benjamin recrq 1807; Deborah gct Corn. 6-1845 with ch, B. Franklin; parents dis 1829 (H)
Benjamin T. gct Corn. 4-2-1845 (clear)
Caleb rocf Chesterfield, N. J. 4-7-1774, rec 7-6-1774
Caleb rocf Chesterfield 4-2-1794 (clear), rem some time since
Colville rocf Hardshaw West 12-29-1859; mo before 10-1864; mbrp relinquished for mo 12-1864
Cyrus B. (nm); m 8-25-1927 Mabel Frances MARINE, dt Arlando & Viola B., b 5-6-1893
Ch: Patricia Brown b 11-1-1929
Patricia recrq of parents 11-1-1933
Daniel d 5-10-1881; m Ann S.,-----
cf Chap. 1834 for Ann S.; cf Corn. 1834 for Daniel; ct Chap. 4-11-1840 for both; cf Chap. 11-13-1845 for Daniel; cf Chap. 3-13-1834 for Ann S.
David rocf Corn 6-26-1834
Deborah M. gct Corn 6-4-1845 (clear)
Dorcas m before 7-3-1805 ----- WHARTON; dis mo 1805
Dorothy (nm), dt Lester W. & Irene M.; m 1908 Victor GARRETT (H)
Elizabeth d 3-19-1805 ae 66y 4m bHS; cf Shrewsbury 3-7-1785 (clear)
Emma d 3- 9-1852 ae 90y; m before 1810 Edward DUDLEY (nm); after long dealings dis mo 1-3-1810; rst 5-3-1815
Esther (late Lawrence) dis mo 2-1-1797
Esther, w Isaiah, rocf Ama. 1-9-1846
Esther A. (nm), dt Amasa & Nancy (Stewart); m 1849 Charles M. FOLGER (H)
Eunice gct Newport 10-2-1811
Frederick [Clarke] rocf Hardshaw West 12-29-1859; dis 4-1862
G. Whitefield, s G. Fisher & Elizabeth, d 11-25-1913 ae 19y 2m 21d bPP (H)
Gideon W., s Nathaniel, gct ND MM 1-7-1807 (clear); cert ret. 9mo 1808 not rec as he was absent at sea & since ret to N. Y.
Hannah [Clarke] rocf Chesterfield 12-2-1800 (clear)
Isabel Reeder (nm); m 1914 Edwin Bunting MOORE (H)
Jacob, s Nathaniel & Eunice, N. Y.; m N. Y. 12-13-1821 Martha M. LAWRIE, dt John & Abigail MORRIS (both dec), Phila., b Phila. d 1-25-1826 ae 36y
Ch: Morris b 4-22-1822 d 3-20-1823
Henry M. " 4-22-1823 " 2- 4-1824
Walter C. " 11- 1-1825 " 11- 1-1825
Jacob dis 12-1877 was in Cuban trade and failed
Jane m 1850 ----- DIFFENDALE; rocf Corn. 4-25-1845 (clear); mo & ret a mbr; ct Corn. 1856
John [Clarke], s Benjamin, Windsor, N. J.; m Flushing 2 Mo (Apr) 3, 1735 Sarah FIELD, dt Thomas, Flushing
Sarah took ct Chesterfield 10 Mo 4, 1735
Jonathan d 7-16-1799 bHS
Joseph Sill (nm) m Elizabeth Storey JENKS, dt Wm. P. & Bertha C., b 8-12-1906; Eliz. rec-

CLARK, Joseph Sill & Elizabeth Storey, continued
rq of parents 4-1914; ct Abington, Pa. 11-6-1929
Josiah G. & Esther
Ch: Josiah Henry H. b 8- 4-1844
Mary C. " 3-1847
Joseph " 2-20-1849
Josiah B. " 1-17-1851
Amy Jane d 5-24-1854
Ada " 10-10-1855 (nm)
cf Corn. 5-22-1845; Esther rocf Ama. 1846; Josiah G. dis 10-1862 for refusing arbitration; ct Corn. 2-1863 for Esther & ch, cert ret for some reason & reissued 10-1866; new ct Corn. 9-1870 for Esther; Josiah rec by Corn. 1865
Julia rocf Chesterfield 11-5-1799 (clear); dis 2-1-1804
Louise Francis (nm), dt Wm. G. & Betsey (Babson); m 1884 Howard Ellworth THORNE (H)
Malinda mo to ----- GILMORE; cf Corn. 1845; dis mo 11-1849
Maria Louisa, dt Rufus & Sarah (Glover), b White Plains 1-17-1825 d 2-13-1907 ae 82y 27d bPP; m 9-25-1850 William MULLIGAN (nm), of Mulligan & Grimshaw Co.; ret a mbr (H)
Maria T., dt Benj. & Deborah, N. Y., b 1-31-1812; m 1833 George FOX
Mary [Clarke], dt Thomas & Catharine; mo to ----- HOXSIE, having been rpd to Hudson, that MM rpd 8-3-1803 having dis her
Melinda rocf Corn 4-25-1845 (clear); dis 11-1849
Nancy Arabella, dt Rufus & Sarah, d 5-26-1872; m 12-25-1856 Andrew Goold WASHBURN (nm)(H) cf Pur. 7-1830; ret a mbr
Nathan, s Reuben & Mary, Corn.; m N. Y. 9-12-1838 Mary P. HEALEY, dt Jonathan & Sarah BIRDSALL, N. Y.
Mary m 1st Isaac HEALY 1834; ct Corn 7-3-1839 for Mary P.
Nathaniel & Eunice [Clarke]
Ch: Amy
Mary
Rebecca
Sarah
John
Joseph
Dorcas
Nathaniel
Jacob
Gideon
cf Newport 9-27-1791 for all
Nathaniel, s John & Eliz., d 8-22-1809 ae 76y 11m bHS; m Mary -----
Ch: John d 5-12-1803 ae 30y
Owen S. rocf Corn. 1854; mbrp relinquished for mo 11-1863
Rachel rocf Chesterfield 3-3-1795 (clear); ct Chesterfield 9-6-1804 (clear)
Rebecca P. [Clarke], dt Nathaniel & Mary, N.Y.; m 1795 Joseph BYRNES
took ct Bush River 1803 with 3 ch, ret with them
Reuben B. mo before 7-1861, ret a mbr; cf Corn. 1848; ct Melbourne, Australia 10-1861
Richard d at the South (H)
Rufus d 9-13-1859 ae 83y 6m 8d, rem from Morris, Oswego Co. 6-12-1893 bPP; m Sarah G. ----- d 4- 8-1865 ae 84y 13d bPP
Ch: Sarah Rebecca
Amanda Kellogg
Maria Louisa
Nancy Arabella
cf Pur. 2-1832 with 3 ch named; ct R. & P. 12-1840 for parents; cf R. & P. 4-1846 for parents; ct R. & P. 12-1-1847 for parents; cf R. & P. 11-1850 for parents
Samuel, s Thomas & Catharine, b 4-11-1784 d 2-1851; ct Hudson 3-4-1829 (clear); he returned before cert was sent & cert returned to recorder 1-6-1830; dis 12-1830 (O)
Sarah Stansbury (form Clark) dis mo 8-3-1796
Sarah, wd John, rocf Hardshaw West 7-1861, but returned as not attend, again rec 3-1863, she living in Calif. with dt; cert returned to England.
Sarah R. [Clarke] dt Rufus & Sarah G., N. Y.; m 1855 James T. KENNEY (H)
Thomas b Flushing d 6-4-1811 ae 63y 4m bHS; m Catharine HULL, N. Y. (m before 6-4-1783, cert not recorded)
Ch: Samuel b 4-11-1784
Mary " 5- 9-1785
Joseph " 7-28-1788; dis 1824
Thomas " 9-10-1791 d 2-10-1791
Thomas Jr. (or 2nd) b 5-15-1792
John Hull " 2-15-1794
Hull b 3-19-1795 d 1-19-1880
Richard " 12-18-1796
cf Phila. 2-28-1783 (clear)
Thomas, s Thomas & Catharine, b 5-15-1792 ct Hudson 2-3-1830
William David, s Josiah & Eleanor, b Corn. 6-10-1888; rocf Marl. 7-11-1917; ct Marl. 3-1924
----- m Elizabeth Story JENKS, dt Wm. P. & Bertha (C----), b 8-12-1906
Eliz. recrq of parents 4-1911; ct Abington, Pa. 11-6-1929
----- m Helen L. HUBBARD, dt M. A., d 11-26-1877 ae 37y bPP
----- m Mary Ann FARRAND (mo before 1-5-1842) cf Tottenham, Eng. 3-21-1839 with her brother to Pokeepsie, recorded in N. Y. without comment; dis 1-5-1842
----- & -----
Ch: Eliza E. d 8-28-1871 ae 10y bPP

CLARKSON
Helen W., dt Jas. B.& Helen E. (Wonell), b Middletown, Del. 9-7-1865; m 1902 Wm. C. McCLOY (H)
Helen recrq 8-11-1906; Helen & dt relrq 10-11-1926

CLATER
Amelia rocf Pontefract 8-16-1830 (clear); ct Pontefract 8-7-1833 (clear)
Sophia, w William, d 5-25-1832 ae 54y bHS
Ch: (prob) Amelia
cf Pontefract 8-16-1830

CLAY
John, Flushing, d 6 Mo (Aug) 6, 1683
Theodore Wm., s Geo. Harry & Mary Eleanor (Walton), b Rockville Centre 9-6-1897; m 4-14-1923 Alida Alice HOLME, dt Chas. E. & Mary T. (Miller), b Bkn. 1-10-1902 (H)
Ch: Jean b 7- 3-1925
Lois Marie " 12-15-1930
Alide Alice relrq 5-8-1815; both recrq 1-12-1925

CLAYTON
Deborah b N. J. d 11-4-1841 ae 61y (H)
cf Shrewsbury 9-1841
James M. b N. J. d 12-21-1845 ae 24y 1m 4d bHS (m)

CLEMENT
Charles b Dutch. Co. d 1-13-1838 ae 28y 6m
cf N. P. 11-20-1817 (clear); dis 2-1830 (0); dis 4-1836 (H) (widower) (lived in a tavern)
Daniel m Hannah THORN
mo before 2-3-1763, probably dis; Hannah con mo 2-3-1763, accepted; Hannah gct Corn. 8-5-1790, having rem with her h
Elizabeth dis jas 8-2-1820
Henry d 7-30-1800 bHS
Henry, N. Y.; m 1796 Elizabeth -----
Ch: Mary b Wby 8-7-1798 d 3-20-1829
Ann Eliza b 12-15-1801
Charles d 6-15-1806; dis 1829
cf N. P. 4-20-1796 for Henry (clear); ct Pur. 1-5-1796 (clear); Elizabeth rocf Pur. 6-8-1797
Henry, s Jonathan & Deborah (dec), Flushing; m at Ann Leffert's 4-8-1847 Ruth L. WINTRINGHAM, dt Thos. & Ruth, N. Y.
ct Flushing 4-5-1848 (H)
James, Flushing, ltm 8 Mo (Oct) 3, 1700 Abigail FARRINGTON
active mbr from 1676, came as indentured servant of John Bowne; Abigail called wd in m intention
James, Flushing; m 1724 Sarah FIELD, dt Benjamin & Hannah, Flushing, b 6 Mo (Aug) 17, 1704
Sarah was dealt with for mo to a minor 5 Mo (July) 24, 1724; she d while under dealing
Jane rocf Wby 2-21-1785 with 2 dt, Martha & Mary (all clear)
Jonathan d 12-24-1855; m Deborah ----- d Flushing 11-22-1841 (H)
Ch: Mary A.
Henry
cf Pur. 11-1836 for all

Joseph [Clements], Wby; m Jane ----- d 1 Mo. 23, 1721/2
Joseph E. rocf Phila. 1-26-1814, minor; ct Wby 8-1-1821 as Joseph E.
Martha, dt Jane, rocf Wby 2-21-1785 (clear) with sister, Martha, & mother; ct Wby & Jericho 12-2-1829 (0); withdrew 1828 (H)
Mary, dt Jane, dis mo 3-20-1829 ----- Frost; cf Wby 2-21-1785 (clear) with sister, Martha & mother
Mary A., dt Jonathan & Deborah, d 10-29-1892; m 9-13-1844 William H. BOWNE (mo) (H)
Sarah [Clements] (late Doughty) dis mo 2-2-1786

CLEVELAND
Ida, dt Cyrus & Emily P., Yonkers; m 1877 Wm. H. THORNE (H)

CLIBBORN
John
Samuel, s Wm. Cooper, rocf Moate, Leinster, Ire. (clear); ct Shrewsbury 1-7-1829 (clear) cert ret as he not to be found within their limits 10-7-1829

CLIFFORD
----- m Elizabeth E. RANSOME, dt Egbert
Elizabeth recrq of father 7-1903, then aged 9

CLIFTON
Ella, dt William & Sarah (Vail), b Plainfield, N. J. 10-30-1860 d 10-13-1923; m J. D. FURNAS (H)
Henry, Flushing; m Flushing 6 Mo (Aug) 22, 1686 Rebekah ADAMS, dt John & Joan
Ch: Mary b 5 Mo (July) 30, 1687
Henry active mbr from 1684

CLOCK
Elizabeth, wd Abraham, d 2-18-1857 ae 90y 8m 4d bPP (H)
recrq 3-4-1818; dis 11-1830 (0)

CLOSE
Ethel B., dt James & Charlotte, N. Y., b London 9-13-1881; m 1912 John Paul BROOMALL (H)
recrq 6-10-1899
James, s Robt. W. & Ann (Coverdale), b London 7-2-1856 d 8- 8-1922 ae 65y 1m 8d bPP; m 7-17-1878 in London Charlotte CAMPION (nm), dt Wm. & Charlotte, d 6-2-1926 ae 69y
Ch: Ethel Brooks b 9-13-1881
Ethel recrq 6-10-1899

CLOTHIER
Lydia, dt Isaac H. & Mary C. (Jackson), b Sharon Hill 1-22-1878; m 1903 John Rogers MAXWELL, Jr. (H)
Wm. P., s Caleb & Hannah F., Phila.; m at Gouverneur St., N. Y. 12-25-1865 (not under care of N. Y. MM) Jane H. DREW, dt Wm.

CLOTHIER, Wm. P. & Jane H., continued
(dec) & Susan, N. Y. (H)
Ch: Caleb b 9-27-1866 d 11-14-1866
Wm. Penn (Wm. Drew) b 7-23-1868 d 1- 2-1870 bPP
Hannah Fletcher b 7- 6-1870
Isaac H. " 7-11-1873 d 11-19-1873
cf Phila. 3-1864 for Wm. P.; Jane recrq 8-1-1866; ct East Hamburgh 2-4-1874 for parents & Hannah

CLOUGH
Alice H., dt Dana B. & Lucinda E., b Lock Haven Pa. 5-10-1879; m 6-27-1906 Charles Melville WEEKS (H)
Arthur Dana, s Dana B. & Lucinda E., b Lock Haven, Pa. 7-16-1874 d 11-14-1926; m 3-15-1899 Anna Josephine MUNIER, dt Chas. & Mary A. (Rolland), b Bkn. 3-2-1871 d 3-30-1933
Ch: Richard Munier b 8-16-1901
Arthur Dana m 2nd Annie STUYVESANT
both recrq 2-10-1910 (death notice pasted in record says "mother of Richard M. Clough & Charles W. Stuyvesant") (H)
Clarence A., s Dana B. & Lucinda E., b Lock Haven, Pa. 4-3-1883; m 6-27-1906 Ethel KIPP (nm) dt Wm. DeGraw & Eliz. (Nangle) (H)
Dana B., s Jonathan & Hannah (nm), b 11-29-1845 d 4-22-1926 bPP; m 10-18-1873 Lucinda E. EILERT, dt Joseph & Elizabeth, b Mifflinsburg, Pa. 4-16-1843 d 4-27-1926 bPP
Ch: Arthur Dana b Lock Haven, Pa. 7-16-1874
Alice H. " " " " 5-10-1879
Clarence A. " " " " 4- 3-1883
recrq 10-9-1897; Lucinda & 2 ch recrq 10-7-1899 (H)

CLOYD
Edwin C. (nm), s Wm. & Mary Jane, d 3-19-1909 ae 50y 3m 27d bPP; m N. Y. 10-12-1881 Josephine ARNOLD, dt Jos. J. & Sarah E., b Arnoldton, N. Y. 9-3-1858 d 3-3-1926 bPP
Ch: Bessie Arnold d 11-11-1888 ae 2y 5m 25d bPP
Genevieve Campbell d 9-20-1911 ae 27y 9m 14d (H)

COAD
Elsie A. m ----- FOSTER; recrq 1-5-1910, at White House, N. J. 1912; death rpd 4-1928

COAKER (or COKER)
Dorcas, dt Nicholas, N. Y.; m 1688 Richard JONES
Nicholas, Flushing; m Alice ----- d 11 Mo (Jan) 5, 1685/6
Ch: Dorcas

COALE
Shipwith rocf ND MM 10-23-1810 (clear); ct Derr Creek, Va. 7-7-1813 (clear)

COATES
Joseph S., s Samuel & Lydia (dec), Phila.; m N. Y. 6-21-1809 Sarah ROBINSON, dt Wm. T. & Sarah (dec), N. Y.
Joseph brought cert of clear from Phila; Sarah took cert there 6-6-1810
Saunders, s John R. (dec) & Sarah M., Phila.; m at A. Bell's, N. Y. 10-23-1845 Rebecca B. BELL, dt Abraham & Mary C. (dec), d 1-24-1894 (not under care of N. Y. MM)
dis by Phila. MM (O) at request of N. Y. 10-1847 for m by Mayor & attending (H) mtg (O)

COBOURN
Agnes rocf Spruce St., Phila. 6-1837; ct Spruce St., Phila. 7-1843 (H)

COCHRANE
Ira Lee m Florence L. WINTERS, dt Geo. W. & Anna B. (Treadway), b N. Y. 1885 d 11-7-1929 bPP
Ch: Vincent
Florence Louise
Ella Victoria
Gladys
parents rolf Plymouth Church, Bkn., 4-1928; 3 ch recrq of parents 4-1928; Gladys recrq 10-1-1930
Jane H. F. [Cochran], w Wallace L., rocf Scip. 3-1867; ct Chicago 4-1880; cf Chicago 3-1888
----- & ----- (nm) bPP (H)
Ch: Henry Firter d 10-14-1867 ae 5y
Wm. H. " 5-31-1871 ae 9y 19d
Emma A. " 7- 7-1873 ae 6m 13d

COCK
Adonijah, s Rees, Flushing, b 4-7-1776; rocf Pur. 4-8-1790, minor; ct Pur. 5-3-1792
Alice, dt Effingham & Harriet (Haight), b N. Y. 9-28-1866; m 1895 Sherman EVARTS (H)
recrq 12-12-1927
Ambrose & Phebe
Ch: Daniel T.
Henry
Andrew
Mary
John L.
Harriet
Edward
cf Creek 6-21-1816 with first 5 ch; ct Scipio 8-1-1821 with 7 ch named
Amy, dt John & Sarah, m John TITUS (mo before 12-4-1793
cf Wby 5-27-1778 (clear); dis mo 1-1-1794
Amy, dt Stephen & Charlotte, rocf Corn. 1-21-1829 with parents; ct Chap. 2-2-1853 (H)
Andrew, s William, Merchant, N. Y. b L. I. d 6-21-1832 ae 62y; m 12-31-1790 Mary TITUS, dt Henry & Martha, d 5-1-1803 ae 31y
Ch: Anne b 3-25-1793 d 4-13-1796
Rachel " 12-24-1794 " 12- 7-1867

COCK, Andrew & Mary, continued
Ch: Martha b 10-24-1797
Isaac " 11-15-1800
2 others d young
Andrew m 2nd 7-10-1806 Sarah EMBREE, dt George & Abigail, d 11-30-1863
Ch: Effingham
William E.
George E.
cf Flushing 5-5-1825 with his ch, Rachel & Martha (clear) & their ch as named; all dis 1828-1839
Andrew L. (nm) b N. Y. d 9-27-1834 ae 31y 7m bHS
Ann
Ann Augusta, dt Thos. & Eliz. T., N. Y.; m 1834 Edward WILLIS
Adam, s John, d 12-7-1801 ae 2y bHS
Arthur M., s Daniel & Jane M., rocf Scip. with mother 3-3-1852; ct Scip. 7-3-1878 (H)
Benjamin, s John & Sarah, Flushing; m Hannah PRIOR, dt Thomas & Martha, Cedar Swamp
Ch: Abraham
Phebe
Sarah b 10- 4-1790 d 7-29-1795
Amy
cf Wby 4-17-1793 with their ch & aged mother, Sarah Cock
Benjamin Hicks, s Geo. E. & Mary M., b 1-14-1843 (H) (changed to Benj. Embree Hicks)
Charity d 9-15-1874 at N. Plainfield ae 86y 10m recrq 1858
Charles (nm) & -----
Ch: Stephen d 12- 7-1819 ae 19y bHS
Deborah m 2-5-1879 Jordan C. FROST
N. Y. P. M. rpd this m 10-4-1881; no action
twin to Elizabeth; cf Chap. 8-1857; ct Ama. 6-4-1884 (H)
Deliverance d 11-21-1803 bHS
Della d 2-21-1803 bHS
Edmund, s Henry, gct Creek 7-4-1787 (clear)
Effingham, s Andrew; m Harriet HAIGHT (H)
Ch: Effingham Moses b 5-31-1855
Phebe Anna " 12-10-1857
Harriet " 6-25-1859 d 10-12-1864
William Howard " 2-10-1862 " 3-30-1864
Alice " 9-28-1866
cf Chap. 1-1855 for Harriet; ct Chap. 4-5-1871 for all
Elijah, s John & Sarah; m Temperance TOWNSEND (nm), dt George & Rosannah
Ch: Sarah d 1- 7-1803 ae 22y
cf Wby 12-4-1771; dis mo 7-7-1773
Eliza, s Thomas & Elizabeth, N. Y.; m 1831 James B. PARSONS
Elizabeth rocf Wby 9-25-1771
Elizabeth rocf Pur. 11-9-1809
Elizabeth, dt Abraham & Susan; m 1838 Alfred Carman SMITH (mo)
dis mo 9-5-1838
Elizabeth, twin to Deborah, rocf Chap. 8-1857; ct Ama. 6-4-1884 (H)
Elizabeth, dt Thomas & Maria M., b 12-25-1837; relrq 2-1864
Elizabeth L., dt Wm. Embree & Mary E.; m Jacob Harvey BELL (H)
Elizabeth M., dt Geo. E. & Mary M., b 4-30-1845 d 1- 1-1917; m 6-20-1877 Thomas STEWART (nm) (H)
Emily L., dt Thos. & Eliz. T., N. Y.; m 1837 Richard H. BOWNE
George (nm) b N. Y. d 12-8-1810 ae 32y 10m bHS
George E., s Andrew, d 8-24-1889; m Mary M. ----- d 10-12-1892 (H)
Ch: George H. (changed to G. Embree Hicks 1-21-1886) b 5- 1-1841
Benjamin H. (changed to Benj. Embree Hicks 7-25-1875) b 1-14-1843
Elizabeth Mowell b 4-30-1845
Mary H. " 1- 8-1847 d 2-19-1858
Frederick E. " 1-12-1860 " 8- 6-1864
cf Wby 4-1842 for Mary
George Hicks (changed name to George Embree Hicks), dt Geo. E. & Mary M., b 5- 1-1841 (H)
Hannah, dt James & Sarah,Mk.; m 1692 James DELAPLAINE; rem to Phila.
Hannah, dt Samuel & Martha; m Joseph COLES; m 2nd c. 1719 Matthew PRIOR
Henry, s James & Sarah, Mk; m at John Feake's 6 Mo (Aug) 28, 1699 Mary FEAKE, dt John & Elizabeth, d 10 Mo (Dec) 30, 1715
Ch: Joseph b 2 Mo (Apr) 29, 1701
Benjamin " 10 Mo (Dec) 5, 1702
John " 1 Mo (Mar) 22, 1705/6
James " 10 Mo (Dec) 24, 1707
Amey " 12 Mo (Feb) 19, 1708/9
Mary " 8 Mo (Oct) 8, 1711
Henry " 6 Mo (Aug) 10, 1713
Sarah " 10 Mo (Dec) 14, 1715
Elizabeth " 10 Mo (Dec) 14, 1715
Henry m 2nd Martha PEARSALL, dt Nathaniel & Martha
Ch: Thomas b 7 Mo (Sep) 15, 1718
Samuel " about 1720
Henry, s Henry, Mk.; m 12 Mo (Feb) 3, 1736/7 (Wby MM record) Mary BOWNE, dt Thomas & Hannah, Wby
Ch: Thomas b 1 Mo (Mar) 25, 1737/8
Sarah " 11 Mo (Jan) 14, 1740/1
Henry, s John; m Elizabeth ROBBINS, dt Jeremiah & Hannah
Ch: Anna
William
Edmund
Stephen
Charles
Hannah
cf Wby 9-20-1785 for all; Hannah (clear); ct Creek 12-5-1787 for all, William & Anna (clear)
Isaac (nm), b L. I. d 2-6-1814 ae 54y bHS
Isaac rocf Corn. 3-1825; ct Ama. 10-1833 (H)
Jacob rocf Corn. 11-5-1851; ct Corn. 6-1-1859 (H)
James b England d bet. 23 July & 10 Dec 1699;

COCK, James, continued
Sarah ----- d 10 Mo (Dec) 16, 1715
Ch: Mary b N.E. 11 Mo (Jan) 1, 1655/6
Thomas b L. I. 8 Mo (Oct) 15, 1658
Martha " Mk. 7 Mo (Sep) 7, 1661 d 9 Mo 1670
John " " 11 Mo (Jan) 22, 1666/7
Hannah " " 6 Mo (Aug) 5, 1669
Sarah " " 7 Mo (Sep) 20, 1672
James " " 2 Mo (Apr) 4, 1674
Henry " " 2 Mo (Apr) 1, 1678
Martha " " 12 Mo (Feb) 13, 1680/1
James, s James & Sarah, d 3 Mo (May) 28, 1728; m at John Feake's 10 Mo (Dec) 1, 1698 Hannah FEAKE (FEKE), dt John & Elizabeth
Ch: Sarah b 12 Mo (Feb) 24, 1700/01
Samuel " 5 Mo (July) 20, 1702
Joshua " 7 Mo (Sep) 2, 1704
Elizabeth " 9 Mo (Nov) 22, 1706
Josiah " 1 Mo (Mar) 27, 1709
James gct Wby 1787; cf Wby 5-5-1791 (minor)
Jane M., w Daniel F., dt ----- MERRITT (H)
Ch: Arthur M.
Janette d 10- 8-1864
cf Scip. 3-3-1852 with 2 ch; ct Scip. 6-6-1877 for Jane
Jesse, s Isaac & Charity; m Elizabeth PEARCE
Ch: Samuel
cf Pur. 8-13-1795; ct Chap. 5-2-1798 with ch, Samuel
John, s James & Sarah, Mk.; m -----
Ch: Hannah b 8 Mo (Oct) 23, 1689
Thomas " 11 Mo (Jan) 14, 1692/3
John m 2nd Dorothy HARCURT, dt Richard & Elizabeth
Ch: John b 1 Mo (Mar) 25, 1698
Daniel " 8 Mo (Oct) 5, 1699
Meriba " 1 Mo (Mar) 2, 1700/01
Hezekiah " 9 Mo (Nov) 28, 1703
James " 2 Mo (Apr) 27, 1708
John con mo twice, accepted by Wby MM 11 Mo (Jan) 29, 1706/7
John L., s John & Freelove, Grocer, N. Y., d 3-13-1814 ae 34y 11m 25d bHS (m); recrq 5-5-1813
Joseph S. rocf Creek 1-1832; dis 3-1833 (H)
Joshua d 3- 9-1800 bHS
Lydia, w David, gct Wby 5-2-1798
Margaret d 1-13-1848, a wd ae 83y; m ----- (H)
Ch: Sarah Ann
Margaret recrq 4-3-1815 with dt, Sally Ann; Margaret dis 1830 (O)
Margaret, dt Richard & Mary M., b 3-1-1826 d 11-30-1891; m ----- CODDINGTON (nm) (H)
Martha, dt Joshua & Elizabeth, N. Y.; m 1834 Richard Hallock, of Yorktown (H)
cf Chap. 1-1832; ct Ama. 8-1834
Martha, dt Andrew & Mary, d 4-3-1881; m Felix M. WALTERS (H)
Mary, dt James & Sarah, Mk.; m 1693 John BOWNE (3rd w John Bowne)
Phebe, dt Thomas & Martha T., b 6-28-1823; gct Rochester 2-3-1836, with brother, Thomas, minors, rem with father
Phebe, dt Stephen & Charlotte; m 7-5-1842 Levi HUNT (H)
cf Corn. 1-21-1829 with parents
Phebe Anna, dt Effingham; m Robert S. MURREY
Rachel, wd Jesse, dt ----- WEEKS, b Westchester Co. d 8-16-1825 ae 28y bHS
Rees rocf Pur. 4-12-1792; ct Pur. 6-2-1796 (clear)
Rosanna, w Charles, d 9-21-1856; recrq 9-4-1822; dis 12-1-1829 (O)
Samuel, s Job, rocf Chap. 8-14-1818; dis mo 1825
Sarah, dt James & Sarah, Mk.; m 1698 Henry FRANKLIN
Sarah rem to Phila 8 Mo (Oct) 2, 1740
Sarah, dt Henry, Newtown, L. I.; m 1742 Joseph SHOTWELL
Sarah, dt Abraham & Susan; m 1837 Manuel FETTER
dis 9-5-1838
Sarah Ann, dt Margaret, d 12-4-1834; m Morris FRANKLIN (H)
recrq of mother 4-3-1815
Stephen m Charlotte ----- d 7- 2-1844
Ch: Amy
Phebe
cf Corn. 1-21-1829 with 2 ch named (H); cf Corn. 4-24-1830 for same (O); parents dis 1831 (O); ch dis 1840-1849; Stephen dis 10-1836 (H)
Dr. Thomas, s Daniel & Rosannah; m Elizabeth T. ----- d 11-22-1830 ae 55y bHS
Ch: Eliza H.
Ann Augusta
Emily
Thomas T.
the 4 ch recrq of Elizabeth 8-2-1820 (prominent physician)
Thomas m 2nd N. Y. 6-12-1833 Esther C. SEYMOUR, dt Wm. & Esther (both dec), N. Y., d 5-7-1834 ae 38y bHS
Ch: infant stillborn 5- 7-1834 bHS
Thomas m 3rd Maria Margaretta RIEHLE
relrq 11-3-1841
Ch: Elizabeth b 12-25-1837
William R. b 1- 8-1841
Thomas recrq 1829; cf Corn. 11-23-1826 for Esther (clear); cf ND MM 8-23-1836 for M. Margaretta
Thomas m Martha T. ----- d 1827
Ch: Lydia d 12-18-1825
Phebe b 6-28-1823
Israel d 12-21-1824 ae 4d
Thomas, Jr. b 11-18-1825
cf Ama. 4-11-1823 with dt, Lydia; Thomas dis 12-1829 (O) 10-1831 (H)
Thomas m 2nd at Pur. Mary ----- d 1----1829(H)
cf Pur. 6-1828 for Mary
Thomas, s Thomas & Martha T., b 11-18-1825
ct Rochester 2-3-1836 with sister, minors, rem with parents
Thomas & -----

COCK, Thomas, continued
Ch: infant stillborn 5- 5-1832 bHS
Thomas T., s Thomas & Elizabeth H., d 6-1869 ae 86y bPP
dis jas 2-2-1842 (prominent physician)
Townsend (nm) m Elizabeth ----- (nm) b N. Y. d 2-24-1827 ae 36y
Ch: George Townsend d 10-4-1817 ae 5y 2m bHS
Townsend & Hannah
Ch: Isaac
William
Phebe
Henry b 9-25-1830
Margaret b 1-1833
cf Corn. 4-22-1830 with 3 minor ch named; ct Roch. 1-6-1836 for all; ct Rochester 5-1837 for Hannah, w Townsend, & 4 ch named
William, s Henry, rocf Wby 6-29-1782; he was young when he rem
William E., s Andrew & Sarah; m Anna HICKS, dt Silas (H)
gct Flushing 8-1856
William R., s Thomas & Maria M., b 1-8-1841; relrq 5-1863
----- & -----
Ch: Esther d 5-28-1813 ae 13y bHS

COCKS
Elizabeth, dt Rowland & Mary W. (Torrey), mbr of Corn; m 1898 George W. Westall (H)
George H., s Townsend & Harriet (Hollett), b Corn. 7-23-1865; m 1-15-1900 Mary BROWN (nm) (H)
recrq 4-14-1924
Mary, dt Robert & Phebe; m 1855 Daniel C. MILLER (H)
Phebe C. (nm), dt John & Armenia (Conklin); m Daniel E. HAVILAND
cf Yorktown 6-1883 with Daniel & ch
Robert d 9-6-1866; cf Chap. 10-1855 (H)
William, s Robert & Phebe (dec), N. Y., d 11-26-1879; m Henry C. Bowron's 4-12-1859 Sarah BOWRON, dt Henry C. & Deborah, N. Y., b 5-27-1821 d 9-10-1900 (H)
cf Chap. 1-1859
William rocf Chap. 1-1859 (H)

CODDINGTON
Margaret, dt Rich'd & Mary CROMWELL, b 3-1-1826 d 11-30-1891 (H)

COFFEE
George F. (nm) m Grace ----- (nm) b Pa. d 3-19-1844 ae 68y bHS
Ch: Thomas A. b Phila. d 12-20-1845 ae 33y
Thomas listed as a mbr (prob Phila.)

COFFIN
Alexander J., s Eliab & Mary, Athens, N. Y., d 7-31-1897 ae 80y 10m 17d bPP; m N. Y. 4-8-1819 Lydia STRATTON, dt Latham & Phebe, N. Y.
Ch: Joseph J. d 3- 1-1889 ae 68y 1m bPP
ct Hudson 7-7-1819 for Lydia
Anna con mo 3-6-1805
Andrew G., s Jorham & Rebecca M., Nantucket; m at Isaac Sherwood's 5-12-1841 (not under care of N. Y. MM) Elizabeth M. SHERWOOD, dt Isaac & Eliz., N. Y., d 1-10-1856 ae 40y 8m 26d (H)
Ch: William Henry d 3-21-1849 ae 3y 4m bPP
Elizabeth R. " 6-21-1930 ae 79y bPP
Frederick L. " 10-17-1930 ae 55y bPP
Andrew G. m 2nd Sarah L. -----, d 7-22-1880 ae 49y 17d bPP
Arthur, s Robert & Lydia (Bunker), b Hudson 4-12-1851 d 4- 7-1915; m Eva GIBBS (nm) (H)
Avis Anna, dt Alex. J. & Mary S., d 8-30-1897 ae 60y bPP (unm) rocf Oswego 4-7-1875 (H)
Caleb (nm), s Caleb & Ruth (Bradbury); m 6-12-1872 Esther LAWTON, dt Abraham & Sarah (Bancroft), b 2-4-1839 d 3-1921 (H)
cf Hudson 11-3-1886 for Esther
Charles (nm) b Nantucket d 3-23-1810 ae 31y 9m bHS
Charlotte, dt Zephaniah & Sally (or Hezekiah) cf Nantucket with mother 4-24-1827; dis 10-1840 (H); dis 2-1841 (O)
Cyrus J. rocf Hudson 12-3-1845; dis 8-1850 (H)
Elizabeth M. d Calif. 1-10-1856; recrq 8-2-1848(H)
Emily B., dt Hezediah & Sally, rocf Nantucket with mother 4-24-1827; dis 2-1841 (O); dis 9-1841 (H)
Emma L. d 11-22-1875 ae 30y 4m 7d bPP (nm) (H)
Eunice d Hudson; m Timothy W. BUNKER (H)
Francis W. (or Frank W.), s Robt. & Lydia, b 5-11-1840 Hudson; m Carrie B. WINANS (nm)(H)
Ch: Frank d 4- 4-1879 ae 4y bPP
Wilbur " 7- 4-1882 ae 2y bPP
joined U. S. Army during the late war 7-3-1867; case dismissed 10-2-1867; he will never do so again & regrets it
Hazadiah (Hezediah) (nm) d 8-29-1855 ae 71y 11m 7d bPP; m Sarah -----
Ch: Emily B. d 11-29-1902 ae 84y bPP
Mary C. " 5-22-1899 ae 75y bPP
Lydia b Bkn. d 1-15-1830 ae 1y 6m bHS
Sarah b " " 8-18-1831 ae 16d bHS
Harriet M. " 3-24-1912 ae 76y bPP
Henry, s Salmon & Anna (both dec), Bkn.; m at Henry Everitt's 6-19-1867 Susannah V. EVERITT, dt Henry & Sarah Ann (Kirby), Bkn., b 12-21-1835 d 11-4-1931 (H)
Ch: stillborn 3- 1-1876 bPP
cf Oswego 2-5-1868 for Henry
Homer T. m Lena WEST
Ch: Charles West b 8- 9-1911
cf Oskaloosa 2-6-1907 for Homer; Lena recrq 3-6-1907
I. Sherwood (nm), s Andrew G. & Eliza. S.; m 6- 1-1881 Ida WILLETS, dt Joseph & Esther (Griffin), b Bkn. 9-10-1856
Ch: Adele d 4-10-1911 ae 40y bPP

COFFIN, I. Sherwood & Ida, continued
Ch: Andrew d 6-11-1877 bPP
cf Wby 11-5-1884 for Esther
Joseph (nm) & Elizabeth (nm)
Ch: Ella d ae 11m bPP
Rollin J. " 5-15-1864 ae 6y 4m 3d bPP
Judith rocf Nantucket 5-27-1830 (clear); ct Nantucket 12-4-1833
Lydia (nm), b Nantucket d 11-3-1811 ae 47y 3m 5d bHS
Mark & Judith
Ch: George Mitchell
Mary d 1- 6-1801
Benjamin b 1- 1-1803 d 3- 1-1803
cf Nantucket 4-2-1801 with 2 ch, George Mitchell & Mary; George placed in N. P. Boarding School; ct Creek 1803 with George & Mary
Mary rocf Oswego 12-16-1829; dis 12-1832
Merab (nm), dt Eliab & Mary, d 10-13-1878 ae 87y 8m bPP (unm) (sister of Alexander J.) (H)
Nathaniel M. rocf Troy 10-1-1845; mbrp cancelled 1-13-1906 (H)
Robert, s Salmon & Ann (Mitchell), d 4-28-1891; m 9-26-1838 Lydia B. BUNKER, dt Timothy M. & Eunice (Coffin), b Hudson 11-11-1818 d 9-18-1903 (H)
Ch: Francis W. b 5-11-1840
Eunice Anna " 3- 4-1842 d 4-22-1916
Robert M. " 11-17-1848
Arthur " 4-12-1851
cf Hudson 8-1858 for all
Sally, w Hezediah (or Heradiah, Zephaniah) d 1-20-1871
Ch: Emily B.
Charlotte
cf Nantucket N. Dist. 4-24-1827 with ch; Sally dis 4-1831 (O)
Sarah A. (nm), b Newport d 2-14-1812 ae 39y bHS
T. Homer m Lena WEST
Ch: Charles West b 8- 9-1911
Margaret b Portland, Ore. 9-2-1914
cf Oskaloosa, Iowa 2-6-1907 for T. Homer; Lena recrq 3-6-1907; letter to First Presbyterian Church, Portland, Ore. 7-1915 for all
Thomas d 4-12-1893 ae 83y 5m bPP; cf Oswego 6-2-1880 (unm)
William Henry b Athens, Md. 3-1-1838 d 4-26-1908; rocf Hudson 10-1858 (H)

COGGESHALL
Caleb d 1-1-1847 ae 89y; m Elizabeth ----- d 6-20-1851
Ch: Job d 8-22-1835 ae 38y 3m
Giles H.
Deborah b 12- 7-1804 (or 12-7-1805)
Geo. Dillwyn b 1-13-1808
Caleb " 8-16-1812; dis 10-1836
cf Newport 11-24-1803 for Caleb & Eliz. with ch, Job & Giles; parents dis 1829 (H)
Caleb, s Caleb & Elizabeth, b 8-16-1812; dis mo 11-2-1836; d & bHS, rem from HS to PP 4-3-1874
Deborah, dt Caleb & Eliz., N. Y.; m 1827 Ellwood WALTER
Edwin W., s Giles H. & Marianna (Walter), Bloomfield, N. J., b 7-26-1842 (or 7-22-1842 d 3- 3-1929; m Bkn. 6-8-1870 Anna WALTER, dt Ellwood & Deborah (dec), b 1-20-1841 d 3-21-1894, Englewood, N. J. (H)
Ch: Sarah Walter b 7- 4-1872
Emma, dt Giles H. & Marianna, b 4-25-1836 d 2-15-1867; m 4-2-1863 Wm. M. FRANKLIN (H)
Florence, dt Geo. D. & Emma, b 7-19-1858; relrq 10-1-1879 (H)
George (nm) & -----
Ch: Infant stillborn 4- 7-1835 bHS
Frances b N. Y. d 11-3-1837 ae 1y 3m bHS
George D., s Caleb & Elizabeth, d 11-5-1891; m Emma ----- d 1-16-1888
Ch: Florence b 7-19-1858
Frederick L. " 1- 8-1861 d 2- 1-1911
ct SD MM 1-5-1825, apprentice; cf Radnor 5-1855 for Emma (H); dealt with 9-9-1930 (O) at rq of SD MM for being Hicksite
Giles H., s Caleb & Elizabeth; m Elizabeth M. ----- b R. I. d 3-12-1832 ae 22y (H)
Ch: Walter b 5-18-1831 d 1- 8-1832
ct Phila. 9- 9-1818; cf Phila. 3-25-1824
Giles H. m 2nd Marianna ----- b 10-13-1805 d 5- 9-1891 (Giles H. b 6-20-1802 d 2-21-1885)
Ch: Walter b 9- 6-1834
Emma " 4-25-1836 d 2-15-1867
Charles Thompson b 11-21-1837 d 12-24-1865
Mary Rhoades b 9- 7-1840
Edwin W. " 7-22-1842
Morton C. " 9-28-1848
cf Radnor 5-1834 for Marianna
Job, s Caleb & Eliz., d 8-22-1835 ae 38y 3m bHS
rem cert to Corn. as a minor apprentice 9-2-1812; dis mo to first cousin 8-1-1821
Mary R., dt Giles & Marianna, Bloomfield, N.J., b 9- 7-1840; m 10-15-1868 Emor K. JANNEY (H)
ct Phila. 7-7-1869
Morton C., s Giles H. & Marianna, Bloomfield, N. J., b 9-28-1848; m at Bloomfield, N. J. 10-15-1874 Harriet T. CRANE, dt Jason & Araminta, Bloomfield, N. J. (not under care of N. Y. MM (H)
relrq 3-1-1882
Walter, s Giles H. & Marianna (Walter), N. Y., b 9- 6-1834 d 8- 3-1906; m at Samuel J. Barry's 11-17-1859, Sarah Emily HAYDOCK (nm), dt Wm. M. & Emily W. (dec) (not under care of N. Y. MM)(H)
Ch: Emma d 11-10-1868 ae 9m 26d bPP
----- & -----
Ch: William W. b N. Y. d 9- 5-1841 ae 2y 8m bHS

COGSWELL
Abby S. d 5-1857; cf Scip 1854

COHU
Aaron B., s Joseph S. & Eliz. J. (Williams), b 5-14-1843 d 9- 1-1904 ae 61y 3m 18d bPP; m 11-29-1866 Eugenie Lecordier TOUSSAINT (nm), d 12-6-1889 ae 42y bPP (H)
Ch: Wm. McC d 11-15-1885 ae 11y 3m 26d bPP
Anna Louise m Arthur Wm. KENWORTHY d 2-17-1931 ae 69y bPP (both nm) (H)
Henry M., s Joseph S. & Eliz. J. (Williams) b 1-16-1851 (or 1-16-1850); m 12-9-1891 Annabell TURCK (nm), dt Solomon & Charlotte
Ch: La Motte b 9-23-1895
Henry Wallace b 2-18-1897
ch recrq of parents 8-8-1908 (H)
Henry S., s Peter, b 12-8-1821 d 5-4-1883 bPP cf R. & P. 3-1846 (H)
Joseph (nm) & -----
Ch: William b N. Y. d 9-24-1845 ae 1y 2m bHS
Elizabeth W. d 7- 5-1861 ae 8y bPP
Joseph S., s Peter, d 1-11-1887 ae 67y 3m 8d bPP; m Elizabeth J. WILLIAMS, d 12-3-1882 ae 62y bPP (H)
Ch: Aaron B. b 5-14-1842
Anna S. " 12-31-1846 d 1-17-1926 White Plains
Henry M. " 1-16-1851 (or 1-16-1850)
Elizabeth " 3-20-1853 d 7- 5-1861
Lydia L. " 1-10-1856
cf Chesterfield 5-1846 with Aaron B.
Lydia L., dt Joseph & Elizabeth J., N. Y., b 1-10-1856; m 1886 Robert W. HULL (H)
Peter & -----
Ch: Joseph S. (nm)
Henry S.
recrq 10-7-1812; ct R. & P. 9-3-1817 (clear)
Rachel H., dt William, d 7-11-1841 ae 31y 1m; m ----- LOWERRE (all nm)
William rocf R. & P. 8-10-1821; ct R. & P. 2-6-1824 (clear); cf R. & P. 7-1830; dis 10-1834
William (nm) & -----
Ch: Julia b N. Y. d 1-12-1841 ae 2y bHS
Harriet b N. Y. d 7-4-1841 ae 4y 6m bHS
Rachel H. b L. I.; m ----- LOWERRE
----- & -----
Ch: William b N. Y. d 4-16-1836 ae 3y 5d bHS

COLDEN
Ann dis mo 8-6-1767
Mary Ann (late Lawrence) dis mo 8-3-1814

COLE
Joseph B. rocf Green St., Phila. 6-1858; mbrp cancelled 5-11-1912 (H)
M. Laura (nm), dt Frank Wm. & Clara (Dodman); m 1905 Henry F. HAVILAND
Henry's name entered by comm 10-10-1886; Henry relrq 7-12-1920
Martha C. d 4- 3-1880; rocf Phila. 3-6-1878(H)

COLEMAN
Abraham B., s Nathan & Phebe, rocf Hudson 12-20-1825 with mother; dis 9-1836 for non-attendance (H); dis mo 7-11-1838 after long dealing (O) (m by M. E. Minister)
Anna, wd John, b Nantucket d 10-24-1812 ae 80y bHS
cf Marl. 7-27-1809 as w of John
Anna E., dt George & Eliza (Bunker), b 7-4-1834 d 8-1909; m 10-7-1859 Timothy M. INGRAHAM (H); cf Hudson with parents 7-1843
Anna M., dt ----- DORLAND; rocf Farm. 12-1-1875
Archibald, s Silas B. & Rebecca B., b Detroit 5-29-1877; m 6-7-1899 in Detroit, Annie NORTHROP (nm), dt Eaton B. & Anna; relrq 9-14-1925; joined Episcopal Church (H)
Benjamin (nm) b Nantucket d 10-19-1810 ae 53y bHS (m)
Bethia Y., dt Chas. I. & Sophia B., N. Y.; m 1863 Frank ANGEVINE (H)
Caroline, dt David & Avis (Bunker), b 6-27-1824; m 1861 I. PERKINS (H)
cf Hudson 3-1846; name removed 11-9-1925 as long unknown
Charles S., s Nathan & Phebe, d 11-1858; m Sophia B. (perhaps YELLOTT)(H)
Ch: Charles d 9- 6-1841 ae 4d
Louisa Y. b 10- 3-1843
Bethia Y. recrq of mother 3-1844
Maria B. d 12- 1-1846 ae 1y
Francis B. Troy d 6-14-1847 ae 1y 6m
Sophia recrq 3-1842; cf Hudson 12-20-1825 with mother; dis 5-1845; ct Troy 2-1848 for Sophia & ch
Clarissa, dt David & Avis B., N. Y.; m 1842 Robert M. FOLGER (H)
Deborah, dt Nathan, d 3-22-1866 ae 65y 11m bPP; dis 2-10-1832 (O)
Donald Whitaker (nm), s Abraham & Mary Eliz., d 4-19-1926 ae 24y bPP (H)
Edward B., s Nathan & Phebe, d 12-18-1885 ae 75y bPP; rocf Hudson 8-22-1826, minor (H)
Emily, dt ----- MATLACK; gct Roch. 6-1841 (H)
Emily Montgomery, dt Silas B. & Rebecca B., b 9-11-1872; m 3-12-1902 Wm. Alonzo CRABTREE (H)
name entered by comm. 1-19-1881; name dropped 5-14-1834
George d 10-13-1867 ae 65y 8m 16d; m Eliza BUNKER, d 11-14-1891 ae 86y 5m 19d bPP
Ch: William B. b 5- 2-1825
Almira B. " 3-31-1830 d 2-27-1908 bPP
Anna E. " 7- 4-1834
Ferdinand T. " 11-21-1837 d 2-19-1911 bPP
James Macy " 12-20-1839
Silas " 7-29-1843
cf Hudson 4-24-1827; dis 1830-1831 (O); ct Hudson 2-1-1837; cf Hudson 7-1843 for all
James Macy, s Geo. & Eliza, b 12-20-1839, Hudson; d 11-27-1911 bPP; m 10-4-1866 Mary

COLEMAN, James Macy, continued
Elma TOWNSEND (nm), dt Leander W. & Anna E. (Wood), d 6-24-1898 ae 58y bPP (H)
cf Hudson with parents 7-1843
John (nm) b Nantucket d 3-25-1810 ae 78y (m)
Leighton P., s Robt. & Rosalie, d 4-19-1914 ae 40y bPP; m Mabel ----- (H)
Louisa Y. d 4-15-1874; m Aaron C. MACY, Jr. (H)
Maria m ----- VAN EVERY (H)
cf Hudson 8-1840 as Van Every; in Calif. 1858
Mary W., w Samuel S., dt Hannah MATLACK, d 11-24-1877 (H)
Ch: Samuel M. b 9-23-1842
Washington b ------1845
cf Balt. 10-11-1833 with mother; ct Alexandria (not found); cf Alexandria 8-1851 with 2 ch named
Nathan (nm) d 10-23-1845 ae 69y 11m 12d bPP
Phebe, w Nathan, d 3-1-1862 ae 87y 1m 14d bPP
Ch: Robert B. (or A.) d 1-10-1838 ae 2y 7m 7d
Edward B.
Deborah d 8-22-1866
Abraham B.
Charles S.,
Samuel S.
cf Hudson 12-20-1825 with her 4 ch first named; cf Hudson 8-22-1826 for Samuel & Edward B.; all dis (O); ct Oswego 7-1839 for Phebe & Deborah; cf Oswego 10-1846 for Phebe & Deborah
Robert B., s Nathan & Phebe; m -----
Ch: Infant stillborn 11-24-1832
Robert A. b N. Y. d 12-13-1838 ae 4m 14d bHS
cf Hudson 7-25-1826 (clear); dis 5-1830 (O); dis 1-1833 (H)
Robert H., s Saul S. & Rosalie H. (Matlack), d 12-24-1924 ae 77y bPP (H)
Samuel M., s Samuel S. & Mary W., b 9-23-1842 d on board U. S. Ship Monongahela 4-28-1875; rocf Alexandria with parents 8-1851 (H)
Samuel S., s Nathan & Phebe; m Mary W. MATLACK (H)
Ch: Sarah M. b 9-23-1842
Washington
cf Hudson 12-20-1825 with mother; Samuel dis 3-1845; ct Alexandria for Mary & ch 5-1845; lived in Washington
Silas B., s George & Eliza (Bunker), b 7-29-1843 d 1-11-1908 bPP; m Rebecca Fitzhugh BACKUS (nm) (m 11-11-1871)
Ch: Emily Montgomery b 9-11-1872
Frederick William b 5-17-1874
Archibald b at Detroit 5-29-1877
cf Hudson with parents 7-1843; ch names entered by comm. 10-11-1881
Silas B. m 2nd Flora B. VAN HUSAN, dt Caleb (m 6-25-1890)
Susan M., dt Jared & Susan (Macy), mbr of Rochester; m 10-4-1877 Washington COLEMAN
cf Alexandria 8-1851 for Washington with parents (H)
Washington, s Sam'l S. & Mary W. (Matlack), b Wash., D. C. 12-12-1844 d 3- 1-1906; m Roch. 10-4-1877 Susan Mary COLEMAN, dt Jared & Susan (Macy)(H)
cf Alexandria with parents 8-1851
William B., s Geo. & Eliza, b N. Y. 5-20-1828 d 2- 8-1902; m 1-1896 Mary Margaret CHRISTIE (nm) (H)
cf Hudson with parents 7-1843
----- & -----
Ch: Francis d 5-29-1844 ae 4m bHS

COLES
Agnes (nm), b N. Salem, N. Y. d 4-30-1811, (after childbirth) ae 33y bHS
Anna recrq 7-1-1818
Caleb d 3-31-1857; recrq 9-6-1815; dis 6-1829 (H)
Ellen Gardner, dt John & Sarah (Willett); m ----- CORLIES, d 3-21-1904 ae 93y 5m bPP (both nm) (H)
Jacob, s Jacob, rocf Wby 7-20-1796, a lad
Marion, dt William & Margaret (Leonard), b 9-19-1903; m 1926 Alan Marple HUGHES (H) both recrq 3-9-1931
Mary, w Jordan, d 12-12-1841; cf Wby 6-17-1795; ct Wby 5-2-1798; cf Wby 4-16-1800; ct Flushing 9-5-1810; cf Flushing 6-3-1813; ct Pur. 7-3-1822; cf Pur. 1-10-1827 (H)
Penelope, dt Joseph, Musketa Cove; m 1725 Thomas THORN
Robert, Mamaroneck; m Flushing 8-11-1774 Hannah THORN, dt Abraham, Rahway, N. J. Hannah gct Pur. 11-3-1774
Samuel & Alice
Ch: Eliza
Mary Ann
James W.
cf Middle MM, Warwickshire 4-1-1818; cert returned with the fam in 1822; ct Buckingham, Eng. 10-2-1822 with 3 ch, Eliza, Mary Ann & James W.
----- & -----
Ch: David R. d 11- 7-1811 ae 3m bHS

COLKET
Elizabeth P., dt J. Hamilton & Ethel (Paxson), b Balt. 12-12-1903; m 5-12-1927 Harold L. WILSON, of Devon, Pa. (H)
J. Hamilton (nm), s Wm. Walker & Jane H.; m 5-11-1901 Ethel PAXSON, dt Wm. Betts & Lydia (Shoemaker), b Phila. 9-3-1874 (H)
Ch: Elizabeth Paxson b 12-12-1903
James Hamilton " 1-18-1907
Carl " 9-29-1916

COLLADAY
Henry S. (nm), s Jacob M. & Julia, d 9-1-1916 ae 81y 11m 1d bPP; m 7-6-1870 Anna FOULKE, dt Daniel & Eliz. C., b Penllyn, Pa. 1-5-1848 d 11-23-1928 bPP (H)

COLLADAY, Henry S. & Anna, continued
Ch: Elizabeth F. b Macon Co., Ill. 5-9-1871
cf Gwynedd 5-13-1918

COLLETT
Dr. Fred m Mary I. ----- d 10-29-1906 ae 34y bPP (mo) (Dr. Fred a nm)
Mary (late Rooke) dis mo 10-7-1801

COLLINS
Abel C. d 7-24-1873; m Mary TABER
Ch: Annie b 1865 d 3-18-1867 ae 2y 3m
cf South Kingston R. I. 7-1863 for both
Mary m 2d 9-9-1879 Edward TATUM
Abel T., s Peter & Deborah, rocf So. Kingston, R. I. 8-23-1841 (clear) with Joseph W.; dis 12-1857
Anna, dt Isaac & Rebecca, N. Y.; m 1871 John R. TABER
Benjamin S., s Isaac & Rachel (dec), Burl., d 8-26-1857; m N. Y. 8-15-1810 Hannah BOWNE dt Robert & Elizabeth, d 9-9-1860 ae 76y

Ch:			
Elizabeth B.		d 4-30-1893	
Robert B.	b 4-18-1813		
William B.	" 9- 3-1815		
Mary	" 7-16-1817	d 6-21-1826	
Rebecca	" 5-19-1819		
Edward	" 2- 2-1821	" 6-18-1837 bHS	
Benjamin	" 11-30-1822	" 2-20-1900	
Richard S.	" 1-13-1825		
Mary	" 5-17-1828	" 8-18-1922	
Charles	" 6- 5-1830	" 10- 2-1918	

Chalkley d 8-18-1849; cf New Hartford 1848
Charles, s Isaac, Trenton, rocf Chesterfield, apprentice with Robert Bowne; took cert of clear to Chesterfield, Pa. 4-1-1801
Charles d 12-27-1843 ae 69y 11m 16d; m Margaret ----- d 10-2-1850

Ch:		
Edith	b 8-13-1803	d 8-25-1873
Rachel	" 1-20-1805	" 7-21-1878
George B.	" 2-14-1807 (or 2-14-1808)	
Edward	" 5- 8-1810	d 2- 2-1817
George B.	d 1- 6-1854	
Infant	" 3-17-1818	d 3-18-1818

cf Chesterfield for Margaret 9-8-1801, rem with her h; parents dis 1829; ch dis 1834-1835
Clarkson T. rocf Bridgewater 5-5-1843 (clear); dis 1845
Cornelia, dt Stacy B. & Mary O., N. Y.; m 1851 Wm. H. HUSSEY, of New Bedford
ct New Bedford 1851
Ellen d 7- 8-1912 in 84th y; recrq 7-5-1899
Elizabeth, dt Isaac & Rachel, N. Y.; m 1797 Robert PEARSALL
cf Chesterfield 11-8-1796 (clear)
Elizabeth rocf Little Egg Harbor, 10-14-1802 (clear); ct Pur. 6-6-1810 (clear)
Elizabeth B., dt Robt. B. & Margaretta, b 9-11-1848; relrq 4-1872
Elizabeth C., dt Ezra & Eunice, d 5-27-1841 ae 27y 3m 19d bHS; m Stephen GAINES (nm)
Emeline, dt John & Eliz., N. Y.; m 1869 Jesse BIRDSALL
Emmeline rocf Hector 1856; ct Hector 1857
Ezra m Eunice ----- d 4-13-1839 ae 56y 9m 2d b bHS

Ch:		
Samuel B.		
George	dis 2-1841	
Content	d 5-28-1837 ae 26y 1m 29d bHS	
Elizabeth		
Isaac B.		
Micajah	" 6-15-1827 ae 13y	
Hannah		
Caroline	" ------1843	

cf Lynn or Salem, Mass. 6-7-1826 with minor ch as named; Ezra dis 2-1832
George B., s Charles & Margaret, b 2-14-1807 (or 2-14-1808); dis mo 3-3-1841
Isaac, s Isaac & Rachel, N. Y.; m Burlington, N. J. 1810 Margaret M. -----

Ch:		
William M.	b 7-21-1811	
Martha Lawrie	" 7-19-1813	
Gulielma Maria	" 8-28-1815	
Wm. Morris	" 7-21-1817	
Henry Hill	" ------1818	
Alfred	" 1-20-1820	
Frederick		
Isaac	" 5- 2-1824	
Theodore		d 9- 4-1826 ae 1m 7d

ct Burl. 9-5-1810 (clear); Margaret M. rocf Burl. 12-3-1810; ct ND MM 7-2-1828 (0) with 7 ch (not including s, Morris)
Isaac Collins, N. Y.; m Rachel BUDD, dt Thomas & Rebecca, d 9-15-1805

Ch:	
Rebecca	b 6- 1-1772
Charles	" 1-14-1774
Sarah	" 4- 2-1775
Elizabeth	" 7-23-1776
Thomas	" 3- 3-1779
Susanna	" 3-17-1781
William	" 8-18-1782
Benjamin Say	" 3- 7-1784
Ann Say	" 3- 6-1786
Isaac	" 10-31-1787
Mary	" 7-27-1789
Stacy	" 1-19-1791
Joseph	" 1-30-1794

cf Chesterfield with their 9 ch 11-8-1796 (all but first 4 named as above); ct Burl. for Isaac with dt, Susannah, Ann & Mary (all clear)
Isaac B. d 6-2-1841 ae 24y 8m 9d bHS; ct Salem, Mass. 6-1-1831 (minor); cf Salem, 9-10-1835; dis 1840
Job, s James & Eliz. (both dec), N. Y.; m N. Y. 4-11-1804 Phebe WEEKS, dt Jesse (dec) & Sarah, N. Y.
cf Jericho 7-17-1800 (clear); ct Jericho 6-2-1803 (clear); Job brought cert of clear from Jericho; Phebe Weeks rocf Chap. 7-9-1802 (clear); Phebe gct Chap. 2-1-1805
John & Anna B.
Ch: Elizabeth B.

COLLINS, John & Anna B., continued
cf WD MM 8-21-1844 with 1 ch named; ct Burl. 10-7-1846 with 1 ch named; this cert returned 2-1867
Joseph dis mo 2-5-1823
Joseph B. rocf Burl. 2-3-1812, apprentice
Joseph B. d 9-16-1867 ae 80y; recrq 5-1861
Joseph W., s Peter (dec) & Deborah, Hopkinston, R. I.; m N. Y 1-10-1849 Emma HAWXHURST, dt Wm. & Mary (dec), N. Y.
Ch: William H. b 11-29-1849 d 8-30-1851
Mary Emma " 2- 6-1851
Joseph H. " 2-24-1853
cf S. Kingston, R. I. 8-23-1841 for Joseph W. (clear); ct Oswego with ch 5-3-1854
Margaretta, dt Robt. B. & Margaretta, b 6- 9-1861; relrq 1-1886
Maria W., dt Richard S. & Sarah (Willets), b N. Y. 11-19-1858; m 1882 Joshua L. BARTON
ct Pur. with parents 8-1860; cf Pur. 11-1885
Mary Foster, dt Isaac & Rebecca, Phila.; m James L. WALTON, of Phila. (m 1867 in N.Y) (H)
Mary S., dt Stacy B. & Mary D., b 11-2-1829; relrq 5-1858
Mary Taber, dt Joseph & Phebe B., N. Y.; m 1879 Edward TATUM
Peter & Sarah
Ch: Thomas Elwood
Elvira
Hannah Elma
Amelia Jane
Mahlon D. b 8-13-1838
Henry H. " 8-31-1841
cf Bridgewater 9-1-1837 with 4 ch named; ct Salem, Iowa, 12-7-1842 with 5 ch (not including Elvira)
Phebe W. d 11-18-1897; cf Chap. 3-7-1866 (H)
Rebecca, dt Isaac & Rachel, N. Y.; m 1804 Stephen GRELLET; cf Chesterfield 11-8-1796 (clear)
Rebecca, w Isaac, a minister, d 4-30-1892
Ch: Anna
Mary Foster
cf WD MM 11-18-1863 for Rebecca; separate cert for dt 11-18-1863
Rebecca, dt Benj. S. & Hannah, Pelham, N. Y.; m 1847 Benjamin TATHAM, Jr.
Richard S., s Benj. S. & Hannah, Pelham, b 1-13-1825; m N. Y. 4-9-1856 Sarah WILLETS (or Willits), dt Stephen & Maria, N. Y., b 12-29-1827
Ch: Maria b 11-19-1858
Charles " 9- 8-1872 d 4-11-1916 bPP
ct Pur. 8-1860 for all
Robert B., s Benj. S. & Hannah, Pelham; m N.Y. 5-13-1846 Margaretta C. MURRAY, dt Lindley & Eliza (both dec), N. Y.
Ch: Lindley M. b 1-23-1847 d 10-11-1875
Elizabeth B. " 9-11-1848
Jane M. " 7-28-1850 " 6- 8-1852
Ch: Margaretta b 6- 9-1861
Margaretta relrq 4-1872; Robert B. released 1-1880
Samuel B., s Ezra & Eunice; dis mo 1-1842
Sarah, dt Isaac & Rachel, N. Y., b 4-2-1775; m 1826 Nathaniel HAWXHURST
cf Chesterfield 11-8-1796 (clear)
Sarah, N. Y. b 1831; m 1876 Joshua H. WORTHINGTON, of Phila.
Stacy B., s Isaac & Rachel (dec), N. Y., d 6-23-1873; m N. Y. 10-11-1821 Mary E. (or D.) DUDLEY, dt Edward & Mary (dec), N. Y., d 6-14-1838
Ch: Emma D. b 5-27-1823 d 1-9-1842 (or 6-14-1842)
Ann Dudley " 6-26-1825 " 1- 7-1834 bHS
Cornelia " 7-27-1827
Mary S. " 11- 2-1829
Sarah " 9-14-1831
Theodore " 9-27-1833 " 12-28-1835 bHS
Edward D. " 10-15-1836 " 1- 1-1838 bHS
cf Burl. 3-6-1809, apprentice
Stacy B. m 2nd Hannah W. ----- d 9- 9-1885
Ch: Stacy B., Jr. b 8- 8-1847 d 2-17-1917
Gertrude d 2----1917
cf Phila. 12-28-1843 for Hannah W.
Theodore, s Isaac, d 9- 4-1826
Thomas m Chesterfield, N. J. 1812 Ann -----
Ch: John b 3-15-1814
Arthur " 10- 3-1815
Charles " 10-29-1817
ct Chesterfield 9-12-1812 (clear); Anna rocf Chesterfield 12-8-1812; ct Burl. 8-5-1818 for all
William gct Phila. 6-5-1816 (clear)
Wm. B., s Benj. S. & Hannah, N. Y.; m N. Y. 7-8-1842 Ann GRIFFEN, dt Solomon & Clarissa, d 3-29-1854
Ch: Emily B. b 9-12-1844 d 4-24-1864 bPP
Lucy " 7-14-1848 " 2-10-1864 bPP
Cornelia " 5-22-1850
ct Ama. 1-1858 for Wm. & ch; cf Pokeepsie 12-1886 for Wm. B.
William B. m 2nd ----- (Wm. B. d 6-24-1890)
ct Pur. 1856 (clear)
William P. rocf Hector 1856; relrq 3-1880
----- & -----
Ch: Caroline b N. Y. d 12-28-1823 ae 21d bHS
Edward d 6-18-1837 ae 16y 4m 7d bHS
Edward S. " 1- 1-1838 ae 1y 2m bHS

COLONS
Margaret m 1837 John Wm. ONDERDONK (H)

COLTON
John Bowne d 1-19-1900; cf Uxbridge, Mass. 6-1873
Samuel Horton, s Reuben & Abigail (both dec), Worcester, Mass.; m N. Y. 12-13-1843 Ann K. KING, dt John & Mary R., N. Y.
ct Uxbridge, Mass. 6-5-1844 for Ann K.

COLVIN
Henry, s John & Jane (Brown), b Lurgan, Ireland 1-10-1858; m 8-2-1882 Alice HASTINGS (nm), dt John S. & Matilda L. (H)
Henry m 2nd 11-5-1924 Amy HILLIARD, dt Henry & Mary Amanda (Brundage), b Ossining 6-20-1872
Henry transferred from Albany 1-8-1816; Amy recrq 1924

COMBS
Albert H., s Martin H. & Dorinda (Wilbur), b Clinton Hollow 11-3-1846; m 8-2-1869 Mary E. HICKS (nm), dt Benj. D. & Elizabeth (Butts) (H)
cf Creek 5-4-1864
Ann, w Amos, rocf Chesterfield 9-6-1825, rem with h; ct Chesterfield 5-6-1829
Frank C. [Combes], Jr., s Frank C. & Mary (Mullin) (nm), b N. Y. 8-15-1896 (H)
Henrietta, dt Martin H. & Dorinda; m 5-16-1871 David DEPUTY; relrq 6-10-1899 (H)
John W., s Martin H. & Dorinda, rocf Creek with parents 5-4-1864; relrq 1-6-1900 (H)
Martin H. & Dorinda
Ch: John W.
Albert H.
Henrietta
cf Creek 5-4-1864 for all; ct Oswego 3-5-1898 for parents (H)
Mary (late Franklin) dis mo 11-3-1785

COMFORT
John took cert of clear 3 Mo (May) 5, 1720; "late an inhabitant in these parts"

COMMONS
Evelyn Alice (or Eva A.), dt W. C. & Caroline TABOR, b 12-1-1879 (w Walter Commons)
ct Stanford 5-7-1902 as Eva A.

COMSTOCK
Albert, s Nathan & Charlotte, b 12-5-1859 d 8-10-1905; m 4-4-1888 Caroline Agnes RANGER
Ch: Infant stillborn 3-10-1889 bPP (H)
Elizabeth, wd, b Westchester d 6-29-1825 ae 86y bHS
Elizabeth Ann, dt Nathan & Ann, b 6-11-1817 d bPP; dis 6-1848 (H)
Elsie, dt Nathan & Charlotte H., Bkn., b 11-24-1854; m 1875 Rudolphus Ritzema BOGERT (H)
George, s Nathan & Ann, rocf Nantucket 5-1-1811 with parents; dis 9-1830 (H); dis 10-1830 (O)
Job S. rocf N. P. 9-18-1823 (clear); dis 4-1827 for failure
John M., s Nathan & Elizabeth, b 11-11-1823; m ----- (H)
Ch: infant stillborn 12-22-1855 bPP
dis mo by a "hireling priest" 2-7-1849
Louisa M., dt Nathan & Eliza., b 2- 2-1825; m ----- PIGGOTT; dis 5-6-1846 (H)
Lucy, dt Nathan & Elizabeth, N. Y.; m 1829 Robert B. HAVILAND (H)
Martha, dt Nathan & Eliz., N. Y.; m 1841 Josiah HOPPER (H)
Mary J., dt Nathan & Ann, b 9-22-1826 N. Y. d 5-12-1901 ae 74y 8m 10d; m Ignatius J. BRIEN (H)
Nathan, s Samuel & Lucy, d 1-30-1859 (or 1-28-1859) ae 82y (or ae 83y); m Elizabeth ----- b Nantucket d 4-30-1818 ae 38y (H)
Ch: Samuel d abroad 2-17-1824
Lucy
William
George
Thomas " 12-22-1855 ae 35y
Phebe b 9-15-1812 d 7-25-1820
Martha " 3-25-1815
Elizabeth Ann b 6-11-1817
Nathan, m 2nd 5-11-1820 Ann MERRITT, dt John & Phebe, N. Y., d 9-13-1860 ae 74y 8m 24d
Ch: Phebe b 3- 2-1821 d 9- 3-1821
John M. " 11-11-1823
Louisa M. " 2- 2-1825
Mary J. " 9-22-1826
Sarah M.
Nathan, Jr.
Nathan rocf Nantucket 5-1-1811 with 5 ch; cf Jericho 7-19-1798 for Ann; dis 1-7-1930 for preventing YM (O) from occupying basement at Hester St.
Nathan, Jr., s Nathan & Ann (Muritt), d 1-18-1897 ae 74y 11m bPP; m 12-24-1853 Charlotte H. CROMWELL, dt Oliver & Sarah (Titus), b Corn. 3-31-1832 d 3- 6-1912 bPP
Ch: Elsie b 11-24-1854
Philip " 6- 5-1858
Albert " 12- 5-1859
Ann E. " d 1860
cf Corn. 3-1857 for Charlotte
Philip, s Nathan, Jr. & Charlotte, b 6- 5-1858; m 9-24-1885 Harriet T. SMITH (H)
relrq 11-11-1911
Sarah M., dt Nathan & Ann; m ----- MOELLING (H)
Thomas, West Greenwich, N. Y.; m Flushing 10-2-1766 Elizabeth HAVILAND, dt Ebenezer & Phebe, Flushing
Ch: Thomas, Jr. d 10-3-1797
Elizabeth gct Greenwich 11-6-1766
William, s Nathan & Ann, rocf Nantucket with parents 5-1-1811; Salem, Mass. requested to deal with him for mo; dis 5-1836 (H); dis 6-1-1836 (O)

CONGDON
Charles rocf Providence 9-29-1830; dis mo 12-4-1833
Ellen L. d 5-11-1886; rocf Providence 2-2-1876
Emma m 1865 Wm. H. S. WOOD
cf Providence 7-1866

CONGERS
Arline (nm) m Howard U. VAN BURKIRK (H)

CONING (or CONNING)
George rocf Guisbro MM, Yorkshire, 6-20-1830 (clear); ct Rochester 1-4-1837 as Conning

CONKLIN
David b West Co. d 11-12-1831 ae 38y bHS
David P. d 11-12-1831; cf Chap. 5-12-1825 (clear); dis 2-1830
Elizabeth R. d 4-11-1878; cf Corn. 1849
Elizabeth T. rocf Wby & Jericho 12-20-1843
Erwin Raymond, s Josiah & Mary L. (Johnson), Pomona, N. Y., b Pomona 5-18-1873; m at J. G. Miller's 5-18-1904 Leah H. MILLER, dt Joseph G. & Isabella T., Pomona, b Bkn. 11-29-1871 (H)
Ch: Isabella Leah b 8-30-1905
Eleanor " 1-24-1907
Margaret Elizabeth b 8-12-1908
Josiah Raymond " 10- 5-1912
Erwin (nm) recrq 9-9-1905; Leah's name entered by comm. 4-3-1888
Jacob & Elizabeth T.
Ch: James
William b 3- 8-1844
cf Ama. 1844 for Jacob & James; cf Wby & Jericho 1844 for Eliz.; ct Wby & Jericho 8-1872 for parents
James, s Jacob & Elizabeth, d 3-1928; m Anna H. ---- d 3-24-1928
Ch: James Arthur b 10-26-1884
cf Ama. with father 1844; Anna recrq 8-1-1877
Jean, dt Enoch & Katherine (Smith), b N. Y. 1-11-1869; recrq 1-9-1922
John rocf Chap. 2-12-1813, minor; dis mo 1825
Josiah [Concklin], s Joseph & Martha; m Mary L. JOHNSON (H)
Ch: Erwin Raymond 5-18-1873
Josiah m 2nd at J. W. Onderdonk's 9-20-1876 Margaret ONDERDONK, dt John W. & Margaret (Colons), N. Y., d 12-4-1929 (H)
Margaret recrq 5-1874
Mary A. d 3-27-1852; cf Chap. 5-3-1848
Mildred Laura [Concklin], dt Erwin R. & Leah (Miller), b Pomona, N. Y. 8-30-1910; m 1935 George S. GUMMERSON (nm) (H)
Phebe, dt Isaac; m ----- KIPP (mo before 5-2-1810)
cf Chap. 12-11-1807 (clear)
Rachel rocf Corn. 1849; ct Corn. 11-1854
William, s Jacob & Elizabeth, b 3- 8-1844; m 6-1872 Ellen C. LADD
Ch: Frank Henry b 3-30-1873
Edward Boote b 8-10-1877 d 11-29-1900
Wm., s Jacob & Eliz., Bkn.; m at Wm. Ladd's 6-13-1872 Ellen C. LADD, dt Wm. H. & Caroline, Bkn.
Ch: Frank Henry b 3-30-1873

CONNERS
Bessie recrq 2-4-1874
Gertrude (nm), dt A. B.; m 1907 Clarence M. HAVILAND (H)
Clarence relrq 7-8-1929
Lewis A. (nm), s Chas. H. & Cath.B. (Atterbury) m 9-27-1923 Leila COSTON, dt Herbert H. & Addie B. (Pinney), b Scranton, Pa., 8-15-1899 (H)
Leila recrq 11-9-1924
Mary A. rocf Providence, R. I. 5-1915; name erased 10-1928
Wallace L. [Conner] recrq 7-11-1934

CONOVER
Mary, Stoughtenburgh, rocf Creek 8-22-1823 with parents; ct Cincinnati 6-5-1862

CONROW
Herman, s Clayton & Mary G. (Collins), N. Y., b Cinnaminson, N. J., 7-3-1874; m at J. W. Hutchinson's 10-12-1898 Emma S. HUTCHINSON, dt John Wm. & E. Eliza, N. Y., b 12-10-1872 Balt.
Ch: Eleanor Hite b Orange 6-8-1900
Barbara Dutton b Orange 11-12-1901
Roger Hunt " Hampton 9-5-1903
Jonathan Hutchinson b Hampton 6-11-1906
cf Chester 5-7-1898 for Herman; cf Balt. 12-5-1877 for Emma with parents; ct Chester at Moorestown 12-8-1906 for all (H)
Jonathan H., s Herman & Emma H., Bkn., b Hempsted 6-11-1906; m Greenwich, Conn. 11-22-1930 Anna L. HANAN, dt Addison G. (dec) & Lillian (McDowell), N. Y., b Bkn. 8-16-1909 (H)
Joseph Wallace, s Howard F. & Eliza (Biddle), b Germantown, 9-25-1887; m Phila. 4-23-1913 Alma E. PAXSON, dt Harvey S. & Eliza. (Murfit), b Solebury, Pa., 2-19-1887 (H)
Ch: Howard Paxson b 4-30-1915
cf Phila. 11-12-1923 for all

CONSTANTIAN
Joseph J. recrq 12-3-1913; jas name erased 8-1920

COOK
Amelia (nm) b Phila. d 10-7-1827 ae 17y 8m 23d bHS (unm)
Caleb C. (nm) & -----
Ch: Infant stillborn 12-10-1830 bHS
Carrie E., dt Cornelius & Caroline (Olson), b Bkn. 12-30-1873; m James F. BUCKWELL (H) recrq 12-10-1928
Charles Gilpin, s Joel & Martha G. (Pearson), b 11-25-1866; m Anna TRAVIS, dt Martin Wm. & Hannah M. (Pierce), b 2-14-1874
Ch: Katharine Elizabeth b 10-29-1904
Mary Gilpin " 12----1906
cf Deer Creek, Md. 6-11-1902 for both
Cornelius, s Ebenezer & Sarah, d 2-7-1929 ae 83y 25d bPP; m Caroline L. OLSEN (H)

COOK, continued
Ebenezer, s Thomas & Ann, d 12-26-1898 ae 76y bPP; m Sarah T. ----- d 11-16-1909 ae 85y bPP (H)
cf Shrews. 6-1844
Elizabeth, dt Lewis P. & Laura J. (Turner), b Bay of Biscay 8-16-1864; m Louis R. LA MONT (nm); m 2nd George W. LILLEY (nm); m 3rd Nelson P. WEBSTER (nm) (m 8-1-1921) ct Alexandria 5-14-1923 (H)
Isaac rocf Easton 11-22-1821 (clear); dis 4-1833 (H); dis 2-1830 (O);

Job W. rocf Shrewsbury 7-5-1813, left in his infancy; ct Shrewsbury 5-3-1837; cf Shrewsbury 8-5-1846; ct R. & P. 4-7-1852 (H)
John A. (nm) b N. Y. d 4-16-1841 ae 31y 2m; m -----
Ch: Sarah B. L. b N. Y. d 1-2-1841 ae 11m bHS
John G. (nm) b R. I. d 8-23-1822 ae 59y bHS (m)
John Gamble d 2-28-1934 ae 68y bPP; m Grace BELLOWS (H)
John W. (nm) b Phila. d 10-19-1828 ae 19y bHS
Joseph Alexander, s C. Alex. & Louise C. (dec), Montclair, N. J.; m 6-19-1912 at David D. Engle's, Marion Fenimore ENGLE, dt David D. & Marg. C., Newark, b about 1890
Ch: Marion Louise
Helen Elizabeth
Margaret I.
Marion F. recrq of her mother 5-6-1903
Joseph H., s Thomas, d 5-19-1893 ae 68y bPP (H)
Lewis P. d Havana 9-24-1870; m Laura J. TURNER (nm) (H)
Ch: Elizabeth b Bay of Biscay 8-16-1864
cf Shrews. 1-4-1854
Martha P. m 1908 Mortimer J. TRAVIS
recrq 3-1-1905
Thomas, s Cornelius W. & Cornelia M., d 6-21-1921 ae 40y bPP; m Dorothy S. ----- (H)
Wm. Wilbur James [Cooke] (nm); m 1910 Jane Levick, wd Edwin JACKSON
----- m Elizabeth F. KLOPP
Elizabeth recrq 3-6-1918; name erased 2-1926
----- & -----
Ch: Harry P. d 9- 8-1839 ae 11m 9d bHS
Caleb Edwin " 11- 5-1839 ae 1y 18d bHS
Joseph H. " 6- 7-1852 ae 10m bPP
Ann E. " 10-14-1857 ae 27d bPP

COOLIDGE
Carrie Louisa, dt J. Howard & Sarah J. WRIGHT, b 12-29-1853 d 5- 8-1889 (w Henry, m 4-9-1873) (H)
Daniel [Cooledge] d 11-1-1847 ae 62y; m Ruth ----- d 9- 6 (or 8) 1863 ae 76y bPP
Ch: Phebe H. dis 7----1837
George F. " 10----1843
William Penn " 4-1844
Phebe
cf Weare 5-10-1821 with 3 ch named parents dis 1829 (H)
George F. [Cooledge], s Daniel & Ruth, d 8-4-1873 ae 57y bPP
cf Weare with parents 5-10-1821; dis 10-1843 for non-attendance
Phebe H. [Cooledge], dt Daniel & Ruth, d 5-17-1881; m ----- METFORD (dis mo 8-2-1837)
William Penn [Cooledge], s Daniel & Ruth, rocf Weare with parents 5-10-1821; dis 4-1844

COOLEY
Catharine m ----- McCALLUM
cf Marl. 1852; dis 1857
Eleanor, dt Justus H. & Mary H., b Corning, N. Y. 2-28-1879 d 10-26-1919; m 1903 Henry C. JENKINS(H)
cf R. & P. 9-9-1905
Samuel H. d 9-19-1905 ae 64y 11d bPP; m Maggie MONTALZO, dt Ramon & Mary, d 8-27-1822 ae 65y bPP (both nm)

COOPER
Ann T., dt Joseph P. & Alice E., b 8-20-1873; relrq 8-4-1897, joined Episcopal Church
Charlotte, dt Joseph P. & Alice E., relrq 8-4-1897, joined Episcopal Church
Eleanor H., dt Joseph P. & Hannah G., b 6-28-1866; ct Pokeepsie 5-1887
Ellen, dt Ellwood & Sarah; m 12-4-1907 R. BAXLEY
cf Phila. with parents 10-1865; in Monticello, Calif. 1912
Ellwood d 12-29-1918; m Sarah P. ---- d 3-13-1908
Ch: Henry
Ellen
Fannie b 4-18-1865
cf Phila. 10-1865 with 2 ch; Elwood, Henry & Fannie in Santa Barbara, Calif. 1912
Fannie, dt Ellwood & Sarah P., b 4-18-1865; m ----- HERON
Hannah, dt David S. & Eliza Ann BOOTH; m 1883 John BELL, of Santa Barbara, Calif.
Henry Richardson rocf Hardshaw East 2-17-1858; mbrp relinquished 3-1880
John (nm) b N. J. d 1-3-1825 ae 51y 1m (m)
John Lister d 6-18-1881; m 1872 Hannah BOOTH, dt David & Eliza Ann
Ch: Elizabeth Proctor b 8-10-1873
Anna Jane " 3-19-1876
Hannah m 2nd 6-5-1883, John BELL; ct Corn. 8-1872 (clear); cf Balby, Eng. 1-30-1854 for John; cf Corn. for Hannah; ct San Jose, Calif. 12-1883 for Hannah & ch; John joined army before 5-1864, case discontinued 5-1866
Joseph Phipps mo before 12-1855, retained mbrp; Joseph Phipps m 2nd Marl. 1861 Hannah G. ----- d 9-28-1866
Ch: Wm. Edward b 1-19-1864
Eleanor H. " 6-28-1866

COOPER, Joseph Phipps & Hannah G., continued
cf Grace Church St., Eng. 7-4-1849 for Joseph; ct Marl 10-1861 (clear)
Joseph Phipps m 3rd Alice E. -----
Ch: Anne T. b 8-20-1873
Charlotte
ct Elba 1-1871 (clear); cf Elba 3-17-1874 for Alice E.; Joseph & Alice relrq 2-4-1891
Mary, w Simon, O. B., active mbr 1685; d 1710
Mary, dt Simon & Mary, O. B.; m 1686 Edward WHITE
Mary, wd, b N. Y. d 7-31-1830 ae 74y bHS
Mary D., dt Samuel & Eliz. D. PAXSON, b 6-2-1836; dis mo 1-1856
Simon, O.B., d 11 Mo (Jan) 11, 1690/1; m Mary -----
Ch: Simon
Mary
Robert d 3 Mo 16, 1707
Simon, s Simon & Mary, O.B.; m Mk. 5 Mo (July) 24, 1693 Martha PRIAR, dt Matthew & Mary, Mk.
Ch: Simon b 2 Mo (Apr) 30, 1694
Mary " 7 Mo (Sept) 17, 1696
Robert " 12 Mo (Feb) 16, 1700/01 d 3 Mo 16, 1707
Joseph b 3 Mo (May) 25, 1705
William (Cowper in cert to Eng.) & Mary
Ch: William
Magdalen
cf ND MM 7-25-1780 with 2 ch; ct Hitching, Harts. 6-4-1783 with 2 ch
Wm. Edward (William T.), s Joseph P. & Hannah G., b 1-19-1864; relrq 10-3-1900

COPE
Anna Ellora (nm), dt Otis M. & Sarah M., Omaha; m 1931 Edward R. STABLER, Jr. (H)

COPELAND, CORBIN, CORLESS, CORLIES (see p. 373)

CORLIES
Deborah (nm), wd, b Shrewsbury d 12-18-1825 ae 45y bur. Shrewsbury
Edmee Alcine, dt Jno. Edgar & Mary B., b 4-18-1882, N. J.; m 12-30-1899 John U. HUSSEY (nm) (H)
Edward Alex., s Jacob & Hannah, b 2-14-1807 d 3-3-1873 ae 66y bPP; dis 4-1841 (H)
Edward Garrigues rocf Shrewsbury 11-5-1810; ct Shrewsbury 5-7-1823 (clear); cf Shrewsbury 6-1835; ct Shrewsbury 1-7-1846
Edward L., s Joseph W. & Lydia, b 6-27-1833 d 4-11-1872; dis 3-1866 for non attendance & going to places of diversion (H)
Emily, dt Joseph W. & Lydia L., b 7-30-1841; m 10-5-1876 M. M. REESE (mo); relrq 7-6-1870
George (nm) m Margaret ----- b L. I. d 11-12-1832 ae 78y bHS
George, Newtown, b 9-25-1752 N. J. d 3-14-1847 ae 92y 5m 17d bHS; dis 7-1829 (0) (H)
George (nm) & -----
Ch: Margaret d 12-18-1818 ae 22y (unm)bHS
George, s Benj. & Phebe, b 1-11-1804; ct Oswego 8-1834; cf Oswego 1-1841; ct Oswego 4-6-1853 (H)
George, Jr. rocf Shrewsbury 5-3-1790
George W., s Jacob & Hannah, b 4-10-1809 d 12-18-1885 ae 79y 8m 10d bPP (mo); dis 8-1848 (H)
Henry De Witt, s Benj. & Phebe; gct Scipio 4-14-1832 (clear) (0); ct Scipio 7-1832 (H); supposed to have d at sea
Henry P. d 4-24-1852 ae 48y bPP; m Elizabeth W. ----
Ch: Sarah Allinson b 5- 3-1838
William Henry " 9-14-1840
Albert " 2-28-1843 d 5-15-1843
Edwin " 2-12-1844
Ellen W. (or Eleanor) b 3-23-1847 d 7-23-1848 (H)
cf Shrewsbury 4-1-1822, he living with John & Joseph W. Corlies; Henry P. dis 8-1830 (0) 4-4-1849 (H); cf Cherry St. Phila. 9-1837 for Elizabeth; ct Phila. 3-2-1853 for her & the ch
Jacob d 9- 4-1834 ae 56y bPP; m Hannah ----- d 7-12-1866 ae 86y 7m bPP (H)
Ch: Edward Alexander b 2-14-1807
George W. " 4-10-1809
Margaret G. " 1- 5-1811 d 9-29-1896 bPP
Patience C. (changed to Caroline) b 1- 9-1813
cf R. & P. 2-22-1804 for Jacob (clear); Hannah rocf Darby 10-31-1805; all dis 1829-1839
Jacob, s George & Elizabeth, Po'keepsie; m at F. Haines' 9-6-1855 Edith W. HAINES, dt Franklin & Abigail B., N. Y. (not under care of N. Y. MM) (H)
dis 12-3-1828 (0) ct Oswego 12-5-1860 for Edith W.
James (nm) & -----
Ch: Elizabeth b Mass. d 8-17-1820 ae 66y bHS
James, Jr. (nm) b N. Y. d 11-22-1826 ae 47y bHS
John & Phebe
cf R. & P. 9-16-1802; ct Shrewsbury 10-5-1808; cf Shrewsbury 3-1-1813 for both; John dis 4-1829; Phebe dis 2-1830 (0); ct Shrewsbury 9-1833 for both (H)
John Edgar, s John W. & Phebe G. (dec), b 8-13-1843 d 6-22-1883; m at J. H. Wright's 12-16-1869 Mary B. WRIGHT, dt John Howard & Sarah Jane (Walton), N. Y., b 5-13-1850 d 12-31-1912 (H)
Ch: Clara W. b 5- 8-1871; m Henry C.
Annie Wright " 8-22-1874[ADAMS 1891
Howard W. " 6-25-1876 d 1- 6-1899
Edmee Alcine " 4-18-1882
John W., s Joseph & Sarah, d 9-11-1872; m Phebe GREEN (m 11-1842) (H)
Ch: John Edgar b 8-13-1843

CORLIES, John W. & Phebe, continued
Ch: Samuel G. b 2- 5-1845
Frederick Joseph b 3-30-1846
Amelia
cf Hudson 3-1843 for Phebe; ct Oswego 8-1848 for all (3 ch); cf Oswego 11-4-1863 for John W. with John E., Samuel G. & Amelia
Joseph rocf Cherry St., Phila. 8-1843; ct Falls, Pa. 5-4-1859
Joseph b N. J. d 3-15-1831 (or 3-17-1831); m Sarah W. WHITE, dt John & Elizabeth
Ch: Infant stillborn 11-26-1816
Albert (or Alfred) b 10-2-1818 d 1-17-1830
John W. b 4-13-1821
Infant stillborn 3-30-1824
Sarah W. m 2nd Charles MARRIOTT (m 12-8-1836)
cf Shrewsbury 3-4-1805 (clear); ct Pur. 11-1-1815 (clear); parents dis 1830-1831 (O)
Joseph N., s Benj. & Phebe, b 9-18-1815; mo 1837; ret a mbr; ct Oswego 1-1855 (H)
Joseph N. (nm) & ----
Ch: Richard Stanton d 4-28-1839 ae 1y 1m 4d bHS
Joseph W. m Esther L. ----- b N. Y. d 2-14-1820 ae 24y 11m 14d bHS
Joseph W., s Briton & Sarah, d 10-25-1860; m N. Y. 7-8-1818 Esther LEGGETT, dt Joseph (dec) & Marion (H)
Ch: Joseph b 4-13-1821
Joseph W. m 2nd Lydia L. ----- d 11-2-1869
Ch: Alfred W. b 12-5-1826 d Chicago 12-26-1872
Joseph William b 3- 1-1829
Elizabeth T. " 6- 6-1831 d 6- 7-1832
Edward L. " 6-27-1833
Cornelia L. " 11- 7-1838; dis mo ----- Earnshaw 4-2-1862
Emily b 7-30-1841
cf Shrewsbury 2-5-1810 for apprentice with Benj. Corlies; ct Shrewsbury 6-2-1813 (clear); cf Shrewsbury 9-4-1820
Joseph Wm., s Joseph W. & Lydia, b 3-1-1829 d Paris, France 6-9-1877; dis 2-1866 for non-attendance & going to places of diversion (H)
Lydia b N. J. d 1-7-1835 ae 79y 3m; m-----
Ch: Edna d 6- 9-1867; dis 2-1830 (O)
Phebe " 7-25-1869
cf Shrewsbury 7-4-1814 with her 2 dt; Lydia marked in pencil "very aged"
Lydia L. rocf Flushing 6-8-1826

Margaret H., dt Joseph & Sarah E. HAGAN (w Edmund W.) d 10-14-1857 (H)
Margaret N., dt Benj. & Phebe, b 2-12-1814 d 5-21-1875; m 1834 Henry STANTON (H)
Mary, w William, b Shrewsbury d 6-19-1828 ae 79y; cf Shrewsbury 12-3-1804; ct Shrewsbury 2-6-1822, cert not delivered & returned
Mary N., dt Benjamin & Phebe, N. Y.; m 1837 William H. BARNEY (H)
Patience C., dt Jacob & Hannah, b 1-10-1813 N. Y. d 3-17-1902; m 1839 George G. HAYDOCK (H)
Samuel G., s John W. & Phebe (Green), b N. Y. 2-5-1845; cf Oswego 11-4-1863 with father (H)
Sarah L., dt Benjamin & Phebe, N. Y.; m 1831 Charles A. MACY (H)
Sarah W., wd Joseph, dt John & Elizabeth WHITE, N. Y.; m 1836 Charles MARRIOTT (H)
cf Pur. 4-11-1816 for Sarah W. Corlies, having rem with her h, Joseph
Walter, s Benj. & Phebe, b 4-11-1817; ct Shrewsbury 3-1-1848 (H)
William, s William, rocf Shrewsbury 7-4-1808, he having left when young; dis 12-1829
William (nm) & -----
Ch: Mary b N. Y. d 11- 8-1822 ae 3m 10d bHS
James b West. Co. d 10-4-1828 ae 15y bHS
William d 1-22-1836 ae 55y 8m; m Hester ----- d 8-28-1874 (H)
Hester recrq 3-1832
William S. (nm) b Shrewsbury d 4-13-1814 ae 72y bHS
William W. rocf Shrewsbury 5-1839; dis 11-1-1848 (H)
----- m Ellen Gardner COLES, dt John & Sarah (Willett), d 3-21-1904 ae 93y 5m bPP (both nm) (H)

CORNEILSON
Thomas R. & Eleanor
Ch: Eleanor Linnie b 7-15-1929
Janice " 12-29-1933

CORNELL
Abigail, dt Comfort (dec) & Eliz.; m ----- DOTY; m 2nd 1810 Israel CORSE
Alice, w Richard, rocf R. I. MM (Newport) 11-24-1842; ct R. I. MM (Newport) 5-4-1859
Anne, dt Richard & Phebe, Flushing; m 1773 Ferris CORNELL
Benjamin, s Benj. (dec) & Abigail, Scarsdale; m N. Y. 5-9-1804 Permelia FARRINGTON, dt John & Mary, Flushing (H)
He brought cert of clear from Pur.; Pamela rocf Pur. 9-6-1804
Benjamin, Jr. d 3-22-1837; m Sarah T. ----- d 12-9-1869
Ch: Mary H. b 7-11-1818
cf Pur. 10-12-1815; failed 1819 but ret mbrp; ct Pur. 6-8-1823 with dt, Mary; cf Pur. 11-1836
Caleb, Hempsted; m 2nd 5 Mo (July) 21, 1743 Phebe HAIGHT, wd John, Flushing, d 2 Mo (Apr) 1750
Phebe took rem cert 8 Mo (Oct) 5, 1743
Caroline, dt Josiah D. & Mary B., rocf Oswego with parents 1846; ct Weare 1854
Charles (nm) & -----
Ch: Infant d 1-21-1859 ae 4d bPP
Charles G. (nm); m Annie W. DELANOY, wd Wm. P.,

CORNELL, Charles & Annie, continued
dt John Edgar & Mary B. (H)
Charles W. & Phebe C. (H)
Ch: David W. b 9-28-1872
Fanny Emily " 8-31-1874 d 7-21-1877
Phebe A. T. " 2-9-1877 " 8-23-1877
Charles W. Jr. " 1-23-1878
John S. " 2-14-1880 " 7- 8-1880
Harold Barclay " 3-28-1881
John F. " 2-15-1884
6 others d young
Charles recrq 4-3-1872; Phebe recrq 2-1862; ct Chap. for all 1-9-1897
Deborah, dt Richard, Cow Neck; m 1723 Matthew FRANKLIN
Deborah, Flushing, b 8 Mo (Oct) 26, 1736
Deborah con mo 8-6-1767
Edward, s David & Susan A.; m 106 Columbia Heights, Bkn., 12-12-1896 Esther HAVILAND, dt David S. & Sarah (Carpenter), b Newark 4-9-1872 (H)
Ch: Willard Haviland b 4-10-1901 (adopted)
Katherine " 2-12-1904
Edward Jr. " 1-10-1906 d 1-1-1909
Geo. Davison " 3-17-1910
Julien Davies " 3-17-1910
Phebe " 1-12-1912
Edward mbr Corn.; Esther rocf Pur. with father 8-7-1895
Elijah (nm) & -----
Ch: Walter b N. Y. d 6-1-1824 ae 5y bHS
Eliza P., dt Rich. & Mary Annette, N. Y.; m 1857 Albert K. SMILEY, of Phila.
ct Spring Creek, Iowa, 6-1-1858
Elizabeth b Flush. d 8-5-1822 ae 70y bHS
Elizabeth dis mo to her brother-in-law 12-4-1754
Elizabeth, dt Josiah & Catharine (Mailer), b Monroe 10-16-1835; m 11-15-1855 Reuben L. BIRDSALL, s Dan'l & Abigail (H)
cf Chap. 12-3-1879 (Elizabeth d 10-3-1918)
Ferris, s Joseph & Phebe, Scarsdale; m Flushing 8-12-1773 Anne CORNELL, dt Richard & Phebe, Flushing
Anne gct Pur. 11-3-1774
Franklin, s James C. & Mary N., d 4-27-1919 ae 61y 1m 5d; m Spring Valley, N. Y. 1-27-1860 d 10-4 (or 5) 1928 Elmhurst, L. I.
Ch: Edgar V. b 3-21-1881
Martha C. " 5-30-1883
Marion H. " 1- 6-1886
Esther S. " 9-14-1892 d 3- 1-1917
Franklin M.
Edgar V.
cf Corn. 9-3-1890
Julien Davies, s Edward & Esther (Haviland), b 3-17-1910; m Swarthmore 6-27-1932 Virginia STRATTON, dt Daniel & Josephine (Graves) (H)
Ch: Julien Martin b 7- 7-1933
ct Corn. 12-11-1933 for all
Katherine, dt Edw. & Esther (Haviland), Central Valley, b 2-12-1904; m 1925 John L. STAINTOR (H)
Marion H., dt Franklin & Sarah R., b 1-6-1896; m Fred H. NYHOLM
Mark, s Jacob (dec) & Mary, N. Y.; m N. Y. 10-9-1828 Anna SINCLAIR, dt John & Elizabeth, N. Y., d 10-23-1842
Ch: Infant stillborn 5- 2-1829
Charles Henry b 11-21-1830
Mark S. gr s of Mark d 12-25-1855 ae 4y 9m 23d (prob s of Charles Henry); cf Creek 10-19-1827 (clear); ct Roch. 2-1837 for Anna & s; Mark dis 9-1836; Mark rst 7-1856; ct Pur. 7-6-1864
Martha C., dt Franklin & Sarah R., b 5-30-1883; m ----- STORY (nm)
cf Corn. 9-3-1890
Martha W. con mo 1-1844 & ret a mbr, referred to Marl.
Mary m 1780 Elijah PELL
Mary (form Willis) dis mo 2-1803
Mary, dt Josiah & Anna; m 1826 Abraham LOCKWOOD
Mary, dt Lot & Hester G. HUNT, dis 7-7-1852 (H)
Mary, wd Elijah, d 2-17-1871; recrq 5-1864
Mary A., dt Richard & Mary A., recrq of parents; ct Providence 11-1865
Mary H., dt Benj. & Sarah T., b 7-11-1818; m Nelson WALBRIDGE; dis 8-3-1853 (H)
Peter (nm) & -----
Ch: Infant stillborn 8-6-1812
Phebe, dt Richard & Phebe, Flushing; m 1761 Thomas PEARSALL, Jr.
Phebe, dt Joshua & Hannah, N. Y.; m 1793 James HALLETT
cf Jericho 5-17-1792 (clear)
Phebe, dt Stephen, rocf Oswego 3-19-1834, minor; dis 12-1839
Phebe R. rocf Plains 5-22-1821 (clear); dis 12-1831 (O); ct Battle Creek 1-5-1848 (H)
Rebecca d 4-16-1877
Reynolds rocf Plains 5-21-1816 (clear); ct Plains 8-11-1819 (clear)
Richard, s Thomas (dec), Hempsted; m Flushing 10 Mo (Dec) 5, 1734 Phebe DOUGHTY, dt Charles, Flushing
Richard rocf Pur. 2-9-1797, minor
Richard m Mary Annette ----- (ro before 1-2-1828
Ch: Eliza P.
Mary A.
Adrien d 4-12-1854
Amy
Albert " 7-30-1840 ae 1y 4m 8d bur Pur.
cf Pur. 4-7-1824, minor; dis 4-1828 for mo; rst 1838; ch recrq of father; Richard dis 4-4-1859
Richardson & Anna
Ch: Alletta K. b 4-25-1817
cf Plains 6-25-1816 for both; ct Plains 8-5-1818 for all 3
Robert C. (nm) & -----
Ch: James Lovett d 10-25-1813 ae 2y 10m bHS
Robert " 1-23-1818 ae 1y 3m bHS
Robert " 8-30-1819 ae 9d bHS

CORNELL, continued
Samuel, Flushing & Hannah
Ch: Hannah b 1 Mc (Mar) 21, 1729/30
 Samuel " 4 Mc (June) 17, 1731
 Sarah " 12 Mc (Feb) 5, 1732/3
 Mary " 3 Mc (May) 4, 1736
Sarah U. gct Flushing 10-2-1816
Silas, s Benj. & Alice (dec), Scarsdale; m N.Y. 12-13-1815 Sarah MOTT, dt Adam & Anne, N. Y.
Stephen d 9-1-1813; m Hannah -----
Ch: Richard b 10-27-1811
 cf Pur. 2-14-1811 for Stephen & Hannah; ct Pur. 8-3-1814 for Hannah & s, Richard; cf Pur. 11-1836 for Hannah; ct Queensbury 8-1838 for Hannah
Stephen S. rocf Pur. 4-1872; mbrp relinquished 5-1880
Thomas, s Ferris, rocf Pur. 6-13-1793, a lad, placed in N. Y.; ct Pur. 12-2-1801 (clear)
Thomas C. having mo Roch. referred it to N. Y. 3-1850; dis 7-1850
William C. & Anna Maria (m Balt.)
Ch: Theodore b 9-30-1831
 Mark " 3-21-1833
 cf Creek 8-1829 (H); cf Creek 6-17-1831 (0); dis 2-1833 (0); cf Balt. 6-1830 for Anna; ct Roch. 11-1835 for all
William T. & Phebe F.
Ch: John Jr.
 Sarah Ann
 Lydia P. d 7-17-1834 ae 1y 2m
 James B. b 10- 4-1836 d 11-26-1836
 Robert d 7-31-1836 ae 8m
 cf Oswego 7-1834 with 3 ch; ct Oswego 7-1837 with 4 ch; cf Oswego 10-1838; ct Roch. 5-1842 (H)
----- & -----
Ch: Jesse b N. Y. d 8-28-1821 ae 6m bHS
 Albert d 7-30-1841 ae 1y 4m 8d bHS

CORNWALL (see CORNELL)

CORNWELL
Mary Ann (form Dickinson) dis 2-1831 (H)
Stephen (nm) b L. I. d 4-19-1834 ae 53y bHS

CORSA
Sarah, Newtown, b 10 Mo (Dec), 23, 1729; con mo 6-5-1760

CORSE
Barney, s Israel & Lydia (dec), N. Y.; m N. Y. 11-12-1823 Mary E. LEGGETT, dt Samuel & Eliza, N. Y.
Ch: Samuel Leggett b 9- 5-1824 d 9-13-1844
 remains rem to Flush. 9-17-1895
 William L. b 4- 1-1827
 Eliza L. " 12-28-1829
 Mary Lydia " 3-11-1833 d 1-21-1837
 remains rem to Flush. 9-17-1895
 Cornelia b 8-15-1836
 Frederick Aug. " 10-11-1840
 both dis 1831,1832 (0); ct Flush. 4-3-1861 for Mary E.
Cornelia, dt Barney & Mary E., b 8-15-1836 d 5-12-1864; m 1861 ----- PELL; dis mo 8-1861 (H)
Eliza L., dt Barney & Mary E., b 12-28-1829; m ----- SAUNDERS
 dis 7-3-1851 (H)
Elizabeth b Maryland d 11-7-1835 ae 68y, a wd
Ch: John B. b Me.
 recrq 1-6-1813; dis 2-1829 (0)
 Elizabeth bHS, transferred to PP (H)
Frederick Augustus, s Barney & Mary, b 10-11-1840; m ----- (H)
Ch: Infant bPP
 joined a military company engaged in the present war, also mo; dis 9-1862
Israel, s David & Elizabeth, N. Y.; m Lydia TROTH, dt William & Lydia, d 9-3-1808 ae 38y (H)
Ch: David b 12-10-1803 d 10-30-1805
 Lydia Ann " 11-30-1805
 Mary dis 12-1839 (0)
 cf Murderkiln, Del. 11-15-1803 for both
Israel m 2nd N. Y. 4-12-1810 Abigail DOTY, dt Comfort (dec) & Eliz. CORNELL
Ch: Israel b 6-18-1811
 Robert " 4-19-1814 d 4- 6-1815
 Israel " 3-20-1816 " 2-22-1817
 Israel " 10-24-1819; dis 12-1840 (0)
 Rights of Abigail's ch protected; Abigail dis 9-1840 (H); Israel dis 1829; Lydia 1839
Israel, s Israel & Abigail b 10-24-1819; dis 12-1840 (0); dis 2-1847 (H)
John rocf Deer Creek 9-1836, minor; ct Deer Creek 6-1843 (H)
John B., s Elizabeth, b Me. d 8-25-1835 ae 35y bHS & rem to PP (m) (H)
Lydia, dt Israel & Lydia; m 1823 Jonathan THORN
Mary, dt Israel & Lydia; dis 12-1839 (0); dis 9-1840 (H)
William & Deborah
Ch: Mary W. b 2-27-1833
 Caroline " 11-23-1836
 Robert Sinclair b 5-21-1838
 cf Wilmington 5-1732 (H); cf Balt. 10-1831 for Deborah (H); cf Wilmington 7-26-1830 (0); dis 11-1831 (0)
Ch: George F. b 12- 8-1839
 Esther S. " 11- 3-1841
 Susan " 8-20-1843
 William J.D. " 7-17-1845
 ct Balt. 8-1845 for all
William L., s Barney & Mary E., b 4-1-1827; m Frankford, Pa. 1856 Laura P. -----
Ch: Josephine b 9-18-1857
 ct Frankford 9-1856 (clear); relrq 2-1862 Orthodox (H); cf Frankford, Pa. 12-1857 for Laura; ct Frankford, Pa. 1858 for all

COSMAN
Eliza d 5- 8-1910; rocf Marl. 9-6-1876

COSTON
Leila, dt Herbert H. & Addie B. (Pinney), b Scranton, Pa. 8-15-1889; m 1923 Lewis R. CONNER (H)
recrq 11-9-1924

COTT
----- & -----
Ch: Sarah d 7- 5-1811 ae 4y 8m bHS

COULEY
Francis, active mbr from 1676; under dealing 1683 nothing further

COURTENAY
James Gibbons d 12-28-1801 ae 28y bHS

COUTANT
Gilbert m Sarah L. ----- d 11-2-1866 ae 47y 5m 1d bPP (both nm) (H)
Grace D ., dt Lawrence B. & Julia R. (Soldan), b Bkn. 6-16-1867; m 1895 Robert UNDERHILL (H); recrq 3-4-1905
Mary V., dt John & Susan FERGUSON, d 9-1842 (w Gilbert) (H)
Henry rocf Marl. 8-22-1804; ct Marl. 7-3-1811
Peter J., s Peter & Susannah, Plattekill, N.Y.; m N. Y. 11-14-1821 Sarah P. HAWXHURST, dt James & Catharine, N. Y., b N. Y. d 11-6-1828 ae 36y; ct Marl. 3-5-1823 for Sarah H.

COVERT
Elizabeth, w Leonard, dt John & Lydia DODGSON (m 8-1839); date of her d not known in 1900 (H)
Jacob (nm) & -----
Ch: Infant stillborn 4-17-1811
----- & ----- (nm)
Ch: Thomas L. d 5-31-1837 ae 9y 3m 29d bHS
Theirlove A. " 11-18-1860 ae 17y bPP

COWDRY
Henrietta, dt John & Amy HULL, d 1-17-1888 (m Samuel Cowdry 1841) (H)
ret a mbr

COWGILL
Ezekiel rocf Duck Creek, Del. 12-9-1809, apprentice; ct Duck Creek 4-3-1811 (clear)
cf Duck Creek 9-1814; ct Duck Creek 5-5-1819 (clear)

COWPER (see COOPER)

COWPERTHWAIT
Elizabeth, Flushing, active mbr from 1676 d 10 Mo (Dec) 15, 1697
Elizabeth, dt John, West Jersey; m 1712 Abraham SHOTWELL, s John
Grace, wd, Flushing; m 1735 Samuel BOWNE
Hugh, Flushing; b Kentmore, Westmoreland, 1648 d 3 Mo (May) 20, 1730 ae about 82y
took cert of clear to N. E. 12 Mo (Feb) 25, 1698/9
Hugh m 2nd Elizabeth ----- d 6 Mo (Aug) 27, 1707
came from England 6-1675, a minister 40 yrs
Hugh m 3rd bet. 11 Mo 5 and 12 Mo 2, 1709/10 Grace BURLING, Flushing
Hugh took cert to place not stated 6 Mo Aug) 29, 1696
Hugh, Flushing, took cert of clear to ----- 5 Mo 5, 1731
John, Flushing, active mbr from 1685
John, Flushing, ltm Sarah Adams, O. B. 9 Mo. (Nov) 29, 1690
Samuel rocf Phila. (clear) 10-26-1764, rec 5-2-1765

COX
Abby Jane rocf Middletown, Pa. 4-8-1825, rem with h
Abel, s Isaac & Phebe, b Yorktown d 9-18-1825 ae 21y bHS (unm)
Abraham L. & Abby Ann
Ch: Mary Newbold b 11-18-1825
cf Upper Springfield 4-6-1825; Abby Ann rocf Middletown, Pa. 1825; parents dis 1829-1830 (ch marked "off" in pencil) (O); joined Presbyterian (H)
Ann d 7-11-1851; recrq 2-3-1806
Anna, dt John & Armenia, b Croton-on-Hudson d 12-11-1903 ae 70y bPP; m Charles C. VARNEY
cf Linington, Me. with h & ch 11-1887; ct Providence 3-7-1894 for all
Annabel B., dt Benoist James & Francelia (Bancher); m 2-20-1901 Geo. Washington DAHL(H)
both recrq 4-13-1925
Benjamin rocf Phila., Spruce St. 11-1844; ct Phila. Spruce St. 9-1850 (H)
Eliza J. m John HUNN (m before 5-1-1816)
cf Muncy 8-21-1822; dis 10-1830 (O); ct Stanford 2-2-1853
Harriett, dt Wm. G. & Sarah (Jones), b Malvern, Pa., 2-8-1867; m 1892 Dr. Charles McDOWELL
cf Goshen, Pa. 1-5-1892 (H)
Henry, s Isaac & Phebe; m Sarah HYATT, dt David M. & Chloe (H)
Ch: Infant stillborn 7-17-1844 bHS
recrq (rst) 9-1845; ct Roch. 6-1847
Henry H., s Henry & Caroline H. (dec), Bkn.; m at A. Underhill's 10-8-1846, Louisa S. UNDERHILL, dt Adonijah & Deborah S., Bkn. (A. Underhill not under care of N.Y.MM) (H)
Henry H. Cox d 11-30-1878 ae 61y (H)
Hope, dt John & Mary N., Chap., b N. Y. 12-22-1901; m 1927 John Lefferts (H)
Jane, dt Stephen & Eliz. N. (Taylor), b 3-28-1855 d 6-18-1917; m 1879 Howard Cassin ROOT (H)
Jesse d 9-30-1825; m Rachel ---- d 8-16-1825
Ch: Isaac
Rachel b 8-10-1825 d 8-25-1825
cf Corn. 11-27-1823 with s, Isaac

COX, continued
John, Jr., s John & Mary (Cunningham), Monroe Co., N. Y.; m at 15th St. 6-30-1900 2 P.M. Mary Alice NICHOLS, dt Benj. F. & Lauretta H(essin), Huntington, Ind., b State Center, Iowa, 8-15-1869 (H)
Ch: Hope b 12-22-1901 N. Y.
Martha " 10-23-1908 Chap.
cf Roch. 9-4-1889 for John; cf Maple Grove, Ind. 5-5-1900 for Mary
Joseph (nm); m Mary ---- (nm), Chenango Co. d 11-18-1831 ae 24y bHS
Ch: Henry b N. Y. d 3-24-1834 ae 2y 4m bHS
Joseph m 2nd Mary ----- (nm) d 12-17-1833 ae 31y 11m 17d bHS
Mary, dt Robert & Phebe, N. Y.; m 1855 Daniel C. MILLER (H)
Phebe, dt Samuel & Sarah, N. Y.; m 1801 Joshua BARKER
cf Burl. 5-4-1801 (clear)
Phebe H., dt Timothy & ----- CARPENTER (m 1844) (H)
retained & ct Ama. 9-3-1845
S. Louisa, dt Adonijah & Deborah UNDERHILL, b 1-6-1820 d 6- 3-1894 (H)
Samuel (nm) & -----
Ch: Infant stillborn 11-17-1820 bHS
Sarah, w Samuel, rocf Burl. 5-4-1801
Stephen, s Isaac & Hannah; m ---- 1843 (mo)(H)
Ch: Infant stillborn 8-21-1847
cf Ama. 6-1845; ct Roch. 6-1850
William d 1855; recrq 1835
William H. d 10-11-1889; rocf Flush. 8-1844 (H)
----- & -----
Ch: William b Yorktown d 1-13-1826 ae 2y 8m 27d
Henry b N. Y. d 2-3-1829 ae 1y

COYKENDALL
Sarah O., dt Wm. L. & Ann TITUS, d 12-21-1900 ae 58y 11m 25d (m 4-3-1861) (H)
cf Corn with parents 11-1853

COZINE
Florence (nm), dt Joseph & Catharine; m 1905 Willis T. STRINGHAM (H)

CRABB
Richard, O. B. d 2 Mo (Apr) 6, 1680; m Alice ----- d 2 Mo (Apr) 24, 1685
active mbr from 1676

CRABTREE
William Alonzo (nm); m 3-12-1902 Emily M. COLEMAN, dt Silas B. & Rebecca B., b 9-11-1872 (H)
Emily's name entered by comm. 1-19-1881; dropped 5-14-1934

CRAFT
Esther, dt James & Hannah, N. Y.; m 1859 Richard M. REYNOLDS (H)
cf Wby & Jericho 5-19-1830 (clear) (O); dis 7-1831 (O)
Mary, dt James & Hannah, N. Y.; m 1831 Rufus REYNOLDS, dt Harrison
cf Wby & Jericho 5-19-1830 (O) (clear); dis 4-1831 (O)
Sarah (nm), b West Chester d 11-16-1810 ae 31y 11m 13d bHS
----- & -----
Ch: Martha b N. Y. d 8-23-1834 ae 1y bHS

CRAGG
Eleanor, dt William, b Eng. 4-22-1835 d Stratford, Canada 2-26-1918; bPP; m Thomas Wynne HOLME; m 2nd Stephen FROST (all nm)

CRAIG
John (nm) b Del. d 1-22-1833 ae 32y bHS (unm)

CRANDELL
Harriett (nm), dt Lewis & Dorothy; m 1869 Eli E. NELSON (H)

CRANE
Amos R., s Elijah & Mary, b 6-14-1816; ct Adrian 5-1-1839 (clear)
Elijah & Mary (m Pur. 1814)
Ch: Matthew T. b 3-10-1815
Amos R. " 6-14-1816
Josiah " 10- 7-1817 d 4-24-1824
Wm. Elijah " 6-12-1819
William " 8-16-1821
Deborah R. " 5-22-1823
Josiah " 5-28-1825 d 8-21-1826
Nathan Selleck b 1-26-1827
ct Pur. 2-2-1814 (clear); Mary rocf Pur. 5-12-1814
Elijah dis 8-1829 (O); ct Adrian 5-1-1839 for Mary with her 3 ch, William E., Deborah R. & Nathan S.; Elijah dis 9-1829 (H); rst 1851 by Adrian
Harriet T., dt Jason & Aramintha, Bloomfield, N. J.; m 1874 Morton C. COGGESHALL (H)
Matthew F. dis mo 9-7-1836; cf Adrian, Mich. 2-1843; ct Adrian, Mich. 12-1843. (H)
William E., having mo Adrian refers it to N. Y. 2-6-1845, retained a mbr; cf Adrian 1845; went in business, failed, dis 4-1847
----- & -----
Ch: Josiah b N. Y. d 4-24-1824 ae 7y bHS

CRAVEN
Evelyn C., dt Ishi & Mary Bunting (Davis); m ----- ROUTLEDGE (nm)
recrq 12-1915

CRAWFORD
Cyril (nm) m Ruth UNDERHILL, dt Abram & Anna T. (Murray)
divorced 1929 or 1930
letter from 1st Presbyterian Church, Ossining 6-2-1919 for Ruth

CREPON
James rocf ND MM 12-27-1825; ct ND MM 1-1832

CRESSON
James H. gct ND MM 1-4-1832 (clear)

CRETTY
Charles & Elizabeth B.
Ch: Leslie A.
letter from Reformed Church, Bkn. Heights 11-1918 for parents; Leslie A. recrq of parents 7-1924
Leslie A., s Charles & Elizabeth B.; m Virginia TERRELL
Leslie recrq of parents 7-1924; Virginia rolf 1st M. E. Church of Queens Village 4-3-1935

CRISSON (CRISPEN)
Jeremiah rem cert to Phila. 1-26-1759; ct Phila. 4-5-1759; ct Phila. 5----1759
Ann (also written Christon) roc 8-5-1756; ct Burl. 2-3-1757

CHRISTON (see CRISPEN)

CROASDALE
Stevenson (nm) m Martha R. ----- d 1-26-1886 ae 77y 9m 3d bPP (H)
Ch: William T. d 8- 9-1891 ae 47y 4m 24d ashes bPP
cf Balt. 1-6-1885 for Martha

CROCKER
Gladys T. (nm) m Lewis Hartley THOMAS (H)
Lewis' name cancelled for lack of interest 3-13-1933

CROMWELL
Alice U., dt Wm. & Caroline, N. Y.; m 1860 Thomas CHASE, of Haverford
ct Radnor, Pa. 4-1863 with ch
Ann m Wm. L. TITUS (H)
cf Corn. 11-1853 with h & 3 ch
Anna, dt David & Rebecca (Bowman), b N. Y. 9-13-1823 d 2-1913; m 1847 Charles M. FIELD (H)
cf Corn. with parents 10-25-1823; ct Corn. with parents 5-1833; cf Corn. 2-1848
Anna, dt John & Sarah M., Bkn., b 1-14-1845 d 4- 5-1887; m 1875 Chas. E. DAVENPORT (H)
Caroline Ann, dt Wm. & Caroline, b 6-12-1833; ct Corn. 2-1871; cf Corn. 11-1883; ct Providence 11-6-1907
Charles m Sarah A---- d 1-26-1823 ae 29y
Ch: Rachel M. b 9-30-1810; dis 12-1839
Israel Anderson b 3-24-1813
cf Pur. 4-12-1810; dis for failure 11-1-1817; rst 3-7-1821
Charles m 2nd Peru 1824 Phebe -----
Ch: Samuel K. b 3-25-1826
ct Peru 8-1829 for all (H); cf Peru 10-28-1824 for Phebe, w Charles; Charles & Phebe dis 1829
Charlotte H., dt Oliver & Sarah (Titus), Corn., b Corn. 3-31-1832; m 1853 Nathan COMSTOCK, Jr.
Daniel (nm), b Harrisons Pur. d 5-29-1813 ae 58y bHS (m)
Daniel J. (nm) b N. Y. d 2-1-1827 ae 21y 2m bHS (unm)
Daniel d 7- 7-1836 ae 80y bPP; m Elizabeth ----- d 12-27-1860 ae 66y 7m bPP
Ch: Charlotte b 5-27-1815 d 3- 2-1888 bPP
Elizabeth " 12- 8-1816
Henry " 2-25-1819 " 10-25-1884
Edward " 5- 1-1821
Daniel, Jr. " 6-20-1825 " 12-15-1866 bPP
Anna " 6-13-1829 " 5-26-1838 bPP
George " 11-11-1833 " 4-11-1838 bPP
Robert " 2-13-1837 " 8-29-1837
cf Corn. 7-27-1815 with their ch, Charlotte
Daniel, s Edward & Martha, relinquished mbrp 3-1880, supposed to be in Chicago
David d 9-14-1857 ae 63y bPP; m Rebecca ----- d 4-22-1886 ae 87 bPP (H)
Ch: James d 9-13-1823 ae 2y 7d
James " 7- 2-1863 ae 24y
William
Anna
Sarah b 10-13-1825
Henry B. " 4-29-1828
Charlotte b 8- 2-1830
Emily d 1- 6-1920 ae 82y bPP
David & Rebecca dis 1829-1830; ch rem to Corn.; cf Corn. 10-23-1823 with 2 ch, William & Ann; ct Corn. 5-1833 for all
Edward, s Daniel & Eliz., N. Y.; m N. Y. 4-9-1848 Martha W. BIRDSALL, dt Wm. & Martha (dec), N. Y.,
Ch: William B. b 4-21-1849
Gertrude " 7-18-1850
Lydia B. " 10-23-1853
Everett Ernest b 4-11-1860
Edward recrq 2-9-1848; Martha recrq of parents 2-1830; Edward relrq 8-1861
Elizabeth, w John J., d 2-14-1833 ae 46y
ct Wby 11-4-1812; cf Wby & Jericho 1829 (O); dis 11-1829 (H)
Elizabeth, dt Daniel & Eliz., N. Y.; m 1839 Thomas WOODWARD, Jr.
cf Wby & Jericho 7-19-1828 (clear)
Elizabeth, dt Joshua T. & Eliz. (Titus), b Highland Mills 4-18-1858 d 6-18-1919; m 1880 Thomas B. HALLOCK (H)
cf Corn 2-11-1911
Everett Ernest, s Edward & Martha, b 4-11-1860; mbrp relinquished 3-1880, at Storm Lake, Iowa
George, s John & Sarah (Merritt), b 10-27-1840 d 8-13-1932; m Isabella HEWITT (nm)

CROMWELL, George & Isabella, continued
(m 6-10-1879) (H)
Ch: Robert H. b 5-28-1880
Robert's name entered by comm. 10-10-1886
George W., s Henry B. & Sarah, b 7-3-1860; mbrp cancelled 10-14-1905 (H)
Gertrude, dt Edward & Martha, b 7-18-1850; mbrp relinquished 3-1880 at Storm Lake, Iowa
Helen, dt Henry & Sarah M., N. Y.; m 1869 John K. SHANNON (H)
Henry b 2-25-1819 d 10-25-1884; mo 12-1845; ret a mbr
Henry B., s David & Rebecca, N. Y., d 4-2-1864 ae 30y 4m bPP; m at Caroline H. Seaman's 6-10-1856 Sarah SEAMAN, dt Wm. (dec) & Caroline H., N. Y. (H)
Ch: George W. b 7- 3-1860
Francis d 2-12-1863 ae 8m bPP
Henry B. Jr. " 5- 1-1896 ae 32y
Henry B. gct Corn. 4-1834; cf Corn. 3-5-1856 for both; Henry relrq 2-7-1863; Sarah relrq 1-6-1869
Israel A., s Charles & Sarah, b 3-24-1813 d 3-1-1882
ct Peru with brother, Samuel K., 8-4-1830 (minors)
James & Charlotte
Ch: Hannah
Rebecca
cf Pur. 4-8-1784 for both with dt, Hannah; ct Pur. with ch, Hannah & Rebecca, 12-7-1785
James, s James, b 8- 1-1824
James, s John & Letitia, b 7-24-1830; m Phebe Jane ---- (H)
Ch: James b 1-21-1852 d 4-12-1862
Cornelia " 7- 7-1856 " 10-27-1857
Emily " 3-10-1859
Elizabeth " 12-27-1867
cf Pur. 11-1853 for Phebe Jane; ct Ama. 3-2-1870 with 2 ch
James M., s Richard & Mary, b 10-6-1820 d 11-12-1862 (mo) ret a mbr (H)
James Wm., s Wm. & Caroline, b 2-10-1842; m ----- (mo before 10-1865, ret mbrp)
Ch: (prob) Charles E. d 1-13-1879 ae 1y 6m
relrq 4-7-1875
John d 6- 5-1799 bHS
John, Jr., N. Y.; m Sarah ----- d 6-24-1848 ae 39y
Ch: Charles b 2-21-1788
Robert " 1-10-1791
Phebe " 10- 9-1793
Anna d 6- 5-1799
Richard " 12-16-1798
William " 9-17-1801
Anne
cf Pur. 4-13-1797 with their 4 small ch, Charles, Robert, Phebe & Anna; ct Pur. 6-5-1805 with 6 ch as named
John & Letitia
Ch: Walter
Ch: James b 7-24-1830
Oliver " 7-24-1831
David " 5-25-1838
cf Corn. 5-27-1830 with their 2 ch named; parents dis 1831 (O); ch dis 1848 (O); ct Corn. 1-5-1848 for all but James
John dis mo 12-6-1837
John, s John & Sarah (both dec), N. Y., d 4-2-1873; m N. Y. 4-12-1837 Sarah MERRITT, dt James & Sarah, N. Y. d 6-24-1848 ae 38y
Ch: Robert b 1-17-1838
George " 10-27-1840
Edward M. " 4-23-1843 d 1-11-1856
Anna " 10-14-1845
Charles " 4- 7-1848 " 8-11-1864
cf Pur. 6-9-1830 (O); dis 1831 (O); cf Pur. 9-1828 (H)
John, s Richard & Mary M., b 3-1-1829 d 1- 7-1910 bPP; m Hannah C. ----- (H)
Ch: (prob) Fannie d 4-18-1869 ae 6y 6m 8d bPP
John m Hannah WEEKS, dt James, d 7-3-1920 ae 79y bPP (H)
Ch: Louise C.
(both nm)
John J. (nm) b N. Y. d 6-28-1827 ae 45y bHS (m)
Louise B., dt James & Anna B. , d 7-2-1916 ae 53y 4m 12d bPP (nm) (H)
Louise C., dt John & Hannah W., d 3- 6-1929 ae 68y 8m 6d bPP; m Benj. C. GLOVER (both nm) (H)
Lydia B., dt Edward & Martha, b 10-23-1851; mbrp relinquished 3-1880
Margaret, dt Richard & Mary M., b 3- 1-1826; ----- CODDINGTON (nm) (H)
Maria d 1860 rem from Corn to PP 4-27-1906 (prob mother of David) (H)
Phebe, dt Oliver & Sarah (Titus), Corn., b Corn. 10-11-1827 d 11-29-1915 (unm) (H)
cf Corn. 9-2-1891
Rachel, dt Chas. & Phebe, gct Chap. 2-1839 (H)
Rachel, wd, d 9-14-1845; recrq 1816
Rebecca, dt James & Charlotte, b Corn. 7-20-1835 d 7-30-1915; m 1856 Valentine SEAMAN (H)
Richard, s John & Sarah, b 12-16-1798 d 2-24-1865 ae 66y bPP; m Ama. 1819 Mary M. ----- d 4-14-1862 ae 42y bPP (H)
Ch: Richard, Jr. b 10- 6-1820 d 11-12-1862 bPP
Margaret " 4- 1-1823 " 4-22-1823
James " 8- 1-1824
Margaret " 3- 1-1826
John " 3- 1-1829
cf Pur. 6-13-1816 (minor); ct Ama. 9-1-1819; Mary rocf Ama. 6-10-1820; all dis (O); Richard dis 4-1831, rst 2-1837
Richard, Jr., s Rich. & Mary M., b 10-6-1820 d 11-12-1862 bPP; m Elizabeth R. WALTON, dt John F. & Ann S., d 9-13-1921 ae 89y bPP
Ch: Frank d 12- 5-1914 bPP (all nm) (H)
Robert b West Co. d 8-26-1832 ae 45y; m Hannah -----
Ch: Phebe Jane

CROMWELL, Robert & Hannah, continued
Ch: Sarah Ann
Solomon H.
cf Pur. 6-13-1816 with dt, Phebe Jane; ct Pur. 10-6-1819 with w, Hannah, & 2 dt, Phebe & Sarah; cf Pur. 6-8-1825 with 3 ch as named; ct Pur. 6-3-1829 with 3 ch named (0); ct Pur. with same 5-1829 (H)
Robert, s John & Sarah (Merritt), b 1-17-1838 d 10-9-1918; m 6-29-1876 Mollie A. SMITH (nm) (H)
Robert H., s Geo. & Isabella, b 5-28-1880; m Ruth ---- (H)
name entered by comm 10-10-1886
Samuel K., s Charles & Phebe, gct Peru 8-4-1830 with brother, Israel A. (minors); cf Peru 3-1834 (H); ct Peru 12-6-1848; cf Peru 6-6-1849 (H)
Sarah, dt David & Rebecca, b 10-13-1825; ct Corn. 4-1834
Sarah M., dt Sidney BOWNE, d 4-13-1875 (H)
Thomas rocf Corn 10-1844; mo 1845 to nm; relrq 7-4-1860 (H)
William, s David & Rebecca, rocf Corn. with parents 1824; ct Corn. 4-1834
William, s James & Charlotte, N. Y.; m N. Y. 11-9-1825 Caroline UNDERHILL, dt Joshua & Mary (dec), N. Y., d 9-16-1848
Ch: Mary b 11-25-1826 d 12-15-1842
Eliza U. " 1-30-1829 " 3-20-1840 bHS
Caroline Ann b 6-12-1833
Alice U. " 7-15-1836
James William b 2-10-1842
Mary Eliza. " 6- 7-1843 d 11-21-1845
Infant stillborn 3-18-1847
cf Corn. 4-26-1821 for Wm. (clear); ct Corn. 2-1871 with ch
William A. d before 1900; rocf Norwich, Canada 4-1838(H)
William B., s Edward & Martha, b 4-21-1849; mbrp relinquished 3-1880
William D. (nm) & -----
Ch: Infant stillborn 2-8-1848 bHS
----- m Anna BARTON, dt Richard, d 12-30-1900 ae 60y 5m 13d bPP (both nm) (H)
----- & -----
Ch: Elizabeth d 2-13-1833 ae 46y bHS

CRONE
Sarah A., dt Seth & Anna (Phillips) ARMITAGE; b Canada 7-10-1835; m 3-22-1855 John A. Crone (nm) (H)
cf Yonge Street 2-7-1894; ct East Hamburg 9-10-1910

CROOKER
Elizabeth rocf Wby 5-20-1801 (clear); d on L. I. (wd when she d)
Simeon (nm) b Oyster Bay d 6-17-1815 ae 30y 8m 18d bHS (m)

CROSBY
Charles J. d 6-26-1914 ae 81y bPP; m Ellen ----- d 10-3-1912 ae 77y bPP (both nm) (H)
Mary J., dt Robert & Ann (Root), b Dumfries, Scotland 6-19-1843 d 5- 3-1909 bPP; m James BURNETT

CROSSE
Elizabeth, Exon, Eng.; m at Westchester 1689 Samuel BURDEN, of R. I.

CROSMAN
Charles S. d 12-18-1926; m Sarah FULKE d 2-15-1928
cf Haverford 2-1921
Cornelia A., dt Alfred B. & Mary H., Huntington, L. I.; m 1857 Edward WILLETS, of N. Y. (H)
Elizabeth m 1925 Harry E. RYAN (nm)
cf Haverford 4-1921

CROUCH
Alexander Wilson (nm); m 12-22-1904 Mabel CARVER, dt Wm. A. & Eliz. (Dye), b Troy, O. 1-6-1880 d 3-26-1934
Mabel recrq 6-9-1924 (H)

CROWDER
Samuel R. (nm); m 6-27-1917 Teressa MATTHEWS, dt Jos. B. & Eliz. S. (Jones), b Balt. 4-7-1879 (H)
cf Balt. 12-9-1899 for Teressa

CROZIER
Eva Jennie, dt Hiram B. & Delia, d 4-20-1915 ae 62y 7m 9d bPP; m Franklin BROWN (nm) (H)

CRUTCHFIELD
Frank m Ethel WATKINS
Ch: Philip Jerome b 11-22-1928
Douglas Milton b 8-10-1931
Alfred " 12-19-1933
cf New Garden, N. C. for Frank 3-1928; letter from Woodeville M. E. Church of Mt. Gilead, N. C. for Ethel Watkins 3-1928

CRYGIER
Alice V., dt James H. & Catharine A., b N. Y. 11-5-1858 d Flushing 4-6-1924 bPP; m Charles S. FROST
recrq 1-4-1893

CULVER
James W. d 7-26-1887; m Amy -----
James recrq 6-1871; Amy recrq 7-1871; ct Farm. 5-1873; cf Farm. 5-1875
Mary mo before 6-5-1766, con mo 3-5-1767

CUMMER
Mildred, dt Harry & Mildred (Swartz), b Buffalo 10-14-1886; m 1914 Clement WOOD (H)
both recrq 9-10-1917

CUMMIN
Carrie, w Jos. W., dt John & Mary W. (Hazard) RIDER (m 4-12-1894) (H)
Ch: Melville Porter b 1-29-1895
Melville's name entered by comm. 3-7-1896
Joseph W. (nm), s Jos. H. & J. Louise; m 4-12-1894 Carrie C. RIDER, dt John R. & Mary W. (Hazard), b Monroe, N. Y. 9-7-1871 (H)
Ch: Melville Porter b Bkn. 1-29-1895
Walter Edwin b Corn. 6-24-1899
cf Corn. 8-13-1910 for Carrie
Melville P., s Jos. W. & Carrie (Rider), b Bkn. 1-29-1895; m 12-15-1915 Marian VAN BURKIRK dt Anchor & Emma, b Bkn. 1-21-1897 (H)
Ch: Eleanor Claire b N. Y. 12-6-1916
Jean " Spring Lake, N. J. 7-1-1918 d 7-19-1925
Marian Louise b Mt. Vernon 8- 9-1920
Melville recrq of parents 3-7-1896
Walter Edwin, s Jos. W. & Carrie (Rider), b Corn. 6-24-1899; m 6-24-1923 Ida Beauvais CRAFT, dt Sterling R. & Ida (Beauvais) (nm) (H)

CUMMINGS
Edward rocf ND MM 5-1853; dis 10-1858 for neglect of mtg & attending others

CUNNINGHAM
Abner & Elizabeth
having ack Corn. referred to N. Y. 3-5-1823; rpd adversely 6-4-1823
Anna, dt James & Eliza (Hoyland) b Bkn. 6-28-1888 (H)
recrq 11-12-1928
David & -----
Ch: Girl d 6-22-1803 ae 1y 9m
rq mbrp 9-7-1831; rq returned to him 1-2-1832; again rq mbrp 3-6-1833; rq returned to him 6-5-1833
Eliza rec by ack.; ct Corn. 9-1841
Elizabeth, w Abner, recrq 3-3-1818; dis 7-1830 (O); ct Cincinnati 4-1837 (had m 1795) (H)

CUOMO
Taddeo, s Pietro & Maria (Caridi), b 2-14-1882; recrq 12-11-1915 (H)

CURLL
Daniel Bernard, Jr. (nm), s Dan'l B. & Lillian (Anthony); m 6-9-1933 Priscilla RAWSON, dt Jonathan A. & E. Marion (Nichol), b Metuchin 7-11-1911 (H)
Priscilla recrq 4-11-1932

CURRY
Mary Jane, dt John & Anna (Turner), d 12-31-1922 ae 88y 4m 13d; m John L. ADAMS (H) (both nm bPP)

CURTIS
Anna Louise, dt Geo. D. & Lillian (Tryon), b Willoughby, O., 8-15-1882 (H)
recrq 2-12-1910; ct Swarthmore 4-8-1811; cf Swarthmore 1-10-1914
Charles d 1840; cf Phila. 8-27-1829
E. Lewis B., s Arthur M. & Mary P. (McNair), b Oneonta, N. Y. 4-8-1903; m 8-9-1930 Catharine SIMONE (nm), dt Edw. P. & Margaret (Dore) (H)
Edith G., dt Samuel & Mary A. STICKNEY, b Roch. 1-24-1876 d 12-14-1919 (H)
cf Farm. 4-6-1887
Elizabeth (nm) dt Stephen & Rebecca (Pearce), b Manasquan 2-10-1833; m 1852 Samuel K. JACKSON (H)
recrq with dt 1-6-1892
Ephraim P. (nm) b Phila. d 7-23-1835 ae 34y bHS (unm)
Esther rocf Norwich, Canada 1-14-1824; ct Norwich 11-4-1829 (O)
John (nm) b Eng. d 8- 3-1819 ae 76y bHS (m)
Joseph (nm) & -----
Ch: Infant stillborn 11- 4-1819
Joseph rocf Phila. 8-28-1828, minor; dis mo 7-1837
Thomas rocf Phila. 1-27-1831; ct Phila. 4-4-1838 (clear)
----- & -----
Ch: Albin d 11-29-1809 ae 3y bHS
Albin " 11-10-1812 ae 5m bHS

CUTTEN
----- & -----
Ch: Mary Frances d 4-14-1854 ae 3d bPP

DAHL
Elizabeth B., dt Geo. Wash. & Annabel (Cox), b 6-23-1910 Bayport, L. I.; m 1-17-1931 Henry WARE, Jr. (nm) (H)
Florence Annabel, dt Geo. Work. & Annabel (Cox) b Bkn. 7-22-1901; m 5-23-1926 Moses E. CHENEY (nm) (H)
Geo. Washington, s Harold A. & Gustava S. (Thomson), b Bkn. 6-25-1874; m 2-20-1901 Annabel B. COX, dt Benoist James & Francelia (Baucher), b Bkn. 12-19-1881(H)
Ch: Florence Annabel b 7-22-1901
Harold Arrid Cox " 11- 9-1904
Elizabeth Bancher " 6-23-1910
James Benoist " 9-18-1915
parents & 3 ch recrq 4-13-1925; Elizabeth rec 4-12-1926; James recrq of parents 5-13-1929
Inez H., dt Harold A. C. & Anna C. E., Bkn., b Bkn. 9-23-1887; m 1911 Erik HAMMARSTROM (H)
John C., s Harold A. C. & Anna C. E., b Bkn. 5-30-1886 d 12-13-1913 in an automobile accident; m probably Sandy Spring 6-28-1913 Catharine MILLER, dt Henry H. & Helen G. (H)
John recrq 2-10-1906

DAISLEY
Frank m Alice WALFORD, dt Robert M. G., d 10-17-1920 ae 45y bPP (both nm) (H)

DAKIN
William Henry rocf Quakertown, N. J. 12-1861; ct Quakertown, N. J. 7-5-1865 (H)

DALY
Sarah H., dt Thomas T. & Mary WEEKS, b 5-14-1820; cf Chap. with parents 11-8-1825; relrq 6-1869, absent 5 yrs (H)

DAME
John Ellison, s Moses & Amy Anna; mo before 8-1868 Rebecca MILLER, dt Robert (nm) b 3-1-1822 S.I. d 3-28-1900 bPP
cf Phila. 8-24-1854; dealt with for mo till 8-1877, then case dismissed
Mary rocf R. I. 7-1889; ct Boston 4-5-1911
Moses d 8-24-1880 ae 69y 6m bPP; m Amy Ann ---- d 12-8-1889 ae 74y bPP
Ch: Sarah U. d 6-21-1870
Wm. Birdsall " 12-21-1862 ae 17y 10m bPP
John E. " 2-23-1902
cf Oswego 4-20-1853 with 2 ch; cf Phila. 8-24-1854 for John E.
Owen, s Jonathan, rocf Portsmouth, R. I. 8-25-1853; ct Salem, Mass. 3-6-1861; ct Nantucket 7-1857 (clear)

DANE (see DEAN)

DANBY
Robert m Amy EVANS, dt Lewis & Sarah (Birdsall), b Bkn. 4-21-1861 d 2-19-1935 bPP (both nm)

DANIEL
Dorothea (nm), dt Henry; m 1922 Chester Willets VANDERBILT (H)

DANNAT
Julia (nm), dt William & Susan (Jones); m 1874 Theodore HAVILAND (H)

DARBY
John (nm) b Chester, Eng. d 10-19-1819 ae 64y bHS (m)
John, N. Y. d 4-5-1837; m Kezia ----- b L. I. d 4- 5-1837 ae 73y
Ch: Anne b 5-12-1795
Mary " 3-14-1799
Samuel " 7-14-1801
Phebe "
cf Jericho 5-17-1788 with dt, Anne; ct Pur. 6-6-1810 for Kezia, rem with h; cf Pur. 8-12-1819 with dt, Phebe; ct Pur. for Keziah 2-5-1823; cf Pur. for Keziah 11-1831

DARLING
Hamilton (nm) m Jane ----- (nm) b L. I. d 2-12-1834 ae 36y bHS (a wd)
his ch, Isaac, d 2-23-1804 ae 1y 11m bHS

DARLY
Phebe dis 7-4-1821 for diversion & neglect of mtg
Sarah H. [Darley], dt Thos. T. & Mary WEEKS; relrq 5-6-1869; in Erie Co., Ohio 1855 (H)

DART
Edna, dt Edward & Hester (Wilson), b N. Y. 9-1-1876; m 6-21-1905 Maurice Evans DAVIS (nm) (H)
Edna's name entered by comm. 1-17-1887; relrq 5-14-1910
Hester M. W., w Edward, dt ----- WILSON, Astoria (H)
Ch: Elizabeth Starr b 3-24-1874 d 12-27-1892
Edna " N. Y. 9-1-1876
Hester & Elizabeth recrq 6-7-1876; Edna's name entered by comm. 1-17-1887; Hester relrq 5-14-1910

DAUBLE
Agnes Schissel (Agnes V. in directory) recrq 1-5-1910

DAVENPORT
Ann Eliza, dt Enoch & Sophia CARPENTER (w of Ira M.; m 2-4-1855) (H)
Charles B., s Ira M. & Ann E. (Carpenter), b Oregon, Wis. 6-19-1862 d 1916; m 1-1-1889 Retta PIERCE (nm), dt Lucien B. & Annie (Harman) (H)
Chas. E., s David M. (dec) & Hannah, Bkn. b N. Y. 2-16-1850 d 11-9-1919 ae 69y 8m 23d bPP; m at Richard Field's, Bkn. 9-15-1875 Anna CROMWELL, dt John & Sarah M., both dec, b 10-14-1845 d 4- 5-1887 bPP (H)
Ch: George C. b 7-18-1877
David " 10-23-1879 d 7- 3-1885 bPP
Theodore " 4-28-1882
Dudley " 10-22-1884
cf Duanes. 1-1-1873 for Charles; recrq of mother 7-1855; ct Duanes with mother 7-1861
Charles E. m 2nd Leah WRIGHT (nm), dt Job & Mary A., d 3-7-1922 ae 76y 7m 9d ashes bPP (m 9-28-1889) (H)
David M. d Flush. 10-3-1871; m Hannah BRIGGS
Ch: Charles E. b 2-16-1850
Reuben B. " 3-19-1852
William F. " 3-30-1854
Phebe B. " 9-20-1842
Stephen " 12- 8-1840
cf Duanes. 9-4-1867 for parents & 3 ch; Phebe B. cert 10-1867
Dudley, s Chas. B. & Anna (Cromwell), b Bkn. 10-22-1884; m 12-25-1912 Irene B. WOOD (H)
Eliz. D., dt Wm. D. & Phebe C., Duanesburg; m ----- MILLER; m 2nd 1896 David R. UNDERHILL (H)
Enoch Franklin, s Ira M. & Ann E. (Carpenter), b Oregon, Wis. 12-18-1859 d 1-15-1934; m Miriam K. LYON, dt Henry L. & Hannah S. (Kipp) (H)

DAVENPORT, continued
Esther, w Andrew O., rocf Bridgewater 1833; cf Bridgewater 11-1834
Hannah (late Brantingham) d 3-18-1882
Ch: Lydia B.
Stephen
Phebe C.
Charles Emery
Reuben B.
William Francis
dis mo 3-2-1796, had then left N. Y., ch recrq of mother 7-1855; cf Duanes for Hannah 9-1851; ct Duanes for all 7-1861; cf Duanes 7-3-1872 for Hannah & 2 youngest
Ira M., s Wm. D. & Phebe C., N. Y.; m at Martha G. Lane's 2-14-1855 Ann Eliza CARPENTER, dt Enock, dec, & Sophia, N. Y., b West Co. 2-14-1826 d 3-19-1906 ae 80y 1m 5d
Ch: William H. b 2-20-1858
Enoch Franklin b 12-13-1859
Charles B. " 6-19-1862
Mary T. " 5-17-1864 d 2-14-1892
cf Duanes 2-1855 for Ira; cf Pur. 1-1842 for Ann E. (H)
Mary T., dt Wm. D. & Phebe (Marshall), b Duanes 4-3-1829 d 9-28-1919; m 9-7-1847 Horace Carpenter (nm) (H)
cf Chap. 7-1853
Phebe C., dt David M. & Hannah (Briggs), b Schoharie Co. 9-20-1842 d 12-31-1934 bur Chap. (unm) (H)
recrq of mother 7-1855; ct Duanes with mother 7-1861; cf Duanes with mother 10-1867
Reuben B., s David M. & Hannah (Briggs), b N. Y. 2-19-1852 d 3-10-1932; m 9-15-1874 Sarah N. MILLER, dt Joseph & Hannah (Carpenter), b Ama. 12-25-1845 d 3-16-1912 bPP
recrq of mother 7-1855; ct Duanes with mother 7-1861; cf Duanes with mother 7-3-1872; cf Ama. 3-1-1876 for Sarah
Reuben B. m 2nd 7-30-1911 Marie Louise SAURNEUF (nm), dt Celestin & Maria C.
cf Duanes 7-3-1872
Stephen, s David M. & Hannah (Briggs), b N. Y. 12-8-1840 d 2- 9-1932 (H)
cf Duanes 2-3-1864; ct Duanes 6-3-1874; transferred from Albany 1-8-1916
William Francis, D.D.S., s David M. & Hannah (Briggs), b N. Y. 3-30-1854 d 5- 2-1927; m 3-31-1880; m Julia C. WHEELER, dt B. C. & Julia C. (H)
cf Duanes 7-3-1872

DAVIDS
Benjamin rocf R. & P. 9-20-1810, minor; ct R. & P. 11-6-1816 (clear)
Benjamin (nm) & -----
Ch: Casper M. b N. Y. d 12-25-1825 ae 1y 7m bHS

DAVIDSON
Andrew (nm); m Gretta HUBBARD, dt Edward A. & Margaret C., b about 1864
Ch: Ruth Marie
Ruth recrq of parents 3-1928; Andrew J. recrq 4-3-1929
Loatta m William J. MERRILL (both nm)

DAVIES
Alfred B. rocf Lurgan, Ireland 9-1885; name erased 3-1928
Henry G. rocf Lisburn, Ireland 10-2-1889; erased 3-1928

DAVIS
Anna m Freeman SCALES
cf Washington for both with ch 8-1926
Anna M., dt David H. & Susan M., b N. Y. 5-15-1848 d 12-25-1919; m 1869 William M. JACKSON (H)
Charles (nm) b N. Y. d 2-23-1809 ae 2m 4d bHS
Christy d 12-1901; m Eleanor (or Ellen), death rpd 11-1928
Ch: Abraham Barker d 4-15-1926
cf Salem, Mass. 1857
Clementine m ---- MOORE
cf Corn. 11-23-1843; dis mo 7-1856
Daniel (nm) b N. J. d 5-23-1810 ae 38y bHS
David H. d 3-20-1867 ae 68y bPP; m ----- (H)
Ch: Henry Munson b N. Y. d 3-28-1847 ae 1y 5m bPP
Mary E. d 12-15-1879 ae 29y 3m bPP
cf Cherry St., Phila. 12-1843
Deborah H., w John W., d 12-28-1893; cf Stanford 5-1852; ct Stanford 5-1865; cf Stanford 1-3-1866 (H)
Elizabeth, dt Isaac & Ann PATCHING, London; m 1817 John SUTCLIFF
recrq 1817
Elizabeth Ann, w John C., dt Silas & Phebe SUTTON (m 4-22-1863) (H)
Esther F., dt Horace A. & Hannah N., Hopkinton, Mass.; m 1926 Ralph W. BROWN (H)
Grace Ann, dt Francis, m 1853 d 3-20-1881 (H)
Hallowell, s Horace A. & Anna N., b N. Y. 8-31-1896; m 7-10-1923 Paune ALLEN, dt Wm. Young & Robenia (Gratz) (H)
Harry M., s Wm. & Eliz.(Mills) b 3- 6-1863; m 3-7-1891 Lillian MARSH (nm) (H)
recrq 8-1-1894; mbrp cancelled 5-11-1912, she obtained a divorce
Henry C., s Edward M. & Maria (Mott); m Martha MELLOR d 1864 in Phila. (H)
Ch: Lucy b 6-30-1863
Henry C. m 2nd 6-14-1876, Phila., Naomi LAWTON, dt Abraham & Sarah (Bancroft), b Stanton, Del. 9-24-1842 d 5-21-1918
Ch: Martha b 7-12-1877
(Henry C. b Phila. 9-4-1839 d 1-29-1901 ae 61y 4m 15d)
cf Phila. 4-4-1894 for Henry & Martha; cf Hudson 2-2-1887 for Naomi
Horace Andrew (nm), s Andrew McF. & Henrietta P. H., N. Y.; m at N. P. Hallowell's 11-28-1895 Anna N. HALLOWELL, dt Norwood P. & Sarah W., West Medford, Mass., b 3-20-1871

DAVIS, Horace Andrew & Anna N., continued
W. Medford, Mass. (H)
Ch: Hallowell b 8-31-1896
Horace Bancroft b 8-10-1898
Sarah Haydock " 5-14-1901
Esther Fisher " 9- 1-1876
names of ch entered by MM 6-4-1898, 12-10-1898, 8-10-1901; ch recrq of parents soon after birth
Horace Bancroft, s Horace A. & Anna (Hallowell), b N. Y. 8-10-1898; m 6-22-1925 Marian RUBINS (nm), dt Harry W. & Florence (Hawkins) (H)
Isaac d 6- 9-1898; m Mary A. ----- b 10-10-1806 d 8- 7-1891 ae 84y 9m 28d (H)
cf Goshen, Pa. 5-5-1886 for both
James (nm) & -----
Ch: Julia E. b Phila. d 3-11-1844 ae 6y 2m 24d bHS
James S. rocf Phila. Cherry St. 11-1843; dis 4-5-1848 (H)
John C. (nm) m 4-22-1863 Elizabeth Ann SUTTON, dt Silas & Phebe F. (H)unknown 1900
Jonathan (nm) b Ireland d 10-10-1845 ae 49y bHS (m)
Lucy rocf Phila. 12-7-1887 (H)
Margaret, w Alexander, dt Joseph H. & Mary BEALE, b 2-22-1826 d 1-25-1897 (H)
cf Pur. with mother 3-1853
Mary E., dt John H. & Eliza L., b Whitesville Court House, Ga. 4-18-1864 d 1-3-1910; m Benjamin H. DOANE (H)
Mary not a mbr here; Benjamin recrq 10-1-1911
Maurice Evans (nm), s Harrison F. & Susan M. (Goodman); m Edna DART, dt Edward & Hester (Wilson), b N. Y. 9-1-1876 (H)
Edna's name entered by comm. 1-17-1887; relrq 5-14-1910
Peter gct South Kingston, R. I. 9 Mo (Nov) 5, 1747
Richard Wistar dis 7-1848 by Balt. for failing
Royal J. b Balt. 1878 d 10-20-1934; m Louise STANTON
Ch: Royal Stanton
William Wills
Emily Louise b 4-30-1911
Jane " 3- 2-1916
cf Balt. 11-2-1910 with 2 ch named; Royal Stanton active mbr 4-1925
Samuel rocf Lurgan, Ireland 2-1873; ct Lisburn, Ireland 1-6-1876
Sarah B., dt Joseph & Hannah (Collins), b 3-23-1834 d 3-28-1902; m 1861 William H. OSBORNE (nm) (H)
cf Evesham, N. J. 7-6-1864
Sarah H., dt Horace A. & Andria, N. Y.; m 1828 Clifford H. POPE, of Washington, Ga. (H)
Sarah Haydock, dt Horace A. & Anna (Hallowell), b Dongan Hills, N. Y. 5-14-1901 (H)
Susan M. d 10-27-1876 ae 65y bPP (H)
recrq 11-1875
William (nm) b Waterford, Ireland d 11-23-1815 ae 44y bHS (m)
William d 12-11-1895 ae 58y 9m 5d bPP; m -----
Ch: Edith S. (nm) d 4-27-1911 ae 46y 7m 10d bPP (H)
recrq 11-1-1882
----- & ----- (nm)
Ch: Elizabeth d 3-30-1810 ae 3m bHS
Isaac " 8-25-1812 ae 9y bHS
Henry M. " 3-28-1847 ae 1y 5m bPP

DAWSON
Anna Sarah rocf first Presbyterian Church of Arlington, N. J. 12-1914
Herbert Henry (nm); m 4-21-1894 Ellen ROBINSON, dt Winfield & Caroline (Mann), of Liskeard & St. Austell MM, Corn., b Liskeard, Corn. 8-31-186] (H); cf Neward 8-13-1898

DAY
Edward Munson, s Mahlon & Mary, b 11-22-1824 drowned; relrq 5-1856
Jane R., dt Mahlon & Mary, N. Y.; m 1842 Wm. R. THURSTON
Josephine (form Nolen) rocf Linington, Me. 11-1887; ct Boston 3-7-1894
Mahlon & Mary
Mahlon lost at sea 9-27-1854
Ch: Sarah Ann dis 6-1841
Susan d 8- 4-1819 ae 1y 2m
Susan b 9-20-1822 d 9-27-1854
Jane R.
Susan B." 9-20-1822
Edward Munson b 11-22-1824; rel, drowned
Mary Kerr " 1-18-1829
Anna Braithwaite b 5-10-1830 d 2-14-1911
Mahlon recrq 3-1-1820; Mary recrq 2-2-1820; Sarah Ann recrq 10-3-1821; parents dis 1829 (H)
Mary Kerr, dt Mahlon & Mary, b 1-18-1829; relrq 8-1861
Ruth (nm) m David A. HAVILAND
Sarah Gould d 4- 1-1893; recrq 2-1883
----- (nm) m Grace UNDERHILL, dt Alex. John & Ada L.
Grace recrq of parents 11-4-1903; name erased 3-1928 for jas

DAYBILL
Alfred b Eng. 2-27-1847 d 5-19-1903; m Elizabeth WISEMAN, dt Wm. & Anne (Giles), b Birmingham, Eng. 8-2-1849 d 10-31-1913
Ch: Alfred
William
cf Warwickshire, Eng. 7-1887 for all
Alfred, s Alfred & Elizabeth (Wiseman); m Susie JONES
Ch: Baby b 4-17-1917 d ae 1h bPP
cf Warwickshire, Eng. 7-1887 with parents; letter to Emanuel Bapt. Church, Ridgewood, N. J. 7-1920
William R. m Mabelle J. JACOBS, dt James C. & Emma L., b 6-18-1875 d 3-29-1900 bPP
Ch: Lilian Edna
parents recrq 2-7-1900; Lilian recrq of

DAYBILL, William R. & Mabelle J., continued
parents 2-7-1900; letter to Ocean Ave. Congregational Church, Bkn., 4-1917 for father & dt

DEADMAN
Harold A., s Horace A. & Sarah (both dec), N. Y. m N. Y. 6-27-1904 Bertha Margaret MILLER, dt John B. (dec) & Agatha C., Bronx
Ch: Clara Victoria
Edith b 11-29-1908
Harold recrq 3-3-1897
Bertha recrq 8-7-1907; Clara V. recrq of parents 8-7-1907; ct Chicago for all

DEAL
Peninah (form Weeks) rocf Chap. 1-1835; ct Pur. 11-1837 (H)
Sarah d 3-26-1845; cf Pur. 11-1832 (H)

DEAN
Agnes, dt Israel & Agnes, b 8-30-1824; dis mo 10-1846 to ----- Abbott
Amy Blake (form Dean) rocf Corn. 3-27-1823 (clear); dis mo 1827
Anna, w Daniel S.
Ch: Mary
Hannah
Robert
Sarah
Joseph
Stephen
Garwood
cf Oswego 10-31-1815; ct Oswego 6-3-1818 with 5 minor ch last named
Cornelia, dt Israel & Agnes, d 9-23-1841 ae 25y 2m 28d bHS; m ----- BRINKMAN (mo by Episcopalian minister); dis 4-7-1841
Dane, s Daniel, Flushing, mo before 1 Mo (Mar) 2, 1698/9; con mo 5 Mo (July) 7, 1692
Edward, s Israel & Agnes, dis mo 5-1844
Elizabeth [Deane] active mbr from 1676
Elizabeth, dt Samuel & Sarah PALMER, N. Y.; m 1835 Thomas THORN (H)
cf Oswego 11-1835
George dis by Salem MM, Mass. 11-12-1802; rst 11-3-1813, much correspondence
Henry gct New Bedford 6-7-1798 (clear); Salem referred his case to N. Y. 5-5-1813; rpd 6-2-1813 that he was deranged, but his release from the army procured and he suitbly cared for
Isaac, s Gilbert, d 11-2-1804 ae 33y bHS
Israel m Agnes ----- d 3-21-1854
Ch: Arthur d 8-24-1829
Eliza " 3-31-1861
Mary Ann
Robert
Edward
Cornelia
Valeria b 3-29-1819
Robert A. d 11-9-1820 ae 8y 11m 27d
Joseph Abbott b 3-10-1822
Agnes b 8-30-1824
cf Oswego 11-19-1817 for Agnes with her 6 ch (minors) as named; cf Oswego 6-16-1819 for Israel, who had rem some part with his fam; Israel dis (0) 1832; ch dis 1841-1849 (0); Israel dis 4-1830 (H); Agnes dis 12-1829 (H)
John, N. Y. & Rebecca
Ch: William b 7-23-1775
George " 2-11-1777
Henry Loyd b 12-27-1779

Rebecca b 9- 3-1781
Elizabeth b 2-27-1784
cf Salem, Mass. 7-14-1791 for Rebecca & last 4 ch; ct Salem 6-4-1794 for Rebecca & dt, Rebecca & Elizabeth
Joseph A., s Israel & Agnes, b 3-10-1822; dis mo 12-1849
Lydia rocf Stanford 8-20-1825; ct ND MM 3-6-1844, minister
Mary m Harry S. CARPENTER, death rpd 7-1928
letter from Summerfield M. E. Church, Port Chester, 5-7-1913
Mary Ann, dt Israel & Agnes; m ----- MIDDLECOTT; dis mo 3-1-1843
Miriam cert 1842; d 1845
Robert B., brother of Stephen, rocf Oswego 7-19-1826 (clear); dis 7-1830 (0); name checked off in Reg. 1031 without comment
Samuel [Deane], Jamaica, d 6 Mo (Aug) 28, 1707; active mbr from 1672
Sarah, dt Samuel, Jericho; m 1687 John WAY
Stephen B. rocf Oswego 7-19-1826 (clear); dis 1-1832 (0); dis 4-1836 (H), in Buffalo then
Thomas (nm) b L. I. d 5-5-1812 ae 85y 2m 7d bHS (m)
Valeria, dt Israel & Agnes, b 3-29-1819; m ----- BURGESS; dis mo 11-1845
William, s John, rocf Salem, Mass. 11-11-1790, apprentice; ct Salem, Mass. 11-1-1797 (clear)

DE BOST
----- & ----- (nm)
Ch: John R. b N. Y. d 10-1-1826 ae 4m 14d bHS

DE COST
Caroline, w Franklin, dt Silvanus & Hannah Jenkins, dis mo 11-6-1833; m 2nd ----- COOLEDGE (H)

DECOW
William rocf Upper Springfield 7-8-1795, apprentice with Solomon Pancoast, having mo some time past, referred to Upper Springfield MM in N. J. 4-6-1803; dis mo 9-1-1803 on their report

DE GRAFF
Livineus m Alice FAIR, dt Robert & Ann M., d 12-11-1932 ae 93y bPP (both nm) (H)

DE GRAUW
Sarah T. rocf Shrewsbury 10-1842 d 12-25-1898, Montclair, N. J. (H)

DEGROOT
Sarah (late Brown), rocf Creek 7-1840; dis 1-6-1847

DELAMATER
Ruth S. rocf Oswego 8-1848; d 12-7-1894 (H)

DELANO
Mary H., w Capt.
Ch: Eliza Howland (adopted)
cf New Bedford 1852 with Eliza; ct New Bedford 1856 with Eliza

DELANOY
William C. (nm), s John A. & Emma (Peshine); m 2-5-1895 Annie W. CORLIES, dt John Edgar & Mary B. (Wright), b N. Y. 8-22-1874
Annie m 2nd Charles G. CORNELL between 1916 and 1917 (H)

DELAPLAINE
Charlotte, dt Samuel & Philadelphia, dis 7-1-1831 (O); dis 1-1837 (H)
Elizabeth, dt Nicholas; m 1686 Caspar HOET
Elizabeth [De Laplaine], dt Joseph, N. Y.; m 1780 Isaac MARTIN
Elizabeth d 8-13-1799
Esther dis mo 5-7-1800 to ----- Kimberly
Euphemia d 11-22-1803 ae 55y bHS
James, now of Pa., of Nicola, France; m at John Underhill's, Md. 6 Mo (Aug) 28, 1692; Hannah COCK, dt James & Sarah, Md.
rem to Phila.; James was "late of N. Y."
Joseph d 6-12-1799; m Abigail -----
Ch: Phebe b 11- 8-1752
Elizabeth " 3-17-1756
Joseph
James
Joseph took cert of clear to Burl. 12 Mo 7, 1750; Abigail rocf Burl. 6 Mo (Aug.) 1, 1751; ct Shrewsbury 5-2-1776; Joseph, with w & 4 ch rocf Shrewsbury 4-7-1777, rec 6-4-1777
Joseph m between 6-9 & 7-2-1755 Hannah CHILD
Joseph gct Wby 9-1-1779 (clear)
Joseph [De Laplaine] dis 12-1839 under YM rule of 1839
Joseph d 5- 2-1872 ae 91y (prob s of Joseph & Abigail) (H)
Joshua, Jr., joiner, N. Y., d 10-4-1771; m N. Y. 10 Mo (Dec) 4, 1716 Esther LANE, Hampsted Harbor
Ch: Elizabeth b 3 Mo (May) 14, 1718
Joshua " 8 Mo (Oct) 27, 1721
Joshua took cert of clear to Wby 9 Mo (Nov) 1, 1716 (noted cabinet maker, N. Y. Sun 6-1-1835)
Joshua, Jr., s Joshua & Esther, N. Y., b 8 Mo (Oct) 27, 1720; took cert of clear to Burl. 2 Mo 4, 1744; took cert of clear to Burl. 3 Mo 2, 1745
Joshua rqct Pur. 12-7-1774 to m; comm reports 2-2-1775 that he is not clear of m engagements; dis mo 3-1-1775
Margaret b N. Y. d 8-19-1810 ae 44y bHS
Mary rocf Burl., N. J. 5 Mo (July) 2, 1746
Nicholas active mbr 1686
Nicholas dis mo 10-4-1781
Phebe m 1784 Gilbert EVERNGHIM
Phila. rocf Wby 11-29-1780
Philah Bradley (form Delaplaine) dis mo 4-4-1792
Phila. dis jas 3-6-1816
Samuel m Philadelphia d 8-12-1832 (m Purchase)
Ch: Samuel
Charlotte
took cert of clear to Pur. 5-5-1774; ct Shrewsbury for Samuel 9-6-1781; cf Shrewsbury 9-6-1784 with 2 ch (H)
Samuel (nm) b N. Y. d 11-6-1809 ae 60y bHS
Sarah d 5-17-1829 in childbirth bHS
----- & -----
Ch: Isaac b N. Y. d 9- 7-1821 ae 6m bHS
Collins b N. Y. d 11-17-1823 ae 1y 6m bHS
Collin R. b N. Y. d 7-29-1825 ae 10m 20d bHS
Elias " N. Y. d 10-13-1829 ae 1y 3m bHS

DE LASHURE
Hope rocf Smithfield, R. I. 1847; ct Smithfield, R. I. 5-1851; cf Smithfield, R. I. 7-1861

DELAVALL
John, Merchant, N. Y., d 12 Mo (Feb) 26, 1697/8 m Flushing 3 Mo (May) 31, 1686 Hannah LLOYD, dt Thomas
Ch: Thomas b 12 Mo (Feb) 24, 1686/7 d 6 Mo (Aug) 17, 1687 bur in Friends burying place at Gravesend
----- stillborn 4 Mo (June) 28, 1688 bur same place
Mary b 1689
John active mbr from 1686; treasurer of mtg 1688
Thomas, s John & Hannah, d 6 Mo (Aug) 17, 1781

DE LONG
Marion H. m ----- TERRY (nm)
cf Glens Falls 9-1924; letter to Douglaston, L. I. 6-1928 Community Church

DEMILT
Benjamin (nm) b N. Y. d 4- 2-1835 ae 55y bHS
Elizabeth (nm), b L.I. d 7-15-1809 ae 66y bHS
Peter (nm) b N. Y. d 11-12-1828 ae 92y bHS (m)
Samuel (nm) b N. Y. d 5-23-1845 ae 58y bHS
Thomas (nm) b N. Y. d 3-25-1816 ae 48y bHS (m)

DE MONTALOC
Marie, dt Evaristo & Louise (Leblanc), b 12-15-1884; m 5-26-1906 Effingham C. MURRAY; they were divorced, she m again
recrq 12-8-1900; name removed 3-13-1933 for

DE MONTALOO, Marie, continued
lack of interest (H)

DENLINGER
Dorothy, dt Henry K. & Janet (Sutherland), b 4-28-1902 Bloomington, Ill.; recrq 4-13-1925 (H)

DENNIE
Thomas (nm), s Joseph & Mary; m 1848 Sarah L. WEST, dt Amos & Elizabeth (Coates), b Balt. 1816 d 2-17-1904 ae about 88y (H)
cf Balt. 5-5-1869 for Sarah

DENNIS
Eliza (nm) m James C. BELL, Jr.
Hannah, apparently a mbr 1676
Wilmot rocf Wby 8-14-1811 (clear); ct Flushing 11-3-1813
Winifred M., dt Alfred & Frances (Wyckoff), b N. Y. 5-4-1889; m 1913 Geo. Maychim STOCKDALE (H)

DENNY
John (nm) & -----
Ch: Infant stillborn 1-25-1837 bHS
Sarah rocf Balt. 5-5-1869 (H)

DEONTEROCHE
Abigail (nm) b Bridgetown, N. J. d 4-15-1825 ae 45y bHS

DEPUTY
Henrietta C., w David, dt Martin & Dorinda COMBS (m 5-16-1871)
cf Oswego 5-4-1864 with parents; relrq 6-10-1899 (H)

DE ROSA
Ulysses, s Francesco & Raffaela, b Accadia, Italy 2-13-1892; recrq 6-6-1917; name erased 2-1926

DESPARD
Walter Douglas d 11-27-1923 ae 63y; m Cornelia WHITE, dt Robt. Cornell & Hannah D. (Baker), d 3-11-1924 ae 65y bPP (H)
Ch: Marie Corlies d 4- 2-1924 ae 37y bPP (unm)

DE ST CROIX
Euphemia (nm) d 1-21-1854 ae 83y 6m 12d bPP

DEUELL
Agnes G., w Geo. H., dt Oscar GEORKE; ct Stanford 6-7-1905

DEVERELL
Hannah, dt Abigail HEWSON
cf Dublin 9-23-1851; dis mo 4-1853

DE VEZE
Camille (nm) m Bessie M. BARRETT, dt James T. & Lucy E. BECK
Bessie recrq 5-5-1897

DE VOE
Hannah Augusta m 2-19-1885 J. G. WILKINS
recrq 10-4-1876
Isaac B., s Moses & Eleanor (both dec); m 31 Tiemann Pl., Bkn. 8-18-1924 Elizabeth A. VALENTINE, dt Jos. A. & Sarah E. ARNOLD (both dec), N. Y. (H)
Susan (late Knowles) rpd mo before 1-4-1804; dis not found

DE VOL
Katie A., dt Rowland G. & Amanda B. (Merritt), b Fakton, Md. 1-6-1863; m 1881 James A. HARNED (H)
both recrq 6-8-1907

DEWEES
Ernest Joseph, s Jos. N. & Lucetta V., West Branch, Iowa; m Bkn. 12-27-1917 Ruth F. CAWL, dt Robert C. (dec) & Florence A., Bkn.
ct WD MM for Ruth 11-5-1919

DEYO
Eleanor, dt Charles & Amanda, b Crum Elbow 2-22-1866; m 1892 Irving J. STRINGHAM (H)
recrq 12-3-1892

DEZELL
Franc, s John T. & Alice (Royce), b Howard City, Mich. 2-20-1884; m 1919 Egbert G. JACOBSON (H)
recrq 5-14-1923

DICKERSON
Joseph R., s Valentine, d 4-7-1882 ae 61y 8m 2d bPP; m Emma P. MC CLELLAN, dt Emma, d 3-31-1881 ae 50y bPP (H)
Ann, wd, rocf Wby 6-15-1796 with dt, Mary (both clear); Ann d 8-3-1798

DICKINSON
Carson rocf Wilmington 7-11-1787 with consent of mother; dis mo 4-7-1790
Charles G. (nm) b N. Y. d 11-3-1834 ae 31y 6m bHS
David (nm) b L. I. d 2-15-1825 ae 54y bHS (m)
Edmund, s Samuel, d 1-11-1803 ae 1y 8m bHS
Eleanor Westervelt (form Dickinson) dis mo 1834; cf Corn. 1-1829 (H)
Emma Mary, dt Henry & Grace; m J. Harvey HILL
recrq of parents 1859; ct Balt. 3-1889
Hannah, dt John & Eliz., O. B.; m 1696 Isaac GIBBS
Hannah, Flushing
Henry d 11-9-1895; m Grace ----- d 6-9-1886
Ch: Jeannie (adopted)
Emma Mary
cf Whitewater 11-24-1852 with adopted dt; Emma M. recrq of parents 1859
Isaac (nm) b Dutchin Co. d 4-27-1830 ae 24y

DICKINSON, Isaac, continued
11m bHS
Isabella, dt Reuben & Roxey, rocf Coey. 1-1825; relrq 2-1875 (H)
James Hunt rocf White Water 6-25-1856; ct White water 6-10-1857
Jane rocf Corn. 4-22-1830 (clear) with sister, Marian; dis 6-1831
Jeannie, adopted dt Henry & Grace; m S. G. ELY cf Whitewater 11-24-1852 with Henry & Grace
John m Elizabeth HOWLAND, dt John, of Mayflower Elizabeth active mbr from 1677
John rocf Wby 2-28-1781 (clear); ct Baltimore 6-8-1785 (clear)
John d 9- 4-1801 bHS
John & Susanna
Ch: Margaret
Anna (called Ann Eliza 1813 and later)
Mary
Lydia
Susanna d 9- 3-1801 ae 1y
Susanna b 5-23-1803 d 10-1-1806 ae 3y
cf Corn. 9-24-1801 with 5 ch; ct Flushing 8-1-1810 with 4 ch; cf Flushing 11-4-1819 with 4 dt; ct Cincinnati 3-4-1818 with 4 ch named
John, s Reuben & Roxey, rocf Coey. 1-1825; relrq 2-1875 (H)
John (nm) & -----
Ch: Infant stillborn 8-16-1847 bHS
John M. d 5-15-1857 ae 42y bPP (prob nm)
Jonathan [Dickenson], s Merchant & Jonathan, Phila.; m Flushing 8-3-1716 Hannah RODMAN, dt Dr. John, Flushing
his cert of clear preserved
Jonathan m Shrewsbury -----
ct Shrewsbury 6-6-1773 (clear); joined a few months earlier
Jonathan con mo 1-4-1792
Jonathan & Frances
Frances rocf R. & P. 1-17-1792; ct R. & P. for both 5-2-1798
Jonathan & Anna W. (m Wby 1856)
Ch: Alice Mary b 4-19-1859
Jonathan " 4- 7-1861
cf Whitewater 11-24-1852 for Jonathan; cf Wby & Jericho for Anna 12-17-1856; ct Wby & Jericho for all 3-1866; cert of clear to Wby 9-1856
Leonard K., s Reuben & Roxey, rocf Coey. 1-1825; relrq 2-1875 (H)
Marian rocf Corn. 4-22-1830 (clear) with Jane; dis 3-1831
Mary rocf Wby 9-4-1752
Mary rocf Wby 6-15-1796 with mother, Mary (both clear); ct Plains 10-1-1817 (clear)
Mary, w John, dt John & Ann WEEKS, rocf Wby with parents 5-16-1827; ret mbrp after mo; d before 1900 (H)
Mary Ann m ----- CORNWELL
dis 2-1831 (H)
Reuben L. d in Calif; m ----- ROXEY d 184-
Ch: Isabella
John
Leonard K.
cf Coeymans 7-21-1824 with 2 ch named; ct Lowville 8-4-1830 with same ch (O)
Samuel (nm) & -----
Ch: ----- d 1-30-1803 ae 10d bHS
Maria " 9-25-1804 ae 6m bHS
Sarah, w David, rocf Creek 11-16-1821; dis 11-1830; she d a wd 1-17-1855
Townsend & -----
Ch: Samuel d 11-19-1804 ae 26y bHS
Zebulon, s Joseph, dec, O. B.; m Flushing 7 Mo (Sep) 10, 1747 Mary DOUGHTY, dt Charles (dec), Flushing
----- & -----
Ch: Charles b N. Y. d 5-12-1838 ae 4m 16d bHS
Margaret d 2-20-1848 ae 2y 11m bHS

DIEKER
Henry (nm) & -----
Ch: Elmira d 10-15-1814 ae 3y 10m bHS

DIEM
J. Martin recrq 10-3-1906; name erased 3-1928

DIETRICH
John (nm), s John & Elizabeth (dec), Belvedere, N. J.; m N. Y. 15th St. 7-19-1876 Margaret B. ALING, dt Silvanus & Sarah HAND, Morris Co., N. J. (H)
ct R. & P. 8-1-1877

DIFFENDALE
Jane (form Clarke) rocf Corn. 1845; ret a mbr 2-1850; ct Corn. 1856

DILLINGHAM
Mary m Walter S. EDGE
cf WD MM 7-1-1908

DILLISTON
Hazel, dt Howard P. & Jennie B. (White), b Patterson, N. J. 5-13-1885; m 5-14-1910 Will Wiseman BERDAN (nm) d 2-23-1914; m 2nd Floyd H. BRADLEY (nm), s Wm. J. & Anna R. (m 4-15-1916) (H)
Hazel recrq 12-14-1912
Helen B. [Dillistin], dt Howard P. & Jennie B., Patterson; m 1915 Alan JOHNSON

DINEGAR
Adelaide W., dt Jonas & Hannah, Mt. Vernon, b Livingston, N. Y. 3-21-1842; m ----- FAILES; m 2nd 1901 Thos. T. HILLIARD (H)
recrq 8-10-1901; ct Salem, N. J. 12-6-1902; cf Salem 7-10-1911

DINGEE
Patience rocf Chap. 11-7-1860; ct Marl. 3-1864

DISBROW
Levi (nm) m Mary ----- (nm) b Conn. d 2-17-1831 ae 46y bHS

DISTURNELL
Charles, s Wm. & Jane W., d 9-24-1894 ae 58y 11m bPP; m Matilda R. ----- d 9- 8-1899 ae 63y bPP (H)
Frances, dt Wm. & Jane (Williams), d 12-3-1921 ae 83y bPP; m George JENKINS (both nm)(H)
Jennie d 5-24-1916 ae 51y 7m 4d bPP; m Harry E. STURDEVANT (H)
Mary G., dt William & Jane, d 8-14-1927 ae 82 y 4m bPP; m Furman Black ROGERS (both nm) (H)
William (nm) d 10-26-1859 ae 61y bPP; m Jane W. WILLIAMS, dt Hezekiah, d 12-15-1897 ae 87y 1m 21d bPP
Ch: George William d 3-28-1864 ae 10y 4m 13d bPP
Charles
Thomas W. d 12-20-1899 ae 55y bPP
Anna C. " 4- 9-1856 ae 16y bPP
Elizabeth " 4-22-1871 ae 21y bPP
Frances D.
Mary G.
cf Coey. 7-1836 for Jane

DIVER
Richard m Elizabeth RUSHION (mo before 12-9-1800) she dis mo 2-4-1801; he dis mo 1-7-1801

DIX
James m Jemima ----- d 11-1-1878 ae 80y 8m 6d bPP (both nm) (H)

DIXON
Clara m John A. NASH d 8-12-1907 ae 70y bPP (both nm) (H)

DOANE
Alice Mary, dt Benjamin & Mary; m 1916 ----- LEACH
recrq 1-5-1910
Benjamin H., s Benj. & Maria; m Mary E. DAVIS, dt John H. & Eliza J., b Whitesville Court House, Columbia Co., Ga. 4-18-1864; d Liberty, N. Y. 1-3-1910 bPP
Ch: Alice Mary
Benjamin D.
Benjamin recrq 10-4-1911; Alice recrq 1-5-1910; Benjamin(s) recrq 10-4-1911
Benjamin Hervey m 2nd N. Y. 2-20-1913 Alice Howes UNDERHILL, dt Reuben H. (dec) & Harriet L., b 3-16-1877
recrq 10-4-1911
Mary E. Davis rocf Springfield, N. C. 1-1889; d 1-3-1910

DOBSON
Aleda d 1841; recrq 5-1-1822; ct Le Ray 5-6-1829 (clear); lived with Charles Lawton at Pottsville
Anne, dt Thomas, dec, N. Y.; m 1733 John BURLing
Elizabeth, dt Thomas, N. Y.; m 1765 Thomas Pearsall, watchmaker
Margaret, dt Thos. & Margaret, N. Y.; m 1791 Isaac SHARPLESS
Peter & -----
Ch: Catharine m ----- WILSON; dis mo 1-7-1756
Sarah, dt Thomas & Margaret, N. Y.; m 1781 Henry SHOTWELL
Sarah brought rem cert from Rahway but not clear; comm rpd 7-5-1780 she & the young man have given each other honorable discharge; her cert rec
Thomas, s Thomas (dec), N. Y. d 9-9-1812 ae 93y; m between 7 Mo 2 & 8 Mo (Oct) 6, 1742 (cert not recorded) Elizabeth BOWNE, dt Samuel, Flushing
Ch: Mary b 8 Mo (Oct) 4, 1743
Elizabeth " 10 Mo (Dec) 1, 1744
Hannah " 11 Mo (Jan) 4, 1747/8
took cert of clear to Phila. 5 Mo 3, 1751
Thomas m 2nd Margaret ----- (m Phila. 1751)
Ch: Ann b 11-19-1753 d 5-30-1797
Sarah " 11- 2-1755
Esther " 10-30-1756
Susannah " 11-17-1759
Margaret " 6- 4-1764 d 3-14-1797
Joyce " 12-13-1766
Thomas & Margaret with Ann, Sarah & Margaret, gct Plainfield 5-2-1776, ret. 6-4-1777; cf R. & P. 5-18-1780 with 3 dt, Anna, Sarah & Margaret

DODD
Marion E., dt Charles T. & Rebecca M. (Northall), b 12-16-1882; recrq 1-9-1904 (H)

DODGE
Amy Anna, dt Jos. C. & Martha, b 12-3-1837; m ----- BIRDSALL (H)
cf Chap. 5-1850; dis mo 3-1860
Isaac b N. Y. d 12-1-1819 ae 70y bHS (unm)
James C. m Rosannah BAYLIES (mo before 8-7-1813)
Rosannah con mo 12-1-1813; James con mo after ref. to Troy 5-4-1814; ct Troy for James 5-4-1814; ct Troy for Rosannah 4-6-1814
Joseph C. dealt with for mo to a mbr, ref. to Troy, ret on cert to Troy 5-4-1814
Joseph C. m 2nd Phebe d 1-21-1832
Ch: Rosanna B. d 1-15-1830 ae 15y 3m
Edward (or Edmand) 19 in 1839
Maria 19 in 1839
Joseph b 7-29-1823 17 in 1839
ct Chap. 8-10-1810 (minor); cf Chap. 3-9-1826 with 3 ch last named; Joseph & Phebe dis 1829-1830; ch dis 1839-1849
Joseph C. m 3rd N. Y. 4-11-1833 Martha STIVERS dt Thomas & Kesiah, N. Y.
Ch: Phebe W. b 12-28-1833
Sarah Elizabeth b 3- 7-1835
Amy Anna " 12- 3-1837
ct Chap. 4-1841 for Joseph, Martha & Joseph

DODGE, continued
Maria, dt Joseph C. & Martha (H)
cf Chap. 9-1826 with parents; ct Chap. 7-1841
Martha, w Joseph, dt Thos. & Kezia STIVERS (m 11-1833) (H)
Phebe W., dt Joseph C. & Martha; m ----- STIVERS cf Chap. 5-1-1850; dis 5-1852 (H)
Rosanna B. d 8-24-1829; cf Troy 1-10-1821 (minor)
Sarah E., dt Jos. C. & Martha, b 3- 7-1835; cf Chap. 5-1-1850; relrq 5-2-1866 (H)
Thomas & -----
Ch: Ann d 11- 5-1304 ae 23y bHS

DODGSON
Elizabeth, dt John & Lydia; m 8-1839 Leonard COVERT (H)
John b Eng. d 1-17-1834 ae 54y bPP; m New Bedford 1809 Lydia S. ----- d 1-29-1853 ae 65y bPP
Ch: Elizabeth b 4-10-1811 dis 12-1839
Lydia " 4-22-1814 " 12-1839
cf Kendall, Eng. 12-6-1799 (clear); cert of clear to New Bedford 9-6-1809; Lydia rocf New Bedford 1-16-1810; parents dis 1830 (O)
Lydia, dt John & Lydia; m ----- HOFFMAN; m 2nd 1847 Charles F. MOTT; ct Sara. 8-1852 (H)

DODSON
Charles P., s Wesley & Des demona (Wadsworth), b New Phila., Pa. 8-14-1857 d 1826; m 3-25-1885 Mary F. ----- (nm) (H)
recrq 5-12-1906

DODSWORTH
John rocf Woodbridge 11-1-1753 (clear)

DOEG (see Hope-Doeg)

DOHERTY
Harriett Alida, dt John & Harriett M., b 2-28-1882; m 1918 George NUSE
both recrq 2-10-1930

DOLE
John, shoemaker, Jericho; m at Sarah Williams', Jericho 1 Mo (Mar) 26, 1688 Mary JESSUP, wd
Ch: John b 9 Mo (Nov) 23, 1689
Mary " " " " " "
rem cert (clear) from Bristol, Eng. 6 Mo 20, 1683 " he now residing in Phila."; active mbr

DONALDSON
Henrietta L., dt Isaac & Deborah HADDOCK; relrq 2-5-1896

DONALLY
Mary, dt John & Mary, Phila.; m ----- McDONALD dis mo 8-1-1781

DONCHIAN
Dikran B. d 9-24-1924 Berkeley, Calif. ae 59y bPP; m Virginia A. CONSTANTIAN, dt Avedis, b Constantinople d 10-5-1913 bPP
Ch: Paul Dikran b 2-25-1892
Eugenie " 7- 2-1894
Levorn Peter b 5-28-1899
parents recrq 6-9-1897; ch recorded 5-19-1902
Dikran m 2nd 5-7-1915 Angel Agnes CHOPOURIAN
Ch: Daniel Dikran b 8-1917
Angel Agnes recrq 5-1916
Eugenie, dt Dikran B. & Virginia, b 7-2-1894; ct First Friends Church, Pasadena 5-1920
Levon Peter, s Dikran B. & Virginia, b 5-28-1899; m Suzanne WAYMAN (m at Peter Edwin Wayman's 5-19-1929)
Suzanne recrq 5-1-1929
Paul Dikran, s Dikran B. & Virginia, b 2-25-1892 m Bessie Z-----
Ch: Virginia Christine b 5- 4-1922
Paul Dikran " 11-30-1925
letter from First Congregational Church of Pasadena for Bessie 10-1925; first ch recrq of parents 10-1925

DONLEVY
Alice, dt John & Intaglio & Alice HUGHES, b Manchester, Eng. 1-7-1846 d Nico, France, 3-5-1929 (H)

DORLAND
Andrew (nm) & Rebecca (nm)
Ch: Elizabeth L. d 6-24-1856 ae 19y 7m 3d bPP
Anna, w David S. SAYLOR, rocf Glenn Falls for both with 1 ch 4-4-1906; ct West Lake, Canada 7-3-1912 for all
Anna M. d 11-29-1881; m ----- COLEMAN cf Farm. 12-1-1875
Edward H. rocf Alexandria 10-1858; ct Sara. 9-7-1864; cf Sara. 11-6-1867; ct Phila. 10-1-1883 (H)
Jonathan d 1817; rq rem cert to Oswego 10-1-1817; cf Oswego 7-20-1814 (clear); comm reported 11-5-1817 that he had dec
Philip rocf Sara. 12-1855; ct Sara. 12-7-1870 (H)
Thomas G. & Sarah E.
Ch: Annie
Carlotta
all recrq 3-1872; mbrp for all relinquished 3-1880

DORNIN
Elizabeth Ann, w Oscar, d 6-13-1854; cf Hudson 7-20-1841 (E)

dos SANTOS
Antonio Elias Borges (nm), s Feliciano E. & Secrinka (Borgee); m 4-28-1926 Charlotte BOGERT, dt Rudolphus & Elsie C., b Bkn. 9-22-1880
It transpired that he had a w living at

dos SANTOS, Antonio Elias Borges, continued
time of this m, hence this m void & she resumed her maiden name; name entered by comm 11-18-1884 (H)

DOSTER
Mary Catharine (nm), dt John B. & Grace (Leach) m 1920 Robt. Franklin HULL (H)

DOTY
Abigail, dt Comfort & Eliz. CORNELL; m 1810 Israel CORSE
rights of her ch protected
Charity E. (nm) d 10-13-1867 ae 68y 1m 16d bPP (H)
Elizabeth, w Isaac, rocf Wby 1-17-1810
Elizabeth Holmes (form Doty) rocf Creek 10-1838; dis mo 11-1830 (H)
Isaac d on L. I. 1823; m Elizabeth ----- b Oyster Bay d 9-27-1820 ae 60y
Wby reports that he rq rst 2-5-1823; rst 3-5-1823
Jacob d 11-8-1798 bHS (nm)
Jacob T. (nm) b N. Y. d 6-26-1834 ae 35y bHS (m)
Phebe McKenny (form Doty) rpd mo before 5-2-1804; rocf Jericho 4-18-1791 (clear); dis not found
Phebe d 3-24-1878 ae 81y bPP
Ch: Willet R.
cf Oswego 2-1834; ct Roch. 11-1835; cf Roch. 10-1846 for Phebe
Sarah rocf Pur. 3-28-1781 (wd)

DOUGHERTY
Alexander rocf Pur. 1-13-1814, apprentice; ct R. & P. 9-1-1819 (clear)

DOUGHTY
Benjamin, s Charles (dec), rqc 10 Mo 1, 1737 (of clear)
Benjamin, s Benjamin, Flushing, b 4 Mo (June), 10, 1744 d 8-21-1796; certified mbr 1755
Benjamin dis mo 8-7-1777; rst 11-2-1786
Charles, Flushing, d 7 Mo (Sep) 1735; m Elizabeth ----- d 1-1758 ae near 90
Ch: John
Charles gct Wby 4-1-1761
Charles, s John, Flushing, con mo 10-5-1757; certified mbr 1755, again or another Charles certified 2-3-1758
Charles, s Benjamin, Flushing, b 12 Mo (Feb) 30, 1741/2; m Sarah ----- b 10 Mo (dec) 26, 1738

Ch:		
Margaret	b	3-16-1772
Mary	"	9-16-1773
Benjamin	"	3- 6-1775
Charles	"	7-24-1777
Sarah	"	10-22-1780
Hannah		

Sarah rocf Wby 1-26-1774; ct Wby with w & 3 small ch 10-7-1778; cf Wby with w & 6 sm ch 6-25-1783

Christopher, s John, Flushing, dis mo 7-6-1757
Elizabeth rpd mo before 8-3-1758, result of dealing not found
Elias rem some time since to N. P. & mo referred to that MM 10-7-1778; he had joined a few years earlier
Elias d 12 Mo (Feb) 1, 1746; m Mary -----
Ch: Charles d 5-28-1801 ae 78y
Elias, Jr., s Elias & Sarah, Flushing, b abt 1664 d bet. 1743-1755; m Mary EASTMAN (1tm 4 Mo (June) 5, 1718)
Ch: 7
Elizabeth, dt Benjamin (dec), Flushing; m 1787 William TOWNSEND
ack. 4-2-1788; ct Wby 6-4-1788
Francis, s Elias & Sarah, Flushing, b 1661 d L. I. 1741; m Mary PALMER, dt John & Bricket, Westchester Co.

Ch:		
Elias	b	4 Mo (June) 5, 1687
Palmer	"	7 Mo (Sept) 20, 1689
Frances	"	12 Mo (Feb) 20, 1691/2
Charity	"	12 Mo (Feb) 14, 1693/4
Mary	"	12 Mo (Feb) 4, 1695/6
Obadiah	"	1 Mo (Mar) 20, 1698/9
James	"	12 Mo (Feb) 8, 1701/2
Sarah	"	11 Mo (Jan) 20, 1703/4
Phebe	"	11 Mo (Jan) 20, 1703/4
Elener	"	2 Mo (Apr) 16, 1706

Francis, Flushing, d 12 Mo (Feb) 21, 1741/2
Ch: Rebecca d 7 Mo (Sep) 1747
Hannah con mo 8-7-1735
Hannah, dt Benjamin & Hannah, Flushing; m 1782 John HILL
Isaac T. rocf Pokeepsie 6-1877; ct Pokeepsie 9-1880
Jacob, Flushing; m Ame (Amy)-----
Ch: Abigail b 2 Mo (Apr) 15, 1697; d 12 Mo 27, 1713/14
Mary b 2 Mo (Apr) 17, 1699
Sarah " 11 Mo (Jan) 19, 1700/01
Ame, Amy b 4 Mo (June) 30, 1702
Daniel " 10 Mo (Dec) 17, 1703
Deborah " 6 Mo (Aug) 23, 1705
Elizabeth b 1 Mo (Mar) 17, 1706/7
Esther " 8 Mo (Oct) 17, 1708
Ann " 8 Mo (Oct) 10, 1710 d 2 Mo 13, 1713
Hannah " 2 Mo (Apr) 10, 1712
All rem to Crosswix, N. J. 2 Mo (Apr) 1, 1714
John, s John, Flushing, con mo 8-4-1757
John, s Chas. & Eliz., Flushing, b 8 Mo (Oct) 12, 1722 d 12-31-1757
Ch: John
Charles
Christopher
John, s John, Flushing, d 12-17-1795
took cert of clear to Wby 9 Mo (Nov) 7, 1723; certified mbr 2-3-1758
Joseph, Flushing, d 1732/3
Margaret m 1770 Leonard LAWRENCE
she was his first cousin's dt, both dis 1-1-1771

DOUGHTY, continued
Martha (late Thorne) mo before 10-7-1778; ct N. P. 11-5-1778
Mary m 1730 William BURLING
Mary, dt Charles (dec), Flushing; m 1747 Zebulon DICKENSON
Mary, dt Chas. & Sarah, Flushing; m 1798 Joseph KING, N. Y.
Obadiah & Mary
Ch: Obadiah b 10 Mo (Dec) 30, 1735
Phebe, dt Charles, Flushing; m 1734 Richard CORNELL
Philadelphia, dt Benj., Flushing; m 1762 Nicholas TOWNSEND
Rebecca, dt Francis, Flushing, d 7 Mo (Sept) 7, 1747
Robert rem cert to Phila. (clear) 8-3-1758; returned (clear) 11-24-1758; cf Phila. 11-1-1759; certified mbr 1755
Robert gct Wby 1-7-1766, having rem
Samuel, s Charles (dec), Flushing; m Flushing 1 Mo (Mar) 10, 1747/8 Deborah WILLETS, dt Samuel LAWRENCE, (Deborah a wd)
Ch: William b 1-12-1758
Charles " 12- 1-1760
certified mbr 1755
Samuel, Jr. dis mo 8-4-1785
Sarah, Flushing, an ancient wd d 1726
Sarah, Flushing, recorded same time as Joseph, may be his w
Sarah Clements (form Doughty) dis mo 2-2-1786
Sarah, dt John & Abigail, Bkn.; m 1790 Isaac HICKS, N. Y.
William m Phebe ----- d 1 Mo (Mar) 10, 1714/15
Ch: William b 10 Mo (Dec) 4, 1710
Sarah " 9 Mo (Nov) 21, 1712
William & Ann
dis mo 4-6-1757
William, s Benjamin, Flushing, b 11-17-1755 d 5- 7-1812 ae 56y; m Mary ----- b 8-22-1755
Ch: Benjamin b 12-28-1785
Esther " 4- 6-1789
George Masters b 5- 6-1793
William took cert of clear to Wby 2-3-1785
Mary brought cert from Wby 8-31-1785

DOUGLAS
Benjamin D. & Mary
Ch: Benjamin b 12-21-1806
George W., s Frank H. & Grace C., b Newark, N. J. 1-20-1901; recrq 9-5-1917; ct First Friends Church, Pasadena, 6-6-1934

DOWNER
Esther, w Andrew O., rocf Bridgewater 8-3-1832; ct Bridgewater 11-5-1834

DOWNING
Benjamin d 8-14-1799 bHS
Daniel (nm) & -----
Ch: Abraham d 12-9-1803 ae 1y 4m bHS
Eliza " 12-21-1803 ae 3y
Dora (nm), dt James & Julia (nm); m 10-14-1915 Arthur McDowell CARPENTER (H)
Arthur recrq of parents 10-6-1894
George d 4-6-1842;m -----
Ch: George S. d 8- 4-1818 ae 3y 6m bHS (H)
recrq 5-1835
Jacob & -----
Ch: Eliza A. d 12-21-1803 ae 1y 8m bHS
Mary, dt Stephen & Phebe W., rocf Wby 11-1832 with parents; ct Wby 7-1850 (H)
Richard (nm) & -----
Ch: Rosetta K. b West. Co. d 8-2-1832 ae 10m 2d bHS
Samuel d 1-25-1801
Samuel B. rocf Wby 7-19-1826 (clear); dis 2-1830 (O); dis 1-1834 (H)
Silas rocf Wby 6-1839; ct Wby 6-1847 (H)
Silas & Sarah
cf Oswego 1-1853 for both; ct Oswego 1856 for both
Stephen (nm) & -----
Ch: Isaac b L. I. d 4-8-1832 ae 22y (unm) bHS
Thomas b L. I. d 12-22-1834 ae 26y bHS (unm)
Stephen d 3-21-1840; m Phebe W. ----- d 8-13-1844 (H)
Ch: Mary
Sarah R. d 7-24-1896
John " 8-16-1836 ae 11m 29d
cf Wby 11-1832
William (nm) b Oyster Bay d 1-31-1825 ae 37y (m)
----- & ----- (nm)
Ch: George b N. Y. d 3-11-1834 ae 3y 4m bHS

DOXY (Doxey or Doxsey)
Elizabeth Burk (form Doxy) rocf Oswego 7-17-1816 (clear); dis mo 3-4-1818; rst 1824

DOYLE
Thomas (nm) d 12-1-1881 ae 60y bPP; m (prob) Susan B. ----- d 9-24-1886 ae 60y bPP
Ch: ----- (dt) d 8-11-1863 ae 2y 6m bPP

DRAKE
Augustus & Tabitha (H)
Ch: Susan S. b 7-20-1799 d 5-31-1853
Mary F. " 1-10-1801 d 11-12-1877
Catherine
Celia b 11- 8-1810 d 11-24-1850
cf West Chester 11-1836 for all
Catharine rocf West Chester with parents 11-1836; ct Oswego 2-1840 (H)
Emily E. rocf Wby 6-1873; ct Pur. 8-5-1874
James (nm) & -----
Ch: Infant stillborn 7-26-1810
John (nm) m Rebecca ----- (nm) b Dutchin Co. d 2- 3-1830 ae 25y bHS
Hallock (nm), s Charles & Mary (nm); m 11-10-1857 Phebe B. TITUS, dt William T. & Mercy W. (Hallock), b Corn. 4-2-1839 d 9-29-1906 (H)
cf R. & P. 10-10-1896
Thomas d 9-30-1800 bHS

DRANDT
Otto A. d 2-10-1928; m Ella W. WINGATE, dt Charles & Mary (Robinson), b Bkn. 9-12-1856 d 12-13-1928 bPP in Wingate plot (both nm)

DRESLER
Dorothy E., dt John H. & Sophia F. (Schaeffer), N. Y., b N. Y. 2-18-1876; m 1906 Frederick W. CARPENTER (H)
recrq 5-6-1899

DREW
Jane H., dt Wm. & Susan, N. Y.; m 1865 Wm. P. CLOTHIER, of Phila. (H)

DRINKER
William Waln (nm) d 4- 6-1864 ae 63y 1m 27d bPP; m Joanna ----- (nm)
Ch: Edward d 4-29-1855 ae 21y 8m 12d bPP
Anna M. d 12-27-1855 ae 8y 10m bPP

DRIVER
Richard d 11-28-1803 bHS

DUBOIS
Evelyn Jeanne, dt Lucy M.; a foster child of Thomas & Anna MAIPHY
she was recrq of Lucy M. Dubois 12-6-1906 as Evelyn Jeanne Dubois; she resumed name of Dubois in 1930 & resigned
Gertrude, dt John Coert & Evaline P. (Kimball) b Hudson 4-29-1878; m 8-6-1907 Allan R. CAMPBELL (nm) (H)
recrq 5-9-1927; ct Pur. 5-14-1934
Koert (nm); m 11-25-1842 Mary HYATT, dt James B. & Sarah (Denel), b Stanford 8-31-1822 d 10-30-1914 (H)
cf Stanford 6-1858 for Mary; lived Bangall, N. Y.
Lucy M. m ----- LENT (nm)
recrq 10-3-1906; name erased 2-1926
(this appears to be Lucy's 2nd m, she had dt, Evelyn Jeanne Dubois rec 12-5-1906 on her rq)
Phebe, w Daniel P., dt James & Mary JENKINS (H)
cf Marl. 12-1848; dis 3-1-1859
Tuthill m Caroline TAYLOR, dt Isaac & Jane, d 4-15-1924 ae 80y 1m 22d bPP (both nm) (H)

DUCK
Sarah Elizabeth rocf Balt. 3-9-1848; dis 11-1849 for joining Episcopal Church
Sophia Louisa rocf Balt. 3-9-1848; dis 11-1849 joining Episcopal Church

DUDLEY
Amy (late Clark) dis mo 2-7-1810
Ann S., dt Abrm. & Margaret SHOEMAKER, b 5-15-1800, d 11-21-1889; ct Phila. 2-6-1878 (H)
Edward m Mary -----, of Mount Mellick, Ire., d 6- 3-1845 ae 74y 6m bHS
Ch: Margaret
William E. m 1836 Ann SHOEMAKER
Samuel
Edward b Ireland d 11-18-1835 ae 38y
Mary
cf Mount Mellick 6-24-1812 for the last 3 ch, the mother dec
Edward d 11-18-1835 ae 38y bHS; m Emma CLARK d 3- 9-1852 ae 90y bPP
Edward rocf Mt. Mellick, Ireland 6-24-1912
Emma dis mo 1-3-1814; rst 5-3-1815; dis 12-1839 (O)
Guilford d 11-13-1857 ae 42y bPP (prob nm)
John rocf Phila. 6-23-1814 (minor)
Joshua (nm) & Margaret
Ch: Infant stillborn 1-7-1833 bHS
Margaret, dt Edward & Mary, b Ireland d 1-10-1842 ae 41y; rocf Mount Melick, Ireland 8-23-1815 (clear) (unm)
Mary, dt Edward & Mary, rocf Mt. Mellick, Ire., 6-24-1812
Mary E., dt Edward & Mary, N. Y.; m 1821 Stacy B. COLLINS
Samuel, s Edward & Mary, d 1-10-1853; rocf Mt. Mellick, Ire., 6-24-1812; ct R. & P. 2-5-1823 (clear); cf R. & P. 1-1840
Samuel (nm) & -----
Ch: Edward b N. Y. d 4-9-1842 ae 1y 7m 5d bHS
William E., s Edward & Mary (dec), b Ireland d 8-27-1859 ae 40y bHS; m N. Y. 4-14-1836 Ann SHOEMAKER, dt Abraham & Margaret, N. Y. d 11-21-1889 ae 89y 6m bPP
ct Phila. 2-6-1878 for Ann; cf Dublin 6-13-1815 of tender years; ct R. & P. 2-5-1823 (clear); cf R. & P. 1-20-1830 (O); dis 11-1830 (O); cf R. & P. 8-1835 (H); dis 11-1830 (O)

DUELL
Catharine, dt John HULL, dis 2-1837 (H)
Sarah, w Joseph, rocf Troy 5-1833; ct Troy 3-1835 (H)

DUGAN
Susan Louisa (nm) m 1865 Jacob B. WOOLLEY (H)

DUKESHIRE
----- m Elizabeth O. TABER, dt Wm. C. & Caroline (Battey), b 3-9-1892
letter to Greenwood Baptist Church, Bkn.

DAMARTHARAY
----- (nm) m before 1874 Rebecca WHITFIELD, d 2-1915
Rebecca recrq 2-4-1874

DUMONT
Elizabeth M. (unm) d 5-12-1882 bPP
John B. (nm) m 10-6-1903 Annie A. WRIGHT, dt John Howard & Sarah J. (Walton), b N. Y. 11-3-1857; Annie A. m first Joseph P. MASON 1877 (H)

DUNBAR
Daniel m Naomi HALLETT
Ch: Rebecca b 11-27-1780
Mary " 6- 7-1782
Beulah " 10-15-1785
Naomi dis mo 5-4-1780; rst 2-3-1785
Mary m Daniel A. NEALE (both nm)
Mary, dt Daniel & Naomi, N. Y.; m 1803 Wm. L. SLOCUM
Naomi, wd, b Rahway d 2-21-1816 ae 68y bHS
Rebecca, dt Daniel & Naomi, m 1798 Jordan WRIGHT, N. Y.
----- m Naomi HALLETT
dis mo 5-4-1780

DUNHAM
Jemima (form Way) dis mo 12-3-1800 after ref. to Rahway

DUNLOP
Eleanor rocf Dublin 11-2-1898; name erased

DUNN
Cornelia, w George, dt Oliver C. HULL, b Troy 11-3-1832 (H)
Josiah rocf Woodbury, N. J. 2-10-1801 (clear) mo twice but having been part of the time in Savannah, escaped notice; dis 4-5-1809
Mahlon H., s S. Clifford & Louisa (Hendrickson), b Haddonfield, N. J. 6-20-1890; m 11-1-1913 Eleanor HALLOWELL, dt William & Anna T. (H)
Ch: Mahlon H., Jr. b Trenton 11-16-1915
Elizabeth Louise b Jersey City 11-6-1924
cf Chesterfield for father & s 7-10-1922; Eleanor mbr Horsham, Pa.; Eleanor rocf Horsham, Pa. 11-13-1922 (H)
Mary [Dunns] m George Wm. HUBBICK
cf Darlington, Eng. 1-1928 for both

DUPIN
Louisa recrq 11-1842; relrq 7-5-1871 absent over 5y; in New Orleans 1853 (H)

DURAND
Elizabeth (late Powell) dis mo before 5-7-1817

DURFEE
Anna B. m ----- MEDLOCK (nm)
recrq 8-1925
Bessie, dt Wm. W., b Gloversville, N. Y. 6-9-1884; m Eugene V. IRISH
recrq 3-1916
William W. & -----
Ch: Bessie B.
recrq 6-5-1912; Bessie recrq 3-1916

DURYEA
Ann Evans (form Duryea) dis mo 5-2-1781

DUSENBURY
Joan, perhaps w John, d 7 Mo (Sept) 20, 1703
John [or Dewsbury], Mk., dealt with for extravagance 1688 (perhaps h of Joan)
Mary, dt Henry & Jane, Pur.; m 1795 Penn FROST

DUTTON
Grace, dt Charles & Ellen, East Orange, b Chicago 8-5-1870; m 1904 Henry B. SEAMAN (H)
recrq 3-9-1907
James B., s John B. & Emma (Schooley); m 5-14-1868 Melissa Madeline KRAMER, dt Frederick & Sarah L.
Ch: John F. b Kalamazoo 11-27-1872
cf Fairfax 8-6-1890; John F. recrq 3-7-1894
John F., s James B. & Melissa M. (Kramer), b Kalamazoo 11-27-1872 d 10-26-1923 (or 4-24-1923); m 10-21-1902 Lauretta SMEDLEY, dt Lewis V. & Selina (Cox), b Westtown, Pa. 4-27-1874 (H)
Ch: Dorothy b 7- 2-1904
John Walthon b 10-14-1905
Chester Smedley b 3-16-1909
cf Goshen for Lauretta 8-6-1890; ct Goshen 3-12-1923 for Lauretta & ch

DU VALL
Charles Edward (nm), s Edwin & Emeline Hanah; m 9-21-1889 Mary Ella HULL, dt James C. & Caroline E. (Haviland), b N. Y. 8-2-1861 d 2-27-1928 (H)
Ch: Frank Stuart b 8-12-1890
Edward Harold b 5-24-1893
Edith Eloise " 6- 4-1895
Marguerite b 1- 2-1900
Edith Eloise, dt Chas. E. & Mary Ella (Hull), b Bkn. 6-4-1895; m William J. POTTER (H)
recrq of parents 1-5-1901
Edward Harold, s Chas. E. & Mary Ella (Hull), b Bkn. 5-29-1893 (H)
name entered by com. 5-2-1893; relrq 11-12-1910
Marguerite, dt Chas. E. & Mary Ella (Hull), b Bkn. 1-2-1900 (H)
recrq of parents 1-5-1901; relrq 11-9-1925, affiliated with another religious society
Mary Ella, w Charles E., dt Jas. C. & Caroline E., b 8-2-1861 (m 9-21-1889) (H)
Ch: Frank Stewart b 8-12-1890
Charles Russell b 3-25-1892 d 8-26-1892
Edward Harold " 5-24-1893
Edith Elioise " 6- 4-1895
Marguerite " 1- 2-1900
Edith L. b Bkn.; Marguerite b Hackensack; 3 ch names entered by com; last 2 recrq of parents

DWIGHT
William (nm) m Mary ----- (nm) b West. Co. d 5-22-1831 ae 30y 5m 18d bHS

EAMES
Edward gct Abington 9-5-1821 (clear)

EAMES, continued
Francis L. (nm), s Asa & Harriet (Seabury); m 10-1-1874 Sarah WRIGHT, dt William & Emily (Carpenter), b 2-3-1847 d 5-12-1908 (H)

EARL
John d Newport 11-11-1837; m Elizabeth S. ----- d 11-16-1852
cf Scipio 3-16-1820; dis 2-1831 (O); she dis 2-1841 (O)
Jonathan rocf Uxbridge in N. E. 11-27-1789; ct Uxbridge 12-3-1794 (clear)
Mary M. (nm) (form Orr) m 1897 Herbert W. CLAPP (H)
Oliver took cert of clear to R. I. 5 Mo (July) 2, 1720; he and w gct R. I. 4 Mo (June) 4, 1724
Phebe [Earle] rocf Phila. Cherry St. 2-1840; ct Phila. Cherry St. 7-1845 (H)
Pliny [Earle] rocf Frankford 8-27-1844; ct Uxbridge, Mass. 12-1856
Robert [Earle] & Anna Maria
cf WD MM 1853 for both; ct Oswego 8-7-1861 for both
Sarah, dt John & Dorcas, N. Y.; m 1828 Samuel MOTT (H)
rec without cert 8-1828

EARNSHAW
Cornelia L., dt Jos. W. & Lydia CORLIES, b 11-7-1838; dis mo 4-2-1862 (H)

EARP
Theresa death recorded 4-1928

EASTER
Hamilton, s John & Anne (both dec), Balt.; m at J. C. Haviland's, July 23, 1861 Anna HAVILAND, dt James C. & Phebe, Bkn., d 5-18-1868 (not under care of N. Y. MM) (H)
Ch: Lydia R.
ct Balt. 6-4-1862 for Anna
Lydia (nm), dt Hamilton & Anne (Haviland); m 1884 Edward S. FIELD (H)

EASTMAN
Mary m 1718 Elias Doughty, Jr.
Robt. Felt. (nm), s Howard P. & Sarah, Dayton, O.; m Bkn. 6-16-1917 Ethel P. UNDERHILL, dt Chas. F. & Rachel W., Bkn., b Bkn. 12-19-1885 (H)
ct Green Plains, O. 9-14-1931 for Ethel
Wesley, s James E. & Carrie (Coburn), b Orwell, Pa. 5-13-1900; m 6-27-1925 Beulah CARY (nm) dt Jesse Logan & Rose (Brock) (H)
Wesley recrq 12-10-1930

ECKSTEIN
Wilhelmina (nm), dt Erhardt & Johanna; m 1885 Josiah C. RIDER (H)

EDDINS
Margaret, dt Thos. K. & Clara B. (Russell), b Jonesboro, Ark. 3-9-1904; m 1923 Donald A. ROBERTS (H)
both recrq 1-8-1934

EDDY
Ann, dt Thomas & Hannah, b 11-25-1785; ct R. & P. 8-6-1806 (clear)
Casper Wistar rocf Phila. 11-30-1804; dis mo 2-3-1813
Charles rocf Phila. 2-23-1781, he having rq a cert to Cork & living in N. Y.; ct Cork 10-5-1781 (clear)
Charles rocf SD MM 6-28-1815 (minor); dis mo 11-4-1818
Hannah rocf Farm. 10-1847; ct Chap. 4-1858 (H)
Hannah, Jr., dt Thomas & Hannah, b 8-11-1784; ct R. & P. 8-6-1806 (clear); cf R. & P. 11-4-1808 (clear); ct R. & P. 5-4-1843 with sister & niece, Lucy E. Shipley
Henry rocf Peel, London 7-19-1815, a lad
James rocf SD MM 6-28-1815
Lucy H., dt Thomas & Hannah, b 8-15-1796; ct R. & P. 5-4-1842 with sister, Hannah, & niece Lucy E. Shipley
Thomas, s James & Mary, Merchant, N. Y.; b Phila. d 9-16-1827 ae 69y 11d; m N. Y. 3-20-1782 Hannah HARTSHORNE, dt John & Lucy, d 8-4-1832 ae 72y bHS
Ch: John H. b 3-14-1783 d 12-21-1817 (or 12-22-1817)
Hannah " 8-11-1784
Ann " 11-25-1785
Thomas " 2-25-1792
Lucy " 8-15-1796
Thomas rocf Phila. 11-30-1781 about to m with mother's consent; Hannah rocf Shrewsbury 2-4-1782; Hannah gct Phila. 2-5-1784; Hannah rocf Phila. 9-24-1790 with her 3 ch John, Hannah & Aron; Thomas rocf Phila. 7-29-1791; ct R. & P. 8-6-1806 with 2 ch, Thomas & Lucy; cf R. & P. 11-24-1808 with same 2 ch
Thomas, Jr., s Thomas & Hannah, b 2-25-1792; dis 11-1827 after a yr of dealing re failure

EDGAR
Clementine, dt Amos & Pamelia UNDERHILL; dis mo 4-1833 (H); dis mo 5-1-1833 (O)
Dorcas, dt James & Lydia, rocf Plains with parents 12-22-1829; ct Marl. 8-3-1836, minor, rem with parents
James m Lydia ----- d 1832
Ch: Margaret b 6-16-1825
Dorcas " 6-16-1825
William " 11-17-1829
cf Plains 12-22-1829 with 2 ch named; ct Marl. 8-3-1836 for Margaret & Dorcas; James dis 6-1836
Margaret, dt James & Lydia, rocf Plains with parents 12-22-1829; ct Marl. 8-3-1836,

EDGAR, Margaret, continued
minor, rem with parents
Sarah recrq 5-3-1820; ct R. & P. 2-6-1822
William, s James, b 11-17-1829; unknown for 20 yrs in 1862

EDGE
Walter S. m Mary DILLINGHAM
Ch: Margaret Janet b 8- 6-1908
cf Deer Creek, Md. 8-5-1908 for Walter; cf Phila. W.D. 7-1-1908 for Mary; Margaret active mbr 5-1925

EDGET
Webster rocf Coey. 1851; dis mo 4-1855

EDWARDS
Duncan (nm) m 5-9-1906 Susan W. CARLE, dt John J. & Cornelia R. (Willets), b N.Y. 3-27-1879 (H)
Eliza Ann, w Lewis, dt Chas. & Avis BARNEY, b 3-20-1827 d 9-11-1862 (m 4-29-1857)(H)
cf Nantucket 1-1857
Emma, dt Philo & Clarissa LEWIS; name erased 11-1886
Jane, dt Sarles & Phebe MILLER (H)
dis 5-1834; d 5-6-1835 for mo
John (nm) m Mary ----- (nm) b Sligo, Ireland d 9- 7-1817 ae 42y bHS
Mariana C., dt Wm. H. & Caroline E. LADD
cf Smithfield, Ohio, 5-1867 with parents; ct WD MM 11-4-1891 (Marianna L. in cert to Phila.)
Mary, dt Philo & Clarissa LEWIS, d 5-4-1891
Robert L. d 1-19-1898; m Eliza ----- d 2-28-1876
Robert recrq 6-1868; Eliza recrq 4-1868
----- & -----
Ch: Sarah C. d 12-24-1837 ae 2m 6d bHS

EELS
Rebecca F., w R. F., dt David D. & Sarah BYERLY (H)
ct Phila. 3-4-1874 after m

EGBERT
George F. m Fannie Ray BARRETT, dt Lucy E., b Beverly, Mass. 1878 d Liberty, N. Y. 4-7-1907 bPP (rem from Mt. Olivet Cemetery, L. I.)

EHRMAN
Artis H. (nm), s John & Mary A.; m 10-13-1886 Mary E. ALBAUGH, dt Henry C. & Sarah J. (Hull), b Balt. 11-27-1866 (H)
cf Balt. 10-9-1897 for Mary; name removed 11-9-1925 as she had not been heard of for many years

EILERT
Lucinda E., dt Jos. & Eliz. (Detwiler); m 1873 Dana B. CLOUGH (H)

ELAM
Robert rocf Brighouse MM, Eng., 4-27-1781 (clear); ct Brighouse MM, Eng., 2-5-1784 (clear); cf Brighouse MM, Eng. 5-18-1791; ct Brighouse MM, Eng., 3-1-1797 (clear)
Samuel rocf Brighouse MM, Leeds, 9-19-1777; cert as to his character while at Phila. 11-22-1780; ct Brighouse 4-5-1781 (clear) cf Brighouse, Halifax, 8-31-1781, he having left before his cert rec; ct R. I. 1-7-1793 (clear)

ELDRIDGE
Anna (form Macy) d Nantucket 12-5-1860 (H)
Anna d 9-19-1874; cf Nantucket; ct Duxbury, Mass. (H)
Stacy M. [Eldredge rocf Cherry St., Phila. 4-1848; dis 12-5-1860 (H)

ELLICOTT
Joseph C. b Pa. d 8-19-1826 ae 65y bHS (unm)

ELLIMAN
Mary E., w James B., dt Wm. SMART, rocf Flushing 6-1847; dis 7-4-1849 (H); dis 4-1848 (O)

ELLIOTT
Edmund, s Eli & Sarah B., b 8-18-1843; relrq 12-1-1880 (H)
Eli, s Eli (dec) & Margaret, N. Y.; m N. Y. 9-14-1837 Sarah P. UNDERHILL, dt Samuel (dec) & Eliza B., N. Y., d 5-11-1866 (or 5-18-1866 or 5-19-1866) (H)
Ch: Samuel b 7- 3-1838 d 8-13-1838
Edmund " 8-18-1843
cf Pipe Creek 3-1830
Margaret b Pa. d 12-16-1839 ae 61y bHS (unm)
Margaret (form Haydock) d 12-16-1856 ae 23y bPP
cf Grange, Ireland 12-22-1852; dis mo 4-1855 (prob sister of Sarah Jane Haydock)
Mary b Salem, N. Y. d 6-5-1821 ae 38y bHS (unm)
Wm. L., s Joseph & Isabella (both dec), Balt., Md.; m N. Y. 2-20-1889 Cornelia UNDERHILL, dt Abm. S. & Mary F., N. Y. (both dec)
Cornelia m 2nd William H. S. WOOD

ELLIS
Eliza (form Merritt) dis mo 12-7-1831
Robt. John Robinson (John Robinson later) rocf Darlington, Eng. 11-6-1907

ELLISON
Caroline rocf Oswego 12-1869 with Phebe E. & Sarah; death rpd 7-1920
Elizabeth rocf Burl. 6-6-1803 with her aunt, Eliz. Barker, minor, ct Goshen, Pa. for both 8-1-1810
John d 11-18-1882; m -----
Ch: Phebe E. d 1- 1-1877
Sarah
Caroline
cf Oswego 8-1870 for John; cf Oswego 12-1869 for ch
Phebe E. rocf Oswego 12-1869 with Sarah & Caro-

ELLISON, Phebe E., continued
line
Sarah d 3-21-1897; rocf Oswego 12-1869 with Phebe E. & Caroline
Thomas & -----
Ch: Anthony
Elizabeth
cf Chap. 5-15-1789; ct Chap. 12-2-1789; cf Chap. 11-11-1796 with w, Amy, & 2 youngest ch, Anthony & Elizabeth; ct Chap. 4-4-1798 for Thomas & Amy
William C. rocf Phila. 2-3-1864 d 4-26-1874 (H)

ELTON
Anthony (nm) b Burl. d 3-21-1826 ae 56y bHS
Anthony (nm) m Mary ----- (nm) b N. Y. d 2-29-1844 ae 74y 6m 6d bHS
William (nm) b Phila. d 7-18-1809 ae 16y 7m bHS

ELY
S. G. & Jeannie
Ch: (prob) Grace C. d 9- 5-1870 ae 5m bPP
" Henry S. " 7-30-1877 ae 5m bPP
cf Whitewater for Jeannie with foster parents, Henry & Grace Dickinson, 11-14-1852
----- m Hannah ROBBINS, dt Elizabeth (H)
cf Oswego for Hannah with mother 7-5-1875

EMBLY
Mary gct Phila. 9 Mo (Nov) 2, 1732

EMBREE
Abigail (late Bowne) dis mo 1-1-1772; rst 7-7-1773; ct Pur. 7-6-1774
Charles (nm) & Martha W.
Ch: Charles d 2-25-1853 ae 1y 9m 6d
Egginingham " 3-10-1853 ae 9m
Martha relrq 12-1864
F. Lawrence (nm), s George & Fanny; m 11-7-1899 Marie OGDEN, dt Henry Corbit & Eliz. (Beroman) (nm) b N. Y. 10-5-1870(?) (H)
Marie recrq 1-7-1905
George & Abigail
Ch: Samuel
Sarah
cf Pur. with 2 ch 11-13-1783; ct Pur. with 2 ch 9-1-1784; cf Pur. with dt, Sarah, (clear) 6-8-1797
Hannah b Flushing d 6-14-1817 ae 63y bHS (unm)
John, Flushing, took cert of clear to Wby 3-3-1716; m 2nd Charity DOUGHTY (m bet 4 Mo 2, & 5 Mo (July) 7, 1720
Lawrence, Flushing; m bet. 4-3 and 5-2-1771 (cert not recorded) Sarah PEARSALL
Ch: Nathaniel b 3-16-1776
ct Shrewsbury 1-7-1778 for all; cf Shrewsbury 3-1-1784
Mary (late Lawrence) dis mo 2-7-1781; rst 11-1-1815 & Flushing notified; cf Flushing 3-5-1829 (O)
Mary d 9-16-1831; cf Flushing 9-1829 (H)
Nathaniel, s Lawrence & Sarah, Flushing, b 3-16-1776 d 9- 6-1797
Robert C., s Lawrence E. (dec) & Sarah R., N.Y., m at J. Birdsall's 7-8-1852 Phebe S. BIRDSALL, dt James F. & Avis C., N. Y., b 4-7-1830 (not under care of N. Y. MM) (H)
ct Flushing 4-1862 for Phebe
Samuel, s George & Abigail d 8-4-1802 ae 25 on Island of Hispanola
cf Pur. with parents 11-13-1783; ct Pur. with parents 9-1-1784; cf Pur. as apprentice 2-9-1792
Sarah, Flushing d 3 Mo (May) 17, 1729
----- & -----
Ch: William L. b Flushing d 4- 1-1812 ae 5y 6m 6d bHS
Ann A. " N. Y. d 5-18-1827 ae 1y 2m bHS
William F. " " " " 8-15-1828 ae 1y 3m bHS
Edward " " " " 6-24-1841 ae 2y 7m 8d bHS
Thomas C. " " " " 5- 7-1844 ae 8y bHS
Franklin " " " " 2-20-1845 " 12y 19d bHS

EMERSON
Joseph B. rocf Butternuts 10-28-1835 (minor); ct Bridgewater 10-5-1842
Raymond (nm), s Edw. Waldo & Ames (Keyes); m 4-12-1913 Amelia FORBES, dt J. Malcolm & Sarah C. (Jones), b Milton, Mass. 11-29-1888 (H)
Amelia recrq 2-13-1933
William, Jr. (nm), s Wm. & Susan (Haven), d 2-29-1914; m 11-24-1863 Sarah H. GIBBONS, dt James S. & Abigail (Hopper), b N. Y. 9-19-1835 d 1918 (H)
Sarah ret a mbr

EMLEN
James rocf Chester, Pa. 7-31-1809; ct Chester 9-1-1813 (clear)

EMMANUEL
John M. recrq 8-1-1906; ct Seattle

EMORY
John Comegys (nm), s Stuart R. & Anna (Comegys), N. Y.; m at 253 - 5th Ave., N. Y. 3-13-1886 Sarah Hull LEGGETT, dt Wm. F. & Sarah (Hull), N. Y., b N. Y. 2-1-1843 d 7-15-1926
in Hollywood, Calif. 1900

ENG
----- & ----- (nm)
Ch: Emeline d 9-19-1828 ae 1y 1m bHS

ENGLAND
Rachel rocf Wilmington 1-30-1841; ct Phila.

ENGLAND, continued
----- & -----
Ch: Richard b N. Y. d 10-15-1842 ae 5m 9d bHS

ENGLE
David D. & Margaret C.
Ch: Marion Fenimore 13
William Clothier 11
cf Burl. 6-10-1903 for David; Margaret recrq 5-6-1903; ch recrq of mother 5-6-1903; ct Montclair 2-5-1930 for parents; death recorded 6-1923
Eva H., dt Edith E.; m Oliver PROCTOR (nm)
cf Evesham, N. J. with mother 3-1924
Marion Fennimore, dt David D. & Margaret C., b about 1892 (11 in 1903); m Joseph Alexander COOK
recrq of mother 5-6-1903
----- m Edith E. ----- d 12-1928
Ch: Eva H.
Amos W. d 2-13-1926
Joseph W.
cf Evesham, N. J. 3- 9-1924 for all

ENGLISH
John rocf Cork 4-11-1779 (clear); ct Dublin 7-4-1810 (clear)
William rocf ND MM 11-22-1796 (clear), having brought cf Pontefract 10-8-1795; ct Brighouse, Eng. 3-2-1803 (clear); cf Brighouse 10-21-1803; ct Brighouse 3-2-1808

ENGS
----- & -----
Ch: Philip b N. Y. d 6- 7-1824 ae 3y 1m bHS

EPPENDORFF
Max, s Geo. A. W. & Juliana (Landgraff), b Dresden, Germany 11-4-1820 d 5-21-1906 bPP; m Sarah HOWLAND (perhaps Sarah R., dt John H. & Sarah), d 5-1915 ashes bPP

ERWINE
Dorcas m 1693 Daniel KIRKPATRICK

ESCHWEGE
Nina, dt Herman & Bessie, b London, Eng. 10-24-1874; m 4-25-1903 Herbert H. FIELD in London (H)
recrq 2-8-1926

ESMOND
Eseias, s John, Flushing
Frederick E., s Joseph & Rhoda (Titus), b 1-16-1854 Fulton, N. Y. d 11-9-1904 bPP; m Lulu NASE
Ch: Ethelwynne d 12-15-1904 ae 20y bPP
(both nm)
Jacob, s John, Flushing, d 1735
John, Flushing & -----
Ch: Eseias
Jacob d 1735

ESTABROOK (or Esterbrook)
Richard & -----
Ch: Mary Elsie d 7-29-1867 ae 9m bPP
Thomas & -----
Ch: Alfred d 1-15-1834 ae 8y 11m 8d bHS
John " 10-17-1834 ae 25y bHS

EVALETH
Mary rocf Shrewsbury 7-1842; ct Shrewsbury 1-3-1866 (H)

EVANS
Abigail, dt Crowell & Frances, N. Y.; m 1811 Elijah H. RUNNELLS
Alice, dt Joshua D. & Rebecca G.; m D. F. CARMICHAEL
cf Phila. with mother 2-21-1854; mbrp relinquished 3-1880
Amy, dt Lewis & Sarah (Birdsall), b Bkn. 4-21-1861 d 2-19-1935 bPP; m Robert DANBY (both nm)
Ann, w Lemuel, dt ----- DURYEA
dis mo 5-2-1781; rst 12-1789; ct Burl. as w of Lemuel
Annie E., dt Lewis B. & Sarah J., b N. Y. 9-26-1857 d Boston 6-27-1923 bPP; m Herman T. GILBERT (both nm)
Caleb G., s Joshua D. & Rebecca G., rocf Phila. with mother 2-21-1854; mbrp relinquished 3-1880
Eleanor, dt Joseph & Alice, N. Y.; m 1828 Mordecai BUZBY (H)
Eliza G., dt Joshua D. & Rebecca G., m ----- OTIS (mo)
cf Phila. with mother, this taken as a resignation 1869
Frances rocf R. & P. 2-18-1807, rem with her h
Francis J. recrq 4-1872
George L., s Louis & Sarah (Birdsall), b N. Y. 8-26-1863 d 4-23-1935; m Julia -----
Jessie Viola rocf Chicago 2-1-1905; ct Edgewood, Kans. 10-2-1907
Joel, s John, d 1-18-1804 ae 22y bHS (unm)
John rem 7 Mo (Sep) 4, 1740
Joseph d 2-25-1829; m Alice -----
Ch: William P.
Ellen
Samuel d in Ohio
Wilson
Joshua David rem (O)
Robert E.
cf Balt. WD 7-11-1823 for all but Joshua; Joshua dis 1829-1842 (O); ct Phila. 4-1839 for Alice
Joshua, s Joseph & Alice, gct Burl. 7-4-1832 (minor)
Lewis (prob the Lewis B. who d 4-6-1868 ae 45y bPP) m Sarah J. BIRDSALL d 12-31-1904 ae 70y 3m 2d bPP
Ch: Amy b 4-21-1861 (nm)
George L. " 8-26-1863 (nm)
Lydia J. recrq; ct Burl. 2-1871
Mary Frances m ----- LEACH

EVANS, Mary Frances, continued
recrq 4-1871; ret a mbr after m
Mary K., dt Joshua D. & Rebecca G.; m 1871 Edward PARRISH
cf ND MM 2-21-1854 with mother; relrq 3-1878
Priscilla, dt Mary; m ----- SHARP
recrq 3-1872; ret a mbr
Rebecca B., w Joshua D., d 6-27-1868
Ch: Joshua D., Jr. b 9-30-1852
Eliza G.
Caleb G.
William Gill
Alice
Mary K.
cf ND MM 2-21-1854
Robert E., s Joseph & Alice, rocf Balt. 7-11-1823 with parents; ct Phila. 4-1839 with mother (H)
Samuel gct Middletown, Pa. 7-7-1830 (clear), cert ret as he had ret to N. Y.; ct Fairfield, O., 9-4-1833, ret 1835 as he could not be found
Sarah Jane, dt Geo. H. & Phebe BIRDSALL, b 11-21-1834 d 12-31-1904
ret a mbr
Thomas & -----
Ch: Thomas b N. Y. d 3-26-1831 ae 8m bHS
mbr elsewhere
Wm. Gill, s Joshua D. & Rebecca, rocf ND MM 2-21-1854 with mother; mbrp relinquished 3-1880
William P., s Joseph & Alice, rocf Balt. 7-11-1823 with parents; dis 12-1828 (H); dis 7-7-1830 (O)
Wilson, s Joseph (dec) & Alice; m N. Y. 11-15-1838 Susan SINCLAIR, dt John & Elizabeth, N. Y. d 1-25-1868 ae 46y bPP (H)
Ch: Elizabeth S. b 11-26-1839
Joseph " 2-26-1842
cf Balt. 7-11-1823 with parents; ct Phila. 8-1829; cf Phila. 12-1836; ct Solesbury 6-1843 for all
----- m Mary ----- d 7-22-1875 ae 58y 4m 8d
Ch: Priscilla
Mary & dt recrq 3-1872
----- & -----
Ch: Sarah M. b N. Y. d 2-17-1827 ae 1y 4m 15d bHS
Morris A. b N. Y. d 10-9-1828 ae 2y bHS
Rebecca B. d 3-13-1860 ae 5y 1m bPP
Lewis B. " 4- 6-1868 ae 45y bPP
Jennie " 9-28-1870 ae 4y bPP
(some ch may be Lewis B.'s)

EVARTS
Sherman (nm), s Wm. Maxwell & Helen M., d 10-22-1922; m 4-30-1895 Alice COCK, dt Effingham & Harriet (Haight), b N. Y. 9-28-1866
Alice recrq 12-12-1927 (H)

EVERITT
Amelia, dt Richard & Mary C., Bkn.; m 10-9-1862 Joseph D. SHOTWELL (H)
Ann [Everit], dt Thos. & Eliz., Bkn.; m 1817 John Townsend HALLOCK, of Marlborough
Anna R., dt Valentine & Beulah, Bkn., b 2-6-1848; m 1870 Lawrence HURLBURT (nm), of Utica (H)
relrq 5-2-1894
Caroline L., dt Valentine & Beulah E., Bkn.; m 1858 Josiah MACY, Jr. (H)
Catharine m ----- HICKS (mo before 4-2-1823)
cf Wby 1808 with parents; dis mo 4-2-1823
Edward Augustus, s Valentine & Beulah, b 6-8-1854; relrq 2-3-1886 (H)
George dis mo 6-5-1816
Henry, s Thomas, d 7-20-1885; m Sarah Ann KIRBY d 12-30-1899
Ch: Henry b 4-11-1834 d 2-15-1835
Susannah Valentine b 12-21-1835
Theodore Edgerton b 5- 4-1842 d 1-28-1847 (H)
cf Pur. 12-1833 for Sarah Ann
Jane Elizabeth, dt Richard & Mary C., Rahway, b 3-19-1839 d 1-30-1908; m 12-8-1874 Samuel H. SHOTWELL (H)
Richard, s Thomas & Susanna, Bkn., b 2-27-1798 d 12-13-1880; m N. Y. 11-12-1823 Mary CARLE, dt Jacob & Phebe, d 10-21-1860
Ch: Jane d 11-30-1824 ae 2m
Amelia b 7-14-1827
George W. b 5-22-1834 d 2-11-1835
George H. " 2- 1-1835 (marked dec)
Edward " 11-19-1836 d 12-24-1836
Jane Elizabeth b 3-19-1839
Mary rocf Wby 7-19-1809, minor, left with her gr parents; both dis 1830
Susannah V., dt Henry & Sarah Ann (Kirby), Bkn. b 12-21-1835 Bkn. d 11-4-1931; m 1867 Henry COFFIN (H)
Thomas d 1-26-1846; m Susannah ----- d 1-19-1836 (H)
Ch: Thomas
Ann
George
Richard
Valentine dis 3-1830 (O)
Phebe d 8-31-1854; dis 12-1829 (O)
Catharine
Henry dis 3-1832 (O)
cf Wby 7-20-1808 for all but Thomas, Jr.
Ann (clear); parents dis 1829 (O)
Thomas & Susannah
Ch: Henry b 6-30-1809
Thomas, Jr. dis mo 5-4-1814
Thomas, s Thomas & Susannah, rocf Wby 3-19-1806, apprentice to Samuel Hicks
Thomas, s Valentine & Beulah E., Bkn., b 9-14-1846 d 3- 5-1898; m at Geo. E. BYXBE's, N. Y. 11-5-1862 Carrie A. LANSING, dt Durck C. & Susan F. (both dec), N. Y. (not under care of N. Y. MM) (H)
Valentine, s Thomas & Susannah (dec), N. Y., b 10-10-1800 d 10-23-1874; m Bkn. 2-15-1838 Beulah E. KIRBY, dt Edmond & Sarah

EVERITT, Valentine & Beulah E., continued
(dec), Harrison, b 8-15-1812 d 7-13-1891
(H)
Ch: Caroline Louisa b 12- 9-1838
Thomas " 9-14-1840
Catharine Hicks b 12- 4-1842 d 9-19-1865
William Henry " 3- 9-1845 " 7-27-1846
Anna Ross " 2- 6-1848
Valentine, Jr. " 1-26-1851 " 4-28-1853
Edward Augustus " 6- 8-1854
cf Pur. 12-1837 for Beulah
----- & -----
Ch: Catharine b Bkn. d 1-26-1827 ae 1y 1m bHS
George " " " 7-27-1829 ae 1y 2m bHS

EVERNGHIM
Abigail, dt Gilbert & Phebe, N. Y.; m 1821 Wm. R. THURSTON
Elizabeth M., dt James & Avis, b 7-9-1821; ct Farm. with parents 2-5-1823; cf Roch. 7-1837 (H)
Elizabeth R., dt Joseph & Susan R., b 11-8-1816; m ----- BATES
dis mo 3-1837
Gilbert, s Mary, N. Y., b N. J. d 4-21-1831 ae 73y; m N. Y. bet. 4-7 and 5-6-1784 (cert not recorded, Gilbert had joined the mtg 9-3-1783 Phebe DELAPLAINE b 11-8-1752 N. Y. d 12-5-1834 ae 82y 10m 27d
Ch: Abigail b 5-10-1785
Joseph " 10- 9-1786
Mary " 7-14-1788 d 2-17-1818
James " 7- 5-1790 d 2-28-1792 ae 1y 7m 23d
Gilbert " 8-14-1794
James
Gilbert dis 1830 (O)
Gilbert, s Gilbert & Phebe, b 8-14-1794; mo before 3-1-1820, case discontinued 12-6-1820 ct Farm. 9-3-1823 for Gilbert (O)
Gilbert, s Joseph D. & Susan R., b 8-15-1818; name cancelled 4-9-1904 (H)
Henry, s James & Avis, b 1-3-1819; cf Roch. 7-1837; ct Farm. 9-1839; cf Farm. 8-1843; dis 2-1847 (H)
James, s Gilbert & Phebe, N. Y.; m N. Y. 11-13-1816 Avis B. MOTT, dt Samuel & Elizabeth, N. Y., b West. Co. d 3-18-1831 ae 33y (James b N. Y. d 6-24-1835 ae 43y 2m 28d)
Ch: Maria M.
Henry b 1-30-1819
Elizabeth " 7- 8-1820
Elizabeth " 7- 9-1821 d 1-10-1911
Samuel M. " 5- 8-1825 " 1- 6-1911
Delaplaine " Roch. d 10- 3-1829 ae 1y 6m
James d 2-21-1831 ae 7m
ct Farm. 2-5-1823 with Maria M., Henry & Elizabeth; cf Roch. for Maria M., Henry, Elizabeth & Samuel M. 11-1831
Joseph D., s Gilbert & Phebe, d 4-24-1864 ae 76y 6m 16d bPP; m Susan R. ----- b Blazing Star, N. J. d 6-22-1824 ae 39y (H)
Ch: Margaret R. b 5-11-1810
Phebe Anna d 5-27-1824 ae 13y 7m 18d
Sarah S. d 3-27-1824 ae 10y 3m 12d
Elizabeth R. b 11-8-1816
Gilbert D. " 8-15-1818
Susan R. " 5- 3-1820
Jacob R. " 11-18-1821 d 8-18-1822
Lydia W. " 6-27-1823
cert of clear to R. & P. 6-7-1809; Susan rocf R. & P. 1-17-1811
Joseph D. m 2nd N. Y. 7-12-1827 Louisa WILSON, dt Ebenezer & Hepzibah, N. Y., d 11-18-1889
Ch: Helen Louisa b 4- 4-1828
Delaplaine d 10-3-1829
Phebe Anna b 12- 3-1839
Julia Ross " 3- 3-1832 d 2-18-1837
William Thurston b 2-24-1834
Mary Josephine " 3-25-1836
Louisa recrq 1825; Joseph D. dis 5-1829 (O)
Louisa dis 8-1830 (O); ct R. & P. 4-1-1846 4-2-1846; cf R. & P. 6-1851 for Joseph & Louisa
Margaret R., dt Joseph S. & Susan, b 5-11-1810; dis mo 10-1833 (H) to ----- BELL; dis 1-1832 (O)
Maria M., dt James & Avis; m ----- LEEDS (H) cf Roch 7-1837; dis mo 5-1838
Samuel, s James & Avis B., rocf Roch. 7-1837 (H)
Susan R., dt Jos. D. & Susan, b 5- 3-1820; m ----- WILSON (H)
dis mo 9-1844
Unity (late Pancoast), rocf Upper Springfield 1-6-1796 with her 3 ch, Asa, Thomason & Hannah Pancoast; ct N. P. 6-5-1800 (clear)

EVERS
Elizabeth (late Whitehead) dis mo before 5-7-1806

EVES
Edward, s William & Deborah, rocf Edenderry, Ire., 5-23-1816, apprentice to master of a trading vessel of N. Y.

EWER
Edward m Anna RUSHMORE
Ch: Edith Rushmore
Paul R. b 11-27-1899
Edmund R. " 6-23-1901
cf Sandwich, Mass. 4-4-1894 for Edward; Anna recrq 7-6-1898; Edith R. recrq of parents 7-6-1898; ct Sandwich 4-1-1908 for all

EYRE
Edward D. rocf Phila. 10-1862; ct Phila. 12-1863 (H)
Jacob & Elizabeth Ann
Ch: Harriet b 6-30-1806

FAILES (see also FAYLES)

FAIR
Alice, dt Robert & Ann M., d 12-11-1932 ae 93y bPP; m Levvineus DE GRAFF
Ch: Emeline d 12- 9-1850 ae 1y 10m bPP (H)
Robert (nm) d 2-16-1857 ae 44y bPP; m Ann M. ----- d 7-26-1899 ae 86y 9m 27d bPP
Ch: Infant stillborn 4-20-1839 bHS
Thomas b N. Y. d 2- 4-1846 ae 3y 6m bHS
Emeline d 12- 7-1851 ae 1y 10m bPP
William John d 12-30-1859 ae 14y 6m 3d bPP
Alfred H. " 9-19-1860 ae 4y 8m bPP
Alice
Thomas d 5-14-1854 ae 74y bPP; m Ann ----- b Ireland d 10-29-1847 ae 83y (H) (Ann may be w of another Thomas) cf Corn. 5-28-1828 for Thomas; dis 3-1832 (O) for non attendance

FAIRBANKS
Henry rocf Balby 5-14-1835; dis mo 3-1838

FAIRLAMB
Francis rocf SD MM 6-26-1811 (clear); marked absent & off

FAIRLEE
Eliza Ann b N. Y. d 7-27-1830 ae 17y bHS

FALCONER
Samuel m Hester ----- b Middletown, N. J. d 1-29-1820 ae 44y 4m 12d bHS
Samuel m 2nd at Mamaroneck 4-15-1824 Rachel M. CARPENTER, dt Samuel & Rebecca W., Plains, d 9-8-1871
Samuel recrq 8-1798; cf Pur. 9-7-1824 for Rachel M.; Samuel dis 4-1829 (O); Rachel M. dis 2-1841 (O); Rachel M. relrq 4-5-1865 (H); Rachel recrq 4-1865 (O)

FALES
Adelaide, dt Jonas & Hannah DINEGAR, Mt. Vernon, m 10-30-1901 Thomas T. HILLIARD, s Jos. & Ann, Salem, N. J. (Adelaide, wd, b Livingston, N. Y. 3-21-1842) (H)
recrq 8-10-1901
Emily J., dt Geo. & Mary, Thomaston, Me.; m 1864 John I. ROBERTS, of Bkn. (H)

FANCHER
Esther E. rocf Corn. 3-1883; relrq 10-5-1892

FARLEY
Elizabeth, dt Peter & Eliz. VAN COTT; dis 3-1830 (H)

FARO
Jarvis, Springfield, N. J.; m at Hope Willits' 11 Mo (Mar) 1701 Elizabeth WILLITS, dt Hope & Mary, Wby
rem to N. J.

FARQUHAR
Mary Anna, dt Edmund & Phebe S. UNDERHILL, b 7-1-1821; dis mo 11-1842

FARRAND
James, s Matthew, Eng., rocf Tottenham, Eng., 3-21-1839; ct Poughkeepsie with brother & sister recorded in N. Y. without comment; ct Oswego 1850
Jane, w Matthew, dt ----- FARRINGTON, d 9-1848 bPP
Mary Anne, dt Matthew, Eng.; m ----- CLARK cf Tottenham, Eng. 3-21-1839 with brother & sister to Poughkeepsie, recorded in N. Y. without comment; dis mo 1-5-1842
Matthew, s Matthew, Eng.; m 10-1843 Jane T. MARSH, dt E. FARRINGTON, b 4-25-1803 d 10-2-1848
Ch: Mary Anne dis 1842 (O)
James
cf Tottenham, Eng. 3-21-1839 with brother & sister, to Poughkeepsie, recorded in N. Y. without comment; Matthew dis 1-1851
Sarah Harvey Van Norsdal (form Farrand) dis mo 4-1851

FARRELL
John D. d 10-23-1878 ae 53y bPP; m Mary Ann ----- d 2-1891
Ch: Alice b 1-26-1862 d 8-31-1862
John recrq 10-5-1859; Mary Ann recrq 12-1866; ct Dublin, Ireland 4-1865; cf Carlow, Ireland, 1-1868 forwarded to Pokeepsie & then held 8 yrs while they lived near Troy & other places, returned to N. Y. 5-1876 as they were in N. Y. as he had rq in another religious society his mbrp is relinquished & Carlow rq to send cert for Mary Ann; Carlow could not give cert as mbrp had ceased 8 yrs ago; Mary Ann recrq 2-1877
----- & -----
Ch: Mary L. d 10-1885 ae 30y bPP

FARRINGTON
Abigail, Flushing; m 1700 James CLEMENT
Abigail called wd in m intention
Abigail, Flushing; m 1714 Thomas HEDGER or Hedges
Abigail Lawton (form Farrington) dis mo 8-4-1785
Amelia, dt Geo. & Eliz. (dec), N. Y.; m 1845 John D. WRIGHT (H)
Amos White, s Ezra & Hannah, b 8-15-1813; ct Battle Creek 4-1856 (H)
Ann, dt Ezra & Hannah; m ----- HIGBY; dis 4-1831 (O); dis 12-1835 (H)
Anna, Flushing; m 1743 Edward BURLING
Anna M., dt Margaret, d 6-25-1905 ae 73y 1m 11d; m Thomas H. GARNER (both bPP) (nm) (H)
Bridget, Flushing; m 1718 John RIDER, Jr.
Catherine b L. I. d 10-11-1839 ae 79y 2m; m 1781 Thomas TOM; dis mo 1-4-1781; rst 2-3-1819; dis 12-1829 (O)
Charity, dt Ezra & Hannah (Hyde), b Bkn. 7-20-1816 d 1-12-1901; m 1835 Richard PLATT

FARRINGTON, Charity, continued
dis 3-1836; recrq 2-1840 (H)
Charles dis mo 4-4-1784
Charles W., s Ezra & Hannah, b 11-28-1819 (H)
In St. Louis 1856
Deborah Nelson (form Farrington) dis mo 3-7-1787
Dorothy, Flushing, rpd mo before 10 Mo (Dec) 8, 1676
Edward, Flushing; m Frances SMITH, Wby
Ch: Ann b 8 Mo (Oct) 28, 1733
cert of clear to Wby 7 Mo (Sep) 7, 1732; ct Pur. 5-3-1759
Ezra d 4-29-1860 ae 84y bPP; m Hannah ----- d 4-29-1866 ae 87y bPP
Ch: Sally D.
Ann
Maria
Amos White b 8-15-1813
Charity " 3-22-1816
Charles W. " 11-28-1819 d 1894
con mo Wby sends cert to N. Y. 5-18-1808; all dis (O)
George dis mo 12-6-1780; rst by Flushing 3-5-1817
Hannah, dt Matthew, Flushing; m 1722 Moses MOLINEAUX
Hannah, dt Thomas, Flushing; m 1751 Samuel THORN
Hiram (nm) m Margaret ----- d 5-11-1849 (H)
Margaret recrq 10-1838
Jane, dt Geo. & Elizabeth, N. Y.; m 1838 Joseph WILLETS (H)
Jane, dt E.; m ----- MARSH; m 2nd 10-1843 Matthew FARRAND (H)
Jesse rocf Ama. 12-14-1787 (clear); ct R. & P. 10-6-1790 (clear)
Jesse b West. Co. d 8-9-1835 ae 65y; cf Flushing 3-4-1813 (clear); dis 1-1830
John, Flushing; m Elizabeth ----- d 4 Mo (June) 1, 174-, N. Y.
John active mbr from 1693 to 1701
Ch: Elizabeth d 1715
John " 12 Mo (Feb) 4, 1715/16
Marcy (or Marey) d 12 Mo 8, 1715/16
Sarah d 1721
John, s Thomas, Flushing; m Flushing 9 Mo 9, 1749 (Nov) Mary BOWNE, dt Samuel, dec, Flushing
John, Flushing, & -----
Ch: Sarah Fowler b 1 Mo (Mar) 22, 1724/5
Mary " 12-12-1763
Kexia took cert 6-4-1752 (may be w of Thomas)
Lydia, dt Thomas, rocf Pur. 9-10-1767
Lydia gct Pur. 8-6-1761; rocf Pur. 12-3-1767
Margaret (nm) d 8-22-1851 ae 88y bPP (H)
Maria recrq 5-1-1822
Maria, dt Ezra & Hannah, dis 11-1829 (H); dis 2-1833 (O)
Maria rocf Flushing 12-1841; d 3-26-1857
Mary, dt Matthew, Flushing; m 1735 William PHILLIPS
Mary (nm) d 8-22-1851 ae 88y bPP
Mary d 8- 9-1835; rocf Flushing 12-4-1806; dis 12-1829 (C)
Mary recrq; m; dis 5-1833
Matthew, s Matt., Flushing;m Flushing 7 Mo (Sep) 20, 1716 Hannah HEDGER, dt Hannah, d 9 Mo (Nov) 1740 (Matthew d 9 Mo (Nov) 1728)
Ch: Sarah b 9 Mo (Nov) 18, 1689
Nathan " 5 Mo (July) 4, 1693
Edward " 10 Mo (Dec) 30, 1695
Hannah " 9 Mo (Nov) 14, 1698
Mary " 4 Mo (June) 6, 1701
Joseph " 10 Mo (Dec) 21, 1703
Benjamin " 9 Mo (Nov) 14, 1705
James " 9 Mo (Nov) 10, 1709
Thomas " 3 Mo (May) 29, 1712
Matthew, Flushing; m Hannah ----- d 2-4-1788
Permelia, dt John & Mary, Flushing; m 1804 Benjamin CORNELL
Samuel con mo 7-7-1755
Sarah, dt Matthew, Flushing; m 1725 Samuel VAIL
Sarah, dt Thomas, Flushing; m 1740 James THORN
Sarah m 1770 Benjamin HAVILAND
Sarah b Bridgetown, N. J. d 3-9-1812 ae 36y bHS
Sarah D., dt Ezra & Hannah, N. Y.; m 1839 Daniel S. THORN; m 2nd Benjamin LEWIS (nm) (H)
recrq 1824; dis 1831 (O)
Thomas, s Thomas (dec), Bayside, Flushing; m Sarah WAY, Jr., dt John & Sarah (ltm 7 Mo (Sep) 6, 1716
Ch: Samuel b 2 Mo (Apr) 28, 1718
Abigail d 4 Mo (June) 3, 1740
(Thomas, the father, d 8 Mo (Oct) 19, 1732)
Thomas m Elizabeth ----- d 10 Mo (Dec) 9, 1747
Thomas, Flushing & Kezia
took cert of clear to Pur. 7 Mo 7, 1749;
Kezia brought cert from Pur. 1 Mo 1, 1750
Timothy rocf Wby 11-16-1803; ct Oswego 11-4-1807
Walter, s John (dec) & Mary), Flushing; m Flushing 12-9-1784 Amy SEAMAN, dt Gilbert & Mary
Walter m 2nd Flushing 11-8-1787 Mary FIELD, dt Caleb (dec)
Ch: Sarah b 10-20-1790
Anne " d 5-22-1791
Anne " 12-25-1793
William, Flushing & Susannah
Ch: Elizabeth b 10 Mo (Dec) 30, 1732

FARWELL

Joseph rocf Richhill, Ireland 10-29-1833 to Hudson MM, recorded in N. Y. without comment (clear)

FASSETT

Emma (nm) m 7-13-1881 Daniel J. CARPENTER (H)

FATHERLY

Robert E. rolf M. E. Church, Hollis, N. Y. 1-2-1929; ct Wby MM 8-6-1930 (H)

FAUSTMAN
Monica (nm) m George GOERKE

FAYLE (see also Failes)
Joshua rocf Grange MM, Ire., 11-20-1822
(clear) (long absent)

FAZER
----- & -----
Ch: Eliza b N. Y. d 4-14-1842 ae 8m bHS

FEAKS
Deborah, Mk. m 1716 Thomas WHITSON, Jr.
Elizabeth, dt John, Mk.; m 1710 Benjamin FIELD
Hannah [Feake], dt Robert; m 1656 Mk. John BOWNE
Hannah [Feek, Feake], dt John & Eliz.; m 1698 James COCK
John [Feake], s Lt. Robert, of N. E., Mk., b N. E. 1639 d 3 Mo (May) 1724; m at Matt Priar's 7 Mo (Sep) 15, 1673 Elizabeth PRIAR, dt Matt, d 11 Mo (Jan) 25, 1701/2
Ch: Elizabeth b 4 Mo (June) 9, 1674
Hannah " 8 Mo (Oct) 6, 1675
Mary " 2 Mo (Apr) 30, 1678
John " 5 Mo (July) 10, 1679; d 1-18-1683/4
Robert " 4 Mo (June) 22, 1683
Sarah " 12 Mo (Feb) 17, 1685/6
Martha " 8 Mo (Oct) 27, 1688
Abigail " 6 Mo (Aug) 7, 1691
Deborah " 11 Mo (Jan) 5, 1695/6
active from 1672
Martha [Feake], dt John & Eliz. (dec), Mk.; m 1713 John CARPENTER
Mary, dt John & Elizabeth; m 1699 Henry COCK
Mary [Feake], Mk., rem 7 Mo (Sep) 4, 1740

FELLOWS
Thomas & Alice
Ch: James
Thomas
John
William
cf Pur. 5-11-1820 with 3 ch named; ct Hardshaw East 5-7-1823 with 4 ch named

FENNYERE
----- & Ruth
Ch: John T. death rpd 12-1928
Wilfred H.
Ruth recrq 4-3-1907; ch recrq of mother 7-3-1912

FERGUSON
Albert (nm), s George & Hannah, d 10-15-1892 ae 50y 8m bPP (H)
Amelia A. d 11-25-1925; rocf Cork 10-2-1907
David, s George, Jr., d 2-7-1909 ae 74y 10m 23d bPP; m Helen ----- (nm)
Ch: Edward W. d 3- 2-1896 ae 32y bPP
Ellen " 7-23-1895 ae 20y 11m 27d
George A.
Deborah, dt George & Sarah, d 1-16-1908 ae 84y m ----- BAUWIS (bPP) (H)
Eliza (prob Elizabeth, dt Geo. & Sarah), dt George; m Charles H. GRIFFEN (H)
cf Plains 5-1816; dis 8-3-1854 (H); dis 1-4-1832 (O) (mo)
Elizabeth J., dt John C. & Elizabeth (Pierce), b North Castle 2-5-1844 d 1-8-1924; m 1866 Philip VAN EVEREN (H)
cf Chap. 10-7-1868
George d 11-20-1849 ae 77y 7m bPP; m Sarah ----- d 5-17-1862 ae 88y 3m bPP (H)
Ch: Hannah d 4-18-1853 ae 58y 6m bPP
John
Mary " 12-28-1849 ae about 20
Deborah
Sarah H. b 12-23-1799 d 7-10-1870 bPP
George " 9- 3-1801
Israel " 2-17-1804 " 8-14-1819
Elizabeth b 10- 9-1806
Rachel " 2-16-1809
Ann " 7-22-1817 d 10-24-1858 bPP
Sarah rocf ND MM 8-28-1798; ct Marl. 7-1-1812 with 8 ch; cf Plains 12-26-1815 with 6 minor ch; all dis (O); cf R. & P. for George 11-15-1798
George, Jr., s George & Sarah, b 9-3-1801 d 4-6-1868; m Hannah L. ----- (nm) d 11-26-1885 ae 75y 9m 26d bPP
Ch: David R. b N. Y. d 4-12-1833 ae 1y 2m bHS
George F. b N. Y. d 2-17-1842 ae 5y 6m bHS
Charles " " " " 2-20-1842 ae 3y 4m bHS
George d 7- 5-1847 ae 3y 11m 5 d bHS
David
dis mo to first cousin 8-3-1831
George A., s David & Helen, d 3-27-1917 ae 49y 6m 27d bPP; m Elsie L. ----- (H)
James (nm) b N. J. d 1-26-1830 ae 54y bHS
John m Susan ----- b Fishkill d 5-25-1824 ae 29y
Ch: Sarah L.
Mary V.
cf Plains 5-21-1815 for parents; Mary V. & Sarah L. dis 2-1841 (O); John dis 4-5-1820 for attending theater and neglect
John (nm) b Phila. d 2-27-1837 ae 40y 2m bHS & -----
Ch: Infant stillborn 8-16-1833 bHS (mbr)
John H. (nm), s George & Julia, d 7-1-1904; m 6-20-1895 Mary E. VAN EVEREN, dt Philip F. & Elizabeth J., b Bkn. 1-27-1870 (H)
Ch: Elizabeth b Bkn. 4-17-1896
name entered by com 6-4-1890; ct Orange Grove, Calif. 5-9-1921 for Mary & Elizabeth; Elizabeth recrq of parents 1-7-1899
Mary Effie, w John H. (nm), dt Philip F. (nm) & Eliz. J. VAN EVEREN, b 1-27-1870
Ch: Elizabeth Van Everen b 4-17-1896
Mary E. name entered by com. 6-4-1890; Elizabeth V. name entered by MM
Mary V., dt John & Susan, d 9-1842; m Gilbert COUTANT (H)
Rachel, dt George & Sarah; m ----- SHERWOOD

FERGUSON, Rachel, continued
dis mo 12-1836 (H); dis 2-1841 (O); recrq 1-1859 (H)
Sarah L., dt John & Susan; m ----- CONTANT (H) dis mo 6-1837 (H); dis mo 2-1841 (O)
William (nm) m Amelia Anne ATKINS, dt William & Kathleen (Kingston), b Ireland 5-6-1845 d 11-27-1925 bPP
Amelia bur as a mbr but no record found
William B. (nm) b Phila. d 12-25-1828 ae 34y bHS (unm)
William B., s Peter, b 12-5-1823 d 7-29-1908 in Jersey City bPP (m)
----- & -----
Ch: Louise C. d 7-10-1861 ae 28y bPP
Charles Elgar d 9-16-1861 ae 2m 26d bPP

FERRIS
Ann (or Anna), dt Dr. Valentine & Anna SEAMAN, b 3-18-1812; dis 12-1843 (H)
Anna H., dt John & Jane W., Throg's Neck; m 1851 Augustus TABER
Anne, dt John & Anna, N. Y.; m 1794 Dr. Valentine SEAMAN
Cornell rocf Pur. 6-2-1784, a lad, apprenticed; ct Pur. 1-2-1788 (clear)
Deborah (nm) m 1913 G. Edmund STRATTAN (H)
G. Edmund gct Moorestown 5-9-1921
Elijah rst 4-7-1819, dis not found; Pur. notified; Pur. accepted him as mbr 10-6-1819
Elijah, s John & Anna, of Westchester, Merchant, N. Y.; m N. Y. 1-2-1791 Phebe HAVILAND, dt Ebenezer & Jane, N. Y. d 5-19-1801 ae 30
Ch: Anna b 2-26-1793 d 6-19-1805 ae 12y 3m
Phebe Jane b 9- 6-1797
John Haviland b 11-17-1799
Elijah rocf Pur. 6-10-1790 (clear)
Erastus (nm) m Mary Abby YEATES, dt Samuel & Jane (minard), b 1-16-1844 (m 2-22-1886) (H); Mary ret a mbr
John, Flushing, Westchester Co., d 1715; m 2nd Grace ----- d Flushing 12 Mo (Feb) 28, 1715/16
John active 1684-1700
John, Westchester Co., gct Oblong 2 Mo (Apr) 6, 1748
John & Ann (or Anna)
Ch: Elizabeth
cf Pur. 6-13-1793; ct Pur. 3-5-1800; Elizabeth clear
John H., s Elijah & Phebe (dec), N. Y., d 9-4-1862; m N. Y. 6-8-1825 Jane UNDERHILL, dt Joshua & Mary (dec), N. Y., b 11-23-1801 d 8-8-1877
Ch: Infant stillborn 2-22-1826
Anna H. b 4- 6-1827
John H. Jr. b 12-22-1829 d 6-28-1850
Infant stillborn 12-10-1837 bHS
ct Pur. 6-6-1810 for John H. with sister, Phebe J.; cf Pur. for John H. 5-12-1824; parents dis 1829 (H)

Jonathan rocf Pur. 8-3-1792 (clear); dis mo 12-2-1803
Lindley Murray con mo 11-2-1836; cf Pur. 5-9-1832 (clear); ct Corn. 2-5-1840; cf Marl. 10-1860; relrq 7-1889
Lindley Murray, dt Elijah (dec) & Amelia, Throgg's Neck; m N. Y. 4-12-1854 Mary MURRAY, dt Robert I. & Eliz. C. (dec), N. Y.
L. Murray Jr., s Lindley M. & Caroline (dec), N. Y., b 9-27-1839; m N. Y. 11-12-1861 at Paulina Sands' Martha I. SANDS, dt David (dec) & Paulina, N. Y., d 1-9-1880
Ch: David Sands b 8-13-1863 d 8-19-1915
Caroline " 2-28-1865 " 3- 7-1865
cf Marl. 10-1860 for Lindley M.
Mabel L., dt Robert M. & Mary A. T., Pokeepsie, b 8- 6-1873; m 1907 Edward N. MENNELL, of Shirly, Eng.
Mary m 1686 Nathaniel UNDERHILL
Mary, Westchester d 1704 (perhaps dt John & Mary)
Phebe, dt John & Mary, Westchester; m 1700 Edward BURLING
Phebe J., dt Elijah & Phebe, gct Pur. 6-6-1810 with brother, John H.
Philip Livingston, s T. & Sophia (Neave), b 7-28-1909 N. Y., glt Presbyterian Church, Dobbs Ferry 4-1925; active mbr 4-1925
Robert M. m Mary Anna T. ----- d 8-29-1877
Ch: William Taber b 7-16-1866
Caroline Murray b 10-20-1870
Mabel " 8- 6-1873
Robert Murry, Jr. b 1876
cert of clear to New Bedford 9-6-1865; cf Marl. 11-7-1860 for Robert; cf New Bedford 11-1866 for Mary; ct Pokeepsie 4-6-1878 for father, Caroline M. & Robt. M. Jr.
Sands rocf Pur. 8-11-1791, apprentice to John White
Sarah, dt John & Mary, Westchester; m 1719 Samuel HARRISON
William L. d 8-13-1886; rocf Pur. 6-8-1825, minor; ct Pur. 12-1829; cf Pur. 1-1865
William Taber, s Robt. M. & Mary Anna, b 7-16-1866; m 6-1-1905 Sophia NEAVE, d 8-16-1916
Ch: Philip Livingston b 7-28-1909
Francesca " 4- 6-1912
William Jr. " 4-30-1913
cf Cheshire, Eng. 8-31-1905
Zachariah gct Wilmington 3-3-1758
Zachary rem to Newark MM, Pa. 4 Mo (June) 6, 1745
----- & -----
Ch: Reed b Albany d 9-23-1823 ae 8y bHS
Mary Louisa " 3- 2-1876 ae 5y 2m 22d bPP

FETTER
Sarah, w Manuel, dt Abraham & Susan COCK (m 1837); dis 9-5-1838

FICKETT
Phebe M. rocf Flushing 8-4-1825, rem with h

FICKETT, continued
Samuel (nm) b Me. d 11-15-1842 ae 74y bHS;
m Hannah ----- (nm) b Cape Elizabeth, Me. d 2-24-1822 ae 49y bHS
Samuel m 2nd Phebe ----- b L. I. d 6-3-1830 ae 50y bHS
Scott H. (nm) b Portland, Me. d 10-4-1829 ae 33y

FIEHN
Arthur, s Carl & Louisa (Bachhoffer), b Bkn. 2-22-1884; m 9-2-1908 Clara SCHLICHT, dt Otto & Caroline (Bogemann), b Bkn. 12-31-1885 (H)
both recrq 8-13-1917

FIELD
Aaron, s Richard & Deborah M.; m Charlotte C. ----- d 4-24-1862 ae 31y (H)
Ch: Fannie E. b 4- 3-1856
Henry C. " 12-30-1857
Edward S. " 11-12-1860
cf Corn. 8-1854 for Charlotte
Aaron m 2nd at J. C. Haviland's 12-11-1865 Lydia S. HAVILAND, dt James C. & Phebe, Bkn., b Jericho 4-28-1838 d 11-12-1917
Ch: Herbert H. b 4-25-1868
Hamilton Easter b 4-21-1873 d 4- 9-1922 bPP (unm)
Anna Haviland b 10-5-1875 d 5-26-1883 bPP
cf Jericho 7-1844 for Lydia (Aaron, the father, d 4- 9-1897 ae 67y 7m 19d bPP)
Abigail con mo 3-1-1759
Abigail rocf Hudson 2-24-1797, minor, to live with a relation; ct Ama. 8-3-1803 (clear)
Abigail (or Abby Jane), dt Charles & Martha, b 5-24-1806 N. Y. d 8-26-1837 ae 31y 2m bHS; m ----- YOUNG (mo)
ct Pur. 2-1-1809 with mother
Ambrose gct Corn. 9-6-1809 (clear); cert returned as he lived in Albany; cert endorsed to Coey. 6-5-1811
Ann, dt Caleb & Ann, Flushing; m 1783 John BOWNE, s John & Dinah
Anna H., dt Edw. S. & Lydia R. E., Bkn., b Bkn. 9-13-1885; m 1913 Howard S. FLETCHER, of Boston (H)
recrq of parents 5-5-1900
Anne d 8- 9-1796
Anthony, s Benjamin, Flushing; m Flushing 6 Mo (Aug) 13, 1730 Hannah BURLING, dt William, Flushing
rem to Pur. 1 Mo (Mar) 6, 1739/40
Benjamin, Flushing; m Experience ALLEN, Shrewsbury (1tm 6 Mo (Aug) 27, 1692)
Experience brought cert of clear from Shrewsbury
Benjamin, s Anthony & Susannah, Flushing, d 10 Mo (Dec) 1, 1732; m Flushing 9 Mo (Nov) 30, 1691 Hannah BOWNE, dt John, d 10 Mo (Dec) 30, 1707
Ch: Benjamin b 12 Mo (Feb) 1692/3
John b 11 Mo (Jan) 13, 1694/5
Samuel " 8 Mo (Oct) 10, 1696
Anthony " 5 Mo (July) 28, 1698
Hannah " 5 Mo (July) 20, 1700 d 10 Mo 30, 1707
Joseph b 4 Mo (June) 12, 1702
Sarah " 6 Mo (Aug) 17, 1704
Robert " 7 Mo (Sep) 7, 1707
Benjamin m 2nd at Flushing 12 Mo (Feb) 23, 1709/10 Elizabeth FEAKS, dt John, d 1724
Benjamin active mbr from 1684
Benjamin, s Benj. & Hannah, Flushing, b 12 Mo (Feb) 5, 1692/3 d before 1734; m Flushing 2 Mo (Apr) 13, 1727 Sarah TAYLOR, d 1734
Caleb, s Thomas & Hannah, Flushing, b 11 Mo (Jan) 5, 1705/6 d 2-10-1769; m at Flushing 9 Mo (Nov) 13, 1746 Ann RODMAN, dt Thomas & Elizabeth, Flushing
Ch: Thomas b 7 Mo (Sep) 28, 1747 d 1-26-1772
Caleb certified mbr 1755
Catharine rocf Oblong 2-12-1798, minor, gone with her mother
Charles gct Pur. 4-4-1810
Charles d 8-2-1862 (or 8-3-1862) ae 77y bPP; m Martha ----- d 12-8-1855
Ch: William
Abigail b 5-24-1806
Hannah
cf Pur. 4-10-1806 for both; ct Pur. 2-1-1809 for Martha with 2 ch, William & Abigail, rem with her h; cf Marl. 12-1830 with dt, Hannah; Charles & Martha dis 1836 for non-attendance; Charles restored 4-1857
Charles M., s Richard & Deborah, b 3-19-1823 d 2-12-1885; m 11-9-1847 Anna C. CROMWELL, dt David & Rebecca (Bowman), b N. Y. 9-13-1823 d 12-25-1912 bPP (H)
Ch: Henrietta C. b 8-16-1848 d 12-29-1851 bPP
Richard B. " 9-18-1850
Caroline " 1-21-1852 d 12-30-1890 bPP
Frederick C. " 7-18-1854 " 10- 7-1866 bPP
William D. C." 11-29-1858
Charles M. " 12-28-1860
Charlotte C. " 11-23-1862 d 1-21-1887
cf Corn. 2-1848 for Anna
Charles Merritt, s Charles M. & Anna (Cromwell) b Bkn. 12-28-1860 d 9-26-1916 ae 55y 8m 26d bPP; m 10-15-1896 Anna P. LYNES (nm) dt Stephen C. & Caroline S. (H)
Deborah rocf Pur. 5-7-1752
Deborah, dt Robert; m ----- BETTS
dis mo 8-7-1760
Deborah, dt William & Hannah, N. Y.; m 1797 John PIERCE
cf Oblong 12-12-1796 (clear)
Deborah, dt Peter, b 9-17-1781; ct Oswego 6-4-1808 (clear)
Edward d 7-29-1882 ae 70y 8m 12d bPP; m Josephine L. ----- d 8- 7-1907 ae 74y 11m 22d bPP (H)
cf Ama. 10-1852
Edward S., s Aaron & Charlotte C., b 11-12-1860 Bkn.; m 9-10-1884 Lydia R. EASTER, dt

FIELD, Edward S., continued
Hamilton & Anne (Haviland)
Ch: Anna Haviland b Bkn. 9-13-1885
Katherine Hamilton b Great Neck b 8- 5-1894 (8-4-1894)
Infant b 7-12-1896
Elizabeth, Flushing, b 10 Mo (Dec) 7, 1750
Elnathan, s Susannah, Newtown; m -----
Ch: Elizabeth b 4 Mo (June) 24, 1696
Robert " 3 Mo (May) 12, 1698
Elnathan " 9 Mo (Nov) 19, 1700
Elnathan m 2nd Elizabeth BULLOCK, late of Barbados (m at his mother's 5 Mo (July) 9, 1701
Fannie E., dt Aaron & Charlotte, Bkn., b 4-3-1856; m 1879 Henry E. GRIFFEN (H)
Gilbert certified mbr 1758
Hannah, dt Benjamin, Flushing; m ----- HAVILAND, of Rye
Hannah d Rye 9 Mo (Nov) 26, 1721
Hannah, Flushing, b 10 Mo (Dec) 6, 1728
Hannah m 1763 Ebenezer RAYMOND
(probably dis for m by priest)
Hannah con mo 1-1-1772
Hannah, dt Charles & Martha; m Charles MOUNTAIN dis 5-6-1863 (H)
Harriet, dt Wm. H. & Mary (Carpenter), b Port Chester 1-20-1872; m 1903 Wm. Halleck SNYDER (H)
recrq 3-11-1916
Henry C., s Aaron & Charlotte C., b 12-30-1857 d 11-14-1885 bPP; m 9-14-1881 at S. L. Haviland's Adelaide H. HAVILAND, dt George & Sarah Louise (Childs), b Bkn. 4-21-1862 (H)
Ch: Louise b 2- 2-1883
Henry C. b 1- 4-1886
Adelaide & Louise rec 5-6-1885
Henry C., s Henry C. & Adelaide (Haviland), b Bkn. 1-4-1886; m Helen FREEMAN (nm) (H)
Herbert H., s Aaron & Lydia S. (Haviland), b Bkn. 4-25-1868 d 4- 5-1921; m in London 4-25-1903 Nina Sefton ESCHWEGE, dt Herman (nm) & Bessie, b London, Eng. 10-24-1874 (H) Nina recrq 2-8-1926
Jacob, s Thomas & Hannah, Flushing, certified mbr 1755
Jerusha rocf Pur. 12-13-1837; ct Ama. 2-1863
Jesse & Phebe
Ch: Richard
Rebecca
cf Pur. 7-14-1791; ct Chap. 4-3-1793 with ch (not named)
John, s Benjamin, Flushing, d 3-23-1773; m Flushing 11 Mo (Jan) 12, 1720/1 Elizabeth WOOLLEY, dt John, Shrewsbury, d 6-1-1769
Ch: Hannah d 3-20-1773
John
John, s John & Eliz., Flushing, certified mbr 1758
Joseph, s Thomas & Hannah, Flushing; m Flushing 6 Mo (Aug) 16, 1750 Mary RODMAN, dt Thomas & Elizabeth, d 8 Mo (Oct) 30, 1751 ae about 22
Joseph dis mo 5-2-1754
Joseph Coles (nm) b Putnam Co. d 7-24-1813 ae 43y 11m 2d bHS (m)
Josiah, s Uriah & Mary; m Hannah G. ----- d 8-30-1824
Ch: Phebe
Sarah
Maria M. dis 2-1830
Richard Mott d 10-23-1819 ae 5y 8m 7d
cf Chap. 10-11-1816 with 4 ch named; Josiah dis 1829 (H)
Josiah m 2nd in N. Y. 10-11-1827 Sarah HALLETT, dt James & Phebe, N. Y.
ct Oswego 2-1869 for Sarah
Katherine H., dt Edw. S. & Lydia R. E., Bkn., b Great Neck, L. I, 8-5-1894 (or 8-4-1894); m 1917 Guy Carlton HESTER (H)
recrq of parents 5-5-1900
Louisa M., dt Richard & Deborah M., Bkn., b 8-3-1826 d 2-12-1914; m 1859 Edward H. STABLER (H)
ct Balt. 1-1860; cf Balt. 2-1866
Maria M. m ----- BOWRON (mo) (H)
cf Chap 11-1816; dis 2-1832
Marielma, dt Henry C. & Mary (Schureman); m 1876 Solomon HAVILAND
Mary, dt Caleb, Flushing; m 1787 Walter FARRINGTON
Mary, dt George E. & Ann (Stevens), b Cincinnati, O. 1880; m 1913 Lemuel E. PARTON (H)
both recrq 7-13-1931
Moses rocf Chap. 2-12-1796, a lad
Nathan, s Thomas & Hannah, Flushing; m Flushing 12 Mo (Feb) 10, 1725/6 Elizabeth JACKSON, dt James & Rebecca, Flushing
Nathaniel, Newtown; m Patience BULLOCK, late of Bermuda(ltm 5 Mo (July) 3, 1701); they took cert 6 Mo 6, 1702 to Burl or elsewhere
Oliver (nm) b Pur. d 11-18-1826 ae 61y bHS (m)
Peter & Phebe
Ch: Zebulon b 4-16-1780 d 8-19-1801 ae 21
Deborah " 9-17-1781
Peter " 10-21-1783
Ambrose " 7- 9-1785
Phebe " 11-10-1789
Maria " 7-10-1796
Walter " 7-16-1798
cf Coey. 10-23-1800 for all, Deborah clear; ct Oswego with their 3 minor ch, Phebe, Maria & Walter
Peter (nm) m Rachel b Bridgeport, Conn. d 11-20-1821 ae 17y bHS
Ch: Thomas S. d 3-30-1821 ae 4m bHS
Edward " 7- 1-1832 ae 16y bHS
Phebe, dt Joshua & Hannah, N. Y.; m 1826 Josiah BARNES
cf Chap. with parents 10-11-1816; ct Pur. 5-1827
Phebe d 1-28-1891; m David R. UNDERHILL (H)
Richard, s Aaron & Jane, d 11-23-1875 ae 83y; m N. Y. 12-11-1816 Deborah MERRITT, dt John & Phebe, d 10-8-1875 ae 78y bPP
Ch: Charles M. b 3-19-1823

FIELD, Richard & Deborah, continued
Ch: Louisa M. b 8- 3-1826
Aaron " 8-21-1829
cf Pur. 4-9-1812 (clear); Richard & partner, John Haviland, dis failure 10-7-1817; rst 5-1-1822; all dis (0)
Richard C., s Charles M. & Anna (Cromwell), b Bkn. 9-18-1850 d 3-22-1921; m 1-7-1874 Mary C. MANNING, dt Richard H. & Mary (Weeks) (H)
Ch: Richard Manning b 8-29-1882
Richard C. m 2nd Helen G. FRASER (nm) (m 4-3-1901)
Richard Manning, s Richard C. & Mary C. (Manning), b Bkn. 8-29-1882; m 3-26-1908 Eleanor SMITH, dt Wm. T. & Annie T., b Bkn. 2-1-1887 (H)
Ch: Phebe Titus b Maplewood, N. J. b 3-30-1910
Donald M. d 5- 4-1910 ae 1y 3m 23d bPP
Richard relrq 2-13-1928; Eleanor's name entered by com. 12-3-1890
Richard Mott, s Josiah, d 10-28-1819 ae 5y 8m 7d
Richard T. rocf Ama. 5-16-1812 (clear); dis mo 9-1-1813
Robert, s Robert & Charity, Newtown; m Susannah -----
Ch: Robert (active mbr from 1689)
Robert, s Robert & Susannah, Newtown, d 2 Mo (Apr) 13, 1701; m at Edmund Titus', Wby 12 Mo (Feb) 24, 1689/90 Phebe SCUDDER, wd Samuel, dt Edmund TITUS, d 1 Mo (Mar) 10, 1742/3; abt to rem to Mamaroneck (Pur) 1 Mo (Mar) 5, 1729/30
Robert, s Benjamin & Hannah, Flushing; m Flushing 9 Mo (Nov) 13, 1729 Rebeckah BURLING, dt William, Flushing, d 12 Mo (Feb) 2, 1736/7
recorded twice; rem to Horseneck (Lloyd's Neck, O.B.) where Rebecca d
Rodman con mo 2-5-1783 (mc 1781)
Samuel, S. Benjamin, Flushing; m Flushing 1 Mo (Mar) 7, 1718/19 Mary PALMER, dt William (dec), Mamaroneck
Sarah, dt Benjamin & Hannah, Flushing; m 1724 James CLEMENTS
Sarah d 1724
Sarah, dt Thomas, Flushing; m 1735 John CLARKE took rem ct Chesterfield, Pa. 10 Mo (dec) 4, ----
Sarah (prob dt Josiah & Hannah), d 4-22-1852 ae 50y bPP (H)
Josiah & Hannah rocf Chap. 10-11-1816 with ch including Sarah)
Sarah S., dt Josiah & Hannah G., N. Y.; m 1821 John S. BOWRON
Stephen (nm) d 6-27-1821 ae 22 bHS (unm)
Susannah, Newtown; m 1700 Isaac MERRITT
Thomas d 1- 3-1761 ae 87y; m Hannah ----- d 2-2-1761 ae 81y
Ch: William b 10 Mo (Dec) 22, 1701
Nathan " 9 Mo (Nov) 30, 1703
Caleb " 11 Mo (Jan) 5, 1705/6
Ch: Jacob b 5 Mo (July) 23, 1708
Mary " 10 Mo (Dec) 30, 1710
Sarah " 7 Mo (Sep) 6, 1712
Hannah " 5 Mo (July) 24, 1715
Thomas " 9 Mo (Nov) 28, 1719 d 10 Mo 9, 1748
Joseph " 2 Mo (Apr) 29, 1722
had been m nearly 60y
Whitehead dis mo & giving money to pay for men to go into the war against the French, 5-1-1760
William, s Thomas, Flushing, b 10 Mo (Dec) 22, 1707 d 3- 4-1759
William m Hannah VAN WYCK bet. 6-7- & 7-4-1764 (cert not recorded)
William m Hannah BURLING
Ch: Peter
William
Stephen
John
cert for all including Hannah's ch, Ann & Phebe Burling, to Oblong 5-4-1775
William D. C., s Charles M. & Anna (Cromwell), b Bkn. 11-28-1858 d 12- 6-1916 ae 58y bPP; m 5-15-1890 Violet V. HINRICHS (nm), dt C. F. A. & Louisa (Dotten) (H)

FIELDING
William, s Thos. Peter & Ann (Fearuley), b Haddonfield, Yorkshire, 7-29-1841 d 1-1-1927; m 3-7-1863 Ann FLEMING, dt Thomas & Sarah (Hartley), b Halifax, Eng. 3-11-1843 d 2-28-1916 (H)
both recrq 2-8-1913

FINCH
Hannah B. W., d 10-9-1879; m ----- (H)
Ch: William Y.
cf Shrews. 2-4-1885 for Hannah; William recrq of Hannah 5-6-1885
John W. d 12-15-1933; m Charlotte ----- (H)
John transferred from Albany 1-8-1916
lived Rider's Mills, Columbia Co.
Thomas Ellwood, s David L. & Eliza (Coffin), b Chatham 1-12-1849 d 9-14-1926; m 1-12-1874 Anna M. PALMER, dt Samuel L. & Sarah E. (Caine), b Milford, N. H. 4-25-1851 d 10-23-1929 (H)
Thomas rocf Hudson & Chat. 4-25-1900; Anna recrq 3-13-1909
Willie M., s Orville & Ocelia, d 10-3-1919 ae 57y bPP; m Ada M. ----- Jr. (all nm) (H)
William Y., s Richard S. H. & Hannah B. W. (Cook), b N. Y. 8-14-1871; m 4-25-1900 Jennie QUICK (nm), dt David R. & Emma R. (H) recrq of mother 5-6-1885

FINK
Emil (nm), s Ernest & Anna; m 10-2-1874 Ada BYRON, wd of -----, dt Seth & Sally (Osborn) PANCOAST, b Phila. 11-6-1853
Ch: Herbert H. b Jersey City 4-12-1883
Helen

FINK, Emil & Ada, continued
cf Phila. 7-13-1912 for Ada; ct Phila. 11-14-1932 for Ada
Helen, dt Emil & Ada P., Phila., b Jersey City 8-11-1878; m 1908 Abner P. WAY (H)
recrq 2-10-1912; ct Pur. 4-12-1935 with h & s
Herbert H., s Emil & Ada Byron, b Jersey City, 4-12-1883; m 2-24-1917 Eunice BEATTIE (nm), dt James W. & Gertrude B. (H)
recrq 6-12-1915

FIRMIN
Arthur E. recrq 12-6-1882; mbrp cancelled 4-9-1904 as long unknown (H)

FIRTH
Sidney (nm) m Mary A. BOWRON, dt John S. & Sarah, b 10-16-1842 d 12-12-1893 bPP (mo)
dis mo 2-6-1887 (H)

FISH
Mary, w Preserved, rocf New Bedford 6-19-1810; ct Hardshaw West. 5-1827; cf Hardshaw West. 1829; dis 12-1829; d 11-13-1839

FISHER
Anna W., dt Redwood & Rebecca, rocf Phila. 2-21-1833 with other ch, minors, living with parents; dis 12-1839
Edward (nm) m 5-31-1862 Susan BIRDSALL, dt Samuel & Susan A., b 11-27-1844 d 8-13-1864 bPP (H)
Francis Rotch, s Redwood & Rebecca, rocf Phila. 2-21-1833 with other ch, minors, living with parents; marked "off" in pencil
Grace gct Phila. 12-2-1756
Henry rocf Brighouse, Eng., 8-19-1836; ct Hardshaw West. 1-2-1839 (clear)
Joshua rocf Brighouse, Yorkshire, 7-17-1835; ct Hardshaw West. 1-2-1839 (clear)
Lamar W., s Redwood & Rebecca, rocf Phila. 2-21-1833 with other ch, minors, living with parents; marked "off" in pencil
Mary Ann d 6-19-1871; rocf Scip. 2-1871
Miers, s Redwood & Rebecca, rocf Phila. 2-21-1833 with other ch, minors, live with parents; marked "off" in pencil
Phebe, w Nicholas, d 10-19-1874; rocf Chap. 6-1832 (H)
Susan, w Edward, dt Samuel & Susan A. BIRDSALL, b 11-27-1844 d 8-13-1864 (m 5-31-1862) (H)
----- m Josephine WRAY, dt Joseph B. & Hannah B., b 2-27-1885

FITCH
Hezekiah b Salisbury, Eng., d 8-4-1828 ae 59y
m Sarah BELDEN, d 4-22-1852 ae 50y
cf Stanford 7-23-1825 for both

FITZGERALD
Margaret, dt Gerald & Amelia, Pur.; m 1791
Isaac SHERMAN
cf Pur. 4-8-1790 (clear)

FITZPATRICK
---- m Bessie WINDER, dt Alfred & Martha L., d 3-28-1925 ae 47y (all nm) (H)

FITZ RANDOLPH (see also RANDOLPH)
Caroline Eliza, dt John L. & Eliza, N. Y.; m 1845 Josiah L. HARVEY
Edward, s Edward, Woodbridge; m Flushing 8 Mo (Oct) 3, 1734 Phebe JACKSON, dt James, Flushing
Eliza [Fitz Randolf]
Dr. John Lindley, s Robert & Phebe, Annapolis Royal, N.E.; d Nova Scotia 1823; m N. Y. 9-12-1811 Eliza WILLIS, dt William & Jane, N. Y.
Ch: James Cornwall b 4-24-1814
Edmund d 7-31-1834
----- & -----
Ch: Edmund d 7-31-1834 ae 17y 10m 21d bHS

FLANDREAU
Letitia d 8-11-1849; cf Pur. 8-13-1845
Nelson Eugene (nm); m Eleanor TOWNSEND, dt George & Frances (Buchanan), b Tarrytown 10-11-1881 (H)
Ch: Frances b New Rochelle 7-3-1913
Eleanor recrq 4-6-1901; Frances recrq of parents 7-12-1920

FLANSBURGH
Catharine H., dt John H. & Maria (Bradt), b New Salem, N. Y. 2-18-1847; m 1868 Charles WOOD (H)
both transferred from Albany 1-8-1916

FLASH
Edward (nm), s Alexander & Rachel; m 12-21-1853 Frances SERRILL, dt Pearson & Rachel (Starr), b Phila. 9-2-1830 d 12-11-1906 (H)
cf Darby 5-1856 for Frances

FLEMING
Ann, dt Thomas & Sarah (Hartley), b Halifax, Eng., 3-11-1843 d 2-28-1916; m 1863 William FIELDING (H)
both recrq 2-8-1913
Thomas, s James & Sarah (Ainley), b Halifax, Eng. 11-8-1818 d 11-18-1913 ae 95y; m 1840 Sarah HARTLEY (H)
recrq 4-8-1905

FLETCHER
Albert W. rocf S. 8th St., Richmond, Ind. 4-6-1910; letter to M. E. Church, Lenore, Okla. 2-1917; in Texas 1912
Althea (nm), dt Alfred P. & Katharine (Leahy); m 1932 C. Gayton POSTLETHWAITE (H)
Howard S. (nm), s Edw. C. & Ruth, dt Elizabeth (Stetson), N. J.; m at 106 Columbia Hts., 9-20-1913 Anna H. FIELD, dt Edw. S. &

FLETCHER, Howard S. & Anna H., continued
Lydia R. C., Bkn., b Bkn. 9-13-1885 (H)
Ch: Howard Stetson, Jr. b Brookline May 8-5-1914
Anna recrq of parents 5-5-1900
Thomas rpd mo; rocf Waterford, Ireland 4-23-1857; mbrp relinquished 5-1880
----- m Londa STEBBINS, dt Alfred & Edith (Lange), b Alameda, Calif. 5-30-1872 (H)
Londa recrq 4-14-1924

FLOURNOY
John Herbert (nm), s Nathaniel & Laura, d 4-22-1926; m 6-30-1897 Florence WILSON, dt Jesse & Rebeca (Stratton), b Springfield, O., 10-18-1875 (H)
Florence recrq 11-8-1926

FLOYD
Robert Wentworth (nm) m 12-4-1901 Adelaide O. WILLITS, dt Wm. H. & Ella (Osborne), b 7-21-1878 (H)

FLYNN
Selina A. (nm), dt Maurice; m 1909 Virgil C. PIATTI (H)

FOLGER
Alexander C., s Robt. C. & Susan M., b 7-20-1831 d 7-29-1902 (H)
ct Hudson 1-2-1839 with parents; cf Hudson 11-1845 with parents; lived Bridgeport, Calif.
Benjamin (nm) b Nantucket d 4- 8-1837 ae 68y bHS
Charles M., s Robert C. & Susan (Macy), b 9-24-1818 d 9-30-1902; m 11-15-1849 Esther A. CLARK (nm), dt Amasa & Nancy (Stewart) (H)
ct Hudson 1-2-1839 with parents; cf Hudson 11-1845; in Calif. 1859 and thereafter at Sacremento
Edward, s Robt. C. & Susan M., b 9-12-1825; ct Hudson 11-2-1839 with parents; cf Hudson 11-1845 with parents (H)
Emily B. (form Swain) ret a mbr; ct Salem, Mass. 1-1863
Francis R., s Robt. C. & Susan M., b 6-18-1823 d 4- 6-1891; cf Hudson 12-1845; in Calif. 1859-1886 (H)
Franklin (nm) m Diodamia ----- (nm) b Nantucket d 4- 3-1831 ae 50y bHS
Frederick Wm. (nm) b Nantucket d 3-22-1824 ae 30y bHS (m)
Phebe, w Reuben, rec by ack. 12-1833
Robert C. d 8-15-1849 ae 58y bPP; m Susan M. ---- d 7-25-1862
Ch: William J. b 11-1-1816 d 6-1875
Sarah J. " 11-1-1816
Charles M. " 9-24-1818
Robert M. " 10- 9-1820
cf Hudson 7-20-1819 with first 3 ch; parents dis 1830; ch dis 1836-1848 (0)
Ch: Francis R. b 6-18-1823
Ch: Edward R. b 9-12-1825
Alexander C. " 12-28-1827 d 8-23-1830
Samuel W. " 11-24-1829 " 8-21-1830
Alexander C. " 7-20-1831
ct Hudson 1-2-1839 for parents & 4 ch; cf Hudson 11-1845 with Edward & Alex.
Robert M., s Robt. C. & Susan M., Bkn., d 7-5-1899 ae 78y 8m 16d; m at Avis B. Coleman's 5-10-1842 Clarissa COLEMAN, dt David & Avis B., N. Y., b Hudson 11-26-1821 d 8-30-1901 ae 79y 11m 4d (H)
Ch: Avis C., b N. Y. d 12-2-1843 ae 9m 24d
cf Hudson 4-1842 for Clarissa; in Calif. 1859, and thereafter at Modesto
Sarah J., dt Robt. C. & Susan, b 11-1-1816; m ----- OSBORN (mo)
cf Hudson with parents 12-1819; dis mo 12-1835 (H); dis mo 8-3-1836 (0)
Susannah, wd William, rocf Nantucket 9-2-1830; dis 4-1839
----- & -----
Ch: Reuben b Eastchester d 9-29-1821 ae 1y 9m 6d bHS

FOLSOM
Morris W. (nm) m 10-21-1891 Annie MILLER, dt Ezekiel H. & Phebe C. (Underhill), b Bkn. 11-21-1865 (H)
Annie relrq 5-9-1921; in Lincoln, Neb. 1899 & thereafter
Chas. S., s Wm. & Rebecca, Phila.; m N. Y. 6-14-1821 Ann LAWRENCE, dt Richard E. & Hannah, N. Y.
ct ND MM 1-2-1822 for Ann L.

FOLWELL
Edward rocf Chesterfield 1-3-1826, minor, placed; ct Chesterfield 8-1830
John G. rocf Chesterfield 10-1825; ct WD MM 1-4-1832 (clear)

FONDERWHITE
Walter J., s Benj. F. & Louisa Maria (Dieter), b Port Carbon, Pa. 1-16-1887 (H)
recrq 4-14-1924

FORBES
Amelia, dt J. Malcolm & Sarah C. (Jones), b Milton, Mass. 11-29-1888; m 1913 Raymond EMERSON (H)
recrq 2-13-1933

FORD
Elizabeth, dt Thomas, Flushing; m 1728 David HUMPHREY
Esther, Flushing, an ancient wd, d 2 Mo (Apr) 1723
Thomas, Jr., Flushing, d 3 Mo (May) 11, 1699; m Sarah BOWNE (dmi 9 Mo (Nov) 28, 1696)
Thomas d 1743; active mbr from 1697
Thomas rpd mo before 1 Mo (Mar) 6, 1701/2

FORFAR
Grace Louise, dt Robt. & Mary I., b Bkn. 11-16-1879; m 1896 Dr. Edward PARRISH (H) recrq 4-13-1931

FORMAN
Mary M., dt George & Catharine, had m ----- MINOR before coming here; cf SD MM 10-26-1825

FORRESTER
Charlotte rocf Concord 9-1-1757
Elizabeth temporary ct Phila. 7-3-1776

FORSTER
Miles, N. Y. m Rebecca -----
Ch: Thomas d 6 Mo (Aug) 20, 1689
Elizabeth d 8 Mo (Oct) 30, 1690
rem to N. J.; active mbr from 1692 till 1700
Thomas B. (nm) d 11-25-1880 ae 70y 9m 28d; m 10-26-1844 Margaret SINCLAIR, dt John & Elizabeth (Williams), b Balt. 6-12-1824 d 2-6-1906 bPP (H)
Ch: Anna S. d 11-14-1900 ae 53y bPP
ct Flushing 5-1857; cf Flushing for Margaret 10-5-1870

FOSDICK
David & Rebecca (H)
Ch: Samuel T.
cf Coey. 5-21-1823 with ch, Samuel; David dis 5-1830 (O); Rebecca 6-1833 (O); ct Coey. 11-1831
Hamilton (nm) & -----
Ch: Deborah b N. Y. d 12-8-1848 ae 1m 14d bHS
Tamar (or Thamar), w Henry C.
Ch: Moses
Abigail
Epenetus
Eliza
David
cf Duanes. 7-24-1824 with 4 ch; ct Coey. 9-5-1827 with 4 ch named; cf Coey. not found; ct Marlbro. O. 7-1828 for Thamar & 4 ch
Underhill (nm) & -----
Ch: Infant stillborn 12-1-1841 bHS

FOSTER
Ann (form Griffen) rocf Chap. 7-9-1835 (clear) dis mo 4-7-1841
Anna M., dt Israel & Alice E. WHITALL, rocf Phila. 12-1854 with parents; dis mo 11-1856
Frank Bryn (nm), s Jos. B. & Matilda (Wheeler); m 1-27-1904 Mabel W. LATTIMER, dt Thos. Henry & Margaret (Speer), b Wilmington, Del. 2-17-1880 (H)
Mabel recrq 3-14-1921
George W. rocf Evesham 2-1-1826; ct Mt. Holly 12- 5-1827 (clear)
Hallie (nm), dt Reuben & Betsy; m 1878 Benjamin W. FOSTER (H)
John (nm) m 9-4-1854 Elizabeth T. BIRDSALL, dt Jacob & Amy (Dodge), b Chap. 3-18-1837 d 3-4-1920 bPP (H)
cf Chap. 12-3-1856; ct Chap. 7-4-1868; cf Chap. 4-5-1876 for Eliz.
John B. & Maria E.
Ch: Mary
William H.
Martha d 1-23-1864
Othniel
cf South Kingston, R. I. 12-25-1837 (clear); Maria & ch recrq 12-1860; ct Chap. 3-1868; John B. mo before 1-1843, ret a mbr
Mary, dt John B. & Mary E., Flushing; m 1865 Oscar F. BROWNING
Robert, s Robert N., d 3-6-1894 ae 67y 2m bPP; m Augusta S. SWAIN, dt Charles F. & Mary T., d 12-22-1914 ae 80y 6m 5d bPP (H)
Ch: Lillian d 11-12-1897 ae 37y 9m 24d bPP (all nm)
William d 9-13-1893 at Ocala, Fla.; m Celia C. ----- d 12-15-1883 at South Lake Weir, Fla.
Ch: Reuben B. d 11- 7-1895
Lizzie M. " 6- 6-1885
William P. d 5-13-1887 at South Lake Weir, Fla.
Parents recrq 4-1877; 2 ch recrq of parents 9-1878; William P. recrq 8-1886
----- & -----
Ch: Margaret d 10-27-1845 ae 17y bHS
----- & Elsie A.
Elsie recrq 1-5-1910; death rpd 4-1928

FOULKE
Anna, dt Daniel & Eliz. C., b Penllyn, Pa. 1-5-1848 d 11-23-1928; m 1870 Henry S. COLLADAY (nm) (H)
James, s Edward & Matilda (Green), b Quakertown, Pa. 9-3-1847 d 3- 4-1920 (H)
cf Richland, Pa. 11-4-1885 (unm)
Judith (late Way) dis mo 6-1803; rst by R. & P. & rem cert to N. Y. 2-20-1820; cf R. & P. 6-16-1824, rem with her fam; dis 1-1834 (O); ct Flushing 10-1837 (H)
Lydia, dt Edwin M. & Elva (Jones), b Montgomery Co., Pa. 8-3-1884; m 1910 J. Hibberd TAYLOR (H); cf Birmingham for both 1-14-1911
Thomas, s Joseph & Elizabeth, Montgomery Co., Pa., b 5-28-1817 d 1-25-1890 bPP; m at Abraham Shoemaker's 11-5-1840 Hannah SHOEMAKER, dt Abm. & Margaret, N. Y., d 10-6-1876 ae 72y bPP (H)
Ch: Infant stillborn 8-21-1846
Edwin b 8-21-1846 d 10- 6-1876
William D. " 11-19-1848
Edwin M. d 3-19-1850 ae 3y 6m 29d bPP
cf Gwynedd 2-1844; principal Friends Seminary
William Dudley, s Thomas & Hannah, b 11-19-1848 d 5-30-1935 at Richmond, Ind. (H)
ct Whitewater, Richmond, Ind. 7-2-1878

FOWLER
Abigail d 12-21-1865 ae 89y (prob w Isaac P.)
Ch: Jane d 11-21-1866 ae 64y 4m bPP
Martha E. b Dutch. Co. d 5-11-1834 ae 27y 10m 21d
cf Hudson 5-22-1827 for all (clear) (H)
Alice A. b 1-5-1844 d 1-13-1900; recrq 2-6-1895 (H)
Alice Maria rocf New Hartford 1845; rem to Chap. 1853
Ammon d 1830 at Hyde Park; mo before 6-2-1830
cf Creek 9-21-1827 (clear); death recorded in both H & O 9-1-1830; the com. to inform him of his dis rpd his d (O)
Catharine d 8-28-1882 ae 89th yr; recrq 6-1865
Charles (nm) & -----
Ch: Infant stillborn 7-2-1836 bHS
Dorinda F., dt Gilbert; m 1845 John T. H. BRADY, s Lydia C. (H)
cf Creek 10-1833
Edward, s Weeden & Phebe, rocf Creek 9-1829; dis 9-4-1850 (H)
Eliza B., dt Borden & Ruth B. CHASE, dis mo 10-5-1831
Freelove (form Thorn) dis mo 5-1836 (H)
Gilbert & Sarah (H)
cf Creek 4-1839; ct Clear Creek 6-7-1848
Gilbert, Jr. d 5- 9-1840; m ----- (H)
Ch: Catharine Ann b N. Y. d 10-8-1839 ae 1y 11m
cf Creek 1-1840
Hannah con mo 5-5-1757
Henry (nm) b Marl. d 12-25-1827 ae 28y 5m 21d bHS
Henry & Jane
Ch: Alice Maria d 3-28-1838 ae 1y 3m 11d bHS (all nm)
Hester (nm) b N. Y. d 10-27-1836 ae 23y bHS; m -----
Ch: (prob) Benjamin d 10-26-1836 ae 1y 3m bHS
Isaac P. d 11-18-1866 ae 66y 1m 17d (prob 1st m) Abigail -----
Ch: Alice A. d 1-13-1900 bPP (bur in same grave as Jane, dt Abigail)
Henry H. d 8-6-1866 ae 17y 10m 20d bPP
Isaac P. m (prob 2nd m) Ethelinda D. ----- d 4-18-1889 ae 72y 2m 5d bPP (H)
Isaac rocf Hudson 12-1828
James & Lydia (H)
Ch: Lydia Ann
Isaac d 12-15-1841
cf Oswego 7-1832; ct Creek 12-1843; cf Creek 6-1844; dis, all, 1-5-1848
John, Rye, m Mary TATEM, dt Samuel, Flushing (ltm 7 Mo (Sep) 5, 1717)
John P., having mo Balt. refers to N. Y. 3-4-1847, ret a mbr; cf Balt. 8-10-1848; ct Balt. 1850
L. Frank (nm) m 2-1-1890 (or 2-20-1890) Sarah H. RIDER, dt John R. & Mary W., b 2-29-1855 (H)
cf Corn. 12-1-1880 for Sarah with mother
Lydia, dt Moses & Mary, rocf Chap. with mother 12-7-1837; dis 10-1842 (H)
Martha E. (nm) d 1842, tombstone in PP (H)
Martha, dt Horace & Mary (T----), d 9-10-1894 ae 70y 10m 6d bPP; m Dr. Wm. J. BANER (H)
Mary, w Moses, d 8-7-1853 (H)
Ch: Maria d 2-22-1857 ae 39y 3m bPP
Susan
Lydia
cf Chap. 12-7-1837 with ch
Moses C. (nm) b N. Y. d 12-7-1847 ae 65y; m ----
Ch: William b Stanton Hill, N. Y. d 11-18-1829 ae 17y 6m bHS
Caleb b Dutchen Co. d 12-10-1829 ae 14y
Susanna b N. Y. d 9-24-1845 ae 25y 3m 4d bHS (unm)
Rebecca Morrell (form Fowler) dis mo 10-2-1771
Susan, dt Moses & Mary, rocf Chap. with mother 12-7-1837; dis 10-1842 (H)
Susan B. Brady (form Fowler) dis mo 4-1837; rocf Creek 11-1834 (H)
Weeden & Phebe (H)
Ch: Jonathan d 12-28-1847
Edward
cf Creek 9-1829; ct Pur. 10-6-1852
William D. (nm) m 3-24-1873 Martha MACY, dt John I. & Jane (Hall), b Greenport, N. Y. 12-13-1850 d 2-1920 (H)
cf Hudson & Chatham 12-5-1896 for Martha
----- & ----- (nm)
Ch: Deborah b West. Co. d 12-16-1835 ae 9y bHS
Cornelia " 2-13-1836 ae 1y 6m bHS
Benjamin d 10-26-1836 ae 1y 3m bHS
Maria " 2-28-1838 ae 1y 3m 11d bHS
Henry B. " 2- 9-1840 ae 1y 2m 1d bHS
Martha b N. Y. d 12-20-1842 ae 5m bHS

FOX
Abraham m Mary SHOTWELL
Ch: Hester d 3-13-1810 ae 56y
Anna M., dt George & Rebecca L., b 3-31-1827 d 1- 5-1905; m 1873 Augustus SCHELL (H)
Edward B. d 7-26-1915; rocf WD MM 5-1-1901
Eliza L., dt George S. & Rebecca L., N. Y.; m 1854 Benjamin MERRITT; m 2nd 1874 Jonathan THORN (H)
Esther, dt George S. & Rebecca L., N. Y.; m 1849 James W. TUCKER (H)
George, s Jonathan & Deborah (dec) Tartor, N.Y. d 9-20-1803 ae 47y bHS; m Lydia -----
Ch: William b 9-26-1783
George rocf Burl. 2-7-1785 had rem in minority, had mo & con mo
George m 2nd N. Y. 5-10-1786 Esther SHOTWELL, dt Abraham & Mary, Essex Co., N. J., d 3-13-1810 ae 56y
Ch: Deborah b 8-24-1789
Elizabeth " 5-25-1792 d 12- 2-1792
Abraham " 9-30-1796
George S. " 9-30-1796
Esther gct R. & P. (not found); Esther rocf

FOX, George & Esther, continued
R. & P. 2-3-1808 with 2 ch, Deborah & George; Deborah clear; Esther rocf R. & P. 2-15-1785 (clear)

George, s Wm. W. & Charlotte L., N. Y., b 11-6-1809 d 5- 9-1865; m N. Y. 10-9-1833 Maria T. CLARK, dt Benj. & Deborah M., N. Y. d 7-8-1836 bur at Po'keepsie
Ch: William W. Jr. b 8-22-1834 d 3- 9-1871
Sarah Clark " 12-23-1835 " 5-22-1836 bHS

George Henry, s George S. & Rebecca, b 10-10-1824 d 3-27-1865 (H)

George S., s George & Esther, b 9-30-1796 d 6-29-1864; m Pur. Rebecca L. ----- b 2-7-1799 d 4-14-1878 (H)
Ch: Esther b 6-29-1820
Eliza L. " 8-10-1822
George Henry b 10-10-1824 d 3-27-1865
Ann Mott " 3-31-1827
William James b 11- 4-1828 d 8-12-1888
cf R. & P. 7-15-1819 for George; cf Pur. 3-9-1820 for Rebecca; parents dis 1830 (O); ch 1841-1849 (O)

Mary L., dt Wm. W. & Charlotte, b 3-15-1816; m ----- TIFFANY (dis mo 3-1-1837 (O)

Sarah rocf Upper Springfield, N. J. 11-3-1784 (clear); ct Upper Springfield, N. J. 4-4-1787 (clear)

William (not a mbr in N. Y.) b Hanover, N. J. d 6-13-1823 ae 70y bHS (m)

Wm. Henry m Catharine T. D---- [6-5-1929
Catharine recrq 6-1928; Wm. Henry recrq

William W., s George & Lydia (both dec), N.Y., d 3-1-1861; m N. Y. 6-9-1808 Charlotte LEGGETT, dt Thomas & Mary (dec), N. Y., d 6-1-1871
Ch: George D. b 11- 6-1809
Thomas Leggett b 10- 6-1811
Mary Lydia b 3-15-1816; dis 3-1837
Mary dis 3-1837 (O); all others dis 1829-1832 (H)

FOY

Phebe rocf Nantucket 10-30-1786 to tarry a while with her uncle, William Johnson; ct Nantucket 4-6-1791 (clear)

FRACE

Clara m ----- BENSON
recrq 4-2-1902

FRAME

Jesse, s David & Catharine, N. J.; m N. Y. 12-12-1798 Mary LEGGETT, dt Joseph & Miriam, N. Y.
Ch: Catharine D.
Joseph
Maria
Thomas
Eliza b 11-12-1811
cf R. & P. 3-15-1798 for Jesse (clear); ct R. & P. 3-6-1799 for both; cf R. & P. 5-24-1810 with their 4 ch; ct Flushing 10-5-1814 with 5 ch named

Joseph L., s Jesse, rocf Flushing 4-3-1823, minor; dis 7-1830 (O); dis 9-1833 (H)

Mary d 2- 2-1853; m ----- (H)
Ch: Catharine
Maria
Eliza
Benjamin
William
cf Flushing 4-5-1832, Catharine & Maria clear; ct Flushing 1-1834

Thomas L. rocf Flushing 7-7-1825, apprentice; dis 1830 (O); dis 1-7-1863 (H) for non-attendance

FRAMPTON

William, N. Y. m Elizabeth P----
took cert of clear to Phila. 4 Mo (June), 27, 1680 to m; no rem cert for Elizabeth
Ch: Elizabeth b 5 Mo (July) 26, 1681
by 1684 they were in Phila. & signed a cert there)
William active mbr from 1677; William & Mary took cert to Antigna 3-6-1703; this was a cert of unity

FRANCE

Sanford Dewey (nm), s Wm. Stewart & Maria (Borst); m 6-14-1909 Jane MILLER, dt Jos. Richardson & Helen A. (Munger), b Amherst, O. 3-25-1886 (H)
Ch: Helen b Bkn. 10-2-1912
Susan b Bkn. 4-15-1914
Jane recrq 12-12-1927; ch recrq of parents 12-12-1927

FRANCHE

F. William (nm) m Marie EMBREE, dt Henry Corbit & Eliz. B. OGDEN, wd Lawrence F. Embree (H)

FRANCIS

Alfred Tench, s Lloyd W. (dec) & Edna D. (Smith), Yorktown Hts.; m N. Y. 10-18-1922 Dorothy T. TURNER, dt Frank & Ella F. (both dec), N. Y. (H)
recrq 4-11-1908

Augustus T., s Wm. Albert & Grace Ann (West), b N. Y. 9-7-1838 d 11-12-1927; m Anna LLOYD (H)
Ch: Lloyd West. b N. Y. 9-20-1867
recrq 4-11-1908

Grace Ann d 3-20-1881; m 1853 ----- FRANCIS
cf Balt. 2-1835; ret a mbr (H)

Lloyd West, s Aug't T. & Anna (Lloyd), b N. Y. 9-20-1867; m 9-16-1896 Edna D. SMITH, dt Alfred & Melvina H. (Cook), b Vineland, N. J. 10-1-1870 (H)
Ch: Alfred Tench b 6-23-1897
Philip Ward " 10-22-1900
all recrq 4-11-1908

Philip Ward, s Lloyd W. & Edna (Smith), b 10-22-1900; m 2-24-1923 Edith Agnes ALBERTSON

FRANCIS, Philip Ward & Edith Agnes, continued
(nm), dt Geo. Fitz R. & Agnes E. (Green)
(H)
recrq with parents 4-11-1908
----- & -----
Ch: Grace b N. Y. d 9-10-1837 ae 1y bHS
William A. b Balt. d 9-28-1840 ae 8y bHS

FRANKLIN
Abraham (nm) d 2-12-1826 ae 58y 10m bHS
dis mo 6-4-1788
Abraham (nm) d 12-10-1841 ae 39y 9m 27d bHS
Almira (nm) d 11-1-1832 ae 18y bHS
Amelia, dt Thos. & Mary, N. Y.; m 1831 John T.
S. SMITH
Ann M., w Walter M., dis 4-1846 for attending
parties where there was music
Anthony dis mo 2-4-1790; rst 12-3-1794
Benjamin H. dis mo 7-1845
Deborah M., dt Thos. & Sarah P., N. Y.; m 1810
Benjamin CLARK
Edward, s Thomas & Mary, b 11-7-1803; m Almira
----- (nm) d 11-1-1832 ae 18y bHS (mo)
Ch: Emily d 3-10-1866 ae 25y bPP
dis mo 2-6-1831
Elizabeth Townsend (form Franklin) dis mo 10-5-
1803
Emma, w Wm. M., dt Giles H. & Marianna COGGE-
SHALL (m 4-2-1863)(H)
Francis, Jericho, d 10 Mo (Dec) 23, 1687; m
Mary ----- d 11 Mo (Jan) 23, 1687/8
Ch: Mary d 12 Mo (Feb) 6, 1686/7
George N., s Thomas & Mary, d 7-28-1864 ae 54y
bPP; dis mo 10-2-1833
Henry, s Matthew, Flushing; m 3 Mo (May) 27,
1689 Dorothy BOWNE, dt John, Flushing;
d 9 Mo 26, 1690
Henry m 2nd Sarah COCK, dt James & Sarah, Mk.
(ltm 12 Mo (Feb) 26, 1697/8), d 8 Mo. 24,
1750
Ch: Matthew b 12 Mo (Feb) 19, 1698/9
Sarah " 6 Mo (Aug) 31, 1700
Henry " 7 Mo (Sep) 30, 1702
Thomas " 11 Mo (Jan) 20, 1703/4
Elizabeth b 12 Mo (Feb) 10, 1706/7
Henry active mbr from 1681
Henry, Flushing & Mary
Ch: Matthew b 11-6-1773 d 1-9-1815 ae 42 (d
of apoplexy while preaching)
Richard b 2- 6-1775 d 9- 3-1805 ae 30y 5m
William " 7-22-1777 d 5-24-1809 ae 31y
10m bHS
Henry dis mo 2-6-1794
Henry (nm) d 4-3-1838 ae 67y 5m 19d bHS; m -----
Ch: Louisa b N. Y. d 2-18-1816 ae 21d bHS
Henry J. m Wby 1762 Mary -----
cf Pur. 8-7-1760 (clear); cert of clear to
Wby 10-6-1762; cf Wby for Mary 10-26-1763
John d 8-30-1801 bHS; m Phila. 1756 Deborah

Ch: Sarah
Thomas
Mary
Ch: Elizabeth
Anthony
Rebecca
Walter b 6-15-1773
cert of clear to Phila. 6-3-1756; Deborah
rocf Phila. 10-6-1756; ct Phila. with w &
7 ch 9-5-1781; cf Phila. with w & 7 ch
11-26-1783; the ch clear
John, s Thomas & Mary, Merchant, N. Y.; m
N. Y. 5-13-1789 Letitia UNDERHILL, wd Ben-
jamin, N. Y.
Ch: John (prob) d 8-30-1801 bHS
John, Jr. dis mo 1-6-1796
John C. (nm) d 12-26-1831 ae 29y 10m 7d bHS
Joseph F. (nm), s Jos. L. & Mary (Fitch);
m 12-5-1854 Miriam L. LEGGETT, dt Thos.
H. & Francis Vant (Pleasants), b N. Y.
8-25-1826 d 10-10-1912 (H)
Miriam recrq 2-5-1898
Maria, dt Thomas & Sarah P., gct Corn. 6-4-
1845 (clear)
Matthew, Owens Co., d 7-31-1777; m at Cow
Neck (Manhasset) L. I. 1 Mo (Mar) 14,
1722/3 Deborah CORNHILL (CORNELL), dt
Richard, Cow Neck
Took cert of clear 11 Mo (Jan) 3, 1722/3
Mary rocf Wby 2-2-1764
Mary rocf Phila. 5-3-1764
Mary m 1764 Caspar WISTAR, of Phila.
Mary Combs (form Franklin) dis mo 11-3-1785
Mary Osgood (form Franklin) dis mo 7-5-1786
Mary E. (form Spencer) dis mo 6-1848
Morris, s Thomas & Mary, b 10-20-1801; m
Sally Ann ----- (nm) b N. Y. d 12-4-1834
ae 30y 6m bHS (mo)
Morris dis 2-5-1834
Phebe Hauxhurst (form Franklin) rpd mo 1794
Peter B., s Geo. N. (dec) & Catharine C., West
Farms; m 11-8-1866 Mary HICKS, dt Elias
(dec) & Sarah H., N. Y. (H)
(Not under care of N.Y. MM)
cf Wby 11-2-1870 for Mary
Phila. d 3-3-1838 ae 69y 8m 14d bHS; dis 7-1829
(H)
Rebecca Townsend (form Franklin) dis mo 4-3-
1793
Samuel, s Thomas & Sarah, N. Y., d 9-3-1807
ae 70; m Phila. 1762 Esther MITCHELL, dt
Abraham & Sarah, Phila., d 4-28-1804 ae 61y
Ch: John b 2-28-1775
cert of clear to Phila. 5-6-1762; Esther
Franklin rocf Phila. 8-27-1762
Sarah, Jr. m 1716 Samuel BOWNE
Sarah, dt Samuel & Esther, N. Y.; m 1781 Wm. T.
ROBINSON
Sarah m 1784 Samuel MOTT, N. Y.
Sarah Robbins (form Franklin) dis mo 9-2-1789
Thomas, s Henry, Rye Woods, d 12-25-1773;
m Wby 12 Mo (Feb) 8, 1727/8 Mary PEARSALL,
dt Nathaniel, Wby
Ch. Walter b 10 Mo (Dec) 11, 1728
John d 8-29-1801 ae 69y
Thomas, with w & ch roc 10-4-1752

FRANKLIN, continued
Thomas & -----
Ch: Benjamin
Ann
Walter
Samuel
cert of clear to Phila. 11-3-1763; ct ND MM 7-1-1778 with w (not named) & 4 ch
Thomas, s John & Deborah, Merchant, N. Y., b N. Y. d 5-3-1830 ae 72y bHS; m Sarah P. -----
Ch: Deborah M. b 11-18-1784
Maria " 1-12-1787 d 1869
Thomas m 2nd N. Y. 6-12-1793 Mary HAVILAND, dt Benjamin & Sarah, N. Y., d 6-20-1854
Ch: ----- d 5- 7-1796
Benjamin b 5-29-1798 d 4- 3-1809 ae 11y
William H. b 11-23-1799
Morris " 10-20-1801; dis 11-1834
Edward " 11- 7-1803; dis 1-1833
Rebecca T. " 7- 7-1805 d 8-19-1805
Amelia " 8-22-1806
George N. dis 9-1833
------ stillborn 4-3-1809
all dis 1829 (H)
Thomas (nm) d 4-3-1838 ae 67y 5m 19d bHS
Thomas, Jr. dis mo 4-7-1784; rst 1-4-1792
Thomas M., s Wm. H. & Hannah, b 11-6-1825; dis mo by a priest 11-1848
Walter, s Thomas, Merchant & Newtown, N. Y., d 8-6-1780; m Flushing 5-12-1774 Mary BOWNE, dt Daniel, Flushing, d 3-7-1813 ae 77y bHS
Ch: Maria b 11-21-1775
Sarah " 10-4-1777
Hannah " 1- 8-1780
Walter (nm) b N. Y. d 12-11-1817 ae 20y bHS (unm)
Walter m Ann M. MOTT, dt William F. & Phebe, b 9-18-1813
Ch: Louisa d 2-10-1841 ae 1y 19d bHS
Ann M. dis 4-1846 for attending parties of music & dancing
Walter, Jr. dis mo 3-4-1795
William H., s Thomas & Mary, N. Y.; m N. Y. 9-12-1822 Hannah C. REDMOND, dt John C. & Letitia, N. Y.
Ch: Benjamin H. b 7-25-1823; dis 6-1845
Thomas Morris b 11-26-1825; dis 11-1848
Wm. H. dis 3-1832; Hannah 12-1842 (O); both dis 1829 (H)
----- & -----
Ch: Anna T. d 7-4-1835 ae 1y 9m bHS
Anna " 8-29-1836 ae 6m 14d bHS (dt Walter)
Louisa d 2-10-1841 ae 1m 19d bHS

FRASER
Helen G. (nm) m 4-3-1901 Richard C. FIELD
----- m Dorothy Gladys SPICER, dt J. Lindley & Phoebe (Washburn), b 11-3-1893
ct Po'keepsie with parents 12-7-1904; rolf First Presbyterian Church, Po'keepsie for h & w, Dorothy G. 9-1920

FRAZEE
Henry (nm) b N. J. d 9-20-1832 ae 24y bHS
Ch: Rufus b N. Y. d 9-25-1832 ae 2y 2m bHS

FREAR
Frank Burroughs (nm) m 4-18-1888 Carrie L. VONDER SMITH, dt William & Caroline (Birdsall), b 12-15-1868 d 1-15-1923 bPP (H)
Carrie's name entered by com. 11-24-1875

FREEBORN
Benjamin, s Thomas & Alice, b 10-15-1809 (H)
rel 7-5-1871, absent over 5y
Elizabeth, dt Thomas & Alice, d 8-8-1884 at Yarmouthville, Mass. (H)
George, s Thomas & Alice, b 3-4-1801 d 11-24-1863 (H)
dis 5-1833 after long dealing for not being plain in dress and address & non-attendance
Gideon, s Thomas & Alice, b Nantucket d 5-31-1846 ae 48y bHS
Ch: Joseph S. d 8-21-1823 ae 1y 2m bHS
Infant stillborn 3-17-1824 bHS
Alice (prob) b N. Y. d 1-15-1835 ae 1y 6m bHS
dis mo 1-6-1819
John W., s Thomas & Alice, b 3-1818 d 2-11-1870
Mary, dt Thomas & Alice, b 8-10-1805; m Raymond L. JONES (H)
was at Fox Lake, Wis. 1857; Wasiago, Minn. 1864-1879; unknown thereafter; name cancelled 4-9-1904
Susanna, dt Geo. & Susanna, d 5-23-1802 ae 30; m Barzilla HUSSEY
Thomas d 12-8-1846 ae 60y bPP; m Alice ----- d 4-13-1848 bPP
Ch: Gideon L.
Elizabeth M. d 12- 8-1884
George b 3- 4-1801
Susan P. " 6-19-1803 d 1841
Mary " 8-10-1805
Caroline " 7-19-1807 d 8-29-1808
Benjamin " 10-15-1809
William " 11----1811
Ann Louisa b 12-22-1813 d 10-29-1885
John W. " 2----1818 d 2-11-1870
parents dis 1829-1830; ch 1832-1839 (O); cf Nantucket 4-2-1801 with ch, Gideon & Elizabeth; Thomas dis 7-1830 (H)
William, s Thomas & Alice, b 11-1811 (H)
long unknown; name cancelled 4-9-1904

FREEMAN
Blanche F. (nm) m 1917 Nathaniel THAYER (H)
Jackson rocf R. & P. 2-18-1807, apprentice; ct R. & P. 7-5-1809 (clear)

FREIDEL
Frank Burt, s Grant & Mary E. (Quinby), b Bkn.

FREIDEL, Frank Burt & Edith M., continued
8-5-1895; m 4-28-1915 Edith M. HEACOCK, dt Wm. A. & Lucretia M. (Robinson), b Alliance, O., 4-20-1898 (H)
Ch: Frank B., Jr. b 5-22-1916
Richard Grant " 1-16-1919
Doris Edith " 2-27-1920
Audrey Mary " 1- 4-1923
Frank recrq 5-9-1914; cf Chap. for Edith 12-11-1915; ct Chap. for all 8-13-1923
Grant (nm), s Conrad & Phebe (Hoffman); m 12-24-1894 Mary Eliz. QUINBY, dt Edward S. & Eliza (Field), b New Castle 2-9-1863 d Chatham, N. Y. 5-12-1935 (H)
Ch: Frank Burt 3-5-1895 (8-5-1895)
Nelly, dt Elizabeth, d 4-5-1905 ae 4y 20d bPP (nm) (H)

FRENCH
Rachel rocf Pur. 6-8-1825 (clear); dis 5-1828 for assisting in managing a theater
Shepherd rocf Morley, Eng. 4-28-1824 aged about 14; dis mo 12-1836

FRISBIE (or Frisbee)
Elizabeth W., w Lawrence, dt ----- Longbotham, 1924 (H)
Ch: (prob) Willard C. d 3-4-1862 ae 7m 17d bPP
Ida V. m Frank JOYCE
cf Chatham 8-1851
Ida V., dt Lawrence & Elizabeth (Longbotham) d 3-25-1898 ae 45y bPP; m Frank JOYCE (H)

FRIIS-HOLM
Dr. Gudson, M.D., s Edw. Holm & Astrid E. (Pauken), b Copenhagen 5-20-1867; recrq 1-13-1919 (H)

FROST
Aaron rocf Creek 5-17-1816 (clear); ct Scipio 8-1-1821 (clear)
Abraham rocf Ama. 4-10-1813 (clear); dis 7-5-1815
Anna H. m Moses HALSTER (H)
cf Creek & Stanford 9-6-1876 with h
Caleb gct Wby 5-4-1796
Caleb H. gct Ama. 8-7-1822, minor rem with parents
Caroline A. b 9-19-1838 d 2-24-1898; cf Oswego 12-4-1895 (H)
Catharine, dt Stephen & Sarah Ann; m 7-2-1887 at Topeka, Kans. Silas B. PATTON
recrq of parents 3-1872; ct Friendswood, Texas, 1-6-1897
Charles Seely (nm), s Stephen & Sarah Ann, d 1-23-1932; m Alice V. CRYGIER, dt James H. & Catharine A., b N. Y. 11-5-1858 d 4-6-1924 Flushing bPP
Charles recrq of parents 6-1870; Alice recrq 1-4-1893; letter to Christian & Alliance Church, Bkn. 1-1927 for Charles
David M., s Isaac C. & Phebe Jane (Miller), b Bkn. 8-11-1849 d 1825 or earlier (letter returned 3-1825 marked "dec"); m 7-4-1876 Lilla J. PIERCE, dt Merritt & Amanda (H)
lived East Putneys, Vt.
Eleanor, wd ----- HOLME, recrq with her two dt 5-1887; ct Marl. 6-12-1895; cf Marl. 10-2-1901; Eleanor's d rpd 1-2-1929
Elizabeth M., dt Obediah & Phebe, N. Y.; m 1-2-1840 James C. HALLOCK (H)
cf Ama. 8-1831 with mother
Gideon & Mary W.
Ch: Leonard T.
cf Wby 7-19-1815, minor, to live with brother, Leonard; ct Wby 7-5-1820 (clear); cf Wby 7-14-1824; cf Scipio 11-18-1824 for Mary W., w Gideon; both dis 1829-1830 (O); ct Wby 11-1843 for all 3
Harriet F., dt Solomon V. & Abigail (Smith), b Pokeepsie; m 1866 Richard P. MERRITT (H)
Isaac & -----
Ch: Matilda d 10- 2-1820 ae 8m bHS
Infant stillborn 1-12-1829
Isaac C. d 3-14-1854 ae 27y 10m 25d bPP
cf Chap. 10-11-1805 (clear); dis mo 3-6-1816
Isaac C., s Stephen & Phebe, N. Y., d 10-7-1858 ae 39y 3m bPP; m at Stephen Miller's 1-4-1844 Phebe Jane MILLER, dt Stephen & Leah H., Bkn. (H)
Ch: Stephen M. b 1- 5-1847 d 2-26-1849 bPP
David M. " 8-11-1849
William H. " 12- 4-1852 " 4-10-1926
lived Berwick, Me.
cf Wby 6-1833 for Phebe Jane; she m 2nd ----- BROOKS
J. Sheldon, s John D. & Phebe E. (Sheldon), b Renss'ville 12-1-1864 d 5-12-1932; m 10-15-1902 Dorothy GOULD (H)
transferred from Albany 1-8-1916
Jacob m Sarah M. ----- b West Co. d 1-6-1830 (or 1-3-1830) ae 31y 4m
Ch: Hannah Matilda
Phebe Elizabeth
John Hicks
Sally Ann C.
Phebe b 12-21-1829 d 1- 4-1830
cf Ama. 3-12-1830 with his 4 minor ch (O); cf same 11-1828 (H); Jacob dis 5-1831; ch 1839-1842
Jacob, s Obadiah (dec) & Phebe, N. Y.; m 2nd 3-12-1834 Jane Ann LOCKWOOD, dt Walter & Martha (H)
Ch: Walter L. b 7- 3-1835 d 7-16-1835
Mary D. " 7-22-1837
ct Milton, Mich. 3-1839 for all living
Jacob rocf Whitewater, Ind. 8-1829; ct Wby 3-1838 (H)
Leonard J. d 7-12-1822 ae 30y; m 1816 Sarah Ann ----- (mo)
Ch: William S.
Edward S. dis 12-1848
Charles L. b 6-16-1821; dis 12-1848
cf Wby 4-19-1815 (clear); their ch recrq of parents 3-6-1822; dis mo 5-1-1816; rst 9-7-

FROST, Leonard J. & Sarah Ann, continued
1820; Sarah Ann recrq 9-7-1820; dis 3-1858
Margaret, w Jacob, d 1-10-1865, wd; recrq 6-6-1820; dis 6-1830
Marquis Chester (nm), s Samuel & Susan; m 7-1-1858 Josephine B. MILLER, dt Stephen & Leah (Hubbs), b Peekskill 10-28-1835 d 1-25-1923 (H)
cf Ama. 2-1856 for Josephine with mother
Martha (nm) d 9-19-1831 ae 62y bHS under Orthodox com.
Matilda, dt Robert & Naomi BOWNE; dis mo 5-4-1842
Mary (nm) b Dosoris, L. I. d 10-12-1813 ae 31y 4m bHS
Obadiah m 1755 Hannah UNDERHILL
Obadiah m 2nd 3-3-1819 Phebe HALSTEAD, dt Stephen, d 5-7-1855 ae 85y bPP (mo)
Ch: Richard K. d 8-31-1839 ae 25y 11m 4d
Elizabeth M.
Samuel
Hannah d 9-17-1813 ae 17y
cf Chap. 7-12-1805; cf Oswego 7-15-1812 for Obadiah (clear); Obadiah dis 5-5-1819; ct Ama. for Phebe 8-7-1822; cf Ama. 8-1831 with Richard & Elizabeth
Penn, s Wright & Freelove (dec), Mk.; m N. Y. 6-10-1795 Mary DUSENBURY, dt Henry & Jane (dec), Pur.
Mary gct Wby 8-5-1795
Phebe, w Stephen
Ch: Isaac C.
ct Wby 8-7-1822
Phebe, w Thomas, recrq 11-5-1845; ct Oswego 2-5-1862 (H)
Philemon H. & ----- (H)
Ch: Amelia b N. Y. d 9-19-1834 ae 4y 4m
cf Whitewater, Ind. 10-1829; dis 3-1830
Samuel, s Obadiah & Phebe, d 8-19-1884; dis 1-1830
Samuel, s Samuel & Anna (both dec), Clinton, N. Y.; m at Alex. B. Week's 9-9-1846 Semantha WEEKS, dt Nathaniel & Hannah MEAD (both dec), N. Y. (H)
Semantha rocf Oswego 10-11-1843 with dt, Phebe Jane
Sarah, w William, d 3-26-1853; cf Wby 10-18-1815; dis 12-1829
Sarah d 9-28- (or 29) 1898 ae 78y bPP; m Joshua W. BROWN (H)
cf Scip. 6-4-1845 with dt
Semantha d 4-25-1881; cf Creek 3-1850 (H)
Smith P., s Stephen & Sarah Ann, recrq of parents 3-1872; name erased
Solomon V. & Abigail
Ch: Mary S.
Eliza b 3-26-1817
Charles
cf Creek 6-16-1815 with their infant ch, Mary; ct Oswego 6-14-1820 with 3 ch named
Stephen d 1-25-1819 ae 29y 6m 17d bHS; dis mo 4-14-1813 (b Somers)
Stephen rocf Renss. 7-22-1819 (clear); ct Scipio 6-14-1820 (clear)
Stephen rocf Wby 6-17-1818; dis mo 2-6-1822
Stephen m Eleanor CRAGG
Eleanor was wd Thos. Wynne HOLME; Eleanor recrq with ch 5-1887; Eleanor gct Marl. 12-1895
Stephen m Sarah Ann ----- d 8-22-1889 bur Elevation Cem. Topeka, Kans.
Ch: Charles Seely
Smith P.
Emily C. d 8-30-1889 bur Topeka, Kans.
Catharine P.
Stephen recrq 4-1863; Sarah roc; ch recrq of parents 3-1872; ct Marl. 4-4-1894 for Stephen
Susan, wd b N. Y. d 6-17-1833 ae 43y 4m bHS
William & -----
Ch: Elizabeth d 2-10-1805 ae 3y 6m bHS
William S., s Leonard J. & Sarah Ann, gct Richmond, Ind. 3-3-1838 (clear) (H); ct Richmond, Ind 4-4-1838 (O)
Wright d 8-14-1799 bHS; m -----
Ch: Mary Ann d 4-23-1804 ae 14y bHS
Wright (nm), s Samuel & Mary (Cock), b Westchester 2-3-1765 d 3-30-1811 ae 45y bHS; m Martha SMITH, dt Philip & Mary A. (Golden), b 7-13-1771 d 9-19-1831 ae 62y bHS (6 ch)
----- & -----
Ch: Mary b N. Y. d 3-31-1812 ae 1y 5m 9d bHS
Phebe A. d 1-27-1819 ae 2y 2m 16d bHS
Sarah b N. Y. d 8-29-1823 ae 1y 4m 19d bHS
Jane W. b N. Y. d 12-23-1829 ae 1y 4m 10d bHS
Edward b N. Y. d 7-4-1840 ae 2m bHS

FROTHINGHAM
----- m Helen POST
Ch: Infant stillborn 3-19-1903 bPP (all nm)

FRY
Clifford S. (nm) m 2-5-1930 Bessie M. WAIBEL, dt ----- & Marion, wd John Llewellen TILLEY
Bessie recrq of mother 12-4-1901
Eleanor Priscilla, dt W. Raymond & Lillian; m 1923 Frank Edwin RANSOME
recrq of father 9-7-1910; active mbr 7-1923
John, s ----- (dec) & Frances, Jericho, d 1 Mo (Mar) 9, 1714/15; m Jericho 1 Mo (Mar) 7, 1686/7 Mary WILLITS, dt Richard & Mary, Jericho, d 1 Mo (Mar) 1, 1714/15
Ch: John b 11 Mo (Jan) 15, 1687/8
John active mbr from 1682; shoemaker
John, s John, O.B.; m Wby 10 Mo (Dec) 19, 1711 m Mary URQUHART, dt John, now of E. Jersey, from L. I.
Joseph, s John & Mary, rocf Mountmelick MM, 7-22-1801 (clear)
Martha b 12 Mo (Feb) 16, 1712/13
Mary, dt William & Thomasin; m 1708 William GLADING
Thomas E. rocf Bolton, Mass. 9-1860; ct Chicago 4-1867

FRY, continued
Walter Raymond & -----
Ch: Eleanor Priscilla
cf Darlington, Eng. 10-3-1894 for Walter
Eleanor recrq 9-7-1810
William contributor 1685

FUHRER
Harry & Marie
Ch: Ethel 10
Lillian 9
Harry recrq 6-12-1901; Marie recrq 2-6-1901; ch recrq of parents 6-12-1901; all names erased 3-1928

FULKE
Sarah d 2-15-1928 m Charles S. CROSMAN
cf Haverford 2-1921 for both

FULKERSIN
Wesley (nm) m Ora Lucille ORVIS, dt Francis W. & Emma G., b 8-6-1887

FULLER
Hannah rocf Scipio 1836 (minor); ct Scipio 11-1837
James, Jr. rocf Scipio 1844; dis mo 3-3-1847 after reference to Bristol, Eng.
Samuel rocf Scipio 4-13-1836 (minor); ct Scipio 11-1-1837 (clear)

FULLERTON
Florence Mott recrq 11-1920

FULTON
Amelia, dt John & Jessie, b Bkn. 2-11-1888; name erased 3-1928
Dorcas, dt John & Jessie; m ----- MOFFITT
cf Lurgan, Ireland with parents 8-1888
John m Jessie ----- d 11-4-1903
Ch: Joseph Sidney
Dorcas
Amelia b 2-11-1888 in Bkn.
Nellie
John
Robert
cf Lurgan, Ire. 8-1888 with 2 ch named; John relrq 3-2-1898
John, s John & Jessie, recrq 6-12-1907; joined Methodists name erased 3-1928
Joseph Sidney, s John & Jessie, rocf Lurgan, Ire. with parents 8-1888; name erased 3-1928
Nelly, dt John & Jessie; m a Catholic
name erased
Robert, s John & Jessie, joined Methodists; name erased

FURNAS
Elizabeth, dt Davis & Jane (Satterthwaite), b Waynesville, O. 8-10-1855; m 1884 Joseph A. Bogardus (H)
cf Miami 6-4-1884; ct Swarthmore 6-11-1923
John D., s Davis & Jane; m Ella CLIFTON, dt William & Sarah L. (Vail), b Plainfield, N. Y. 10-30-1860 d 10-13-1923 (H)
Ch: Rachel Dakin b 9- 9-1892
Mary Louise " 1-1-1894
Sarah Jane " 2- 1-1897
cf Miami, O. 10-10-1908 for Ella & ch; h dec mbr
Mary Louise, dt John D. & Ella (Clifton), b L. I. 1894; m 1921 John J. KIRWAN (nm) (H)
Paul J. rocf Indianapolis 2-1920; ct Woodbury, N. J. 12-1925
Sarah Jane, dt John D. & Ella (Clifton), b 2-1-1897; m Howard Van VOLKENBURG (H)
cf Miami, O. 10-10-1908

FUSSELL
Bartholomew, s Bart. & Rebecca, Phila; m at Owen Churchman's 9-1-1841 Rebecca C. HEWES, dt Edw. & Reb. CHURCHMAN, Del. Co., Pa. (H)
Rebecca C. resident in N. Y.
George D., s M. Howard (or Howard Milton) & Sarah E., Phila.; m at John Wm. Hutchinson's 6-30-1915 Eliz. D. HUTCHINSON, dt John Wm. & E. Eliza, Hampsted, N. Y., b N. Y. 7-2-1887 (H)
ct Phila. 2-12-1916 for Elizabeth
Jacob rocf Balt. 1-1867; relrq 1-1880
Mordecai, s Jacob, recrq 5-1871; ct Ashton, Md. 3-2-1904
Rebecca O. (or C.), w Bartholomew, dt ----- HEWES (m 9-1841) (H)
recrq 6-1841; ct Phila. Cherry St. 1-1842

GAIL
Elizabeth, dt Thomas & Abigail, Jamaica; m 1723 James BURLING
Thomas, s Abel & Dinah, Jamaica, L. I., d 1 Mo (Mar) 14, 1728/9; m Flushing "on instant day of" 11 Mo (Jan) 1704/5 Abigail SMITH, dt Alex. (dec) & Mary, Jamaica
Ch: Elizabeth b 6 Mo (Aug) 20, 1706

GAINES
Frances, wd James, d 11-1-1897; recrq 10-1867
Stephen (nm) m Elizabeth C. COLLINS (nm), dt Ezra & Eunice, d 5-27-1841 ae 27y 9m 19d bHS
Ch: Elizabeth d 6-22-1840 ae 2y 11m bHS
Stephen m 2nd -----
Ch: Elizabeth W. d 5-1859 ae 11y bPP

GALE
Moses (nm) (Moses Gale, Jr. b Goshen, N. Y. d 6-19-1825 ae 46y bHS, probably same person); m -----
Ch: George d 9- 6-1817 ae 5d bHS
Infant stillborn 4-30-1818 bHS
Susan d 5- 5-1863 ae 78y bPP
----- & -----
Ch: Caroline b N. Y. d 7-21-1824 ae 1y 3d bHS

GALLAGHER
Benjamin b Dublin d 6-21-1828 ae 69y; con mo 3-5-1794
Sally, dt Henry Newcomb & Harriet (Carpenter), b Bkn. 11-24-1883; recrq 4-12-1926 (H)

GALLAWAY
Daniel A. recrq 1-1879; d 9-17-1880 (H)

GAMBLE
Richard rocf Dublin 7-11-1797 (clear)

GAMMON
Harold W. & Amelia J. WOOTON
Ch: Howard W. Jr. b 1- 2-1929
Amelia rolf Nortrand Ave. M. E. Church, Bkn. 3-4-1903 as Amelia J. Wooton; Harold rolf St. George Episcopal Church, Bkn. 11-1928

GANNETT
Charlotte Katharine (nm), dt Wm. C. & Mary T. L.; m 1919 Edwin Carleton MCDOWELL (H)

GARD
Annie (nm), dt David A. & Mary (Sherwood); m 1902 Lewis A. ROBINSON (H)

GARDHAM
Christopher Walker (nm), s Jos. & Mary E. (Walker); m 12-31-1903 Frances M. TERHUNE, dt James & Mariette (Ross), b Woodside, L. I. 4-20-1882 (H)
Ch: Andrie Frances b N. Y. 4-21-1919
Frances recrq 12-13-1926; Andrie recrq 11-14-1932

GARDINER
Ellen rocf Brighouse 6-1882; ct Brighouse 11-4-1891

GARDNER
Alice m ----- ARMSTRONG
recrq 6-1887
Anna D. W., dt Ernest H. & Mary Ella, b Mt. Vernon 3-21-1895; m ----- McNEILE
Anna Deacon Wills Gardner in birth record; Anna Gordon (Gardner) McNeile is given later; b given later 3-25-1895
Archelus, s Seth, rocf Oblong 4-18-1785 (clear); ct Phila. 12-7-1785 as apprentice to Jas. Star
Asa d 11-30-1839; rocf Oswego 5-19-1830 (clear); dis non attendance 2-1836 (0); relrq 7-6-1859 (H)
Benjamin S. m Sarah E. ----- d 2-11-1879 ae 80y bPP; cf Swansea, Mass. 9-30-1844
Cordelia A., dt Rowland H. & Mary Ann; m 1852 Samuel H. ROSS (H)
Demaris rocf Hudson 12-27-1837 (clear); ct Frankford 10-1864
Dinah recrq 1801 d on Nantucket 1825
Elnathan, s Lewis & Sarah (Teft), b Beekman Town 3-16-1833 d 10-10-1908 bPP; m 12-3-1860 Hannah LYNCH (nm), dt William & Elizabeth, d 5-5-1918 ae 80y bPP (H)
cf Oswego 12-5-1903
Ernest H. m Mary Ella ----- d 7-21-1929
Ch: Charles William b 4- 5-1884 d 5-19-1884
Harper Wills " 11-16-1891 d 2-28-1892
Anna Dean Wills b 3-21-1895
Ernest recrq 6-1881; cf Burl. 7-1882 for Mary b Mt. Vernon; cert of clear to Burl. 1-1882; Ernest glt Chestnut Hill M. E. Church, Mt. Vernon 11-1921
Frederick d 10-26-1847; rocf Oswego 6-17-1835 (clear) (0); cf Oswego 1-1839 (H); relrq 3-1880
George F. rocf Oswego 1-1839; d 1-25-1846 (H)
George G. b Nantucket d 1-25-1846 ae 60y bHS (m) (prob mbr of Nantucket)
Hannah, dt Seth, rocf N. P. 9-15-1784 (clear); ct Creek 1-7-1789 (clear)
Hezekiah Barnard rocf Nantucket 10-3-1799; ct ND MM 2-6-1805 (clear)
Jacob, s Smith, rocf Le Ray 2-7-1839, minor; ct Oswego 11-4-1840
James, having mo, Nantucket refers it to this MM 9-3-1801, on a sea voyage 10-7-1801, rpd to Nantucket 11-1802 that he resides in France
Jane gct East Hoosac 12-2-1835 (clear), rem with parents; returned as they did not live there
Laban & -----
Ch: Infant d 6-12-1820
(mbr prob elsewhere)
Lydia m 5-1835 Willett SECOR
ct Jericho 7-4-1804, minor; cf Flushing 3-5-1829 (clear) (0); cf Flushing 12-1828 (H); dis 1831 (0)
Nathaniel, s Seneca & Sarah, d 9-12-1884; m 4-20-1871 Sarah Elizabeth SUTTON, dt Aaron & Anna (Haight), b N. P. 3-9-1840 d 3- 3-1934 ae 94y (H)
Sarah Elizabeth m 2nd 4-24-1902 Edward H. MAGILL (H)
cf Oswego 3-1856 for Nathaniel; cf N. P. 12-4-1872 for Sarah; she d St. Petersburg, Fla., ashes interred Salisbury, Pa.
Noah, N. Y. m Wby 1786 Sarah -----
Ch: Lydia b 9-16-1787
cf Wby 4-28-1784 (clear); Noah took cert of clear to Wby 10-4-1786; Sarah rocf Wby 6-6-1787
Noah (nm) & -----
Infant stillborn 2-16-1810
Phebe, w Laban
Ch: Jane
cf Troy 6-9-1810; ct East Hoosac 12-2-1835, rem with h, ret as she did not reside there (0)
Ruth, dt Seth, rocf N. P. 4-20-1785; ct N. P. 5-12-1787
Ruth S. rocf Oswego 5-21-1877; d 10-26-1884
Sarah E., dt Aaron & Anna H. SUTTON, b 3-9-

GARDNER, Sarah E., continued
1840 d 3- 3-1934; m 1902 Edward H. MAGILL wd Nathan; she adopted John W. Reynolds, he d 4-1-1887 ae 27y 4m 16d bPP (H)
Seth rocf N. P. 6-15-1785, an elder; d 9-17-1800 bHS
Susannah L., dt Geo. L., d 7-6-1900 ae 86y 9m 27d bPP (nm) (H)
Thomas W. (nm) b Stonington, Conn. d 12-26-1825 ae 27y bHS; m -----
Ch: Infant stillborn 4-14-1825 bHS
----- & ----- (nm)
Ch: Benjamin A. d 5-13-1872 ae 72y bPP

GARFORD
Samuel (nm) d 7-31-1838 ae 72y bHS

GARNER
Thomas H., s Thomas H., d 2-25-1918 ae 89y 8m 28d bPP; m Anna M. FARRINGTON, dt Margaret, d 6-25-1905 ae 73y 1m 11d bPP (nm)
William H. d 9-28-1880 ae 26y 7m 8d bPP (nm)

GARONE
August m 2-5-1930 Margaret SCALES, dt Edw. S. & Alice L., b Glens Falls 2-5-1897
Ch: Barbara Grace b 1-4-1933
August rocf Marl. 1-1924; Margaret rocf Glens Falls 2-5-1906; active mbr 10-1914

GARRETT
Alice Biardot, dt Thomas & Mary (Groff), b 2-20-1887; m 12-23-1920 Norris Folger HALL (nm); name entered by com. 9-3-1890 (H)
Helen, dt Thomas & Mary (Groff), b 9-5-1883; m 1905 Keith SMITH (H)
name entered by com. 9-3-1890
Henry A., dt Alexander & Amelia, Niagara, d 12-23-1874; m at Sarah Loines 5-24-1843 Sarah K. LOINES, dt Rich. & Sarah, N. Y. (not under care of N. Y. MM) (H)
Laura B., dt Maris & Eliz. (Kinsey), b Phila. 2-26-1868; rocf Balt. 10-12-1912; relrq 5-12-1919 (unm) (H)
Sarah K., w Henry A., dt Richard & Sarah LOINES b 8-17-1816 d 12-23-1874 (H)
Thomas, s Thos. & Mary (Groff), b Wilmington, Del. 7-26-1877; m 5-10-1907 Dorothea E. KOBBE. (H)
Thomas m 2nd 2-24-1934 Lucile E. STIM (nm), dt Louis A. & Natalia M. (H)
Thomas' name entered by com. 9-3-1890
Thomas S., s Henry & Cath. Ann (Canby), b Wilmington, Del. 10-2-1851 d 10-1-1923; m 5-4-1876 Mary GROFF (nm) (H)
Ch: Thomas b 7-26-1877
Victor " 12-14-1881
Helen " 9- 5-1883
Alice Biardot b 2-20-1887
cf Wilmington 3-6-1889 for Thomas; names of ch entered by com. 9-3-1890
Victor, s Thomas & Mary (Groff), b Wilmington, Del. 12-14-1881; m 11-27-1908 Dorothy CLARK (nm), dt Lester W. & Irene M. (H)
Ch: Irene Marie b 4- 2-1911
Dorothy Clark b 1-20-1913
Alice " 3-30-1917
Victor's name entered by com. 9-3-1890; ch recrq of parents 5-13-1918

GARRIGUES
Mary Higginbotham (form Garrigues) dis mo 4-3-1811; cf SD MM 7-26-1809

GARRISON
Hester Atwaide, dt John, d 10-31-1902 ae 73y 10m 27d bPP (H)

GASKILL
Joshua W. & Caroline E.
Ch: Alfred R.
Rodman C.
Joshua Howard
Caroline
Henry K.
cf Phila. Green St. 9-3-1873 for all; ct Phila. Race St. 10-6-1875 for all (H)

GATCHELL
Alice, wd, d 10-6-1908; recrq 4-1857
Henry rocf Hardshaw West 10-1850; rel 3-1880

GATES
Horatio Hamilton recrq 3-1881; relrq 3-2-1904
Merrill E., Jr. (nm) m Mary U. WOOD, dt Wm. H. S. & Emma (Congdon), b N. Y. 7-19-1881; Mary relrq 1-1-1919
Samuel J. (nm) s Philip; m 8-27-1917 Mildred KAHN, dt I. Robert & Hattie (Rice), b Chippewa Falls, Wis. 1894 (H)
Mildred recrq 5-13-1918

GAUNT
Ann R. m 1838 ----- RYSDICK (H)
cf Upper Evesham, N. J. 8-8-1827; dis 11-1830 (O)
Delaplaine m Jane W. ----- b L. I. d 6-10-1833 ae 27y 11m
Ch: William
Jane
cf Upper Evesham, N. J. 5-1826; dis 7-1830 (O); ct Corn. 8-5-1835 (H); ct Corn. 6-1-1836 for 2 ch named
Jefferson [Gauntt] rocf Phila. 3-24-1836; dis 10-1837
Stacy T. rocf Green St., Phila. 1-17-1828; ct Green St., Phila. 5-1829; cf Green St., Phila. 8-1837; dis 8-4-1830 for m in (H) mtg in Phila; dis 6-6-1849

GAWTHORP
Thomas rem to Condel MM, Westmoreland, Eng. 7 Mo (Sep) 3, 1747, may be cert of unity

GAY
Roland & Grace

GAY, Roland & Grace, continued
Ch: Roland E. b 3- 5-1919
Dorothy L. b 8-19-1921
Grace V. b 5- 7-1922
parents recrq 11-6-1929; ch recrq of parents 11- 6-1929; Roland E. active mbr 5-1-1935

GEDDS (or GEDDES)
Susan rocf Balt. 9-1834; ct Alexandria 8-4-1847 (H)

GEDNEY
----- & -----
Ch: Caleb b Tioga Co. d 7-20-1828 ae 5m 21d bHS
Emma " N. Y. d 10-26-1829 ae 17y bHS

GEE
Too Shaw recrq 3-6-1907 (chinese)

GEIGER
Mabel Elizabeth, dt Otto John & Nancy M. (Tillotson), b Cleveland 9-13-1906 d 5-4-1934; m 1932 Chauncey O. REINHART (H) recrq 2-12-1934

GEIS
Henry F. recrq 1-1917; name erased 5-1928

GELSTON
Anna rocf Hudson 8-24-1819
Eliza C., Hudson sends her ack. 6-30-1829, accepted a mbr here

GENHERT
Ethel, dt Wolf & Rene (Rafell), b Man. 10-11-1891; m 1906 Abraham Marks GOFFEN (H) recrq 4-11-1932; ch recrq of mother

GERLAGER
Henry (nm) & -----
Ch: Frederic b Flush. d 2-1-1830 ae 5m bHS

GERMOND
Earl m Selma G. GOERKE, dt Oscar & Selma
Ch: Earl Goerke b 2- 6-1918
Norman Maurice b 8-20-1919
Selma Belle " 3-16-1921
Earl recrq 10-1-1930; Selma recrq 4-1-1903; ch recrq of parents 10-1-1930
Samuel (nm) & -----
Ch: Henry b N. Y. d 10-16-1816 ae 8m bHS
----- & ----- (nm)
Ch: William d 3-30-1813 ae 4m 11d bHS

GERNHARDT
Marie Josephine (nm), dt Jos. Henry & Anna (Cogne); m 1915 Cornelius Bertram TITUS (H)

GEROW
Lucy Ann gct Marl. 6-7-1843
William P. d 6-14-1859; m Sarah ----- (H) cf Scipio 9-1855 for both; ct Scipio 1-4-1865 for Sarah

GEST
Joseph Haywood, s Guion M. & Lillian (Haywood), b Cincin. 6-29-1895; m 5-8-1930 Pauline STAFFORD (nm), dt Roy E. & Jennie (Davis) recrq 12-11-1933 (H)

GETCHELL
William (nm) d 4-13-1870, rem from Newark to PP

GEUREKIAN
Bedras T. & Mary
Ch: Arman
Huart b 4-12-1913
parents recrq 4-3-1912; Arman recrq of parents 5-1-1912; all relrq 5-3-1916

GIBBINS
Bevington Henry m Edith Susan ----- d 11-4-1903
Bevington Henry rocf Southern Div. Wales, 9-1883; Edith Susan rocf Worcester & Shropshire 10-1885

GIBBONS
Charles, s Wm. & Rebecca, Phila.; m N. Y. 6-12-1839 Eliza C. HULL, dt Wager & Eliz., N.Y. ct SD MM 9-4-1839 for Eliza C.
Daniel, s Joseph & Phebe (Earle), b Bird-in-Hand, Pa. 11-7-1860 d 10-7-1929 (H) cf Phila. Spruce St. 1-8-1898 (unm)
Francis rocf Phila. 11-1855; ct Phila. 4-1859 (H)
James S., s William & Rebecca, Phila.; m N. Y. 2-14-1833 Abigail HOPPER, dt Isaac T. & Sarah (dec), N. Y. (H)
Ch: William b 1-16-1834 d 12-17-1855
Sarah Hopper b 9-19-1835
Julia b 6-21-1837 d 12-28-1889
Lucy " 10-30-1839
Isaac H. b 9-9-1841 d 3-29-1847
James dis 8-1841; Abigail rel 8-1842
Lucy, dt James S. & Abigail H., b 10-30-1839; m 1870 James Herbert MORSE (H) ret a mbr
Sarah Hopper, dt James S. & Abigail (Hopper), b 9-19-1835 N. Y. d 1918; m 11-24-1863 William EMERSON (nm) (H) ret a mbr

GIBBS
Abel & Elizabeth
Ch: Haydock
cf R. & P. 4-16-1794; ct R. & P. 7-6-1798 for Elizabeth & her two small ch, Hannah & Phebe
Charlotte dis jas 8-6-1817
Elizabeth & ----- (H)
Ch: Hannah
cf Shrews. 1-4-1813 with dt, Hannah; dis 1829 (O); ct Shrewsbury 12-1833 (H)
Eva (nm) m Arthur COFFIN (H)
Grace Carol, dt Dr. Sam'l & Grace C. (McCord), b N. Y. 6-19-1899; m 1924 Elton Verner SMITH (nm) (H)

GIBBS, Grace Carol, continued
recrq of parents 4-13-1912; relrq 3-13-1933
Hannah, dt Abel & Eliz., N. Y.; m 1818 Robert WHITE
Isaac, s Richard & Sarah, Bkn.; m Flushing 8 MO (Oct) 22, 1696 Hannah DICKENSON, dt John & Elizabeth, O.B.
Isaac d 3-7-1799 bHS
Isaac, s Joshua & Hannah, d 5-21-1802 ae 28y bHS; cf Upper Springfield 4-8-1795 (clear); con mo 6-8-1797
Mary R., w John, dt Obadiah & Eliz. WILLETS, d 3-18-1886 (she was wd Edmund KIRBY) (H)
Miles H. rocf Upper Springfield 1-9-1793 (clear)
Richard active mbr 1681-1693
Samuel E., M.D. (nm), dt Samuel T. & Eliz. Mary, d 9-27-1933 ae 90y 7m 14d bPP; m 10-28-1897 Grace Carcline MCCORD, dt Willet & Grace (Willet), b Cssining 9-10-1861 d 5-20-1922 bPP
Ch: Grace Caroline b 6-19-1899
Samuel T. " 12-18-1900
Grace recrq 5-7-1898; ch recrq of parents 4-13-1912 (H)

GIFFORD
Annie W., dt Ruth B.; m ----- LAWRENCE
cf Swansea,Mass.with mother 6-1874; relrq 3-1887
Rebecca rocf Sandwich, Mass. 10-6-1858; ct Sandwich, Mass. 5-1873
Ruth B. & -----
Ch: Annie W.
cf Swansea, Mass. 6-1874 for both; ct Swansea 2-1-1899
Sarah S. (nm), dt Wm. & Rebecca; m 1849 Chas. MILLER, DD.S (H)
----- & -----
Ch: Elma d 7- 2-1872 ae 70y bPP

GILBERT
Herman T. d 8-7-1897 ae 42y bPP; m Annie E. EVANS, dt Lewis B. & Sarah J., b N. Y. 9-26-1857 d Boston 6-27-1923 bPP (both nm)
Walter C. & -----
Ch: Gertrude Francis
cf Kingston, Eng. 4-1889 for both; both joined another religious society, names rem 12-3-1904; he had joined Flushing (H) MM

GILCHRIST
Mina, dt Samuel & Martha T., d 4-1-1916 ae 46y 5m 15d bPP; m J. Brinton KETCHIN (both nm) (H)

GILDERSLEEVE
Alfred Mosher, s Henry B. & Jane (Haight), b 9-12-1861 d 6-28-1924; recrq 3-11-1916 (H)
Florence L. m Bertram SMITH
recrq 3-4-1891; relrq 1-8-1902
Mary J. recrq 4-1882 d 6- 2-1890

GILFORD
Ann (late Myers) dis mo 3-6-1782 (mbr of Kingwood)

GILLESPIE
Sarah (form Howland) dis mo 3-6-1839

GILLINGHAM
Edward C. rocf Phila. 7-24-1834; dis non-attendance 4-1838
Henry W., s Warrington & Mary Ann (Roberts), N. Y., b 9-24-1862 Union Bridge, Md.; m at Sarah Carpenter's 3-31-1897 Sarah CARPENTER dt Robert H. & Amy T. (both dec), N. Y., b N. Y. 1-31-1867 (H)
Ch: Sarah Norbury b 8-18-1899
Edith Leslie " 1-29-1902
cf Alexandria 8-7-1895; parents relrq 12-9-1905
Sarah, dt Henry W. & Sarah (Carpenter), b N.Y. 8-18-1899; m Courtney MONSEN (nm) (H)
Theodore T., s Lucas & Elizabeth T., d 10-28-1923 ae 87y 9m 17d bPP; m Elizabeth HALLOWELL, dt Nathan H. & Elizabeth, d 7-31-1929 ae 92y bPP (both nm) (H)

GILMORE
Benjamin (nm), s Benjamin & Mary; m 6-1-1868 Mary WEEKS, dt James & Lydia (Hoag), b So. Salem, N. Y. 12-23-1821 d 4-25-1909 (H)
cf Ama. 10-1825 for Mary with parents
John recrq 12-1885; name erased 3-1928
Lucy recrq 12-1885
Malinda (form Clark) rocf Corn. 1845; dis mo 11-1849
Thomas Henry granted cert of clear to Wby 8-1871; cf Lisburn, Ireland 3-15-1860; relrq 6-1874
William W. rocf Lisburn, Ireland 3-15-1860; ct Balt. 3-1871; recrq 4-1889; ct Wby 11-1924 (these items may not all pertain to same person)

GILPIN
Charles, s George & Sarah, gct Marl. 11-3-1830, minor (0); ct Marl. 8-1831, minor (H)
George m before 6-3-1807 Sarah DUNHAM, dt Benjamin & Jane, b Mt. Holly, N. J. d 1-17-1815 ae 35y bHS (mo)
Ch: Elizabeth b 12- 1-1809 d 3-11-1833
George " 10-28-1810
Charles " 5-18-1812
cf Phila. 5-30-1806 (clear); dis, rst 9-6-1809; Elizabeth recrq of parents 1-11-1815
George b Maryland d 5-8-1820 ae 54y 5m; m 2nd 1816 Lucy PAGE, dt Rebecca, d 6-12-1855 ae 71y 2m 3d bPP
George took cert of clear to R. & P. 10-2-1816; Lucy rocf R. & P. 12-18-1816
George, s George & Sarah, b 10-28-1810; cf R. & P. with father 1-1817; went to sea in 1831, not heard from 1851, supposed d
John (nm) m Sarah ----- (nm) b N. Y. d 8-2-1818

GILPIN, John & Sarah, continued
ae 23y 7m 9d
Joseph D. [Gilpen] (nm), s George, b Del. d 1-7-1820 ae 27y 6m bHS; dis mo 1-5-1814; widower
Maria, dt George, rocf Phila. 3-26-1807, having rem with her father
Rachel, dt George & Rachel, N. Y.; m 1820 Rowland T. ROBINSON, of Ferrisburg, Vt. cf Wilmington 3-10-1808

GILSO
----- & ----- (nm)
Ch: William d 7-19-1826 ae 21d bHS
Benjamin d 5- 5-1832 ae 8m bHS

GIMBERLING
Adelaide, dt Horace E. & Juliet (Bradbury), b Albion, Mich. 4-30-1880; cf Mt. Holly, N. J. 6-12-1915 (H)

GLADING
William, late of Burlington, N. J.; m at Wm. Fry's 12 Mo (Feb) 23, 1707/8 Mary FRY, dt William & Thomasin, O.B.

GLAENTZER
Helen (nm) m 1929 Ralph George GREATER

GLASER
Myron (nm), s Sam'l Jerome & Henrietta (Herzog); m 12-15-1931 Carolyn C. BUCKWELL, dt Jas. F. & Carrie E. (Cook), b Westfield, N. J. 1-16-1907 (H)
Carolyn recrq 2-10-1919

GLASSFORD
Esther K., dt James & Catharine HULL, rocf Pur. 9-4-1850 with parents; relrq 5-3-1876 (H)

GLAZIER
Elizabeth C., dt Richard B. & Anna, rocf Hudson with parents 3-20-1821; ct Adrian 6-3-1835 with brother & sister, rem with father
George G., s Goddard & Lydia, rocf Hudson 3-20-1827 with mother; dis (H)
Goddard b 12-22-1766 d 11-15-1854 bPP; m Lydia W. ----- b Nantucket d 12-14-1846 ae 75y 1m 19d
Ch: Lydia mo 1823
Russell W. d 11-15-1856 ae 51y bPP
George G.
Edward
cf Hudson 5-21-1822 for Lydia with 4 ch named; ct Hudson (not found); cf Hudson 3-20-1827 for Goddard, having lived some time in N. Y.; Lydia & 3 ch dis 1832-1840 (O)
Lydia, dt Goddard & Lydia; m before 11-5-1823 ----- TAFFAN (or Tappan) (dis that date for mo)
Mary, dt Richard B. & Anna, gct Adrian 6-3-1835 with brother & sister, rem with father
Nathaniel S. (nm) b "in U.S." d 8-21-1845 ae 49y 6m bHS
Richard B. & Anna
Ch: Robert Barclay
Elizabeth C. b 12-23-1820
Edward d 12-9-1822 ae 7y 7m
Lydia B. b 6-17-1822 d 8-8-1823
Mary
Richard, Jr.
cf Hudson 3-20-1821 with their 2 ch named; ct Adrian 6-3-1835 (O) for Robert B., Elizabeth C. & Mary, rem with father; parents dis 1829 (O); ch gct Adrian 6-1835 (O); ct Nankin, Mich for all 2-1835, including Richard, Jr. (H)
Robert Barclay, s Richard B. & Anna, rocf Hudson with parents 3-20-1821; ct Adrian 6-3-1835 with sisters, rem with father
Russell W., s Goddard & Lydia, d 11-15-1856 ae 51y; rocf Hudson with mother 5-21-1822; dis non-attendance 3-1832 (O); dis non-attendance 1-1833 (H)
----- & -----
Ch: Sarah K. b N. Y. d 3-6-1824 ae 13y 9m bHS
George " " " " 11-19-1842 ae 5y 4m bHS

GLOVER
Beatrice L., dt Benjamin G. & Louisa C., d 10-16-1918 ae 32y 4m 10d bur in vault PP (nm) (unm) (H)
Benjamin C. m Louise CROMWELL, dt John & Hannah W., d 3-6-1929 ae 68y 8m 6d bPP (H)

GODDARD
Arthur H. rocf New Bedford 5-1925

GODET
Margaret W. rocf Oswego 4-5-1848; ct Gwynedd 11-6-1867 (H)

GOERKE
Agnes, dt Rudolph & Paulina, d 1-11-1931; m Louis SCHISSELL (nm)
recrq of parents 1860
Agnes, dt Oscar; m George H. DEUELL
Benjamin, s Rudolph & Paulina, b Bkn. 7-31-1858 d 11-9-1904 bPP; m Phebe MEYER, dt George & Phebe, b Bkn. 9-1-1860 d Central Park, L. I. 6-8-1922 bPP
Ch: Infant s d 6-1886 bPP
Infant s " 9-1886 bPP
Edmund, s Oscar, b 6-5-1889; m Marguerite -----
Ch: Gerald George
Edmund, Jr.
Marguerite Elizabeth
Edmund recrq of parents 8-5-1896; ch recrq of parents 12-1928; Marguerite recrq 12-1928; Marguerite active mbr 4-1935
Dr. Francis C., s Oscar & Selma; m Ada THOBIN (or Thoben), dt Frederick H. & Caroline (Fuchs)
Ch: Evelyn T.
Francis C. Jr.
Francis recrq of parents 12-2-1898; Ada

GOERKE, Dr. Francis C. & Ada, continued
recrq 3-1928; ch recrq of parents 3-1928;
Evelyn active mbr 4-1935
Frank, s Rudolph & Paulina, relinquished mbrp 3-1880
George, s Rudolph & Paulina, relrq 10-4-1876
George, s Oscar & Selma (Schissell), b Bkn. 4-25-1886 d 6-12-1935 bPP; m Monica FAUSTMAN (nm)
Isabella, dt Oscar, b 1-5-1879; m Albert W. LINTON
name entered 8-5-1896
Martha B., dt Rudolph & Paulina, b 10-8-1860; m ----- WICK (nm); name erased 4-1928; unknown 1912
Mary, dt Rudolph & Paulina, d 7-25-1893; m ---- METZ
recrq of parents 11-5-1862
Oscar, s Rudolph & Paulina, d 3-17-1895 bPP; m Selma SCHISSELL, dt Francis & Louisa, b Ger. 12-13-1850 d 11-27-1926 at Monclair bPP
Ch: Isabella b 1- 5-1879
Agnes " 10-11-1881
Oscar " 1-10-1883
Walter " 9-13-1884 d 3-14-1935
George " 4-25-1886
Edmund " 6- 5-1889
These ch entered according to disc. 8-5-1896
Francis C.
Selma, Jr.
child d about 1891 bPP
Oscar recrq of parents 11-5-1862; Selma recrq 12-2-1908; Francis recrq 12-2-1908; Selma, Jr. recrq of parents 4-1-1903
Oscar, s Oscar & Selma (Schissell), b 1-10-1883 d 12-12-1934 bPP; m Sophia SUMLEADER
Ch: Hazel Arline b 6-17-1913; active mbr 4-1935 as Arlene
Oscar's name entered according to Disc. 8-5-1896; Sophia recrq 12-2-1908
Paulina, dt Rudolph & Pauline, b 2-22-1872 d 4-3-1921 bPP; m James LEHMAN
Rudolph m Paulina ----- d 9-12-1896 ae 70y bPP
Ch: Oscar
Agnes
Frank d about 1896 bPP
Mary
George
Benjamin d 11- 9-1904
Rudolph b 9-19-1866 d rpd 1920
Martha B. " 10- 8-1860
Paulina " 2-22-1863
Rudolph recrq 2-4-1857; Paulina recrq 6-1860 ch recrq of parents 1860-1862; Rudolph relrq 10-1869; Rudolph rec again 1-1870; Rudolph relrq 10-7-1874
Selma G., dt Oscar & Selma; m Earl GERMOND (nm) recrq 4-1-1903
Walter, s Oscar & Selma, b 1884 d Orange, N.J. 3-14-1935 bPP; m Helen MILLER (nm)

GOETZ
Frederick Carl, s Carl & Katherine, b N. Y. 7-16-1855 d Woodhaven, L. I. 12-14-1933 bPP; m Ottillie GUYER, b 12-13-1859 d Woodhaven, L. I. 7-18-1935 bPP (both nm)

GOFFEN
Abraham Marks (nm), s Daniel & Deborah S.; m 11-6-1906 Ethel GENHERT, dt Wolf & Rene (Rafell), b Mass. 10-11-1891 (H)
Ch: Bernard S. b 1-22-1915
William " 11-25-1909
Ethel recrq with first ch 4-11-1932;
William recrq of mother 5-19-1932

GOLDEN
Jane gct Scipio 5-1835 (H)
Jane M. rec by ack 1827; dis 1830 (O); ct Scipio 9-1832 (H)

GOLDSMITH
Elijah gct Hudson 7-1-1812 (clear)

GOODBODY
Agnes Eliz., dt Robt. & Margaret Jane, rocf Dublin 9-1886 with parents; name erased, having jas 9-1920
Dora, dt Robt. & Margaret Jane, rocf Dublin with parents 9-1886; jas name erased 9-1920
John Lister, s Robt. & Margaret Jane, rocf Dublin with parents 9-1886; name erased 4-1924
Marcia B., dt Marcus & Lydia, London; m 1929 Daniel J. CARROLL (nm) (H); under care of N. Y. MM (H) at rq of Dublin MM
Maurice F., s Robt. & Margaret Jane, rocf Dublin 9-1886 with parents; name erased 4-1924
Robert d 4-13-1911; m Margaret Jane -----
Ch: Isabella Sophia b 9- 6-1873 d 3-24-1929
Hannah Frances " 5-20-1875 " 2- 4-1931
Marcus " 11-20-1876
Thomas Pim " 6- 4-1878
cf Dublin 9-1886 with 4 ch
John Lister
Dora
Maurice F. F.
Agnes Elizabeth
Robert
Thomas & Susan (nm)
Ch: Infant d 11-3-1872 ae 4m bPP
cf Mt. Mellick, Ireland 3-24-1854; ct Mt. Mellick, Ireland 1855; cf Mt. Mellick 1-1870; ct Mt. Mellick, Ire. 2-1877
Thos. Pim, s Robt. & Margaret Jane, b 6-4-1878; cf Dublin 9-1886 with parents; name erased 4-1924

GOODE
John recrq 12-1916; d 8-8-1934

GOODENOUGH
Alice, dt Thos. & Nancy A. (Kelley), b New

GOODENOUGH, Alice, continued
Bedford, Mass. 5-28-1881; m 1905 Chas. E. WHITE, d 1-5-1933 (H)
recrq 1-13-1930

GOODMAN
Daniel (nm), s John & Elizabeth; m in Chicago Anna Smith YEATES, dt Samuel & Jane (Minard) (H)

GOODRICH
Elizabeth Barker rocf Providence 5-3-1893
Stanley W. recrq 4-1909; name erased 3-1928
----- m Elizabeth BARKER
Elizabeth rocf Providence, R. I. 5-3-1893; name erased 2-1926

GOOKIN
May (nm) m Edward Carpenter THORNE (H)

GORDON
Clementina b Strathdon, Scotland d 2-14-1825 ae 33y bHS (unm) (nm)
----- & -----
Ch: Joseph B. b N. Y. d 12-19-1840 ae 5y bHS

GORHAM
Pamelia (late Reed) dis mo 12-4-1811
----- & -----
Ch: George b N. Y. d 2-22-1824 ae 2y 4m bHS

GORM
Elizabeth (nm) d 5-17-1857 ae 60y bPP

GORTON
Alice May (nm), dt Horace Simmons, of Hartford, Conn.; m 1904 Samuel B. VON DER SMITH (H)
Charles rocf Winnesheitt, Iowa 5-1886; d 11-29-1899

GOSLIN
Eleanor (nm), b Flush. d 2-4-1821 ae 87y bHS (wd)

GOUDY
Bernice A. recrq 4-1-1931

GOUGH
Adna H., dt John M. & Sarah, d 1-19-1876; rocf Corn. 3-24-1842, minor, with brother
Ann Eliza, dt John & Sarah, rocf Corn. 10-1847 with mother; ct Marl. 12-1861 with mother
Mary H., dt John M. & Sarah, N. Y.; m 1849 Aaron SUTTON
cf Corn. 10-1847 (clear)
Richard, s John M. & Sarah, rocf Corn. 3-24-1842, minor, with brother; ct Corn. 2-1-1843, minor; cf Corn. 1847; d in Calif.
Sarah, w John
Ch: Ann Eliza
Adna H.
Mary H.
cf Corn. 10-1847, with ch named; Minister; ct Marl. 12-1861

GOULD
Dorothy (nm) m 10-15-1902 J. Sheldon FROST (H); he transferred from Albany 1-8-1916
Gladys Kinghorn (nm), dt Thos. & Florence; m 1926 Dudley S. MAC KENZIE (H)
John, s Daniel & Wait, R. I.; m at Matthew Pryer's 6 Mo (Aug) 30, 1686 Sarah PRYER, dt Matthew & Mary, Mk.

GOW
John (nm) b Scotland d 8-29-1835 ae 24y bHS

GRACEY
Raymond Rossiter (nm), s Jas. Travilla & Ella (Reinhardt); m 11-6-1921 Winola D. CARPENTER, dt Wm. N. & Sarah F., b N. Y. 11-25-1892 (H)
Winola recrq of parents 10-6-1894

GRAHAM
Andrew J., s Lemuel (dec) & Hannah, N. Y.; m at 80 Madison St., May 6, 1856 Caroline ROSS, dt Samuel & Sarah, N. Y. (H)
Ch: Infant stillborn 4-26-1867 bPP
Caroline rocf Phila. 1841 ae 14
Caroline Ross, w Andrew J., dt Samuel ROSS, d 5-1-1900 in 75th yr. (H)
Robert recrq 9-1854; ct Norwich, Canada 4-1858 (H)
William John rocf Pontefract, Eng. 3-1859; rel 2-1864 (mo)

GRANDY
Elinor, spelled Grundy, con mo 8-2-1753, nothing further, but apparently accepted; Elinor Grandy's misconduct noted 12-5-1770, succeeding minutes missing

GRANGER
Wm. L. (nm), s Arthur L. & Annie W., Pelham; m Carmel Country Club 9-15-1934 Mariana CHAPMAN, dt Chas. H. & Mary P., Pleasantville, b Bkn. 7-12-1909 (H)

GRANT
Delaplain rocf Evesham, N. J. 12-10-1825

GRAVES
Gordon H. rolf First Ber Church, Fort Collins, Colo. 10-1-1913; letter to Central Presbyterian Church, Lafayette, Ind.

GRAY
David Howard (nm), s Percy R. & Emma (King); m 9-4-1931 Phebe T. FIELD, dt Richard M. & Eleanor (Smith), b Maplewood, N. J. 3-30-1910 (H)
John, N. Y. & Elizabeth
Ch: Robert U. b 8-14-1799
James " 1- 2-1801

GRAY, John & Elizabeth, continued
cf Ama. 9-14-1799, infant not mentioned; ct Hopewell, Va. 8-1-1804 for Elizabeth & 2 ch

GREATER
Harold H. recrq 11-5-1919; relrq 1-4-1933
Ralph George m 8-31-1929 Helen GLAENTZER (nm)
Ch: Stephen Arlene b 10-28-1934
Ralph George m 2nd Mildred LEWIS
recrq 11-1921

GREEN
Almira, dt Stephen & Lydia (Chase), b So. Starksboro, Vt. 3-28-1836 d 10-19-1914 bPP; m Cyrus PRINDLE (nm)
Almira not in Register of mbrp but listed in 1909 Directory as mbr
Ann rocf Corn. 10-23-1845 (clear); d 5-4-1869
Ann R., dt Israel & Phebe; m ----- MEAD
cf Corn. 5-27-1830 with parents; ct Cedar Creek 4-6-1836 rem with parents (0); ct Corn 3-4-1846 (H)
Arthur B. [Greene] b Bkn. 8-6-1904; stepson of Arthur N. Waring; recrq 9-5-1917; name changed to Waring rpd 3-1928
Caroline, dt Israel & Phebe; m 1857 ----- COTTON (mo)
cf Corn. 5-2-1830 with parents (0); ct Cedar Creek, Va. 4-1836 (0); dis mo 6-3-1857
Caroline rocf Ama. 2-3-1864; d 12-1-1887 (H)
Charles, s Dr. Israel & Phebe, rocf Corn. with parents 5-27-1830; ct Cedar Creek, Va. 1-6-1836, minor, to live with parents at Portsmouth; dis mo 6-4-1862
Elizabeth, dt Stephen & Lydia C., b So. Starksboro, Vt. 3-31-1843 d Richmond Hill, L. I. 8-14-1922 bPP; m Joshua B. UNDERHILL
Enoch rocf Weare 5-13-1841; ct Chap. 8-5-1846
Frances R., dt Dr. Israel & Phebe (Townsend), b 4-20-1836 (or 4-17-1836); m 1856 Augustus E. POTTER (nm) (H)
relrq 5-9-1921; Green Bay, Wis. 1895-1900
Griffen (nm) & -----
Ch: William G. d 3-30-1832 ae 1m 14d bHS
Gurnell Crafton rocf Canterbury & Folkestone 5-4-1904; ct Westminster & Longbord 8-1-1906
Helen L., dt Alva E. & Ann Eliza LAING, d 4-2-1899 ae 84y (w Frank E.) (H)
Isaac rocf Corn. 1-22-1835 (clear); dis failure 7-1837
Dr. Israel in Wis. for Friends Mtg 1848; d 7-30-1886; m Phebe ----- d 8-20-1873
Ch: Ann R.
Charles
Townsend d 1-26-1858
William
Caroline
Frances b 4-17-1836
Edward " 2-28-1838 d 8-11-1838
cf Corn. 5-27-1830 with 5 ch named (0); cf Corn. 10-1831 (H)
James rocf Corn. 2-22-1844 (clear); dis mo 11-1857
Jemima, w Oliver, rocf Chap. 5-12-1797; ct Chap. 5-2-1798
John, having been transported to L. I. for declining the test or affirmation made by the Governor, cf Pur. 2-11-1779, hoping that a way may open for his return to his fam; ct Pur. 4-2-1784; ct Chap. 7-13-1810 (clear); ct Oswego 7-3-1816 (clear)
John T. [Greene] d 8-26-1879; m before 7-1851
Lucy T. ----- d 7-3-1852 (mo)
cf Corn. 2-27-1845 (clear); dis mo 1855; rst 8-4-1875; cf Salem, Mass. 1851 for Lucy
Martha [Greene] rocf Corn. 10-23-1845
Rufus [Greene] rocf New Bedford 7-20-1802 (clear); dis mo 6-4-1803
Sarah (late Lawrence) dis mo 12-2-1795; con mo 8-1-1798
Sarah, wd, N. Y., dt Caleb & Sarah LAWRENCE; m 1797 Caleb NEWBOLD
Sarah A. rocf Dublin 7-5-1893; relrq 2-4-1903
Thomas [Greene] rocf Corn. 1-22-1835 rem with his fam; dis failure 7-1837
Thomas A. [Greene] b 12-19-1873 d 12-14-1867
rocf Nantucket 10-1847 (H)
Townsend, s Israel & Phebe, gct Cedar Creek, Va. 1-6-1836, minor, to live with parents at Portsmouth
William, s Israel & Phebe, rocf Corn. with parents 5-27-1830; ct Cedar Creek, Va. 1-6-1836, minor, to live with parents at Portsmouth; dis 10-1858 (H)
William Henry (nm), s Wm. & Rachel (Bennett); m 4-30-1902 Aimee RUGGLES, dt James Henry & Susan (Blair), b Bkn. 1869 (H)
Aimee recrq 12-11-1922; ct Pur. 7-13-1925
----- m Eva Ella SHERPICK, dt Eugene A. & Eva
Eva Ella recrq as Green 6-6-1934
----- & -----
Ch: Temperance b N. Y. d 7-28-1827 ae 5y 5m bHS
William G. " " " " 11-21-1827 ae 2y 9m bHS

GREENBERG
Julius R., s Jacob & Louisa (Sauner), b N. Y. 6-7-1894; m Palma ----- (H)
Julius recrq 12-10-1917; rem by overseers 3-13-1933 for lack of interest

GREENOAK
Ann, b N. Y. d 2-17-1826 ae 22y 7m 3d bHS

GREENWOOD
Mary rocf Sedbergh MM, Westmoreland, Eng. 3-25-1828 (clear); ct Marl. MM, Ohio 10-4-1843

GREER
Jane, of Belfast, Ire., con mo 3-3-1841; referred to Lisburn, Ire., Lisburn rpd having reconsidered her case & had restored her; ct Lisburn
Samuel dis mo 4-7-1802, had brought rem cert

GREER, Samuel, continued
from Lisburn MM, Ire., the previous month; rem cert not recorded

GREGG
William Henry (nm); m Sarah A. ----- (nm), d 9-29-1856 ae 24y 2m bPP
Ch: Walter d 11-15-1855 ae 3m 29d bPP

GRELLETT
Joseph, now in London, rq rst 2-5-1823, com. rpd 3-5-1823 having examined the minutes of dis, rpd to Grace Church Street MM favorable, if they accept, he to be their mbr
Stephen, s Gabriel (dec) & Susannah, Limoges, France; m N. Y. 1-11-1804 Rebecca COLLINS, dt Isaac & Rachel, N. Y.
Ch: Rachel b 12-21-1810
cf ND MM 4-23-1799 (clear); ct Burl. 2-5-1812 for Rebecca & dt, Rachel; cf Burl. 4-3-1815 for Rebecca & Rachel; cert of unity 1807 and 1811 for Stephen; ct Burl. 3-5-1823 with their dt, Rachel

GRIFFEN
Aaron & Charlotte C. (H)
Ch: Fannie
cf Chap. 2-1844 for both; ct Pur. 4-7-1875 for both
Abigail, wd
Ch: Susan Mott
cf N. P. 7-17-1817 for Abigail & minor dt, named; ct Scip. 8-1829 for Abigail (clear)
Alice, dt Stephen & Jane A., b 7-7-1863; m 1900 Joseph N. BUNTING (H)
Amy, dt John, Flushing; m 1718 Thomas CARLE
Amy T., dt Thos. T. & Mary M., N. Y.; m 1853 Robert H. CARPENTER
Ann, dt Solomon & Clarissa, N. Y.; m 1842 Wm. B. COLLINS
cf Pur. with parents 7-11-1811
Ann Foster (form Griffen) rocf Chap. 7-9-1835 (clear); dis mo 4-7-1841
Anna, w John, rocf Marlbro 5-21-1806 (Ann, wd John, d 1-6-1819 ae 67y bHS)
Anna T. V., dt Charles & Sarah A., Bkn., b N.Y. 5-17-1854; m 1880 Richard L. WALKER (H)
Charles b West. Co. d 7-25-1831 ae 31y bHS
cf Pur. 4-11-1816, apprentice; dis 1830 (O) (m) (H)
Charles, s Edmund & Abigail F., b 9-2-1830, Harrison, N. Y. d 3-1-1910 bPP; m at Stephen Valentine's 11-4-1852 Sarah A. VALENTINE, dt Stephen & Ann (Titus), b 1-7-1829 d 12-6-1894 bPP (H)
Ch: Anna T. V. b 5-17-1854
Henry E. " 10- 1-1856
Edith C. " 1-21-1863 d 7- 6-1925 bPP
David, having ack. for what dis, Pur. referred to N. Y. 3-11-1815; rst 6-7-1815
Deborah, dt Ezekiel, gct Marl. 1-5-1842 (clear)
Edmund d 8-9-1841; m Abigail T. ----- d 1-7-1879
Ch: Hannah T. b 11-17-1822; lost on board S. B. "Eni" 1841
John T. b 3- 2-1824
Henry " 10- 7-1825
Charles " 9- 2-1830
Esther " 8-22-1834
cf Pur. 6-9-1830 with 3 ch named
Edmund Field, s Stephen & Jane A., b 5-18-1870, Windsor Locks, Conn.; m 10-20-1895 Minnie Victoria LEAHY (nm), dt Dennis & Mary A. (Temple), of San Francisco (H)
relrq 5-9-1921
Eliza (probably Elizabeth, dt George & Sarah Ferguson), w Charles H., rocf Plains 6-1816; dis 8-2-1854 (H); dis 1-4-1832 (O)
Elizabeth V., dt Henry & Martha V., Bkn., b 2-16-1853; m 1874 James S. HAVILAND, of Harrison (H)
ct Pur. 6-2-1875
Ellwood B., s John D. & Anna B., Pur.; m N. Y. 4-20-1932 Eliza D. SAVAGE, dt Jose R. F. & Mary H., Jackson Hts., b Hempstead 9-20-1907 (H)
Emily H., dt John L. & Sarah H., N. Y., b 6-1-1848; m 1866 Wm. Wilson UNDERHILL (H)
Esther, dt Edmond & Abigail T., Williamsburgh; m 1854 Joseph WILLETS (H)
Esther L., dt John & Mary E., b 1-24-1852; ct Phila. Race St. 2-5-1868 (H)
Ezekiel m Ann Smith (m Wby)
he took cert of clear to Wby 7 Mo 7, 1727
Ezekiel & Sarah
Ch: Joseph T.
Martha dis 4-1839
Deborah
Elnathan d 4-11-1838 ae 20y 6m 2d bHS
James dis 10-1847
Phebe M.
cf Chap. 5-13-1830; ct Marl. 11-3-1841 with minor dt, Phebe M.
George S., s John & Mary E., b 1-11-1854; ct Phila. Race St. 2-5-1868 (H)
Hannah gct Pur. 11-1-1820 (clear)
Hannah, dt Henry & Martha V., Bkn., b 12-17-1850 Bkn. d 4-9-1910; m 1870 Daniel WILLETT (H)
Hannah, dt Stephen & Jane A., N. Y., b 3-18-1865 Bkn.; m 1886 William Moore, of Phila. (H)
cf Phila. for Wm. 5-7-1884; ct Presbyterian Church for all; Los Gatos, Calif. 2-10-1917
Henry m Sarah R. ----- d 1-9-1854 ae 36y 3m 22d bPP (H) (both nm)
Henry, s Edmond (dec) & Abigail F., N. Y., d 10-5-1888; m at Stephen Valentine's 2-7-1850 Martha VALENTINE, dt Stephen & Ann (Titus), N. Y., b N. Y. 6-23-1826 d 10-21-1914 (H)
Ch: Hannah b 12-17-1850
Elizabeth b 2-16-1853
Henry E., s Charles & Sarah A., Bkn., b 10-1-1856 N. Y. d 6-12-1930 ae 74y 8m 12d bPP; m at Aaron Field's 10-1-1879 Fannie C. FIELD, dt Aaron & Charlotte C. (dec) Bkn.,

GRIFFEN, Henry E. & Fannie C., continued
b 4-3-1856 Bkn. d 6-12-1830 ae 74y 1m 9d
bPP (H)
Ch: Charles, Jr. b 1-19-1882 d 7- 6-1883 bPP
Henry E. Jr. " 2-27-1884 " 3- 4-1887 bPP
Charlotte Field b 1- 9-1890 d 6- 4-1890
bPP
Edward Ellis b 1-27-1892
Charles Field (or Richard) b 3-5-1893
Sarah A. b 2-19-1895
Margaret C. " 8-17-1896
Henry R., s John & Mary E., b 8-23-1857; ct
Phila. Race St. 2-5-1868 (H)
Jacob rocf Chap. 7-9-1835, minor; dis mo 4-1841
James, s Ezekiel & Sarah, dis mo 10-1847
James Henry, s Henry Jesse & Thirzah H., b Yorktown, 1-13-1862; m 11-6-1883 Ella HYATT
(nm), dt Milton & Jemima (H)
recrq 10-6-1886; ct Chap. 5-14-1910
Jeannie H. (or Jane), dt John L. & Sarah H.,
N. Y. b 10-13-1852 N. Y. d 5-8-1930; m 1883
S. Raymond ROBERTS (H)
Job, N. Y. & Phebe
Ch: Marcia b 10-21-1815 d 4- 7-1816
cf Pur. 8-10-1809 for both; failed in bus.
but retained a mbr 5-3-1875; ct Pur. 6-5-1819 for Job & Phebe; cf Pur. 2-12-1823 for
Job & Phebe; Job dis 4-1835 (0) parents dis
1829-1830 (H)
John, Mamaroneck & Hannah
Ch: John b 5 Mo (July) 29, 1713
Hannah " 12 Mo (Feb) 14, 1715/16
Joseph " 6 Mo (Aug) 25, 1717
Jemima " 1 Mo (Mar) 21, 1718/19
Mary " 8 Mo (Oct) 27, 1720
Hannah, having ack. Pur. ref. to N. Y. 3-3-1812, rpd favorably 4th mo; the 5 ch recrq
of Hannah 5-4-1814
John, Flushing, d 1 Mo (Mar) 30, 1741/2; m
Elizabeth ----- d 10 Mo (Dec) 1740
Ch: John
John b Ulster Co. d 1-28-1809 ae 58y 9m 6d bHS
(H)
John, s John (dec) & Esther S., N. Y.; m N.Y.
5-10-1837 Esther LEGGETT, dt Reuben (dec)
& Mary, N. Y. d 4-16-1849 (H)
Ch: Mary L. b 7-29-1838
Esther H. b 8- 5-1840 d 9- 5-1841 rem
from Ft. Greene to PP
Henry S. b 5- 9-1842 d 9-27-1844
Robert N. b 9-13-1844 d 9- 7-1867
cf Chap. 6-1835 for John
John, s John (dec) & Esther S., Safe Harbor,
Pa., late of Mamaroneck, b 8-23-1826; m 3-6-1851 at Thos. H. Brown's Mary E. LEGGETT
dt Reuben & Mary (H)
Ch: Esther L. b 1-24-1852
George S. " 1-11-1854
Clara R. " 9-28-1855 d 6-26-1857
Henry R. " 8-23-1857
These ch b in Phila.; John relrq 7-4-1860;
Mary relrq 2-5-1868
John C. (nm), s Henry Clay & Josephine (Blair),
m 6-4-1925 Beatrice J. CARPENTER, dt Wm.
H. & Sarah F., b N. Y. 2-28-1887 (H)
Beatrice recrq of parents 10-6-1894
John D. d 2-13-1836; m Martha WOODWARD, dt Thomas & Elizabeth
Ch: John D.
Daniel M. d 12-20-1838 ae 4y 6m bHS
cf Pur. 2-7-1827, minor; dis 1830 (0);
Martha dis 2-1844 (0); ch John D. rec (0)
John D., s John D. & Martha; m Elizabeth -----
(mo before 1-1860, ret a mbr); John recrq
of mother; relrq; Elizabeth nm
John F., s Edmond (dec) & Abigail F., N. Y.;
m at Daniel G. Haviland's, Bkn. 2-7-1850
Mary MEKEEL, dt Isaac & Phebe, Somers,
N. Y. (not under care of N. Y. MM) (H)
Mary dis mo 11-1850 (0); ct R. & P. 9-4-1867
John L., s John (dec) & Hannah, N. Y., b 1-26-1820 d 8-31-1898 bPP; m at Wm. M. Haydock's 5-13-1847 Sarah HAYDOCK, dt Henry &
Sarah, both dec, N. Y., d 3-25-1894 (H)
Ch: Emily H. b 6- 1-1848
Louisa " 12-20-1850 d 1-24-1851 bPP
Jane H. " 10-13-1852
Walter H. " 11- 2-1855
Alice L. " 9-12-1862 d 7-15-1914 bPP
Joseph & ----- (H)
Ch: Sarah Ann b 7-14-1838 d 10-9-1840
cf Pur. 5-11-1831 (clear); ct Pur. 2-1837;
cf Pur. 1-1838; ct Pur. 3-1849
Joseph d 3-15-1870; m Elizabeth ----- d 1-2-1904
cf Ama. 10-1864
Joseph T., s Ezekiel & Sarah, mo before 7-1834
retained a mbr
Ch: Mary Jane d 1-2-1835
ct Oswego 8-4-1838
Letitia rocf Chap. 7-9-1835 (clear); d 1836
Martha (form Hall) dis mo 5-1845
Mary, dt John, Flushing; m 1718 Thomas CARLE
Mary J., dt Thos. T. & Mary M., N. Y.; m 1854
Benj. C. ARNOLD, of Arnoldtown, N. Y. (H)
Mary L., dt John & Esther (Leggett), Phoenixville, Pa., b N. Y. 7-29-1838 d 6-23-1920;
m 5-12-1858 Wyatt W. MILLER (nm), of Safe
Harbor, Va. (H)
Oliver m Cornelia A. WILLETS, dt Jacob & Susan
A., d 9-21-1894 ae 73y 8m 26d bPP (H)
Ch: George J. d 8-9-1883 ae 22y 4m 28d bPP
Phebe M., dt Ezekiel & Sarah; m ----- BRYANT
(dis mo 6-1849)
Richard F. (or Charles), s Henry E. & Fannie
C. (Field), b Bkn. 3-5-1893; m 6-30-1922
Marguerite SAWYER, dt John Tilton & Florence (Streeter) (H)
Ch: Deborah b 5-26-1926
Robert rocf Pur. 1-11-1810 (clear); cert of
clear to Chap. 4-7-1813; ct Pur. 10-6-1813
Robert C., s Stephen & Jane (Arnold), b 8-14-1867; m 7-16-1901 Leila LAMAR (nm) (H)
Samuel (nm) b Stamford, Conn. d 12-16-1810 ae
21y 8m bHS

GRIFFEN, continued
Sarah, w Henry (nm), dt Richard & Sarah TITUS, d 1-9-1854 ae 36y 3m 22d (H)
Sarah A., dt Henry E. & Fannie T., Great Neck; m 1924 Cyrus C. TURNER, Jr. (nm) (H)
Sarah Clark, dt Cornelia H., d 7-18-1904 ae 47y 9m 22d bPP; m ----- BROWN (H) (both nm)
Sarah Elizabeth, dt Thos. T. & Mary M., N. Y., b 5-10-1834; m 1855 Joseph Arnold, Jr., of Arnoldton
Solomon & Clarissa
Ch: William b 5-31-1814 d 11-16-1816
Ann " 5-15-1817
cf Pur. 7-11-1811 for Solomon & Clarissa; parents dis 1829 (H); ct Ama. 1855 for both
Stephen, s Thomas T. & Mary (Miller), b N. Y. 9-30-1826 d San Jose, Calif. 3-29-1901 in 76th yr.; m 9-3-1857 Jane A. ARNOLD, dt Joseph & Dorcas (Cornell), b Rifton, N. Y. 8-1-1831 d 1-26-1906 (H)
Ch: Thomas T. b 5-27-1858 d 10-18-1864 bPP
Joseph Arnold b 6-30-1860 d 9-25-1888 bPP
Alice b 7- 7-1863
Hannah " 3-18-1865
Robert Cornell b 8-14-1867
Edmund Field b 5-18-1870
cf Plains 11-1858 for Jane A.
T. T.s Stephen d 10-18-1864 ae 6y 4m 21d
Thomas P. rocf Pur. 8-9-1826
Thomas T., s Stephen & Jerusha, Scarsdale, d 1-1-1881; m N. Y. 11-10-1825 Mary MILLER, dt Charles & Amy (dec), N. Y. d 12-21-1887 ae 84y 3m 9d bPP (H)
Ch: Stephen
Amy T. b 8- 2-1829
Mary Jane " 1-10-1831
Sarah Elizabeth b 5-10-1834
Caroline " 1-12-1839 d 2- 1-1923 bPP
Hannah b 4- 2-1844 d 12-19-1849
Thomas rocf Pur. 1826
Thomas W., s Samuel & Abigail; m 5-16-1850 Eliza B. CARPENTER, dt David & Mary (Harcourt), b Barkerville 5-22-1817 d 6- 4-1903 (H)
cf Albany 9-5-1866 for Thos.; cf Sara. 12-5-1866 for Eliza; Thomas dis 11-6-1872 for failure in commission business
Walter H., s John L. & Sarah H., b 11-2-1855 d 12- 6-1898 bPP; m 7-15-1896 Ann D. SOUTHWICK (nm), d 7-4-1895 ae 31y 5m 23d bPP (H)
William J., s Jesse H. & Eliza H. (Miller), b Yorktown 7-4-1861; m 1-25-1888 Alice JORDAN (nm), dt Wm. H. & Margaret, d 10-29-1824 ae 59y 2m 19d bPP (H)
Ch: Eliza M. d 9-14-1893 ae 2y 10m
cf Ama. 12-6-1893
Wm. Jay (nm), s Henry & Josephine; m 2-21-1912 Elizabeth CARPENTER, dt Wm. H. & Sarah F., b N. Y. 2-28-1887 (H)
Elizabeth recrq of parents 10-6-1894
----- & -----
Ch: Mary Jane d 1- 2-1835 ae 9m bHS
Ch: Daniel M. d 12-20-1838 ae 4y 6m bHS

GRIFFITH
Isaac (or Griffiths) rocf Green St., Phila. 8-22-1822; ct West Grove 3-17-1827 (clear)
Sarah Emily, w Walter, rocf Chap. 2-1857; ct Chap. 2-3-1869 (H)

GRIGGS
----- & -----
Ch: Eliza T. b Orange Co. d 1-1-1834 ae 7m 11d bHS

GRIMES
James d 7-15-1877 ae 58y bPP; m Frances ----- b Eng. 11-5-1814 d 11-1-1897 bPP
both recrq 10-1867; 12-1867

GRIMM
Edward Eugene b N. Y. 1855 d 4-13-1920 ae 65y bPP (unm) (nm)

GRIMSHAW
Ann Eliza, dt Samuel & Hannah, d 1-17-1879; rocf Newcastle, Eng. with mother 8-14-1833; ct Scipio 2-2-1848; cf Scip. 9-1855; visited on behalf of Scip & dis 11-3-1858 (O)
Benjamin, s Samuel & Hannah, rocf Newcastle, Eng. with mother 8-14-1833; mo, referred to Scipio, retained a mbr by that MM 7-1844
Catharine, dt Samuel & Hannah, recrq of mother 10-1837; ct Scipio 2-2-1848; cf Scipio 1856; dis 9-2-1857
Elizabeth, dt Samuel & Hannah, mo before 6-1847 to ----- TALLMAN
cf New Castle, Eng. 8-14-1833 with parents; dis mo 6-1847
Emma gct Ferrisburgh 8-7-1844; cf Ferrisburgh 9-1-1852 (clear); d 1-5-1878
Emma R., dt John & Emma, N. Y.; m 1851 Benj. S. HAVILAND
rec on ack. 4-1842; ct Ferrisburgh 8-7-1844
George rocf Peel MM, London 1-19-1831 (clear); dis 10-1832
Hannah, w Samuel, d 3-1846
Ch: Benjamin
Ann
John d 9-1838
Elizabeth dis 6-1847
Henry Holmes
Hannah Holmes
Catharine
cf Newcastle, Eng. 8-14-1833 with 5 ch named; two more ch recrq of mother 1834-1837
Hannah Holmes, dt Samuel & Hannah, recrq of mother 10-21-1834; ct Scipio 2-2-1848
Henry Holmes, s Samuel & Hannah, rocf Newcastle, Eng. with mother 8-14-1833; ct Scipio 2-2-1848
Sarah recrq 7-1-1818; dis mo 2-2-1820 to -----

GRIMSHAW, Sarah, continued
O'BRIEN

GRINNELL
Cornelius, Jr. m New Bedford, Mass. 1808 Eliza TALLMAN
Ch: Eliza b 7- 3-1809
cf New Bedford 12-20-1803, apprentice with Post & Russell; cert of clear to New Bedford 5-4-1808; Eliza rocf New Bedford 5-4-1808; all rem to New Bedford 5-1-1811; cert of 1811 not recorded
Henry rocf New Bedford 12-26-1816 (minor); dis mo 10-2-1822
Joseph d New Bedford 2-7-1885; m Sarah ----- d 7-27-1862 (H)
Pres. of Wamsuta Mills Corp. of New Bedford cf New Bedford 10-26-1815 for both; dis 1831,1832 (O)
Susan R. dis 1-1849; ct Scipio 4-23-1846 (clear) cert returned, she having returned; cf New Bedford, endorsed by Scipio 11-1847
William rocf New Bedford 8-24-1815, apprentice to his brother, having mo New Bedford referred to N. Y. 5-1-1822, after correspondence, New Bedford rpd adversely and N. Y. dis him 12-4-1822; erroneously placed on our Reg. 2-1850 (H)

GRINYER
Samuel recrq 1-1885; relrq 5-1888

GRISCOM
Daniel rocf Phila. Cherry St. 6-1839; ct Phila. Cherry St. 5-1842; cf Phila. Cherry St. 3-1843; ct Phila. Green St. 5-1849 (H)
David rocf Salem, N. J. 11-27-1809; ct Salem 1-11-1815 (clear)
David, having mo Frankford refers to N. Y. 12-1-1841; dis 4-6-1842
Edward, s John & Abigail, b 11-12-1811; ct Hudson 3-7-1832 (clear)
John m Abigail ----- b Burl., N. J. d 4-3-1816 ae 42 bPP (or 4-4-1816) (m Burl.)
Ch: Elizabeth D.
Mary H.
Susanna
William H. b 6-14-1807 d 12-1871 bPP
John Hoskins b 8-14-1809 d 4-28-1874
Edward b 11-12-1811
Ruth Anna b 7-13-1813
Abigail " 3-1816
cf Burl. 5-4-1807 with 3 ch named; ct Providence 7-3-1833 for John, with 4 dt, Elizabeth D., Mary H., Ruth Ann & Abigail, dt (clear) (O); parents & Susan dis 1827 (H)
John H., s John & Abigail, b 8-14-1809 d 4-28-1874 bPP; m before 10-1835 Henrietta ----- (mo)
Ch: Infant stillborn 10-8-1836 bPP
ret a mbr 12-1835
Mary H., dt John & Abigail, gct Burl. 10-2-1816 (minor); cf Burl. 2-7-1820
Susan (or Susanna), dt John & Abigail, rocf Burl. with father 5-4-1807; ct Radnor 11-6-1839
----- & -----
Ch: Edward P. d 11-19-1867 ae 27y bPP
Grand ch of Dr. Griscom, d 10-25-1868 ae 5m 10d bPP

GROFF
Mary (nm) m 5-4-1876 (prob in Wilmington) Thomas S. GARRETT (H)

GROSHON
Amelia, w Henry, dt William & Ann WAGSTAFF, mo & retained a mbr; ct Kingston, Eng. 1-1857

GROVES
Florence M. recrq 3-4-1931
Jennie recrq 3-4-1931

GRUBB
Thomas m Limerick, Ireland 1870 Susanna ----- cf Dublin 9-1867 for Thomas; cert of clear to Limerick, Ireland 7-1870; cf Limerick 11-10-1870 for both; both relrq 8-1873
Wm. M. dealt with at rq of Phila. for misconduct; rpd to Phila. 9-5-1832 he now living in Burl.

GRUNDY
Alfred Allen & Alice
Ch: Alfreda Elizabeth
recrq 10-4-1911; ct Germantown for all 12-1920; Alfreda recrq of parents 4-6-1910
Alfreda Elizabeth recrq 4-6-1910

GUERNSEY
Mary H., w Sam'l B., dt John & Abigail HOSIER, b 3-17-1826 d 7-16-1879 (m 1-6-1869) (H)

GUION
Mary, dt Benjamin & Sarah, b Pelham d 11-15-1809 ae 26y 2m 9d bHS

GULAGER
Henry (nm) & -----
Ch: Louisa b N. Y. d 12-19-1834 ae 2y 2m bHS

GUMMERE
----- & -----
John d 4-22-1833 ae 8m 8d bHS

GUMMERSAL
Thomas, cert for him, addressed and sealed as a letter, lately arrived in the Diana, Wilton, Liverpool, as agent or factor from Brighouse MM, Yorkshire 10-25-1771

GUMNERSON
George S. (nm), s Geo. J. & Alice T.; m Pomona 5-25-1935 Mildred Laura CONCKLIN, dt Erwin

GUMNERSON, George S. & Mildred Laura, continued
& Leah H. (Miller), b Pomona, N. Y. 8-30-1910 (H)

GURNEE
Margaret E., wd Francis W., dt Henry & Eliz. M. MEAD, Kakiat, N. Y., b Saddle River, N. J. 10-29-1829 d 1920; recrq 6-4-1884; lived Mt. Ivy, N. Y. (H)
Myra E., dt Frances W. & Margaret E. (Mead), b Bloomingdale, N. J. 12-3-1870; m 1892 Stephen H. SMITH (nm) (H)
recrq 7-6-1901

GUTHRIE
Helena Elizabeth rocf Dublin 11-5-1902; ct Dublin 11-6-1907

GUY
John Henry rocf Westminster & Longford 3-2-1904; name erased 11-1928; rst. 6-1930; ct Jordans, Eng. 6-4-1930
Mary, dt Percy C. & Abigail Susan; m ----- MURDOCK
cf Westminster & Longford 7-11-1906 with parents; ct Phila. 3-1927
Percy C. & Abigail Susan
Ch: Mary
Bertha
cf Westminster & Longford 7-11-1906 for all

GUYER
Ottillie b 12-13-1859 d Woodhaven, L. I. 7-18-1935 bPP; m Frederick Carl GOETZ (both nm)

GWYER
Gwendolyn (nm) m Robert I. WALKER (H)

HABBICK
George Wm. m Mary DUNNS
cf Darlington, Eng. 1-1928

HACKETT
Edna Wallace (nm), dt Wm. N.; m Sidney H. CARPENTER (H)
Sidney recrq of parents 10-6-1894

HADAWAY
Wm. Stratton (nm), s Frank T. & Anna (Stratton) m 3-7-1925 Dorothy KINKEAD, dt Wm. L. & Amy T. (Scantlebury), b Paterson, N. J. 10-31-1902 (H)
Dorothy recrq 1-8-1923; ct Montclair 7-8-1929

HADDOCK
Catharine (form Marsh) gct Battle Creek 7-1852 (m 1847) (H)
Henrietta L., dt Isaac & Deborah, b 9-9-1852; m ----- DONALDSON
relrq 2-5-1896
Isaac d 3-24-1884; m Frankford, Pa. 1851 Deborah ----- d 2-28-1864
Ch: Henrietta Louisa b 9- 6-1852
Lydia Ann " 3-13-1855
Frederick Wm. " 6-15-1857 d 3-14-1876
Robert James " 11-18-1861
cf Dublin 1848 for Isaac; cf Frankford 1852 for Deborah; cert of clear to Frankford 11-5-1851
Isaac m 2nd Sarah Ann ----- b Clinegal, Ire. 12-10-1835 d 2-23-1915 bPP (mo before 5-1868, ret a mbr)
Ch: Edwin Joseph b 6-13-1868 d 4-1917 bPP
Deborah Chapman b 10-30-1869
ch marked "not mbr" in Reg. hence Sarah Ann probably nm
Lydia Ann, dt Isaac & Deborah, b 3-13-1855; relrq 7-1889
Robert J., s Isaac & Deborah, b 11-18-1861; name erased 10-1928
William J. d 4-23-1891; recrq 6-5-1872 (H)
----- & -----
Ch: Nathaniel d 3-17-1876 ae 18y bPP

HADLEY
Ross A. rocf Oskaloosa 10-7-1908; ct West Richmond, Ind. 5-3-1916

HADWIN
James brought rem cert from Barbados; took cert back 2 Mo (Apr) 15, 1714

HAFFORD
Eloise Ada rocf New Bedford, Mass. 9-1914; ct First Friends Church, Pasadena, 12-4-1929

HAGAN
Arthur Tyson, s Olive & Sarah, rocf Devonshire House 9-5-1860; ct Roch. 4-1880
Austin Alexander, s Olive & Sarah, rocf Devonshire House with mother 9-5-1860; ct Roch. 5-1871
Eliz. Leedom, dt Joseph & Sarah E., N. Y., b 10-15-1842; m 1865 Chas. Lambert RATHBORNE (H)
James (nm) & -----
Ch: John d 10-18-1803 ae 7d
James Wallace, s Jos. & Sarah E., b 1-31-1840; cf Chap. 6-1858; dis 8-5-1863 for joining Episcopal Church (H)
John rocf Troy 1-7-1846; dis 3-3-1847 (H)
Joseph, s Margaret, d 5-14-1887; m Sarah ----- d 5-18-1867 (H)
Ch: Phebe C. b 8-18-1828
Margaret S. " 4-13-1831
Sarah Jane " 9-23-1833
James Wallace " 1-31-1840
Elizabeth Leedom b 10-15-1842
cf Troy 9-1843 with their ch; ct Chap. 1-18-1856 with 3 ch; cf Chap. 3-7-1860 with 2 ch, Sarah J. & Eliz. L. (H)
Margaret, w -----
Ch: Joseph
James
William

HAGAN, Margaret, continued
Ch: John
 Jane
 Eliza Ann
 cf Lisburn to Wilmington 11-12-1801 with ch, Joseph, endorsed to N. Y. 5-6-1802 with her ch, Joseph & James, the latter b Wilmington; her four ch recrq of mother 4-7-1813; ct Troy with 6 minor ch named 2-7-1816; cf Troy 11-4-1846 (H)
Margaret, d 6-23-1894; m 2nd James THOMPSON (nm) cf Troy 11-4-1846 (H)
Margaret S., dt Joseph & Sarah E., d 10-14-1857; m Edmund W. CORLIES (H)
Olive m Sarah ----- d 7-20-1865 ae 45y bPP (mo before 10-1867
Ch: William Levell d 12-25- (or 27) 1863 ae 15y
 Austin Alexander
 Arthur Tyson
 Benjamin Olive
 Mary Henrietta
 cf Reading & Warborough, Eng. 3-4-1863 for Olive; cf Devonshire House 9-5-1860 for Sarah & ch named; ct Roch. 5-1871 for Olive, Austin, Benjamin & Mary
Phebe C., dt Joseph & Sarah Elizabeth, N. Y.; m 1848 Robert CARPENTER (H)
Robert & -----
Ch: George
 Elizabeth
 Robert
 Sarah
 cf Wilmington 6-7-1804 for these four minors, endorsed to Easton 8-1-1804 as it is found that they live there
Sarah Jane, dt Joseph & Sarah E., N. Y., b 9-23-1833; m 1878 Webster Lane, of Chap. (H) ct Chap. 10-2-1878

HAIG
William, Antigua, W. I.; m Flushing 7 Mo (Sep) 1, 1702 Mary MASTERS, dt George & Mary, N. Y.
Ch: Mary b 6 Mo (Aug) 11, 1704
 William prc of clear from Antigua; he & w took cert there 9 Mo (Nov) 25, 1704

HAIGHT
Amy rocf Creek 11-6-1850; relrq 5-27-1852 (H)
Anna, dt Franklin C. & Caroline A. (Quinby), b Little Rest, N. Y. 3-6-1872; m 1898 Charles L. McCORD (H)
 cf N. P. 12-9-1899
Samuel Carleton, s Stephen & Mary A., rocf Chap. with parents 4-5-1876; relrq 9-2-1896
Charles d 7-28-1890; m Emeline ----- d 2-9-1887 (H)
 cf Chap. 1-1844; Emeline recrq 7-3-1872
Edward rocf Chap. 2-12-1846; relrq 1-1868
Eliza L. (or Hait), w Selah, dt James J. & Mary JENKINS; rocf Marl. 12-1848; at Milton, then at Lloyd, Mich. 1859; relrq 6-8-1901
Israel A., s Aaron & Phebe A., rocf Chap. 5-11-1843, minor; dealt with by Chap. for mo & rec by them 7-1847; ct Chap. 1853
Jacob gct Pur. 3 Mo (May) 3, 1744
John, Flushing, m at Robt Field's, Newtown, 1 Mo (Mar) 14, 1716 Phebe TITUS, dt Samuel, Wby.
Ch: Elizabeth b 11 Mo (Jan) 5, 1716/17
 Charity " 6 Mo (Aug) 3, 1718
 Elizabeth " 10 Mo (Dec) 14, 1720
 Phebe " 11 Mo (Jan) 14, 1722/3
 Sarah " 1 Mo (Mar) 6, 1725/6
 Mary " 7 Mo (Sep) 10, 1727
 Samuel " 8 Mo (Oct) 1, 1729
Mary, dt Samuel, Flushing; m 1711 David HEUSTIS of Westchester

Mary Evelyn, dt Stephen & Mary A., rocf Chap. with parents 4-5-1876; relrq 9-2-1896
Nicholas, s Samuel & Sarah, Flushing; m Wby 3 Mo (May) 5, 1704 Patience TITUS, dt Edmund & Martha, Wby
Ch: Martha d 10 Mo (Dec) 29, 1725
Phebe, dt Samuel (dec), Flushing; m 1719 Anthony BADGLEY
Phebe, Flushing, m 1739 Jonathan HOLMES
Phebe, wd John, Flushing, dt Samuel TITUS; m 1743 Caleb CORNELL
Phebe dis 1-5-1763
Samuel, Flushing, d 7 Mo (Sept) 1712 m -----
Ch: Samuel, Jr. d 5 Mo (July) 1712
 active mbr 1681 to 1702 or later
Samuel L., s Samuel & Phebe; m Pur. 1-14-1835 Elizabeth HAVILAND d 3-14-1837
Ch: Stephen S. b 3-6-1836
 cf Chap. 6-17-1832 for Samuel (clear); cf Pur. 12-9-1835 for Elizabeth
Samuel L. m 2nd N. Y. 2-14-1844 Deborah UNDERHILL, dt Andrew & Deb. (both dec), N. Y.
 cf Chap. 6-17-1832 for Samuel (clear); ct Chap. 12-2-1846 for both
Sarah, dt Samuel & Sarah, Flushing; m 1704 Silas TITUS
Stephen S. & Mary A.
Ch: Mary Evelyn
 Samuel Carleton
 cf Chap. 4-5-1876 with 2 ch named; Mary A. relrq 3-1881; Stephen relrq 12-7-1892
Susan A., dt Jacob T. & Sarah (Griffen), b Macedon, 12-22-1836 d 7-24-1909; m 9-22-1853 John H. HILL (nm) (H)
 cf Duanes 12-4-1889; matron of Orphan Asylum, Bkn.
----- & -----
Ch: Jane d 7-19-1866 ae 78y bPP

HAINES
Edith C., dt Samuel B. & Rebecca, b 9-7-1866 N. Y.; m 1896 E. Norman NICHOLS (nm) (H)
Edith W., dt Franklin & Abigail B., N. Y., b 8-7-1830; m 1855 Jacob CORLIES, of Po'keepsie (H)
Franklin, s Geo. & Edith, Northampton, N. J.,

HAINES, Franklin, continued
d 9-25-1871; m N.Y. 11-12-1829 Abigail BOWNE, dt Samuel (dec) & Hannah, N. Y., d 6-14-1876 (H)
Ch: Edith W. b 8- 7-1830
Samuel B. b 4-23-1834
Hannah B. " 1-17-1836
cf Burl. 2-5-1827; Abigail rocf Flushing 9-1825; dis 1830; Abigail & Hannah gct Oswego 6-1873
Franklin, s Samuel B. & Rebecca M., b N. Y. 6-29-1862; m 2-11-1885 Frances C. WAY (nm), dt Geo. Pierce & Carlene A. (Dobuert) (H)
Malinda Elkinton, Malvern, Pa.; m 11-17-1904 William E. STAFF
William E. took cert to R. & P. 8-1-1906 (Malinda probably took cert from Malvern to R. & P.)
Reuben, s Caspar W. (dec) & Hannah, Phila.; m N. Y. 5-13-1812 Jane BOWNE, dt Robert & Elizabeth, N. Y.
Jane B. gct Phila. 12-2-1812
Richard R., s Jervis & Elizabeth, d 3-20-1897; m 2-13-1856 Harriet T. TOWNSEND, dt Edward & Ann C., b Phila. 12-12-1833 (H)
Ch: Edward T. b 9-17-1858 d 10- 8-1874 bPP
Richard R. d 11-17-1864 ae 1y 2m 27d bPP
Elizabeth b 5-1-1865 d 8-13-1865
Frank b 12-12-1868 d 2-24-1899
cf Phila. Green St. 5-1864 with 2 ch; cf Phila. 11-7-1903 for Harriet
Samuel B., s Franklin & Abigail (Bowne), b 4-23-1834 N. Y. d 10-10-1913; m 10-25-1859 Rebecca M. ROWLAND, dt Samuel & Mary L., d 3-1-1895 (H)
Ch: Mary Rowland b 11-11-1860
Franklin " 6-29-1862
Edith C. " 9- 7-1866
Simeon rocf Phila. 5-27-1824; dis 1826
William Mickle, s Jos. C. & Caroline, b Bethlehem, Pa. 3-7-1863; m 4-19-1888 Alice D. SELLECK, dt James W. & Eliz. M. (Beth), b Bkn. 9-13-1864 (H)
both recrq 12-9-1929

HALE
Caleb (nm) & -----
Ch: Elizabeth b N. Y. d 11-14-1840 ae 8m bHS
Philip rocf Miami, O. 2-5-1890; mbrp cancelled 1-13-1906
Philip (nm) b Phila. d 5-1-1832 ae 26y bHS (unm)

HALFDAN-NIELSON
Regnor & Deborah
Ch: Ellen
all recrq 5-1925; ct Detroit for all 7-1926

HALL
Alice L., dt Isaac, Jr. & Emma L., b 3-4-1866; m 6-22-1893 Franklin PHILLIPS (nm)
Elizabeth, dt Edward & Mary (Pease), b Colgary, Can. 3-25-1907; m 1934 Winifield G. HORNER, 3d (H)
cf Boston 9-10-1934; Winfield recrq 1-14-1935
Emma L., wd Isaac, dt Israel L. & Susan J. LUKENS; m 2nd 6-25-1891 Samuel S. THOMPSON
cf Phila. Green St. 4-1861 with mother; relrq 2-4-1863 (H); recrq 6-1863 (O); ct WD MM 2-1-1893 (O)
Hannah Macy (form Hall) dis mo 1-1-1840
Isaac, Jr. d 11-8-1883; m Emma L. LUKENS, dt Israel L. & Susan J.
Ch: Alice L. b 3- 4-1866
Charles Lyman b 3-12-1868 d 11-10-1885
Isaac mo before 6-1844 by priest, ret a mbr
cf Hudson 7-24-1839 (clear); Emma L. recrq 6-1863; Emma m 2nd 6-25-1891 Samuel S. THOMPSON
John & Ann
Ann recrq 10-3-1810
Lillian (nm), dt John & Mary F.; m Theodore McDOWELL (H)
he relrq 5-9-1921
Martha Griffen (form Hall) dis mo 5-1845
Norris Folger (nm), s Lyman B. & Carolyn (Ladd); m 12-23-1920 at Thos. Garrett's Alice Biardot GARRETT, dt Thomas & Mary (Groff), b 2-20-1887 (H)
Ch: Helen G. b Cambridge, Mass. 9-29-1921
Carolyn Ladd b Cambridge, Mass. 1-20-1923
name of Alice entered by com. 9-3-1890; ch recrq of parents 2-11-1935
Rachel W., w Charles C., dt Samuel & Mary SMITH, b 12-6-1838
cf Wby & Jericho 11-1873; relrq 3-1885
Rebecca B., dt Stephen & Jane, b 1-12-1811 d 4-15-1899 bPP; m William HANNA (both nm)
Theodore G., s Theodore & Mary L. (Grueniski), b Poland, Russia, 12-4-1874 d 12-12-1918 bPP; m Henrietta HUDSON
Ch: Theodore H. d 7-13-1919 ae 22y bPP (both nm)
----- m Georgia BAILEY, wd Chas. H., dt Hiram & Esther RHODES
recrq of parents 4-1872

HALLENBACH
Fred W.'s name erased 5-1928; lived 146 Quincy St., Bkn.

HALLETT
Abraham S. b New Town d 2-19-1826 ae 52y bHS; dis mo 12-7-1808
Amy, dt Richard, Newtown; m 1746 Benjamin SHOTWELL, of Elizabeth Town
Ann m 1781 William WEBSTER, of Plainfield
both dis mo 10-4-1781
Eliza W. (nm) b R. I. d 11-4-1809 ae 28y 3m bHS
Esther, dt Thomas & Phebe, Newtown; m 1803 Joseph TOWNSEND
Hester rocf R. & P. 6-2-1794 (clear); ct N.P. 9-4-1800 (clear); cf N.P. 2-12-1803 (clear); Esther gct Balt. 9-1-1803

HALLETT, continued
Gideon, Newtown, b 12-8-1773; con mo 6-8-1797; ct R.& P. 5-1-1805; cf Flush. 8-3-1815; ct R.& P. 7-3-1816; cf R. & P. 8-23-1820; ct Flush. 3-3-1824; ct Flush. 5-1837, this cert returned as a previous one sent 1824 & rec 1826 (H)
Hannah (nm) b N. Y. d 9-30-1818 ae 21y 10m (unm)
Israel, N. Y. & Newtown, d 10-1-1776; m 1765 Naomi -----
Ch: James b 5-18-1772
Abraham S. b 10-2-1774
cert of clear to Woodbridge 11-7-1765; Naomi rocf Rahway 4-2-1766; Naomi Hallett dis mo 5-4-1780 to ----- DUNBAR
James, s Israel (dec) & Naomi, cabinet maker, N. Y.; m N. Y. 7-10-1793 Phebe CORNELL, dt Joshua & Hannah (dec), N. Y., d 7-22-1851
Ch: Mary C. b 4-17-1794 (or 9-17-1794) d 1-12-1870
Sarah " 2-27-1796
William " 1-12-1792
Phebe Ann d 3-30-1840
Child " 3- 6-1800
Phebe Cornell rocf Jericho 5-17-1792 (clear); all dis 1830-1832 (0)
Lydia m 1767 Abraham SHOTWELL, of Plainfield
Mary m before 10-3-1783 Henry BURNETT, N. Y. (mo)
Mary, dt Richard, d 6-14-1876
Naomi, wd Israel, N. Y. rocf R. & P. 2-19-1766
Naomi Dunbar (form Hallett) dis mo 5-4-1780 (perhaps dt Israel & Naomi)
Phebe, Queens Co., m 1787 Edward MOORE
cf Rahway 11-16-1763
Phebe rocf R. & Plainfield 6-15-1796 (clear); ct R. & P. 8-4-1802 (clear)
Richard, Flushing; m Flushing 9 Mo (Nov) 14, 1717 Amy BOWNE, dt John & Mary, d 9 Mo (Nov) 7, 1733 (Richard d 5-19-1769)
Ch: Mary b 11 Mo (Jan) 12, 1719/20; d 10 Mo. 1724
Richard " 10 Mo (Dec) 31, 1721 d 5-13-1757
Sarah " 6 Mo (Aug) 5, 1723
William " 12 Mo (Feb) 10, 1725
Amy " 9 Mo (Nov) 5, 1727 d 9-15-1759
killed by falling tree
Richard m 2nd Ann -----, of Pennsylvania d 9-15-1759 bur at Flush.
Ch: Thomas b 1 Mo (Mar) 24, 1739/40
Lydia " 7 Mo (Sep) 12, 1741
Israel " 9 Mo (Nov) 5, 1742
Richard took cert of clear to Concord, Pa. 2 Mo (Apr) 26, 1739; John & Isaac Miller, s of Richard Hallett's w, gct Concord 1-10 & 1-9-1744
Richard, s Richard, Newtown; m between 9 Mo-1- & 10 Mo (Dec) 6, 1744 Mary WAY, dt Samuel
Richard S. d 12-5-1849 ae 83y bPP; m Chesterfield, N. J. 1791 Sarah ----- d 4-1-1849 ae 81y 5m bPP
Ch: Mary b 2-13-1792 d 6-14-1878 bPP
Israel C. b 3-22-1793 d 1- 9-1820 [PP
Rachel C. b 5- 5-1796 d 5-11-1837 rem to
Richard b 11-24-1799
Joseph D. b 1-16-1803 d 7-14-1834; rem from HS to PP
Richard granted cert of clear to Chesterfield 4-6-1791; Sarah rocf Chesterfield 8-2-1791; all dis 1830-1831 (0)
Sarah, Newtown, L. I.; m 1745 William WEBSTER
Sarah, dt James & Phebe, N. Y.; m 1827 Josiah FIELD
Thomas, New Town, d 8-22-1780; took cert of clear to Woodbridge 9-1-1763
Thomas C. (nm) & -----
Ch: Hannah Ann d 3-17-1839 ae 16d bHS
Jeremiah " 6-16-1840 ae 1y 3m bHS
Wm. Paxson & -----
Ch: (Prob) Elizabeth C. b N. Y. d 5-30-1825 ae 3y 9d bHS
dis mo 3-1-1820
----- & -----
Ch: Hannah Ann d 3- 9-1839 ae 16d bHS
Jeremiah " 6-16-1841 ae 1y 3m bHS

HALLIDAY
John Green rocf Lisburn, Ire. 12-1883; name erased 11-1886

HALLOCK
Aaron B. rocf Mt. Holly 7-1834; ct Honey Creek, Ill. 3-7-1849 (H)
Alice J. gct South Starksboro, Vt. 12-1914
Allen C. rocf Mt. Holly 10-1832; ct Honey Creek Ill. 3-7-1849 (mo 6-1836) (H)
Ann L., w Henry J., dt ----- HARRIS, b Somers 5-1-1824 (m 2-20-1856) (H)
Ann L. m 1st Thomas H. HARRIS 8-2-1843
cf Ama. 4-1844; in Kalamazoo 1900 & thereafter
Anna W., dt Thomas B. & Sarah W., b 11-26-1874, Bkn.; m 1895 Ernest A. HOHOFF (nm) (changed to Hallock by court)
Catharine, dt John & Abigail; m 1706 Thomas WILLITS
Daniel & Ann
Ch: Samuel
William
cf Chap. 1849; ct Chap. 1852 for all
David & Jane (H)
Ch: Elizabeth b 3-28-1836
William " 1-18-1843
cf Ama. 8-1834; ct Ama. 4-1854 with 2 ch named
Edward B., s Allan C. & Eliz. P. (Stoddard), b Evansville, Ind. 10-20-1858; recrq 5-9-1914; letter returned marked "dec" but no date on letter (H)
Elinor rocf Corn. 3-1832; d 1-21-1863
Elizabeth C., dt Henry B. & Anna B., b Bkn. 4-18-1874; m 1924 John Eldridge WRIGHT (nm) (H)
Elizabeth M., w James C., dt Phebe FROST,

HALLOCK, Elizabeth M., continued
b 1-2-1840 (H)
Emma Amelia d 7-17-1873 bPP (nm) (H)
George d 2-25-1888; m Mary W. ----- d 5-4-1888 (H)
Ch: Reuben L. b 4- 5-1834
Sarah " 1-16-1837 d 6- 8-1838 at Bay City, Mich.
Isaac P. b 3- 3-1840 d 9-12-1877
Sarah Jane
cf Ama. 3-1836; ct Ama. 7-5-1848 with 3 ch; cf Ama. 1-1866 for parents & Sarah J.; ct R. & P. 11-5-1884 for parents
George D., s Reuben L. & Mary M., b 12-10-1861; gct R. & P. 11-5-1884 (H)
Grace, dt Burling & Mary Emma (Scofield), b Peakskill 10-27-1875; m 1911 Thomas L. NOBLE (H)
Henry d 9-10-1853; m Phebe -----
Ch: Phebe H. Underhill, adopted dt., d before cert rec
cf Ama. for Henry; cf Ama. for Phebe; ct Ama. 1856 for Phebe
Henry B., s Reuben & Mary (Birdsall), b 11-2-1832 W. Somers d 9-26-1918 bPP; m 6-11-1868 Anna B. BARNES, dt David H. & Naomi C. (Haviland), b White Plains 8-10-1834 d 11-8-1925 bPP (H)
Ch: Henry Lindsley b 10-24-1869
Marianna " 6-20-1871
Sarah Emily " 1- 8-1873 d 7-17-1873 bPP
Elizabeth A. " 4- 8-1874
Henry rocf Ama. 7-1838 with parents; cf Pur. 3-3-1869 for Anna B.
Henry G. rocf Marl. 1851
Henry L., s Henry B. & Anna (Barnes), b 10-24-1869 Bkn. d 11-18-1915 bPP; m 10-14-1896 Josephine VAIL, dt Geo. F. & Clara M. (Ross) (H)
Ch: Dorothy Vail b 7-19-1901 (nm)
Israel, affairs unsettled, Oswego refers to N.Y. 6-5-1816, rpd favorably 7-3-1816; having mo Oswego refers to N. Y. 6-3-1878; had held military surgeons commission, no wish to retain mbrp, rpd to Oswego 7-1-1818
James d 3-6-1800 bHS
James C., s John & Lydia (dec), N. Y., d 10-5-1895 ae 75y 10m 2d bPP; m at Samuel Frost's 1-2-1840 Elizabeth M. Frost, dt Obediah (dec) & Phebe, N. Y., d 3-18-1867 ae 62y bPP
Ch: Lydia C. b 4- 7-1842
Phebe Francena b 12-17-1843
James Jr. b 9-26-1846 d 5-30-1929 bPP (unm)
Richard Frost b 8-13-1849
cf Little Egg Harbor for James C. 1831 (O); rec without cert 11-1831 (H); dis 5-1833 (O); James was founder of the N. Y. Clearing House
James C. m 2nd Phebe ----- d 8-16-1872
cf Buckingham 10-4-1871
Dr. James C., s James C. & Eliz. M. (Frost), b N. Y. 9-26-1846 d 5-30-1929 (H) (unm)

John rocf Mt. Holly 6-1838; ct Honey Creek, Ind. 3-1839 (H)
John Townsend, s James & Eliz., Marlboro; m N.Y. 9-11-1817 Ann EVERIT, dt Thos. & Susannah, Bkn.
ct Marl. 11-3-1819 for Ann
John W. rocf Little Egg Harbor 5-9-1822, placed with Oliver Hull; d 9-7-1830
Lydia C., dt James C. & Eliz. M., b 4-7-1842 N. Y. d 4-4-1932; m 7-6-1882 Richard M. NEWHALL (H)
Margaret, dt John & Abigail; m 1705 John POWELL
Marianna, dt Henry B. & Anna B., Bkn., b 6-22-1871 N. Y. d 10-19-1913; m 1898 Franklin NOBLE (H)
P. Francena, dt James C. & Eliz. M. (Frost), b N. Y. 12-17-1843 d 1-30-1927; m 1864 Malcolm T. MAINE (nm) (H)
Philadelphia, dt Nathaniel & Ann, b 5-9-1844, Milton, d 10-20-1920; name entered by comm. 11-30-1885; in Wilmington 1900 & thereafter (H) (unm)
Reuben, s Jesse & Elizabeth, d 9-9-1856 ae 57y 6m 14d; m Mary B. ----- d 1-28-1864 ae 67y 4m 29d (H)
Ch: Henry B. b 11-2-1832
Sarah Elizabeth b 8-20-1835 d 1-15-1926 at Plainfield bPP
cf Ama. 7-1838 for all
Reuben L., s George & Mary M., b Yorktown 11-5-1834 d 5- 8-1910; m Mary M. ----- (H)
Ch: George D. b 12-10-1861
cf Ama. 4-1857 for both; in Denver 1900 & later
Richard, s Richard & Sarah, Yorktown; m N. Y. 4-9-1834 Martha COCK, dt Joshua & Elizabeth N. Y. (H)
Richard B. rocf Phila. Green St. 7-1836; ct Honey Creek, Ill. 3-7-1849 (H)
Richard F., s James C. & Eliz. M. (Frost), b 8-13-1849 d 11-6-1893 bPP; m Hannah L. ----- (nm) (H)
Ch: Guildford d 10-8-1891 ae 2y 1m bPP
----- (probably) stillborn 2-2-1885 bPP
Sarah, dt John, Jr., Brookhaven; m 1737 Caleb HUNT
Sarah b N. Y. d 8-4-1809 ae 3y bHS
Sarah Jane, dt George & Mary W.; m 5-24-1860 Albert FLEWELLIN (H)
relrq 7-7-1900
Stephen & Mary (H)
Ch: Henry James
William Penn b 12-12-1831 d 9- 1-1832
Isaac C. b 9- 6-1834
cf Ama. 11-1831; ct Roch. 9-1836
Sybil J. Noyes (form Hallock) rocf Ferrisburg 6-6-1906
Thomas B., s Nathaniel & Ann, Marlboro, b Milton 7-19-1838 d 5-21-1924; m at Ellwood Walter's 11-25-1863 Sarah WALTER, dt Ellwood & Deborah (Coggeshall) (dec), b Westchester 10-7-1836 d 1918

HALLOCK, Thomas B. & Sarah, continued
Ch: Anna Walter b 11-26-1874
Thomas Burling b 12-18-1877
cf Marl. 7-2-1873 (O); when Marl. MM (H) laid down 1847 & mbr attached to N. Y., name of Thos. omitted by chance
Thomas B., s Thomas B. & Sarah (Hunter); m 11-10-1880 Elizabeth CROMWELL, dt Joshua T. & Eliz. S. (Titus), b Highland Mills 4-18-1858 d 6-18-1919 (H)
cf Corn. for Elizabeth 2-11-1911
Thomas Burling, s Thos. B. & Sarah (Walter), b Bkn. 12-18-1877; m Rebekah SAYR (nm)
Ch: Thomas B. 3d b Seaside, L. I. 10-28-1908; recrq of parents 2-8-1913
Valentine H. & Henrietta B. (H)
Ch: Anna
Edward b 10-29-1850
cf Marl. with 2 ch 12-1848; ct N. P. with 3 ch 2-1852
William, s James & Eliz., Marlborough; m N. Y. 10-14-1818 Phebe Ann HULL, dt John & Anna, N. Y.
ct Marl. for Phebe Ann 4-5-1820
----- & -----
Ch: Patience d 7-21-1810 ae 9m 27d bHS
Charles B. d 1-19-1838 ae 1y 1m bHS

HALLOWELL (see also Hollowell)
Anna N., dt Norwood P. & Sarah W. (Haydock), West Medford, Mass., b 3-20-1871; m 1895 Horace A. DAVIS, of N. Y. (H)
Eleanor, dt William & Anna T.; m 1913 Mahlon H. DUNN (H)
mbr of Horsham, Pa., cf Horsham, Pa. 11-13-1922; Mahlon brought cert from Chesterfield 7-10-1922
Elizabeth, dt Nathan H. & Elizabeth, d 7-31-1929 ae 92y bPP; m Theodore GILLINGHAM (H) (both nm)
Esther F., dt Norwood P. & Sarah W., W. Medford, Mass., b W. Medford, Mass. 3-21-1881; m 1907 Arthur H. MORSE, of Kansas City (H)
Frederick T., s J. W. & Abbie, b Goldsboro, N. C. 11-29-1889; cf Oak Grove, N. C. 9-5-1917
James R., s Rich. L., rocf Greensboro, N. C. 10-2-1907; ct Greensboro 8-1914
John W., s Richard L., rocf Greensboro, N. C., 10-2-1907; ct Greensboro 8-1914
John White, s Norwood & Sarah (Haydock), b W. Medford, Mass. 12-24-1878; m 10-10-1905 Marian H. LADD (nm), dt William J. & Anna (Watson) (H)
Ch: William Ladd b 8-18-1906
John White, Jr. b 1-22-1909
Roger Haydock b 12- 7-1910
Eleanor " 5-13-1914
Philip " 11-14-1917
ch recrq of parents 5-12-1924; all b W. Medford
Joseph G., s Rich. L., rocf Greensboro, N. C. 10-2-1907; ct Greensboro 8-1914
Norwood P., s Morris L. & Hannah P., N. Y., b Phila. 4-13-1839 d 4-11-1914; m at Robert Haydock's 1-27-1868 Sarah W. HAYDOCK dt Robert & Hannah W., N. Y., b 1-22-1846 N. Y. d 6-10-1934 (H)
Ch: Anna Norwood b 3-20-1871
Robert Haydock b 6-30-1873
Norwood Penrose, Jr. b 7- 3-1875
John White b 12-24-1878
Esther Fisher b 3-21-1881
Susan Morris b 12-19-1883
live West Medford, Mass.
Robert H., s Norwood P. & Sarah (Haydock), b W. Medford, Mass. 6-30-1873; m 10-7-1902 Rebecca B. JACKSON (nm), dt James (H)
Ch: Robert Haydock, Jr. b 8-31-1903
Samuel Haydock " 5-15-1905
Francis Jackson b 11- 5-1906
ch recrq of parents 4-9-1910
Susan M., dt N. P. & Sarah W., Medford, Mass., b W. Medford, Mass. 12-19-1883; m 1912 Lawrence G. BROOKS, of Cambridge (H)

HALSEY
George A. (nm) m Edith VANDERBILT, dt Isaac S. Jr. & Carrie (Willets) b N. Y. 6-18-1899 (H)

HALSTED
Catharine T., w John F., dt Sam'l & Lucy THOMPSON (m 1854); relrq 11-1860 (H)
David F., s Moses & Anna (Frost), b Dutch Co. 8-13-1843 d 7-11-1903; m 7-1-1874 Catharine Ann CHAMBERLAIN (nm), dt Gilbert & Eleanor (Howard) (H)
cf Creek & Stanford 3-4-1874
Hannah C. (or T.), dt Barnabas WRIGHT, rocf Corn. 8-27-1842 with father; ct Chap. 11-1863 (H)
John [Halstead], s Samuel & Sophia (dec), Peekskill; m N. Y. 5-13-1830 Mary HUNTER, dt John & Tamar, N. Y. (H)
Mary rocf Chap. with parents 1826; ct Chap. 8-1830
John F., s Ezekiel & Ann B. (dec), N. Y.; m at S. Thompson's 6-8-1854 Catharine THOMPSON, dt Samuel & Lucy, Bkn. (H)
Catharine relrq 11-1860
Jonathan [Halstead] rocf Creek 1-1833; d 4-10-1856 (H)
Moses d 2-12-1891; m Anna H. FROST d 2-7-1882 (H)
Ch: David F. b 8-13-1843
cf Creek & Stan. 9-6-1876 for both; cf Stan. for David 3-4-1874
Phebe [Halstead], dt Stephen, d 5-7-1855 ae 85y; m 1819 Obadiah FROST
Sophia [Halstead] (late Peters) dis mo 4-6-1808
----- & -----
Ch: Amanda b N. Y. d 12-18-1827 ae 5m bHS
Stephen b N. Y. d 9-2-1829 ae 17d bHS

HAMBLETON
Joseph W. d 12-30-1894 ae 67y bPP; m Sarah SCANTLEBURY, dt Samuel & Sarah (Wray), b Albany 10-12-1832 d 12-10-1921 bPP (H)
cf Scip. 8-7-1850 for Sarah; at Chicago 1859-1893, Yonker 1899

HAMBURGER
Margaret recrq 1-5-1910 d rpd 4-1928

HAMILTON
Mary Ann (nm) (form McDowell) d 12-26-1853 ae 56y bPP

HAMMARSTROM
Erik (nm), s Carl Johan (nm) & Maria C. Koping, Sweden; m at Harold A. C. Dahl's 5-31-1911 Inez H. DAHL, dt Harold A. C. & Anna C. E., Bkn., b Bkn. 9-3-1887 (H)
Inez recrq 2-10-1906

HAMMOND
Abigail b N. Y. d 3-8-1847 ae 78y bHS (wd)
Elizabeth d 1-9-1855 ae 43y bPP
Elizabeth M., dt Arthur & Elizabeth (Onderduck) d 7-17-1914 ae 75y 3m 7d bPP (H) (unm)
Jemima rocf N. P. 3-17-1842 (clear); d 2-8-1858 ae 63y 2m

HAMPTON
Adam (nm) b 10-1-1800 d 9-8-1870; m 12-30-1826 Ann JACKSON, dt Hugh & Rebecca, b 2-25-1801 d 11-30-1891
Ch: Emeline b N. Y. d 1-14-1834 ae 5y bHS
Mary " " " " 2- 3-1834 ae 3y bHS
Adam H. " " " " 6-26-1841 ae 5y 4m 9d bHS
Elwood " 7-19-1838 d 7- 7-1907
Elizabeth b N. Y. d 7-3-1841 ae 1y bHS
John " 6- 9-1842 d 4- 3-1877
Ann recrq 5-1834; Ann had been dis mo; none of the ch were mbr, names here given by rq of descendants
John (nm) b N. J. d 11-7-1833 ae 63y bHS (m)
Joseph rocf R. & P. 7-17-1794 (clear); ct R. & P. 10-4-1797 (clear)
Lovicia E., dt Elwood & Katherine T. (Clark), b N. Y. 11-24-1873; recrq 7-12-1913 (H)
Mary rocf R. & P. 1-1851; d 4-21-1861 ae 72y 10m 5d bPP (H)
Sarah rocf R. & P. 8-19-1795 (clear); ct R. & P. 1-4-1797 (clear)

HANAN
Addison G. (nm), s John H. & Henrietta F., d 6-16-1923; m 4-29-1902 Lillian J. McDOWELL, dt Joseph & Anna L. (Stone), b Jersey City 10-10-1878 (H)
Ch: Leonard McDowell b 7-31-1903
Richard Addison " 5-20-1905
Charles Burton " 4-21-1915
Anna Livingston " 8-16-1909
Lillian m 2d Junius C. ROCHESTER
ch recrq of parents, two 11-11-1905; two 2-12-1916
Anna L., dt Addison G. & Lillian (McDowell), N. Y., b Bkn. 8-16-1909; m 1930 Jonathan H. CONROW (H)

HANCE
Amy L. m 2-24-1864 John MOORE (H)
cf R. & P. 11-6-1850
Angelina, dt Hannah B.; m ----- CONOVER (H)
cf Shrews 8-1-1849; ct Shrews 4-5-1854
Anselm B., s Thomas & Rachel, d 8-25-1873; Ellen ----- (H)
Ch: Ellen Coddington d 10-2-1896
Sarah Ann
Rachel Rebecca
Jane Eliza
Anselm recrq 4-1832; ch recrq of father 11-1842
Anselm B. m 2nd at Mary M. Leggett's 11-2-1842 Hannah L. MIDDLETON, dt Wm. (dec) & Jane, N. Y., d 7-16-1884 (not under care of N. Y. MM)
Hannah L. recrq 3-1-1843
Elizabeth A. d 5-23-1898; recrq 5-7-1884 (H)
Hannah B. & ----- (H)
Ch: Angelina
Susan Woolley
Robert William
cf Shrews. 8-1-1849 for all; ct Shrews. 4-5-1854 for all
Jane Eliza, dt Anselm B. & Ellen; m 1876 Walter Henry BORDEN (H)
ct Shrews. 10-2-1878
Jemima rocf Chesterfield 5-7-1805 (clear); ct Chesterfield 7-13-1808 (clear)
Rachel rocf Shrewsbury 7-1827; dis 5-1831 (0); ct Shrewsbury 2-1830 (H)
Rachel Rebecca, dt Anselm B. & Ellen, d 6-26-1904; m 10-6-1863 Chauncey WRIGHT (H)
recrq of father 11-1842
Revo C. & -----
Ch: Obadiah b N. Y. d 4-23-1830 ae 1y 5m 10d bHS
Revo C. b N. Y. d 3-9-1834 ae 1y 6m bHS
cf Shrews. 9-6-1813; dis mo 1-3-1816
Sarah Ann, dt Anselm B. & Ellen, d 1-8-1911; m 11-21-1871 John M. NICHOLS (H)
recrq of father 11-1842
Susan B., dt Benj. B. & Sarah Lavinia, b Red Bank 6-22-1864; m 1896 Henry M. HAVILAND (H)
recrq 5-7-1884
Sarah Lavinia rocf Shrewsbury 3-4-1885; d 9-1-1888 (H)

HANCOCK
John, s Simon & Ann (both dec), N. Y. d 12-18-1851; m N. J. 10-12-1820 Sarah MILLS, dt Stacy & Hannah, Mt. Holly, N. J., d 7-23-1864 ae 70y bPP
John recrq 1806
cf Burl. 4-5-1819 for Hannah; John dis

HANCOCK, John & Sarah, continued
1829 (H)
Maria d 1882; rocf Lisburn, Ireland 8-17-1826 (clear)
Robert (nm) m Ann ----- d 4-21-1876 ae 71y bPP
Ann recrq 10-1845
----- & -----
Ch: Sarah b N. Y. d 8-6-1829 ae 1y 6m bHS

HAND
Margaret B., dt Silvanus & Sarah, Morris Co., N. J.; m ----- LAING; m 2d 1876 John DIETRICK (H)

HANDLEY
Jacob (nm) & -----
Ch: Infant stillborn 6-25-1828 bHS
Infant stillborn 12-24-1829 bHS
Charles d 7-30-1831 ae 8m bHS
Theodore W. d 6- 5-1838 ae 5y 11m 21d bHS
Infant stillborn 3-27-1842 bHS

HANES
Elizabeth, mbr Pilesgrove, N. J., s Thomas & Mary; m William TAYLOR (H)
Margaret S., dt Wm. & Elizabeth; m 1923 Dr. Bert G. SIMMONS, he d 1926; m 2d 1929 Wm. Alexander TAYLOR (H)

HANKINSON
Ambrose C. rocf R. & P. 11-17-1796, minor
Ann (late Copeland) dis mo 11-4-1779

HANKS
John rocf Limerick, Ire. 7-1823; cert returned as his residence unknown; cert again from Limerick 11-8-1829; he lives at Point Pleasant, Bucks Co., Pa.; cert to be sent to MM in whose compass he lives

HANNA
William (nm) d 3-30-1863 ae 44y bPP; m Rebecca B. HALL, dt Stephen & Jane, b 1-12-1811 d 4-15-1899 bPP
Ch: Malcolm B. b 2-24-1893 d 5-3-1914 bPP

HANNEMAN
William J., s Frdk. Wm. John & Eleanor Rebecca, b 11-25-1875; recrq 3-1926

HANSEN
Anna C., dt C.F.A.& Olivia, d 9-20-1911 ae 23y bPP; m George F. ROGERS (H)
Caroline [Hanson], dt Nathaniel & Keziah, d 1-24-1914 ae 71y bPP (H) (nm)
Harold R. [Hanson] rocf Providence 7-11-1906; d rpd 1920; in Phila. 1912
Rudy & Hazel
Ch: Dorothy C. b 1911
Robert B. " 1917
Hazel rolf Lafayette Ave. Presbyterian Church 3-1920; her 2 ch recrq of mother same date; Hazel m 2d Raymond E. MENDENHALL ct Wilmington, O. 7-10-1935; Hazel & ch as associates
Rudy C. [Hanson] recrq 5-1924 (dec)

HARBERT
Felix (nm) b Shrews. d 6-29-1818 ae 80y (widower)
Mary [Harbart] d 9-10-1798 bHS (nm)

HARDEN
Agnes (form Harrison) recrq 4-1879; d 8-1888
John & -----
Ch: ----- d 11-5-1798 bHS

HARDIN
Abigail con misconduct 12-3-1767
James, Flushing, rqc of clear 12 Mo (Feb) 9, 1716/17

HARDING
Elizabeth d 4-8-1891 ae 83y bPP (nm) (H)

HARE
Elizabeth (nm) b Rye d 9-23-1811 ae 47y bHS (wd)

HARFORD
Samuel rocf Somersetshire N. Division 9-14-1836; d 7-3-1838 ae 72y (killed in B'way)
Virgil (nm) b West. Co. d 5-19-1830 ae 26y bHS
Ch: Lorretta b N. Y. d 5-27-1830 ae 4m 27d bHS

HARGIS
Morton L., s Merton L. & Amanda (M----), b San Francisco 12-19-1883; recrq 6-6-1917; name erased 10-1928

HARKINS
Caroline M., dt John & Mary J., d 7-16-1917 ae 49y 9m 4d bPP (unm) (nm) (H)
Susan G., dt John & Josephine (Kesley), b Boston 1874; recrq 12-4-1897 (H)

HARKNESS
David, s Adam & Thankful, Peru, N. Y.; m Manhattanville, N. Y. 6-4-1818 Mary CHADWICK, dt Daniel & Phebe WILLIS (dec), N. Y.
ct Peru 12-2-1818 for Mary

HARLAN (or Harland)
Josephine G., dt Joseph G. & Anna B. (both dec) Haverford, Pa.; m 1878 J. Kent WORTHINGTON, of Phila.
cf Radnor 3-1860, minor, with Edward Tatum; ct WD MM 2-1880

HARNED
Ada K., dt Andrew J. & Marion U. (Whipple), b Dix Hills, N. Y. 8-8-1862; recrq 8-13-1910 (unm) (H)
Anne (or Anna) ack. accepted by R. & P. & so accepted here; cf R. & P. 10-7-1812
Eunice Adams (form Harned) dis mo 1-4-1781

HARNED, continued
Helen m William H. PELLOWE, d 7-21-1918 (H)
Helen mbr of R. & P.; William recrq 6-13-1914
Irving Alfred, s Jas. A. & Katharine A. (De Vol), b Kissimmee, Fla. 8-3-1884; m at John Wm. Hutchinson's 9-8-1909 Edith C. HUTCHINSON, dt John Wm. & E. Eliza, N. Y., b N. Y. 7-2-1887 (H)
Ch: Wm. Hutchinson b Hempstead 7-26-1910
Irving Alfred, Jr. b Hempstead 7-26-1910
James A., s Hugh W. & Margaret K. (Vail), b Green Brook, N. J. 10-17-1859 d 8-13-1913; m 3-17-1881 Katie A. DE VOL, dt Rowland G. & Amanda B. (Merritt), b Falston, Md. 1-6-1863 (H)
Katie m 2d Charles D. V. HEATH; both recrq 6-8-1907
Marion Virginia, dt Andrew J. & Marion U. (Whipple), b Melville, N. Y. 3-12-1870 d 12-16-1917; recrq 8-13-1910 (unm) (H)
Mary Younghusband (form Harned) dis mo 7-4-1782
Phineas rocf R. & P. 9-21-1780

HARNETT (or Hornett)
Anna dis 11-2-1803

HARPER
Elizabeth rocf Phila. Green St. 11-1850; ct Burl. 2-1856 (H)
Nathan & Sarah P.
Ch: Elizabeth W. d 3-21-1855 ae 7y 5m 13d bPP
Anna M.
Franklin d 8-30-1854 ae 3m 22d bPP
Joseph M. b 9-20-1856
cf Phila. Spruce St. 9-1844; ct Green St., Phila. 1-1847; cf Green St., Phila. 1-1-1851; ct Balt. 2-5-1862 for parents & 2 ch

HARRINGTON
Harry G., s Joseph & Anna C. (Weiss), b Newark 10-27-1877; recrq 10-8-1917 (H)

HARRIS
Agnes m S. Marshall BUSSELLE
cf Toronto 2-7-1900 for Agnes; ct Toronto 9-1913 for both & s
Ann L., dt Isaac & Patience CARPENTER, b Somers 5-1-1824; m 2d 2-20-1856 Henry J. HALLOCK cf Ama. 4-1844 (m 1st 8-2-1843 Thomas H. HARRIS) (H)
Arthur, s Abram C. & Sarah M. (Young), b 5-12-1872 Plainfield; m 1-8-1896 Caroline PEENE (nm), dt George & Jennie E. (H)
recrq of mother 12-5-1883; name rem 3-13-1933 for lack of interest
Caroline, dt Geo. E. & Lucia BROWN, b 5-10-1856 d 12-23-1886 (w Frederick Harris, nm) (H)
Caroline S., w James N., dt James O. & Julia HAWXHURST (m 7-30-1867); cf Jericho with parents 10-1857, ret a mbr; d 8-7-1879 (H)
Channing Page, s Charles & C. Esther, Bridgeport; m 11-4-1901 at David G. Alsop's, Haverford, Pa. Esther ALSOP, dt Samuel, Jr. (dec) & Esther K., Denver, Colo.
Ch: Rachel Griscom
Estelle Kite
Margaret Alsop
cf WD MM 4-3-1901 for Esther; ch recorded as associates on rq of parents 12-1909; ch active mbr 1922-1924; Channing P. recrq 12-1919
Cornelia M., w Richard, dt Silvanus J. & Caroline MACY, b 9-16-1865; relrq 7-2-1890 (H)
Helen S., dt Abram & Sarah M. (Young), N. Y., b 9-10-1870 Plainfield, N. J.; m 1897 Isaac M. SUTTON (nm) (H)
recrq of mother 12-5-1883; relrq 5-10-1902
Henry Knight rocf Kingston, Eng. 3-1887; ct Kingston, Eng. 7-1889
J. Wistar rocf Ypsilanti, Mich. 12-2-1908; d rpd 11-1928
James W. rocf Balt. 3-1842; rel 7-5-1871, absent over 5y (H)
Mary P. rocf Ypsilanti, Mich. 11-4-1914; d 10-8-1917
Samuel & Sarah
Ch: Samuel, Jr. b 18-1846
cf Providence 8-30-1845; ct Hudson 8-5-1846 with ch, Samuel
Sarah, wd Daniel HOLDER; dis mo 5-1-1844
Sarah M., wd Abram C., dt John S. & Sarah M. YOUNG, b 1-4-1849 d 12-27-1901 (m 9-9-1869 (H)
Ch: Helen S. b 9-10-1870
Arthur " 5-12-1872
Sarah recrq 3-7-1883; ch recrq of Sarah 12-5-1883

HARRISON
Agnes Harden (form Harrison) recrq 4-1879; d 8-1888
Daniel (nm) m Sarah ----- b Eng. d 5-16-1835 ae 41y bHS
Ch: Bernard d 7-28-1830 ae 7m 11d bHS
Rachel rocf Lisburn, Ireland 2-2-1910 (William with cert same date, probably brother)
Roger, Little Egg Harbor, m Wby 6 Mo (Aug) 3, 1726 Mary WEEKS, wd George, Queens Co. recorded as Richard Harrison
Samuel, Merchant, late of Phila.; m 10 Mo (dec) 8, 1719 Sarah FERRIS, dt John & Mary, Westchester
Ch: Mary b 7 Mo (Sep) 27, 1720
John " 12 Mo (Feb) 26, 1721/2
Margery " 2 Mo (Apr) 1, 1724
Sarah " 9 Mo (Nov) 18, 1725
Samuel " 7 Mo (Sep) 9, 1727
Elizabeth b 8 Mo (Oct) 30, 1729
Hannah " 8 Mo (Oct) 2, 1732
cert of clear from Phila. Friends (not from the mtg) 9 Mo (Nov) 27, 1719; rem to Boston 4 Mo (June), 5, 1729, about to rem
Sarah m 1735 Solomon PALMER, of Mamaroneck
William rocf Lisburn, Ireland 2-2-1910 (Rachel

HARRISON, William, continued
with cert same date, probably sister); names of both erased 3-1928
----- & -----
Ch: Francis b N. Y. d 3-29-1835 ae 1y 6m bHS
Rebecca b N. Y. d 12-5-1836 ae 5y 4m bHS

HART
Frances, dt Hastings H. & Laura (Love), b St. Paul 11-14-1894; m 2-4-1922 Arthur BURKE (H)
Nellie E. (nm), dt Fred I. & Nettie (Hilers); m 1910 Howard U. VAN BURKIRK (H)

HARTLEY
Sarah (nm) m 1840 Thomas FLEMING (H)
Thomas recrq 4-8-1905

HARTSHORNE
Hannah, dt John & Lucy, Shrews.; m 1782 Thomas EDDY, N. Y.
Hugh brought rem cert from R. & P. 8-24-1803 (clear); took cert of clear to R. & P. 6-4-1806; Hugh took rem cert to R. & P. 12-2-1807
John, Jr. rocf Shrews. 1-4-1819, apprentice to George Gilpin; dis 1-1830 (O); dis 12-1829 (H)
Pattison (or Patterson) rocf Alexandria 12-21-1809 (clear); ct Balt. W. Dist. 9-1-1819 (clear)
Robert rocf Alexandria 6-26-1806 (clear); rem some time since to Halifax; dis mo 7-2-1817
Robert H. & Sarah
Ch: Richard b 10-22-1810
Sarah, w Robert, d 11-11-1809 ae 86y bHS
William d 7-25-1833 in 85th y bHS m -----
Ch: Mary L. b Shrews. d 7-13-1821 ae 23y bHS
cf Shrews. 8-13-1821; dis 1829 (H)

HARVEY
Jacob, s Joseph & Rebecca, Limerick, rocf Limerick, Ire. 5-14-1816, apprentice; dis mo 4-1829 (O); dis mo 4-1829 (H)
Josiah L., s Isaac Jr. & Agnes, Phila.; m N.Y. 10-8-1845 Caroline Eliza FITZ RANDOLPH, dt John L. (dec) & Eliza, N. Y.
ct WD MM for Caroline E. 5-6-1846
Sarah b Pa. d 3-25-1838 ae 65y bHS; cf Phila. 12-24-1811; dis 5-4-1814

HASHAGEN
Lillian B., dt Henry O. & Caroline (Steiger), b N. Y. 1-5-1883; m 1906 Alexander J. WALL (H)
recrq with h & s 4-11-1932

HASKINS
John B. (nm) & -----
Ch: John B. b N. Y. d 7-12-1830 ae 17y bHS
Henry " " " " 10-31-1838 ae 5m bHS
Mary (perhaps) (see Mary Peterson)

----- m Sarah Elizabeth RAYNOR, dt Susan W., b 5-10-1881
Sarah's name recorded as per Disc.

HASSINGER
----- (nm) m Hazel D. STANLEY
cf Westfield, Ind. 12-6-1905 for Hazel

HASTINGS
Alice (nm), dt John S. & Matilda L.; m 1882 Henry COLVIN (H)
Ernest C., s Wm. P., rocf Friendsville, Tenn. 6-12-1895 with father; name erased 10-1928
William P., dec, & Luzena B., dec.
Ch: Ernest E.
William W.
cf Friendsville, Tenn. 6-12-1895 with Ernest E.; cf same for brother, Wm. W. 9-4-1895
William W., brother of William P., rocf Friendsville, Tenn. 9-4-1895; letter to First Presbyterian Church, Jacksonville, Fla. 10-3-1917

HATCH
Isaac, s Isaac & Latitia (both dec), N. Y.; m N. Y. 7-14-1819 Phebe WOOD, dt Samuel & Mary, N. Y. d 2-21-1864 ae 81y bPP (Isaac d 12-11-1841 ae 65y bHS
Ch: Samuel W. b 6-20-1820 d 10-17-1821
Isaac S. " 1-28-1822
Mary W. " 10- 8-1824 d 5-10-1845
Isaac recrq 9-3-1817; Isaac dis 1830 (O); Isaac dis (H); Phebe dis 1829 (H)
Isaac S., s Isaac & Phebe, b 1-28-1822; dis mo 12-1849

HATFIELD
Sarah rocf Hudson 9-21-1831 (O); dis 2-1832 (O)
cf Hudson 2-1831 (H); dis 1832 at Ghent

HATHAWAY
Benoni d 11-13-1836; m Phebe HAVILAND, dt Benjamin & Phebe, Pur.
Ch: Elizabeth b 12-11-1831
Benjamin H. b 8-14-1834
cf Chap. 8-11-1831 for Benoni; cf Pur. 8-10-1831 for Phebe; she m 1843 Abraham WANZER
Esther rocf Farm. 4-5-1876 d 5-27-1876
Geo. Smith dis mo 1-4-1809
Harriet E. rocf Farm. 3-1-1876; d 3-5-1884
Henry B. rocf Farm. 10-1870; ct Farm. 8-1914
Smith rocf New Bedford 12-21-1802, apprentice to a Friend
Stephen, Jr. d New Bedford 1822; m Lydia S. -----
Ch: Mary b 1-24-1813
Sarah " 1-24-1813
Caroline b 12-24-1815 d 11-20-1816 bHS
Susan B. " 7-26-1817
Stephen
Lydia Ann

HATHAWAY, Stephen, Jr. & Lydia S., continued
Ch: William S.
cf New Bedford for both 7-18-1809; ct New Bedford 3-16-1822 for Lydia with 6 ch named

HATTON
Edward, s Robert & Constance, of Cork, d 7-25-1911 at Los Angeles in his 81st yr.; cf Hardshaw West. 11-1866; his name had been erased

HAUGHTON
Eliza L. (form Lowerre), d 4-13-1845 ae 54y bPP (apparently dt Thomas & Mary Lowerre)

HAVENS
Elizabeth rocf Pelham, N. C. 8-1829; ct Pelham, N. C. 1-1843 (H)
Joseph & Eliza (nm) (probably dt Thomas & Anna Hazard d 11-4-1851 ae 48y 19d bur in same grave as T. Hazard)
Pelham asks that he be dealt with for mo 9-3-1829; rpd adversely; dis 1-5-1831 by Pelham & N. Y. served it on him 4-6-1831

HAVILAND
Aaron, s Stephen & Sarah, b 8-15-1828; mo before 7-1872, ret a mbr; relinquished mbrp 3-1880
Aaron m Pur. Rebecca SUTTON, dt George & Amy, d 4-21-1884
Ch: Emma S. d 9-9-1874
A. Walter b 2-24-1852; rpd 1920 as prob dec
cf Pur. 11-10-1841 (clear); Rebecca recrq of mother 1825
Aaron G., s John & Ann C.; m 1-20-1848 Elizabeth C. WILLETS, dt Samuel & Hannah (Carpenter), b N. Y. 11-4-1824 d 7-9-1903 (H)
Ch: S. Willets b 4-29-1852 d 12-29-1910
John A. b 6-16-1854 d 5-31-1902
cf Pur. for Elizabeth & ch 1-5-1870
Adelaide, dt George & Sarah Louise (Childs), b Bkn. 4-21-1862; m 1881 Henry C. FIELD (H)
Albert E., s Daniel E. & Phebe C., rocf Yorktown 6-1883; name erased 3-1928
Alfred, s William & Esther (Seaman), rocf Pur. 7-7-1869 with parents; relrq 5-2-1877; d 5-2-1910 ae 60y 10m 20d bPP
Alice, dt Robt. B. & Rebecca (Hull), b 7-8-1855; m 7-5-1882 Uldrich THOMPSON (nm) (H) in Honolulu since 1899
Ann rocf Pur. 3-12-1818 (clear); dis 11-1829 (H); d 1842
Anna, dt James C. & Phebe, Bkn.; m 1861 Hamilton EASTER, of Baltimore (H)
cf Jericho 7-1844 with parents; ct Balt. 6-4-1862
Anna, dt John G. & Mary H., b 6-26-1862; relrq 8-3-1887 (H)
Anna Griffen d 2-9-1868 ae 88y bPP (nm) (H)
Anna M., dt Mary (Cooley), b 10-8-1816; m Ellwood WALTER (H)
cf N. P. 6-5-1867

Anthony B. rocf Pur. 5-12-1791, minor; ct Pur. 9-3-1801, rem with his uncle; cf Pur. 7-12-1826 (clear); ct Pur. 3-3-1830 (clear (O); d 5-26-1836 at Pur.
Arthur, s Daniel G. & Hannah (Quinby), b Bkn. 3-8-1848 d 6-13-1919; bPP; m 11-11-1888 Margaret A. BURT (nm), dt John & Mary J. (Martin), d 9-23-1930 ae 77y bPP (H)
Benjamin, Rye, d 7 Mo (Sep) 31, 1726
Benjamin, Flushing, active mbr 1701
Benjamin, s Ebenezer (dec), New Rochelle, N. Y. d 9-8-1862 ae 71y bPP; m Flushing 8-9-1770 Sarah FARRINGTON, dt John & Mary, Flushing
Ch: Mary b 11-26-1773
John " 8-25-1776
Abigail b 12-21-1781
Catharine b 12- 1-1783
Benjamin b 2-25-1787 d 1- 6-1789
Benjamin
Benj. rocf Pur. 5-9-1771; ct Pur. 6-4-1777 cf Pur. 5-14-1778 with w & 2 small ch, Mary & John; ct Pur. 6-4-1801 with 3 ch, Abigail, Catharine & Benjamin; cf Pur for Benj. 1825
Benjamin H. b 5-23-1905; m Grace -----
Ch: Stewart Benjamin b 3-25-1933
Wallace J. b 6-20-1935
cf Po'keepsie 6-1925
Benjamin S., s Stephen & Sarah, N. Y., d 1-19-1880; m N. Y. 6-11-1851 Emma R. GRIMSHAW, dt John (dec) & Emma, N. Y., d 9-3-1888
Ch: William R. b 6-21-1852
Gertrude " 4-23-1855
Franklin " 7-19-1858
Cornelia " 3- 1-1860
Emma R. recrq 4-1870; she had resigned 3-1866
Caroline, dt Daniel G. & Hannah, Bkn.; m 1857 John D. HICKS, of Wby. (H)
cf Pur. 9-7-1825 (clear)
Caroline, dt Robert, gct Pur. 7-2-1834, minor with brother rem with parents
Caroline, dt Edwin & Louisa, b 11-25-1858; relrq 12-6-1882 (H)
Catharine, dt Stephen & Sarah, rocf Pur. 7-13-1825 (clear); d 4-21-1862 ae 74y 4m bPP
Charity, dt Thomas (dec), rocf Pur. 10-10-1793 to live with a Friend in N. Y.
Charles F., s Robert B. & Lucy, b 8-11-1832; m ----- (H)
Ch: Maurice R.
relrq 11-3-1858
Clarence M., s Edwin & Louisa (Merritt), b Bkn. 6-6-1866; m 12-18-1907 Gertrude CONNOR (nm) dt A. B. (H)
relrq 7-8-1929
Clement, s George, d 12-27-1897 ae 37y 10m bPP; m Mary Abbie SLOCUM, dt Henry Nason & Abbie, d 7-21-1935 ae 76y bPP (H) (both nm)
Cora, dt David S. & Sarah A., Bkn.; m 1898 John L. CARVER (H)
ct Alton, Southampton & Poole 10-8-1928

HAVILAND, continued
Cornelia, dt Robert B. & Lucy, b 12-27-1836; relrq 7-3-1861 (H)
Cornelia, dt Benj. S. & Emma R., b 3-1-1860 d 8-1-1888; m ----- PADDOCK
Daniel rocf Pur. 8-7-1844, minor (recorded in Reg. 295 as David with note to see Daniel E. for correct name)
Daniel C. b 7-26-1831 d 7-14-1900 ae 68y 11m 18d; rocf Pur. 5-1858 (H)
Daniel E., s Ebenezer & Phebe (Haight), b Chap. 2-6-1826 d 3-23-1894, rem from Croton-on-Hudson to PP; m before 1849 Phebe C. COCKS, dt John & Armenia (Conklin), b 1829 Croton-on-Hudson d 8-7-1918 Newark, N. J. bPP (mo, ret a mbr)
Ch: Armenia b 7-15-1849 d 5-31-1850 bPP
Frederick A. b 12-1-1863 d 2-14-1864 bPP
John E. d 7-22-1809 bPP
Mary b 4-13-1851 Croton-on-Hudson d 9-4-1911 bPP
Annie b 6-6-1856 Croton-on-Hudson d 2-21-1919 bPP
Walter D. b 8-10-1867 Croton-on-Hudson d 3-8-1916 bPP
Albert E.
cf Pur. for Daniel 1844; ct Ama. for Daniel 1852; cf Yorktown 6-1-1883 for all
Daniel G., s William & Anna, d 7-30-1864 ae 64y bPP; m Hannah QUINBY, d 4-1-1864 ae 61y bPP (H)
Ch: Mary Jane d 1-4-1833 ae 2y 6m 25d bPP
Caroline b 4- 4-1832
Richard " 2-13-1835 d 2-28-1842 bPP
George " 11-11-1833
Albert " 1-20-1837 d 4- 8-1839 bPP
Mary " 4- 1-1844 d 12-15-1901 bPP
Arthur " 3- 8-1848
cf Chap. 9-13-1827 (clear); dis 11-1838 (O)
Hannah rocf Chap. 2-1839
David d 12-13-1879 at Limoges, France; m Mary C. ----- d 11-13-1902 at Limoges, France (H)
Ch: Charles E. b 1- 7-1839 d 3-15-1921
Theodore " 8-12-1842
Emma " 7-21-1844 (or 7-24-1844)
Albert " 1-30-1846 d 2-1817
Mary Anna " 3-14-1848
Louisa " 12-12-1856
Henry Louis b 11-15-1859 d 11-1919
cf Chap. 3-1838 for David; cf Pur. 5-1839 for Mary C.; all went to Limoges, France where Haviland china was made
David A. rocf Pur. 2-1839; dis 2-2-1848 (H)
David A., s Solomon & Marielma (Field), b N.Y. 11-6-1881; m Ruth DAY (nm) (H)
David S., s Wm. Jr. & Esther (Seaman), b 7-13-1841 Jericho d 1-2-1915 bPP; m 9-4-1867 Sarah A. CARPENTER, dt Joseph & Charlotte d 4-7-1879 ae 38y bPP (H)
Ch: Charlotte b 1-29-1870
Esther " 4- 9-1872
Cora " 1-29-1874
Ch: Mary S. b 10-30-1876 d 7-31-1932 (or b 10-30-1875)
Willard d 8- 3-1879 ae 4m bPP
ct Pur. 8-1848 with parents; cf Pur. 8-7-1895 for David
Deborah rocf Oblong 8-14-1837 (clear); dis 12-1839
Ebenezer, s Ebenezer, of Westchester Co.; m N. Y. 2-7-1770 Jane BURLING, dt John & Ann, N. Y.
Ch: Phebe b Westchester 11-27-1770
Ann " N. Y. 1-4-1774
Ebenezer & Jane rocf Pur. 6-11-1771; rec 7-1-1772; ct Pur. 6-4-1777; cf Pur. 3-8-1781 with w, Jane, & 2 small ch; ct Pur. 5-7-1800 with dt, Ann.
Edmund, s William & Anne, d 2-20-1844, ae 45y 3m 20d bPP; m Emily W. -----
Ch: Sarah W. b 12-12-1839
cf Pur. 4-11-1816, minor; cf WD MM 9-18-1839 for Emily W.; ct WD MM 1-1847 for Emily & dt; Edmund dis 1829 (H)
Edward, s Wm. Jr. & Esther (Seaman) b 5-20-1851 Pur. d 6-8-1931 Bkn.; m 6-5-1888 Jemima WATSON (nm) (H)
Ch: Elsie b 3-26-1889 Bkn.
cf Pur. 7-7-1869; Elsie's name entered by com. 11-5-1890; in Ohio 1899
Edwin, s James C. & Phebe (Seaman), Bkn., b Jericho 10-6-1833 d 1-10-1911 bPP; m at N. S. Merritt's, Bkn. 9-22-1857 Louisa MERRITT, dt Nathaniel S. & Mary K., Bkn., d 3-18-1870 ae 30y 8m bPP (H)
Ch: Caroline b 11-25-1858
Charles M. " 12-19-1860 d 12-6-1861 bPP
Edwin Jr. " 10- 9-1863
Clarence M. " 6- 6-1866
Edwin, Jr., s Edwin & Louisa (Merritt), b 10-9-1863; relrq 5-9-1908 (H)
Elizabeth, dt Ebenezer & Phebe, Flushing; m 1766 Thomas COMSTOCK
Elizabeth rocf Creek 10-1843 d 5-22-1845 (H)
Elizabeth C. b 11-4-1824, w ----- (H)
Ch: Anna C. b 9-20-1849 d 6- 6-1887
S. Willets " 4-29-1852
John A. " 6-16-1854
Emma S. " 9-12-1856
Elizabeth W. " 2-20-1859 d 10-3-1876
Ella, dt William & Esther, gct Pur. 8-1848 with parents; cf Pur. 6-2-1869 (H)
Elsie, dt Edw. & Jemima, Bkn., b Bkn. 3-26-1889; m 1913 Francis W. ATKINSON, of Moorestown, N. J. (H)
Emily & -----
Ch: Sarah W.
ct WD MM 1-6-1847 with 1 ch named
Emma, dt David & Mary C., b 7-24-1844 d 1932; m 1-1873 Gustave BOUTELLAU (nm) (H)
Emma S., dt Aaron G. & Elizabeth (Carpenter), b 9-12-1856; m Dr. J. Hull PLOTT (nm) (H)
Esther, dt David S. & Sarah C., Bkn. b 4-9-1872; m 1896 Edward CORNELL (H)
Esther G., dt William & Anna G., rocf Chap.

HAVILAND, Esther G., continued
12-1852 (H)
Esther P. rocf Oblong 6-1833 (H)
Frank, s Wm. & Esther (Seaman), Bkn., b Pur. 9-12-1847 d 1-6-1920; m at 137 - 2d Ave. Bkn. 11-27-1878 Kate L. HYDE (nm), dt Barnabas B. (dec) & Cath. A., N. Y., d 3-9-1897 ae 45y 2m 27d bPP (H)
Ch: Bruena d 3- 2-1886 ae 6y 5m 6d bPP
Frank Bernard d 3-15-1886 ae 2y 2m 13d bPP
Frank m 2nd 8-8-1906 Elizabeth SEAMAN (nm), dt Horace & Elvira M. (Foster)
cf Pur. 8-4-1869
Franklin, s Benj. S. & Emma R., b 7-19-1858; mbrp relinquished 3-1880
Frederick, s Robt. R. & Rebecca (Hull), b 8-5-1847; relrq 10-6-1875 (H)
George, s Daniel G. & Hannah, b 3-8-1848 d 9-3-1874 bPP; relrq 12-1862 (H)
Gertrude, dt Benj. S. & Emma R., b 4-23-1855 d 1907; m ----- PADDOCK
Hannah, Flushing, d 3 Mo (May)--- 1712
Hannah B., wd Daniel
Ch: Mary B. m Dan'l Trimble
Hannah dis 5-1830 (O)
Henrietta, dt Robt. B. & Rebecca (Hull), b 11-21-1848; relrq 10-6-1875 (H)
Henry, s James C. & Phebe, b 1-15-1827 N. Y. d 9-3-1902 bPP; m 11-3-1852 Sarah MORRIS, dt Anthony P. & Anna H., b Phila. 6-26-1826 d 9-20-1910 bPP
Ch: Anthony M. b 8-10-1853 d 3-17-1855 bPP
A. Morris d 3-17-1855 ae 1y 7m
Anna M. b 1- 1-1857 d 8-21-1863 bPP
Maria " 1- 2-1859 " 8-23-1863 bPP
Henry M. b 1- 5-1863
Margaret M. b 8-23-1865 d 7-25-1891 bPP
ct Wby & Jericho 8-6-1834 with sister, Maria, minors (O); ct Jericho with parents 5-1835 (H); ct Phila. 4-6-1853 for Sarah M.
Henry F., s Solomon & Marielma (Field), b N.Y. 2-15-1880; m 11-30-1905 M. Laura COLE (nm) dt Frank Wm. & Clara (Dodman) (H)
name entered by com. 10-10-1886; relrq 7-12-1920
Henry Morris, s Henry & Sarah M., b 1-5-1863 Bkn.; m 6-18-1896 Susan B. HANCE, dt Benj. B. & Sarah Lavinia, b Red Bank, N. J. 6-22-1896 (H)
Ch: Margaret b 9- 4-1897
Herbert Hance b 9- 4-1900 d 4-14-1901 bPP
Elizabeth b 10-19-1906
Isaac rocf New Bedford 6-1887
James, s William, rocf Chap. 8-14-1818, apprentice
James C. d 7-20-1870 ae 68y 9m bPP; m Jericho Phebe SEAMAN, dt David, Jericho, d 9-20-1863 ae 65y 2m 25d bPP
Ch: Anna
Maria
Henry b 6-15-1827
Ch: William S. b 9-21-1831 d 12- 4-1915
Edwin " 10- 8-1833
Sarah
Lydia S.
cf Chap. 11-1818 with cert of clear to Jericho 4-2-1823; Phebe rocf Jericho 5-1835; ct Wby & Jericho 8-6-1834 for Maria & Henry (O); parents dis 1829-30 (O); cf Jericho 8-1844 for all
James C. m 2d Sarah C. -----
cf Byberry 7-4-1866 for Sarah; ct Green St. Phila. 10-4-1873 for Sarah
James S., s Wm. T. & Sarah Ann, Harrison; m at Daniel Willet's, Bkn. 1-14-1874 Elizabeth V. GRIFFEN, dt Henry & Martha V., Bkn., b 2-16-1853 (H)
ct Pur. 6-2-1875
James V., s Benj. H. & Catharine; m 1-11-1842 Phebe Ann HAVILAND, dt John & Hannah, b Paterson, N. Y. 12-28-1820 d 11-17-1909 (H)
cf Oblong for Phebe 4-1845
Jane rocf Pur. 5-17-1770; cf Pur. 6-11-1772
Jane d 1-27-1893; rocf Pur. 7-6-1859 (H)
John, N. Y. & Anne (or Anna) F.
Ch: Mary
Jane
Richard
Phebe b 7-25-1815 d 12-17-1815
cf Pur. 3-9-1815 with their 3 ch named; He & partner Rich. Field dis for failure 10-1-1817; ct Pur. 10-4-1820 for Anna & 2 dt, Mary & Jane
John, s Robert, gct Pur. 7-2-1834 with sister, rem with parents
John G., s Robert & Esther, d 9-5-1882; m Mary H. HULL, dt Wager, Jr. & Keziah (Cooley), b Bethlehem, N. Y. 11-9-1828 d 10-29-1911 (H)
Ch: John Howard b 1- 1-1856 d 2-20-1859
Carrie " 7- 4-1858 " 3- 5-1859
Mary Amelia " 3-28-1860 " 4-11-1861
Anna " 6-26-1862
William Robert " 11-23-1863
John rocf Chap. 5-1851 with these 2 ch; Mary rocf Corn. 6-1855
Louise, dt James S. & Elizabeth (Griffen), b Pur. 10-1-1875; m 1910 J. Bernard WALTON (H)
cf Pur. 12-10-1910; ct Swarthmore 3-10-1917 with h & ch
Lydia S., dt James C. & Phebe, Bkn.; m 1865 Aaron FIELD (H)
cf Jericho 7-1844 with parents
Lyman (nm); m Sarah ----- (nm) b Orange Co. d 10-4-1837 ae 30y bHS
Margaret, dt Henry M. & Susan (Hance), b Bkn. 9-4-1897; relrq 12-10-1929 to join Episcopal Church (H)
Margery, dt Walter & Eliz. (Jones), b Glen Ridge, N. J. 10-10-1886; relrq 5-6-1905 (H)
Maria, dt James C. & Phebe, gct Wby & Jericho

HAVILAND, Maria, continued
8-6-1834 with brother, Henry, minors
Maria Louisa, dt Rich'd F. & Matilda (Hicks), b 11-28-1846 Bkn. d 10-7-1920; m 11-28-1865 Erastus B. BARKER, s David D. & Julia A. (Barnes) (H)
cf Chap. with father 1-1851
Mary, dt Benjamin & Sarah, N. Y.; m 1793 N.Y. Thomas FRANKLIN, Jr.
Mary, dt Thos. & Helena, Pur. b 1-23-1778; m 1796 Solomon PANCOAST
Mary Anna, dt David C. & Mary C., b 3-14-1848; relrq 9-5-1857 (H)
Mary B., dt Daniel & Hannah; m Daniel TRIMBLE (H)
Mary E., dt William & Esther, gct Pur. 8-1848 with parents; cf Pur. 6-2-1869 (H)
Mary Elizabeth, dt Solomon & Marseilma, b N.Y. 10-11-1877; m 1905 Dr. Percy Beecher THOMPSON (H)
Maurice R., s Charles F., d 12-30-1889 ae 26y bPP, rem to France 12-30-1890; m Annie S. ----- d 1-4-1890 ae 22y bPP, rem to Newport, R. I. 3-29-1892 (H) (both nm)
Nellie Elma, dt Solomon & Marielma (Field), b N. Y. 1-17-1887; m Dr. Clinton J. HYDE (nm) (H)
name entered by com. 10-10-1886
Paulina, w Lyman, rocf Creek 8-1-1849 d 1-17-1892 (H)
Phebe, wd, d 9-19 (or 9) 1860 ae 88y, rem from PP to Sleepy Hollow 1884
Ch: Sarah
cf Ama. 10-10-1823 with minor dt, Sarah (clear); Phebe dis 1829 (H)
Phebe, dt Ebenezer & Jane, Westchester; m 1791 Elijah FERRIS, N. Y.
Phebe, dt Benj. & Phebe, Pur.; m Benoni HATHAWAY; m 2d 1843 Abraham WANZER
cf Pur. 8-10-1831 for Phebe Hathaway
Phebe Ann, dt John & Hannah, b Paterson, N. Y. 12-28-1820 d 11-17-1909; m 1842 James V. HAVILAND (H)
cf Oblong 4-1845
Phebe S., dt Stephen & Sarah, b 11-16-1834 in Toledo
Richard F. d 10-4-1898 ae 78y 9m 29d bPP; m Matilda HICKS d 3-3-1884 ae 59y 3m 17d bPP (H)
Ch: Maria Louisa b 11-28-1846
Robert H. " 10-21-1850
cf Chap. 1-1851 for Richard & ch; cf Wby 12-1852 for Matilda
Robert & Esther
Ch: Caroline b 6-30-1826
John G.
Hannah
cf Pur. 2-8-1826 for Robert; cf Chap. 2-9-1826 for Esther, his w; parents dis 1830 (0) 1832; ch gct Pur. 7-1834 (0); ct Pur. 7-1833 for all (H)
Robert B., s Wm. & Anna G., N. Y., d 9-1-1885 ae 81y 9m 10d bPP; m N. Y. 9-10-1829 Lucy COMSTOCK, dt Nathan & Eliz. (dec) N. Y., d 4-17-1839 ae 33y bPP
Ch: Edward E. b 7-22-1830; drowned San Francisco 9-9-1850 bPP
Charles T. b 8- 1-1832
Robert B. b 2-22-1835 d 3-29-1837 bPP
Cornelia " 12-27-1836
Eugene d 2-5-1931 ae 76y bPP
cf Chap. 6-1822, minor; dis 11-1831 for hiring a pew in a church & owning & employing slaves (0); lives Augusta, Ga.
Robert B. m 2d at Amy Hull's 10-8-1846 Rebecca HULL, dt John & Amy, N. Y., d 2-25-1861 ae 42y 9m bPP
Ch: Frederick b 8- 5-1847
Henrietta " 11-21-1848 d 1-29-1832 bPP (ashes bPP)
Howard b 8-31-1852 d 12- 9-1878 bPP
Eugene " 1-15-1854 " 2- 5-1931 bPP
Alice " 7- 8-1855
Robert B. m 3d Martha C. ----- d 4-7-1893 ae 80y bPP
dis mo by priest 11-5-1862
Robert H., s Richard F., b 10-21-1850 d 2-16-1899 bPP; m Catharine QUINN (H)
joined a military company before 6-5-1872 dis 8-7-1872
Samuel D. d 3-18-1887; rocf Scipio 11-17-1841, w dec
Sarah, w Stephen, d 9-16-1844 ae 92y 11m 8d
Ch: Catharine
Benjamin
cf Pur. 7-13-1825; Catharine, her dt, rocf Pur. same date; Sarah & dt dis 1829 (H)
Sarah, dt Phebe, rocf Ama. with mother 1823; dis 5-1833
Sarah S., dt James C. & Phebe, Bkn.; m 1853 Edward MERRITT (H)
Sarah Eliz., dt Stephen & Sarah, b 10-22-1842; m David D. WEBSTER
ret a mbr
Solomon J. (nm), s David A. & Elizabeth; m 10-18-1876 Marielma F. FIELD, dt Henry C. & Mary (Schureman), b White Plain 10-7-1852 (H)
Ch: Mary Eliz. b 10-11-1877
Henry F. " 2- 5-1880 (or 2-15-1880)
David A. " 11- 6-1881 (or 11-16-1881)
Nellie Elma" 10- 6-1883
Henrietta B. b 11-11-1885
cf Pur. 7-2-1884 for mother; ch names entered by com 10-10-1886 (3); 1-17-1887 (2)
Stephen d 6-8-1874; m Sarah ----- d 3-4-1877
Ch: Benjamin
Aaron b 8-15-1828
Phebe S. " 11-16-1834 d 10-1923
Sarah Elizabeth b 10-22-1842
cf Pur. 8-8-1827 with ch, Benjamin; parents dis 1829 (H)
Theodore, s David & Mary E., b 8-12-1842 N. Y. d 12-17-1919; m 6-1874 Julia DANNOT (nm) dt William & Susan (Jones) (H)
Thomas & Helena

HAVILAND, Thomas & Helena, continued
Ch: Mary b 1-23-1778
Anthony " 2-20-1780
Charity " 6-15-1781
Anthony B. b 5-1783
having mo & rem to Oblong it is referred to that MM 8-6-1778; ct Oblong 9-2-1778; cf Oblong for Thomas & s, Anthony Bartow 8-18-1783; ct Pur. for Thomas & Helena with ch, Anthony, Mary & Charity; cf Pur. 4-8-1784 for Helena with 2 dt, Mary & Charity
Walter rocf Chap. 12-10-1835, minor; dis 4-1842 for attending another religious society
Walter, s Wm. & Esther (Seaman), Bkn., b Bkn. 9-27-1842 d 7-29-1933 bPP; m at L. M. Jones' 6-15-1882 Elizabeth H. JONES (nm), dt Linda L. (dec) (or Lysander) & Ann M. Bkn., d 10-10-1896 ae 45y 4m 26d bPP (H)
Ch: Elizabeth b 5- 2-1883
Margery " 10-10-1886
Walter m 2d 9-26-1914 Eleanor Hortense TERRY (nm), dt David D. & Eleanor A. (Bliss);
Walter m 3d 7-22-1922 Agnes Maude MEGGS (nm), dt Jos. & Ann S. SUTCLIFFE
William & Anne
Ch: Edmund d 2-20-1844 ae 45y
Daniel d 5-13-1828 ae 2d
cf Pur. 5-9-1797 with Edmund, infant; ct Pur. 6-5-1800 with ch, Edmund & Daniel
William & Esther
Ch: David S. b 7-13-1841
Walter " 9-27-1842
Mary E. " 11-21-1843 d 12- 8-1920 bPP
Ellen " 3- 6-1846
Francis " 9-12-1847
cf Chap. 7-1839 for William; cf Jericho 3-1841 for Esther; ct Pur. 8-1848 for all
William d 2-3-1889 bPP; m Esther SEAMAN d 8-25-1891 ae 82y 4m 3d bPP
Ch: Alfred
Edward
cf Pur. 7-7-1869 for all
Wm. C., s Charles C. & Mary C., White Plains; m White Plains 4-5-1920 Grace A. CAPRON, dt Jacob & Jane E., N. Y., b N. Y. 1-22-1878 (H)
ct Pur. for Grace 1-10-1921
William R., s Benj. S. & Emma R., b 6-21-1852; mbrp relinquished 3-1880
Wm. Robert, s John G. & Mary (Hull), b N. Y. 11-23-1863; m 9-28-1893 Grace R. WOOD (nm), dt Robert & Stella (Read) (H)
relrq 6-14-1913
----- (nm) m Grace SQUIRE, dt Charles & Ida
cf Marl. 10-1-1930 for Grace

HAWESON
Ebenezer d 11-15-1807 ae 23y

HAWKINS
Cornelia C., dt Lewis M. & Sarah (Bull), b Goshen 12-17-1862; cf Corn. 7-1915
Emelene W., dt Lewis W. & Sarah, b 3-5-1869; m 1894 George R. ANDREWS (H)
cf Corn. 10-3-1895
Harry A., s Lewis W. & Sarah (Bull) b Goshen 5-7-1860, recrq 7-6-1881 (H) (unm)
Jane Bull, dt Lewis W. & Sarah (Bull), b Goshen 7-10-1861; cf Corn. 7-1915 (H)
John m Mary J. KEELEY, dt John & Josephine, d 7-29-1913 ae 64y 11m bPP (H) (both nm)
Lewis W. (nm) m Sarah BULL (mbr Corn)
Ch: Harry A. b 5- 7-1860
Jane Bull b 6-10-1861
Cornelia C. b 12-17-1862
Emeline W. " 3- 5-1869
ch b Goshen; Jane & Cornelia rocf Corn. 7-1915 (H)
Martha L. (nm), dt Chas. B. & Martha (L----); m 1866 Alfred WINDER (H)

HAWKS
George W. rolf 2d Presbyterian Church, Newark, N. J. 11-1921

HAWXHURST
Amy, dt Daniel & Hannah, N. Y.; m 1819 Joseph F. CARROLL
Amy d 11-9-1856 ae 56y bPP (apparently not a mbr here)
Ann recrq 1-1829; ct Wby 5-1843 (H)
Benjamin m Hannah ----- d 5-10-1805 ae 83y 4m
Ch: Hannah d 12-13-1815 ae 62y
----- " 7- 4-1799
cf Wby for Hannah & their ch 6-26-1765; ch not named, but those of yrs of discretion are orderly
Caroline S., dt James O. & Julia, d 8-7-1879; 7-30-1867 James N. HARRIS (nm) (H)
cf Jericho 10-1857 with parents; ret a mbr
Catharine, dt James & Catharine, gct Oswego 8-1833 (H)
Daniel rocf Pur. 4-12-1792, he being rst, having con form misconduct
Daniel m Hannah ----- d 7-4-1799 bHS
Ch: Daniel b 12-23-1784
Sarah " 3-16-1789
Amy " 8-28-1791
Mary B. " 11- 3-1793
cf Wby 8-1-1765 (for some Hannah)
Daniel (nm) (some Daniel S. d 5-9-1835 ae 41y bHS) & -----
Ch: stillborn 3-9-1814
Daniel (prob) b N. Y. d 8-25-1832 ae 17y bHS
Daniel K. d 5-19-1887; m Maria S. THOMAS (H)
Ch: John Thomas b 2-29-1876 d 3- 7-1904
Mary K. b Norristown 9-18-1878
Jennie K.
cf Race St. Phila. 3-2-1887 for Daniel & 3 ch named
Daniel S. dis mo 5-2-1821 (prob s Daniel & Hannah b 12-23-1784)
Edmund, s Wm. & Mary, b 3-12-1813 (or 12-3-1813)

HAWXHURST, Edmund, continued
dis mo 4-1838
Elisha rocf Jericho 11-1848; ct Wby 8-5-1857 (H)
Emma, dt Wm. & Mary, N. Y.; m 1849 Joseph COLLINS
Hannah b L. I. d 12-13-1815 ae 61y 8m 18d (wd)
Hannah B. d 7-26-1845
Hannah S., dt James & Catharine, gct Oswego 8-1833 (H)
James, s Benj. & Hannah, Merchant, N. Y., b L. I. d 11-22-1827 ae 68y; m 1-13-1790 Catharine SEACORD, dt James & Catharine (dec), b New Rochelle d 5-22-1823 ae 62y
Ch: Martha b 10-16-1790
Sarah P. b 1-27-1792
Jane S. " 3- 4-1793 d 1- 9-1825
Deborah
Hannah S.
Catharine
Maria
James G.
ct Pur. 1-7-1801 with their 6 ch as named; cf Pur. 4-14-1814 with 8 ch, the dt clear; all dis 1830-1832 (C)
James C. d 9-23-1869; m Julia E. STARKINS, d 9-29-1900 (H)
Ch: Phebe C. b 1- 5-1844
Caroline S.
cf Jericho 10-1857 for parents & 2 ch named
James J. (or G.), s James & Catharine, dis 4-1838 (H)
Jane recrq 10-1853; d 12-21-1897 (H)
Jennie K., dt Daniel K. & Maria S. (Thomas), b 8-8-1874; m John S. STETSON (nm) (H)
cf Phila. with father 3-2-1887
John m Jane KISSAM d 1-5-1895 (H)
Ch: Timothy S. K. b 7-27-1853
Jennie K. " 3- 6-1856
cf Alexandria 6-1-1887 for Jane & 2 ch named; ch b Fairfax, Va.
Maria, dt James & Catharine, gct Oswego 8-1833 (H)
Martha P., dt James & Catharine, b 10-16-1790; ct Oswego 8-1833 (H)
Mary B., dt Daniel & Hannah, N. Y.; m 1825 Daniel TRIMBLE
Mary S. Barnard (form Hawxhurst) rocf Jericho 2-1831; dis mo 11-1836 (H)
Nathaniel d 1847; m before 4-6-1794 Phebe FRANKLIN b N. Y. d 8-12-1824 ae 59y (mo, con mo 10-1-1794)
Ch: Walter b 2-26-1795
Mary F. " 11-27-1796 d 11-1857 ae 60y bPP
Nathaniel Jr. b 1-4-1799
Robert d 8-7-1810 ae 8y 10m 9d
Franklin " 9-25-1804 ae 1y 3m
Nathaniel m 2d N. Y. 7-13-1826 Sarah C. COLLINS b 4-2-1775 d 3-24-1855
Nathaniel, Jr., s Nathaniel & Phebe, b 1-4-1799 d 3-3-1874; m Phebe M. -----
Ch: Sarah M. b 8-11-1826
Phebe F. b 4- 8-1828
Mary " 12-29-1829
Caroline " 6-20-1831
Ann " 7-19-1833
Walter " 8- 5-1835 d 7-29-1837
Richard F. " 2-17-1837
Walter " 1-13-1839 d 1-19-1845
cf Ama. 5-12-1826 for Phebe M.; all dis 1830-1849 (O); ct R. & P. 5-1858 for parents; ct R. & P. 10-1862 for all ch except Richard F.
Nathaniel & Sarah
Ch: Mary F. d 11-23-1857
parents dis 1829-(H)
Penelope (form Burt) dis mo to first cousin 11-1828 (O); dis mo 11-1829 (H)
Phebe C., dt James C. & Julia E.; m 11-11-1863 Moses B. HOUSTON (nm); m 2d 1-30-1882 James S. BODEN (nm) (H)
cf Jericho with parents 10-1857; ret a mbr
Rachel Searing (form Hawxhurst) rocf Jericho 2-1831; dis mo 4-1833 (H)
Richard F., s Nath. Jr. & Phebe M., b 2-17-1837; joined U.S. Army during the late war; min 7-3-1867; dis 5-6-1868 (H)
Sarah rocf Wby 2-23-1774, rec 4-6-1774; ct Pur. 6-6-1781 (clear); cf Pur. 6-10-1784 (clear); ct Pur. 10-5-1785; cf Pur. 12-13-1792
Sarah Marshall (form Hawxhurst) dis mo 12-4-1811; rst 5-1816; d 7-21-1874 (dt of H.B., perhaps Hannah B.)
Sarah P., dt James & Cath., N. Y.; m 1821 Peter J. COUTANT
Seaman (nm) b Westchester Co. d 8-22-1811 ae 28y bHS
Thomas d 10-6-1843 ae 91y 6m 29d; m Sarah ----- d 10-28-1837 ae 80y 10m 16d
Ch: Phebe b 1-10-1785 d 12-11-1868
Wright " 2-11-1790
Daniel " 4-15-1792
Amy " 10- 5-1795
ct Pur. 9-1-1790, he having been long since dis by Pur. & now his ack. accepted by Pur. cf Wby 12-17-1800 for the 4 ch; Thomas, Phebe & Amy dis 1829 (H)
Thomas rocf Wby 8-20-1800
Thomas (nm) m Sarah ----- d 10-28-1837 ae 80y 10m 6d bHS
Ch: Wright b White Plains d 7-30-1819 ae 29y bHS (unm)
Timothy S. K., s John & Jane (Kissam), b Fairfax Co., Va. 7-27-1853 d 12-21-1928; m 7-1-1897 Daisy Eliz. ORMEROD, dt John & Elizabeth, b Bkn. 12-3-1876 (H)
cf Alexandria 6-1-1887 for Timothy; Daisy recrq 9-4-1897
Walter, s Nathaniel & Phebe, b 2-26-1795; m ----
Ch: Hariet d 8-26-1837 ae 11m 15d bHS
ct Starksborough, Vt. 12-5-1821 (clear); cf Starksborough 1840; ct Salem, Iowa 9-1845

HAWXHURST, continued
William d 9-28-1851; m Mary ----- d 1-27-1819 ae 23y bHS
Ch: Edmund b 3-12-1813 (or 12-3-1813); dis 4-1838
Almy " 3- 4-1815; (or 4-3-1815)
Peter " 12- 6-1816 d 8-12-1817
William d 3- 4-1819 ae 6m
cf Wby 9-15-1813 with young ch, Edmund; William dis 1829 (H)
Wright dis 4-1-1818
----- & -----
Ch: Harriet d 8-26-1837 ae 11m 15d bHS

HAY
Catharine, dt Wm. C. & Mary C. (Vinson) PLEASANTS, b Maryland 1864 d 6-11-1925; recrq 4-8-1916 (wd George W. Hay) (H)
Maud Jarvis recrq 12-1928; relrq 7-10-1935
Sarah R., w Frank, (form Seaman) recrq of mother 6-4-1817; m 6-27-1855 by a J.P., ret a mbr (H)

HAYDOCK
Anna Maria, dt John & Jane, b 4-2-1836; m ----- SHOEMAKER
Charlotte Louisa, dt John & Jane, b 4-9-1839; m ----- VAN ETTEN; ret a mbr
Clara N., dt Edward M. & Catharine (Noyes), d 9-13-1928 ae 59y 11m 12d bPP (unm)(H)
Eden rocf R. & P. 4-7-1793 (clear); dis mo 8-2-1791
Edith, dt Rich. & Sarah Anne, N. Y.; m 1897 Russell Benj. HOBSON
Edmund, s Richard & Sarah Ann; m Mary LIDBETTER
Ch: Richard b 1-4-1913
cf Lisburn, Ireland with parents 11-6-1895; cf Holm, Eng. for Mary
Edward M., s Henry & Martha B. (Mott), b N. Y. 12-21-1834 d 4-26-1914 Locust Valley bPP; m 7-20-1865 Kate J. NOYES (nm) d 2-28-1884 ae 49y bPP (H)
Eleanor, dt Robert & Rebecca, Flushing; m 1746/7 Jacob SHOTWELL
Elizabeth b L. I. d 7-8-1831 ae 73y 6m; dis 1829 (O) (wd) (H)
Ephraim, s John & Jane, b 11-8-1840 d 1-11-1915; m before 12-1863 Annie ----- d rpd 7-1920 (mo)
Annie recrq 3-1870
George Guest, s Samuel & Sarah, d 4-6-1898 ae 83y 10m: m 10-25-1839 Patience Caroline CORLIES, dt Jacob & Hannah, b 1-10-1813 N. Y. d 3-17-1902
cf Phila. 10-30-1834, minor; dis 12-1839 (O); cf Phila. 3-1837 (H)
Hannah, dt Henry & Hannah, N. Y.; m 1789 Richard LAWRENCE
Hannah T., dt John W. & Eliz., N. Y.; m 1812 George T. WHITE
Henry, s Robert & Rebecca, Flushing; m Flushing 5 Mo (July) 3, 1746 Mary BOWNE, dt Robert (dec) & Margaret, Flushing, d 1757 in N.Y.
Henry brought cert from Newark MM, Chester, Pa., late from Eng. but last from Pa. 4 Mo. (June) 6, 1745
Henry d 8-27-1798; m Katharine RODMAN, dt Thomas & Eliz., Flushing, b 12 Mo (Feb.) 29, 1731/2 d 7-15-1760
took cert of clear to Phila. 10-6-1762
Henry m 2d Hannah ----- d 3-31-1791
Ch: William b 4-26-1764 d 8-10-1764
Mary " 5-29-1765
Rebecca " 12-14-1766
Hannah " 12-14-1766
Henry " 7-20-1768
Elizabeth Moode b 9-24-1770
Eleanor b 7-16-1772
Jane " 11-11-1774 d 8-28-1798
Robert " 1-14-1777 " 8-11-1778
Hannah rocf Phila. 3-3-1763
Henry, s Henry (dec) & Sarah, N. Y., b 9-3-1803 d 7-29-1884; m N. Y. 7-12-1827 Martha B. MOTT, dt Samuel & Elizabeth (dec), N. Y. d 4-10-1858 ae 55y bPP
Ch: Henry R. b 9-15-1828 d 12-23-1879 bPP
Barnard M. " 2- 2-1830 " 12-15-1831
Elizabeth B." 3-28-1832 " 4-21-1901 bPP
Edward M. " 12-21-1834
Samuel Mott " 10-26-1843 " 4- 6-1903 bPP
cf Wby 11-14-1821, apprentice; parents dis 1830-1831 (O)
Henry & Margaret
Henry recrq 5-1836; Margaret recrq 6-1837; ct Grange, Ire. for both 10-3-1838
Henry m Sarah ----- d 5-9-1846 (H)
Ch: Mary
Elizabeth b 4-29-1812 d 1-23-1906
Jane " 1-29-1816 " 9-22-1901
Sarah J.
Richard L. d 8-24-1898
cf Wby for Sarah with 5 ch 8-20-1834
Henry gct Wby 8-5-1801 (clear)
Henry, Jr., s Henry & Hannah (dec), Merchant, N. Y.; m N. Y. 12-11-1793 Margaret B. PEARSALL, dt Joseph & Hannah, N. Y. d 5-26-1799 bHS
Ch: ----- d 8-1-1797
Isaac d 3-22-1884 ae 70y; m Deborah ----- d 3-2-1864 ae 39y bPP
Ch: ----- (adopted dt) d 6-1865 ae 9y bPP (all nm)
James gc of clear to Woodbridge 3-4-1756
James Jr. rocf R. & P. 6-15-1785 (clear)
John, s Robert, late of Eng. (dec), Rahway, N. J.; m between 2 Mo. 3 & 3 Mo (Mar) 2, 1751 (cert not recorded) Jane BOWNE, dt Robert, N. Y.
Ch: Margaret
ct Phila. 3 Mo (May) 7, 1747; cf Phila. 12 Mo 7, 1750 (clear)
John gct Woodbridge (R. & P.) 12-4-1765
John rocf Hardshaw MM, Lancashire, 1-21-1772 (clear); Mery & Lois, same date and place
John d 4-19-1867 ae 80y bPP; m before 10-1-1828 Jane ALLEN, d 1858 (mo)

HAYDOCK, John & Jane, continued
Ch: Sarah b 12-21-1830 d 1-17-1834 bHS
Elizabeth b 2-19-1833 d 3-30-1864 bPP
Joseph " 10-24-1834
Ann Maria " 4- 2-1836
Sarah Jane b 11-22-1837
Charlotte Louisa b 4- 9-1839
Ephraim " 11- 8-1840
John Jr. " 5-19-1842 d 9-23-1843
Isaac Henry " 3- 3-1845
cf Grange MM, Ire. 7-24-1822 (clear); ct R. & P. 4-4-1827 (clear); cf R. & P. 6-20-1827; dis 1-1829 (0); rst 9-1830; Jane rocf Richhill, Ire. 8-21-1828
John & Sarah
their remains rem from Po'keepsie Rural Cem. to PP 3-21-1901
John W. d 9-18-1798; m Elizabeth ----- d 9-2-1798 bHS (H)
Ch: Sarah b 6-13-1781
Hannah T. " 3-27-1791
William Titus b 9-17-1793
cf Wby for Elizabeth 1-26-1780, w John
Joseph rocf R. & P. 2-18-1795 (clear)
Joseph, s John & Mary, d 11-20-1802 ae 28, at Rahway
Joseph, s John & Jane, b 10-24-1834; mo before 1-1863, ret a mbr; erased 11-1886
Lois, dt William, of Eng.; cf Hardshaw MM, Eng. 3-17-1772 with sister, Mercy; dis 5-6-1773
Margaret, dt John & Jane, Rahway, took cert to Rahway 4-5-1769
Margaret Elliot (form Haydock) rocf Grange, Ireland 12-27-1852; dis mo 4-1855 (probably sister of Sarah Jane)
Maria W., dt Robert H. & Mary W., N. Y.; m 1869 Wm. I. PHILLIPS (H)
Mary, dt Henry & Hannah, N. Y.; m 1793 Edmund PRIOR
Mary rocf Phila. 11-24-1825; dis 1828 (0)
Mary Ann (nm) d 1-17-1850 ae 44y bPP
Mary Ann d 9-28-1854
Mary B., dt Robert & Hannah, N. Y., b 3-13-1849; m 11-24-1874 Grinnell WILLIS (nm) (H)
Mercy, dt William, of England; m 1774 ---- HUNT (mo)
cf Hardshaw, Eng. 3-17-1772 with sister, Lois; con mo 12-6-1775
Rebecca, dt Robert, Flushing; m 1755 Aaron HUNT
Rebecca, dt Henry & Hannah, N. Y.; m 1801 John BARROW
Richard L. & -----
Ch: Joseph W. d 9-5-1866 ae 1y 1m 23d bPP (H) (nm)
Richard R. b 10-5-1901; m Sarah Anne -----
Ch: Henry
Edmund
Herbert
Amelia
Edith
cf Lisburn, Ireland 11-6-1895 for all but Edith; cf same for Edith 12-2-1896
Robert & -----
Ch: Henry
Eleanor
John
James
Rebecca
Robert with w & 4 younger ch rocf Newark MM, Pa. 6 Mo (Aug) 1, 1745
Robert, N. Y. & -----
Ch: Rebecca
James
John
with w (not named) & 2 ch, rem to Woodbridge 3 Mo (May) 7, 1747, returned with w & dt, Rebecca, 4 Mo (June) 6, 1751
Robert gct Darby, Pa. 6-7-1753
Robert (nm) & -----
Ch: Angeline d 1-29-1839 ae 1m bHS
Robert, Jr. b 12-2-1807 d 1-30-1894 bPP; m Hannah W. ----- b 3-6-1818 d 7-15-1893 bPP (H)
Ch: Samuel b 5-30-1844 d 12- 6-1870 bPP
Sarah Wharton b 1-22-1846
Mary Barker " 3-13-1849
Robert Roger " 6- 6-1856
cf Phila. 4-26-1827 for Robert, minor; cf Phila. 6-1843 for Hannah; Robert dis 2-1832 (0)
Robert H., s Henry; m ----- (H)
Ch: Infant stillborn 11-21-1832
cf Wby 9-18-1822, placed; dis 1830 (0); ct Wby 8-2-1871
Robert Roger, s Robt. & Hannah W., b 6-6-1856 d 5-11-1928 ashes bPP; m Annie HEYWOOD (H)
Ch: Edith b 11-21-1884
Eleanor Lowe b 11-18-1886
Robert Jr. " 8-25-1888
Louisa Low " 11- 5-1890
George G., Jr. b 9-15-1894
Names of ch entered by com. 1884-1890 (4); name of George Jr. entered by MM 12-5-1894; ct Phila. Green St. for all 4-9-1898
Samuel b Phila. d 4-18-1842 ae 63y bHS (widower)
Sarah, dt John (dec) & Eliz., N. Y.; m 1801 Samuel HICKS
Sarah, dt Henry & Sarah, N. Y.; m 1847 John L. GRIFFEN (H)
cf Wby 2-8-1834 with mother
Sarah B., dt Robt. J. & Hannah, b 1-22-1846; m Norwood P. HALLOWELL (H)
Sarah Emily, dt Wm. M. & Emily W.; m 1859 Walter COGGESHALL (H)
Sarah J., dt Henry & Sarah; m 1847 John L. GRIFFEN (H); cf Wby 2-8-1834 with mother
Sarah Jane, dt John & Jane, b 11-22-1837 d 1-12-1906; m ----- BRYAN (or Brien)
Sarah Jane rocf Grange, Ire., 12-22-1852; ct Oswego 1856 (probably sister of Margaret)

HAYDOCK, continued

William (nm) & -----
Ch; Margaret J. d 10-26-1819 ae 9m bHS
    Walter b N. Y. d 8-31-1833 ae 6m bHS
William Moode rocf Wby 8-15-1827, minor, placed; dis 1-1832 (O); d 7-19-1863 (H)
William W. d 1831; m Maria Ann ----- (H)
Ch: John W. b 3-2-1820
    dealt with for lack of plainness & attending theater 1817, case discontinued; cert of clear to Troy 5-3-1820; Maria Ann rocf Troy 12-6-1820; ct Troy 4-6-1825 with ch, John; cf Troy for all 3-8-1830; ct Troy for all 8-1834 (H)
----- & -----
Ch: John d 8- 8-1830 ae 1y 9d bHS under (O) com.
    Isaac d 9- 3-1856 ae 11y 6m bPP
    Isaac Jr. d 8-16-1873 ae 13d bPP
    Sarah d 9-16-1873 ae 16d bPP
    a niece of Isaac d 2-22-1881 ae 4m bPP

HAYES
Gertrude, dt Henry H. & Marietta E. (Walton), b Unionville, Pa. 10-11-1876; m Sharpless L. BAKER (nm) 4-5-1899; m 2d 4-26-1927 James J. BARRA (nm), s Gesto & Filipino (H)
    recrq 8-14-1909
Walter W. [Hays] recrq 4-1915; ct 1st Friends Church, Los Angeles 8-1924

HAYTON (see Heaton)
    prcf 2 weeks Mtg, Grace Church St. 2-6-1772, next mo took it to Phila, apparently brought it here again as it was returned to London with endorsement 12-2-1772 (clear)

HAYWARD
Lydia R., dt Sarah W., rocf Balt. 11-1864; mbrp relinquished 3-1880

HAZARD
Ann Catharine rocf Troy 9-1828; d 1830 (H)
John & Martha C. (H)
Ch: Thomas W.
    cf Corn. 4-1833; ct Roch. 4-1837
John d 11-21-1797 bHS
Mary W., dt James & Sarah (Cornell), b Central Valley, N. Y. 6-18-1830 d 1-3-1914; m 1850 John R. RIDER (H)
    cf Corn. 12-1-1880
Samuel (nm) d 2-4-1850 ae 59y 4m 29d bHS, rem to PP; m Rebecca ----- (nm) b S. Carolina d 12-15-1832 ae 32y 7m 15d bHS, rem to PP
Sarah B. rocf Nantucket 11-3-1847 d 4-11-1861 (H)
Sarah W., w Eli B.
Ch: Margaretta E. d 1----1874
    Lydia R.
    cf Balt. 11-1864 with 2 ch named; relrq 10-1872
Thomas, Jr. b R. I. d 7-24-1828 ae 69y 8m 9d bHS, rem to PP; m Anna R. ----- b Newport, R. I. d 6-14-1845 ae 82y 11m 20d bHS, rem to PP (H)
Ch: Edward d 3-28-1820 ae 19y 3m 3d bHS, rem to PP (unm)
    Eliza (prob) m Joseph EVANS
    cf New Bedford 11-23-1815 with ch, Edward; Anna dis 1829 (O)
Thomas R. gct Liverpool 2-6-1811 (clear)
William & Margaret C.
Ch: Charles H. b 10-10-1855
    Margaretta " 12-25-1853 d 3-17-1854
    Mary Alice b 1-20-1852 d 9-23-1852
    cf Corn. 1852 for both; ct Corn. with Charles H. 6-8-1859

HEACOCK
Edith M., dt Wm. A. & Lucretia M. (Robinson), b Alliance, O. 5-20-1898; m 1915 Frank Burt FREIDEL (H)
Emma G. b 9-30-1859 d Hackensack 1-10-1930 bPP; m Francis W. ORVIS
    cf Muncie, Pa. 12-1885 for Emma
William W. & Clara
    cf WD MM 2-1924 for Wm.; letter from 1st R. D. Church of Bkn. for Clara 2-1924; ct Muncie MM, Pa. 3-7-1934

HEAD
Mary con mo before 7 Mo (July) 6, 1744

HEALY
Abigail d 3-8-1885; m -----
Ch: Edwin
    David C.
    Mary S.
    cf Coeymans 3-27-1839 with 3 minor ch
David C., dt Abigail, rocf Coey. 3-27-1839 with mother; dis mo by priest 8-1851 (a minor when m)
Edward H., s William & Renhama, b 12-24-1847; ct Wby 8-2-1854; cf Wby 9-1857; name removed 12-13-1926 as he cannot be located (H)
Edwin, dt Abigail, rocf Coey. with mother 3-27-1839; mo before 12-1849, ret a mbr; dis 7-7-1858 for failure & non-attendance
Hannah rocf Coey. 11-23-1825 (clear); dis 4-1848 (O)
Isaac m Mary P. BIRDSALL, dt Jonathan & Sarah
    cf Coey. 6-24-1834 for Isaac; cf Ama. 9-12-1834 for Mary; Mary m 2d Nathan CLARK, 1838
John d Evansville, Ind., rocf Falls 6-9-1842; at Evansville, Ind.; dis mo 10-1855
Joshua rocf Coey. 8-24-1829 (clear); dis 10-1830
Mary P. [Healey], dt Jonathan & Mary BIRDSALL, N. Y.; m 1838 Nathan CLARK, of Corn.
Mary S., dt Abigail, rocf Coey 3-27-1839 with mother; dis 1-1854
Samuel V., s William, b 4-28-1840; in dealings for mo he said his w belonged to another

HEALY, Samuel, continued
religious society; cf Wby 9-1857; dis 6-1866; had joined a military society before 5-2-1866 (H)
Sarah Ann, dt William, rocf Wby 9-1857 (H)
William & Reuhama (H)
Ch: Mary W. b 12-13-1835 d 2- 3-1852
Samuel " 4-28-1840
Sarah Ann " 7- 3-1843 d 2- 8-1877
Edward Hicks b 12-24-1847
cf Troy 11-1835 for parents; ct Wby 8-1854 for mother & ch; William dis 5-7-1851

HEATER
Guy Carlton (nm), s Nelson E. V. & Minnie H. (Aber) (dec), Waterbury, Conn.; m at E. S. Field's 10-2-1917 Katherine H. FIELD, dt Edw. S. & Lydia R. E., Bkn., b Great Neck, L. I. 8-4-1894 (H)
Katharine recrq of parents 5-5-1900

HEATH
Charles DeVol (nm), s Charles & Lydia; m 5-29-1918 Katharine D. DE VOL, dt Rowland G. & Amanda B. (Merritt), b Falston, Md. 1-6-1863, wd James A. Harned (H)
Noble, s Sarah; m Hannah -----
Ch: John Hardy d 3-16-1832 ae 1y 8m 3d bHS
cf Newcastle on Tyne to Falmouth, Me., he having rem to Westbrook, 1-17-1821 (clear); recorded in N. Y. without endorsement or note; ct Birmingham, Pa. 12-5-1838 (O); dis 1829 (H)
----- m Sarah ----- d 8-4-1833 ae in 56th y bHS
Ch: Noble
(all nm)
----- & -----
Ch: John H. d 3-16-1832 ae 1y 8m 3d bHS

HEATON
Eliza m James Russell TABER
cf Po'keepsie 8-1878 with h
Elizabeth Williamson (form Heaton) dis mo 12-1849
John d 5-13-1884, Flushing; m Elizabeth ----- d 5-12-1871
recrq 5-1845; Elizabeth recrq 5-1863
Maggie J., w Adnah (form McCormick) recrq 5-1886; ct Po'keepsie 1-7-1891

HEDGER
Adeline E., w Wm. N., dt Abraham C. & Eliz. UNDERHILL, b 12-21-1831 d 12-31-1898 Rutherford, N. J. (m 9-24-1853)
at Seneca, Ill. 1858, near Ottowa 1859
Amy, Flushing, b 3 Mo (May), 20, 1725 d 7-3-1792; Amy had ct Shrewsbury 8-7-1766; cf Shrewsbury 12-5-1785 (clear)
Ann m 1762 Daniel LATHAM
Deborah, dt Thomas, d 10-28 (or 29) 1801 ae 85; con mo 5-5-1757
Eliakim, Flushing, m Susannah ----- d 1 Mo (Mar) 27, 1728
Ch: Mary b 8 Mo (Oct) 28, 1711 d 11 Mo 1715/16
Elizabeth b 9 Mo (Nov) 8, 1713
Eliakim " 3 Mo (May) 1, 1716
Joseph " 6 Mo (Aug) 31, 1718
Benjamin " 1 Mo (Mar) 16 1719/20
Sarah " 1 Mo (Mar) 2, 1721/2
Samuel " 3 Mo (May) 26, 1723
Mary " 1 Mo (Mar) 13, 1725/6
rem to Woodbridge 7 Mo (Sep) 5, 1728
Elizabeth rocf Shrewsbury 8-7-1766
Hannah, Flushing; m 1700 Dereck AARSON
Hannah, dt Hannah; m 1716 Matthew FARRINGTON
Keziah, dt Joseph, Flushing; m 1730 William WOOD, of Dartmouth
Mary, Flushing, d 8-22-1770; an old maid, according to best accounts, aged 96 or 97
Mary rpd mo before 9 Mo (Nov) 5, 1747
Stephen dis 5-5-1763, had fetched a priest to m two couples
Thomas, Flushing, d 1 Mo (Mar) 1707
Thomas, Flushing, m Flushing 2 Mo. (Apr) 22, 1714 Abigail FARRINGTON, d 4-1758
active mbr from 1692
Thomas gct Shrewsbury 12-4-1766, having rem to Middletown, N. J.
Thomas d 11-10-1800 bHS
Thomas & -----
Ch: George d 4-10-1804 ae 10m bHS
----- & -----
Ch: Benjamin b N. Y. d 5-9-1813 ae 11y 5m bHS

HEES
Gertrude (nm), dt Albert F. & Amelia (nm); m Charles W. BILLIN (H)

HEFFERNAN
James B. J., s Wm. & Anne C., b N. Y. 2-25-1893; recrq 6-6-1917; name erased 10-1928

HEGEMAN
Jane, w Jonah, recrq 3-1872; d recorded 4-1928
John C. (or Hegerman) (nm) b N. Y. d 6-25-1825 ae 28y bHS (m)
Peter (nm) b L. I. d 7-24-1844 ae 75y bHS
Sarah (probably w of John C.)
Ch: Louisa b N. Y. d 2-15-1832 ae 11y bHS

HEIGHES
Alice, dt John Intaglio & Alice (nm) b Manchester, Eng. 1-7-1846 d Nico, France 3-5-1929; m ----- DONLEVY (H)

HELLENCAMP
Elizabeth rocf Wby & Jericho 7-1861

HELMCAMP
----- & -----
Ch: Augustus d 7-13-1840 ae 6y 11m 24d bHS

HELMS
Rachel (late Burling) dis mo before 6-5-1771

HENDERSON
Almira (nm), dt Jas. & Almira (Haskell); m 1881 Isaac N. MERRITT (H)
Ethel recrq 10-1-1902; ct Chesterfield 3-4-1903
Robert & Margaret C.
Ch: Robert d 11-27-1834 ae 11d bHS
Margaret rec on ack. 7-1831; ct ND MM 1-2-1837 for both

HENDLEY
Ann rocf Third Haven 5-1830; ct Third Haven 1-1833 (H)

HENDRICKSON
Samuel m Julia Ann ----- b Stony Brook, N. J. d 1-6-1814 ae 44y 10m 15d bHS (both nm)

HENRY
Frances Maria gct Balt. 4-1870
John C. m Marietta Bellows WILSEY, dt Wm. & Marietta, d 1-13-1925 ae 70y bPP (both nm) (H)

HERBERT (see also Harbert)

HERON
----- (nm) m Fannie COOPER, dt Ellwood & Sarah P., b 4-18-1865

HERR
Frank S. (not a mbr here), s Henry C. & Fanny A., Moorestown, N. J.; m at Benj. Smith's 3-26-1895 Frances B. SMITH, dt Benjamin & Eliz., Newtown, Pa., b Doylestown, Pa. 8-2-1870 (H)
Ch: Ruth E. b 4-24-1896
cf Buckingham with parents 6-6-1877 for Frances; ct Chester, N. J. 2-12-1910

HERRICK
Emily (nm), dt George & Charlotte; m 8-11-1887 Dr. Edward C. RUSHMORE (H)

HESTON (or Herton)
Gilbert (nm) b Pa. d 7-27-1832 ae 28y bHS (unm)

HEWES (see also Hughes)
Rebecca C., dt Edw. & Reb. CHURCHMAN, of Del. Co., Pa.; m 9-1841 Bartholomew FUSSELL (H)
recrq 6-1841; ret a mbr & ct Phila. 1-1842

HEWITT
Isabella (nm); m 1879 George HEWETT

HEWSON
Abigail & -----
Ch: Hannah
Margaret
cf Dublin 9-23-1851 with minor dt, Margaret; Hannah, cert same date; ct Carlow, Ireland 8-1862 with Marg.
Hannah Deverell (form Hewson) dt Abigail, rocf Dublin 9-23-1861; dis 4-1853

HEWSTIS (see also Huestis, Hustis, Hustes)
David, Westchester; m Flushing 2 Mo (Apr) 13, 1711 Mary HAIGHT, dt Samuel, Flushing
Elizabeth, dt Robert, Westchester; m 1692 Horsman MULLINEX
James, Pur. informs "active in war" & mo before 2-5-1783; dis 4-3-1783
Jonathan, Carpenter, Westchester; m Flushing 2 Mo (Apr) 9, 1709 Mary BRANDRETH, dt Timothy West Jersey
rem to West Jersey 2 Mo (Apr) 6, 1710
Robert [Heustis] active mbr 1684 to 1762 or later

HICKOK
Cornelius C. (nm) & -----
Ch: Gerardine d 7-27-1867 ae 6m bPP (H)

HICKOX
William B. (nm) m 10-9-1890 Zaydee B. KEESE, dt Samuel T. & Phebe (Merritt), b 4-6-1866 d 8-6-1902 (H)

HICKS
Austin m Wby -----
Austin took cert of clear to Wby 7 Mo 19, 1728
Benjamin, s Benjamin, Wby; m Flushing 8 Mo. (Oct) 11, 1739 Elizabeth RODMAN, dt Thomas, Flushing, d 8 Mo (Oct) 14, 1750 ae 31y
Ch: John b 5 Mo (July) 19, 1740
Margaret b 9 Mo (Nov) 8, 1742
Thomas b 8 Mo (Oct) 1, 1745
Benjamin b 12 Mo (Feb) 15, 1747
Elizabeth b 7 Mo (Sep) 13, 1750
Benjamin & Mary
Ch: Elizabeth
Silas
Sarah
Mary
Temperance
Benjamin
Phebe
cf Wby 5-15-1793, Elizabeth clear; ct Wby 5-7-1795 for all, Elizabeth clear
Benjamin rocf Wby 11-6-1861; d 9-20-1872 (H)
Benjamin d 2-22-1891; m Martha ----- d 1-27-1896 (H)
Ch: Joshua T. b 12-11-1861
cf Wby 10-3-1888 for all
Benjamin D., s Isaac (dec) & Sarah, N. Y., d 9-17-1835; m N. Y. 4-10-1823 Elizabeth T. HICKS, dt Whitehead & Margaret, N. Y. (H)
Ch: Marianna b 7-31-1829 d 2-15-1894
Benjamin D. b 2-24-1836
cf Wby 8-14-1822 (clear); dis 1829-1831 (O);
Elizabeth gct Wby 6-7-1865
Benjamin D., s Benjamin D. & Elizabeth T., b 2-24-1836; ct Wby 5-3-1865 (H)
Benjamin Embree, s Geo. E. & Mary COCK, b 1-14-1843 N. Y. (H)

HICKS, Benjamin Embree, continued
changed name from Benjamin Hicks Cock 7-25-1875; ct Wby 10-14-1905
Catharine (late Everitt) dis mo 4-2-1823
Catharine, dt Whitehead & Margaret; m James M. HICKS (dis mo 11-14-1848)(H)
Deborah, Flushing, d 4 Mo. (June) 1712
Elias, s Valentine & Abigail, N. Y., d 1-9-1853; m N. Y. 6-8-1836 Sarah H. HICKS, dt Robert & Mary, N. Y. (H)
Ch: James b 10-22-1837 d 8-31-1838
Mary " 9- 4-1839
Elias " 3-26-1843 d 4- 6-1860
Caroline b 5- 6-1850
Elias rocf Jericho 9-1833; Sarah H. rocf Wby with parents 2-19-1817; Sarah H. gct Wby with ch 11-2-1870
Eliza, dt Samuel & Sarah, b 4-6-1806 d 5-20-1855; m Pierre RIEBEN (H)
dis as Hicksite 4-1849 (0)
Elizabeth Toms (form Hicks) dis mo 10-6-1773
Elizabeth, dt Robert M. & Rose Anna; m 12-28-1865 Aaron L. BROWN (H)
m by Mayor, ret a mbr
Elizabeth S. rocf Coey. 7-1837; ct Verona 9-1849 (H)
Elizabeth T., dt Whitehead & Margaret, N. Y.; m 1823 Benjamin D. HICKS
George certified mbr 1755
George, s Thomas, d 1-21-1817
George Embree, s George E. & Mary M. (Hicks) COCK, b 5-1-1841 N. Y. d 8-22-1903; m 9-17-1889 Louise FIRTH (nm), dt William (H)
George Embree changed name 1884 from George H. Cock
Gilbert d 1-14-1827 ae 31y bHS; m -----
Ch: Infant stillborn 5-4-1824 bHS
con mo 3-3-1822
Henry, s Samuel & Sarah H.; m Sheffield, Eng. 4-22-1830 Frances SANDERSON (H)
Ch: Eliza Sanderson b 8-16-1831
Samuel " 12-27-1832
Sarah " 11-11-1834
John Haydock, Jr. b 6-16-1836
Henry William " 9-15-1839, at New Brighton, Cheshire, Eng.
Edward Fisher Sanderson b 10-1-1845
Henry W., s Samuel & Sarah, b 12-8-1803 d 9-24-1867 bPP; dis 7-1831 (0); dis 8-1841 (H)
Isaac, s Samuel & Phebe, Wby.; m N. Y. 5-12-1790 Sarah DOUGHTY, dt John & Abigail, Bkn.
Ch: John D. b 3-20-1791
Robert " 3-15-1793
Benjamin " 2-11-1798
Isaac " 4-16-1802
Isaac rocf Wby 5-27-1789; ct Wby 6-5-1805 with 3 ch
James M., s Robert & Mary, d 11-24-1880; m Catharine HICKS, d 10-14-1848 (H)
cf Wby with parents 2-19-1867; Catharine dis 11-14-1848 for mo
Jane rqct Phila. 4 Mo (June) 6, 1743; com to prepare cert
Dr. John (nm) b New Field, L. I. d 3-27-1813 ae 73y bHS (widower)
John D., s John D. & Sarah R., Wby., b 11-13-1829; m at D. G. Haviland's, Bkn. 10-13-1857 Caroline HAVILAND, dt Daniel G. & Hannah, Bkn. (H)
Ch: Albert b 10-20-1858
George b 7-10-1860 d 8-30-1860
cf Wby 2-1851; ct Wby 8-5-1863 with 1 ch
John Haydock, s Samuel & Sarah, b 10-17-1802 d 10-21-1857; dis 5-1831 (0); dis 8-1841 (H)
Joseph (nm) b Queens Co. d 4-30-1812 ae 25y 6m bHS (unm)
Joshua T., s Benjamin & Martha (Titus), b Roslyn, 12-11-1861; m 12-25-1892 Grace A. BENNETT (nm), dt Benjamin & Emma T. (H)
cf Wby 10-3-1888; ct Wby 8-12-1911
Margaret rocf Wby 10-27-1773; ct Oblong 4-17-1786 (clear)
Margaret, dt Gilbert & Mary, Flushing; m 1788 Samuel PEARSALL
Margaret , dt Whitehead & Margaret; m 1838 ----- TERRY (H)
dis mo 12-1838
Martha, Wby; m 1739 Nathaniel TOWNSEND
Martha (nm) b L. I. d 8-10-1809 ae 25y 4m bHS
Martha M., dt Willet & Mary, N. Y.; m 1814 John C. CHEESEMAN
Mary, dt William; m 1734 Samuel RODMAN
Mary (nm), b N. Y. d 5-8-1821 ae 38y bHS (wd)
Mary, dt Elias & Sarah H., N. Y., b 9-4-1839; m 1866 Peter B. FRANKLIN (H)
cf Wby 11-2-1870
Mary C. (nm), dt Benj. D. & Elizabeth (Butts); m 1869 Albert H. COMBS (H)
Matt. & Esther (nm)
Ch: Infant stillborn 6-9-1802
cf Wby 5-27-1789; dis mo 6-2-1796
Oliver certified mbr 1755
Rachel Ann d 6-16-1838 ae 42y; m 1819 Cornelius LAWRENCE
dis mo 5-5-1819
Robert d 5-26-1849; m Mary N. ----- d 10-30-1862 (H)
Ch: Ann Mott d 1- 8-1817 ae 2d
James M.
Sarah H.
cf Wby 2-19-1817; all dis 1829-1839 (0)
Robert M. m Rosanna F. LEGGETT d 12-23-1868 ae 69y
Ch: Maria L. b 4-17-1823
Matilda " 11-15-1824
Benjamin L.
Willet H. " 11- 4-1831
Elizabeth
cf Wby 9-20-1815, minor, to live with brother; cert of clear to Pur. 8-7-1822; Rosanna F. rocf Pur. 4-9-1823; all dis 1830-1849 (0); ct Wby for all 11-1835 (H); cf Wby for Rosannah & Elizabeth 1-1853
Robert T. dis 9-5-1821
Ruth (nm) b Queens Co., d 8-10-1821 ae 60y bHS

HICKS, Ruth, continued
(wd)
Samuel, Hempstead, d before 1739; m Martha ----
Martha m 2d Nathaniel TOWNSEND
Samuel certified mbr 1755
Samuel, s Samuel & Phebe (dec), of Wby, b L.I. d 10-12-1837 ae 59y bPP; m N. Y. 10-14-1801 Sarah HAYDOCK, dt John W. (dec) & Eliz., N. Y., b N. Y. d 12-4-1832 ae 52y bPP (H)
Ch: John Haydock b 10-17-1802
Henry W. " 12- 8-1803
Elizabeth (or Eliza) b 4-6-1806
Jane b 6-17-1809 d 8-13-1809 at Havana
Infant d 11- 3-1810 ae 7d
cf Wby 4-16-1796, apprentice
Sarah H., dt Robert & Mary; m 1836 Elias HICKS
Silas, s Benjamin, rocf Wby 4-18-1798 (clear)
Silas m Flushing, Sarah -----
Ch: Benjamin T. b 12-16-1817 d 2- 5-1821
Elizabeth T. b 8- 6-1819 d 2-10-1821
Edward M. " 3-20-1821
William T. " 3-24-1823 d 3-24-1865
Benjamin I. " 12-23-1824 " 6-19-1825
Anna " 9- 5-1826
Silas Jr. d St. Louis 3-17-1868
Mary Elizabeth
cert of clear to Flushing 2-5-1817; Sarah T. rocf Flushing 9-4-1817; all dis 1829-1849 (O); ct Flushing for all 7-1833 (H)
Silas, Jr., s Silas & Sarah, gct Flushing with parents 1833; cf Flushing 10-1849; dis 5-1858 (H)
Smith, s John, d 2-13-1802 ae 7y bHS
Stephen R., s John D. & Sarah R.; m 9-17-1845 Hannah UNDERHILL, dt Thomas & Sarah (Whitson), b N. Y. 12-10-1825 d 1-26-1916 (H)
Ch: Mary P. b Old Wby 10-29-1863
Julia " " " 12-25-1867
cf Wby 4-9-1898 for Hannah & dt; ct Wby for dt 11-22-1923
Susan, dt John, d 5-19-1802 ae 1y 3m
Thomas certified mbr 1755
Valentine m Jericho 1804 Abigail -----
Ch: Phebe b 12-24-1804
Mary S. b 8-17-1806
Caroline b 11-7-1808
Infant
cf Wby 7-15-1801; cert of clear to Jericho 2-11-1804; Abigail rocf Jericho 9-20-1804; ct Jericho with their 4 ch 8-5-1812
Whitehead d 4-1-1834; m Wby 3-26-1795 Margaret TITUS d 5-9-1836 (H)
Ch: Gilbert b 2- 8-1796
Robert T. b 3-18-1798
Mary " 10- 1-1800 d 2-13-1838
Elizabeth T. b 10-21-1803
Jane " 6- 7-1805 d 6-13-1825
Elizabeth " 1-21-1806
Margaret
Susan " 10-12-1810 d 1-28-1831
Anna " 3- 1-1813 d 4-15-1832
infant stillborn 2-28-1815
Ch: Catharine
Henrietta b 4- 5-1822 d 11-30-1846
rem cert from Flushing for Whitehead 7-17-1793; rem cf Wby for Margaret 9-16-1795; all dis 1828-1839 (O)
Willett, s Silas (dec) & Rachel, of Wby, b L.I. d 4-10-1845 ae 79y; m N. Y. 5-9-1792 Mary MATLACK, dt White & Mary, b N. Y. d 9-18-1831 ae 56y (H)
Ch: Martha b 3- 6-1795
Rachel " 8-20-1798
Willett rocf Wby 4-29-1789 (clear); both dis 1829-1830 (O)
William, s Silas & Rachel, rocf Jericho 4-18-1791 (clear); d 9-28-1807 ae 38y
William T. rocf Flushing 7-1844; dis 7-2-1845 (H)
----- & -----
Ch: Walter b Bkn. d 1-11-1824 ae 21d bHS

HIGBY
Phebe dis mo 8-6-1767

HIGGINBOTHAM
Mary (late Garrigues) rocf SD MM 7-26-1809; dis mo 4-3-1811

HIGGINS
Bethany, w Dr., dt Sarah TILSON, dis 5-4-1853 (H)
John Hale, s John & Mary (Petet), b Eng. 1844 d 10-26-1933; m Jane TRUSTAM (nm), dt Frederick & Mary L., b Eng. 9-11-1846 d 3-31-1933 bPP
John recrq 5-7-1930

HIGGINSON
Wm. John (nm), s Frederick & Agnes (Duncan); m Ethel HINDS, dt William & Julia (Bouren), b Wash., D. C. 5-3-1900 (H)
recrq 5-13-1935

HILL
Deborah (nm) bPP
Elizabeth R. recrq 12-7-1892; d 4-7-1901
Ellen, w Edward, rocf Weare 10-1867; mbrp relinquished 3-1880
Emma D., w J. Harvey, dt ----- DICKINSON (perhaps dt Henry & Grace), gct Balt. 3-1889
Emma Mary, dt Henry & Grace DICKINSON, recrq of parents 1859
John, s John (dec), of Buckingham, Pa.; m Flushing 4-11-1782 Hannah DOUGHTY, dt Benj. & Hannah, Flushing
ct Buckingham, Pa. 3-4-1878; cf Buckingham 1-7-1782 (clear); cf Buckingham 6-5-1782 for Hannah
John Jr. rocf Buckingham, Pa. 12-2-1782, a minor; ct Buckingham 10-6-1789
John m Elizabeth RUNKELL, dt John, b 12-27-1815 Flemington, N. J. d 4-6-1901
Ch: Mary E.
both nm

HILL, continued
John recrq 8-1805; mbrp relinquished 3-1880
Lauretta C. B. rocf Indianapolis 6-11-1890; letter to Friend's Church, Whittier, Calif. 6-1-1932; in Reading, Conn. 1912
Mary E., dt John & Elizabeth (Runkell), b 1-3-1840 Woodsville, N. J. d 9-16-1907 at Wilmington, Vt., bPP; m James W. McDERMOTT (both nm)
Susan A., dt Jacob T. & Sarah (Griffen) HAIGHT, b Macedon 12-22-1836 d 7-24-1909 (m 9-22-1853) (wd John H., nm) (H)
cf Duanes 12-4-1889; matron of Orphan Asylum, Bkn.
----- & -----
Ch: Susan F. d 4-27-1880 ae 45y bPP
Charles E. d about 1893 bPP

HILLARD
Mary (nm), Bkn.; m 1872 Stephen LOINES (H)

HILMKAMP
----- & ----- (nm)
Ch: John d 4-15-1838 ae 2y 2m 15d bHS

HILYARD
Adelaide W., w Thos. T., dt Jonas & Hannah DINEGAR, Mt. Vernon (H) (m 10-30-1901) wd of ----- FAILES or Fales; recrq 8-10-1901
Alice Emily, dt Geo. D. & Eliz. R., b 8-28-1866; m ----- THORNTON
relrq 12-2-1903
Amelia, wd Joseph W., Jr.; m 2d Charles E. NORTON
mbrp relinquished 3-1880; in St. Louis, Mo.
Amy Mary [Hilliard], dt Henry & Mary Amando (Brundage), b Ossining 6-20-1872; m 11-5-1924 Henry COLVIN (H)
recrq 1924
George D., s John & Ann, b 11-20-1867; m 1864 Elizabeth R. WILLS d 4-13-1879 ae 45y 3m bPP
Ch: Alice Emily b 8-28-1866
George D. Jr. b 6-13-1809 d 1-5-1834 Merchantsville, N. J. bPP
John b 2- 3-1874 d 7- 2-1898 bPP
cf Burl. 4-8-1853 for George; cf Burl. 3-10-1864 for Eliz. R.
George D. m 2d 1-4-1883 at Allen Fenimore's, Mt. Holly, N. J. Anna D. WILLS, dt Micajah R. & Martha M., b Medford N. J. 9-22-1844 d 7-7-1927 Medford N. J. bPP (George D. d 1-28-1898)
James m Rachel W. ----- d 7-17-1849
Ch: John W. b 2-16-1839
Elizabeth W. b 5-31-1842
James, Jr. b 1- 5-1846
Rachel Louisa b 1-29-1849
cf Burl. 6-4-1827 for James; cf Burl. 9-3-1838 for Rachel; James dis 1829 (H); ct Burl. 12-4-1850
John, s Jonathan & Mary, Northampton, N. J., d 7-28-1838 ae 39y 7m 12d bHS; m N. Y. 4-8-1829 Ann WHITSON, dt Joseph & Hannah, N.Y.
Ch: George D. b 3- 8-1830
Mary " 5- 4-1833
Anna Maria
Emily " 3-24-1838
cf Burl. 2-5-1827 for both; ct Evesham 8-7-1833 with 2 ch named; cf Evesham 11-11-1836 with 3 ch named; ct Burl. 9-2-1840 for Ann W. (clear) & her 4 ch named; John dis 1829 (H)
Joseph Seth, s Jos. W. & Amelia, b 9-23-1869; relrq 7-6-1904
Joseph W. & Hannah T.
Ch: Mary T. b 7-21-1840
Martha W. " 12-19-1841
Joseph " 11-15-1843
Jonathan Henry b 3-31-1845
James Franklin b 10-31-1847
cert of clear to ND MM 9-4-1839; cf Burl. 8-4-1828 for Joseph W.; cf ND MM 1-28-1840 for Hannah S.
Ch: (continued)
Ann b 7-20-1850
Sarah T. " 5-29-1852
Emily H. " 9-11-1854
Cornelia " 5- 6-1857
ct Burl. 9-1870 for parents & last 6 ch
Joseph W., Jr., s Joseph W. & Hannah, b 11-15-1843 d 6- 7-1871; m Amelia -----
Ch: Joseph Seth b 9-23-1869
Amelia recrq 6-1869; Amelia m 2d Chas. E. NORTON
Martha W., dt Joseph W. & Hannah, b 12-19-1841 d 6-25-1872; m Morton SMITH
ret a mbr
Mary T., dt Joseph W. & Hannah T., N. Y.; m 1861 Henry WALKER, of Scarboro, Eng.
Thomas T. [Hilliard], s Joseph & Ann, Salem, N. J.; m at A. W. Failes' 10-30-1901 Adelaide W. FAILES, dt Jonas & Hannah DINEGAR, Mt. Vernon, b Livingston, N. Y. 3-21-1842 (H)
Adelaide recrq 8-10-1901; ct Salem, N. J. 12-6-1902; cf Salem 7-10-1911

HINCHMAN
Elizabeth, w John, gc 9 Mo (Nov) 2, 1749; cf Haddonfield 12-11-1780, this was lost on the way from women's mtg to Recorder; ct Haddonfield 9-3-1783

HINDS
Ethel, dt William & Julia (Bousen), b Wash., D. C. 5-3-1900; m Wm. John HIGGINSON (H)

HINES
Elizabeth (nm), dt James & Elizabeth (Gordon), d 3-31-1935 bPP; m John Wm. TRAVIS

HINMAN
Sarah rocf Wby 4-1845; d 6-24-1865 (H)

HINRICKS
Violet V. (nm), dt C.F.A. & Louisa (Dotten); m 1890 William C. FIELD (H)

HINSDALE
Anna B., dt Henry & Mary, N. Y., b 5-9-1816; m 1835 Henry WOOD
Deborah C., dt Henry & Mary, N. Y., b 12-13-1817; m 1859 Richard H. THOMAS, of Baltimore
ct Balt. 5-4-1859
Henry d 6-23-1845; m Burl., N. J. 1815 Mary ----- d 10-1-1864 ae 70y bPP
Ch: Anna B. b 5- 9-1816
Deborah C. " 12-13-1817
Stephen G. " 6-18-1819 d 10- 8-1877
Rebecca " 3-31-1821 " 7-24-1822
Henry " 10- 2-1822 " 8-14-1823
Samuel " 12-23-1823 " 3-12-1824
Daniel D. " 2- 1-1825 " 7-14-1825
recrq 1809; cert of clear to Burl. 4-5-1815; Mary rocf Burl 8-7-1815; parents dis 1829 (H); Mary gct Balt. 5-4-1859
Stephen G., s Henry & Mary, b 6-18-1819 d 10-8-1877; having mo Wilmington refers to N.Y. 9-1844, rpd favorably 10-1844

HINSHAW
David S. (nm) & Augusta W.
Ch: Robert
Sarah
Augusta & ch recrq 6-1928, the ch as associate

HOAG
Abbie A., dt Ira W. & Sarah I., d 2-7-1906; m 11-27-1904 Gideon Baxter TRAVIS
cf Oblong 11-5-1902; at Manila, Phillipines
Ada Hepzibah, dt Edwin W. & Alice A. (Ishom), b Plattsburgh, N. Y. 9-22-1873; m 1916 Gilmore E. THEW (H)
Ann Eliza (or Ann Maria) rocf Chap. 4-9-1829 with father; ct Chap. 11-4-1835 with sister, Phebe, ret with parents (clear)
Anna Maria, dt John; m 10-3-1849 Joshua W. BOWRON (mo) (H)
cf Chap. 8-1829 with father; ct Chap. 8-1835 with father
Charles B. (nm), s Merritt & Jane; m 11-25-1869 Elizabeth WILBUR, dt Allen E. & Jane (Lawton), b No. Easton 12-29-1850 d 11-29-1932 (H)
cf Easton 12-4-1897; Charles was janitor 15th St.
Elizabeth A., w Charles (nm), rocf Easton 12-4-1897 (H)
Elma H., dt David & Sarah H., Bkn.; m 1861 William U. WILLETS (H)
cf Ama. 11-1859
Emily, dt William & Amy H. (Gurney), b New Balt. 3-7-1855 d 9-25-1934; m Wm. H. PARSONS (nm) (H)
transferred from Albany 1-8-1916
Esther, w Sanford, d 11-19-1856 (H)
Ch: Phebe
cf Chap. 10-1-1851
Fannie, dt William & Amy (Gurney), b New Balt., N. Y. 12-2-1861; m 9-23-1885 Jurdenette CARR (H)
Fannie transferred from Albany 1-8-1916; Fannie relrq to join Christian Science Church at Medway
Hannah H., dt Lindley M. & Huldale, Wolburg, N. H.; m 1855 Thos. H. LEGGETT, Jr.
cf Sandwich, N. H. 1852 for Hannah
Ira W. d 10-1916; m Sarah H. ----- d 3-11-1929
Ch: Abbie A.
Olive I. d 7-18-1893
Mary K.
parents rocf Oblong 2-1-1911; cf Oblong for Abbie 11-5-1902; cf Oblong for Olive 11-5-1902; cf Oblong for Mary 11-5-1902
Israel G., s John, rocf Chap. with father 8-1829; ct Chap. 12-2-1835 (clear)
John & ----- (H)
Ch: Phebe T.
Israel G.
Ann Maria
cf Chap. 8-1829 with 3 ch; ct Chap. 8-1835 with 2 dt
John S. rocf Chap. 4-9-1829 (clear); dis 5-1830 (O); dis 1-1832 (H)
Lindley M. rocf Sandwich, N. H. 1848; ct Sandwich, N. H.
Lydia transferred from Albany 1-8-1916 (H)
Mary E. rocf Oblong 12-1921; d 12-9-1925
Phebe, dt John, rocf Chap. 4-9-1829 with father; ct Chap. 11-4-1835 with sister, Ann Eliza, returned with parents (clear)
Phebe, dt Sanford & Esther, Bkn.; m 1856 Thos. H. BROWN (H)
Sanford Hoag form of Newcastle
Phebe E., dt Charles & Elizabeth, recrq 5-4-1890; relrq (H)
Phebe F. rocf Chap. 7-7-1855; ct Chap. 10-7-1868; cf Chap. 2-3-1869; d 11-7-1884 (H)
Sanford (nm) m Esther ----- (nm) d 11-20-1856 ae 73y 1m 22d bPP (wd)
Sarah H., w David, d 9-27-1860 (H)
Ch: Elma
Sarah Sanford
Louisa L. d 12-23-1876
Sarah Sanford, dt David & Sarah H., rocf Ama. 11-1859 with mother; ct Ama. 10-7-1868 (H)
William E. m Mary K. ----- d 4-5-1872
Ch: Kempton b 3-27-1872 d 12-9-1923
cf Falmouth 9-1868 for Wm.; cf New Bedford 6-1870 for Mary; William relrq 8-6-1902

HOAGLAND
Susan, dt Isaac & Margaret (Johnson), b Troy, O. 2-5-1873; recrq 2-12-1922 (H)
----- & ----- (nm)
Ch: Caroline [Hoogland] b N. Y. d 3-13-1842 ae 16y 2m 2d bHS

HOBABY
Johanna (nm) b Germany d 7-30-1831 ae 31y on board ship Sully bHS (unm)

HOBSON
Charles M. recrq 4-1889; d 3-14-1906
George Henry rocf Grange, Ireland 1-1870; ct Grange 5-1879
Homer H. m Sarah HOOVER
Ch: Helen Hargrave b 4-6-1918
Frances Adeline b 1-13-1920
Marcia Morris b 3-6-1921
parents recrq 3-1917
John, having mo ND MM refers it to this MM 4-2-1800, rpd favorably 7-2-1800
John Linton's name erased
Mary Elizabeth rocf Norwich, Conn. 3-1-1876; ct Norwich, Conn. 2-1882
Russell Benj., s Wm. & Eliz. C., London, Eng.; m N. Y. 12-15-1897 Edith HAYDOCK, dt Rich. & Sarah Anne, N. Y., b Bessbrook, Ireland 11-23-1874 d 9-7-1902 bPP
Ch: Edith Dorothy b 9-25-1898
cf So. Division of Wales 11-1888 for Russell B.
Russell Benjamin m 2d 3-16-1907 Elizabeth Anna Ethel KERR
Ch: William Russell b 10-17-1908
Arthur Kerr b 10-15-1910 (marked associate)
Russell B. Jr. b 10-28-1918
John Milburn b 4-13-1924
Howard Wooding b 4-13-1924
cf Waterford, Ireland 9-6-1905 for Elizabeth
Sophia rocf Richhill, Ireland 10-1870; relrq 7-1872
Wm. Russell, s Russell & Eliz. A. (Kerr), b 10-17-1908; went to sea in a small boat 1930 & never heard from

HODGES
Caleb Horatio, s Samuel H. & Emma (Hilton), b 3-16-1887; m Florence E. -----
Ch: Catharine Emma
Samuel Horatio, 2d
Caleb recorded a mbr 8-7-1901; ct Marl. 3-7-1906; cf Alliance, Ohio, 3-6-1912 with w & 2 ch named associates; letter for Caleb to Presbyterian Church, Champlain, N. Y., 7-1914; names of Florence & ch erased 9-9-1931
Catharine Emma, dt Caleb H. & Florence (E----) rocf Alliance, O. 3-6-1912 with parents; name erased 7-9-1931
Fanny (nm) b Eng. d 7-30-1833 ae 16y 10m bHS (unm)
Joseph Taber, s Samuel H. & Emma, b 5-15-1892; recorded a mbr 8-7-1901; letter to M. E. Church, Arlington, N. J. 12-4-1912
Mary Hilton, dt Samuel H. & Emma, b 1-1-1889; recorded a mbr 8-7-1901; ct R. I. 12-4-1907
Phoebe, dt Samuel H. & Emma, b about 1881; recorded a mbr 3-5-1902; name erased
Samuel Horatio m Emma HILTON
Ch: Samson
Phebe 18 in 1903
Caleb Horatio b 3-16-1887
Mary Hilton b 1- 1-1882
Martha Dodrell b 3-28-1890
Joseph Taber b 5-15-1892
John Crossley b 10-28-1894
Ruth Emma " 5-12-1901
parents recrq with 5 ch 2-3-1892; ct Boston 12-7-1892 for all; parents recrq 6-12-1901; ch recorded 8-7-1901 except Phoebe; Phoebe recorded 3-5-1902; ct Morean 7-6-1904 for parents, Martha D., John C. & Ruth R.
Samuel Horatio 2d, s Edgar T. & Florence, rocf Alliance, O. 3-6-1912 with parents; name erased 9-9-1931

HOE
Mary E. d 9-1887 ae 49y bPP

HOELESTRA
Alice, dt Jacob A. & Eliza A. (all nm), N. Y.; m 1920 Willets CARPENTER (H)

HOET
Caspar, N. Y., m at Thos. Lloyd's, N. Y., 6 Mo. (Aug) 12, 1686 Elizabeth DELAPLAINE, dt Nicholas, N. Y.
Ch: Jacob b 3 Mo (May) 1687
Elizabeth b 8 Mo (Oct) 19, 1688
contributor 1686

HOFFMAN
Beulah (late Murray) dis mo 2-4-1790
Harry N., s Geo. & Sarah M., Elmira; m 11-19-1890 at Chris. Wray's, Anna M. WRAY, dt Christopher & Sophia J., N. Y., b 10-29-1863
Anna M. rel by letter to First Presbyterian Church of Elmira, 1-8-1908
Jonathan & Catharine (H)
cf Phila. Green St. 6-1839 for both; ct Phila. Green St. 10-1839 for both
Joseph R. (nm) b Chester Co., Pa. d 11-2-1833 ae 24y bHS (widower)
Lydia, w -----, dt John & Lydia DODGSON; m 2d 1847 Charles F. MOTT (H)
ct Sara. 8-1852
Lydia A. (nm), dt Wm. A. & Charlotte (Cese); m 1890 Edwin RIDER (H)

HOGG
Charles Edward (nm), m 10-9-1895 Emily A. MEAD, dt George V. & Mary (Birdsall), b N. Y. 1-30-1871 (H)
Emily's name entered by comm. 3-13-1883

HOHOFF
Ernest A. (changed name to Hallock in court), s Ernest A. & Carrie (Pierce); m 9-18-1895 Anna W. HALLOCK, dt Thomas B. & Sarah W., b 11-26-1874 Bkn. (H)
Ch: Therese Marie b 7-3-1898
name of ch entered by MM 9-9-1899
Therese Marie [Hohoff-Hallock], dt Ernest A. & Anna (Hallock), b N. Y. 7-3-1898; m 1919 Lewis E. WELSH (H)
recrq of her parents 9-9-1899
Therese Marie m 2d 1931 Arthur H. TORREY (nm) (H) name removed 3-13-1933 for lack of interest

HOLBROOK
Robt. Russell (nm), s Robt. & Ruth (Harbert); m 1-23-1916 Anna Lily CARPENTER, dt Wm. H. & Sarah F., b N. Y. 11-3-1894 (H)
Ch: Robert Russell Jr. b 2-3-1923 at Ocean Grove
ch recrq of parents 2-10-1930

HOLCOMB
Eleanor Maxwell, dt Wm. Penn. & Eliz. (Miller), b 5-22-1892 d 12-27-1912; m 1911 George ROBINSON (nm) (H)
Jacob gct Buckingham, Pa. 10 Mo (Dec) 4, 1746
Margaret (form Wanzer) dis mo 12-1853
Wm. Penn, s Oliver H. & Cynthia S., Newtown, Ia.; m at A. K. Miller's 12-30-1886 Elizabeth Clark MILLER, dt Dr. Chas. (dec) & Amanda, Bkn., b Bkn. 1-26-1852 (H)
Ch: John Miller b 3- 3-1888
Eleanor Maxwell b 5-22-1892
Elizabeth recrq 10-6-1886; Wm. P. mbr Swarthmore

HOLDER
Charles W., s Daniel & Sarah, rocf Salem, Mass. with parents 8-14-1828; dis mo by a priest 2-3-1842
Daniel & Sarah
Ch: Charles Warren
Richard Houghton
Sarah m 2d ----- HARRIS & dis 5-1-1844 having failed, Salem MM referred to N.Y. 7-2-1823; rpd favorably 12-3-1823; cf Salem 8-14-1828 with w & ch named; parents & Charles dis 1836-1844
Joseph B. d 2-28-1888; m Emily A. -----
Ch: Charles Frederick d 10-10-1915
cf Salem, Mass. 8-1872 with ch named
Richard Houghton, s Daniel & Sarah, rocf Salem, Mass. 8-14-1828 with parents; cert of clear to Uxbridge, Mass. 11-1-1854, he being then in Ill., at Bloomington; ct Vermillion 3-1855; had been in the San Francisco trade 1847

HOLE
Edgar T. & Adelaide W.
Ch: Lena May
Marlan N.
cf Cleveland 9-6-1911 for Edgar; cf Cleveland 6-7-1911 for Adelaide; Adelaide & 2 ch named associates
Leona May, dt Edgar T. & Adelaide W.; m 1927 Orville E. MILES
cf Cleveland 9-6-1911
Leonard Hanna d 7-7-1910; m Sarah Belle ----- d 10-1920
Ch: Lemuel Homer
Ralph J.
cf Western Springs, Ill. 7-13-1904 with 2 ch named
Morlan N., s Edgar T. & Adelaide W., rocf Cleveland 6-7-1911 with mother; ct First Friends Church, Detroit 5-1927

HOLLAND
Sarah roc 4-2-1766 for a short stay
Ruth gc 10-6-1756 (rem)
Thomas L. & Elsie
Ch: Joshua Hudilson (associate)

HOLLETT
Mary Jane Ohmstead (form Hollett) dis mo 1856

HOLLEY
Ella E., dt Samuel P. & Ann Eliza (Whitson), b Bkn. 11-17-1886; m 1905 William BELL (H)
recrq 4-8-1905; ct Flush. 1-13-1906
Florence Amelia (nm), dt Lemuel P. & Ann Eliza; m 1901 Albert E. MARSHALL, Jr. (H)

HOLLIDAY
Clyde Cecil, s Wm. R. & Eliz., Upland, Ind.; m N. Y. 10-8-1904 at Edw. M. Wray's, Cranford, N. J., Edith Sophia WRAY, dt Joseph B. & Hannah B. (both dec), N. Y., b 1-19-1878
ct Upland, Ind. 1-4-1905 for Edith

HOLLOWELL
David T., s Richard L., rocf Greensboro, N.C. 11-6-1907 for David with father; name erased 1-2-1929
Richard L. & -----
Ch: David T.
Walter P.
Richard L.
John W.
William E.
Joseph G.
James R.
cf Greensboro, N. C. 12-5-1906 for Richard; cf Greensboro 10-2-1907 for ch
Richard L. m 2nd Hettie O. -----
cf Woodland, N. C. 10-26-1907 for Hettie O.; ct Greensboro, N. C. 8-1914
Richard L. Jr., s Rich. L., rocf Greensboro, N. C. 12-5-1906 with father; ct Wilmington, Del. 9-1922
Walter P. (or R.), s Richard L., rocf Greensboro, N. C. 11-6-1907 with father; name erased 1-2-1929

HOLLOWELL, continued
Wm. C., s Richard L., rocf Greensboro, N. C. 10-2-1907; ct Greensboro 8-1914
Henry O. (nm) d 11-15-1871 bPP (perhaps h of Sarah W., both in one grave)(H)

HOLMAN
Nathan d 8-27-1860 ae 3y bPP; gr s of James Lafetra (perhaps s of Henry O. & Sarah W., bur in one grave)
Sarah W., dt James & Sarah LAFETRA, d 2-5-1875 ae 36y bPP (perhaps w of Henry O., both in one grave) (H)

HOLME
Alida Alice, dt Chas. E. & Mary T. (Miller), b Bkn. 1-10-1902; m 1923 Theodore CLAY (H) relrq 5-8-1915; both recrq 1-12-1925
Amy, dt Eleanor; m Edward JONES, Jr. recrq of mother 5-1887
Charles E., s Thomas W. & Eleanor (Cragg), b Sedgwick, Eng. 1-5-1865; m at Jos. G. Miller's, Bkn. 9-6-1888 Mary T. MILLER, dt Joseph G. & Isabella T., b Bkn. 10-8-1870
Ch: Ethel Mary b 6- 4-1889
Charles E. Jr. b 9-15-1892 d 7-23-1908 bPP
Arthur Joseph b 3-12-1894 d 12-5-1894 bPP
Edith M. " 4-12-1895
Eunice A. " 4-29-1899
cf Kendall, Eng. 10-1886 (O); both relrq 12-6-1899 (O); ch relrq of parents 12-6-1899 (O); both recrq with ch 3-10-1900 (H)
Charles recrq 3-3-1886 (H); relrq 2-2-1887 (H)
Ch: (continued) (H)
Alida Alice b 1-10-1902
Marion Florence b 9-24-1907 d 12-24-1925 bPP
Charles O., s Chas. E. & Mary T. (Miller), b Bkn. 9-15-1892; relrq 5-9-1908 (H)
Edith M., dt Chas. E. & Mary T. (Miller), b Bkn. 4-12-1895; relrq 4-10-1909 (H)
Effie, dt Eleanor, b Eng. d Springtown, N. Y. about 1896 bPP; m Wilson ROBINSON
Ethel M., dt Chas. E. & Mary T. (Miller), b Bkn. 6-4-1889; relrq 3-9-1907 (H)
Eunice A., dt Chas. E. & Mary T. (Miller), b Bkn. 4-29-1899; relrq 2-8-1913 (H)
Thomas Wynne m Eleanor CRAGG
Ch: Margaret Alice d 8-21-1893 in Loho, China
Amy J.
Effie b Eng.
Eleanor m 2d Stephen FROST
Eleanor recrq 5-1887 with dt; ct Marl. 6-12-1895

HOLMES
Eliza D., dt Thos. D. & Sarah L. (Griscom), b Moorestown, N. J. 8-26-1870; m 1899 Reuben Grant BENNETT (H)
James (nm) & -----
Ch: Infant d 9-8-1887 ae 7m bPP
Jonathan, Flushing; m Flushing 9 Mo (Nov) 8, 1739
took rem ct Pur. 8 Mo (Oct) 5, 1743
Samuel, R. I., dmi Hannah DICKENSON at 2d m intention Edward Stevenson objected as she was promised to him. Not allowed to pass. John Rodman appealed to QM but no further mention
----- m Juliette NASH, dt Margaret, d 8-10-1893 ae 55y bPP (H) (both nm)
----- (nm) m Ann BURLING d 6-19-1859 ae 61y bPP Ann dis 1-5-1814 for mo

HOMMEDIEN
Charlotte L. (nm) d 7-11-1852 ae 31y 8m 4d bPP

HONEYWELL
Phebe (nm), wd James, b N. Y. d 9-1-1814 ae 48y bHS

HOOVER
Sarah m Homer H. HOBSON both recrq 3-1917

HOPE DOEG
Amelia C., dt Jno.& Phebe CORLIES (m 4-20-1873) relrq 12-9-1899 (H)

HOPKINS
Alfred (nm) & -----
Ch: Infant stillborn 7-4-1836 bHS
Ann rocf Balt. 2-1830; d 1-24-1851(H)
Catharine Stewart (form Hopkins) dis mo 5-3-1809
Charles F. m 9-23-1878 Georgina DYMOND, dt George F. & Jane, b Eng. 3-30-1854 (H)
Ch: Edna D. b 1-26-1880
Miriam D. " 8-23-1882
Rebecca " 2- 3-1887 (or 2-2-1887)
parents recrq with ch 9-4-1889; Charles relrq 10-7-1899
Daniel (nm) b L. I. d 10-13-1833 ae 50y bHS
Ch: Sidney W. b L. I. d 9-5-1832 ae 12y bHS
Edna, dt Chas. T. & Georgina (Dymond), b 1-26-1880; m 1907 Merrill Clark SLUTES (nm) (H) recrq of parents 9-4-1889; relrq 3-9-1912 to join with h in Ohio
Edwin (nm) & -----
Ch: Saul Alley b N. Y. d 8-16-1842 ae 1y 9m bHS
Elizabeth, b Phila., rocf Wrightstown 11-6-1816; dis 3-1829 (O); d 12-26-1832 ae 67y 9m bPP in grave with Rich. Loines
Frances, dt Elizabeth HOUSTON, rocf Lurgan, Ireland 3-1888 with mother; at Elizabethport 1912
George, s Samuel, rocf ND MM 3-24-1795, apprentice to William Shotwell; ct R. & P. 8-6-1800 (clear)
Gerard (nm) d 7-16-1864 ae 58y bHS, rem to PP; m Arin E. ----- (nm) d 1-24-1851 ae 41y 2m 17d bHS, rem to PP
Ch: Elizabeth d 8- 6-1846 ae 16y 8m 17d bHS, rem to PP
Carrie d 9-20-1851 ae 4y 5m 23d bHS, rem to PP

HOPKINS, Gerard & Arin E., continued
Ch: John Chandlee d 2-13-1863 ae 21y 9m 1d bHS, rem to PP
Sarah B. d 5-11-1865 ae 33y 9m 6d bHS, rem to PP
Frank C. " 1- 2-1900 ae 52y rem from Hillside Cem. Plainfield, Conn.
Hannah Stewart (form Hopkins) dis mo 1-1-1812
John (nm) & -----
Ch: Lawrence d 9-16-1803 ae 17y bHS
Joseph, s Wm. & Hannah, of Botley, Yorkshire, d 7-19-1803 ae 33 bHS; m N. Y. 4-13-1791 Catharine BURLING, dt Thos. & Sarah, N.Y.
Ch: Sarah b 12-31-1791
Hannah " 8-23-1793
Mary " 9- 3-1795
Ann " 6-11-1798 d 4- 8-1804 bHS
William John b 8-15-1802
cf Brighouse, Leeds 6-23-1788 (clear); William & Hannah were of Botley, Yorks
Leonard (nm) b Oyster Bay d 6-6-1825 ae 42y bHS (m)
Mary b North Castle d 11-6-1825 ae 52y bHS; rocf Chap. 5-10-1816 (clear)
Mary Stewart (form Hopkins) dis mo 6-5-1816
Mary H., w Edwin, dt Isaac T. & Hannah HOPPER (m 9-5-1858) (H)
ct Wby 8-4-1875
Phebe (nm) & -----
Ch: Isaac b N. Y. d 3-1-1834 ae 4y 6m bHS
Pine (nm) & -----
Ch: Laura Jane d 4-12-1815 ae 1m 22d
Rebecca, dt Chas. F. & Georgina, b Norwood, O. 2-2-1887; m 11-28-1917 Merritt Alfred BOYLE (H)
name dropped 1932
Richard b Maryland d 8-17-1822 ae 29y bHS
cf Balt. E. Dist. 8-9-1810 (minor) (unm)
Samuel, Jr. rocf ND MM 11-22-1796, minor; ct R. & P. 2-3-1802
Sarah Stewart (form Hopkins) dis mo 11-1-1809
Sarah b 11-3-1786 d 11-27-1869; m 1813 Richard LOINES (H)
Thomas (nm) b West. Co. d 7-17-1834 ae 51y bHS (unm)
Wm. J. b N. Y. d 6-8-1834 ae 31y bHS; attended theater & joined military Co., dis 6-2-1822
----- m Frances HOUSTON, dt Elizabeth
Frances rocf Lurgan, Ire. 3-1888; name erased 12-7-1932
----- & ----- (nm)
Ch: Lot d 2-28-1811 ae 3m bHS
Jane " 8-30-1814 ae 11y bHS
Edgar " 8-14-1821 ae 21d bHS
Isaac R. b N. Y. d 12-9-1826 ae 1y bHS
Rowland F. d 3-17-1853 ae 2y 4m 26d bPP
Abigail, dt Isaac T. & Sarah, N. Y.; m 1833 James S. GIBBONS, of Phila. (H)

HOPPER
Isaac Tatem, s Levi, d 5-7-1852; m Sarah TATUM d 6-18-1822 (m 9-18-1795) (H)
Ch: Josiah
Rachel
Abigail
Edward
John
Susanna d 12-15-1908 ae 91y 10m
Isaac " 12-10-1887
cf Phila. 11-1829
Isaac Tatem m 2d 2-4-1824 Hannah ATTMORE d 1-5-1868 (or 1-6-1868)
Ch: Thomas d 2- 8-1832 ae 3y 6m
Elizabeth " 8-26-1872
Mary
Hannah b 1831 d 2-10-1832
cf Phila. 11-1829 for all but Abigail; Isaac dis 8-1841 to the great discredit of the MM. Note. Some of the ch may be assigned to the wrong mother
John, s Isaac T. & Sarah; m Rosalie DE WOLF (H)
Ch: DeWOLF actor b 3-30-1858
changed from William d 9-23-1935
cf Phila. with father 11-1829; rel 7-1842
Josiah, s Isaac T. & Sarah (dec), N. Y.; m at Nathan Comstock's 5-6-1841 Martha COMSTOCK, dt Nathan & Eliz. (dec)., N. Y. (H)
cf Phila. 10-1835 for Josiah; Josiah rel 7-1842
Mary, dt Isaac T. & Hannah; m 9-5-1858 Edwin HOPKINS (H)
Rachel, dt Isaac T. & Sarah, N. Y.; m 1832 Samuel BROWN (H)
----- & -----
Ch: Charles d 5-12-1855 ae 2y bPP

HORNER
Isaac, O.B. m O.B. Mtg House 1 Mo (Mar) 17, 1683/4 Lydia WRIGHT, dt Peter
Ch: Deliverance b 1 Mo (Mar) 26, 1685
rem to N. J. 1685; active mbr from 1676
Isaac, Mansfield, N. J.; m Flushing 8 Mo (Oct) 9, 1718 Eleanor BOWNE, dt Samuel & Mary, Flushing
Eleanor took rem ct Chesterfield, N. J. 6 Mo (Aug) 6, 1719
Mary rocf Kingwood 6-10-1773; ct Kingwood 3-2-1774
Mary rocf Phila. 7-1-1885; d 11-22-1898 (H)
Thomas (nm) b Eng. d 3-18-1844 ae 60y bHS (unm)
Winfield G. 3d, s Winfield G. 2d & Naomi E. (Rice), b Gettysburg, Pa. 1-7-1908; m 3-19-1934 Elizabeth HALL, dt Edward & Mary (Pease), b Calgary, Canada 3-25-1907
Ch: Winfield Grier 4th b N. Y. 6-30-1935
Winfield recrq 1-14-1935; cf Boston 9-10-1934 for Eliz.

HORNET
Anna rocf R. & P. 8-18-1802 (clear)

HORNIMAN
Annie Smith rocf Lewes & Chichester, Eng. 7-11-1906; name erased 10-1928

HORSKINS
Jane granted rem cert 10-6-1756

HORSLEY
Peter N. (nm) d 1-6-1890 ae 71y in Jersey City bPP

HORSNAL
Annie G. m ----- VELLMER (H)
cf Chesterfield for Annie G. 1-10-1921

HORTON
Anna (late Reynolds) d 12-15-1868 ae 75y 7m 5d bHS
Ch: Edward b Mamaroneck d 5-7-1825 ae 3y 4m bHS
dis by Pur. MM 12-6-1820
Joseph (nm) b White Plains d 8-31-1823 ae 34y 10m 4d bHS (m) (H)
Pamelia recrq 9-6-1871; d 4-29-1882 (H)
Phebe rocf Corn. 2-1847; d 3-31-1848
William (nm) & -----
Ch: George b N. Y. d 9-19-1836 ae 2y 5m bHS
Wm. Henry (perhaps) b N. Y. d 5-9-1838 ae 3m 6d bHS

HOSFORD
James rocf Albany 3-7-1849; d 4-9-1862

HOSIER
Benjamin B., s Samuel P. & Margaret, d 4-22-1911 ae 81y 4m 22d bPP; m Ann JERUSHA (nm) d 2-16-1921 ae 92y bPP (H)
cf Corn. with parents 11-1835; relrq 3-1-[1876
Catharine rocf Pur. 6-12-1817 (clear); ct Pur. 7-13-1822 (clear)
Catharine B., dt John & Abigail, rocf Oswego with parents 9-1828; dis (H)
Elizabeth b R. I. d 7-12-1829 ae 82y 11m 3d; rocf R. I. MM (Portsmouth) 6-27-1816 (clear) (H)
Hannah, dt John & Abigail, b 8-10-1817 d 1-29-1902; m 1-6-1869 Isaac OSBORN (prob nm) (H)
Jane (or Hosher), wd, Rye; m 1724 Thomas NICHOLS
John d 12-1-1857; m Abigail ----- d 3-16-1865
Ch: Catharine B. b 8-13-1815
Hannah " 8-10-1817
Ann Eliza " 2-22-1819 d 11-6-1828
Edward Hicks " 6-23-1823 d 6-14-1847
William Bowne b 6-23-1823 d 6-14-1847
Mary " 3-17-1826
John Burling " 1-14-1830 d 3-16-1896
cf Pur. 7-10-1817 for both with ch, Catharine; ct Oswego with 3 ch 7-5-1820; cf Oswego with 6 ch 9-1828
Ch: (continued)
Susan Amelia b 2- 6-1834
Wilson Merritt b 8-14-1836
date of Wilson M. Hosier's d not known 1900
Maria, w William, rocf Corn. 5-8-1825; dis 5-1830 (O); dis 2-2-1853 (H)
Mary H., dt John & Abigail, b 3-17-1826 d 7-16-1879 ae 73y 3m 29d; m 1-6-1869 Samuel B. GUERNSEY (H)
Samuel P., s John & Catharine; m Margaret ----- d 10-22-1840 (H)
Ch: Benjamin Burling
cf Corn. 11-1835 with s
Samuel P. m 2d at Nathaniel Weeks', Bkn. 8-7-1862 Lydia T. ALLEY, dt Rowland & Sarah TITUS, Bkn. d 11-25-1895 bPP (H)
(Samuel P. d 1-25-1866 ae 65y bPP
Susan Amelia, dt John & Abigail; m Leander SARLES (H)

HOTBLACH
Mary b N. Y. d 10-21-1828 ae 28y 6m bHS

HOTCHKISS
Agnes (nm) m Joseph S. LEGGETT (H)

HOTSON
John Leslie, s John Hastie & Lillie (Swayze), b Delhi, Ont. 8-16-1897; m 12-25-1919 Mary May PEABODY, dt Frederick W. & Anna G. May, b Dorchester, Mass. 9-29-1896 (H)
both recrq 6-13-1921

HOUGHTON
Eliza (probably dt of Thos. & Mary LOWERRE), rocf Flushing 8-1833; d 4-13-1848 ae 54y bPP (all nm) (H)
Nestor recrq 6-1850; d 10-24-1863 (H)
William A. (nm) m Eliza L. ----- (nm), b Flushing d 4-13-1848 ae 54y bHS

HOUSTON
Elizabeth d 11-1891 m -----
Ch: Frances
Elsie
cf Lurgan, Ireland 3-1888 with 2 ch named
Elsie, dt Eleanor; m ----- ROSS
cf Lurgan, Ireland 3-1888 with mother; in Dunellen, N. J. 1912
Frances, dt Elizabeth; m ----- HOPKINS (nm)
cf Lurgan, Ireland 3-1888 with mother; name erased 12-7-1932; at Elizabethport, N. J. 1912
Mary (form Wright) rocf Jericho 6-1842 (H)
Phebe C., w Moses B. (nm), dt James C. & Julia E. HAUXHURST (m 11-11-1863); m 2d 1-30-1882 James S. BODEN (H)
cf Jericho with parents 10-1857; ret a mbr

HOVEY
Elizabeth Hunt rocf Plains 7-1846; d 5-28-1861 (H)

HOWARD
Asa rocf Short Creek, Ohio 2-23-1830; dis 11-1836
Benjamin, s John G. & Julia O., d 3-16-1909 ae 48y bPP (unm) (nm) (H)
Elma, w Hugh B., dt Charles & Sarah WOOD (H)
cf N. P. with parents 9-1843; ct N. P. 9-1852

HOWARD, continued
John rocf Core Sound, N. C. 8-6-1796, minor, desirous of a useful trade, with consent of his guardian; ct Concord N. W. Territory 6-3-1802 (clear)
John (nm) b Eng. d 11-21-1826 ae 38y bHS
Richard rocf Chatham 3-27-1823 for Richard & his fam (not named); dis 1825
Sarah M. b N. Y. 11-25-1807; rocf Pur. 10-1848; d 7-15-1887 (H)
William (nm) & -----
Ch: Infant d 12-8-1837 ae 1/4 hr bHS

HOWELL
Elizabeth, dt Isaac Q. & Mary UNDERHILL, b 10-29-1820 d 6-5-1879 (H)
George T. (nm), s Joseph B. & Mary, N. J.; m at Wm. B. Coffin's, Geneva, Neb. 1-1-1872 Phebe H. SUTTON, dt Henry & Hannah, Bkn. (not under care of N.Y. MM)(H)
Ch: George F. Jr. b 9-22-1878
    Mary Sutton " 12-14-1875
    ch names entered by com.; ct Race St. Phila. 12-4-1889
John Brazier m Ama. 1804 Elizabeth ----- cert of clear there 3-7-1804; Elizabeth rocf Ama. 5-12-1804; ct Easton 5-1-1805 with their apprentice, Wm. S. King
Ruth rocf Green Plains, Ohio 2-1888; name erased

HOWEY
Alfred, s Jacob & Eliz. T. (Ogden), b Swedesboro, N. J. 5-14-1841 d 7-25-1914; cf Woodbury 4-6-1870 (H)

HOWISON
Ebenezer rocf Edinburgh, Scotland 7-21-1803 (clear)

HOWITT
Thomas (nm) b Heanor, Derbyshire d 4-25-1823 ae 36y bHS (m)

HOWLAND (see also Holland)
Allen d 8-20-1801 bHS
Eliza, adopted dt Mary H. Delano, ct & cf New Bedford 1852-1856 with foster mother
Emma, w Henry J. (or I.) rocf Hudson 3-2-1859; ct Hudson 2-3-1875 (H)
Gideon rocf Wyanoke, Va. 7-5-1823; dis 9-1831 (O); dis 10-1840 (H)
Gilbert Jr. rocf Dartmouth 6-23-1824, apprentice; dis 11-1830 (O); at New Bedford 1850; rel 7-5-1871, absent over 5y
Hannah H. rocf New Bedford 5-1882; d 9-11-1889
Isaac, s Wm. P. & Hannah (Hathaway), b New Bedford, Mass. 6-21-1839 d 3-29-1918 bPP; m Martha A. ----- d 1-13-1920 ae 85y bPP cf New Bedford 6-1887
John H. & Sarah
Ch: William Hazard
    Algermon Sydney d 8-23-1813 ae 4y 6m 13d
    Martha Hazard
    Mary Rodman b 11-26-1810
    John Jr. " 11- 2-1812; relrq 1-1857
    Sarah R.
    all dis 1830-1839 (O); all dis 1830-1838 (H); Sarah had joined Episcopal Church; cf New Bedford 5-22-1810 with 3 ch first named
Mary R., dt John H. & Sarah; m ----- PELL (mo) dis mo 3-1831 (H); dis mo 4-6-1831 (O)
Pontius d 5-6-1857 ae 50y 7m 18d bPP (H)
Richard G. rocf Nantucket N. Dist. 6-23-1824; ct Balt. 1-17-1826 (clear)
Robert Bowne recrq 12-6-1905; ct Chap. 9-4-1912
Sarah Gillespie (form Howland) dis mo 3-6-1839
Sarah R., dt John H. & Sarah; (perhaps) m Max EPPENDORFF
    perhaps d 5-1915 ashes bPP
Tenta rocf N.P. 12-20-1827 (clear); sister of Jos. Brown's w; d at Buffalo (H)
Thomas C., s Wm. P. & Hannah (Hathaway), b 11-1842 d 4-12-1918 bPP (not a mbr here)
William H. rocf New Bedford 1-25-1816, apprentice with Hicks Jenkins & Co.; dis 12-1830
William W. d 6-16-1869 ae 70y 11m 19d bPP; m ---- (mo) (H)
Ch: Charles H. d 6-20-1849 ae 2y 4m 21d bPP
    Wm. W. Jr. d 6-3-1857 ae 13d 10m bPP
    Eliza H. d 6-23-1849 ae 2y 4m 21d bPP
    dis mo 5-1843
----- & -----
Ch: Ann Eliza b N. Y. d 9-11-1827 ae 2m 4d bHS
    Joseph T. d 10-30-1873 ae 1m 5d bPP

HOWLEY
Jane, w Henry, rocf Knaresbro, Eng. 2-1-1836; dis 3-1841

HOWNKS
Franziska (nm), dt Walter & Franziska; m 1920 Dr. Francis S. ONDERDENK, Jr. (H)

HOXIE
Christopher (nm) b New Bedford d 9-7-1842 ae 79y bHS (widower)
Ellen, dt Isaac Upton & Hannah (Anthony), b Adams, Mass. 6-27-1833 d 10-18-1904; m 1855 Lucien B. SQUIER (H)
    cf Easton 8-1857

HOXSIE
Lodowick, s Zebulon & Sarah, Beekmans; m Oswego Mtg House 4-24-1777 Dorcas ADAMS, dt Abel & Abigail, Marlborough
Mary (late Clarke), having mo referred to Hudson which rpd 8-3-1803 having dis her

HOXSLEY
Eliza C. (nm) d about 1895 bPP

HOYLAND
Elizabeth, dt Wm. & Mary; m 1802 Thomas WALKER ct ND MM from Birmingham, Eng. 6-13-1798;

HOYLAND, Elizabeth, continued
(clear); recorded without endorsement of Phila.
Jane, dt Wm. & Mary, N. Y.; m 1798 Samuel MELLIS cf Lamworth, Warwickshire 4-12-1797 (clear)
James (nm) b Eng. d 10-10-1840 ae 55y 7m bHS (m)
John (nm) b Sheffield, Eng. d 8-10-1819 ae 73y 4m 4d bHS (m)
Mary (nm) d 11-7-1834 ae 82y 8m 25d bHS

HOYT
Edith Lilian, dt George A. & Emeline, b 4-2-1881; m Stephen Maurice UNDERHILL
Emeline, wd George A.; m 2d George MEKEEL (not a mbr here)
recrq 10-1877; ct Minneapolis 6-1920
George A. d 4-13-1902; m Emeline -----
Ch: Lyda Imogene b 12-21-1877 d 6-18-1882
Edith Lilian " 4- 2-1881
Mabel M. " 3-21-1883
Emeline m 2d George Mekeel & was in Minneapolis; George recrq 10-1877; Emeline same date
Georgia (or Georgina) m ----- PEARSON
recrq 11-1883; ct Minneapolis 4-1-1896
Mabel M., dt George A. & Emeline, b 3-21-1883; m ----- CAHALEY (nm)
In Minneapolis 1912; ct Minneapolis 6-1920
S. Olivia d rpd 7-1928; m ----- STRICKLAND
recrq 1-6-1897; in Albany 1912

HUBBARD
Abbie L., dt Sylvester & Mary Ann, d 4-18-1880 ae 30y 2m 25d bPP; m ---- BECKWITH (H) (all nm)
Abigail S. (nm) d 10-4-1872 bPP (H)
Charles S. F., s Sylvester S. & Mary Ann, d 12-12-1916 ae 72y 3m 5d bPP; m ----- (H)
Ch: Clifton Travis d 10-27-1874 ae 5y 3m 18d bPP
Pervilla Bell " 6- 8-1868 ae 2y bPP (rem from Bellport, L. I.
recrq 6-1-1881; mbrp cancelled 1-13-1906 as long unknown
Clarence, s William & Sarah E. (Brundage), b Greenwich, Conn. 10-15-1843; m 7-31-1865 Josephine H. NOE (nm), dt James H. & A. L. (Perigow)
recrq 8-9-1913; relrq 9-13-1920
Edward A. d 1888; m Margaret C. ----- d 1-2-1908
Ch: Gretta aged 13
Walter Harper b 3- 8-1879
Clarence " 7- 9-1883 d 5-1915
Laura V.
Frank H.
both recrq 4-1877; Gretta recrq of parents 8-1877
Frank H., s Edward A. & Margaret C.; m Isabelle -----
Frank not originally recorded, but acknowledged a mbr 8-1920; Isabelle recrq 3-1928
Frank W. (nm) m 11-18-1891 Grace KEESE, dt Samuel T. & Phebe M., b 1-5-1869 (H)
ct Flush. 3-4-1905 for Grace
Gretta, dt Edward A. & Margaret C., b about 1864; m Andrew DAVIDSON (nm)
recrq 8-1877
Helen L., dt M. A., d 11-26-1877 ae 37y bPP; m ----- CLARK (H)
Mary Ann, dt Sylvester S., d 5-12-1879 ae 70y 4m 12d bPP (H) (unm) (nm)
Milton, s Walter Harper & Mary E., name erased 12-6-1833
Sylvester S. (or F.) (nm), d 3-16-1885 ae 71y 3m bPP; m Mary Ann SWAIN, d 5-12-1879 ae 70y 4m 12d bPP (H)
Ch: Abbie L.
Charles F.
cf East Hamburg for Mary Ann 8-1859
Walter Harper, s Edw. A. & Margaret C., b 3-8-1879 d 11-8-1933; m Mary E. -----
Ch: Walter E.
Milton
Ruth Marie b 6-26-1918
Harold James b 10-10-1919
Mary E. recrq 3-1928; Ruth & Harold active mbr 4-1935
William H. (nm) d 3-8-1873 ae 25y 6m 18d bPP (H)

HUBBS
Amaziah, s Christopher & Charity, attended theater, but will not go again, case discontinued 4-7-1819; dis 2-1827 (0)
Amy, w Robert, b L. I. d 8-3-1832, a wd, ae 65y 9m
Charles (nm) m Fanny ----- (nm) b Portland, Me. d 7-25-1829 ae 25y 2m bHS
Charles F., s Mary F., recrq of mother 12-1837; dis 11-2-1859, he was engaged in theatrical performances and could get no other work (H)
Christopher b Westchester Co. d 6-11-1825 ae 57y; m Charity ----- d 8-30-1860 ae 88y bPP
Ch: John d 11-30-1814 ae 12y
Joseph d 11-31-1814
Amaziah
Leah
David d 1-29-1828 ae 2d
Joseph b 5- 9-1816 d 3- 1-1818
cf Pur. 1-11-1816 with 3 ch; Charity gct Ama. 2-1835 (0);
David (nm) b L. I. d 8-10-1840 ae 52y 10m bHS (m)
Leah, dt Christopher & Charity, N. Y.; m 1820 Stephen MILLER, of Somers
Mary, w Amos, rocf Wby 8-15-1798; ct Ama. 8-3-1808
Mary B. Hunt (form Hubbs) rocf Jericho 4-1841; dis 4-1846 (H)
Mary F. d 5-3-1876 ae 74y bPP m ----- (H)
Ch: Charles F.
Mary F. rst 5-1837; Charles F., minor, rec-

HUBBS, Mary F., continued
rq of mother 12-1837
Mercy, dt Jacob & Phebe, rocf Little Egg Harbor 7-10-1794, a minor; ct Little Egg Harbor 2-3-1796 (clear)
Phebe Ann, dt Thomas, rocf Wby 7-1837; ct Wby 2-3-1875

HUDSON
Henrietta m Theodore G. HULL (both nm)
Sarah b Corn. d 4-16-1827 ae 46y bHS
Wm. J. D., s Thos. A. & Sarah (Grieg), b Belfast, Ireland 12-8-1848 d 9-28-1924 bPP; m Eleanor G. HANNA, dt William & Rebecca, b N. Y. 5-18-1847 d 1-26-1920 bPP (both nm)

HUESTIS (see also Hustes, Hewstis)

HUGHES (see also Hewes)
Alan Marple, s Chas. C. & Eliz. R. (Wills), b Wayne, Pa. 11-19-1900; m 6-5-1926 Marion COLES, dt William & Margaret (Leonard), b 9-19-1903 (H)
Ch: Mildred M. b 6-23-1932
parents recrq 3-9-1931
Celia b Bristol, Eng.; rocf Kingston, Eng. 3-19-1873; d 10-31-1900 ae 72y bPP (unm)
Emma, w Isaiah, rocf Peel 1-22-1845; ct Devonshire House 10-1854
John Peter rocf Bristol, Eng. 10-27-1801 (clear), endorsed to Bristol 6-2-1803 (clear)
Sarah [Hues] rocf Mt. Holly, N. J. 8-8-1781 to live with her h; ct (probably Mt. Holly) 7-5-1786

HULL
Anna E., dt Samuel G. & Elizabeth, N. Y.; m 1884 A. Lincoln CARPENTER (H)
Caroline C. rocf Haddonfield 6-8-1829
Carrie Louise, dt James C. & Caroline E., N.Y., b 7-8-1865 d 2-28-1889; m 1884 Hartley G. PELLETIER, of Boston (H)
Catharine m 1783 Thomas CLARK, of Phila.
Catharine, dt John & Amy; m ---- DUELL (mo)
cf Stanford 12-1833 with parents; dis 2-1837 (H)
Charles Edward, s Jas. C. & Caroline E., b 9-9-1856; relrq 11-7-1877 (H)
Charles Wager, s John C. & Caroline C., b 3-7-1830; dis mo 2-1856; cf Corn. 9-1863; relrq 6-7-1876
Cornelia B., dt Oliver C., b Troy 11-3-1832; m George DUNN (H)
error of form Recorder, as her mother not a mbr (W.H. Macy)
Damaris gct Newport 8-3-1786
David rocf Scipio 3-16-1826 (clear); dis 12-1827
David A. rocf Marl. 1-23-1828 (clear); ct Marl. 8-6-1834 (clear) (O); ct Marl. 5-1837 (H)
Marl mbr annexed to N. Y.; ct Oswego 10-1-1862 (H)

Edward rocf Stanford 9-22-1827, minor; dis 5-1829 (O); dis 7-1828 (H)
Eliza E., dt Wager & Eliz., N. Y.; m 1839 Charles GIBBONS, of Phila.
Emma T., dt Oliver C., b 11-22-1838 (H)
error of form Recorder as her mother was not a mbr (W.H. Macy)
Esther K., dt James C. & Caroline E., b 6-1-1847; m before 7-1-1868 ----- GLASSFORD (mo) (H)
cf Pur. 9-4-1850 with parents; ret a mbr 11-1868
Freelove, dt Jos. & Phebe, N. Y.; m 1790 John MANN
George D. rocf Marl. 8-1845; ct Oswego 10-1-1862 (H)
Henrietta, dt Oliver & Penelope; m 1781 Thomas BURLING
Henrietta, dt John & Amy; m 1841 Samuel COWDRY (H)
cf Stanford 12-1833 with parents
Henry C., s Charles W. & Hannah, Catskill; m N. Y. 4-9-1835 Phebe B. YOUNG, dt Alexander & Eliz., N. Y.
cf Stanford 8-21-1830; ct Stanford 11-2-1831 (clear) (O); ct Hudson 7-1835 (H)
Henry Cohn, s Robt. W. & Lydia (Cohn), b Bkn. 4-16-1892; m 6-26-1922 Eugenia SAALFIELD (nm), dt Richard A. & Lizzie T. (Cohu) (H)
Jacob m Harriet ----- (nm) d 12-18-1844 ae 50y 22d bHS (wd)
dis mo before 11-6-1811
James, s Joseph & Phebe, b 3-5-1774; ct Creek 2-1-1787 to live with his brother John
James rocf Marl. 12-1848; d 6-1858 (H)
James C. d 6-10-1890; m Caroline E. ----- d 1-31-1897 (H)
Ch: James F. b 11- 4-1844
Esther K. " 6- 1-1847
Robert W. " 12-20-1852
Charles Edward b 9- 9-1856
Mary Ella " 8- 2-1861
Carrie Louisa " 7- 8-1865
Caroline E. with first 2 ch rocf Pur. 12-1844 & ret 12-1-1847; cf Pur. 9-4-1850 for parents & 2 ch
James Frank, s Jas. C. & Caroline E., b 11-4-1844; rocf Pur. with mother 12-1844; relrq 5-3-1876 (H)
John, s Joseph, rocf Oblong 4-18-1785 (clear); ct Creek 2-1-1787 (clear); ct N. Y. 7-22-1796 (clear); cf Creek 8-18-1797, he having ack.; ct Creek 9-6-1798 (clear)
John (nm) d 11-30-1798 bHS, rem to PP 11-10-1865 [another d 9-27-1800 bHS]
John & Mary
Ch: Sarah
Penelope
Robert
Mary
Abigail
Oliver
Catharine

HULL, John & Mary, continued
Ch: ----- d 11-30-1798
ct Creek 4-2-1800 for all
John & Anna (mo before 8-1-1781) (H)
Ch: Jacob b 1- 1-1788
Joseph " 9-17-1790
Elizabeth " 3-22-1793
Phebe Anna b 1- 1-1797
John Jr. " 1802 d 8- 4-1803 ae 1y 1m
John W. " 4-25-1804
Oliver C. " 2-20-1807
Edward " 10-22-1809 d 7-31-1820
ack. accepted 7-3-1793; ct Corn. 6-6-1799 with their 4 ch; cf Corn. for same 12-23-1799; ct Hudson 5-1-1811 with 6 ch not including Jacob; cf Hudson 1-23-1817 with 4 younger ch; ct Marl. 10-1834 for John & Anna
John d 8-11-1840 ae 78y bPP, rem from HS; m Amy ----- d 6-19-1850 ae 71y 9m 10d bPP, rem from Mamaroneck (H)
Ch: Rebecca
Henrietta
Catharine
Penelope, w John, d bur in same grave as this John (probably 1st w); cf Stanford for parents with these ch 12-1833
John Cox, s Wager & Elizabeth, d 8-1858; m Haddonfield, N. J. Caroline COOPER
Ch: Charles Wager b 3- 7-1830
Richard Cooper b 10- 3-1832
Robert Bowne " 1-21-1834
William L. " 11-11-1836
Infant stillborn 5-6-1838
John Cox b 5- 3-1839
Caroline " 3- 1-1842 d 10-23-1844
Effingham B. " 6- 1-1845 " 9- 5-1846
Wager " 4- 1-1847
Alfred C. " 4-21-1849
cf Haddonfield 1829 for Caroline; Caroline dis 5-4-1859
John F. (nm) m Georgiana ----- (nm)
Ch: Eugene Foster d 1-15-1857 ae 2y 11m bPP
Joseph d 10-1-1798 bHS; m Phebe -----
Ch: James b 3-15-1774
Joseph " 8- 4-1776 d 5-13-1791
Wager " 3-19-1779
Phebe " 5-11-1781
Freelove
Sarah
cf Oblong for Joseph & 3 s 9-15-1784; cf Oblong for Phebe & 3 dt 9-15-1784; ct Hudson 1-5-1814 for Phebe; Phebe Jr. same date & destination; cf Hudson 7-22-1817 for Phebe & dt, Phebe, both ministers
Joseph (nm), s John W. b N. Y. d 2-21-1846 ae 56y 5m bHS; m -----
Ch: Ann d 9- 2-1820 ae 3y bHS
Mary Ann b N. Y. d 12-19-1843 ae 15y 9m bHS
Mary, dt Wager Jr. & Keziah (Cooley), b Bethlehem, N. Y. 11-9-1828 d 10-29-1911; m John G. HAVILAND (H)
cf Corn. 6-6-1855
Mary Ella, dt Jas. C. & Caroline E., b 8-2-1861 N. Y. d 2-27-1928; m 9-21-1889 Charles E. DU VALL (H)
Mary Florence, dt Wm. F. & Emily L., b 4-6-1866; relrq 2-1-1888 (H)
Oliver, s Joseph, rocf Oblong as apprentice 5-12-1783; ct Phila. Middle Dist. 7-6-1791 to reside with an apothecary (called Oliver Jr. in this cert, perhaps a different person)
Oliver & -----
Ch: Joseph
Henrietta
Catharine
John
Penelope d 9-19-1848
cf Oblong for all 5-19-1774, rec 9-7-1774
Oliver, s John & Damaris, d 8-1-1803 ae 72 (in R. I.); m Hannah ---- (m Pur)
Ch: Catharine Field
cf Stanford 8-15-1810, apprentice; Oliver took cert of clear to Pur. 11-2-1796; Hannah brought cf Pur. 2-9-1797; ct Duanesbury 2-9-1807 for Hannah & dt, Catharine Field, latter clear
Oliver & -----
Ch: Infant d 1-29-1832 ae 12h bHS
Frederic b N. Y. d 9-23-1835 ae 6m 3d bHS
cf ----- 1810, minor; dis 1825
Oliver C., s Stephen, d 6-1889 (H)
Penelope, dt Liddeman Jr. & Anna, dis 1829 (H)
Phebe b Mamaroneck d 8-8-1818 ae 79y 9m bHS; m -----
Ch: Wager m Elizabeth -----
Phebe, dt Joseph & Phebe, N. Y.; m 1830 William RENOUF, of Rensselaer (H)
Phebe rocf Marl. 12-1848; dis non-attendance 5-1829 (O); d 8-12-1885 ae 87y 4m 6d bPP (H)
Phebe Ann, dt John & Anna, N. Y.; m 1818 William HALLOCK
Phebe C., dt Wager & Elizabeth, b 4-25-1819; m 1842 Edward H. WOOD
Rebecca, dt John & Amy, N. Y.; m 1846 Robert B. HAVILAND (H)
Richard Cooper, s John C. & Caroline, b 10-3-1832; dis 1856
Richard Randolph, s John Y. & Sarah Ann (Travis) b Waterloo, N. Y. 9-11-1844 d 12-25-1906 bPP; m 4-19-1893 Anna M. F. RIEHL, dt Ernst A. & Anna (Haack), b N. Y. 8-15-1862 (H)
cf Ama. 5-3-1865; ct Ama. 12-4-1878; this last cert cancelled by MM 6-6-1888; Anna recrq 1-2-1895
Robert rocf Stanford 9-22-1827, minor; dis 6-1830 (O); dis 9-1833 (H)
Robert Bowne, s John C. & Caroline C., b 1-21-1834; in Army; mbrp relinquished 3-1880
Robert Franklin, s Robt. W. & Lydia L. (Cohu), b Bkn. 2-5-1889; m 2-19-1920 Mary Catharine DOSTER (nm) dt John B. & Grace (Leach) (H)
Robert W., s James C. & Caroline E. (Haviland), Bkn., b 12-20-1852 N. Y. d 2-25 (or 15)

HULL, Robert W., continued
1923 bPP; m at J. S. Cohu's 9-8-1886 Lydia E. COHU, dt Joseph S. & Eliz. I. (Williams) (dec), N. Y., b 1-10-1856 N. Y. d 1-16-1934 bPP (H)
Ch: Robert Franklin b 2- 5-1889
Henry Cohu " 4-16-1892
Sarah Piggott (form Hull) dis mo 9-7-1791
Sarah Frances, dt Samuel G. & Elizabeth, b 12-29-1855; m 1883 Wm. Henry CARPENTER (H)
Tiddeman & -----
Ch: Tiddeman
Sarah
Ruth
Henry
John
Demaris
Elizabeth
Tiddeman & w rocf Pur. 5-17-1770; ct N.P. for all 4-2-1777
Tiddeman Jr., s Tiddeman; m Anna -----
Ch: Amy
Penelope
George
Anna
Solomon
Sarah
cf N.P. 4-20-1792 with 5 ch; ct Creek 11-7-1793 with 6 ch
Wager, s Phebe; m Elizabeth -----
Ch: Oliver C. d 9-12-1802 ae 14d
Susan " 5- 1-1813 ae 6y 5m 17d
Phebe " 8- 1-1812 ae 1m
John Cox "
dis mo 12mo-1801; rst 11-6-1805; Phebe recrq 1811
Ch (continued)
Sarah dis 3-1834
Elizabeth b 9-25-1813
Infant d 8-12-1816
Ann C. b 11-18-1817; dis 5-1842
Phebe C. b 4-25-1819
Infant d 9- 4-1820 stillborn
Infant " 7-16-1823 stillborn
William F.
parents of John C. dis 1829 (H)
Wager, s John C. & Caroline, b 4-1-1847; mbrp relinquished 3-1880
William, s John, rocf Stanford 2-19-1825, minor; dis 6-1830 (O); dis 3-1832 (H)
William F., s Wager, d 10-31-1900 ae 74y 1m 22d; m 10-1-1863 Emily L. STRATTON, dt Enoch & Amy I. (H)
Ch: Mary Florence b 4- 6-1866
cf Corn. 9-1863 for Wm. F.; Emily relrq 3-1880; Emily rocf Phila. 10-1848 with parents

HUMANN
Herman recrq 6-8-1898; d 9-9-1908

HUMPHREY
David, s Benj., Merion, Pa.; m Flushing 1 Mo (Mar) 20, 1727/8 Elizabeth FORD, dt Thomas, Flushing
cf Merion, Pa. (clear) he being home to visit his parents 6 Mo (Aug) 13, 1724
Elsworth (nm) b Morristown, N. J. d 11-17-1827 ae 17y bHS (unm)
Samuel rem 7 Mo (Sept) 4, 1740
Thomas brought cert of clear from Tortola, W. I. 8-1-1754; took cert back 10-2-1754

HUNN
Jacob W. (nm) b Greene Co. d 9-1-1832 ae 44y bHS (m)
John (nm) m Sarah ----- b L. I. d 12-9-1833 ae 45y bHS
Ch: Susan Hester b N. Y. d 5-3-1834 ae 14y 5m 14d bHS
Infant stillborn 8-25-1838 bHS
John b R. I. d 8-17-1840 ae 78y; m before 5-1-1816 Eliza J. COX (mo) (H)
Ch: Infant stillborn 2-27-1817; bHS
Jonathan d 5-22-1822 ae 4y bHS
cf R. & P. 5-24-1804, apprentice; dis mo 6-5-1816; Eliza rocf Muncy 8-21-1822; Eliza gct Stanford 2-2-1853
Susannah b Kent Co., Del. d 10-5-1819 ae 75y 1m 2d bHS (wd)
Susannah rocf R. & P. 6-18-1817; d 10-5-1829
----- & -----
Ch: Martha W. b N. Y. d 1-26-1824 ae 1y 9m 2d bHS

HUNT
Aaron, Westchester; m Flushing 2-7-1755 Rebecca HAYDOCK, dt Robert, Flushing
Rebecca took cert 9-4-1755
Alsop rocf Pur. 12-10-1772 with brother, James; ct Pur. for Alsop 9-6-1781; d 9-16-1803 ae 20y bHS
Alsop (nm) b Westchester d 6-16-1816 ae 67y bHS (m)
Benj. Lawrence, s Chas. Lindley & Cath. M. (both dec); m at G. A. McDowell's 10-16-1897 Fannie McDOWELL, dt Geo. A. & Mary J. (dec), N. Y., b N. Y. 1-16-1872 (H)
Ch: Lawrence Alexander b 11-12-1903
Charles Howland " 1-23-1909
Katherine " 1 -14-1911
Fannie's name entered by com. 1873; Fannie & ch gct Chap.; cf Chap. for all 5-9-1921; ct Chap. for all 2-13-1922
Benjamin W., s Benj. W. & Mary (Quinby), b Chap. 5-18-1848 d 6-26-1934; m 5-8-1876 Louise PRUDDEN (nm), dt Sidney C. & Isabella S. (H)
cf Chap. 1-1866; lived & d at Eastontown, Ga.
Caleb, s Josiah, Eastchester, N. Y.; m Wby 6 Mo (Aug) 30, 1737 Sarah HALLOCK, dt John Jr., Brookhaven, N. Y.
Ch: Josiah d 9-6-1802 ae 55y bHS
Catharine gct N. P. 1-11-1815
Edmund L. rocf Ama. 7-13-1822 (clear); dis

HUNT, Edmund L., continued
1830 (O); d 1831
Hannah, dt Richard & Mary, dis 1823
Hester G., wd Lot, d 2-11-1868 (H)
Ch: William L. b 2-11-1815
Mary " 5-14-1817
Lott G. " 6-21-1821
Hester G. "12-22-1823 d 3- 9-1847
Phebe Jane " 9-19-1826
cf West Chester (Pur.) 11-1836 for all
Isaac, N. Y. d 9-15-1798 bHS; m Catharine -----
Ch: Rebeckah b 9- 2-1770
Charlotte " 9-19-1784
Marian " 5-20-1786
Luke " 4- 3-1788 d 10-12-1798
cf Pur. 6-9-1791 with fam, Rebecca (clear)
James, with brother, Alsop, rocf Pur. 12-10-1772; rec 3-3-1773; d 10-13-1801 bHS
James W. d 7-13-1879; m Sarah Frances -----
d 3-7-1876 (H)
Ch: Lewis b 8-10-1863
cf Chap. for all 11-1-1871
James W., s Lewis P. & Charlotte, N. Y.; m at Oliver Mathews', Greenwich, Conn. 4-3-1879 Helen T. MATHEWS, dt Jacob & Ann Eliza, Greenwich (H)
Josiah, Westchester & Abigail
Ch: Jacob b 9 Mo (Nov) 6, 1696
Rebekah b 1 Mo (Mar) 25, 1698
Caleb " 10 Mo (Dec) 10, 1699
Esther " 5 Mo (July) 1, 1701
Rachel " 1 Mo (Mar) 6, 1703/4
Solomon b 2 Mo (Apr) 6, 1705
Tabitha " 7 Mo (Sep) 25, 1707
Lidiah (Lydia) b 8 Mo (Oct) 22, 1700
Josiah D. rocf Ama. 11-1845; dis 7-1853 (H)
Levi m 7-5-1842 Phebe COCK, dt Stephen & Charlotte
ct Chap. 2-1853 for Phebe
Lewis, s James W. & Sarah Frances, b 8-10-1863; cf Chap. with parents 11-1-1871; mbrp cancelled 5-11-1912 (H)
Lott G., s Lot & Hester G., b 6-21-1821; cf W. Chester with mother 11-1836; dis 4-1850 (H)
Luke d 10-12-1798 bHS
Mary b Liverpool, Eng. d 12-19-1814 ae 71y 10m bHS
Mary, dt Lot, b 5-14-1817; m 1845 ----- CORNELL (H)
cf W. Chester with mother 11-1836; dis 7-7-1852
Mary B. (form Hubbs) rocf Jericho 4-1841; dis 4-1846 (H)
Moses rocf Pur. 11-11-1790, apprentice; dis mo 3-1-1797
Percival, s Chas. H. & Louisa, b Cornwall, Eng. 8-14-1884; recrq 7-11-1917; relrq 11-1928
Phebe H., dt Lewis P. & Charlotte (Weeks) b Chap. 1-30-1840; m 1862 Peter J. CARPENTER (H)
Phebe Jane, dt Lot & Hester G., b 9-19-1826; m ----- VELTMAN (H)
cf W. Chester with mother 11-1836; dis 5-7-1851
Philena rocf Creek 5-22-1801 (clear); ct MM (not stated) 1-3-1810 (clear), she to live a while at Brothertown, in fam of John Dean, with a hope she may be useful in promoting the concern of Friends relative to the Indians; ct Butternuts 7-5-1815 as previous one 1810 was lost
Rebecca gct N. P. 10-7-1812 (clear)
Richard & Mary
Ch: Hannah
cf Pur. 4-11-1816 with infant ch, Hannah
Richard L., s Wm. L. & Elizabeth (Powell), b West Chester, Pa. 8-18-1853; m 1-25-1877 Rebecca KERR (nm), dt William & Cornelia (H)
Richard relrq 1921
Roger d 8-30-1798; m Elizabeth ---- (m Phila.)
Ch: Joseph
Roger rocf Pur. 11-11-1790; Roger took cert of clear to ND MM 9-3-1795; Elizabeth brought cert from ND MM 11-24-1795; Elizabeth gct R. & P. 1-1-1800 with infant s, Joseph
Sarah (nm) b Marl. d 3-1-1812 ae 67y 10m 20d bHS (wd)
Stevenus, Westchester; m Flushing 6 Mo (Aug) 8, 1745 Lydia LAWRENCE, Flushing
Lydia took rem cert 8 Mo (Oct) 2, 1745
William L., s Hester G.; m Elizabeth POWELL, d 11-23-1895 (H)
Ch: Joseph G. b 8-31-1843 d 11-23-1895
William L. b 4-23-1847
Esther G. " 1-27-1849 d about 1879
David " 10-25-1851 " 10-31-1851
Richard L. " 8-18-1853
Emily " 10-20-1855 d about 1880
John Lawrence b 10-6-1857
Moses " 5- 2-1864 d 12-19-1931
cf Wby 10-1-1845 for Elizabeth; ct Jericho 6-4-1879 for all, but cert returned 8-6-1879
----- m Margaret STEER, dt William & Mary
Mary recrq 5-4-1932 as Hunt

HUNTER
Anna, dt John & Elizabeth (Brown), b Woodbury Falls, N. Y. 11-25-1849 d 3-28-1930; m 1869 Washington MEAD (nm) (H)
recrq 3-7-1894
Gulielma, dt James & Mary, rocf Lisburn, Ire. 1848
Henry & Hannah
Ch: Elizabeth
Henry
Deborah
James
Thomas
William
cf Chap. 7-14-1825 with 6 ch named; ct Chap. 8-2-1826 with same 6 ch
Isabella, dt James & Mary, rocf Lisburn, Ire.

HUNTER, continued
James, s James & Mary, rocf Lisburn, Ire. 1848
John & Tamar
Ch: Mary
cf Chap. 5-11-1826 with 2 (not named) & 1 ch named; dis 1830 (O); ct Chap. 4-1830 (H)
Jonathan came from Co. Wicklow, Ire. 1717 with sister, Susanna; dis 7 Mo (Sep) 4
Joseph gct Pickering 8-1866
Leander & Ayton (mo before 5-1864, ret a mbr, engaged when he joined)
Ch: William b 11-1-1865 d 12- 2-1865
Matilda " 12- 6-1869
Henry L." 12-29-1863
George " 12-23-1866 d 4-17-1887
Matilda " 12- 6-1869
Leander recrq 11-5-1862; Ayton recrq 10-1863; ct Chap. 4-1887 for all living
Mary (late Robinson) dis mo before 9-6-1804
Mary, dt John & Tamar, N. Y.; m 1830 John HALSTEAD, of Peekskill (H)
cf Chap. with parents 5-11-1826; ct Chap. 8-1830
Mary, wd James
Ch: James
Isabella
Susanna
Gulielma
Mary Jr.
cf Lisburn, Ireland 1848; ct Burl. 1851 with Isabella, Mary & Susanna, but Reg. 295 shows all included in this cert
Rachel D., dt Isaac & Patience CARPENTER, N.Y.; m 1856 Elisha H. POWELL (H)
cf Ama. 3-2-1853
Susanna, N. Y.; m 1717 John SLOCUM
Susanna, dt James & Mary, rocf Lisburn, Ire. 1848
William m Amy ----- d 7-31-1854 ae 68y 5m 8d bPP (H)
William recrq 5-1844; Amy rocf Verona 1-1843; William dis 5-3-1848

HUNTINGTON
Eunice rocf N. P. 10-4-1865; d 7-22-1880 (H)
Prescott B. (nm), s Francis C. (dec) & Susan Louisa; m N. Y. 1-11-1930 Sarah H. POWELL, dt Wilson M. & Elsie (Knapp), N. Y., b N.Y. 1-11-1906 (H)
Sarah recrq of parents 10-9-1909 (as mother was not yet a mbr)

HURLBURT
Lawrence (nm), s Hiram & M. Antoinette, Utica; m at Valentine Everitt's 4-7-1870 Anna R. EVERITT, dt Valentine & Beulah E., Bkn. (not under care of N. Y. MM) (H)
Anna R. relrq 5-2-1894

HURVEY
Sarah Ann, w Charles, dt John T. & Sarah CARPENTER (H); mo before 7-6-1864; joined Congregational Church in Milwaukee; name erased 9-7-1864

HUSBAND
Hannah, dt Thos. J. & Mary R.; m 1863 Samuel H. SEAMAN (H)

HUSSEY
Benjamin B., s James & Bethiah, Charleston, S. C.; m N. Y. 7-9-1834 Mary D. WOODWARD, dt Thos. & Eliz., N. Y., d 10-1837 (or 1-14-1838 ae 35y 4m 27d)
drowned from on board steamboat "Home" stone in PP
Edmee A., w John U., dt Jno. Edgar & Mary B. CORLIES (m 12-30-1899) (H)
Edward rocf Ratcliff, London 3-19-1801, the Mtg for Sufferings, under whose care are the Friends at Dunkirk, having rq it; ct Nantucket 2-6-1805 (clear)
George b Nantucket d 12-24-1811 ae 33y bHS
George Enion (nm) b Balt. d 12-21-1836 ae 45y bHS (m)
George F., s Samuel & Susan; m Hetty -----
Ch: William H. b 1-24-1824
Abby H. " 4- 4-1826
John B. " 4- 4-1826
Elizabeth Bowne b 1-21-1831
George Jr. " 11-24-1828
Sarah H. " 1-10-1834
Mary B. " 8-24-1837 d 12-15-1839 bHS
cf New Bedford 2-28-1822 for both; ct New Bedford 6-7-1843 with 6 ch named; parents dis 1829 (H)
George F. m 2d N. Y. 11-13-1839 Gertrude Colden MURRAY, dt Robt. I. & Eliz. C. (dec), N.Y., d 9-13-1848
Ch: David C. d 11-12-1859
Infant stillborn 11-16-1840
Murray b 10-21-1845 d 1-31-1849
ct New Bedford 6-3-1840 for Gertrude C.; cf New Bedford 1-25-1844 for both with 1 ch named
George F. m 3d N. Y. 3-12-1851 Margaret CLAPP, dt John & Phebe H., N. Y., d 10-2-1878 ae 52y bPP (George F. d 12-9-1859)
Ch: Phebe C. b 12-6-1851 d 3-14-1852
John Clapp b 9-3-1855 d 11-29-1870 bPP
George Frederick b 9-24-1859
Margaret relrq 12-1861
George F., s Geo. F. & Margaret, b 9-24-1859 d 4-27-1894; m Katharine M. -----
Ch: Margaret Clapp b 1-2-1893
Geo. gct Balt. 4-1880; cf Balt. 5-7-1890 for Geo.; Margaret C. recrq of parents 6-7-1893
George Fitch d 12-9-1859 ae 48y bPP; m before 1841 Mary ----- (nm) b N. Y. d 1-6-1842 ae 28y 5m bHS (mo)
Ch: Infant stillborn 1-6-1842
having mo, Nantucket refers it to this mtg 8-27-1841, rpd unfavorably 11-3-1841; lived Bkn.

HUSSEY, continued
John U. (nm) m Edmee CORLIES, dt John Edgar & Mary B. (Wright), b N. Y. 4-18-1882 (H)
Margaret Clapp, dt Geo. F. & Katharine M., b 1-2-1893; recrq of parents 6-7-1893; name erased 2-1924
Martha rocf New Bedford 7-20-1827 (clear); dis 1829 (H); d 11-4-1844 ae about 72y
Mary W., w Benjamin B., d 1837
Obed rocf Nantucket N. Dist. 8-30-1826; ct Cincinnati 9-7-1831 (clear) (0)
Susanna, w Barzilla, dt George & Susanna FREELOVE, rocf Nantucket 12-3-1801; d 5-23-1802 at Dunkirk, France
Wm. H., s Geo. & Hetty H., New Bedford, Mass.; m N. Y. 4-16-1851 Cornelia COLLINS, dt Stacy B. & Mary D. (dec), N. Y.
Ch: Mary
George B. b 3-10-1863
cf New Bedford 1855 for Wm. H.; ct Corn. 12-1857 for all
----- & -----
Ch: Mary B. d 12-25-1839 ae 2y 4m bHS

HUSSON
Hannah B., wd, dt Samuel & Eliza UNDERHILL, d 3-31-1886 ae 72y 1m bPP; m 3-10-1845 John S. SHAPTER (H)
John (nm) d 2-1-1842 ae 27y 7m 6d bHS (d in Italy)
Ch: (prob) Hannah Louisa b N. Y. d 12-20-1841 ae 1y 9m 6d bHS

HUSTED (Huestis)
Robert, Westchester, d 9 Mo (Nov) 23, 1704; active mbr from 1684

HUTCHINGS
Elizabeth recrq 4-4-1821; dis 8-1829 (0); ct Nankin, Mich. 2-1835 (H)
Joshua [Hutchins] d 3-3-1803 ae 73y bHS
Lucy rocf Weare, N. H. 5-12-1831; ct Falmouth 8-7-1839 (clear)
Mary [Hutchin], w William, rocf Phila. 6-23-1831, rem with h
William [Hutchin] d 1833; m Mary B. ----- at Phila.
Ch: Elizabeth W.
cf Chesterfield 1-3-1826 for Wm.; cf Phila. 1831 for Mary B.; ct Phila. 4-1834 for mother & dt

HUTCHINSON
Alfred W. (nm) b N. Y. d 12-15-1820 ae 23y bHS (unm)
Anna, dt John & Sarah W., b 8-17-1828; cf Nantucket with parents 5-1837; ct Spruce St. Phila. 4-1843 (H)
Anna C., dt John Wm. & E. Eliza, Hampstead, b N. Y. 11-11-1878; m 1904 Lionel WURTS (H)
Barclay H., s Jno. Wm. & E. Eliza (Dutton), b N. Y. 6-3-1884; m 6-29-1911 Elsie Margarita BAHLER, dt Martin & Annie L., b N. J., 3-28-1888 Summit (H)
Ch: Martin Hite b 8- 3-1912
John D'Espau " 10-19-1915
Macdonald Hough " 5-17-1917
Roy Cadmus " 12-19-1918
Alan Bahler " 5-18-1925
Elsie M. recrq 4-13-1912; ct Plainfield 11-12-1917; cf Newark 8-13-1928
Edith C., dt John Wm. & E. Eliza, N. Y., b N.Y. 7-2-1887; m 1909 Irving Alfred HARNED, of Denver (H)
Edward D., s Jno. Wm. & E. Eliza, b Balt. 12-5-1868 d 3-11-1929 bPP (H)
ct R. & P. 5-8-1897
Elizabeth D., s John Wm. & E. Eliza, Hempstead, b N. Y. 7-2-1887; m 1915 Geo. D. FUSSELL, of Phila. (H)
ct Phila. 2-12-1916
Emma S., s John Wm. & E. Eliza, N. Y., b 12-10-1872; m 1898 Herman CONROW (H)
cf Balt. 12-5-1877 with parents
George C. d 11-15-1908 ae 40y bPP; m Elizabeth ----- (H)
Hannah b N. Y. d 12-23-1823 ae 24y bHS (unm)
John (nm) b Ireland d 12-7-1817 ae 50y bHS (m)
John (nm) bPP
John Jr. d 4-19-1842 ae 54y 9m 3d bPP; m Sarah W. ----- (H)
Ch: Joseph Pierce b 11-21-1823
Mary " 11-21-1823
John Finnister b 5- 3-1826
Anna " 8-17-1828
William Savory " 12- 7-1830
Sarah Pierce " 1-18-1837
cf Nantucket 5-1837 for all but last ch; Sarah W. gct Spruce St., Phila. 5-1843 with 4 ch
John Finister, s John & Sarah W., b 5-3-1826; cf New Bedford 1-26-1837, minor with brother & sister; ct Wby & Jericho 4-5-1843 (0); ct Cherry St. Phila. 9-1846 (H)
John W. m Jessie BELKNAP, dt August & Julia, d 3-26-1930 ae 66y bPP (H) (both nm)
John Wm., s James & Mary (Hamilton), b 7-8-1843 Newburg, N. Y. d 9-21-1920 bPP; m 12-27-1866 Emma Eliza DUTTON, dt John B. & Emma (Schooley), b 8-16-1844 Wheatland, Va. d 2-26-1921 bPP (H)
Ch: Edwin Dutton b 12-25-1868
John William Jr. b 10-26-1870
Emma Schooley b 12-10-1872
Mary Elizabeth b 3-21-1875
Anna C. b 11-11-1878
Barclay H. b 6- 3-1884
Edith C. b 7- 2-1887
Elizabeth D.b 7- 2-1887
cf Balt. 12-5-1877 with first 4 ch
John Wm. Jr., s Jno. Wm. & E. Eliza. b Balt. 10-26-1870; m 9-17-1896 Ann Louise CLARK (nm), dt Henry T. (H)
cf Balt. with parents 12-5-1877; name removed for lack of interest 3-13-1933

HUTCHINSON, continued
Joseph Pierce, s John & Sarah W., b 11-21-1823; cf Nantucket with parents 5-1837; ct Uwchlan with sister, Mary, 9-1840 (H)
Mary, dt John & Sarah W., b 11-21-1823; cf Nantucket with parents 5-1837; ct Uwchlan 9-1840 with brother Joseph P. (H)
Mary E., dt John Wm. & E. Eliza, N. Y., b 3-2-1875; m 1899 Jose F. F. SAVAGE (H)
Mary Pierce, dt John, rocf New Bedford 1-26-1837, minor with brother
Sarah P., dt John & Sarah, b 1-18-1837; ct Spruce St., Phila. 4-1843 (H)
Thomas recrq 4-1927
William Savory, s John & Sarah, b 12-7-1830; cf Nantucket with parents 5-1837; ct Spruce St., Phila. 4-1843 (H)

HYATT
Abraham rocf Chap. 10-14-1830 (minor)
Abraham rocf Chap. 6-14-1832 (clear); dis mo 6-3-1835
Adam b Westchester Co. d 11-8-1815 ae 35y 8m 3d bHS (m) mbr Westchester Co.
Alvin (or Alvan), dt Alvan & Letitia, d 11-8-1815 ae 36y; m Wby 1810 Sarah -----
Ch: Isaac b 1-21-1814
cf Pur. 2-11-1808; cert of clear to Wby 9-5-1810; Sarah rocf Wby 12-18-1811; ct Wby 12-5-1817 for Sarah (clear) with s, Isaac
Eliza, w Carpenter, dis 1832 (H)
Ella (nm), dt Milton & Jemima; m 1883 James Henry GRIFFEN (H)
James H. recrq 10-6-1886
Mary, dt James B. & Sarah (Deuel), b Stanford 8-31-1822 d 10-30-1914; m 1842 Koert DUBOIS (H)
Mary, dt Thos. & Eliz. BURKE, recrq of mother 1824; dis mo 11-1849
Morgan rocf Chap. 12-1849; ct Chap. 7-2-1851; cf Chap. 5-1854; ct Chap. 8-1859 (H)
Stephen rocf Chap. 1832; dis mo 7-1835
Thomas (nm) & -----
Ch: David d 11-26-1813 ae 1y 8m bHS

HYDE
Dr. Clinton J. (nm); m Nellie Elma HAVILAND, dt Solomon & Marielma (Field), b N. Y. 1-17-1887 (H)
Nellie's name entered by com. 10-10-1886
George P. (nm) m Anna G. WALKER, dt Rich'd L. & Anna (Griffen), b Bkn. 8-14-1891 (H)
Anna's name rem 9-14-1925
Kate L., dt Barnabas B. & Cath. A., N. Y.; m 1878 Frank HAVILAND (H)
Louise, dt Jos. Von Hoegler & Johanna (Schavoir) m 4-8-1812, wd Charles Hyde (nm), b Germany 2-16-1886 (H)
recrq 5-14-1923
Lydia rocf Renss. 9-7-1836; d 8-19-1852 (H)

HYNARD
Eliza T., w Benj. F., rocf Ama. 2-2-1853; d 10-1887 (H)

IDDINGS
Frances Harrison rocf Cherry St., Phila. 3-1839; ct Cherry St. Phila. 8-1849 (H)

IMLAY
Maria b N. J. d 11-18-1829 ae 47y bHS; cf Mount Holly 11-9-1826, a minister, this cert returned to Burl. at their rq 12-3-1828 (O) as Mt. Holly laid down

ING
William d 6-13-1800 bHS

INGRAHAM
Edward (nm), s Andrew (dec) & Mary E., Cambridge, Mass.; m at W. M. Powell's 2-3-1912 Elsie POWELL, dt Wilson M. & Sarah H. (Brown), N. Y., b N. Y. 5-20-1875 (H)
Mary C. rocf Oswego 2-4-1852; dis 8-1850 (H)
Timothy M. (nm), s Geo. & Mary, d 11-4-1894 ae 74y; m 10-7-1859 Anna E. COLEMAN, dt George & Eliza (Bunker), b Hudson c. 1835 d 8-1909 bPP (H)
Ch: Clymene D. d 6-30-1875 ae 17d bPP
Anna E. gct New York with parents 7-1843

INGRAM
Mary Titus, dt Henry T. & Alice G. SHOTWELL, b 1-5-1887 (m 11-28-1908); name recorded as per Disc. 3-5-1896; letter to Lafayette Ave. Presbyterian Church, 4-5-1922

IRISH
Caroline M. (nm) b N. Y. d 8-8-1842 ae 20y 3m 24d bHS (unm)
Edmund rocf Oblong 7-1846; d 8-15-1850 (H)
Eliza (nm) b L. I. d 12-28-1839 ae 31y 2m 10d bHS (unm)
Elizabeth d 10-22-1801 bHS
Esther (late Kimberly) b N. Y.; dis mo 1-4-1804; d 11-16-1841 ae 61y 2m 2d bHS
Eugene V., s Wm. A. & Lucy, b Potsdam, N. Y. 7-29-1884; m Bessie DURFEE, dt Wm. W., b Gloversville 6-9-1884
Eugene recrq 7-4-1917; Bessie recrq 3-1916
Frederick (nm) & -----
Ch: Charles b N. Y. d 11-10-1832 ae 1y 10m bHS
Joseph rocf Oswego 6-1829 (H); dis 1-7-1846 (H); Oswego sent ct N.P. which was referred to N. Y. 7-20-1831, rpd adversely 9-1831 (mo)(H)
Ruth (nm) d 6-15-1850 ae 83y 7m 18d bPP
Thomas & -----
Ch: Mary d 7-26-1804 ae 1m bHS

IRWIN
Samuel (nm) b Ireland d 10-10-1834 ae 25y 7m bHS

IVERS
----- & -----
Ch: Amelia d 7- 7-1811 ae 1y 6m bHS
Charles d 7-11-1823 ae 11m bHS

IVES
Catharine H., w David, rocf ND MM 12-23-1834; lives at Jersey City
Elizabeth (nm), wd, b Bridgetown, N. J. d 12-29-1825 ae 37y bHS
----- & -----
Ch: Adaline b N. Y. d 4-30-1826 ae 1y 2m bHS

IVESON
John (nm) b Eng. d 10-11-1841 ae 30y bHS (unm)

JACKSON
Ann, dt Hugh & Rebecca, b 2-25-1801 d 11-30-1891; m 1826 Adam HAMPTON (H)
recrq 5-1834
Anna M., dt Wm. M. & Anna M., N. Y., b N. Y. 12-27-1881; m 1910 Charles F. BRANSON (H)
name entered by com. 3-4-1882
Constance, dt Chas. Lincoln & Martha (Pogue), b Melrose Highlands, Mass. 3-14-1899; m 1923 Raymond W. WARDELL (H)
both recrq 7-12-1926
Edwin A. d 2-24-1896; m 1869 Jane L. LEVICK dt Samuel J. & Ellen (Foulke), b Quakertown, Pa. 1842 d 10-1-1914 (H)
Ch: Jane infant d 1-3-1871
Edwin L. b 7-27-1875 d 12-22-1876
Jane m 2d 1910 Wm. Wilbur James COOKE (nm)
cf Richland 11-7-1870 with infant ch
Elizabeth, dt James, Flushing; m 1725/6 Nathan FIELD
Elizabeth, dt Gilbert, d 3-21-1803 ae 22y
Elizabeth A., w George, dt Hannah UNDERHILL(H)
ct Flushing 8-1841
Ella L., dt Samuel K. & Elizabeth (Curtis); m 9-10-1891 Franklin BURDGE, s Ira & Harriet (H)
recrq 1-6-1892
Florence L., dt Wm. M. & Anna M., N. Y.; m 1891 Andrew J. McINTOSH (nm) (H)
Gilbert (nm) b Queens Co. d 8-4-1823 ae 82y bHS; m Elizabeth ----- (nm) b Staten Is. d 7-28-1823 ae 75y bHS
Halliday m Caroline H. ----- d 6-28-1851 (H)
Ch: Thomas H.
cf Salem, N. J. 11-27-1850; ct Birmingham, Pa. 11-1-1854 with s
Harriet M., dt Francis & Eliza (Copeland), b Boston 1825 d 5-12-1912; m 1848 Charles PALMER (H)
James, Flushing & Rebecca
either this James or his s dealt with 4 Mo 3, 1730 for too hasty m with 2d w, dis 3 Mo 6, 1731; James dealt with 9 Mo 3, 1726 for attending a dt's m to nm
James, s James & Rebecca, Flushing, d 8 Mo (Oct) 1735; m Flushing 12 Mo (Feb) 10, 1725 Sarah THORNE, dt Joseph & Mary, Flushing
Jane E. rocf Jericho 1-5-1887; d 5-28-1896
Mabel Asche, dt Rev. C. L. & Martha (Pogue), b Albany 12-23-1891; m 2-21-1911 Aelian Arnold BELING (nm) (H)
Mabel recrq 7-12-1926
Mary, dt James, Flushing; m 1717 Jacob WILLITS
Mary H. rocf Phila. 4-1855; ct Middletown, Pa. 5-1859 (H)
Peter b N. Y. d 11-8-1829 ae 38y bHS m -----
Ch: William B. b N. Y. d 1-6-1822 ae 3m bHS
Infant stillborn 2-3-1826 bHS
Edward d 6-20-1828 ae 9m bHS
ch nm; cf Shrewsbury 10-7-1816; dis 11-1831 (O)
Rebecca, w James, Sr., Flushing, d 2 Mo (Apr) 12, 1730
Rebecca B. (nm), dt James; m 1902 Robert H. HALLOWELL (H)
Samuel K., s James M. & Mary A. (King), b Phila. 10-9-1829 d 8-29-1915; m 8-4-1852 Elizabeth CURTIS, dt Stephen & Rebecca (Pearce), b Manasquan 2-10-1833 d 4-26-1913 (H)
Ch: Ella L.
Samuel mo but ret a mbr; cf Richland, Pa. 2-1849 for Sam'l; Ella L. recrq 1-7-1892; Elizabeth C. recrq 1-7-1892
Sarah Smith, dt Morris, rocf Chesterfield 4-7-1829, minor; dis 12-1839 (O); d 1844
Susan P., dt Amos & Eliz. (Coates) WEST (wd Henry m 1848) b Balt. 10-1813 d 3-25-1905 ae 91y 5m; cf Balt. 8-4-1869 (H)
Thadeus & Eunice
Ch: Infant d 11-5-1903 ae 1hr. bPP
Leslie T. b 1909 d 8-7-1910 ae 8m bPP
both nm
Thomas H. rocf Middletown, Pa. 11-1831; dis 6-1833 (H)
William gct New Garden, Pa. 7-5-1781 (this is a cert of unity)
William rocf ND MM 4-26-1814; ct ND MM 4-3-1816 (clear)
William (nm) m Ann ----- d 8-23-1847 ae 51y 4m 28d bHS
Ch: Susan B. b N. Y. d 7-9-1831 ae 1y 5m bHS
Elizabeth A. b N. Y. d 10-5-1838 ae 4d bHS
Asa b N. J. d 3-27-1839 ae 16y 3m bHS
William Morris, s Jas. M. & Mary Ann (King), b Phila. 4-7-1837 d 7- 8-1919 bPP; m 8-18-1869 Anna M. DAVIS, dt David H. & Susan M., b N. Y. 5-15-1848 d 12-25-1920 bPP (H)
Ch: Florence L.
William W. b 5-27-1872
Mary Anna d 2- 6-1881 ae 5y 4m 28d bPP
Anna M. " 12-27-1881
cf Whitewater, Ind. 8-7-1878 for William & 3 ch; Anna recrq 2-5-1890; Anna M. entered by com. 3-4-1882 (H)
William Walter, s Wm. M. & Anna M., b Richmond, Ind. 4-27-1872; m 6-7-1896 Fanny H. BACON, dt George B. & Lavinia, b Bkn. 1-24-1872 (H)
Ch: Morris Bacon b 5-27-1898 d 10-27-1918 bPP

JACKSON, William Walter & Fanny H., continued
Ch: George Bement b 4- 4-1900
Katharine King d 5-27-1920 ae 14y ashes bPP
Wm. W. rocf Whitewater 8-7-1878 with father; Fanny recrq 1-8-1922; ch recrq 5-14-1917
Zipporah d 6-29-1828 bHS
----- & -----
Ch: John D. b N. Y. d 12-24-1823 ae 7m bHS
William C. F. b N. J. d 8-9-1826 ae -- bHS
Moses b Shrewsbury d 8-19-1826 ae 6y 3m bHS
Edward b N. Y. d 5-24-1835 ae 3m bHS

JACOB
A. Gertrude & -----
Ch: (adopted)
Lois Antoinette b 5-11-1931; adopted 11-20-1933
Edith Gertrude b 9-14-1932; adopted 12-22-1933
cf New Garden, Pa. 4-5-1905; adopted ch recrq of foster mother 4-4-1934
Edith Gertrude b 9-14-1932; adopted Surrogates Court, Jamaica 12-22-1933 by A. Gertrude; recrq of foster mother 4-4-1934
Lois Antoinette b 5-11-1931; adopted Surrogates Court, Jamaica 11-20-1933 by A. Gertrude; recrq of foster mother 4-4-1934
Louis rocf Newcastle, Eng. 4-13-1864; ct Cork 7-1871
James C. (nm) m Emma LAWSON, dt Matthew U.B. & Elizabeth, d 9-11-1900 ae 48y bPP (d at Stamford, Conn)
Emma L. recrq 4-1871; letter to Lexington Ave. Congregational Church 12-3-1890
Mabelle J., dt James C. & Emma L., b 6-18-1875 d 3-29-1900 bPP; m William R. DAYBILL both recrq 2-7-1900
----- m Emma LAWSON
Ch: Edna b 1878 d 10-22-1899 ae 21y bPP
Emma recrq 4-1871; letter to Lex. Ave. Congregation Church, Bkn. 12-3-1890
----- & -----
Ch: Walter S. d 12-27-1876 ae 3y bPP

JACOBSON
Egbert G. (nm), s Gustav & Matilda (Drexter); m 8-23-1919 Franc DEZELL, dt John T. & Alice (Royce), b Howard City, Mich. 2-20-1884 (H)
Franc recrq 5-14-1923

JACOBUS
Mary, dt Samuel & Cath. MEDLAR; dis mo 5-4-1831

JACOBY
Herman Murray, s Dr. Eugen & Henrietta (Franck) m 8-2-1920 Catharine MURRAY (H)
Ch: Elaine b 1-22-1922
Beatrice b 1-28-1926
Herman Murray recrq 11-12-1917; ch recrq of parents 5-8-1922 & 6-14-1926

JACOCKS
George (nm) b Dutch Co. d 10-7-1841 ae 25y bHS (unm)
William T. (nm) b West. Co. d 12-26-1837 ae 48y 6m bHS
----- & -----
Ch: Thomas R. b Northeast, Dutchus Co. d 3-20-1823 ae 12y 11m bHS

JAGGER
Louise M., dt John & Sarah E., Bkn.; m 1857 George MERRITT (H)

JAMES
Abel rocf ND MM 1-23-1798 (clear); ct Burl. 2-5-1806
Abigail con mo 5-5-1763; ct Phila. 9-1-1763, having rem some years ago
Andrew recrq 3-7-1934
Atticus S. d 11-2-1808; m Alice L. M-----
Ch: Ethel M.
cf Newbury, Ohio 3-1878 for Atticus & Ethel M.; Alice recrq 3-1-1876; Mother & dt's names erased 3-1928
Dinah rem to East Nottingham, Pa. 6 Mo (Aug) 4, 1743
Harriet R. recrq 1835; d 7-1865 ae 56y bPP; matron on Ward's Island
Henry m Ethel Mae STAFFE
Henry recrq 7-1927; Ethel rocf Germantown 6-1927
John (nm) d 5-4-1832 ae 34y 9m 26d bHS
Joseph & Mary
Ch: Rebecca
Samuel
Hannah
Sarah
Chalkley
Ann
cf Phila. 4-25-1794; ct R. & P. 9-3-1801, with their 6 small ch as named
----- & -----
Ch: Mary Elizabeth d 6-22-1841 ae 2m 11d bHS

JAMISON
Helen L., dt Wm. S. & Eliz. M. (Kinsey), b Phila. 1-7-1888 (H)
recrq 4-11-1922; ct Race St. 1-10-1927; parents (at date of rq) mbr of Race St. Phila. (H)

JANNEY
Emmor K., s Thos. & Mary K. (dec), Phila.; m at Giles Coggeshall's 10-15-1868 Mary R. COGGESHALL, dt Giles H. & Marianna, Bloomfield, N. Y. b 9-7-1840 (H)
ct Phila. 7-7-1869 for Mary
Frances, dt Stephen T. & Harriet, Jr.; m 1877 in Pa. Wilmer A. BRIGGS (H)
cf Makefield 8-1-1888
Samuel M., s John & Eliza F. (Coffin), d 7-11-1932; m 12-29-1889 Margaret E. MILLER, dt Francis & Caroline H. (H)

JANNEY, Samuel M. & Margaret E., continued
Ch: Samuel M. Jr. b 1-12-1892 d 6-4-1929 Victorville, Calif.
cf Goose Creek 9-1-1886 for Samuel; cf Sandy Spring 8-6-1890 for Margaret; ct Wilmington, Del. 3-13-1933 for Margaret

JAQUES
E. (nm) & -----
Ch: Moses b N. Y. d 4-9-1830 ae 3y bHS
----- & ----- (nm) (apparently all ch of Moses)
Ch: Gideon d 9- 6-1811 ae 1y 2m bHS
Elizabeth d 8- 8-1812 ae 10m bHS
Margaret " 8-10-1812 ae 6y 6m bHS
Elias " 1-21-1815 ae 10m bHS
Charles A. d 7-22-1826 ae 6y bHS
Julia Anna d 10-17-1831 ae 2m 24d

JEFFERSON
Thomas (nm) & -----
Ch: Jane b N. Y. d 7-23-1848 ae 2y 6m bHS

JEFFREYS
Louisa J. (nm), dt Charles & Mary Anna; m 1855 John B. SCANTLEBURY (H)

JENKINS
Caleb J. recrq 3-6-1895; ct Corn. 6-12-1895
Caroline, dt Silvanus & Hannah, b 8-21-1814; m Franklin DECOST (mo); m 2d ----- COOLEDGE (H)
ret a mbr; dis 2-1845
Catharine D. m Charles S. KNOWLES (H)
Charles transferred from Albany 1-8-1916
Charles, s Jonathan & Mary, b 3-27-1823; dis mo by a priest 11-5-1862; had long attended another denomination (H)
Charles Alexander, s Jas. Jr. & Mary, mbrp cancelled 6-9-1900; he had joined the other branch of Friends (H)
Edward Y., s Jas. Jr. & Mary, relrq 2-10-1900 (H)
Eliza, dt James; m Selah HAIGHT (H)
at Milton, then at Lloyd, Mich. 1859
Eliza L., dt Silvanus & Hannah, N. Y.; m 1827 Wm. H. MACY
Eliza L., dt James Jr. & May; m Selah HAIGHT (H)
cf Marl 12-1848; at Milton, then at Lloyd, Mich. 1859; relrq 6-8-1901
Eliza L., w Silvanus F., dt Silvanus J. & Caroline MACY, relrq 2-4-1885 (H)
Elizabeth H., dt Henry C. & Eleanor (Cooley), b N. Y. 10-8-1904; m 1926 Herbert L. MORRIS (H)
cf R. & P. 9-9-1905 with mother
George m Hannah JAMES
Ch: Elizabeth
George Francis
cf ND MM 12-7-1825; dis 10-1830 & 3-1831 (O); cf Nottingham 3-17-1826; ct Phila. 5-1830 for all
George Edward, s James Jr. & Mary (Smith), b Milton, N. Y. 7-2-1847; m 12-11-1870 Mary BROADHEAD (nm), dt Jeptha & Anna, b Eng. 3-13-1850 (H)
cf Marl. 12-1848 with parents; mbrp cancelled 6-10-1911
Henry, s Jonathan & Mary, relrq 7-6-1864
Henry C., s Thos. W. & Mary Frances (Carpenter) b Bkn. 5-4-1880; m 10-14-1903 Eleanor COOLEY, dt Justus H. & Mary H., b Corning, N. Y. 2-28-1879 d 10-26-1919 bPP (H)
Ch: Elizabeth Haviland b N. Y. 10-8-1904
Silvanus Waterman b Plainfield 6-12-1908
Oliver C. b 2- 6-1910
Henry C. recrq 12-7-1901; cf R. & P. 9-9-1905 for Eleanor with Elizabeth H.
Henry C. m 2d 10-9-1923 Estelle B. LOESER (nm) dt Mathilde (H)
James (nm) b Eng. d 9-19-1844 ae 64y 2m 15d bHS (m)
James Jr. d 2-6-1885; m Mary ----- d 12-12-1876 (H)
Ch: Phebe Ann
Lydia W.
Sarah T.
Eliza L.
Edward Y.
Seth Smith b 7-20-1838
Charles Alexander
George Edward b 7- 2-1847
cf Marl. 12-1848 for all
Jonathan d 2-1865; m Mary ----- d 9-25-1849 (H)
Ch: Judith B.
Adelia (or Delia) d 9- 9-1866
Henry
Francis
Charles L. b 3-27-1822
William B. dis 8-1834
Henry relrq 7-6-1864
cf Hudson 2-20-1816 with 3 ch named; all dis 1830-1849 (O)
Joshua & -----
Ch: Ann b Phila. d 4-29-1829 ae 7y 11m 20d bHS
Judith, dt Jonathan & Mary; m 1829 ----- MILDEBURGER (H) (mo)
dis mo 1-1830 (H); dis mo 9-2-1829 (O)
Lydia W., dt James Jr. & Mary; m William F. TILSON (H)
cf Marl. 12-1848 with parents
Mary K., dt Thos. W. & Caroline K., N. Y.; m 1856 Henry BARROW (H)
Matthew having mo, Nantucket rq N. Y. to deal with him 4-6-1808; rpd adversely 5-4-1808
Phebe rocf Hudson 5-26-1807 (clear); dis 2-6-1812
Phebe, dt Jos. S. & Deborah SHOTWELL, b 10-11-1809 d 1833 (w Wm. L.)
Phebe d 3-13-1898 ae 75y 8m 22d bPP; m Justus PHELPS (H)
(both nm)
Phebe Ann, dt James J. & Mary; m Daniel P. DUBOIS (H)
cf Marl. 12-1848; dis mo 3-1-1859
Sarah, wd Jonathan, d 6-1844 at Nantucket (H)

JENKINS, Sarah, continued
Ch: Thomas W.
Ann (or Nancy) dis 1825
cf Nantucket 9-23-1818 (both clear)
Sarah, dt Thomas W. & Caroline K., N. Y.; m 1851 Samuel P. TITUS (H)
Sarah T., dt James Jr. & Mary; m James PALMER (H)
cf Marl. 12-1848; joined Orthodox 3-1859
Seth Smith, s James Jr. & Mary (Smith), b Milton 7-20-1838 d 8-1-1903; m 4-13-1864 ----- ANGUS, dt Thomas & Catharine; m 2d ----- DEYO, dt Ewing & Aletta (m 3-20-1879)
cf Marl. 12-1848 with parents (H)
Silvanus, s Thos. W. & Caroline (King), b N.Y. 5-17-1841 d 3-24-1918 (H) (unm)
Silvanus F., s Jonathan & Sarah, Nantucket, d 12-23-1818 ae 36y 5m 27d bHS; m N. Y. 10-12-1803 Hannah LEGGETT, dt Joseph (dec) & Mirriam, N. Y., b 2-1-1781 d 7-3-1878
Ch: William H. (or Wm. Leggett) b 8-23-1804 d 9-30-1805
William L. b 10- 9-1806
Mary d 5-15-1809 ae 10m 14d
Child " 3- 4-1810
Eliza " 6-30-1808
Mary " 6-30-1808 d 12-25-1828
Infant stillborn 3-1-1810
Sarah d 4-22-1813 ae 3d
Caroline b 8-21-1814
Silvanus F." 11-25-1818 d 2-10-1820 bHS
Silvanus F.
cf Nantucket 5-1-1799, apprentice to Isaac Hicks; all dis 1829-1840 (O)
Silvanus F., s Silvanus F. (dec) & Hannah, b N. Y. 11-25-1818 d 11-27-1908 ae 90y 2d; m at Isaac Walker's Jan. 12-1848 Augusta WALKER (nm), dt Isaac & Gulielma, N. Y. (H) (not under care of N.Y. MM)
Silvanus, Jr. m 1885 Eliza L. MACY
she joined another religious society; name erased 2-4-1885
Simeon rocf Berwick, Me. 8-1873; name erased 11-1886
Thomas W., s Jonathan & Sarah, Nantucket, b 11-22-1794 d 11-24-1849 bPP; m N. Y. 11-11-1824 Caroline KING, dt John & Mary R., N.Y. d 11-25-1883 ae 79y 11m 23d bPP (H)
Ch: Thomas Jr. b 8-4-1825 d 9-8-1826
Sarah " 4-15-1828
Mary K. " 8- 4-1829
Eliza " 7-25-1831 d 4- 3-1881 bPP
Caroline " 9-17-1833 d 6-20-1883 bPP
Thomas W. Jr. b 5-18-1836
both dis 1830-1839 (O)
Ch: (continued)
William M. b 3- 8-1838 d 2- 9-1839
Ann K. " 11-13-1839 " 12-13-1839
Sylvanus " 5-17-1841 " 3-24-1918
Avis " 3-18-1844 " 5- 2-1894 bPP
cf Phila. 7-8-1807 to live with his brother Silvanus F.
Thomas W., s Thos. W. (dec) & Caroline K., b 4-18-1836 d 10-8-1917; m at D. J. Willets' 12-8-1859 Anna WILLETS, dt Daniel & Eliz. F., b 6-26-1839 d 4-10-1867 bPP (H)
Ch: Edward W. b 3-25-1863 d 4-12-1863 bPP
Infant stillborn 3-29-1867 bPP
Thomas W. m 2d 11-27-1877 Mary Frances CARPENTER (nm) d 4-3-1912 ae 66y 10m 20d bPP
Ch: Henry C. b 5-4-1880
William B., s Jonathan, rocf Hudson 2-25-1823, minor; dis mo by a priest 3-2-1836
William L. m Phebe SHOTWELL d 1833 (H)
William dis 9-1839
William Levitt rocf Lynn, Eng. 8-1-1838; dis 8-1843 (O)
----- & ----- (nm)
Ch: Frederick Z. b Phila. d 11-27-1843 ae 4y 9m bHS

JENKS
Barton Loag (nm), s Llewellyn H. & Emma (Loag) Rutherford, N. J.; m at G. R. Andrews' 6-23-1921 Elizabeth H. ANDREWS, dt Geo. R. & Emeline W. (Hawkins), b Goshen 9-7-1895 (H)
Elizabeth recrq of parents 1-7-1899
Elizabeth Storey, dt Wm. P. & Bertha, b 8-12-1906; m ----- CLARK
recrq of parents 4-1714; ct Abington, Pa. 11-6-1929
Josephine, Jr., dt Wm. P. & Bertha, b 12-30-1903; m ----- WARREN
Wm. Pearson & Bertha
Ch: William b 12-12-1902 d 1- 9-1921
Josephine J. b 12-30-1903
Elizabeth Storey b 8-12-1906
George Cooke " 2-27-1908
Priscilla " 10-10-1909
Randolph " 3-17-1912
Nicholas Cooke " 12- 8-1916
cf WD MM 4-1914 for Wm.; Bertha recrq 4-1914; ch recrq of parents 4-1914

JENNER
Mary Elizabeth, dt Solomon & Elizabeth; m 1846 ----- MILLARD (H) (mo)
dis mo 11-1846
Sarah, dt Solomon & Elizabeth; m 1847 ----- JOHNSON (mo) (H)
dis mo 7-7-1847
Solomon & Elizabeth
Ch: Edward b 2- 9-1825
William b 4-19-1826
Sarah " 11- 8-1827
Mary Elizabeth b 3-24-1829
Phebe Maria b 7-24-1833
cf Corn. 11-25-1824; parents dis 1830 (O)
Solomon m 2d Margaret WEBSTER, wd Wm. S.
Margaret relrq 2-1866
Solomon (nm) & -----
Ch: Infant stillborn 12-25-1840 bHS
William, s Solomon & Elizabeth, b 4-19-1826; rel 11-1844 (H); dis 12-1848 (O)

JENNINGS
Gertrude S. recrq 5-1-1935
James (nm) & -----
Ch: dt d 8-23-1814 ae 4m bHS
Sarah (prob) d 7-13-1827 ae 8m 24d bHS
Mary Emeline " 7-28-1830 ae 7m 28d bHS
James C. (prob) d 7-9-1839 ae 7y 8m bHS
James E. (nm) d 1863; m Mary ----- (nm) d 7-15-1856 ae 59y bPP

JERVIS
Martin, Phila., m at Mary P. Willets', Jericho, 7 Mo (Sept) 11, 1698 Mary CHAMPION, Wby. He brought cert of clear from West Jersey

JESSUP
Mary, wd; m 1688, Jericho John DOLE
Richard b Ireland d 7-9-1819 ae 23y bHS he was from Ireland; drowned while bathing in North River
Susan Ann rocf Ama. 12-1-1847; ct Ama. 7-1856 (H)
Thomas (nm) b Ireland d 10-2-1828 ae 35y bHS (drowned)

JESTER
Simeon Van Trump, s P. C. & Rachel, b Md. 12-15-1883; recrq 5-14-1910; ct Moorestown 6-14-1920 (H)

JEWETT
James J., having mo Balt. refers to N. Y. 2-9-1832; rpd adversely 6-5-1832
Thomas L. rocf Wilmington 9-1830; dis 5-1836 (H)

JOHNSON
Anna con mo 7-4-1787
Alan, s John A. & Selina, Newark, b Hyannis, Mass. 9-19-1876; m at H. P. Dillistin's 6-5-1915 Helen B. DILLISTIN, dt Howard P. & Jinnie B. W., Paterson, N. J., b Paterson, N. J. 4-14-1887 (H)
Ch: Joy Dilliston b Ogdensburg 8-7-1917
Alan Dilliston b Newark 6-20-1919
Alan recrq 6-11-1917; Helen recrq 4-11-1914; ct Montclair for all 3-10-1930
Amy, having mo Chap. refers it to this MM 11-5-1800, rpd favorably 1-7-1801, rst; cf Chap. 4-10-1801; ct Troy 1-5-1814 (clear)
Asa, s David (dec) & Abigail, b 4-22-1787; ct Upper Springfield 8-2-1797, minor
David, N. Y. & Abigail
Ch: Keziah
Thomas
Asa b 4-22-1787
Mary " 2-12-1790
Elizabeth b 8-17-1792
cf Burl. for David & Abigail with 2 ch, Keziah & Thomas 3-5-1787; ct Upper Springfield 6-3-1802 for Abigail with 2 ch, Elizabeth & Mary
Edward rocf Deep River 4-7-1806; ct Deep River MM, N. C. 11-3-1820, minor, placed with a [Friend
Edward (nm) & -----
Ch: Infant stillborn 1-8-1818
Elijah (nm) b N. Y. d 1-29-1811 ae 28y 3m 3d bHS (m)
Elizabeth Margaret, dt William; m Harry Hilary BELL, Jr.
recrq of father 9-1867
Emma, dt Mordecai & Samuella, rocf Dublin 11-13-1855 with mother; relrq 4-7-1875
Emma Teresa, dt William, recrq of father 9-1867; relrq 1-1880
Franklin (nm) m Priscilla WEBB d 11-5-1882 ae 52y bPP
Ch: son d 2-27-1864 ae 3y bPP
Mary " 9-27-1867 ae 1y 4m bPP
cf Dublin for Priscilla 8-16-1864 as Webb (they being unaware of her m)
George m Frances DISTURNELL, dt Wm. & Jane (Williams), d 12-3-1921 ae 83y bPP (H)
Henry (nm) d 7-11-1854 ae 43y bPP; m -----
Ch: Mary d 2-22-1846 ae 1y 3m 11d bHS
Henry C. d 9-11-1878 ae 35y bPP (H)
Ida recrq 10-5-1910; d recorded 4-1928
James B. rocf Clear Creek, Ind. 4-1883; d in the West
Joseph (nm) b Canada d 10-30-1832 ae 20y 10m bHS (unm)
Joseph dis enlisting as a soldier 6-6-1821
Keziah, dt David (dec) & Abigail, gct Upper Springfield 8-2-1797, placed with a Friend
Louisa Grace, dt Mordecai & Samuella, rocf Dublin 11-13-1855 with mother; relrq 4-7-1875
Margaret H. H. rocf Wilmington, Del. 1-1922; ct Uwchlan MM 9-1928
Maria (nm) b Conn. d 4-22-1831 ae 30y bHS (unm)
Mary A.; m 4-25-1856 Reuben Bigelow BURTON (H) cf Phila. Spruce St. 9-1842; in Vt. 1858
Mordecai d 1890; m Samuella ----- d 8-25- (or 28) 1863 ae 40y bPP
Ch: Louissa Grace
Emma
Mordecai recrq 9-1883; Samuella rocf Dublin 11-13-1855 with 2 ch
Phebe Jane, w Willard B., dt John T. CARPENTER, in Milwaukee 1859; joined Congregational Church there; dis 9-7-1864 for mo (H)
Richard d 9-12-1798 bHS (H) (nm)
Rowland, s Samuel (dec) & Jenette, Phila., b 5-24-1816 d 9-25-1886; m at H. W. Wolcott's 6-30-1852 Henrietta WOLCOTT (nm), dt Henry W. & Sybillah, Monmouth, N. J. (not under care of N.Y. MM) (H)
cf Green St. Phila. 6-1851; dis 9-1853; rst by QM
Dr. Samuel John, s William & Elizabeth, d 6-10-1902 ae 51y 29d bPP; m Emma W. ----- (nm) d 11-11-1904 ae 40y bPP
recrq of father 1-1864; lived in Mt. Vernon
Sarah M., dt Wm. & Anna, N. Y.; m 1813 John W. POWELL
Sarah Rebecca, dt Rich. A. & Eliz. (Hampton),

JOHNSON, Sarah Rebecca, continued
b Darlington, Pa. 2-27-1857 d 4-19-1935; m 1875 A. Andrew WEMMELL (nm) (H)
Thomas, s David (dec) & Abigail, gct R. & P. 8-2-1797, minor
Thomas (nm) d 3-11-1869 ae 21y bPP "brother of William, prob nm"
William, s Wm. & Eliz., of Chesham, Eng., b Essex, Bucks Co., Eng. d 10-17-1815 ae 70y bHS; m N. Y. 9-13-1786 Anna MARSHALL, dt Jos. & Phebe, Nantucket
Ch: Edward b 6-19-1789
Phebe " 12-21-1790
Sarah " 7-11-1792
Joseph Marshall b 8-28-1794
Mary " 2-17-1797
William Marshall b 8-16-1800
Anna rocf Dartmouth 11-21-1785 (clear); William's parents were of Chesham, Bucks Co., Eng.; all dis 1828-1840 (O); Anna gct Wby 4-1834 with Mary (H); others dis 1829-1830
William dis 10-1-1817 for attending theater; rst as Wm. M. Johnson 7-7-1819
William, s John & Teresa (Richardson), b Dublin 11-18-1819 d 4-9-1902 bPP; m 8-12-1848 Elizabeth STREIGHT, dt John & Margaret, d about 1890 bPP (H)
recrq 8-1-1894
William & -----
Ch: Samuel John
Eliz. Margaret
Emma Teresa
William Henry d 11- 6-1863 ae 3y bPP
recrq 1860; dis 5-1873; ch recrq of father 1864 & 1867
William, Jr. rocf MM at Wickham in Bucks Co., Pa. to Phila. 3-2-1778, sometime resident in Phila. now "with his father here" (clear)
----- & -----
Ch: Phebe b N. Y. d 2-11-1826 ae 1y 7d bHS
Jennie d 2-25-1870 ae 22y bPP
Jane " about 1890 ae -- bPP

JOHNSTON
Albert T. (nm) & ----- (H)
Ch: Charles d 3-11-1882 ae 5m bPP
Charles L., M.D.; m Ruth A. BATTEY, dt Jonathan & Anna, b Bkn. 3-31-1862 d 1-12-1921 bPP
Ch: Grace L. b 6- 2-1890
Charles Lindley b 12- 9-1890
Thomas Elmer " 7- 8-1894 d about 1895 bPP
cf Winthrop, Me. 8-1895; parents rel 1-17-1897 by letter to Lafayette Ave. Pres. Ch.
Charles Lindley, Jr., s Chas. L. & Ruth A. (Battey), b 12-9-1892 Bkn. d Newburgh, N.Y. 11-19-1930 bPP; m Ruth -----
jas & name erased 11-6-1907
Eliza recrq 5-2-1906; name erased 3-1928, having jas
Grace L. b 6-2-1890; jas & name erased 11-6-1907

James W. (nm) d 2-15-1865 bPP in grave with Phebe Weeks
Jane, w Richard, rocf Lurgan MM, Ire. 12-17-1796
Jane d 5-15-1878 ae 82y 9m 5d bPP (H)

JOHNSTONE
Mary Ellen (form Perkins) rocf Warwickshire North 9-1-1897; name erased 2-1926 as Perkins

JONES
Aquilla rocf Phila. 3-24-1842; dis 1-1844
Benjamin m Mary ----- b N. J. d 10-15-1846 ae 80y 8d bHS (a wd)
Caroline M. rocf Balt. 7-9-1898 (H)
Catharine (nm) d 9-19-1866 bPP (H)
Charles (nm) m Delilah Ann ----- (nm) d 6-10-1863 ae 26y
Ch: Elvira Olinsha d 4-29-1856 ae 1y 7m 16d bPP later 4-30-1868 rem to Kensico
Dorothy W. d 10-5-1855 ae 79y 2m 12d bPP
Edward, Jr. m Amy J. HOLME, dt Eleanor
Ch: William H. b 10-13-1901
Harry Raymond b 9- 8-1906 d 2- 2-1907 bPP
Edward recrq 5-3-1899; Amy recrq 5-1887; letter to Calvary Bapt. Ch. 5-3-1916 for Amy; Edward & Wm. H. names erased 3-1928 for jas; lived Hopewell, N. J.
Eliza F. rocf Butler 3-1869; ct R. & P. 5-1877
Elizabeth H., dt Linda & Ann M., Bkn.; m 1882 Walter HAVILAND (H)
Evan, Jamaica m Mary ----- d 6 Mo (Aug) 19, 1745
Ch: John b 3 Mo (May) 10, 1729
Thomas b 3 Mo (May) 16, 1733
Evan con mo before 6-7-1753
Harvey D. m Alice Cynthia SCALES, dt Edward S. & Alice L., b 1-15-1908 (m 6-22-1922)
Ch: Nancy Lora b 1-24-1932
Linda Cary b 10- 5-1935
Margaret Cynthia b 10- 5-1935
cf China, Me. 4-1928
Henry R., s Oliver & Meriam; m ----- (mo before 2-1871; ret a mbr)
Henry R. m 2d 2-6-1901 Eliza MILLER, dt Abrm. E. & Mary (Briggs), b N. Y. 11-26-1858 d 12-11-1935 bPP
cf Pur. 1865; ct Peace MM 4-1880 (Kansas?)
Jane S. rocf Troy 9-1831; ct Troy 10-1833
John, s Charles & Phebe; m 5-11-1844 Caroline PECK, dt George & Sarah (Ritter), b Danville, Pa. 11-6-1824 d 4-12-1909 (H)
Caroline m 2d Wm. ROTHWEILER 3-4-1885
John B. rocf Oblong 7-1861; d 4-8-1878
Joseph & Sarah S.
Ch: Emily Clara b 1-25-1856
cf Haddonfield 4-1854; ct Exeter, Pa. for all 7-2-1856
Joshua Sharpless rocf Phila. 10-1855; d 7-12-1885 (H)
Louisa, w Henry, dt Daniel C. & Ann Eliza MILLER, d 10-23-1897 (m 5-13-1869)

JONES, continued
Mary, w Raymond T., dt Thomas & Alice FREEBORN, b 8-10-1805 (H)
Mary rocf Jericho 1823 (clear); ct Wby & Jericho 2-1-1832 (clear); ct Jericho 9-1830 (H)
Mary rocf R. & P. 6-1844; d 10-5-1846 (H)
Mary E. gct Balt. 2-1917
Oliver & Meriam
Ch: Ella M.
Oliver W.
Henry R. separate cert; cf Pur. 4-1866 with 2 ch; ct Pur. 6-1869 with 2 ch
Phebe L., w Benjamin P., rocf Albany 6-1847; ct Oswego 9-4-1861 (H)
Raymond T. m Mary FREEBORN, dt Thomas & Alice (H) Mary a mbr at time of Separation 1828; her name cancelled 4-9-1904; unknown since 1879; she was then at Wasiaga, Minn.
Richard, Merchant, N. Y.; m Dorcas COAKER, dt Nicholas, Mariner of N. Y. (m at John Delavall's 5 July 1688
Ch: Esther b 1 Mo (Mar) 7, 1690/1
Dorcas " 10 Mo (dec) 21, 1692
active mbr from 1688 to 1693
Samuel, Flushing, b 3-9-1765; m Elizabeth ----- ct Jericho 5-2-1793
William gct Burl. 9-1-1779 (cert of unity)
William rocf Darby, Pa. 1-27-1824; marked "absent" in Reg. 294
----- & -----
Ch: William d 2-18-1832 ae 63y
Williamsburg, Bkn.
----- m Caroline L. SHEPP, dt Samuel & Mary, b Frankford, Ind. 7-2-1843 (m 1864)
Caroline recrq 5-20-1917; name erased 3-1922
----- & Grace -----
Ch: James
Grace recrq 4-5-1933; James recrq of mother 4-5-1933

JORDAN
Alice (nm), dt Wm. H. & Margaret; m 1888 William J. GRIFFIN (H)
Robert, Flushing rqc of rem 10 Mo (Dec) 6, 1722; com. approved, no further mention

JOWETT
Sarah (form Lockwood) relrq 3-4-1857 (H)

JOY
Alexander, s Levi & Margaret, rocf Hudson with mother 1-20-1818; dis mo 1824
Margaret, w Levi
Ch: Sarah dis 1825
Alexander " 1824
Reuben
Maria
cf Hudson 1-20-1818 with ch, Alex., Sally & Reuben; ct Hudson 5-2-1827 for Margaret; ch all dis (0)
Reuben rocf Hudson 7-1818; d lost at sea
Sarah, dt Levi & Margaret, rocf Hudson with mother 1-20-1818; dis 1824

JOYCE
Frank m Ida V. FRISBIE, dt Lawrence & Elizabeth (Longbotham), d 3-25-1898 ae 45y bPP (H)
Ch: Florence Estelle d 5-10-1881 ae 1y 5m 22d bPP
Willard Creighton d 7- 9-1879 ae 1y 11m 22d bPP
Jane Susanna rocf Lewes & Chester, Eng. 7-7-1897

JUDGE
Hugh d 8-16-1799 bHS
another d 8-4-1800 bHS
Hugh & Susannah
Ch: Thomas
Hannah
Susanna
Margaret
Phebe
Hester d 10-10-1803 ae 14
Rachel
Rebecca
Child d 8-16-1799 (minister)
cf Pur. 6-8-1797 for both with their 8 ch, those of marriageable age (clear); ct Gunpowder, Md. 8-1-1804 with 2 dt, Phebe & Rebecca; Phebe (clear)
Margaret, dt Hugh & Susannah, gct Gunpowder, Md. 6-5-1805 (clear)
Rachel, dt Hugh & Susannah, gct Gunpowder, Md. 1-2-1805, minor
Susannah, Jr., dt Hugh & Susannah, gct Gunpowder, Md. 8-1-1804 (clear)

KAHN
Mildred, dt I. Robert & Hattie (Rice), b Chippewa Falls, Wis. 1894; m 1917 Samuel J. GATES (nm) (H)

KAMP
Thomas (nm) & -----
Ch: John Helm d 4-15-1838 ae 2y 2m 15d bHS
Augustus Helm d 7-13-1847 ae 6y 11m 24d bHS

KAPHAELIAN
Vargin, dt Melkis & Arden, Jersey City; m 1887 Sarkis BASMAJIAN (Armenians)

KASHOW (or Kershow)
Abraham m Mary ----- b West. Co. d 4-10-1833 ae 54y (H)
Ch: Abraham
George D. dis 3-1839 (H)
rel 6-2-1875 (said to be dec many yrs)
cf Wby 7-14-1824; parents dis 1830 (0); ch dis 1840 (0)
George D., s Abraham & Mary, rocf Wby 7-14-1824; dis 3-1839 (H)

KAUFMAN
Helen (nm) m Alfred ROSSITER (H)

KAUFMAN, continued
Joseph H. [Kauffman], s Emanuel & Clemenda (Hall), b 1870, Pa. d 5-19-1930 bPP; m Emma L. -----
Ch: Harriet G. b 8-25-1909 d 9-26-1915 bPP

KAULFUSS
Ettiel W. (nm) m 1918 Albert E. MARSHALL, Jr. (H)

KEARNS
Elizabeth (late Bowne), wd, dis mo 8-6-1800; cf Fairfax, Va. for her s, William & Josiah Bowne, 3-28-1801
Wilmer R., s John P. & Henrietta (Rhamstine), b Beavertown, Pa. 1-17-1882; m 6-8-1904 Edna BUCKMAN, dt Chas. H. & Mary B. (H)
Ch: Serena Buckman b 8- 3-1905
Wilma D. " 11-12-1920
Wilmer recrq 5-6-1905; cf Green St. 4-10-1909 for Edna; ct Gwynedd for all but Serena B.

KEATES
William J. R., s Harry, recrq 2-7-1906; name erased 10-1928

KEEFER
David Holcomb, s Wm. & Helen (Holcombe); m 4-11-1906 Grace MACY, dt Chas. W. & Ella A. (Wichwin) SANDERS, b Rahway 8-18-1870 (H) wd John H. Macy, Jr.; Grace recrq 1-14-1911; name changed to Macy 4-11-1916 by Court order

KEELER
Eleanor Caroline, dt Henry W. & Emilia (Braun), b Phila. 5-18-1885; m 1910 Eugene H. STRINGHAM (H)
Eleanor recrq 7-10-1911; ct Jenkintown, Pa. for Eugene
Hannah (form Carpenter) rocf Pur. 6-10-1859 as Carpenter; ct Pur. 5-6-1868 as Keeler (H)

KEELEY
Mary J., s John & Josephine, d 7-29-1913 ae 64y 11m bPP; m John HAWKINS (H) (both nm)

KEENE
Anna, dt Samuel & Rebecca J., b Lancaster Co., Pa. d 7-8-1894; m Dr. Charles H. BUSHONG (H)
recrq 11-6-1889
Nora E., dt Samuel & Rebecca J., b Lancaster Co., Pa. 4-21-1868 d 3-14-1930; m 5-25-1899 Dr. Charles H. BUSHONG (his 2d w) (H)
recrq 7-8-1899

KEESE
Catherine Voker (or Volker) (form Keese) dis mo 3-4-1772
Elizabeth, dt Wm. & Mary, Flushing; m 1782 Gideon SEAMAN
George M., s Samuel T. & Phebe (Merritt), rec 4-10-1909 (H)
Grace W., dt Samuel T. & Caroline, b 1-5-1869; m 11-18-1891 Frank W. HUBBARD (H)
Herman Bancroft, s Sam'l T. & Phebe (Merritt), b 9-12-1867; relrq (H)
Jemima, dt Wm. & Jemima (Baldwin), b Peru 12-30-1823 d 6-13-1913; rec 4-8-1905 on recommendation of Overseers (H)
John, Flushing, m Flushing 11 Mo (Jan) 14, 1719 Mary BOWNE, d 4-4-1773
Ch: William
John
Mary con allowing dt to mo; William & John Jr. dealt with for same
John (nm) & -----
Ch: Eliza H. d 7-23-1863 ae 20y 9m bPP
John, Jr., s John & Mary, Flushing; m Elizabeth -----
John dealt with 1753 for aiding sister to mo; John took cert of clear to Wby 12 Mo. 1, 1749; Elizabeth rocf Wby 6 Mo. 12, 1750; ct ----- 4-2-1760
John, Jr. gct N. P. 9-6-1781, he had mo & gone into military service (perhaps s John S. & Elizabeth)
Pamela Allen (form Keese) dis mo 3-4-1772
Pauline Stoddard, dt Rich. P. & Anna (Hauxhurst), b Keesville, N. Y. 6-6-1870; name entered on proposal of Overseers 4-13-1907; father mbr Peru; mother mbr Plainfield
Phebe F. rocf Hudson 2-25-1817 (clear); dis 1-1831 (0); ct Coey. 5-1835, returned 4-1841; ct Oswego 7-1841 (H)
Samuel T. (or Y.), s Peter & Mary; m Caroline M. ----- d 5-8-1863 ae 35y 7m bPP (H)
Ch: Mary T. (or Y.) b 3-29-1853 d 3- 6-1863
William Merritt b 6-26-1854 d 12-6-1857
cf Peru 12-1853 for Samuel; cf N.P. 7-1854 for Caroline
Samuel T. (or Y.) m 2d at J. J. Merritt's 6-15-1805 (Samuel T. (or Y.) d 10-17-1890); Phebe B. MERRITT, dt John J. & Hannah B., Bkn., b 12-14-1843 d 5-17-1878
Ch: Zaydee Bancroft b 4- 6-1866
Herman Bancroft " 9-12-1867
Grace Waldron " 1- 5-1869
George M. (perhaps s of 1st m)
Phebe relrq 7-7-1869
William, s John & Mary; m Mary -----
Ch: Elizabeth
cert of clear to Pur. 6-2-(Apr) 1743; dealt with 1753 for aiding sister to mo; Mary, w of William, with dt, Mary, gct Wby 7-7-1768; cf Wby 9-25-1771 for Mary
William m Jemima BALDWIN (H)
Ch: Pamelia d 3-18-1899 ae 83y bPP
Jemima b Pem. 12-30-1826
Zaydee Bancroft, dt Sam'l T. & Phebe M., b 4-6-1866 d 8-6-1902; m 10-9-1890 Wm. B. HICKOX (H)

KELLERS
Harriet H., dt Bohl & Hattie Lavinia (Henry), b Jersey City 3-21-1869; m 1889 J. VAN VECHTEN WARING (H)
both recrq 5-7-1890

KELLY
Edward G. rocf New Bedford 7-28-1836, minor; ct Nantucket 11-1-1837 (clear)
Florence, dt Wm. D. & Caroline B. (Bonsall), b Phila. 9-12-1859 d 2-17-1932; m -----(H)
Ch: Nicholas b 7-12-1885
m name not given, she resumed her maiden name after separation; cf Phila. 11-14-1827 for Florence
Helen (nm) m 12-29-1917 Chas. Wm. BAYLIS (H) separated
John E. m Maude THOMPSON
Ch: Rose Marie
Andre Lorraine
John recrq 11-6-1929; Maude recrq 7-1923; ch recrq of parents 12-1928
Nicholas, s Florence (Kelly), b Zurich, Switzerland 7-12-1885; m 6-19-1909 Augusta L. MAVERICK (H)
Nicholas recrq 12-13-1926; parents separated mother & s took name of Kelly

KELSEY
Luman P., s Rollo E. & Dora (Callender), b Denver, 1-6-1906; m 5-8-1930 Dorothea STOREY, dt Creighton R. & Sadie (Bogue), b Kingston, N. Y. 8-30-1893 (H)
Ch: Peter Storey b 1-7-1935 d 3-30-1935
both recrq 8-13-1934

KELSO
----- (nm) m Sarah VAN NOTE (nm), dt James & Clementine, b N. J. d 2-2-1840 ae 36y bHS

KEMBLE
Ann rocf Byberry, Pa. 3-30-1824; ct Byberry, Pa. 12-7-1825

KEMP
Thomas rocf Balt. W. Dist. 9-7-1827; ct Balt. W. Dist. 8-1831; dis by Balt. 5-1834
William (nm) b Maryland d 5-13-1842 ae 43y 3m 6d bHS; m -----
Ch: (prob) William T. b N. Y. d 3-28-1837 ae 6m 15d bHS

KEMPTON
John d 1-2-1881 ae 54y bPP; m -----
Ch: Infant d 1-13-1868 ae 2y 6m bPP
William W. d 1-7-1873 ae 3y 4m bPP
recrq 4-1873

KENDALL
Henry rocf Hardshaw 3-24-1795 (clear); cert endorsed to Balt. 3-2-1796 (clear)
Lydia (form Wistar), w Edward H., rocf WD MM 5-1879; relrq 12-6-1893

Myra Mae, dt Chas. H. & Winifred E. (Bergen), b Ausable Forks, N. Y. 11-7-1875; m 1900 Edwin Oscar SMITH (H)

KENNEDY
Alexander, s John & Jessie (Russell), b Broxburn, Scot. 7-6-1881; m Jessie AITKEN, dt John & Jane (Stoddart), b Edinburgh, Scot. 7-28-1884
Ch: John Neil b Bkn. 5-31-1912
Margaret Stoddart b 3- 6-1916
Alexander Jr.
parents recrq 9-14-1917; ch recrq of parents 9-14-1917
Henry C., s Sam'l W. & Cath. A., Ridgeway, b 6-27-1863; m Mary C. ----- b 5-5-1864 d 11-6-1894 (H)
Ch: Elizabeth C. b 5-29-1889
Franklin Wm. " 10-20-1890
Edwin Craft " 8-31-1892 d 12-17-1898
Martha H. " 5-10-1894 " 11-23-1894
cf Phila. 3-4-1891 with 2 ch
Henry C. m 2d 4-12-1897 Elizabeth M. GRISCOM (nm), dt Geo. H. & Frances H.
all relrq 10-12-1925
Maria A. (nm), dt James & Charity; m 1866 Thomas Edgar VALENTINE (H)
----- & -----
Ch: Joseph d 4-29-1841 ae 2y 10m 16d bHS
nephew of John Swinerton

KENNER
Anna E. rolf Mott Ave. M. E. Ch., N. Y. 11-1923
name erased 11-1928 (prob sister of Esther R. D.)
Esther R. D. rolf Mott Ave. M. E. Ch., N. Y. 11-1923; name erased 11-1928 (prob sister of Anná E.)

KENNY
Daniel (nm) d 10-19-1851 ae 51y (or 11-14-1850) bPP; rocf Balt. 9-1843 (H)
David (nm) & -----
Ch: Sarah W. b N. Y. d 12-17-1848 ae 8y bHS
Eleanor, w Daniel, b Pa. d 12-17-1843 ae 80y (H)
Ch: Eleanor Ann
cf Balt. 8-1828 for both; ct Balt. 1-1829 for mother (prob mbr Balt.)
Eleanor Ann, dt Daniel & Eleanor, N. Y.; m 1829 William RICHARDS, of Phila. (H)
cf Balt. 8-1828 with mother; ct Phila. 1-1829
Ellen Maxwell, dt Jas. T. & Jane; m O. B. MATTHEWS (H)
James F., s Daniel & Eleanor, d 9-30-1862 ae 57y 2m 8d bPP; m Jane A. ----- d 6-1-1853 ae 45y 3m 9d bPP (H)
Ch: Ellen Maxwell b 4-15-1833
Sarah Glover " 7-10-1834 d 6-22-1911 bPP
Isabella C. " 5-27-1839 " 11-24-1846
Maxwell " 6-10-1840
Infant stillborn

KENNY, James F. & Jane A., continued
cf Balt. 11-1827; ct Phila. ND 4-7-1830 (clear); cf ND MM 2-1834; ct R. & P. 12-1840; cf R. & P. 3-1844; Jane recrq 4-1838
James F. m 2d at Rufus Clarke's 9-12-1855 Sarah R. CLARKE, dt Rufus & Sarah G., N. Y., d 9-3-1882 ae 62y bPP (H)
Ch: Ellen Richard (adopted dt)
cf R. & P. 1844 d 1-6-1855
Maxwell [Kenney] rocf Balt. W. Dist. 11-10-1826; ct Balt. 2-3-1830 (clear)
Maxwell rocf Balt. 1-1827; ct Phila. 9-1831 (H)
Maxwell, s James F. & Jane, b 6-10-1840; dis 8-5-1863 (H)
Sarah Ann, w David, dt Matthias & Sarah WALL, d 6-9-1844 (H)
Sarah G., dt James F. & Jane A., b 7-10-1834; relrq 7-3-1872 (H)

KENT
Alice M., dt Benj. Lundy & Sarah (Cutken), b Goshen, Pa. 4-1-1867; m David C. REID (nm) (m 1888) (H)
cf Wilmington 8-10-1901; ct Wilmington 3-7-1903
Mary (nm) b Corn. d 3-21-1836 ae 39y 1m bHS

KENWAY
Gawen Pearse rocf Warwickshire North 4-6-1892; name erased 3-1928; in Chicago 1912
Sophia, w Peter, rocf Tottenham, Eng. 3-1869; ct Tottenham 7-1871

KENWORTHY
Arthur William, s James K. & Elizabeth (Atlie), d 2-17-1931 ae 69y bPP; m Anna Louise COHU

KENYON
James dis mo 10-6-1813
William, s David, of Liverpool, N. Y.; m between 4-1- and 5-7-1778 (cert not recorded) Abigail BOWNE, dt Samuel, N. Y., b N.Y. d 8-31-1822 ae 68y
Ch: Samuel b 3- 6-1780 d 9- 6-1803 bHS
William b 8- 7-1784
James " 8-20-1791
cf Hardshaw 2-3-1774; William rocf Hardshaw MM, Lancashire 9-9-1777 (rem cert); rem some time since

KERR
Elizabeth Anna Ethel m 1907 Russell B. HOBSON
cf Waterford, Ireland 9-6-1905
Jane (nm) b Eng. d 10-31-1823 ae 66y bHS (wd)
Jane rocf Darlington, Eng. 8-7-1901; ct Lewiston, Me. 4-6-1904; cf Lewiston, Me. 12-6-1905; d 6-12-1909
Rebecca (nm), dt William & Cornelia; m 1877 Richard L. HUNT (H)
Richard relrq 1921

KERWEIN
Edith Anne, dt John R. & Henrietta (Dawson), b Montreal 11-3-1901; recrq 11-10-1924 (H)

KETCHAM
David, s David (dec) & Sarah, N. Y.; m at Alexander N. Weeks' 10-21-1850 Phebe Jane WEEKS, dt Rich. (dec) & Semantha, Bkn., b Milton, N. Y. 11-21-1828 d 1-12-1908 (H)
Phebe rocf Oswego 1-1844 with mother; Phebe Jane in Toledo 1901
Hannah, dt Joseph & Sarah P., rocf Corn. 12-1833 (clear); d 11-11-1886 ae 84y 11m 17d bPP (H)
James recrq 3-6-1816; dis 7-1829 (O); d 8-22-1854 ae 70y 11m 13d bPP (H)
Mary, dt David, d 8-21-1824
Phebe, dt Thomas & Mary, b 8-22-1826; ct Pur. 3-5-1835 with sister, Sarah Ann, minors
Phebe P. (or A.) rocf N. P. 12-1862
Samuel (nm) [Ketchum] & -----
Ch: Mary Ann b N. Y. d 2-20-1830 ae 1y 20d bHS
James Sand (prob) b N. Y. d 2-6-1837 ae 8m 15d bHS
Sarah Ann, dt Thomas & Mary, rocf Pur. with parents 6-9-1824; ct Pur. with sister, Phebe, 3-5-1835, minors
Thomas & Mary
Ch: Sarah Ann
Phebe S. b 8-22-1826
Dorcas S. b 3-19-1831
cf Pur. 6-9-1824 with 1 ch Sarah Ann; ct Pur. 3-5-1834 for Sarah Ann & Phebe, minors; parents dis 1830 (O); Sarah & Phebe gct Pur. 3-1834 (O); ct Pur. 12-1833 for all (H)
----- & ----- (prob Thomas)
Ch: Mary d 8-21-1824 ae 10d

KICHERER
John C. & Alice
both recrq 10-1923

KIDD
Samuel, having mo Longford MM, Eng. rq N. Y. to deal with him 10-2-1822, rpd 2-5-1823 unable to find him

KIKER
Elizabeth rocf Shrewsbury 9-2-1793 (clear)

KILPATRICK
Sarah (nm), wd, b N. J. d 9-23-1830 ae 35y bHS

KIMBALL
Florence Chevy (nm), dt Francis W. & Florence M.; m 1912 Percival C. SMITH (H)
Wm. Lockwood (nm), s Wm. C. & Blanche L. (Read) d 4-14-1926 ae 49y 8m 13d bPP; m at Bkn. 3-25-1903 Martha P. ROBERTS, dt John H. & Sarah B. Williams, Flatbush, b Camden 3-6-1878 (H)
Martha m 2d 9-18-1931 Albert T. MILLS
ct R. & P. 9-10-1917 for Martha; cf Newark 8-13-1928

KIMBER, continued
Anna, dt Joshua & Rachel, relrq 6-1862 (or 1-6-1876)
Amie M. (or H.), dt Geo. D. & Harriet Ann, b 3-22-1850 (or 10-6-1851); m ----- SPENCER name erased 2-7-1900
George D., s Joshua & Rachel, Flushing, b 3-27-1824; m Harriet Ann -----
Ch: Amie M. b 3-22-1850
Anna M. " 10- 6-1851
William
Louisa
George D. relrq 1-1869; Harriet rocf Pur. 6-13-1849
Joshua m Rachel ----- d 2-16-1865
Ch: Anna
Joshua Jr.
William G. b 1-30-1826 d 3- 8-1827
Sarah
Lydia G. b 1- 3-1828
George D. b 3-27-1824
Louisa, dt Geo. D. & Harriet A.; m ----- WOOD name erased 5-1886
Phebe M. m Samuel H. CLAPP
Sarah, dt Joshua & Rachel, Flushing; m 1851 Thos. Ellwood ROBERTS, of Phila.
Thomas d 12-23-1790; m Mary S. SHERMAN, dt Davids & Hepsa H., b 7-25-1838 d 3-14-1921 bPP
His rq ref. to Rep. Com. as follows: Now residing Burl., relrq from a MM in Phila., rq here; well known & believed convinced, Rep. Com. decision favorable, he rec 1-1877; ack. a minister 10-1878; Mary recrq 1-1877

KIMBERLY
Esther (form Delaplaine) (late Irish) mo before 11-2-1803, "& does not appear to have any knowledge of her first h's dec."; dis 1-4-1804; mo before 4-2-1800; dis 5-7-1800; rst 5-6-1801

KING
Ann rocf Nantucket ---27-1792 to settle with her s; informed from Dartmouth that she lived some time in Nova Scotia (prob. mother of John & Reay)
Ann rocf Westminster, London 5-16-1793 (clear); ct Newcastle on Tyne 7-3-1811 (clear) returned to her native land; cf Fishing Creek, Pa. (Muncy MM) 5-18-1814, not recorded but endorsed to N. P. 9-7-1814 (clear); sometimes called "Jr."
Ann gct Ferrisburgh 6-5-1822 (clear)
Ann, dt John & Mary R., N. Y.; m 1843 Samuel Horton COLTON
rocf N. P. 2-17-1820 (clear)
Caroline, dt John & Mary R., N. Y.; m 1824 Thomas W. JENKINS
Catharine M., dt John & Mary R., N. Y.; m 1834 Stephen WOOD
Christine Lois recrq 12-2-1892
Eleanor, N. Y.; m 1796 William R. THURSTON
cf Nantucket 4-30-1792
Ellen, dt John & Mary R., N. Y.; m 1846 Benjamin BUFFUM, of Worcester
Elias & Catharine
Ch: Rachel b 3- 3-1791
Phebe " 2-11-1793
David Sands b 10-11-1796
Eliza " 4- 5-1798
Harriet " 11-22-1800
Mary " 6-17-1803
Eliza gct Concord, Ohio 12-2-1812 (clear)
(Jane King same date & destination)
Elizabeth, dt John & Mary R., N. Y.; m 1840 Henry WOOD
Hannah, dt John & Mary R., N. Y.; m 1821 William T. (or S.) MERRITT
Harmans gct Chesterfield, N. J. 5 Mo (July) 7, 1699 (rem cert)
Irving & Alta Florence
Ch: Philip Burk
Robert E. b 9-20-1906
Edward Joshua b 6- 4-1916
cf Chicago 11-2-1904 for parents & Philip
In Iowa City, Iowa 1912; letter to Presbyterian Ch., Iowa City, 6-4-1924 for all
James, Jr. rocf Little Britain, Pa. 4-11-1812; ct Little Britain 7-7-1813 (clear)
Jane rocf Ratcliff MM, London 4-25-1793 (clear)
Jane gct Concord, Ohio (clear) 12-2-1812
Eliza King same date & destination)
Jane rocf Richhill, Ireland 12-24-1835 (clear)
John (prob s of Ann) rocf Nantucket 4-30-1792, with Reay (both clear); had brought cf Halifax; d 8-16-1800 bHS
John, s John & Dorothy (both dec), of Satterforth, Yorkshire; m N. Y. 2-13-1799 Sarah RUSHTON, dt Benj. & Sarah (both dec), of Bradford, Yorkshire, d 3-17-1806 ae 43y
Ch: Joseph b 12-29-1801
Sarah " 6-27-1804
John " 7-29-1803 d 8- 9-1803 (or 8-10-1803)
John, s Joseph & Ann, of New Castle, Eng., d 12-29-1835 ae 68y bHS; m N. Y. 5-13-1801 Mary R. BOWNE, dt James & Caroline, Flushing, d 4-6-1834 ae 57y 6m 25d bHS (or 4-4-1834 in 294 only)
Ch: Hannah b 4-13-1802
John Bowne " 7-29-1803
Caroline m T. W. JENKINS
Mary b 11-30-1805; m N. S. MERRITT
Samuel rem to Balt. 1826
Elizabeth m H. WOOD
Catharine M. m S. WOOD
Ann m S. I. H. COLTON
Walter d in Bloomingdale
Eleanor b 6- 3-1822; m B. BUFFUM
rem cert (clear) from Brighouse MM, Yorkshire 7-20-1798; rem with w & 6 ch to Concord, Ohio 1-6-1813, returned with w & 8 ch 6-23-1819 (not including last two); parents dis 1829 (H)
John & Mary

KING, John & Mary, continued
Ch: Samuel
Elizabeth
ch recrq of parents 5-6-1812
John Bowne, s John & Mary, b 7-29-1803; ct R. & P. 9-5-1823, apprentice; cf R. & P. 3-19-1828; ct Nantucket 6-2-1841 (clear)
Joseph, s Joseph & Ann (dec), Newcastle on Tyne; m Flushing 1-11-1798 Mary DOUGHTY, dt Charles & Sarah, Flushing
Ch: Charles b 10-14-1798
Caroline b 12- 2-1803 (recorded as dt of John & Mary)
cf Newcastle MM, Eng. 10-10-1796 (clear), a mariner
Joseph gct Hudson 2-5-1817
Joseph, Jr. gct Balt. W. Dist. 9-6-1815 (clear)
Joseph B. d 10-19-1905; m Katharine J. ----- (apparently w of Joseph)
cf Greenwich, R. I. 12-6-1899; Katharine recrq 11-1-1899
Joseph H. (prob. s John & Sarah, b 12-29-1801) mo before 7-1839; expected to attend mtg when not accompanying his w; dis 10-2-1839
Laura (nm) m Henry H. CARPENTER (H)
Mary Ann, dt John & Mary R., N. Y.; m 1825 Nathaniel S. MERRITT
Mary Ann, dt Joseph & Mary, Flushing; m 1832 Lindley MURRAY
Reay m Phila. 1794 Anna -----
Ch: William Nelson
Eleanor
Abigail
Joseph
Mary
cf Nantucket 4-30-1792 with John (both clear), had brought cert from Halifax; took cert of clear to Phila. 12-3-1794; Anna brought cert from Phila. 4-24-1795; they took ct Phila. 3-2-1796 with a s (Reay prob s of Ann); cf Burl. 8-6-1810 for Anna with ch, Wm. Nelson, Eleanor, Abigail, Joseph & Mary; ct Burl. 7-1-1812 with same ch, rem with h
Samuel d 10-28-1845; m before 12-1830 Eliza GARDNER d 2-16-1879 ae 81y 4m 23d bPP, rem to Cypress Hills 4-3-1888 (mo)
Ch: John d 12-13-1834 ae 4m 1d bHS
John d 2- 1-1836 ae 2m 14d bHS
cf Grange MM, Ire. 4-18-1827 (clear); ret a mbr 5-1831
Samuel, s John & Mary, gct Balt. 12-6-1826, minor; cf Balt. 11-4-1830, minor; d at Frankford Asylum 1854
Stephen (nm) & -----
Ch: Fanny d 8-17-1803 ae 1y bHS
Wm. Sutcliff rocf Brighouse, Eng. 5-14-1802, a youth; ct Easton 5-1-1805 for John B. Howell & w & their apprentice, William S. King

KINGSLAND
Daniel (nm) & -----
Ch: Mary Jane b West. Co. d 3-18-1831 ae 8y 6m bHS
Mary J. (or I. dt Wm. H. & Eliza L. MACY (w Wm. M.) (m 9-16-1847)
relrq 1863 (H)
----- & ----- (nm)
Ch: Henry d 8-13-1829 bHS

KINGSLEY
Isabella (nm), wd, b Scotland d 12-14-1814 ae 77y bHS
Zephania (nm) b Scotland d 9-13-1843 ae 76y bHS (m)

KINKEAD
Dorothy, dt Wm. L. & Amy T. (Scantlebury), b Paterson, N. J. 10-31-1902; m 1925 Wm. Stratton HADAWAY (H)
Wm. Lloyd (nm), s Maxwell & Cath. J., Altoona, Pa.; m at E. Scantlebury's 6-13-1899 Amy T. SCANTLEBURY, dt Edward & Mary Anna, Bkn. b 9-1-1872 Bkn. (H)
Ch: Dorothy b Paterson, N. J. 10-31-1902
Edward Maxwell d 11-25-1904 ae 1d bPP

KINNY
David m Sarah Ann ----- b N. Y. d 6-9-1844 ae 32y bHS
Ch: Helen Eliza b N. Y. d 9-6-1844 ae 1y 29d bHS
mbr prob. elsewhere
James F. [Kinney] & -----
Ch: Arabella C. b N. J. d 11-23-1846 ae 7y bHS
mbr prob in N. J.

KINSEY
Mootry rocf R. & P. 7-16-1795, minor

KIPP
Amy, w Thomas, rccf Chap. 6-14-1816; dis 4-1830 (O); ct Chap. 4-6-1859 (H)
Eden (nm) & -----
Ch: Emma J. b N. Y. d 6-22-1830 ae 1h bHS
Ethel (nm), dt Wm. De Graw & Eliza. (Nangle) (nm); m 6-27-1906 Clarence A. CLOUGH (H)
Griffanna, w Caleb, rocf Chap. 4-12-1816; ct Chap. 12-3-1817
Isaac (nm), s Thomas (nm), b St. John's, New Brunswick d 3-4-1847 ae 61y 10m 5d bHS (widower)
Jane Sleight (form Kipp) rocf Creek 10-21-1831; dis mo 8-1834 (H)
Josiah F. (nm) m Rachel I. ----- (nm) d 5-14-1864 ae 57y 4m 3d bHS, rem to PP
Mary M. rocf Creek 10-21-1831 (clear); ct Oswego 8-5-1840 (H)
Mary M., dt Abraham, d 5-6-1885 ae 74y 23d bPP; m Daniel VAN CLIEF (H) (both nm)
Phebe gct Chap. 1-5-1811
Phebe H. rocf Creek 10-21-1831; ct Oswego 10-1838
Samuel d 12-21-1804 ae 39y bHS (nm)

KIPP, continued
Thomas d 2-22-1799 bHS
Thomas (nm) b Mount Pleasant, N. Y. d 9-1-1823 ae 68y 1m bHS; m Abigail ----- b West. Co. d 3-17-1839 ae 81y 4m 7d bHS
Ch: Isaac (prob)
----- & ----- (nm)
Ch: Emma Jane b N. Y. d 3-3-1835 ae 2y 5m bHS

KIRBY
Beulah E., dt Edmond & Sarah, Harrison; m 1838 Valentine EVERITT (H)
cf Pur. 12-1837
Edmund, s Willet & Hannah (dec), Jericho, N. Y., m Flushing 10-13-1803 Sarah LOINES, dt Wm. (dec) & Sarah, N. Y., d 6-16- (or 8-17-) 1816 ae 36 yr bHS
Ch: William b 8-11-1804
Edmund " 8- 7-1806
Gilbert R. b 12-31-1807 d bPP
Sarah Ann " 4-26-1810
Beulahelma Twining b 8-15-1812
Willet T. b 8-29-1814
Jacob d 8-19-1816 ae 4m
Edmund rocf Wby 10-26-1785; cf Hudson 2-24-1801 for Sarah (clear)
Edmund m 2d N. Y. 3-9-1820 Maria ROBINS, dt John & Deborah WHIPPO, N. Y.
Ch: Deborah b 12-29-1820
Henry
Rem to Pur. 10-1-1823 with ch Edward, Gilbert R., Sarah Ann, Beulah, Elmy T., Willet T., Deborah & Henry
Edmund b L. I. d 8-7-1842 ae 74y bHS (m)
Edmund d 6-23-1851; m Mary WILLETS, dt Obadiah & Elizabeth (H)
Mary m 2d John GIBBS 1857; cf Flushing 10-1839
Edward rocf Pur. 3-1865; d 7-17-1878 (H)
Joseph Mason, s Jas. Jackson & Sarah Ann, d 3-28-1916 ae 79y 2m 1d bPP; m Anna E. ----- (both nm) (H)
Maria rocf Pur. 4-1856; d 10-16-1866 (H)
Mary, dt Obadiah & Eliz. WILLETS; m 4-20-1857 John GIBBS (wd Edmund Kirby) (H)
Perry (nm) b Westport, Mass. d 5-27-1824 ae 22y bHS (m)
Sarah Ann m Henry EVERITT (H)
Willett T. d 4-19-1849; m ----- (H)
Ch: Infant stillborn 10-31-1847
cf Pur. 5-1839 for Willet
William S. dis 2-1835 (H)

KIRCHOFF
Regina Henrietta (nm) m 1886 Alfred WALTER (H)

KIRK
Henry Ecroyd, s Henry E. & Gertrude P., Pennsdale, Pa.; m N. Y. 4-26-1924 Enid Mary RICHARDSON, dt Henry & Henrietta M., Parsaic N. J.
Enid rocf Warwickshire North with parents 3-1-1905; Enid gct Muncie, Pa. 1-1926

John gct Phila. 9-6-1781 (clear) as John Jr.; cf Wby 8-25-1773 (clear)

KIRKPATRICK
Daniel, Flushing, m Dorcas ERWINE (dmi 2 Mo (Apr) 6, 1693)
Daniel m 2d at his house 2 Mo (Apr) 25, 1696 Dinah YEATS (Yates)
Ch: Sarah b 9 Mo (Nov) 19, 1697
Daniel b 7 Mo (Sep) 26, 1699
Anna " 12 Mo (Feb) 9, 1703/4
Samuel b 12 Mo (Feb) 9, 1703/4
Daniel active mbr from 1701 or later

KIRWAN
John J. (nm) m 7-9-1921 Marie FURNAS, dt John D. & Ella (Clifton), b 7-1-1894 (H)
cf Miami, O. 10-10-1908 for Mary Louise (Marie changed from Mary Louise)

KISSAM
Jane m John HAUXHURST (H)
cf Alexandria 6-1-1887 for Jane & 2 ch
Natilie W., dt Albert W. & Margaret C. (Woolley), b N. Y. 3-29-1892; m 1918 Wm. Henry SCHOFIELD, Jr. (nm) (H)
recrq 7-9-1917
Albert W. (nm), s Benj. & Sarah S.; m 6-17-1891 Margaret WOOLLEY, dt Wardell & Mary V., b 8-16-1859 (H)
Ch: Natilie Wardell b 7-9-1917

KITCHIN
J. Brinton, s Samuel C. & Martha T., d 5-18-1911 ae 48y 4m 21d bPP; m Mina GILCHRIST, dt William & Mary, d 4-1-1916 ae 46y 5m 15d bPP (H) (both nm)
Jennie C., dt Sam'l Carey & Martha T. (Wilson), b Solebury, Pa. 8-14-1862 d 6-19-1928 (H)
recrq 3-7-1894

KITCHING
Pennington rocf York, Eng. 11-1866; dis 1-1870

KITE
Abbie rocf WD MM 1-1880; ct ----- 2-5-1919 (perhaps resignation instead of cert)

KLAMT
Henrietta E., dt Wm. L. & Ann C. TITUS (w Henry E., nm) b Cornwell 1851 d 7-12-1919 (m 1883)
cf Corn. 11-1853 with parents (H)
(Henry E. b 1848 in Germany)

KLOPP
Elizabeth F. m ----- COOK (nm)
Harvey Leeson, ch by her form m to Klopp d rpd 3-1924; recrq 3-6-1918; name erased 2-1926; Harvey recrq of mother 3-6-1918

KNAPP
Elsie, dt Shepherd & Emma (Benedict), b N. Y. 9-12-1879; m 1902 Wilson M. POWELL (H)

KNAPP, Elsie, continued
recrq 12-14-1925 (Elsie a nm)
Fannie M. (nm) d 7-12-1909; m 1856 Thomas Fair McDOWELL (H)
Gertrude, dt Milton & Paula (Von K.); m 1926 Philip Nichols RAWSON (H)

KNIFFEN
Algernon Sidney (nm), s Edgar & Sarah Ann; m 4-10-1890 Ella RIDER, dt John & Mary W. (Hazard), b 10-10-1859 d 6-18-1914 (H)
Ch: Hazel Hazard b 8-29-1895
cf Corn. 12-1-1880 for Ella; Hazel's name entered by com. 2-4-1896
Emelane C., dt A. Sidney & Eliz. C., Bkn.; m 1879 Josiah C. RYDER (H)

KNIGHT
Dorothy, dt Harry P. & Charity Ellen, b 3-1-1918; m ----- MATTHES (nm)
E. C. bur in grave with Elizabeth L. Antrim who d 1855 bPP (H)
Emmor m Mary W. WILDE, dt John & Eleanor
cf ND MM 11-24-1835; Emor dis 7-1840; Mary W. gct Wilmington 8-1845
Eva Helen, M.D., dt Geo. Henry & Annie K., b Cincin. 11-18-1864 d 1-17-1921 bPP (unm) (nm)
George Henry, s George & Sarah, b London, Eng. 6-26-1819 d 2-25-1903 ashes bPP; m Anna K. ----- d 5-28-1919 ae 89y bPP "Beloved Minister"
Ch: Mary E.
George Henry Jr.
cf Cincinnati 3-1899 for mother & ch; ct Salem, O. 10-4-1893 for same; cf Salem same 3-2-1898; cf Salem 10-1-1902 for George
George Henry, Jr., s Annie K., rocf Cincinnati with mother 3-1889; ct Salem, O. with mother 10-4-1893; cf Salem, Ohio 10-1-1902; relrq 2-7-1906
Harry K., s Harry S. & Charity Ellen, b about 1900 (or 1903); recrq of parents 4-1-1903; letter to Central Cong. Ch., Bkn. 4-1-1931
Harry Palmer & Charity Ellen
Ch: Harriet Elizabeth 4
George Palmer 3
Harry K. b 6-24-1903
Dorothy
parents recrq 4-1-1903; Harriet & George recrq of parents as associated 4-1-1903; parents, having jas, name erased 3-1928
Henry (nm) d 3-16-1855 ae 34y bPP; m -----
Ch: (prob)
Ezekiel Hunn d 10-27-1836 ae 3m
Cooper D. " 8-11-1852 ae 3y 10m
Edna
(all nm)
Joshua & Sarah
Ch: Priscilla
Jacob
Sarah rocf Abington 4-30-1781 with 2 ch; Priscilla rem from Abington, Pa. 4-30-1781 (clear); Jacob quite young
Mary Esther, dt Geo. Henry & Anne, N. Y.; m 1898 Preston Hamilton BREED
cf Cincinnati 3-1889; ct Salem, Mass. 10-4-1893
Mary W. rocf Wilmington 8-6-1845
Stephen & -----
Ch: Infant d 9-27-1836 ae 3m bHS
having mo before 1-1836, Phila. WD refers to N. Y.; rpd adversely 4-6-1836

KNOWLES
Abigail Cannon (form Knowles) dis mo 1805
cf New Bedford 12-21-1802
Charles S. d 1-20-1916; m Catharine D. JENKINS (H)
Ch: Eunice E. b Germantown, N. Y. 9-1-1873
Charles transferred from Albany 1-8-1916; Eunice transferred from Albany 1-8-1916
Mary Wilson (form Knowles) dis mo 3-7-1804
Sarah D. Smith (form Knowles) rocf Oblong 7-17-1815, had rem when a minor; dis mo 3-6-1816
Susan DeVoe (written Debooe) (form Knowles) rpd mo before 1-4-1804
Tabitha, dt Lot & Susanna TRIPP, b R. I. 4-1756 d 4-12-1809 ae 53y 8m 11d bHS
Dr. William (nm) b Conn. d 1-31-1815 ae 56y bHS

KNOWLTON
Cynthia A., dt Robt. & Sarah A. M. (Sutton), b Mt. Kisco 10-9-1863 d 10-5-1926 (H)
recrq 5-7-1884
Elizabeth, dt Robt. & Sarah A. M. (Sutton), b Mt. Kisco 3-8-1866; m Norie KOMORI (H)
Ch: Phyllis b Brockley, London 8-23-1898
recrq 5-7-1884; Phyllis recrq of mother 12-14-1912
----- m Maria Amelia BOWRON, dt Dr. John S. & Sarah, b 2-23-1829 d 3-21-1900 bPP (H)
Maria m 1st William TOLFREY (or Tolfree) (nm); Maria dis 5-6-1868 for non-attendance

KNOX
George recrq 5-1881; d 6-28-1906
Sarah rocf Green St., Phila. 5-20-1824; ct Phila. 5-6-1829

KOBBE
E. Dorothea (nm) m 1907 Thomas GARRETT (H)

KOESTING
Charles C. (nm), s Chas. C. (dec) & Elizabeth, Bkn.; m Bkn. 11-9-1927 Helen C. BUCKWELL, dt Jas. F. & Carrie E., Bkn. b Bkn. 6-8-1903 (H)
Helen recrq 4-12-1926

KOMORI
Elizabeth, w Norie, dt Robt. & Sarah KNOWLTON, b Mt. Kisco 3-8-1866; recrq 5-7-1884 (H)

KOMORI, continued
Phyllis, dt Norie & Elizabeth (Knowlton), b Brockley, London 8-23-1898; m 1927 Maurice A. SELLERS (nm) (H)
recrq of mother 12-14-1912

KRECKER
R. Hoffman recrq 2-5-1930

KROLL
Margaretha Magdalena (nm), dt Carl & Margaretha m 1878 Gilbert Lee MAC MASTER (H)

KRUGER
Helena (nm), w Capt. John UNDERHILL
Theodore H. [Krueger], s Karl & Sophia, b Ponce, Neb. 5-7-1889; m Cecelie MOORE, dt Howard B. & Mathilde, b Bkn. 10-7-1889
Ch: Alfred P. b Hooper, Neb. 3-18-1891
Karl A. b Atchison, Kans. 1-19-1894
both recrq 5-4-1917; ch recrq of parents 7-4-1917

KUBLER
William H., s Herman & Louise (Rach), b Hoboken 5-2-1903; recrq 12-8-1924 (H)

KUGELMANN
Wilhelmine, dt Wilhelm & Eliz. (Lankhant) b Frankfort-on-Main 4-17-1896 (H); recrq 2-10-1928; relrq 1-11-1932 (H)

KUHN
Brenda, dt Walt & Vera (Spier), b N. Y. 6-13-1911; recrq 8-12-1935 (H)

KUIRKJIAN
Sarkis T. rocf Constantinople, Turkey 11-1884; transferred under name of Basmajian

KUNZ
Christine Lois recrq 11-2-1892
Edith T., dt Jacob & Caroline (Weiss), b Erie, Pa.; recrq 11-14-1932 (H)

LACEY
Florence Ruth (nm), dt Leroy & Mary; m 1907 Frederick Aldrich RIDER (H)

LADD
Benjamin W., s Wm. H. & Caroline E., rocf Smithfield, Ohio 5-1867 with parents; name erased 11-6-1907, having jas
Ellen C., dt Wm. H. & Caroline, Bkn.; m 1872 William CONKLIN
cf Smithfield, O. 5-1867 with parents
Isaac G., s Thomas W. & Hannah P., rocf Cincinnati with parents 1-19-1865; ct Providence 2-1883
Mariana C. (or L.), dt Wm. H. & Caroline E.; m ----- EDWARDS
cf Smithfield, Ohio 5-1867 with parents; ct WD MM 11-4-1891
Marian H. (nm) m John White HOLLOWELL (H)
Thomas W. d 12-12-1882; m Hannah P. -----
Ch: Walter J.
Isaac G.
cf Cincinnati 1-19-1865 with ch; Hannah gct Providence 3-2-1892; Walter J. gct Providence 11-6-1907
Walter J. (mbr of Orth. Branch), s Thomas W. & Hannah P.; m 12-5-1883 Kate E. MACY (mbr Hicksite Branch), dt Josiah Jr. & Caroline Louisa, b 4-6-1863
cf Cincinnati 1-19-1865 with parents; ct Providence 11-6-1907 (O); Kate relrq 12-5-1883 (H)
William C., s Wm. H. & Caroline, rocf Smithfield, Ohio with parents 5-1867; ct WD MM 2-3-1897
William H. d 5-31-1890; m Caroline ----
Ch: Ellen C.
Benjamin W.
Mariana C.
Charles F. C. d 11-22-1883
William C.
cf Smithfield, O. 5-1867 for all; ct WD MM 3-4-1891 for Caroline

LAFETRA
Amy d 1833; rocf Shrewsbury 3-3-1800 (clear); ct Phila. 9-11-1816 (clear); cf Phila. 1-28-1823; dis 1829 (O)
James, s Samuel & Elizabeth, b 3-19-1808 d 12-25-1883; m 5-29-1831 Sarah L. WOLCOTT, dt Joseph & Mary (Lewis), b Eatontown, N. J. 8-20-1813 d 8-12-1901 bPP (H)
Ch: Joseph W. b 11- 6-1833
Nathan A. b 7-10-1836 d 3-29-1863
Sarah " 6- 5-1839
James " 10-26-1842 d 7-22-1907 bPP
George F. b 11-18-1846 d 8-18-1865
cf Shrews. 5-1839 for both
Joseph W., s James & Sarah L. (Wolcott), b 11-6-1933; m ----- (H)
Ch: Infant stillborn 6-14-1868 bPP
Sarah, dt James & Sarah; m ----- HOLMAN (nm)(H)
Ch: Nathan d 8-27-1860 ae 3y
Tylee (nm) & -----
Ch: David b N. Y. d 1-20-1837 ae 13y 1m 6d bHS
----- & ----- (nm)
Ch: Mary b Shrewsbury d 8-12-1822 ae 1y 1m 4d bHS
Elizabeth b N. J. d 4-6-1834 ae 15y bHS

LAGERBLOM
Joseph N. recrq 5-3-1893; name changed to Milton 3-10-1899 by order of Kings Co. Court, Bkn.

LAGUES
----- (nm) m Wilhelmina LISTER
cf MM in Colo. as Lister 10-1918; name erased 12-1922

LAING
Aaron G. d 8-11-1874; m Margaret B. HAND, dt Silvanus & Sarah (H)
cf R. & P. 11-5-1873 for both; Margaret m 2d John DIETRICH 1876
Alec Edgar, s William & Martha (dec), Phila.; m N. Y. 7-12-1838 Ann Eliza UNDERHILL, dt Adonijah & Deborah S., N. Y., d 12-21-1880 ae 69y bPP (H)
Alfred D., s Hugh & Catharine, rocf R. & P. 3-1820; dis attending Episcopal Church 8-1833 (H)
Alva Edgar m Ann Eliza UNDERHILL, d 12-21-1880 (H)
Ch: Howard E. b Phila. 4-7-1845
William lost at sea, Pacific Ocean 5-1866
Helen
cf R. & P. 3-1865 for all; ct R. & P. 6-6-1883 for Alva E.
Daniel (nm) & -----
Ch: Albert d 1-11-1846 ae 2d bHS
Helen L., dt Alva E. & Ann Eliza, d 4-2-1899 ae 84y; m Frank E. GREEN (nm) (H)
Howard E., s Alva Edgar & Ann Eliza (Underhill), b Phila. 4-7-1845 d 3-1911; m Sarah A. ----- (H)
Hugh & Catharine
Ch: Albert D. dis 1833
Benjamin Davids b 9-22-1824
cf R. & P. 2-23-1820; Hugh dis 1825; Catharine dis 1826.
Joseph rocf Kingwood 1-10-1788, apprentice to William Webster on L. I.; ct Hardwick 5-5-1791 (clear)
Margaret B., dt Silvanus & Sarah HAND, Morris Co., N. J., wd Aaron G. Laing; m 1876 John DIETRICH, of Belvedere, N. J. (H)
ct R. & P. 8-1-1877
----- m Louise PEELE, dt Caleb & Maria W., b Macedon, N. J.
cf Farm. 11-1888 for Louise with parents

LA LOSETTE
Paul (nm) & -----
Ch: Infant stillborn 12-11-1826 bHS

LAMAR
Leila (nm) m 1901 Robert C. GRIFFEN (H)

LAMB
Alvah Newby, s Wm. H. & Mary A., Belverdere, N. C.; m N. Y. 12-22-1915 Anna Alice TALBOTT, dt Wm. M. & Mary E. (both dec) Mt. Pleasant, O.
cf Piney Woods, N. C. 6-4-1913; cf Damascus, O. 1-1915 for Anna

LAMBERT
Samuel W., s Edward W. & Martha W.; m at 15th St. 10-21-1893 Elizabeth WILLETS, dt John T. & Amelia, N. Y. (H)
----- & -----
Ch: Emeline b N. Y. d 4-4-1826 ae 5y bHS

LA MONT
Louis R. m Elizabeth COOK, dt Lewis P. & Laura J. (Turner), b Bay of Biscay 8-16-1864
Elizabeth m 2d George W. LILLEY; Elizabeth m 3d Nelson P. WEBSTER 8-1-1921 (H)
ct Alexandria for her 5-14-1923

LAMSON
Martha V. B. (nm) d 3-28-1870 ae 49y bPP

LAN
Yung recrq 3-6-1867 (chinese)

LANCASTER
Aaron, Wby, rocf Abington 9-5-1765 but forwarded with endorsement to Wby, he living there
Elizabeth, dt Phebe WAY, gct Richland, Pa. 10-2-1765
Joseph b London d 10-24-1838 ae 62y bHS, rem to Greenwood
school teacher, over 5 pages in Smith's Catalogue, of items, books, etc. by and about the Lancasterian system of instruction; run over by horse and wagon; had been dis in London

LANCROFT
Mabel, dt Henry S. & Cornelia (Luttle), b Fair Haven, Conn. 5-20-1888; m Malcolm R. THORP both recrq 6-6-1917

LANE
David H. rocf Pur. 9-1844; ct Chesterfield 9-2-1874 (H)
Ebenezer, s Gilbert, rocf Oblong 5-16-1814 (clear); dis mo 9-6-1815, rst 8-6-1817; dis 5-5-1819, then at Charleston, S. C.
Esther, Hempsted Harbor; m 1716 Joshua DELAPLAINE
Gilbert & Susan A. (H)
cf Pur. 8-1840; ct Pur. 8-1843
Maltby G. rocf Oblong 2-13-1832 (H); cf Oblong 3-17-1834 (O), was minor when living there; dis 9-1839 (O); dis 2-1838 (H)
Park H., s Gilbert, rocf Oblong 10-14-1816, minor, placed; ct Oblong 8-2-1820
Susan U., w W. J., dt Alex. & Phebe A. UNDERHILL, b 5-15-1843 (m 1871)
ct N. P. 5-1872
Webster, s Peter & Deborah, Chap.; m at Chas. L. Rathborn's 1-15-1878 Sarah Jane HAGAN, dt Joseph & Sarah E. (dec), N. Y. (H)
ct Chap. 10-2-1878 for Sarah Jane
Wm. J., s Wm. & Mary, Washington, Dutchess Co.; m at Alex. Underhill's 10-5-1871 Susan UNDERHILL, dt Alex. & Phebe A. (dec) Bkn.
Susan gct N. P. 5-1872

LANG
Mary (late Lawrence) dis mo 3-3-1784

LANGDON
Abigail Clark (form Langdon) dis mo 9-5-1810

LANGDON, continued
John rocf Wby 3-19-1794; dis 3-6-1799; d 8-21-1801 bHS
John recrq 5-1835; ct Nantucket 9-1841; cf Nantucket 11-1845; d 11-26-1848 (H)
Martha con mo 10-5-1768
Martha gct N. P. 7-5-1781, she having rem several years ago, & then young; cf Corn. 2-20-1797; ct Bridgewater 1-1-1823; cert returned 2-1-1824
"Rachel Langdon resides Bridgewater, supposed to be Martha Langdon"
Mercy m 1696 Hope WILLITS
Rachel supposed to be a mbr, resides at Bridgewater

LANGE
Kate (nm), dt Edward & Susan; m 1900 Frank A. RAY (H)

LANGLEY
George, Flushing, d 10 Mo (Dec) 26, 1703; active mbr from 1696

LANSING
Carrie A., dt Durck C. & Susan F., N. Y.; m 1862 Thomas EVERITT (H)

LAPHAM
Anson d 10-26-1876 ae 72y 7m bPP; m Anna D. ----- d 4-28-1848 ae 38y 10m 27d bPP (H)
Ch: Samuel T. b 2-15-1833 d 5----1856
Elizabeth A. b 9-13-1839 d 12-30-1864 bPP
Phebe Anna b 10-3-1841 d 2-28-1843 bPP
cf Danby 1-1833; Anna rocf N.P. 1-1839; ct Scipio 2-6-1861
Anson m 2d Ann F. WILLETS, wd Wm. J.
cf Scip. 4-2-1856 for Annie; ct Scip. 2-6-1861 for both; ct Scip. 4-1-1863 for Elizabeth but she d before it was rec
Hannah D. d 8-13-1799 bHS
Henry G., s Jesse & Elizabeth; m 12-22-1846 Semantha VAIL, dt John & Ruth (Rogers), b Danby, Vt. 4-26-1826 d 1-4-1905 (H)
cf Danby 11-1855 for Semantha
Stephen mo before 12-4-1799 & resides within MM of Great Egg Harbor & Cape May; dis 2-5-1800

LARGE
Mary H., dt Samuel & Elizabeth, Hoboken; m 1864 Samuel W. SMEDLEY
Samuel d 11-18-1874; m Elizabeth C. ----- d 5-14-1873
Ch: Mary H.

LARRABEE
Daniel m Ama. Anna (or Ann) -----
cf Salem, Mass. 10-4-1794 (clear); Daniel took cert of clear to Ama. 9-6-1798; Anna brought cert from Ama. 12-15-1798; they took ct Baltimore 10-2-1799; ct Balt. 10-2-1799 for both

LARZELERE
Charles T. (nm), s Nicholas H. & Ida (Loch), Norristown, Pa.; m at Walter Mendelson's 11-8-1912 Frances W. MENDELSON, dt Walter & Mary (Wharton), b N. Y. 4-17-1889 (H)
Ch: Nicholas Henry 2d b 11-18-1913
Mary Wharton " 8-29-1916
Frances W. name entered by com. 8-7-1889; Nicholas recrq of parents 4-14-1914; Mary W. recrq of parents 5-12-1919; ct Norristown, Pa. 10-10-1921 for mother & ch

LATCHMORE
Edwin rocf Nottingham & Mansfield, Eng. 7-20-1864; ct Nottingham & Mansfield 10-1865

LATHAM
Abigail Roorbach (form Latham) dis mo 10-3-1787
Benjamin, the younger, rocf Hitchin, Herts. 6-30-1841
Daniel, s John & Mary, Cow Neck, d 1-24-1801 ae 83y (or 1-26-1801) con mo 3 Mo (May) 4, 1749; certified mbr 1755
Daniel, N. Y. m Ann HEDGER (m between 3-4- & 4-7-1762, cert not recorded)
Daniel Jr., Phila., had rem before 8-1-1781 without cert & since mo; ct Phila. 9-6-1781
David (nm) b N. Y. d 7-12-1831 ae 77y bHS (widower)
Elizabeth con mo 10 Mo 4, 1746
Hope D. rocf Smithfield 10-30-1845 (clear)
John dis mo 11-6-1782 & helping to build ships of war
Joseph m Jane SINGLETON (m license 2 Feb. 1697/8 from wills)
Ch: William b 1 Mo (Mar) 23, 1706/7
Margaret b 12 Mo (Feb) 17, 1708/9
Jane " 10 Mo (Dec) 18, 1710/11
Hannah " 8 Mo (Oct) 23, ----
Sarah " 4 Mo (June) 18, 1718
Joseph, s John, Cow Neck, d 12-24-1804 ae 85y bHS; m -----
Ch: Margaret
Margaret, dt Joseph, Cow Neck; m 1724 Robert BOWNE
Stephen (nm) b N. Y. d 11-29-1827 ae 65y bHS; m -----
Ch: James d 11-8-1804 ae 1y 9m bHS
Dt. " 4-19-1809, stillborn bHS
Infant stillborn 2-12-1810 bHS
Thomas gct Phila. 2-4-1779 (clear)
----- & -----
Ch: George d 10-7-1811 ae 12y 6m bHS
James " 9-13-1819 ae 1y 4m bHS
Delia b N. Y. d 4-19-1827 ae 11y bHS

LATOURETTE
----- (nm) a stillborn ch bur 4-4-1830 in HS

LATOURETTE, continued
cemetery, the first Orthodox burial there after the Separation

LATTIMER
Mabel W., dt Thos. Henry & Margaret (Speer), b Wilmington, Del. 2-17-1880; m 1904 Frank Bryn FOSTER (H)
recrq 3-14-1921

LATTIMORE
Florence, dt Samuel & Ellen F. (Larabee) ALDEN, b Roch. 4-24-1876 (H)
recrq 6-13-1921

LATTIN
Mary (prob Latting) rocf Plains 10-21-1823 (clear); ct Plains 2-1-1826

LAVENDER
Sarah R., w Thomas, dt Wm. & Jane WILLIS, gct Chesterfield 8-4-1841

LAWRENCE
Alfred N., s John B. & Hannah N., b 10-7-1813 dis 11-1837 (H)
Alice, dt Rich. R. & Hannah, N. Y.; m 1834 Joshua T. UNDERHILL
Amelia (nm) m Caleb Pierce CARPENTER (H)
Amos (nm) m Hannah BOWNE, dt Robt. L. & Naomi, d 4-11-1858 ae 41y 7m bPP
Hannah dis 12-1846
Ann, wd, b Westchester Co. d 2-14-1821 ae 86y bHS (mbr prob Pur)
Ann Van Clacke (form Lawrence) dis mo 9-4-1771
Ann, dt Richard R. & Hannah, N. Y.; m 1821 Charles S. FOLWELL, of Phila.
Anna, dt John & Ann, N. Y.; m 1793 Thomas BUCKLEY
Annie, dt Ruth B. GIFFORD, rocf Swensea, Mass. with mother 6-1874; relrq 3-1887
Caleb con mo 3-5-1752
Caleb, s Richard, Flushing, d 11-19-1799 bHS; m Flushing 6-7-1754 Sarah BURLING, dt James (dec) & Eliz., d 2-23-1809 ae 79y bHS
Ch: Hester b 5-12-1775
Sarah
Child d 12-11-1796
Child " 3-22-1798
Caleb, a distant buyer for his firm 11-1823; lived at Oswego; d 1842
Carolina Augusta, dt John B. & Hannah N., b 8-18-1815 d 4-20-1841; m Wm. LAMOND (H)
Charles W. d 1917; m 2-9-1888 Alletta Bement WARRING (nm)
recrq 5-1871
Charlotte d 12-6-1798 bHS
Cornelius (nm) m Rachel Ann HICKS b N. Y. d 6-16-1838 ae 42y bHS
Ch: Henry b N. Y. d 8-27-1831 ae 11y bHS
Daniel, Flushing, d 1757; took cert of clear 6 Mo (Aug) 2, 1706 to place not stated
Deborah, dt Samuel, Flushing; m 1734 John WILLITS
Deborah, dt Samuel, Flushing; m ----- WILLETS; m 2d 1748 Samuel DOUGHTY
Edward (nm) d 4-16-1832 ae 76y bHS (this date may be for another person); m Matilda ---- (nm) b N. Y. d 2-13-1832 ae 35y bHS
Edward N., s John B. & Hannah N., b 2-12-1805 d 10-21-1839 at Liverpool, Eng., bur here (H)
Effingham W. rocf Flushing 2-1-1816, minor; dis mo 1-1824
Eliza (Elizabeth), dt Richard & Mary, b 8-16-1795
Eliza dis 11-1829 (H)
Eliza gct Scip. 6-1863
Elizabeth, Flushing; m 1714 John BOWNE
Elizabeth, dt Richard & Hannah, Flushing, b 4 Mo (June) 14, 1719; rpd mo before 12 Mo. (Feb) 7, 1739/40
Elizabeth rocf Wby 8-26-1789 (clear)
Elizabeth & -----
Ch: Mary
Ann
Effingham
cf Flushing 12-4-1806 with 3 ch named; ct Flushing 9-2-1807 with 3 ch named
Elizabeth T. d 4-10-1801 bHS
Elizabeth W. rocf Phila. 9-25-1795
Elizabeth W. rocf Flushing 2-5-1816 (clear)
Elizabeth W. & -----
Ch: Anna
ct Flushing 9-1-1819 with dt, Anna
Esther Clark (form Lawrence) dis mo 2-1-1797
George d 9-18-1798 bHS
George N., s John B. & Hannah N., b 10-20-1806; dis 3-1835 (H)
Hannah, Flushing; m 1745 Moses MULLENEX
Hannah, dt Norris (dec), gct Pur. 9-5-1787 (clear)
Hannah, dt John; m 1780 ----- SCHEIFELIN (mo) dis mo 10-5-1780
Hannah (late Underhill) dis mo 10-3-1793
some Hannah d 2-4-1799
Hannah, dt Robt. L. & Naomi BOWNE; dis mo 12-1846
Hannah H., dt Rich. R. & Hannah, N. Y., b 9-26-1795; m 1833 Robert J. WALKER
Henry H., N. Y. & Mary T. (m Phila. 1817)
Ch: William Henry b 11-20-1818 d 9-30-1825
Susan F. " 6-12-1822
Richard " 10- 7-1824 d 9-22-1847 bHS, rem to PP
John F. b 12-25-1828 d 4-15-1838
Henry " 11-30-1832
Mary " 12-20-1837
Anna " 1-15-1840
Albert " 5-15-1844
cert of clear to Phila. 5-7-1817; Mary F. rocf Phila. 11-27-1817; parents dis 1829 (H);Henry dis 5-1849; Mary F. & ch gct Phila. 1850
Henry, s Henry & Mary F., N. Y., b 11-30-1832; m N. Y. 4-8-1857 Caroline WHITALL, dt

LAWRENCE, Henry & Caroline, continued
dt Israel F. & Alice, N. Y.
cf Phila. 2-21-1854 for Henry; cf Phila. 12-1854 for Caroline with her parents; ct Greenwich, N. J. 12-2-1857 for both
Jacob & -----
Ch: Caleb d 9-19-1804 ae 1y 7m bHS
Jane, dt John & Ann, d 8-25-1854; m before 7-6-1791 ----- LIVESEY (mo)
dis mo 1-4-1792; rst 6-3-1802
Jane, dt Richard & Mary, b 7-5-1798; m Charles McCULLY (or McCaulley)
Jane H. (nm) b Ballston, N. Y. d 8-4-1828 ae 35y 6m bHS
John, s Richard & Hannah (dec), Queens Co.; m N. Y. 8-13-1755 Ann BURLING, dt John, distiller, & Ann, N. Y.
Ch: Edward B. b 6-13-1756
Hannah " 7- 8-1758
Effingham " 6- 6-1760
Mary " 9-11-1762 d 11-13-1762
Mary " 10-17-1763
Catharine " 5-15-1766 d 5- 9-1834 bHS
Jane " 10- 2-1768
Phebe " 12-24-1770 d 7- 2-1771
Anna " 5-22-1772
John " 10-31-1774
Phebe " 3-17-1778 d 8- 8-1780
Cornelia " 3-17-1778 " 3-27-1778
John rocf Shrewsbury 8- 2-1784; ct Corn. 5-5-1791; called a carpenter in index to cert
John B. d 10-1844; m Upper Springfield, N. J. Hannah N. ----- b N. J. d 9-2-1832 ae 54y bHS (H)
Ch: Edward N. b 2-12-1805
George N. " 10-20-1806
Newbold " 10-23-1809 d 10-12-1885
Alfred N. " 10- 7-1813
Caroline Augusta b 8-18-1815
John B. b 12-30-1817 d 3-13-1887
Thomas N. (or John N.) b 1-15-1820 d 7-9-1889
John took cert of clear there 1-4-1804; Hannah brought cert from there 5-9-1804; all dis 1831-1842 (O)
Jonathan rocf Hudson 1-22-1822 (clear); dis 1-1829 (O); dis (H)
Joseph 's acknowledgment accepted 4-6-1791
Leonard, Flushing m 1770 Margaret DOUGHTY (mo)
Leonard dis 1-1-1771 for m a young woman too near kin (The QM recently decided on rq of Flushing PM that a first cousin's dt was too near kin);Leonard rst 9-3-1788
Lydia, Flushing; m 1745 Stephanus HUNT, of Westchester
Margaret con mo 10-4-1797
Mary Embree (form Lawrence) dis mo to first cousin & by a priest 2-7-1781
Mary Lang (form Lawrence) dis mo 3-3-1784
Mary m 1784 Burling MARTIN
Mary, dt Daniel, Flushing; m 1734 James THORN
Norris, Flushing, d 10-7-1769; m Ann -----, Pur. b 10 Mo (Dec) 23, 1743
Ch: Mary b 10- 9-1765
Hannah b 9-21-1767
Norris " 2-15-1769
cert of clear to Pur. 12-5-1764; Ann brought cert from Pur. 12-4-1766; Norris gct Pur. 8-4-1785
Norris, s Norris & Ann, Pur.; rocf Pur. 8-9-1786, as apprentice to Robert BOWNE
Obadiah, Flushing, d 9 Mo (Nov) 30, 1732 a minister
Phebe, s Joseph, Flushing, b 9 Mo (Nov) 14, 1740
Phebe (form Loines) dis mo 10-1829 (H)
Richard, s Joseph, Flushing; m Flushing 2 Mo (Apr) 6, 1717 Hannah BOWNE, dt Samuel, Flushing, d 7 Mo 1, 1748
Ch: Mary b 2 Mo (Apr) 3, 1718
Elizabeth b 4 Mo (June) 15, 1719
Joseph " 9 Mo (Nov) 10, 1721
Caleb " 12 Mo (Feb) 1, 1723/4
Hannah " 2 Mo (Apr) 2, 1726
Lydia " 7 Mo (Sep) 27, 1728
John " 11 Mo (Jan) 31, 1730/31, lived 9 das.
John " 11 Mo (Jan) 22, 1731/2
Effingham " 12 Mo (Feb) 11, 1734/5
Norris " 11 Mo (Jan) 6, 1737
Joseph " 6 Mo (Aug) 23, 1741
Richard & Hannah ack. allowing dt, Elizabeth, to mo 2 Mo 3, 1740
Richard d 9-7-1798; m Mary ----- b M. Cove, L. I. d 6-17-1819 ae 58y 4m bHS
Ch: William L. b 9- 3-1781
Caleb L. " 7-22-1784
Richard L. " 3- 4-1788
Mary Ann " 9-26-1790
Sarah " 4-22-1793
Elizabeth " 8-16-1795
Jane " 7- 5-1798
Richard mo before 12-6-1780 & dis; rst 7-1-1795; ct Butternuts 10-17-1812 for Mary with dt, Eliza & Jane; cf Butternuts 4-29-1818 for Mary & 2 dt last named; all clear
Richard d 7- 2-1822
Richard d 2- 8-1891 bPP; m Ellen ----- d & bur HS, rem to PP
Ch: Hannah d 7-25-1842
Charles W.
Robert W.
Hannah recrq of father 1839; Richard dis 5-1849; rst 5-1872; two sons recrq of father 5-1872
(prob this Richard mo before 2-1837 & ret a mbr)
Richard L., s Richard & Mary, b 3-4-1788; ct Butternuts 10-7-1812 (clear)
Richard R. d 8-18-1799 bHS
Richard R., s Richard & Alice, of Shrewsbury, d 7-2-1822 ae 57y; m N. Y. 5-13-1789 Hannah HAYDOCK, dt Henry & Hannah, N. Y., d 3-22-1841 ae 74y 3m 8d bHS
Ch: Ann b 1-28-1790
Henry Haydock b 8-25-1791

LAWRENCE, Richard R. & Hannah, continued
Ch: Hannah b 9-26-1795 d & bur HS, rem to PP
Richard " 6-12-1800
Jane H. " 8-20-1802 d 3-21-1870 bPP
Alice " 11-20-1804
Child d 8-19-1799
Richard rocf Shrewsbury 1-3-1785, as apprentice to Robert Bowne
Robert W., s Rich. & Ellen (dec), N. Y., d 10-24-1906 ae 63y bPP; m 4-11-1882 at Paulina Sands', Agnes C. SANDS, dt Dr. David (dec) & Paulina, N. Y., b 11-24-1851 d 4-21-1931 bPP
recrq 5-1871
Samuel, Black Stump, d before 1776; m Mary ---- d 4-17-1776
Samuel rocf Shrewsbury 5-3-1813; dis mo 12-1-1819 (mo before 7-7-1819, referred to Flushing, they rpd adversely)
Sarah m 1707 Joseph RODMAN
Sarah, Flushing; m 1735 Joseph BOWNE
Sarah, Flushing, wd, d 1 Mo (Mar) 26, 1740
Sarah Green (form Lawrence) dis mo 12-2-1795
Sarah, dt Caleb & Sarah, N. Y.; m ----- GREEN; m 2d 1797 Caleb NEWBOLD, of Burl.
Sarah b N. Y. d 2-23-1809 ae 79y bHS (unm)
Sarah gct Butternuts 10-7-1812 (clear)
Sarah (late Mann) dis mo 10-4-1815
Smith rocf Plains 9-1828; mo 9-19-1835; dis 12-1851 (H)
Stephen, Flushing, m Flushing 5 Mo (July) 4, 1734 Amy BOWNE, dt Samuel, Flushing
Ch: Summerset b 3 Mo (May) 7, 1735
Lanselot " 4 Mo (June) 7, 1737
Deborah " 6 Mo (Aug) 8, 1739
Leonard " 7 Mo (Sep) 17, 1741
Tamar (or Thamar), w William, recrq 10-3-1821; ct Chap. 9-4-1822, rem with h; dec
Theron (nm) m Mary Louise ANGEVINE, dt Frank & Bethia Y., b Bkn. 8-18-1864
Mary L. recrq of parents 11-27-1878
Walter, s James, rocf Shrewsbury 8-3-1807; cert of clear to Cornwall 12-2-1812; ct Cornwall 7-7-1813
William rocf Phila. 4 Mo (June) 30, 1732 (cert of rem & clear)
William, Flushing, m Deborah ----- d 1 Mo (Mar) 28, 1743
William active mbr 1697
(Deborah may be wd of a son, Wm.)
William dis mo before 9-2-1812
----- & -----
Ch: Sarah d 4-11-1811 ae 11m bHS
Harriet b N. Y. d 2- 4-1825 ae 8y 11m bHS
John b N. Y. d 2-14-1825 ae 8m bHS
Charles b N. Y. d 3-2-1825 ae 3y 1m bHS
Sarah b N. Y. d 7-30-1829 ae 1y 7m bHS
John b N. Y. d 1-22-1836 ae 9y bHS
John F. b N. Y. d 4-15-1838 ae 9y 3m bHS
Willet b N. Y. d 5-24-1840 ae 18y bHS

LAWRIE
Caroline H. rocf Corn. 8-7-1895; d 4-10-1919
George G. rocf Chesterfield 2-3-1829; ct Phila. 11-4-1829
Martha M., dt John & Abigail MORRIS, Phila.; m 1821 Jacob B. CLARKE
rocf Upper Springfield (no date but in latter half of 1816)
Thomas rocf Pilegrove, N. J. 6-27-1826; dis 10-1831 (O); d Pilesgrove (H)

LAWS
Thomas (nm), s Ludowick & Anna, Jersey City; m Mary Ann ----- (nm) b Va. d 11-6-1839 ae 39y 3m bHS
Thomas m 2d at Freelove Mann's 4-7-1842 Phebe H. MANN, dt John (dec) & Freelove, N. Y. (Thomas d 6-1882) (H)
Ch: Thomas M. (adopted) b Phila. d 7-27-1848 ae 7m 12d
Thomas recrq 10-1841; ct H. & R. 5-1853 for both; cert returned; ct R. & P. 8-7-1861

LAWSON
Elizabeth M., wd ----- BLANVELT, dt Geo. H. & Phebe BIRDSALL
ret a mbr 1853
Emma L., dt Matthew K. B. & Elizabeth, d 9-11-1900 ae 4y bPP; m James C. JACOBS (nm)
recrq 4-1871; letter to Lex. Ave. Cong. Ch., Bkn. 12-3-1890

LAWTON
Abigail (late Farrington) dis mo 8-4-1785; rst 6-6-1820; dis non-attendance 7-1831 (O) d 2-14-1836 ae 72y bHS
Albert R., s Abraham A. & Phebe P. (Giles), b 12-25-1858 d 9-29-1930; m 12-25-1889 Emily W. WILSON, dt Jesse S. & Rebecca D., b 10-31-1861 d 1-1-1935 (H)
Ch: Louise M. b 1-19-1891
Elizabeth Campbell b 1-24-1895
cf Scip 3-5-1890 for Albert; cf Goose Creek 9-2-1891 for Emily
Charles & Sophia
Ch: John W.
Alfred
Mary
Matilda
Charles, Jr.
Catharine
Charles recrq (or rst) 6-6-1820; their ch rec on their rq 5-2-1821; ct Le Ray 5-4-1829 with 10 ch (O)
Ch: (continued)
Joseph G. b 2-14-1822
Sarah H. " 5-14-1823
Walter Farrington b 10- 8-1824
Amelia
William d 7-25-1820 ae 3m
Augustus
all dis except John, Walter & Augustus (H),

LAWTON, Charles & Sophia, continued
who had ct Exeter, Pa. 5-6-1846
Elizabeth C., dt Albert R. & Emily W., b N. Y. 1-24-1895 d 4-1-1931; m 1924 Raymond A. WOOD (H)
Raymond mbr Pokeepsie (O)
Elizabeth, w Wm. T., dt Daniel T. & Eliza. WILLETS, b 1-4-1844 (m 6-20-1866) (H)
Esther, dt Abraham & Sarah (Bancroft), b 2-4-1839 d 3-1921; m 6-12-1872 Caleb COFFIN (nm) (H)
cf Hudson 11-3-1886; sister of Naomi L. Davis
George Augustus, s Chas. & Sophia; name cancelled 4-9-1904 as long unknown; nothing ascertained 1900 (H)
John W., s Charles, dis 12-1839 (O); d 1865
Louise Marie, dt Albert R. & Emily W., b N. Y. 1-19-1891; ct Phila. 1-14-1918; cf Phila. 12-12-1921 (H)
Naomi, dt Abraham & Sarah (Bancroft), b Stanton, Del. 9-24-1842 d 5-21-1918; m 6-14-1876 in Phila. Henry C. DAVIS (H)
cf Hudson 2-2-1887
Phebe, dt William & Phebe; m ----- BRADBURY
Ruth m 1808 Thomas WINTRINGHAM (H)
cf N. P. 11-17-1808

LEA
Alexander (nm) b Scotland d 4-23-1839 ae 46y bHS (unm)
John Bentley, s Henry Tyson & Edith Helen (Bentley), b 6-13-1881; m 8-27-1913 Helen VAN INGEN, dt Dudley W. & Eliz. S. (Bunker) b Bkn. 1-1-1880 (H)
Ch: Elizabeth Starbuck b Syracuse 3-16-1915
cf Sandy Spring 1-10-1927 for John; Helen recrq with dt 7-8-1929

LEADBEATER
Peter, s Peter & Agnes, Chester, Eng., rocf Newton MM, Eng. 10-5-1760 (clear); cert rec 3-7-1765

LEACH
Mary Frances (form Evans) recrq 4-1871; ret a mbr after m; name erased 3-1928
Merritt, s William & Charlotte, N. Y.; m N. Y. 10-10-1838 Susan W. MERRITT, dt Wilson (dec) & Mary B., N. Y.
Ch: James M. b 3- 3-1841
William b 10-20-1842
Infant stillborn 12-3-1839 bHS
cf Hudson 7-4-1838 for William; ct Queensby 10-1844 with fam
----- m Alice Mary DOANE, dt Benjamin & Mary (m 1916)
Alice recrq 1-5-1910
----- & -----
Ch: Mary Jane d 4-27-1839 ae 4y 3m 2d bHS (dt of Wm.)

LEAHY
Minnie Victoria (nm), dt Dennis, San Francisco; m 10-20-1895 Edmund Field GRIFFEN (H)

LEAVEY
Bertha C., dt Samuel & Rose (Uprumney) b N.Y. 7-14-1893; m 1918 Edgar H. WOODWARD (H)
recrq 6-12-1933

LEAVITT
Sarah E., dt Jacob WILLETS, d 5-28-1884 ae 61y 17d bPP (nm) (H)

LEBER
Robert Edward, s Edward & Mathilde C. (Badenhausen), b Hoboken 3-18-1876; m 12-5-1907 Alma BIELE, dt Charles F. & Friedericke (Prediger), b N. Y. 8-12-1884 (H)
both recrq 12-12-1921

LECAUST
----- rocf Marl. 11-22-1809; ct Oswego 1-6-1813

LE DUC
Alex. N. (nm) m 6-3-1885 Nannie BELL, dt Wm. & Ann (Thomas), b 6-10-1861 (H)
Ch: John Spencer b 3-8-1886 d 2-10-1905
Lewin Bell " 12- 8-1887 d 12-11-1919
names of ch entered by com. 11-28-1888

LEE
Deborah T., w Joseph, dt Richard & Sarah (Udall) TITUS, b 8-11-1815 d 12-23-1905 ae 90y 4m 12d (H) (m 8-1-1845, corrected 1900 to 9-10-1844)
Edward (nm) d 5-27-1811 ae 60y bHS (m)
Elizabeth (nm) m Howard R. ROBINSON
George W. (nm) m 11-23-1898 Helen THROSSELL, dt Jos. E. & Emily C., b Newark, N. J. 8-13-1887
Ch: Norman b 11-2-1901
Helen & s recrq 9-5-1917
John & Sarah
Ch: William b about 1791
cf Limerick 4-14-1795 with w, Sarah, & s, Wm, 4 years old; dis mo 5-1-1799
Mary recrq 11-8-1913; d 9-22-1928 (H)
Sarah (nm), b Rahway d 6-8-1816 ae 63y bHS (wd)

LEEDOM
Benjamin J. & Priscilla B. (H)
Ch: Hannah B.
John Moore
Infant stillborn 3-18-1845
cf Phila. Cherry St. 10-1844; ct Phila. Cherry St. 11-3-1847
Elizabeth rocf Phila. Cherry St. 2-1847; d 6-22-1866 (H)

LEEDS
Deborah rem 8 Mo (Oct) 2, 1740 (place not stated)
William B. rocf Whitewater 7-7-1847; d 7-7-1894

LEEDS, William B., continued
w a nm (H)

LEES
Ann gct Uxbridge, Mass. 3-6-1839
Anna rocf Marsden, Lancashire 1-27-1831 (clear) John Bright among the signers; ct Uxbridge, Mass. 3-1839

LEFEVRE
Thomas & Sarah
cf Longford MM, Middlesex, Eng. 3-15-1820; cert returned to Longford MM, Middlesex, Eng. 1-15-1821

LEFF
Viola Susan (nm), dt Wm. & Janet; m 1929 Ralph Robert SHAW (H)
Ralph recrq 4-9-1934

LEFFERTS
Anna, wd Samuel, d 12-30-1852 ae 73y 8m 26d bPP
Ch: Martha
cf Jericho 8-9-1819; dis 2-1829
John, s Leffert & Abby L., Bkn.; m Chap. 12-31-1927 Hope COX, dt John & Mary N., Chap. b N. Y. 12-22-1901 (H)
Martha, dt Martha, recrq 10-1826; dis (O); d 7-10-1868 (H)
Samuel (nm) b L. I. d 4-14-1838 ae 65y; m -----
Ch: Sarah T. d 3-12-1821 ae 21y 11m 12d bHS (unm)
Aaron, s Joseph & Miriam, b 11- 4-1792 d 2-28-1860 ae 65y bPP
dis 7-1829 (O); dis 2-1834 (H)

LEGGETT
Abraham W. (nm) d 12-6-1899 ae 85y bPP; m Phebe B. ----- d 9-7-1886 ae 70y 5m bPP (H)
Ch: Henry d 5- 6-1841 ae 16d bPP
Anna " 11-26-1857 ae 8y 3m 26d bPP
John " 6-22-1909 ae 74y 20d bPP
cf Sara. 1-19-1839
Ann, dt Thomas & Mary, N. Y.; m 1814 Samuel F. MOTT
Caroline H., dt Wm. F. & Sarah, b 1-30-1836 d 4-7-1867; m ----- Mitchell (H) (mo) ret a mbr
Catharine T., dt Thomas, Jr. & Ann, b 1-23-1821 d 3-25-1901 ae 81y (H)
ct Flush. with parents 11-4-1846; cf Flush. 10-6-1873
Charlotte, dt Thomas & Mary, N. Y.; m 1808 William W. FOX
Eliza, dt Dr. Valentine & Anna SEAMAN, b 3-18-1812; ct Wby 10-1843; dis mo 7-5-1837 (O) (w Augustus)
Elizabeth, w Joseph, rocf ND MM 10-29-1806
Elizabeth H., dt Wm. F. & Sarah, b 11-2-1837; m before 1-3-1866 ----- MILLS (mo) (H)
dis 3-7-1866
Esther, dt Joseph & Miriam, N. Y.; m 1818 Joseph W. CORLIES
Esther, dt Reuben & Mary, N. Y.; m 1837 John GRIFFEN (H)
Frances V. rocf Phila. 12-26-1822
George F. (nm), s Wm. H. & Margaret (Wright) West Farms; m at C. A. Macy's, Pokeepsie, 12-13-1852 Charlotte L. MACY, dt Chas. A. & Sarah L. (Corlies), Po'keepsie, b N. Y. 9-6-1834 (not under care of N. Y. MM) (H)
Ch: Sara F.
Hannah, dt Joseph & Miriam; m 1803 Silvanus T. JENKINS
James Kent, s John & Sarah, b 11-8-1828 d 7-17-1885 bPP; dis 6-5-1872 for non-attendance (H)
James S., s Joseph & Eliza, rocf Pur. 3-1831 with parents; dis 1-1839 (H)
John d 1-28-1849 ae 57y 29d bPP; m Sarah H. ----- d 7-25-1873 (H)
Ch: Maria A. b 1-29-1825 d 5-24-1891 bPP
Mary B. b 9-9-1826 d 1-23-1887 bPP
James Kent b 11- 8-1828
Elizabeth A. b 11-11-1830 d 6-26-1839 bPP
Isaac G. b 8-13-1833 d 10-23-1887 bPP
cf Butternuts 12- 2-1818 (clear); Sarah rocf Troy 7-7-1824; all dis 1830-1849 (O)
Joseph d 9-25-1803 bHS; m Miriam ----- b West. Co. d 10- 5-1833 ae 83y 5m 22d bHS
Ch: Mary
Hannah b 2- 1-1781
Phebe
Sophia
Thomas b 10-26-1787
Reuben " 1-29-1790
Aaron " 11- 4-1792
Esther " 3-31-1793
cf Pur. 4-9-1795, Esther b there; cf Ama. to Pur. 9-5-1794 for parents with all but Mary & Esther
Joseph & Eliza (H)
Ch: Sally Ann
James Shaw b 9-14-1809
Caroline " 4-15-1811 d 1- 4-1833
William Jenkins b 7-17-1813
Mary Haight " 7-17-1813
ct Pur. 1-1-1817 with their 5 ch as named; cf Pur. 3-1831 for all but William J.; ct Phila. 12-1846 with Sally Ann
Joseph B. & ----- (H)
Ch: Henry Atkins d 8-8-1869 ae 6m bPP, rem to Po'keepsie 1-7-1902
cf Sara. 7-4-1855; dis mo by a "hireling" minister 11-4-1868; he felt it best to attend the mtg his w prefers
Joseph R. d 2-15-1802 ae 35d
Joseph S., s Reuben & Mary M.; m Agnes HOTCHKISS (w not a mbr) (mo) (H)
Lindley Hoag, s Thos. H. Jr. & Hannah H., b 1-3-1870; m 3-8-1894 Frances Chase BIRDSALL, dt Geo. H. Jr. & Phebe
Ch: Lindley Hoag, Jr. b 12- 8-1894
George Harold " 3- 6-1896
Francis Chase " 2-19-1900

LEGGETT, Lindley Hoag & Frances Chase, continued
cf Stanford 4-6-1892 for Lindley H.; all rel by letter to First M. E. Church of Westfield, N. J. 10-4-1911; Frances recrq 7-1886
Louisa, dt Wm. F. & Sarah (Hull), b 5-4-1845; m 1886 Henry RANSOME (H)
Mary, dt Joseph & Miriam, N. Y.; m 1798 Jesse FRAME
cf Chap. 6-13-1794
Mary d 11-27-1804 ae 41y 9m bHS
Mary, w Joseph, rocf Wby 2-15-1809, rem with her h
Mary, dt Joseph & Eliza; m Lewis STURDEVANT, of Boston (H)
cf Pur. with parents 3-1831
Mary, dt John & Sarah, d 7-21-1849 (H)
Mary, dt Thomas & Ann (Farrington), b N. Y. 2-5-1823 d 10-13-1905; m 1851 Wm. B. PARSONS (H) cf Flush. 6-3-1874
Mary E., dt Samuel & Eliza, N. Y.; m 1823 Barney CORDE
Mary E., dt Reuben & Mary M., N. Y.; m 1851 John GRIFFEN, of Safe Harbor, Pa. (H)
Miriam L., dt Thos. H. & Frances (Pleasants), b N. Y. 8-25-1826 d 10-10-1912; m 1854 Joseph F. FRANKLIN (H)
recrq 2-5-1898
Phebe Ann, dt Reuben & Mary M.; m 1840 Thomas H. BROWN (H)
Phebe G., s Isaac & Judith, Bkn.; m 1869 Paul BUNKER (H)
cf Pur. 11-1836
Reuben b Mt. Pleasant, N. Y. d 8-15-1826 ae 36y 6m 2d bPP; m Mary M. ----- d 1-24-1853 ae 66y 5m 4d bPP
Ch: Phebe Ann b 4- 1-1815
Infant stillborn 3-17-1816
Alfred " 2-20-1817
Joseph Samuel b 5- 9-1821
Reuben
Esther
Mary E. b 8-23- (or 24) 1826
cert of clear to R. & P. 5-1814; Mary rocf R. & P. 8-24-1814; all dis 1830-1849 (0)
Reuben, s Reuben (dec) & Mary M., N. Y., d 9-13-1866; m at Mary G. Ogden's, New Haven, Feb. 26-1861 Ann Maria OGDEN, dt Chas. (dec) & Ann Maria, N. Y. (not under care of N. Y. MM) (H)
Rosanna F. d 12-23-1868; m Robert M. HICKS (H)
Samuel d 1847; m Eliza ----- (mo before 4-3-1805) (H)
Ch: Mary E.
William F.
Charlotte F.
Martha
Margaret d 10-11-1831 ae 5y 10m 2d
Samuel Jr. b 9-10-1828
Rebecca F. (not a mbr)
Samuel con mo, first 4 ch recrq of father 4-7-1819; Eliza recrq 4-4-1821; all dis 1829-1839 (0)
Sarah rocf Sara. 2-1863; d 5-14-1875 ae 83y 1m 19d bPP (bur in same lot as Abraham Leggett & his s, John) (wd John)
Sarah, dt Wager & Elizabeth HULL, dis mo 3-5-1834; d 7-25-1873 ae 78y bPP
Sarah F., dt Thos. Jr. & Ann, b 6-23-1830; ct Flush. with parents 11-4-1846; cf Flush. 10-6-1873 (H)
Sarah Hull, dt Wm. F. & Sarah (Hull), N. Y., b 2-1-1843 N. Y. d 7-1-1826; m 1886 John Comegys EMORY (H)
Sara F. (nm), dt Geo. F. & Charlotte, N. Y.; m 1880 Edward D. THURSTON
Silvanus J., s Thos. H. & Avis J., b 9-30-1812; dis mo 11-7-1838
Thomas rocf Sara. (Easton) 4-19-1787
Thomas & Mary (mo before 7-5-1781)
Ch: Samuel b 10-4-1782
Joseph " 1- 5-1785 d 9-25-1803
Charlotte b 8-12-1787
Wm. Haight b 4-15-1789
Mary " 2-23-1791 d 6- 4-1802
a ch d 8-27-1798
Thomas con mo 3-3-1784 (when he left home (Sara.) he was engaged, had since m a mbr by a priest)
Ch: (continued)
Thomas b 1-30-1793
Ann " 8- 2-1795
Rebecca b 7- 2-1799
James F. b 12-26-1800 d 6- 4-1802 (or 6-11-1802)
Mary " 1-13-1803
Elizabeth b 10-24-1809 d 1-25-1834
Jacob d 12-1890
Mary's ack. for mo accepted by Pur.; Mary rocf Pur. 7-11-1782; ct Pur. 1-3-1810 with their 3 ch, Mary, Rebecca & Elizabeth; cf Pur. 11-1836 for both with s, Jacob
Thomas, Jr., s Thomas & Mary (dec); m Flushing 4-11-1816 Ann FARRINGTON, dt Walter & Mary; d 1833 (or 1832) (H)
Ch: Walter Farrington b 1-26-1817
Sarah " 10- 5-1818
Katharine T. b 1-23-1821 d 3-25-1901 bPP
Sarah F. " 6-23-1830 d 10-10-1909
Anna F. " 1832 d 2-10-1833
cf Flush. 6-5-1817 for Ann F.; father & ch dis 1829-1841
Thomas, Jr., s Thomas & Mary; m 2d 10-26-1836 Patience H. ----- (H)
Ch: Ann Farrington b 8-10-1837
Caroline H. " 9-11-1842
Susan H.
Patience rocf Phila. 3-1837; ct Flushing 11-4-1846 for all but Walter F.
Thomas H. m Nantucket 1811 Avis J. ----- b Nantucket d 2-24-1817 ae 29y bHS
Ch: Silvanus Jenkins b 9-30-1812 d 6- 8-1840
Alfred " 12- 5-1814 d 6-25-1815 bHS
cert of clear to Nantucket 5-6-1811; Avis

LEGGETT, Thomas H. & Avis J., continued
rocf Nantucket 11-27-1811
Thomas H. m 2d Frances V. ----- d 6-15-1876
(m Phila. 1822)
Ch: Avis J. b 11-14-1823
Charles Pleasants b 12- 1-1824
Miriam b 8-24-1826 (or 8-26-1829)
Thomas H. Jr. b 5-14-1828
Pemberton " 10- 8-1831
Frances Pleasants b 8-24-1834
Nancy Emlen " 12- 5-1836
cert of clear to Phila. 9-4-1822; Frances V. rocf Phila. 4-1823; all dis 1829-1849 except Thomas H. Jr. (O); ct Flushing 7-7-1852 for all (H); Frances V. rst 3-1873; Thomas H. d 6-29-1867 ae 80y
Thomas H. Jr., s Thomas H. & Frances V., Flushing; m N. Y. 2-14-1855 Hannah H. HOAG, dt Lindley M. & Huldah (dec), Wolfburg, N.H.
Ch: Pemberton b 12- 6-1855
Annie Sands " 4-25-1858
Wm. Penn "
Lindley Hoag " 1-30-1870
cf Sandwich, N. Y. 1852 for Hannah; ct Oswego with 2 ch 2-1860; cf Oswego 5-1866; ct Stanford 5-1879 for all
Tripp, s Samuel, d 6-14-1802 ae 1y 10m bHS
Walter F., s Thomas Jr. & Ann, b 1-26-1817; ct Little Falls, Md. 3-1845 (H)
William F., s Samuel; m Sarah C. HULL, dt Wager, d 7-27-1876 (H)
Ch: Margaret b 11- 4-1834 d 6- 6-1851
Caroline H. b 1-30-1836
Elizabeth H. b 11- 2-1837
William F. Jr. b 4-12-1839 d 3-30-1910
Sarah H. " 2- 1-1843
Louise " 5-24-1845
Charlotte S. " 3-24-1847 d 8- 7-1849
Samuel " 9-15-1848 d 8- 6-1849
William F. dis 2-1849
William H., s Thomas & Mary, b 4-15-1789 d 12-26-1863 ae 78y 8m 8d bPP; m -----
Ch: Wm. H. Jr. d 6-8-1829 ae 1y 8m 6d bHS (nm)
dis mo 3-1-1815 (Note. Age as given does not agree with dates)
----- & -----
Ch: Clayton N. b N. Y. d 1-23-1839 ae 3m bHS
Caroline b L. I. d 2-11-1842 ae 3y 6m bHS

LEHMAN
James m Pauline L. GOERKE, dt Rudolph & Paulina b Bkn. 2-22-1872 d 4-3-1921 ae 49y bPP

LEICESTER
Mary (nm), w Stephen, b Norwalk, Conn. d 12-12-1820 ae 27y bHS
Thomas rocf N. P. 7-15-1824 (clear); ct Hardshaw West, Eng. 8-5-1829 (clear)

LEIGH
Florence m George E. PEASLEY
letter from Hampden Bapt. Ch., Springfield, Mass. 3-1916

LENOX
David b Piscataway, N. J. d 2-25-1815 ae 65y 10m 26d bHS; m 1782 Susannah WEBSTER b Westfield, N. J. d 3-1-1815 ae 62y 28d bHS (mo)
Ch: Lydia b 7-10-1787
James R. b 2- 3-1790
Hugh W. " 2-15-1793
Susanna dis mo 6-5-1782; rst; Susanna rocf R. & P. 12-16-1795
David, s James R. & Christiana, b 4-19-1831; m Margaret ----- d 12-15-1869 ae 40y bPP (H) dis non-attendance 6-6-1860 (H)
Hugh W. b 2-15-1793; name erased 3-1880; d 1850, deranged (H)
James R., s David & Susanna (both dec), N. Y.; m N. Y. 3-13-1823 Christiana RUSHTON, dt James & Hannah, N. Y., b 11-18-1793 d 6-20-1867, a wd bPP
Ch: Susanna b 1- 5-1824
James R. Jr. b 11- 4-1828 d 6-22-1849
David " 4-19-1831
Hannah R. " 9- 9-1833 d 2-24-1856 bPP
Hugh
both dis 1830 (O); James R. dis 1-1834 (H)
Joseph d 10- 6-1798 bHS
Leontine J., dt Narcisse & Mary J. REMOND, Bkn.; m 1872 Levi N. LOCKWOOD, of Po'keepsie (H)
Lydia, dt David & Susannah, N. Y., b 7-10-1787; m 1828 Joseph THORNE, of Po'keepsie (H)
dis 1829 (O); ct Oswego 1-1829 (H)
Susannah, w David, dt John & Anna WEBSTER, d 3-1-1815 ae 62y
Ch: Lydia b 7-10-1787
Susanna, dt James R. & Christiana, b 1-5-1824; relrq 2-1-1896 (H)

LENT
----- (nm) m Lucy M. DUBOIS
Lucy recrq 10-3-1906; name erased 2-1926

LEONARD
Priscilla (nm), b L. I. d 8-12-1819 ae 36y bHS (wd)

LEROY
Benjamin (nm) d 12-31-1857 ae 52y bPP
Catharine rocf Oswego 7-1836; ct Hudson 2-1859 (H)

LESTER (or Lister)
Elizabeth rocf York, Eng. 4-28-1824 (clear); dis 10-1829 (H)
Emanuel (nm) & -----
Ch: Ida Maria b N. Y. d 12-8-1846 ae 5m bHS
Gertrude m Bernard ROWNTREE
cf WD MM 2-1914; divorced 3-1932
Jedediah (nm) & -----
Ch: Phebe b N. Y. d 2-21-1821 ae 5y bHS

LETCHWORTH
William P. rocf Scipio 11-1846; ct Ham. 7-4-1849

LEVICK
Jane, dt Samuel J. & Ellen (Foulke), b Quakertown, Pa. 1842 d 10-1-1914; m 1869 Edwin A. JACKSON; m 2d 1910 Wm. Wilbur James COOKE (nm) (H)
cf Richland 11-7-1870 with infant ch

LEWIS
Alexander d 9-22-1836 in 73d yr; m Frances (or Fanny) b West Co. d 12-10-1848 ae 78y 6m (H)
Ch: Nathaniel
cf Pur. 2-10-1820 with ch, Nathaniel; parents dis 1830 (O)
Annie, dt Elias, Jr. & Mary U., Bkn.; m 1878 Stephen VALENTINE, Jr. (H)
Dorothy con mo 10 Mo 3, 1730
Elias, Jr. (nm) m 8-2-1853 Mary UNDERHILL, dt Thomas & Sarah (Whitson) b N. Y. 11-17-1829 d 1-26-1906 (H)
cf Wby for Mary 12-1855
Elizabeth, dt Job & Sarah, d 1-23-1910 ae 86y; m Samuel TOWNSEND (H)
both nm
Emma, dt Philo & Clarissa; m ----- EDWARDS
name erased 11-1886
Fred B. recrq 11-1-1911; name erased 3-1928
Gilbert (nm) b Ulster Co. d 8-14-1833 ae 33y bHS
Hannah, dt Alexander & Fannie; m 1821 ----- COOPER (mo)
cf Pur. 2-10-1820 having rem with parents; dis mo 7-4-1821
Hannah, dt Philo & Clarissa, b 1-24-1820; m ----- UNDERHILL (mo)
dis mo 9-1-1841
James S. (nm) & -----
Ch: Infant stillborn 8-18-1838 bHS
Mary b N. Y. d 8-11-1848 ae 2y bHS
John W., s Philo & Clarissa, recrq 10-1830; dis 4-1841 (H)
Mary d 4-11-1800 bHS
Mary, dt Philo & Clarissa, b 3-22-1826; m ----- EDWARDS
name erased 11-1886
Mary E., w James L., dt Timothy & Jemima CARPENTER, dis 12-1839 (O); ct Chap. 12-1-1875 (H)
Mildred m Ralph George GREATER
Mordecai & Elizabeth
Ch: Joseph Smith b 9-18-1810
Charles Smith b 4-11-1812
James
cf Phila. 10-26-1809 with their infant, Jas. Smith Lewis; ct SD MM 11-3-1813 with 3 ch, James, Joseph & Charles
Nathaniel, s Alexander & Frances, rocf Pur. with parents 2-10-1820; dis neglecting mtg & not plain in dress & address 8-1827
Phebe d 3-31-1802 ae 39y bHS
Philo d 1-15-1843; m Clarissa L. ----- d 9-2-1860
Ch: Elizabeth b 11-26-1817 d 12-1-1870
Hannah b 1-24-1820
David " 3----1822 d 3- 5-1832
Mary " 4-18-1824 d 8- 1-1825
Mary " 3-22-1826
Emma " 6- 8-1828
John W. d 9-29-1830 ae 3m
Clarissa
Wheeler b 11-30-1831 d 9-27-1832
Clarissa recrq 9-1816; she attended Henry St. Orthodox Mtg; Philo joined Henry St. Mtg 7-1839
Sarah (nm) b N. Y. d 1-23-1812 ae 71y bHS
Sarah, dt Henry; m ----- SIPHER
(Sarah d 5-11-1804 ae 33 bHS)
Sarah, w Benjamin, dt Daniel & Sarah THORN (H)
Sidney Ann, w Evan
Ch: James
Edward
Enoch
Sarah
cf Pur. 11-11-1829 with 4 ch named; ct WD MM 11-2-1831 with same ch, rem with h

LIDDELL
John Anderson, s Andrew & Margaret (Wallace), b Scotland 3-20-1882; m 7-2-1907 Agnes NEILSON, dt Archibald J. & Agnes (Wilson), b Scotland 4-11-1884 (H)
Ch: Agnes Wilson b Scotland 9-10-1908
Raymond Neilson b N. J. 1-10-1911
John Anderson b N. J. 12-29-1915
Elizabeth Lindsay b N. Y. 8-24-1921
parents & ch all recrq 10-9-1922
Supt. of Friends Seminary & 15th St. MH

LILLEY
George W. (nm) m Elizabeth LA MONT, wd Louis R., dt Lewis P. & Laura J. COOK, b Bay of Biscay 8-16-1864 (H); Elizabeth m 3d Nelson P. WEBSTER 8-1-1921; ct Alex. for Elizabeth 5-14-1923

LIM
Lan recrq 4-1928; returned to China

LIN
Yen (Paul) m Ruth ----- d 11-1917
Ch: John
Lucy E. B.
Yen recrq 7-1-1903; Ruth recrq 4-1914; ch recrq of parents 4-1914
Yen m 2d Fannie -----
Ch: Helen b 10-1922
Bessie Gloria b 1-1924
Evelyn Doris
Fannie recrq 10-1922
Yen recrq 4-1928
Young (John) recrq 7-1-1903 (or 3-6-1907) (chinese)

LINDELL
William m Louisa M. ROBERTS, dt Edw. C. & Eleanor M., b 1-10-1874 d 2-17-1913 bPP (H)
Louisa relrq 4-2-1890

LINDLEY
Joseph d 10-23-1813 ae 62y bHS (unm); rocf Phila. 3-27-1778 (clear); ct MM at 4 Mile Creek, Va. 10-5-1785 (clear), he having rem some time past; cf Henrico Co. MM, Va. 7-7-1792 (clear)
Susannah rocf Phila. 12-7-1774; d 10-6-1812 ae 87y bHS (wd)

LINDSAY
Chas. Seton (nm), s Wm. (dec) & Jene L., Elizabeth, N. J.; m London, Eng. 6-19-1878 Mary Lewin BELL, dt Wm. & Nannie T., N. Y., b 3-11-1855 (H)
Ch: Lewin Seton b 6-1-1829
Harvey Bell b 7-3-1880
cf Balt. 11-1855 for Mary L.; ch names entered by com. 1880-1882; Mary L. relrq 5-9-1921
David Henry rocf Richhill MM, Dublin, Ire. 2-3-1909; name erased 3-1928
Lewin Seton, s Chas. S. & Mary L., b 6-1-1879; relrq 2-14-1921 (H)

LINNEKIN
Harold V. (nm) m 9-3-1932 Ruth Eleanor CARTLAND, dt Alfred L. & Jennie M., b 1-5-1910
Ruth active mbr 1-1922

LINNETT
Edith K., dt John Wm. & Maria Louisa (Allen) (nm), b Chester, Eng. 3-31-1871 (H)
recrq 3-11-1916

LINTON
Albert W. m Isabella GOERKE, dt Oscar
Ch: Eloise Beatrice b 2- 3-1904
Dorothy Selma " 7-28-1906
Grace " 1910
cf Center, Ohio 10-6-1897 for Albert; ch associates; parents glt Bkn. Central Congregational Ch. 4-1920
David Hector, s Ralph & Marg. A. (McIntosh), b Chicago 7-20-1923 (H)
cf Moorestown, N. J. 5-13-1935
Dorothy Selma, dt Albert W. & Isabella (Goerke) b 7-28-1906; m ----- WALSHEID (nm)
Eloise B., dt Albert W. & Isabella (Goerke), b 2-3-1904; letter to Bkn. Central Cong. Ch. 3-1921
Grace, dt Albert W. & Isabella (Goerke), b 1910; m 1930 ----- RUTTY
Margaret rocf Wyanoke, Va. 5-5-1821; ct Cork, Ireland 1-3-1827 (clear)
Ralph, s Isaiah W. & Mary E. (Gillingham); m 1-28-1922 Margaret Anne McINTOSH, dt Andrew J. & Florence L. (Jackson), b 11-6-1892(H)
Ch: David Hector b Chicago 7-20-1923
Ralph mbr at Moorestown; Margaret's name entered by com. 3-22-1893; Margaret got divorce

LINVILLE
Alice R., dt Asahel W. & Lydia R. (Moore), b New Garden, Pa. 10-27-1881; cf Swarthmore 4-8-1911 (H)

LION (see also Lyon)
Elizabeth, w William, rocf Ama. 5-16-1807

LIPPINCOTT
Charles E., Phila. MM having dis him, rq N. Y. to show him a copy 4-6-1808, rpd having done so
Elisha (nm) b N. J. d 2-5-1844 ae 50y 11m 15d bHS (m)
Ella H., dt Rich. Robt. & Ella (Hansell), b Rancocas, N. J. 10-11-1875; m 1899 Richard Downing WILLIAMS (H)
Ellwood, s Jehu & Elizabeth, rocf Chesterfield with parents 4-2-1844; ct Chesterfield 4-2-1862 (H)
Hannah b Shrewsbury d 1-29-1814 ae 75y
cf Shrewsbury 11-6-1786 (clear) (unm)
Jehu, s Jehu & Achsah, d 10-24-1882; m 3-17-1836 Elizabeth D. PITMAN, dt Caleb & Elizabeth (Marlin), b 3-15-1815 d 12-21-1903 (H)
Ch: Ellwood
Mary Ellen
Achsah b 12-31-1846 d 6-27-1848
Anna " 5-10-1851 " 10-25-1852
Wendella " 10-12-1856
cf Shrewsbury 7-6-1795 for both; John dis 7-1829 (O); cf Chesterfield 2-1844 with 2 ch; ct Chap. 10-6-1873 for parents & Wendella; cf Chap. 12-5-1877 for parents
John d 3-22-1831; m Elizabeth ----- d 12-21-1829 ae 64y (Elizabeth b N. J.) (H)
John b N. J. d 3-21-1831 ae 68y bHS (widower, mbr probably in N. J.)
Mary rocf R. & P. 12-19-1804 (clear); ct Upper Springfield 12-5-1810 (clear)
Mary, dt Samuel & Sarah (Acton), b Salem, N.J. 2-21-1857; m 1876 Samuel W. MILLER (H)
cf Salem 11-5-1879
Mary Ellen (or Mary L.), dt Jehu & Elizabeth; m 12-25-1862 Ebenezer SCOFIELD (nm) (H)
cf Chesterfield 2-1844 with parents; relrq 5-3-1893
Orphy, s Samuel & Hannah, b N. J. d 12-12-1810 ae 40y bHS (mbr)
Wendella, dt Jehu & Eliz. D. (Witman), b N. Y. 10-12-1855 d 3-25-1923; m 1877 Stephen B. SEARLES (nm) (H)
recrq 10-8-1910

LISTER (or Lester)
Elizabeth rocf York, Eng. 4-24-1824 (clear); dis 10-1829 (H); d 4-20-1841 ae about 60y bHS
Wilhelmina m ----- LAGUES (nm)
cf MM in Colo. 10-1918; name erased 12-1922

LITCHFIELD
Mary Ten Eyck m Richard L. WALKER, Jr. (H)

LITTLE
Charles, having accepted commission in U.S. Army, Balt. refers it to N. Y. 9-1834, dis 3-4-1835
David recrq 4-1877; ct Stanford 2-1884

LIVESEY
Ezra con mo 3-7-1821; Middletown MM, Pa. sends copy of dis to be shown him 9-5-1821
Jane, dt John & Ann LAWRENCE, dis mo 1-4-1792; rst 6-3-1802; dis 1829 (H); d 8-25-1854

LIVINGSTON
Ada m Alexander UNDERHILL
Elizabeth (form Underhill) dis mo 11-1829 (H)

LLOYD
Anna (nm) m Augustus T. FRANCIS (H)

LOBDELL
Ethel (nm), dt George G.; m 1908 Frederick C. SEAMAN (H)

LOCKE
Florence Kate rocf Alton, Southampton & Poole, Eng. 11-6-1912; d 11-1918

LOCKWOOD
Abraham, s Walter & Mary, N. Y., d 6-17-1864 ae 68y 10m 19d bPP; m N. Y. 5-10-1826 Mary CORNELL, dt Josiah & Anna, N. Y., d 7-26-1868 ae 67y bPP (H)
Ch: Alfred Cornell b 2-25-1827
George Truman b 7-22-1830 d 10-15-1832
Charles Penn " 6-20-1832
George Truman " 8- 1-1834
William Abraham b 9-12-1836 d 6- 7-1911 bPP
Anna Mary " 9-12-1836 " 8-10-1921 bPP
cf Plains 6-20-1820 (clear); Mary rocf Plains 9-24-1872 (clear); both dis 1830 (O) ct Milton, Mich. 8-1839 for all living; cf Battle Creek 8-1854 for Abraham
Arthur (nm) d 11-18-1896 ae 77y bPP, rem to Po'keepsie 1-17-1902; m -----
Ch: Amy Jr. d 12- 2-1864 ae 11y 7m 7d bHS
Anthony rocf Lick Creek, Ind. 10-20-1827 with Edward & Stephen Lockwood; ct Lick Creek 6-2-1830, minor; name on Hicksite reg. until 1850 when marked Orthodox
Edward rocf Lick Creek 10-20-1827 with Anthony & Stephen Lockwood; ct Chap. 11-5-1828, minor
Edward, s John & Amy A., rocf Oswego with parents 1-1835; joined U.S. Army for 30 das during late war 7-3-1867, ret a mbr; d 11-23-1871 bPP (H)
Helen Augusta, dt Neely & Eliza, b 7-6-1835 d 3-10-1907 bPP; m Joseph SOMERS (H) relrq 12- 9-1899
Jane Ann, dt Walter & Martha; m 1834 Jacob FROST (H)
John, d 11-10-1859 ae 66y bPP, rem to Pokeepsie 1-17-1902; m Amy A. ARNOLD, d 5-26-1892 ae 95y 8m bPP, rem to Pokeepsie (H)
Ch: Arthur d 11-17-1896 bPP, rem to Pokeepsie 1-17-1902
Levi A. b 8-29-1822 d 1-23-1883 bPP, rem to Pokeepsie 1-17-1902
Lydia A. b Pokeepsie 3-25-1825 d 6-15-1908 bur Pokeepsie
John Jr. b 7-13-1827
Edward
Jane d 11-12-1830 ae 18d
Walter Field b 12-27-1834 d 3-12-1840 bPP, rem to Pokeepsie 1-17-1902
Martha Jane b 8- 3-1838 d 12- 9-1861 bPP, rem to Pokeepsie 1-17-1902
cf Oswego 1-1835 with 5 ch
John, s John & Amy A., b 7-13-1827 d 12-24-1901; m Emily ----- d 8-28-1874 ae 37y 7m 23d bPP, rem to Pokeepsie (H)
Ch: John Franklin d 12-31-1873 ae 2y 11m 27d bPP, rem to Pokeepsie
cf Oswego with parents 1835; joined U.S. Army during late war 7-23-1867, ret a mbr
Joseph W., s Walter & Martha, b Dutchess Co. d 3-7-1845 (or 3-19-1845) ae 53y; m Mary H. ----- (H)
Ch: Walter J. (or H.) b 6-5-1826
Daniel
Sarah b 7-27-1841
Jane
cf Plains 6-25-1822 with infant dt, Sarah; all dis 1829-1849 (O); Mary H. & Walter gct Cincinnati 1852-1853; Daniel not a mbr, b before mother joined; Joseph dis 7-1833
Levi H., s John (dec) & Amy, Po'Keepsie; m at Wilber B. Maben's, Bkn. 8-29-1872 Leontine J. LENOX, dt Narcisse Remond & Mary J., Bkn. (H)
Neely, s Walter & Martha, N. Y., d 10-2-1869 ae 67y 2m 2d bPP; m N. Y. 4-11-1833 Eliza. BOWNE, dt Richard (dec) & Penelope, N. Y., d 5-24-1865 ae 57y 11m 23d bPP (H)
Ch: Edward Pearsall b 3-19-1834 d 1-22-1840 bPP
Helen Augusta " 7-6-1835
Hester " 7- 6-1835 (?)
Virginia " 5-24-1839 d 10-20-1865 bPP
Clara A. " 3- 8-1843 d 2-29-1910 bPP
Neely dis 8-1-1860
Phebe, dt Walter & Martha, N. Y.; m 1839 Charles SUTTON (H)
cf Plains with parents 1825; ct Oswego 11-1831 (O) (clear); ct N.P. for Phebe, w Charles 5-5-1841 (H)

LOCKWOOD, continued
Sarah m ----- JOWETT (H)
relrq 3-4-1857
Stephen dis 6-1836 (H); cf Lick Creek 10-20-1827 with Anthony & Edward Lockwood; ct Lick Creek, Ind. 10-5-1831 as Stephen U. (O)
Walter d 3-6-1849 rem to PP 11-10-1865; m Martha ----- b Dutch. Co. d 3-22-1838 ae 70y 1m 3d (H)
Ch: Mary b Dutches Co. d 8-21-1825 ae 28y bHS
Jane Ann
Elias d 2-11-1868
Phebe
Joseph W.
cf Plains 5-31-1825; all but Phebe dis 1829-1841 (O)
Walter Jr. d 2-27-1885; m Hannah C. HALL d 6-6-1861 ae 56y 9m 3d
Ch: Mary b 12-21-1840 d 7-31-1842
cf Plains 5-25-1826 (clear); dis 3-1830 (O)
Walter H. (or J.), s Walter & Mary, b 6-5-1826; ct Cincinnati 10-1852 (H)

LOE
Joshua, about to rem, com to prepare cert 12 Mo. (Feb) 6, 1717/18

LOESER
Estelle B. (nm), dt Mathilde; m 1923 Henry C. JENKINS (H)

LOINES
Alice, dt John (dec) & Mary B., Bkn.; m 1860 Edward S. BUNKER (H)
Anna, dt William & Sarah; m 1792 Thomas ROSS
Charles W. b N. Y. d 1-25-1834 ae 28y bHS; m -----
Ch: Charles b N. Y. d 9-28-1829 ae 5y 11m bHS
dis mo 11-7-1821
Elizabeth H., dt Richard & Sarah, N. Y.; m 1840 William S. CARPENTER (H)
James, s William & Sarah; m -----
Ch: William b 10- 4-1782
Joseph " 1- 5-1785
Charlotte b 8-12-1787
Wm. Haight b 4-15-1789
James m 2d Jericho, Phebe WRIGHT, dt John & Phebe, d 2-28-1804 ae 32 bHS
Ch: Mary Ann b 3-8-1801
James took cert of clear to Jericho 1-5-1791; Phebe brought cert from Jericho 12-15-1791
James b L. I. d 5-16-1847 ae 78y bHS; m -----
Ch: Infant stillborn 2-17-1817
Harriet b N. Y. d 9-8-1826 ae 15y 6m bHS
Emma b N. Y. d 11-28-1847 ae 32y bHS (unm)
cf Wby 5-27-1789 (clear); dis mo 9-2-1807
John, s Stephen (dec) & Sybel, N. Y.; m at Reuben Bunker's 6-14-1843 Mary BUNKER, dt Reuben & Abigail (dec), N. Y., d 7-7-1868 (H) (John d 3-5-1854 ae 36y bPP)
Ch: Alice b 9- 5-1844
Stephen b 9-28-1846
Walter " 5-10-1849 d 3-18-1907
Mary rocf Hudson with parents 2-24-1824
Mary Ann Byrnes (form Loines) dis mo 6-6-1820
Mary B., dt Richard & Sarah, N. Y., b N. Y. 7-31-1823 d 10-2-1903; m 1844 Robert F. MATTHEWS (H)
ct Pur. 4-6-1853; cf Pur. 3-6-1861
Phebe Lawrence (form Loines) dis mo 10-1829 (H) & (O)
Rebecca bPP
Richard, s William & Sarah, b L. I. d 8-23-1832 ae 58y bPP; m Wrightstown, Pa. 1813 Sarah HOPKINS b 11-3-1786 d 11-27-1869 (H)
Ch: William Hopkins b 7-31-1814
Sarah K. " 8-17-1816
Elizabeth H. " 12-23-1818
Sarah K.
Anna R. " 6-21-1821 d 1-30-1906
Mary B. " 7-31-1823
Richard A. " 12-17-1825 d 6-20-1907
cf Wby 5-27-1789 (clear); cert of clear to Wrightstown, Pa. 2-3-1813; Sarah rocf Wrightstown 6-9-1813; all dis 1829-1848 (O)
Richard A., s Rich. (dec) & Sarah, N. Y.; m at Adelia Carpenter's 10-31-1849 Mary Elizabeth CARPENTER, dt Aaron B. (dec) & Adelia A., N. Y. (not under care of N. Y. MM) (H)
Richard S. (nm) & -----
Ch: Clarence d 3-9-1861 ae 1y 8m bPP
Robert L., s Stephen & Sybil, d 11-18-1858 at Davenport, Iowa (H)
dis 10-1828 (H); dis 12-1830 (O) (b here)
Sarah, dt Wm. & Sarah; m 1803 Edmund KIRBY
cf Hudson 2-24-1801 (clear)
Sarah rocf Wby & Jericho 12-18-1833 (clear); dis 1-1835
Sarah K., dt Richard & Sarah, N. Y., b 8-17-1816 d 12-23-1874; m 1843 Henry A. GARRETT, of Niagara (H)
Sarah W., dt Stephen, rocf Wby 11-2-1836; ct Wby 3-1844 (H)
Stephen m Sybil ----- d 9-10-1866 a wd (H)
Ch: Infant stillborn 12-21-1815 (H)
William
Robert L.
John
Jonas P.
cf Wby 10-18-1815 with minor s, William; Stephen dis 6-6-1822; ct Jericho 6-6-1821 for Sybil with ch, John & Jonas; cf Jericho 1-17-1828 with same 2 ch; all dis 1830-1842 (O)
Stephen, s John & Mary (Bunker, b 9-28-1846 d 1-15-1919 bPP; m at Harriet L. Hillard's Bkn. Oct. 10-1872 Mary HILLARD (nm), dt John & Harriet (Low), Bkn. (not under care of N. Y. MM) (H)
Ch: Russell Hillard d 12-27-1922 ashes bPP
William b L. I.; m Sarah ----- d 2-1-1825 ae 77y

LOINES
William & Sarah, continued
Ch: Anne
Sarah
James
Richard
cf Wby 5-19-1790; Anne clear but not so plain as agreeable; ct Hudson 10-4-1797 for Sarah, Sr. (clear); cf Hudson 1801 for Sarah (not recorded)
William gct Scipio 8-4-1824; ct Wby 11-1843 (H)
William (nm) & ----- (H)
Ch: William H. d 1-7-1862 ae 3y bPP
Helen A. " 2-11-1862 ae 5y 3m 2d bPP
Mary M. " 2-15-1862 ae 1y 3m bPP
William H., s Richard (dec) & Sarah, N. Y., b 7-31-1814 d 6-30-1889; m at J. Aitkin's 1-12-1848 Elizabeth L. AITKEN (nm), dt John & Lydia, N. Y. (not under care of N. Y. MM) dis 11-4-1818, gone to South America

LONG
Mary B., dt George C. & Phebe C. (White) BAKER, b 4-20-1849 d 4-28-1904 (m 7-7-1869, w Thomas H., nm) (H)
lived Flushing

LONGBOTHAM
Edward C., s Wm. G. & Eliz. W. (Marshall), b Hudson 7-26-1820 d 2-28-1910; m 6-23-1850 Sarah Ann MILLER (nm), dt Samuel & Eliz. (Bedell) (H)
cf Chatham 5-1850
Elizabeth W. d 9-9-1860 ae 63y bPP; m -----
Ch: Elizabeth W.
Mary
cf Chatham 8-1851 with 2 ch (H)
Elizabeth W., dt Eliz. W.; m ----- FRISBIE (H)
cf Chatham 8-1851 with mother
Joseph C., s Wm. G. & Eliz. W. (Marshall), b Chatham 8-8-1829 d 8-8-1902 bPP (H)
Ch: James F. d 12-4-1914 ae 59y bPP
cf Chatham 9-1851
Mary, dt Eliz. W.; m J. P. BYRNE; d 12-17-1861

LOOF
Anthony, Flushing, a contributor 1686

LOOFBURY
Abraham rocf R. & P. 5-17-1792; ct R. & P. 5-2-1793 (Luffbury)

LOPEZ
Virgil G. (nm) m Edna Russell TABER, dt Jas. R. & Eliza (Heaton), b 5-30-1885
Ch: Barbara A.
Lila
Barbara recrq of parents 8-1896; Lila recrq of parents 1-2-1929

LORENZ
William A. (nm), s Chas. & Leocadie B. (nm); m 12-6-1916 Phebe Anna BUNKER, dt Edw. S. & Alice A. (Loines), b Bkn. 12-18-1863 (H)
In Hartford, Conn. 1924

LORING
James (nm) & -----
Ch: Gilbert d 4-11-1814 ae 28d bHS

LORTON
Amy Eliza, w Eugene V., rocf Pur. 4-1870; relrq 3-3-1880 (H)

LOUDERBACK
Walter, s Andrew J. & Matilda, b Valparaiso, Ind. 2-3-1887; m Nell BROOKE, dt Orson Holloway & Lu (Smith), b 6-19-1887, Chicago both recrq 6-6-1917; Walter's name erased 2-1928

LOUNSBURY
Phebe rocf Pur. 1-1824 (H)

LOVELL
George & Margaret
Ch: George
Robert
Ignatius
Marcus d 6-24-1836 ae 4y 10m 21d bHS
Infant stillborn 3-27-1834 bHS
cf Bristol, Eng. 11-5-1833 with 4 ch; ct Eng. 2-1838, not recorded

LOWERRE
Arthur H. (nm) d 7-6-1895 ae 82y 3m 1d; m Elizabeth S. ----- d 1-2-1893 ae 73y (H)
cf Wby 9-4-1850 for Elizabeth
Caroline, dt Arthur H. & Eliz. S. (Titus), b Bkn. 9-9-1848; recrq 8-13-1923 (unm) (H)
Frances Gertrude, dt Benj. H. & Anna M., N.Y.; m ----- RUSHMORE; m 2d 1888 Silas A. UNDERHILL
Josephine, dt Arthur H. & Eliz. S. (Titus), b N. Y. 9-2-1846; recrq 8-13-1923 (unm) (H)
Mary, wd, d 1-10-1845 (or 1-11-1845) ae 80y 7m 20d (H)
Ch: (prob) Eliza L. m ----- HAUGHTON
cf Flushing 8-1833
Sarah Embree [Loweree] (nm) b L. I. d 11-24-1842 ae 37y 3m 27d bHS, rem to PP in same grave as Rachel (Cohu) Lowerre (unm)
Thomas (nm) m Mary ----- (nm) d 1-11-1845 ae 80y 7m bPP
Ch: (prob) Eliza bur in same grave with Mary (all nm)
Walter & -----
Ch: Joseph b Patterson d 5-3-1834 ae 7m bHS
cf Flushing 6-3-1813; dis mo 8-7-1816
William R. (nm) d 3-9-1844 ae 68y 4m 11d bPP; m Sarah W. BURLING (nm) d 9-21-1858 ae 82y bPP (H)
William W. (nm) b Flush. d 3-9-1844 ae 68y 4m 12d bHS (m)
----- m Rachel H. COHU (nm), dt William, b L.I. d 7-11-1841 ae 31y 10m bPP

LOWNES
Jane rocf Frankfort 1-1823; marked Orthodox 2-1850 (H)
Jane (or Janes) rocf Frankford, Pa. 9-27-1822; marked "off" in pencil in Reg. 294

LOWNSBURY
Phebe, w John, rocf Chap. 9-11-1823, rem with h; ct Chap. 5-6-1829, rem with h

LOYD (Lloyd)
Anna Maria, dt Isaac S. & Rebecca S., rocf WD MM 11-20-1844, minor; ct Chesterfield 10-6-1847, minor
Elizabeth, dt Isaac S., rocf WD MM 11-20-1844, minor; ct Chesterfield 10-6-1847, minor
Hannah m 1686 N. Y. John DELAVALL
Joseph, s Isaac S. & Rebecca S., rocf WD MM 11-20-1844, minor; ct Chesterfield 10-6-1847, minor
Rebecca S., s Isaac S. & Rebecca S., rocf WD MM 11-20-1844, minor; ct Chesterfield 10-6-1847, minor
Susan, dt Isaac S. & Rebecca S., rocf WD MM 11-20-1844, minor
Thomas [Lloyd], of Phila., Pa.; m Patience STORY, wd Robert, N. Y. (ltm 10 Mo (Dec) 27, 1684, Flushing; 1st intention at Phila. m cert not recorded, nor cert to Phila.) Patience & ch rem to Phila.
Thomas, s Isaac S. & Rebecca S., rocf WD MM 11-20-1844, minor; ct Chesterfield 10-6-1847, minor

LUDLAM
Elizabeth, w Henry, dt Abm. & Mary SHOTWELL, rocf Plainfield 12-21-1774; mo & ack.; ct R. & P. 8-5-1795 with h; cf R. & P. 10-17-1804, wd of late Henry; d 6-15-1807 ae 61y
James d 10-11-1800 bHS
Sarah b N. Y. d N. Y. 11-12-1841 ae 60y cf R. & P. 10-17-1804 (clear); dis 12-1830 (0); ct Shrews. 8-1839 (H)
Sarah W. recrq 7-7-1813; ct Cincinnati 6-12-1820 (clear)

LUFF
George (prob) m Rebecca ----- b Springfield, Pa. d 3-31-1827 ae 34y 2m 28d bHS
Ch: Elizabeth b N. Y. d 5-8-1827 ae 2y 6m bHS cf ND MM 11-25-1806 (clear); dis 3-6-1822

LUFFBURY (See Loofbury)

LUKENS
Anna, M.D., dt Reuben & Catharine (Wood), b Phila. 10-29-1844 d 6-16-1917 (H) cf Gwynedd 1-3-1877 (unm)
Emma L., dt Isaael & Susan J.; m Isaac HALL (nm); m 2d Samuel S. THOMPSON 6-25-1891 (nm)
cf Phila. Green St. 4-1861 with mother (H) relrq 2-4-1863 (H); recrq 6-10-1863 (0); ct WD MM 2-1-1893
Harriet L., dt Dr. Israel & Susan J., b Phila. 12-12-1837 d Germantown 4-3-1922 bPP; m Reuben H. W. UNDERHILL
Sarah rocf Burl. 8-12-1859; ct Chesterfield 4-1863
Susan rocf Phila. Green St. 4-1861 with dt, Emma; ct Salem 10-5-1864; cf R. & P. 4-1-1891; d 11-7-1898 (H)

LUNDY
Ebenezer dis mo 2-3-1808
Eleazer rocf Middletown 4-5-1804 (clear); ct R. & P. 1826 (C)
Eleazer (nm) b Nantucket d 5-2-1818 ae 35y bHS (m)
Eleazer, s Rachel, recrq of mother 12-1818; ct R. & P. 1-4-1826, apprentice; cf R. & P. 8-20-1835, minor; dis 1842 (0); d 1853
Elizabeth Meldrum (form Lundy) rocf Middletown 9-4-1800; dis mo 1-6-1802
Elizabeth (nm) b N. Y. d 2-14-1842 ae 27y bHS (unm)
Hannah Ferguson (form Lundy), dt Rachel, recrq of mother 12-1818; dis mo 5-1831; dis 2-1829 (0)
Rachel, wd, d 7-10-1864 ae 80y bPP, in same grave with James Vickers (H)
Ch: Sally Ann
Hannah
Elizabeth d 2-14-1842
Eleazar
Charles
Rachel, Jr. d 12-2-1844 ae 26y
Rachel recrq 4-1818; six ch recrq of mother 12-1818; all but Eleazar & Rachel, Jr. dis 1829-1849 (0); cf Upper Springfield 5-4-1803 (clear); ct Wrightstown, Pa. 2-4-1806 (clear)
Sally Ann, dt Rachel; m ----- BARRY (mo) (H) recrq of mother 12-1818; dis mo

LUPINSKI
Hugo Houghton (his mother, Clementine (Houghton) d at b of Hugo H., he desired his step-mother's name recorded in m cert), s Hugo (dec) & Lucy J., Liberty, N. Y.; m at Jacie P. Willets' 10-17-1916; Martha E. S. WILLETS, dt Robert R. (dec) & Tacie P., Harrison, b N. Y. 11-14-1885 (H)
Martha relrq 5-12-1919

LUPO
Victor A. & Juliette
Ch: Victor E.
all recrq 4-1-1931

LYDECKER
Frederick A. (nm), s H. F. & Letitia (Ackerman); m Mary CARPENTER, dt Chas. B. & Anna T. (Reimer), b Bkn. 10-24-1885 (H)
Mary recrq 6-13-1908; ct Montclair 9-9-1929

LYDIG
Rosalie, dt Philip M. & Catharine M., d 4-27-1925 ae 82y 2m 13d bPP; m John J. STAPLES (H) both nm

LYNCH
Hannah (nm), dt William & Elizabeth; m 1860 Elnathan GARDNER (H)

LYNES
Anna P. (nm), dt Stephen C. & Caroline S.; m 1896 Charles M. FIELD, Jr. (H)

LYON (See also Lion)
Anna M. [Lyons] d 11-12-1894; recrq 5-4-1881
Asahel gct Oblong 6-4-1783
Elizabeth, w William, gct Pur. 9-7-1820, rem with h; cf Pur. 1-12-1825, rem with h; rel 7-5-1871, absent over 5y
Hannah K. rocf Wby 7-2-1851; d 7-24-1859 (H)
Miriam K., dt Henry L. & Hanna S. (Kipp); m Enoch Franklin DAVENPORT (H)
Miriam a mbr (not in N.Y.)
Phebe recrq 5-1-1822; marked "off" in pencil in Reg.
Rudolph G. recrq 9-14-1932
Sener, Flushing, b 2-21-1752
Sylvanus (nm) m Hannah T. ----- (nm) d 7-24-1859 ae 32y 9m 18d bPP, rem to Milburn, N. J. 11-3-1880

McAFEE
Helen D. (adopted), dt Jas. R. & Effie D., b N. Y. 5-19-1910; m 9-18-1934 Walter S. BECK (nm) (H)
Helen recrq of foster parents 5-10-1917
James, Renwick, s Archibald & Annie (Ritzie), b 5-31-1871 d 2-23-1923; m 6-21-1905 Effie L. DANFORTH, dt Horace P. & Emma (Butterworth), b Butterworth, O. 10-24-1873 (2nd w James)(H)
Ch: (adopted) Helen D. b 5-19-1910
" Nancy Irwin b 12-26-1915
James recrq 11-8-1913; cf Miami 7-13-1907 for Effie; ch recrq of parents (foster) 2-10-1917 & 3-8-1920

McANNALLY
Mary Jane, dt Wm. S. & Abigail WOOD; dis mo 8-1846

McCALL
Thomas rocf Pur. 8-9-1826 (clear); ct Pur. 1-5-1831

McCAULLEY (or McCULLY)
Jane, w Charles

McCLAY
Donald b Scotland d 8-8-1825 ae 70y bHS; m (prob) Euphemia ----- b Scotland d 8-29-1834 ae 43y bHS (a wd)

McCLELLAN
Emma (nm), mother of Emma P., d 10-13-1866 ae 70y bPP (H)
Emma P., dt Emma, d 3-31-1881 ae 50y bPP; m (prob) Joseph R. DICKENSON, s Valentine, d 4-7-1882 ae 61y 8m 2d bPP (both nm) (H)

McCLOY
Wm. C. (nm), s Wm. & Amelia (Conrad); m 6-6-1902 Helen W. CLARKSON, dt Jas. B. & Helen E. (Worrell), b Middletown, Del. 9-7-1865
Ch: Helen W. C. Jr. b Bkn. 6-6-1904
mother recrq 8-11-1906; dt recrq of parents 10-13-1906; both relrq 10-11-1926 (H)

McCLURE
Graham Traquain, s Jas. T. & Eliza H. (Lang), b Phila. 8-5-1884; m 9-14-1912 Agnes SWAIN, dt M. L. (H) (Agnes nm)
Ch: Thomas T. b Boston 8-30-1914
James Graham b Boston 8-29-1913
Graham recrq 10-10-1927; ch recrq of parents 10-10-1927
----- (nm) m Edna M. ROACH, dt Mary
Edna recrq 11-7-1906; letter to Union Cong. Ch., Tuckahoe 7-1920

McCOBB
Charles m Louise R. ----- d 6-21-1923 ae 86y bPP (H) (both nm)

McCOLLAM (or McCollum)
Anthelia rocf Marl. 4-1866; mbrp relinquished 5-1880

McCONAUGHY
James (nm), s David & Leana, d Germantown 12-5-1934 ashes bPP; m Eleanor UNDERHILL, dt Reuben H. & Harriet L., b Bkn. 8-7-1861 d Germantown 3-13-1926 ashes bPP
James m 2d Mary WENTWORTH (nm)
letter for Eleanor from West Side Presby. Ch., Germantown, 4-3-1918; letter to same ch. 3-1924
Katharine, dt Eleanor; m ----- BAILEY
recrq 5-1915

McCORD
Chas. Luther, s Willet & Grace Caroline (Willets), b Ellenville, N. Y. 5-27-1867; m 10-12-1898 Anna HAIGHT, dt Franklin C. & Caroline A. (Quinby), b Little Rest, N. Y. 3-6-1872 (H)
Ch: Herbert Franklin 3-21-1902
C. Bertram b 3-19-1911
Charles recrq 2-6-1895; cf N. P. for Anna 12- 9-1899
Grace Caroline, dt Willet & Grace C. (Willets); m 1897 Dr. Samuel E. GIBBS (H)
recrq 5-7-1898
Jason, having mo, Creek referred to N. Y. 12-1859; mbrp relinquished by mo 5-1860
Willet m Grace Caroline WILLETS, dt Jacob &

McCORD, Willet & Grace Caroline, continued
Susan A., d 9-12-1925 ae 63y 7m 3d bPP (H)
Ch: Grace Carolyn
Wm. Rufus
Chas. Luther
cf Chap. 2-7-1883 for Caroline, a wd
William Rufus, s Willet & Grace Caroline, b 1-30-1864, Sing Sing, N. Y.; m 3-18-1907 Hilma Kindlund NORDBY (nm) (H)
recrq 2-6-1895

McCORMICK
Clara Hayes (nm); m 1879 Edward Rudolph STRATTAN (H)
Kate M. recrq 4-1887; ct Pokeepsie 4-6-1892
Lydia (nm) b Phila. d 3-16-1826 ae 49y bHS
Maggie J. m Adnah HEATON
recrq 5-1886; ct Pokeepsie 1-7-1891

McCOUBREY
James (nm) m Daisy I. BIRD, dt William & Frances Emma (Hyatt), b Chap. 10-14-1885
Ch: Lucilla Bird b 1-26-1917
Daisy recrq 3-1922
Lucilla recrq of mother 3-1922

McDERMOTT
James W., s Wm. & Maria (O'Connor), b Dublin, Ireland 12-5-1835 d 12-30-1916 bPP; m Mary E. HILL, dt John & Elizabeth (Runkle), b Woodville, N. J. 1-3-1840 d 9-16-1907 Wilmington, Vt. bPP (James W. nm)

McDONALD
Alexander & -----
Ch: Sarah Maria b N. Y. d 7-18-1838 ae 1y 2m 26d bHS
listed as a mbr (prob elsewhere)
Mary (late Donally) rocf Phila., but dis mo 8-1-1781
Mary b Cork, Ireland d 11-3-1825 ae 49y; cf Lurgan, Ireland 5-19-1821 (clear)
Thomas A. recrq 7-1853; rel 6-2-1875 absent over 5y (H)

McDOWELL
Alexander d 11-15-1877 ae 77y 5m 29d bPP; m Sarah ----- d 4-7-1883 ae 84y 7m 19d bPP (H)
Ch: Joseph T. b 8-16-1825
Elizabeth Ann b 8-18-1827
Thomas F. " 8- 4-1829
Henry W. " 9- 9-1831 d 3-15-1850 bPP
James T. " 11-29-1833
Sarah Maria " 4-22-1837 " 7-18-1838
George Alexander b 10-21-1840
cf Corn. 4-1836 with ch; ct Corn. 6-2-1857 with last 2 ch; cf Corn. 9-1866 for parents
Alexander H., s Geo. A. & Mary J. (Secord), b N. Y. 11-29-1876; m 11-6-1905 Mary Dell VAIL, dt James H. & Georgie S., b Balt. 9-11-1883 (H)
Ch: Ella Vail b Bayonne 12-20-1906 d 3-13-1907 bPP
Caroline Carpenter b N. Y. 2-22-1908
Phebe Haviland b Woodbury, N. J. 11-26-1909
Geo. Alexander, 2d b Ruxton, Md. 6-19-1911
James Vail b Ruxton, Md. 10-31-1914
cf Balt. 11-10-1906 for Mary; ct Balt. 2-12-1917 for all
Dr. Charles, s Joseph T. & Isabella M. (Stratton), b 9-30-1857 N. Y.; m 9-3-1891 Harriett COX, dt Wm. G. & Sarah (Jones), b Malvern, Pa. 2-8-1867 (H)
cf Goshen 1-5-1892
Egbert G., s Joseph T. & Isabella M., N. Y.; m at D. R. Underhill's, Bkn. 6-26-1889 Mary E. SEYMOUR, dt Henry & Esther H. (Underhill), N. Y. (H)
Ch: Wilmer Irving b 10-16-1904
Isabella M. " 5-16-1908
Mary recrq 8-1-1888; ct Montclair 8-18-1833 for all
Edwin Carleton, s Jos. T. & Annie L. (Stone), b N. Y. 9-8-1877; m 9-20-1919 Charlotte Katharine GANNETT, dt Wm. C. & Mary T. L. (H)
Elizabeth, dt Alex. & Sarah, N. Y.; m 1853 Mordecai BUZBY, of Phila. (H)
Fannie, dt Geo. A. & Mary J., N. Y., b 1-16-1872; m 1897 Benj. Lawrence HUNT (H)
George A., s Alexander & Sarah, b 10-21-1840 N. Y. d 3-13-1924; m Mary Jane SECORD (nm) d 2-6-1882 ae 37y 5m 23d bPP (H)
Ch: Ella B. b 11-16-1809 d 9-28-1899 bPP
Fannie " 1-16-1872
Alexander H. b 11-29-1876
George T. d 4- 6-1876 ae 1y 2m 12d bPP
cf Corn. 8-1863 for George; ch names entered by com. 1873-1877
George A. m 2d at James E. Carpenter's 10-21-1884 Jane CARPENTER, dt Wright & Hannah (Hallock) (both dec), N. Y., b Ama. 5-8-1841 d 3-4-1930 bPP (H)
cf Corn 8-1863 for George; cf Ama. 8-7-1897 for Jane
George Alexander 2d, s Alex. H. & Mary D. (Vail), b Ruxton, Md. 6-19-1911 (H)
ct Balt. 2-12-1916
James T., s Alex. & Sarah, b 11-29-1833 d 3-13-1897 bPP; m Sarah F. ----- (nm) d 10-6-1918 ae 75y 9m 9d bPP (H)
Ch: Cora May d 11-10-1895 ae 25y 4m 18d bPP
cf Corn. 9-1866; relrq 12-3-1873
James Vail, s Alex. H. & Mary D. (Vail), b Ruxton, Md. 10-31-1914 (H)
ct Balt. 2-12-1916
Joseph T., s Alex. & Sarah (Thompson), N. Y., b 8-16-1825 Corn. d 8-25-1910 bPP; m at Enoch Stratton's 5-6-1852 Isabella M. STRATTON, dt Enoch & Amy T., N. Y., d 8-26-1872 ae 41y 4m 7d bPP (H)
Ch: Cora b 7-23-1854 d 8-14-1854 bPP
Henry M. b 3- 9-1856 d 8- 9-1859 bPP

McDOWELL, Joseph T. & Isabella M., continued
Ch: Charles b 9-30-1857
Theodore L. b 12-1-1860
Arthur b 12- 7-1862 d 11-30-1863 bPP
Egbert Guernsey b 6-29-1865
Joseph T. m 2d Annie L. STONE, dt Jas. H. & Martha Ann (Scott) (m 9-24-1874) (H)
Ch: Mary Stone b 3-22-1876
Lilian Josephine b 11-10-1878
Edwin Carlton b 9- 8-1887
cf Sandy Spring for Annie 7-7-1875
Lillian J., dt Joseph T. & Annie L., N. Y., b Jersey City 11-10-1878; m 1902 Addison G. HANNAN; m 2d 1927 Junius C. ROCHESTER (H)
Mary Ann d 12-26-1853 ae 56y bPP; m ----- HAMILTON (nm) (H)
sister of Alexander McDowell
Theodore, s Jos. T. & Isabella (Stratton), b N. Y. 12-1-1860; m 12-23-1885 Imogene SWEET (nm), dt Almond E. & Sarah A. (H)
Theodore m 2d Lillian M. HALL (nm), dt John & Mary F. (H)
relrq 5-9-1921; lived Jetmore, Kans.
Thomas F., s Alex. & Sarah (Thompson), b 8-4-1829 Corn. d 3-25-1910 ashes bPP; m 9-8-1856 Fannie M. KNAPP (nm) d 7-12-1909 ashes bPP ae 71y 6m 13d (H)
Ch: Frank d 9-19-1858 ae 1y 1m
Walter Thomas
w nm; Frances Mary in burial rq
Walter Thomas, s Thos. F. & Frances M., d 5-15-1918 ae 60y 9m 21d bPP; m Ida MILLER, dt Anton M. & Matilda S., d 3-7-1921 ae 61y 5m 3d bPP (H)

McFARLAN
Elizabeth b Dutch. Co. d 3-8-1848 ae 31y bHS

MacFARLAND
Elijah P. & Evelyn
Ch: Allegra V.
both rec 10-1923

McGINNIS
John rocf Marl. 11-1888
Mary Ann d 9-4-1878 ae 72y bPP
William (nm) d 6-3-1860 ae 52y bPP

McINTOSH
Andrew J., (nm) s Hector & Martha Ann, Phila., b 1-8-1866 Phila. d 10-13-1928 ashes bPP; m at Wm. M. Jackson's 10-8-1891 Florence L. JACKSON, dt Wm. M. & Anna M., N. Y., b Richmond, Ind. 8-27-1870 d 3-20-1919 bPP (H)
Ch: Margaret Anne b 11-6-1892
Andrew J. recrq 1-9-1922; Florence rocf Whitewater, Ind. with father 8-7-1878; Margaret's name entered by com. 3-22-1893
Andrew J. m 2d 12-22-1921 Harriet T. CARSWELL, dt John N. & Susan (Townsend), b Wilmington, Del. 4-11-1887 (H)
Ch: Andrew James Jr. b N. Y. 12-28-1922
Ch: Susan Stokes b Phila. 12-4-1925
Harriet rocf Phila. 11-10-1924
Margaret Anne, dt Andrew J. & Florence (Jackson), b 11-6-1892; m Ralph Linton, mbr Moorestown, N. J. (m 1-28-1922) (H)
Margaret Anne got divorce; Margaret's name entered by com. 3-22-1893

McKAY
Donald, s Kenneth & Mary (Campbell), b Glasgow, Scotland 9-16-1880; m 4-6-1909 Mary BROWN (nm), dt William & Mary B. (H)
Donald recrq 11-12-1917; name rem for lack of interest 3-13-1933

MacKELLAR
Walter, s Archibald & Jeannie (Malcolm), b 11-19-1897; recrq 3-2-1932

McKENNY
Phebe (late Doty) dis mo 5-2-1804

MacKENZIE
Dudley Shannon, s Dudley S. & Eleanor T. (Gould), b Falmouth, Mass. 1-23-1905; m 4-3-1926 Gladys Kinghorn GOULD (nm), s Thomas & Florence (H)
Ch: Dudley S. Jr. b Newtown, Mass. 1-11-1927
Father recrq 12-12-1926; s recrq of father 6-1-1927
James & Agnes
Ch: Jean (first recorded as Georgina)
parents recrq 7-1924; Jean rec as associate 7-1924; Jean active mbr 11-1932

McKEON
Peter Joseph (nm), s Terence & Maria (McKittrick); m 4-8-1911 Ellen RUSHMORE, dt Edward & Clara S. (Riley), b Corning 1-20-1874 (H)
Ch: Ellen Sidney b 1-17-1917
cf Balt. for Ellen 6-14-1920; Ellen S. recrq of parents 8-9-1920

McKEWEN
Mabel Alberta recrq 10-1885

McKIM
Sarah A., w J. Miller, rocf Phila. 3-1-1871; d 1-9-1891 (H)

McKINNON
Alexander recrq 10-1915

MacLAY
Charles (nm) & Emily C.
Emily recrq 6-3-1931

McLEA
Donald rocf Edinburgh Two Months Mtg 2-14-1822; rem nearly 4y ago; d 8-8-1825

MacMASTER
Gilbert Lee, s Arch. Alex. & Sophia (Lee), b Poland, Ohio; m 12-6-1878 Margaretta Magdalena KROLL, dt Carl & Margaretta (H)
recrq 1-10-1921; ct Germany 4-12-1926

McNEILE
----- (nm) m Anna GARDNER, dt Ernest H. & Mary Ella

McPHERSON
George recrq 10-12-1907; d 4-5-1919 (H)

McVAUGH
Roy, s C. Frank & Ruth A. (Eastburn), b Hockessin, Del. 5-18-1880; m ----- (H)
Ch: Infant stillborn 5-19-1906 bPP
recrq 5-6-1905

MABBETT
Joseph, Flushing, & Hannah
Ch: Susannah b 6 Mo (Aug) 3, 1719 d 6 Mo. 19, 1719
Ruth, w Samuel, rocf N.P. 3-19-1779; ct N. P. 1-7-1784
----- & ----- (nm)
Ch: Adlina S. b N. Y. d 8-23-1828 ae 2y bHS

MACK
Rachel Y., w Henry Q., dt William & Mary D. BIRDSALL, b 2-24-1834 d 12-5- (or 6) 1862 ae 28y bPP

MACKIE
James, Jr., s James & Ann; m N. Y. 3-14-1838 Maria THOMPSON, dt George & Elizabeth (dec) d 1-13-1840 ae 43y 7m bHS
Ch: George Wm. b 1-11-1840 d 1-27-1840 ae 16d bHS
ct Goshen, Pa. from Richhill, Ireland 10-25-1832 (clear); recorded in N. Y. without comment; cf Lisburn, Ireland 1-18-1816 for Maria; ct Grange, Ireland 2-6-1841 (clear)

MACOMBER
Anna B. rocf R. I. 12-5-1906; d 4-28-1910

MACY
Abraham W., s George & Deborah (Shepherd), b Ghent 12-29-1844 d 2-24-1931 bur South Livonia, N. Y.; m 7-12-1876 Ella VAN SICKLE (nm), dt John & Alexina (H)
transferred from Albany 1-8-1916
Adaline, dt John J. & Jane H., b Greenport 11-13-1843 d 2-23-1913; m 9-23-1894 Peter BUCKHOUT (H)
cf Hudson & Chatham 12-5-1893
Ann, w Hiram, rocf Hudson 9-21-1831; ct Hudson 1-2-1833
Ann Eliza, dt Josiah & Lydia, N. Y.; m 1839 Isaac MACY (H)
Anna, dt Francis H. & Lydia, b 12-17-1849; m before 11-1878 D. Henry SMITH (mo by a hireling minister (H)
rel 12-4-1878; mbr of Dr. Hall's Ch. for some time
Benjamin b N.P. d 2-27-1824 ae 44y 3m; m Lydia BUNKER, dt Silas & Deborah (H)
Ch: Silas
Hepzibah F. dis 1823
Caroline d 12- 7-1825
Charles B.
Robert B.
Elizabeth B.
Hezekiah B. (or Kezia) d 11----1861
James C. d 9-18-1836
Frederick B. dis 9-6-1854
Henry B. b 7-20-1825
cf Hudson 3-26-1816; Lydia m 2d Hezekiah WILLIAMS; Lydia m 3d Nathaniel STARBUCK, 1851
Caroline (nm) b Hudson d 11-8-1825 ae 21y bHS (wd)
Charles d 1-25-1852; m Anna -----
Ch: Lucretia
mbr at Nantucket 3-3-1847 (H); cf Nantucket 9-25-1828 (O); all dis 1830-1837 (O)
Charles A., s Josiah & Lydia, N. Y., b 7-3-1808 d 7-21-1875; m N. Y. 1-12-1831 Sarah L. CORLIES, dt Benjamin & Phebe, N. Y., b 7-20-1808 d 5-7-1886 (H)
Ch: Benjamin C. b 10-12-1831 d Ya. City, Idaho 7-25-1864
Charlotte L. b 9- 6-1833
Margaret S. " 11-25-1836
Charles A. Jr. b 12-26-1840
Francis H. Jr. b 7-30-1843
cf Nantucket 7-1823 for Charles; ct Oswego 2-7-1855 for all except Charlotte; cf Oswego 9-1-1870 for parents
Charles B., s Benjamin & Lydia, rocf Hudson with parents 1816; dis 10-1835; d 2-11-1869 (H)
Charlotte L., dt Charles A. & Sarah L., Pokeepsie, b N. Y. 9-6-1834; m 1852 George F. LEGGETT, of West Farms (H)
Cornelia T., dt Wm. H. & Eliza L., N. Y., d 5-15-1897; m 12-10-1856 Isaac Henry WALKER (H)
Cornelia W., dt Silvanus J. & Caroline, b 9-16-1865; m 10-23-1889 Richard B. HARRIS (H)
relrq 7-2-1890
Edwin rocf Hudson 4-5-1865; d 12-7-1884 (H)
Eliza L., dt Silvanus J. & Caroline, b 4-29-1860; m Silvanus J. JENKINS, Jr. (H)
relrq 2-4-1885 as Jenkins, jas (erased in Min.)
Elizabeth, dt Wm. & Phebe (Starbuck), b Nantucket d 11-14-1903 ae 88y 2m 2d bPP
cf New Bedford 8-25-1836 (clear) (unm)
Francis H., s Josiah & Lydia, N. Y.; m at A. Underhill's 10-8-1846 Deborah UNDERHILL, dt Adonijah & Deborah S., Bkn., d 10-12-1891 (H)
Ch: Louisa b 5-24-1847

MACY, Francis H. & Deborah, continued
Ch: Anna b 12-17-1849
Francis H. Jr., s Chas. A. & Sarah L., N. Y.; m at C. G. Macy's 1-12-1869 Mary NELSON, dt Henry A. & Cath. A. (both dec) (H)
George H., s Silvanus J. & Caroline (Ridgway), b 3-25-1858 N. Y. d 10-2-1912; m 1-12-1880 Kate CARTER (nm), dt Oliver S. & Eliz. (Cooley) (H)
Hannah Hull (form Macy) dis mo 1-1-1840
Harriet H., dt John I. & Jane (Hall), b Grenport, N. Y. 1837 d 1-2-1920; m 1888 Horace PAYNE (H)
Hezekiah B., s Benjamin & Lydia, rocf Hudson 6-1816; d 11-1861 (H)
Isaac, s Thomas & Eliz. (dec), Nantucket; m at Josiah Macy's 11-6-1839 Ann Eliza MACY, dt Josiah & Lydia, N. Y., d 4-26-1882 (H)
Ch: Lydia H. b 8- 3-1840 d 5-30-1841
Lydia H. " 11-20-1841 " 4-15-1910
Thomas Jr. b 4- 9-1844 d 12- 1-1920
Isaac Augustus b 3- 4-1850 d 12-11-1923; recrq of mother 11-1858
ct Nantucket 4-2-1845 for Ann Eliza & Lydia H.; Thomas' cert returned 10-7-1846
Isaac Hall, s John J. & Jane, b Greenport, N.Y. 5-8-1840 d 3-4-1907; rocf Hudson & Chatham 10-21-1896; rec 6-8-1901 (H)
Isabel, w Samuel H., rocf Nantucket 10-28-1824
Jared rocf Nantucket 6-27-1844 (clear); dis 3-1849 for non-attendance after ref. to Swansea; he at Fall River
John Hicks, s Josiah M. & Lydia, b 7-2-1825 d 6-23-1870; m at H. M. Carpenter's 10-20-1846 Caroline CARPENTER, dt Henry M. & Abby Jane (dec), d 1-10-1852 ae 24y 5m 1d (H)
Ch: Howard d 1-27-1859 ae 8y 11m 19d
Charles Jr. d 1- 4-1852 ae 2m 27d
John Hicks m 2d Sarah A. ARCHER b 6-14-1834
Ch: William H. Jr. b 2-28-1854 d 3-14-1891
John H. Jr.
cf Pur. 6-1-1859 for Sarah & Wm. H. Jr.
John H. relrq 1-7-1857; Sarah relrq 12-5-1866
John H. Jr., s John Hicks & Sarah (Archer); m 11-7-1894 Grace SANDERS, dt Chas. W. & Ella A. (Wickwire), b Rahway 8-18-1870 (H)
Grace m 2d 4-11-1906 David H. KEEFER; Grace recrq 1-14-1911; her name changed to Macy 4-11-1916 by court order
Jonathan (prob. mbr in Nantucket) m Rose ----- b 2-22-1858 d 11-7-1853 ae 95y 8m 15d
cf Nantucket 11-27-1828; rec by Orthodox Mtg, but dis 2-1830; rec without cert 11-1828 (H)
Josiah b 2-25-1785 d 5-15-1872; m Lydia ----- b 11-6-1786 d 9-25-1861 ae 74y 10m 19d (H)
Ch: William H.
Charles A.
Josiah G.
Lydia H.
Ann Eliza
Francis H. b 10-22-1822
John Hicks b 7- 2-1825
cf Nantucket 5-28-1823 with 6 ch named; all dis 1829-1848 (O)
Josiah, Jr., s Wm. H. & Eliza L., N. Y., b 7-15-1838 d 10-5-1876; m at Valentine Everitt's, Bkn. 12-9-1858 Caroline L. EVERITT, dt Valentine & Beulah E., Bkn., b 12-9-1838 d 12-31-1898 (H)
Ch: Mary Kingsland b 11-14-1860
Kate Everit " 4- 6-1863
V. Everit " 3-23-1871
Josiah G., s Josiah & Lydia, dis 4-7-1847 (H)
Kate Everit (H), dt Josiah Jr. & Caroline L., b 4-6-1863; m 12-5-1883 Walter G. LADD (O) relrq 12-5-1883
Louisa m 1859 Robert M. STRATTON (H)
Louisa, dt Francis H. & Deborah, b 5-24-1848; m before 11-1878 Joseph Augustine (mo by a hireling minister) (H)
rel 12-4-1878; attended Dr. Hall's Church
Louisa C. (or Y.), w Aaron C., Jr. (form Coleman) d 4-15-1874 (H)
Lydia, dt Silas & Deborah BUNKER; m 1849 Hezekiah WILLIAMS (H)
Lydia H., dt Josiah & Lydia; m 1836 H-- STANTON (mo) (H)
dis 4-3-1837
Lydia S., dt Wm. W. & Phebe S., N. Y., b 1815; m 1841 Nestor H. SANBORN
cf New Bedford 8-25-1836 (clear)
Martha, dt John I. & Jane (Hall), b Greenport, N. Y. 12-13-1850 d 2-1920; m 1873 Wm. D FOWLER (nm) (H)
cf Hudson & Chatham 12-5-1896
Mary A., dt John, Jr., b Greenport, N. Y. 1848 d 2-25-1835; transferred from Albany 1-8-1916 (unm) (H)
Mary B., w Thomas M., rocf Nantucket 11-30-1826; dis 7-1830
Mary J., dt William H. & Eliza L., b 11-10-1828; m 9-16-1847 Wm. M. KINGSLAND (H) relrq 1863
Mary Kingsland, dt Josiah J. & Caroline L., N. Y., b 11-14-1860 d 5-12-1893; m 1-20-1886 Howard WILLETS (nm), s John T. & Amelia (H)
Reuben d 10-15-1870; m Hannah ----- d 4-22-1859 (H); cf Nantucket 11-1847
Robert B., s Benjamin & Lydia, rocf Hudson 6-1816; rel 6-2-1875, absent over 5y (H)
Sarah (nm) b Hudson d 5-30-1819 ae 23y bHS
Sarah G., w Samuel H., b Nantucket d 4-11-1827 ae 35y (marked as nm in 1040)
Sarah R., dt Silvanus J. & Caroline (Ridgway), b 11-10-1861 N. Y.; m Rochester 6-1-1880 E. Franklin BREWSTER (nm); Sarah R. m 2d 10-7-1915 James MARWICK (nm) (H)
relrq 6-3-1885; rst 1-10-1921; ct Alexandria 4-11-1921
Silas dis mo 9-3-1823
Silvanus J., s Wm. H. & Eliza L., b 7-28-1833; m 10-27-1853 Caroline RIDGWAY, dt Thomas, d 7-4-1869 (H)

MACY, Silvanus J. & Caroline, continued
Ch: Charles Wood b 11- 6-1855 d 3-22-1876
George H. " 3-25-1858
Cornelia W. " 9-16-1865
Eliza L. " 4-29-1860
Sarah Ridgway b 11-10-1861
Silvanus J. Jr. b 10-15-1868 d 7-12-1869
cf Phila. 12-1854 for Caroline; Silvanus relrq 12-1-1869
Thomas H. (nm) b Nantucket d 5-29-1838 ae 44y 2d bHS (m)
Valentine Everit, s Josiah, Jr. & Caroline L. (Everit), b 3-23-1871 d 3-21-1930; m 2-18-1896 Edith CARPENTER (nm), dt Miles B. & Josephine E., d 1925 (H)
Wm. H., s Josiah & Lydia, N. Y., b 11-4-1805 d 5-19-1887; m N. Y. 10-10-1827 Eliza L. JENKINS, dt Silvanus F. (dec) & Hannah (Leggett), N. Y., b 6-30-1808 d 7-22-1901 ae 93y 22d (H)
Ch: Mary J. b 11-10-1828
Cornelia Trimble b 8- 1-1831
Silvanus J. b 7-28-1833
Sarah " 11- 3-1834
William H. Jr. b 1-15-1836
cf Nantucket 7-1823; dis 1830,1831 (O)
Ch: (continued)
William Henry, Jr. b 1-15-1836
Josiah, Jr. " 7-15-1838
George Trimble " 6-20-1843 d 3-31-1851
Charles Marshall " 6-19-1847 " 9-3-1848
Wm. H., Jr., s Wm. H. & Eliza, b 1-15-1836; m (prob.) before 11-6-1867 Cornelia FOSTER (H)
Ch: (prob) Josiah, Sr. b Babylon, L. I. d 9-20-1935 ae 52y at Memphis, Tenn.
dis 9-1868, his w an Episc. and they attend that Ch.
William W. m Catharine ----- d Nantucket
Ch: Mary S. b Nantucket d 5-20-1828 ae 9y 5m
William W. d 2-20-1838 ae 51y 1m bHS; m 2d Nantucket Phebe S. ----- d 4-15-1831 ae 44y 4d bHS
Ch: Anna Hussey d 5-20-1828
Lydia Starbuck b 1815
Elizabeth Hussey b 1815 d 11-14-1903 ae 88y 2m 2d bPP
Edward Starbuck b 10-1-1825 d 8-27-1828
Phebe S. d 4-15-1831
cf Nantucket for parents & first 3 ch here named, also with Mary; parents dis 1829 (H); Wm. W. gct New Bedford 2-6-1833 with ch (clear)
----- & -----
Ch: Uriah b Hudson d 8-19-1818 ae 1y bHS
Caroline b N. Y. d 3-26-1827 ae 1m 14d bHS
Eliza b Hudson d 1-5-1828 ae 16y bHS

MADDANS
Paul, s Ingo & Julia Willets (Meade), b Bkn. 6-13-1913; recrq 6-11-1934 (H)

MAGER
Simeon, N. Y. & -----
Ch: Maria b 2-25-1820

MAGILL
Allen H., s Edgar R. & Katie (Holcomb); m 9-10-1932 Grace WOODROW, dt Henry H. & Eliza. (Watson), b Easton, Pa. 5-22-1904 (H)
Grace recrq 12-11-1933; Allen mbr Solesbury, Pa.
Edw. H., s Jonathan P. & Mary W., N. Y.; m at 128 W. 43d St. 4-24-1902 Sarah Eliz. GARDNER, dt Aaron & Anna H. SUTTON, N. Y., b N. P. 3-9-1840 d 3-3-1934 ae 94y 4m 22d at St. Petersburg, Fla. (H)
wd Nathaniel Gardner; she adopted John W. Reynolds, he d 4-1-1887 ae 27y 4m 16d; cf N.P. 12-4-1872; ashes interred Salisbury, Pa.

MAGINIS
Mary Ann recrq 5-1837; d 9-4-1876

MAGUIRE
Rebecca, dt John & Mary V.D. b Bkn. 9-27-1839 d 1-31-1926 bPP; m James M.H. ALLEN (both nm)

MAHLER (See also Mailor)

MAI
Shinji I. b Japan d 10-29-1902 in Lincoln Hospital bPP (nm)

MAILOR (see also Mahler)
Jamima & ----- (H)
Ch: Mary Ann
cf Corn. 7-23-1829 with dt; ct Corn. 7-4-1849 for Jemima
Mary Ann Mapes (form Mailor), dt Jemima, rocf Corn. with mother 7-23-1825; dis mo 8-1830 (H)
William rocf Corn. 8-1831; dis 7-1838 (H)

MAINE
Elizabeth F., dt Malcolm T. & Phebe F., Bkn., b 11-3-1869; m 1894 Wm. M. ROUNTREE (H)
Frederic E., s Malcolm T. & P. Francena (Hallock), b Bkn. 8-30-1874; m 11-14-1906 Josephine F. CHILD (nm), dt Agnetus & Josephine (H)
Ch: Frederic C. b 5-20-1911
Frederic E.'s name entered by com. 10-10-1886; Fredric C. recrq of parents 6-14-1928
Hallock R., M.D. (nm), s Malcolm T. & Phebe F. (Hallock), d 6-13-1902 ae 37y 1m 20d bPP (H)
Malcolm T. (nm), s Horace S. & Minerva B., d 9-26-1909 ae 68y 11m 29d bPP; m at Jas. C. Hallock's 7-26-1864 (not under care of N. Y. MM) Phebe Francena HALLOCK, dt James C. & Eliz. M. (Frost), b 12-17-1843 N.Y.

MAINE, Malcolm T. & Phebe Francena, continued
d 1-30-1927 bPP (H)
Ch: Elizabeth F. b 11- 3-1869
Frederick E. " 8-30-1874
Malcolm T. Jr. (nm) d 1-7-1919 ae 52y bPP
John D. d 3-16-1902 ae 1m 6d bPP
Hallock R. d 3-14-1882 ae 5y 10m bPP
Eleanor d 7-21-1882 ae 1y 6m 26d bPP
names of 2 ch entered by com. 10-1886

MAIPHY
Evelyn Jeanne, dt Lucy M. DUBOIS, & foster ch of Thomas F. & Anna Maiphy; joined as Evelyn Jeanne Dubois 12-5-1906 by rq of parents; resumed name of Dubois 1930 & rel- [rq
Thomas F. & Anna W.
both recrq 10-3-1906; in France by 1909

MAITLAND
Robert, s John Martin & Mary Eleanor (Crewdson) b Ulverston, Eng. 11-22-1875; m 11-5-1901 Louise ATKINSON, dt Amos & Isabella Hutchinson, b Newcastle-on-Tyne, Eng. 9-23-1870 (H)
Ch: Mary b London 1-31-1903
Ralph Waldo b London 2-28-1904
parents recrq 7-8-1918; ch recrq of parents 7-8-1918

MALCOMSON
Abraham Bell, having con mo Hardshaw West rq care 10-1858, rst & cf Hardshaw West 4-28-1859; mbrp relinquished 3-1880; lived Bkn.
John rocf Lurgan, Ireland 2-19-1831; ct Hardshaw West. 7-3-1844 (clear); cert returned 12-1844 as he had returned to N.Y.; dis mo & lack of interest 1-1856; at Mobile, Ala.

MALONE
Ruth Ann Winifred, dt Jas. Ellias & Anne F. (Brown), b N. Y. 4-14-1903; m 10-27-1923 Wm. P. BURNS (nm) (H)
separated & resumed maiden name; recrq 2-9-1931

MANDEVILLE
Elizabeth, w Giles, wd Edw. K. VON BRUNT; m 3d 1-19-1893 Wm. H. MOREHOUSE (H)
cf Phila. 2-1859

MANEY
James H. rocf Corn. 2-22-1844; d 1872

MANGHAM
Ruth, w John, rocf Ama. 10-12-1824; dis 12-1831 (O); ct Chap. 1-1854 (H)
----- & -----
Ch: Phebe b Westchester Co. d 12-24-1822 ae 9y bHS

MANN
Adrian S. recrq 12-6-1933
George H. d 6-13-1874 ae 23y 2m 27d bPP (H)
George M. (nm) m Kate NASH (nm), dt Margaret, d 12-4-1900 ae 74y bPP
Ch: George B. N. Y. d 11-11-1847 ae 1m 12d bHS
Henrietta Boyles d 11-30-1854 ae 1y 8m 26d bPP
John, s Matthias (dec) & Sarah (now Stanbury) d 1-11-1841; m N. Y. 8-11-1790 Freelove HULL, dt Joseph & Phebe, N. Y., b R. I. d 4-20-1846 ae 82y (H)
Ch: John, Jr. b 5-15 (or 13) 1791
Sarah " 11-17-1793
Phebe " 5- 5-1798
Joseph " 11-20-1800
all dis 1829-1830 (O)
John, Jr., s John & Freelove, b 5-15-1791 (or 5-13-1791); m before 12-6-1820 Eliza ----- b N. Y. d 5-20-1821 ae 22y bHS (mo)
dealing for mo discontinued 3-7-1821
John, Jr. m 2d Phebe -----
Ch: James b 2- 9-1825
John
cf Marl. for Phebe 4-27-1825; all dis 1830-1848 (O); ct Hardwick 8-1829 for all (H)
Joseph, s John & Freelove, dis 9-3-1845 (H)
Phebe H., dt John & Freelove, N. Y.; m 1841 Thomas LAWS, of Jersey City (H)
Sarah, dt John & Freelove, N. Y., b 11-17-1793; m before 9-6-1815 ----- LAWRENCE (mo) dis mo 10-4-1815
Susan P., dt Buel H. & Louise D., b 1843 d 8-31-1915 bPP; m George W. WINGATE

MANNING
Anna M. (nm) d 12-17-1859 ae 68y 6m 1d bPP
Mary C. (nm), dt Richard H. & Mary (Weeks); m 1-7-1874 Richard C. FIELD (H)

MANNY
Benjamin B., having mo Marl. ref. to N. Y. 6-25-1851; dis 4-2-1852
John W., having mo Marl. ref. to N. Y. 6-25-1851; dis 2-1852

MANSFIELD
Edward recrq 8-6-1919; name erased 4-1928

MAPER
Joseph, Southold, desired a mtg established there once a yr 1700

MAPES
Mary Ann, dt Jemima MAILOR, rocf Corn. 7-23-1829; dis 8-1830 (H)

MARCELLINE
Edward (nm) & -----
Ch: Mary D. b N. Y. d 8-5-1832 ae 1y 5m bHS

MARCH
Samuel rocf Brighouse MM, Leeds, Eng. 6-21-1791 (clear)

MARCLINE
Caroline, dt Wm. T. & Mary SLOCUM; dis 11-1830 (H)

MARINE
Arlando, s William & Hannah; m Viola BROWNE, dt J. J. & Rose
Ch: Elinor Graves b 8-25-1891
Mabel Frances " 5-25-1893
James Sydney " 6- 2-1894
cf Cleveland 7-1889 for Arlando; cf Indianapolis 5-7-1890 for Viola
Eleanor Graves, dt Arlando & Viola (Browne), b 8-25-1891 Bkn.; m 1929 Alexander W. ALLEY (nm)
Mabel Frances, dt Arlando & Viola B., b 5-6-1893; m 1927 Cyrus B. CLARK (nm)

MARIS
Edward, s Jesse I. & Mary, Edgmont, Pa.; m N.Y. 10-14-1857 Eleanor K. WOOD, dt Stephen & Catharine M., N. Y.
Jesse J. rocf Deer Creek, Md. 2-1871; d 12-20-1871

MARK
Emily rocf Dublin, Ireland 4-6-1904; ct Dublin, Ireland 3-1927

MARLATT
Mary Eliz., dt Jacob & Rachel (dec), Newark, N. J.; m 1874 Wm. D. WILLIAMS (H)

MARR
William G. (or S.), s Robert & Georgina F., d 4-14-1923 ae 57y bPP; m Lissie ----- (H) both nm

MARRIOTT
Charles, s Henry & Margaret (both dec), Claverack; m N. Y. 12-8-1836 Sarah W. CORLIES, dt John & Eliz. WHITE (both dec), N. Y., b N. Y. d 4-15-1846 ae 62y (H)
cf Hudson 8-1840 for both; Charles dis 11-1841; Sarah was wd of Joseph Corlies
Henry rocf Creek 9-8-1818 (clear); ct Creek 8-1-1821 (clear)
Maria rocf Hudson 7-20-1819; ct Scipio 7-5-1826 (clear)
Susannah rocf Marsden, Lancashire 8-8-1793 (clear); voyage chiefly account of health, advised by Dr.; ct Creek 1-7-1795 (clear) at first intended to go to Phila. but now to your mtg; cf Muncy, Pa. 12-19-1810 (clear); ct Scipio 5-3-1820 (clear)

MARSH
Ann dis 9-5-1781
Benjamin rocf R. & P. 10-16-1782 (clear); ct R. & P. 4-7-1784 (clear), he living at Amboy
Catharine m 1847 ----- HADDOCK (apparently dt Jane F. Marsh); rec 1-1833; ct Battle Creek 7-1852 (H)
Eden rocf R. & P. 8-21-1816, minor; ct R. & P. 2-5-1823 (clear)
Elias (nm) & -----
Ch: Infant stillborn 12-7-1836 bHS
Francis rocf Kingston, Eng. 11-1881; ct Kingston, Eng. 12-1884
Fred D. recrq 2-1921
Hannah F., dt Jane F.; m ----- STRATTON, d 7-21-1854 (H)
recrq 1-1833
Jane F., Farrington; m ----- MARSH; m 2d 10-1843 Matthew FARRAND (H)
John, Flushing, contributor 1681
Lillian (nm) m 3-7-1891 Harry M. DAVIS, s Wm. & Eliz. (Mills) (H)
Harry recrq 8-1-1894; mbrp cancelled 5-11-1912; she obtained divorce (H)
Maria F. (apparently ch of Jane F.) rec 1-1833; ct Battle Creek 7-1852 (H)
Samuel dis mo 5-2-1793
Victor b Belfast, Ire. 1886 d 10-26-1918 ae 32y bPP; cf Lisburn, Ireland 5-6-1908
William & Sarah
Ch: William b 8 Mo (Oct) 6, 1711
----- & ----- (nm)
Ch: Priscilla b Bridgtown, N.J. d 1-25-1812 ae 11y bHS

MARSHALL
Albert E., s Asa & Mary (Birdsall), b N. Y. 10-7-1843; m 12-10-1863 Charlotte J. MILLER, dt Abraham & Catherine (Wright) (H)
Ch: Clarence b 1-15-1866
Gertrude " 9-17-1868
Albert E. Jr. b 8-16-1881
Infant stillborn 5-12-1876 bPP
cf Pur. 3-4-1874 for Albert; Charlotte recrq 5-4-1892; Albert E. Jr. recrq of parents 5-4-1892; others entered by com. 11-18-1884; ct R. & P. for Charlotte 3-11-1911
Albert E., Jr., s Albert E. & Charlotte J. (Miller), b N. Y. 8-16-1881; m 7-16-1901 Florence Amelia HOLLEY (nm), dt Lemuel P. & Ann Eliza (H)
Albert E. m 2d 6-15-1918 Ettiel W. KAULFUSS (nm) (H)
Albert recrq of parents 5-4-1892
Andrew, s Asa & Mary, rocf Chap. 9-9-1830 with mother; mbrp relinquished 3-1880
Andrew & Anna (H)
Ch: Henry G. b 5-5-1854
Andrew rocf Chap. 7-1852; Anna rocf Ama. 12-1853; ct Ama. 5-1855 (H)
Ann Eliza, dt Nathan; m ----- HAGEN (mo) (H)
cf Concord 5-1829; dis 2-1847
Anna, dt Jos. & Phebe, Nantucket; m 1786 Wm. JOHNSON
cf Dartmouth 11-21-1785 (clear)
Aquilla Bolton, dt Nathan, dis 8-1846; cf Phila. 7-1830; ct Phila. 12-1835; cf Phila. 3-1836; ct Phila. Cherry St. 3-1845; cf Phila. Cherry St. 6-1845 (H)

MARSHALL, continued
Asa & -----
Ch: Laura F.
    Sarah Adelia
    Phebe C. d 3-24-1857
    Albert E.
    Walter W.
    cf Chap. 10-1833; ct Duanes 7-1836; cf Duanes 7-1853 with 5 ch
Asa m 2d Mary B. -----
    cf Chap. 3-10-1853
Benjamin (nm) m Niobe ----- (nm) b N. Y. d 1-30-1823 ae 34y bHS
Caroline, dt Nathan & Mary, rocf Concord, Pa. 12-1-1829, minor; dis 1849 (O)
Clarence, s Albert E. & Charlotte, b 1-15-1866; name entered by com. 11-18-1884; relrq 5-6-1891 (H)
Daniel, s Sarah H., recrq of mother 2-1823; dis 2-1841 (H)
David (nm) & -----
Ch: Sarah d 3-17-1831 ae 1y 6m bHS
Edward J., s Edw. & Sarah, Sheffield, Eng.; m N. Y. 10-9-1844 Anna Maria BUSSELL, dt George & Elizabeth, d 8-17-1862
Ch: Sarah Elizabeth b 9-13-1845
    cf Balby, Eng. 1-16-1840; Ann Maria rocf Bristol with parent 6-13-1820
Edward Jr. m 2d Mary E. -----
    cert of clear to Muncy, Pa. 9-5-1866; cf Muncy 5-1867 for Mary; ct WD MM 9-1-1869 for both
Edwin, s Asa & Mary, rocf Chap. 9-9-1830 with mother; mbrp relinquished 3-1880
Edwin, s Asa & Mary B., N. Y., d 10-21-1890; m at Joseph G. Miller's 5-10-1854 Mary A. MILLER, dt Joseph & Hannah, Bkn. (dec), b Ama. 9-7-1834 d 3-12-1924 ae 89y 6m 5d
Ch: Charles E. b 10-9-1859 d 9-14-1908 (b N.Y.)
    Dr. Eugene W. b N. Y. 3-7-1868
    Edwin rocf Chap. 10-1-1856 (H); Mary rocf Chap. 11-1852 (H)
Elihu, s Obed, rocf Nantucket 5-28-1792; ct Nantucket 8-7-1799 (clear); Nantucket rpd to this MM 11-4-1801 that he left there some time previous to the American War, entered the army, obtained a commission, mo, & now resides in N. Y.; he now holds a place in the Naval Department of War.
Eliza rocf SD MM 5-29-1844; ct London, Eng.
Eliza Jane, s Asa & Mary, rocf Chap. 9-9-1830 with mother; mbrp relinquished 3-1880
Elizabeth, dt Sarah, d 10-11-1843; m Charles BABER (H)
Dr. Eugene W., s Edwin & Mary A. (Miller), b 3-7-1868 d 5-17-1933 bPP (H)
Gertrude, dt Albert E. & Charlotte J., Bkn., b 9-17-1868 Bkn.; m 1896 Norman D. STRINGHAM (H)
    her name entered by com. 11-18-1884; ct R. & P. with Norman & ch 3-11-1911
Harold A., s Andrew & Florence (Tompkins), b Bkn. 1-31-1900; m 10-23-1922 Lottiebelle TOMPKINS, dt Stanley & Carrie Belle (Williams), b Mt. Kisco 10-15-1899 (H)
Ch: Elizabeth b 6-21-1923
    Shirley " 6-21-1923
    parents recrq 4-12-1926; ch recrq of parents 4-12-1926
Henry G. rocf Ama. 7-2-1884; relrq 12-1-1880 (H)
Isaac S. rocf Scip. 3-1852; ct Scip. 9-4-1867
Jonathan (nm) b Pa. d 6-25-1843 ae 47y bHS; m Martha ----- (nm) b N. J. d 3-15-1837 ae 41y bHS
Ch: Almira b N. Y. d 11-4-1833 ae 3m 3d bHS
Justus (nm) b Mamaroneck d 9-10-1822 ae 25y bHS (unm)
Laura F., dt Asa & Mary B., N. Y.; m 1854 Benjamin C. MILLER (H)
    cf Duanes 7-1853 with father
Mary, w Asa
Ch: Edwin
    Eliza Jane
    Andrew
    cf Chap. 9-9-1830 with 3 ch named
Mary, dt Sarah, d 2-1837; m ----- MOORE 1836 (H)
Mary B. rocf Pur. 3-4-1874; d 10-26-1870 (H)
Moses & -----
Ch: Benjamin d 8-5-1804 ae 1y 1m bHS (nm)
Myra T., w Geo., dt Wm. C. & Beulah T. BAKER (H) relrq 6-4-1898
Nathan d 8-23-1849; m Mary BOLTON d 7-30-1851 (H)
Ch: Susanna C. b 11-10-1811 d 12-20-1909 ae 98y 1m 10d
    Carolina S. d 9-15-1896
    Mary " 3-20-1896
    Aquilla Bolton
    Ann Eliza
    cf Concord 6-1829 with first 2 ch named; separate cert for last 2
Phebe, w Thomas, rocf Chap. 10-1823; dis 10-1830 (O); ct Duanes 5-1833, ret. 6-1842; ct Duanes 9-3-1845 (H)
Sarah rocf Concord 8-1829; d 11-9-1853 (H)
Sarah Adelia, dt Asa & Mary B., rocf Duanes 7-1853; ct Ama. 8-1859 (H)
Sarah Elizabeth, dt Edward & Ann Maria, b 9-13-1845; ct WD MM 1-1872
Susanna, dt Nathan & Mary, rocf Concord, Del. 12-1-1829, minor; dis 1849 (O)
Walter W. rocf Pur. 3-4-1874; relrq 6-4-1884 (H)
William (nm) b Pa. d 7-18-1845 ae 71y 8m 18d; m Ann ----- (prob) b West. Co. d 10-23-1848 ae 69y bHS
Ch: Eliza d 5-23-1815 ae 2y bHS
William (nm) b N. Y. d 7-28-1848 ae 43y bHS (m)
----- m Sarah HAUXHURST, dt H. B., d 7-21-1874 ae 85y 4m 5d (H)
Ch: Elizabeth
    Daniel H.
    Mary

MARSHALL, ----- & Sarah, continued
Ch: Hannah
Sarah dis mo before 12-4-1811; rst 5-1-1816; ch recrq of mother 2-5-1823; all dis 1830-1839 (0)
----- & ----- (nm)
Ch: Benjamin d 11- 4-1812 ae 2y 3m bHS
Nathan b N. Y. d 11-12-1834 ae 3m bHS

MARTENS
Bahne recrq 3-1837; dis 9-1838
Terese L., dt Carl & Josephine (Weeks), b N. Y. 1-2-1880; m 1901 Henry B. WILSON (H)

MARTIN
Abbie d 4-11-1911 ae 78y 3m bPP; m Charles H. RAYMOND (H)
Abigail gct R. & P. 3-1-1786 (clear)
Agnes B. [Marton] (nm), dt George & Elizabeth; m 1906 Rowland MATHER (H)
Ann, dt Isaac & Eliz., N. Y.; m 1782 Richard SHOTWELL
Burling, s Isaac (dec) & Mary, N. Y.; m Flushing 5-10-1784 Mary LAWRENCE, dt Norris (dec), Flushing
ct Pur. 6-3-1778 with others of his father's fam (clear); cf Pur. 6-10-1779
Delaplaine, dt Catharine, rocf Shrews. 2-1829 with mother; dis 1-1838 (H)
Gulielma rocf Pur. 3-8-1781
Isaac, N. Y.; m 1754 Elizabeth ----- (mo)
Ch: Burling b 1-6-1755
Mary " 7-1-1756
Isaac " 1-16-1758
Elizabeth b 2-19-1764
Isaac & Elizabeth con mo 5-28-1755
Isaac, s Isaac & Eliz., N. Y.; m N. Y. 4-12-1780 Elizabeth DeLAPLAINE, dt Joseph, N.Y.
Ch: Joseph b 1-20-1781
Isaac " 10-24-1782
ct Pur. 8-7-1777; cf Pur. 6-10-1779; ct R. & P. 10-6-1784 with w & s, Isaac
Isaac, Jr., s Isaac & Elizabeth, b 10-24-1782; cf Wby 4-18-1804 (clear); ct R. & P. 7-3-1805 (clear)
Jessie (nm), dt Wm. Logan & Mary (Leet) (nm) m Eugene P. BILLIN (H)
Joseph L. rocf Shrews 4-1838; dis 6-1849 (H)
Maria d 5-20-1877 ae 70y bPP (H)
Mary m 1782 Richard SHOTWELL
Mary gct Phila. 7-5-1809 (clear)
Mary Ann, dt Isaac & Sophia UNDERHILL; dis mo 10-6-1841
Mary Rankin, dt James & Anna M. (Eakin), b Beaver Falls, Pa. 1-16-1888; m 1909 Robt. Canfield MAYER (H)
both recrq 11-12-1917; he d & her name rem 3-13-1933 for lack of interest
Norris L. dis mo 8-7-1816
Robert W., s Catharine, rocf Shrews. with mother 2-1829; d 12-9-1879 ae 68y 11m bPP (H)
----- m Catharine WHITE d 3-31-1872 ae 82y bPP (H)
Ch: Robert W.
Delaplaine
cf Shrews. 2-1829 for Catharine & ch
----- & -----
Ch: Phebe b Scarsdale d 8-27-1821 ae 1y 10m bHS

MARVEL
Josiah P. rocf Whitewater, Ind. 6-5-1929

MARWICK
James (nm) m 10-7-1915 Sarah R. BREWSTER, wd E. Franklin, dt Silvanus J. & Caroline R. MACY, b N. Y. 11-10-1861 (H)
she took ct Alexandria 4-11-1921

MASON
Annie Augusta, w Jos. P., dt J. Howard & Sarah J. WRIGHT, b 11-3-1857 (m 11-13-1877) (H)
Elizabeth Smart Southwick (form Mason) rocf York, Eng. 12-18-1839 with brother; had rem 1833; dis mo 1-1848
Emily rocf Carlow, Ireland 11-24-1859; ct Waterford, Ireland 7-5-1876
John W. dis mo 3-1850
John William & H. Maria
Ch: William b 5- 6-1850
Mary Thompson b 6- 4-1855
cf York, Eng. 12-18-1839 with sister; had rem 1833; parents relrq 11-3-1858
Joseph P., s Joseph & Sarah R., Worcester, Mass.; m at J. H. Wright's 11-13-1877 Annie A. WRIGHT, dt John Howard & Sarah Jane, N. Y., b 11-3-1857 (H)
Mary Thompson, dt John Wm. & H. Maria, b 6-4-1855; mbrp relinquished 3-1880
William, s John Wm. & H. Maria, b 5-6-1850; mbrp relinquished 3-1880

MASTERS
George, tailor, N. Y. d 9 Mo (Nov) 8, 1685 bur Gravesend; m Mary WILLIS, dt Henry (m at Henry's in Wby 9 Mo (Nov) 27, 1678)
Ch: Mary b N. Y. 7 Mo (Sep) 15, 1679
Philadelphia b N. Y. 5 Mo (July) 14, 1684
George b N. Y. d 7 Mo (Sep) 15, 1702, tailor, N. Y.
active mbr from 1676
Helen B. m 1894 Samuel Bussell WRAY
she brought cf WD MM 5-6-1896
Mary, dt Geo. & Mary; m 1702 William HAIG
Philadelphia, dt Geo. & Mary; m 1708 Jeremiah WILLIAMS
Thomas, Jr., s Thomas, Phila.; m Flushing 8 Mo. (Oct) 10, 1723 Elizabeth RODMAN, dt John, Flushing d 10 Mo (Dec) 22, 1724
cert of clear from Phila. 7 Mo (Sep) 27, 1723

MASTERTON
Avis, w Robert M. (m 6-24-1875), dt Willet & Mary SEAMAN, d 3-31-1899 (H)
Thomas (nm) & -----
Ch: Infant boy d 7-4-1848 bHS

MATHER

Rowland, s Joseph & Anna (Row), b Langhorne, Pa. 4-14-1879; m 6-12-1906 Agnes B. MARTON (nm), dt George & Elizabeth (H)
cf Middletown, Pa. 4-5-1902; relrq 3-13-1922

MATHEWS

Albert Frederic, s Robt. & Anna (Valentine), b Pt. Pleasant 8-16-1900; recrq 5-14-1917 (H)

Caroline J. [Matthews], dt Jos. B. & Eliz. S. (Jones), b Balt. 9-19-1888; m Cornelius A. WILSON (H)

Caroline J. m 2d 6-20-1925 Glen H. NOYES, s T. Wilson & Clara G., divorced him & took name of Wilson (H)

Charles (nm) & -----
Ch: Frederick d 2-5-1858 ae 12y 13m 4d bPP, rem 6-3-1864

Elizabeth S. [Matthews], d 6-13-1899; m -----
Ch: Elizabeth
John Jones
Caroline Jones
cf Balt. 7-9-1898 for all; Teressa Roberta a separate cert 12-9-1899

Ellen M. [Matthews], w O. B., dt James T. & Jane KENNY; relrq 8-1874 (H)

Eunice rocf Wby 4-6-1783 (clear); ct Wby 1-4-1804, infirm

Frederick L. (nm), s Robert F. & Mary B., Bkn. d 2-5-1914 ae 63y 3m 5d bPP; m at S. T. Valentines 1-21-1874 Mary Anna (or Ann V.) VALENTINE, dt Samuel T. & Anna (Kirk), Bkn., b 11-23-1848 N. Y. d 9-16-1913 bPP
Ch: Robert Valentine b Bkn. 10-11-1874
Robert V.'s name entered by com. 3-20-1899

Helen T., dt Jacob & Ann Eliza, Greenwich; m 1879 James W. HUNT (H)

Henry C. (nm) m Mary Ellen ----- (nm) d 1-6-1855 ae 20y 9m bPP

John Jones [Matthews], s Jos. B. & Eliz. S. (Jones), b Balt. 3-19-1886; m 10-7-1919 Rachel C. SHOEMAKER (nm), dt Owen & Greta J. (H)
cf Balt. with mother 7-9-1898

Mary Anna V., w Frederic L., dt Sam'l T. & Anna (Kirk) VALENTINE (H)
Ch: Robert Valentine b 10-11-1874
Robert's name entered by com. 3-20-1889

Oliver B., s Oliver & Mary F., d 1-3-1882 ae 48y 6m 2d bPP; m Ellen M. MAXWELL d 5-17-1890 ae 57y 1m 2d bPP (H)

Robert F. (nm), s Oliver & Mary F., Greenwich, Conn., d 8-2-1893 ae 77y 4m 23d bPP; m at Sarah Loines 5-8-1844 Mary B. LOINES, dt Rich. (dec) & Sarah (Hopkins), N. Y., b N. Y. 7-31-1823 d 10-2-1903 (H)
Ch: Frederick L.
Emily A. d 7- 9-1920 ae 74y bPP
Clara A. " 1-21-1926 ae 69y bPP
cf Pur. 4-6-1853 for Mary B.; cf Pur. 3-6-1861 (Sarah Loines not under care of N.Y. MM)

Rob't Valentine, s Frederic L. & Anna V., b 10-11-1874 Bkn.; m 10-25-1899 Martha STEINER (nm), d 4-30-1912 ae 36y 11m 2d (H)
Ch: Albert Frederic b Point Pleasant, N. J. 8-16-1900
recrq 5-14-1917

Sarah Ann, dt Amos & Ann WHITE, b 9-10-1810 d 11-13-1883 ae 67 (?) (H)

Teressa Roberta [Matthews], dt Jos. B. & Eliz. S. (Jones), b Balt. 4-7-1879; m 6-27-1917 Samuel R. CROWDER (nm) (H)
cf Balt. 12-9-1899

William [Matthews] d 10-25-1799 bHS

MATLACK

Armistead G., s Hannah, rocf Balt. with mother 10-11-1833; ct Alexandria 11-3-1847 (H)

Elizabeth S., dt Hannah; m ----- BLACKWELL (H)
cf Balt. with mother 10-11-1833

Emily, dt Hannah; m ----- COLEMAN (H)
cf Balt. 10-11-1833 with mother; ct Roch. 6-1841 (H)

Hannah, dt White & Mary, b 7-21-1783; ct Flushing 5-5-1819 (clear); cf Flushing 5-3-1827 (clear); d 7-27-1866 bPP

Hannah d 8-25-1875; w ----- (H)
Ch: Emily
Elizabeth S.
Mary W.
Armistead G.
cf Balt. 2-1834 with ch named; ct Roch. 6-1841 for Emily; ct Alexandria 1-7-1846 for Hannah; ct Alex. 11-3-1847 for Armistead; cf Balt. 6-1852 for Hannah [HICKS,N.Y.

Mary, dt White & Mary, N. Y.; m 1792 Willett

Mary W., dt Hannah; m Samuel S. COLEMAN (H)
cf Balt. with mother 10-11-1833

Rebecca rocf Phila. 5-28-1784, a minor, to live with her uncle, White Matlack; ct Phila. 5-7-1789

Samuel (nm) b N. J. d 5-31-1836 ae 53y bHS (m)

Timothy, s White & Mary, b 9-1-1791 d 8-4-1845; ct Flushing 5-5-1819 (clear)

White m 1768 Mary ----- (mo)
Ch: Mary
White Jr. b 2-16-1778
Hannah " 7-21-1783
John " 10-24-1785
Timothy, Jr. " 9- 1-1791
cf Phila. 1-3-1767; con mo 12-7-1768; ct Phila. 2-27-1784 with 3 ch named; cf Phila. same yr (not recorded); ct Flushing 6-5-1819 for Mary, rem with h

White, Jr., s White & Mary, b 2-16-1778 d 1-25-1833 ae 56y bHS; dis mo 8mo-1804

MATTHES

----- (nm) m Dorothy KNIGHT, dt Harry P. & Charity Ellen, b 3-1-1918

MAURICE

Charles, s Ch. Camilla & Sarah E. (Green), b

MAURICE, Charles, continued
b Katonah, 1-21-1876; m 6-30-1908 Florence BROWN, dt Geo. Evans & Mary E. (Taylor), b Bedford Villege 12-5-1881 (H)
both recrq 9-8-1919

MAXWELL
John Rogers, Jr., s John R. & Maria Louise (Washburn), b Bkn. 7-6-1875; m in Phila. 10-24-1903 Lydia CLOTHIER, dt Isaac H. & Mary C. (Jackson), b Sharon Hill, Pa. 1-22- [1878 (H)
Ch: John Rogers 3d b Bkn. 12-27-1904 d 4-11-1932
Morris Clothier b N. Y. 4-29-1907
Lydia b N. Y. 3-15-1909
Edith b N. Y. 2-12-1915
John recrq 9-10-1904; cf Phila. for Lydia 3-4-1905

MAYER
Andrew (nm), s Andrew & Mary A. (McDonald), d 2-18-1933 ae 78y 9m 8d ashes bPP; m 11-27-1877 Ella TOWNSEND, dt Sam'l W. & Eliz. F. (Lewis), b Phila. 4-6-1856 d 9-23-1924 bPP (H)
Ch: Andrew Jr. b 1- 3-1880
Wilson Townsend b 11-23-1881
MacDonald " 9-17-1884
cf Phila. 11-5-1890 for Ella; ch names entered by com. 1890
Andrew, Jr., s Andrew & Ella T., Bkn., b 1-2-1880; m at Stephen Valentine's 10-12-1904 Mary L. VALENTINE, dt Stephen & Annie (Lewis), Bkn., b Bkn. 3-7-1880 (H)
Ch: Mary Virginia b Bkn. 12-26-1917
Andrew's name entered by com. 11-5-1890; Mary L. recrq of parents 5-4-1887
August rocf Newcastle, Eng. 1-1867; ct Newcastle, Eng. 9-1-1869
Emily rocf Minden, Germany 11-6-1864 (clear); mbrp relinquished 3-1880
MacDonald, s Andrew & Ella (Townsend), b Phila. 9-17-1884; name entered by com. 1890; relrq 8-10-1912, then living in Portland Ore. (H)
Robert Canfield, s Robt. & Augusta (Werner), b N. Y. 12-2-1882 d 4-25-1930; m 12-15-1909 Mary Rankin MARTIN, dt Jas. & Anna M. (Eakin), b Beaver Falls, Pa. 1-16-1888 (H)
both recrq 11-12-1917; Mary's name rem 3-13-1933 for lack of interest
Wilson Townsend, s Andrew & Ella (Townsend) b 11-23-1881 d 4-19-1923; m Katharine ----- (nm) (H); name entered by comm. 1890

MAYNARD
Cornelia, w Edwin, dt Geo. F. & Hannah WHITE, b 5-24-1833 (m 12-23-1862 (H)

MAZEAN
Camille recrq 5-4-1892; name erased

MEAD
Asenath d 1-2-1875 ae 80y 3m 27d bPP (H)
Charles L. (nm) & E-----
Ch: Nathaniel S. d 7- 2-1852 ae 1y 9m 12d bPP
Julia A. " 8-13-1854 ae 11m 5d bPP
Daniel Independence, s Abraham & Mary (Fritts), b Woodbury Falls, N. Y. 7-4-1826 d 12- 6-1893; m Marietta AUSTIN (nm) (m 11-1852) (H) recrq 12-6-1893
Emily A., dt Geo. V. & Mary B., b 1-30-1871 N. Y.; m 10-9-1895 Edward Charles HOGG (nm) (H) name entered by com. 3-13-1883
Florence L., dt Geo. V. & Mary (Birdsall), b 4-28-1877 d 1-10-1923; m 1900 Wilbur Leed WRIGHT (H)
name entered by com 3-13-1883
George Livingston, s Geo. V. & Mary (Birdsall), b N. Y. 11-3-1872 d 12-15-1829; m 12-8-1896 Bertha VAN NOSTRANS (nm) d 2-19-1931 (H)
George V. (nm), s Ch. L. & Eleanor J.; m 6-23-1868 at Chas. L. Mead's (not under care of N.Y. MM) Mary BIRDSALL, dt Reuben & Sarah, b N. Y. 6-23-1840 d 8- 9-1916 (H)
Ch: Emily Acheson b 1-30-1871
Geo. Livingston b 11- 3-1872
Mary Birdsall " 11-16-1875
Florence Louise " 4-28-1877
Ida May " 4-19-1879
Harold Hallock d 2-21-1885 ae 6m
ch's names entered by com. 3-13-1883
Ida May, dt Geo. V. & Mary (Birdsall), b N.Y. 4-19-1879 d 6-19-1934; m 1913 Harry BENNETT (nm) (H)
Mary Birdsall, dt Geo. U. & Mary, b 11-16-1875; m 4-27-1898 Fred'k Hirleman SCHNEER (H)
name entered by com. 3-13-1883
Phebe d 12-31-1829 ae 49y 2m bPP; m Latham STRATTON
apprenticed to Benjamin & Judith Stratton to learn tailoring; in their rem cf Creek 4-17-1795; rem to Creek 6-8-1797
Semantha, dt Nathaniel & Hannah, N. Y.; m Richard WEEKS; m 2d 1846 Samuel FROST (H)
Washington (nm) m 3-1869 Anna HUNTER, dt John & Elizabeth (Brown), b Woodbury Falls, N. Y. 11-25-1849 d 3-28-1930 (H)
Anna recrq 3-7-1894
William Elmore rocf High Point, N. C.; name erased 4-1928
----- & -----
Ch: Mary E. d 8-20-1875 ae 1y bPP (perhaps ch of Asenath)

MEADER
Albert O. mo before 10-1867, ret a mbr; cf Dover, N.H. 10-1862 (Alfred O. in min.)
William F. rocf Providence 3-1871; ct Minneapolis 4-1880

MEAGHY
John & Anna Mary
John recrq 11-7-1900; Anna rocf Lisburn, Ire. 10-3-1900; ct Preston & Blackburn,

MEAGHY, John & Anna Mary, continued
Eng. 5-1-1907 for both

MEALY
Ethel (nm) m 1924 Wm. P. SMITH (H)

MEARS
Martha (nm) b Pa. d 1-5-1811 ae 66y bHS
Mary (nm) b Pa. d 10-26-1824 ae 37y bHS (unm)
Richard (nm) b Pa. d 7-20-1812 ae 66y bHS (widower)

MEDLAR
Mary,Jacobus (form Medlar), dt Samuel & Catharine, dis mo 4-1831 (H); dis mo 5-4-1831 (O)
Samuel m Catharine ----- d 12-20-1856 (H)
Ch: Infant d 5-17-1814 stillborn
William S. d about 1838
Mary
Samuel J. dis 1846 (H)
both recrq 3-3-1813; their ch recrq of parents 1-3-1816; all dis 1829-1839 (O); Samuel in Ill. & dis 5-1839 (H)

MEDLOCK
---- m Anna B. DURFEE
Anna recrq 8-1925

MEGIRIAN
Jacob, s Stephen & Marian, b Constantinople 1855 d 10-23-1918 bPP; m Acabe STEPHANIAN
Ch: John
Joseph
Rosa
Zareh
cf Westminster & Longford 6-6-1906 for parents & 2 younger ch (2 elder ch separate cert)
John, s Jacob & Acabe, rocf Westminster & Longford 1-4-1905
Joseph, s Jacob & Acabe, rocf Westminster & Longford 10-4-1905; d 7-1-1935
Rosa, dt Jacob & Acabe, d 1-11-1921; m 1918 Benjamin SHEKEYIAN (or Shekerjian) (nm)
cf Westminster & Longford 6-6-1906
Zareh, s Jacob (dec) & Acabie, N. Y.; m N. Y. 10-3-1923 Della Louise YARUS (nm), dt Westley F. & Edna Louise, East Orange
cf Westminster & Longford 10-4-1905 for Zareh, with mother

MEKEEL
Caleb & Maria
Ch: Anna U.
cf Scipio 5-17-1843 with 1 ch; ct Scipio 8-7-1844 with 1 ch named
George (not a mbr here) m Emeline HOYT, wd
George A.
Emeline recrq 10-1877; ct Minneapolis 6-1920
Jacob, Jr. rocf Ama. 1856; ct Ama. 7-1857
Mary, dt Isaac & Phebe, Somers; m 1850 John F. GRIFFEN (H)
dis mo 11-11-1850 (O)

MELDRU
Elizabeth (late Lundy) dis mo 1-6-1802

MELICK
Addie (nm), dt J. M. & Anna H.; m 1880 Wethered B. THOMAS (H)
Virginia A., dt Elmer Ellsworth & Annie (Miller), b Media 10-8-1904; m 1928 Henry Chandlee TURNER, Jr. (H)
cf Swarthmore 2-10-1930

MELLIS
Catharine, s John & Sarah, of Polisworth, Warwickshire; m 1804 William TILTON
Samuel, s John & Sarah, Northcastle; m N. Y. 12-6-1798 Jane HOYLAND, dt Wm. & Mary, N. Y.
cf Chap. 2-15-1799 for Samuel; Jane brought cf Lamworth, Warwickshire 4-12-1797 (clear)
ct Chap. 4-1-1801 for both

MELLOR
Martha m Henry C. DAVIS d 1864 in Phila. (H)
Walter (nm), s Alfred & Isabella (Latham), Germantown, Pa.; m at Walter Mendelson's 10-11-1919 Eliz. Wharton MENDELSON, dt Walter & Mary W., N. Y., b N. Y. 3-7-1886 (H)
Walter recrq 9-12-1910; Eliz.'s name entered by com. 10-6-1886; ct Germantown 1-10-1921

MENDELSON
Anna W., dt Walter & Mary (Wharton), b N. Y. 8-13-1895; recrq of parents 12-4-1895; ct Germantown 1-10-1921 (H)
Dorothy, dt Walter & Mary (Wharton), b N. Y. 5-26-1890; m Magnus SWENSON (nm) (H)
name entered by com. 12-3-1890
Elizabeth, dt Walter & Mary W., N. Y., b N. Y. 3-7-1886; m 1919 Walter MELLOR (nm), of Germantown (H)
Frances W., dt Walter & Mary (Wharton), N. Y., b N. Y. 4-17-1889; m 1912 Charles T. LAZELERE, of Norristown, Pa. (H)
name entered by com. 8-7-1889; ct Norristown, Pa. with ch 10-10-1921
Lewis, s Walter & Mary (Wharton), b N. Y. 2-14-1892; name entered by com. 7-6-1892; ct Germantown 1-10-1921 (H)
Dr. Walter (nm), s Simon & Rebecca (McGarr); m 5-23-1885 Mary WHARTON, dt Wm. Jr. & Anna (Walter), b Phila. 11-8-1858 (H)
Ch: Elizabeth Wharton b 3- 7-1886
Frances " " 4-17-1889
Dorothy " " 5-26-1890
August Lewis " " 2-14-1892
Anna " " 8-13-1895
cf Green St. Phila. for Mary 9-1-1886;
Anna W. recrq of parents 12-4-1895; other

MENDELSON, Dr. Walter & Mary, continued
ch entered by com. 1886-1892; ct Germantown 1-10-1921 for Mary; Walter recrq 2-12-1910; ct Germantown with w & 2 ch 1-10-1921

MENDENHALL
Raymond E. m Hazel HANSEN (m 10-27-1922)
Ch: John Harold b 1-14-1925 d 4- 3-1928
Edith Mildred b 8-31-1928
Hazel had 2 ch by form m; Raymond rocf Stanford 1-1922; Hazel rolf Lafayette Ave. Pres. Ch. 3-1920; ct Wilmington, O. for both 7-10-1935; Hazel was wd of Rudy C. HANSEN
Susan rolf Kimber M. E. Church, Dansville, Ill. 8-1914

MENNELL
Edward Newman, s Henry T. & Maria B., Shirley, Eng.; m Poughkeepsie 2-12-1907 Mabel Livingston FERRIS, dt Robert M. & Mary A. T., Pokeepsie (both dec), b 8-6-1873

MERRICK
Phebe Jane, dt Thos. U. SUTTON, gct Little Falls, Md. 12-7-1859 (H)
Thomas d 9-1-1803 ae 23y bHS

MERRIFIELD
Joseph rocf Pool, Eng. 6-18-1794 (clear); ct Phila. Middle Dist. 2-1-1797 (clear)

MERRIHEW
Frank, s Stephen & Caroline (Starr), b Wilmington, Del. 3-25-1860; recrq 7-4-1903; relrq 2-8-1913 (H)

MERRILL
Charles (nm) m Eliza SQUIRE, dt Samuel & Mary Ann, b 9-16-1851 d 10-17-1898 bPP
Ch: Mary Emma b 3-28-1876 d 5-18-1909 bPP
William J. b 1879
Eliza rel 3-1880
William J., s Charles H. & Eliza (Squire), b 1879 d 2-26-1935 bur in Oliver Hagen plot, PP; m Loatta DAVIDSON
Ch: Elizabeth b Bkn. 1-7-1923 d 8-12-1933 bur in Oliver Hagen plot, PP (all nm)

MERRITT
Albert A., s Edward & Phebe C. (Frost), b Pawling 7-6-1854; rocf Oswego 10-1-1890; ct Oswego 12-26-1914 (unm) (H)
Alice, dt Jesse & Pauline (W----), b Bethpage; m 1924 Victor WILSON (H)
Alice rem Jericho
Amelia E., dt Wilson & Mary, N. Y.; m 1836 Pelatiah P. PAGE
Andrew b N.P. d 11-3-1815 ae 20y 3m 13d bHS (prob. a mbr N.P)
Ann Eliza m ----- ELLIS (H)
cf Plains 7-1829; dis 5-1832
Anna, dt Michael & Phebe M. b 11-20-1799 d 1-22-1896; dis 1-1843 (H)
Anna, dt Richard P. & Harriet (Frost), b Bkn. 10-1-1880; m 1906 Edward Hallowell WORTH, of Coateville, Pa. (H)
ct Wilmington 7-13-1925 for Anna & dt
Anne, dt John & Phebe, N. Y., b 12-19-1785; m 1820 Nathan COMSTOCK
cf Jericho 7-19-1798
Benjamin (nm) & -----
Ch: Jane b Washington Co. d 4-25-1829 ae 19y bHS
Matthew F. b N. Y. d 9-2-1839 ae 25y bHS
Benjamin, s Nehemiah & Phebe (dec), d 3-24-1862; m at Geo. S. Fox's 4-11-1854 Eliza L. Fox, dt Geo. S. & Rebecca L., West Farms (H)
Ch: Infant stillborn 5-14-1859 bPP
Mary P. b 5-23-1861 d 2-26-1865
cf Scipio 7-2-1851 for Benjamin
Daniel, s Nehemiah & Phebe, b 4-3-1801; ct Troy 10-6-1819, apprentice
Daniel d 1-1835 ae 25y; m Hannah -----
Ch: Peter d 5- 5-1834 ae 3y bHS
Phebe Ann
Isaiah
cf Plains 3-25-1834 with 2 ch named; ct Plains 12-2-1835 for Hannah & ch, Phebe Ann & Isaiah
Daniel T., s Isaac & Mary Ann (both dec), Bkn. b Harts Village (now Millbrook), N. Y. 12-21-1856; m at S. J. Valentine's 2-10-1886 Ella VALENTINE, dt Samuel T. & Anna K. Bkn., b 9-5-1862 d 8-24-1893 bPP (H)
Ch: Mary Louise b 1-10-1888 d 3-31-1892 bPP
Daniel Valentine b 5- 6-1891 d 4-24-1893
Daniel V. d 4-24-1893 ae 1y 11m 16d bPP
Daniel T. m 2d 4-25-1901 Fannie Gordon HOWARD (nm)
Deborah, dt John & Phebe, N. Y.; m 1816 Richard FIELD
Deborah rocf Troy 11-1848; d 1-6-1853 (H)
Edward, s Nathaniel S. & Mary (King) Bkn., b 4-23-1827 d 2-11-1911 bPP; m at Samuel Willets' 1-11-1848 Amelia WILLETS, dt Samuel & Sarah H., N. Y., b N. Y. d 11-25-1848 ae 20y 8m 23d bPP (H)
Ch: Infant stillborn 11-16-1848
Edward m 2d at James C. Haviland's 2-16-1853 Sarah HAVILAND, dt James C. & Phebe, Bkn., b 11-21-1835 d 4-27-1890 bPP (H)
Ch: Alfred b 3- 4-1855 d 6- 2-1876 bPP
Charles Edward b 12-22-1856 d 2-22-1876 bPP
James H. b 12- 3-1858
Marshall stillborn 5-12-1876 bPP
Eleanor, dt Nathaniel S. & Mary K., Bkn., b 7-2-1845; m 1872 Edward C. ROBERTS (H)
Eliza (perhaps Ann Eliza, dt Wilson) m ----- ELLIS (mo)
dis 12-7-1831
Eliza L., w Joseph, gct Oswego 10-1829 (H)
Eliza F., dt Geo. S. & Rebecca L. FOX, N. Y.;

MERRITT, Eliza F., continued
m 1874 Jonathan THORN (H)
Elizabeth, dt Michael & Phebe, b 6-1-1810; dis 4-1838 (H)
Elizabeth C., w Joseph, gct Oswego 11-1829
George, s John J. & Hannah B., Bkn.; m at J. Jaggers 6-4-1857 (not under care of N.Y. MM) Louise M. JAGGER, dt John & Sarah E., Bkn. (H)
Ch: Harry G. d 12-3-1863 ae 15m 10d bPP
George relrq 10-6-1869
Grace Frost, dt Rich. P. & Harriet (Frost), b Bkn. 2-12-1878; relrq 5-12-1919 (H)
Hannah B., w John J., rocf Ama. 5-9-1828 (dup) rem with h
Isaac, Burl., N. Y.; m Susannah FIELD (1tm 12 Mo (Feb) 1, 1699/1700)
He prcf Burl., N. J. (clear)
Isaac & Eliza H. (m N.P. 1821)
Ch: Amelia H.
Philip H.
cert of clear to N.P. 4-4-1821; Eliza H. rocf N. P. 11-15-1821; ct N.P. 8-3-1825 with ch, dt & infant s named
Isaac N., s Isaac & Eliza (Hart), b Millbrook 7-24-1838 d 6-16-1923 bur N.P. Cem.; m 10-25-1881 Almira HENDERSON (nm), dt Jas. & Almira (Haskell) (H)
cf N.P. 7-8-1911
Jacob T. dis 4-1837 (H)
James d 3-13-1800 bHS
James b Webb Co. d 11-25- (or 11-24) 1836 ae 74 3m; m Sarah ----- d 9-10-1854 ae 87y 4m 9d bPP
Ch: Nathaniel b 8-26-1789
Richard " 6- 7-1792
Mary " 6-17-1795
Phebe " 3- 6-1798
Joseph " 9- 1-1801
Anne " 5-15-1805 d 1-22-1896
Sarah
cf Jericho 6-19-1794 with their 2 ch, Nathaniel & Richard; ct Ama. 12-2-1807 with 6 ch named; cf Ama. 5-9-1828 with dt, Ann & Sarah (both clear); all dis 1829-1832 (O)
James & Anne
Ch: William G.
Sarah Ann
cf Pur. 5-9-1811; ct Chap. 11-1-1815 with 2 ch named
James H., s Edward & Sarah S., b 12-3-1858 d 3-17-1914 ashes bPP; m Adele OVINGTON (nm), s Theodore T. & Louise, d 9-4-1933 ae 72y 2m 2d ashes bPP (H)
Ch: Charles Ovington b 2-27-1886 d 5-22-1886
Edward Haviland " 5-27-1887
Louise " 3-27-1894
Edward's name entered by com. 3-13-1889 & Louise's name entered by MM 9-9-1899
James N., s Wilson & Mary; m ----- (mo)
Ch: Infant stillborn 11-3-1841
cf Plains with parents 7-21-1829; dis 7-7-1841
Jane, dt Michael & Phebe, b 8-23-1807; dis 4-1838 (H)
John & Mary
Ch: Child d 3-25-1796
Child " 8- 5-1796
Mary " 1-28-1807 ae 29
John b West. Co. d 10-26-1833 ae 75y 6m; m Phebe I. WEEKS d 4-14-1838 at Phila. ae 72y 11m (H)
Ch: Ann b 12-19-1785
Phebe b 3- 1-1789
Deborah b 5-12-1797
Louisa " 12-19-1799 d 12- 7-1818
Nathaniel S. b 3-17-1802
John I. " 5-30-1804
Sarah L. " 4- 3-1807 d 4-25-1827
cf Jericho 4-18-1793 with ch, Phebe & Joseph; Dorothy Weeks, her sister, young, in same cert; all dis 1829 (O)
John, s John J. & Hannah B., b 12-22-1845; had joined U. S. Army during late war (7-3-1867) dis 10-2-1867
John C., s Michael & Phebe, dis 12-1831; d 5-3-1849 (H)
John J., s John & Phebe J., b 5-30-1804 d 1-4-1871; m Hannah B. ----- b 10-14-1808 (H)
Ch: Sarah b 11- 4-1828 d 5-19-1866 bPP
George b 4- 3-1831
Mary " 9-25-1835
Phebe " 11- 9-1838 d 12-18-1839
John " 4- 8-1841 " 1-25-1842
Phebe B. b 12-14-1843
John " 12-22-1845
Hannah rocf Ama. 8-1828; both dis 1830 (O); John J. dis 10-1867, appealed & dis confirmed; his preaching disturbed mtg
Joseph rocf 1822; dis 1826
Joseph, s James & Sarah, b 9-1-1801; cf Ama. 1-12-1822, minor
Joseph (nm) & -----
Ch: Isaac b N. Y. d 12-11-1825 ae 3d bHS
Lemuel (nm) & -----
Ch: Mary b N. Y. d 4-16-1816 ae 9y bHS
Rachel d 8-21-1816 ae 5m bHS
Louisa, dt Nathaniel S. & Mary K., Bkn.; m 1857 Edwin HAVILAND (H)
Louise, dt James H. & Adele O., Bkn. 3-27-1894; m 5-20-1926 Eugene Walker CALLIN (nm) (H)
recrq of parents 9-9-1899; name dropped 5-14-1934
Margaret, dt Michael & Phebe, b 3-10-1812; dis 4-1838 (H)
Maria B., w Richard, rocf Ama. 6-15-1822, rem with h; dis 1-1832 (O); d 7-17-1873 (H)
Mary, dt John, rocf Pur. 7-12-1798 (clear)
Mary, dt John J. & Hannah B., b 9-25-1835; m 9-23-1862 Edwin A. STUDWELL (nm) (H)
relrq 7-7-1869
Mary, dt Benj. A. & Hannah (White), b Pinelawn, N. Y. 6-14-1879; m 1900 Herman H. SMITH (H)
recrq 5-11-1907
Mary S., dt Wilson & Mary; m ----- MESSEROE (mo)
cf Plains 7-21-1829 with parents; dis mo

MERRITT, Mary S., continued
1-1847
Matthew Franklin b 3-2-1815 d 5-10-1896; m 1839 ----- (mo, ret a mbr) (H)
cf Scip. 9-1836 (H); cf Scipio 1-14-1835, minor clear (O); dis 3-1839 (O) for mo
Michael b Burl., N. J. d 6-8-1822 ae 54y; m Phebe M. ----- d 5-25-1855 (H)
Ch: William b 8- 9-1795
John C. " 10-26-1797
Anna " 11-20-1799
Allen C. b 7- 3-1802 d 9-26-1804
Jane " 8-23-1807; dis 4-1838 (H)
Elizabeth b 6- 1-1810 " "
Margaret " 3-10-1812 " "
Phebe rocf Pur. 1-8-1795; all dis 1829-1839 (O); Michael rocf Easton 3-16-1797
Nathaniel S., s John & Phebe J., b 2-12-1802 d 1-20-1890 bPP; m N. Y. 10-13-1825 Mary Ann KING, dt John & Mary R., d 9-27-1880 ae 74y 10m 27d bPP (H)
Ch: Edward b 4-23-1827
Walter " 1- 7-1831 d 1-26-1836
Charles b 5-15-1834 d 6- 6-1858 bPP
Louisa " 7-21-1839
Ellen (changed to Eleanor) b 7- 2-1845
all dis 1830-1839 (O)
Nehemiah m Phebe N. ----- b Washington, Dutchess Co. d 1-30-1823 ae 49y 9m 27d
Ch: Maria
William
Isaac
Daniel b 4- 3-1801
Sarah " 9-12-1804 d 9-22-1810 ae 6y 10d
Jacob " 2-12-1808; dis 1-1831 (O)
Benjamin " 4-16-1810
Matthew Franklin b 3- 2-1815
cf Oblong 2-16-1801 with 3 ch, Maria, William & Isaac; ct Scipio 6-6-1827 with his 3 ch, Maria, Benjamin & Matthew Franklin; Maria (clear)
Phebe, dt John & Phebe, N. Y.; m 1807 Wm. F. MOTT
cf Pur. 11-13-1794 (clear)
Phebe Morris (form Merritt) dis mo 5-6-1812
Phebe A., dt Benj. A. & Hannah E. (White), b Pinelawn, L. I. 10-13-1880; m 2d 1930 Herman H. SMITH (H)
Phebe A. m 1st ----- THOMPSON
Phebe B., dt John J. & Hannah B., Bkn., b 12-14-1843; m 6-15-1865 Samuel T. KEESE (H)
Phebe Jane, dt Thos. U. & Martha H. SUTTON, b 10-29-1834 (w James) (H)
ct Little Falls, Md. 12-1859 as Merritt
Philip H. rocf N.P. 1-1855; ct N.P. 8-2-1871 (H)
Richard (nm) & -----
Ch: Charles b N. Y. d 10-28-1827 ae 1y 2m bHS
Caroline b N. Y. d 6-23-1829 ae 5y 6m bHS
Richard P., s Isaac & Eliz. (Hart), d 9-25-1895; m 4-26-1866 Harriet FROST, dt Solomon V. & Abigail (Smith), b Pokeepsie d 10-20-1918 (H)
Ch: Richard Jr. b 5-21-1872 d 12-13-1876
Eliza Hart " 3-22-1876
Grace Frost " 2-12-1878
Anna Vail " 10- 1-1880
cf Oswego 11-5-1870 for Harriet
Robert (nm) & -----
Ch: Frances b N. Y. d 1-4-1828 ae 1y bHS
John Jr. b N. Y. d 1-16-1828 ae 8y bHS
Sarah, dt John, rocf Pur. 11-13-1794 (clear); dis 10-4-1797
Sarah, dt James & Sarah, N. Y.; m 1837 John CROMWELL (H)
cf Ama. 1828 with parents
Susan W., dt Wilson & Mary B.; m 1838 Merritt LEACH
Thankful rocf Troy 8-9-1815; dis 4-1829 (O); ct Troy 1-1831; d 5-1845 (H)
Titus (nm) d 9-12-1920 ae 93y 2m 27d bPP; m Adaline ----- (nm) d 7-20-1864 ae 29y 7m 5d bPP
Wm. Henry, s Wm. T. & Hannah, b 2-24-1822 d 3-1-1873, drowned in the Steamer Atlantic
William T., s Nehemiah & Phebe, N. Y.; m N. Y. 4-12-1821 Hannah KING, dt John & Mary R., N. Y. (H)
Ch: William Henry b 2-24-1822
Mary " 2-10-1824
Caroline " 7-1829
Phebe b 5-24-1830 d 10-28-1831
Thomas J. b 5-10-1833 d 9-19-1833
all dis 1830-1849; ct N.P. 2-1840 for all but Wm. H.
Wilson d 9-27-1836 ae 53y 1m 3d; m Mary B. ----- d 7-24-1868 ae 79y bPP, rem to Greenwood
Ch: Ann Eliza
Susan W.
Amelia E.
Joseph W. d 5-16-1830 ae 12y bHS
James N.
Mary S.
cf Plains 7-21-1829 with 6 minor ch named; all dis 1830-1847 (O)
----- & -----
Ch: William b N. Y. d 12-25-1811 ae 3y 9m bHS
Daniel d 1- 1-1835 ae 25y bHS
Wilson " 9-27-1836 ae 53y 1m 3d bHS

MERRYWEATHER
William (nm) d 11-12-1833 ae 25y bHS

MESSEROE
Mary S., dt Wilson & Mary MERRITT, rocf Plains 7-21-1829 with parents; dis mo 1-1847

MESSNER
Charles W. & Ida
Ch: Mary Elizabeth
cf Swansea 9-1925; Mary E. associate; letter to Con. Ch. East Canaan, Conn. 3-1927 for all
Henry L., s Martin A. & Clara (Kieffer),

MESSNER, Henry L., continued
b Roaring Branch 2-6-1885; m 6-12-1916 Hannah WALTON, dt Wm. E. & Ellen (Janney), b Genoa, Neb. 10-1-1884 (H)
Ch: Shirley Anne b 2-25-1919
Henry L., Jr. b 6-26-1921
cf Swarthmore for Henry 2-9-1925; cf Balt. for Hannah & ch 3-9-1925

METFORD
Francis (nm) & Phebe
Ch: Infant stillborn 12- 7-1838 bHS
Phebe H., dt Daniel & Ruth COOLEDGE, dis mo 8-2-1837; rst 7-1848; d 5-17-1881
Seymour d 7-4-1844 ae about 24
Thomas Bevan rocf Poole & Southampton, Eng. 8-6-1840; d 7-4-1844 ae about 26

METZ
Herman (nm) m Mary GOERKE, dt Rudolph & Paulina, d 7-25-1893 bPP
Ch: (prob) Pauline b 4-15-1890 d 4-4-1901 bPP
Frank William b 12-3-1883 d 7- 5-1828 Union City, N. J. bPP

MEYER
Ellen C. recrq 6-12-1901; d 5-17-1906
Phebe (nm), dt George & Phebe, b Bkn. 9-1-1860 d Central Park, L. I. 6-8-1922 bPP; m Benjamin GOERKE

MIDDLEBERGER
Judith (form Jenkins) dis mo 9-2-1829 (O); dis mo 1-1830 (H)

MIDDLEBROOK
Mary Ann (nm) (form Seaman) b N. Y. d 10-16-1831 ae 21y 3m bHS

MIDDLECOTT
Mary Ann, dt Israel & Agnes DEAN; dis mo 3-1-1843

MIDDLETON
Hannah L., dt Wm. & Jane, N. Y.; m 1842 Anseln B. HANCE (H)
Joseph H. rocf ND MM 10-1850; rel 3-1880
Mary S. (form Perkins) dis mo 12-4-1839

MILDEBERGER
----- & ----- (nm)
Ch: Emeline b N. Y. d 12-5-1836 ae 1y bHS
Adelia " " " 7- 4-1838 ae 4y 7m 7d bHS
Emeline " 10-27-1845 ae 11d bHS

MILES
Orville E. m 8-17-1927 Leona May HOLE, dt Edgar T. & Adelaide W.
Orville rocf West Richmond, Ind. 1-7-1931; Leona rocf Cleveland 9-6-1911

MILLER
Abraham C. (nm) d 2-26-1892 ae 66y bPP; m Mary ------ (nm)
Ch: Ida d 9- 4-1863 ae 1y 11m bPP
Mary " 8-24-1900 ae 73y bPP
Edwin " 2-15-1866 ae 1y 8m bPP
Frederick " 10- 6-1884 ae 15y 11m 9d bPP
Eugene " 3- 7-1867 ae 1m 10d bPP
Clara
all nm
Ada recrq 11-1883; ct Glens Falls 2-1888
Albert E., s Benj. C. & Laura F. (Marshall), b 2-17-1863 d 6-19-1924; m Jennie E. SMITH (nm)
Amaziah (nm) & -----
Ch: William d 12-13-1855 ae 2y 1m 2d bPP
Sarah Jane d 12-17-1859 ae 68y 6m 1d bPP (Prob some error regarding age of Sarah Jane, pencil figures clearly written over with ink, perhaps was 18)
Anna R. rocf Phila. 12-4-1878; relrq 12-3-1884 (H)
Annie, dt Ezekiel & Phebe (Underhill), b 11-21-1865; m 1891 Morris FOLSOM (H) relrq 5-9-1921
Benjamin C., s Joseph & Hannah (Carpenter) (dec), b Ama. 5-10-1832 d 3- 7-1909; m at Asa Marshall's 5-9-1854 Laura F. MARSHALL, dt Asa & Mary B., N. Y., b Duanes 7-6-1834 d 11-7-1910 (H)
Ch: Francis W. b 4-28-1855 d 10-6-1891 bPP
Emma " 10-29-1857 d 12-13-1857 bPP
Edwin " 1-12-1861 " 12-20-1863 bPP
Albert E. " 2-17-1863
Phebe C. " 8-20-1867
cf Ama. 9-1852 for Benjamin
Benjamin G. rocf Ama. 4-1849 d 8-29-1860 (H)
Carolyn A., dt Henry W. & Eliz. D., Bkn., b N. Y. 11-5-1866; m 1896 D. Frederick CARVER (H)
Catharine rocf Hard. & Randolph 10-5-1820; dis 1-1829 (O)
Catharine Mills (form Miller) rocf H. & R. 2-1821; dis 1-1829 (H)
Catharine, dt Henry H. & Helen G.; m 6-28-1913 John C. DAHL (H)
Charles, s Abraham & Phebe, of Rye; m Chap 10-18-1806 Amy CONKLIN, dt Jacob & Amy, Mt. Pleasant
Ch: Ann A.
Jacob
Daniel H.
Charles C.
Mary
Edward
Phebe
cf Pur. 8-11-1796, apprentice; ct Pur. 2-4-1801 (clear); cf Pur. 11-8-1804 (clear); cf Chap. 12-12-1806 for Amy
Dr. Charles (nm) d 1-10-1854 ae 37y 3m 13d bPP; m Amanda K. CLARK, dt Rufus, d 5-13-1895 ae 73y 5m 8d bPP (H)
Ch: Elizabeth Clark

MILLER, Dr. Charles & Amanda K., continued
Ch: George W.
Grace C. d 5- 7-1850 bPP in same grave with Charles
Amanda YM Clerk; Elizabeth recrq 10-6-1886
Charles, D.D.S., s Abraham & Elizabeth (Griffen), b 3-23-1821 Ama. d 6-28-1909; m 10-20-1849 Sarah S. GIFFORD (not a mbr in N.Y.), dt Wm. & Rebecca (H)
cf Ama. 8-1848; lived in N. Falmouth, Mass.
Charles D. rocf Pur. 4-1835; d 1-18-1858 (H)
Charlotte J., dt Abraham & Catharine (Wright), b N. Y. 7-23-1843; m 1863 Albert E. MARSHALL (H)
ct R. & P. for Charlotte 3-11-1911
Clara, dt Abraham C. & Mary, d 2-27-1903 ae 48y bPP; m (prob. Charles) SMALLEY (H)
Daniel C., s Daniel & Abigail, d 9-29-1882; m Ann Eliza ----- d 7-12-1852 (H)
Ch: Mary b 12-25-1837
Phebe W. " 5-26-1840
Forman W. " 9-11-1842
Louisa " 12- 2-1844
James E. " 7-10-1846 d 10-24-1849
Edgar " 5- 7-1851 d 6-19-1852
cf Ama. 4-1838 for Daniel C.; Ann Eliza recrq 10-1837
Daniel C. m 2d at Robert Cox's 11-10-1855 Mary COX, dt Robert & Phebe (dec), N. Y. (H)
Mary rocf Chap. 9-1855; Mary gct Ama. 6-4-1884
Daniel H. & Abigail
Ch: Stephen
cf Pur. 4-12-1798 for both; ct Pur. 5-1-1799 with s, Stephen
Daniel H. rocf Pur. 9-1840; dis 4-4-1849 (H)
David H., s Sarah, d 12-5-1908 ae 87y bPP; m (prob) Sarah E. ----- (nm) d 5-29-1907 ae 76y 8m 16d bPP (H)
cf Ama. 11-1843; dis 5-1854
Eliza, dt Abm. & Mary (Briggs), b N. Y. 11-26-1858; m 2-6-1901 Henry R. JONES
Elizabeth d 6-19-1858; m ----- (H)
Ch: Mary Emily
cf Ama. 6-1850 with dt
Elizabeth, dt Hyman G. & Mary (Roberts), b Bkn. 6-8-1902; m 1923 C. Norman STABLER (H)
Eliz. Clark, dt Dr. Chas. & Amanda K., Bkn.; m 1886 Wm. Penn HOLCOMB (H)
Elizabeth recrq 10-6-1886
Eliz. D., dt Wm. D. & Phebe C. DAVENPORT, Bkn.; m 2d 1896 David R. UNDERHILL (H)
Elizabeth K. recrq 6-1888; death recorded 4-1928
Ethel A. m ----- MOMBELLY (nm); recrq 1923
Ezekiel H., s Richard & Sarah Ann (Hoag), Somers Tp., N. Y. 9-11-1837 d 4-24-1910; m 2-1-1861 Phebe H. (or C.) UNDERHILL, dt Alfred & Jane (H)
Ch: Ida b 4- 2-1864
Annie " 10-20-1865
Irving Underhill b Nyack 8-17-1883
cf Ama. 4-1-1846 with parents; cf Chap. 3-1862 for Phebe
Ezekiel H. m 2d 7-20-1901 Henrietta WEEKS (nm), of Wby (H)
Forman W., s Daniel C. & Ann Eliza, b 9-11-1842 relrq 3-6-1889 (H)
George F. W., s Charles & Amanda K. (Clark), b 11-15-1850 d 8-5-1926 Bkn. bPP; recrq 10-10-1921 (unm) (H)
Grace Halsey, dt David & Sarah, d 1-20-1929 ae 74y 7m 20d bPP (unm) (H)
Hannah rocf ND MM 10-24-1826; ct Troy 8-1834
Hannah rocf Phila. 1827; dis 1-1832
Hannah rocf Pur. 11-1836; d 4-2-1853 (H)
Helen (nm) m Walter GOERKE
Henry G., s Richard & Sarah Ann; m Amie Jane ----- (H)
Ch: Margaret b 12-13-1870
cf Ama. 4-1-1846 for Henry; cf Chap. 3-5-1862 for Amie; ct Chap. 7-3-1878 for all
Henry W. d 2-17-1879 ae 38y 11m 17d bPP; m Elizabeth D. ----- (H)
Ch: Carolyn Alice b 11-5-1866
cf Ama. 7-1852 for Henry; cf Duanes 3-1855 for Elizabeth; ct Ama. 2-6-1861 for both; cf Pur. 8-1-1866
Herbert & Emma
Ch: Martha
Herbert James
Charles Edward
Ada
all recrq 4-1909, 3 younger ch as associates
Hyman G., s Alex. & Ella (Church), Jericho, Vt. b Jericho, Vt. 10-11-1873; m at J. H. Roberts 10-5-1898 Mary W. ROBERTS, dt John H. & Sallie B. (Williams), Bkn., b 3-3-1875, Camden, N. J.
Ch: Elizabeth b 10-12-1900
Mildred Thorn b 6- 8-1902
Hymen recrq 1-8-1898; Mary rocf Chester with parents 10-7-1891; ct Makefield 8-1814 for all but Elizabeth
Ida, dt Ezekiel & Phebe C., b Bkn. 4-2-1864 d Chap.; m 10-14-1899 David Lane BARNUM (nm), of Stansbury & Phebe, Jr. (H)
Isaac gct Concord, Pa. (or to Gorsham) 10 Mo. (Dec) 1, 1744
Jacob d 5-26-1897; m Mary ----- d 5-13-1890 (H)
Ch: Anna b 7-14-1835 d 3-13-1842
cf Pur. 9-1829 for Jacob; cf Pur. 11-1834 for Mary
James E. rocf Ama. 5-1841; relrq 7-6-1864 (H)
James H. (nm) d 11-5-1877 ae 29y bPP (H)
Jane, dt Sarles & Phebe; m ----- EDWARDS (H)
dis 5-1834; dis 5-6-1835 (O) (for mo)
Jane, dt Jos. Richardson & Helen Adeline (Munger), b Amherst, O. 3-25-1886; m 1909 Sanford Dewey FRANCE (H)
recrq 12-12-1927
Jemima rocf Cornwall 4-22-1830 (clear); dis 6-1831 (O)
Jesse, Chap. m 1782 Elizabeth ----- (mo)
Jesse mbr at Chap; Elizabeth dis mo 12-4-1782

MILLER, continued
John rem to Concord, Pa. 10 Mo. (Dec) 1, 1744
John rocf Pur. 2-13-1806, apprentice; ct Ama. 4-3-1811 (clear)

John T. (nm), s Jacob & Ellen, d 12-18-1896 ae 70y bPP (H)
Joseph d 1-6-1888; m Hannah ----- (H)
Ch: Mary A.
cf Ama. 11-1852 with ch
Joseph G., s Joseph & Hannah (Carpenter), b Ama. 9-8-1837 d 10-21-1913 bPP; m London 10-3-1866 Isabella THOMSON, dt James & Mary (Tulla) b London 3-26-1839 d 2-20-1906 bPP
Ch: Olive d 10-11-1869 ae 1y 8m bPP
Hannah " 7-23-1869 ae 3m bPP
Leah H. b 11-29-1871
Amy J. " 4- 2-1874 d 7-29-1917 bPP
Laura Belle b 9-22-1881
cf Ama. 8-1859; relrq 1-2-1867; both recrq 9-1-1886; ch entered by com. 4-3-1888
Josephine B., dt Leah, b Peekskill 10-28-1835 d 1-25-1923; m 7-1-1858 Marquis C. FROST (H)
cf Ama. 12-14-1855 with mother
Katherine (nm), dt John & Margaret; m Milton ROBBINS (H)
Leah H., dt Joseph G. & Isabella T., b Bkn. 11-29-1871; m 1904 Erwin R. MILLER (H)
Louisa, dt Daniel C. & Ann Eliza, b 12-2-1844 d 10-23-1879; m 5-13-1869 Henry JONES (nm) (H)
Margaret E., dt Francis & Caroline H.; m 1889 Samuel M. JANNEY (H)
cf Sandy Spring 8-6-1890; ct Wilmington, Del. 3-13-1933
Mary (nm), d 3-8-1810 ae 40y 3m after childbirth
Mary, dt Charles & Amy, N. Y.; m 1825 Thomas T. GRIFFEN, of Scarsdale
Mary, dt Sarles, rocf Plains 8-23-1825 (clear)
Mary, dt Daniel & Ann Eliza, b 12-25-1837 d 1909; m 4-22-1857 Benjamin B. PATTERSON (nm) (H)
Mary A., dt Joseph & Hannah, Bkn.; m 1854 Edwin MARSHALL (H)
cf Ama. 11-1852
Mary Emily, dt Abraham & Elizabeth, b Ama. 3-27-1830 d 1-1-1907 bPP (unm) (H)
cf Ama. 6-1850
Mary T., dt Joseph G. & Isabella T.; m 1888 Charles HOLME
Mary T. recrq 6-1884 (O);
Phebe, dt Daniel & Ann Eliza; m Henry WHITSON (H)
Phebe C., dt Benj. C. & Laura F., b 8-30-1867 Bkn.; m 10-25-1888 John C. SMITH (nm) (H)
Phebe C. m 2d 8-16-1912 John A. BARNS (nm)
Phebe Jane, dt Stephen & Leah, Bkn.; m 1844 Isaac D. FROST; m 2d ----- BROOKS (H)
cf Ama. 10-1843
Phebe W., dt Daniel C. & Ann Eliza, b 5-26-1840; m 4-22-1857 Henry WHITSON (mo, ret a mbr (H)

Phila G., w Joseph, rocf New Bedford 1851; ct Sandwich, Mass. 5-1870
Rebecca (nm), dt Robert, b S. I. 1822 d 3-28-1900; m 1868 John Ellison DAME
both bPP
Richard m Sarah Ann ----- d 10-18-1850 (H)
Ch: Henry G.
Ezekiel H.
cf Ama. 4-1-1846 with 2 ch; ct Ama. 6-1-1859 for Richard
Richard Jr. (nm) b N. Y. d 2-5-1844 ae 22y 7m 20d bHS
Robert rocf Ama. 8-1848 d 4-6-1887 (H)
Samuel W. (nm), s Samuel & Anna; m 5-11-1876 Mary LIPPINCOTT, dt Samuel T. & Sarah Jane (Acton), b Salem, N. J. 2-27-1857 (H)
Ch: Harold Acton b 10-14-1882
Alvar Edward " 5-19-1886 d 12-30-1889
cf Salem 11-5-1879 for Mary; ch's names entered by com. 3-29-1887
Sarah, w Thomas, b N. J. d 8-25-1842 ae 69y 11m 25d; recrq 1-1838 (H)
Sarah Ann (nm), dt Samuel & Eliz. (Bedell); m 1850 Edward C. LONGBOTTAM (H)
Sarah H. gct Ama. 5-2-1821
Sarah H., dt Joseph & Hannah (Carpenter), b Ama. 12-25-1845; m 9-15-1874 Reuben B. MILLER (H)
cf Ama. 3-1-1876
Sarah S., w Charles, rocf Sandwich, Mass. 7-1851
Sarles b West. Co. d 2-18-1832 ae 50y; m Phebe ----- b No. Salem d 9-4-1823 ae 44y (H)
Ch: Sarah Ann
Olcha dis 10-1832
Henry
Daniel dis 2-1842
Philip dis 9-1842
Amy d 12-3-1823 ae 8y
Jane
Hannah " 4- 4-1824 ae 3y
Mary U.
Samuel stillborn 5-2-1822
cf Plains 3-25-1823 with 8 ch named, also Mary Underhill
Sarles m 2d Amy ----- d 9-6-1829
Ch: Mody
cf Chap. 1-13-1825 for Amy, w Sarles, with dt, Mody
Stephen, s Daniel & Abigail, Somers, N. Y.; m N. Y. 10-12-1820 Leah HUBBS, dt Christopher & Charity, N. Y., d 2-28-1863 ae 61y 20d bPP
Ch: Josephine B.
cf Ama. 12-14-1855 for Leah & Josephine
Wyatt W. (nm) m Mary L. GRIFFEN, dt John & Esther (Leggett), b N. Y. 7-29-1838 d 6-23-1920 (m 5-12-1858) (H)
----- & -----
Ch: Charles b N. Y. d 1-20-1827 ae 2d bHS
Amy b N. Y. d 3-1-1827 ae 10d bHS

MILLER, continued
----- & ----- (nm)
Ch: Robert E. d 5-4-1858 ae 1y 2m bPP
Robert " 10-12-1866 ae 52y bPP

MILLINGTON
Frederick recrq 4-6-1910; name erased 5-1928
Wm. Henry, s Wm. Henry & Alice (Smith), b Birmingham, Eng. 11-16-1899 d 4-16-1918 bPP (nm)

MILLS
Albert T., s Abel & Elizabeth (Wilson); m 9-18-1931 Martha R. KIMBALL, wd Wm. L., dt John & Sarah ROBERTS, b Camden 3-6-1878 (H)
ct Clear Creek, Ind. 9-1932 for Martha
Catharine (form Miller), b N. J. d 7-22-1829 ae 40y bHS (H)
cf H. & P. 2-1821; dis 1-1829
Eldon H. & Florence
Ch: Sidney A.
Dorothy G.
Eldon H. Jr. b 1-24-1923
Marilyn
cf Dartmouth, Mass. 11-1922 for parents & 2 ch; ct Indianapolis 7-1925 for all; cf Indianapolis for all including Marilyn 10-2-1929; letter to Bkn.-Nassau Presbytery for father 4-6-1932 (Pastor Bkn. Mtg)
Elizabeth, dt Wm. F. & Sarah C. LEGGETT, b 11-2-1837; dis mo 3-7-1866 (H)
Hannah (late White) d 10-11-1826 ae 44y; dis mo 1-2-1811
James took cert of clear to sail abroad 8 Mo (Oct) 5, 1699
James & Adeline (H)
Ch: Madeleine d 7-27-1884 ae 11m 28d
Cromwell " 4-26-1885 ae 3y 18d
Adelaide " 1- 2-1890 ae 1y 2m 5d
Infant stillborn 8-7-1890
all nm bPP; Madeleine rem from Greenwood 4-27-1885
Phebe con mo 11-3-1757
Phebe Jane rocf Oswego 10-1865; ct Minneapolis 6-12-1873
Sarah, dt Stacy & Hannah, Mount Holly, N. J.; m 1820 John HANCOCK
cf Burl. 4-5-1819
Walter Jr. recrq 5-1924; name erased 4-1928
----- & -----
Ch: William F. d 5-23-1882 ae 61y 9m bPP

MILNER
Arthur recrq 2-1869; membrp relinquished 3-1880
Joseph rocf Balby 2-9-1854
William [Millner] rocf Brighouse MM, Shewbroad, Eng. 7-24-1789 (clear); dis mo 12-6-1797

MILTON
Alfred Day, s Nathaniel & Mary Ellen (Sharrock) b 1908; name erased 11-1928
Alfreda Amelia, dt Nathaniel & Ellen (Sharrock) b 12-11-1916; name erased 11-1928
Alice Florence, dt Nathaniel & Mary Ellen (Sharrock), name erased 11-1928
Joseph Nathaniel (name changed from Lagerblom 3-10-1899 by order of Kings Co. Court, Bkn. m 1906 Mary Ellen SHARRACK (or Sharrock)
Ch: Robert Heaton b 1907
Alfred Day " 1908
Alice Florence
Ruth Elizabeth b 12-11-1916
Alfreda Amelia
Mary recrq 3-1-1905; Joseph recrq 5-3-1893; names of all but Robert erased 11-1928
Mary, Jr. rocf Grange, Ireland 4-21-1824 addressed to Phila. (clear); cf Phila. 11-24-1824, added, as she lives in N. Y.
Robert Heaton, s Jos. & Mary E., b 1907; name erased 4-3-1929
Ruth Elizabeth, dt Nathaniel & Ellen, name erased 11-1928

MINARD
Carrie m ----- ANTHONY
cf Marl. 6-1886; rel 11-2-1898, jas
John (mbr of Lobo. Ontario), s David & Margaret; m 6-19-1856 Serena A. CARPENTER, dt James & Mary A. (Jube), b N. Y. 3-1839 d 4-4-1912, Lobo (H)
Ch: Mary Frances
cf Lobo 1-7-1899 issued 9-4-1898; ct Lobo 10-14-1911
Mary Frances, dt John & Serena (Carpenter); m 1891 Wm. Mudge TITUS (H)
Mary mbr Lobo, Ont.
Stephen (nm) & -----
Ch: daughter stillborn 5-18-1809
infant stillborn 11-27-1811 bHS
Walter W. m 6-10-1923 Caroline E. UNDERHILL, dt Eliz. G.
Caroline rocf Hartland 5-4-1898; Caroline gct Scip. 11-1923

MINOR
Mary M., dt George & Cath. FORMAN, rocf SD MM 10-26-1825
----- & ----- (nm)
Ch: Letitia Marsh d 3-1-1811 ae 12y bHS

MINTURN
Benjamin G., Jr. (nm) d 11-6-1832 ae 27y bHS
John recrq 1803; dis mo 9-1838 (O); lived New Orleans
Jonas & -----
Ch: Eliza Ann d 3-16-1803 ae 2y 9m bHS
Mary (late Bowne) dis mo 6-4-1794
Penelope, w William, b Newport, R. I. d 4-6-1821, a wd, ae 74y 4m 14d
Ch: Hannah b New Port, R. I. d 3-1-1817 ae 44y bHS (unm)
William b New Port, R. I.
William (nm), s William & Penelope b R. I. d 11-18-1818 ae 43y bHS (m)
Sarah (late Bowne) dis mo 1-7-1801

MITCHELL
Andrew mo before 2-1853, ret a mbr; cf WD MM 4-26-1843, minor; dis non-attendance & attending those of another society 2-1857
Ann Elizabeth rocf Nantucket 1851; d 2-10-1859 ae 45y bPP
Caroline L., dt Wm. F. & Sarah LEGGETT; mo, ret a mbr; d 4-7-1867 (H)
Daniel Thornton, s James, rocf Nantucket 1-26-1843, minor; ct Salem, Mass. 4-1858
Edwin rocf Creek 2-1864; ct Pokeepsie 7-2-1873
Elizabeth, w Francis, gct Edinburgh, Scotland 7-5-1815, rem with h
Elizabeth (late Travers) dis mo 8-5-1812; rst 4-5-1815
Esther, dt Abraham & Sarah, Phila.; m 1762 Samuel FRANKLIN, cf N. Y.
Eunice, wd David, rocf Nantucket 8-25-1831; d 12-2-1872
Ferris A. (mbr New Garden, Pa.), s Abner & Jane T., b 3-24-1869 d 1908; m 6-8-1899 Jeannette SUTTON, dt Silas H. & Mary (Gager) b Chenoa, Ill. 8-12-1869 (H)
Jeannette recrq 5-6-1899
Hannah D., dt Frank; m 9-10-1899 Jehu C. MOORE cf Smithfield, O. for both with 2 ch 6-1887
James (nm) & -----
Ch: Catherine b Cow Neck, L. I. d 3-20-1830 ae 43y bHS (unm)
Jethro & Mercy
Ch: Henry
Rachel
Mary d 1-21-1827 ae 18y
Rowland G.
Franklin
Sarah
Jethro Jr.
Eliza.
Walter
Thomas G.
cf Nantucket for Mercy 7-28-1824 with her 10 ch named; ct Cincinnati 12-7-1831 for her with 9 ch, not including Mary, elder ones clear; Mercy dis 10-1831 (H); all Orthodox
Jethro rocf N. P. 8-19-1819 for Jethro (clear); ct N.P. 10-1-1823 for Jethro (clear)
John C. rocf Nantucket 1-26-1843; ct Nantucket 12-6-1843
Matthew & Susan
Ch: Samuel S. d 8-8-1837 ae 4y 7m bHS
parents of Hudson (perhaps on visit)
Minnie (nm), dt Meriot & Delia; m 1872 Caleb UNDERHILL (H)
Phebe H., w Obed
Ch: Amelia
Henrietta
cf Nantucket 12-26-1839; ct WD MM 6-3-1846 with 2 ch named
Richard H. rocf Coey. 8-2-1849; ct N.P. 9-4-1850; cf Creek 10-16-1863
Sarah, dt Joseph BROWN; m 1760 ----- (mo) cf Wby 4-2-1760 for Sarah Brown
Sarah rocf Wby 4-2-1760; dis 1-7-1761; ct ----- 5-1-1768; cf Wby 3-3-1772; cf Wby 2-24-1773 (clear)
----- & ----- (nm)
Ch: Samuel S. d 8-10-1837 ae 4y 7m bHS

MOELLING
Sarah M., w Theodore, dt Nathan & Ann (Merritt) COMSTOCK, b N. Y. 2-14-1828 d 4-29-1907 (m 8-27-1863); in Phila. 1899 (H)

MOFFITT
Dorcas, dt John & Jesse FULTON, rocf Lurgan, Ireland with parents 8-1888; name erased 4-1828
John (nm) & -----
Ch: Frederic b N. Y. d 11-20-1830 ae 14d bHS
John L. [Moffatt] (nm) & -----
Ch: John L. b N. Y. d 2-12-1832 ae 14y 2d bHS
Eugene b N. Y. d 7-6-1833 ae 7m bHS
----- & ----- (nm)
Ch: Anthony G. b N. Y. d 5-26-1825 ae 3m bHS
Howard A. b N. Y. d 2-26-1827 ae 1y 7m 7d bHS
Isabella F. b N. Y. d 7-12-1828 ae 5m 21d bHS
Elizabeth b N. Y. d 4-25-1829 ae 11hrs bHS

MOGER (See also Mosher)
Ann C. recrq 5-1843; d 6-13-1878 (H)
Simmons G., s Simmons & Hannah, rocf Chap. 10-1833 with mother; dis 4-7-1847 (H)
Simmons, Jr. d 10-5-1825; m Hannah -----
Ch: John I.
Maria Ann b 2-25-1815
Ezra C.
Simeon G.
cf Chap. 6-13-1817; ct Chap. 8-8-1827 for Hannah with 4 ch named; cf Chap. 10-1833 with s, Simmons G.; Hannah m 2d B. UNDERHILL & dis 1-1838

MOLINEAUX (See Mullenex)

MOLLAYAN
Zaker & Nazena
Ch: Krekor (George) b 12-18-1909
Alice b 12-23-1912
Alice Elizabeth b 12-27-1914
Virginia " 5-10-1920
Parents recrq 4-1909

MOMBELLY
----- (nm) m Ethel A. MILLER
Ethel recrq 1923

MONROE
Sarah (nm) b N. Y. d 12-23-1843 ae 49y bHS (wd)

MONSEN
Courtney (nm) m Sarah GIBBS, dt Samuel E. & Grace C. (McCord), b N. Y. 8-18-1899 (H)

MONTALZO
Maggie, dt Ramon & Mary, d 8-27-1922 ae 65y bPP (H)

MONTGOMERY
Edwin H. recrq 5-1923; name erased 4-1928

MOODY
Eleanor (Elioner Noode rocf Phila. 11-1-1764)

MOON
Elizabeth (nm), dt Thomas H. (nm) b N. Y. d 10-25-1815 ae 27y 1m bHS (unm)

MOORE
Abigail [More] rpd mo before 7-7-1756
Albert R., s Jehu & Hannah D. (Mitchell), b Ohio 4-29-1863 d 1-1-1909 bPP; m Minnie MOREHOUSE (nm)
Alice L. D., dt Thos. R. & Lydia B. (Davenport) b Duanes 6-24-1871; recrq 11-9-1907 (H)
Amy L., w John (form Hance) rocf H. & R. 11-6-1850; ct R. & P. 8-6-1879 (H)
Ann granted rem cert 10-6-1756
Carrie Willets, dt Thos. R. & Lydia B. (Davenport), b Duanes 4-17-1867; cf Duanes 11-9-1907 (H)
Cecelia, dt Howard B. & Mathilde, b Bkn. 10-7-1889; m Theodore H. KRUEGER
both recrq 5-4-1917
Charles F. R. recrq 9-2-1891; d 8-23-1895 (H)
Charles Harrison [Moor] rocf Dublin 4-1886; name erased 10-1928
Clementine (form Davis), rocf Corn. 11-3-1843; dis mo 7-1856
Cornelia (nm) b N. Y. d 1-27-1832 ae 21y bHS (unm)
Earl rocf Wilmington, Ohio 4-3-1907; name erased 10-1928
Edward, Woodbridge, N. J., m Newtown 10-10-1787 Phebe HALLETT, Queens Co.
he produced cert of clear from Rahway; Phebe rocf R. & P. 2-1-1788
Edwin Bunting, s Joseph C. & Jennie R. (Bunting) b N. Y. 11-16-1888; m 6-4-1914 Isabel Reeder CLARK (nm) (H)
Franklin J., s Jehu C. & Hannah D. (Mitchell) b Ohio 1861 d New Brunswick, N. J. 10-17-1923 ae 62y bPP (both nm)
Frederick, s Jehu C. & Hannah D., rocf Smithfield, O. with parents 6-1887; name erased 4-1928
Hannah H., dt Sarah H. MARSHALL, recrq of mother 2-1823; dis 9-1840 (H)
Howard L., s Howard B. & Matilda, b Bkn. 10-7-1893; recrq 6-4-1917
James rocf R. & P. for Hardwick 10-3-1799, endorsed to N. Y. 2-19-1800; ct Creek 1-7-1801 (clear)
Jane R., w Joseph (not a mbr here), dt Chas. T. & Phebe M. BUNTING, b 1-6-1847 (H)
Jehu C., s Joshua & Nancy (Stratton), b Clinton Co., O. 12-24-1836 d 10-24-1915 bPP; m Hannah D. MITCHELL, dt Frank, d 9-10-1899 bPP
Ch: Frederick
Albert R. b Ohio 4-29-1863
Mary b Wilmington, O. 7-11-1860
Franklin J. b Ohio 1861
cf Smithfield, Ohio 6-1887 with 2 ch first named
Job, Jr. rocf Little Egg Harbor 7-14-1809 (clear); ct Burl. 7-11-1810 (clear), ret as he did not live there; ct Phila. Middle Dist. 2-6-1811 (clear)
John, s John & Hannah (dec), Marksboro, N. J.; m at Amy L. Hance's, N. Y. 2-24-1864 Amy L. HANCE, dt Sylvanus & Sarah, N. Y. (not under care of N.Y. MM) (H)
Joseph F. (mbr Radnor, Pa.), s Edwin & Phebe, d 2-25-1909; m 4-27-1887 Jennie R. BUNTING, dt Charles T. & Phebe M. (Burdsall), b 1-6-1847 d 7-10-1926 (H)
Ch: Edwin Bunting b 11-16-1888
Ellwood Burdsall b 11-21-1890
Libbie m Robert UNDERHILL (H)
Lindley Murray & Abigail
Ch: Edward M.
Gilbert H. b 7-29-1816
Anne Mott " 6-19-1818
cf R. & P. 11-23-1815 with their infant s, Edward; ct Flushing 8-1-1821 with 3 ch named
Margaret d 2-18-1802 ae 35; m -----
Ch: ----- d 2-18-1802 ae 5d bHS
Mary m Joseph White TILTON (H)
cf Sandy Spring 11-6-1897
Mary B., dt Sam'l & Eliz. UNDERHILL, b 3-23-1799; dis mo 6-1-1837
May, dt Jehu & Hannah S. (Mitchell), b Wilmington, O. 7-11-1860 d 4-1-1911 bPP; m Horace G. SMITH (nm)
May not a mbr here
Naomi d 10-6-1801 bHS
Rebecca B. [Moores] mbr at Nantucket 3-3-1847; d 3-10-1850 (H)
Susannah, dt John; m before 8-1-1804 ----- PRICE (mo)
cf R. & P. 4-15-1801, minor; dis 1804
Thomas (nm) b N. Y. d 10-27-1829 ae 17y bHS (unm)
Thomas Hayes (nm) b Eng. d 2-9-1841 ae 66y bHS
Ch: Hannah b N. Y. d 9-5-1833 ae 24y 8m 13d bHS (unm)
Thomas, form of Chesterfield, Eng., found dead in bed, inquest, bleeding of lungs
William, s Jonathan R. & Sarah (Lea), b Roxborough, Pa. 3-18-1851; m at S. Griffen's 11-18-1886 Hannah GRIFFEN, dt Stephen & Jane (Arnold), N. Y., b 3-18-1865 Bkn. (H)
Ch: Jennie Arnold b N. Y. 8-16-1895
William Lea b White Pl. 1-4-1898
Robert Griffen b White Pl. 1-9-1903
cf Phila. 5-7-1884 for William; ct Presby. Ch., Los Gatos, Calif. for all 2-10-1917

MOREHOUSE
Elizabeth m Edward K. VAN BRUNT; m 2d Giles MANDEVILLE; m 3d 4-19-1893 Wm. H. MOREHOUSE (H)
Minnie (nm) m Albert R. MOORE
William H. (nm) m 4-19-1893 Elizabeth VAN BRUNT, wd Edward K. (H)
cf Green St. Phila. for her 2-1859; name removed 11-9-1925; not located for many years

MORELAND
Jane (or Jennet), dt John & Eleanor WILDE; dis mo 9-4-1839

MOREY
Fannie, dt Gardner P. & Lydia (Robinson), b Nassau 3-4-1823; m 6-27-1900 Albert B. BRADLEY (H)
transferred from Albany 1-8-1916
Frederick R. transferred from Albany 2-12-1916; relrq 4-8-1916 (H)
Hannah B., w Amos, rocf Hudson 5-1846 (H)
James S., s Levi & Jemima, b 4-19-1865; m 7-17-1890 Nettie Estelle MOREY, dt Gardner & Lydia (Robinson), b Nassau, N. Y. 4-12-1863 d 8-7-1915 bPP (H)
cf Hudson & Chatham 1-5-1901 for Nettie
Nettie Estelle, dt Gardner & Lydia (Robinson), b Nassau, N. Y. 4-12-1863 d 8-7-1915; m 1890 James S. MOREY (H)
cf Hud. & Chatham 1-5-1901

MORGAN
Ann Maria, w Francis (form Wing) dis 12-3-1856 (H)
Ann Merritt, dt E. Robins & Helen M., recrq 8-6-1930
Chester O. recrq 1-8-1902
Elias S. d 10-29-1881 ae 87y 4m 11d bPP; m Rhoda B. ----- d 6-17-1878 ae 82y 2m 17d bPP (H)
Ch: Thomas M.
cf Plains 8-1853 for all; ct Jericho 4-1858 for all; cf Jericho 5-7-1862 for all
Hannah (nm) b L. I. d 2-13-1814 ae 55y bHS
Isabella recrq 8-7-1822; dis 1-1831 (O); dis 11-1830 (H) [bHS (wd)
Jemima (nm) b L. I. d 3-15-1810 ae 77y 9m 2d
William B. rocf Phila. 1851; d 8-3-1854
Thomas (nm) & ----- (H)
Ch----- d 7-18-1880 bPP

MORRELL
Judith, dt Jonathan; m 1745 Joseph BOWNE; m 2nd 1757 Joseph RODMAN
Rebecca (late Fowler) mo before 10-2-1771, dis
Sarah Ann rocf Phila. Cherry St. 2-1850; d 9-23-1858 ae 43y 6m 18d bPP (H)

MORRIS
Abigail, w James, rocf R. & P. 5-23-1805; ct R. & P. 8-5-1807, rem with h
Edward, s Edward & Alice M. (Hannah), b Bkn. 8-21-1893 (H); recrq 7-16-1910
Herbert L. (nm) m 5-17-1926 Elizabeth H. JENKINS, dt Henry C. & Eleanor (Cooley), b N. Y. 10-8-1904 (H)
cf R. & P. 9-9-1905 for Elizabeth with mother
Ida Margaret, dt Thos. Gurley & Julia (Pier) b Blue Rapids, Kans. 11-10-1871; recrq 4-13-1912 (H)
Col. Lewis b Eng. d N. J. 12 Mo (Feb) 14, 1690/1; m Mary ----- d 12 Mo (Feb) 21, 1690/1 active mbr from 1676 till rem. to N. J.

Martha, dt John & Abigail, Phila., m ----- LAWRIE; m 2d 1821 Jacob B. CLARKE
Phebe (form Merritt) b West. Co. d 11-16-1833 ae 62y bHS; dis mo 4-1-1812
Sarah, w Dr. M. R. (form Rogers) rocf Jericho 6-1842; ct Wby 4-2-1856 (H)
Susanna gct Abington 9 Mo (Nov) 2, 1732

MORRISON
Alexander C. recrq 4-1881; d 12-1-1891
John & Margaret
Ch: Annie C. L. b 5-14-1904
William John b 4-24-1910
all recrq 9-7-1910; ch marked associates
Louis A. & Mary M.
both recrq 4-3-1929
Phebe (late Merritt) dis mo 5-6-1812

MORSE
Arthur H. (nm), s Charles F. & Ellen (Holdrege) Kansas City; m at N.P. Hallowell's 8-8-1907 Esther F. HALLOWELL, dt Norwood P. & Sarah W., W. Medford, Mass. b W. Medford Mass. 3-21-1881 (H)
Ch: Susan Hallowell b W. Medford 9-12-1911
Charles Fessenden b Weston, Mass. 11-20-1922
ch recrq of parents 5-11-1912 & 3-12-1923
Fred Callender, s Fred A. & Mary (Heband), b Roch. 7-12-1882; m 12-4-1911 Irene PHILLIPS (mbr E. Hamburg), dt Reuben Eves & Mary Emily (Hull), b Farm. 5-1-1884 (H)
Fred C. recrq 7-10-1933; cf E. Hamburg 11-13-1933 for Irene
James Herbert (nm), s Augusta & Lucinda; m 5-12-1870 Lucy GIBBONS, dt James S. & Abby (Hopper), b N. Y. 10-30-1839 (H)
Waldo J. & H. Kate (H)
Ch: Raymond Vere d 2-26-1879 ae 4y 25d bPP
all nm

MOSELEY
Catharine (nm) b N. Y. d 12-11-1811 bHS ae 58y

MOSES
Richard P.

MOSHER (See also Moger)
Abraham E. rocf Chatham 8-1849; d 5-20-1859 (H)
Avis L. rocf Corn. 3-1851; ct Pur. 3-6-1861 (H)
Eliza rocf Pokeepsie 6-1885; ct South Cong.

MOSHER, Eliza, continued
Ch. Bkn. 11-4-1903
Henry H. d 7-16-1874 ae 78y bPP
cf Rochester 5-24-1839 (clear)
Joseph & Olive
Ch: Smith
Edwin
Julia Ann d 5-10-1830 ae 6y 5m
Nelson b 1831
Seth " 1833 d 4-14-1838
cf Hudson 7-27-1831 with 3 ch (0); all dis 1832-1848 (0); cf Chatham 9-1828 with same (H)
Smith, s Joseph & Olive, d 6-23-1849 bHS; m ----- (H)
Ch: Olive Ann d 10-6-1842 ae 2d bHS
cf Chatham 10-1833 with parents; dis 9-1840
----- & ----- (nm)
Ch: Oscar [Mozier] d 6-18-1843 ae 2y 11m 7d bHS
Adelaide b N. Y. d 11-6-1843 ae 1y 6m bHS

MOSS
Sarah Eliza, dt John & Eliza, N. Y.; m 1864 Samuel Daw BUSSELL
cf Dublin 8-11-1863
William C. rocf Phila. 1850; dis

MOTT
Abigail gct N.P. 6-5-1816 (clear)
Abigail rocf Coey 8-27-1834; ct Coey 4-5-1837 (H)
Adam d 1-1849; m Ann ----- d 8-5-1852
Ch: Sarah
Richard
cf Pur. 8-10-1815 with ch, Sarah & Richard; parents dis 1829 (H)
Alfred A., s Benjamin, recrq of father 8-4-1813; dis 12-1837 (H); dis 12-1839 (0)
Andrew U. gct Farm. 5-12-1819 (clear)
Ann M., dt Wm. F. & Phebe, b 9-18-1813; m Walter FRANKLIN
Annetta H. & -----
Ch: Albert Edwin b 12-16-1884 d rpd 4-1928
Annetta recrq 5-7-1890; Albert E.'s name recorded as per Disc. 9-22-1897
Avis B., dt Samuel & Elizabeth, N. Y.; m 1816 James EVERNGHIM
Benjamin b Great Neck d 10-21-1816 ae 52y bHS; m -----
Ch: Benjamin A. dis 3-1833
Alfred A. " 12-1839
cf Wby 12-30-1789 (clear); dis mo 3-6-1799; s, Alfred A. recrq 8-4-1813
Benjamin A., s Benjamin, dis 3-1833 (0); dis 9-1834 (H); d 12-1838
Charles, s Samuel & Elizabeth, gct Phila. 4-7-1830 (clear)
Charles E. d 8-3-1931 ae 71y bPP; m Susie M. PRICE, dt John & Hannah, d 10-4-1923 ae 62y bPP (H)
Charles E. m 2d Marie ----- (H) both nm
Deborah, w Jacob, b Oyster Bay d 1-18-1826 ae 68y 6m 17d
Elizabeth Brewster (form Mott), dt Samuel & Elizabeth (H)
Elizabeth A. (nm) b Rye d 3-18-1812 ae 27y bHS
Gulielma rocf Pur. 10-5-1870; d 12-22-1891 (H)
Hannah rocf Wby 4-18-1804, she having con her form mo
Hannah, dt William & Elizabeth, d 2-8-1805 ae 51y 9m bHS
Hannah B. gct Pur. 6-6-1828 (clear) (0)
Hannah D. (nm) b L. I. d 11-2-1815 ae 86y bHS (unm)
Dr. Henry, s Wm., Wby; m Wby Jane ----- d 4-12-1834 (H)
Ch: John W.
Way
Valentine
Esther W. d 3-20-1854
Eliza " 4- 1-1866
Maria
ct Wby 6-6-1781 (clear); cert as apprentice from Wby 9-24-1771; all dis 1829-1830 (0); cf Wby with w & 5 ch 6-20-1798; ct Wby (not found); cf Wby 8-3-1815 with their 3 dt, Esther, Eliza & Maria
Henry Franklin, s Wm. F. Jr. & Jane, b 1-10-1847; mo before 10-1875, ret a mbr; relrq 3-1883; lived where there was no Friends Mtg 1875
Isaac d 9-18-1842 bur Albany (H)
cf Coey 11-1840
Israel & Charity (m Pur.)
Ch: William
Solomon
cf Pur. for Israel 4-14-1796; Israel took cert of clear to Pur. 3-1-1797; Charity brought cert from Pur. 5-11-1797; ct Pur. 3-5-1800 with their 2 ch
Jacob (nm) b Bethpage d 1-8-1820 ae 65y bHS (widower)
Jacob (nm) b Hempstead d 8-16-1823 ae 66y 1m 16d bHS (m)
Jacob L. gct Chap. 8-3-1814
James, Mamaroneck, m Flushing 3 Mo (May) 9, 1717 Jane BURLING, Flushing
James & Mary
James & Mary rocf Wby 1-6-1766; James with 5 small ch to Pur. 8-1-1776
James rocf Wby 5-28-1766
James d 5-9-1823 ae 81y bHS (not a mbr in N.Y.) (widower)
Jane, dt Adam & Mary; m 1693 Richard SEAMAN
John d 10-16-1801 bHS
John, s William, b Great Neck, L. I., d 11-20-1823 ae 68y bHS; cf Wby 9-29-1779 (clear)
John roc 9-1824, minor; dis 7-1830
John d 9-13-1887 ae 79y 10m 23d bPP; m Gulielma ----- d 12-22-1891 ae 86y 8d bPP (H)
Ch: Phebe S. b 4- 2-1830
Henry " 2- 9-1833
Walter " 2-15-1836
Robert " 1838
cf Pur. 6-9-1824, minor; cf Chap. 7-1829 for Gulielma; ct Chap. 11-1843 for all
John B. rocf Plains 1852; d 12-3-1892

MOTT, continued
John BOWNE, s Wm. F. Jr. & Jane, b 9-23-1842 d 1890 bPP; mo before 2-1-1861, ret a mbr; mbrp relinquished 3-1880
John C. & Caroline
Ch: Infant stillborn 5-6-1838 bHS
all nm
John W., s Henry & Jane, rocf Flushing 8-2-1810 (clear)
Joseph rocf Wby 5-14-1794 (clear); dis mo by a Baptist preacher 7-3-1799; d 12-5-1801 ae 39y bHS
Joseph L., s Abigail (now Griffen) gct Scipio 11-5-1828 (clear)
Joseph S. rocf N.P. 8-1817; ct Scip. 9-1830 (H)
Lillian U. recrq 11-1920
Louisa, dt Samuel F. & Ann, b 9-11-1820; m ---- RING (mo)
dis mo 2-3-1841
Louise m George W. PRINDLE
both nm
Lydia Butler (form Mott) dis 1-5-1842
Lydia, dt John & Lydia DODGSON; m 2d 1847 Charles F. MOTT (H)
ct Sara. 8-1852
Maria, dt Wm. F., Jr. & Jane, b 5-8-1851; m 1879 ----- PERRY
mbrp relinquished 3-1880
Martha B., dt Samuel & Eliz., N. Y.; m 1827 Henry HAYDOCK
Mary rocf Wby 5-28-1766
Mary, w William, recrq 6-1809; d 8-5-1842 (H)
Mary, dt Daniel, rocf Bridgwater 10-9-1835; ct Coey. 5-1839 (H)
Mary F., dt Wm. F. & Phebe, b 2-27-1809; m 1829 Alfred WILLIS
Matilda Cahoon (form Mott), dt Samuel & Elizabeth; dis mo 8-1831 (H)
Phebe rocf Coey. 8-27-1834; ct Coey 4-5-1837 (H)
Richard rocf Wby 10-16-1793 (clear)
Richard, s William, d 6-2-1919 ae 82y bPP; m Annetta H. -----
both nm
Richard, Jr., s Adam & Anne, N. Y.; m N. Y. 11-12-1828 Eliz. M. SMITH, dt Elihu & Mary, N. Y.
Ch: Mary S. b 3-11-1831
Caroline S. b 3-29-1835
cf Pur. with parents 8-10-1815; ct Adrian 11-1-1837 with 2 ch named
Robert, s James & Mary, d 3-23-1804 ae 36y 6m bHS; m Lydia -----
Ch: Edward
Arthur
Alfred
Jennette b 6-10-1803
cf Pur. 3-10-1791; dis mo before 6-3-1795; rst 3-4-1801, as mbr of Pur.; Lydia P. gct Pur. 12-4-1805 with 4 small ch as named
Robert F. d 1826 Mamaroneck; m Hannah B. -----
Ch: Richard F., Jr. b 5-10-1825
cf Pur. 8-13-1818 (clear); Hannah B. rocf Burl. 10-4-1824; ct Pur. 7-1828 (0); ct Pur. 6-1838 (H)
Robert S., s John & Gulielma, b 1838 d 4-4-1906 bPP; m Phebe E. EGBERT (nm), dt John & Phebe, d 1-20-1919 ae 81y 11m 18d bPP (H)
Ch: Charles E.
Robert perhaps mbr Pur.; ct Pur. with parents 1843
Samuel, s William, N. Y.; m Sarah FRANKLIN, dt Henry & Mary, d 11-12- (or 13) 1801 ae 35y (mo)
Ch: William F. b 1-11-1785
Walter " 12- 4-1786
Samuel F. " 2- 7-1789
Sarah " 9-25-1791
Samuel dis mo 7-7-1784; Sarah con mo 12-1-1784; ch recrq of mother, wd; Samuel rocf Wby 9-29-1779
Samuel dis 11-2-1814; rst 5-6-1818
Samuel m Elizabeth ----- b Nantucket d 3-12-1826 ae 48y bHS
Ch: Matthew Bernard d 1-21-1817 ae 21y 6m 6d bHS
Avis
Andrew
Charles
Martha
Samuel d 4- 3-1881
Elizabeth
Matilda
Martha B.
cf Pur. 10-12-1809 with 8 ch as named
Samuel, s James & Mary (dec), N. Y.; m 2d 10-8-1828 Sarah EARL, dt John & Dorcas (dec), d 1-22-1846 (H)
Sarah rec without cert 8-1828; Samuel & ch dis 1829-1839 (0); Sarah gct Scipio 1-1845
Samuel (nm) m Phebe ----- (nm) b Westchester Co. d 3-4-1822 ae 51y bHS
Samuel, Jr. (nm) m Ruth ----- (nm) d 1-6-1851 ae 36y bPP
Ch: Eliza A. d 5-1-1926 ae 80y bPP (unm)
Infant stillborn 1851
Samuel F., s Samuel & Sarah (both dec), N. Y., b 2-7-1789 d 6-7-1859 bPP; m N. Y. 5-11-1814 Ann LEGGETT, dt Thomas & Mary (dec), N. Y., d 9-24-1854
Ch: Caroline b 3-26-1815 d 2-20-1830
Infant stillborn 2-8-1817
Margaret b 9- 8-1818; dis 1839 (0)
Louisa " 9-11-1820; " 1841
Henry (Samuel F. in Reg.) b 9-22-1822; dis 1844
Charlotte F. b 8- 9-1824 d 8- 1-1826
Ann Elizabeth b 3-17-1835 d 1-19-1842 bHS
parents dis 1829 (H)
Samuel F., Jr. (Henry in Reg.), s Sam'l F. & Ann, b 9-22-1822; dis mo 1-1845
Samuel N. (added letter N. to his name 1-1-1811) b L. I. d 7-18-1838 ae 76y 2d bHS; m -----
Ch: Samuel G. d 7-24-1818 ae 26y bHS
rq rst, Wby referred to N.Y. 12-5-1798;

MOTT, Samuel N., continued
rpd favorably 3-6-1799; cf Wby 4-17-1799; dis 1826
Sarah, dt Adam & Anne, N. Y.; m 1815 Silas CORNELL, of Scarsdale
Sarah, dt Samuel & Sarah, N. Y.; m 1816 John WOOD
Stephen & Sarah (H)
cf Jericho 8-1855 for both; ct Wby 5-5-1858 for both (H)
Susan, dt Abigail, now Griffen, gct Scipio 3-4-1829 (clear)
Susan M. rocf N.P. 8-1817; ct Scip. 8-1829 (H)
Dr. Valentine, s Henry & Jane, con mo 9-1-1819; dis non-attendance 1825
Valentine, s Stephen & Sarah, O.B.; m at R. M. Reynolds' 2-6-1851 Ann Eliza REYNOLDS, dt Rich. & Ann C., N. Y. (H)
Ch: Daniel W. b 7-4-1853
Valentine rocf Jericho 5-1852; Valentine dis 8-6-1862; ct Flushing 8-5-1868 for mother & s
Walter, s Samuel & Sarah, b 12-4-1786 d 3-27-1871; recrq of mother
William, Great Neck, & -----
Ch: Elizabeth d 12 Mo (Feb) 25, 1721/2
desired mtg at his house 1702
William rocf Wby 6-29-1774 (clear)
William dis mo 3-3-1790
William rocf Pur. 8-8-1822 (clear); dis 7-1830 (0); ct Pur. 11-1844, returned 7-2-1845; ct Pur. 4-4-1860 (H)
William d 3-8-1886 ae 88y 1m 17d bPP; m Ann BOOTH, d 10-5-1903 ae 89y 2m bPP (H)
Ch: Ann Eliza d 3-14-1919 ae 78y 3m 1d bPP
all nm
William F., s Samuel & Sarah (both dec), N.Y., b 1-11-1785 d 5- 3-1867 bPP; m N. Y. 12-10-1807 Phebe MERRITT, dt John & Phebe, N. Y., d 8-20-1859 ae 70y 5m bPP
Ch: Mary F. b 2-27-1809
Ann M. " 9-18-1813
William F. Jr. b 8-17-1820
Edward " 11-15-1822 d 1-28-1824
Maria " 5-15-1835 d 9- 4-1847
parents dis 1829 (H)
Wm. F., Jr., s Wm. F. & Phebe, N. Y.; m N.Y. 10-13-1841 Jane BOWNE, dt John L. & Eliza H. (dec), N. Y.
Ch: John Bowne b 9-23-1842
William F. Jr. b 4-29-1845
Henry Franklin b 1-10-1847
Maria " 5- 8-1851
Wm. F. 3d, s Wm. F. Jr. & Jane, b 4-29-1845; mbrp relinquished 3-1880
----- & -----
Ch: Caroline D. d 3-3-1813 ae 11m 10d bHS
Franklin b N. Y. d 2-2-1824 ae 2y 3m 15d bHS
William W. d 1-8-1831 bHS

MOULSON
Deborah rocf Phila. 6-1833; ct Chap. 8-1835; d Phila. (H)

MOUNTAIN
Charles H. (nm) d 4-11-1858 ae 47y bPP; m Hannah B. FIELD, dt Charles & Martha, d 8-30-1876 ae 60y bPP (H)
Hannah dis non-attendance 5-6-1863

MOXHAM
John, Jr. rocf Southwark, London 6-12-1810 (clear); ct Bristol, Eng. 3-1-1815 (clear)

MUIRHEAD
William d 7-26-1892 ae 51y bPP; m Clara W. PEARSALL, dt Wm. & Mary (Wilson), d 9-7-1920 ae 76y 3m 1d bPP (H)
both nm)

MULLEN
Thomas rocf Nantucket 4-6-1832 (clear); he ret to Ire. & this cert sent to Mt. Melick, 10-3-1832.

MÜLLER
Bertha Margaret (nm), dt John B. & Agatha C., Bronx, N. Y.; m 1904 Harold A. DEADMAN

MULLIGAN
Maria Louisa, w William (form Clark), of Mulligan & Grimshaw Co. (H)
ret a mbr
William (nm), of Mulligan, Grimshaw & Co., d 4-2-1882 ae 74y; m 9-25-1850 Maria Louisa CLARK, dt Rufus & Sarah (Glover), b White Plains 1-17-1825 d 2-13-1907 ae 82y 7d bPP (H)
Maria ret a mbr

MULLINEX (Molineaux)
Horsman, Westchester, m at Robert Hewstis' 9 Mo (Nov) 30, 1692 Elizabeth HEWSTIS, dt Robert, Westchester
Ch: Moses b 7 Mo (Sep) 8, 1693
John " 5 Mo (July) 7, 1695
Jesse & Phebe [Mollinex]
Ch: Henry
Sarah
cf Jericho 5-21-1801
Moses, s Horseman, Westchester, d 8 Mo (Oct) 1725; m at Flushing 3 Mo (May) 10, 1722 Hannah FARRINGTON, dt Matthew, Flushing
Ch: Mary b 1 Mo (Mar) 26, 1723
Joseph b 7 Mo (Sep) 5, 1724
----- b 10 Mo (Dec) 5, 1726
Moses m 2d Flushing 8 Mo (Oct) 9, 1746 Hannah LAWRENCE, Flushing
Susanna [Mullinaux] rocf Wby 9-14-1803 (clear)

MUMBY
Joseph H. (nm), s Robt. & Rachel; m 3-8-1854 Tabitha TAGG, dt George & Anna (Claiborn), b Phila. 3-28-1827 d 10-11-1905 (H)
cf Phila. 1-1855 for Tabitha

MUMFORD
Ann (late Pearsall) dis mo 10-3-1787

MUNIER
Anna Josephine, dt Chas. & Mary E. (Rolland), b Bkn. 3-2-1871 d 3-30-1933; m 3-15-1901 Arthur Dana CLOUGH (H)
both recrq 2-10-1910; death notice, pasted in, says mother of Richard M. Clough and Charles W. Stuyvesant

MUNNETT
Abigail, form dis by Wby, her ack accepted & referred to N. Y. 2-5-1812, apparently rec here

MUNROE
James (nm) b West. Co. d 6-22-1839 ae 52y bHS (m)
Thomas [Monro], s Alex. A. & Mary E. (Spaulding), b Omaha 2-15-1897; recrq 5-14-1917; relrq 10-10-1921 (H)

MURDOCK
----- (not a mbr here) m Mary GUY, dt Percy C. & Abigail Susan
cf Westminster & Longford for Mary with parents 7-11-1909; ct Phila. 3-1927

MURPHY
Timothy, s Daniel, d 8-12-1802 ae 1y 9m bHS

MURRAY
Ann Eliza, dt Lindley & Eliza, b 2-11-1814; dis 2-1838 as Hicksite
Anna T., dt Robt. Lindley & Ruth S., Chap., N. Y. 9-27-1854; m 1877 Abraham S. UNDERHILL, of Newcastle
Beulah, dt Robert & Mary; m before 1-6-1790 ----- HOFFMAN
dis 2-4-1790
Catharine (nm) m 1920 Herman Murray JACOBY (H)
Catharine B., dt Lindley & Eliza, b 8-12-1816; m ----- BATTELLE (mo by Episc. minister)
dis mo 3-1-1843
David Colden, s Robt. I. & Elizabeth C., b 10-10-1821; dis mo 8-1854; dis 1859 (?)
Edward L., s Lindley & Mary Ann, Flushing, b 5-11-1842 d 12-11-1864
had joined the army before 12-2-1864; comm. to deal with him rpd 4-5-1864 that they had been informed of his death
Effingham C., s Robt. I., Jr. & Phebe Anna (Cock), b N. Y. 10-11-1884; m 3-26-1906 Marie de MONTALVO, dt Evaristo & Louise (Leblanc), b 12-15-1884 (H)
he obtained a divorce; she m again; she recrq 12-8-1900; name removed 3-13-1933 for lack of interest
Gertrude Colden, dt Robt. L. & Eliz., N. Y.; m 1839 George F. HUSSEY, of New Bedford
Hannah con mo 12-3-1767
Hannah, Jr. gc (prob. London) 6-5-1771
Harriet C., dt Robt. I. & Phebe Anna, Chap.; m 1903 Alfred BUSSELLE
Jane M., dt Lindley, b 5-17-1823; jas & dis 10-1848
John, Jr., s Lindley & Eliza, b 12-26-1827
John, Jr., s Robert & Mary, N. Y.; m Flushing 11-13-1783 Catharine BOWNE, dt James (dec) & Caroline, d 9-14-1834 ae 71y bHS
Ch: Mary b 10-17-1784
Robert b 2-13-1786
Caroline b 3- 3-1788 d 1-12-1792
Lindley " 1- 5-1790
James " 5-30-1791 d 10-1-1791
----- d 2- 2-1797
Catharine dis 1829 (H)
Joseph K., s Lindley & Mary Ann, b 1-17-1836; mo before 11-1867, ret a mbr
Lindley & Hannah (mo)
ct Phila. as apprentice 12-3-1761; con mo 12-3-1767; ct Wby with w, Hannah, 8-6-1778; ct Devonshire House 1-5-1785 with w, Hannah
Lindley, s John & Catharine, N. Y.; m N. Y. 4-15-1813 Eliza CHEESEMAN, dt Forman & Ann, N. Y., d 5-29-1830 ae 40y bHS
Ch: Ann Eliza b 2-11-1814
Catharine B. " 8-12-1816
Margaret C. " 9-23-1818 (or 9-13-1818)
Lindley Jr. " 1-11-1821 (or 8-20-1821)
Jane M. " 5-17-1823
Hannah " 9-26-1825 d 6- 7-1845
John Jr. " 12-26-1827
Infant d 7-16-1830 ae 19d
parents dis 1829 (H)
Lindley m 2d N. Y. 8-9-1832 Mary Ann KING, dt Joseph & Mary, Flushing, d 5-6-1872
Ch: Mary K. b 11-14-1834 d 11-12-1920
Joseph K. b 1-17-1836 d 1- 3-1916
William " 4- 9-1839
Edward L. " 5-11-1842 d 12-11-1864
Lindley Jr., s Lindley & Eliza, b 1-11-1821 (or 8-20-1821); cert of clear to Balt. 9-7-1842; dis mo by a priest 11-1-1843
Lindley, with w, rocf Devonshire House, 12-4-1771
Louisa recrq 10-1877; name erased 5-1886
Margaret C., dt Lindley & Eliza, N. Y.; m 1846 Robert B. COLLINS
Mary, dt Robert & Mary, N. Y., mo before 5-2-1771 ----- BARNETT; testification sent to London, where he had gone
Mary Willits (form Murray) dis mo 4-6-1796
Mary, dt John & Catharine, N. Y.; m 1806 Benjamin D. PERKINS
Mary, dt Robert I. & Eliz. C., N. Y.; m 1854 Lindley Murray FERRIS, of Coldenham
recrq; ct Marl. 1854
Robert, N. Y. certified mbr 1755
Robert gct London 10-3-1759, sent after he had sailed; he had joined about 2 yrs. before
Robert, London, & Mary
Ch: John
Beulah
Susannah
Mary
cert for all but Mary to Grace Church St. 5-2-1771; brought cf Devonshire House,

MURRAY, Robert & Mary, continued
London 6-8-1774, rec 9-7-1774
Robert I., s John Jr. & Catharine; m Elizabeth C. ----- b Coldenham, N. Y. d 1-13-1827 ae 32y
Ch: Mary
Gertrude b 9-25-1817
David Colden b 10-10-1821
Robert Lindley b 11-9-1824
ch recrq of father
Robert I. d 1-28-1858 ae 71y bPP; m 2d N. Y. 3-10-1830 Hannah W. SHOTWELL, dt Wm. & Sarah, N. Y. d 5-13-1877
Ch: Infant stillborn 7-26-1831 bHS
Mary (?)
Sarah S. b 6-12-1834
Robert I., Jr., s Robt. Lindley & Ruth, b 6-6-1851 d 3-5-1803; m Chap. at home of Effingham Cock 6-13-1878 Phebe Anna COCK, dt Effingham & Harriet H.
Ch: Harriet C.
Robert Lindley b 5- 7-1882 d 8-14-1882
Effingham C. " 10-11-1884
Ruth S. " 12- 8-1885
David Colden " 7-11-1890
Sara S. " 7-22-1899
Roberta I. " 1-31-1903
Phebe Anna recrq 8-1880; Harriet C. recrq of parents 2-17-1897; ct Chap. 10-1914 for Phebe Anna
Roberta I., dt Robt. I., Jr. & Phebe Anna (Cock), b N. Y. 1-31-1903; ct Chap. 10-1914
Robert Lindley, s Robt. I. & Elizabeth C., b 11-9-1824 d 8-29-1874; m Ned Bedford 1849 Ruth S. -----
Ch: William Taber b 1-16-1850 d 8-25-1851
Robert I. Jr. b 6- 1-1851
Charles Taber b 1- 4-1853 d 4-16-1913
Anna Taber " 9-27-1854
William T. " 3- 2-1858 d 6-24-1860 bPP
D. Colden " 11-26-1860 " 10-15-1861 bPP
Elizabeth Colden b 8- 6-1862
Frances K. " 5-14-1864
Agnes Taber " 10-29-1866
cf Ned Bedford 10-1849 for Ruth; ct New Bedford 12-1879 for Ruth & 3 young ch.
Ruth S., dt Robt. I. Jr. & Phebe Anna (Cock), b N. Y. 12-8-1885; ct Chap. 4-1913
Sarah S., dt Robt. I. & Hannah, b 6-12-1834; relrq 8-1889
Sara S., dt Robt. I. Jr. & Phebe Anna (Cock), b N. Y. 7-22-1899; ct Chap. 10-1914
Susannah Willets (form Murray) dis mo 11-4-1784
William, s Lindley & Mary Ann, b 4-9-1839; relrq 6-1869

MYERS
Ann Gilford (form Myers) dis mo 3-6-1782; a mbr of Kingwood MM
Josie, dt John W. & Margaret Alice (Sidwell), b Johnsville, Md. 4-26-1871; m 1896 Frank J. RUSSELL (H)
cf Alexandria 4-10-1877

MYNOTTE
Edwin J. m Frances D. ----- d 1-24-1895 ae 25y 11m 19d bPP (H) (both nm)

NABHOLZ
Paul V. & Mary H.
Ch: Hedwig Mary b 9- 6-1828
Roland Paul b 11-5-1929
Paul rolf Friends' Council for International Service, London 7-1925; Mary recrq 6-1925; ct Washington, D. C. 1-3-1934 for all

NAFTEL (or Naphtal)
Joseph, s Nicholas & Mary (dec), rocf Witham MM, Eng. 2-27-1822 (clear) addressed to Friends in Pa. or elsewhere; ct Witham 5-7-1823 (clear)

NASE
Lulu m Frederick E. ESMOND (both nm)
M. Helena, dt Wm. Augustus & Mary (Parker), recrq 6-1884
William Augustus (nm), s Wm. & Emeline (Talmadge), b So. Amenia, N. Y. 3-21-1831 d 4-1-1917 bPP; m Mary G. PARKER, dt John & Grace S., b Nottingham, Eng. 7-30-1832 d 8-4-1921 bPP
Ch: Mary Helen (changed to M. Helena)
cf Oswego 11-1866 for Mary G.; Mary H. recrq 6-1884

NASH
Francis, N. Y. & Susanna, Wby.
they rem to Wby 12-7-1752; brought cert of clear to live in N.Y. from Phila. 9 Mo. (Nov) 2, 1749; took cert of clear to Wby 2 Mo. 3, 1751; Susanna brought cf Wby 6 Mo 1, 1751
George F. (nm), s Isaac, b N. Y. d 9-17-1847 ae 25y bHS
Ch: John A. d 8-9-1846 ae 4m bHS
Isaac d 3-15-1870 ae 77y bPP (H)
John A., s Margaret, d 9-5-1900 ae 79y 1m 11d bPP; m Nellie ----- (H) (both nm)
John A. m Clara DIXON, d 8-12-1907 ae 70y bPP (H) (both nm)
Juliette, dt Margaret, d 8-10-1893 ae 55y bPP; m ----- HOLMES (H) (both nm)
Kate C., dt Margaret, d 12-4-1900 ae 74y bPP; m George M. MANN (H)
Margaret d 4-16-1885 ae 86y 6m 14d bPP; m ----- (H)
Ch: John A.
Juliette
Theodore d 3- 7-1909 ae 78y bPP
Isaac (perhaps)
cf Oswego 10-1847 for Margaret
----- & ----- (nm)
Ch: Theodore b N. Y. d 9-18-1826 ae 9m 9d bHS

NAYLOR
Catharine T., dt Job Rogers & Eliz. (Norcross) b 1881; recrq 5-7-1930
Madge N., dt Job Rogers & Eliz. (Norcross), b 1884; recrq 5-7-1930

NEALE
Daniel A., s John & Caroline (Sanband), b Boston 1-1848 d 5-28-1908 bPP; m Mary DUNBAR
Lydia M. rocf Berwick, Me. 8-17-1855; d 9-30-1859
Sarah recrq 5-1842; relrq 12-1863 (H)

NEILSON (see Nelson)
Agnes, dt Archibald J. & Agnes (Wilson), b Scotland 4-11-1884; m 1907 John Anderson LIDDELL (H)

NELSON
Andrew (nm) d 4-21-1882 ae 89y 7m bPP; m Mary ----- d 12-28-1869 ae 74y bPP
cf Corn. 4-25-1822 for Mary
Deborah (written Neilson) (late Farrington) mo before 3-7-1787 & dis; rst 2-2-1820 as Nelson; Flushing notified & rpd rec her 6-6-1820
Eli E., s Thomas & Caty (Bedell) b Greene Co., N. Y. 2-2-1828 d 5-20-1906; m 6-23-1869 Harriett CRANDELL (nm), dt Lewis & Dorothy (H); cf Wby 2-2-1887
Eliza, dt Thomas & Caty (Bedell), b 12-6-1825; rocf Wby 8-17-1853; d 11-22-1903
Henry Augustus, s James & Hester, d 12-13-1861 ae 57y bPP; m Catharine ----- (nm) d 9-1857 ae 48y bPP
Ch: Eugene d 3-16-1835 ae 4y 14d bHS
Horatio b 2-2-1847 d 5- 2-1908 bPP
cf R. & P. 6-17-1812 with parents; dis 9-1826, having mo before 4-5-1826
James d 3-14-1842; m Hester (Esther) ----- d 2-11-1851
Ch: Henry Augustus dis 9-1826
Mary
ct R. & P. 1-7-1807; cf R. & P. 6-17-1812 with w, Hester, & 2 ch, named; parents dis 1829 (H)
John C. recrq 12-1920; name erased 10-1928
Lucy, w Thomas, d 4-26-1862 (H)
Ch: Eliza
cf Wby 8-17-1853; Eliza separate cert, same date
Mary, dt Henry A. & Catharine A., N. Y.; m 1869 Francis H. MACY (H)
Mary, dt James & Hester; m Edward WRIGHT (mo) ret a mbr
----- & -----
Ch: Wright d 6- 2-1881 ae 46y bPP

NERHOOFF
John, came from Germany, d 11 Mo (Jan) 16, 1732/3; left by will £10 for poor among Friends

NEUENSCHWANDER
Wm. J. Jr. (nm), s W. J. (dec) & Maud (Thistle) Sisterville, W. Va.; m N. Y. 6-20-1928 Ramona T. SAVAGE, dt Jose R. F. & Mary (HUTCHINSON), Bkn., b N. Y. 8-12-1904 (H)

NEVILL
Joseph & Susanna
Ch: Agnes about 14
James " 12-1/2
Joseph Watts about 11
Benjamin Greenwood about 9-1/2
Alfred about 6-1/2
Elizabeth about 4
Edward about 9m
cf England, Hardshaw West. 6-1843; ct Cincinnati 7-1843

NEVINS
Thomas rocf Brighouse, Yorks. 4-17-1807 (clear); ct Brighouse 7-11-1810 (clear); Carlisle MM, England informs that he has mo & neglected mtg; dis 5-1-1811

NEVITT
Jemima & -----
Ch: Matilda
Charles Henry
cf Pardshaw, at Whitehaven, Eng. 8-21-1849 with 2 ch named; ct Carlisle, Eng. 12-3-1851 with same ch

NEWBOLD
Caleb, s Caleb (dec) & Sarah, Burl., N. J.; m N. Y. 3-13-1799 Sarah GREEN, dt Caleb & Sarah LAWRENCE, N. Y.
he brought cert of clear from Upper Springfield; Sarah took cert from Upper Springfield 5-1-1799
Clayton, s George & Mary, b 2-3-1813; dis jas 4-4-1838
Emily, dt John & Susan, d 10-5-1909 ae 66y 2m 8d bPP; m Caleb BARKER (H) (both nm)
George d 1858; m Phila. Mary E. ----- d 5-10-1820 ae 32y 8m
Ch: Mary Ann b 9- 9-1808
James Emlen b 3-22-1810 d 4- 7-1811
Susannah d 5-17-1812 ae 3m
Clayton " 2-23-1813; dis
James E. " 3- 3-1815 d 8-27-1859
Emily d 8-27-1843
cf Upper Springfield 7-5-1797, placed with a Friend; cert of clear to Phila. 9-2-1807; Mary brought cert from Phila. 12-7-1807; George dis 2-1830 for mcd (O)
Mary Ann, dt George & Mary, b 9-9-1808; m 1835 ----- LAWRENCE (H)
dis mo 3-1835 (H); dis 4-1835 (O)

NEWBURY
Anna K., dt Jonathan & Anna, relrq 9-2-1878; attended Bapt. Ch. with h
Charles E., s John & Phebe, d 7-29-1933 ae 76y

NEWBURY, Charles E. & Anna B., continued
bPP; m Anna B. -----
Nelson b Bkn 4-1892 d Pittsburg 10-15-1918 bPP (nm)
Walter [Newberry], s Walter (dec), of R. I.; m Flushing 1 Mo (Mar) 11, 1707 Ann RODMAN, dt Dr. John, Flushing

NEWBY
Elva D. & Mary Christine
Elva rocf Westland, Ind. 12-4-1912; Mary rolf Zion's Evang. Ch., New Palestine, Ind. 12-4-1912
Exum Jr. rocf Piney Woods, N. C. 7-5-1806; ct Piney Woods 1 -2-1811 (clear)
Mary Christine rolf Zion's Evang. Ch., New Palestine, Ind. 12-4-1912

NEWCOMB
John d 10-21-1862 ae 83y 5m bPP; m Mary ----- d 6-4-1870 ae 74y bPP (H)
John recrq 9-1836; Mary recrq 9-1841

NEWHALL
Elizabeth H., w Joseph P., (form Parker) rocf R. I. 1859 (m 1-4-1866)
Joseph P., s Estes & Miriam, Lynn, Mass.; m Bkn. 1-4-1866 Eliz. H. BARKER, dt Abraham & Margaret B., Tiverton, R. I.
ct Salem, Mass. 12-1866 for Elizabeth
Richard W. (nm), s Richard & Betsey, d 12-23-1908 ae 67y bPP; m 7-6-1882 Lydia C. HALLOCK, dt James C. & Elizabeth (Frost), b N. Y. 4-7-1842 d 4- 5-1932 ae 90y bPP(H)
Ch: Edwin R. d 2-26-1896 bPP

NEWHOUSE
Walter Scott, Jr., s Walter S. & Florence Anna, b 9-18-1907; recrq 12-10-1923 (H)
Silas b North Castle d 4-19-1818 ae 77y bHS; m Ethland ----- b North Castle d 4-17-1818 ae 79y bHS

NEWMAN
Walter rocf Ama. 3-12-1824; dis 6-1830 (O); d 2-28-1849 (H)
----- & -----
Ch: Edwin b No. Salem d 7-14-1823 ae 8m bHS

NEWSOM
Edith A., dt Everett & Elizabeth, rocf Sand Creek, Ind. with parents 3-6-1907; relrq 1-1920
Everett H. & Elizabeth R.
Ch: Edith Armstrong
cf Sand Creek, Ind. 3-6-1907 with 1 ch named; Elizabeth relrq 1-1920; Edith relrq 1-1920

NICHOLAS
Mary Jane, w Robt. B., dt Stephen & Anna B. SUTTON, b 11-27-1834 d 6-13-1892 (m 11-30-1865) (H)

NICHOLS
Dr. Charles H. rocf Balt. 10-1878; d Washington, D. C. 12-16-1889
Elizabeth P. recrq 7-11-1877; ct Chap. 5-1877
Erickson Norman (nm), s Wm. I. & Eliza E.; m 2-18-1896 Edith HAINES, dt Samuel B. & Rebecca M. (Rowland), b N. Y. 9-7-1866 (H)
Ch: Ruth (nm) (the aviatrix)
Ernest Lee m Winifred RIGGS
Ch: Lindley Kendall b 11- 4-1916
Herbert Lee " 4-24-1919
Ernestine Agnes " 11-28-1920
Esther Jean
parents recrq 1-1916; ch recrq of parents before 1921; letter to M. E. Church, Fairmount, W. Va. 12-1925; Ernest & ch rocf Wichita, Kans. 6-7-1933; Winifred recrq 6-6-1934
John M. d 4-28-1881 ae 40y bPP; m 11-21-1871 Sarah Ann HANCE, dt Anselm B. & Ellen, d 1-8-1911 ae 80y bPP (H) (both nm)
Sarah recrq 11-1842
Marion [Nicholl], dt Thos. J. & Avis M. (Townsend), b Scotch Plains, N. J. 6-24-1878; m 1907 Jonathan A. RAWSON, Jr. (H)
recrq 7-9-1923
Mary, Mk., d 11 Mo (Jan) 27, 1715/16
Mary A., dt Benj. F. & Lauretta H., Huntington, Ind.; m 1900 John COX, Jr. (H)
rocf Maple Grove 4-14-1900
Thomas Fuller, Westchester; m Flushing 3 Mo. (May) 8, 1724 Jane HOSHER (or Hosier), wd, Rye
----- & -----
Ch: James d 8-11-1811 ae 1m 7d bHS

NICHOLSON
Elizabeth R. m Joseph R. WOOD
cf New Bedford with parents for Joseph R. 11-1883; ct WD MM 2-2-1898 for Joseph R.
Isabella rocf Lisburn, Ireland 1848; ct Burl. 1851
John (nm) d 1-20-1858 ae 45y bPP (last figure of year not clear, may be 6)
Lancelot rocf Devonshire House 3-7-1906; name erased 11-1928
Lydia & -----
Ch: Sarah
Anna
Jane
Huldah
Charlotte
cf Lisburn, Ire. to Wilmington 9-17-1801, endorsed to N. Y. 5-6-1802; ct Lisburn 7-7-1802
Mary, dt Joseph & Abigail, N. Y.; m 1819 Joseph H. BEALE
cf Richhill, Ire. 4-23-1818 for Mary (clear); parents were of Cook, Ire.
Meadows Taylor rocf Lurgan, Ire. 2-17-1822, young lad, cert not rec till 1835; d 1891
Richard L., s Lindsey & Abigail P. (dec); m N. Y. 4-8-1857 Elizabeth VAN HOESEN,

NICHOLSON, Richard L. & Elizabeth, continued
dt Leonard (dec) & Mary, N. Y.
Elizabeth rocf Hudson 1835 with mother; ct SD MM 3-1858
Ruth (nm) d 2-12-1836 ae 45y at Bloomingdale Asylum bHS
S. Edgar d 4-17-1934; m Rhoda Elma -----
cf West Richmond, Ind. 2-1926 for both
Samuel Greer rocf Hardshaw West 10-1872; d 8-1-1877
Thomas rocf Lurgan, Ire. 4-18-1818 (clear); ct Stroudsburg, Pa. 8-2-1820 (clear)

NICKERSON
Adelaide, dt Stephen & Sarah, d 11-13-1915; m Martin D. ALLEN (H)
both nm bPP

NILSON
Harold L., s Richard S. (dec) & Ellen Y., Devon, Pa.; m at 44 Monroe Pl., Bkn. 5-12-1927 Eliz. Paxson COLKET, dt Jas. H. & Ethel P., Bkn. (H)

NIVEN
----- & -----
(prob all ch of George)
Ch: Mary b N. Y. d 8-14-1818 ae 2y bHS
Robert b N. Y. d 3-4-1822 ae 7y 9m 9d bHS
Jeannette, dt George, d 5-29-1832 ae 2y 1m bHS

NOBLE
Ann, Flushing d 3 Mo (May) 14, 1699
active mbr from 1676
Emily Lucile, dt Franklin & Marianna (Hallock), b Bkn. 2-24-1899; ct Phila. 10-13-1919 (H)
Franklin, s Samuel W. & Eliz. H. (Mather) (both dec), N. Y.; mat 15th St. 3-16-1898 Marianna HALLOCK, dt Henry B. & Anna B., Bkn., b 6-22-1871 N. Y. d 10-19-1913 (H)
Ch: Emily Lucile b 2-24-1899
Lindsley Hallock b 10-28-1901
Elizabeth Hallock b 8-16-1909
cf Phila. 5-9-1896 for Franklin
Lindsley Hallock, s Franklin & Marianna (Hallock), b Bkn. 10-28-1901; ct Haddonfield, N. J. 7-10-1922 (H)
Thomas L., s Samuel W. & Elizabeth (Mather); m 4-29-1911 Grace HALLOCK, dt Burling & Mary Emma (Scofield), b Peekskill 10-27-1875 (H)
Ch: Leroy Eugene b Jenkintown 6-13-1913
Thomas Burling b Bkn. 10-4-1917
cf Abington 1-12-1920 for all
William active mbr 1681-1691; his will, 1691, arbitrated by a comm.

NOE
Josephine H. (nm), dt James H. & A. L. (Perigow) m 1865 Clarence HUBBARD (H)
Clarence recrq 8-9-1913; Clarence relrq 9-13-1920

NOLEN
Josephine m ----- DAY
cf Linington, Me. 11-1887; ct Boston 3-7-1894

NOODE (See Moody)

NORDBY
Hilma Kindlund, wd, m 1907 Wm. Rufus McCORD (H)

NORRIS
Eugene Wesley (nm) m 2-1-1935 Frances FLANDREAU, dt Nelson E. & Eleanor (Townsend), b New Rochelle 7-3-1913 (H)
Frances recrq of parents 7-12-1920

NORTHROP
Annie Claire (nm), dt Eaton B. & Anna (nm); m 6-7-1899 Archibald COLEMAN (H)
Archibald relrq 9-14-1925, joined Epis. Ch.
Sarah Ann [Northrup], dt John & Eleanor WILDE, rocf Plains with parents 12-22-1829; dis mo 6-1848

NORTON
Amelia, w Charles E., wd Joseph W. HILYARD, Jr. recrq 6-1869; mbrp relinquished 3-1880
Gains m Mary ----- b West. Co. d 8-6-1833 ae 53 bHS
Mary, w Gains, d 8-6-1833 (H)
Ch: Hannah d 7-6-1870
cf Troy 12-9-1818; Mary dis 11-1830 (0); Hannah 1-1832
Robert (nm) b West. Co. d 7-15-1833 ae 31y bHS (widower)

NOTMAN
Josephine R. (nm), dt Henry T.; m Joseph H. SEAMAN (H)

NOTTINGHAM
Joseph rocf Rounds MM, Norts, 8-3-1778 (clear); ct Wellingborough, Norts, 9-1-1779 (clear)
Samuel & Mary
Samuel took ct Willingbury, Norts, Eng. 1 Mo (Mar) 5, 1747 with w; cf Tortola 8-1-1754; they ack ct Tortola 12-4-1755, nothing further; they, with fam, ct Tortola 5-4-1758, ret. from Tortola 5-29-1763; cf Phila. 10-25-1771; ct Bristol, Eng. 9-1-1777 for Samuel & Mary

NOYES
Glen H. (nm), s T. Wilson & Clara G.; m 6-20-1925 Caroline MATTHEWS, dt Joseph B. & Edith S. (Jones), b Balt. 9-19-1888 (H)
she was wd of Cornelius A. Wilson; divorced Glen H. Noyes & resumed name of Wilson
Kate J. (nm) m 1865 Edward M. HAYDOCK (H)
Lucinda (nm), dt Henry T. & Lucinda (Chamberlain); m 1913 James M. WILLIAMS (H)
----- (nm) m Sybil J. HALLOCK

NOYES, ----- & Sybil J., continued
Sybil rocf Ferrisburg 6-6-1906

NUSE
George, s Charles & Mary (Hopper), b N. Y. 7-28-1892; m 11-9-1918 Harriett Alida DOHERTY, dt John & Harriett M., b N. Y. 12-28-1882 (H)
both recrq 2-10-1930

NUTT
Sarah recrq 8-1837; ct Wby 5-2-1855 (H)

NYHOLM
Fred H. & -----
Ch: Frederick Howard, Jr.
Lillian Florence
Hannah Marie
father & ch recrq 4-2-1919; 3 ch recrq of father 4-2-1919
Fred H. m 2d Marion H. CORNELL, dt Franklin & Sarah R. (Southerland), b 1-6-1886 d 4- 9-1931, Jamaica, L. I.
Marion rocf Corn. with parents 9-3-1890
Hannah Marie, dt Fred H.; m ----- BRITHS recrq 4-2-1919

OAKLEY
Sarah (nm), wd, b White Plains d 4-9-1817 ae 84y bHS

O'BRIEN
Ignatius Jerome (nm) m 9-11-1869 Mary J. COMSTOCK, dt Nathan & Anne (Merritt), b N. Y. 9-11-1826 d 5-12-1901 bPP (H)
Sarah (late Grimshaw) dis mo before 2-2-1820

ODDIE
Robert rocf Creek 4-22-1796 (clear); ct Balt. 4-4-1798 (clear)
William rocf Westminster & Longford, Eng. 4-4-1906; name erased 2-1926

ODELL
Gabriel & Hannah
Ch: Daniel
Jacob
Benjamin
Sarah d 10-13-1815 ae 1y 10m bHS
cf Corn. 7-27-1815 with 4 ch named; ct Corn. 9-11-1816 with their 2 ch, Daniel & Jacob
Hannah D. recrq 12-1860; d 3-17-1861 (H)
William (nm) b Brunswick, N. J. d 11-11-1822 ae 56y bHS
----- m Florence TABER
Florence recrq 6-10-1908

OFFLEY
Daniel granted cert of unity to SD MM 10-5-1783

OGDEN
Ann Maria, dt Charles & Ann Maria, N. Y.; m 1851 Reuben LEGGETT (H)
Anna F., w Francis J., rocf R. & P. 4-1-1874; ct Chicago 12-9-1899 (H)
Gilbert rocf Jericho 5-21-1795; d 9-17-1798 bHS
Henry Corbit d 7-29-1891; m Elizabeth Beroman (nm) (H)
Ch: Marie
cf Phila. 3-6-1878 for Henry
Marie, dt Henry Corbit & Eliz. (Beroman), b N. Y.; m 11-7-1899 Lawrence F. EMBREE; m 2d T. William FRANCHE (H)

O'HARE
----- & -----
Ch: James d 1-17-1862 ae 4y bPP

OHNEMUS
Frank H. recrq 5-1925

OLCOTT
Maria C., dt Stephen & Phebe C. UNDERHILL, dis mo 5-1832 (O); retained (H); relrq 1-4-1871

OLMSTEAD
Mary Jane [Ohmstead] (form Hallett) complaint from Corn 11-1852 (not found); dis 1856
William B. d 8-6-1881 ae 73y bPP; m Louisa -----; Louisa ----- d 6-29-1882 ae 57y bPP (H) (both nm)

OLER
Hazel m George H. WOOD
cf Indianapolis 10-1-1919 with George & ch; ct Hartland 1-1-1925 for both with ch

ONDERDONK
Elizabeth, dt John W. & Margaret (Colons), N. Y. b N. Y. 6-18-1852 d 11-16-1930; m 1875 Wm. I. STRATTON (H)
Wm. rocf Phila. 10-1848 for Wm. with parents; Eliz. recrq 8-3-1881
Fanny (nm) d 4-6-1861 ae 78y bPP
Francis S., Jr., s Francis S. & Bertha (Ornstein), b Bkn 10-18-1893; m 1-11-1920 Franziska HOWNKS (nm), dt Walter & Franziska (H)
Ch: Elizabeth S. b Vienna, Aus. 4-18-1922
Adrian C. b 4- 3-1924
Francis recrq 2-13-1928; ch recrq of parents 4-9-1928
John Wm., s John & Fanny (Odell), b N. Y. 7-1-1817 d 3-22-1906 bPP; m 9-24-1837 Margaret COLONS, d 1-31-1886 ae 68y bPP (H)
Ch: Margaret Jr.
John recrq 8-1850; Margaret recrq 7-1-1885; Margaret Jr. recrq 5-1874
Margaret, dt John W. & Margaret (Colon), N.Y.; m 1876 Josiah CONKLIN, of Pomona, N. Y. (H) recrq 5-1874
----- & -----
Ch: Mary F. d 12-15-1852 ae 3y 5m bPP

O'NEILL
Agnes, dt Gregory, b N. Y. 1-18-1869 d 9-9-1925; m 1896 Stephen TITUS (H)
recrq 2-2-1887

ORDWAY
Joshua (nm) b New Hampshire d 2-5-1845 ae 26y (m)

ORMEROD
Daisy Elizabeth, dt John & Eliz., b Bkn. 12-3-1876; m 1897 Timothy S. K. HAUXHURST (H)

ORT
Evalena m William TRUMAN (nm)
recrq 6-12-1901; relrq 7-10-1918

ORTLOFF
Frank rolf St. Thomas P. E. Ch., Bkn. 5-2-1934

ORVIS
Francis W. (nm) m Emma G. HEACOCK, dt Samuel & Susanna (Winner), b 9-30-1855 d 1-9-1931
d Hackensack 1-10-1930
Ch: Ora Lucile b 8- 6-1887
Eugene Luvois b 9-26-1888
Harold Heacock b 3-22-1891
Edward Ernest b 11-26-1892
cf Muncy, Pa. 12-1885 for Emma; ch recorded mbr 5-5-1897
Ora Lucille, dt Francis W. & Emma, b 8-6-1887; m Wesley FULKERSIN

OSBORNE
Celia d 7-2-1835 ae 53y bHS
Ella, dt Abner & Sarah, b 8-18-1850 d 4-20-1933; m 1877 William H. WILLITS (H)
recrq 6-5-1878
Isaac (prob nm) m 1-6-1869 Hannah HOSIER, dt John & Abigail, b 8-10-1817 d 1-29-1902 (H)
Richard [Osburn], Wby; m at Nathaniel Pearsall's 11 Mo (Jan) 5, 1698/9 Jane BATES
William [Osborn] recrq 1835; ct Oswego 4-1-1840 (clear)
Sarah J., dt Robt. C. & Susan FOLGER, rocf Hudson with parents 12-1819; dis mo 12-1835 (H); dis mo 8-3-1836 (O)
William G. (nm) d 8-20-1836 ae 76y bHS
William H. (nm), s Sealey; m 12-12-1861 Sarah B. DAVIS, dt Joseph & Hannah (Collins), b 3-23-1834 d 3-28-1902 (H)
Ch: Infant d 6- 4-1867 ae 2d bPP
Grace Lee (prob) (gr dt Sarah Gardner) d 8-26-1872 ae 4m bPP
----- m Sealey ----- d 7-2-1835 ae 53y bHS
Ch: William H.
all nm

OSGOOD
Mary (late Franklin) dis mo 7-5-1786

O'SHUFF
Aaron (nm) d 10-24-1832 ae 35y 9m 14d bHS
same day

OSTRANDER
Maurice d 11-2-1922; m Mary ----- d 6-8-1904
Maurice recrq 11-5-1862; Mary recrq 5-3-1876
Sarah (late Woolsey) dis mo before 1-1-1812
----- & ----- (nm)
Ch: Hetty b N. Y. d 9-10-1812 ae 16d bHS

OTIS
Bethiah B. rocf Providence 2-24-1841
Eliza G., dt Joshua D. & Rebecca G. EVANS (mo) cf Phila. with mother 2-21-1854; called a resignation 1869

OVERDELL
Albert Eugene, s Otto & Martha E. (Travis); m Elizabeth -----
recrq of mother 5-1909; relrq 1-3-1934
Otto (nm) m 7-30-1908 Martha E. TRAVIS, dt Mortimer W. & Hannah (Cook), b before 1866
Ch: Albert Eugene
Martha recrq of parents 3-1872; Albert, recrq of mother 5-1909

OVINGTON
Adele (nm), dt Theodore T. & Louise; m James H. MERRITT (H)

OXTOBY
William b Yorkshire d 11-29-1837 ae 88y 8m bHS; m Mary Ann ----- b Eng. d 7-19-1840 ae 75y bHS (a wd)

OZBUN
James & Esther
cf Salem, Iowa 3-1882 for both; both relrq 11-1884

PACKARD
Winnie (nm) m Cloyd Hampton VALENTINE (H)

PADDOCK
Cornelia, dt Benj. S. & Emma HAVILAND, b 3-1-1860 d 8-1-1888
Gertrude, dt Benj. S. & Emma HAVILAND, d 1907

PAGE
Annie S., dt Pilatiah P. & Amelia, N. Y.; m 1861 Wm. W. TITUS
David G., having mo by a priest, Weare refers to N. Y. 8-11-1853; rpd adversely 10-1853
Edward T. rocf Yorktown 10-1887; in West Phila. 1912; d 8-1921
George, s John & Hannah; mo, ret a mbr; rocf Corn. with parents 8-25-1825; rem to Wisconsin & dis 9-1860
John m Hannah ----- d 11-11-1842
Ch: Louisa
Emeline Smith
George
cf Corn. 8-25-1825; all dis (O); Hannah

PAGE, John & Hannah, continued
dis 11-1829 (H)
Louisa, dt John & Hannah, rocf Corn. with parents 8-25-1825; dis 10-1827
Lucy, dt Rebecca; m 1816 George GILPIN
Lydia Ann, dt Pelatiah & Amelia; m 1861 Wm. W. TITUS
Pelatiah P., s Enoch & Peace (dec), N. Y.; m N. Y. 5-11-1836 Amelia C. (or E.) MERRITT, dt Wilson & Mary, N. Y., d 8-4-1897
Ch: Wilson M. b 2-20-1838
Lydia Ann b 5-30-1841
cf Salem MM, Mass. 8-13-1835 (clear)
Rebecca b Franklin, Del. Co. d 10-17-1818 ae 63y bHS
Ch: Lucy m Geo. GILPIN
Wilson M., s Pelatiah & Amelia, b 2-20-1838; ct Wby & Jericho 8-1858

PAIGE
Alice Browning m 9-7-1910 Henry Alva WHITE, of High Point, N. C.
cf Salem, Mass. 11-6-1907; ct High Point, N. C. 11-2-1910

PAINE
Experience rocf Chap. 6-15-1792, having rem with h

PALAMOUNTAIN
Bennett [Palimountain] b Eng. d 12-28-1831 ae 41y bHS
David, s Bennet, rocf N.P. 5-1828; ct Hamburgh 10-1843; afterward to Phila. 11-1844 (H)
Isaac Thorn, s Bennet, rocf N.P. 5-1828; ct Oswego 10-1843; cert returned as he Orthodox (H)

PALMER
Alice Smedly, dt Eli & Marianna (Smedley), b West Chester, Pa. 5-12-1870; recrq 5-12-1924 (H)
Anna M. (nm), dt Samuel L. & Sarah B. (Caine); m 1-12-1874 Thomas Ellwood FINCH (H)
Caroline Rapelye (form Palmer), dt Martha, dis mo 7-7-1841
Charles, s Jonathan & Sarah (Hopper), b Phila. 11-9-1824 d 3-11-1907 bPP; m 12-16-1848 Harriette M. JACKSON, dt France & Eliza (Copeland), b Boston 1825 d 5-12-1912 ae 87y bPP (H)
cf Phila. 11-4-1863 for Charles; Harriet M. recrq 4-8-1905
Clarissa, dt Nathan, rocf Pur. 1-1826; d 4-17-1879 (H)
Daniel, s Joseph & Sarah, Westchester, b 3 Mo. (May) 2 (or 3) 1680; rem cert to Pa. or thereaway 10 Mo (Dec) 2, 1708
Edith A., dt Edward Maria Theresa (Van Horne) b Dover, N. J. 2-9-1852; recrq 4-10-1897; ct Newark, N. J.; cf Newark, N. J. 7-12-1926 (H)
Edmund (nm) m Sarah ----- (nm) d 5-14-1855 ae 61y 10m bPP
Ch: Infant d 9-20-1836 ae 3m bHS
John B. d 5-10-1858 ae 40y 9m
Edward, s Obadiah & Hannah, b 3-1-1814; rocf Corn. 9-23-1824 with parents; dis mo 5-2-1838
Edward dis mo 2-1856
Edward A. (nm) & -----
Ch: Infant stillborn 7-20-1837 bHS
Caroline E. d 2-12-1845 ae 4m 1d bHS
Edward Pennock, s Edw. & Ellen P. (Marshall) (dec), b Doe Run, Pa. 7-17-1884; m N. Y. 5-20-1916 Aliph Gertrude SMITH, dt Chas. H. & Rebecca (Rosecrans) (dec), Spring Valley, N. Y., b Spring Valley, N. Y. 5-20-1916 d 1-21-1931 (H)
Ch: Edward Pennock, Jr. b N. Y. 3-14-1917 d 3-22-1917 bPP
Elizabeth Smith b Mt. Vernon 8-30-1918
Edward rocf Fallowfield 5-11-1912; Aliph recrq 1-13-1917
Elizabeth, dt Samuel & Sarah, N. Y.; m ----- DEAN; m 2d 1835 Thomas THORN (H)
Emily, dt Martha, rocf Pur. 1-9-1839 with mother; dis 12-1855
Esther, dt Joseph & Sarah, Westchester, b 2 Mo. (Apr) 24, 1678; being now at Phila. cert issued 2 Mo 3, 1707; cert of clear issued 3 Mo (May) 1, 1712
Florence, dt Eli & Marianna (Smedley), b West Chester, Pa. 8-5-1879; m 1915 Frank Meade STERRETT (H)
Francis J., s Charles & Harriet M.; m Edith N. ----- d 5-16-1886 ae 21y 3m 12d bPP (H) both nm
Francis J. d 9-16-1923 ae 65y 7m 25d ashes bPP; m 2d Sarah H. ----- (H) (both nm)
Hannah, dt Harrison & Phebe, N. Y.; m 1825 Charles BRUFF; m 2d 1854 Abel ADAMS
Harrison (nm) b Westchester Co. d 5-11-1814 ae 62y bHS (m)
Harrison m Phebe ----- d 1-9-1849 ae 82y
Ch: Richard d 12- 8-1824
Harrison
Hannah F.
cf Wby 7-28-1773; ct N.P. 1-6-1779 (clear); Pur. MM reports having dis him 4-13-1781; cf Chap. 4-15-1803 for Phebe & 3 ch named; cf Pur. not found; Phebe, wd, dis 1829 (H)
Harrison dis 5-3-1820
Henry rocf Phila. 2-1863; d 12-6-1886
Israel D. d 11-25-1830 ae 38y bHS (not a mbr here)
Japheth rocf Pur. 2-9-1797, placed not with a Friend; ct Pur. 7-7-1802 (clear)
Jonathan rocf Middletown, Pa. 7-7-1785 (clear); ct Falls MM 2-5-1786 (clear)
Joseph, Westchester, d Flushing 12 Mo (Feb) 14, 1726/7 (this may be date of s's d); m Sarah ----- d Flushing 2 Mo (Apr) 18, 1711
Ch: Sarah b 3 Mo (May) 20, 1666
Joseph b 10 Mo (Dec) 28, 1667
Mary " 1 Mo (Mar) 8, 1669/70
John " 11 Mo (Jan) 22, 1671
Martha " 7 Mo (Sep) 17, 1674

PALMER, Joseph & Sarah, continued
Ch: Esther b 2 Mo (Apr) 24, 1678
Daniel " 3 Mo (May) 2 (or 3) 1680
ch b Westchester, Westchester Co.
active mbr 1678-1701 or later
Maria, dt Martha, d 10-12-1832
Martha, w -----
Ch: Caroline dis 6-1841
Hannah
Emily dis 12-1855
cf Pur. 1-9-1839 with 3 ch named; ct Hector for Martha 3-4-1863; cert returned from Hector; ct Minneapolis 2-1864 for Martha & Hannah
Mary, dt Wm., Mamaroneck, m 1719 Samuel FIELD gr dt of Samuel Palmer
Mary Ann (form Allen) rocf Ireland 1852; dis mo 10-1856
Mary C., dt Dorinda Bouten, sister of Samuel A. Palmer, rocf Oswego 6-1828; ct Oswego 7-4-1849 (H)
Nathan, s Nehemiah & Jane, b 5 Mo (July) 10, 1717; ct Pur. 5-7-1772
Nathan m Deborah ----- d 12-26-1851 (H)
Ch: Clarissa
Ebenezer C., 30 yrs old in 1840; dis 6-1840 (H)
cf Pur. 11-9-1825 with 2 ch named; all dis 1829-1840 (O); Nathan dis 1-1842 (H)
Nehemiah, Mamaroneck, m Jane ----- d 2 Mo (Apr) 13, 1726
Ch: Drake b 7 Mo (Sep) 30, 1713
Aaron " 5 Mo (July) 23, 1715
Nathan b 5 Mo (July) 10, 1717
Mary " 8 Mo (Oct) 11, 1719
Sarah " 5 Mo (July) 17, 1721
Elihu " 5 Mo (July) 5, 1723
Nehemiah b 6 Mo (Aug) 5, 1725
Obadiah & Hannah
Ch: Edward b 3- 1-1814
William
Benjamin
cf Pur. 12-14-1809 for both; ct Cornwall 7-4-1821 with their s, Edward; cf Cornwall 9-23-1824 with 2 ch named; all dis 1832-1846 (O); all dis 1829-1852 (H); Obadiah holding a pew in Univ. Ch. (O)
Richard, s Harrison (dec) & Phebe, N. Y., b North Castle d 12-8-1824 ae 35y; m Westchester 4-17-1816 Eliza -----, dt John (dec) & Elizabeth, Westchester, d 6-21-1857 (H)
cf Wby 12-1-1773 with parents; ct Pur. 12-5-1821 for both; cf Pur. 8-8-1816 for Eliza; Eliza dis 1830 (O)
Samuel, Mamaroneck, Westchester, d 2 Mo (Apr) 1, 1716; m Mary ----- d 1728
Ch: William b 5 Mo (July) 23, 1675
Obadiah " 4 Mo (June) 25, 1680
Nehemiah b 8 Mo (Oct) 22, 1683
Samuel " 4 Mo (June) 3, 1686
Silvanus " 7 Mo (Sep) 13, 1688
Solomon " 9 Mo (Nov) 10, 1692
active mbr from 1684-1692
Samuel A., s Dorinda Bouten, brother of Mary C. Palmer, rocf Oswego 6-1828; dis 1-7-1857 (H)
Samuel H., having mo by J.P., Marl. ref. to N.Y. 2-21-1855, ret a mbr & Marl. notified
Sarah T., w James, dt James, Jr. & Mary JENKINS, rocf Marl. 12-1848; joined Orthodox before 3-1859 (H)
Solomon, Mamaroneck, m N. Y. between 6 Mo 7, & 7 Mo (July) 4, 1735 (cert not recorded) Sarah HARRISON, N. Y.
Susannah, dt Silvanus & Mary (dec), rocf Pur. 9-8-1763
William dis mo 3-3-1763
William, s Obadiah & Hannah, rocf Corn. 9-23-1824 with parents; dis mo by a priest 7-1846
----- & ----- (nm)
Ch: Peter D. d 2-17-1826 ae 11y bHS
Maria " 10-12-1832 ae 17y 2m bHS
Rosaline " 11- 5-1841 ae 6d bHS
Isaac Allen d 4-2-1862 ae 1y 8m bPP

PALMGREEN
Antoinette d 2-22-1885; m -----
Ch: Oluff d 12-23-1879
Margaret d 2-23-1897
cf Providence 4-7-1875 for Antoinette & dt, Margaret; separate cert for s, Oluff

PANCOAST
Ada, dt Seth & Sally, b Phila. 11-6-1853; m ----- BYRON; m 2d 1874 Emil FINK (H)
cf Phila. 7-13-1912; ct Phila. 11-14-1932
Asa, s Unity, rocf Upper Springfield 1-6-1796 with mother (minor)
Hannah, dt Unity, rocf Upper Springfield 1-6-1796 with mother (minor) ct N.P. 6-3-1802, had rem in her minority
Joseph, Jr. & Unity (nm)
Ch: Mary m ----- WILLETS
Hannah d 12-1-1804 ae 18y bHS
cf Upper Springfield 2-4-1795 (clear); dis mo 6-8-1797; his ack. 7-5-1809 ref. to Scipio
Mary m 1797 Thomas WILLETS (mo)
cf Burl. 1-6-1794 (clear); con mo by priest 2-7-1798
Mary rocf Frankford 1-1-1839; d 10-19-1844 ae about 69y
Sarah rocf Burl., N. J. 10-1-1798 to reside with her mother (clear)
Solomon d 4-18-1799 bHS
Solomon, s Jos. (dec) & Unity, Burl., d 4-3-1801 (or 4-4-1801) ae 31y; m N. Y. 11-9-1796 Mary HAVILAND, dt Thomas & Helena (both dec), Eastchester, b 1-23-1778
Ch: ----- d 4-18-1799
Walter b 3-21-1799
Solomon b 5-11-1800 d 4- 4-1801
Mary rocf Pur. 1-13-1791, a minor; Solomon rocf Burl. 7-4-1791 (clear); dis 4-3-1822

PANCOAST, Solomon & Mary, continued
for jas
Thomasin, dt Unity, rocf Upper Springfield 1-6-1796 with mother (minor); ct Creek 6-4-1801 (clear)
Unity & -----
Ch: Asa
Thomasin d 12-22-1802 ae 21
Hannah
Unity rocf Upper Springfield 1-6-1796 with 3 ch named; m ----- EVERINGHAM (mo)
Walter dis jas 10-4-1820

PARK
Mary T., w Joseph, rocf Pur. 12-5-1860; ct Pur. 1-1-1862 (H)

PARKELY
Timonson d 12-21-1803 bHS (nm)

PARKER
Abigail & -----
Ch: Asher
Daniel
Margaret
Sarah
Elizabeth
Marjory
cf Shrews. 8-6-1792 with 6 ch
Abigail rocf Shrews. 2-1-1813; ct Shrews. 9-11-1816 (clear)
Benjamin rocf Shrews. 2-1-1813; ct Shrews. 12-2-1818 (clear)
Elizabeth (prob. dt of Abigail) d 9-25-1798 bHS
Elizabeth rocf R. & P. 3-15-1821
Elizabeth rocf R. & P. 4-1821; d 6-30-1832 ae 62y 2m 25d bHS
George rocf Shrews. 8-7-1786 as apprentice to Geo. Fox; dis mo 5-7-1795
George & Hannah
Ch: ----- stillborn 1-6-1803
Charlotte d 12-9-1803 ae 3
Eliza
cf R. & P. 8-18-1802 with infant ch, Charlotte; ct R. & P. 7-3-1805 with infant ch, Eliza
George Howard (nm), s Geo. W. & Martha; m 6-15-1894 Louise M. STABLER, dt Edward H. & Louisa M. (Field), b Bkn. 2-27-1868 (H)
Gilbert d 8-17-1801 bHS
John, s Peter, rocf Shrews. 8-4-1783, 8 yrs. old, placed as apprentice with John White
John S. & Grace
Ch: Mary Grace
Phebe Anna
Elizabeth Slatie
cf Uxbridge, Mass. 3-1-1850 for John, minor; cf same 1-30-1852 for Grace & ch; John dis 1855; ct N.P. 11-6-1856 for Grace & ch
Linfoot F., s Elmer E. & Lucy A., b Waterbury, Conn. 12-19-1892; recrq 6-6-1917
Mary b Shrews. d 6-25-1828 ae 71y bHS (wd)
Mary G., dt John & Grace S., b Nottingham, Eng. 7-30-1832 d 8-4-1921 bPP; m Wm. Augusta NASE (nm)
cf Oswego 11-1866 for Mary G.
Ruth Louise rolf Union Ch. of Bay Ridge, Bkn. 9-14-1932
Sidney rocf Shrews. 12-5-1796 (clear); d 9-11-1798 bHS
Tyler William rocf Shrews. 2-4-1846, apprentice; dis mo 9-1851
----- & ----- (nm)
Ch: Sarah d 9-27-1810 ae 1y 6m bHS

PARRISH
Caroline L., dt John C. & Sarah H. (Wilson), b Oxmead, N. J. 12-25-1866; rocf Woodbury 12-3-1884; relrq 3-14-1927 (H)
Clemmons, s Edward & Margaret S. (Hunt), b Phila. 8-1-1848 d 3-31-1912 bPP; m 2-3-1872 Emma POWELL (nm), dt Alexander & Elizabeth, d 12-25-1912 ae 70y 9m 22d bPP (H)
Ch: Edward b Phila. 1-30-1873
Edward rocf Phila. 6-4-1884 (H)
Edward, s Edward & Margaret S. (Hunt), b Phila. 2-24-1850 d 6-9-1935; m 12-27-1871 Mary K. EVANS (nm), dt Joshua D. & Rebecca G. (H)
cf Phila. 7-4-1884
Edward, M.D., s Clemmons & Emma (Powell), b Phila. 1-30-1873; m 9-29-1896 Grace Louise FORFAR, dt Robt. & Mary I., b Bkn. 11-16-1879 (H)
Ch: Edward Jr. b Bkn. 12-4-1916
Edward recrq 11-11-1911; Grace recrq 4-13-1931; Edward Jr. recrq 3-13-1933
Mary K., w Edward, dt Joshua D. & Rebecca EVANS, rocf ND MM 2-21-1854 with mother; relrq 3-1878
William G. rocf Phila. 7-2-1862; ct Woodbury 3-1-1865; cf Woodbury 7-1879; d 1-25-1892 (H)

PARRY
Elijah rocf Burl. 2-5-1827; d 1-23-1854
Hannah rocf Phila. 1848; ct Burl. 1-1854
Joseph S., s Thomas & Lydia C. (both dec); m at Lydia P. Willets' 3-31-1897 Sarah WILLETS, dt Robert R. & Tacey (Parry), N.Y., b 3-12-1872 N. Y. d 2-26-1909 (H)
Ch: Amelia W. b 12-13-1897
Joseph S., Jr. b 2- 5-1899
Tacy W. " 1- 6-1901
Lydia " 1-13-1903
Maria Willets " 2-26-1905
Ch b Harrison
ct Pur. 6-1914 for all ch; Joseph mbr of Horsham, Pa.
Ruth, dt Charles C. & Minnie H.; m 1932 Austin Harris CHURCH (H)

PARSONS

Augustus Taber, s Edw. W. & Mary F. (Taber), b 2-21-1883; name erased 8-1920; he jas

Edith Augusta, dt Edw. W. & Eliza F., Flushing, b 7-9-1878; jas, name erased

Edward Willis, s James B. & Eliza F., Flushing; m N. Y. 10-5-1876 at Aug. Taber's Mary F. TABER, dt Augustus & Anna F., Throgs Neck
Ch: Edith Augusta b 7- 5-1878
    Augustus Taber b 2-21-1883
    Edward W. relrq 9-2-1896

Elizabeth rocf Pur. 5-7-1752

Elizabeth, dt Stephen & Rosanna (Croswell), b New Balt. N. Y. 8-18-1862; m 1908 Benjamin I. CASHART (H)

Elizabeth F., dt Jas. B. & Eliza F., b 5-26-1832; relrq 6-1860

Emily L., dt Jas. B. & Eliza F., b 4-17-1836; relrq 7-1861

James, s Thomas (dec), of Oxford, Pa.; m Flushing 14 Dec. 1721 Jane YATES, dt John, Flushing
    James rocf Abington where he had served apprenticeship 9 Mo (Nov) 27, 1721 (of clear & rem.); James took ct Abington 2 Mo 5, 1722

James, s James, Phila., b 4 Mo (June) 17, 1736 d 4-12-1779; m N. Y. 7-10-1765 Mary BURLING dt John & Ann, b 6 Mo (Aug) 13, 1737
Ch: John b 7-15-1767
    James b 1-22-1772
    Samuel b 8- 8-1774
    ct Pine St. MM, Phila. for all 3-5-1777; cf ND MM for all 4-21-1778

James & Jane (m 1780 Wby)
Ch: James Jr. d 8-27-1799
    James " 10-1810 ae 7y at Flushing
    cf Wby for Jane 12-27-1780; cert of clear to Wby 10-5-1780; cf 2 Weeks Mtg, London (clear) after a short stay 3-12-1764; ct Jericho 1-6-1819 for Jane, beloved Friend

James B., s Samuel & Mary, N. Y., d 9-2-1894; m N. Y. 6-8-1831 Eliza T. COCK, dt Thomas & Eliz. (dec), N. Y., d 7-25-1902
Ch: Elizabeth F. b 5-26-1832; relrq 6-1860
    John Bowne " 3-27-1834 d 6-24-1845
    Emily " 4-17-1836; relrq 7-1861
    Catharine B. b 1- 3-1838 d 5-31-1844
    Mary " 3-25-1843
    James B. "10-30-1845 d 1-29-1861
    Robert William b 8-22-1848
    Edward Willis " 12-19-1850

Jane, sister of Wm. B. & Mary B., d 7-10-1862

John dis mo 3-7-1754

John d 8-28-1798

Julia Frances, dt Robt. Wm. & Julia (Russell), b N. Y. 2-3-1878 d 2-4-1878 bPP, rem to Greenwood 6-28-1880; m 1902 Henry S. REDMOND (nm) (H)

Mary d 6-21-1880 ae 77y, w -----
Ch: Jane Ann d 11-29-1926
    George " 7-20-1903
    cf Whitewater, Ind. 3-1867 for mother & ch

Mary, dt James B. & Eliza, b 3-25-1843; m ----- BOLLER
    relrq 6-1868

Mary B., Flushing, sister of Wm. B. & Jane, d 11-26-1878

Melvin Herschel (nm), dt Kenyon & Helen Mary, of E. Setanket, b Bkn. 8-6-1905; m Bkn. 1-24-1930 Katharine TURNER, dt Henry C. & Charlotte, b Bkn. 3-27-1904 (H)
Ch: Katharine Pansy b Bkn. 3-2-1931
    Martha Turner b Bkn. 4-8-1934
    M. Herschel recrq 11-9-1930

Robert W., s James B. & Eliza F., Flushing, b 8-22-1848 d 5-1934; m at Jane C. RUSSELL'S 3-14-1877 Julia Frances RUSSELL (nm) dt Isaac (dec) & Jane C., N. Y. d 2-4-1878 (H)
Ch: Julia Frances b 2- 3-1878
    Julia's name entered by com. 1-14-1879

Samuel, s James & Mary, b 8-8-1774 d 1-20-1841 bur Flushing; m Mary -----
Ch: James
    Infant d 4- 2-1811 ae 3 wks.
    Mary J. d 4-27-1812 ae 27days
    Mary B. b 5- 6-1813
    John Bowne b 9-10-1815 d 12-15-1830 bur Flushing
    Anna b 12-24-1817
    Samuel
    ct Flushing 9-3-1806; cf Flushing with w, Mary, & ch, James; ct Flushing 5-5-1819 with last 4 ch named; Samuel "made his own black walnut coffin"

Samuel, s Sam'l B. & Susan H., b 1844 d 2-3-1923; mo before 1-1867, ret a mbr

Samuel B. d 1-4-1906; m Susan H. ----- d 8-9-1854
Ch: Samuel b 1844
    Susan H. " 2- 8-1847; relrq 9-1872
    George H. " 3-17-1849 d 4-14-1898
    John B. " 3-24-1851 " 10-14-1854
    cf New Bedford 12-22-1842

Samuel B. m 2d ----- (mo, ret a mbr)

William B. (nm) m 6-4-1851 Mary LEGGETT, dt Thomas & Ann (Farrington), b N. Y. 2-5-1823 d 10-13-1905 bPP (H)
    cf Flush for Mary 6-3-1874

William B., Flushing, mo before 12-1852, ret a mbr (had sisters, Mary B. & Jane)

PARTON

Lemuel E. (or F.), s Geo. & Eliz. (McCutcheon), b Plattsfield, Colo. 1880; m 6-1913 Mary FIELD, dt George B. & Ann (Stevens), b Cincinnati, O. 1880 (H)
    both recrq 7-13-1931

PARTRIDGE

Harry W. m Ella May BEDELL, dt Caleb C. & Martha, d 9-14-1923 ae 54y 8m 1d bPP (H)
    both nm

Margaret H. (nm), dt Mason H. & Ella (Miller); m Henry Edmund WALKER (H) (divorced)

PARVIN
Benjamin C. (nm) b Phila. d 7-1-1832 ae 38y bHS
Hannah rocf Phila. 5-24-1827; dis 11-1830 (O); ct Phila. 8-1829
John (nm) b Phila. d 2-8-1845 ae 45y 7m 6d bHS (m)

PATCHING
John F. rocf Warwickshire 2-1-1893; d 11-1928

PATIN
William rocf Renss. 12-1839; dis 1-1856 (H)

PATTERSON
Benjamin B. (nm), s Robt. L. & Ellen M.; m 4-22-1857 Mary MILLER, dt Daniel C. & Ann Eliza (Wright), b Bkn. 12-25-1837 d 1909 (H)

PATTISON
Cornelia, w Godfrey, dt Francis & Mary THOMPSON, b 1818 d 12-30-1885 (H) (ret a mbr)
James (nm) d 1907; m Jane THOMPSON, dt Francis & Mary (Wright), b 3-27-1816 (H)
relrq 6-8-1901; lived Ulverscroft, Scotland 1900

PATTON
Catharine, w Silas B., dt Stephen & Sarah A. FROST; m 7-2-1887 at Topeka, Kans.
recrq of parents 3-1872; ct Friendswood, Texas, 1-6-1897

PAULL
Gideon rocf Southwark, Eng. held by com. a long time, but unknown 1-6-1836; cert returned to Southwark

PAXSON
Alma E., dt Harvey S. & Eliz. (Murfit), b Solebury, Pa. 2-18-1887; m 1913 Joseph Wallace CONROW (H)
cf Phila. 11-12-1923 with h & ch
Elliott D., s Howard & Mary (Small), b Bucks Co., Pa. 1855 d 6-29-1921 in Phila. (H)
cf Phila. 6-6-1894
Frances, sister of Samuel C. (prob mbr in Phila.) d 5-28-1858 ae 51y 2m bPP (unm)
Frances, dt Sam'l C. & Eliz. D., b 5-19-1839; relrq 3-1860
Mary D., dt Samuel C. & Eliz. D., b 6-2-1836; m ----- COOPER (mo)
dis mo 1-1856
Samuel C. & Elizabeth D.
Ch: Henry Drinker b 10-1-1829 d 1-8-1830
Hannah Drinker b 3-26-1831 d 5- 8-1833 bHS
William " 11-22-1833
Ann b 7-31-1834 d 3-31-1837 bHS
Mary Drinker b 6- 2-1836
Frances " 5-19-1839
Elizabeth " 11-24-1841
Hetty D. d 8-30-1844
cf SD MM 2-21-1827 for Samuel; cf SD MM 11-28-1827 for Elizabeth D.; parents dis 1854 (O); Mary D. dis 1856 (O); Elizabeth 3-1862; William & Frances rel 1854,1859; Samuel dis 1829 (H); Samuel had a pew in a Ch. 1854
William (nm) d 9-3-1858 ae 79y bPP
William (or William, Jr.), s Samuel C. & Eliz. D., b 11-22-1833; jas & offered resignation; rel 3-1854
----- & -----
Ch: Ann d 3-31-1837 ae 2y 8m bHS

PAYNE
Horace (nm) m 11-15-1888 Harriet H. MACY, dt John I. & Jane (Hall) b Greenport, N. Y. 1837 d 1-2-1920 (H)

PAYNTER
Richard rocf Phila. 8-7-1794 (clear); ct Phila. 12-3-1794 (clear)

PEABODY
Mary May, dt Frederick W. & Anna G. May, b Dorchester, Mass. 9-29-1896; m 1919 John Leslie HOTSON (H)
both recrq 6-13-1921

PEACE
Charlotte A., w George, recrq 8-1878; name erased

PEACO
Mary Louise recrq 4-1888; relrq 9-1889

PEACOCK
Daniel & Elsa Margaret
Ch: Levy L.
Hans G.
Francis G.
Ella C.
cf Whitewater, Ind. 9-6-1911 with ch named, as associates; ct Richmond, Ind. 11-1920 for all

PEARMAN
James gct Linton MM, Herts. 7-3-1833 (clear)

PEARSALL
Alfred E., s Phineas C. & Katherine (Morgan), b Bkn. 4-18-1847 d 4-28-1919 (H)
Amy, dt Thomas & Anne, gct Jericho 3-3-1790, living with her sister there; cf Jericho 4-20-1797 (clear)
Amy Stoddart (form Pearsall) dis mo 10-4-1815
Ann, dt Henry & Mary, m Silas WILLIS; m 2d Matthew PRYER
Ann Mumford (form Pearsall) dis mo 10-3-1787
Antoinette Graham, dt Gilbert H. & Eliza (Frame) b Flush. 11-17-1847 d 7-10-1922
cf Flush. 3-7-1894 (unm) (H)
Charles W. rocf Jericho 10-15-1818, apprentice
Charlotte T., dt Thos. W. & Mary L., N. Y.; m 1857 Edwin THORN (H)
Daniel gct Upper Springfield 4-3-1811, appren-

PEARSALL, Daniel, continued
tice
Edmund, s Thos. & Ann, Flushing; m Flushing 12-11-1794 Rachel WILLETS, dt Thos. & Leah, b L. I. d 10-7-1830 ae 57y
Ch: Thomas W. b 12-8-1795
Charles W. b 8-13-1802
Mary " 11-19-1805 d 5-10-1833
Robert W. d 1834
ct Flushing 11-4-1807 for Rachel & 3 ch named; cf Jericho 8-19-1819 for Rachel with ch, Mary & Robert
Eliza, dt Wm. & Elizabeth, N. Y.; m 1828 Edward BALLINGER (H)
Elizabeth, dt Thomas & Elizabeth, N. Y.; m 1793 James BYRD
George, s William & Elizabeth, b 2-28-1811; dis 5-1835 (H)
Hannah, dt Thos. & Eliz., N. Y.; m 1789 Samuel BOWNE, N. Y.
Israel, s Thomas & Freelove, Wby; m 11-17-1774 Mary BOWNE, dt John & Dinah
Israel rocf Wby (clear); Mary gct Wby 3-1-1775
Jane Stratton (nm), dt Wm. & Mary (Wilson), d 7-21-1918 ae 85y 11m 18d bPP (unm) (H)
Joseph m 1771 Hannah BOWNE (mo)
cf Wby 9-1-1757; ct Phila. 10-5-1757; cf Phila. (clear) 7-3-1760; dis mo to first cousin 10-2-1771; Hannah's ack. accepted after reference to Y.M. 6-5-1772; Joseph's ack. accepted 9-1-1779; ct Wby 12-1-1779
Ch: (continued)
Margaret
Nathaniel d 12-7-1801 (or 12-10-1801)
Mary
ct Wby 12-1-1779; cf Wby 5-27-1789 with w, Hannah & 3 ch, Margaret, Nathaniel & Mary; ct Butternuts 3-5-1817 for Joseph & Hannah
Julia L., dt William, recrq 5-3-1882; d 6-1-1886 ae 59y bPP (H)
Katharine F., dt Gilbert H. & Eliza (Frame), b Flush. 8-10-1844 d 3-19-1930 ae 86y; cf Flush. 8-3-1892 (unm) (H)
Margaret B., dt Joseph & Hannah, N. Y.; m 1793 Henry HAYDOCK, Jr.
Margaret H. b 4-24-1810; cf Flush. 6-1847; d 5-12-1885 (H)
Martha C., dt William, d 7-16-1820
Mary, dt Nicholas & Sarah, Flushing; m 1664 John THORN
Mary, dt Nathaniel, Hempstead; m 1728 Thomas FRANKLIN
Mary rocf Shrews. 1-5-1784
Mary, dt Thomas & Ann, Flushing; m 1796 Samuel TITUS
Mary, dt Joseph & Hannah, N. Y.; m 1803 Wm. P. ROBINSON
Mary, dt William & Eliz., N. Y.; m 1815 Augustine BARIGHT, of Pleasant Valley
Mary W. (nm) d 10-19-1886 ae 83y 7m bPP (H)
Nathaniel, Hempstead, d 8 Mo (Oct) 24, 1703; m -----
Ch: Nathaniel d 11 Mo. 30, 1679
Hannah " 4 Mo. 20, 1699
Phebe " 1 Mo. 14, 1702/3
Nathaniel " 4 Mo. 17, 1701
active mbr 1701
Nathaniel d before 1767; m Mary -----
Ch: Sarah
Jean
Mary
Hannah
ct Wby for Mary & 4 dt 7-29-1767 (all clear)
cf Wby for Mary 10-16-1799
Rachel C., dt Robert & Eliz., N. Y.; m 1821 John J. SMITH, of Phila.
Richard, Wby. & Martha
Ch: Nathaniel b 11 Mo (Jan.) 27, 1676/7
Thomas " 4 Mo (June) 18, 1679
Martha " 10 Mo (Dec) 10, 1681
Hannah " 1 Mo (Mar) 22, 1683/4
Sarah " 5 Mo (July) 1, 1686
Elizabeth " 8 Mo (Oct) 28, 1688
Hannah " 12 Mo (Feb) 14, 1690/1
Phebe " 10 Mo (Dec) 20, 1693
Samuel " 12 Mo (Feb) 18, 1695
Nathaniel " 7 Mo (Sep) 11, 1699
Mary " 2 Mo (Apr) 30, 1703
Richard Franklin, s Gilbert H. & Eliza (Frame), b Flush. 1-5-1850 d 12-7-1924; m 12-21-1899 Anna Arabella ROSSITER (nm), dt Thos. & Margaret (H)
Richard O. dis 11-1819
Robert, s Nathaniel (dec), rocf Wby as apprentice to his brother in N. Y. 10-29-1766, rec 2-5-1767
Robert, s Thos. & Eliz., Flushing; m N. Y. 12-13-1797 Elizabeth COLLINS, dt Isaac & Rachel, N. Y.
Ch: Robert, Jr. b 11- 9-1798
Rachel C. " 12-29-1800
Mary
Rebecca G. " 6-15-1805
Elizabeth " 9-16-1812
ct Jericho 1-7-1793, apprentice; cf Jericho 12-19-1793 with 4 ch named; ct Phila. WD 2-7-1827 with 3 ch, Mary, Rebecca G. & Elizabeth, she a minor, the others (clear)
Robert, Jr., s Robert & Elizabeth, b 11-9-1798; ct Phila. 5-7-1823 (clear)
Robert W., s Thos. W. & Mary L., N. Y.; m at T. W. Phelps' 7-2-1860 Elizabeth PHELPS, dt Thos. W. & Eliz. B., N. Y. (H) (T.W. Phelps not under care of N.Y. MM)
Rowland & Mary (H)
Ch: Hannah
Sarah B.
Mary Ann b 7-15-1825 d 1-11-1828
Eliza Ann b 4-11-1831
Martha " 7- 1-1828
Mary A. " 4-25-1834
Emeline D.
cf Corn. 9-25-1823; all dis 1830-1843 (O); ct Corn. for all 8-1839

PEARSALL, continued
Samuel, s Thos. & Ann, Flushing; m Flushing 12-11-1788 Margaret HICKS, dt Gilbert (dec) & Mary, Flushing, b 3-8-1767
Ch: Mary H. b 1-15-1790 d 11-26-1828
Ann " 8-29-1791
Sarah m 1771, Flushing Lawrence EMBREE
Sarah, dt Thomas & Ann, N. Y.; m 1781 Patrick CAMPBELL (mo)
Sarah, w John, rocf Oswego 3-1829; d 8-7-1856 (H)
Silas (nm) b L. I. d 4-2-1834 ae 72y 11m 15d bHS
Thomas, s Nathaniel (dec) & Martha, Wby; m Wby 9 Mo (Nov) 25, 1709 Sarah UNDERHILL, dt John & Mary, Mk.
cf Wby 5-26-1762 (clear)
Thomas, Merchant, N. Y., b 8 Mo (Oct) 2, 1725; m Ann ----- b 6 Mo (Aug) 31, 1733
Ch: Sarah b 8 Mo (Oct) 18, 1746
Samuel b 2- 5-1764
Jacob " 2-15-1767
Edmund " 4-29-1768
Mary " 5-29-1770
Esther " 3-18-1772
Robert " 10-16-1776 d 12-1-1805
Thomas, s Nathaniel, of Cow Neck, N. Y., watch-maker; m N. Y. 11-13-1765 Elizabeth DOBSON, dt Thomas, N. Y.
Ch: Elizabeth b 5- 1-1767
Sarah " 4-23-1772
Robert " 6-25-1774
cf Wby 7-7-1762
Thomas, s Thos. & Freelove, of O.B., d 3-18-1807 ae 71; m Flushing 2-12-1761 Phebe CORNELL, dt Richard & Phebe, Flushing, b L. I. d 12-1-1810 ae 74y bHS.
cf Wby 1-28-1761 (clear)
Thomas & Ann
Ch: Sarah
Samuel
Jacob
Edmund
Mary
Esther
Amy
Robert
cf Wby 4-26-1786 for all; Sarah, Mary & Samuel (clear)
Thomas, Jr. rocf Jericho 8-19-1802 (clear); ct Pur. 7-6-1803 (clear)
Thomas W., s Edmund & Rachel, d 2-21-1866 ae 70; m 4-14-1824 Mary L. LEGGETT, d 7-20-1878 ae 75y 6m 2d (H)
Ch: Charlotte b 1- 3-1825
Anna M. " 7-29- (or 9) 1826 d 11-26-1828
Caroline " 4- 9-1828 d 7-1832
Edward " 4- 4-1830 " 6- 6-1832
Robert " 8-31-1833 " 5-29-1871
Thomas W. Jr. b 6-10-1838
cf Flush. 7-3-1817 (clear); Mary L. rocf Pur. 9-8-1824; both dis 1831-1838 (O)
Thomas W. (nm) & -----
Ch: George H. d 12-17-1856 ae 12y 8m 2d bPP, rem to Woodlawn 10-15-1866
Thomas W., Jr. b 6-10-1838; dis mo 12-1867 (H)
William d 3-29-1841 ae 81y; m Elizabeth ----- d 8- 5-1849 (H)
Ch: Samuel G. b 8-19-1787 d 10-13-1811
Amy " 12- 4-1788
Richard " 1-22-1791
Jane " 10- 8-1792 d 7-29-1793
Daniel " 7-17-1795
Mary " 3-13-1797
John G. " 3- 5-1799 d 9-22-1825
Elizabeth " 2-11-1800
Martha d 7-16-1820 ae 17y 10m 10d
William " 11- 1-1804
Edward " 5-13-1807 d 1833
George " 2-28-1811
cf Jericho with their ch, Samuel, Amy & Richard, 7-19-1792; all dis 1828-1831 (O)
William (nm) & -----
Ch: Richard O. d 3-1-1820 ae 29y bHS (unm)
George b N. Y. d 10-14-1843 ae 32y bHS
William, s William & Elizabeth, b 11-1-1804 d 3- 6-1868 ae 64y bPP; dis mo 10-1826

PEARSON
Alicia d 9-15-1886; m Charles M. HOBSON
cf Richhill (Brighouse) Ireland 7-1872
Georgiana (or Georgia) (form Hoyt) recrq 11-1883; ct Minneapolis 4-1-1896
Jacob J. rocf Grange, near Charlemont,(Eng.?) 5-22-1816 (clear); ct Lynn 4-4-1821 (clear)
Mary d 6-21-1880 in 77th yr;
Ch: Jane Ann
George d 7-20-1903
cf Whitewater 3-1867 with 2 ch named

PEASE (or Peace)
Mary m Henry WILLIS, Mk.
Phebe (late Barnard) dis mo 11-2-1808

PEASELEY
George E. m Florence LEIGH
Ch: Edgar Everet
cf Boston 6-1914 for George & Edgar; letter from Hampden Bapt. Ch., Springfield, Mass. 3-1916 for Florence; Edgar active mbr 7-1925
Rachel [Peasley] rqc 6 Mo (Aug) 3, 1738 (no further mention)

PEBBLES
Nelson recrq 5-1848; dis 3-1855

PECK
Caroline, dt George & Sarah (Ritter), b Danville, Pa. 11-6-1824 d 4-12-1909; m 5-11-1844 John JONES (H)
cf Balt. 7-9-1898 (wd); m 2d 3-4-1885 Wm. ROTHWEILER (nm)
William (nm) b N. Y. d 11-29-1828 ae 20y bHS (unm)

PECKHAM
Errol D. & Mary A.
Ch: Errol Kellogg b 2- 4-1917
cf Fremont, Neb. for father; cf North Loup, Neb. for Mary; son b after they came here; ct Po'keepsie for all 9-1920
James D. , after residing here some months, he took back to Westport, Mass. the minute which he had brought (2-2-1820)
Mary (nm), dt William G.; m 10-7-1901 Josiah T. TUBBY (H)

PECKOVER
Octavius rocf Newcastle, Eng. to R. & P. 2-13-1804 (clear), endorsed to Southwark, 5-1-1804; cf Southwark, Eng. 2-12-1805; his stay there very short

PEDLEY
Sarah, Great Neck; m 1705, Flushing John CHAPPEL

PEDLOW
James Green rocf Lurgan, Ireland 9-1885; name erased 4-1928
Sinton rocf Lurgan, Ireland 9-2-1881; name erased 4-1928

PEDRICK
Elihu having mo, Salem, N. J. refers to N. Y. 2-1-1843; dis by Salem 6-28-1843 & N. Y. notified (0); cf Phila. 5-1841 (H); ct Green St. 12-1851 (H)

PEELLE
Caleb Morris, s Henry B. & Mary (Morris), b Ind. 6-12-1843 d 10-11-1911 bPP; m Maria W. SMITH, dt James & Sarah, d 12-3-1928 ae 86y 1m 27d bPP
Ch: Louise W.
Sarah S.
Frank d 1890 bPP
James Walter b Cambridge, N. J. 3-25-1872 d 12-12-1908 Summit, N. J. bPP
cf Farm. 11-1888 with 2 ch named
Henry E. & Inez B. [Peele] (Inez sister of Arthur L. Allen's w)
Ch: Robert B. b 5-26-1919
Frances Charlotte b 9-24-1920
Henry Edmund b 11-1-1922
Inez Marilyn b 12-16-1925
Henry rolf Presbyterian Ch., Rock Stream, N. Y. 1-1914; Inez rclf Calvary Bapt. Ch., Roch. 8-1920; Robert recrq of parents 8-1920
Louise [Peele], dt Caleb & Maria W., b Macedon, N. Y.; m ------ LAING (nm)
cf Farm. 11-1888 with parents
Sarah S., dt Caleb & Maria W.; m 6-11-1903 Hugh B. PITCHER
cf Farm. 11-1888 with parents

PEENE
Caroline (nm), dt George & Jinnie E.; m 1896 Arthur HARRIS (H)

PEGLOW
Walter & Elfriede
both recrq 4-5-1933

PELL
Aaron, s Caleb, rocf Pur. 11-9-1785 as apprentice; dis mo 1-7-1795
Abraham & -----
Ch: Elizabeth d 4-13-1818 ae 9m
Benjamin m Mary
Ch: Sands b 3- 1-1786
Gilbert b 2-15-1788
Ferris " 8-15-1790
cf Corn. 4-20-1789 for Benjamin & w, Mary, & two sons, Sands & Gilbert
Benjamin m 2d Wby 2-25-1795 Mary TITUS, dt William & Sarah, Wby, b 1-8-1769 d 9-20-1803 ae 34y
Ch: Gilbert 1-1-1797
cert of clear to Wby 2-5-1795; Mary rocf Wby 5-20-1795
Benjamin & Rebecca
Benjamin m Nantucket 1808 Susannah F. (or Susan) ----- (H)
Ch: Susan Rebecca b 10-22-1812
Edward Howland b 3- 5-1815; recrq of mother 3-6-1816
cert of clear to Nantucket 4-6-1808; Susanna brought cf Nantucket 8-31-1808; mother dis 1829 (0); Edward H. dis 1840 (0)
Benjamin dis 2-2-1814
Cornelia, dt Barney & Mary E. CORSE, dis mo 8-1861 (H)
Edward H., s Benjamin & Susan, gct Oswego 1-6-1830, minor, cert returned 8-4-1830 as he had returned
Elijah d 9-2-1798; m between 12-6-1780 & 1-4-1781 Mary CORNELL
Ch: Mary C. b 8-12-1785
cert of clear 1780; cf Pur. 7-12-1781
Gilbert Titus gct Cornwall 1-5-1816; cert returned 8mo-1818 as he now in N. Y.; dis mo 11-7-1827, he now living in Ill.
Isaiah rocf Pur. 1-9-1794, apprentice to one not a mbr; his father nm
Josiah gct Pur. 9-3-1801 (clear)
Mary, dt William & Sarah TITUS, d 9-21-1803 bHS
Mary gct Flushing 2-6-1811 (clear)
Mary R., dt John H. & Sarah HOWLAND, b 11-26-1810; mo; dis 3-1831 (H); dis 4-6-1831 (0) (H)
Phebe con mo 3-6-1755; ct Pur. 9-6-1775
Susan Rebecca, dt Benjamin & Susan, b 10-22-1812; ct Nantucket 9-1829 (0); ct Nantucket 1-1835 (H)

PELLETIER
Hartley G., s Eugene A. & Abbey S., Boston;

PELLETIER, Hartley G., continued
m at J. C. Hull's 8-9-1884 Carrie Louise HULL, dt James C. & Caroline E., N. Y. (H)

PELLOWE
William H. d 7-21-1918; m Helen HARNED (H)
William recrq 6-13-1914; Helen mbr of R.& P.

PEMBERTON
Henry rocf Phila. 7-22-1794, apprentice to Richard R. Lawrence; ct ND 11-5-1800 (clear)

PENDLETON
Estelle (nm), dt Nathan; m 1897 Joseph Baker WHITE (H)

PENNELL
Francis W. rocf Chester, Pa.; ct Chester, Pa. 9-1921
Mary [Penel] rem 8 Mo (Oct) 2, 1740 (place not stated

PENNY
Mary rocf Marl. 12-1820; dis 1830 (O); d 5-27-1854 ae 70y bPP (H)

PENROSE
Geo. Pike b Waterford, Ire., d 6-8-1825 ae 31y bHS; m -----
Ch: William b N. Y. d 9-3-1825 ae 2y bHS
John C. b N. Y. d 9-23-1826 ae 5y bHS
Waterford MM in Ire. rq care 2-5-1817, he having mo & rem to America; dis from Waterford shown him & rpd 2-4-1818

PERCY
John C., s Geo. R. & Abbey (Crocker), Chatham, N. Y., b Chatham, N. Y. 6-29-1875; m at 15th St. 6-28-1904 Elizabeth SUTTON, dt Silas (dec) & Mary (Gager), Denver, b Chenoa, Ill. 10-6-1879 (H)
Ch: Sarah E. b Chatham 4-15-1905
Elizabeth recrq 5-6-1899; John recrq 12-4-1912; Sarah recrq of parents 3-14-1908
Sarah Eliz., dt John C. & Eliz. S., Salisbury, Conn.; m 1927 Wm. D. ROGERS, of Milford, Mass. (H)

PEREIRA
Lillie P., dt Russell & Lillie (Swimney) b Bkn. 2-26-1890; m 6-8-1912 Wm. Raymond BURLING (H)
recrq 3-13-1928

PERERA
Charles A., s Lionello & Carolyn (Allen); m Westtown, Pa. 2-20-1932 Ruth Hoops BRINTON
Ch: Sylvia Brinton b 12-30-1932
John Brinton " 6-10-1934
Charles recrq 12-2-1931; ch recrq of parents 3-1-1933 & 7-11-1934; Ruth rocf Westtown 2-6-1935

PERKINS
Benjamin D., s Elisha & Sarah (both dec), N.Y., b Conn. d 10-13-1810 ae 35y bHS; m N. Y. 4-9-1806 Mary MURRAY, dt John & Catharine, N. Y.
Elisha & Sarah of Plainfield, Conn.
Benjamin D., s Benjamin & Mary, b 12-21-1806 d 1831; m -----
Ch: Lindley Murray
Benjamin D.
ct Flushing 5-2-1827 (Flushing MM combined with N.Y. 1830); ct ND MM 2-5-1840 for 2 ch named
Benjamin D., s Benjamin D., gct ND MM 2-5-1840 with brother (minors)
I---- (nm) m 1-3-1861 Caroline COLEMAN, dt David & Avis (Bunker), b 6-27-1824 (H)
cf Hudson for Caroline 3-1846; name removed 11-9-1925 as unknown for many years
Lindley Murray, s Benjamin D., gct ND MM 2-5-1840 with brother (minors)
Lucretia S. W. recrq 8-1921
Mary b N. Y. d 4-1892 ae 44y (wd Benjamin D.)
Ch: Benjamin D. b 12-21-1806 d 1831 bHS
Caroline d 11- 2-1826 ae 17y 6m bHS
Mary Ellen Johnstone (form Perkins) rocf Warwickshire North 9-1-1897; name erased 2-1926 as Perkins
Mary S. Middleton (form Perkins) dis 12-4-1839 (mo)

PEROT
Francis Jr. rocf Phila. 3-4-1885; relrq 3-9-1901; 2942 Oakland Ave., Minneapolis in 1900 (H)

PERRY
Lydia rocf Jericho 8-1852; ct Wby 5-1858 (H)
Maria, dt Wm. F. & Jane MOTT; m 1879

PETERS
David having mo, WD MM refers it to N. Y. 7-22-1846; rpd adversely 5-1847
Deborah Hamilton (form Peters) dis mo before 6-5-1816
John b L. I. d 5-22-1817 ae 35y bHS (widower)
Mordecai C. b Pa. d 5-15-1824 ae 20y in explosion of Steamboat Etna bHS (m) (mbr in Pa.)
Sophia Halstead (form Peters) dis mo 4-6-1808
William m Anne ----- d 1-28-1814 ae 51y bHS
Ch: Ruth d 3-31-1811 ae 27y bHS
Sophia
Mariam Julia d 2- 2-1816 ae 27y bHS
Sarah T. " 2-17-1811 ae 16m bHS
Valentine
Deborah
Jane Ann " 8-15-1813
Amy " 1-28-1814
cf Creek 11-21-1800 for all; Ruth (clear)
William b Hempstead d 1-7-1821 ae 56y 6m 24d bHS; m -----
Ch: Ann Sophia d 5-22-1817 ae 1y 4m bHS
dis mo before 2-7-1816

PETERSON
Anna E. recrq 4-5-1933
Mary (nm) bPP in grave with John B. Harkins
(perhaps his dt)

PETTIT
Jeannette, dt John & Mary Frances, b Hempstead
11-14-1863; m 9-28-1890 Charles Stebbins
BATES (nm)
recrq 4-14-1924
John m Mary Frances PAGE
Ch: Jeannette A. b Hempstead 11-14-1863
Jeannette recrq 4-14-1924

PHARO
Joseph W. rocf Little Egg Harbor 1842; ct Little
Egg Harbor 1-1858

PHELPS
Elizabeth W., dt Thos. W. & Elizabeth B., N.Y.;
m 1860 Robert W. PEARSALL (H)
Joseph James rocf Dublin, Ire. 1848; in Australia 1854; rel 3-1880
Justus (or Justis, Justise) M. m Phebe JENKINS
d 3-13-1898 ae 75y 8m 22d bPP (H)
Ch: Jessie S.
all nm

PHILLIPS
Charles C. (nm), s John P. & Sara; m 5-8-1890
Maria Louise WILLIAMS, dt Jacob R. & Jane
M. (Betts), b N. Y. 9-16-1852 (H)
Maria recrq 10-1868
Elizabeth, Jericho, m 1690 Thomas POWELL
Franklin (nm) m 6-22-1893 Alice L. HULL, dt
Isaac Jr. & Emma L., b 3-4-1866
Ch: Marguerite b 4- 8-1895
Frederick Morris b 5- 2-1901
Marguerite recorded 1-18-1899; Frederick
recorded 8-6-1902; ct Phila. 10-1920 for
mother & ch
Hannah (nm), w -----
Ch: Frances b N. Y. d 2-9-1837 ae 5y 7m bHS,
rem to PP
Henry, s Samuel & Jane, gct Hudson 1-5-1825,
apprentice; dis mo 12-2-1829 (O)
Irene, dt Reuben Enos & Mary Emily (Hull)
b Farm. 5-1-1884; m 1911 Fred Callender
MORSE (H)
cf E. Hamburg 11-13-1933
Julian, s Samuel & Jane, rocf Oswego with
parents 1-14-1824; dis 5-1827
Maria Louise, w Chas. C., dt Jacob R. & Jane
M. (Betts) WILLIAMS (m 5-8-1890) (H)
Mary, dt Daniel & Susan (Young), b Newmarket,
Ont. 8-25-1869; m 1893 John Jay WATSON (H)
recrq 5-9-1908
Pardon, s Samuel & Jane, dis 12-2-1829 (O)
Samuel & Jane
Ch: Pardon
Henry
Julian
Catharine
Jane
Mary
Sally Burlingham d 1829
William Augustus b 8-19-1825
cf Oswego 1-14-1824 with 7 ch as named;
parents dis 1827
Thomas dealt with 1680 at rq of some mtg not
named; a follower of Thos. Case
Thomas d 3 Mo (May) 17, 1688; m Marcie -----
Ch: Thomas d 7 Mo. 17, 1688
Thomas recrq 4-1877
William, s William, of Denby, Pembrokeshire,
Wales; m Flushing 3 Mo (May) 18, 1721 Ruth
TATEM, dt Samuel & Mary, Flushing, d 7 Mo.
(Sep) 1734
William m 2d between 9 Mo. 6 & 10 Mo. (Dec) 4,
1735 (cert not recorded) Mary FARRINGTON,
dt Matthew (dec), Flushing
William I., s Simeon & Rebecca A. (dec), N. Y.;
m at Robert H. Haydock's 1-6-1869 Maria
W. HAYDOCK, dt Robert H. & Mary W., N. Y.
(not under care of N. Y. MM) (H)
----- & -----
Ch: unnamed boy b N. Y. d 3-27-1827 ae 1y 7m 7d
bHS
Francis d 2- 9-1837 ae 5y 7m bPP

PIATTI
Virgil C., s Patrizio & Antonia (Tantardini),
b N. Y. 7-20-1868; m 4-28-1909 Selina A.
FLYNN (nm), dt Maurice (H)
recrq 1-13-1930

PICKETT
George (nm) b London d 5-29-1809 ae 42y bHS

PICKFORD
Sarah E. recrq 1-7-1891; name erased

PIER
John, s Matthew, Mk., b 12 Mo. (Feb) 1650/1
d 4 Mo. (June) 2, 1698; m Elizabeth BOWNE,
dt John & Hannah, d 12 Mo (Feb) 14, 1721
Ch: John b 7 Mo (Sep) 16, 1679 d 1748
Hannah " 11 Mo (Jan) 22, 1681
Elizabeth b 8 Mo (Oct) 9, 1683
Mary " 11 Mo (Jan) 4, 1685
Sarah " 8 Mo (Oct) 19, 1687
Matthew " 1 Mo (Mar) 21, 1690/1
Samuel " 7 Mo (Sep) 15, 1692
Joseph " 8 Mo (Oct) 20, 1695

PIERCE
Abigail (late Robinson) dis mo 12-6-1820
Abraham rocf Chap. 4-10-1812 (clear)
Abraham dis mo 9-4-1816
Alfred rocf Wilmington 9-28-1829 (minor); (mo)
dis 2-1836 (O); dis 3-1834 (H); came with
parents
Alice H., dt Elias H. & Rebecca (Jacobs),
b Lake Mohegan, N. Y. 10-13-1859 d 10-4-1935; recrq 11-8-1920 (H)
Caleb D., s Eli & Martha, Phila.; m at Samuel

PIERCE, Caleb D., continued
Churchman's 4-14-1853 Phebe CHURCHMAN, dt Joseph (dec) & Hannah, N. Y. (H)
Phebe rocf Green St. 1-20-1853
Ezekiel, Flushing, b 2-17-1752; m Mary ----- b 1 Mo (Mar) 18, 1746/7
Francis H. recrq 3-1-1876; ct Collins 7-1888
Isaac (nm) & -----
Ch: Emeline b N. Y. d 8-13-1831 ae 1y 1m bHS
James rocf Chap. 6-14-1832 (clear); dis 12-1839 (O)
Jane rocf Chap. 12-10-1830 (clear); dis 4-1831
John, s Wm. & Deborah, of Dutchess Co., N. Y.; m N. Y. 3-8-1797 Deborah FIELD, dt Wm. & Hannah, N. Y.
Ch: Mary b 9-29-1798
William " 11-29-1802
John rocf Pur. 8-14-1794 (clear); ct Coey. 8-6-1806 with their 2 ch named
Lilla J. (nm), dt Merritt & Amanda; m 7-4-1876 David M. FROST (H)
Mercy L., w Isaac (H)
Ch: Sarah E.
Alfred (not included in cert)
cf Wilmington 10-29-1830 with dt; ct Salem, Ohio 3-1841
Myra rocf New Hartford 4-3-1846 (clear); d 4-1873
Retta (nm), dt Lucien B. & Annie (Harmon); m 1-1-1889 Charles B. DAVENPORT (H)
Reuben rocf Chap. 2-11-1830, minor; d 1834
Sarah E., dt Isaac & Mercy L., rocf Wilmington 10-29-1830 with mother; ct Salem, Ohio, 3-1841 with mother (H)
Sarah W. d 1-17-1895; m David UNDERHILL (H)
Thomas L. m Dorothy ----- d 12-1835 (H)
Ch: Infant stillborn 6-9-1835
cf Chap. 8-1833 for Thomas; cf Pur. 9-1835 for Dorothy; ct Chap. 9-1837 for Thomas

PIERMAN
James rocf Oswego 12-16-1829 (clear); ct Eng. 7-1833

PIERSON
Catherine C., dt Arthur N. & Sadie F., Westfield, N. J.; m 1930 Howard H. TURNER (H)

PIGGOTT
Elizabeth A. (nm) b N. Y. d 3-18-1812 ae 19y bHS (unm)
George d 8-22-1799 bHS; m -----
Ch: Maria d 7-8-1803 ae 1y 3m bHS
Samuel (nm) m Sarah ----- (nm) b Put. Co. d 9-22-1834 ae 62y 5m 10d bHS
Sarah (late Hull) dis mo 9-7-1791
----- & -----
Ch: Charles b N. Y. d 7-12-1829 ae 26y bHS

PIKE
James rocf Dublin 4-11-1854; ct Dublin 1-2-1856

PILLAR
Alfred Ernest rocf Dublin 1-6-1904; ct Dublin 11-6-1907
Francis, Dublin asks care 1-16-1849, rpd 6-1849 that he had ret. to Ire.

PIM
Henry rocf Dublin 9-13-1831 (clear); ct Dublin 7-1832
John rocf Phila. 1-27-1831; dis 10-1832

PINE
Gilbert G. rocf Marl. 1850; ct N.P. 1856
Mary, dt William & Cath. Jane (Popenoe) b Cincinnati 1-8-1876; m 1903 Charles H. CHAPMAN (H)
recrq 2-10-1919 (her mother not a mbr)
Samuel, Wby. m Wby 4 Mo. (June) 1, 1723 Rachel ZANE
Sarah Ann, dt Smith & Catharine, rocf Plains with mother 1851; mo
Smith & Catharine
Ch: Sarah Ann
Elizabeth G.
Isaac
cf Plains for all 1851; ct Marl. 1855 for all but Sarah Ann

PINKHAM
Fanny S. rocf Salem, Mass. 10-6-1875; ct Marl. 12-1881
Libny rocf N.P. 7-18-1798 [1857; d 1867 (H)
Ruth, w Frederick, rocf Scip. 9-1845; in Calif.
Sarah rocf Jericho 4-9-1798 to live with her h

PINKNEY
William recrq 1-3-1816; dis 11-4-1818

PINTARD
Mary rocf Shrews. 11-5-1787 with dt, Ann; ct Shrews. 7-7-1790 with dt, Ann (both clear)

PIPER
Harry L. b Canada d 9-15-1921 ae 82y bPP; m Janet H. ----- (both nm)

PITCAIRN
Robert Brower (nm), s Robert & Martha; m 3-4-1856 Mary WING, dt Oliver H. & Rachel H. (Ketcher), b N. Y. 12-11-1833 d 8-11-1903 (H)
cf Stanford for Mary 3-1-1871
----- & -----
Ch: Emma C. d 9-12-1859 ae 4m bPP

PITCHER
Hugh B. (nm) m 6-11-1903 Sarah S. PEELE, dt Caleb & Maria W.
Ch: Clinton b 1-18-1905 d 1-26-1912 bPP
cf Farm. 11-1888 for Sarah with parents

PITMAN
Elizabeth, dt Caleb & Elizabeth (Marlin) (nm)

PITMAN, Elizabeth, continued
b 3-15-1815; m 1836 Jehu LIPPINCOTT (H)
cf Chap. 12-5-1877

PITT
William R., s John B. & Charlotte (Rafford), d 4-28-1931 ae 85y bPP; m Anna SUTTON, dt George Thomas & Margaret (Dodge), d 9-30-1932 ae 63y 3m 10d bPP (H) (both nm)

PIXLEY
John H. (nm) m Ann ----- (nm) b Harrison's, Pur. d 6-20-1816 ae 27y bHS
Ch: Thomas b Horse Neck, Conn. d 6-8-1815 ae 4m

PLACE
Isaac I. (nm) b Dutchess Co. d N. Y. Hosp. 2-2-1814 ae 45y bHS
Joseph (nm) & -----
Ch: Infant stillborn 12-21-1835 bHS
----- & -----
Ch: Mary Ann b N. Y. d 7-15-1810 ae 4m 18d bHS

PLANKINHORN
Susanna rocf Phila. 2-21-1827; dis 6-1830 (0); ct Phila. 7-1829 (H)

PLATT
Eleanor (nm) b Rye d 9-13-1811 ae 28y 2m 16d bHS
J. Hull, M.D. (nm) m Emma S. HAVILAND, dt Aaron G. & Elizabeth (Carpenter), b 9-12-1856 (H)
Mary rocf Phila. 9-1845; ct Phila. 12-1846 (H)
Richard (nm) d 4-7-1847 ae 36y bPP; m 10-29-1835 Charity FARRINGTON, dt Ezra & Hannah (Hyde), b Bkn. 7-20-1816 d 1-12-1901 bPP (H)
----- & -----
Ch: Elizabeth d 7-29-1811 ae 4m 21d bHS
Esther Ann d 8-11-1811 bHS

PLUMMER
William T. (nm) d 8-18-1851 ae 49y 2m 24d bPP

POHL
Francis Julius, s Fred'k Joseph & Adelaide (Von Nordroff); m 5-14-1926 Josephine POLLETT (nm), dt Chas. F. & Lulu (McIlvaine) (H)
cf Wilmington, Del. for Francis 2-9-1920

POILLON
Margaret b Ireland d 3-16-1839 ae 51y bHS (wd)

POLLETT
Josephine McIlvaine (nm), dt Chas. F. & Lulu (McIlvaine); b 1926 Francis Julius POHL (H)

POLLOCK
Ruth Isabella, dt James R. & Eugenia (Parkinson), b Bkn. 11-19-1910; recrq 7-8-1929; ct Wby 7-13-1931 (H)

POOLE
Clark, s Milo Randolph & Sophronia Ellen, b 10-26-1879; rolf Bapt. Ch. of Redeemer, Bkn. 12-1921
Samuel [Pool] (nm) m Maria L. SWAIN, dt Chas. F. & Mary T., d 1-26-1900 ae 58y bPP
Ch: Eugene d 7-18-1863 ae 11m 9d bPP
(Arthur, s Samuel & Eliza, d 3-2-1898, ae 38y bPP)

POPE
Clifford Hillhouse, s Mark C. & Harriet H., Washington, Ga.; m Lewisboro, N. Y. 9-8-1928 Sarah H. DAVIS, dt Horace A. & Anna N., N. Y., b Dougan Hills, N. Y. 5-14-1901 (H)
Daniel N. rocf Salem 4-10-1823 (clear); dis 2-1834 (0); dis 6-1836 (H)
James rocf Salem, Mass. 11-10-1825 (minor); d Mexico 1833 (at Tabasco, Mex.) (H)

PORTER
Eleanor rocf Phila. 4-24-1772; she had come there from Burl & is young (clear)
Eliza Ann, dt Sam'l & Harriet ROBBINS, rocf Phila. with parents 6-21-1814; dis mo 3-4-1835
George (nm) & Mary T.
Ch: (prob) Joseph F. d 2-7-1867 ae 6y bPP
Mary rocf New Bedford 5-1868; relrq 7-1872
John (nm) & -----
Ch: Infant s stillborn 7-9-1875 bPP
John G., s William & Amelia (Giles), b Whitable Kent, Eng. 1-2-1843 d 7- 8-1926 bPP; m Sarah STEVENS, dt John & Sarah, b Kent, Eng. 9-10-1841 d 12-11-1928 bPP (Sarah nm) recrq 12-1868
Thomas & -----
Ch: Thomas C. G. b Eng. d 6-21-1893 ae 23y 7m 15d bur Woodlawn rem to PP (both nm)

POSSONS
Elizabeth Mary, dt Wm. H. & Emily (Hoag), b Stanton Hill, Greene Co. 4-18-1882; recrq 7-11-1914 (H)
William H. (nm), s George & Elizabeth, d 1890; m Emily HOAG, dt William & Amy H. (Gurney), b New Balt. 3-7-1855 d 9-25-1934 (H)
Emily transferred from Albany 1-8-1916

POST
Helen m ----- FROTHINGHAM (both nm)
Helen Bulkley, dt Morgan B., b 10-19-1908; m after 1928 Frank SILOR (nm)
Helen recrq of father 9-1922
Henry, s Henry, rocf Wby. 6-16-1790 (apprentice)
Henry & -----
Ch: Infant stillborn 12-18-1815
Henry (nm) & -----
Ch: Caroline P. d 3-23-1821 ae 1yr 11m bHS

POST, continued
Henry R., s Edmund (dec) & Mary N., Hempstead, b about 1818; m N. Y. 10-11-1843 Elizabeth C. WOOD, dt John & Martha, N. Y.
recrq of parents 12-1828, ae about 10; ct R. & P. 10-2-1844 for Elizabeth C.
Mary R. rocf Westbury 1-1-1896; d 7-26-1902
Morgan B. b Bkn. 9-7-1877 d 1-17-1929 Pelham, N. Y. bPP; m Sarah H. -----
Ch: Agnes Morgan b 3-20-1907
Helen Bulkley b 10-19-1908
Caroline Bulkley b 11-12-1912
Margaret Morgan " 11-12-1912
all recrq 9-1922
Phebe b L. I. d 10-15-1825 ae 70y bHS (unm)
Richard, s Jotham , b L. I. d 8-8-1813 ae 78y bHS; rocf N.P. 1-16-1793; ct N.P. 12-4-1793; cf N.P.
Robert F. rocf Oblong 12-7-1921
Samuel & Mary U.
Ch: Mary Jane b 11-27-1825
Amelia " 1833
cf Wby 3-20-1816 (clear); cert of clear to Stanford 11-7-1821; cf Stanford 12-21-1822 for Mary U.; ct Wby & Jericho with minor dt named (O); ct Roch. 11-1835 with 2 ch named
Smith recrq 8-1858; ct Jericho 4-2-1862 (H)
Stephen R. b 5- 3-1830 d 12-24-1899 bPP; m before 10-1867 Caroline BULKLEY (nm) b Ind. 1844 d W. Nyack, N. Y. 1935 bPP
Stephen rocf Wby & Jericho 3-1861
Willis having mo Hudson ref. to N. Y. 4-1-1818, rpd adversely 8-5-1818

POSTLETHWAITE
C. Gayton, s Clarence E. & Charlotte (Stratton) b Sewickley, Pa. 2-1-1902; m 6-11-1932 Althea FLETCHER (nm), dt Alfred P. & Katharine (Leahy) (H)
Clarence E. (nm), s J. A. J. & E. J.; m 3-27-1890 Charlotte L. STRATTON, dt Geo. W. & M. Virginia, b Altoona, Pa. 3-27-1865 (H)
Ch: C. Gayton b Sewickley, Pa. 2-1-1902
Charlotte recrq 5-4-1887; Gayton recrq 4-9-1923

POTTER
Augustus C., s Elisha & Ruth; m 1856 Frances R. GREEN, dt Israel & Phebe (Townsend), b 4-20-1836 (H)
relrq 5-9-1921; In Green Bay, Wis. 1900
Elizabeth took cert of general clearness "to whom it may concern" 6 Mo (Aug) 26, 1677
Frances, w Augustus E., dt Dr. Israel & Phebe GREEN (m 1856) (H)
William J. (nm) m Edith Eloise DUVALL, dt Chas. E. & Mary Ella (Hull), b Bkn. 6-4-1895 (H)
Ella recrq of parents 1-5-1901 (H)

POTTS
Dorothy recrq 3-3-1836 (rst); d 10-26-1865
Mary, Newtown, m 1742 Abraham SHOTWELL

Thomas, Bristol, Pa., m Flushing 6 Mo. (Aug) 14, 1712 Judith SMITH, Flushing
Judith took rem ct Abington 7 Mo. (June) 4, 1712

POULTNEY
Benjamin m Eliza ----- d 11-9-1850
Ch: Maria b 1-10-1846, rem to Balt. 1856
cf Balt. E. & W. Dist. 12-8-1836 (minor); cf Wilmington 8-2-1845 for Eliza; Benjamin dis 11-1852
Jane T. E., w -----
Ch: Hannah
cf Wilmington 8-2-1845 with 1 ch named; ct Balt. 2-1853

POUND
Samuel S. rocf R. & P. 6-1844; ct E. Hamburgh 11-6-1850; cf E. Hamburgh 10-6-1869; d 1-25-1885 (H)

POWELL
Abigail, dt Thomas, Jericho; m 1690 Richard WILLITS
Abigail (nm) b L. I. d 11-11-1825 ae 43y 5m bHS (wd)
Amy recrq 4-1830; d 12-11-1844 bPP (H)
Anna L., dt Jonathan R. & Anna (Morrell), b Chatham, N. Y. 9-18-1866; recrq 5-10-1920 (H)
Bethany b Dutchess Co. d 2-7-1821 ae 44y 6m 6d bHS
recrq 12-4-1816; wd
Cornelius & Rachel
Ch: Reuben
Christopher
Elizabeth W.
cf Wby 3-14-1827; ct Wby 4-2-1828
Edith rocf Wby 4-17-1816 (clear)
Elisha H., s Thos. & Cath. (both dec), Greenville, N. Y.; m at Caleb P. Carpenter's 1-2-1856 Rachel D. HUNTER, dt Isaac & Patience CARPENTER, N. Y. (H)
cf Ama. 3-2-1853 for Rachel D.; ct Coey. 6-1856 for Rachel D.
Eliza, w Abraham, rocf Jericho 10-1837; ct Jericho 8-1842 (H)
Elizabeth, dt Thomas; m 1691 Samuel TITUS
Elizabeth b Fishkill d 2-26-1812 ae 68y bHS
Elizabeth Durand (form Powell) dis mo 5-7-1817
Elizabeth m William L. HUNT (H)
Elsie, dt Wilson M. & Sarah H., N. Y., b N. Y. 5-20-1875; m 1912 Edward INGRAHAM (nm) (H)
Emma (nm), dt Alexander & Elizabeth; m 1872 Clemmons PARRISH (H)
Frederick (nm) b Greene Co. d 6-6-1841 ae 21y bHS (unm)
George Townsend, s Townsend & Catharine (Macy), b Clinton Corners 3-18-1843 d 5-21-1927; m 12-2-1868 Marcia CHACE, dt Wm. Henry & Marcia (Alger), b Jersey City, 3-23-1845 d 7-27-1932 (H)
both transferred from Albany 1-8-1916

POWELL, continued
Jacob & Hannah
Ch: Israel
Samuel
Abigail
John
cf Jericho 3-21-1805 with their 4 small ch as named; ct Coey. 4-2-1806 with 4 small ch named
James, s Moses (dec) & Catharine, Clinton, N. Y.; m N. Y. 4-5-1804 Martha TOWNSEND, dt John & Susanna, Middlesex, N. J.
Martha rocf R. & P. 1-19-1804 (clear); he brought cert of clear from Creek; Martha took ct Creek 5-2-1804
John, Bethpage, m at John Hallock's 11 Mo (Jan) 9, 1704/5 Margaret HALLOCK, dt John & Abigail, Brookhaven
Ch: John b 10 Mo (Dec) 24, 1705
Philenah b 10 Mo (Dec) 12, 1707
Clements " 12 Mo (Feb) 27, 1709/10
Mary " 8 Mo (Oct) 22, 1713
Phebe " 2 Mo (Apr) 13, 1716
Amy " 1 Mo (Mar) 6, 1718/19
Rachel " 3 Mo (June) 1, 1720
Sarah " 2 Mo (Apr) 18, 1723
Hannah " 6 Mo (Aug) 17, 1725
John, Flushing, b 10 Mo (Dec) 27, 1740
John m Wby 1804 Phebe -----
cf Wby 4-26-1786; he took cert of clear to Wby 5-2-1804; Phebe brought cf Wby 9-19-1804
John D. & Ann (H)
Ch: Jacob
Elizabeth
Sarah d 6-12-1828
Anna
Daniel
cf Creek 6-16-1826 with 2 ch named; all dis 1830-1848 (0); ct Farm. 7-1835 with 5 ch named (H)
John W., s Joshua & Phebe, Wby; m N. Y. 11-10-1813 Sarah M. JOHNSON, dt Wm. & Anna, N.Y., b N. Y. d 6-12-1828 ae 36y
Ch: Mary b 5-12-1814
Mary, Jr. b 12- 6-1815
Sarah Ann " 9- 1-1816
Matilda
Emily " 9- 5-1825
William J. (nm) d 8- 6-1829 ae 1y 2m 1d
Phebe (nm) (note. entered by error, her father dis before her b)
cf Wby 5-20-1807, lad, placed with a Friend; dis 9-2-1818; ct Wby & Jericho 6-4-1834 for 3 ch, Mary J., Sarah & Matilda
Jonah & -----
Ch: William S. d 9-10-1804 ae 6y bHS
Ethalenda b Wby d 8-18-1826 ae 11m bHS
Jonathan P., s Henry J. & Judith (Rider), b Chatham, N. Y. 2-2-1828 d 1917; m 10-4-1859 Phebe POWELL, dt Cyrus, b New Balt. 7-1823 d 1-1918 (H)
Jonathan R. rocf Chatham 8-2-1871; ct Chatham 8-3-1881 (H)
Jones d 7-13-1801 bHS (nm)
Mary, dt Wm. N. & Mary N., b 8-26-1849; ct Oswego 4-6-1859 (H)
Mary J., dt John W. & Sarah M., gct Wby & Jericho 6-4-1834 with sisters (0); ct Wby 3-1834 with sister (H)
Matilda, dt John W. & Sarah M., gct Wby & Jericho 6-4-1832 with sisters (0); ct Wby 5-1836
Phebe (nm) b L. I. d 11-16-1833 ae 57y 6m bHS (unm)
Phebe, dt Cyrus, b New Balt. 7-1823 d 1-1918; m 1859 Jonathan P. POWELL (H)
Ruth Alice, dt Walter & Lucy G. (Harned), b Bethpage 12-15-1886; m 1909 Clifford Burr WHITE (H)
cf Jericho 2-8-1913
Sarah Ann, dt John W. & Sarah M., gct Wby & Jericho 6-4-1834 with sisters (0); ct Wby 3-1834 with sister (H)
Sarah H., dt Wilson M. & Elsie (Knapp), b N.Y. 10-9-1906; m 1930 Prescott B. HUNTINGTON (nm) (H)
recrq of parents 10-9-1909 (as mother not yet a mbr)
Solomon certified mbr 1755
Stephen (nm) b Westchester Co. d 1-6-1810 ae 45y bHS
Stephen (nm) b Westchester Co. d 5-11-1827 ae 45y 6m 9d bHS (widower)
Tabitha rocf Ama. 12-1-1847; ct Ama. 7-1856 (H)
Thomas, Bethpage, O.B., m 2d Wby 9 Mo (Nov) 2, 1690 Elizabeth PHILLIPS, Jericho
active mbr from 1685
Thomas, s Thomas, Bethpage, m at Thomas Willets' 9 Mo (Nov) 6, 1691 Mary WILLETS, dt Thomas, Jericho
Ch: Thomas b 5 Mo (July) 30, 1693
Deborah " 11 Mo (Jan) 4, 1694/5 d 2 Mo (Apr) 1695 (recorded at end of list)
Abigail b 12 Mo (Feb) 13, 1695/6
Mary " 3 Mo (May) 18, 1697
Wait " 9 Mo (Nov) 22, 1698
Amey " 9 Mo (Nov) 5, 1700
Moses " 5 Mo (July) 14, 1702
Richard " 1 Mo (Mar) 27, 1704
Elizabeth " 10 Mo (Dec) 11, 1705
Hannah " 7 Mo (Sep) 1707
Joshua " 5 Mo (July) 18, 1709
Martha " 6 Mo (Aug) 29, 1713
Thomas T. (nm) b Dutchess Co. d 3-6-1826 ae 26y bHS (m)
Timothy (nm) b Ama. d 12-23-1825 ae 44y bHS (m)
Wilson M., s Henry J. & Judeth (Rider), N. Y., b Chatham, N. Y. 12-7-1834 d 5-22-1915 bPP; m at Samuel Brown's 6-11-1861 Sarah H. BROWN, dt Samuel & Rachel, Bkn., b N. Y. 4-5-1840 d 5-24-1905 bPP-(H)
Ch: Samuel B. N. Y. 3-1-1863 d 2- 3-1869 bPP
Rachel H. b N. Y. 10-30-1864 [bPP
Henry J. " N. Y. 11-23-1868 d 12-10-1887
Wilson M. Jr. b 5- 7-1872

POWELL, Wilson M. & Sarah H., continued
Ch: Elsie b 5-20-1875
Melville R. b N. Y. 4-30-1881 d 8-19-1886 bPP
cf Chatham 4-3-1861 for Wilson
Wilson M., s Wilson M. & Sarah (Brown), b N.Y. 5-7-1872 d 8-17-1935 bPP; m 10-23-1902 Elsie KNAPP, dt Shepherd & Emma (Benedict) b N. Y. 9-12-1879 (H)
Ch: Wilson Marcy b 7-18-1903
Sarah Hopper " 10- 9-1906
Elsie Knapp " 12-14-1925
ch recrq of parents 10-9-1909; Elsie recrq 12-14-1925
Wilson Marcy, s Wilson M. & Elsie (Knapp), b N. Y. 7-18-1903; m 10-25-1930 Fredrika T. RICHARDSON, dt Frederick A. (H)
Ch: Wilson M. 3d b Cambridge, Mass. 6-24-1932
Fredrika mbr Boston
----- & -----
Ch: Rachel A. d 10-23-1839 ae 2y 8m 7d bHS

PRATT
Charles Barton m Jessie Emma BARTON, dt Jesse & Anna M. C.
Ch: Loraine Ethel b 5-30-1919
Walter B.
Charles associate 5-1917; Jessie recrq of parents 12-2-1903; parents gct First Bapt. Ch. Ossining 7-10-1929; Walter B. recrq of parents 6-1928
Walter rocf Warwickshire North 3-6-1907; ct Warwickshire North 5-1-1912

PRETLOW
Abbie, dt Robt. E. & Emma T.; m 1914 Franklin R. CAWL
cf Wilmington, O. with parents 9-5-1906; ct Providence 5-7-1919 with h
Robert E. d 1-12-1929; m Emma T. -----
Ch: Robert T.
Abbie
cf Wilmington, Ohio 9-5-1906 with 2 ch named; ct Seattle 7-2-1913 for parents; cf Seattle 1-1924 for Robt. E. & Emma T. (Pastor of Bkn. Mtg)
Robert T., s Robt. E. & Emma T., rocf Wilmington, O. with parents 9-5-1906; letter to First R. D. Church, Lebanon, Pa. 3-1917

PRICE
Charles Coale, s John F. & Rebecca W. (Walton); m ----- (H)
Ch: Thornton Walton b 11-10-1887
Elizabeth Evans b 9-24-1889
John Morris " 12-25-1891
Charles Coale b Fallstown, Md.; m 2d 12-8-1896 Alice ALBERTSON, dt William & Mary W. (Gillam), b Phila. 2-8-1866 (H)
cf Race St., Phila. 1-5-1901 for Charles & Alice with 3 ch of first w; ct Race St. 6-7-1902 for all
Farrington (nm) d 12-28-1809 ae 2y 4m bHS
Ichabod (nm) d 2-22-1862 ae 81y bPP (or 80y); m -----
Ch: Margaret C. b N. J. d 8-9-1832 ae 18y 9m (unm)
Ann W. b N. Y. d 6-29-1835 ae 16y 9m bHS
Katharine, dt Wm. Lightfoot & Emma (West); m 1923 Edward Sidney RAWSON (H)
Katharine mbr Race St. (both dec)
John & Mary
Ch: William
Daniel
Keziah
cf Plains 6-23-1818 for all, William (clear); ct Plains 6-7-1820 with their minor ch, Daniel & Keziah
Marsia Anne (nm), dt Frank O. & Florence; m 1935 Merlin A. WATSON (H)
Phebe O. (nm) d 11-30-1868 ae 58y bPP (H)
Susan, w Ichabod, recrq 5-1839; d 5-3-1871 ae 88y bPP (H)
Susannah (late Moore) rocf R. & P. 4-15-1801; dis mo before 8-1-1804
William dis enlisting as a soldier in the State Prison Guard 10-4-1820
William (nm) b Klinekill d 6-5-1824 ae 26y bHS (m)

PRIN
Mary (nm) bPP

PRINCE
Ann, Flushing, b 12 Mo (Feb) 15, 1734/5; con mo 5-2-1754
Rebecca (late Willis) dis mo 9-4-1800

PRINDLE
Anna Louise b Charlotte, Vt. 10-30-1863 d Richmond Hill 7-14-1918 bPP; m Edgar S. WRIGHT (both nm)
Cyrus (nm) m Almira L. GREEN, dt Stephen & Lydia (Chase), b So. Starksboro, Vt. 3-28-1836 d 10-19-1914 bPP
Almira not in Reg. of mbr but listed in 1909 Directory as mbr
Elmira L. rocf Cleveland; d 10-19-1914
Henry W. (nm), s Wm. P. & Mary W.; m 7-16-1921 Clara R. BAYLIS, dt Chas. W. & Elma C., b N. Y. 9-11-1894 (H)
Ch: Judson b Orange, N. J. 6-14-1922

PRINIT
John gct Phila. 7 Mo (Sep) 3, 1747

PRIOR
Edmund, s Joseph & Mary, N. Y.; m Wby 1779 Phebe ----- d 9-29-1791
cert of clear to Wby 11-4-1779; Phebe had cf Wby 12-27-1780
Edmund m 2d N. Y. 10-9-1793 Mary HAYDOCK, dt Henry & Hannah (dec), N. Y., b 5-29-1765 d 10-22-1836 (or 10-23-1836) ae 71y 5m
Ch: Hannah b 9-11-1794
Phebe " 12-14-1796

PRIOR, Edmund & Mary, continued
Ch: Eleanor H. b 6-12-1798
Elizabeth M. b 8-30-1800
Edmund H.
Sarah
ct Wby 1-6-1808 with their 4 ch named; cf Wby with their 3 minor ch, Phebe, Eleanor H. & Edmund H.; ct New Bedford 11-1-1837 for Edmund; parents dis 1829 (H)
Edmund H., s Edmund & Mary, rocf Wby 1825; d 10-16-1888
Eleanor H., dt Edmund & Mary, b 6-12-1798; cf Wby 1-6-1808 with parents; dis 11-1828
Elizabeth, dt Matt.; m 1673 John FEAKE, Mk.
Esther gct Coey. 6-1-1808 (clear)
Hannah [pryor] rocf Burl. 8-4-1788 with ch, William
Henry d 9-5-1805 ae 49y 11m; m Esther -----
Ch: Anne
Mary
Telitha b 2-25-1804
cf Wby 6-15-1803 for both with 2 ch, Anne & Mary
Horace rocf Wby 6-1842; dis 10-1851
John, s Matthew, Mk. d 2 Mo (Apr) 4, 1698; m Elizabeth BOWNE, dt John & Hannah, Flushing active mbr from 1676
John, s James, rocf Wby 9-18-1805, apprentice to a Friend; ct Wby 10-5-1808
John & Elizabeth
Ch: Philemon F. (or Philenor F.)
Phebe W.
John Augustus
Sarah F.
Henrietta W.
cf Jericho 7-20-1826 with 3 ch named; parents dis 1830 (O); ct Scipio 2-4-1835 for the 3 ch, minors, including Philemon F. (O); ct Scipio 5-1834 for all (H)
John Augustus, s John & Elizabeth, gct Scipio 2-4-1835 with sisters, minors
Joseph [Prier] d 1 Mo (Mar) 28, 1728; m Deborah -----
Ch: Elizabeth b 12 Mo (Feb) 2, 1722/3
John b 2 Mo (Apr) 13, 1725 [Simon COOPER
Martha, dt Matt. & Mary, Mk., d 1717; m 1693
Martha rocf Wby 5-14-1794; inability of body had prevented much attendance of mtg
Mary, dt Matt, Mk.; m 1668 John UNDERHILL, Jr.
Mary [Pryer] d 5 Mo (July) 4, 1700
Mary [Pryor] (nm) d 10-23-1836 ae 71y 5m bHS
Matthew [Priar, Prier, Prior] b Eng., Mk.; [m Mary -----
Ch: John b 12 Mo (Feb) 1651/2
Mary " 1 Mo (Mar) 1652/3
Elizabeth b 6 Mo (Aug) 1656
Sarah " 8 Mo (Oct) 1664
Martha " 8 Mo (Oct) 1672
Matthew & Mary active mbr from 1676
Matthew [Preyer, Priar], s Matthew & Hannah, b 1 Mo (Mar) 6, 1728/9; m 1754 Ann WILLIS, wd Silas, dt Henry & Mary PEARSALL
Ch: Henry b 9-18-1755
James " 4-23-1757
Matthew m Hannah COLES, wd Joseph, dt Samuel & Martha COCK
Ch: Hannah b 4 Mo (June) 26, 1720
Mary " 11 Mo (Jan) 2, 1723/4
Matthew b 1 Mo (Mar) 6, 1729/30
Phebe d 5-1-1806 ae 73y (not identified)
Phebe gct New Bedford 6-6-1828 (clear)
Phebe W., dt John & Elizabeth, gct Scipio 2-4-1835 with brother & sister (minors)
Philenor T., s John & Elizabeth, gct Scipio 2-4-1835 with brother & sister (minors)
Samuel rocf Wby 8-16-1826 (clear)
Samuel [Prier], s James & Theodosia, N. Y., d 10-6-1829; m N. Y. 10-11-1827 Mary Ann SINCLAIR, dt John & Eliz., N. Y. (H)
Ch: Amelia b 2-27-1829
cf Balt. 12-10-1824 for Mary Ann Sinclair; Mary Ann dis 3-1831 (O); Mary Ann m 2d ----- DOWNING & had ct Roch. 11-1837; ct Wby 11-1840 for Amelia
Sarah [Pryer], dt Matthew & Mary, Mk.; m 1686 John GOULD
Sarah d 7-4-1841 ae 88y
William b Burl., N. J. d 9-24-1829 ae 49y m -----
Ch: William Jr. d 8-28-1816 ae 1y bHS
William " 8-20-1818 ae 7m bHS
dis mo 3-6-1816

PRITCHARD
Alfred George, s John C. & Emily, b 2-10-1878; letter to R. D. Ch. of Westwood, N. J. 9-5-1906
John Charles (Beloved Minister) b Bristol, Eng. 9-22-1848 d 7-5-1926 bPP; m Emily C. ----- b Bristol, Eng. 12-14-1842 d 1-13-1922 bPP
Ch: Clara Emily b 10-11-1876
Alfred George b 2-10-1878
Edith Hannah b 7-27-1880
parents recrq 6-14-1876

PROCTOR
Isaac rocf Peel MM, London 6-19-1793 (clear), a young man, cert addressed to Phila.; ct Balt. 7-6-1796 (clear) [7-1868
Mary rocf Roch. 12-1861; ct Carlow, Ireland,
Oliver (nm) m Eva H. ENGLE, dt Edith E. cf Evesham, N. J. for Eva with mother 3-1924
Sarah rocf Pickering MM, Yorkshire 2-23-1796 (clear); ct Balt. 6-4-1801 (clear)

PROUD
Amy rocf New Bedford 12-17-1799 (clear); ct New Bedford 6-5-1805 (clear)

PROUDFOOT
Andrew (nm) m Jeannette ----- (nm) b Scotland d 1-27-1830 ae 45y bHS-

PRUDDEN
Louise (nm), dt Sidney C. & Isabella S.; m 1876 Benjamin W. HUNT (H)

PUGH
Esther rocf Cincinnati 2-1879; ct Cincinnati 12-1883

PUGSLEY
Elizabeth rocf Pur. 10-10-1793 to live with relatives; ct Pur. 5-7-1806

PULLWITZ
Edward Mitchell (nm), s Henry & Edith (Mitchell); m 6-22-1923 Eunice BROWNING, dt Clarence P. & Eva S., b 2-26-1897 (H)
Eunice recrq 6-9-1906 (H)

PURDY
James Garfield, s Theodore & Juliette (Hallock) b West Somers 3-4-1881; m Alice Roberta -----, dt Robert (H)
cf Ama. 1-8-1816 for James; relrq 6-1-1935 to join Ch. in Ossining
Julia D., dt Alex & Alchie, d 12-30-1912 ae 74y 3m 8d bPP; m James S. CARMAN (H) both nm)
Monmouth d 10-19-1798 bHS
Monroe (nm) & -----
Ch: Infant stillborn 1-22-1835 bHS
----- & ----- (nm)
Ch: Adamile (girl) d 10-30-1810 ae 2y 10m bHS (b Mamaroneck)
----- & ----- (nm)
Ch: George H. b N. Y. d 1-8-1841 ae 5y 5m 9d bHS

PURHAM
Sarah (form Underhill) dis mo 5-6-1840

PURINTON
Sarah & ----- (H)
Ch: Avis
cf Sara. 8-1841 with dt; ct Chesterfield 2-1854 with dt

PUSEY
Caleb rocf N.P. 1-18-1810 (clear); ct Linden Grove, Pa. 7-4-1810
Mary Albino, dt Joseph M. & Elizabeth (Phillips), b Hockessin, Del. 9-18-1853; m 1876 Frank Thomas WEBB (H)

P-----
Elizabeth, dt Phila; m 1680 William FRAMPTON

QUEST
----- (nm) m Harriet R. WOOTEN, dt Wilfrid E.
Harriet recrq of father 3-1903; name erased 11-6-1929

QUICK
Jennie (nm), dt David R. & Emma R.; m 4-25-1900 Wm. Y. FINCH (H)

QUINBY
Aaron J., s Moses I. & Esther, d 12-28-1894 ae 66y bPP; m Margaret L. ----- (nm) d 8-15-1880 ae 47y 10m 17d bPP (H)
Ch: Frances Eugene d 11-27-1878 ae 3y 15d bPP
George W. d 7-26-1879 ae 22y 1m 28d bPP
Esther F. " 1- 4-1893 ae 33y 1m 26d bPP
cf Chap. 11-1832 with parents
Azariah rocf Chap. 5-11-1826 (clear); ct Chap. 4-7-1830 (O) (clear); ct Wilmington, Del. 5-6-1846 & 1-5-1848 (H)
Caleb & Eliza
Ch: Edward
cf Chap. 4-9-1829; both dis 1830-1831 (O); ct Chap. 2-1834 with ch named (H)
Daniel, Westchester, m Flushing 5-13-1756 Mary THORNE
Mary gct Pur. 8-4-1757
Daniel rocf Chap. 3-9-1826 (clear) (mo) dis 10-1831 (O); dis 1-1831 (H)
Elijah P. rst on ack. rec from Pur. 7-3-1822; ct Roch. 5-3-1826
George W., s Moses I. & Esther F., b 9-27-1822; m ----- BOWNE, dt Scott (H)
cf Chap. 11-1832; ct Flush. 7-2-1851
Hannah d 1864; m Daniel G. HAVILAND (H)
Isaiah & Amy (H)
Ch: Joshua S.
Valentine
cf Chap. 11-1827; parents dis 1830 (O); ch gct Chap. 3-1841 (O); ct Chap. 1-1833 (H) for all; cf Chap. 1850,1851 for all; ct Chap. 1852 for parents; 1-1854 for Joshua S.
John & Esther (H)
Ch: Mary Jane
Phebe b 8-13-1832
cf Chap. 5-8-1828; all dis 1830-1849 (O); ct Chap. for all 7-1834 (H)
John, Jr., s Isaiah & Mary, rocf Chap. 8-1850; ct Chap. 4-1859
Joshua, s Isaiah & Amy, gct Chap. 2-3-1841 with brother; cf Chap. 7-1850; ct Chap. 1-1854
Josiah, Westchester, d 1728; m Mary ----- d 1728
Josiah desired cert 3 Mo (May) 2, 1723 before next MM adjourned 2 wks & comm. appointed 3 Mo 16, to hear him & act as needful; no rpt
Josiah & Amy
Ch: Joshua
Valentine
cf Chap. 8-9-1827 with 2 ch named
Josiah H., s William; m N.P. Deborah -----
Ch: Caroline b 4-10-1818
William " 4-17-1820
Charles " 10- 7-1821 d 7-19-1823
Phebe Jane b 4-12-1825
Mary Elizabeth b 2-19-1826
John Jagger
ct Chap. 9-10-1812 (clear); ct N.P. 11-5-1828 for all living (O); ct N.P 8-1828 (H); cert of clear to N.P. 12-4-1816;
Deborah rocf N.P. 7-17-1817
Mellicent d 3-29-1839 ae 89y 7m

QUINBY, continued
Mary, w Isaiah (H)
Ch: John Jr.
Eliza F.
cf Chap. 3-1851 with dt, ct Chap. 4-1859 with Eliza only
Mary Elizabeth, dt Edward S. & Eliza (Field), b New Castle 2-9-1863; m 1894 Grant Freidel (nm) (H)
Mary Jane, dt Moses I. & Esther F., b 7-14-1837; m 11-5-1857 Isaac W. RUSHMORE (H)
Moses I. d 4-6-1843; m Esther F. ----- d 1-19-1852
Ch: Walter U. b 10-28-1817
Moses I. (or Jr.) b 2-17-1820 d 1822
George W. b 9-27-1822
Aaron J. d 12-28-1894
Mary Jane b 7-14-1837
cf Pur. 6-14-1816 for Moses J.; ct Chap. 5-3-1826 with w & s, Walter U. & George W. (0); cf Chap. 11-1832 with 3 ch
Sarah rocf Roch. 11-1866; d 7-9-1869 (H)
Valentine H., dt Isaiah & Amy, gct Chap. 2-3-1841 with brother; cf Chap. 8-1850
Walter U., s Moses I. & Esther F., rocf Chap. 11-1832 with parents; dis 8-1837 (H)
William (nm) d 3-20-1839 ae 89y 7m bHS
----- & -----, Westchester
Ch: Josiah b 1 Mo (Mar) 31, 1693/4

RAINSTEIN
Mae (nm) m Stephen G. CARPENTER (H)

RAKE
Ann d 11-3-1801 ae 52y bHS
John Dyke, s Samuel & Mary, N. Y.; m N. Y. 3-13-1822 Alice BOWRON, dt Joshua & Agnes (both dec), N. Y. (H)
Ch: Infant d 3-18-1823 stillborn
John recrq 1-2-1822; cf 2 Weeks Mtg, Glasgow 2-11-1819 for Alice; John dis 10-1828 (H) and 12-1828 (0)

RALE
John prcf Falmouth, Corn., Eng. 10-6-1756 (clear)

RAMSEY
William recrq 5-1856; ct N.P. 5-6-1858, altered to Grange, Ire. 1-6-1858
William J. [Ramsay] rocf Grange, Ireland 5-1889; ct Grange, Ire. 5-4-1892

RAMSON
Louisa, w Henry, dt Wm. F. & Sarah H. LEGGETT, b 5-24-1845 (H)

RANDOLPH (See also Fitzrandolph)
Caroline Eliza, dt John L. F. & Eliza F.; m 1845 Josiah L. HARVEY
Hannah S. F., st John F. & Mary, dis 1823
Harriet Ann F. (or S.F.), dt John F. & Mary, b 9-31-1806; ct Pur. 11-4-1829 (H); ct Pur. 9-2-1829 (0) (clear)
James C. F., s John L. F. & Eliza F., b 4-28-1814; dis mo 9-1844; d 1844
James F. dis mo 11-7-1821
John L. F. d in Nova Scotia; m Eliza F. -----
Ch: William W. F. b 11-16-1812
James C. F. " 4-28-1814 d 2- 3-1844
Edmund F. " 9- 9-1816 " ------1834
John R. F. " 4- 1-1820
Caroline Eliza
cf Sandwich 12-8-1807, minor; Eliza gct Chesterfield 4-1848
John R. F., s John L. F. & Eliza F., b 4-1-1820; dis 1-1842 (0)
John T. d in N. J. 7-30-1837; m Mary ----- b N. J. d 1-24-1826 ae 58y
Ch: Joseph 6
King 5
Sidney
James
Harriet S. F. 9-31-1806
Edmund F. b 9- 1-1808 d 7- 3-1809
Hannah S. F.
Sarah K. F.
cf R. & P. 10-16-1805 with 4 minor ch & Hannah Skinner
John T. rocf R. & P. 3-20-1806, apprentice; ct R. & P. 4-4-1810 (clear)
Joseph K. F., s John, b Somersett Co., N. J. d 4-24-1819 ae 23y; dis 10-7-1817 (note: this may be a confusion of two persons)
Mary F., w John, d 1-25-1826
Samuel F. rocf R. & P. 3-18-1819, apprentice; dis 7-1831 (H)
Sarah K., dt John F. & Mary, gct Pur. 9-2-1829 (clear); ct Pur. 11-4-1829 (H)
Sidney Wilcox (form Randolph) dis mo 11-5-1823
William W. F., s John L. F. & Eliza F., b 11-16-1812; dis 3-1844 (0)

RANKIN
Abigail rocf Warrington, Pa. 10-7-1780; ct Warrington, Pa. 8-3-1784

RANSOM
Catharine H., w Benj., rocf Stanford 7-1850; ct Oswego 7-1865 (H)
Egbert [Ransome] & -----
Ch: Frank Edwin
Eliza Elizabeth
cf Kingston, Eng. 4-1-1903 for Egbert; ch recrq of father
Elizabeth E. [Ransome], dt Egbert; m ----- CLIFFORD (nm)
recrq of father 7-1903 aged 9; active mbr 7-1925
Frank Edwin [Ransome], s Egbert & Blanch G., Mountain View, N. J.; m N. Y. 9-20-1923 Eleanor Priscilla FRY, dt W. Raymond & Lillian, Wading River, L. I.
Ch: Frank Fellows b 9-19-1924
John Fry " 12- 2-1927

RANSOM, Frank Edwin & Eleanor Priscilla [Ransom], continued
Frank recrq of father
Henry [Ransome] (nm) m 1886 Louisa LEGGETT, dt Wm. F. & Sarah (Hull), b 5-24-1845 (H)

RAPELYE
Caroline, dt Martha PALMER, dis mo 7-7-1841

RASMUSSEN
Christian W. (nm) m 6-26-1907 Bertha C. VAN BURKIRK, dt Andrew & Emma (Underhill), b N. Y. 7-21-1885 d 10-30-1918 (H)
Bertha's name entered by comm. 1-19-1886

RATE
John rem out N. Y. 8-4-1757, cert to be prepared (no further mention)

RATHBONE
Anna D., dt Francis & Susan; m ----- WHITE
cf Creek with mother 4-1861; ct Raysville, Ind. 4-1880
Francis H., s Francis & Susan, mo 12-1865, ret mbrp; cf Creek with mother 4-1861; mbrp relinquished 2-1881; rem to Providence 1866 & rqc but had returned & comm. dismissed 7-1866
Susan, wd Francis
Ch: Anna D.
Francis H.
cf Creek 4-1861 with 2 ch named; moved away

RATHBORNE
Charles Lambert (nm), s Rich. (dec) & Ann Maria, N. Y.; m at Joseph Hagan's 6-13-1865 Eliz. Leedom HAGAN, dt Joseph & Sarah E., N. Y. b 10-15-1842 d 12-31-1890 (H)

RAUB
Henry (nm) m Margaret YOUNG, dt Geo. F. & Mary Amanda (Frick), b Easton, Pa. 2-12-1900
Margaret recrq 7-9-1917

RAVIS
Nathaniel, Devonshire House MM had sent his dis some time since, but unable to find him, rpd to Devonshire House 6-1823
Peter, s Nathaniel (a tailor) rem cert from Dorking MM, Surry, Eng. 1-4-1760, he being apprenticed to Robert Murray, of N. Y.
Peter rqct Grace Church St. MM 8-3-1769 (minute missing till 1771)
Thomas rocf Peel MM, London 9-24-1806 (clear); ct Balt. 11-4-1807 (clear)

RAWLINGS
Alfred rocf Devonshire House 11-6-1838; dis mo 1-1847
John Edward rocf Westminster & Longford 7-7-1897; name erased 12-1922

RAWSON
Arthur Joy, s Edward B. & Marianna (Smith), b Lincoln, Va. 1-13-1896; m 9-29-1923 Margaret BYRD, dt Philip G. & Ella R. (dec) (H); Margaret m ----- SWARTHMORE
Edward B., s Edward Joy & Eliz. A. (Hall), b Dover, Mass. 7-31-1860; m 8-27-1891 Marianna S. SMITH, dt Edward J. & Mary H. (Brown), b Lincoln, Va. 1-7-1871 (H)
Ch: Arthur Joy b 10-13-1896
Edward Sidney b 2-23-1901
Philip Nichols b 10-26-1903
cf Goose Creek 2-3-1892 for parents; ct Goose Creek 11-12-1917 for all; Principal of Friends Seminary
Edward Sidney (name ch from Sidney Perne on rq of father), s Edward B. & Marianna (Smith) b N. Y. 2-3-1901 d 11-6-1926; m 7-16-1923 Katharine PRICE, dt Wm. Lightfoot & Emma (West) (H); Katharine mbr Race St., Phila.
Eliza F. rocf Chat. 4-4-1877; ct Sandy Spring 2-4-1892 (H)
Jonathan A. Jr. (nm), s Jonathan A. & Charlotte (Fletcher); m 6-15-1907 Marion NICHOLL, dt Thomas J. & Avis M. (Townsend), Scotch Plains, N. J. 6-24-1878 (H)
Ch: Priscilla Alden b Metuchen, N. J. 7-11-1911
Marion recrq 7-9-1923; Priscilla recrq 4-11-1932
Philip Nichols, s Edward B. & Marianna (Smith) b N. Y. 10-26-1903; m 5-21-1926 Gertrude KNAPP, dt Milton & Paula (Von K.) (H)
Gertrude mbr Westfield
Priscilla A., dt Jonathan & Marian N., N. Y., b Metuchen 7-11-1911; m 1933 Daniel B. CURLL, Jr., Wayne, Pa. (H); recrq 4-11-1932

RAY (See also Reay & Wray) (Name changed to Wray)
Anna C., dt Wm. Anthony & Lucy W. (Shepherd), b Rayville, N. Y. 3-12-1873; transferred from Albany 1-8-1916 (H)
Francis H. rocf Phila. 4-1859; d 1-18-1862 (H)
Frank A., s Wm. Anthony & Lucy W. (Shepherd), b Rayville, N. Y. 10-6-1871 d 11-26-1926; m 12-25-1900 Kate LANGE (nm), dt Edward & Susan (H); transferred from Albany 1-8-1916
Margaret (nm) b Scotland d 2-22-1842 ae 28y bHS (wd)
Martha, dt Christopher & Elizabeth

RAYMOND
Caroline E., dt George & Maria L. (Dorland), b Bkn. 4-25-1861 d 11-12-1923; name entered by comm. 1-2-1884 (unm) (H)
Charles H. m Abbie MARTIN d 4-11-1911 ae 78y 3d bPP (H) (both nm)
Ebenezer m Hannah FIELD (mo 1763, dis not found)
Ellwood H., s George & Maria L. (Dorland), b Bkn. 1-14-1855 d 3-17-1931 (unm) (H)
cf Sara. 1-2-1884
Florence d 10-11-1901 ae 28y bPP; m George T. ROGERS (H)

RAYMOND, continued
John Wm., s Chas. H. & Abby B. (Martin), Bkn., b Bkn. 9-25-1864 d 1-3-1933 bPP; m at S. T. Valentine's 2-11-1891 Hannah T. VALENTINE, dt Samuel T. & Hannah (Kirk), Bkn., b 5-14-1866 N. Y. d 8-5-1903 bPP (H)
Ch: John Wm. Jr. b 12-12-1891
Valentine Kirk b 6-16-1897
Richard Valentine b 1-29-1899
Olney Martin b 12-16-1902
recrq 11-4-1891
John Wm., Jr., s John Wm. & Hannah T. (Valentine), b Bkn. 12-12-1891; m 4-24-1918 Marguerite REEVES, dt Andrew C. & Sara A.C. (H)
Ch: Jacqueline b 9-14-1918
Marguerite a mbr of Chesterfield, Pa.
Lewis (nm) m Maria ----- d 5-14-1866 ae 68y bPP (H)
Ch: Judith b Athens, N. Y. 1-3-1829 d 1-8-1911 bPP
cf Hudson 1-1859 for Maria; Judith a separate cert same date
Lewis d 4-24-1885 ae 85y bPP; m 2d Maria L. DORLAND, dt Andrew, d 4-12-1886 ae 65y bPP
Ch: Carrie E. d 12-12-1923 ae 62y 6m 17d bPP (unm)
Elwood H. " 3-16-1931 ae 77y bPP (unm)
Maria L. rocf Sara. 12-1855; all nm but Maria
Lillie T. (nm) m 1887 Wm. Clinton BURLING (H)
Valentine Kirk, s Jno. Wm. & Hannah (Valentine) b Bkn. 6-16-1897; m 5-11-1929 Eleanor B. ANDREWS (nm), dt Wm. Arthur & Ellena (Bedle) (H)

RAYNOR
George (nm) d 1895; m Susan WHITFIELD d 5-5-1919 bPP
Ch: Sarah Elizabeth b 5-10-1881
Mary Rebecca
cf Lurgan, Ire. 5-1870; mo but ret a mbr; ch recorded as per Disc. 5-12-1896
Mary R., s Geo. & Susan W., Sheffield, Eng.; m 6-5-1906 Geo. W. SEGAR, of Brisco, N.Y. recorded as per Disc. 5-12-1896
Sarah Eliz., dt Susan W., b 5-10-1881; m ----- HASKINS (nm)
name recorded as per Disc. 5-12-1896

READ
Caroline Seaman, dt Sam'l H. & Hannah SEAMAN, b 6-3-1868; relrq 7-10-1897 (H)
James rocf Balt. 3-10-1926; marked "absent" in Reg.
Luther (nm) & -----
Ch: William d 9-3-1803 ae 1y 6m bHS
William [Reid] & -----
Ch: Pamela
Alexander
Martha
cf Creek 5-16-1800 with his 3 small ch; ct Yonge St., Canada 6-7-1809 with 2 ch, Alexander & Martha

REARDON
Ella (nm), dt Ralph & Mary J. (Curry); m 1886 Edward E. WRIGHT (H)

REAY
John (or Ray) rocf Allen Dale, Norts 3-23-1790 (clear) to Friends of Nova Scotia

REDMAN
Edith M., w Neighbor Geo.
Ch: Holly b 12-6-1884
cf Folkestone, Eng. 11-7-1894; ct Folkestone, Eng. 4-5-1899; Holly recorded as per Disc. 5-12-1896 & included in cert 1899

REDMOND
Hannah, dt John C. & Letitia, N. Y.; m 1822 Wm. H. FRANKLIN
Henry S. (nm) m 1-8-1902 Julia Frances PARSONS, dt Robt. Wm. & Julia (Russell) b N. Y. 2-3-1878 (H)
Julia's name entered by comm. 1-4-1879
Jas. Norton, s John C. & Letitia, N. Y., d 4-14-1886; m N. Y. 3-13-1828 Ann BOWNE, dt Richard (dec) & Penelope, N. Y., d 6-8-1881
Ch: Cornelia (or Caroline) b 3-10-1829
Mary Eliza " 5-14-1830
Charles Philip " 9-24-1832
Morton " 6-20-1836
rec a mbr 2-1816; ct Chesterfield 11-7-1838 (O); ct Chesterfield 10-1840 (H); cf Chesterfield 4-1868 for parents
John C. m Letitia ----- d 6- 4-1868
Ch: Hannah
Maria
James M.
Charles P. d 10-30-1832 ae 18y 7m bHS
John C. Jr. b 5- 7-1817
cf Wby 7-19-1815 for both; 4 ch recrq of parents 2-7-1816; ct Frankford 7-4-1832 with dt, Maria; parents dis 1829 (H); all Orthodox; cf Chesterfield 7-1856
John C. Jr., s John C. & Letitia, b 5-7-1817; m Abigail B. ----- d 9-5-1871
Ch: William F.
Samuel G.
Anna G. b 6-26-1852
Philip d 4-14-1872
ct Chesterfield 11-4-1846 (clear); cf Chesterfield 7-8-1851 with w & 2 ch
John C. Jr. m 2d ----- ; mo before 11-1863, ret a mbr
Maria rocf Chesterfield 7-1856; d 4-22-1888
Samuel G., s John C. Jr. & Abigail B., rocf Chesterfield with parents 7-8-1851
William E., s John C. Jr. & Abigail B., d 12-14-1934; m 12-22-1881 Hannah T. CARPENTER cf Chesterfield 7-8-1851 with parents
----- & -----
Ch: Charles P. b L. I. d 7-29-1812 ae 3y 9m bHS

REDMOND, continued
Ch: John d 10-3-1832 ae 18y 7m bHS

REED
Luther, of Ware, N. H. but for sometime a resident in N. Y., dis mo before 10-1-1800
Pamelia Gorham (form Reed) dis mo 12-4-1811

REESE
Annie J. [Rees], dt Jonah L. & Anna J., rocf Cincinnati 2-6-1884; ct Hopewell 3-5-1898 (H)
Delia rocf R. I. 12-5-1906; d 12-1918
Emily, w M. M., dt Joseph W. & Lydia L. CORLIES (m 10-5-1876) (H)
Jonah L. & Anna J. (H)
Ch: Mary Alice
Annie Jackson
cf Cincinnati 2-6-1884 for all; ct Hopewell for parents
Mary Alice [Rees], dt Jonah L. & Anna J.; m 1892 James O. STEER (H)
cf Cincinnati 2-6-1884 with parents
William W. recrq 1-1860; d 10-20-1894 ae 80y bPP (H)

REEVES
Marguerite, dt Andrew C. & Sara G. C.; m 1918 John Wm. RAYMOND, Jr. (H)
Marguerite a mbr of Chesterfield

REFFORD
John T. recrq 12-7-1887; cancelled 4-9-1904 as long unknown (H)

REGENHARD
Olga M. m 1925 R. Solomon TICE (nm)
letter from St. Trinitatas Evan. Luth. Ch., Jersey City 6-1925; ct Yorktown 3-1926; name dropped

REGNIER
Agnes, dt Charles F. & M. Abby (Bowlsby), b West Liberty, Iowa, 1-11-1872; m 1894 Percy RUSSELL (H)

REID
Daniel (nm) m 10-10-1888 Alice M. KENT, dt Benj. Lundy & Sarah A. (Aitken), b Goshen, Pa. 4-1-1867 (H)
Alice rocf Wilmington, Del. 8-10-1901; ct Wilmington, Del. 3-7-1903 (H)
Herbert Wesley (nm), s Wm. Henry & Ida (Dixon); m 10-15-1919 Anna BURLING, dt Edw. F. & Alice G., b Bkn. 4-1-1891 (H)
recrq of parents 5-9-1903; relrq 10-11-1932
James rocf Balt. 5-1827 (H)
William & Mary
Ch: Pamela Rebecca b 10-31-1789
Alexander " 9- 8-1791
Martha " 12-13-1794
----- (nm) m Marjorie WILLIAMS, dt Chas. & Lilla F., b 11-29-1899

REIMER
Anna Therese (nm), dt Carl H. G. & Anna; m 6-5-1878 Charles B. CARPENTER (H)

REINHART
Chauncey, s Chauncey R. & Mary M. (Spillett), b Elizabeth, N. J. 10-15-1906; m 2-14-1932 Mabel Elizabeth GEIGER, dt Otto John & Nancy M. (Tillotson), b Cleveland 9-13-1906 d 5-4-1934 (H)
Ch: Loraine b Roselle, N. J. 2-27-1934
Rolfe Ormond b Roselle, N. J. 10-10-1935
Chauncy recrq 6-?-1930; Mabel recrq 2-12-1934

REMINGTON
Alcy A. rocf Providence 1-24-1849; ct Swansea
Joseph P. rocf ND MM 4-1869; ct WD MM 2-4-1874

REMOND
Leontine J., dt Narciss & Mary, Jr., Bkn.; m ----- LENOX; m 2d 1872 Levi N. LOCKWOOD (H)

RENOUF
Martha rocf Troy 5-1855; ct Troy 8-1-1860; cf Troy 1-1865; d 3-19-1869 (H)
Mary R., dt Wm. & Hannah, b 2-23-1810 d 3-31-1901; m Wm. BLANCHARD (H)
cf Troy 8-4-1847
William, s Thomas & Martha (dec), N. Y.; m N. Y. 4-11-1804 Hannah BALDWIN, dt Benj. (dec) & Eliz., N. Y.
Ch: Martha
Mary R. b 2-23-1810
cf Farm. 8-7-1805 with ch, Martha; Thomas & Martha of Island of Guernsey
William m 2d N. Y. 4-15-1830 Phebe HULL, dt Joseph & Phebe (both dec), N. Y., d 10-22-1869 (H)
cf Troy 1-1865

RESCOE
Mary gct Burl. 3-4-1812, a minister (clear)

REYNOLDS (See also Runnells)
Abigail & -----
Ch: Ann Maria
ct Chap. (not found); cf Chap. 5-13-1814 with little dt named, ret after a short residence there
Abraham (nm) b Del. d 8-14-1819 ae 57y bHS (m)
Ann rocf Pur. 6-12-1817
Ann Horton (form Reynolds) mo referred to Pur., Pur rpd 12-6-1820 having dis her
Ann, w Richard, rocf Wby 5-16-1827
Ann Eliz., dt Richard & Ann C., N. Y.; m 1851 Valentine MOTT, of O.B. (H)
Charles rocf Wilmington 7-1829; dis 1-1831 (H)
Dr. Charles H. (nm) b 2-15-1851 d Po'keepsie 7-20-1930 bPP; m Lydia K. BATTEY, dt Jonathan & Anna G., b Keesville, N. Y. 11-12-

REYNOLDS, Dr. Charles H. & Lydia K., continued
1853 d Po'keepsie 10-15-1925 bPP
ct Marl. for Lydia K. Reynolds 5-3-1905
Elias rocf Ama. 6-13-1807 (clear); ct Chap. 6-6-1810 (clear); cf Chap. 12-13-1811 (clear)
Esther m Edward C. UNDERHILL
cf Chap. as Underhill 8-1885; relrq 6-8-1892
Francis Henry rocf Wilmington 7-2-1830, minor; ct Wilmington 5-3-1837 (H)
Henry rocf Corn. 8-27-1801; ct Corn. 2-7-1810
John W., adopted s Sarah E. Gardner, d 4-1-1887 ae 27y 4m 16d bPP (H)
Justice (or Justin) (nm) & Elizabeth (nm)
Ch: Naomi H. d 12-17-1862 ae 67y 6m 3d bPP
Margaret gct Hudson 12-1833; cf Pur. 1-9-1800 (Clear; ct Hudson 1-4-1809 (clear); cf Troy 6-7-1815 (clear); dis 4-1829 (0); d Athens, N. Y. 1842 (H)
Mary A., dt Rich. & Penelope BOWNE, b 3-10-1815; dis mo 12-7-1836
Nancy rocf Ama. 12-1848; dis 4-5-1854
Naomi H. rocf Pur. 12-6-1817 (clear); ct Wby 5-2-1821 (clear); cf Wby 1-15-1823 (clear); dis 6-1830 (0)
Rhoda, w Henry, rocf Corn. 9-25-1800; ct Corn. 6-12-1809; rem with h each time
Richard C., s Rich. M. & Ann C., b 4-4-1835; relrq 8-1-1866 (H)
Richard M. m Ann C. ----- d 7-6-1857 ae 60y 3m 7d bPP (H)
Ch: James C. b 8-25-1828 d 9-18-1830 bPP
Ann Elizabeth b 6-22-1832
Richard C. b 4- 4-1835; relrq 8-1-1866
cf Pur. 5-8-1817, minor, placed; both dis 1830 (0)
Richard M., dt Justus & Eliz. (both dec), N.Y., d 1-21-1875 ae 76y 3m 24d bPP; m 2d at Rich. M. Reynolds' 2-3-1859
Esther CRAFT, dt James & Hannah (both dec) d 3-6-1863 ae 67y 3m bPP (or 3-9-1863)
cf Pur. 5-8-1817, minor, placed
Rufus, s Justus (dec) & Phebe, Harrison, N. Y.; m N. Y. 4-14-1831 Mary CRAFT, dt James & Hannah (both dec), N. Y. (H)
Sally, w Abraham, rocf Hudson 7-21-1807 having rem with h; dis 6-6-1820
Samuel dis mo 9-6-1798
Sarah m Peter TITUS (mo)
cf Pur. 9-10-1823 (clear); dis 1-1830 (0)

RHODES
Georgia, dt Hiram & Esther, b 9-21-1865; m Charles H. BAILEY; m 2d ----- HALL
recrq of parents 4-1872
George H. (nm), s Richard Utter & Louisa (Battey), b Warwick, R. I. 1-22-1842 d New Bedford, Mass. 6-1-1925 bPP; m Cornelia WOODWARD, dt Thos. Jr. & Eliz. (Cromwell), b N. Y. 9-29-1855 d New Bedford, Mass. 11-11-1923 bPP
Cornelia relrq 6-14-1876
Hiram, s Josiah & Eliza (Warner), b N. Y. 1-10-1836 d 9-23-1915 bPP; m Esther BIRDSALL, dt George H. & Phebe, b 9-15-1840 West Co., N. Y. d 1-22-1895 bPP
Ch: Harry (or Henry) B. d 2-13-1886 ae 26y bPP
Georgia b 9-21-1865
Grace D. " 12-13-1869 d 8- 9-1870 bPP
Edith Lee b 1-14-1872
Stanley Pumphrey b 9-25-1881
Hiram & ch recrq 4-1872
John [Rhoads] rocf WD MM 1-22-1845; ct WD MM 12-2-1846
Phiannah, w Cornell, recrq 1833; d 7-27-1881 (or 10-26-1881 ae 70y)
Selina, dt Ira & Anna Eliza (Phoebus), b Milton, N. Y. 8-31-1867 d 12-12-1928; m 1885 George E. SUTTON (H)
Thomas rocf Cork, (clear) 7-18-1811; ct Simonds Creek, N. C. 7-7-1813 (clear)
----- & -----
Ch: Martha Ann d 5-17-1867 ae 30y bPP

RICE
Edward & Frances
Ch: (prob) Eleanor Jane d 8-22-1867 ae 30y bPP
having mo, Poole & Ringwood MM, Eng. rq care 9-5-1821; rpd 12-4-1822 that he is about to return; Frances recrq 11-6-1822; ct Pool & Ringwood for her 5-7-1823; she had ct Pool & Ringwood

RICH
James B. rocf Green St., Phila. 9-1861; d 6-18-1864 (H)

RICHARDS
Isaac W. rocf Richland 10-1853; in N. J. 1859; rel 6-2-1875, absent over 5y (H)
Philip, of Barbados, having lived here several years, rem cert to Barbados 1680 (clear); probably returned soon; contributor 1681, 1684,1685; active 1687
Samuel & Ann
Ch: Frederick Burge
Emma
Hannah Burge b 3-15-1830
cf Bristol, Eng. 8-26-1828 with 2 ch named; ct Wilmington 7-3-1833 for Ann with ch, Frederick & Emma B., rem with h; Samuel dis 1833 (0)
William, s Samuel (dec) & Mary, Phila.; m N.Y. 11-13-1828 Eleanor Ann KENNY, dt Daniel (dec) & Eleanor, N. Y. (H)
cf Balt. with mother 8-1828; ct Phila. 1-1829 for Eleanor

RICHARDSON
Deborah rocf Dublin to Phila. 12-13-1853; recorded in N. Y. without comment; ct Whitewater 3-5-1856
Enid M., dt Henry & Henrietta P., Passaic, N. J.; m 1924 Henry Ecroyd KIRK
cf Warwickshire North with parents 3-1-

RICHARDSON, Enid M., continued
1905; ct Muncie, Pa. 1-1926
Francis, Mariner, N. Y. d 5 Mo (July) 15, 1688; m Rebeckah -----
Ch: Francis b 9 Mo (Nov) 25, 1681
Rebeckah, Jr. b 1 Mo (Mar) 16, 1683/4
d 7 Mo (Sep) 18, 1684
Rebeckah, Jr. b 9 Mo (Nov) 2, 1685
they took rem ct London, Newcastle, or elsewhere 4 Mo (June) 27, 1680, but returned; Francis active mbr 1676-1688
Fredrika T., dt Frederick A.; m 1930 Wilson Marcy POWELL (H)
Fredrika mbr Boston
Henry b Lichfield, Eng. 9-19-1868; m Henrietta Mary BURTT, dt Henry & Anne (Holmes)
Ch: Hubert Townsend
Enid Mary
Ingram Henry b 6-29-1906
Philip Burtt " 5-21-1911 (at Passaic, N.J.)
cf Warwickshire North 3-1-1905 with first 2 ch; last 2 ch recorded as associates
John, s Robert & Anne, rocf Mountmelick, Ire. 5-19-1802 (clear); ct ND MM 3-7-1804 (clear)
Mary gc 9 Mo (Nov) 2, 1749
Philip Burtt, s Henry & Henrietta (Burtt), b 5-21-1911; ct Montclair 11-5-1930
Rebecca took cert, kind & destination not stated 5 Mo (July) 4, 1689
Samuel W. rocf Lisburn, Ire. 12-1879; relrq 3-1886
Thomas d 3- 3-1865; rocf Lisburn, Ire. 10-13-1836; ct WD MM 1-2-1839 (clear); cf WD MM 4-27-1842; mo before 8-1846 to a mbr, ret a mbr
William, Westchester, m Deliverance -----, d on board ship at anchor N. Y. 12 Mo. (Feb) 10, 1675/6
William m 2d Amy ----- d 12 Mo (Feb) 5, 1683/4
Ch: William b 11 Mo (Jan) 15, 1678/9
Thomas " 7 Mo (Sep) 10, 1680
John " 10 Mo (Dec) 10, 1683 d 5 Mo 1688
William active mbr from 1677; took cert of clear 10 Mo (Dec) 29, 1677

RICKETSON
Annie, dt Shadrach & Mary, b 2-14-1839, Chestnut Ridge, N. Y. d 7-17-1912; m 5-8-1859 William C. BARKER (nm), s S. G. & Edith, Castlebury (H)
cf Oswego with parents 8-1854; at Hennepin, Ill. 1900
Shadrach d 3-5-1893; m Mary BARMORE d 1-21-1892 (H)
Ch: Anna (or Annie) b 2-14-1839
Susan " 10-30-1841
cf Creek 4-18-1806 (clear); ct Easton 12-2-1812; cf Oswego 8-1854; Shadrach in Ill. 1859
Susan, dt Shadrach & Mary, b Clove, N. Y. 10-30-1841; m 10-5-1859 Theodore TAPPEN; m 2d 5-23-1873 John J. ANDERSON (H)
cf Oswego 8-1854 with parents

RICKMAN
William gct Wby 3-1-1780 (clear)

RICKERS
William gct Partners Mill, Lincolnshire, 12-6-1858, prob returning unity minute but not before noticed

RIDER
Carrie, dt John R. & Mary W. (Hazard), b Monroe, N. Y. 9-7-1871; m 1894 Joseph W. CUMMIN (nm) (H)
cf Corn. 12-1-1880 with mother; ct Corn; cf Corn. 8-13-1910
Catharine, dt Charles C. & Mary Ann, b Corn. 8-17-1865 (H)
cf Corn. 10-3-1877 with parents; ct Wilmington 10-9-1897
Catharine M., dt Chas. C. & Mary Ann (Cornell), b 8-17-1865 Mountainville, N. Y. (H)
cf Wilmington, Del. 1-14-1911
Charles C. b 11-26-1823 d 3-20-1899; m Mary Ann ----- b 9-14-1828 (H)
Ch: Josiah C. b 8- 1-1849
Edwin " 2- 2-1852
Anna " 8-27-1854
Charles Henry " 12-22-1856
James C. " 3- 2-1859
Catharine M. " 8-17-1865
cf Corn. 6-1850 with 1 ch; ct Corn. 5-1859 with all ch; cf Corn. 10-3-1877 with all ch; ct Corn. 10-9-1897 for parents
Charles Henry, s Chas. C. & Mary Ann, b 12-22-1856 N. Y. d 3-17-1931; m 10-26-1884 Catharine W. ALDRICH, dt Eli S. & Margaret Ann, b Cornwall-on-Hudson 6-30-1857 (H)
Ch: Frederick Aldrich b 9-23-1885
Edwin Hanford b 1-27-1888 d 7-26-1928
cf Corn. 10-3-1877 for Charles with parents; Katharine recrq 2-3-1886; ch's names entered by comm. 10-10-1886
Edna C., dt George W. & Ella L. (Cecil), b Bkn. 1-1-1891; recrq 6-10-1911 (H)
Edwin, s Charles C. & Mary Ann (Cornell), b N. Y. 2-2-1852 d 9-26-1928; m 1-29-1890 Lydia A. HOFFMAN (nm), dt Wm. A. & Charlotte (Cese) (H)
Egbert S. rocf Corn. 1-6-1857; ct Corn. 3-6-1861 (H)
Ella, dt John R. & Mary W., b 10-10-1859 d 6-18-1914; m Algernon Sidney KNIFFEN (nm) (m 4-10-1890) (H)
cf Corn. 12-1-1880 with mother
Franklin, s John R. & Mary W. (Hazard), b Monroe, N. Y. 5-6-1852 d 1-16-1926; cf Corn. 11-3-1880 (unm) (H)
Frederick Aldrich, s Chas. Henry & Catharine W. (Aldrich), b Bkn. 9-23-1885; m 5-1-1907 Florence Ruth LACEY (nm), dt Leroy & Mary (H)
George W., s Henry & Mary H. (Gahagan), b

RIDER, George W., continued
Middletown, N. Y. 10-8-1866; m 10-8-1890 Ella L. CECIL, dt Alfred & Margaret, b Bkn. 12-8-1868 (H)
George recrq 8-4-1880; Ella recrq 4-14-1924
James, Jr. rocf Corn. 4-4-1859; relrq 1-1805
James C., s Charles C. & Mary Ann, b Corn. 3-2-1859; cf Corn. with parents 10-3-1877; ct Corn. 2-3-1892 (H)
John, Jr. m Bridget FARRINGTON, Flushing (ltm 4 Mo (June) 5, 1718)
John R. (mbr Corn.) m 10-15-1850 Mary W. HAZARD, dt James & Sarah (Cornell), b Central Valley, N. Y. 6-18-1830 d 1- 3-1914 (H)
Ch: Franklin b 4-16-1852 d 1-16-1926
Sarah H. " 2-29-1855
Ella
Carrie
cf Corn. 12-1-1880 for Mary & ch; cert for Franklin 11-3-1880
Josiah C., s Chas. C. & Mary Ann (Cornell), b Corn. 8-1-1849 d 2-20-1910; m 6-3-1885 Wilhelmina ECKSTEIN (nm), dt Erhardt & Johanna (H)
cf Corn. 11-7-1877
King, Jr. having mo, Corn. referred to N. Y. 3-28-1850; dis 3-1851 & Corn. notified
Mary W. dt ----- HAZARD (H)
Ch: Sarah H.
Ella
Carrie
cf Corn. 12-1-1880 with 3 ch named
Sarah H., dt John R. & Mary W., b 2-29-1855; m 2-1-1890 (or 2-20-1890) Luther Frank FOWLER (H)
cf Corn. 12-1-1880 with mother

RIDGELEY
Eugenia, dt Dan'l M. & Ellen (Madden), b Wyoming, Del. 9-4-1884; m 1917 John R. ARNOLD
cf Wilmington 12-12-1921

RIDGES
R. Virginia rocf Reading, Eng. 2-7-1934

RIDGWAY
Aden (nm) b Trenton, N. J. d 4-27-1815 ae 37y 1m 19d bHS (m)
Caroline m 10-27-1853 Silvanus J. MACY (H)
Elizabeth, dt Thos. (dec) & Eliz., N. Y.; m 1811 Aaron BAKER
cf R. & P. 11-19-1807
Henry, Jr. rocf Waterford, Ireland 7-28-1818 (clear); ct Waterford, Ire. 11-5-1828 (clear) (O); ct Waterford, Ire. 7-1829 (H)
James & Henrietta
Ch: Evelyn Ruth
Elaine Agnes
parents recrq 7-5-1933; ch recrq of parents 7-5-1933; Evelyn active mbr 4-1935
Joseph rocf R. & P. 11-19-1801, minor; form dis, his ack. referred to Scipio 12-1-1813; Scipio rpd rec him as a mbr 5-4-1814
Mary rocf R. & P. 1-17-1805 (clear); dis 5-1843 (O); ct Scip. 5-1831 (H)
Richard, s Richard, Springfield, N. J.; m at Hope Willits' 8 Mo (Oct) 9, 1701 Mary WILLITS, dt Hope & Mary, Jerusalem in Hempstead
rem to N.J.
Robert rocf ND MM 7-24-1804 (clear); dis mo at Wysox, Pa. 10-1-1806
Sarah rocf R. & P. 1-15-1801 (clear)
Sarah Ann rocf Green St., Phila. 11-17-1825; ct Little Egg Harbor, 2-3-1830; marked Orthodox (H)
Thomas rocf R. & P. 8-21-1805, apprentice; dis 9-3-1823

RIEBEN
Pierre m Eliza HICKS, dt Samuel & Sarah, b 4-6-1806 d 5-20-1855 bPP (H)
Eliza dis 4-1849 (O)

RIEHL
Anna M. F., dt Ernst & Anna (Haack), b N. Y. 8-15-1862; m 1893 Richard Randolph HULL (H)
recrq 1-2-1895

RIESON
Mary con mo 5-7-1767

RIFFORD
John T. recrq 11-1868; name erased 5-1886

RIGGS
Winifred m Ernest Lee NICHOLS
both recrq 1-1916; letter to M. E. Church, Fairmont, W. Va. 12-1925 with ch

RIKER
Agnes S., dt William A. & Rachel, rocf Chesterfield 2-3-1846 with parents; relrq 11-1863
Elizabeth b Shrews. d 12-25-1817 ae 67y bHS (wd)
Joseph m Delia ----- d 4-1-1860 ae 35y bPP (H)
both nm; Delia a niece of David S. Brown
Lucy A., dt Wm. A. & Rachel, rocf Chesterfield with parents 2-3-1846; relrq 11-1863
Rachel S., w William A., d 1873
Ch: Ruth Anna relrq 11-1863
Agnes S. " "
Lucy A. " "
Oliver Stokes relrq 6-3-1874
Alice b 7-26-1847 (marked "off" in reg. as father was dis before her b)
cf Chesterfield 2-3-1846 with 4 ch named
Ruth Anna, dt Wm. A. & Rachel S., rocf Chesterfield with mother 2-3-1846; ct Upper Evesham 2-6-1850; cf Upper Evesham 4-7-1855; relrq 11-1863

RING
David Sands dis mo 10-7-1818
Elias & Catharine
Ch: Rachel b 3-13-1791
Phebe " 2-11-1793
David Sands b 10-1-1796
Eliza " 4- 5-1798
Harriet " 11-22-1800
Robert Elam " 8-17-1806
Clemintina Sands b 4-17-1811
Catharine Elam " 7-16-1815
George Washington d 8-1830
Charles Henry
cf Corn. 3-19-1798 with their 3 small ch, Rachel, Phebe & Sands; Elias dis 4-3-1816; ct Charles City, Va. 8-5-1818 for Phebe & Eliza (clear); ct Corn. 3-4-1829 for Catharine with 3 minor ch, Clementine, Catharine & Charles Henry
Eliza, dt Elias & Catharine, gct Charles City, Va. 8-5-1818 (clear); cf Charles City, Va. 7-7-1827 (clear); dis 3-1834 (O); marked Orthodox (H)
Franklin Mott, s John & Louisa, b N. Y. 10-13-1841 d E. Orange, N. J. 10-5-1922 bPP (nm) (unm)
George Stewart (nm), s Geo. W. & Evelyn (Stewart), b 1874 d 11-11-1929, Orange, N. J.; m Henrietta -----
George W. (nm) m Louise MOTT, dt Samuel F. & Ann, b 9-11-1820
Ch: George W. b 1-31-1842
Infant stillborn 8-15-1840 bHS in Caroline Mott's grave, but stated ch of "George W. Ring & Margaret his w". Louise Mott dis mo 2-3-1841; her sister, Margaret, dis 11-1839
George W. (nm), s George W. & Louise (Mott), b Quaker Ridge, N. Y. 1-31-1842 d Orange, N. J. 11-7-1914 bPP; m Evelyn STEWART, d 1934 bPP
Ch: George Stewart b 1874
Harriet, dt Elias & Catharine, b 11-22-1800; m ----- SMITH (mo); dis 10-7-1829 (O)
Louisa, dt Samuel F. & Ann MOTT, dis mo 2-3-1841
Martha G. rocf Corn. 1853
Phebe, dt Elias & Catharine, gct Charles City, Va. 8-5-1818 (clear)
Rachel gct Corn. 8-3-1831 (clear); marked Orthdox (H)
Rachel W. rocf Corn. 9-5-1877; d 9-19-1884
Robert Elam, s Elias & Catharine, b 8-17-1806; ct Corn. 2-4-1829 (clear)

RINO
Elias & Catharine
Ch: Mary d 9-7-1804 ae 1y 3m bHS

RITCHIE (or Richie)
Sarah M. dec

ROACH
Amy Jane, dt Egbert P. & Anna E. STOVER, b 1872; rocf Corn. with parents 5-1883; letter to Presby. Ch. Corn. on Hudson 5-3-1899
Edna M., dt Mary E.; m ----- McCLURE recrq with mother 11-7-1906; letter to Union Cong. Ch. Tuckahoe, 7-1920
Mary E., w ----- d 8-11-1829
Ch: S. Ruby
Edna M.
Mary recrq 11-7-1906, ch included
S. Ruby, dt Mary E.; m Karl John WEIMER rec with mother 11-7-1906

ROAKE
Mary, Jr. rocf Ama. 1-11-1800 (clear)

ROBBINS
Clara, dt Wm. M. & Elizabeth, b 3-24-1847; relrq 6-2-1869 (H)
Daniel C., dt Elizabeth; m Matilda L. -----
Ch: Ernest b 8-20-1847 d 1-15-1849
Louisa Matilda b 2-9-1849
Charles Allen " 6-19-1852
Jessie Anna " 11-23-1857
Mabel " 7-25-1860
Herbert Daniel " 10-14-1862
Russell Frost " 3-11-1867
cf Oswego 12-17-1834 with mother; cf Scip. 10-1848 for Matilda; Daniel relrq 7-1-1868; Matilda & all ch relrq 1-7-1880; cf Oswego 12-18-1833 for Daniel, minor (O); dis 12-1840 (O)
Edith P., dt Silas T. & Susan H., b Bkn. 9-14-1879; m 12-26-1904 Joseph Henry BURDETT (nm) (H)
Elizabeth d 2-27-1861, w ----- (H)
Ch: Daniel C.
William M.
Hannah M.
cf Oswego 12-17-1834 with 3 ch named
Eliz. Ann, dt Samuel & Harriet; m ----- PORTER (mo); cf Phila. 6-21-1814 with parents; dis mo 3-1835 (O)
Ella, dt Silas T. & Susan H. (Seaman), b Bkn. 2-13-1868; m 1887 Harry W. WINTER (nm) (H)
Forman C., s Samuel & Harriet, b 4-22-1803; ct Phila. 4-7-1830 (clear) (O); dis 3-1832 (H)
Hannah rocf Oswego 4-15-1835, minor, with brother, William; dis 5-1843 (O)
Hannah M., dt Elizabeth; m ----- ELY (H) cf Oswego 7-1835 with mother; rel 7-5-1875
Jeremiah rocf Oswego 4-15-1835 (clear); dis 12-1839
John Elliott, s Samuel & Harriet, rocf Phila. with parents 6-21-1814; dis 1-1832 (O); dis 4-1833 (H)
Margaret S. rocf Winthrop, Me. 2-6-1907
Maria [Robins] recrq 12-1-1819
Maria, dt John & Deborah WHIPPO, N. Y.; m 1820 Edmund KIRBY
Mary, dt Samuel & Eliz., Pur.; m 1794 Flushing William BOWNE
cf Wby 12-29-1784, she having rem & settled with her uncle, Isaac Underhill

ROBBINS, continued
Milton, s Silas T. & Susan H., b 4-3-1875 d 6-5-1931; m Katherine MILLER (nm), dt John & Margaret, d 10-23-1933 ae 52y
Samuel m Harriet; d at Jericho
Ch: Forman b 4-22-1803 (?)
Valentine b 9- 6-1803 (?)
Elliott dis 1-1832
Elizabeth Ann dis 3-1835
ct Wby for both 10-3-1804 with 2 small ch as named; cf ND MM 6-21-1814 for Harriet with 4 ch named

Sarah (late Franklin) dis mo 9-2-1789 (some Sarah Robbins d 9-17-1798 bHS)
Silas T., s Edward & Rachel W. (Titus), b Roslyn, L. I. 9-13-1837 d 11-25-1915 bPP; m 11-29-1865 Susan H. SEAMAN, dt Samuel & Phebe P., b Corn. 8-15-1840 d 9-27-1924 bPP (H)
Ch: Ella b 2-13-1868
Willet S. b 7-16-1870
Silas T. Jr. b 1-29-1873
Milton " 4- 3-1875
Sarah E. " 5- 7-1877 d 2-22-1923 bPP
Edith P. " 9-14-1879
cf Jer. 2-1863 for Silas; cf Corn. 3-1-1871 for Susan
Valentine, s Samuel & Harriet, rocf Phila. 6-21-1814 with parents; marked Orthodox 1850
Willett d 12-3-1855; m Esther ----- (m Jericho 1805)
Ch: Mary
William S. b 11-27-1808
Elizabeth " 2-28-1811 d 6- 2-1815 ae 3y
Edward " 7-1813
Matthew Franklin b 3-30-1815
cf Jericho 5-21-1801 (clear); cert of clear to Jericho 12-4-1805; Esther brought cf Jericho 7-17-1806; ct Jericho with their 4 ch named; cf Jericho 6-1843 for Willet S.
Willet d 1898; m Hannah W. WILLETS, dt Isaac & Amy, b 9-20-1836 d 12-4-1901 (H)
cf Wby 8-3-1864 for Willet; cf Jer. 9-4-1867 for Hannah
William M., s Elizabeth, d 10-23-1877; m Elizabeth ----- d 9-29-1875 (H)
Ch: Clara b 3- 4-1847
William C. b 9- 6-1849 d 4- 9-1883
Alice " 11-18-1851 d 9-13-1852
cf Oswego 4-15-1835 with sister, Hannah, minors; dis 12-1840 (O); cf Wby 1-1853 for Elizabeth
----- & ----- (nm)
Ch: Angelina d 9-18-1811 ae 7y bHS
Edwin " 4-12-1813 ae 9m 11d bHS

ROBERTS
Alfred rocf Dublin 8-16-1853; ct Dublin 3-7-1855
Anna B., dt John H. & Sallie B. (Williams), b Camden, N. J. 11-13-1885; m 1910 Cyrus J. WILSON (nm) (H)
cf Camden with parents 10-7-1891
Anna C., dt John S. & Anna, Bkn.; m 1859 Richard F. BROWN (H)
David (nm) & -----
Ch: Lucinda b Stamford, Conn. d 5-13-1815 ae 1y
Donald Alfred, s Alfred Jas. & Mary B. (McClellan), b N. Y. 11-13-1897; m 6-21-1923 Margaret EDDINS, dt Thos. K. & Clara B. (Russell) b Jonesboro, Ark. 3-9-1904 (H)
Donald recrq 1-8-1934; Margaret recrq 1-8-1934
Edward C., s John S. & Sarah Ann (dec), Bkn., b 6-1845 d 4-29-1908 bPP; m at N.S. Merritt's 3-26-1872 Eleanor MERRITT, dt Nathaniel S. & Mary K., Bkn., b 7-2-1845 d 9-26-1924 bPP (H)
Ch: Infant stillborn 1- 5-1873 bPP
Louisa M. b 1-10-1874
Mary K. " 9-23-1880
Edward relrq 1-2-1884; Eleanor relrq 1-2-1884
Elizabeth W., dt John H. & Sarah, Flatbush, b Camden, N. J. 7-19-1876; m 1904 Walter R. WILLETS (H)
Ellwood, s Thos. Ellwood & Sarah H., rocf Phila. with mother 2-20-1855; relrq 6-1874
John H., s Reuben & Hannah, b 7-4-1847, Fellowship, N. J.; m 2-19-1874 Sallie B. WILLIAMS, dt Isaac & Mary H. (Borton), b 7-10-1852 Chestnut Hill, Pa. d 3-28-1912 bPP (H)
Ch: Mary W. b 3- 3-1875
Elizabeth M. b 7-19-1876
Martha P. " 3- 6-1878
Anna B. " 11-13-1885
cf Chester for all 10-6-1891
John S., s John & Sarah (both dec), N. Y.; m N. Y. 6-11-1834 Sarah Ann CHURCHMAN, dt Owen & Mary, N. Y., d 12-2-1860 ae 44y 5m 20d bPP (H)
Ch: Mary Pennell b 1- 4-1836
Anna C. " 10-10-1837
Frances " 3-14-1841 d 2-10-1866 bPP
William Pennell b 5-27-1843
Edward C. b 6----1845
Alfred C. " 5-11-1847 d 12-20-1847 bPP
Caroline " 8- 3-1850 " 1- 1-1852 bPP
Henry S. " 12-28-1852 " 7-11-1862 bPP
John S. d 5- 4-1872 ae 65y 10m 2d bPP; m 2d at David B. Everitt's (not under care of N. Y. MM) 6-15-1864 Emily J. FALES, dt Geo. & Mary, Thomaston, Me., d 9-24-1907 ae 84y bPP (H)
(William B., s John S. d 3-23-1907 ae 68y bPP. This puts his b 4 y earlier than Wm. Pennell); John S. dis 9-6-1854
Louisa M., dt Edw. C. & Eleanor M., b 1-10-1874; m William LINDELL (H)
relrq 4-2-1890
Martha P., dt John H. & Sarah, Flatbush, b Camden, N. J. 3-6-1878; m 1903 Wm. L.

ROBERTS, Martha P., continued
KIMBALL; m 2d 1931 Albert T. MILLS (H)
ct Clear Creek, Ind.
Mary, Newtown, b 2 Mo (Apr) 13, 1725
Mary con mo 4-2-1766
Mary (nm) m David K. WARNOCK (H)
both nm
Mary K., dt Edward C. & Eleanor M., b 9-23-1880; relrq 8-5-1899 (H)
Mary P., dt John S. & Sarah Ann; m 1856 Edward H. BROWN (H)
Mary W., dt John H. & Sallie B., Bkn., b 3-3-1875 Camden, N. J.; m 1898 Hyman G. MILLER (H)
cf Chester, N. J. 10-7-1891; ct Makefield 8-1914
Matthew (nm) d 8-9-1855 ae 40y bPP
S. Raymond, s Spencer & Louisa J. (Raymond), Phila., b 8-30-1845 Phila. d 8-19-1928; m at John L. Griffen's 2-13-1883 Jeannie H. GRIFFEN, dt John L. & Sarah (Haydock), N. Y., b 10-13-1852 N. Y. d 5-8-1930 (H)
Ch: Walter Ernest b 8-30-1885
Edith Adeline " 6- 8-1887
Mildred Louise b 3-29-1891
ct Phila. 9-3-1884 for Jeannie; cf Phila. 9-3-1890 with 2 ch
Sarah rocf Pur. 6-13-1816 (clear); dis 9-1829 (H); d 3-18-1855 ae 66y
Thomas Ellwood, s Jesse & Rachel, Phila.; m Flushing 10-9-1851 Sarah KIMBER, dt Joshua & Rachel, Flushing
Ch: Ellwood Walter
ct Phila. for Sarah (not recorded); cf Phila. for Sarah with infant s 2-20-1855; Sarah relrq 10-6-1858
W. Glenn, s John T. & Alva (Button), b 4-3-1898; m Katharine -----
Ch: Rachel Elizabeth
cf Fairfield for all 12-1928; ct Mooresville, Western YM 9-13-1933 for mother & dt
Walter Ernest, s S. Raymond & Jeannie (Griffen) b N. Y. 8-30-1885; m 10-12-1912 Jean Margaret WILLIAMSON (H)
Wm. Pennell, s John S. & Sarah A., b 5-17-1843; dis 3-7-1877 (H)

ROBINSON
Abigail rocf Newport 9-30-1794, our esteemed Friend; absent longer than expected at time of her sudden departure; ct Newport 4-1-1795
Abigail m 1820 ----- PIERCE, of Salem, Mass. (mo) dis mo 12-6-1820
Alice Gertrude, w Edw. Fraser, dt Sam'l & Phebe H. BURLING (m 1897) (H)
Ch: Eleanor b 5-14-1901
Ann, dt Wm. T. & Sarah, b 8-14-1791; dis 10-1826
Anna Burling, dt Edw. F. & Alice G., b Bkn. 4-1-1891; m 10-15-1819 Herbert Wesley REID (H)
recrq of parents 5-9-1903; relrq 10-11-1932
Charles, s Wm. P. & Mary, gct Corn. 5-5-1841
(clear); cf Corn. 7-24-1845 (clear); dis 6-9-1852
Edward, s John S.; m Sarah Jane ----- (nm)
d 1-6-1858 ae 38y bPP
dis 10-1837 (H); dis 12-1839 (O)
Edward C. m ----- (mo before 2-1844, ret a mbr)
Ch: Alida d 10-14-1863 ae 1y 5m bPP
cf Linnington (Windham), Me. 2-28-1840 (clear); dis 9-1846
Edward F. (nm), s Edmond C. & Sarah J. (both dec), Bkn.; m at S. Burling's 4-14-1897 Alice Gertrude BURLING, dt Samuel & Phebe (Haviland), Bkn., b Bkn. 8-3-1870 (H)
Ch: Anna Burling b Bkn. 4-1-1896
Eleanor " " 5-14-1901
ch recrq of parents 5-9-1903
Eleanor, dt Edw. F. & Alice G., b Bkn. 5-14-1901; recrq of parents 5-9-1903; relrq 1-10-1921 (H)
Eliza gct Concord, Pa. 9-1-1813 (clear)
Ellen, dt Winfield & Caroline (Mason), b Liskeard, Cornwall 8-31-1861; m 4-21-1894 Herbert Henry DAWSON (nm) (H)
Emma, dt William T. & Sarah, b 9-7-1803; dis mo 1826
Esther, dt Wm. T. & Sarah, b 11-28-1781; m ----- MINTURN (mo)
dis mo 1-7-1801
Franklin, s William T. & Sarah, b 9-18-1797; dis 1827
George rocf R. & P. 3-21-1838, minor; ct Devonshire House 10-7-1840 (clear); returned to this mtg as he had left Eng. 4-1841; ct Dublin 4-1852
George rocf Phila. Cherry St. 4-1844; d New Orleans 8-9-1853 (H)
George m Eleanor M. HOLCOMB, dt Wm. Penn & Eliz. M., b 5-22-1892 d 12-27-1912 (m 1911) (H)
George Brown, s Philip, Newport, rocf Newport 3-27-1798, apprentice; ct R. I. MM 7-13-1808
George H. m Elizabeth ----- b N. Y. d 3-21-1828 ae 69y
Ch: Abigail b 4----1802
Samuel " 6-21-1804
Catharine
Mary
cf ND MM 2-25-1800 (clear); George took cert of clear to R. & P. 4-1-1801; ct ND MM 5-3-1809 with their 3 ch, Abigail, Catharine & Mary; cf R. & P. 8-19-1801 for Elizabeth; cf Shrews. 12-1-1817 for Elizabeth
Hannah, w -----
Ch: Elizabeth Phelps
Sarah
Hannah Louisa
cf R. & P. 1-15-1840 with 3 ch named, rem with h; ct R. & P. 8-1848 with same ch
Henry d 12-13-1858; m Elizabeth L. -----
Ch: Mary P. b 9- 7-1851
Sarah R. " 10-18-1848

ROBINSON, Henry & Elizabeth, continued
Ch: Emily L. b 11-27-1853
    Wm. T. (in pencil)
    cf R. & P. 3-21-1838; ct R. & P. 10-7-1846 (clear); ct R. & P. 1851 with w; ct R. & P. 8-1859 for all but Wm. T.
Howard Richards, s Jos. & Emma (Richards), b Wilmington, Del. 2-27-1858; m Elizabeth LEE (nm) (H)
    cf Wilmington 3-6-1895
James, s Philip, rocf Newport 11-27-1800, minor, rem with father
James P., s John S., dis 12-1848 (O); dis 11-1840 (H)
John E. rocf Scip. 6-1833; ct Roch. 1-1848 (H)
John S., s Philip, d 9-3-1849; m -----
Ch: Edward
    Reuben B.
    Mary B.
    James P.
    cf Newport 5-28-1799 to live with a Friend; dis mo 6-5-1811; rst 9-4-1816; 4 ch recrq of father 1-20-1821; William S. d 2-18-1822 ae 5m 20d
Lewis A., s Andrew A. & Virginia (Fries), b Winchester, Va. 2-15-1866; m 9-15-1902 Annie GARD (nm), dt David H. & Mary (Sherwood) (H)
    Lewis rocf Hopewell, Va. 2-10-1917
Margaret, dt Wm. P. & Mary, gct Phila. 6-4-1845 (clear)
Mary Hunter (form Robinson) dis mo 1804
Mary B., dt John S.; m ---- SLOCUM (H) (mo) dis mo 3-1836
Mary Elizabeth, dt Wm. P. & Mary, b 1-20-1817; ct Phila. 1848
Mary P. d 10-18-1894 ae 86y 1m bPP; m Charles WINGATE
Ch: Ella W.
    both nm)
Nathaniel rocf Corn. 11-7-1860; relrq 6-1862
Phebe, w Capt., dt David & Mary BIRDSALL; rocf Chap. with parents 2-11-1830; rel 3-1880
Reuben B., s John S., dis mo by a priest 1-1837 (O); dis 10-1836 (H)
Robert Fennell mo before 11-1846, ret a mbr; rocf Hardshaw West. 6-30-1842; dis non-attendance 6-1857
Rowland, s Thomas, rocf Newport 5-28-1782, under age (clear)
Rowland R., s William T. & Sarah, b 2-2-1796; dis 4-1827
Rowland T., s Thos. R. & Jemima, Ferrisburg, Vt.; m N. Y. 9-13-1820 Rachel GILPIN, dt George & Rachel (both dec), N. Y.
    ct Ferrisburgh 1-22-1821 for Rachel
Samuel, s Wm. P. & Mary, gct R. & P. 1-4-1826, apprentice
Samuel T., s Philip, rocf Newport 11-27-1800, minor, rem with father
Sarah, dt Wm. T. & Sarah, N. Y.; m 1809 Joseph S. COATES, of Phila.
Sarah, dt George & Phebe (both dec), rocf Newport 11-26-1829, minor, to live with her aunt, Sarah Mott
Sarah E. d 6-29-1841; m ----- CHICHESTER (H)
    rec without cert 3-1833
Susan (nm) b Eng. d 12-22-1815 ae 35y bHS
Thomas (not mbr here) d 4-11-1801 bHS; m -----
Ch: Rowland
    (Amy, dt Thos. & Sarah; m Robt. L. BOWNE)
Willett & Esther
Ch: Mary b 11-25-1800
William, having served apprenticeship to 2 Friends in N. Y., ct Newport, R. I. 2-5-1778 (clear); cf Newport 9-28-1780 (clear)
William P. (or S.), s Philip & Eliz. (dec), Merchant, N. Y.; m N. Y. 5-11-1803 Mary PEARSALL, dt Joseph & Hannah, N. Y., b Nantucket d 9-29-1821
Ch: Nathaniel b 3- 6-1804
    Hannah " 3-16-1805 d 1845
    Margaret " 1-19-1807
    Samuel
    Charles
    Mary Elizabeth b 1-20-1817
    James d 9-4-1813 ae 35d
    Infant " 4-11-1820
    Joseph d 7-31-1821 ae 2m 2d
    cf Portsmouth, R. I. 8-26-1794, apprentice; ch marked Orthodox (H)
William R(ichardson), s Wm. T. & Sarah, b 8-29-1799; ct Cincinnati 4-3-1844
William T., s Thomas & Sarah, Newport, R. I., b R. I. d 7-10-1825 ae 45y; m N. Y. 1-10-1781 Sarah FRANKLIN, dt Samuel & Esther, d 1-14-1806 ae 42y
Ch: Esther b 11-28-1781
    Sarah " 4-15-1784
    Mary " 1-11-1786
    Thomas " 7- 6-1787
    Elizabeth b 12-17-1788
    Abigail " 2-16-1790
    Ann " 8-14-1791
    Catharine Wistar b 12-26-1792 d 8-17-1793
    Samuel Franklin b 2- 2-1794
    Rowland " 2- 2-1796
    Franklin " 9-18-1797
    William Richardson b 8-23-1799
    Emma " 9- 7-1803
    Rowland R. "
    William gct Newport 2-6-1777; this cert lost, another issued 2-1778; cf Newport 9-28-1780
William T. & ----- (probably same as above)
Ch: Infant stillborn 1-29-1816
    " " 4-11-1820
Wilson m Effie HOLME, dt Eleanor, b Eng. d Springtown, N. Y. about 1896 bPP
----- & ----- (nm)
Ch: Bertha M. d 2-14-1889 ae 2y bPP

ROBSON
Leonard rocf Brighouse, Eng. 4-1915

ROCHESTER
Junius C. (nm), s George A. & Julia (Gwynne), Seattle; m 1222 Albemarle Rd., Bkn. 6-15-1927 Lillian J. HANAN, wd Addison G., dt Jos. T. (dec) & Anna L. McDOWELL, Bkn., b Jersey City 11-10-1878 (H)

ROCHFORD
Hope (nm), dt John; m 1922 Charles WALKER (H)

ROCKWELL
Benjamin E., s Franklin & Maria A., rocf Phila. Arch St. 7-3-1912

RODGERS
Burton (nm), s James B. & Ann (Bigelow); m 12-24-1920 Marie HESS, dt Jean Jacques & Mary M. (Ellicott), b Fribourg, Switzerland 9-19-1894 (H)
Marie recrq 12-10-1917; ct Birmingham

RODAKIEWICZ
Erla recrq 12-1918

RODMAN
Ann, dt Dr. John, Flushing; m 1707 Walter NEWBERRY
Ann, dt Thomas & Eliz., Flushing; m 1746 Caleb FIELD
Caroline, dt Thos. & Eliz., Flushing; m 1762 James BOWNE
Catharine, dt Thos. & Eliz., Flushing; m 1759 Henry HAYDOCK
Eleanor d 8-3-1792
Elizabeth "the first", Flushing, d 8 Mo (Oct) 1701 N. Y. (prob dt of John & Mary, from Barbados)
Elizabeth, dt John, Flushing; m 1723 Thomas MASTERS
Elizabeth, dt Thomas, Flushing; m 1739 Benjamin HICKS
George (nm) & -----
Ch: Lawrence b N. Y. d 2-27-1845 ae 2y 4m bHS
Harriet b N. Y. d 3-17-1845 ae 2m 3d bHS
Hannah, dt Dr. John, Flushing; m 1716 Jonathan DICKENSON
John d 1723 (not identified)
Dr. John, s John & Elizabeth, of Ireland & Barbados, Flushing, b 1653 d 7 Mo (Sep) 10, 1731; m Mary SCANNON b 1662 d 11 Mo (Jan) 21, 1747/8 aged 85y 1m
Ch: John b Barbados 3 Mo (May) 3, 1679
Mary " " 5 Mo (July) 5, 1681 d 12 Mo 1682 R. I.
Samuel b Barbados 6 Mo (Aug) 6, 1683
Joseph b R. I. 2 Mo (Apr) 11, 1685
William b R. I. 3 Mo (May) 20, 1687 d 3 Mo. 23 1704
Ann b Block Is. 2 Mo (Apr) 11, 1689
Thomas b Flushing 12 Mo (Feb) 1691/2 d 8 Mo 1693
Mary b Flushing 10 Mo (Dec) 20, 1693
Elizabeth b Flushing 11 Mo (Jan) 24, 1695/6
Ch: Thomas b Flushing 11 Mo (Jan) 9, 1697/8
Hannah b N. Y. 6 Mo (Aug) 5, 1700
Elizabeth b Flushing 1 Mo (Mar) 7, 1701/2
came to Flushing 6-1690; John active mbr from 1691 & Clerk
John, s John & Mary, Flushing, b 3 Mo (May) 3, 1679; m Margaret GROSSE, dt Thomas & Eliz., Boston, d Flushing 2 June 1718
Ch: John b Flushing 1714 d 1795
Thomas b Flushing 1716; rem to Burl.
Mary m ----- JOHNSON
John m 2d Mary WILLETT, dt William, Cornell's Neck (m between 5 Mo 2 and 6 Mo (Aug) 5, 1719, cert not recorded)
Ch: William b 1720
Anne " 1722
Scammon " 1723
Hannah " 1726
Samuel " 1729
Margaret " 1731
Elizabeth " 1734
John rem to Burl. 3 Mo 5, 1726; a physician
Joseph, Flushing; m Sarah LAWRENCE (ltm 1 Mo (Mar) 6, 1706/7)
Ch: Joseph b 8 Mo (Oct) 6, 1708
Ann " 2 Mo (Apr) 17, 1711 d 9 Mo 13, 1713
William b 1 Mo (Mar) 17, 1712 d 8 Mo 22, 1713
Samuel " 12 Mo (Feb) 6, 1714/15
Mary " 12 Mo (Feb) 1, 1716/17
Sarah " 7 Mo (Sep) 24, 1719
William " 8 Mo (Oct) 31, 1721
Deborah " 11 Mo (Jan) 2, 1725/6
Ann " 2 Mo (Apr) 30, 1728
Joseph, New Rochelle, N. Y.; m Flushing 3-10-1757 Judith BOWNE, dt Jonathan MORRELL, Flushing
Judith wd Jos. Bowne; ct (prob) Pur. 5-5-1757
Joseph, New Rochelle, m Flushing 11-9-1758 Helena WILLETT, dt Abraham (dec), Flushing
Mary, dt John, Flushing; m 1714 John WILLETS
Mary, dt Thomas & Eliz., Flushing; m 1750 Joseph FIELD
Penelope, dt Thos. & Elizabeth; m 1764 Anthony SHOEMAKER
Samuel, s Thomas, N. Y.; m Flushing 3 Mo. (May) 16, 1723 Mary WILLETT, dt Col. Thos., Flushing
Samuel, s Joseph, New Rochelle; m Flushing 8 Mo (Oct) 1734 Mary HICKS, dt William, d 10 Mo (Dec) 20, 1751
Ch: Sarah b 12 Mo (Feb) 20, 1738/9
Joseph b 2 Mo (Apr) 29, 1740
William b 7 Mo (Sep) 15, 1742
Samuel b 9 Mo (Nov) 28, 1744
Mary " 8 Mo (Oct) 28, 1746
Charles b 9 Mo (Nov) 4, 1748 d 7 Mo (Sep) 18-1751
Samuel, s Dr. John, of Burl., d 5-4-1761 ae 32y
Samuel rem ct Pur. 9-13-1859
Thomas, s John & Mary, Flush.; m Elizabeth ----
Thomas gc of clear 9 Mo (Nov) 7, 1717

RODMAN, Thomas & Elizabeth, continued
Ch: Elizabeth b 7 Mo (Sep) 25, 1719
Anne " 10 Mo (Dec) 6, 1721
Hannah " 12 Mo (Feb) 4, 1723/4
John " 6 Mo (Aug) 8, 1726
Mary " 5 Mo (July) 31, 1729
Katharine " 12 Mo (Feb) 29, 1731/2
Caroline " 8 Mo (Oct) 6, 1734
Penelope " 2 Mo (Apr) 5, 1737
Thomas " 12 Mo (Feb) 3, 1739/40
----- & ----- (nm)
Ch: Sarah d 4-28-1841 ae 21d bHS

ROE
----- m Ada UNDERHILL
Ada recrq 11-3-1932

ROGERS
Charlotte recrq 8-1-1883; relrq 9-3-1884 (H)
Clarkson, s James C. & Agnes G., at 10 in 1903 letter from M. E. Ch., Bradford, Canada, with mother 3-4-1903; ct Fairmount, Ind. 1-1915
David Jr., doctor, recrq 9-1-1819; dis 7-1830 (O); d 1841 (H)
Elizabeth, w Elisha T.
Ch: James Swift
cf Uxbridge, Mass. 12-1853 with 1 ch; ct Uxbridge, Mass. 3-5-1856 with same ch
Furman Black d 5-29-1916 ae 72y bPP; m Mary G. DISTURNELL, dt Wm. & Jane, d 8-14-1927 ae 82y 4m bPP (H)
Ch: Frank Hellutt d 1- 5-1906 ae 22y 5m bPP
Infant stillborn 2-11-1865 bPP
all nm
F. P. (nm) & -----
Ch: Infant d 2-4-1865 bPP
George F. m Anna C. HANSEN, dt C. F. A. & Olivia, d 9-20-1911 ae 23y bPP
both nm
George T. m Florence RAYMOND, d 10-11-1901 ae 28y bPP (H)
Henry B. d 2-24-1977; m -----
Ch: Mary Ward (later changed to Muriel)
cf Salem, Mass. 5-6-1891 with 1 ch named
James Clark & Agnes G.
Ch: Clarkson Van Duzen 10
Horace Kingsley 6
cf Maripora, Canada 3-4-1903 for James; letter from M. E. Ch., Bradford, Canada 3-4-1903 for Agnes & ch; ch recrq of parents, rq later transferred to full mbrp; letter to Ontario St. M. E. Ch., Buffalo for parents 1-1923
Mary, late of Nantucket; m 1723 Edward BURLING
Mary Ward, dt Henry B.; m ----- STEINHAUSER
Moses F. rocf Boston 12-3-1890; lived in Newark, N. J.
Muriel (Mary Ward form) m ----- STEINHAUSER (nm)
cf Salem, Mass. with father 5-1891
Richard took cert of clear to Westchester 12 Mo 1, 1727/8; ct Westchester (Pur) 12 Mo (Feb) 4, 1727/8; cf Pur. 9-1-1757

Rowland Cotton (nm) b Eng. d 9-26-1812 ae 93y 10m bHS
Sarah m Dr. M. R. MORRIS (H)
cf Jericho 6-1842; ct Wby 4-2-1856
Wm. Davis, s Edward & Anna L., Medford, Mass.; m Swarthmore, Pa. 6-6-1927 Sarah Eliz. PERCY, dt John C. & Eliz. S., Salisbury, Conn. b Chatham, N. Y. 4-15-1905 (H)
Ch: William D. Jr. b Camden 1-14-1928
John Edward b 10-27-1929

ROOKE
Mary Collett (form Rooke) dis mo 10-7-1801

ROORBACK
Abigail (late Latham) dis mo 10-3-1787
John O. [Rooraback] (nm) & -----
Ch: William d 8-14-1821 ae 3y 1m bHS
Benjamin C. d 8-25-1821 ae 19y bHS
Alfred b N. Y. d 2-11-1833 ae 3y bHS
Mary F. b N. Y. d 12-7-1841 ae 18y bHS (unm)
Mary F. (nm) d 2-26-1860 ae 72y bPP (prob w of John O.)

ROOT
Howard Cassin (nm) m 6-3-1879 Jane J. COX, dt Stephen & Eliz. N. (Taylor) b 3-28-1855 d 6-18-1927 (H)
cf Green St., Phila. 3-5-1890

ROSCO
Mary rem ct Burl. 3-4-1812

ROSS
Anna B. rocf Easton 9-5-1860; ct Wapsainonock, Iowa 8-2-1871
Anna L. rocf Middletown, Pa. 10-1817; d 6-24-1850 (H)
Caroline, dt Samuel & Sarah, N. Y.; m 1856 Andrew J. GRAHAM (H)
cf Phila. MM 12-22-1840 with brother, rem with parents; dis 4-1849 (O) (H)
Cephas rocf Wrightstown 5-6-1794 with brother (clear); con mo 6-8-1797; ct Buckingham, Pa. 10-4-1797, he having rem
Edward, s Samuel & Sarah, rocf Phila. 12-22-1840 with sister, rem with parents (O); dis 12-1848 (O); cf Phila. Green St. 12-1842 (H); dis 1-5-1848 (H)
Elsie, dt Elizabeth HOUSTON, rocf Lurgan, Ire. 3-1888 with mother; name erased 4-1928; in Dunellen, N. J. 1912
Henry W., s Samuel & Sarah, rocf Green St., Phila. with parents 8-1840; ct Phila. 7-4-1894
Samuel d 5-5-1857 ae 60y 1m 17d bPP; m Sarah H. ----- d 9-21-1854 ae 55y bPP (H)
Ch: Caroline
Samuel Holcomb
Henry W.
Edward H.
cf Phila. Green St. 8-1840 for all but Edward H. who brought cert 12-1842

ROSS, continued
Samuel H., s Samuel & Sarah, N. Y.; m at Wm. B. Humbert's, N. Y. 3-23-1852 (not under care of N. Y. MM) Cordelia A. GARDNER, dt Rowland H. (dec) & Mary Ann, N. Y. (H)
Samuel relrq 5-1858
Thomas gct Buckingham, Pa. 10 Mo (Dec) 4, 1746
Thomas, s Thomas & Anna (dec), Hatter, N. Y.; m N. Y. 5-9-1792 Anna LOINES, dt Wm. (dec) & Sarah, N. Y.
cf ND MM 12-23-1788 (clear), had served apprenticeship; gr s of Thomas Ross; ct Buckingham, Pa. 8-7-1794 with w, Anne; Thomas & Anna, of Salsbury, Pa.; cf Middletown 9-4-1817 for Anna L.; Anna dis 5-1829 (O)
William, s Thomas & Anna, N. Y., rocf Wrightstown 5-4-1790, apprentice to his brother, Thomas; ct Buckingham 4-3-1793 (clear); cf Buckingham 4-7-1794 (clear); ct ND MM 4-5-1796 (clear)
----- & ----- (nm & mbr)
Ch: Augustus W. d 10-21-1855 ae 8m 6d bPP

ROSSITER
Alfred, s Sigmond H. & Helena (Schmalz); m Helen KAUFMAN (nm) (H)
Ch: Jonathan b N. Y. 10-8-1920
Alfred & Jonathan recrq 6-10-1929
Alfred, b Frankfort, Germany 1-2-1882; m 2d 6-5-1929 Nettie STOUT (mbr Lawrence, Kans.) dt John W. & Lucetta (H)
Anna Arabella (nm), dt Thos. & Margaret; m 1898 Richard F. PEARSALL (H)

ROTHWEILER
William (nm) m 3-4-1885 Caroline JONES, wd John, dt Geo. & Sarah (Ritter) PECK
b Danville, Pa. 11-6-1824 d 4-12-1909 (H)
cf Balt. 7-9-1898

ROUTLEDGE
----- (nm) m Evelyn C. CRAVEN, dt Ishi & Mary Bunting (Davis)
Evelyn recrq 12-1915

ROWE
Beatrice Alice, dt Alfred Tennyson & Elsie E. (Klingsmith) (nm), b 11-12-1913 Woodhaven, N. Y.; m 1932 John Curlin ALLEN
Beatrice recrq 10-12-1931; divorced
Martha, having mo long since, dealt with 7-5-1769 to 11-2-1769, still under care of comm but nothing further

ROWNTREE
Anna Mary rocf Springdale, Iowa 12-1880; ct Chicago 12-1885; (prob sister of Hannah E. who had cert same dates)
Bernard m Gertrude E. LESTER
Ch: Cedric b 7-13-1911
cf Chicago 5-3-1911 for Bernard; cf WD MM for Gertrude 2-1914; divorced 3-1932
Hannah Elizabeth rocf Springdale, Iowa 12-1880; ct Chicago 12-1885 (prob sister of Anna Mary, who had certs same dates)
Henry m Hannah W. RAY, dt Christopher & Elizabeth (mo)
Ch: Joseph W.
Robert W.
William B.
Joseph W.
John H.
Henry, Jr.
Hannah Elizabeth
Anna Mary b 9-14-1851
cf Balby, Eng. 9-12-1833; dis mo, con mo 5-5-1841; ct Corn. 8-2-1843 with w & 1 ch, Joseph; ct Scipio 11-1853 for all named; Henry a minister; ct Red Cedar, Iowa 1856, 1857 for all except Joseph W.
Robert W., s Henry & Hannah, rocf Scip. with parents 11-1853; dis 5-1862 for joining the Navy
Wm. M. [Rountree] (nm), s Wm. F. & Julia J., Newberne, N. C.; m at M. T. Maine's 10-10-1894 Elizabeth F. MAINE, dt Malcolm T. & Phebe F. (Hallock), Bkn. 11-3-1869 (H)
Ch: Maine Mitchell b 5-5-1898
Isabella M. d 2-17-1897 ae 1y 7d bPP
Elizabeth's name entered by comm. 10-10-1886; Maine recrq of parents 8-10-1901

ROY
Harold E., s Frank A. & Eugenie (Woodbridge), b N. Y. 8-6-1889; cf Swarthmore 2-12-1910; relrq 4-10-1915 (H)
Lincoln & Alice C. [Roys]
cf Durham, Me. 5-1915 for both

RUBINS
Marian (nm), dt Harry W. & Florence (Hawkins); m 1925 Horace Bancroft DAVIS (H)

RUDOLPH
Gladys M. (nm), dt Wm. Henry; m 1914 Daniel D. STREETER (H)

RUGGLES
Aimee, dt James Henry & Susan (Blair), b Bkn. 1869; m 1902 Wm. Henry GREEN (H)
recrq 12-11-1922; ct Pur. 7-13-1925
Augustus G. m Emily B. ----- d 10-20-1896 ae 66y 6m bPP (both nm) (H)

RULAN
Elizabeth bPP in same grave with her 2 young ch

RULON
Henry recrq 3-1872; d 9-25-1885

RUNNELLS
Abigail gct R. & P. 7-5-1815 (clear)
Elias [Runnels] rocf Chap. 3-4-1812 (clear)
Elijah H., s Robert (dec) & Ann, N. Y.; m N.Y.

RUNNELLS, Elijah H. & Abigail, continued
3-14-1811 Abigail EVANS, dt Crowell & Frances, N. Y.
Ch: Anna Maria b 12-26-1811
cf Chap. 4-13-1810 (clear); ct Chap. 1-5-1814 with w, Abigail & infant named

RUSHMORE
David Barker, s Jno. Howard & Julia A. (Barker) b Old Wby 8-21-1872; recrq 1-14-1929 (H)
Deborah rocf Jericho 4-1837; ct Wby 9-4-1850 (H)
Dr. Edward C., s John U. & Sarah (Drake), b Cooksburg, N. Y. 3-21-1862; m 8-11-1887 Emily HERRICK (nm), dt George & Charlotte (H)
cf Renss. 8-7-1895
Ellen, dt Edward & Clara S. (Riley), b Corn. 1-20-1874; m 1911 Peter Joseph McKEON (nm) (H) cf Balt. 6-14-1920
Frances Gertrude, dt Benj. H. & Anna M. LOWERRE, N. Y.; m 1888 Silas A. UNDERHILL
Gertrude recrq 2-1883
Hannah d 4-28-1820 ae 5m bHS
Isaac W. rocf Wby & Jericho 4-1857; relrq 3-3-1875
Dr. Mary D., dt John U. & Sarah (Drake), b Cooksburg, N. Y. 11-12-1866; cf Renss. 9-4-1895; ct R. & P. 10-14-1911 (unm) (H)
Mary Jane, w Isaac, dt Moses I. & Esther QUINBY b 7-14-1837; marked as attending Orthodox 1861
Samuel W. rocf Wby & Jericho 3-1861; d 4-1871

RUSHTON
Benjamin G., s James & Hannah, b 8-29-1809; m Hannah ----- (nm) d 12-2-1831 bPP (mo)
Ch: Harriet E. d 8- 6-1847 ae 9m 28d bPP
David " bPP
dis mo 1-1834 (H); dis mo 4-2-1834 (O)
Christina, dt James & Hannah, N. Y.; m 1823 James R. LENOX
Elizabeth m Richard DIVER (mo)
cf York, Eng. 10-2-1799 (clear); dis mo 2-4-1801
Hannah, dt James & Hannah, d 11-16-1804; m 1828 ----- MARSHALL (mo)
dis mo 12-1828
Hannah, b Eng. d 12-2-1834 ae 20y bHS
James m Hannah ----- b Eng. d 12-17-1836 ae 68y 2m 18d (a wd)
Ch: Christiana
Joseph
Hannah b 11-16-1804
Sarah " 7-11-1807
Benjamin G. b 8-29-1809
Mary Ann " 5-18-1812
Abraham " 11-22-1815 d 3-22-1819
cf Knaresbro, Eng. for James & w & ch, Christiana & Joseph 6-14-1802; James dis 1824; others dis 1828-1834 (O)
Mary Ann, dt James & Hannah, b 5-18-1812; dis 10-1837 (H)
Sarah, dt James & Hannah, N. Y.; m 1837 Andrew WILLETS (H)
cf Brighouse MM, Eng. 7-20-1798 (clear)
----- & -----
Ch: David T. b N. Y. d 11-29-1843 ae 4m 2d bHS
Hannah d 4-28-1821 ae 5m bHS

RUSSELL
Charles R., s Percy & Agnes (Regnier) b Bkn. 9-1-1900; cf Pipe Creek with parents 2-8-1902; ct Swarthmore 6-12-1922 (H)
Charlotte H. recrq 2-1886; d 11-1-1916
Everett DeWitt, s Worthington & Ellen E. (Tanner), b 7-9-1896; recrq of parents 2-1910; name erased 2-1924
Frank J., s Thos. W. & Mary (Englar), b Union Bridge, Md. 12-28-1869 d 2-6-1914; m 4-25-1896 Josie M. MYERS, dt John W. & Margaret A. (Sidwell), b Johnsville, Md. 4-26-1871 (H)
Ch: Roger Sidwell b 5-13-1901
Alice Englar " 7- 7-1905
Lawrence Myers b 4-21-1908
Frances stillborn 10-9-1903 bPP, rem to Union Bridge 12-22-1904
Frank rocf Pipe Creek, Md. 1-9-1897; Josie rocf Alexandria 4-10-1897; ct Balt. 8-13-1917 for Josie & ch
Gilbert E. rocf New Bedford 7-12-1806, minor, now with Post & Russell; joined a military corps 10-12-1814; absent 12-7-1814; dis 5-3-1815
Hannah, w Abraham, rocf Dartmouth, Mass. 4-22-1818; ct Dartmouth 2-2-1820
Hannah R., w Benjamin
Ch: Maria
Thomas S.
Louisa
cf New Bedford 8-24-1837 with 3 ch named; ct New Bedford 2-3-1841 with 3 minor ch, named
Henry R. b 4-23-1832 d 1-5-1899; m Elizabeth S. -----; cf Woodbury 4-9-1898 for both; ct Goose Creek 11-10-1900 (H)
Isaac (nm), s Emanuel & Elizabeth; m 11-26-1840 Jane C. BURDSALL, dt Richard & Frances (Crowell), b Trenton, N. J. 8-24-1817 d 1-5-1902 (H)
Ch: Julia F.
cf R. & P. for Jane 2-1842; ct Pur. for Jane, 1-1845; cf Pur. 2-1851 with ch
Isaac D. (nm) d 8-18-1871 ae 64y 3m 15d bPP, rem to Woodlawn 6-28-1880 (H)
John W. dis mo 8-5-1807
John Wady, s Humphrey, rocf Dartmouth 5-19-1800, apprentice to a Friend
Jonathan S. rocf New Bedford 6-11-1811, apprentice to John W. & Gilbert Russell
Josiah (nm) b Nantucket d 10-5-1830 ae 42y bHS
Julia Frances, dt Isaac & Jane C., N. Y., d 2-4-1878 ae 36y bPP, rem to Greenwood 6-28-1880; m 1877 Robert W. PARSONS, of Flushing (H) cf Pur. with mother 2-1851
Lewis J., s Percy & Agnes (Regnier), b New

RUSSELL, Lewis J., continued
Market, Md. 2-26-1896; m 2-5-1916 Bertha P. WHITESIDE (nm), dt Frederick W. (H) cf Pipe Creek with parents 2-8-1902; ct Balt. 3-13-1922
Nancy b Ireland d 2-5-1833 ae 75y, a wd (H)
Percy, s Isaac S. & Lucie S. (Buckingham), b New Market, Md. 11-12-1867; m 7-11-1894 Agnes REGNIER, dt Charles F. & M. Abby (Bowlsby), b West Liberty, Iowa 1-11-1872 (H)
Ch: Lewis J. b New Market 2-26-1896
Charles R. b Bkn. 9-1-1900
cf Pipe Creek, Md. 2-8-1902 for all
Phebe Ann, dt Thos. W. & Mary (Englar), b Union Bridge, Md. 4-7-1868; cf Pipe Creek 4-8-1905; ct Pipe Creek 2-10-1912 (H)
Seth (nm) d 9-7-1837 ae 70y 11m bHS
Shubael, having mo, Nantucket refers it to this MM 8-5-1801; comm. rpd 9-3-1801 he was gone from here; left with com.
Solomon B. rocf Marl. 9-22-1847 (clear); dis mo 3-1856
Stanley Seaton, s Worthington & Ellen E. (Tanner), b 7-13-1894; recrq of parents 2-1910; name erased 2-1924
Stephen (nm) m -----
Ch: Walter d 6-1-1848 ae 1y 10m bHS
Thomas John, having mo, Moate, Ireland, refers it to N. Y. 7-1848, rpd 12-1848 as not found here
Wm. Tallman rocf New Bedford 8-20-1805, placed under care of Henry Post & John Wady Russell, of N. Y.; ct New Bedford 10-3-1810 (clear)
Worthington S., M.D. (nm) m Ellen Eliza TANNER, dt Wm. J. & Ellen E., b 4-28-1871 d 1914
Ch: Stanley Seaton b 7-13-1894
Everett De Witt b 7- 9-1896
ch recrq of parents 2-1910
----- & -----
Ch: Mary B. b New Bedford d 11-9-1836 ae 4y bHS

RUTTER
Thomas rocf Bristol, Eng. 2-25-1806 (clear); dis 12-7-1814

RUTTY
----- (nm) m Grace LINTON, dt Albert W. & Isabella (Georke) b 1910 (m 1930) (rpd 2-5-1930)

RYAN
Harry E. (nm), s George W. & Nellie W., b Omaha 11- 4-1888 d St. Petersburg, Fla. 5-8-1925 bPP; m 1925 Elizabeth CROSMAN
cf Haverford for Elizabeth 4-1921

RYDER
Josiah C., s Charles C. & Mary H., Bkn.; m at A. SIDNEY Kniffen's 5-7-1879 Emelane C. KNIFFEN, dt A. Sidney & Eliz. C., Bkn. (H)
Mary Ann recrq 6-6-1820; ct Corn. 11-1-1820 (clear)

RYSDYK
Ann (nm) b N. J. d 1-28-1841 ae 33y bHS (wd)

SAALFIELD
Eugenia (nm), dt Richard A. & Lizzie T. (Cohn); m 1922 Henry Cohu HULL (H)

SACKET
Phebe con mo before 3 Mo (May) 2, 1751; d 3-20-1797

SAFELY
Henry (see Santell)

SALTUS
Lloyd (nm) m 10-15-1902 Sarah SEAMAN, dt Samuel H. & Hannah (Husband), b Bkn. 8-21-1875 (H)
Sarah relrq 7-13-1907

SAMPSON
Alden d 4-16-1878; m Sarah T. ----- d 2-19-1871
Ch: Maria H.
Esther P.
Sarah E.
Mary
Alden
cf Litchfield, Me. 2-1869 for all
Alden m 2d Phebe J. -----
cert of clear to Scip. 12-1873; Phebe rocf Scip. 6-1874; Phebe gct Scip. 8-5-1885
Alden, s Alden & Sarah, rocf Litchfield, Me. with parents 2-1869; relrq 1-1887
Maria H., dt Alden & Sarah, N. Y.; m 1869 Wm. R. THURSTON, Jr.

SANBORN
Nestor, s Nestor H. & Lydia S. (Macy), b 8-11-1843 N. Y. d 12-1-1935 ae 93y bPP; m Caroline V. -----
relrq 7-1868
Nestor H., s James (dec) & Mary H.; m N. Y. 7-14-1841 Lydia S. MACY, dt Wm. W. & Phebe S. (both dec), d 12-19-1855
Ch: Nestor b 8-11-1843
Ann Augusta b 10-7-1845 d 2- 4-1865 bPP
Nestor rocf Weare 7-1838 (clear); Lydia rocf Nantucket with parents 6-30-1825; Nestor dis 7-1846

SANDERS
Amos, s David & Mary (Horton), b 5-30-1845 Valley Mills, Md. d 3-22-1907 in Los Angeles bPP; m R. Anna ----- d 7-4-1903 ae 57y 11m 7d bPP
Ch: Harold A.
cf Noblesville, Ind. 12-5-1906 for all
Charles (nm) b Pa. d 12-7-1832 ae 34y bHS (m)
Grace, dt Chas. Walton & Ella A. (Wickwire) b Rahway 8-18-1870; m 1-7-1894 John H. MACY

SANDERS, Grace, continued
Jr.; m 2d 4-11-1906 David Holcomb KEEFER (H)
recrq 1-14-1911; name changed to Macy 4-11-1916 by Court Order
Harold, s Amos & R. Anna; m Edith BELL
Ch: Harold A. Jr.
Robert Bell
Harold rocf Noblesville, Ind. 12-5-1900; Edith rolf First Presby. Ch., Milton, N.Y. 4-5-1911; ct Pasadena, Calif. 2-1920 for all

SANDERSON
Catharine rocf Balt. W. Dist. 2-12-1812; ct SD MM 3-6-1816 (clear)

SANDS
Agnes C., dt David & Paulina, N. Y., b 11-24-1851; m 1882 Robert W. LAWRENCE
Anna P., dt David & Paulina, b 5-12-1842; relrq 9-1862
Catharine, w Richard, recrq 1811; dis 12-1830
Daniel C. (nm), s Daniel (dec) & Phebe F., N. Y.; m at Katurah Titus' 11-13-1874 Martha S. TITUS, dt Peter S. (dec) & Keturah, N. Y., b 2-9-1849 N. Y. d 4-8-1926 (H)
Ch: Daniel C. Jr. b 11-22-1875 N. Y.
Martha recrq of mother 3-1862; ch recrq of mother 3-13-1877
David (nm) b N. Y. d 10-26-1809 ae 2y 1m bHS
David & Betsy
Ch: Elizabeth Ann
David Jerome
Reuben
Samuel
cf Ama. 6-10-1821 with 4 ch named; ct Chap. 8-1-1821 with 3 ch named
David d 7-31-1859; m Paulina ----- d 7-14-1882
Ch: Nathaniel D. b 2-26-1835 d 8-16-1835
Emma " 4- 5-1836 " 4-12-1837
Martha Jane " 9-27-1839
Infant stillborn 5-13-1841
Anna P. b 5-12-1842; relrq 9-1862
David " 7-21-1844 d 7-24-1845
Abraham " 6-20-1846 d 3-20-1847
William L. " 6-27-1848 d rpd 7-1920
Sarah " 7- 9-1849; relrq 2-1870
Agnes " 11-24-1851
cf Corn. 9-25-1834; cf Oblong 9-15-1834 for Paulina
Emily Augusta, dt John A. & Pamelia, rocf Pur. 11-7-1860 with parents; mbrp relinquished 3-1880
Gulielma d 1- 6-1800 bHS
John Quincy m Permelia (or Pamelia) ----- d 6-4-1885
Ch: Phebe Ann
Emily Augusta
William
cf Pur. 11-7-1860 with 3 ch named; John Q. relrq 8-1869
Martha I., dt David & Paulina, N. Y.; m 1861
L. Murray FERRIS, Jr.
Mary rocf Jericho 11-20-1794
Mary H. rocf Chap. 8-1844; d 11-2-1847 (H)
Paulina, wd Daniel, d 7-14-1882
Ch: William L. b 6-27-1848
Agnes C. " 11-24-1851
cf Oblong 1834
Phebe Ann, dt John Q. & Pamelia, rocf Pur. 11-7-1860 with parents; ct Morean 4-1880, a minister
Thomas & Anna G.
Ch: Sarah Elizabeth b 7- 7-1833
Mary " 3- 4-1836
cf Chap. 7-10-1823 (clear); cf N.P. 5-19-1831 for Anna G.; he dis 6-1830 (0); she dis 5-1843 (0); ct Creek 8-1838 for all
Treadwell & -----
Ch: Theodocious d 4- 9-1804 ae 2m bHS

SARAFIAN
Gadar, dt George & Solomon (both dec); m 1890 Sarkis BASMAJIAN

SARLES
Susan Amelia, w Leander, dt John & Abigail HOSIER, d 9-26-1875 (H)

SATEL, SANTELL
Henry, Newtown, active mbr from 1676; d 11 Mo. (Jan) 13, 1703/4; frequently written Safely

SATTERTHWAIT
Asa M. m Hannah B. ----- d 10-8-1866 (H)
Ch: William E.
Hannah M. b 8-11-1856 d 2- 1-1858
Job " 11-23-1861 d 12-30-1861
Josepha Y. b 12-19-1863
cf Phila. 9-1855 for Asa; cf Chesterfield same date for Hannah & William; ct Chesterfield 8-4-1869 for Asa, William & Josepha

SAUNDERS
Edward A. (nm) m Elizabeth ----- (nm)
Ch: Edward W. d 9-13-1849 ae 2y 4m 16d bPP, rem to Flush. 9-17-1895
Lillie d 3-21-1861 ae 5y 11m 20d bPP, rem to Flush. 9-17-1895
Edwin rocf Southwark 11-14-1837; dis 3-1843
Eliza L., dt Barney & Mary CORSE, b 12-28-1829; dis 9-3-1851 (H)
Elizabeth Clark, dt John & Hannah, rocf Wilmington 8-3-1827; dis 8-1831 (0); ct Phila. Spruce St. 1-1838
Frederick rocf Kingston, Eng. 2-25-1854; absent 3-1868; d 1-28-1876
Hannah, w John
Ch: Elizabeth Clark
Mary Ann
cf Wilmington 8-3-1827; all dis 8-1831 (0); ct Spruce St., Phila. 1-1838 for Hannah (H)
Mary Ann b Del. d 10-5-1833 ae 31y 10m bHS; cf Wilmington 8-3-1827; dis 8-1831

SAURNEUF
Marie Louise (nm), dt Celestin & Marie C.; m 7-30-1911 Reuben B. DAVENPORT (H)

SAVAGE
Charity gct Flushing 2-12-1812; cf Wby 1-15-1817; ct Flushing 10-3-1821; cf Flush. 5-1843; d 8-19-1863 ae 82y bPP
Crossfield rocf Strickland MM, Westmoreland, Eng. 7-19-1810 (clear); dis mo 1-7-1818; rem to Savannah
Eliza D., dt Jose R. F. & Mary H., Jackson Hts, b Hempstead 9-20-1907; m 1932 Ellwood G. GRIFFEN, of Pur. (H)
Jose R. F. (nm), s Edw. & Teresa F. (both dec); m at 15th St. 10-18-1899 Mary Eliz. HUTCHINSON, dt John Wm. & E. Eliza, N. Y., b 3-21-1875, Balt. (H)
Ch: Ramona Teresa b N. Y. 8-12-1904
Eliza Dutton b Hempstead 9-20-1907
Ramona T., dt Jose R. F. & Mary H., Bkn., b N.Y. 8-12-1904; m 1928 Wm. J. NEUENSCHWANDER, Jr. (nm), Sistervill W. Va. (H)
Robert & Sarah
Robert form dis; Sarah mo before 2-1-1811, ret mbrp & took rem ct Flushing 2-12-1811
Robert, having been dis by Hull MM, Eng., N.Y. rq to show him copy; rpd having done so 11-4-1812
Samuel & Hannah
cf Scipio 12-20-1827 for both; ct Scipio 12-2-1829 for both (O); Samuel dis 1829 (H)

SAWYER
Benaiah rocf Nantucket 6-29-1814 (clear); ct Balt. W. Dist. 2-6-1822 (clear); cf Balt. W. Dist. 12-9-1825; dis 1-1830 (O)
Marguerite (nm), dt John T. & Florence (Streeter); m 1922 Richard GRIFFEN
Moses G. rocf Weare, N. H. 9-11-1845 (clear); ct Weare 1-6-1847 (clear)
Viola m David S. TATUM
recrq 11-1923
Walter rocf Dover, N. H. 2-27-1811 (clear); he having lived 2 years past in Nantucket, cf that MM had been sent to Dover; ct Dover, N. H. 10-1-1823 (clear)

SAYLOR
David Sutton m Anna DORLAND
Ch: Parry Dorland
cf Glens Falls 4-4-1906 with 1 ch named; ct West Lake, Canada 7-3-1912 for all

SAYMAN
Abraham, White Plains, rocf Whitewater, Ind. 12-1883; cannot be found; name erased 8-1920

SAYRES
Abigail, w Isaac, gct R.& P. 6-4-1817; cf R.& P. 3-15-1843; dis joining M.E. Ch. 11-1851
Rebekah [Sayr] (nm) m (prob. 1906 or 1907) Thomas Burling HALLOCK (H)

SCALES
Alice Cynthia, dt Edward S. & Alice L., b 1-15-1908; m 1922 Harvey D. JONES
cf Glens Falls 12-5-1906 with parents; active mbr 12-1923
Edward S. m Alice L. CARY, dt Jervis & Sarah (Eddy), b Glens Falls 9-30-1866 d 12-1-1926 bPP
Ch: Harold E. b 3-25-1894
Margaret L. b 2- 5-1897
Alice Cynthia b 1-15-1908
cf Glens Falls 12-5-1906 with 2 ch named
Freeman m Anna DAVIS
Ch: Elizabeth b 9-30-1911
Ruth " 3-12-1914
cf Washington 9-1926 for all
Harold E., s Edward S. & Alice L., b 3-25-1894; cf Glens Falls 12-5-1906 with parents; letter to Richmond Hill Bapt. Ch., N. Y. 7-1915
Margaret L., dt Edw. S. & Alice L., b Glens Falls 2-5-1897; m 1930 August GARONE

SCANTLEBURY
Alfred L., s Edward & Mary A., b 8-10-1855 d 1935; relrq 5-7-1898; joined Episc. (H)
Amy T., dt Edw. & Mary Anna, Bkn., b 9-1-1872; m 1899 Wm. Lloyd KINKEAD (nm) (H)
Edward, s Samuel & Sarah (Wray), b Albany, 3-5-1831 d 12-12-1914; m at Enoch Stratton's 10-11-1854 Mary Anna STRATTON, dt Enoch & Amy (Thorn), N. Y., b Phila. 5-9-1833 d 1-11-1924 ae 90y bPP (H)
Ch: Alfred L. b 8-10-1855
Joseph " 4-18-1858 d 3-12-1861 bPP
Edward T. " 2-23-1871 " 2-24-1872 bPP
Amy T. " 9- 1-1872
Sarah Wray b 11-19-1874 d 4-17-1875 bPP
Mary Anna rocf Phila., Green St., 10-1848 with parents
Emilie L., dt Enoch & Amy T.; m William F. HULL (H)
cf Phila. Green St. with parents 10-1848
John B., s Samuel & Sarah (Wray), b Kips Bay, N. Y. 5-29-1829 d 1-14-1906; m 11-15-1855 Louisa J. JEFPEYS (nm), dt Charles & Mary Anna (H)
Ch: Infant stillborn 10-14-1856 bPP
was at Proffit, Va. 1900
Joseph rocf Leicester, Eng. 2-19-1824 (clear); dis 4-1830 (O); ct Scipio 7-1831 (H)
Samuel m Sarah RAY, dt Christopher (H)
Ch: (prob) John b N. Y. d 4-27-1827 ae 1y
John Barlow b 5-29-1829
Edward " 5- 3-1831
Sarah J. " 10-10-1832
Thomas " 1-22-1835
Elizabeth " 10- 5-1836 d 4-24-1840
Ann " 9- 2-1840 d 10-25-1907 bPP
Joseph " 10- 7-1842
cf Hudson 8-22-1826 for both; ct Coey. 9-

SCANTLEBURY, Samuel & Sarah, continued
1834 (H); dis 1832,1835 (O); cf Coey. 3-1838; ct Scip. 7-1846; cf Scip. 8-7-1850 for all
Sarah, dt Samuel & Sarah (Wray), b Albany 10-12-1832 d 12-10-1921; m 1855 Joseph W. HAMBLETON (nm) (H)
both bPP
Thomas, s Samuel & Sarah, b 1-22-1835 d 8-1-1864; Lieutenant in Army, killed at White River (H)
Sarah, dt Samuel & Sarah; m ----- HAMBLETON (H) was at Chicago 1859

SCARBOROUGH
John gct Buckingham, Pa. 3-3-1757

SCHANK
Susanna Stansbury (form Schank) rocf R. & P. 11-19-1812; dis mo 4-2-1823

SCHELL
Augustus (nm) m 3-25-1873 Anna M. FOX, dt George & Rebecca L., b 3-31-1827 d 1-5-1905 (H)

SCHENCK
Sarah, dt Peter & Parmelia STOUGHTENBURG, rocf Creek with parents 8-22-1823 d 5-16-1860
Susan (or Screnck) (nm) b Rahway d 1-10-1828 ae 39y bHS

SCHIEFFELIN
Jacob d 8-8-1800 bHS

SCHISSEL
Louis (nm) b 1838 d 7-23-1899 ae 61y; m Agnes GOERKE, dt Rudolph & Paulina, d 1-11-1931 ae 81y bPP
Ch: Edmund b 12-4-1883 d 7-12-1912 Newark, N. J. bPP
Agnes V.
Agnes recrq of parents 1860; Agnes V. recrq 1-5-1910
Selma, dt Francis & Louisa, b Ger. 12-13-1850 d 11-27-1926 at Montclair bPP; m Oscar GOERKE
Selma recrq 12-2-1908

SCHLICHT
Clara, dt Otto & Caroline (Bogemann), b Bkn. 12-31-1885; m 1908 Arthur FIEHN (H)
both recrq 8-13-1917
Julius, s Otto & Caroline (Bogemann), b Bkn. 12-6-1883; m 6-23-1906 Antonia WEBLUS, dt John C. & Helen (Hartwig), b Hoboken 9-27-1886 (H)
both recrq 8-13-1917

SCHMUCK
Edward W. rocf H. & R. 4-5-1848; ct H. & R. 2- 2-1853 (H)

SCHNEER
Frederick Hirlman (nm) m 4-27-1898 Mary B. MEAD, dt George V. & Mary (Birdsall), b 11-6-1875 (H) Mary's name entered by comm. 3-13-1883

SCHNEIDER
Margaret, dt Christopher F. & Louisa E. (Westbrook), b Altoona, Pa. 4-25-1869; m 1906 George W. STRATTAN (H)
recrq 2-9-1907

SCHOCKE
Arthur (nm) m Alice E. UNDERHILL, dt Alexander & Ada A. (Livingston), b 8-11-1893 Bkn. d 9-21-1915 Bkn bPP
Alice recrq of parents 11-4-1903

SCHOFIELD
Edith, dt Frank & Harrietta (Broadbent) b Bolton, Eng. 1-7-1883; m 1926 Adrian U. TREADWELL (H)
Wm. Henry, Jr. (nm), s Wm. H. & Ellen B.; m 9-5-1918 Natilie W. KISSAM, dt Albert W. & Margaret (Woolley), b N. Y. 3-29-1892 (H)
Natilie recrq 7-9-1917

SCHOLEFIELD
George, resided in Exeter, Eng., went to London then to N. Y., lived 110 Broadway; dis 3-1851

SCHURMAN
Charles F., s Frederick & Jane, b N. Y. 1-24-1884; recrq 6-17-1917; name erased 4-1927

SCHWARTZ
Annie recrq 2-5-1930; ct First Friends Church, Los Angeles, 1-4-1933

SCHWEIKERT
William, s Wm. & Emma, b Bkn. 2-4-1893; letter from Bapt. Temple, Bkn. 6-4-1917; name erased 4-1927

SCIFFINGTON
George granted rem cert 3 Mo (May) 1, 1701

SCOFIELD
Mary L. (or Mary Ellen), dt Jehu & Eliz. LIPPINCOTT (w Ebenezer, m 12-25-1862) relrq 5-3-1893 (H)
Rebecca rocf Chap. 12-1873; ct Chap. 2-7-1883

SCOTT
Austin Allen, s Jas. Thos. & Abbie Rebecca W. (Walton), b Wilmington, Del. 12-8-1890; m 6-1-1918 Wally B. BECK (nm), dt Adam & Marie (Vox Arx) (H)
cf Wilmington 5-10-1926; ct Wby 9-9-1929
Jane gct Shrews. 8-3-1786 (clear)
Joseph & Sarah
Ch: Sarah b 6 Mo (Aug) 12, 1742
Joseph b 4 Mo (June) 18, 1744
John b 12 Mo (Feb) 20, 1747/8

SCOTT, Joseph & Sarah, continued
Ch: Catharine b 2 Mo (Apr) 14, 1749
rem ct Plaistow MM, Eng. 6-6-1754; cf Phila. 5-25-1781, he having heard of the d of his dt & concerned for gr ch; ct Phila. for Joseph 12-5-1781 (clear)
Lamphear H. (nm), s John W. & Jane P., Cadiz, Ohio; m at J. R. Williams' 7-17-1901 Julia Matilda WILLIAMS, dt Jacob R. & Jane Maria (Beth), Newark, N. J., b 9-10-1856 d 1-27-1924 (H)
Julia recrq of parents 10-1868
Mary, dt Job, rocf Providence 7-25-1810 (clear) ct Renss. 8-2-1826 (clear)

SCRIBNER
Maria (nm) d 11-11-1820 ae 26y 1m 5d bHS, w -----
Ch: Mary Ann d 5-1-1821 ae 6m

SCRIVEN
James rem to South Kingston, R. I. 12 Mo (Feb) 6, 1745/6

SCUDDER
Henry, Hempstead, d 11 Mo (Jan) 29, 1731/2
Samuel d 11 Mo (Jan) 1688/9; m Phebe -----
Phebe m 2d 1690 Robert FIELD

SEAMAN
Amy, dt Gilbert & Mary, Flushing; m 1784 Walter FARRINGTON
Ann (or Anna), dt Dr. Valentina & Anna, b 3-18-1812; m ----- FERRIS (H)
dis 12-1843
Avis L., dt Willet & Mary, b 10-4-1816; m 6-24-1875 Robert M. MASTERTON (H)
ret a mbr
Ayree Cromwell, s Henry B. & Grace (Dutton), b Bkn. 8-1-1905; m 2-4-1932 Ann M. STEWART (nm), dt Hugh & Susanna (Moran) (H)
Benjamin active mbr 1701
Benjamin m 1815 Phila. -----
cert of clear to Phila. 10-4-1815
Benjamin R. d 1-30-1824 ae 42; m Amy ----- d Flushing 1825
Amy rocf Flushing 11-7-1816
Caroline H., dt Dr. Wm. & Hannah H., b 6-3-1868; m William A. READ (nm) (H)
relrq 7-10-1897
Clarissa b N. Y. d 1-30-1824 ae 42y bHS
Cora, dt Wm. Henry & Laura Eliz. (Carpenter), b N. Y. 4-1-1869 d 1- 2-1936; recrq 4-8-1899 (H)
David (nm) & Sarah (nm)
Ch: Lydia d 1-15-1864 bPP
Edmund, s Jacob & Hannah; m 10-16-1865 Mary S. WILLITS, dt Edward S. & Esther (Whitson), b Wby 2-10-1832 d 1-10-1928 ae 96y (H)
Ch: Elizabeth b Wby 12-30-1870
Mary rocf Wby 3-7-1903 with Elizabeth
Elias H. rocf Jericho 10-1852; ct Jericho 4-7-1858 (H)
Eliza, dt Dr. Valentine & Anna, b 5-9-1815; m ----- LEGGETT (mo)
dis 7-5-1837
Elizabeth recrq 4-3-1816 d Hempstead, L. I. (H)
Elizabeth, w James, d 9-11-1855 ae 81y bPP
Ch: Sarah R.
Thomas M.
recrq 4-2-1817; Sarah R. & Thomas recrq of mother 6-4-1817; all dis 1830-1833 (O)
Elizabeth m Jesse BALDWIN
cf Corn. 8-25-1825 (clear); dis 6-1831 (O)
Elizabeth, dt Jonathan & Martha, N. Y.; m 1832 Jesse Baldwin, Jr. (H)
Elizabeth, dt Edmund & Mary S. (Willits), b Wby 12-30-1870; cf Wby 3-7-1903 (H)
Elizabeth (nm), dt Horace & Elvira M. (Foster) m 1906 Frank HAVILAND (H)
Elizabeth H., wd William, dt Isaac HICKS, of Matinecock, rocf Wby 10-1824; ct Wby & Jericho 9-2-1829 (clear) (O); ct Wby 7-1829 (H)
Frederick Augustus, s Willet & Mary J., b 4-7-1811; dis 3-1-1848 (H)
Frederick C., s Valentine H. & Rebecca (Cromwell), b 10-6-1880 d 1-19-1910; m 4-4-1908 Ethel LOBDELL (nm), dt George G. (H)
George (nm) & -----
Ch: Eliza b N. Y. d 9-22-1834 ae 25y bHS (unm)
John W. b N. Y. d 2-2-1840 ae 33y 8m bHS (unm)
George W. d 7-11-1821 ae 13d
Gideon, s Thomas & Hannah, Wby; m Flushing 2-14-1782 Elizabeth KEESE, dt Wm. & Mary (dec), Flushing
Elizabeth gct Wby 5-5-1782
Gilbert & Mary
Mary rocf Wby 7-28-1773
Gulielma Matilda, dt Willet & Mary J., b 7-10-1809 d 1847; m ----- SMITH (H)
dis 10-1831 (H); dis (O)
Hannah mo before 9-2-1762 (H)
Hannah P. rocf Corn. 11-1851; ct 3-2-1859
Harriet d 2-2-1810 ae 2y bHS
Henry B., s Valentine H. (dec) & Rebecca, b N. Y. 1-20-1861; m at Charles Dutton's 4-7-1904 Grace DUTTON, dt Charles & Ellen M., East Orange, b Chicago 8-5-1870 (H)
Ch: Ayres Cromwell b 8- 1-1905 Bkn.
Henry B. Jr. b 3-30-1908 Bkn.
Grace recrq 3-9-1907
Henry Jenkins, s Willet & Mary, Jr., b 7-13-1813; dis 4-1853 (H)
Jacob & Ann
Ch: Jemima
cf Wby 6-29-1774; dt (clear); ct Wby with w, Ann, & dt 5-7-1778; Jamima (clear) 1778; cf Wby with w & young s, James 7-26-1780
Jacob, Jr. gct Devonshire House 3-3-1784 (clear), he on business; cf 2 weeks mtg, London 9-12-1785 (clear)
Jacob gct Jericho 3-6-1793 (clear)
James, s Obadiah, d 8-20-1799 bHS; cf Wby 9-25-1782; dis 8-5-1790

SEAMAN, continued
James d 7-4-1800 bHS; another d 6-26-1801 bHS
James (nm) b Glen Cove d 4-16-1823 ae 61y 3m bHS (m)
James (nm) b N. Y. d 3-6-1826 ae 23y bHS (m)
Dr. James V., s Valentine & Anna, b 3-1-1799; dis mo 1824
John F. (changed name from Walter), s Dr. Valentine & Anna, b 3-22-1801; dis 5-1837 (H)
John G., s Zebulon & Mary, N. Y.; m N. Y. 11-12-1835 Ann R. WALL, dt Humphrey & Edith (dec), N. Y. (H)
Ch: William H. b 11- 1-1836
cf Jericho 6-1829 for John; cf Chesterfield 6-1830 for Ann; ct R. & P. 11-1852 for all
Joseph H., s Samuel H. & Hannah (Husband), b Bkn. 2-28-1865; m Josephine R. NOTMAN (nm), dt Henry T. (H)
Lydia rocf Jericho 8-1844; d 1-15-1864 (H)
Martha H., dt John & Amy (Pearsall), b Monroe 8-10-1834 d 4-25-1931; m 1878 George S. BRINKERHOFF (H)
cf Corn. 1-1-1879
Mary, Flushing, b 2 Mo (Apr) 6, 1737 d 12-4-1792
Mary, dt Willet & Mary, N. Y.; m 1815 Wm. Richardson THURSTON
Mary (nm) b Eng d 2-29-1848 ae 86y 7m 13d bHS (wd)
Mary, w Samuel, recrq 7-3-1833; ct Farm. 6-3-1839, cert ret 2-20-1840; d 9-19-1841 ae 62y 10m 28d
Mary Ann m ----- MIDDLEBROOK (H); d 10-16-1831
Nathaniel, Hempstead, m at Henry Willis' 8 Mo (Oct) 9, 1695 Rachel WILLIS, dt Henry & Mary
Ch: Rachel b 5 Mo (July) 26, 1696 d 11 Mo 25, 1702
Nathaniel b 11 Mo (Jan) 18, 1699/00
Hester " 9 Mo (Nov) 8, 1701
Jacob " 8 Mo (Oct) 10, 1703
Abraham " 11 Mo (Jan) 10, 1706
Rachel " 1 Mo (Mar) 9, 1708/9
Hezekiah " 3 Mo (May) 11, 1711
Thomas " 11 Mo (Jan) 2, 1713
Samuel " 4 Mo (June) 13, 1715
Nathaniel active mbr from 1698
Obadiah & Mary
Ch: James
Richard
cf Wby 6-2-1788 for Mary, indisposed; cf Wby 9-25-1782 for James & Richard who had gone with their father when young
Obadiah rocf Wby, rem some yrs past 6-24-1789
Percival, s Dr. Valentine & Anna, dis (H)
Phebe m ----- WILLIAMS
cf Corn. 9-22-1825 (clear); dis 9-1830 (0); ct Ama. 5-1837 (H)
Richard, s Richard, Wby; m Jane MOTT, dt Adam & Mary
Ch: Richard b 11 Mo (Jan) 31, 1694/5
Thomas " 10 Mo (Dec) 17, 1696
Tamar " 5 Mo (July) 21, 1699
Ch: Jane b 8 Mo (Oct) 16, 1701
Adam " 7 Mo (Sep) 11, 1704
Sarah b 1 Mo (Mar) 4, 1706/7
Richard, s Obadiah, rocf Wby 9-25-1782; dis 5-7-1795
Richard (nm) & -----
Ch: ----- d 3- 1-1803 ae 3d bHS
Samuel & Kezia
Ch: Thomas
cf Newport 9-28-1780 with w & s; ct Wby 9-5-1781 for Samuel & w, Kezia, & young s, Thomas, having again returned to Wby
Samuel & -----
Ch: Henrietta b Manhattonville d 3-13-1830 ae 10y bHS
(mbr elsewhere)
Samuel (nm) d 8-30-1841 ae 52y 7m 15d bHS; m Mary ----- (nm) d 9-19-1841 ae 62y 10m 28d bHS
Ch: Gideon b Bloomingdale, N. Y. d 9-21-1813 ae 1y 4m bHS
Mary b Manhattanville d 8-1-1815 ae 1y 10m bHS
Samuel rocf Jericho 1-1844; d 9-26-1850 (H)
Samuel H., s Dr. Wm. & Caroline, b 11-26-1838 N. Y. d 1-25-1901 bPP; m 9-15-1863 Hannah HUSBAND, dt Thos. J. & Mary R., b Phila. 10-21-1837 d 7- 4-1912 bPP (H)
Ch: Joseph H. b Bkn. 2-28-1865
Mary Thomas b L. I. 7-13-1872 d 5-10-1931 at Morristown bPP
Sarah b Bkn. 8-21-1875
Franklin d 8- 7-1896 ae 26y bPP
Sarah (late Bowne) dis mo before 7-3-1811
Sarah gct Cornwall 8-2-1820 (clear)
Sarah, dt Wm. & Caroline H., N. Y., d 12-30-1913 ae 77y bPP; m 1856 Henry B. CROMWELL; m 2d ----- BENEDICT (H)
Sarah, dt Samuel H. & Hannah (Husband), b Bkn. 8-21-1873; m 1902 Lloyd SALTUS (H)
relrq 7-13-1907
Sarah R., dt James & Elizabeth; m 6-27-1855 Frank HAY (nm) by J.P. (H)
recrq of mother 6-4-1817; ret a mbr
Susan H., dt Samuel & Phebe P., b Corn. 8-15-1840 d 9-27-1924; m 1865 Silas T. ROBBINS (H)
cf Corn. 3-1-1871
Thomas, s Obediah, rocf Wby 6-30-1779
Thomas (nm) b Westchester Co. d 11-1-1821 ae 30y 21d bHS (widower)
Thomas, s James & Elizabeth, d 8-16-1883 ae 73y bPP (H)
Thomas, Jr. rocf Wby 11-19-1800; dis 6-7-1815
Thomas M., s James & Elizabeth, recrq of mother 6-4-1817; dis 3-1845 (H)
Dr. Valentine, s Henry & Hannah (dec), N. Y., b 4-2-1770 d 6-27-1817 bHS; m N. Y. 5-7-1794 Anna FERRIS, dt John & Anna, b 12-8-1771 d 11-5-1854
Ch: ----- d 3-23-1796
William F. (Dr.) b 2- 3-1797
James V. (Dr.) b 3- 1-1799

SEAMAN, Dr. Valentine & Anna, continued
Ch: Walter (changed to John F.) b 3-22-1801
Valentine (Dr.) b 9-30-1802
Percival " 10-11-1804
Willet J. " 6- 9-1808
Mary Anna " 4-20-1810
Anna " 3-18-1812
Eliza " 5- 9-1815
all dis 1828-1839 (0)
Dr. Valentine, s Valentine & Anna, b 9-3-1802 d 3-29-1899; m 1838 Anna Amelia FERRIS, dt Elijah & Amelia
dis 2-1839 (H)
Valentine H., s Dr. Wm. & Caroline, b 6-9-1834 N. Y. d 9-27-1902 bPP; m 10-7-1856 Rebecca CROMWELL, dt James & Charlotte (or David & Rebecca), b Corn. 7-20-1835 d 7-30-1915 bPP (H)
Ch: William b 7- 5-1857 d 2-26-1892
Caroline H. b 2-23-1859 d 11-18-1859 bPP
Henry B. " 1-20-1861
Edwin H. " 10- 5-1862 d 8-25-1863 bPP
Howard " 11-23-1863 d 8-26-1883
Valentine H., Jr. b 5- 3-1872 d 4- 5-1931 bPP
Emily C. b 3- 5-1876
Frederick C. " 10- 6-1880
cf Corn. 4- 1-1857 for Rebecca & s
Wait B. rocf Corn. 6-1850; ct Chap. 6-3-1885 (H)
Walter (nm) d 1- 3-1831 ae 75y bHS; m -----
Ch: Infant stillborn 4-10-1822 bHS
cf Wby 7-28-1773, rec here 12-1-1773; dis 9-7-1774
Willet, s Samuel & Martha, N. Y., d 5-4-1807 ae 69; m Mary ----- d 6- 8-1813 ae 73y 11m 3d (H)
Ch: Gulielma b 3- 4-1772 d 3-18-1791
Mary " 9-14-1776
Rachel " 2-15-1779 d 7-30-1831
Willet " 6- 7-1781
Samuel " 3-17-1783 d 1-27-1803
Benjamin " 7-15-1787
Willet rem cf Wby 9-24-1777
Willet, s Willet & Mary, N. Y., b 6-7-1781 d 4-10-1864 ae 83y bPP; m Mary J. ----- b 4-8-1786 d 7-14-1880 (H)
Ch: Gulielma Matilda b 7-10-1809
Fred'k Augustus " 4- 7-1811
Henry Jenkins " 7-13-1813
Avis Leggett " 10- 4-1816
William K. " 8- 5-1818 d 1-24-1852 bPP
Willet Jr. b 7-10-1820 d 12- 7-1909
Mary J. " 3-30-1827 " 10-22-1829
all dis 1829-42 (0); cf ND MM 11-2-1808 for Mary J.
Willet H. rocf Jer. 8-1-1860; ct Jer. 4-5-1865 (H)
Willet J., s Dr. Valentine & Anna, b 7-10-1820; dis 4-1831 (0); dis 2-1847 (H) rst 3-3-1847 (mo)
Dr. William d 4-19-1855 ae 58y bPP, rem from Jericho 6-23-1868; m Caroline H. ----- d 2-2-1868 ae 60y bPP (H)
Ch: Valentine H. b 6- 9-1834
Sarah " 9-26-1836
Samuel H. " 11-26-1838
cf Jer. 11-1832 for Caroline
Dr. William m 2d 8-1863 Hannah H. -----
Ch: Joseph H. b 2-28-1865
Caroline H. b 6- 3-1868
Franklin b 12-23-1869 d 8- 8-1896
Mary " 7-13-1872
Sarah " 8-21-1875
Dr. William F., s Dr. Valentine & Anna, b 2-3-1797 d 1-12-1827; m Elizabeth H. -----
Ch: William F. d 3-26-1825 ae 10m
Sarah H. b 11-26-1825
cert of clear to Wby 9-4-1822; Elizabeth H. rocf Wby 4-14-1824; Elizabeth gct Wby & Jericho 9-1829
Wm. Valentine, s Willet & Mary, Jr. b 8-5-1818 d 1-24-1852 ae 33y 5m 19d; relrq 6-6-1849 (H)

SEARING
Elizabeth, dt John, rocf Pur. 7-4-1803 (clear)
John, Jr., N. Y. & Mary
Ch: Sarah b 8-24-1790
Phebe
cf Wby 5-18-1791 for John & Mary with ch, Sarah; ct Oblong for Mary with 2 ch 6-3-1795
Rachel (form Hauxhurst) dis mo 4-1833 (H)

SEARLES
Stephen B. (nm) m 5-7-1877 Wendella LIPPINCOTT, dt Jehu & Eliz. (Pitman), b N. Y. 10-12-1855 d 3-25-1923 (H)
Wendella recrq 10-8-1910

SEARS
Abigail rocf R. & P. 6-20-1798, having rem with her h

SECKLE
Harry Lee b 6-18-1864 d 10-4-1919 bPP; m Anna M. ----- (both nm)

SECOR
Benjamin B. & Sarah
Ch: Hannah
Joseph
Mary
Benjamin b 12-20-1825
Thomas
Elizabeth
cf Corn. 12-22-1825 with 3 ch named; ct Corn. 7-7-1830 with 4 ch named (0); ct Corn. 4-1831 for all (H)
Hannah, dt Benjamin & Sarah, Seneca, Mich.; m 1845 Joseph H. SMITH (H)
Hannah R., dt Willet & Hannah, rocf Jericho with father 8-1834; relrq 4-6-1834 (H)

SECOR, continued
Mary b New Rochelle d 2-7-1830 ae 63y 9m bHS (unm)
Phebe rocf Ama. 9-1859; ct Ama. 11-4-1863 (H)
Rebecca rocf Chap. 2-1842; ct Chap. 7-4-1849 (H)
Willet, s James & Hannah; m Hannah R. REYNOLDS
Ch: Elizabeth C.
Sarah Ann d 3-15-1836 ae 17y 9m
Obediah W.
Gilbert W. b Huntington, L. I. 4-18-1827 d 12-25-1916
Hannah R.
cf Pur. 10-12-1815 with ch, Elizabeth C.; ct Wby 6-2-1819 for all but last named; cf Wby 1-5-1823 with their dt, Sarah Ann; ct Jericho 5-3-1826 with first 2 ch
Willet m 2d N. Y. 5-13-1835 Lydia GARDNER, dt Noah & Sarah, N. Y., d 3-9-1867 (H)
cf Jer. 8-1834 for Willet & ch; cf Flush. 12-1828 for Lydia

SECORD
Catharine, dt James & Catharine; m 1790 James HAUXHURST
Mary Jane (nm) m George A. McDOWELL (H)

SEDGWICK
Anthony rocf Lisburn MM, Ire. 4-16-1801 (clear)

SEE
John d 7-25-1838 ae 70y m Maria -----
Marie recrq 12-5-1832 (O); John rq mbrp 1821, returned to him 9-3-1821; recrq 2-5-1823; dis 1829 (H)

SEED
Emma C., dt Joseph & Sarah (Green), b Eng. 1852 d 3-29-1935 bPP; m John WALKER (both nm)
John Hartley (nm), s Joseph & Elizabeth, b 8-12-1843, Maidstone, Eng. d Red Bank, N.J. 7-28-1918 bPP; m Mary Louise ALLEN, dt Isaac H. & Susan W., b N. Y. 8-1850 d 1-15-1909 bPP
Mary recrq of parents 1859
Joseph H. (nm) d 1-10-1905 ae 79y 5m 14d bPP; m Elizabeth -----
Ch: John Hartley
Mary Louisa, dt Isaac H. & Susan W. ALLEN, recrq of parents 1859; name erased 2-7-1900

SEELY
Harriet V. S., dt Wm. S. & Abigail WOOD, rocf Marl. with parents 1-21-1835; ct Haddonfield 2-5-1840, minor; cf Haddonfield 5-10-1841; dis mo 3-1849
Sands [Seeley], nm, b Stamford, Conn. d 12-1-1811 bHS ae 23y

SEERY
Hannah B., w -----
Ch: Hector
Hannah recrq 2-1885; Hector recrq of mother 2-1886; Hector's name erased 2-7-1900

SEGAR
George W. (nm), s Ormalo (or possibly Climalo) (dec) & Romalie, Brisco, N. Y.; m 6-5-1906 at 308 E. 44th St. Mary R. RAYNOR, dt Geo. (dec) & Susan W., Sheffield, Eng.
Mary recorded as per Disc. 5-12-1896

SELLECK
Alice D., dt James W. & Eliz. M. (Betts), bBkn. 9-13-1864; m 1888 Wm. Mickle HAINES (H)
both recrq 12-9-1929
Sands [Sellick] d 5-7-1883; m Anna ----- d 8-8-1909
Sands recrq 9-1871; Anna recrq 5-1884

SELLERS
Maurice A. (nm), s Albert & Hannah (Laraby); m Phyllis KOMORI, dt Norie & Elizabeth (Knowlton), b Brockley, London 8-23-1898 (H); Phyllis recrq of mother 5-7-1884

SEMMLER
Fritz & Alta
Ch: Henry Charles b 12-31-1929
parents recrq 7-6-1932; s recrq of parents 7-6-1932

SERRILL
Frances, dt Pearson & Rachel (Starr), b Phila. 9-2-1830 d 12-11-1906; m 1853 Edward FLASH (nm) (H)
cf Darby 5-1856

SESSIONS
James d 3 Mo (May) 7, 1687

SEXAUR
William, s Ernest & Hedwig, b L. I. City 5-5-1894; recrq 5-21-1917; name erased 4-1927

SEYMOUR
Drake rocf Corn. 7-27-1815; ct Corn. 1-2-1822 (clear)
Esther E., dt Wm. & Esther, N. Y., d 1834; m 1833 Thomas COCK
cf Corn. 11-23-1826 (clear); dis 1829 (H)
Manning L., s Levi & Huldah, Johnstown, N. Y., b Conn. d 2-12-1826 ae 34y; m N. Y. 6-5-1823 Mary WOOD, dt Samuel & Mary, N. Y.
Ch: William W.
ct Galway 12-3-1823 for Mary W.; cf Galway 5-11-1826 for Mary with s named; Manning L. d after rqc 1826; Mary dis 10-1844; William dis 3-3-1847; Mary W. withdrew 1828 (H)
Mary E., dt Henry & Esther, N. Y.; m 1889 Egbert G. McDOWELL (H)
recrq 8-1-1888
William W., s Manning L. & Mary, rocf Galway with mother 5-11-1829; dis 3-3-1847 (O)

SHAFFER
Louise (nm), dt Thos. & Amanda HAZARD; m 1872 Henry H. WEEKS (H)

SHANNON
John K., s Elwood & Mary, Phila.; m at Henry CROMWELL's 9-2-1869 Helen CROMWELL, dt Henry & Sarah M., N. Y. (Henry Cromwell not under care of N. Y. MM) (H)

SHAPTER
John S. d 2-12-1871 ae 55y 5m 5d bPP, rem from Greenwood; m 3-10-1845 Hannah UNDERHILL, dt Samuel & Eliza, d 3-31-1886 ae 72y 1m bPP (H) Hannah m 1st ----- HUSSON
Rebecca, w -----
Ch: Evangeline
    Wilberforce
    cf Chap. 11-5-1862 with 2 ch named; ct Chap. 3-1866 with same

SHARP
Benjamin, having mo, WD MM ref. to N. Y. 1-1859; ack rec & cf WD MM 12-1859; ct Frankford 8-1861; cf Frankford 10-1861; ct WD MM 1-1866
Hannah, w Benjamin, rocf Phila. 4-1858; ct Phila. 10-7-1868 (H)
Priscilla, dt Mary EVANS, recrq 3-1872; ret a mbr; name erased

SHARPLESS
Aaron d 8-26-1798, N. Y.; m Mary ----- d 3-16-1797
Ch: Rebecca b 4- 9-1785 d 6-10-1786
    John " 5-17-1787 " 11-11-1787
    Sarah " 10- 2-1788
    Joseph " 5-12-1790
    Mary
    cf Falls 4-5-1786 for Aaron & Mary; ct Wilmington for Sarah, Joseph & John, 4-3-1799
Isaac, s Benj. & Sarah (dec), of Phila.; m N.Y. 4-13-1791 Margaret DOBSON, dt Thos. & Margaret, N. Y., d 10-18-1834 ae 73y (wd)
Ch: Hannah b 9-21-1793
    Edith " 9-17-1795
    Thomas " 2-23-1797 d before 1813
    Anne " 10- 7-1798
    Mary " 2- 8-1801
    Isaac " 4- 6-1803 d 7-16-1803 ae 3m
    Isaac D. b 1-20-1805
    Isaac rocf Wilmington 7-11-1787 (clear); ct Corn. 4-14-1813 for both with 5 ch
Mary rocf Phila. 1-25-1799 (clear); ct ND MM 6-3-1802
Mary D. rst 3-1839; ct WD MM 3-3-1841 (clear)
Thomas gct Chesterfield 4-14-1813, apprentice

SHARRACK (or Sharrock)
Mary Ellen m 1906 Joseph Nathaniel MILTON recrq 3-1-1905

SHAURMAN
Emily L. (nm), dt Isaac & Amanda (Avery); m 1853 Nelson SMITH (H)
    Nelson recrq 3-14-1914

SHAW
Annie (nm) d 8-18-1909 ae 70y bPP (unm) (H)
Frank Stinson (nm), s Wm. R. & Jennie R. (Stinson) (dec), Bath, Me.; m at Stephen Valentine's 3-15-1816 Helen Elise VALENTINE, dt Stephen & Annie (Lewis), Bkn., b Bkn. 10-27-1890 (H)
Joseph O'Neill recrq 12-4-1907
Maria b Flushing d 10-27-1810 ae 34y 1m 6d bHS
Mary rocf R. & P. 10-1868; d 2-10-1878 (H)
Mary rocf Lisburn, Ireland 5-1-1929
Ralph Robert, s Max & Pauline (Sandbing), b Detroit, 5-18-1907; m 11-27-1929 Viola Susan LEFF (nm), dt Wm. & Janet (H)
    Ralph recrq 4-9-1934

SHAY
Francis L. recrq 1809; dis 2-1832 (O); d 4-23-1852 (H)

SHEARBACK
Rose B. recrq 6-12-1901; name erased 4-1928

SHEARMAN
Almira (nm) b N. Y. d 10-23-1809 ae 1y 4m bHS
David S. rocf WD MM 12-7-1904
Samuel M. rocf Cincin. 7-2-1902

SHEARON
Richard recrq 4-3-1935

SHEFFIELD
Edward rocf So. Kingston, R. I. 12-25-1848; dis mo 3-1851
George Haviland m Sarah Louise CHILD, dt Wm. & Anna (Thomas), d 3-27-1931 ae 89y bPP (H)
John rocf South Kingston, R. I. 5-25-1818 (clear); ct South Kingston, R. I. 2-2-1820 (clear)
Rebecca rocf Marl. 12-1848; d 5-2-1870 (H)

SHENCK
----- & -----
Ch: John S. b Shrews. d 8-21-1824 ae 1y bHS

SHEPHERD
Albert G. recrq 4-3-1901; ct Stanford 10-7-1908
Allen (nm) b New Bedford d 10-10-1824 ae 53y bHS (m)
Caleb W., s Wm. R. & Eliza Ann (Keese), b Saratoga 10-4-1841 d 10-14-1917; m 10-8-1879 Sarah WILLETS, dt Edmund & Martha (Whitson) b Flush. 4-7-1838 d 10-30-1918 (H)
    cf Sara. 10-3-1888 for Caleb; cf Wby 8-3-1887 for Sarah
Eliza Ann rocf Hudson 11-1879; d 12-21-1894

SHEPHERD, continued
Jonathan b New Bedford (nm) d 11-13-1825 ae 45y bHS (unm); rocf New Bedford 2-18-1800, apprentice to Isaac Hicks; dis 5-1-1816
Mary rocf Stackport, Eng. 11-27-1805 (clear); ct Corn. 6-7-1809 (clear); cf Corn. 10-22-1812 (clear)
Sarah, gr dt Joseph Scott, of Phila., while rem cert for her & other gr ch was being considered, she mo before 1-5-1785; other 2 gone with father to Nova Scotia
Sarah W. rocf Wby 8-3-1887 (H)
William , having mo, New Bedford ref. to N.Y. 4-6-1814; rpd favorably 5-4-1814

SHEPP
Caroline L., dt Samuel & Mary, b Frankford, Ind. 7-2-1843; m 1864 ----- JONES
recrq 5-20-1917; name erased 3-1922

SHERMAN
Isaac, s Samuel & Sarah (both dec); m N. Y. 4-20-1791 Margaret FITZGERALD, dt Gerald & Amelia, Pur.
Margaret Fitzgerald rocf Pur. 4-8-1790 (clear); Samuel & Sarah were of Stratford, Conn.; Margaret gct Jericho 6-8-1796
John D., s David S. (dec) & Hepsah H.; m at David M. Adams 1-18-1865 Emma ADAMS, dt David M. & Hannah C.
Ch: Charles b 7-17-1866
Mabel Adams b 10-21-1868
cf Balt. 1864 with parents for Emma; cf New Bedford 7-1863 for John D.; ct WD MM 4-1871 for all
(Name written Shearman in minutes)
Mary S., dt David S. & Hepsa H., b 3-25-1838 d 3-14-1921 bPP; m Thomas KIMBER

SHERPICK
Eugene Arthur & Nell
Ch: Ann Elizabeth
Wm. Edwards
Eugene A., Jr. bur 12-4-1932 ae 12y, auto accident
ch recrq of parents 4-5-1933

SHERWOOD
Elizabeth M., dt Isaac & Elizabeth, N. Y.; m 1841 Andrew G. COFFIN, of Nantucket (H)
Henry, s Isaac & Elizabeth (McCartae), b N. Y. 10-23-1823 d 6-9-1906; m ----- d 1873 (H)
recrq of parents 4-1836; lived at Tipton, Iowa
Isaac (nm) & -----
Ch: Peter b N. Y. d 6-27-1829 ae 20y 2m bHS
William b N. Y. d 10-11-1830 ae 18y 2m bHS
Robert b N. Y. d 10-17-1831 ae 5y 4m bHS
Lydia Catharine b N. Y. d 12-27-1844 ae 26y 11d bHS
Isaac d 1-13-1850 ae 70y 11m 6d bPP; m Elizabeth ----- d 2-7-1853 ae 65y 10m 5d bPP (H)
Ch: Lydia C. d 12-29-1844 ae 26y 13d bPP
Peter McCarty b 2-14-1833 d 10-23-1884 bPP
Isaac, Jr. recrq 4-1836
Henry " "
Mary M. " 8- 2-1848; d 4-18-1887 ae 72y 4m 14d bPP
cf Third Haven 12-16-1804 (clear); con mo 1-4-1809; dis 7-1829 (0)
Isaac, Jr., s Isaac & Elizabeth, recrq of parents 4-1836; ct Wby 6-6-1855 (H)
James rocf Third Haven, **Md.** (clear); dis mo before 12-4-1811
Mary (nm) b N. C. d 1-11-1842 ae 38y 8m bHS
Rachel F., w William, dt George & Sarah FERGUSON, dis mo 12-1836; recrq 4-1859; ct Pur. 1-3-1866; cf Pur. 7-7-1875 for Rachel F.; d 6-1-1885 (H)
William (nm) & -----
Ch: Infant stillborn 3-15-1839 bHS
----- & ----- (nm)
Ch: William d 10-12-1811 ae 10m bHS
John b N. Y. d 11-12-1834 ae 1m 27d bHS
Catharine b N. Y. d 2-18-1835 ae 5y 2m bHS

SHEY
Francis L. dis 1-4-1832 as Hicksite (0)

SHIPLEY
Ann M., dt Morris & Sarah, gct Cincinnati 6-7-1843 with parents; cf Cincinnati 1856; d 1-8-1875
Hannah rocf Warrington MM at Hardshaw, Eng., to Abington 8-19-1794 (clear); cf Abington 5-25-1794 endorsed on above cert
Hannah, dt Morris & Ann, b 6-24-1813 d 2-27-1837; m ----- VANDEVEER
John W. b 7-2-1810; ct Centre MM, Ohio 7-1833 (clear)
Joseph M., s Morris & Ann M., gct SD MM 11-7-1838 (clear)
Lucy E., dt Morris & Ann, b 1-24-1822; ct R. & P. 5-4-1842 with aunts, Hannah & Lucy H. Eddy
Morris m Ann ----- b Shrews. d 7-23-1824 ae 35y
Ch: Hannah 12 d 6-12-1805 ae 23y
Mary 11
Morris 9
Thomas Eddy b 11-10-1809 d 11-20-1830 bHS
William L. b 8- 6-1811 d 8-23-1837 bHS
Hannah " 6-24-1813 d 2-27-1837 bHS
Joseph Morris b 11- 5-1815 (or 5-11-1815)
Robert
Lucy Eddy b 1-24-1822
Ann M. " 6-27-1824
A ch of Morris' d 8-6-1796;Ann rocf Hardshaw Eng. 8-19-1794 to Abington with 3 ch, Hannah 12, Mary 11, Morris 9, endorsed to N.Y. 5-25-1795; Morris gct Abington from Phila. 4-24-1795, endorsed to N. Y. 5-25-1795; ct Oswego 10-2-1797 for Ann & same 3 ch; cf Oswego 11-18-1807 for Ann (clear); ct Centre MM, Ohio, 6-1-1831 for Ann, minister
Morris, s Morris (dec) & Ann, d 6-14-1859; m N. Y. 1-12-1826 Sarah H. SHOTWELL, dt Wm.

SHIPLEY, Morris & Sarah H., continued
& Sarah
Ch: Ann M.
Murray
Infant stillborn 12-22-1828
Morris rocf Oswego 12-17-1806 (clear); ct Cincinnati 6-7-1843 with minor ch, Ann M. & Murray; cf Cincinnati 1856
Morris m 2d N. Y. 2-14-1856 at Westchester, Mary SHOTWELL, dt Wm. & Sarah (both dec)
Morris J., s William & Phebe; m Susan M. MAKEEL
Ch: Jacob M. b 1830
Phebe Ann b 9- 6-1833
Hannah " 5-24-1838
cf Ama. 1-11-1833 for Susan; ct Ama. 6-7-1843 with 3 ch named
Robert, s Morris & Ann, dis mo by a priest 5-1845
Thomas C., s William & Phebe, b 5-16-1807; ct Centre MM, Ohio, 6-1-1831 (clear)
William & Phebe
Ch: Morris
Thomas C. b 5-16-1807
Child stillborn 5-23-1809
John W. b 7- 2-1810
Ann " 9-14-1812
Elizabeth C.
Mary P. b 2- 3-1820
Caroline " 9-16-1822
Henry " 4-19-1825
Jane " 4-19-1825
William " 8-29-1827
ct Oswego 2-3-1802 (clear); cf Oswego 10-14-1807 for both with 2 ch, Mofris & Thomas; ct Butternuts 6-7-1815 with first 4 ch named; cf Butternuts 7-2-1817 with 5 ch named; cf Butternuts 7-2-1817 with 5 ch named; ct Centre MM, Ohio 6-1-1831 with last 6 ch named

SHOEMAKER
Abraham d 9-4-1857 ae 91y 2m 5d bPP; m Margaret ----- d 1-28-1853 ae 91y 4m 18d (H)
Ch: Mary b 4-19-1795 d 2- 4-1849 bPP
Isaac L. " 4- 2-1797
Ann " 5-15-1800
Thomas L. b 9-28-1802 d 9-17-1803 ae 11m
Hannah " 2-25-1804
cf R. & P. 12-18-1793 for both; ct Gwynedd 4-6-1808 with 4 ch named; cf Green St., Phila. 8-20-1818 with their 2 minor ch, Ann & Hannah; all dis 1829-1831 (O)
Ann, dt Abraham & Margaret, N. Y., b 5-15-1800 d 11-21-1889; m 1836 William E. DUDLEY (H) ct Phila. 2-6-1878
Anna Maria, dt John & Jane HAYDOCK, b 4-2-1836; ct R. & P. 10-1862 (parents' name Haddock in one case)
Anthony, s Benj. & Eliz., of Pa., Merchant, N. Y.; m 11-8-1764 Penelope RODMAN, dt Thos. (dec) & Elizabeth
Ch: Elizabeth b 6-28-1765
Benjamin b 9-11-1766
Ch: Thomas Rodman b 1-19-1768 d 8-18-1770
John Rodman " 2-20-1770
cf 2 weeks mtg, London 3-26-1764, he lately came from Pa. on account of trade & now embarks for your parts (clear); consent of Benj. & Eliza to Anthony's m 9-11-1764; ct Goshen, Pa. for Penelope & ch, Eliz. & John 12-4-1782; ct Corn. 11-4-1790, her cf Goshen lost
Edward, s Samuel, gct Devonshire House or elsewhere 3-2-1785, having embarked with his father, a minor; had come with his mother from Phila.
Elizabeth, dt Anthony & Penelope, b 6-28-1765 d 10-23-1858 ae 93y 2m
Hannah, dt Abm. & Margaret, N. Y.; m 1840 Thomas FOULKE (H)
Isaac L. b 4-2-1797 d 9-30-1867 bPP; cf Green St. Phila. 6-8-1818
Mary, dt Abraham & Margaret, b 4-19-1795; cf Green St., Phila. 7-23-1818
Rachel C. (nm), dt Owen & Greta, Jr.; m 1919 John Jones MATTHEWS (H)
Rebecca, w Samuel
Ch: Edward
cf ND MM 6-27-1780 with s; ct ND MM 7-1-1784

SHOLL
John, from Eng., dis 6-2-1841 & rpd to Devonshire House

SHOTWELL
Aaron, Newtown, b 4-7-1775; cf R. & P. 6-16-1790, apprentice on L. I.; ct R. & P. 2-4-1794, apprentice lad, included in cert for William & Susannah Webster
Abel rocf R. & P. 4-18-1798; ct R. & P. 12-2-1801 (clear)
Abraham, s John, of Staten Island; m Flushing 10 Mo. (Dec) 5, 1712 Elizabeth COWPERTHWAIT, dt John, of West Jersey
Abraham, of Elizabeth Town, N. J.; m Newtown 9 Mo. (Nov) 10, 1742 Mary POTTS, Newtown, L. I.
Ch: Elizabeth m ----- LUDLUM
Mary took rem cert 8 Mo (Oct) 5, 1743
Abraham, Plainfield, m between 10-7 & 11-5-1767 (cert not recorded) Lydia HALLETT
cf Plainfield (clear); Lydia gct Woodbridge 2-4-1768
Abraham rocf R. & P. 1-16-1794, a minor
Amelia E., w Jos. D., dt Richard & Mary EVERITT (m 10-19-1862); ct R. & P. 4-1865 (H)
Amy T. d 5-26-1904, w -----
Ch: Walter F.
Henry T.
cf Wby. 9-1885 with 2 ch named
Benjamin, s John & Mary, Elizabeth Town; m between 8 Mo. 1 & 9 Mo. (Nov) 6, 1746, cert not recorded Amy HALLETT, dt Richard, Newtown
Amy took ct Woodbridge 1 Mo 5, 1747

SHOTWELL, continued
Catharine, dt David (dec), rocf R. & P. 4-17-1798, with sister, Charlotte, minors; ct R. & P. 8-6-1800 (clear)
Charlotte, dt David (dec), rocf R. & P. 5-17-1798 with sister, Catharine, minors; ct R. & P. 8-6-1800 (clear)
Eden, s Hannah, rocf Rahway, as apprentice, s of a mbr of N. Y. Mtg 9-16-1772, rec 12-2-1772; ct Rahway 3-1-1775; cf R. & P. 11-19-1777 (clear); ct Phila. Middle Dist. 1-4-1786 (clear)
Edward (nm) & -----
Ch: Infant stillborn 5-23-1836 bHS
Elizabeth b Phila. d 2-24-1827 ae 73y bHS (wd) (mbr prob. in Phila.)
Esther, dt Abm. & Mary; m 1786 George FOX, N.Y.
George T., s Joseph S. & Deborah, b 1-28-1819; ct Scipio 3-7-1838
Hannah, w ----- b Rahway d 7-10-1826 ae 77y 4m
Ch: Eden
Joseph
Elizabeth d 2-24-1827
Catharine
cf R. & P. 6-19-1793 with 4 ch, having rem with her h; ct R. & P. 2-4-1801 with dt, Catharine; cf R. & P. 12-18-1811
Hannah W., dt Wm. & Sarah, N. Y.; m 1830 Robert I. MURRAY
Harvey & Louisa
Ch: Ann Fitz Randolph
Sarah R.
William b Bkn. d 3-21-1831 ae 9m 1d
Harvey " 4- 2-1831 ae 11d
cf R. & P. 2-21-1821; cert of clear to R. & P. 12-3-1823; cf R. & P. 12-21-1825 for Louisa; ct R. & P. 3-6-1829 with 2 minor ch named, returned 11-24-1830 as they had returned (O); all dis 1831-1849 (O); ct R. & P. 9-1834 (H)
Henry, s Joseph & Sarah, of Rahway; m N. Y. 7-18-1781 Sarah DOBSON, dt Thos. & Margaret, N. Y.
Ch: Joseph Dobson b 4- 6-1782
Sarah " 1- 2-1784
cf Plainfield 8-18-1773 (clear); ct R. & P. 6-3-1778; ct R. & P. 7-7-1784 with w, Sarah, & 2 ch
Henry T. & Alice G.
Ch: Mary Titus b 1- 5-1887
Willets Haviland b 1-31-1889
cf Wby 9-1885 for Henry; ch recorded as per Disc. 8-5-1896
Isaac d 9-24-1798 bHS; m -----
Ch: Dt d 7-26-1797
cf R. & P. 11-17-1796
Jacob, s John & Mary, Elizabeth Town, N. J.; m Flushing 11 Mo. (Jan) 8, 1746/7 Eleanor HAYDOCK, dt Robert & Rebecca, Flushing
Jane Eliz. w Samuel H., dt Rich'd & Mary EVERITT (m 12-8-1874) (H)
Jeremiah dis mo 8-1-1781
John, Staten Is., m Flushing 9 Mo (Nov) 8, 1709 Mary THORN, dt Joseph, Flushing
cert of clear from Woodbridge
John Jr. rocf R. & P. 8-17-1796 (clear); ct R. & P. 7-3-1799 (clear)
Joseph, Elizabeth Town, N. J., m Newtown 1 Mo (Mar) 10, 1741/2 Sarah COCK, dt Henry, Newtown, L. I.
Joseph, s Joseph, Woodbridge, cert as apprentice to Haydock Bowne, 4-18-1764; ct Rahway 5-3-1769
Joseph dis mo 3-6-1782
Joseph, s Isaac, rocf R. & P. 8-7-1794 (clear); dis mo 6-7-1798
Joseph d 9-17-1798 bHS (H)
Joseph Jr., s John, rocf R. & P. 1-20-1803, apprentice to a Friend; ct R. & P. 5-14-1806 (clear)
Joseph D., s Henry R. & Margaret G., Rahway, N. J.; m at Richard Everitt's 10-9-1862 Amelia EVERITT, dt Richard & Mary C. (dec), Bkn. (H)
Joseph F., s Joseph S. & Deborah, b 1-30-1827; ct W & Jericho 1849
Joseph H. & -----
Ch: George b N. Y. d 12-8-1815 ae 2d (prob. mbr in N. J.)
Joseph Smith d 9-14-1848; m R. & P. 1808 Deborah ----- d 8-20-1862
Ch: Phebe b 10-11-1809
Walter T. " 9-28-1811
Esther " 2-28-1817
George F. " 1-28-1819; rem to Scipio 3-1838
Robert " 8-20-1821 d 9- 3-1821
Mary " 12-31-1822
Rebecca Fox b 7-22-1825
Joseph F. " 1-30-1827
Augustus F. d 4-25-1864
dis 1838-1839 (O); Joseph cert of clear to R. & P. 9-7-1808; Deborah rocf R. & P. 1-4-1809; Joseph rocf R. & P. 2-19-1806, apprentice, with a Friend; Deborah rocf R. & P. 12-21-1808
Lydia rocf R. & P. 11-21-1793; ct R. & P. 6-7-1798 (clear)
Mary, dt Joseph S. & Deborah, N. Y.; m 1845 Abraham S. UNDERHILL
Mary, dt Wm. & Sarah, West Farms; m 1856 Morris SHIPLEY
Mary Titus, dt Henry T. & Alice H., b 1-5-1887; m 11-28-1908 ----- INGRAM
name recorded as per Disc. 8-5-1896; letter to Lafayette Ave. Cong. Ch. 4-5-1922
Phebe, dt Jos. S. & Deborah, b 10-11-1809 d 1833; m William L. JENKINS
Richard, s Benjamin, of Rahway, N. Y.; m N.Y. 4-10-1782 Mary MARTIN, dt Isaac (dec) & Mary, N. Y.
cert of clear from Rahway 3-21-1782 recorded; Mary gct R. & P. 12-4-1782
Samuel Emlen m Sarah CARLILE
cf ND MM 4-25-1815; cert of clear to Middletown, Pa. 1-1-1817; cert from Middletown,

SHOTWELL, Samuel Emlen & Sarah, continued
Pa. 5-8-1817 for Sarah Carlile, his w; ct R. & P. 4-7-1819 for both
Samuel H., s Benj. (dec) & Mary (Hunt), Gloversville; m at John D. Shotwell's, Rahway, 12-8-1874 Jane E. EVERITT, dt Richard & Mary (Carle) (dec), Rahway, b 3-19-1839 d 1-30-1908 (H)
Ch: Joseph R. d 12-6-1817 ae 2d
Sarah H., dt Wm. & Sarah, N. Y.; m 1826 Morris SHIPLEY
Sarah W. rocf R. & P. 12-1861; ct R. & P. 8-7-1867 (H)
Thomas rocf R. & P. 1-17-1799, minor, placed with Willet Hicks
Thomas L. gct R. & P. 1-4-1804 (clear)
Walter F., s Joseph S. & Deborah, gct Scipio 3-7-1838 (clear)
Walter F., s Amy T., d 8-3-1913; m Phebe T. -----
Ch: Samuel T.
Joseph W. d 4-26-1899
cf Wby 9-1885 with mother; Phebe T. & 2 ch recrq 8-3-1898
William b Rahway 1762, m Sarah HOPKINS, d 4-19-1850
Ch: Sarah H. b 9-25-1788
Hannah W. " 3- 5-1790
Samuel " 7-20-1792 d 7-27-1792 ae 7d
William
Mary " 8-15-1796
Elizabeth d 9-15-1803 ae 4
Phebe " 3-30-1802 ae 1
Anna H. " 11-17-1802 d 5- 5-1875
Joseph d 4-16-1807 ae 1
Eliza " 10-24-1803 d 8-10-1804 ae 8m
Joseph " 5-13-1806
Samuel Wilson b 11-26-1810 d 12-9-1810
w called Mary for first 3 ch; William rem from R. & P. 3-18-1784 (clear); returned there with 3 & 3 ch 5-4-1796, came back with w & 6 ch 3-18-1802; all dis 1829 (H)
William, s William & Sarah, d 2-16-1851; m Eleanor KING (m Burl., N. J. 1832)
cert of clear to Burl. 7-1832; Eleanor rocf Burl. 7-1-1833; Elenor gct Burl. 1851

SHOVE
Asa & Harriet A.
cf Swansea, R. I. 3-1874 for both

SHREVES
Elizabeth sent in a cert some time ago, comm. to inspect her circumstances 12-2-1762

SHRIEVE
Thomas brought rem cf Middletown, Pa. 8 Mo. (Oct) 4, 1749 (clear); con mo 8-2-1753

SHRIGLEY
Mary d 9-22-1857; m -----
Ch: Rebecca Allen
recrq 3-6-1816; her dt, Rebecca Allen Shrigley recrq of mother 7-2-1817; Mary dis 4-1830 (O)

SHUFF
Aaron P. (nm) d 10-24-1832 ae 35y 9m 14d bHS

SHUPE
Walter H. recrq 11-6-1872; dis 4-2-1884 (H)

SIBELL
Elizabeth recrq 11-1820; dis 11-1829 (H)

SICKELS
Jesse S. & Anna J.
Ch: Ethel May b 3-29-1894
parents recrq 2-3-1893; parents released to Epworth M. E. Ch. of Bkn. 4-5-1899; Ethel's name erased, jas

SIDDONS
Abigail rocf Phila. 10-29-1784 (clear); ct Phila. 7-4-1787 (clear)

SIFTON
John (nm) m Caroline ----- b Me. d 5-8-1831 ae 32y bHS
Ch: Infant stillborn 5-8-1831 bHS

SIGMAN
Ida G. (nm), dt Abram & Susan; m 1875 Isaac E. STEER (H)

SILL
Henry (nm) b Eng. d 7-16-1848 ae 45y bHS (unm)

SILOR
Frank (nm) m Helen B. POST, dt Morgan B.
Helen recrq of father 9-1922

SIMKIN
Robert L. m Margaret L. ----- d 1922
Robert L. m 2d 1923 Margaret T. ----- (nm)
cf Scip. 2-3-1904 for Robert; Margaret recrq 9-5-1906

SIMMONS
Amelia dis mo 11-1830 (H)
Dr. Bert G. (not mbr here) d 1926; m Margaret S. HANES, dt Wm. & Elizabeth; Margaret m 2d 1929 Wm. Alex. TAYLOR
Stephen m Harriet A. ----- d 12-8-1889 ae 49y bPP (H)

SIMONE
Catharine (nm), dt Edw. P. & Margaret (Dore);

SIMONE, Catharine, continued
m 1930 E. Lewis B. CURTIS (H)

SIMONS
Deborah, dt Solomon & Eliz., Wby; m 1703 Joseph WILLETS
Sarah (late Brantingham) dis mo 8m-1803

SIMONSON
Catharine Ann recrq 8-1835; ct R. & P. 6-5-1867 (H)

SIMPSON
Henrietta (form Carman) dis mo by Bapt. Minister 3-6-1861; cf Oswego 10-1856 (H)
Sarah Eliz., dt Robert & Martha (Janney), b Pineville, Pa. 1-5-1837; m 1867 Benjamin SMITH (H)
cf Buckingham with h 6-6-1877; ct Gwynedd with h 12-8-1906
----- (nm) m Fannie J. STRATTON, dt Robert M., d 2-10-1875 ae 40y bPP (H)
----- & ----- (nm)
Ch: ----- d 5-27-1824 ae 3y 3m bHS
Maria b N. Y. d 7-30-1824 ae 1y 6m bHS
Jane P. b Sheffield, Eng. d 2-21-1829 ae 15y 5m bHS
George L. b N. Y. d 2-23-1829 ae 10y bHS

SINCLAIR
Anna, dt John & Elizabeth, N. Y.; m 1828 Mark CORNELL (H)
Emma Roberts (form Sinclair), dt John & Elizabeth, dis 10-1844 (H)
James Kennedy, s Edw. P. & Cath. J. A. (Spohn) b Rutherford, N. J. 11-1-1898; m 6-24-1920, 57 Pierrepont St., Rutherford, N. J. Sarah Louise ANDREWS, dt Geo. R. & Emeline W. (Hawkins), b Goshen 8-21-1898
Ch: Harry Addison b Rutherford 7-9-1922
James K., Jr. " Passaic 9-9-1925
Sarah recrq of parents 1-7-1899; ch recrq of parents 1-8-1923 & 1-4-1926; James recrq 5-9-1927
John d 10-13-1862 ae 87y bPP; m Elizabeth ----- d 9-21-1861 ae 84y bPP (H)
Ch: Mary Ann
Anna S.
John T. dis 2-1833
Emma
Joseph
Susan
Margaret S.
cf Balt. W. Dist. 12-10-1824 for all; all dis 1829-1849 (O)
John F., s John & Elizabeth, rocf Balt. with parents 12-10-1824; dis mo 2-1833 (H)
Joseph, s John & Elizabeth, gct Balt. 3-1833; returned from Balt. 2-1840; dis 10-1844 (H)
Margaret, dt John & Elizabeth, b Balt. 6-12-1824 d 2- 6-1906; m 1844 Thomas B. FORSTER (mo)
ct Flushing 5-1857
Mary Ann, dt John & Eliz., N. Y.; m 1827 Samuel PRIER; m 2d ----- DOWNING
cf Balt. W. Dist. 12-10-1824, resides with parents
Susan, dt John & Eliz., N. Y.; m 1838 Wilson EVANS (H)

SINTON
Margaret roc 1821; ct Cork, Ire. 1-3-1827

SIPHER
Sarah, dt Henry LEWIS, d 5-11-1804 ae 33

SISSON
Abigail (nm) b New Bedford, Mass. d 11-25-1822 ae 63y bHS (unm)

SITGREAVES
----- (nm) & Jessie L.
Ch: Garry Loveridge
Helen Burgess
letter from St. Paul's Luth. Ch., Easton, Pa. for Jessie 2-6-1907; ch recrq of mother; all names erased 4-1928

SHEKEYIAN (or Shekerjian)
Benjamin (nm) m Rosa MEGIRIAN, dt Jacob & Acabe, d 1-11-1921
cf Westminster & Longford 6-6-1906 for Rosa

SKELTON
Abram & Hannah
cf Brighouse MM, Eng. to Boston 3-23-1801, endorsed to N. Y. 5-13-1802; Hannah gct Brighouse 5-4-1814 (clear)
Abraham (nm) b Cumberland, Eng. d 3-19-1809 ae 37y bHS (prob h of Sarah)
Sarah (late White) (prob. w Abraham) rocf Shrews. 2-2-1801 (clear); dis mo 8-4-1802

SKINNER
Charles L. (nm) m 5-5-1852 Matilda H. SUTTON, dt Wm. & Charlotte (Hunt), b Mt. Kisco 5-5-1923 d 11-26-1902 (H)
Ch: Thomas Edgar b 12-21-1857
cf Chap. 9-4-1850 for Matilda; name of ch entered by comm. 1873
Thomas Edward, s Chas. L. & Matilda (Sutton), b N.Y. 12-21-1857 d 3-28-1919; m 12-13-1882 Gertrude I. VAN DOLSEN (nm) (H)

SLACK
Harry Casleton (nm), s Harrison & Anna (Corbett); m 10-16-1896 Mary BROWN, dt Edward H. & Mary, b Bkn. 11-26-1872 (H)
Mary relrq 2-14-1921

SLAUIK (or Slanik)
Frank recrq 8-1917; name erased 2-1926

SLEEM
R. B. m Elsie BANK

SLEFM, R. B. & Elsie, continued
Elsie recrq 5-5-1909; ct Po'Keepsie for Elsie 3-1928

SLEIGHT
Jane (form Klpp) rocf Creek 10-21-1831; dis 8-1834 (H)

SLOAN
Joseph (nm) & -----
Ch: William H. d 8-17-1851 ae ly 6m bPP
(prob) Anna Cora d 7-30-1853 ae 9m 16d bPP

SLOCUM
Caroline, dt Wm. T. & Mary, b 8-1-1809; m Marceline ----- (H)
dis 11-1830
Charles, s Christopher & Eliz., gct Abington [3-2-1814
Christopher M. & Elizabeth
Ch: Marshall b 5-1-1807
Emmeline M. b 10-12-1809
Charles
cf Portsmouth, R. I. 12-30-1794 (clear), apprentice; Christopher dis 9-2-1812; ct Abington 3-2-1814 for 3 ch named
Elizabeth Flowers rocf Phila. 9-26-1806 having rem with h; dis 9-2-1812
Emeline M., dt Christopher & Eliz., b 10-12-1809; ct Abington 3-2-1814
John, ship carpenter, N. Y., m Flushing 2 Mo (Apr) 6, 1717 Susanna HUNTER, dt Peter & Joan, N. Y.
Susanna brought cert (clear) from Ballicane MM, Co. Wicklow, Ireland
Marshall C., s Christopher & Eliz., b 5-1-1807; gct Abington 3-2-1814; cf Frankford 6-29-1830; dis 3-1843
Mary Abbie, dt Henry N. & Abbie, d 7-21-1935 ae 76y bPP; m Clement HAVILAND (H) (both nm)
Mary B., w Charles, gct Phila. 8-3-1836
Robert F. (nm) m Hypacia M. ----- d 12-15-1897 ae 88y bHS (H)
Ch: Edward E. b N. Y. d 9-7-1847 ae ly 17d bHS
Robert F., s Wm. T. & Mary, b 5-21-1813 d 2-9-1880 bPP (H) rel 6-2-1875, absent over 5y
Thomas Stelle rocf Newport 7-31-1798 (clear); ct Hudson 5-5-1802 (clear)
William T., s John & Martha (dec), Newport, R. I., b R. I. d 5-10-1840 ae 73y; m N. Y. 2-9-1803 Mary H. DUNBAR, dt Daniel (dec) & Naomi, N. Y., b Newtown, L. I., d 1-18-1824 ae 42y (H)
Ch: Dr. John H. b 11-17-1803 d 10-16-1831
William " 3-11-1805 " 12-30-1823
Edward " 11-15-1806 " 1835
Caroline " 8- 1-1809
Mary " 7-14-1811 " 12- 6-1830
Robert F. " 5-21-1813
cf Portsmouth 10-28-1802 (clear); all dis 1838-1839 (O)
----- & -----
Ch: Edward M. b N. Y. d 8-17-1841 ae ly 9m 19d bHS

SLUTES
Merrill Clark (nm), s Wm. Laurence & Julia (Clarke); m 6-29-1907 Edna HOPKINS, dt Chas. T. & Georgina (Dymond), b 1-26-1880 (H)
Edna recrq of parents 9-4-1889; Edna relrq 3-9-1912 to join with h in Cincinnati, Ohio

SMALLEY
Charles (prob) m Clara MILLER, dt Abraham C. & May (H)
Ch: Elizabeth d 7-14-1881 ae 3m 12d bPP

SMART
Catharine, dt Wm.; m ----- CARTER
dis 4-1849 as Hicksite
Elizabeth E., Bkn., d 12-3-1848 ae 86 (wd); m -----
Ch: Mary
Hannah
cf New Hartford (Bridgewater MM) 5-2-1845, with 2 ch named (all clear)
Hannah, dt Elizabeth E., rocf New Hartford, with mother; ct Po'keepsie
Mary, dt Elizabeth E., rocf New Hartford with mother 1845; ct Po'keepsie
Mary E., w Jas. ELLIMAN, dt Wm. Smart; dis as Hicksite 4-1849 (O); dis 7-4-1847 (H)
William & -----
Ch: Lucy A.
Mary E. m ----- ELLIMAN
Catharine m ----- CARTER
all dis as Hicksites 4-1849

SMEDLEY
Lauretta, dt Lewis V. & Selina (Cox), b Westtown, Pa. 4-27-1874; m 1902 John F. DUTTON (H); cf Goshen 8-6-1890; ct Goshen with ch 3-12-1923
Samuel W., s Wm. & Rebecca (dec), Middletown, Pa.; m N. Y. 6-15-1864 at Samuel Large's, Mary LARGE, dt Samuel & Eliz. C., Hoboken; Mary L. gct WD MM 6-1865

SMILEY
Albert K., s Daniel & Phoebe (dec), Vassalborough, Me.; m N. Y. 7-8-1857 Eliza P. CORNELL, dt Rich. & Mary Annette (dec), N.Y.

SMITH
Abel rocf Chatham 10-25-1827; dis non-attendance 5-1829 (H)
Abel (nm) & -----
Ch: Infant stillborn 3-30-1836 bHS
Abel S. d 4-1-1867 ae 65y bPP; m Bethany ----- d 12-21-1886 ae 85y bPP
Ch: (as indicated)
a gr dt, infant, d 12-5-1886
cf Chatham for Abel 1828; Bethany never had a cert
Abigail, dt Alex & Mary; m 1705 Thomas GAIL
Abraham witnessed m cert 1683-1687
Abraham, Jr. rocf New Bedford 5-17-1803, under care of his brother, Stephen

SMITH, continued
Albert E., s Samuel & Ellen Augusta, d 4-13-1904 ae 40y 23d bPP; m Eve R. ----- d 12-2-1892 ae 25y bPP (all nm) (H)
Albert E. m 2d Jessie S. PHELPS, dt Justice M., d 8-6-1930 ae 69y bPP
Ch: Lauretta Phelps stillborn 10-3-1902 bPP
Alexander (nm) m 10-2-1876 Mary L. THOMAS, dt Wm. George & Mary L. (Wethered), b Balt. 11-19-1841 d 3-18-1917 (H)
cf Balt. for Mary 4-2-1879
Alice, Eastchester, d 1727, a wd
Alice C., dt Thos. T. & Sarah B., b Bkn. 1-15-1868; m 1902 James C. T. BALDWIN (H)
relrq 1-13-1917
Aliph G., dt Chas. H. & Rebecca R., Spring Valley, b Spring Valley, N. Y. 3-2-1881 d 1-21-1931 (H); m 1816 Edward P. PALMER
recrq 1-13-1917
Ann rocf Coey. 8-1853; d 8-18-1865 (H)
Anna rocf Wby 7-19-1826 (clear); dis 2-1830
Anna, dt Francis H. & Lydia MACY (w D. Henry) (mo); mbr Dr. Hall's Ch. for some time; released 12-4-1828 (H)
Anna W. rocf Frankford 1852; ct Wby & Jericho 1854
Asa, s Abraham & Zeriah, of Ned Bedford; m Westchester 4-17-1816 Abigail HAVILAND, dt Benjamin & Sarah, Westchester
cf New Bedford 8-24-1815 (clear); cert of clear to Pur. 4-3-1816; Abigail rocf Pur. 11-14-1816; Asa gct New Bedford 8-7-1822 (clear)
Benjamin, Wby, rqc of clear 12 Mo (Feb) 4, 1719/20
Benjamin, s Jonathan & Elizabeth, b Pineville, Pa. 8-1-1840; m 10-3-1867 Sarah Elizabeth SIMPSON, dt Robert & Martha (Janney), b Pineville, Pa. 1-5-1837 (H)
Ch: Frances B. b 8- 2-1870
Clarence W. b 4-30-1872
Herbert T. " 4-19-1874
cf Buckingham 6-6-1877 for all; ct Gwenedd 12-8-1906 for parents
Bethany, wd Abel S., d 12-21-1886 (0); cf Plains 9-1828; dis 11-1829 (H)
Caroline E., dt Elihu & Mary, d 10-12-1851 ae 43y 3m bPP; dis 4-1845 (H)
Charles (nm) b London d 4-23-1829 ae 29y bHS (neck broken in fall) (widower)
Charles A. d 11-21-1900; cf Balt. 3-1-1871 (H)
Charles F., s Jacob & Deborah, d 2-18-1883; m Judith C. ----- d 10-12-1852 (H)
Ch: Elizabeth P. b 12-18-1829
Phebe B. " 3- 8-1832
Caroline " 9- 5-1833 d 8- 7-1834
Samuel 2d " 11-18-1836
Charlotte b L. I. d 6-17-1829 ae 54y 6m bHS (wd)
Clarence, s Benj. & Sarah E. (Simpson), b Doylestown, Pa. 4-30-1872; cf Buckingham 6-6-1877 with parents; ct Chester, N. J. 4-13-1912 (H)
David P., s Jacob & Deborah (both dec), N. Y., d 8-17-1872; m at Phebe Archer's 11-5-1840 Phebe T. ARCHER, dt Thomas & Abigail (dec) THORN, d 12-7-1885 (H)
David P. rq mbrp 8-1813, not accepted 11-3-1813; rec 12-6-1815; dis 6-2-1929 (0)
Deborah, Oblong ref. to N. Y. her ack. 8-6-1817; rpd favorably 9-3-1817
Deborah (nm) b N. Y. d 10-3-1830 ae 43y bHS (J. L. Mott's sister written in pencil)
Edna, dt Alfred D. & Malvina, b Vineland, N. J. 10-1-1870; m 1896 Lloyd West FRANCIS (H)
all recrq 4-11-1908
Edward, Eastchester, d 6 Mo (Aug.) 6, 1723
Edwin Oscar, s Oscar & Ida Clair (Pope), b Albany 12-12-1871; m 11-27-1900 Myra Mae KEANDALL (nm), dt Chas. N. & Winifred E. (Bergen), b Ausable Forks, N. Y. 11-7-1875 (H)
Elener, Flushing, d 7 Mo (Sep) 28, 1724 (wd)
Eleanor, dt Wm. T. & Annie (Titus), b Bkn. 2-1-1887; m 1908 Richard Manning FIELD (H)
name entered by comm. 12-3-1890
Elihu b New Bedford d 10-3-1825 ae 54y 2m; m Mary ----- d 9-27-1812 ae 33y 6m 14d bPP
Ch: Elizabeth Mitchell
John T. Slocum
Caroline
cf New Bedford 9-18-1810
Elihu m 2d Catharine F. ----- d 12-4-1856 ae 72y 8m 26d bPP
Ch: Jane F. b 12-2-1816 (or 2-12-1816 d 8-19-1858 ae 8y 17d
Maria F. b 10-1818 d 1-16-1896 in 78th yr.
Thomas Thorn b 7-5-1820 (or 5-7-1820)
cert of clear to Flushing 11-2-1814; Catharine rocf Flushing 5-4-1815: Catharine & last 4 ch dis 1831-1842 (0)
Elizabeth d 9-7-1800 bHS
Elizabeth, w Alfred Carman, dt Abraham & Susan COCK; dis mo 9-5-1838
Elizabeth (nm) d 8-15-1858 ae 74y 10m bPP
Elizabeth rocf Providence 2-2-1876; d 8-20-1880
Elizabeth M., dt Elihu & Mary, N. Y.; m 1828 Richard MOTT, Jr.
Elizabeth P., dt Charles F. & Judith C., N. Y., b 12-18-1829; m 1857 Stephen R. SMITH
parents (H)
Ellen A. (nm), dt John & Elizabeth M.; m 1859 Samuel SMITH (H)
Elton Verner (nm), s Thos. Richpoole & Jerusha (Bratton); m 2-2-1924 Grace Carol GIBBS, dt Samuel E. & Grace C. (McCord), b N. Y. 6-19-1899 (H)
Grace's name entered by comm. 4-13-1912; relrq 3-13-1933
Emeline M. Bingham (form Smith) dis mo 7-1848
Emma recrq 6-2-1880; d 5-11-1882 (H)
Emma, dt Wm. & Caroline (Becker), b Seneca Falls, N. Y. 9-4-1848 d 1-23-1931; m William A. SMITH (H)
both recrq 1-10-1919
Esther, dt Abraham, O. B.; m 1693 "Mill" John

SMITH, Esther, continued
TOWNSEND, of O.B. (mo)
dis mo 12 Mo 22, 1694/5; wit m cert 1687
Ezekiel wit m cert 1705
Florence L., w Bertram, dt ----- GILDERSLEEVE, recrq 3-4-1891; relrq 1-8-1902
Frances m 1732 Edward FARRINGTON
Frances, dt Benjamin & Elizabeth; m 3-26-1895 Frank S. HERR (H)
cf Buckingham 6-6-1877 with parents
Frederick P., s John T. S. & Amelia, b 12-5-1840; joined a military organization before 2-1866; dis 4-1866
Gulielma Matilda, dt Willet & Mary J., seaman, b 7-10-1809; dis 10-1831 (H); dis (O)
Hannah, dt Jasper & Margery, Flushing; m 1709 Samuel BOWNE
wit m cert 1701
Harriet, dt Elias & Catharine RING, b 11-2-1800 (mo); dis 10-7-1829 (O)
Harriet T. m 1885 Philip COMSTOCK (H)
Harry E. & Louise A.
Ch: Esther Louise (later Esther)
all recrq 1-5-1910; names of all erased 4-1928
Helen Gertrude, dt Fred'k D. & Agnes (Clark), b N. Y. 7-13-1892; m 1912 Ernest Anton TROEGER (H)
Henry H. rocf Creek 6-1845; cancelled 4-9-1904, long unknown; cousin of Isaac Sands; in Calif. 1859 (H)
Henry Mitchell, s John T. S. & Amelia, b 4-24-1835; dis 1856
Herbert T., s Benj. & Sarah Eliz. (Simpson), b Doylestown, Pa. 4-19-1874; cf Buckingham with parents 6-6-1877; ct Chester, N. J. 7-13-1912 (H)
Herman H., s S. W. & Anna M. SCHMIDT (name changed to Smith 1-10-1919) b Hoboken 3-2-1876; m 6-23-1900 Mary MERRITT, dt Benj. A. & Hannah (White), b Pinelawn, N. Y. 6-14-1879 (H)
Ch: Marritt S. b 4-8-1901
Herman recrq 4-8-1911; Mary recrq 5-11-1907; ch recrq of parents 4-8-1811
Herman H. m 2d Phebe A. MERRITT, dt Benj. A. & Hannah E. (White), b Pinelawn, L. I. 10-13-1880 (m 8-9-1930); Phebe m 2d Geo. G. THOMPSON
cf Wby for Phebe 12-8-1930 with 2 ch
Horace G. (nm), s Dill A. & Mary J. (H----), b Pittsburg 7-27-1850 d Newton, Mass. 10-22-1920 bPP; m May MOORE, dt Jehu C. & Hannah D. (Mitchell), b Wilmington, O. 7-11-1860 d 4-1-1911 bPP
May not a mbr here
Isaac m Elizabeth UNDERHILL, dt Capt. John
Ch: Jacob b 10 Mo (Dec) 8, 1790
Isaac witnessed m cert 1686-1693; Elizabeth witnessed m cert 1698-1702
Isaac rocf New Bedford 12-19-1809 (minor); ct Bridgewater 5-7-1820 (clear)
J. Clarence m Hannah EASTBURN
Ch: Eastburn Richey
recrq 11-7-1906, the s as an associate; letter to Plymouth Cong. Ch. 11-1917 for all
Jacob witnessed m cert 1691
Jacob b N. Y. d 3-8-1838 ae 73y 3m 12d; m Deborah ----- b West. Co. d 3-14-1838 ae 67y 11m 3d (H)
Ch: William d 8- 7-1801
David P. bHS
Charles F.
Sarah E. d 5- 8-1866
Joseph H.
William d 8-13-1803 ae 10m bHS
all dis 1830-1833 (O); Deborah rec in mbrp 9-1817; David P. rec in mbrp 12-1815; Jacob withheld keys of bur. ground from (O) 1929
James rocf Knaresbro 3-11-1822 (clear); dis 10-1831
James B. rocf Corn. 3-1846; relrq 7-3-1867 (H)
James G. recrq 3-7-1821; dis 1824; rst 7-1858; d 11-6-1862
Jasper, Flushing, d 11 Mo (Jan) 22, 1696; m Margery -----
Ch: John d 2 Mo (Apr) 18, 1728
Judith
Hannah
witnessed m cert 1679-1691
Jemima rocf SD MM 7-23-1788, having rem with her h; ct Phila. 8-2-1797
Jennie E. (nm) m Albert E. MILLER (H)
Jesse (nm) b Coram, L. I. d 12-19-1823 ae 24y bHS (unm)
John witnessed m cert 1701
John C., Smyrna rq N. Y. to visit him; dis 4-1861 by Smyrna
John C. (nm) d 1-18-1906 ae 47y bPP; m 10-25-1888 Phebe C. MILLER, dt Benjamin C. & Laura F. (Marshall), b Bkn. 8-30-1867 (H)
Ch: Irving J. d 8-11-1891 ae 4m 25d bPP
Phebe C. m 2d 1912 John A. BARNES; all nm but Phebe C.
John J., s John (dec) & Gulielma, Phila.; m N. Y. 4-12-1821 Rachel C. PEARSALL, dt Robert & Eliz., N. Y.
ct Phila. 8-1-1821 for Rachel P., rem with h
John M. (nm) m Mary C. ----- (nm) d 8-31-1854 ae 34y 10m 4d bPP
John T. S., s Elihu & Mary (both dec) N. Y.; m N. Y. 3- 9-1831 Amelia FRANKLIN, dt Thos. & Mary, N. Y., d 1-14 (or 17) 1864 ae 57y bPP
Ch: Infant stillborn 12-17-1831 bHS
Thomas Franklin b 4-26-1833
Henry Mitchell " 4-24-1835
Mary " 6- 4-1837
Frederick P. " 12- 5-1840
Sarah H. " 12- 5-1840
John dis 6-29-1829 (H), eet 7-1-1829 (O); John dis 1-1844 (O) for non-attendance
Joseph witnessed m cert 1704-1706

SMITH, continued
Joseph, having mo, Ama. refers it to N. Y. 3-10-1848; dis 8-1848; Ama. notified 9-1848
Joseph H., s Jacob & Deborah (both dec); m at Benjamin Secor's, Seneca, Mich. 6-23-1845 Hannah SECOR, dt Benjamin & Sarah (dec), d 2-22-1842 (H) (Benj. Secor not under care of N. Y. MM)
Ch: Willet b 10- 8-1836 d 8- 9-1850
Silas " 1- 4-1841 " 10-24-1843
Sarah Jane b 12-20-1846
cf Corn. 2-1838 for Hannah; cf Corn. 1-7-1846 for Hannah; ct Adrian, Mich. 8-[illegible]-1851 for all
Judith, dt Jasper & Margery, Flushing; m 1712 Thomas POTTS, Bristol, Pa.
Judith C., w Charles, rocf Hudson 12-21-1831; dis 12-1832
Keith (nm), s Frank W. & Fannie M.; m 12-1-1905 Helen GARRETT, dt Thomas & Mary (Groff), b 9-5-1893 (H)
Helen's name entered by com. 9-3-1890
Lewis T., d 5-26-1854 ae 43y 8m bPP; m ----- (H)
Ch: Norman D.
Mary Elizabeth
cf Roch. 3-1853
Louisa M. (nm) d 7-14-1864 ae 20y 2m 4d bPP (H)
Lydia C. (nm) d 3-17-1877 ae 72y bPP (H)
Margery, Flushing, d 9 Mo (Nov) 14, 1703, wd Jasper; witnessed m cert 1689-1701
Maria W., dt James & Sarah, d Boonton, N. J., 12-3-1928 ae 86y 1m 27d bPP
Marianna, dt Edward J.& Mary H. (Brown), b Lincoln, Va. 1-7-1871; m 1891 Edward B. RAWSON (H)
cf Goose Creek 2-3-1892 with him; ct Goose Creek 11-12-1917 with him & ch (H)
Marjorie rolf First Presbyterian Ch., Bkn. 11-1928
Marmaduke, m Elizabeth ----- d 8-15-1858 ae 74y 10m 9d bPP (H) (both nm)
Martha witnessed m cert 1714
Martha W., w Morton, dt Joseph W. & Hannah HILYARD, b 12-19-1841 d 6-25-1872
ret a mbr
Mary witnessed m cert 1690
Mary, dt Edward & Ailse, Flushing; m 1722 Henry CHARLICK
Mary, a poor girl that Friends maintained many years, d 1 Mo (Mar) 18, 1740
Mary, dt Asa, rocf New Bedford 1-23-1817 (clear); ct New Bedford 7-4-1821 (clear)
Mary, w Samuel
Ch: Ann
Deborah
Thomas dis as (H)
cf Hudson 2-22-1832; cf Hudson 12-26-1832 for her 3 ch named; ct Wby & Jericho 1-7-1846 with 2 ch, Anna W. & Deborah
Mary, dt John T. S. & Amelia, b 6-4-1837; m ----- COOK (mo) [attending mtg mbrp relinquished 2-1865 for mo & not
Mary, w Joseph, dt Benj. & Mary CARPENTER, rocf Ama. 8-1846; ct Ama. 10-1859 (H)
Mary, w -----
Ch: Caroline
Rachel W.
cf Wby & Jericho 1852 with 2 ch; ct Wby & Jericho 7-1860 with 2 ch
Mary, d 3-3-1883; m -----
Ch: Caroline d 3-1910
cf Wby 11-1873
Mary Anna, dt Clarkson & Deborah TABER
Mary Eliz., dt Lewis, rocf Roch. 3-1853; ct Albany 8-1856 (H)
Mary L. T. rocf Balt. 4-2-1879 (H)
Matilda Rutland m ----- BACON (nm) (after coming to America)
cf Thaxted, Eng. 4-5-1905; rel to jas 2-1922
Maude Elizabeth, dt Chas. H. & Rebecca (Rosecrans) b Spring Valley, N. Y. 10-2-1883 (H)
recrq 11-12-1917; relrq 4-11-1927
Molllie A. (nm) m 1876 Robert CROMWELL (H)
Morris, Jamaica, L. I. & Bethia
Ch: Morris b 1 Mo (Mar) 19, 1664/5
Abraham b 7 Mo (Sep) 28, 1667 d 5 Mo 1688
Isaac " 12 Mo (Feb) 14, 1668 d 2 Mo 21, 1682
Jacob " 10 Mo (Dec) 20, 1671
Mary " 9 Mo (Nov) 12, 1674
Martha " 3 Mo (May) 19, 1677
John " 2 Mo (Apr) 10, 1680
Morris active mbr from 1676; Morris witnessed m cert 1678-1687; Bethia 1678-1679
Morris, Jr., s Morris & Bethia, b 19 Jan. 1664; mo before 2 Mo (Apr) 5, 1688
Nathaniel & Abigail
recrq 8-6-1817; ct Flushing 2-3-1819 with w, Abigail; she recrq 7-2-1817
Nehemiah rocf Corn. 8-24-1795, apprentice
Nellie M., dt Alfred Holbrook & Susan, b Bkn. 1-19-1876; recrq 6-13-1921 (H)
Nelson, s Samuel & Rachel (Yaple), b Margaretville, N. Y. 9-29-1828 d 2-28-1916; m 12-20-1853 Emily L. SHAURMAN (nm), dt Isaac & Amanda (Avery) (H)
Ch: (not mbr)
Marion
Nelson, Jr.
Anne Elizabeth
Nelson recrq 3-14-1914
Norman D., s Lewis, rocf Roch. 3-1853; d 10-18-1863 (H)
Obed (nm) b 11-2-1772 d 4-17-1831 ae 58y 5m 15 bHS
Patience rocf Roch. 5-1844; ct Albany 8-4-1858 (H)
Percival C., s Thomas T. & Sarah B. (Cromwell) b N. Y. 1-12-1862; m 11-12-1912 Florence Chevy KIMBALL (nm), dt Francis W. & Florence M., d 8-10-1929 ae 53y bPP (H)
Ch: Mary b 3-29-1915 d next day bPP
Phebe, w -----, dt Dr. NOLE, sister of Rachel, b Bkn. d 9-12-1830 ae 33y bHS (H)

SMITH, Phebe, continued
cf Wby 1-14-1818 (clear); dis 5-1829
Phebe B., dt Chas. F. & Judith C., N. Y., b 3-8-1832; m 1855 John C. THORNTON (H)
Phebe C., w John C., dt Benj. C. & Laura F. MILLER, b 8-30-1867 (m 10-25-1888
Phebe C. m 2d 8-6-1912 John A. BARNES (nm)
Rachel, w Jacob, of Wby, d 12-23-1836 (H)
Ch: Anna d Wby 8-19-1841
cf Wby 7-19-1826; sister of Phebe
Rachel W., dt Samuel & Mary, b 12-6-1838; m Charles C. HALL
cf Wby & Jericho 11-1873; relrq 3-1885
Samuel & Mary
Ch: Anna b 5-28-1822
Deborah b 4-29-1824
Thomas W. b 2-19-1830 d 3- 5-1852 bPP
William " 10-21-1832
Caroline " 11- 6-1835
Rachel W. " 12- 6-1838
recrq 5-4-1814; ct Hudson 5-6-1818 (clear); cf Hudson 1-1832 for both with 3 ch; ct Jericho 2-1848 for Samuel & William; the others marked Orthodox
Samuel (nm) & -----
Ch: Infant stillborn 9-17-1829
Samuel rocf Jericho 3-3-1852; d 11-3-1872 (H)
Samuel (nm) & -----
Ch: Lucretia B. d 7-24-1860 ae 9y bPP
Samuel, s Chas. F. & Judith C. (Bunker) (dec), b N. Y. 11-18-1836 d 3- 7-1905; m at Geo. F. Badger's (not under care of N. Y. MM) Bkn. 1-5-1859 Ellen A. SMITH, dt John & Elizabeth M. (dec), d 3-24-1914 ae 73y 6m 17d bPP (H)
Ch: Albert E. (nm)
Samuel & ----- (H)
Ch: George J. B. d 7- 6-1870 ae 5m bPP
Gilbert Badger d 6-23-1878 ae 7m bPP
Frank " 2- 7-1875 ae 5m bPP
Elizabeth Hitchings d 4- 8-1873 ae 1y 3m 8d bPP
Lucretia B. d 7-24-1860 ae 7m bPP
Sarah A. " 6- 4-1869 ae 5m bPP
Samuel Archibald, s Sam'l W. & Frances A. (Jones), b Milton, N. H. 11-27-1870; m 9-6-1898 Isabelle BLACKBURN, dt Alexander & Margaret E. (Hail), b Chicago 3-9-1874 (H)
cf Wby 12-10-1934 for both
Samuel B. recrq 3-1851; d 5-1867 ae 76y bPP
Samuel B. rocf Pur. 4-4-1888; relrq 7-1-1891 (H)
Samuel E. mo before 1-1867, ret a mbr; cf Ferrisburgh 9-2-1863; ct Ferrisburgh 5-1867
Samuel I., s Silvanus & Jane (dec), N. Y.; m at Rich. W. Titus', N. Y. 10-2-1845 Ruannah WATERBURY, dt Azariah & Mary (both dec), N. Y. (H)
Ruannah recrq 12-1840; ct Jericho for Ruannah 10-7-1846
Sarah, dt Edward, Westchester, dmi with Benjamin CLAPP 1722, but not passed
Sarah, w Benjamin, of Trenton, took ct Trenton 11 Mo (Jan) 5, 1737/8
Sarah gc 3-7-1770
Sarah (late Knowles) dis mo 3-6-1816
Sarah H., dt John T. S. & Amelia, b 12-5-1840; dis 6-1869
Stephen rocf New Bedford 12-18-1798 (clear); cert of clear to Hudson 3-2-1814
Stephen gct Hudson 3-1-1815; cf Hudson 10-22-1816 (clear); ct De Ruyter 5-2-1827 (clear)
Stephen gct New Bedford 12-1-1819
Stephen H. (nm) m 10-13-1892 Myra E. GURNEE, dt Frances W. & Margaret E. (Mead), b Bloomingdale, N. J. 12-3-1870 (H)
Myra recrq 7-6-1901
Stephen R., s Henry & Maria, Flushing; m N. Y. 6-17-1857 Elizabeth P. SMITH, dt Charles F. & Judith C. (dec), N. Y., b 12-18-1829
cf Eng. 1855 for Stephen; Elizabeth P. (her parents being (H); joined (O) 3-1859; ct Chap. 3-1871 for both
Thomas Franklin, s John T. S. & Amelia, b 4-26-1833; dis jas 4-1854
Thomas R. (nm) & -----
Ch: Infant d 8-26-1818
Thomas T., s Elihu & Catharine, b 7-5-1820 (or 5-7-1820) d 8-4-1883; m Sarah B. CROMWELL d 12-30-1878 ae 52y bPP (H)
Ch: Catharine b 7-21-1850 d 9-14-1853 bPP
Cornelia " 8-10-1852 " 9-20-1853 bPP
William T. b 7-10-1854
Augustus C. b 5- 9-1859 d 8- 4-1861 bPP
Percival C. " 1-24-1862
Alice C. " 1- 5-1868
cf Corn. 4-1850 for Sarah
William "that came late from England" d Flushing 1 Mo (Mar) 28, 1722
William A., s Seth & Charity (Finch), b Union Springs, N. Y. 5-9-1852; m Emma S. SMITH, dt Wm. & Caroline (Bocker), b Seneca Falls, N. Y. 9-4-1848 d 1-23-1931 (H)
both recrq 1-10-1919; Wm. relrq 3-14-1932
William C. rocf Corn. 2-4-1846; ct Corn. 4-7-1858 (H)
William H. (nm) d 7-11-1871 bPP (H)
William P., s Wm. T. & Annie (Titus) b Great Neck 6-5-1890; m 2-1924 Ethel MEALY (nm) (H)
Wm. R., s Asa B. & Hannah C., Farington, N. Y.; m N. Y. 9-7-1832 Eliza WRIGHT, dt John W. (dec) & Eliza, N. Y.
ct Farm. 12-5-1832 for Eliza
Wm. T., s Thos. T. & Sarah B. (Cromwell) Bkn., b N. Y. 7-10-1854 d 12-17-1929 bPP; m at E. Lewis Jr.'s 10-3-1878 Annie TITIS, dt John V. (dec) & Phebe W., Bkn., b Wby 5-15-1852 d 6-14-1935 bPP (H)
Ch: Thomas T. b 4-26-1881 d 11-5-1927 bPP
Sarah B. " 7-20-1883 d 5-10-1907 bPP
Eleanor b 2- 1-1887
Annie C. b 10-18-1888 d 10-17-1918 bPP
William P. b 6- 5-1890

SMITH, Wm. T. & Annie, continued
Annie recrq 5-9-1896; ch recrq of parents 5-9-1896
William W. (nm) b L. I. d 8-2-1834 ae 28y 4m bHS
----- & ----- (nm)
Ch: William b Bkn. d 8-18-1821 ae 1y 1m 13d bHS
Louisa d 7-14-1864 ae 20y 2m bPP
Ira G. " 11- 6-1862 ae 61y bPP

SMYTH
Jane recrq 2-1870; d 6-19-1877
Rebecca [Smythe] (nm) b Pa. d 2-17-1847 ae 78y bHS (wd)
Thomas H. [Smythe] (nm) d 9-22-1873 ae 57y bPP

SNIFFEN
Catharine M. (nm), dt John, d 1-5-1906 ae 90y bPP (H)

SNOW
Asa d 10-8-1887; m Harriet -----
cf Swansea, R. I. 3-1874; ct Greenwich, R. I. 9-1888 for Harriet
Martha E. recrq 4-1871; in Michigan

SNYDER
Wm. Halleck, s Thos. J. & Mahitable H.; m 6-18-1903 Harriet FIELD, dt Wm. H. & Mary (Carpenter) b Port Chester 1-20-1872 (H)
Ch: Mary Carpenter b 8-16-1904 Bkn.
Richmond F. " 10-19-1907 "
Katharine L. " 4-30-1910 "
Harriet recrq 3-11-1916; ch on rq of parents 3-8-1926

SOMERS
Joseph m Helen A. LOCKWOOD, dt Neely, b 7-6-1835 d 3-10-1907 ae 69y 8m 3d bPP (H)
Ch: Clarence d 11-1-1882 ae 6y 10m 2d bPP
Infant stillborn 9-5-1873
Walter d 4-23-1875 ae 8m 12d bPP
all nm except Helen A., she resigned 12-9-1899

SOUTHERLAND
Andrew & Phebe d 1872
Ch: William dis 9-1846
Maria " 2-1848
John " 9-1847
James Jr. b 9-30-1824 d 10-1858
Uriah " 3- 7-1828; dis 4-1858
Phebe Jane b 11-10-1831; dis
cf Corn. 10-26-1823; parents dis, Phebe 1829; Andrew 1835 (H); Andrew dealt with 1829 for paying military fine
James, s Andrew & Phebe, b 9-30-1824 d 10-1858; mo before 12-1847, ret a mbr
John P., s Andrew & Phebe, dis mo 10-1847
Maria, dt Andrew & Phebe; m ----- WOOD; dis mo 2-1848
William, s Andrew & Phebe, dis mo 9-1846

SOUTHWICK
Anna L. (nm) m 7-15-1896 Walter H. GRIFFEN (H)
Elizabeth S. (form Mason) rocf York, Eng. 12-18-1839 with brother; dis mo 1-1848
Geo. William, s Thos. M. & Matilda, rocf Troy 9-1838 with mother; rel 8-1850 (H)
Julia Ann, dt Thos. M. & Matilda, rocf Troy 9-1838 with mother; dis 5-1841 (H)
Matilda, w Thomas M., d 10-13-1867 (H)
Ch: Julia Ann
George William
cf Troy 9-1838 with 2 ch named
Mary, late of R. I., m 1701 Samuel TATUM
brought rem cert from R. I. 8 Mo. (Oct) 14, 1701 (clear)

SOWLE
Eliza M., dt Jethro & Mary (Grinnell), b Little Compton, R. I. 9-7-1849 d 2-23-1922; m 1880 Henry W. WILBUR (H)
recrq 7-7-1900

SPARKS
----- m Anna Irene BARTON, dt Jesse & Anna M.
Anna recrq 4-4-1906

SPEAKMAN
John rocf Phila. 11-30-1804 (clear); ct SD MM 1-7-1807 (clear)

SPENCER
Amie H. (or Annie M.), dt Geo. D. & Harriet A. KIMBER, name erased 2-7-1900
Charles L., s Chris. V. & Anna L., dis mo 12-1854
Christopher V. d 1-19-1866; m Anna Louisa -----
Ch: Sarah A.
Christopher V.
Charles L.
Mary E. dis 6-1848
Samuel A.
Anna Louisa
James A.
Thomas H. rel 2-1862
William Penn
cf Greenwich MM at Coventry 5-1-1843 with 9 ch named; ct R. & P. 2-1869 for Anna L. & dt, Anna L.; all dis except as noted 1853-1861
Christopher C. V., s Chris V. & Anna L., rocf Greenwich MM at Coventry with parents 5-1-1843; dis mo by a priest 10-1850
Jonathan J. rocf Gwynedd 1-30-1817; ct Chester, N. J. 2-4-1818 (clear)
Mary E., dt Christopher V. & Anna L.; m ----- FRANKLIN
dis mo 6-1848
Phebe Ann rocf Corn. 11-1861
Samuel A., s Chris. V. & Anna L., dis mo 7-1856
Sarah A., dt Chris. V. & Anna L., dis attending mtg of another religious Society 7-1853

SPENCER, continued
Wm. Penn, s Chris. V. & Anna L., joined a military organization before 8-1861; dis 11-1861
----- & -----(nm)
Ch: Clarence d 1-24-1877 ae 43y bPP

SPICER
Dorothy Gladys, dt J. Lindley & Phoebe (Washburn), b 11-3-1893; m ----- FRASER
ct Po'Keepsie 12-7-1904 with parents; letter from First Presby. Ch., Po'keepsie, 9-1920
Eber Grant, s J. Lindley, rolf First M. E. Ch., Greenwich, N. Y. 8-3-1892; ct Westtown, Pa. 12-1918
J. Lindley & -----
Ch: Eber Grant
cf Morean 4-1889 for J. Lindley; letter from First M. E. Church, Greenwich, N. Y. 8-3-1892 for Eber G.
J. Lindley d 5-18-1928; m 2d Phebe WASHBURN
Ch: Lindley Milton b 11-24-1889 d 3-29-1900 at New Dorp., Staten Island
Dorothy Gladys b 11- 3-1893
cf Morean 4-1889 for J. Lindley; Phebe recrq 12-4-1889; Lindley M. recrq of parents 3-2-1892; ct Po'keepsie 12-7-1904 with dt; cf Po'keepsie 12-6-1911 for parents
Samuel, Gravesand, L. I.; m O.B. 3 Mo (May) 21, 1665 Esther TILTON, dt John
Ch: Abraham b 8 Mo (Oct) 27, 1666 d 5-25-1679
Jacob " 1 Mo (Mar) 20, 1668
Mary " 8 Mo (Oct) 20, 1671
Sarah " 4 Mo (June) 19, 1674 d 1-5-1677
Martha " 11 Mo (Jan) 27, 1676 d 2 Mo 29, 1677
Sarah 2d b 12 Mo (Feb) 16, 1677/8
Abigail " 1 Mo (Mar) 26, 1683
Samuel active mbr from 1676; Esther active mbr from 1676

SPINK
Katherine, dt Thomas H. & Eliza (Gillen), b N. Y. 7-31-1883; m 12-1914 Charles M. CARPENTER (H)

SPRAGUE
Enos T. having mo, Plains ref. to N. Y. 2-2-1831; dis 1-2-1832 & Plains notified
Lydia (form Birdsall) rocf Chap. 2-11-1830; rem with parents (clear) 2-11-1830; dis mo 1-2-1833

SPRINGER
Bess (nm), dt John & Bell (Rummel), b Atlanta, Ga. 2-11-1888; m 1910 Norris B. STRINGHAM (H)
recrq 7-10-1911

SQUIER
Bertrand Wintringham, s Lucien B. & Ellen (Hoxie), b Orange, N. J. 7-15-1898; rel 9-14-1925 & joined Episc. Ch. (H)
Lucien B., s Gardner & Caroline M. (Howe), b Delphi, N. Y. 12-20-1829 d 1-4-1904; m 1-1-1855 Ellen H. HOXIE, dt Isaac Upton & Hannah (Anthony), b Adams, Mass. 6-27-1833 d 10-18-1904 (H)
Ch: Lucien B. Jr. b 5-4-1867
Benjamin B. b 10-11-1868 d 12-25-1921
Lucien recrq 2-4-1855; cf Easton for Ellen 4-8-1857; ch names entered by comm. 5-17-1880
Lucien B. Jr., s Lucien B. & Ellen H., Bkn., b 5-4-1867 d 3-10-1911; m at J. Wintringham's 2-25-1891, Helen Eliz. WINTRINGHAM, dt Jere. & Eliz. V., Bkn., b 2-28-1863 d 1-1917 (H)
Ch: Bertrand Wintringham b Orange, N. J. 7-15-1898
Infant stillborn 5-16-1892 bPP

SQUIRE
Eliza, dt Samuel & Mary Ann, b 9-16-1851 d 10-17-1898 bPP; m Charles MERRILL
both nm; Eliza rel 3-1880
Grace, dt Charles & Ida, b 5-27-1907; m ----- HAVILAND
cf Marl. 10-1-1930
Samuel d 10-22-1883 ae 69y rem from Greenwood to PP; m ----- Mary Ann -----
Ch: Thomas
Mary Ann
Emma b 10-13-1842
Edward L. b 11-22-1847
Sarah
Eliza " 10-16-1851
cf Southwark 11-12-1839 to Phila. MM with 2 ch named; recorded in N. Y. without comment; Mary Ann dis 1855; ct Eng. for Edward L. & Sarah, cert ret. 1858, reissued 10-1860; Samuel & ch rel 3-1880

STABLER
Anna M., dt Francis, rocf Balt. with father 3-5-1879; relrq 9-7-1881 (H)
C. Norman, s Chas. M. & Ida (Palmer), b George Sch., Pa. 1-13-1901; m 9-22-1923 Elizabeth MILLER, dt H. Griffen & Mary W. (Roberts), b Mt. Vernon 10-12-1900 (H)
Ch: Chas. N. Jr. b 1-31-1925
Griffen Miller b 2- 3-1927
Edward Palmer " 5-30-1929

STABLER, C. Norman & Elizabeth, continued
Ch: John Roberts b 1932
cf Swarthmore 9-10-1928 for father & 2 ch; cf Newtown, Pa. 5-13-1929 for Elizabeth
Charles M. rocf Balt. 8-1-1888; ct Sandy Spring 10-7-1891 (H)
Cornelia, dt Francis, rocf Balt. with father 3-5-1879; ct Makefield, Pa. 10-9-1897 (H)
Edward H., s Edward & Mary (both dec), Balt., b N. Y. d 2-2-1877 ae 64y bPP; m at Richard Field's, Bkn. 6-15-1859 Louisa M. FIELD, dt Richard & Deborah M., Bkn., b N. Y. 8-2-1829 d 2-12-1914 (H)
Ch: Mary C. d 12-10-1869 ae 7y bPP
Edward L. b 4-20-1865
Louise Merritt b 2-27-1868
ct Balt. 1-1860 for Louisa; cf Balt. 2-1866 for both with 2 ch
Edward L., s Edward (dec) & Louisa M. (Field), Bkn., b 4-20-1865; m at J. Tubby's 6-12-1890 Elizabeth TUBBY, dt Josiah T. & Phebe Anna (Bunker), Bkn., b Bkn. 8-2-1866 (H)
Ch: Eleanor M. b 9-27-1892
Anna Bunker b 12-18-1901
Howard Parker b 10-26-1903
Edward Russell b 9-14-1906
Eliz.'s name entered by com. 6-4-1890
Edw. Russell, s Edw. L. & Eliz. T., Greenwich, b Bkn. 9-14-1906; m Ann Arbor, Mich. 9-12-1931 Anna Ellora COPE (nm), dt Otis M. & Sarah M., Omaha (H)
Eleanor M., dt Edw. L. & Eliz. T., Bkn., b 9-27-1892; m 1914 Charles F. BROOKS (H)
Francis d 6-30-1885; m ----- (H)
Ch: Cornelia
Anna M.
Norman d 8-30-1889
Howard Parker, s Edward L. & Eliz. (Tubby), b Bkn. 10-26-1903; m 4-5-1932 Margaret A. VAN ALSTYNE (nm), dt Wm. B. & Harriet (Kelley) (h)
Louise M., dt Edward H. & Louisa M., b 2-27-1868 Bkn.; m 6-15-1894 George Howard PARKER (nm) (H)
Walter rocf Balt. 4-2-1879; relrq 8-3-1881 (H)

STACKHOUSE
Hastings d 1-28-1800 bHS

STAFFE
Ethel Mae m Henry JAMES; cf Germantown 6-1927
William E. [Staff] m 11-17-1904 at Malvern, Pa. MH, Malinda HAINES, of Elkinton; Wm. recrq 8-3-1904; ct R. & P. 8-1-1906

STAFFORD
Pauline (nm), dt Roy E. & Jennie (Davis); m 1930 Joseph Haywood GEST (H)

STAIGER
A. David & Sophie K.
Ch: Gladys Helen
David La Shell
David rocf Coatesville, 9-1925; Sophie K. recrq 1-7-1931; ch recrq of parents 1-7-1931

STAINTON
John L., s Robt. S. & Eldora, Chester, Pa., b Chester, Pa. 10-24-1898; m Central Valley 6-20-1925 Katherine CORNELL, dt Edward & Esther, Central Valley, b 2-12-1904 (H)
Ch: Katherine b 10-22-1929
ct Corn. 6-1930 for all
Margaret N., w Henry, dt Benj. & Phebe CORLIES, b 7-12-1814 d 5-21-1875 (H) (m 1834)

STANLEY
Hezel D. m ----- HASSINGER (nm)
cf Westfield, Ind. 12-6-1905 with Pearl B. (prob. sister)
Pearl B. m ----- AMESS
cf Westfield, Ind. 12-6-1905; ct Los Angeles 1-4-1933 (prob. sister to Hazel)

STANSBURY
Frances (nm) b Bridgetown, N. J. d 1-15-1817 ae 57y 10m bHS
Susan's mother
Joseph Albert d 2-1-1809 ae 6y 11m 10d bHS (perhaps ch of Sarah)
Sarah (late Clark)
Ch: (perhaps) Joseph A. d 2-1-1808 ae 6y 11m 10d bHS
dis mo 8-3-1796
Susanna (form Schank) rocf R. & P. 11-19-1812; dis mo by a priest 4-2-1823

STANTON
Daniel gct Phila. 2 Mo (Apr) 3, 1745
Henry (nm) & -----
Ch: Infant stillborn 11-19-1834 bHS
Jonathan H. (nm) & -----
Ch: Lydia M. b N. Y. d 1-23-1843 ae 4y 6m 8d bHS
Louise m Royal J. DAVIS
cf Balt. with h & ch 11-2-1910
Margaret, w Henry (form Corlies) (H)
Martha, w John, rocf Newport 11-20-1818; ct Newport 8-1-1821
Mary (nm) b N. J. d 2-28-1836 ae 55y bHS (wd)

STAPLES
John J., s Wm. J. & Hannah W., d 8-20-1900 bPP; m Rosalie LYDIG, dt Phillip M. & Catharine M., d 4-27-1925 ae 82y 2m 13d bPP
William J. (or Wm. T.) (nm) m Hannah W. ----- d 8-3-1858 ae 40y bPP (nm)
Ch: Amelia d 8- 4-1851 ae 3m bPP
John Jr.
all nm

STARBUCK
Nathaniel & Merab
Ch: Mary
Hannah
Stephen

STARBUCK, Nathaniel & Merab, continued
Ch: Benjamin
cf Easton 8-21-1817; ct Troy 6-3-1818 with all named, the dt (clear)
Nathaniel, s Benj. & Hepzibah (both dec), Troy, N. Y.; m at Nathaniel Starbuck's 4-3-1851 Lydia A. WILLIAMS, dt Silas & Deborah BUNKER (both dec), d 11-11-1870 ae 72y bPP (H)
Lydia A. m 1st Benjamin MACY; m 2d 1849 Hezekiah WILLIAMS
ct Troy for Lydia 9-3-1851

STARKINS
Julia E. d 9-28-1900; m James C. HAWXHURST (H)

STARR
John rocf ND MM 7-27-1824
Mary M. gr dt Wm. & Phebe L. BUNTING, d 3-1-1921 bPP (ashes) (unm) (H)

STEARNS
Lutie B., s Isaac H. & Catharine (Guild), b Stoughton, Mass. 9-13-1866; recrq 8-12-1919 (H)
Winthrop, s J. Milton & Marie (Kissam), b Bkn. 3-19-1887; m 7-4-1915 Nella WHITNEY, dt Chas. B. & Katie Gould (Robinson), b Chelsea, Mass. 1-10-1889 (H)
Ch: Winthrop 2d b 5-25-1916
Barbara " 1-22-1918
Paul Adams " 9-6-1919
Whitney Kneeland b 10-3-1923
Winthrop recrq 3-9-1925; Nella recrq 11-12-1928; ch recrq of parents 11-12-1928

STEBBINS
Londa, s Alfred & Edith (Large), b Alameda, Calif. 5-30-1872; m ----- FLETCHER (H)
recrq 4-14-1924

STEELE
Catharine (nm) b Maryland d 9-29-1835 ae 52y bHS rem to PP (unm)
Thomas [Steel] gct Dublin 3-9-1783 to visit his aged parents, left his w & ch here; cf Dublin 1-9-1784; ct Redstone MM 7-7-1790 for Thomas, he rem to Kentucky

STEER
Isaac E., s Samuel L. & Harriet A. (Taylor) b Balt. 9-2-1847 d 10-14-1909; m 2-24-1875 Ida G. SIGMAN (nm), dt Abram & Susan (H)
cf Fairfax 8-3-1881
James D., s Franklin M. & Mary F., Wash., D. C. m at N. Y. 8-11-1892 Mary A. REES, dt Jonah L. & Anna T., N. Y. (H)
cf Fairfax 6-6-1873 for James; ct Alexandria 3-4-1891 for James; ct Alexandria 12-7-1892 for Mary
Margaret, dt Wm. & Mary; m ----- HUNT
recrq 5-4-1932 as Hunt

STEHL
George Christopher, dt Edward Rich's & Wilhelmine, b N. Y. 12-29-1870; m -----
Ch: Richard E. b 4-20-1894
George recrq 5-23-1917; Richard recrq of father, same date; name erased 6-7-1933

STEINER
Ina (nm) m 6-3-1911 Thomas Smith BUCKMAN (H)
Martha (nm) m 10-25-1899 Robt. Valentine MATHEWS (H)

STEINHAUSER
----- (nm) m Mary (changed to Muriel R.) ROGERS, dt Henry B.
cf Salem, Mass. 5-1891 with father 5-6-1891

STELLING
Lydia b Balt. d 1-30-1843 ae 39y 1m bHS

STEPHANIAN
Acabe m Jacob MEGIRIAN

STEPHENS
----- & ----- (nm)
Ch: Frederick S. b Phila. d 10-3-1827 ae 8y 1m bHS
Emily d 3-12-1832 ae 45y 4m 5d bHS

STERN
Hettie, dt Louis & Rosalie, Mt. Vernon; m 1906 Alfred Henry WALDMEIER

STERRETT
Frank Meade, s Jas. W. & Margaret W. (Mann), b Phila. 9-26-1863; m 5-29-1915 Florence PALMER, dt Eli & Marianna (Smedley), b West Chester, Pa. 8-5-1879 (H)
Ch: James Woods b 4- 6-1916
both recrq 4-8-1929 with James W.

STETSON
Jennie K., w John, dt Daniel K. HAWXHURST (H)
cf Phila. with father 3-2-1887
John S. (nm) m 8-13-1896 Jennie K. HAWXHURST, dt Daniel K. & Maria S. (Thomas), b 8-8-1874 (H)
Ch: Sherman Hawxhurst b 11-17-1897
Walter Kissam b 6- 9-1905 d 10-1918
Sherman Hawxhurst, s John S. & Jennie K. (Hawxhurst) b 11-17-1897; ct Chicago 4-11-1922 (H)

STEVENS
Charles J. rocf Kingston, Eng. 3-1881; d Port de Paix, Haiti, 7-17-1900
Edward grantee in deed of land for the first MH in N. Y. 1696; photostat in "Quakerism in N. Y."
Edward Jr., s Edward, grantee in deed of land for the first MH in N. Y. 1696; photostat in "Quakerism in N. Y."
Emily, w Benjamin, rocf ND MM 10-23-1807; d 3-

STEVENS, continued
12-1832
Sarah (nm), dt John & Sarah, b Kent, Eng. 9-10-1841 d 12-11-1928 bPP; m John G. PORTER (nm)
----- (nm) m Sarah ----- b 1813 d 1-3-1899 bPP
Ch: Fanny b 12-26-1852 d 1-6-1899 bPP

STEVENSON
Ann, dt Thomas & Ann, Newtown; m 1715 Samuel THORN
Edward, Newtown, d 8 Mo (Oct) 12, 1700
Grace W. (nm), dt Morris & Lydia (Walton); m 1-23-1909 A. Wright CHAPMAN (H)
John, Westchester, d 3 Mo (May) 2, 1728; m ----
Ch: John
took cert of clear to West Jersey 12 Mo. 7, 1705
John, s John, Newtown; m between 2-9 & 10 Mo (Dec) 7, 1738 (cert not recorded)
Thomas, Sr., s Thomas, Newtown, d 2 Mo (Apr) 6, 1725; m Elizabeth LAWRENCE
Ch: Elizabeth d 9 Mo 27, 1703
Thomas
William
John
Susannah
Ann
3 others
Thomas active mbr from 1696
Thomas, Sr., Newtown, m 2d Ann -----
Thomas took cert of clear to West Jersey 12 Mo 7 1705
Thomas, Jr., Newtown, & Sarah
took cert of general clearness to W. Jersey 2 Mo (Apr) 6, 1699; mbr 1702
William, Newtown, took cert of clear to ----- 9 Mo (Nov) 2, 1699

STEVES
Egbert O. (nm) m 10-5-1899 Jennie M. WILLIAMS, dt Morris R. & Eleanor (Hanna), b N. Y. 1-19-1852 d 3-2-1923 (H)
she was wd of Lee WITHY; recrq 5-8-1915

STEWART
Ann M. (nm), dt Hugh & Susanna (Moran); m 1932 Ayres Cromwell SEAMAN (H)
Catharine (late Hopkins) dis mo 5-3-1809
Hannah (late Hopkins) dis mo 1-1-1817
Isabel rocf Lisburn, Ire. 2-5-1908; name erased 4-1928
Sarah (late Hopkins) dis mo 5-3-1809
Thomas (nm) d 1-15-1912; m 6-20-1877 Elizabeth M. COCK, dt Geo. E. & Mary M., b 4-30-1845 d 1-1-1917

STEYMETS
Mary d 3-17-1797

STICKNEY
Adaline, dt John T. & Sarah CARPENTER, mo before 7-6-1864 to Frank Stickney (H)
rel 4-4-1866; in Milwaukee 1859 (prob. joined Cong. Ch. there)
Anna, dt Samuel C. & Mary A. (Webster), b Roch. 1-24-1876; m ----- CURTIS (H)
cf Farm. 4-6-1887; Anna d 12-14-1919
Byron, s Samuel C. & Mary A. (Webster), b Picton, Ont. 9-26-1868; cf Farm. with mother 4-6-1887; relrq 3-5-1904 (H)
Samuel C., s Walter & Phebe; m 12-13-1867 Mary A. WEBSTER, dt John B. & Edith (Eves), b Whitechurch, Canada 11-27-1846 (H)
Ch: Byron b Picton, Ont. 9-26-1868
Edith Goodrich b Roch. 2-24-1876
cf Farm. 4-6-1887 for Mary; Samuel mbr Bloomfield, Ont.

STILWELL
William d 10-6-1842 bHS, rem to PP; m Mary ---- d 10-19-1841 bHS, rem to PP (H)
cf Jericho 4-19-1798 for both; he dis 8-1829 (O)

STIM
Lucille E. (nm), dt Louis A. & Natalia M.; m 1934 Thomas GARRETT (H)

STINARD
Emily rocf Pur. 11-1836; dis 4-1837

STIRRIDGE
Zachary (called Zachariah in last cert) rocf 2 weeks mtg, London, 9-1-1783 to Phila. MM (clear); a mbr of Grace Church St. MM with father's consent; James Stirridge one of the signers, endorsement by Phila. MM 10-27-1785; ct Grace Church St. 10-5-1785

STITT
William (nm) & -----
Ch: Infant stillborn 11-9-1844 bHS

STIVERS
Martha, dt Thomas & Kesiah, N. Y.; m 11-1833 Joseph C. DODGE (H)
Thomas (nm) b L. I. d 5-16-1827 ae 71y bHS
Thomas, Jr. d 1-7-1852 ae 75y bPP; m Kezia ----- d 3-19-1850 (H)
Ch: Martha
cf Wby 7-17-1816, minor; all dis 1829-1830 (O); Thomas refused to open basement at Hester St. 1828 for YM (O)

STOCKDALE
George Maychim, s Fairbank B. & Sarah Ann (Maychim); m 6-30-1913 Winifred M. DENNIS, dt Alfred & Frances (Wyckoff) (H)
Ch: George Fairbanks b Spencerport, N. Y. 7-13-1921
Winifred recrq 2-12-1934; ch recrq of mother 2-12-1934

STODDART
Amy (late Pearsall) b Oyster Bay d 1-26-1820

STODDART, Amy, continued
ae 31y bHS; dis mo 10-4-1815

STOKES
Abraham m Hannah -----, a minister, d 12-21-1836 ae 65y bHS
cf Chesterfield 7-2-1811; Abm. dis 5-3-1815; Hannah dis 1829 (H)
Samuel rocf Phila., Cherry St. 4-5-1848; ct Phila. 10-1852; cert ret. with information of his d; d 9-14-1852 (H)
Thomas, Waterford, N. J.; m Wby 7 Mo (Sep) 1, 1715 Rachel WRIGHT, dt Job (dec) & Rachel, O. B.
----- & ----- (nm)
Ch: Serena b N. Y. d 2-4-1829 ae 1y 10m bHS

STOKEY
Isaac (nm) & -----
Ch: Catharine b N. Y. d 1-31-1830 ae 6m bHS

STONE
Annie L. m Joseph T. McDOWELL (H)

STONEHILL
William M., s John & Sarah (Wilson), b Oxford, Eng. 2-28-1855 d 2- 5-1908 bPP; m E. Daisy -----

STOREY
Dorothea, dt Creighton R. & Sadie (Bogue), b Kingston, N. Y. 8-30-1893; m 1930 Luman P. KELSEY (H)

STORRS
Joseph rocf Nottingham, Eng. 10-6-1802; d 10-5-1803 ae about 25 bHS
Patience, wd Robert, N. Y.; m 1684 Thomas LLOYD
Patience active mbr from 1676

STORY
Robert d 10 Mo (Dec) 29, 1683, N. Y.; m Patience -----
Ch: Mary b 11 Mo (Jan) 9, 1677/8
Mary " 10 Mo (Dec) 21, 1679
Enoch b 12 Mo (Feb) 12, 1680/1
Patience m 2d Thomas LLOYD (1tm 10 Mo. Dec. 27, 1684
cert of clear from Phila; rem to Phila.; active mbr 1676
----- (nm) m Martha C. CORNELL, dt Franklin & Sarah R., b 5-30-1883
cf Corn. 9-3-1890 for Martha

STOTHARD
James & -----
Ch: Eliza d 10-19-1839 ae 2y 6m 10d bHS
all nm

STOUGHTENBURGH
David [Stoutenburgh] (nm) m Mary Ann ----- b Eng. d 11-18-1842 ae 20y bHS

James V., s Peter & Parmelia, rocf Creek 8-22-1823 with parents; ct Chap. 11-1864 (H)
Joseph, s Peter L. & Parmelia, rocf Creek 8-22-1823 with parents; dis 4-5-1848; joined U. S. Army in Mexico before 3-1-1848 (H)
Mary, dt Peter L. & Parmelia; m ----- CONOVER (H) cf Creek 8-22-1823 with parents, ret a mbr; ct Cincinnati 6-5-1862
Peter L. b Dutchess Co. d 12-21-1831 ae 45y; m Pamelia ----- d 1834 (H)
Ch: Jacob F. d 6-11-1879
Samuel V.
Wright F.
James V.
Joseph dis 4-5-1848
Edwin d 12-19-1824
Sarah b 9-11-1825
Mary " 12-25-1828
cf Creek 8-22-1823; all dis 1830-1848 (O)
Samuel V., s Peter L. & Parmelia, rocf Creek 8-22-1823 with parents; ct Chap. 3-1860 (H)
Sarah, dt Peter L. & Parmelia, d 5-16-1860; m ----- SCHENCK (H)
cf Creek 8-22-1823 with parents
Wright F., s Peter L. & Parmelia, rocf Creek 8-22-1823 with parents; ct Ama. 7-1870 (H)

STOUGHTON
Bradley (nm), s Chas. B. (dec) & Ada R., New Haven, b 9-21-1874; m at Bkn. 1-4-1899 Grace Abbie VAN EVEREN, dt Philip F. & Eliz. J., Bkn., b Bkn. 9-21-1874 d 1-16-1905 (H)
Ch: Philip Van Everen b 2-20-1900 in Chicago
Grace's name entered by comm. 6-4-1890;
Philip's name recrq of parents 9-7-1901
Philip Van Everen, s Bradley & Grace A. (Van Everen), b Chicago 2-20-1900; m Lenore BLANCHARD (nm) (H)
Ch: Lenore Maple b 6-21-1931
Philip recrq of mother 9-7-1901; Lenore M. recrq of parents 9-14-1931

STOUT
Nette (mbr Lawrence, Kans.), dt John W. & Lucetta; m 1929 Alfred ROSSITER (H)

STOVER
Amy Jane, dt Egbert P. & Anna E., b 1872; m ----- ROACH
cf Corn. with parents 5-1883; letter to Presby. Ch. Corn. on Hudson 5-3-1899
Egbert P. d 7-21-1911; m Anna E. ----- d rpd 4-1928
Ch: Amy Jane 11
Egbert P. Jr. 16 mos.
cf Corn. 5-1883
Egbert P. Jr., s Egbert P. & Anna E., rocf Corn. 5-1883 (then 16m old) with parents 5-1883; name erased 4-1828
S. Elizabeth, dt Adam J. & Charity A. (Snyder), b Norwich, Ont. 5-24-1863 d 11-10-1918; recrq 6-3-1891; assistant Principal Friends

STOVER, S. Elizabeth, continued
Seminary (unm)

STRANGMAN

William rocf Waterford, Ire. 7-11-1784, he about to voyage to N. Y., thence to Phila. & return within a yr.

STRATTAN

Benjamin W., s Jos. P. & Martha W. (Jefferies) b Richmond, Ind. 8-13-1834; m 1-30-1878 Hallie FOSTER (nm), dt Reuben & Betsy (H)
cf Milford, Ind. 9-7-1864; ct Chicago 1-11-1911 (H)

Edward Rudolph, s Enoch & Amy (Thorn), b N. Y. 2-11-1850; m 2-20-1879 Clara Hayes McCORMICK (nm) (H)
Edward long unknown, name cancelled 4-9-1904

Emily L., dt Enoch & Amy T.; m 1863 William E. HULL (H)
cf Phila. 10-1848 with parents

Enoch, Jr. m Amy T. THORN (H)
Ch: Isabella M.
Mary Anna
George W. b 1-26-1836
Virginia T.
Emilie L.
William Irvine b 9-14-1845
Edward Rudolph " 2-11-1850
cf Everham 7-8-1826; dis 10-1830 (O); ct Phila. 8-1829 (H); cf Phila. Green St. 10-1848

Fannie J., dt Robert M., d 2-10-1875 ae 40y bPP; m ----- SIMPSON (H)

G. Edmund, s Geo. W. & M. Virginia (Satterthwaite), b Altoona, Pa. 10-3-1873; m 11-20-1913 Deborah FERRIER (nm)
Edmund's name entered by comm. 3-29-1887; ct Moorestown 5-9-1921

George W., s Enoch, Jr. & Amy T., b Phila. 1-26-1836 d 4-14-1917; m 9-24-1863 M. Virginia SATTERTHWAITE (nm), dt Samuel & Hannah A., d 2-10-1897 (H)
Ch: Charlotte L.
Clement T. b 5-29-1868 d 7-22-1889
G. Edmund b 10-29-1873
Virginia M. d 2-10-1897
cf Phila. Green St. 10-1848 with parents; ch's names entered by comm. 3-29-1887; M. Virginia recrq 5-4-1887

George W., s Enoch, Jr. & Amy (Thorn); m 2d 8-30-1906 Margaret SCHNEIDER, dt Christopher F. & Louisa E. (Westbrook), b Altoona, Pa. 4-25-1869 (H)
Margaret recrq 2-9-1907

Isabella M., dt Enoch & Amy, N. Y.; m 1852 Joseph T. McDOWELL (H)

Latham, s Benjamin & Judith, d 3-18-1849 ae 72y 8m 8d bur Troy, rem to PP 9-27-1899; m Phebe MEAD, d 12-31-1829 ae 49y 2m bur Troy, rem to PP 9-27-1899 (H)
Ch: Phebe Ann d 11-13-1831 ae 14y 10m 9d bur Troy, rem to PP 9-27-1899
all nm here

Mary Anna, dt Enoch & Amy T., N. Y., b Phila. 5-9-1833 d 1-11-1924; m 1854 Edward SCANTLEBURY (H)

Virginia T., dt Enoch Jr. & Amy (Thorn), b Phila. 3-20-1838 d 3-9-1914; m 6-8-1859 George BILLIN (nm) (H)
cf Phila. Green St. with parents 10-1848

Wm. Irvine, s Enoch Jr. & Amy (Thorn), b Phila. 9-14-1845 d 10-21-1920; m 6-17-1875 Elizabeth ONDERDONK, dt John W. & Margaret (Colons), b N. Y. 6-18-1852 d 11-16-1930 (H)
William rocf Phila. 10-1848 with parents; Elizabeth recrq 8-3-1881

STRATTON

Benjamin, s Caleb & L---- b Nantucket d 5-3-1810 ae 73y 1m bHS; m Judith ----- d 6-24-1799 bHS
Ch: Latham d 1849 bPP
cf Creek 4-17-1795 with their s, Latham, & Phebe Mead apprenticed to learn tailoring

Benjamin, Jr., s Benj. & Judith, Dutchess Co., N. Y.; m N. Y. 8-13-1794 Ann WILLIS, dt Wm. & Amy, Summerset Co., N. J.
Ch: William W. b 12-21-1800
Enos Alley " 9-30-1802 d 7-21-1803 ae 9m
Samuel W.
Benjamin W. b 5-17-1813
Joseph
Eliza
cf Creek 8-16-1793 (clear); ct Duanes 4-1-1807 for Ann with 2 ch named, Wm. W. & Samuel W.; cf De Ruyter 6-26-1811 for Benjamin & Ann with 4 ch, William, Samuel, Joseph & Eliza; ct ND MM 11-1-1815 with 5 ch

Benjamin W., s Benj. Jr. & Ann, b 5-17-1813; ct ND MM 11-1-1815 with parents (H)

Charlotte L., dt Geo. W. & M. Virginia, b Altoona, Pa. 3-27-1865; m 1890 Clarence E. POSTLETHWAITE (nm) (H)
Charlotte recrq 5-4-1887

Elizabeth rocf Creek 4-17-1795 about to rem with her parents (clear); ct Hudson 7-7-1813 (clear)

Hannah M. (nm) d 12-5-1869 ae 46y bPP (H)

Hannah F., dt Jane MARSH, rec 1-1833; d 7-21-1854 (H)

Latham & Phebe
Ch: Lydia b 7- 5-1798
Hannah " 6-19-1800
Robert M. " 5-22-1803
Nathaniel M. b 2-20-1807
Cinthia " 10-19-1809
Alexander " 1-20-1813
Phebe Ann " 1- 5-1817
Latham took cert of clear to Creek 9-7-1797; Phebe rocf Creek 1-19-1798; ct Oswego 8-2-1820 with 6 minor ch, not including Lydia

STRATTON, continued
Lydia, dt Latham & Phebe, N. Y.; m 1819 Alexander J. COFFIN, of Athens, N. Y.
Robert M. b 1803; m Jane WILSON, d 8-11-1858 ae 53y 3m 29d bPP
Ch: Robert M. b 2-13-1844
Mary Lois d 6-30-1829 ae 4y 2m bPP
Robert M. b 5-23-1803 d 4-10-1874 bPP; m at R. M. Stratton's 10-6-1859 (not under care of N. Y. MM) Louisa MACY (H)
cf Oswego 1-15-1823 (clear); dis 1824; rst 5-1842
Robert M., s Robt. M. & Jane W., b 2-13-1844 N. Y. d 5-29-1911 bPP; recrq 8-7-1897 (H); relrq 8-10-1907 (H); recrq 8-7-1907 (O) (unm)
Virginia (mbr of Swarthmore), dt Daniel & Josephine (Graves); m 1932 Julien Davies CORNELL (H)
ct Corn. 12-11-1933 with h & ch
----- (nm) m Hannah WHITE, dt Amos & Ann, b 6-2-1818 (H)

STREET
John G. (nm) d 1-13-1882 ae 70y 11m ; m Lydia S. WRIGHT, dt Joseph, d 4-24-1866 ae 50y 2m 7d (H)
cf New Garden, O. 7-1847 for Lydia S.

STREETER
Daniel Denison, s Milford B. & S. Maria (Wyckoff), b Bkn. 1-27-1885; m 6-10-1914 Gladys M. RUDOLPH (nm), dt Wm. Henry (H)
Ch: Catharine b 1-23-1917
Daniel D. Jr. b 2-8-1925
Samuel Schuyler b 5-19-1926
Sarah Ann " 4-24-1931
cf Wby for Daniel & 3 ch 11-10-1930; Sarah Ann recrq of parents 9-14-1931

STREIGHT
Elizabeth, dt John & Margaret; m 8-12-1848 Wm. JOHNSON (H)
Eliz. prob nm

STRINGHAM
Ernest J., s Jas. C. & Gertrude (Van Keuren), b Hyde Park, N. Y. 3-24-1876; m 3-19-1902 Adis H. WALFORD (nm), dt Robert & Sadie (H)
Ernest recrq 7-8-1899
Eugene H., s John & Ann Eliza (Barnes), b Hyde Park, N. Y. 8-2-1873; m 10-19-1910 Eleanor Caroline KEELER (nm), dt Henry W. & Emilia (Braun) (H)
Ch: Altheas b 10-3-1911
cf Creek with parents 11-3-1891; ct Jenkintown, Pa; Eleanor recrq 7-10-1911
Irving J., s John & Ann Eliza (Barnes), b Crum Elbow 12-18-1867; m 2-29-1892 Eleanor DEYO, dt Charles & Amanda b Crum Elbow 2-22-1866 (H)
Ch: Marion b 5-17-1898
Ch: Ralph Irving b 4-4-1900 d 5-10-1912
Lydia " 2-28-1909
Irving rocf Creek with parents 11-3-1891; Eleanor recrq 2-3-1892; ct Wby 11-9-1912 for all
James C., s David & Lydia (Barnes), b Clinton, N. Y. 9-22-1835 d 2-2-1925; m 12-20-1865 Gertrude VAN KEUREN, dt Benj. & Mary Ann, b Clinton, N. Y. 10-16-1842 d 12-25-1917 (H)
Ch: Willis T. b 7-31-1869
Ernest J. " 3-24-1876
Norman D. " 1-18-1874
Gertrude M. b 9-17-1868
Winifrid " 12-22-1896
Leroy Marshall b 10- 9-1898
cf Creek 2-16-1900 for James; Gertrude recrq 4-7-1900
John, s David & Lydia (Barmore), b 9-22-1835 Clintontown, N. Y. d 12-31-1915; m 9-3-1857 Ann Eliza BARNES, dt Henry & Emily (Wildey), b 10-16-1835 Clinton, N. Y. d 1-14-1913 (H)
Ch: Irving J. b 12-18-1867
Eugene H. " 8- 2-1873
Norris B. " 9- 4-1880
cf Creek for all 11-3-1891
Norman D., s James C. & Gertrude, Bkn., b Crum Elbow 1-18-1874; m at A. E. Marshall's 8-4-1896 Bkn. Gertrude MARSHALL, dt Albert E. & Charlotte J., b 9-17-1868 Bkn. (H)
Ch: Winnifred b 12-22-1896
Leroy Marshall b 10-19-1898
Norman recrq 3-1-1893; Gertrude's name entered by comm. 11-18-1884; ct R. & P. for all 3-11-1911
Norris B., s John & Ann Eliza (Barnes), b Hyde Park, N. Y. 9-4-1880; m 1-1-1910 Bess SPRINGER (nm), dt John & Bell (Rummel), b Atlanta, Ga. 2-18-1888 (H)
Ch: Elliot Barnes b Roslyn, L. I. 8-13-1912
Norris rocf Creek with parents 11-3-1891; Bess recrq 7-10-1911
Samuel, Flushing, d before 1774; m Hannah ----- d 7-30-1774
Ch: Samuel d 5-31-1794
Sarah
Sarah, dt Samuel & Hannah, Flushing; m 1746 Daniel BOWNE
Willis T., s Jas. C. & Gertrude (Van Keuren), b Crum Elbow 7-31-1869 d 6-6-1921; m 4-19-1905 Florence COZINE (nm), dt Joseph & Catharine (H)
Willis recrq 3-1-1893

STROPE
Diana (nm), w -----
Ch: Julia b Hudson d 4-1-1848 ae 8y 11m bHS

STUBBS
Edith B., dt Horace R. & Lucretia (Williamson), b Bkn. 2-8-1915; m 1935 Elwood A. CHINSLEY (H)

STUBBS, continued
Horace R., s Howard L. & Lizzie (Reister), b Oxford, Pa. 9-7-1887; m 4-7-1913 Laurette W. WILLIAMSON, dt Frank H. & Anna L. (Hieweg), b Lincoln Union, Pa. 12-25-1886 (H)
Ch: Louise R. b 1-28-1914
Edith B. " 2- 8-1915
Elizabeth R. " 4- 4-1916
Jean W. " 9- 2-1918
Horace rocf Nottingham MM 12-13-1920; Laurette W. recrq 1-8-1920; ch recrq of parents 1-8-1920

STUDWELL
Mary, w Edwin A., dt John Jr. & Hannah B. MERRITT (H) (m 9-23-1862)
relrq 7-7-1869

STURDEVANT (or Sturtavant)
Harry E., s Edgar D. & Augusta, d 3-2-1923 ae 50y bPP; m Jennie D. DISTURNELL, d 5-24-1916 ae 51y 7m 4d bPP (H)
----- (nm) m Mary LEGGETT, dt John & Sarah, d 7-21-1849 (H)

STURGE
Edw. Pease, s Wilson & Sara (both dec) Hampstead, Eng.; m Pur. 6-5-1926 Grace Lower WARREN, dt Geo. W. & Mary Alice, Harrison, N. Y.
Ch: b in England
Grace recrq 11-6-1912; ct Westminster & Longford, Eng. 9-1926

STYMETS (or Stimets)
Mary gct Pur. 8-5-1779; cf Chap. 6-10-1784

SUMLEADER
Sophia m Oscar GOERKE
Sophia recrq 12-2-1908

SUTCLIFF
John, s Abm. & Sarah (both dec), N. Y., b Eng. d 9-11-1828 ae 66y; m N. Y. 10-9-1817 Elizabeth DAVIS, dt Isaac & Ann PATCHING, London, b Eng. d 2-24-1839 ae 68y 5m (H)
cf Balby, Eng. 6-9-1803 (clear); Elizabeth Davis recrq

SUTHERLAND
Charlotte recrq 4-1-1931
Charlotte P., dt Anna Ella, recrq of mother, 6-12-1901; name erased 4-1928
Donald, s Anna Ella, recrq of mother 6-12-1901; name erased 4-1928
Herman G. & Caroline Anna
Ch: Donald Grant
letter from Webb Horton Memorial Ch., Middletown, N. J. 2-6-1918 for parents; Donald recrq of parents same date
----- (nm) & Anna Ella
Ch: Charlotte P.
Ch: Donald
Anna recrq 6-12-1901; ch recrq of mother 6-12-1901

SUTLIFF
Mary L., dt Timothy M. & Martha (Barnard), b Rensselaer, N. Y. 2-11-1865; recrq 4-15-1918 (unm) (H)

SUTTON
Aaron & Martha
cf Chap. 5-9-1817
Aaron & Melissa
Ch: Charles
ct Queensboro 11-3-1819 with infant Charles
Aaron, s Isaac & Sarah, N. Y.; m N. Y. 5-9-1849 Mary H. GOUGH, dt John M. & Sarah, N. Y.
Ch: Aaron Franklin b 3-10-1850
Adrea H. " 1-28-1852
John M. " 11-30-1854
cf Adrian 1848 for Aaron; cf Corn. 10-1847 for Mary H. (clear); Aaron dis 1854; ct Marl. 3-1864 for the others
Abby Jane (nm) m Thomas THORNE (H)
Abraham m Jane M. ----- d 6-1845 (mo 12-1835)
cf Chap. 3-13-1819; dis 2-1830 (O); Jane recrq 3-1840; ct N. P. 8-1840
Albert, s Joshua, rocf Pur. 6-4-1856; ct Pur. 8-1864 (H)
Alfred m Phebe ----- d 6-25-1855 (H)
Ch: Sarah Jane
Charles T.
cf Chap. 10-1852 for all; ct Pur. 2-5-1857 for father & 2 ch named
Amy, w George, d 6-27-1872
Ch: Rebecca 6y 3m when rec
rst 2-1825; Rebecca recrq of mother 11-2-1829; dis 10-1829 (H)
Ann (nm) d 11-20-1834 ae 35y bHS
Ann M. (nm) d 12-17-1851 ae 54y 7m 14d bPP
Anna, dt George Thomas & Margaret, d 9-30-1832 ae 63y 3m 10d bPP; m William R. PITT (H) (both nm)
Anne H. rocf Stanford 4-1886; d 5-1-1900
Caleb d 12-11-1835 ae 86y 1m bHS; m Hannah ----- b Pa. d 8-10-1819 ae 75y
Ch: Abigail
Hannah (or Anna) d 11-26-1834 bHS
cf Corn. 9-26-1811, ch clear; Caleb dis 6-1829 (H)
Caleb rocf Chap. 5-10-1811, a lad
Caleb U. dis mo 3-5-1817
Caleb U. Jr. d 6-14-1825 ae 44y 6m bHS (prob same person as one before)
Carrie m Stephen H. BROOKS d 3-13-1911 ae 52y 1m 4d bPP (both nm) (H)
Charles, s Aaron & Melissa (dec), Washington, N. Y.; m at John Lockwood's 12-4-1839 Phebe LOCKWOOD, dt Walter & Martha (dec), N. Y. (H)
Daniel H., s Henry, joined U. S. Army of own free will & served until disabled, dis 5-1-

SUTTON, Daniel H., continued
1860; cf Alexandria 1-2-1861 with father; in Chicago 1866 (H)
Edgar, s Stephen & Anna B., b 5-26-1840; cancelled 5-11-1912 (H)
Edmund rocf Chap. 12-14-1826 (clear); dis 3-1830 (O); ct Battle Creek 9-3-1856 (H)
Eliphalet W., s Jacob H. & Ann Louisa, rocf Scipio 3-1855 with parents; ct Ham. 11-1862 (H)
Elizabeth, dt Silas H. & Mary (Gager), b Chenoa, Ill. 10-6-1879; m 1904 John C. PERCY (H)
recrq 5-6-1899
Elizabeth Ann, dt Silas & Phebe F., b 8-12-1836; m 4-22-1863 John C. DAVIS (nm); (H)
unknown 1900
Elizabeth P., wd Thomas, rocf Pur. 6-6-1859; d 6-22-1883 (H)
Florence K., dt Thos. G. (d 1904) & Emeline (d 1928) (Rapp), b Pur., N. Y. 1874; recrq 12-10-1934; Thomas once mbr of Pur. (H)
Freelove rocf Chap. 1827; d 8-23-1843 (H)
George A., s Geo. T. & Margaret (Dodge); m Leila N. ----- d 11-8-1884 bPP (H)
Ch: Infant stillborn 10-30-1884
George A. d 6-8-1917 ae 63y 21d bPP; m 2d Nellie THORNELL (all nm) (H)
George E., s Alfred & Mary, d 2-4-1920 ae 72y 11m 27d bPP; m 1-19-1885 Selina R. RHODES, dt Ira & Anna Eliza (Pheobus) (or Pheonbus) b Milton, N. Y. 8-31-1867 d 12-12-1928 (H)
Selina rocf N.P. 2-11-1918; Geo. E. mbr N.P.
George Thomas d 8-3-1899 ae 77y 11m 21d bPP; m Margaret DODGE, d 2-11-1907 ae 80y 5m 20d bPP (H)
Ch: Anna m Wm. R. PITT
Amelia Dodge d 11-14-1896 ae 31y 7m 16d bPP
George A.
recrq 3-6-1897; all nm
Hannah W. (nm) d 4-24-1860 ae 52y bPP
Helen, dt Abram & Sarah M. HARRIS, b 9-10-1870 (m 1897 Isaac Sutton)(H)
Henry d 10-26-1881 ae 82y 9m 5d bPP; m Hannah WEEKS d 4-24-1860 ae 53y bPP (H)
Ch: Daniel H.
Mary B. b Croton Valley 11-3-1850
Louisa M. b 9-30-1836 d 1-10-1925
Phebe H.
cf Alexandria 1-2-1861 for Henry & ch
Isaac & Sarah U.
Ch: Townsend b 2-12-1812
William " 5-11-1814
Ann " 2-21-1816
Asa
Edward
cf Chap. 5-10-1811 for Isaac & Sarah; ct Scipio 3-5-1820 with 5 ch named
Isaac M. (nm), s Franklin & Olive, Po'keepsie; m at Arthur Harris', Mt. Vernon 6-2-1897 Helen S. HARRIS, dt Abram C. (dec) & Sarah M. (Young), N. Y., b 9-10-1870 Plainfield, N. J. (H)
Helen recrq of mother 12-5-1883; relrq 5-10-1902
Jacob H. d 3-14-1866 ae 63y 3m 3d bPP; m Ann Louisa WHEELER(?), d 11-7-1869 ae 66y 11m 26d bPP (H)
Ch: Eliphalet W. d 1-30-1832 ae 3m
Mary W.
Sarah Jane
cf Chap. 8-14-1818 (clear); ct Pur. 10-1-1823 (clear); cf Pur. 8-9-1826 as Jacob H. (clear); ct Scipio 11-1833; cf Scipio 3-1855 with w & 3 ch named
James gct Pur. 5-5-1768
Jeannette, dt Silas H. & Mary (Gager), b Chenra, Ill. 8-12-1869; m 6-8-1899 Ferris A. MITCHELL (H)
recrq 5-6-1899
John rocf Pur. 4-11-1811 (clear); ct Charles City, Va. 9-1-1819 (clear)
John & Matilda
Ch: Susan Matilda b 8-15-1830
cf Pur. 8-9-1826 for both; ct Pur. 4-7-1830 for both (O)
John Joseph, s Silas & Phebe F., b 10-11-1839; ct Pur. 9-5-1879; cert ret. 1-6-1886 (H)
Joshua b 11-20-1793 d 1-17-1880; m Phebe B. ----- b 1-26-1802 d 7-15-1881 (H)
Ch: Joshua B. b 6-18-1829
Samuel A. " 7- 9-1831
Albert " 5-20-1833
cf Chap. 7-12-1816 (clear); cf Pur. 5-7-1828 for Phebe B., both dis 1830-1832 (O) ct Pur. 9-1835 for all; cf Pur. 11-1855 for parents
Joshua B., s Joshua & Phebe B., b 6-18-1829 d 7-6-1868; ct Pur. 9-1835 with parents; cf Pur. 5-1856 (H)
Joshua W., s Henry & Hannah W. (dec), N. Y., b 5-3-1839 d 8-28-1906 bPP; m at Wm. T. Carpenter's 11-27-1866 Maria Louisa CARPENTER, dt Wm. T. & Esther Jane (dec), Bkn., b 3-2-1841 d 12-26-1922 bPP (H)
Ch: William Henry b 9- 7-1868
cf Chap. 10-4-1854 for Joshua
Lucretia (nm) b New Paltz d 11-6-1810 ae 30y bHS
Mary b 3-20-1794 d 12-18-1867 (wd); m Isaac A. UNDERHILL (H)
Mary Ann, w David, recrq 9-5-1821; dis 4-1839 (O); dis 1-1854 (H); rst 2-1862; d 4-8-1873
Mary B., dt Henry & Hannah (Weeks), b 11-3-1850; cf Alexandria with father 1-2-1861; ct Alexandria 2-11-1911 (H)
Mary Jane, dt Stephen & Anna B., b 11-27-1834 d 6-13-1892; m 11-30-1865 Robert B. NICHOLAS (H)
Mary W., dt Jacob H. & Ann Louisa, d 5-1-1879 bPP; m 11-15-1859 Wm. B. ALLEN (nm) (H)
cf Scipio 3-1855 with parents
Matilda E., dt Wm. & Charlotte (Hunt), b Mt. Kisco 9-1850 d 11-26-1902; m 1852 Charles L. SKINNER (nm) (H)
cf Chap. 9-4-1850; ret a mbr

SUTTON

Milissa, dt Aaron & Anna H., rocf N. P. 1-7-1891; ct N. P. 8-4-1900 (H)

Moses J. rocf Chap. 6-1863; ct Chap. 4-5-1876

Phebe, w Charles (form Lockwood) gct N. P. 5-1841 (m 1839) (H)

Phebe H., dt Henry & Hannah, Bkn.; m 1-1-1872 George T. Howell, of N. J., at Geneva, Neb. (H)
cf Alexandria 1-2-1861 with parents

Phebe Jane, dt Thos. U. & Martha H., b 10-29-1834; m James MERRICK (H)
ct Little Falls, Md. 12-7-1859

Rebecca (nm) b Westchester Co. d 3-1-1813 ae 29y 10m 3d bHS

Rebecca, dt George & Amy; m Aaron HAVILAND

Rebecca K. recrq 5-7-1851; d 6-19-1881 (sister of ----- Kingsland) (H)

Richard B., s Stephen & Anna B., b 4-12-1838; dis mo by hireling minister 5-6-1868 (H)

Samuel A., st Joshua, rocf Pur. 5-1856; d 7-1893 (H)

Sarah (nm) b Maryland d 2-11-1823 ae 46y bHS

Sarah Eliz., dt Aaron & Anna H., N. Y., b N.P. 3-9-1840 d 3-3-1934 in 95th yr; m 1st Nathaniel GARDNER 1871; m 2d Edward H. MAGILL 1902 (H)
cf N.P. 12-4-1872; Sarah Eliz. d St. Petersburg, Fla., ashes interred Salisbury, Pa.

Sarah Jane, dt Jacob & Ann Louise, rocf Scip. 3-1855 with parents; cancelled 6-11-1912, long unknown (H)

Silas d 2-11-1871; m Phebe ----- d 9-15-1872

Ch: Elizabeth Ann b 8-12-1836
John Joseph b 10-11-1839 d 6-26-1908
Jesse " 8- 9-1832 d 2- 9-1833
cf Pur. 6-9-1830 (clear) (0); dis 1-1831 (0); cf Pur. 10-1833 for both

Stephen d 10-11-1861 (or 10-12-1861); m Anna B. ----- d 8-9-1886 (H)

Ch: Mary Jane b 11-27-1834
William Henry b 9-19-1833 d 12-21-1833
George W. " 1-25-1837 d 6- 3-1837
Richard B. " 4-12-1838
Edgar " 5-26-1840
Stephen I. " 11- 3-1842 d 4-16-1843
Samuel B. " 3-29-1844 d 10-14-1863
cf Chap. 12-14-1826 (clear); dis 3-1830 (0)

Thomas U. m Martha H. ----- d 9-7-1841

Ch: Phebe Jane b 9-29-1827 d 4-22-1833
Robert " 8-28-1830 d 1-24-1856
Phebe Jane " 10-29-1834
George W. " 6-20-1837 d 12-2-1854 bPP
Infant stillborn 3-7-1836
cf Chap. 8-11-1825; ct Chap. 8-1-1827;
cf Chap. 4-1833 with first 2 ch

Thomas U. d 9-28-1880 ae 81y 5m 25d bPP; m 2d Mary R. ----- d 8-31-1858 ae 34y bPP

Ch: Eugene d 2-20-1854 ae 4y 1m 15d bPP
Margaret R. d 3-23-1854 ae 2y bPP

William A. rocf Pur. 8-4-1869; d 10-23-1893 (H)

----- & ----- (nm)

Ch: Caroline b N. Y. d 3-10-1827 ae 1m bHS
Albert d 12-11-1861 ae 54y bPP
Mary D. d 4-31-1866 ae 66y bPP

SUYDAM

Phebe rocf Jericho 2-21-1822 (clear); dis 1-1830

SWAIN

Aaron, having mo, Nantucket refers it to N.Y. 9-27-1839; rpd adversely 7-3-1839

Agnes (nm), dt M. L.; m 1912 Graham T. McCLURE (H)

Ann C., mbr at Nantucket 3-1-1848; d 10-5-1857 ae 77y 6m 7d bPP (H)

Augusta S., dt Charles F. & Mary T., d 12-22-1914 ae 80y 5m 6d bPP; m Robert FOSTER (H) all nm

Charles F. b Nantucket 1806 d 1-3-1896 ae 89y 4m bPP; m Mary T. ----- d 3-28-1885 bPP

Ch: Augusta S.
Maria Louisa
Charles E. d 9-28-1883 ae 43y 8m 22d bPP
name entered by MM 7-2-1873; having mo, Nantucket ref. to N. Y. 5-23-1832; rpd 11-1832 to Nantucket that he not inclined to give satisfaction but intends to attend mtg; he gives clear explanation of his dis by Nantucket for mo 6-4-1873 (0); had since attended Rose St.; cf Sara. 2-1863 for Mary

Edith Neal [Swayne], dt Edward & Mary D. (Walton), b E. Fallowfield, Pa. 10-20-1887 d 1-14-1919 (H)

Edwin J. [Swayne] & Ruth J. (H)

Ch: Bertrand E. b 8-6-1875 d 8-17-1876
Lawrence P. " 7-16-1879
parents & Lawrence relrq 4-6-1881

Elizabeth (nm) d 8-10-1852 ae 72y bPP

Emily B. m ----- FOLGER
ret a mbr; ct Salem, Mass. 1-1863

James Harvey rocf Nantucket 9-1865; mbrp relinquished 3-1880; d 6-2-1888 ae 67y 2m 24d bPP

Lucien B. rocf Nantucket 4-1857, minor; joined the Army before 5-1864, ret a mbr 11-1864; d 1868, said to be in Calif. (Lucius B. in minutes)

Mary, wd Valentine, mbr at Nantucket 11-1847; d 1855 (H)

Mary Ann, sister of Chas. F.; m Sylvester S. (or F.) HUBBARD (Mary Ann d 5-12-1879 ae 70y 4m 12d bPP) (H)

Mary T. rocf Sara. 5-1844; ct Sara. 3-2-1859 (H)

Richard (nm) m Ann ----- (nm) b N. J. d 11-25-1830 ae 24y bHS

Ch: George F. b N. Y. d 6-30-1830 ae 4m 15d bHS

Robert B. d 4-15-1872 bPP

Sarah recrq 1-1839; d 1845

Susan b Nantucket d 8-22-1828 ae 20y bHS (prob mbr Nantucket)

William A., having paid a substitute in a military parade, Nantucket ref. it to N.Y.

SWAIN, William A., continued
4-6-1836, rpd favorable; cf Nantucket 10-27-1836 (O); dis non-attendance 4-1838 (O); rec without cert from Nantucket 4-1837 (H); dis 2-1842 (H)
----- & ----- (nm)
Ch: George d 11-24-1863 ae 84y bPP

SWAN
Frederick Asa m Helen WOOD
Ch: Frederick Wood b 7-20-1907
Gulielma Coffyn b 4-18-1910
Mary Elizabeth b 12-16-1915 d 12-4-1915
cf Boston 4-6-1907 for both
Frederick Wood, s Fred'k Asa & Helen (Wood), b 7-20-1907; ct Westtown, Pa. 1-3-1934

SWART
Deborah, dt John & Deborah, Middletown, N. J.; m 1822 Timothy H. BURGER
recrq 2-7-1821
----- & ----- (nm)
Ch: John b Shrews. d 8-3-1819 ae 17y 2m 14d bHS
Francis b N. Y. d 9-30-1823 ae 1y 8m bHS

SWARTZ
Roberta T., dt Wm. King & Carrie (Teale), b Bkn. 6-9-1903; m 1929 Gordon Keith CHALMERS (H)
recrq 1-11-1926

SWEET
Dodge d 9-16-1835; m Rachel ----- (H)
Ch: Hermes M.
Jervis C.
Betsey b 9-1833
cf Sara. with 2 ch 7-1833; ct Phila. 4-1841 for Rachel & Betsey
Hermes M., s Dodge & Rachel, rocf Sara. 7-1833 with parents; rel 6-2-1875, absent over 5y (H)
Imogene (nm), dt Almond E. & Sarah A.; m 1885 Theodore McDOWELL (H)
Jervis, s Dodge & Rachel, rocf Sara. 7-1833 with parents; ct Phila. 2-1845 (H)
Margaret (late Cheeseman) mo before 12-4-1822, ref. to Oswego, which rpd adversely; dis mo 4-2-1823
----- & ----- (nm)
Ch: George W. d 3-8-1855 ae 13y 11m 14d bPP

SWENSON
Magnus (nm) m Dorothy W. MENDELSON, dt Walter & Mary (Wharton), b N. Y. 5-26-1890 (H)

SWIFT
Zebulon, having joined a military Co., Oswego ref. to N. Y. 11-18-1863; com. rpd 4-6-1864 that he was out in that service a short time, & now feels disposed to go on a national war vessel; we suppose he has now left; rpd to Oswego 5-1864

SWINNERTON
Elizabeth, dt John, recrq of father 11-1838; dis 1-2-1856 (H)
John (nm) m ----- b Ireland d 4-7-1818 ae 35y bHS
Ch: Infant stillborn 3-24-1818 bHS
John b Ireland d 11-20-1841 ae 63y; m 2d ----- (H)
Ch: John William d 1-26-1841 ae 2y 6m bHS
Sarah
Elizabeth
Joseph
John recrq 7-1834 (prob rst); ch recrq of father 11-1838
Joseph, s John, recrq of father 11-1838; dis 8-2-1854 (H)
Richard (nm) b Ireland d 2-11-1826 ae 17y bHS (unm)
Sarah, dt John, recrq of father 11-1838; relrq 10-4-1854 (H)
William, s John, recrq of father 11-1838; dis 11-4-1846 (H)
----- & ----- (nm)
Ch: Robert b Manhattanville d 3-14-1827 ae 1y 2m bHS
Richard b Harlem d 9-4-1837 ae 22d bHS
John W. (prob s John) d 1-26-1841 ae 2y 6m bHS

SYBELL
Elizabeth W., wd Frederick, recrq 11-1-1820; d 11-16-1854, a wd

SYKES
Anna (late Barnard) dis mo 11-4-1801 & rpd to Hudson

SYLVESTER
Rachel M. recrq 1833; d 10-21-1852
William T. (nm) d 10-28-1859 ae 20y 9m bPP

SYMMES
William A. d 1-1-1882; m Margaret W. -----
Ch: Ernest L. d 7-27-1925
William Edward b 1-3-1881 d 7-21-1881
cf Pine's Wood, N. C. 5-1880 with 1 ch named; ct Greensboro, N. C. 10-2-1907

TABER
Augustus, s Wm. C. & Hannah T., New Bedford, Mass., d 4-6-1898 bur Woodlawn Cem.; m N.Y. 5-15-1851 Anna H. FERRIS, dt John & Jane U., Throg's Neck, b 4-6-1827 d 9-13-1911 at Saratoga, Calif., bur Woodlawn Cem.
Ch: Mary F. b 3- 9-1852
Cornelia b 4-11-1858 d 3- 1-1929
cf New Bedford 1-1853 for Augustus
Carol E., dt Wm. C. & Caroline L. (Battey), b 10-5-1883; letter to West Side Congregational Church, Ridgewood, N. J. 10-1918
Clarkson & Deborah
Ch: Samuel S. b 10-28-1852
Mary Anna " 10- 4-1854

TABER, Clarkson & Deborah, continued
Ch: Wm. Clarkson b 2-28-1857
Carrie " 1- 9-1862
Frank " 10-22-1864 d 7-19-1865 bPP
Mellie
infant
cf Litchfield, Me. 1854; ct Toledo 1-7-1874 for all but 2 eldest
David S., s Wm. C. & Hannah T. (dec), N. Y., d 12-31-1914 bur Woodlawn; m 10-21-1869 at Wm. H. S. Wood's Elizabeth U. WOOD, dt Wm. & Mary S., N. Y., b 4-7-1842 d 2-10-1922
Ch: Augustus Frederick b 1-16-1871 d 6-26-1872
David Shearman " 6- 5-1873
William Wood " 8-19-1878 d 1-22-1879
Eleanor Wood " 4-30-1884
cf New Bedford, Mass. 12-1862 for David S.
David Shearman, s David S. & Elizabeth (Wood), b N. Y. 6-5-1873; m Charlotte BLISS
Ch: David Shearman, Jr. b 9-29-1917
Charlotte recrq 1-2-1934
Deborah C. recrq 12-1880; ct Sterling, Kans. 3-1889
Edmund B. d 4-1915; m Mary H. ----- d 11-22-1887
both recrq 11-1884
Edna Russell, dt James R. & Eliza H., b 5-30-1885; m Virgil G. LOPEZ (nm)
Eliza H., dt James R. & Eliza (H-----); m 1907 Wm. Clark ADAMS
Eliza S. rolf Millville, N. Y. M. E. Church 12-5-1906; letter to Millville, N. Y. 2-6-1907
Elizabeth D., dt Wm. C. & Caroline B., b 3-9-1892; m ----- DUKESHIRE (nm)
letter to Greenwood Bapt. Ch., Bkn. 3-1892 (manifest error)
Evelyn Alice, dt Wm. C. & Caroline L., b 12-1-1879; m Walter COMMONS
ct Stanford 5-7-1902 as Eva A.
Florence R. m ----- O'DELL (nm)
recrq 6-10-1908
Harold Earle, s Wm. C. & Caroline L.
James Russell, M.D., b Milton, N. Y. 12-18-1851 d 2-21-1921 bPP; m Eliza HEATON
Ch: Marian H. b 4-6-1882
Edna Russell b 5-30-1885
cf Pokeepsie 8-1878 for parents; James R. relrq 8-1886
John R., s Wm. C. & Hannah F. (dec), N. Y., d 11-1-1922; m 9-26-1871 at Rebecca Collins', Anna COLLINS, dt Isaac & Rebecca, N. Y., d 5-25-1924
Ch: Marion Russell b 5- 4-1875
Josephine C. " 5-16-1879
cf New Bedford, Mass. 12-1862; Anna rocf WD MM 11-18-1863
Jonathan Clarkson, s Wm. C. & Caroline L. (Battey), b 3-1-1896; relrq 11-1920
Josephine C., dt John R. & Anna (Collins), b 5-16-1879; m Dorr VIELE (nm)
relrq 2-1923
Marian H., dt James R. & Eliza H., b 4-6-1882; m Wm. Clark ADAMS (nm)
Martha, dt Samuel T., d 1912; m William Henry TABER (H)
Mary m Abel C. COLLINS; brought cert with him from S. Kingston; m 2d 9-9-1879 Edward TATUM
Mary Anna, dt Clarkson & Deborah, b 10-4-1854; m ----- SMITH
name erased 5-1886
Mary F., dt Augustus & Anna F., Throgs Neck; m 1876 Edward H. PARSONS
Nellie rocf Sterling, Kans. 3-1887; relrq 4-1889
Paul Hoag, s Wm. C. & Caroline L. (Battey), b 1-2-1898; letter to Flatbush Presby. Ch., Bkn. 7-1923
Samuel S., s Clarkson & Deborah, b 10-28-1852; relrq 1-1884
William Battey, s Wm. C. & Caroline L., b 10-20-1881
William C. m Caroline L. BATTEY, dt Jonathan & Anna (Battey), b N. Y. State 12-20-1857 d 3-9-1935 bPP
Ch: Evelyn Alice b 12-1-1879
William Battey b 10-20-1881
Harold Earle " 7- 4-1884
Anna Keese " 4-1886
cf Sterling, Kans. 12-1884 for Wm. C.;
cf Peru 10-1864 for Lois C. with parents
Ch: (continued)
Anna Ruse b 4- 1-1886
Elizabeth D. " 3- 9-1892
Carrol Emma " 10- 5-1893
Jonathan Clarkson b 3- 1-1896
Paul Hoag " 1- 2-1898
(Caroline L. changed name from Lois C.)

TAGG
George m Anna CLAIBORNE
Ch: Mary b Phila. 10-5-1823 d 12-12-1906
Tabitha b Phila. 3-28-1827
John M.
Wilmot
Eliza
last three ch may be by 2nd w; George recrq 5-1834 (H)
George m 2d Susanna -----
Ch: Mary b Phila., 11
John M. 10
these two ch may be by first wife
Wilmot 8
Eliza 5
George Jr. 2
last three ch may be by 2d w
Susanna rocf Balby, Eng. 12-15-1831 with ch aged as shown (O); ct Adrian for Susanna & ch 9-2-1835 (O); Susanna & ch rec without cert 7-1832 (H); cert for all to Nankin, Mich. 3-1835 (H)
Tabitha, dt Geo. & Anna (Claiborne), b Phila. 3-28-1827 d 10-11-1905; m 1854 Joseph H. MUMBY (H)

TAGG, Tabitha, continued
cf Phila. 1-1855

TALBOTT
Anna A., dt Wm. M. & Mary E., Mt. Pleasant, O.; m 1915 Alvah N. LAMB
cf Damascus, O. 1-1915

TALCOTT
Daniel & Rebecca
cf Scip. 1-1853 for both; ct Ama. 7-1857 for both
George rocf Scip. 9-1865; moved away - Oswego, N. Y.
Richard, s Joseph & Sarah, Scipio; m N. Y. 5-10-1815 Mary VALENTINE, dt Jacob & Phebe, N. Y.
ct Scipio 10-4-1815 for Mary

TALLMAN
Charity rocf Chesterfield 7-4-1828; ct Shrewsbury 2-2-1842
Eliza, New Bedford, m 1808 Cornelius GRINNELL
Elizabeth, dt Sam'l & Hannah GRIMSHAW, rocf New Castle, Eng. 8-14-1833 with parents; dis mo 6-1847
James & Charity (m Shrews.)
Charity, w James, rocf Shrews. 6-3-1811; ct Shrews. 8-3-1814 for Charity
James [Talman] (nm) & -----
Ch: Augusta b N. Y. d 1-23-1832 ae 4y 3m bHS
Mary [Talman] dis mo 10-4-1769
Samuel (nm) b L. I. d 7-5-1811 ae 57y bHS (m)

TALMADGE
Daniel (nm), s Daniel & Hanna; m 11-1-1882
Mary B. VAILL, dt Timothy D. & Isabel
Mary (Breck), b Bkn., 6-15-1858 (H)
Mary recrq 5-8-1922
Clementina [Tallmage] rocf Corn. 12-1883

TANNER
Edward William, s Wm. Jr. & Ellen, b 9-28-1861; relrq 12-5-1900
Ellen Eliza, dt Wm. J. & Ellen E., b 5-28-1871; m 9-12-1893 Dr. Worthington S. RUSSELL
William J. d at Banstead Downs, Eng. 8-28-1884; m Ellen E. ----- d 9-30-1905
Ch: Edward Wm. b 9-28-1861
Wm. Joseph Jr. d 2-13-1877 ae about 11y bPP
Ellen Eliza b 5-28-1871
Emma Louisa " 5-30-1874 d 4-14-1881 bPP
William recrq 4-1857; Ellen recrq 4-1857

TAPPAN
Lydia (late Glazier) dis mo 11-5-1823
Susan, w Theodore, dt Shadrach & Mary RICKETSON; m 2d John J. ANDERSON (H)

TATHAM
Benjamin, Jr., s James & Mary (both dec), d 12-25-1885 ae 70y bPP; m Westchester 6-10-1847 Rebecca COLLINS, dt Benj. S. & Hannah, Pelham, N. Y., d 5-31-1901 ae 82y bPP
Ch: Hannah H. b 5- 7-1848 d 7- 9-1867 bPP
William " 7-10-1850 " 9-10-1913 bPP
Charles " 9- 3-1854
Fanny " 12-12-1852 d 1-29-1853
Francis " 3-28-1858
Edwin " 11-18-1859 " 1- 1-1933
cf Hitchin, Eng. 1841
Francis, s Benj. Jr. & Rebecca (Collins), b 3-28-1858 N. Y. d 1935 Orangeburg State Hospital; name erased 12-1928 (unm)

TATUM
Charles rocf WD MM 5-1856; dis 1859; mo before 3-1874, ret a mbr
David S., s Wm. E. & Hannah L.; m Viola SAWYER
David rocf Chicago, Ill. 11-1923; Viola recrq 11-1923
Edward, s Josiah & Rachel; m Anna COOPER d 4-22-1876
Ch: Charles Albert d 11-14-1920
Edward Jr. " 3-29-1891
cf Greenwich, N. J. 11-1857 with 2 ch named
Edward d 5-15-1883; m 2d N. Y. 9-9-1879 at Mary T. Collins' Mary Taber COLLINS, dt Joseph & Phebe B., N. Y., d 11-18-1926
Elizabeth, Flushing, d 10 Mo (Dec) 4, 1699
Patience, dt Samuel, Flushing; m 1717 Richard WILDEY
Ruth (or Tatem), dt Samuel & Mary, Flushing; m 1721 William PHILLIPS
Samuel, Flushing, m Mary SOUTHWICK, late of R. I. (m Flushing 10 Mo (Dec) 13, 1701)
Mary brought cf R. I. MM clear; Samuel active mbr 1700,1701

TAUNTUM
Benjamin T. (nm) b Burl. d 2-20-1826 ae 18y 1m 3d bHS (unm)

TAYLOR
Alida French, dt Jno. M. & Julia (Le Comte), b S. Orange, N. J. 4-10-1909; recrq 12-14-1935 (H)
Anita, w William, dt ----- UNDERHILL, rocf Washington, D. C. 11-1-1911
Caroline, dt Isaac & Jane, d 4-15-1924 ae 80y 1m 22d bPP; m Tuthill DU BOIS (both nm) (H)
Edgar J., s Thomas & Sophia (Dewstoe), b Bkn. 8-24-1862; m 10-9-1900 Mary E. WHITSON (mbr Wby), dt Samuel & Phebe J. (H)
Elizabeth roc 7-4-1753
Elwood, having mo, Upper Springfield refers it to N. Y. 1-8-1845; rpd adversely; dis by Upper Springfield & N. Y. notified 7-1845 lived Tompkinsville, L. I.
George Clarence (nm) m 6-8-1887 Estelle V. VONDERSMITH, dt Wm. B. & Caroline (Birdsall), b 9-9-1861 (H)
Ch: Florence Estelle d 3-4-1889 ae 2m 16d bPP
Estelle's name entered by comm. 11-24-1875
Hannah rocf East Branch, N. C. 6-1921

TAYLOR, continued
Henry, Flushing, & Sarah
Ch: Sarah b 3 Mo (May) 12, 1688
    Phebe " 1 Mo (Mar) 9, 1690/1
Henry M. rocf Wilmington, Del. 3-5-1884; ct Wilmington, Del. 6-12-1909 (H)
Isaac d 3-23-1867 ae 53y bPP; m Jane ----- (nm) d 7-4-1857 ae 37y bPP
Ch: Victoria S. d 10-1-1851 ae 5y 3m 17d bPP
    Emily J. " 7-25-1853 ae 2y 1m 7d bPP
    Caroline
    having mo, Upper Springfield, N. J. refers it to N. Y. 1-8-1845; rpd adversely; dis by Upper Springfield & N. Y. notified 7-1845; lived 19 Oliver St., N. Y.
J. Hibberd, s Caleb M. & Susan W. (Jones), b Del. Co., Pa. 3-27-1878; m 9-17-1910 Lydia FOULKE, dt Edwin M. & Elva (Jones), b Montgomery Co., Pa. 8-3-1884 (H)
    J. Hibberd rocf Birmingham MM, 1-14-1911; Lydia rocf Birmingham MM 1-14-1911
Jane recrq 5-7-1845; d 7-4-1757 (H)
Margaret S., dt William & Elizabeth (Hanes), b Woodstown, N. J. 8-16-1878; m 1929 William Alex. TAYLOR (H)
    cf Woodstown 12-14-1932
Mary (nm), w Edward, b Middletown, N. J. d 2-5-1814 ae 25y bHS
Robert b Yorkshire d 7-5-1811 ae 58y (unm)
Sarah, Flushing, m 1727 Benjamin FIELD
Sarah S. rocf R. & P. 8-21-1823, lives with h
    Sarah, w Samuel d 1832
Theodore (nm) m Alice S. VONDER SMITH, dt Wm. B. & Caroline (Birdsall), b 9-24-1864 d 8-31-1923 (H)
    Alice's name entered by com. 11-24-1875
William, s William & Elizabeth (Hood), b Nottingham, Pa. 11-18-1839; m Elizabeth HANES (mbr Pilesgrove), dt Thomas & Mary (H) cf Pilesgrove, N. J. 10-7-1899 for Wm.; ct Orange Grove, Calif. 2-14-1914 for Wm.
William & Anita W.
    Anita rocf Washington 11-1-1911; name erased 11-1928
William Alexander, s Robert & Jessie (McGhie), b Paisley, Scot. 11-23-1873; m 5-3-1929 Margaret S. SIMMONS, dt Wm. & Elizabeth (Hanes), b Woodstown, N. J. 8-16-1878 (H)
    Margaret m 1st Dr. Bert G. SIMMONS 1923, who d 1926; Wm. recrq 12-14-1932; Margaret rocf Woodstown 12-14-1932
----- & ----- (nm)
Ch: Shotwell d 5-27-1834 ae 1y 8m 12d bHS

TEBBETS
Charles E. rocf Whittier, Calif. 11-1920; ct Whittier, Calif. 9-1921

TELNER
Jacob & Susannah
Ch: Susannah
    Jacob active mbr 1685-1688
Susanna, Jr., dt Jacob & Susannah, N. Y.; m 1688 Albertus BRANDT

TEMPLE
Charles (mbr Landsdowne), s Edward B. & Lucy B.; m 8-1-1917 Emily Grace YOUNG, dt Geo. F. P. & Mary A. (Frick), b Easton, Pa. 1-5-1894 (H)
    Emily G. recrq 7-9-1917

TERHUNE
Frances M., dt James & Mariette (Ross), b Woodside, L. I. 4-20-1882; m 1903 Chris. Walker GARDHAM (nm) (H)
    recrq 12-13-1926

TERRY
Anna H., dt Charles M. & Margaret, N. Y.; m 1865 Stephen WOOD (H)
Charles M. (nm) d 1-24-1885 ae 68y 5m 28d bPP; m Margaret H. ----- (nm) d 12-20-1851 ae 43y 8m bPP
Charles M. m 2nd Rebecca F. SMITH, dt Benj. & Margaretta (Coates) b Phila. 2-16-1838 d 10-8-1906 bPP (H)
Ch: Sarah Willets d 12-23-1873 ae 7y 5m 10d bPP
    Rebecca b 1-26-1870
    Frank b 9- 4-1875 d 8-11-1876
    Charles & Rebecca recrq 12-1872; ch, Rebecca, recrq 9-9-1929
Rebeckah m 1675 at Gravesend John TILTON, Jr.
Rebecca, dt Charles M. & Rebecca F. (Smith), b N. Y. 1-26-1870; recrq 9-9-1929 (H)
----- (nm) m Marion H. DE LONG
    cf Glens Falls 9-1924 for Marion; letter to Douglaston Community Ch. 6-1928

THACKER
John (nm) b Eng. d 1-8-1810 ae 45y; m -----
Ch: (prob) Lucy Ann d 11-28-1809 ae 1y 4m bHS

THAIN
David (nm) & -----
Ch: Infant stillborn 4-13-1825 bHS
Jethro [Thane], s Deborah, rocf Providence 1-25-1815 with brother, Samuel, s Deborah Campbell, formerly Thane, to live with their parents, Duncan & Deborah Campbell; ct Nantucket 1-14-1818
Lydia rocf Nantucket, N. Dist. 7-28-1824 (clear); ct Cincinnati 11-6-1833 (clear) (O); ct Cincinnati 8-1832 (H)
Samuel [Thane], s Deborah, rocf Providence 1-25-1815 with brother, Jethro, s of Deborah Campbell, form Thane, to live with their parents, Duncan & Deborah Campbell; ct Nantucket 1-14-1818

THATCHER
Harvey S., s Thos. Jackson & Electa (Trowbridge), b Utica, O., 6-18-1885; cf Chicago 7-9-1923; ct Flush. 10-13-1924 (H)

THAYER

Nathaniel, s Chas. Henry & Etta Reed (Grover), b Chicago 5-12-1892; m 10-5-1917 Blanche F. FREEMAN (nm) (H)
Ch: Aline Arden b Bkn. 8-6-1918
recrq 8-9-1926; Aline A. recrq 6-11-1934
Willard (nm) m Mary ----- (nm) b Vt. d 1-10-1845 ae 53y bHS
Willett (nm) b Vt. d 6-13-1832 ae 45y bHS (m)
----- & ----- (nm)
Ch: Caroline M. b Flush. d 8-4-1823 ae 1y 3m bHS
Ann Maria b Flush. d 10-16-1834 ae 18y bHS (unm)

THEW

Gilmore E. (nm), s Friend A. & Parmelia (Macomber); m 5-27-1916 Ada Hepzibah HOAG, dt Edwin W. & Alice Ada (Ishom), b Plattsburgh, N. Y. 9-22-1873 (H)
Ada recrq 10-8-1928
----- & ----- (nm)
Ch: Mary Ann d 11-12-1933 ae 25y bHS (appoplexy)

THISTLETHWAITE

Theodosius rocf Preston, Eng. 10-9-1856; ct Hardshaw East 4-4-1860

THOBIN (or Thoben)

Ada, dt Frederick H. & Caroline (Fuchs); m Francis C. GOERKE
Ada recrq 3-1928
Frederick H. [Thoben] m Caroline FUCHS, dt John & Marie, d Forest Hills, L. I. 10-18-1828 ae 55y 6m 10d bPP
Ch: Ada
both nm

THOMAS

Davis rocf Burl. 3-8-1807, apprentice
Edward rocf Worcester, Mass. 11-1-1911
Eleazer (nm) m Fanny ----- (nm) b N. Y. d 3-14-1847 ae 94y bHS (a wd)
Evan d 1-28-1905; m ----- (H)
Ch: Evan Barker b 5- 8-1881
cf Balt. 6-4-1879; ch's name entered by comm. 10-10-1882
Lewin Hartley, s Wethered B. & Addie (Melick), b 12-13-1881; m Gladys T. CROCKER (nm) (H)
name entered by comm. 10-10-1882; canceled 3-13-1833 for lack of interest
Ludlow, s Philip & Frances M. (both dec), N. Y. m at S. Thompson's (not under care of N.Y. MM) 9-13-1854 Mary S. THOMPSON, dt Samuel & Lucy, Bkn. (H)
Mary S. relrq 10-7-1857
Margaret con mo 5-4-1758; ct Phila. 6-1-1758; cf Phila. 11-27-1789; ct Gwined 3-5-1794
Maria B., dt Sidney B. & Jemima BOWNE, b 4-9-1824; relrq 6-2-1880 (H)
Maria S. m Daniel K. HAWXHURST (H)
cf Race St. for Daniel & 3 ch 3-2-1887
Mary L., dt Wm. George & Mary L. (Wethered), b Balt. 11-19-1841 d 3-18-1917; m 1870 Alexander SMITH (H)
Nannie, dt Wm. G. & Mary L., Balt.; m 1853 Wm. BELL (H)
cf Balt. 11-1855
Richard H., s John C. & Mary, Baltimore; m N.Y. 2-9-1842 Phebe CLAPP, dt John & Phebe H., N. Y.
ct Balt. 11-2-1842 for Phebe
Richard H. m 2d N. Y. 2-9-1859 Deborah C. HINSDALE, dt Henry (dec) & Mary, N. Y.
ct Balt. 11-2-1842 for Deborah; her mother gc same date
Wethered B., s Wm. Geo. & Mary (Lewin), b Balt. 6-11-1853 d 8-3-1925; m 2-4-1880 Addie MELICK (nm), dt J. M. & Anna H. (H)
Ch: Lewin Hartley b 12-13-1881
cf Balt. 7-2-1879 for Wethered; Lewin's name entered by com. 10-10-1882
William G. d 4-24-1891; m Mary L. W. ----- b 12-2-1812 d 11-10-1898 (H)
cf Balt. 4-2-1879 for both

THOMPSON

Alice, w Uldrick, dt Robt. B. & Rebecca HAVILAND, b 7-8-1855 (m 7-5-1882) (H)
In Honolulu from 1899
Ann rocf Hudson 6-21-1803 (clear), late from Eng., endorsed to ----- MM 9-1-1803 (clear)
Ann Eliza, w James, rocf Troy 5-1841; d 8-5-1847 (H)
Catharine, dt Samuel & Lucy, Bkn., b 12-16-1835; m 1854 John F. HALSTEAD (H)
relrq 11-1860
Christopher rocf Knaresbro, 5-9-1825 (clear); had ret. to Knaresbro & mo; that MM notified 3-3-1830; dis 12-1-1830 & Knaresbro notified
Cornelis, dt Francis & Mary, b 1818; m Godfrey PATTESON (mo)
ret a mbr
David recrq 12-7-1814; dis mo 9-3-1817
Edith Virginia, dt William, d 6-29-1909 ae 31y bPP; m Charles A. WRIGHT (H) (both nm)
Edward, s Francis & Mary, b 4-11-1807 d 11-11-1889 (H)
In St. Louis 1845; was in Ill. from 1875; at Hinckley 1887
Francis, s Jas. (dec) & Mary, Randon, Eng., b Eng. d 7-10-1832 ae 55y; m N. Y. 12-12-1804 Mary WRIGHT, dt Isaac & Sarah, N. Y., d 5-31-1864 (H)
Ch: William W. b 9- 1-1805
Edward " 4-11-1807
Sarah " 3-11-1809
Mary Ann " 7-12-1811 d 9-13-1823
Elizabeth C. b 7-21-1813 d 9- 1-1823
Jane " 3-27-1816
Cornelia " 1818
Hannah " 8- 8-1821 d 10-3-1822
Francis rocf Knaresbrough 2-13-1797 (clear); all dis 1829-1839 (0)
Francis, Jr. rocf Knaresborough 9-14-1818

THOMPSON, Francis, Jr., continued
(clear); ct Phila. 2-2-1825
Frances d 1832 bPP (prob w of Jeremiah) (H)
George (nm) & Elizabeth
Ch: Maria
Sarah
John
cf Lisburn, Ireland 1-8-1816 for their 3 ch; their parents had seceded when the ch were very young, addressed to Salem, Mass., endorsed to N. Y. 8-8-1816 as they & their parents had settled in N. Y.
Grove G., s Geo. G. & Phebe A. (Merritt), b Lynbrook, N. Y. 1-18-1915; cf Wby 12-8-1930 (H)
Hazel, dt Geo. G. & Phebe A. (Merritt), b Lynbrook, N. Y. 3-2-1912; cf Wby 12-8-1930
Phebe A. now Mrs. Herman H. Smith
Helen Ware, dt William, d 2-3-1920 ae 40y bPP; m Herbert Banyon (H) (all nm)
Isabella [Thomson], dt James & Mary (Tullo), b London, Eng. 3-20-1839 d 2-20-1906; m 1866 Joseph G. MILLER (H)
both recrq 9-1-1886
James d 2-5-1895 ae 90y 9m 29d bPP; m Ann Eliza ----- b N. Y. d 8-5-1847 ae 37y bPP (H)
Ch: Infant stillborn 2-23-1844 bPP
Maria Jane d 10-13-1847 ae 6y 10m bPP
James m 2d Margaret HAGAN, wd, d 6-23-1894 ae 80y 4m 20d bPP
cf Troy 11-4-1846 for James
ch bHS & rem
Jane, dt Francis & Mary, b 3-27-1816; m James PATTISON (mo 11-1852) (H)
ct Phila. Spruce St. 4-13-1844; cf Phila. Spruce St. 9-1848; relrq 6-8-1901; in 1900 lived Ulverscroft, Scotland
Jeremiah b Eng. d 11-10-1835 ae 52y bHS rem to PP; prob. m Frances -----
cf Knaresbro MM 7-13-1801 (clear); dis 5-1829 (O); dis 10-1828 (H)
John & Phebe
Ch: George
cf Jericho 4-18-1793 for both; ct Hudson 5-1-1794 with ch, George
John, s George & Elizabeth, rocf Lisburn, Ire., 1-8-1816, minor; dis 8-1840 (H); dis 1-6-1841 (O); lived New Orleans
L. Joshua dis 12-1852
Margaret, w James, dt ----- HAGEN (H)
Maria, dt Geo. & Eliza, N. Y.; m 1838 James MACKIE
cf Lisburn 1-8-1816, minor
Mary S., dt Samuel & Lucy, Bkn.; m 1854; relrq 10-7-1857 (H)
Maude m John E. KELLY
Maude recrq 7-1923
Dr. Percy Beecher (nm), s Geo. S. & Maria B.; m 12-18-1905 Mary Elizabeth HAVILAND, dt Solomon & Marielma (Field), b N. Y. 10-11-1877 (H)
Elizabeth's name entered by comm. 10-10-1886
Philadelphia gct Wby 11-3-1763
Samuel d 1-29-1855; m Lucy ----- d 3-1-1871 (H)
Ch: Elizabeth b 3- 8-1826 d 3- 7-1862
Lucy Jane " 5-18-1829 " 7-13-1829
Charles " 7-21-1830 " 8-13-1830
Mary Smart b 9-20-1833
Catharine " 12-16-1835
cf Knaresborough 9-14-1818 (clear); cf Oswego 3-16-1825 for Lucy; Samuel dis 9-1829 (O); w & dt 1839-1849
Samuel S., s Daniel B. & Mary H. (dec), West Town, Pa.; m 6-25-1891 at Emma L. Hall's, Emma L. HALL, of Bkn., wd Isaac Hall, Jr., dt Israel L. (dec) & Susan J. LUKENS, Rahway
Emma recrq 6-1863; Emma gct WD MM 2-1-1893
Sarah gct Corn. 4-3-1822
Sarah, dt Francis & Mary, N. Y.; m 1832 Joseph WALKER (H)
Thomas [Thomson] gc of rem 1701
Uldrick, s Abrose & Phebe, b Glens Falls 6-9-1849; m 7-5-1882 Alice H. HAVILAND, dt Robert & Rebecca (Hull), b Bkn. 7-8-1855 (H)
Uldrick recrq 3-13-1928; in Honolulu 1899-192-; later in Florida
William rocf Falls 6-1856; d 5-29-1866 (H)
William gc of clear to New Bedford 10-1875; cf Dublin 3-1871; ct New Bedford, Mass. 1-6-1876
William, s Wm. & Elizabeth U., d 5-11-1923 ae 68y bPP; m Virginia C. WARE, dt Wm. P. & Isabel (McKay) d 5-27-1931 ae 71y bPP (H)
Ch: Olive C. d 11-2-1883 ae 11m bPP
both nm
William W., s Francis & Mary, b 9-1-1805; dis 3-1834 (H)
----- & ----- [Thomson] (nm)
Ch: Gerhardus Langdon d 8-6-1812 ae 1y 5m 1d bHS

THORNE

Abigail (nm), b West Co. d 9-21-1832 ae 80y 10m bHS (wd)
Abraham [Thorn], s Joseph Sr., Flushing, rqc of clear 7 Mo 5, 1717
Alida con mo 1-7-1761
Amy [Thorn] d 11-20-1892; m Enoch STRATTAN (H)
Anna [Thorn] roc 1822 (wd)
Ann Pierce (form Thorn) dis mo 2-7-1754
Anne [Thorn] rocf Wby 2-20-1822
Catharin H. Ives (form Thorne) rocf ND MM 12-23-1834 (mo)
Charity [Thorn] dis 2-2-1769 (perhaps for mo)
Daniel [Thorn] rocf Wby 9-16-1801, apprentice to a Friend
Daniel [Thorn] (nm) & -----
Ch: Infant stillborn 9-25-1819
Daniel (nm) m Eliza ----- (nm) b L. I. d 4-11-1838 ae 35y bHS
Daniel S. [Thorn], s Stephen & Eliz. (both dec) Bkn., d 4-24-1846; m Bkn. 6-13-1839 Sarah D. FARRINGTON, dt Ezra & Hannah, N. Y. (H)

THORNE, Daniel S. & Sarah D. [Thorn], continued
Sarah m 2d Benjamin LEWIS; Sarah recrq 5-1824; dis mo 11-7-1810; rst 7-5-1820; dis 5-1829 (O); dis 2-1844 (H); cf Battle Creek 10-1849 for Sarah
Delilah d 9-23-1811 ae 2y 6m 11d bHS
Edgar [Thorn] rocf R. & P. 10-19-1837, minor; ct Redstone, Pa. 4-5-1843 (clear), ret as he had rem to Pittsburgh; cert to be sent there; ct Providence, Pa. 6-1843
Edward Carpenter, s Wm. H. & Ophelia (Carpenter) b 8-28-1862 d 9-4-1906; m May GOOKIN (nm) (H)
Edwin [Thorn], s Jonathan & Lydia Ann, N. Y., b 1-20-1826; m at T. W. Pearsall's 5-6-1857 Charlotte T. PEARSALL, dt Thos. W. & Mary L., N. Y. (H)
Ch: Thomas Pearsall b 7-26-1861
Chester " 11-11-1863
Oakleigh " 7-31-1866
Edwin gct N.P. 1-2-1878 with the 3 ch
Elizabeth Underhill (form Thorne) con mo 6-6-1781
Elizabeth rocf Wby 11-16-1808; ct Wby 1-11-1815 (clear)
Elnathan (nm) b N. Y. d 10-20-1818 ae 31y (m)
Elnathan, s Thomas & Abigail; m -----
Ch: Infant stillborn 3-10-1847 bHS
dis mo 9-3-1823
Freelove Thorn (form Thorn) dis mo 5-1836 (H)
George con mo 10-6-1773
George, s Jacob, d 9-21-1804 ae 23y bHS
Hannah con mo before 8-2-1753
Hannah [Thorn] m 1763 Daniel CLEMENT (prob dis mo by priest)
Hannah [Thorn] rocf Plainfield 12-20-1769
Hannah m 1774 Robert COLES, of Pur.
ct Pur. 11-3-1774
Howard Ellsworth, s Wm. H. & Ophelia (Carpenter), b Bkn. 1-27-1859; m 4-2-1884 Louise Francis CLARK (nm), dt Wm. G. & Betsey (Babson) (H)
Isaac, s Joseph, Flushing, took cert of clear 10 Mo (Dec) 6, 1722; gct Pur. with w 4 Mo (June) 7, 1744
Jacob, Flushing, cert of conversation, etc. 8 Mo (Oct) 4, 1722
James, s Benjamin, Flushing; m Flushing 7 Mo. (Sep) 5, 1734 Mary LAWRENCE, dt Daniel
James [Thorn], s Joseph, Flushing; m Flushing 7 Mo (Sep) 11, 1740 Sarah FARRINGTON, dt Thomas, d 3-24-1794
James, s John (dec) & Mary, Flushing, b 2 Mo. (Apr) 5, 1751; ct Oblong, as apprentice 11-7-1765; cf Oblong, apprenticeship completed 3-16-1769, rec 5-3-1769
James [Thorn] gct N.P. with Joseph 2-3-1774, some time rem
James Frederick, s Levi E. & Anna R., rocf Cincinnati with parents 1-1880; name erased 10-1928
John [Thorn], s William, Flushing; m Flushing 3 Mo (May) 9, 1664 Mary PEARSALL, dt Nicholas & Sarah
Ch: Hannah m Richard CORNELL
Joseph " Martha Johanna BOWNE
Mary " William FOWLER
Sarah " Joshua CORNELL
John [Thorn], Flushing, d 10-7-1764; m Mercy -----
Ch: John b 2 Mo (Apr) 11, 1738
Joanna b 3 Mo (May) 4, 1740
Jordan " 8 Mo (Oct) 1, 1742 d 3 Mo 25, 1745
Joseph " 11 Mo (Jan) 5, 1744/5
James " 2 Mo (Apr) 5, 1751
Mercy, with dt, Joanna, gct Creek 1-2-1788 (clear)
John con mo before 1 Mo (Mar) 6, 1745/6
John & Phebe [Thorn] (H)
Ch: Hannah
Infant d 10-3-1837 ae 1-1/2d
cf Chap. 7-14-1825 with 1 ch named; ct Farm. 5-5-1837 (H); cf Farm. 4-22-1847, parents only; ct Chap. 5-2-1855, parents only
John [Thorn] Jr., s John & Mercy, Flushing, certified mbr 1755 (prob this John dis mo 8-7-1777)
John, Jr. rocf Chesterfield 6-6-1826, apprentice; ct Chesterfield 7-7-1830 (clear) (O); ct Chesterfield 12-1828 (H)
Jonathan, s Samuel & Phebe, Washington, N. Y., b 4-20-1801 d 10-11-1884; m N. Y. 7-9-1823 Lydia Ann CORSE, dt Israel & Lydia, b 12-27-1805 d London 10-14-1872 (H)
Ch: Mary Elizabeth b 5- 2-1824 d 7-27-1843
Edwin " 1-20-1826
Phebe Anna " 2-10-1828
Samuel Jr. " 5-31-1830 d 9-12-1833
William J. " 4-21-1833 " 8-16-1835
Samuel " 9- 6-1835
Jane D. " 12-24-1837 " 3-14-1842
Louisa " 11- 8-1840 " 5-10-1842
Jonathan Jr. " 4- 5-1843
William " 9- 7-1845
George White " 10- 6-1847 d 4-20-1883
Jonathan m 2d at Rebecca L. Fox's 6-6-1874 Eliza T. MERRITT, dt Geo. S. (dec) & Rebecca L. FOX, N. Y., d 4-6-1891 (H)
ct N.P. 2-4-1824 for Lydia Ann; cf N.P. 8-1835 with 8 ch [relrq 12-4-1867 (H)
Jonathan, Jr., s Jonathan & Lydia, b 4-5-1843;
Joseph [Thorn], s John & Mary, Flushing, d 3 Mo (May) 1727; m at Benj. Field's, Flushing, 9 Mo (Nov) 9, 1695 Martha Johanna BOWNE, dt John, b 6 Mo (Aug) 17, 1673 d 6 Mo (Aug) 1, 1750
Ch: Samuel b 5 Mo (July) 12, 1696
Joseph " 8 Mo (Oct) 16, 1698 d 7 Mo 1723
John " 1 Mo (Mar) 4, 1702/3
Thomas " 2 Mo (Apr) 25, 1704
William " 5 Mo (July) 15, 1706
James " 7 Mo (Sep) 2, 1709
Joseph, Flushing m Mary BOWNE, b 1660 d Woodbridge, N. J. 1728
Ch: Hannah b 8 Mo (Oct) 26, 1680
Joseph " 7 Mo (Sep) 22, 1682
William " 9 Mo (Nov) 7, 1684

THORNE, Joseph & Mary, continued
Ch: Mary b 6 Mo (Aug) 22, 1686
Susannah b 4 Mo (June) 18, 1688
John " 8 Mo (Oct) 5, 1690
Thomas " 11 Mo (Jan) 1, 1692/3
Benjamin " 11 Mo (Jan) 6, 1694
Abraham " 7 Mo (Sep) 1, 1696
Isaac " 9 Mo (Nov) 4, 1698
Jacob " 3 Mo (May) 20, 1700
Sarah " 11Mo (Jan) 20, 1702/3
Joseph [Thorn] gct N. P. with James 2-3-1774, some time rem
Joseph, s Thos. & Abigail, rocf Marl. 10-27-1813 with parents; dis 2-1837 (H)
Joseph, s Joseph (dec) & Sarah, Po'keepsie, m N. Y. 11-13-1828 Lydia LENOX, dt David & Susannah (both dec, N. Y. (H)
Josephine A., dt Levi E. & Anna R., d 3-7-1929; m William A. West (nm)
cf Cincinnati 1-1880 with parents
Leonard D. rocf Wby 5-5-1858; ct Granville 9-6-1876; d 3-3-1878 (H)
Levi E. & Anna Rosella
Ch: Josephine Allen
James Frederick
Walter Thomas
cf Cincinnati 1-1880 for all; had been Gen. Agent there for Provident Life & Trust Co.; Levi's name erased 10-1928
Linton [Thorn] rocf Balt. E. & W. Dist. 1-10-1833; ct Balt. E. & W. Dist. 12-5-1838 (clear)
Lydia dealt with 4-3-1754
Lydia (Lilian), dt James P. & Helen A. (Harrington); m 1895 Dr. Albert BOWERMAN (H)
Margaret Hayes (nm), dt Oakleigh; m 6-12-1912 Edward Hicks CARLE (H)
Martha Doughty (form Thorne) mo before 10-7-1778; ct N.P. 11-5-1778
Martha J., dt Thos. & Abigail; m ----- WILLIAMS (mo) (H)
cf Marl. 10-27-1813 with parents
Mary [Thorn], dt Joseph, Flushing; m 1709 John SHOTWELL
Mary, dt Benjamin, Flushing; m 1756 Daniel QUINBY
Mary [Thorn] (late Way) dis mo 11-1-1797
Mary Anna, w Peter, rocf Pur. 3-3-1869 (H)
Moses, s Thos. & Abigail, rocf Marl. 10-27-1813; dis 12-1832 (H)
Oakleigh, s Edwin & Charlotte, b N. Y. 7-31-1866; m -----
Ch: Margaret Hayes (nm) m 6-12-1912 Edward H. CARLE
Parmelia, dt Thos. & Abigail; m ----- HORTON (H) (mo)
cf Marl. 10-27-1813 with parents; dis 4-1832
Peter J. (nm), s James H. & Jane, d 3-28-1906 ae 67y 9m 1d bPP; m 6-10-1863 Mary Annah UNDERHILL, dt David & Sarah W. (Pierce), b Scarsdale 6-7-1838 d 10-2-1911 bPP (H)
Phebe [Thorn], dt Thomas & Abigail, N. Y.; m before 7-3-1822 Josiah ARCHER (mo); m 2d 1840 David P. SMITH (H)
dis mo 7-3-1822; rst 9-1828
Phebe Anna, dt Jonathan & Lydia Carle, b N.P. 2-10-1828 d 8-25-1909 ae 81y 6m 15d (H)
cf N.P. 8-1835 with parents; wealthy Philanthropist (unm)
Samuel [Thorn], s Joseph & Martha, Flushing, d 1759; m at her father's 10 Mo (Dec) 9, 1715 Ann STEVENSON, dt Thomas & Ann, Newtown, d 3 Mo (Mar) 19, 1723/4
Ch: Joseph b 2 Mo (Apr) 19, 1717
Thomas " 7 Mo (Sep) 11, 1719
Nathaniel b 11 Mo (Jan) 14, 1720/1
Samuel " 8 Mo (Oct) 3, 1723
Samuel [Thorn], s Samuel & Ann, Cortlandt Manor; m 5 Mo (July) 11, 1751 Hannah FARRINGTON, dt Thomas, Flushing
Ch: George b 8 Mo (Oct) 11, 1751
Samuel b 2-15-1753 N.S. d Flushing 12-8-1759
William " 11- 9-1755
ack. accepted; certified m 3-2-1758; rem to Dutchess Co.
Samuel con mo 12-7-1774
Samuel, s Jonathan & Lydia Ann, b 9-6-1835; ct N.P. 4-4-1860 (H)
Sarah, dt Joseph & Mary, Flushing; m 1725 James JACKSON
Sarah [Thorn], wd Daniel S.; m Benjamin LEWIS (nm) (H)
Thomas [Thorn, s Joseph, Flushing; m Wby 9 Mo (Nov) 3, 1725 Penelope COLES, dt Joseph, Glen Cove
Thomas (nm) b L. I. d 12-16-1835 ae 83y bHS (widower)
Thomas d 4-2-1840; m Abigail ----- d 5-12-1833 (H)
Ch: Phebe
Elnathan
Charlotte dis 1828
Freelove
Martha J.
Parmelia
Moses
Thomas J.
Joseph
Thomas m 2d N. Y. 12-9-1835 Elizabeth DEAN, dt Samuel & Sarah PALMER, N. Y., b West Co. d 8-11-1839 ae 65y 3m (H)
cf Marl. 10-27-1813 with 7 ch first named; all dis 1829-1839 (O); cf Oswego 11-1835 for Eliz.
Thomas Jr., s Thos. & Abigail, rocf Marl. 10-27-1813; dis 3-1839 (H)
Thomas b N. Y. 6-1-1818 d 9-10-1911 ae 93y; m Abby Jane SUTTON (nm) d 3-27-1897 (H)
Thomas recrq 8-8-1896
Walter Thomas, s Levi E. & Anna R., rocf Cincinnati with parents 1-1880; name erased 10-1928
Webster & Elizabeth [Thorn]

THORNE, Webster & Elizabeth [Thorn] continued
Ch: Jacob
Rebecca
Phebe
Eliza b 9- 1-1801
cf R. & P. 6-17-1801 with their 3 ch as named; ct R. & P. 5-5-1802 with 4 ch as named here
William, s Joseph, Flushing, gct West Jersey 3-3-1705 (rem cert)
William, s Joseph, Flushing; m Woodbridge, -----
Wm. took cert of clear to Woodbridge 1 Mo 6, 1728/9; Wm. & w gct Woodbridge, N. J. 3 Mo (May) 3, 1733
William, s Jonathan & Lydia A., b 9-7-1845; relrq 10-1-1873 (H)
William [Thorn] (nm) & -----
Ch: Infant stillborn 5-20-1858 bPP
William H., s Samuel C. & Maria (Hoagland), N. Y., b Glen Cove 11-7-1831 d 11-21-1916; m at Isaac Carpenter's 3-11-1856 Ophelia CARPENTER, dt Isaac & Abby S. (dec), N. Y., d 8-30-1873 ae 39y bPP (H)
Ch: Howard Ellsworth b 1-27-1859
Edward Carpenter " 8-28-1862
William Lincoln b 10-4-1867 d 5-2-1900
cf Wby 9-3-1856 for both
Wm. H. m 2d at C. Cleveland's 1-24-1877 Ida CLEVELAND (nm), dt Cyrus & Emily P., Yonkers (H)

THORNELL
Nellie m George A. SUTTON, d 6-8-1917 ae 63y 21 d bPP (H)
both nm

THORNTON
Alice Emily, dt Geo. D. & Eliz. R. HILYARD, b 8-28-1866; relrq 12-2-1903
Daniel & Rachel
Ch: Elizabeth M.
Lydia M.
cf Creek 11-17-1837 with 2 ch named; Rachel, a minister; ct WD MM 1-1-1840 for all
Henry, s James & Emma (Gilbert), b 11-3-1861 Byberry, Pa.; cf Mt. Holly 8-7-1895
John C. (nm), s James (dec) & Julia A., of Buffalo; m at Chas. F. Smith's (not under care of N. Y. MM) 10-30-1855 Phebe B. SMITH, dt Charles F. & Judith C. (Bunker), N. Y., b 3-8-1832 (H)
Ch: Charles J. d 7-18-1856 ae 11m 21d bPP
Francis " 12- 4-1865 ae 2m bPP
Phebe's name rem 11-9-1925 as long unknown; in Chicago 1900
Samuel, s James & Emma (Gilbert), b 3-1-1865, Phila; cf Mt. Holly 8-7-1895; ct Phila. 5-8-1909 (H)

THORP
Malcolm R., s Walter & Florence R., b Bristol, Conn., 3-12-1888; m Mabel L. LANCROFT, dt Henry S. & Cornelia (Tuttle), b Fair Haven, Conn. 5-20-1888
both recrq 6-6-1917

THROSSELL
Helen, dt Jos. E. & Emily C., b Newark, N. J., 8-13-1887; m 1898 George W. LEE (nm) recrq 9-5-1917

THURSTON
Abigail rocf Newport 11-24-1808 (clear); d 10-25-1840 (wd) (H)
Anna Day, dt Wm. R. & Jane, b 5-4-1857; released 4-5-1911
Edward Day, s Wm. R. & Jane R. (dec), N. Y., b 3-4-1851; m 11-11-1880 at Geo. F. Leggett's, Sara F. LEGGETT (nm), dt Geo. F. & Charlotte M., N. Y.
Joseph Delaplaine, s Wm. R. & Abigail, b 2-22-1823; ct Flushing 3-1845
Mary Day, dt Wm. R. & Jane, b 5-31-1846; relrq 6-6-1894
Peleg, Portsmouth, & Amy
Ch: William
cf Portsmouth, R. I. for William 6-29-1784
Philip Wanton rocf Portsmouth 10-29-1801 to live with a Friend
William Richardson, s Peleg & Amy (dec), Newport, R. I.; m N. Y. 8-10-1796 Eleanor KING, dt Joseph & Ann (dec), New Castle on Tyne, Eng.
Ch: Eleanor b 5- 2-1797 d 6-12-1797
Eleanor d 9-26-1805 ae 7y 4m
cf Portsmouth, R. I. 6-29-1784
Wm. R. m 2d N. Y. 3-8-1815 Mary SEAMAN, dt Willet & Mary (dec), N. Y., b Hempstead d 4-18-1819 ae 42y 7m 4d bHS
Ch: William Richardson b 5-14-1817 d 4-25-1855
Wm. R. d 4-25-1855; m 3d N. Y. 7-12-1821 Abigail EVERNGHIM, dt Gilbert & Phebe, N. Y., d 6----1851 (H)
Ch: Joseph Delaplaine b 2-22-1823
Edward d 4-5-1830 ae 1-1/2d
Abigail dis 1-1831 (O); Abigail gct Flushing 3-1845 (O)
Wm. R., s Wm. R. & Mary (dec), N. Y., b 5-4-1817 d 10-10-1895 bPP; m N. Y. 11-9-1842 Jane R. DAY, dt Mahlon & Mary, d 11-19-1863 ae 50y bPP
Ch: William R. Jr. b 10-27-1843
Mary Day b 5-31-1846 d 8-22-1921 Grandview, N. Y. bPP (nm)
Edward D. b 3- 4-1851
Anna D. " 5- 4-1857
William R. Jr., s Wm. R. & Jane R. (dec), N.Y., b 10-27-1843 d 10-19-1890; m 11-4-1869 at Alden Sampson's, Maria H. SAMPSON, dt Alden & Sarah, N. Y.
Ch: Wm. Richardson b 7-23-1873
William R. dis 5-1835 (H); Maria relrq 7-1-1874
Wm. R. 2d, s Wm. R. Jr. & Maria H., b 7-23-

THURSTON, Wm. R. 2d, continued
1873 d about 1895 bPP; name erased

TIBBITS
John (nm) & -----
Ch: Howard D. b Columbia Co. d 3-16-1830 ae 5m bHS
----- & ----- (nm)
Ch: John B. b Conn. d 7-6-1829 ae 4y bHS

TICE
R. Solomon (nm) m 6-2-1925 Olga REGENHARD
Olga rolf St. Trinitatas Evan. Luth. Ch., Jersey City 6-1925; ct Yorktown 3-1926

TIERNEY
Bertha Hazard m Frank P. UFFORD
cf Germantown 6-12-1907 as Ufford

TIFFANY
Caroline C. rocf Weare 11-1865; ct Weare 5-1873
Mary L., dt Wm. W. & Charlotte FOX, dis mo 3-1-1837 (0)

TILDEN
Jane (form West) rocf Balt. 3-1852; sister of Eli West; d 11-18-1880 (H)

TILLEY
John Llewellen m Bessie Marion WAIBEL, dt Marion
Ch: Joyce Llewellen b 1-14-1921
Bessie Marion m 2d 1930 Clifford S. FRY; John rolf First Pres. Ch., Stamford, Conn. 5-5-1919; name erased 3-1928; Marion Waibel recrq of mother 12-4-1901

TILSON
Bethany, s Sarah; m Dr. HIGGINS (mo) dis 5-4-1853
Carrie [Tillson], dt Wm. E. S. & Annah, b 10-25-1879; name erased
Edward Hosmer [Tillson], s Wm. E. S. & Annah, b 4-28-1881; name erased
Isaiah S., s Sarah, d 9-4-1855 (H)
Sarah, w ----- d 3-17-1880 (H)
Ch: Bethany
Martha S. d 2-6-1843 (or 2-5-1843) ae 21y 10m
Isaiah
William F.
cf Plains with her 4 ch 7-1834
William E. S. [Tillson] d 12-1888; m Anah ----- d 12-1888
Ch: Carrie b 10-25-1879
Edward Hosmer b 4-28-1881
Phebe R. " 5-14-1886 d 12-23-1886
William P. C. [Tillson], s Timothy & Sarah H.; m 9-11-1850 Lydia JENKINS, dt James & Mary (Smith), b Esopus, N. Y., 8-20-1829 d 12-22-1902 (H)
Ch: Winfield Scott b 10-23-1858 d 1-1-1903
Mary Smith b 6-15-1862 d 9-14-1870
cf Marl. 12-1848 for Lydia with parents

TILTON
Benj. W., s Amos (dec) & Eliz. (White), of Middletown, N. J.; m at Dobel Baker's 11-5-1846 Mary BAKER, dt Dobel & Mary (Corlies), N. Y., b Phila. 12-6-1823 d 10-31-1905 (H)
Ch: Joseph White b N. Y. 1-25-1849
Mary Elizabeth b N. Y. 2-4-1853 d 4-8-1869
Caroline S. L. b N. Y. 8-25-1853
Caroline L. b N. Y. 8-25-1855
Edward L. b N. Y. 10-19-1861
Josephine H. b N. Y. 3-15-1867
Catharine, wd William, d 4-1843 (H)
Ch: Elizabeth B. b 10-11-1804 d 3-20-1887
Sarah
Mellis b 10-25-1810
cf Cincinnati 3-1820 with 3 ch named
Charles Edward, s Edw. L. & Mary (Bigelow), b N. Y. 5-26-1905; recrq of parents 9-8-1924 (H)
Edward L., s Benj. W. & Mary B., b 10-19-1861 N. Y. d 1-5-1933; m 6-5-1901 Mary Eastman BIGELOW (nm), dt Chas. C. & Laura E. (H)
Ch: Charles Edward b 5-26-1905
Architect of over 100 libraries; Chas. Edward recrq of parents 9-8-1924
Esther, dt John, Mk.; m 1665
John, Sr., Gravesend, d 1688; m Mary ----- d 3 Mo (May) 29, 1683
Ch: John b 4 Mo (June) 4, 1640
John active mbr 1672-1683
John, Jr., s John & Mary, Gravesend, b 4 Mo. (June) 4, 1640; m Rebeckah TERRY (m 3 Mo. (May) 12, 1674)
Ch: John b 2 Mo (Apr) 14, 1675
Abraham " 11 Mo (Jan) 14, 1676/7 d 8/9, 1686
Samuel " 1 Mo (Mar) 2, 1678/9
Sarah " 9 Mo (Nov) 4, 1680
Daniel " 10 Mo (Dec) 27, 1682
Thomas " 10 Mo (Dec) 20, 1684
Mary " 8 Mo (Oct) 21, 1696
Hester " 2 Mo (Apr) 17, 1689
John active mbr 1677-1685
Joseph W., s Benj. W. & Mary B., b 1-25-1849 N. Y. d 5-3-1920; m 4-12-1887 Mary MOORE, dt Joseph T. & Anna F. (Leggett), b Whitestone, N. Y. 9-14-1859 (H)
cf Sandy Spring 11-6-1897 for Mary; ct Sandy Spring 4-13-1925 for Mary
Mellis S., dt William & Catharine, b 10-25-1810; rocf Cincinnati 3-1820 with mother; dis mo 5-6-1835 (0); rst; ct Pur. 3-1839 (H)
Sarah M., dt William & Catharine, b 11-25-1807; m ----- HOWARD (mo) (H)
cf Cincinnati 3-1820 with mother; dis 9-1833 (0); dis 5-1831 (H)
Thomas (nm) b Middletown, Conn. d 11-8-1809 ae 32y bHS
Thomas rocf Chesterfield 7-7-1807 (clear); ct

TILTON, Thomas, continued
Shrews. 12-1-1813 (clear); cf Shrews. 10-7-1816; ct Cincinnati 9-3-1817
William, s Thos. & Sarah, of Monmouth Co., N. J.; m N. Y. 1-11-1804 Catharine MELLIS, dt John & Sarah (both dec) of Polisworth, Eng., d 4-1843 (H)
Ch: Elizabeth B. b 10-12-1804 d 3-20-1887
Sarah M. b 11-25-1807
Mary S. " 10-25-1810
cf Burl. 11-9-1801 (clear); ct Cincinnati 9-3-1817 with their 3 ch, Eliz. B., Sarah M. & Mellis S.; Catharine & ch dis 1829-1835 (O)
----- & ----- (nm)
Ch: Thomas b N. Y. d 9-15-1812 ae 5y 10m bHS

TINKER
----- & ----- (nm)
Ch: Catharine b Me. d 9-26-1829 ae 5m bHS

TIPPING
Robert rocf Hardshaw MM, Eng. 9-18-1798 (clear)

TITLEY
Thomas rocf 2 weeks mtg, London, 9-25-1786 (clear)

TITUS
Amelia M., dt Wm. W., b 5-15-1864; mbrp relinquished 3-1880
Amy, w John, dt John & Sarah COCK; dis mo 1-1-1794
Ann recrq 5-6-1818
Ann, dt Samuel & Abigail, N. Y.; m 1818 Stephen VALENTINE
Annie, dt John V. & Sarah W., Bkn.; m 1878 Wm. T. SMITH (H)
recrq 5-9-1896
Austin rocf Hudson 3-23-1819, apprentice; ct Nantucket, apprentice to Barzilla Bunker, 4-5-1820; cf Nantucket 9-30-1824 (clear)
Benjamin rocf Oswego 12-18-1833 (clear); dis 12-1840
Charles d 7-24-1800; m Margaret ----- bHS
Margaret, w Chas., rocf Wby 7-27-1774
Charles (nm) b L. I. d 5-19-1815 ae 78y bHS
Charles F. & Mary F. (H)
Ch: George B. b 12-31-1843
Hannah B. " 3- 6-1850
cf Wby 4-1844; ct Wby 7-4-1855 with Mary F. & ch; Mary F. rocf Pur. 4-1844
Cornelius Bartram, s Stephen & Agnes (O'Neill) b N. Y. 3-28-1893; m 9-5-1915 Marie Josephine GERNHARDT (nm), dt Joseph H. (dec) & Anna (Coyne) (H)
Daniel rocf Wby & Jericho 1850; d 12-12-1896
Deborah, dt Richard & Sarah; m 8-1-1845 Joseph Lee (nm) (H)
Edmond b 1630 d 2 Mo (Apr) 7, 1715 ae 85y; m Martha ----- d 2 Mo (Apr) 1727 ae about 84
Ch: John
Mary
Patience
Samuel
Silas
Phebe
active mbr 1677-1702
Edmund m Elizabeth C. ----- d 9-9-1854
Ch: James C. b 7- 2-1854
Infant stillborn 7-19-1859 bPP
cf Wby & Jericho 1854 for Edmund; cf Oswego 1854 for Eliz.
Edmund d 11-16-1892 m 2d Esther C. -----
Ch: Lizzie b 5-20-1861
Bertha b 1- 2-1866 d 1- 4-1870 bPP
cf Pur. 10-6-1858 for Esther; Esther relrq 9-5-1894
Elizabeth recrq 7-5-1882; d 8-2-1891 (H)
Elizabeth Ann, w Jacob S.
Ch: Martha P.
cf Wby & Jericho 1853 with Martha P; name omitted 2-1881
Esther, w Richard A., d 6-23-1848 (H)
Ch: Thomas W.
Richard A.
Sarah
cf Oswego 11-14-1832 with 2 ch first named
Franklin, s Coles & Phebe, rocf Pur. with parents 4-1828
George b L. I. d 6-30-1832 ae 56y; m Jemima ----- d 9-7-1849 (H)
Ch: Richard D.
Mary Ann d 6-30-1836
Samuel L. d 1864
cf Oswego 9-14-1825 with 3 ch named; ct Oswego 3-4-1835 for Jemima with dt, Mary, both clear (H)
George B. & Marietta (H)
Ch: Alice W.
Mary W.
Georgiana
cf Wby 8-2-1876 for all; ct Wby 8-3-1881 for all
Hannah rocf Pur. 7-12-1810; ct Wby 4-5-1815 (an aged Friend & minister)
Henrietta E., dt William L. & Ann C., b Corn. 1851 d 7-12-1919; m 1883 Henry E. KLAMT b Germany 1848 (nm) (H)
cf Corn. 11-1853 with parents
Henry (nm) & -----
Dt.:----- d 10-28-1809 ae 4m
Henry b L. I. d 4-10-1829 ae 89y; m ----- (H)
Ch: Elizabeth b L. I. d 9-27-1842 ae 72y 9m 15d
cf Wby 2-1797
Henry m Martha SEAMAN, b Wby d 6-5-1816 ae 71y 4m 2d bHS
Ch: Mary b 12-30-1771
Martha rocf Pur. 8-26-1772
Henry rocf Wby & Jer. 1-1861 d 10-1921
Isaac C. rocf Wby & Jer. 3-1871; d 3-29-1928 near Cleveland 1912
Jacob rocf Wby 8-19-1801 (clear)
James (nm) & -----
Ch: Agnes J. d 7-22-1847 ae 11m bHS

TITUS, continued
Jerusia rocf Wby 8-19-1801 (clear)
John, s Edmund & Martha, Wby; m at Henry Willis' 8 Mo (Oct) 9, 1695 Sarah WILLIS, dt Henry & Mary, Wby
Ch: Mary b 4 Mo (June) 13, 1696
John " 5 Mo (July) 28, 1698
Philadelphia b 9 Mo (Nov) 29, 1700
Jacob " 5 Mo (July) 1, 1703
William " 7 Mo (Sep) 23, 1705
Sarah " 1 Mo (Mar) 7, 1708/9
Phebe " 5 Mo (July) 6, 1710
John, Jr., Flushing, b 2-13-1759 d 2-21-1817; m Phebe ----- b 7-20-1761
Ch: Jonathan b 9- 8-1785
Anne " 10-12-1788
Thomas " 2- 5-1795
Phebe " 2- 5-1795
cf Wby 12-26-1787 with w, Phebe, & 2 ch, Jonathan & Anne; ct Corn. 5-5-1802 for both with 3 ch, Ann, Thomas & Phebe
John d 10-13-1880; m Eliza ----- d 1-1-1876 (H)
Ch: Townsend d 8-14-1881
cf Corn. 10-1844 with 1 ch named
John V., s Joshua & Ann; m 9-27-1844 Phebe W. UNDERHILL, dt Thos. & Sarah (Whitson), b N. Y. 4-11-1824 d 4-13-1914 (H)
cf Wby 9-3-1879 for Phebe (wd)
Joseph R. (nm) d 1-14-1892 ae 83y 1m 3d bPP; m Ruth Amelia TITUS, dt Samuel J. & Hannah (Conklin), b Little Rest, N. Y. about 1822 d 2-25-1906 ae 78y 5m bPP
Ch: Adeline C. d 7-26-1851 ae 9y 9m 21d bPP
Albert " 9- 3-1853 ae 2y 8m 24d bPP
Louise Jane " 10-20-1857 ae 5y 2m 7d bPP
Stanley H. " 7-27-1861 ae 17y 5m 8d bPP
Ida " 4- 2-1863 ae 6y 11m 29d "
Stephen
Stanleyetta
George I. b 11-14-1865
Elizabeth I. d 4-15-1896 ae 31y 11m 2d bPP
Joseph rocf Oswego 7-18-1832 (clear); dis 12-1840 (O); Ruth A. recrq 3-4-1885 with ch
Keturah, w Peter S., d 6-10-1893 (H)
Ch: Martha S. b 2-9-1849
cf Corn. 2-1845; Martha recrq 3-1862
Lizzie, dt Edmund & Esther C., b 5-20-1861; relrq 2-1886
Lydia T., dt Rowland & Sarah, Bkn.; m ----- ALLEY; m 2d 1862 Samuel P. HOSIER (H)
Martha, w Edmund, active mbr 1677-1684
Martha rocf Pur. 12-2-1772
Martha rocf Wby 8-19-1812 (clear)
Martha, dt Samuel & Abigail, N. Y.; m 1814 Jacob VALENTINE
Martha C., dt Richard, d 4-8-1826
Martha P., dt Jacob S. & Elizabeth Ann, rocf Wby & Jericho 1853 with mother; name omitted 2-1881
Martha S., dt Peter S. & Keturah, N. Y., b 2-9-1849; m 1874 Daniel C. SANDS (nm) (H)
Martha recrq of mother 3-1862

Mary, dt Edmund & Martha; m 1687 Wby, William WILLIS
Mary, dt Henry & Martha; m 1790 Andrew COCK, of N. Y.
Mary, dt William & Sarah, d 9-21-1803 bHS
Mary, dt George & Jemima, rocf Oswego with parents 9-14-1825; ct Oswego with mother 3-4-1835 (clear)
Mary, dt David & Jane (Colley), b Flush. 2-16-1821 d 9-21-1907 ae 86y 7m 5d (unm) (H)
cf Flush. 8-5-1868
Melle Stanleyetta, dt Jos. & Ruth Amelia, N.Y.; m 1896 Edgar Schell WERNER (nm) (H)
recrq 2-4-1885 (the first woman admitted to the Bar in N. Y. State)
Michael M. d 3-17-1801 bHS
another d 12-18-1802 ae 14d
Oliver C., s Wm. L. & Ann (Cromwell), b Corn. 1-4-1849 d 5-15-1927; m 1-17-1889 Emma WALTON (nm) (H)
cf Corn. 11-1853 with parents
Patience, dt Edmund & Martha, Wby; m 1704 Nicholas HAIGHT
Peggy, Margaret, Wby, m 1795 Whitehead HICKS
Peter b L. I. d 1-5-1843 ae 50y 2m 5d bPP; m Sarah R. ----- d 1-8-1871 ae 79y bPP (H)
Ch: Wm. M. d 12-28-1828 ae 9m bPP
Samuel P.
Elizabeth R. b 9-4-1830 d 12-18-1831
Richard R. ae 13y d 1-23-1846 bPP
Stephen d 1-11-1839 ae 1y 11m 5d
Stephen V. b 2- 7-1837 d 1-12-1839 bPP
Ann Elizabeth " 2-16-1840 d 3- 2-1840
Peter recrq 5-1830; Sarah rocf Pur. 11-1823
Phebe, dt Samuel, Wby; m 1716 John HAIGHT
Phebe, dt Edmond & Martha, Mk., d 1 Mo (Mar) 10, 1742/3; m (1) Samuel SCUDDER; m (2) Robert FIELD
Phebe B., dt William T. & Mercy W. (Hallock), b Corn. 4-2-1839 d 9-29-1906; m 11-10-1857 Drake HALLOCK (nm), s Charles & Mary (H)
cf R. & P. 10-10-1896
Phebe S. rocf Wby & Jericho 1853; d 11-14-1854
Richard rocf Wby 5-25-1763 (clear)
Richard, Jr. d 5-11-1850; m Wby 1810 Sarah ----- d 6-25-1866 ae 81y bPP (H)
Ch: Susan b 8-20-1811 d 3-4-1870 bPP
Mary d 1-13-1875 ae 61y bPP
Deborah
Sarah b 9-17-1817
Richard U. b 10-6-1820
Caroline B. b 2-25-1828 d 12-1-1886 bPP
Richard rocf Wby 6-17-1801 (clear); cert of clear to Wby 10-3-1810; Sarah rocf Wby 3-20-1811; ct Flushing 6-2-1813 with 2 ch; Susan & infant rocf Flush. 1817; cf Flush. 9-1817
Richard (nm) & -----
Ch: Infant stillborn 1-5-1832 bHS
Alonzo b N. Y. d 7-2-1847 ae 3y 6m 6d bHS
Richard, Jr. rocf Oswego 11-16-1831 with Thomas minors; dis 12-1848 [ae 78y bPP (H)
Richard A ., s Richard A. & Esther, d 12-2-1854
cf Oswego 2-1833 with mother; dis 8-1853

TITUS, continued
Richard W. & Mary P. (H)
Ch: John Jr. b 9-24-1840 d 7-19-1846
Richard rocf Wby 8-1840 with 1 ch; ct Jericho 8-1840 for Mary; ct Jericho 1-4-1854 for parents
Robert (nm) b N. Y. d 4-29-1809 ae 2y 8m 20d bHS
Robert S. & Hannah
Hannah S. recrq 7-1853; cf Wby & Jericho 1850 for Robt.; ct Rocksylvania, Iowa, 5-1850 for both
Ruth Amelia, dt Samuel J. & Hannah (Conklin), b Little Rest, N. Y., abt 1822 d 2-25-1906; m Joseph TITUS (H)
Samuel, s Edmond & Martha, Wby; m at Thos. Powell's, Bethpage, 9 Mo (Nov) 6, 1691 Elizabeth POWELL, dt Thomas, Bethpage, d 2 Mo. (Apr) 9, 1704 (or 1705)
Samuel m 2d Elizabeth PRIAR, dt John & Hannah BOWNE, Flushing, d 12 Mo (Feb) 14, 1721/23
Elizabeth m 1st John PRIAR
Samuel, s Henry & Sarah, Harrison, N. Y., d Wby; m Flushing 12-15-1796 Mary PEARSALL, dt Thomas & Ann, Flushing (H)
Ch: Stephen
Elizabeth
Samuel J.
ct Wby 5-3-1797; cf Wby 5-19-1819, with 2 ch named; ct Wby & Jericho 12-2-1829 for Mary with 3 minor ch, Stephen, Elizabeth & Samuel
Samuel rocf Wby & Jericho 5-1873; d 2-25-1894
Samuel C. rocf Wby 12-14-1825, placed; ct Flush. 11-1854; cert returned 2-7-1855; d 7-26-1856 (H)
Samuel L. rocf Oswego 4-1826; d 1864 (H)
Samuel P., s Peter (dec) & Sarah R., N. Y., d 11-19-1855 ae 29y 27d bPP; m at C. K. Jenkins' 2-6-1851, Sarah JENKINS, dt Thos. W. (dec) & Caroline K., N. Y., d 6-22-1893 ae 65y 2m 7d bPP (H)
Ch: Caroline J. b 4-28-1852 d 10-8-1925 bPP
William Mudge b 2-20-1854
Samuel recrq 6-1831
Sarah, dt Richard & Sarah, b 9-17-1817; m Henry GRIFFEN (nm) (Sarah d 1-9-1854) (H)
Sarah, w Peter (form Reynolds) dis 1-1830
Sarah, dt Richard A. & Esther; m ----- WHITNEY (mo) (H)
cf Oswego 9-1833; dis 12-1833
Sarah C., dt Wm. L. & Anna C.; m 4-3-1861 ----- COYKENDALL (nm) (H)
cf Corn. with parents 11-1853
Sarah O., dt Wm. L. & Ann, d 12-21-1900 ae 58y 11m 25d; m ----- COYKENDALL (H)
cf Corn. 11-1853 with parents
Silas, s Edmund & Martha, Wby; m at Flushing 10 Mo (Dec) 8, 1704 Sarah HAIGHT, dt Samuel & Sarah, Flushing
Silas & Elizabeth
Ch: Sarah
William
Ch: Lydia
cf Wby 3-14-1798 with 3 young ch
Stephen d 3-6-1819 ae 14d
Stephen, s Joseph & Ruth Amelia, d 5-4-1898 ae 40y 14d bPP; m 9-29-1896 Agnes O'NEILL, dt Gregory, b N. Y. 1-18-1869 d 9-9-1925 bPP (H)
Ch: Ruth Amelia b 11-26-1887 d 9-27-1903 bPP
Albert " 9- 2-1889
Cornelius Bertram b 3-28-1893
Stephen recrq 9-4-1885; Agnes recrq 2-2-1887
Stephen R. d 2-12-1880; m ----- LEWIS, dt Philo & Clarissa (H)
cf Wby 7-1836 for Stephen R.
Stephen Wm. & Hannah (H)
Ch: Sarah
Elizabeth
cf Jericho 10-15-1818; all dis 1830-1849 (O); Stephen dis 5-1835 (H); Hannah & ch gct Wby 8-1837
Thomas W. rocf Oswego 11-16-1831 with Richard, Jr., minors; dis 2-1842 (O); rel 6-2-1875, absent over 5y
William, s Silas (dec), Hempstead; m Flushing 11-8-1753 Sarah BOWNE, dt Samuel, Flushing
Ch: Mary
William gct Pur. 3-6-1793, his ack. having been rec; cf Pur. 5-12-1796
William C. rocf Wby 12-14-1825 (clear); ct Wby 8-1835; cert ret 12-1836; dis 3-1839 (H)
William L. rocf Flush. 2-2-1826 (clear); cf Flush. 1-1832 (H)
William L. d 4-14-1862; m Ann CROMWELL d 3-30-1892 (H)
Ch: Sarah O.
Henrietta E.
Oliver C. b 1-4-1849
cf Corn. 11-1853 with 3 ch
William Mudge, s Samuel P. & Sarah (Jenkins), b 2-20-1854 d 10-13-1918 bPP; m 6-10-1891 Mary F. MINARD, dt John & Serena A. (Carpenter), of Lobo, Ont. (H)
Mary mbr Lobo MM, Ont.
William W., s Wm. & Phebe W., N. Y., d 3-24-1869; m N. Y. 1-3-1861 at Pelatiah P. Page's, Annie L. PAGE, dt Pelatiah P. & Amelia, N. Y., b 5-30-1841
Ch: Amelia M. b 5-15-1864
cf Wby & Jericho 7-1859 for William; Annie L. relrq 12-1867
----- & ----- (nm)
Ch: Martha C. b Flush. d 4-8-1826 ae 2y 5m 8d bHS
Benjamin b N. Y. d 11-17-1834 ae 2m bHS

TOBEY
Samuel R. Jr. rocf Providence 1-1851; dis 1855

TOBIAS
Phyllis b Conn. d 7-3-1844 ae 70y; cf Troy 3-1819 (prob same as Priscilla)
Priscilla rocf Troy 12-9-1818

TODHUNTER
Joseph Massey Howey & Frances Ann
Ch: Ellen Frances b 2-7-1873
Edith Rebecca " 7-16-1874
cf Dublin 9-1871 for parents; ct Hardshaw East 6-14-1876 for all
Joshua Edmundson rocf Dublin 3-14-1854; ct Dublin 4-1863; cf Dublin 9-1864; d in Dublin 3-14-1881

TOLFREE
William (nm) m Maria Amelia BOWRON, dt John S. & Sarah (H)
Ch: Sarah A. d 7-19-1859 ae 1y 7m bPP
Mary Bowron d 12-4-1862 ae 2y 5m bPP
Maria dis 5-6-1868 for non-attendance

TOLLERTON
Robert & -----
Ch: (prob) Charlotte Ann d 8-28-1831 ae 8y 11d bHS
cf Chap. 8-12-1803; dis 9-2-1818

TOMS
Elizabeth (late Hicks) dis mo 10-6-1773
Thomas [Tom] (nm) b L. I. d 3-7-1816 ae 73y bHS; m Catharine FARRINGTON b L. I. d 10-11-1839 ae 79y 2m (H)
Catharine dis 1-4-1781 for mo; rst 2-3-1819; dis 12-1829 (O)

TOMPKINS
Charity, w James, rocf Chap. 6-13-1817; ct Rochester 11-7-1827
Coles d 1844; m Phebe ---- d 1858
Ch: Franklin
Julian b 4-17-1840
Phebe near 16y
cf Pur. 2-13-1828 with 1 ch
Daniel H. (nm) & Eliza (nm)
Ch: Frank d 7-11-1853 ae 2y 5m 29d bPP
Elijah rocf Pur. 1-13-1814 (clear); ct Pur. 2-3-1819 (clear)
Eliza, dt Wm. & Jane WRIGHT, b 12-4-1810; dis mo 1-1-1834
Elizabeth S. recrq 8-2-1893; relrq 11-6-1897 (H)
Joseph & Mary
Ch: John H. b 4-3-1828
Catharine
Phebe Ann
cf Pur. 9-1828 for parents; ct Galway 10-1835 for all, ret 12-1836; all marked (O) 2-1850
Lottie belle, dt Stanby & Carrie Belle (Williams), b Mt. Kisco 10-15-1899; m 1922 Harold A. MARSHALL (H)
both rec with ch 4-12-1926
Noah rocf Pur. 4-12-1826, apprentice; dis 7-1834

TONG
Jow recrq 5-2-1906 (chinese)
Yet recrq 3-1-1905 (chinese)

TOPPING
David rocf Kingston, Eng. 12-5-1906; name erased 2-1926

TORREY
Arthur H. (nm), s Lucien E. & Maude (Haviland); m 7-8-1931 Therese Marie HOHOFF -HALLOCK, dt Ernest A. & Anna (Hallock), b N. Y. 7-3-1898 (H)

TOSTEVEN
John d 1-16-1857 ae 64y bPP; m Martha ----- d 11-9-1856 ae 62y bPP
Ch: Thomas
David
Rachel b 2-9-1825
Peter recrq of parents
cf Southampton, Eng. 10-6-1836, having rem from Island of Gurnsey; ct Salem, Iowa, 4-4-1849 (apparently ret)
Malene recrq 5-1851; ct Burl. 2-1853
Peter, s John & Martha, recrq of parents 1836; dis mo by a priest 1-1851
Rachel, dt John & Martha, b Isle of Guernsey, 2-9-1825 d 10-24-1907 bPP; m George UNDERHILL (nm)

TOTHILL
Charles Jr. rocf Bristol, Eng. 7-2-1844; cert ret. to Bristol 11-1846 as he had ret.
Edward rocf South Division, Wales 10-1851; d 1854

TOTTEN
Hannah d 7-20-1832 bHS
Robert gct Phila. 9-6-1781; had resided in Pur.

TOUSSAINT
Eugenie Lecordier m 1866 Aaron B. COHU (H)

TOWELL
Joseph rocf Ireland 1834; d 11-6-1852

TOWER
Ambrose (nm) & -----
Ch: Franklin F. stillborn 8-12-1862 bPP

TOWNSEND
Abraham & -----
Ch: Anne d 7-4-1835 ae 1y 9m bPP
Arthur (nm) & -----
Ch: James b N. Y. d 1-8-1832 ae 6d bHS
Benjamin (nm) & -----
Ch: Infant stillborn 3-21-1818
Christopher gct R. I. 12-2-1756
Deborah signed m cert 1676-1681; d 1 Mo (Mar) 30, 1798
Edwin, s Samuel & Phebe, rocf Pur. 4-13-1820 with parents; dis 3-1-1848 (H)
Eleanor, dt George & Frances (Buchanan),

TOWNSEND, Eleanor, continued
b Tarrytown, 10-11-1881; m 1913 Nelson Eugene FLANDREAU (H)
recrq 4-6-1901
Elizabeth gct Wby 7-2-1788
Elizabeth (late Franklin) dis mo 10-5-1803
Epinetus (nm) & -----
Ch: Infant stillborn 8-14-1828 bHS
Harriet d 10-12-1830 ae 1y 1m 21d bHS
John G. b N. Y. d 6-23-1833 ae 1m 14d [(H)
Frederick E. (nm) d 10-1-1866 ae 41y 2m 27d bPP
George (nm), s Benj. & Elizabeth, b L. I. d 9-20-1841 ae 78y bHS; m Elizabeth BOWNE, dt James & Caroline, b L. I. 1772 d 3-14-1841 bHS
Ch: Caroline d 5-8-1802 ae 2m bHS
Walter
James
dis mo 6-2-1796
Harriet, dt Edward & Ann C., b Phila. 12-12-1833; m 1856 Richard R. HAINES (H)
cf Phila. 5-1864; ct Phila. 11-7-1903
Henry (nm) & -----
Ch: John d 4-15-1838 ae 9y 3m bHS
Hester (Esther) (form Smith), O.B., w Mill John Townsend (nm)
John m 1768 Susannah -----
John took cert of clear to Woodbridge 3-3-1768; Susannah rocf Woodbridge 7-6-1768; both gct Woodbridge 8-3-1769
John d 3-30-1799 bHS
John (nm) b Oyster Bay d 9-4-1823 ae 58y bHS (widower)
John (nm) m Rebecca ----- b N. Y. d 5-18-1822 ae 51y bHS (nm)
John P. & Catharine T.
cf Albany 3-6-1861 for John; cf Phila. 3-3-1875 for Catharine; ct Phila. 5-7-1884 for both (H)
Joseph, s John & Joanna (dec), Balt.; m N. Y. 6-3-1803 Esther HALLETT, dt Thomas (dec) & Phebe, Newtown
Ester gct Balt. 9-1-1803; John & Joanna, of East Bradford, Pa.
Martha gc 9 Mo (Nov) 2, 1749
Martha, dt John & Susanna, Middlesex, N. J.; m 1804 James POWELL
cf R. & P. 1-19-1804 (clear)
Mary Elma (nm), dt Leander W. & Anna E. (Wood); m 1866 James Macy COLEMAN (H)
Nathaniel, O.B., m between 9 Mo 1, & 10 Mo (Dec) 6, 1739 Martha HICKS, wd Samuel, of Hempstead
Nathaniel & -----
Ch: Nathaniel
Martha
Almey
cf Wby for the 3 ch rem some yrs ago, very young 9-30-1761
Nicholas, Wby, m between 2 Mo 12, 1762 & 5 Mo 1, 1763, Philadelphia DOUGHTY, dt Benjamin, Flushing
Ch: Hannah
Ch: Elizabeth
Philadelphia
cert of clear from Wby 12-2-1762; cf Wby 8-28-1765; ct N.P. with w & 3 ch 10-6-1779
Phebe, dt Thomas, Hempstead, d 12 Mo (Feb) 26, 1726/7
Philadelphia gct Wby 8-4-1763
Rebecca (late Franklin) dis mo 4-3-1793
Richard Mott, s Samuel & Phebe, rocf Pur. 4-13-1820 with parents; dis 7-1848
Samuel b Franklin, Dutchess Co. d 5-7-1826 ae 39y 7m 9d; m Phebe ----- d 9-14-1868 (H)
Ch: Sarah Ann
Edwin
Abigail Mott d 12-11-1853
Richard M. d 8- 6-1819 ae 1y 8m
Richard Mott b 3-25-1820
Gilbert G. (or R.) b 12-22-1822 d 10-27-1826
Samuel A. b 8-9-1825
cf Pur. 4-13-1820 with 4 ch; all dis 1830-1840 (O); d at sea
Samuel m Elizabeth F. LEWIS, dt Job & Sarah Z., d 1-23-1910 ae 86y (both nm) (H)
Samuel (nm) & -----
Ch: Daniel d 2-1-1832 ae 1y 8m bHS
Samuel A., s Samuel & Phebe, b 8-9-1825; name cancelled 4-9-1904 as long unknown
Sarah rocf R. & P. 6-16-1802 (clear); ct R.& P. 6-3-1835 (O); dis 1829 (H)
Sarah Ann, dt Samuel & Phebe, rocf Pur. 4-13-1820 with parents; dis 2-1838 (H)
Solomon & -----
Ch: Solomon d 3-2-1804 ae 2y 8m bHS
Stephen rocf Creek 12-19-1800 (clear); took cert of clear to Stanford 5-1-1805; ct Stanford 9-4-1805
Tappen rocf Albany 10-1853; relrq 10-1854 (H)
Temperance (nm), dt Geo. & Rosannah; m 1773 Elijah COCK
Walter B. (nm) & -----
Ch: Infant stillborn 8-11-1827 bHS
Elizabeth d 2-24-1832 ae 3y bHS
Infant stillborn 2-13-1841 bHS
James B. N. Y. d 10-1-1841 ae 10y bHS
William, s Thomas (dec), N. Hempstead; m Flushing 3-15-1787 Elizabeth DOUGHTY, dt Benj. (dec), Flushing
Elizabeth's ack. forwarded, accepted 4-2-1788; ct Wby 6-4-1788
William rocf Corn. 11-1845; ct Corn. 11-5-1873 (H)
----- & ----- (nm)
Ch: Edward b N. Y. d 8-14-1822 ae 1y 3m bHS
Francis A. b Bkn. d 11-4-1842 ae 10m bHS
William H. d 3-13-1871 ae 4y 8m bPP

TRACE
Clara m ----- BENSON
recrq 4-2-1902

TRAVIS
Abbie A., w Gideon Baxter, dt Ira W. & Sarah I.

TRAVIS, Abbie A., continued
HOAG, d 2-7-1906 (m 11-27-1904)
(at Manila, Phillipines)
Anna, dt Mortimer Wm. & Hannah (Pierce), b 2-14-1874; m Charles Gilpin COOK
cf Deer Creek, Md. for both 6-11-1902
Elizabeth Mitchell (form Travis) rocf Pur. 3-13-1806 (clear); dis mo 8-5-1812
Elizabeth, dt Mortimer J. & Martha (Cook), jas, name erased 21-1928
Jesse Heaton, s Mortimer J. & Martha (Cook), jas, name erased 3-1928
John Wm., s Mortimer J. & Martha P. (Cook); m Elizabeth HINES (nm), dt James & Elizabeth (Gordon), d 3-31-1935 bPP
Josiah m Phebe G. ----- d 3-24-1883
Ch: Mary Eugenia
Mortimer W.
cf Ama. 2-1869 with 1 ch named
Martha d 9-21-1802 ae 76y bHS
Martha E., dt Mortimer W. & Hannah; m 1908 Otto OVERDELL (nm)
recrq of parents 3-1872; jas, name erased 3-1928
Mary Eugenia, dt Josiah & Phebe, Bkn.; m 1870 Albert UNDERHILL
cf Ama. 2-1869 with parents
Mortimer J., s Mortimer W. & Hannah (Pierce), d 8-1927; m Amy J. WESTON (nm), dt Samuel & Amelia, b Parkville, N. J. 5-30-1864
d 1-5-1901 bPP
Ch: Emma stillborn 1-26-1896
Ralph M. b 1- 4-1898
Mortimer J. m 2d 7-30-1908 Martha P. COOK, d 4-3-1934
Ch: John Wm.
Elizabeth
Jesse Heaton
Martha Elizabeth
Ruth Clara b 11-13-1919
Mortimer recrq of parents 5-1872; Martha recrq 3-1-1905; Ralph M. recrq of father 12-4-1901; Mortimer relrq 3-7-1894; Mortimer recrq 12-4-1901; left friends shortly before his death
Mortimer W. d 1-7-1924; m Hannah M. PIERCE, dt Thomas L. & Martha E. (Cox), b 11-7-1844
d 3-5-1878 ae 34y bPP
Ch: Martha Elizabeth
Mortimer Josiah
Anna Edith b 2-14-1874
cf Ama. 5-1872 for Mortimer; Hannah recrq 3-1872; 2 elder ch recrq of parents same date
Mortimer W., b Ama. 3-23-1837; m 2d Matilda -----
Matilda Travis recrq 4-3-1912
Mortimer W. (nm) m Caroline M. SPRAGUE, dt John & Ann (Irish), b N. Y. 5-9-1844 d 3-30-1916 bPP
Nehemiah rocf Ama. 7-2-1845; ct Ama. 11-4-1846

TREADWELL
Adrian U., s Leman B. & Augusta (Ward), b Ardsley, N. J. 1-17-1869; m 11-16-1926 Edith SCHOFIELD, dt Frank & Harrietta ((Broadhent) b Bolton, Eng. 1-7-1883 (H)
both recrq 10-10-1927; both relrq 11-14-1932 to join Christian Science Church; both rec again 8-13-1934 (H)
Anna, w Samuel, rocf Pur. 12-10-1834; dis 11-1844 (O)
Dorothy [Tredwell] (late Carpenter) dis mo 11-4-1818
Joseph (nm) b Conn. d 7-17-1823 ae 29y 3m bHS; m -----
Ch: Ellsworth d 7-31-1820 ae 11d bHS
Letitia [Tredwell] rocf Pur.; d 1-7-1855 (H)
Mary, w Edwin, dt Abraham WHITSON, rocf Flush. 3-1847; d 3-26-1861 (H)

TRIMBLE
Daniel, s Daniel (dec) & Ann, N. Y., d 10-9-1851 ae 50y 7m 22d bPP; m N. Y. 2-9-1825 Mary B. HAWXHURST, dt Daniel & Hannah, N.Y., d 7-22-1879 ae 86y bPP
cf Falls, Va. 6-9-1820, minor; both dis 1830 (O); Daniel dis 5-1832 (H)
George F., s Richard, b 8-17-1793 d 5-16-1872; m ----- (H)
Ch: Richard d 7-3-1827 ae 1y 7m (nm)
George rocf Corn. 5-23-1811; George mo before 7-2-1823, ret a mbr (H); dis 1830 (O)
George T. (nm) & -----
Ch: George b N. Y. d 8-19-1845 ae 12y 11m 26d bHS

TRIMM
Madella H. recrq 7-1925

TRIPP
Elizabeth (nm) b Stonington, Conn. d 12-18-1828 ae 50y bHS (unm)
James (nm), s James, b Providence d 9-4-1831 ae 83y 5m bHS
James (nm) b Conn. d 8-7-1834 ae 47y bHS
Lot & Susannah
Ch: Tabitha b 4----1756
Lot d 2-19-1805 ae 57y 8m bHS; m 2d Eunice ----
cf N.P. 1-20-1792 for Lot, minister; cf Creek 1-20-1792 for Eunice
Peleg b Mass. d 12-18-1831 ae 69y 3m; Sandwich MM ref. his ack. to N.Y. 11-5-1823; rpd favorable 1-7-1824; rst that date & accepted by N.Y.

TROEGER
Ernest Anton, s John F. R. & Amalia (Becker), b N. Y. 5-19-1887; m 10-22-1912 Helen Gertrude SMITH, dt Fred'k D. & Agnes (Clark), b N. Y. 7-13-1892 (H)
Ch: Robert Ernest b 11-17-1913
Helen Gertrude b 8- 5-1916
all recrq 1-12-1925
John F. R., s Frederick & Wilhelmina W., d 7-

TROEGER, John F. R., continued
22-1926 ae 74y bPP; m Amelia Louise BECKer, dt William & Fredericka (Whormann), d 10-10-1928 ae 78y bPP (H)
Ch: Ernest Anton b 5-19-1887
Ernest recrq 1-12-1925 (both nm)
George & Catharine
Ch: Anna
Mary M.
cf SD MM 12-29-1824 with 1 ch named; ct ND MM 7-5-1826 with 2 ch, Mary M. & Anna. It was found that they were in Abington instead & this cert endorsed thereto 8-2-1826

TRUMAN
----- (nm) m Evalena ORT
Evalena recrq 6-12-1901; relrq 7-10-1918

TRUSTAM
Jane (nm), dt Frederick & Mary L., b Eng. 9-11-1846 d 3-31-1933 bPP; m John Hale HIGGINS

TUBBY
Elizabeth, dt Josiah T. & Phebe Anna, Bkn., b 8-2-1866; m 1890 Edward L. STABLER (H)
Elizabeth's name entered by com. 6-4-1890
John recrq 3-3-1836; ct Oswego 8-1842 (H)
Josiah T., s John & Mary (Green), b Eng. 2-17-1828 d 12-2-1909; m 10-7-1857 Phebe Anna BUNKER, dt Paul & Almira (Starbuck), b Boston 1-8-1832 d 1-27-1922 ae 90y 19d (H)
Ch: Almira B. b 3-21-1860 d 4-12-1926
Elizabeth " 8- 2-1866
Mary d 3-28-1867 ae 2y 7m 9d
Elsie b 8-25-1869 d 1-29-1893
Josiah T. Jr. b 6-2-1875
Edward J. d 10-25-1873 ae 2m 17d bPP
cf Oswego 2-6-1850; Phebe recrq 4-1878; ch names entered by com. 6-4-1890
Josiah T. Jr., s Josiah T. & Phebe A., b 6-2-1875 Bkn.; m 10-7-1901 Mary PECKHAM (nm), dt Wm. G. (H)
ct R. & P. 8-13-1910 for Josiah
Daniel B. & Phebe
Daniel recrq 5-11-1822; ct Licking Creek 12-4-1822 (clear); cf Licking Creek 4-15-1826 for Phebe; cf Licking Creek for Daniel 8-5-1829; ct Lick Creek for Daniel & his fam 11-4-1835; cf Lick Creek 12-19-1841 for Daniel; ct Salem, Iowa, 5-4-1853 for Daniel & his fam; Lick Creek states that Daniel had mo before 1-29-1829; rpd his ack. & accepted 8-5-1829

TUCKER
James W., s James W. & Sarah A. (both dec), N. Y.; m at Geo. S. Fox's, Jan. 11-1849, Esther FOX, dt George S. & Rebecca L., N. Y., b 6-29-1820 (H) (Geo. S. Fox not under care of N.Y. MM)
Phebe, w James, rocf Ama. 6-16-1810; ct Licking Creek, Indiana, 5-2-1821; cf Lick Creek, Indiana 4-15-1826
Susan recrq 6-6-1834; name canceled 10-14-1905 for lack of interest (H)
Thomas m Burl., N. J. 1807 Ann S. -----
Ch: Mary E. b 7-10-1808
Benjamin S. b 3-3-1810
Hannah " 6-20-1811
Elizabeth " 3-11-1813
George " 2- 7-1815 d 2-21-1817 bHS
William
cf Burl. 11-5-1804 (clear); cert of clear to Burl. 9-2-1807; Ann S. brought cert from Burl. 12-7-1807; ct Cincinnati 9-3-1817 with their 5 ch as named
Thomas S. rocf WD MM 5-17-1815, minor; ct WD MM 2-4-1818

TUNISON
Mary V., dt Hardenburg & Sarah (King), b 6-29-1818 d 7-13-1906; m 1841 Wardell WOOLLEY (H)
recrq 6-3-1863

TURCK
Annabel (nm), dt Solomon & Charlotte; m 1891 Henry M. COHU (H)

TURNER
Cyrus C. Jr. (nm), s Cyrus C. (dec) & Mary H., N. Y.; m Great Neck 8-28-1924 Sarah A. GRIFFEN, dt Henry E. & Fannie T., Great Neck, b Bkn. 2-19-1895 (H)
Ch: Sallie Jouett infant d 11-5-1930 bPP
Dorothy T. (nm), dt Frank & Ella Frances; m 1922 Alfred Tench FRANCIS (H)
Francis rocf Ireland forwarded by Phila. MM, but returned, as he was living in N.P. 8-3-1775
Henry C., s Richard T. Jr. & Martha E. (Birch), Bkn., b Betterton, Md. 10-16-1871; m at N. H. Chapman's 10-11-1899 Charlotte H. CHAPMAN, dt Noah H. & Marianna W., Bkn., b 9-16-1877 Glendale, O. (H)
Ch: Henry Chandlee Jr. b 4-24-1902
Katharine " 3-27-1904
Howard Haines " 4-12-1906
Robert Chapman " 7-22-1913
James Sinclair " 5- 9-1917
Henry's name entered by MM 5-6-1899; Charlotte rocf Cincinnati 2-2-1881
Henry Chandlee, Jr., s Henry C. & Charlotte, b Bkn. 4-24-1902; m 8-16-1928 Virginia A. MELICK, dt Elmer Ellsworth & Annie (Miller) b Media 10-8-1904 (H)
Ch: Virginia Ann b 9-24-1929
Mary Charlotte b 2-16-1933
cf Swarthmore for Virginia 2-10-1930
Howard H., s Henry C. & Charlotte C., Bkn.; m at A. N. Pierson's 6-11-1930, Catherine C. PIERSON, dt Arthur N. & Sadie F., Westfield, N. J. (H)
Katharine, dt Henry C. & Charlotte C., Bkn., b Bkn. 3-27-1904; m 1930 Melvin Herschel

TURNER, Katharine, continued
PARSONS (H)

TURPIN
William (nm) b Mass. d 1-21-1835 ae 80y 2m bHS

TURTLE
Alfred rocf Lurgan, Ireland 10-7-1891; d 3-1908
Henry F. rocf Dublin 12-4-1889; relrq 7-5-1905
Herbert S. & Emily L.
Ch: Lancelot James b 3-27-1905
Arabella " 11-1906
cf Lurgan 5-2-1894 for Herbert; Emily recrq 7-5-1905; Lancelot's name recorded 6-19-1905; ct Lisburn, Ireland 11-6-1912 for all

TUTHILL
Sylvester Davis (nm) m 4-27-1903 Elma W. BAYLIS, dt Chas. W. & Elma C., b N. Y. 8-5-1889
Elma recrq of parents 3-26-1890

TWEEDY
David (nm) m 4-16-1859 Elizabeth Ann WALKER, dt Thos. E. & Ann, d 7-7-1906
rq mbrp 1-1-1823, ret. to him 8-1823; cf West Chester 11-1836 for Elizabeth
Mabel, dt Richard & Mary Ann, b Yorkshire 3-8-1884; recrq of parents 5-4-1898; with parents joined Clinton Ave. Cong. Ch. & name erased 6-3-1906; letter from Memorial M.E. Church, Troy, N. Y. 9-30-1917; ct Po'keepsie 11-1922
Richard & Mary Ann
Ch: Mabel
Richard recrq 9-4-1895; Mary Ann recrq 6-12-1895; Mabel recrq 5-4-1898; all joined Clinton Ave. Cong. Ch. & names rem 6-3-1906

TYLEE
Elizabeth rocf Oblong 5-12-1783 to rem with her h
Elizabeth, dt Thomas & Eliz., of Shrews. d 4-4-1805 ae 85y

TYLER
Edward B. rocf Kingston, Eng. 10-1880; name erased 8-1920
W. Russell, s Wilson M. & Elizabeth M. (Powell) b Easton, Md. 7-24-1889; cf Third Haven, Md. 2-10-1912; ct to some place West about 1915 (Secretary N.Y. MM)

TYSON
Mary J. rocf ND MM 7-23-1833; dis 12-1839 (0); ct Phila. 2-1835 (H)
Sarah Ann rocf Phila. 9-1833; ct Phila. 12-1834; cf Phila. 6-1840; ct Phila. 10-1843 (H)

UDALL
Charles d on L. I. 1826; m Wby 1816 Catharine ----- b Islip, L. I. d 6-20-1823 ae 27y 5m 10d
Ch: Susan
Sarah b 11-10-1817
John C. " 7- 7-1819
Maria
Deborah d 4- 7-1823 ae 1m 21d
cf Wby 8-19-1812 (clear); cert of clear to Wby 11-6-1816; cf Wby 2-18-1818 for Catharine & dt, Susan
Charles gct Wby & Jericho 4-4-1832 (minor)
Hannah b N. Y. d 9-24-1818 ae --y 10m 14d bHS mbr & m
John C., s Charles & Catharine, b 7-7-1819; ct Wby & Jericho 4-4-1832 (0); ct Wby 1-1834 (H)

UFFORD
Charles Wilbur, s Frank P. & Bertha (Tierney), b N. Y. 2-15-1900; recrq of mother & consent of father, 4-2-1913; active mbr 4-1925; ct Germantown 5-6-1931
Frank P. (nm) m Bertha H. TIERNEY
Ch: Charles Wilbur b N. Y. 2-15-1900; active 4-1925
Elizabeth Hazard b N. Y. 2-12-1908
cf Germantown for Bertha 6-12-1907; ch recrq of mother & consent of father 4-2-1913

UNDERHILL
Aaron, s Amos, d 1836 (H)
Aaron C. rocf Ama. 7-10-1835 (clear); ct N.P. 4-1864
Aaron T. rocf Chap. 7-10-1845 (clear); mo by a priest before 12-1849, ret a mbr 2-1850; dis 1854
Abigail K., w Ira B., rocf Burl. 8-5-1839
Abraham, s John & Mary, Mk., d 11 Mo (Jan) 27, 1713/14
Abraham C., s Daniel, d 7-18-1887; m Elizabeth B. BUCKLEY, d at Kingston 8-2-1837 (H)
Ch: Amanda M. b 4-27-1825
Alonzo " 12-14-1827 d 5-31-1830
Adeline E." 12-21-1831
Louisa " 3- 2-1835
cf Chap. 12-12-1822 (clear); cf Ama. 2-11-1825 for Elizabeth B.; all dis 1830-1849 (0)
Abraham S., s Joshua & Mary (both dec), N. Y., d 12-12-1881; m N. Y. 2-12-1845 Mary F. SHOTWELL, dt Joseph S. & Deborah, N. Y., d 1-20-1886
Ch: Cornelia W. b 3-15-1846
Frederick Shotwell b 6-10-1856 d 3-27-1876
Abram S., s Jesse H. & Eliza S., New Castle; m 5-24-1877 at Ruth S. Murray's, Anna T. MURRAY, dt Robt. Lindley (dec) & Ruth S., New Castle, b 9-27-1854
Ch: Margaret B.
Ruth M.

UNDERHILL, Abram S. & Anna T., continued
ct Chap. 9-5-1877 for Anna T.; letter from First Presby. Ch., Ossining for Abram 6-2-1919 with 2 dt
Ada m ----- ROE
recrq 11-3-1932
Adelia A., w David L., dt Townsend & Phebe CARPENTER (H)
Adeline E., dt Abm. C. & Eliz. B., b 12-21-1831; d 12-31-1898; m 9-24-1853 Wm. N. HEDGE (or Hedger) (H)
at Seneca, Ill. 1858; near Ottawa 1859
Adna, dt Isaac & Sophia, dis mo 2-6-1833 by M. E. Minister
Adonijah d 10-27-1848 ae 60y 8m 10d; m Deborah SUTTON d 4-17-1874 ae 87y bPP (H)
Ch: Jane S. b 1-14-1810
Ann Eliza b 8- 4-1811
Harriet G. b 6-25-1817 d 7-14-1901 at Liverpool, ae 84y 20d
Louisa S. b 1- 6-1820
Adonijah Jr. b 10-22-1825 d 6-26-1832
Deborah Jr. b 6-16-1828
Henry S. d 1-28-1898
cf Chap. 5-12-1809; all dis 1829-1839 (O)
Adonijah, s Richard & Pamela, N. Y., b 2-17-1788 d 3-23-1848 ae 60y 2m 18d bPP; m N.Y. 9-11-1822 Sarah UNDERHILL, dt Israel & Sophiah, N. Y., d 10-14-1857 ae 64y 5m 21d bPP (H)
Ch: Mary b 10-26-1825 d 1-29-1865 bPP
Adonijah b N. Y. d 6-21-1832 ae 6y 7m
Walter d 3-20-1828 ae 7m
Child stillborn 5-16-1829
Sophia b 5-23-1830
Charlotte b 10-27-1832 d 4-25-1834
cf Pur. 7-12-1804, minor, placed with a Friend; both with ch, Mary, dis 1830 (O)
Adonijah (nm) m Sarah U. ----- (nm) d 10-14-1857 ae 64y 5m 21d bPP (a wd)
Ch: Mary d 1-29-1865 bPP
Adonijah J. d 6-27-1854; m Phebe H. ----- d 6-23-1852 (H)
cf Jericho 1-16-1817, minor; ct Jericho 11-1-1820 (clear); cf Jericho 10-18-1827 with w, Phebe H., both dis 1830-1831 (O)
Albert, s Alex & Phebe (dec), Bkn., d 11-20-1906 bPP; m at Josiah Travis' 10-12-1870 Mary Eugenia TRAVIS, dt Josiah & Phebe, Bkn.
Ch: John Alexander (changed to Alexander John) b 8- 1-1871
Edward Albert b 12-31-1873 d 12-18-1901 bPP
cf Ama. 2-1869 for Mary E. with parents
Alexander m Phebe ----- b Roslyn, L. I. 2-6-1819 d 2-9-1847, rem from Yorktown to PP 5-13-1899
Ch: Caroline b 9- 5-1841 d 2-26-1842
Silas A.
Susan b 5-15-1843
Albert b 2- 8-1845
Alexander Jr.
cf Ama. 7-10-1835 (clear); m dec w's sister before 8-1849, dis 12-1849, rst 5-1861; Alex. Jr. recrq of father 5-1861
Alexander m 2d Anna C. ----- (sister of first w) before 8-1849
cf Ama. 2-1868 for Anna
Alexander Jr., s Alex. & Phebe, d 5-4-1891; m Emma C. ----- d 5-2-1901
Alex. recrq of father 5-1861; Emma rocf Ama. 2-1868; cert of clear to Ama. 2-1865
Alexander m Celia F. ----- (nm) b Va. 1847 d 7-3-1921 ae 74y bPP
Alexander Jr. d Tucson, Arizona, 2-10-1928 ae 56y bPP
Alexander John, s Albert & Mary E., b 8-1-1871; m Ada L. LIVINGSTON
Ch: Alice Eugenia 10
Grace 5
Ada recrq 11-4-1903; ch recrq of parents 11-4-1903
Alfred & ----- (H)
Ch: Hannah M. d 9-2-1868 ae 45y bPP
both nm
Alfred, s Richard & Pamela; m 1-21-1830 at Newcastle, Jane UNDERHILL, dt Solomon & Phebe (H)
Ch: Caroline b 4-30-1831
Solomon " 5-16-1837
Infant stillborn 3-27-1835
Infant stillborn 1-16-1836
Phebe C.
cf Wby 7-19-1826 (clear); dis 5-1830 (O); ct Chap. with 2 ch named 2-1841
Alfred, s Samuel & Eliza (Bowne), b N. Y. 4-2-1821 d 10-15-1901 bPP; m 12-21-1858 Anna HOPKINS (nm), dt Gerard & Ann H. (Chandler) d 10-18-1921 ae 87y 5m 3d bPP (H)
Alice E., dt Alexander & Ada L., b about 1893 d 9-21-1915; m ----- SCHOEKE (nm)
recrq of parents 11-4-1903
Alice H., dt Reuben & Harriet L., N. Y., b 3-16-1877; m 1913 Benjamin H. DOANE
Amanda M., dt Abm. C. & Elizabeth, b 4-27-1825; m 9-22-1857 David L. CARPENTER (nm), dt Abm. & Ruth (H)
cf Corn. for her mother dated 2-11-1825, rec N. Y. 6-1825; Amanda considered as included therein
Amelia (or Permelia), dt Amos & Parmelia, b 1-24-1809; m 1830 ----- SIMMONS (mo) (H)
dis mo 11-1830 (H); dis 2-1831 (O)
Amelia, dt Samuel & Hannah W., N. Y.; m 1858 John T. WILLETS
Amelia mbr (O); John T. mbr (H)
Amos dis mo 6-1-1774
Amos m Parmelia (or Amelia) ----- d 9-30-1822
Ch: Robert d 12- 7-1865
Maria
Edmund b 10-10-1805 d 12-18-1805
Eliza " 10-29-1806
Permelia b 1-24-1809
Emmeline b 9-27-1810
Clementina b 3-31-1813
Amos " 12-16-1814 d 12-10-1815

UNDERHILL, Amos & Pamelia, continued
Ch: David
Amos, Jr. rocf Wby 7-7-1768; son, Robert, recrq of parents 5-6-1812, aged about 15 ct Pur., not found; cf Pur. 5-13-1802, with infant dt, Maria
Amy rocf Marl. 6-1-1831 (clear); dis 5-1832
Andrew m Wby 1774 Deborah -----
Ch: Samuel b 9-11-1775
James
Ann " 11- 3-1780
Elizabeth b 1-27-1733
James " 5-16-1737
Deborah b 1794; m ----- HAIGHT; d 12-14-1874
Andrew rocf Wby 5-29-1771, rec 7-3-1771; cert of clear to Wby 10-5-1774; ct Wby 9-2-1778; cf Wby 7-28-1779 with Deborah & s, Samuel & James; ct Pur. 1-5-1796 for Ann, Eliz., James & Deborah, ch Andrew (dec)
Ann gct Pur. 4-6-1808 (clear)
Ann rocf Chap. 4-13-1826 (clear) with Mary (clear); ct Chap. 1-6-1830 (clear) (0); ct Chap. 3-1829 (H)
Ann rocf Marl. 6-1-1831 (clear); dis 6-1832 (0)
Ann Eliza, dt Adonijah & Deborah S., N. Y.; m 1838 Alec. Edgar LAING, of Phila. (H) ct Phila. 3-1839; cf R. & P. with h & ch 3-1865
Annie, dt Robert & Sarah W., rocf Chicago with mother 7-1871; relrq 12-2-1874
Augusta, dt Geo. & Sarah Ann, b 2-33-1848; relrq 4-1866
Augustus rocf Ama. 9-4-1861; d 5-15-1864 (H)
Benjamin, s Amos & Eliz. (Seaman), b 11-26-1736 d N. Y. 1-10-1788; m N. Y. 4-29-1763 by Pres. Minister Letitia TOWNSEND, dt Silvanus & Susannah (Hedger), b 12-26-1738 d 8-24-1804
Ch: two (nm)
cf Wby 5-29-1765, he having rem some years ago; mo & took up arms; cert rec 10-2-1765
Caleb, s Isaac Q. & Mary (Sutton), b N. Y. 8-22-1824 d 12-28-1903; m 5-21-1872 Minnie MITCHELL (nm), dt Minct & Delia (H)
Caroline, dt Joshua & Mary; m 1825 William CROMWELL
Caroline, dt Stephen & Phebe C., b 1-14-1822; jas & dis 6-1853 (H)
Caroline E., dt Eliz. G.; m 1923 Walter W. MINARD
cf Hartland 5-4-1898; ct Scip. 11-1923
Charles & -----
Ch: Maria b 11-10-1820
Charles F., s Elias H. & Elizabeth, N. Y., b 4-17-1856 N. Y. d 8-30-1928; m at Peter I. Thorne's, Bkn. 1-24-1883 Rachel W. UNDERHILL, dt David (dec) & Sarah, Bkn., b Mamaroneck, 10-7-1844 d 11-23-1923 at Springfield, O.; both bPP (H)
Ch: Ralph Irving b 11-19-1883
Ethel " 12-19-1885
Charles W. roc 10-12-1821 (clear); dis 6-1830 (0); dis 6-1834 (H); d 3-21-1889 ae 89y 5d bPP
Charlotte, dt Israel & Zeruiah, N. Y.; m 1833 Charles M. CARPENTER (H)
Charlotte, w Joshua, dt Thos. & Abigail Underhill, d 6-6-1857 (H)
Ch: Theodore d 10-13-1856
Charlotte dis 1828
Clarkson, s Josiah J. & Hannah, b 10-15-1821; cf Scip. with parents 2-1835; ct Oswego 5-5-1858 (H)
Clementine, dt Amos & Parmelia, b 3-31-1813; m 1833 ----- EDGAR (mo) (H)
dis 5-1833 (0); dis 4-1833 (H)
Cornelia W., dt Abraham S. & Mary F., b 3-15-1846; m 1889 William L. ELLIOTT; m 2d 1907 William H. S. WOOD
Cyrus rocf Ama. 2-1854; d 9-8-1889 (H)
Daniel, s John & Helena, Mk., d 12 Mo (Feb) 9, 1713/14
Daniel, s Levi & Elizabeth, rocf Alexandria 10-1835 with parents; dis 1-1844 (H)
Daniel C. rocf Chap. 5-13-1814 (clear); ct Chap. 10-7-1829 (clear); cert ret. 3-1830; dis 1-1831 (0); dis 1-1834 (H)
Daniel H., s Stephen & Phebe C., b 12-13-1825; dis 12-1848 for non-attendance (0)
David, s Amos & Eliz., Flushing, b 2 Mo. (Apr) 2, 1743 d 2-7-1811 ae 67y 10m bHS; m Elizabeth ----- b 2 Mo (Apr) 5, 1747 d 9-1829
Ch: William b 11- 9-1774
Benjamin
Elizabeth b 5- 2-1784; dis 6-1830 (0); d 3-4-1855 (H)
Merriam b 4- 8-1786
David took cert of clear to Wby 11-4-1773; cf Wby 2-26-1783 with w & s, William & Benjamin
David gct Wby 4-6-1774
David d 7-13-1870; m Sarah W. PIERCE d 1-17-1895 (H)
Ch: Hannah
Elizabeth b 3-21-1822
Martha " 7-31-1828
Phebe Jane d 3- 6-1824
John " 9-15-1828 ae 3hrs.
Thomas " 9-17-1830 ae 11m 28d
Phebe Jane " 3- 1-1834 ae 10y 20d
Sarah b 10-10-1831
Rachel " 10-17-1844
cf Chap. 3-15-1822 with little ch, Hannah; all dis 1830-1849 (0); ct Pur for all living 8-1834; cf Pur. 3-3-1869 for parents
David R., s David & Sarah; m Phebe F. FIELD, d 1-28-1891 (H)
Ch: Emma b 2- 3-1859
John T. b 3- 8-1865 d 7-23-1869
Caroline b 1-18-1867
cf Pur. for both 2-1857
David R. m 2d at 15 Jefferson Ave., Bkn. 1-15-1896 Eliz. D. MILLER, dt Wm. D. & Phebe C.

UNDERHILL, David R. & Eliz. D., continued
(Marshall) DAVENPORT (both dec), Bkn., Duanesburgh, b Duanes. 8-20-1833 d 5-14-1923 (H)
Elizabeth m first Henry W. Miller
Deborah, dt Andrew & Deborah, N. Y.; m 1844 Samuel L. HAIGHT
cf Pur. 6-8-1825 to live with Uncle Thomas Underhill
Deborah, dt Adonijah & Deborah S., Bkn.; m 1846 Francis H. MACY (H)
Edmund, Flushing, b 2-1-1754; m 1783 ----- (mo) dis mo 3-6-1782; rst 1-2-1788
Edmund & Phebe J.
Ch: John b 1818
Marianna b 7-10-1821
Mary A. " 7- 1-1821
Edmund R. b 4- 5-1828 d 1- 9-1833
Elijah Ferris b 6- 2-1830
cf Ama. 7-10-1813 (clear); cert of clear to Pur. 3-5-1817; John F. & Mary A. dis 1841-1842 (O); parents dis 1829 (H); ct Ama. 4-1861 for Samuel & Phebe
Edwin, s Stephen & Phebe C., b 8-9-1833; dis 8-1856 (H)
Eleanor, dt Reuben H. & Harriet (Lukens), b Bkn. 8-7-1861 d Germantown 3-13-1926; m James McCONAUGHY (nm)
letter from Eleanor from West Side Presby. Ch., Germantown 4-3-1918; letter to same ch 3-1924
Elias, s Solomon & Phebe C., d 6-8-1858; m at Thomas Carpenter's 12-27-1842 Jane CARPENTER, dt Thomas & Phebe, N. Y., d 4-24-1900 in 78th yr. (H)
Ch: Mary C. b 10-3-1843
cf Chap. 11-1838 for Elias
Elias H., s James & Lydia (dec) (Carpenter), N. Y., b Yorktown, N. Y. 7-17-1825 d 10-7-1905; m at Robert Underhill's 4-8-1852 Elizabeth UNDERHILL, dt David (dec) & Hannah, N. Y., d 9-6-1892 (H)
Ch: Robert b 11- 4-1853
Charles Frederick b 4-17-1856
Lydia b 8-12-1859 d 2-1-1867
cf Ama. 11-1-1848 for Elias; cf Creek 2-2-1848 for Elizabeth
Elijah Ferris, s Edmund & Phebe, Jr., b 5-2-1830; dis mo & non-attendance 10-1858
Eliza, dt Amos & Parmelia, b 10-29-1806; dis 7-1829 (H) for joining Shakers; dis 1828 (O) for joining Shakers
Elizabeth Livingston (form Underhill) dis mo 11-1829 (H)
Elizabeth, dt Joshua & Mary, N. Y.; m 1840 John R. WILLIS
Elizabeth, dt David & Hannah, N. Y.; m 1852 Elias H. UNDERHILL (H)
Elizabeth, dt Isaac A. & Mary, b 10-29-1820; m John HOWELL (mo) (H)
Elizabeth (nm) d 4-3-1855 ae 72y bPP
Elizabeth (nm), dt James, d 7-24-1870 ae 37y bPP, rem to Pur. 11-28-1886 (H)
Elizabeth A., w George JACKSON, dt Hannah, b 6-3-1817; ct Flushing 8-1841 (H)
Elizabeth G., d 1-27-1922; m -----
Ch: Caroline E.
cf Cleveland 12-7-1804 for Eliz., a minister
Caroline E. rocf Hartland 5-4-1898
Elizabeth W. gct Middletown 8-1-1804 (clear)
Elizabeth Yeates, dt Levi & Eliz., rocf Alexandria 10-1835 with parents; dis 2-1855 (H)
Emeline C., dt Lydia BRADY; recrq 1-1833; ct Clear Creek 5-7-1845 (m 1843) (H)
Emma, dt Isaac & Sophia, dis joining M. E. Ch. 12-1831
Emma, dt David R. & Phebe F., N. Y., b 2-3-1859; m 1884 Andrew VAN BUSKIRK (nm) (H)
Ephraim rocf Chap. 1-1831 (H); cf Chap. 1829 (O); dis 1-1831; dis 5-1832 for non-attendance (H)
Esther R., w Edward C., dt ----- REYNOLDS, rocf Chap. 8-1885; relrq 6-8-1892
Ethel, dt Chas. F. & Rachel W. (Underhill), Bkn. b Bkn. 12-19-1885; m 1917 Robert F. EASTMAN, of Dayton, O. (H)
ct Green Plains, O. 9-14-1931
Eugene rocf Ama. 5-2-1860; relrq 8-2-1876 (H)
Euphemia, dt Josiah T., rocf Scipio 2-15-1837 (clear), rem with parents; dis after 1849
Francis Lawrence, s Josh. S. & Alice, b 9-15-1843; m Mary Augusta -----
cert of clear to Chap. 4-1870; cf Chap. 6-1874 for Mary; ct Chap. 4-1882 with w
George, s Robert & Mary, N. Y., d 4-16-1868 ae 72y 9m bPP; m N. Y. 5-9-1822 Sarah Ann WARING, dt Wm. & Ann (dec), N. Y., d 11-29-1872
Ch: George W. b 2-19-1823
Infant stillborn 2-14-1825
William Waring b 2- 8-1826
Anna C. b 11- 8-1827 d 8- 7-1861 bPP
Robert " 1829
James Edward b 7-11-1831
cf Ama. 11-15-1817 (clear); parents dis 1829 (H) (head of a big cloth business)
Ch: (continued)
Mary Jane b 7-18-1833 d 4-18-1903
Frederick " 4-24-1836 d 8-12-1849
Lydia Willis b 6-1838
Augustus " 5-22-1842 d 7- 2-1843
Augusta " 2-23-1844
Franklin " 7-21-1848 d 4-12-1881
Sarah " 7-1828
George (nm) m Rachel TOSTEVIN, dt John & Martha (Provost), b 2-9-1825 Isle of Guernsey d 10-24-1907, Greenville, N. J. bPP
George W. & Mary S.
Ch: Frederick A. b 7- 3-1856
Caroline S. " 6-22-1860
George Jr. " 1-26-1863 d 7- 9-1864 bPP
Hubert " 2- 4-1866
cf Chap. 1855 for Mary; ct Chap. 7-1867 for all living
Grace, dt Alex. John & Ada , recrq of parents

UNDERHILL, Grace, continued
11-4-1903; m ----- DAY (nm); name erased for jas 3-1928
Hannah, dt John (dec), Mk.; m 1717 Thomas BOWNE
Hannah, dt Samuel, m before 9-4-1793 ----- LAWRENCE (mo)
dis mo 10-3-1793
Hannah, w Josiah J., b 5-9-1791
Ch: Phebe T.
Elizabeth A. b 6- 3-1817
Clarkson b 10-15-1821
Mary F. " 5-21-1823
Aaron J. " 8- 7-1825
Anna " 8-28-1828
cf Scipio 2-1835 with 6 ch named; ct Oswego 2-7-1844 (H)
Hannah, dt Philo & Clarissa LEWIS, b 1-24-1820; dis mo 9-1-1844
Hannah, dt Thomas & Sarah (Whitson), b N. Y. 12-10-1825 d 1-26-1916; m 1845 Stephen R. HICKS (H)
cf Wby with dt 4-9-1898
Hannah, w B., wd Simmons MOGER (H)
Hannah B., dt Samuel & Eliza B., b 3-1-1814; m 1836 ----- HUSSON (mo); m 2d 3-10-1845 John S. SHAPTER (H)
dis mo 4-6-1836 (0); dis (H); rst
Hannah Louisa, dt Abraham C. & Elizabeth B., b 3-2-1835 d 12-18-1924; m 1853 Charles E. YEOMANS (H)
Henry rocf Ama. 6-1863; d 1-29-1923
Henry H., s Joshua S. & Alice, b 5-27-1841; cert of clear to Ama. 10-1868; ct Ama. 2-1870
Henry S., dt Adonijah & Deborah, d 1-28-1898 at Riverside, Conn.; m ----- DOTY (mo) (H)
Howard Lawrence, s Josh. S. & Alice, b 2-11-1846 d 5-6-1905; m M. Ida TALLCOT
cert of clear to Yorktown 5-2-1883
Ira B. d 10-1857 ae 58y bPP; m Burl. 1838 Abigail K. ----- d 2-20-1888, wd
Ch: William Wilson b 9-13-1839
cert of clear to Burl. 10-1838; Abigail K. rocf Burl. 1839; ct Burl. 3-2-1842 with 1 ch named; Abigail rocf Corn. 4-4-1859 with same ch
Isaac, Flushing, b 5 Mo (July) 21, 1732; m Mary ----- b 9 Mo (Nov) 5, 1730
Isaac & Mary
Isaac & Mary rocf Wby 7-27-1768, rec 10-5-1768
Isaac rocf Chap. 11-10-1825 (clear)
Isaac recrq 1826; dis 11-1829
Isaac d 9-25-1852; m Sophia ----- d 2-21-1845
Ch: Sarah
Phebe
Adna
Emma
Morris
John
Mary Ann
Caroline d 7-22-1831 ae 1y 3m
Jane Elizabeth d 2-2-1832 ae 4y 9m 18d bur in grave with sister, Caroline
Ch: Anna d 6-27-1837
cf Wby 2-17-1802, apprentice; dis mo 6-7-1809; cf Plains 8-27-1830 with ch named; 3 eldest clear; all dis 1831-1847 (0)
Isaac, Sr. dis 6-1839
Isaac m 2-1830 Jane S. UNDERHILL, dt Adonijah & Deborah, b 1-14-1810 d 7-14-1884
cf Chap. 2-8-1827 (clear); Isaac dis 4-1831 (0); Isaac dis 10-1833 (H); at Peoria. Ill. 1848
Isaac Q. m Mary SUTTON b 3-20-1794 d 12-18-1867, a wd (H)
Ch: Elizabeth b 10-29-1820
William Penn b 6-15-1822 d 8-23-1840
Caleb " 8-22-1824
Thomas " 4-16-1828 d 8-31-1885
cf Pur. 12-5-1824 with 2 ch named; all dis 1829-1848 (0); Isaac Q. dis 2-1829 (H)
Israel b Mt. Pleasant d 7-15-1828 ae 58y 6m; m Zerviah (or Sophia) ----- b West. Co. d 2-5-1832 ae 63y (H)
Ch: Sarah b 4-23-1793
Abijah b 1- 6-1795
Phebe " 4-23-1797
Edmund b 11-29-1800 d 8-21-1801
Elizabeth b 8- 3-1802
Eliza
Charlotte
cf Chap. 6-12-1795 with Sarah & Abijah; Zerviah & Eliza dis 1829-1830 (0)
Israel rocf Chap. 2-1825; dis mo 2-1829 (0); dis mo 6-1831 (H)
Jacob (nm) & Elizabeth
Ch: Edward d 1-25-1852 ae 2y 8m 3d bPP
James gct Pur. 7-11-1810; cf Pur. 2-1-1824 (clear); dis 3-1830 (0); d 11-29-1887; ct Pur. 12-1832; cf Pur. 1-1867
James rocf Chap. 7-10-1845 (clear); d 1845
James Edward, s Geo. & Sarah Ann; m Phebe T. -----
ct N.P.; cf N.P. 7-1857; Phebe recrq 5-1868; ct Balt. 7-11-1877 for both
Jane, dt Joshua & Mary, N. Y.; m 1825 John H. FERRIS
Jane, dt Adonijah & Deborah, N. Y.; m 1830 Isaac UNDERHILL (H)
at Peoria, Ill. 1848
Jay Hoyt, s Stephen M. & Edith (Hoyt), rec as associate on rq of parents 6-7-1911; name erased 3-2-1932
Capt. John, b Eng. d Mk. 7 Mo (Sep) 21, 1672; m Helena KRUGER (nm)
Elizabeth bapt. 14 Feb. 1636; John bapt. 24 Apr. 1642 aged 13d
Capt. John m 2d Elizabeth -----
Ch: Deborah b 9 Mo (Nov) 29, 1659
Nathaniel b 12 Mo (Feb) 22, 1663/4
Hannah " 10 Mo (Dec) 2, 1666
Elizabeth " 5 Mo (July) 2, 1669
David " 2 Mo (Apr) 1673
very active mbr 1673-1692
John, s John & Helena, Mk., b 11 Apr. 1642 bapt.

UNDERHILL, John & Mary, continued
Boston 24 Apr. d 10 Mo (Dec) 28, 1692;
m Mary PRIAR, dt Matthew & Mary, d 1 Mo
(Mar) 29, 1698 (m 8 Mo (Oct) 1668)
Ch: John b 5 Mo (July) 1, 1670
Daniel b 9 Mo (Nov) 3, 1672
Samuel " 12 Mo (Feb) 18, 1674/5
Mary " 2 Mo (Apr) 26, 1677
Abraham b 6 Mo (Aug) 28, 1679
Deborah " 2 Mo (Apr) 11, 1682
Sarah " 6 Mo (Aug) 17, 1687
Jacob " 10 Mo (Dec) 16, 1689 d 3 Mo 1798
Hannah " 1 Mo (Mar) 23, 1690/1
John & Elizabeth
Ch: Thomas
John
Anne
cf Wby 4-17-1793
John d 9-15-1828
John, s Isaac & Sophia, dis mo 9-1844
John F., s Edmund & Phebe, dis mo 7-1-1840
Joseph rocf Pur. 7-10-1800 (clear); dis mo 9
Mo 1805
Joshua d 2-15-1839 ae 73y 7m 5d bHS; m Mary
----- d 7-12-1820 ae 53y (Mary b Somers)
Ch: Elizabeth b 9-15-1790
Anna " 4-25-1793 d 1-13-1873
Walter " 3-12-1795
Joshua Sutton b 11-14-1796
Sarah F. " 9- 9-1798 d 3-12-1887
Ira " 3-11-1800
Jane " 11-23-1801
Caroline " 7- 9-1803
Mary " 9- 8-1805
Abraham I. (or S.) b 3-4-1807
Hannah S. b 10-10-1808 d 11-29-1865 bPP
Joshua & Mary rocf Chap. 4-12-1793 with
dt, Eliz.; all dis 1829 (H)
Joshua & ---- (H)
Ch: Abby Jane b N. Y. d 1-1-1834 ae 2y 2m 1d
Joshua B., s Chas. R. & Eliz. C. (Quinby),
b Chap. 9-29-1835 d 6-27-1898; m Elizabeth
GREEN, dt Stephen & Lydia C., Cornwall
Landing, b So. Starksboro, Vt. 3-31-1843
d Richmond Hill, L. I. 8-14-1922 bPP
cf Elba. 11-1-1893 for both; cf Hartland
5-4-1898 for Caroline E.; ct Cleveland 4-
2-1902 for Elizabeth; cf Cleveland 12-7-
1904 for Elizabeth
Joshua L., s Joshua S. & Alice, b 11-23-1838
d 2-11-1872 m Sarah S. ----- d 9-25-1875
Ch: Joshua S. b 6- 4-1866
Lucy " 3----1871
cert of clear to Chap. 6-1864; cf Chap.
1-1866 for Sarah
Joshua L., s Joshua & Mary, N. Y., d 3-13-
1857 ae 61y bPP, rem to Woodlawn; m N. Y.
4-9-1834 Alice LAWRENCE, dt Richard R.
(dec) & Hannah, N. Y., d 10-7-1888
Ch: Richard L. b 7- 4-1837 d 7-11-1832
Infant d 7-13-1837 ae 7d
Joshua Lawrence b 11-23-1838
Henry H. " 5-27-1841
Ch: Francis L. b 9-15-1843
Howard L. " 2-11-1846
Joshua S., s Joshua L. & Sarah, b 6-4-1866; ct
Chap. 2-1877
Letitia, wd Benjamin; m 5-13-1789 John FRANK-
LIN (both bur Mk.)
Levi m Elizabeth ----- d 10-24-1887 (H)
Ch: Sarah
Daniel
Wm. Francis
Elizabeth Yeates
cf Alexandria 10-1835; Levi dis non-attend-
ance 3-1852
Lindley, s Samuel & Eliza B., b 5-5-1819;
dis mo by priest 11-3-1847 (H)
Louisa, dt Abm. C. & Eliz. B., b 3-2-1835;
m 3-23-1853 Charles E. YEOMANS (H)
Louisa S., dt Adonijah & Deborah, Bkn.;
m 1846 Henry H. COX (H)
Lucy, dt Joshua L. & Sarah, b 3-1871; ct Chap.
2-1877
Lydia E., dt Samuel & Eliza B., N. Y., b 8-15-
1826; m 1862 John D. WRIGHT (H)
Lydia Willis, dt Geo. & Sarah Ann, b 6-1838;
relrq 4-1866
Margaret, dt Abram & Anna T. (Murray); m Edward
F. BARRON
Elizabeth Barron (dt) recrq of mother 2-
1922
Maria Van Zandt (form Underhill) dis mo 11-1-
1820
Maria C., dt Stephen & Phebe E., b 3-18-1813;
m ----- OLCOTT (mo) (H)
dis 5-1832 (C); ret a mbr (H)
Martha, dt David & Sarah W. (Pierce), b 7-31-
1828 d 11-26-1911 ae 86y (H); ct Pur. with
parents 8-1834; cf Pur. 3-3-1869 (unm)
Mary d 5 Mo (July) 9, 1698
Mary rocf Plains 3-25-1823 with the fam of
Sarles Miller
Mary, w Samuel J., gct Jericho 1-6-1825
Mary rocf Chap. 4-13-1826 (clear) with Ann
(clear); ct Chap. 1-6-1830 (clear) (O);
ct Chap. 3-1829 (H)
Mary, dt Samuel & Phebe, N. Y.; m 1839 Daniel
C. BROWN (H)
Mary, dt Thomas & Sarah (Whitson), b Mk. 11-17-
1829 d 1-26-1906; m 1853 Elias LEWIS, Jr.
(nm) (H)
cf Wby 12-1855
Mary Ann, dt Isaac & Sophia; m ----- MARTIN (mo)
dis mo 10-6-1841
Mary Anna, dt Edmund & Phebe J., b 7-1-1821;
m before 9-1842 ----- FARQUHAR (mo)
dis mo by Pres. Minister 11-1842
Mary Annah, dt David & Sarah W. (Pierce),
b Scarsdale 6-7-1838; m 1863 Peter J.
THORNE (nm) (H)
Mary B., dt Samuel & Elizabeth, b 3-23-1799;
m before 6-1837 ----- MOORE
dis 6-7-1837
Mary C., dt Elias & Jane, b 10-3-1843; m -----
BOOCOCK (H)

UNDERHILL, Mary C., continued
relrq 5-5-1869
Mary M., w Walter, rocf Nantucket N. Dist. 4-26-1826
Mary S., dt Joshua & Mary; m 1835 William WOOD
Mary S., dt Walter & Mary; m ----- TRIMBLE
dis mo 12-1852
Mira d 2-12-1827
Morris, s Isaac & Sophia, dis mo & non-attendance 9-1847
Moses rec by dealing, on behalf of Chap. 5-1849; d 8-7-1893
Nathaniel, Mk. m Mary FERRIS (ltm 12 Mo (Feb) 27, 1685/6)
Pamela, dt James & Margaret (Rogers), b N. Y. 12-29-1827 d 12-20-1907; recrq 3-4-1874 (unm) (H)
Phebe, dt Israel & Zerriah, N. Y.; m 1821 Thomas CARPENTER
Phebe Baldwin (form Underhill) dis mo 5-6-1835
Phebe rocf Creek 2-2-1848; ct Stanford 8-1850 (H)
Phebe C., dt Alfred & Jane; m 1861 Ezekiel H. MILLER (H)
Phebe J. rocf Pur. 3-12-1818
Phebe T., dt Josiah J. & Hannah; m 1839 John J. YELLOTT (H)
Phebe W., dt Thos. & Sarah (Whitson), b N. Y. 4-11-1824 d 4-13-1914 ae 90y; m 1844 John V. TITUS (H)
cf Wby 9-3-1879
Rachel (nm) b Marl. d 10-2-1809 ae 18y 8m 12d bHS (wd)
Rachel W., dt David & Sarah, Bkn.; m 1883 Charles F. UNDERHILL
Ralph Irving, s Chas. W. & Rachel W. (Underhill), b N. Y. 11-19-1883 d 7-18-1932 bPP; m 6-18-1907 Marion D. MATTHEW, dt Robt. E. & Christine D., b Bkn. 11-25-1882 (H)
Ch: Charles Matthew b Cambridge 12-26-1908
Leslie " 10-15-1913
ch recrq of parents 10-8-1910 & 3-11-1916; Marion recrq 1-1924
Reuben rocf Chap. 11-12-1813 (clear); ct Chap. 8-2-1820 (clear)
Reuben H. W. d 3-8-1908 bPP; m Harriet L. LUKENS, dt Dr. Israel & Susan J., b Phila. 12-12-1837 d 4-3-1927 at Germantown
Ch: Eleanor b 8- 7-1861
Edmund Clarence b 5-30-1865 d 9- 4-1897
Reuben L. " 8-13-1869
Alice H. " 3-16-1877
Grace " 1- 9-1868 d 10- 8-1868 bPP
Frederick H. d 5-17-1873 ae 3m bPP
-----
cf Creek 6-1858 for Reuben; Harriet L. recrq 12-1860
Richard T. rocf Ama. 1-12-1822, minor; ct Ama. 1854 (O); dis 1829 (H)
Richardson, s John & Sarah; m Elizabeth ----- (m at Hudson)
cf Ama. 5-10-1793 (clear); cert of clear to Hudson 4-3-1799; Elizabeth rocf Hudson 4-24-1800
Ch: Frederick Augustus b 3-10-1800
Mary Jenkins " 12-29-1801
ct Hudson 2-1-1804 for Mary & 2 ch as named here
Richardson b West Chester d 10-25-1809 ae 40y bHS
Robert & Martha (H)
cf Creek 9-10-1840; Robert dis 3-7-1849; Martha dis 7-1843
Robert, s Amos & Parmelia, d 12-7-1865 (H)
Robert, s George & Sarah Ann, b 1829; m before 4-1860 Charlotte ----- (mo
Ch: Frances A. b 6-17-1868
ret a mbr; Charlotte recrq 3-1863; ct Ama. 2-1880 for all 3
Robert, s Elias H. & Elizabeth, b 11-4-1853 d 11-16-1922 bPP; m Libbie MOORE (nm) (H)
Ch: Elias Milton b 4-25-1878
Etta Foster " 3- 7-1886
Robert m 2d 10-17-1895 Grace D. COUTANT, dt Lawrence B. & Julia S.
ch's names entered by comm. 1-17-1887; Grace recrq 3-4-1905
Robt. Wales, s Stephen M. & Edith (Hoyt), b N. Y. 8-27-1913; name erased 3-2-1932
Ruth M., dt Abram & Anna T. (Murray); m Cyril CRAWFORD (nm)
letter from First Presby. Ch., Ossining, 6-2-1919; divorced 1929 or 1930
S. Louisa, dt Adonijah & Deborah, b 1-6-1820 d 6-3-1894; m ----- COX (H)
Samuel, s John & Mary, O.B.; m Hannah WILLETS, dt Thomas & Dinah
Ch: Amee b 9 Mo (Nov) 9, 1702
Dinah b 7 Mo (Sep) 20, 1705
Samuel b 9 Mo (Nov) 8, 1708
Abraham b 12 Mo (Feb) 12, 1715/16
active mbr 1695/1703
Samuel, s Samuel & Ann, Flushing, b 7 Mo. (Sep) 26, 1740 d 7-4-1797; m Anna WILLITS, dt Richard & Hannah, O.B., b 10 Mo (Dec) 15, 1748
Ch: Richard W. b 9-18-1772 d 10- 7-1796
Hannah " 2-24-1775
Robert " 2-12-1778
Mary " 5-11-1780
Joseph " 3- 9-1783
Anna " 5-13-1785
Andrew " 3-22-1792
cf Pur. 5-12-1791 with their 6 ch
Samuel, s Andrew & Deborah, Merchant, N. Y.; m N. Y. 5-11-1796 Elizabeth W. BUCKLEY, dt Phineas & Mary (dec), N. Y.
Ch: Mary B. b 3-23-1799
Samuel, s Israel, rocf Wby 12-19-1792, apprentice; ct Wby 1-7-1807 (clear); cf Wby 7-19-1826 (clear); dis 6-1833 (O); dis 5-4-1836 (H)
Samuel, Jr. rocf Wby 6-14-1809 (clear)
Samuel, s Andrew & Deborah, N. Y.; b Cow Neck L. I. d 9-15-1827 ae 38y; m Flushing 1813

UNDERHILL, Samuel, continued
Eliza B. BOWNE, b 3-1814 d 1-29-1861 ae 71y
Ch: Hannah B. b 3- 1-1814 [bPP (H)
Sarah P. " 7-29-1815
Samuel B. " 7- 4-1817
Lindley " 5- 5-1819
Alfred " 4- 2-1821
Edward " 1- 6-1824 d 9- 1-1883
Lydia E. " 8-15-1826
cert of clear to Flush. 5-5-1813; Eliza B. rocf Flush. 1-6-1814; all dis 1830-1849 (O)
Samuel (nm) & Phebe
Ch: John d 12-20-1833 ae 4y 4m 14d bHS
all nm
Samuel B., s Samuel (dec) & Eliza B., New Rochelle; m at Levi Underhill's 1-5-1843 Sarah UNDERHILL, dt Levi & Elizabeth, N.Y. (H)
Sarah rocf Alexandria 10-1835 with parents; ct Pur. 9-1838 (O); ct Pur. 5-3-1843 (H)
Samuel P., s Daniel & Mary (dec), Jericho; m N. Y. 2-12-1824 Mary (or Mary Ann) WILLETS, dt Samuel & Hannah, N. Y., d 10-15-1881
Samuel R. (nm) & ----- (H)
Ch: Frank d 7-17-1777 ae 4y 1m bPP
Samuel S. rocf R. & P. 1-15-1899; d 12-6-1899 (H)
Sarah, dt John & Mary, Mk.; m 1709 Thomas PEARSALL
Sarah rocf Marl. 11-24-1830; d 3-26-1841 ae 80y 11m 20d bHS
Sarah, dt Solomon & Lydia, N. Y.; m 1809 Wm. WARING
cf Wby 2-14-1798 for Sarah, a youth
Sarah, dt Zerviah, N. Y.; m 1822 Adonijah UNDERHILL
Sarah Purham (form Underhill) dis 5-6-1840
Sarah, dt Levi & Eliz., N. Y.; m 1843 Samuel B. UNDERHILL (H)
Sarah Jane, dt Stepehn & Phebe C., b 2-8-1815 dis jas 6-1853 (H)
Sarah P., dt Samuel & Eliza B., N. Y.; m 1837 Eli ELLIOTT (H)
Sarah W. rocf Jericho 11-16-1820, rem with h
Sarah W., wd Robert
Ch: Annie
cf Chicago 7-1871 with dt; ct Chicago 3-4-1874 for Sarah
Silas Albertson, s Alex. & Phebe A., b 1840 d 12-24-1907 ae 66y bPP; m Frances Gertrude ----- d rpd 4-1928
Gertrude recrq 2-1883
Silas A. m 2d 5-15-1888 at her residence Frances Gertrude RUSHMORE, dt Benj. H. & Anna M. LOWERRE, N. Y.
joined army before 5-1864; dis 5-1865; rst 5-1868; relrq 3-2-1892
Solomon b N. Hempstead d 2-5-1827 ae 78y; m Lydia -----
ct Wby 3-1-1775; cf Wby 12-27-1780 for each; ct Wby 6-5-1782, Minister
Sophia, dt Adonijah & Sarah U., b 5-23-1830; m 1867 Henry T. WILLETS (H)
Stephen d 7-18-1854; m Phebe C. ----- d 6-22-1872 (H)
Ch: Maria C. b 3-18-1813
Sarah Jane b 2- 8-1815
Benjamin C. b 10-30-1817 d 1-4-1818
Caroline " 1-14-1822
Stephen C. b 2-10-1824 d 10-20-1827
Daniel H. " 12-13-1825
Stephen Jr. dis 9-1846
Edwin b 8- 9-1833
cf Oswego 12-20-1809 (clear); Phebe rocf Pur. 8-13-1812; all dis 1829-1848 (O);
Stephen Jr., s Stephen & Phebe C., dis 9-1846 (H)
Stephen Maurice m Edith HOYT, dt George A. & Emeline, b 4-2-1881
Ch: Jay Hoyt, associate, recrq of parents 6-7-1911
Robert Wales b 8-27-1913
cf Yorktown for Stephen 6-7-1911; ct Ramona Park Friends Community Ch., Calif. 6-1924 for parents
Susan, dt Josiah T., rocf Scipio 2-15-1837 (clear), rem with parents; dis under rule of YM 12-1839
Susan, dt Alex. & Phebe A., Bkn.; m 1871 Wm. J. LANE, of Washington, N. Y.

Thomas d 1834; m Elizabeth -----; con mo 6-6-1781; ct Pur. 5-7-1789 for Thomas & w, Elizabeth; cf Pur. 12-13-1798 for both with Ann, Elizabeth, James & Deborah, ch of Andrew Underhill, dec; ct Pur. with nieces, Elizabeth & Deborah, minors; cf Pur. 1825 for Thomas & niece, Deborah; Thomas & Deborah dis 1829 (H)

Thomas rocf Wby 11-19-1817 (clear); cert of clear to Jericho 1-5-1820
Thomas rocf Pur. 6-8-1825 (a brother of Andrew) d 1834
Thomas m Sarah W. WHITSON
Ch: Henry W.
Phebe H. b 4-10-1824
Hannah W. b 12-18-1825
Mary b Mk. b 11-17-1829
ct Wby 8-2-1826 with 3 ch named
Townsend d 2-14-1799 bHS
Townsend N. rocf Chap. 8-4-1830 (clear); dis 2-1831 (O); dis 4-1835 for mo (H)
Walter, s Joshua & Mary, b 3-12-1795 d 8-17-1866 bPP; m Nantucket Mary MITCHELL
Ch: Mary S. b 11- 5-1826
Walter M. b 8-1828 d 3-13-1875
Lydia Green b 9-1830; relrq 12-1861
Anna Elizabeth b 11-14-1842
cf Nantucket for Mary; ct New Bedford 6-1869 for Mary M. & Anna Elizabeth
Walter rocf Chap. 4-8-1847 (clear); mo before 8-1853, ret a mbr; dis 1854

UNDERHILL, continued
Walter M., s Walter & Mary, b 8-1828 d 3-13-1875; mo before 2-1874
William dis mo 1-2-1799
William rocf Pur. 6-11-1807, youth (clear); ct Wainoak (Wyanoke), Va. 3-6-1811 (clear); cf Wainoak 3-6-1813 (clear)
William, s Caleb, rocf Ama. 9-16-1809, minor
William, s David & Eliz., Flushing; m Pur. Phebe G. -----
Ch: Sarah b 1-25-1813
William G. b 7-12-1819
Louisa
Andrew b 10-28-1823
Maria d 2-12-1827 ae 1y 16d
cert of clear to Pur. 12-4-1811; Phebe G. rocf Pur. 7-9-1812; ct Ama. with 3 ch named 4-4-1827
William dis mo 8-7-1816; rst by Wby 9-4-1822, who rec him a mbr
William, s Geo. & Sarah Ann, b 2-8-1826; dis mo 3-1856
William Jr. d 7-10-1889; m Miriam -----
Ch: William A. b 4-15-1851 d 1-16-1870 bPP
cf Ama. 12-15-1848 for William; cf Salem 4-12-1849 for Miriam; ct New Bedford 4-1880 for Miriam
William Francis, s Levi & Eliz., rocf Alexandria with parents 10-1835; dis mo 12-1-1863 (H)
Wm. Wilson, s Ira B. (dec) & Abigail K., N. Y., b 9-13-1839 d 6-11-1935; m at John L. Griffen's 10-18-1866 (not under care of N. Y. MM) Emily H. GRIFFEN, dt John L. & Sarah H., N. Y., b 6-1-1848 N. Y. d 7-17-1923
Wm. rocf Corn. with mother 4-4-1859; mo & ret a mbr (O); Emily (H)
----- & ----- (nm)
Ch: Robert b N. Y. d 3-14-1812 ae 1y 9m bHS
Abraham S. b N. Y. d 3-9-1843 ae 1y 1m bHS
Sarah (dt Samuel) d 9-23-1840 ae 15y 11m bHS
----- & -----
Ch: Jane Elizabeth d 2-2-1832 ae 4y 9m 18d
John d 12-20-1833 ae ry 4m 14d
Phebe d 12-17-1833 ae 6y
Sarah d 9-23-1840 ae 15y 11m

UNDERWOOD
Benjamin d 6-4-1880 ae 79y; m Margaret G. ----- d 2-10-1882 ae 71y 1m (H)
Ch: William d 9-1-1883 ae 59y 7m 25d
all nm; all bPP

URQUHART
Mary, dt John, East Jersey; m 1711 John FRY, of O.B.

UTLEY
Sarah D. (nm) d 6-23-1870 ae 32y bPP

VAIL
Addison, s George D. & Martha, d 11-25-1859 ae 45y bPP; m Mary J. SNIFFEN (nm) d 3-12-1869 ae 51y bPP (H)
cf Oswego 7-9-1826 with mother
Benjamin, Hudson MM ref. his case of mo 12-2-1801; rpd 12-7-1803 to Hudson that he lives in Albany, had ack. mo but had taken an oath
Charles rocf Phila. 8-25-1825; at Terre Coupee, Ind. & mo; dis 6-1833 (O); ct Whitewater, Ind. 4-1841 (H)
Eli rocf R. & P. 3-16-1820; d 1827 Isle of Wight
George D. m Martha ----- d 12-25-1856 ae 69y 21d
Ch: Araminta D. d 4-16-1888 ae 77y 8m 18d
Dorinda A. " 4-10-1856 ae 44y
David
Addison
Mary
Egbert d 8- 7-1836
cf Oswego 7-19-1826 for Martha with first 5 ch; all dis 1830-1849 (O); ct R. & P. 2-1852 with first 2 ch; cf R. & P. 11-1854 with same 2 ch
Hugh D. rocf R. & P. 1-20-1836, apprentice; ct R. & P. 11-1-1837 (clear)
John rocf Ama. 1-2-1805 (clear)
Joseph rocf N.P. 11-23-1786; dis mo 11-6-1788
Josephine (nm) m 10-14-1896 Henry L. HALLOCK (H)
Lot, dt Isaac, rocf R. & P. 7-17-1823, apprentice with William Underhill; dis 3-1830 (O) ct R. & P. 1-1838 (H)
Maria L. recrq; d 8-16-1871
Mary, dt George D. & Martha, d 3-9-1864; m John ARCHABALD (mo) (H)
Mary B. [Vaill], dt Timothy D. & Isabel Mary (Breck), b Bkn. 6-15-1858; m 1882 Daniel TALMADGE (H)
recrq 5-8-1922
Mary Dell, dt James H. & Georgie S., b Balt. 9-11-1883; m 1905 Alex. H. McDOWELL (H)
cf Balt. 11-10-1906; ct Balt. 2-12-1916 with Alex. & ch (H)
Samuel, Westchester, m Flushing 2 Mo (Apr) 8, 1725 Sarah FARRINGTON, dt Matthew, Flushing
Semantha, dt John & Ruth (Rogers), b Danby, Vt. 4-26-1826 d 1-4-1905; m 1846 Henry G. LAPHAM (H)
cf Danby 11-1855
Thomas rocf Ama. 12-12-1801 (clear)
----- & ----- (nm)
Ch: Sarah d 8-3-1826 ae 3h bHS

VALENTINE
Anna K., dt Stephen & Annie (Lewis), Bkn., b Bkn. 3-26-1882; m 1906 James WILLITS, of Glen Cove (H)
ct Wby 6-9-1906
Benjamin E. rocf Burl. 5-5-1823; cert of clear to Phila. 12-3-1823; ct WD MM 7-6-1825 having rem

VALENTINE, continued
Benjamin E. rocf Salem, Mass. 3-26-1874; name erased 2-7-1900
Charles, s David, b Hempstead Harbor d 9-11-1823 ae 47y bHS; cf Wby 10-20-1802, apprentice to a Friend; dis mo 2-3-1813
Charles & Keziah H. (H)
Ch: Thomas Edgar b 10-10-1840
Jacob L. " 4-16-1857
cf Wby 6-1839 for parents; ct Jer. 10-5-1864 with Jacob L.
Cloyd Hampton, s John H. & Eliz. (Arnold), b N. Y. 1-25-1894; m Winnie PACKHARD (nm) (H)
Ch: Robert Packard b 11-21-1923
Richard Arnold b 1-31-1937
Daniel K., s Samuel T. & Anna (Kirk), b N. Y. 2-22-1860 d 1-13-1934; m 1-15-1895 Blanche E. WOOD (nm) (H)
Elizabeth, dt Stephen & Ann T., Bkn.; m 1855 Jeremiah WINTRINGHAM (H)
Eliz. A., dt Jos. A. & Sarah E. ARNOLD, N. Y.; m 1924 Isaac B. DEVOE (H)
Elizabeth Ann, w -----
Ch: Charles Morton
s recrq of mother 12-7-1814
Ella, dt Samuel T. & Anna K., Bkn., b 9-5-1862; m 1886 Daniel T. MERRITT (H)
Florence N., dt Stephen & Ann (Lewis), Bkn., b Bkn. 1-11-1888; m 1911 Augustus F. WALDENBURG (H)
George b 4-10-1810 d 1-15-1870 bPP; m Hannah E. ----- d 1-4-1878 ae 81y 8m 9d bPP (H)
Ch: Jacob Doty b 2-11-1846 d 6-26-1889
cf Wby 5-1844 for George; Jacob D. recrq of father 1-1855
Hannah T., dt Samuel T. & Hannah K., Bkn., b 5-14-1866 N. Y. d 8-5-1903; m 1891 John Wm. RAYMOND (H)
Helen Elise, dt Stephen & Annie L., Bkn., b Bkn. 10-27-1890; m 1916 Frank Stinson SHAW (nm) (H)
Henry E. m Sarah E. ----- d 3-4-1901 ae 71y 5m 25d bPP (H)
Ch: Amelia M. d 3-22-1926 ae 77y 7d bPP
Isaac R. rocf Wby 7-19-1826; dis 1-1830 (O); ct Wby 12-1839 (H)
Jacob & Phebe
Ch: Mary
cf Wby 5-15-1793
Jacob (nm) b L. I. d 7-2-1816 ae 53y bHS (m)
Jacob m Phila. 1799 Elizabeth Ann -----
Ch: Beulah S. b 5-11-1800
Benjamin E. b 5-28-1801
William " 10-20-1802
Elliott " 3-17-1804 d 8-24-1807 ae 3y
Elizabeth Ann b 2-14-1808
Harriet d 3-21-1807 ae 9m
Charles Morton
Robert Barclay d 7-21-1815
cert of clear to ND MM 5-1-1799; Elizabeth Ann rocf ND MM 7-23-1799; ct Phila. 9-3-1817 for Elizabeth Ann with 5 ch, including first 3 named, & Eliza & Charles Morton
Jacob, s Lewis & Jane, Glen Cove; m N. Y. 6-8-1814 Martha TITUS, dt Samuel & Abigail (both dec), N. Y.
Ch: Charles
Lewis d 5- 1-1820
Mary " 1-27-1819 ae 24d bHS
cf Wby 8-17-1808; rem cert to Wby 9-5-1810; cert of clear from Wby; Martha took cert there 8-3-1814; cf Wby 4-19-1815 for both with ch, Charles; ct Wby 10-3-1821 with 2 ch named
Jacob D. (nm) & ----- (H)
Ch: Gilbert C. d 1-10-1883 ae 2y 8m 13d bPP, rem to Deposit, N. Y. 12-5-1883
Jacob L., s Charles & Keziah H., b 4-16-1857; ct Jer. 10-5-1864 with father (H)
Jerusha, w Willet, rocf Wby 12-20-1797
John Hampton b 12-25-1867; m 3-21-1892 Elizabeth ARNOLD, dt Joseph Jr. & Sarah, b N.Y. 11-16-1865 (H)
Ch: Cloyd Hampton b 1-25-1894
John recrq 12-5-1888; John's name cancelled 3-13-1933; Elizabeth m 2d Isaac B. DeVOE
Martha A., dt Stephen & Ann T., N. Y.; m 1850 Henry GRIFFEN (H)
Mary, dt Jacob & Phebe, N. Y.; m 1815 Richard TALCOTT, of Scipio
Mary Anna, dt Samuel T. & Anna K., Bkn., b 11-23-1848; m 1874 Frederick L. MATHEWS (H)
Mary L., dt Stephen & Annie L., Bkn., b Bkn. 3-7-1880; m 1904 Andrew MAYER, Jr. (H)
recrq of parents 5-4-1887
Obadiah, s Obadiah, Wby; m Wby 8 Mo (Oct) 22, 1715 Martha WILLITS, dt Richard (dec) & Abigail, O. B.
Richard Kirk, M.D., s Samuel T. & Ann (Kirk), b 5-6-1855 d 3-22-1901; m Alice COURTRIGHT, dt Milton, d 3-1-1911 ae 50y (H)
Ch: Milton C. d 2-12-1889 ae 4y 4m 26d
Samuel T., s Stephen & Ann (Titus), b 8-4-1820 N. Y. d 3-9-1903 bPP; m 10-21-1847 Anna K. KIRK, dt Daniel & Mary T., b 2-4-1822 d 9-8-1899 bPP (H)
Ch: Mary Anna b 11-23-1848
Louise E. " 2-16-1851 d 11-12-1855 bPP
Stephen " 3-23-1853
Richard Kirk b 5- 6-1855
Florence N. b 12-29-1857 d 5-28-1863 bPP
Daniel K. " 2-22-1860
Ella " 9- 5-1862
Hannah T. " 5- 4-1866
Anna K. rocf Wby 3-7-1849
Sarah, dt Geo. & Mary, Pickering, Canada; m 1851 John WRIGHT
cf Yonge St., Canada 1-14-1847 (clear) for Sarah
Sarah A., dt Stephen & Ann T., b 1-7-1829; m 1852 Charles GRIFFEN (H)
Silas rocf Wby 4-19-1815, apprentice to Jacob Valentine; ct Wby 5-6-1818 (clear)
Stephen, s Lewis & Jane (dec), N. Y., b 8-19-1796 d 4-27-1878 bPP; m N. Y. 11-11-1818

VALENTINE, Stephen & Ann T., continued
Ann T. TITUS, dt Samuel & Abigail (both dec), N. Y., d 1-1-1873 ae 76y 7m 11d (H)
Ch: Samuel T. b 8- 4-1820 (or 4-8-1820)
Elizabeth " 8-19-1824
Martha Ann b 6-23-1826
Sarah Ann " 1- 7-1829
cf Wby 2-18-1818 for Stephen (clear); all dis 1830-1849 (O)
Stephen Jr., s Samuel T. & Anna (Kirk), Bkn., b 3-23-1853; m at E. Lewis Jr.'s 9-25-1878 Annie LEWIS, dt Elias Jr. & Mary (Underhill), Bkn., b Bkn. 11-7-1854 (H)
Ch: Mary L. b 3- 7-1880
Anna K. " 3-26-1882
Elias Lewis b 8- 2-1884 d 10-30-1890
Florence N. " 1-11-1888
Helen Elise " 10-27-1890
Stephen Lewis b 4-10-1896
Annie recrq 5-4-1887
Stephen Jr., s Stephen & Annie (Lewis), b Bkn. 4-10-1896; m 6-4-1919 Margery H. BOODY (nm), dt Alvino & Anna L. (Weeks) (H)
Stephen Jr. changed from Stephen Lewis on rq of mother 1907
Thomas rocf Pickering 1849; ct Lisburn, Ireland 2-4-1851
Thomas Edgar, s Chas. & Keziah W., b 10-10-1840 d 6-12-1925 at Freeport, N. Y.; m Maria A. KENNEDY (nm), dt James & Charity (m 4-26-1866) (H)
Ch: John H. b 12-25-1867
Townsend, s David & Hannah d 6-5-1802 ae 22 at Glen Cove
Warren m 9-24-1903 Florence E. BIRDSALL, dt Geo. H. Jr. & Eleanor C., b 8-22-1880
Ch: Eleanor Harriet
Walter Birdsall
Warren recrq 11-7-1900; at Holyoke, Mass. 1912; ct Haddonfield, N. J. 4-1917 for all
William, s Jacob & Elizabeth Ann, b 10-20-1802; mo, rpd to Gwynedd, which rpd dis him 6-5-1833
----- & ----- (nm)
Ch: Jane b N. Y. d 1-6-1812 ae 1y 11m bHS

VAN ALSTYNE
Margaret A. (nm), dt Wm. B. & Harriet (Kelley); m 1932 Howard Parker STABLER (H)
Mary Ann [Van Alstine] (nm) bPP

VAN BRUNT
Elizabeth, wd Edw. K.; m 2d Giles MANDEVILLE; m 3d 4-19-1893 Wm. H. MOREHOUSE (H)
cf Phila. Green St. 2-1859 (H)

VAN BURKIRK
Andrew (nm), s Martin & Hilah Ann, N. Y.; m at D. R. Underhill's 1-23-1884 Emma UNDERHILL, dt David R. & Phebe F., N. Y., b 2-3-1859 d 2-18-1900 ae 41y (H)
Ch: Bertha b 7-21-1885
Howard U. b 11- 9-1888
Ch: Charles Harold b 2-20-1894
Marian " 1-21-1897
Bertha's name entered by comm. 1-21-1886; other ch's names entered by MM 1890-1898
Bertha C., s Andrew & Emma (Underhill), b N.Y. 7-21-1885 d 10-13-1918; m 1907 Christian W. RASMUSSEN (H)
name entered by com. 1-19-1886
Charles Harold, s Andrew & Emma (Underhill), b Bkn. 2-20-1894; m 2-20-1915 Evelyn BYRD (nm), dt Geo. Radcliffe & Amy (Pierson) (H)
Howard U., s Andrew & Emma (Underhill), b N.Y. 11-19-1888; m 9-3-1910 Nellie E. HART (nm), dt Fred I. & Nettie (Hiles) (H)
Howard U. m 2d Arline CONGERS
Howard's name entered by comm. 1-19-1886
Marian, dt Andrew & Emma (Underhill), b Bkn. 1-21-1897; m 1915 Melville P. CUMMIN (H)

VAN CLACKE
Ann (late Lawrence) dis mo 9-4-1771

VAN CLIEF
Daniel m Mary M. KIPP, dt Abraham H., d 5-6-1885 ae 74y 23d bPP (both nm) (H)

VAN COTT
Elizabeth, w Peter (H)
Ch: Eliza Ann
recrq 9-5-1821 with dt; dis 4-1830 (O); ct Corn. for Elizabeth 4-1858
Elizabeth (or Eliza), dt Peter & Elizabeth; recrq of mother 9-5-1821; dis mo 3-1830 to ----- FARLEY (H)
Peter (nm) b Bethpage d 7-3-1824 ae 45y bHS
----- & -----
Ch: Peter d 8-9-1802 ae 4m bHS

VANDERBILT
Chester Willets, s Isaac S. & Carrie (Willets) b N. Y. 10-29-1895; m 12-6-1922 Dorothea DANIEL (nm), dt Henry (H)
Ch: Jane Patricia b E. Orange, N. J. 10-10-1924
Jane recrq of parents 5-14-1928
Edith Judson, dt Isaac S. & Carrie (Willets), b N. Y. 6-18-1899; m George A. HALSEY (H)
Isaac S. Jr., s Isaac S. & Sarah J. (Haddock) b Rockland Co., N. Y. 8-1-1868; m 4-22-1891 Carrie S. WILLETS, dt Wm. U. & Clara (Hitt), b 1-1-1868 N. Y. (H)
Ch: Chester Willets b 10-29-1895
Doris Eleanor " 8-30-1897 d 6-23-1924
Edith Judson " 6-18-1899
Marjorie Gordon " 3-29-1901
Isaac recrq 8-3-1892; Carrie's name entered by comm. 1-10-1879; Isaac's name rem for lack of interest 3-13-1933
Ch: (continued)
Corinne Lucille b 9-14-1902
Ralph Petty " 9-15-1905
Laura Judith " 11-27-1906
Donald Haddock b 5- 1-1910

VANDERBILT, Isaac S. Jr. & Carrie S., continued
Ch: Duncan Stevens b 4- 7-1912
last 3 ch b Maplewood, N. J., other ch b N. Y.

VANDERVOORT
Eunice (late Allen) dis mo before 7-3-1811

VANDEVEER
----- (nm) m Hannah STRIPLEY, dt Morris & Ann, b 6-24-1813 d 2-27-1837 bHS
Ch: Adelaide d 2-11-1837 ae 6d bHS

VAN DOLSEN
Gertrude I. (nm) m 1882 Thomas Edward SKINNER (H)

VAN DUREN
James (nm) b Orange Co. d 11-24-1834 ae 27y bHS (m)

VAN ETTEN
Charlotte Louisa, dt John & June HAYDOCK (Haddock in later entries) b 4-9-1839 d 1915
ret a mbr 12-1861
----- & ----- (nm)
Ch: Gertrude d 9-28-1869 ae 8m bPP

VAN EVEREN
Grace Abbie, dt Philip E. & Eliz. J., Bkn., b Bkn. 9-21-1874 d 1-16-1905; m 1899 Bradley STOUGHTON (nm) (H)
name entered by com. 6-4-1890
Mary Effie, dt Philip F. & Elizabeth J., b Bkn. 1-27-1870; m 1895 John H. FERGUSON (H)
name entered by comm. 6-4-1890; ct Orange Grove, Calif. 5-9-1921 (H)
Philip F., s John & Harriet; m 11-7-1866 Elizabeth J. FERGUSON, dt John C. & Elizabeth (Pierce), b North Castle 2-5-1844 d 1-8-1924 (H)
Ch: Mary Effie b 1-27-1870
Grace Abbie b 9-21-1874
cf Chap. 10-7-1868 for Eliz.; ch's names entered by comm. 6-4-1890

VAN EVERY
Maria (form Coleman) rocf Hudson 8-1840; in Calif. 1858; rel 6-2-1875, absent over 5y; rst on her rq 12-1-1875; d 8-29-1881 (H)

VAN HELDEN
Adrian (nm) m 9-28-1884 Caroline WEST, dt Geo. W. & Mary (Chaffin), b Booneville, Mo. 6-8-1847 (H)
Caroline recrq 6-13-1914; ct Swarthmore 11-11-1918

VAN HOESEN
Catharine, dt Mary, rocf Hudson 1835 with mother; dis 11-1840
Elizabeth, dt Mary; m 1857 Richard L. NICHOLSON
cf Hudson 1835 with mother; ct SD MM 1856
Mary, Hudson, d 2-10-1870, w -----
Ch: Catharine
Mary
Anna d 7-9-1883
Elizabeth
con mo 12-16-1815, forwarded to Hudson; cf Hudson 1835 with 4 ch named, the last 3 minors
Mary, dt Mary; m ----- BYRNES (mo)
cf Hudson 1835; relinquished mbrp 2-1861
Thomas rocf Phila. 1837; dis 11-1839
----- & ----- (nm)
Ch: Mary Ann d 12-10-1842 bHS

VAN HORN
John (nm) & -----
Ch: Infant d 12-26-1845 ae 1d bHS
Charles E. d 12-19-1864 ae 1y 3m bHS
Lydia b 4-26-1825 d 4-20-1893; m ----- (H)
Ch: Charles E. d 12-19-1864
cf Shrews. 6-1846
Mary Ann dis mo 11-2-1831

VAN HOUTON
Mary Ann, dt ----- BURKE, d 1-16-1879
Ch: (adopted) Mary Ella
Mary recrq (or rst) 10-1868; Mary Ella recrq of foster mother 12-1870; relrq 12-1878

VAN INGEN
Adele, dt Wm. & Mary, d 10-12-1917 ae 42y bPP; m Oscar BORGESON (H)
both nm
Helen, dt Dudley W. & Eliz. S. (Bunker), b Bkn. 1-1-1880; m 1915 John Bentley LEA
Helen recrq with ch 7-8-1929
William, s Abraham & Mary (Gifford), d 10-5-1919 ae 70y bPP; m Clarissa M. SUTTON, dt George & Margaret, d 7-8-1925 ae 75y bPP (H)

VAN KEUREN
Gertrude b Clinton, N. Y. 10-16-1842 d 12-25-1917; m 1865 James C. STRINGHAM (H)
recrq 4-7-1900

VAN LOAN
John S., s J. S., d 6-30-1870 ae 12d bPP

VAN NICE
Mary d 6-12-1848; recrq 6-2-1847 (H)

VAN NORSDAL
Sarah Harvey (form Farrand), having mo Oswego ref. to N. Y. 4-1851; dis 5-1851

VAN NOSTRAND
Bertha (nm) d 2-19-1931; m 1896 Geo. Livingston MEAD (H)

VAN NOTE
Henry, s James & Clementine, rocf Shrews. 11-6-1826 with parents; dis 5-1856 (H)
Henry (nm) & -----
Ch: Samuel b N. Y. d 7-30-1847 ae 1y 3m bHS
James b Shrews. d 2-9-1829; m Clementine ----- b N. J. d 3-16-1846 (or 3-15-1846) ae 62y (H)
Ch: Sarah m ----- KELSO; d 2-2-1840
James d 10-15-1828 ae 20y
Peter T.
William
Henry
Infant stillborn 4-3-1827
cf Shrews. 11-6-1826 with 4 ch named; all dis 1830-1842 (O)
Peter T., s James & Clementine, rocf Shrews. 11-6-1826 with parents; dis 1-4-1854 (H)
Sarah, dt James & Clementine, b N. J. d 2-2-1840 ae 36y; m ----- KELSO (mo) (H)
William, s James & Clementine, rocf Shrews. 11-6-1826 with parents; dis 12-1840 (H)

VAN NOY (or Vannuy)
Permelia R. rocf Plains 1827; dis 11-1830 (O)

VAN RIPER
Sallie, dt Jacob & Matilda (Lydecker), b Rutherford, N. J. 7-30-1874; recrq 5-9-1896; relrq 11-9-1907 (unm) (H)

VAN SICKLE
Ella (nm), dt John & Alexina; m 1876 Abraham W. MACY (H)

VAN SICKLIN
Phebe, dt Timothy & Eunice BUNKER, b 8-17-1814 d 8-12-1897; dis mo 5-6-1835; cf Hudson 10-1858

VAN SON
Arthur Leveinus, s Leveinus & Maria VON DER GUMETER, b 9-6-1903; recrq 4-11-1927 (H)

VAN TASSEL
Dorinda Eloise, dt Wright & Phebe, b Mt. Kisco 5-28-1850 d 9-19-1905; m 1865 Sandford H. WEEKS (H)
both recrq 3-7-1894
Howard rolf So. Cong. Ch., Middletown, Conn. 5-2-1934

VAN VALKENBURG
Horace (nm) m Sarah Jane FURNAS, dt John D. & Ella (Clifton), b 2-1-1897 (H)
cf Miami 10-10-1908 for Sarah J.

VAN VLEET
Abby Jane, w John B., rocf Farm. 4-1868; d 3-14-1875

VAN VOORHEES
----- & ----- (nm)
Ch: Asa d 5-4-1841 ae 24d bHS

VAN WAY
Pamelia R. rocf Plains 4-1827; d 10-8-1888 ae 87y 11d bPP (H)

VAN WYCK
Deborah, dt William & Martha, Newtown; m 1757 Edward BURLING
Hannah m 1764 William FIELD
John, s William & Martha, Newtown, d 4-1758; mo before 3 Mo (May) 2, 1751
Mary
Phebe m 1761 Thomas BURLING

VAN ZANDT
----- (nm) m Maria UNDERHILL d 1-3-1834 ae 31y 1m 25d bHS
Ch: Theodore d 3-29-1836 ae 12y 3m 10d bHS
Maria dis mo 11-1-1820

VARNEY
Charles C. m Anna C. COX, dt John & Armenia, b Croton-on-Hudson d 12-11-1903 ae 70y bPP
Ch: Edith b Croton-on-Hudson 7-20-1873 d Los Angeles 6-28-1926 bPP
Charles Arthur
cf Limington, Me. 11-1887 with 2 ch named; ct Providence 3-7-1894 for all
Permelia R. rocf Plains 12-26-1826 (clear)

VARNUM
Eugene (nm) d 11-24-1835 ae 32y bHS

VARTOOGUIAN
Parsegh H. d 8-20-1897 ae 23y; m Heipsime ----- d 1-23-1903 ae 58y (H)
Ch: Lucy d about 1893 bPP
both nm, bPP

VELLMER
Annie G., dt Arthur N. & Horsnal, b 2-1-1897; cf Chesterfield 1-10-1921 (H)

VELTMAN
Phebe Jane, dt Lot & Hester HUNT, rocf W. Chester 11-1836 with mother; dis 5-7-1851 (H)

VETHAKE
----- & ----- (nm)
Ch: Chas. Henry b N. Y. d 1-3-1839 ae 4y 9m 16d bHS
Frederick G. b Dutch. Co. d 1-28-1839 ae 10y 2m 28d bHS
John b N. Y. d 6-19-1841 ae 10m bHS

VICKERS
James (nm) d 5-3-1855 ae 72y bPP (half brother of Israel Corse)

VIELE
Dorr (nm) m Josephine C. TABER, dt John R. & Anna (Collins), b 5-16-1879
Josephine relrq 2-1923

VOKER (Volker)
Catherine (late Keese) dis mo 5-7-1772

VOLENTINE
Thomas Jefferson d 2-2-1900 ae 57y bPP (H)

VOLKMAR
Daniel, s Daniel Peter & Anna (Hartle), b N.Y. 8-25-1877; m 6-22-1909 Nina LOOKER, dt Wm. A. & Sarah (Blackburn), b N. Y. 5-6-1878 (H)
Ch: Daniel S. b 5-25-1910
Nina " 5- 2-1912

VONDERSMITH
Alice, dt Wm. B. & Caroline (Birdsall), b 9-24-1864 d 8-31-1923; m Theodore TAYLOR (nm) (H)
name entered by comm. 11-24-1875
Carrie L., dt Wm. & Carolina (Birdsall), b 12-15-1868 d 1-15-1923; m 1888 Frank Burroughs FREAR (H)
Carrie's name entered by comm. 11-24-1875
Estelle, dt Wm. B. & Caroline (Birdsall), b 9-9-1861; m 1887 George Clarence TAYLOR (nm) (H)
name entered by comm. 11-24-1875
Samuel B., s Wm. B. & Caroline (Birdsall), b N. Y. 6-26-1866; m 6-1-1904 Alice May GORTON (nm), dt Horace Simmons, of Hartford, Conn. (H)
William B. (nm) d 8-22-1889 ae 56y bPP (rem from another cem); m 4-6-1861 Caroline BIRDSALL, dt Samuel & Susan R., b 8-30-1840 d 1-4-1884 bPP (H)
Ch: Estelle b 9-19-1861
Alice S. b 9-24-1864
Samuel B. b 6-26-1866
Carrie L. " 12-15-1868
Anna " 11- 3-1874 d 7-19-1896 bPP

VON HOEGLER
Louise, dt Joseph & Johanna (Schavoir) b Germany 2-16-1886; m 4-8-1912 Charle HYDE (nm) recrq 5-14-1923 (H)

VOTOW
William T. rocf Indianapolis 1-1918

VREDENBURGH
Zipporah b East Chester d 3-13-1826 ae 35y bHS
----- & ----- (nm)
Ch: John d 9-6-1826 bHS

WADE
Louis Francis (nm), s Charles & Mary F.; m 11-14-1882 Mary H. BLANCHARD, dt Chas. Henry & Caroline C. (Yale), b Charleston in Boston 6-23-1860 (H)
Mary recrq 7-14-1924

WAGER
Emma recrq 11-1884; name erased 10-1928

WAGSTAFF
Alexander, s Wm. & Ann, b 11-25-1827 d London 1857
Amelia, dt William & Ann; m Henry GROSHON (mo)
Ch: Infant dt
ret a mbr; ct Kingston, Eng. 1-1857 with information (clear); recrq 1853
Hannah M., dt William & Ann, b 12-26-1821; ct London 1850
John Cheeseman, s Wm. & Ann, b 10-10-1829 d 10-3-1878; ct Kingston, Eng. 1-1857 with mother; cf Kingston 2-1873
Thomas Henry, s William & Ann, b 12-23-1825; dis mo 4-4-1855
William & Ann
Ch: Rachel Maria d 6-10-1819 ae 2y 2m 3d
William R. b 4-16-1820
Hannah M. " 12-26-1821
Amelia " 10-24-1823
Thomas Henry " 12-23-1825
Joseph Alexander b 11-25-1827 d 1843
John Cheeseman b 10-10-1829
George W. " 9- 6-1831
Samuel Harford " 11-15-1833
Francis " 8-19-1837 d 8-21-1837 bHS
parents recrq 1820; William dis 9-1841 (O); Ann gct Kingston, Eng. 1-1857 (O); parents dis 1829 (H); William rst 1-1858; living at Brixton Hill, near London
William R., s William & Anna, b 4-16-1820
----- & ----- (nm)
Ch: Francis d 8-19-1837 ae 2y bHS

WAH
King recrq 5-2-1906 (chinese)

WAIBEL
Bessie M., dt Marion; m John Llewellen TILLEY; m 2d 2-5-1930 Clifford S. FRY
recrq of mother 12-4-1901
Marion, w -----
Ch: Margherita Olivia 8y d 1-1913
Bessie Marion 8m
ch included in mother's rq 12-4-1901;
Marion recrq 12-4-1901

WAKELEY
Charles C. (nm), s Truman & J. B.; m 10-25-1855 Elizabeth B. WANZER, dt Ebenezer L. & Esther (Irish), b Fairfield Co., Conn. 7-12-1831 d 2-27-1902 (H)
cf Scip. 9-1855 for Elizabeth
Elizabeth [Wakely] (form Wanzer) rocf Scip. 9-1855 as Wanzer; ret a mbr (H)

WALDENBURG
Augustus F., s Wm. & Julia F. (dec), Bkn., b Bkn. 10-2-1886; m at 62 - 8th Ave. Bkn. 4-20-1911 Florence N. VALENTINE, dt Stephen & Ann L., Bkn., b Bkn. 1-11-1888 (H)
Ch: Augustus F., Jr. b 1-28-1912
William 2d b 5- 7-1913 d 4-10-1916 bPP

WALDENBURG, Augustus F. & Florence N., continued
Ch: Annie Lewis b 11-23-1915
Stephen Valentine b 11- 8-1922
Florence d 9-6-1920 ae 6d bPP
Eleanor d 8-22-1925 ae 6y bPP

WALDMEIER
Alfred Henry (or Alfred Ilma), s Theophilus & Susanna B. (dec), Syria; m N. Y. 10-31-1906 Hettie STERN, dt Louis & Rosalie, Mt. Vernon
Ch: Viola
Lily
all recrq 4-1926

WALFORD
Adis H. (nm) dt Robert & Sadie; m 1902 Ernest J. STRINGHAM (H)
Alice, dt Robt. M. G., d 10-17-1920 ae 45y bPP; m Frank DAISLEY (H) (both nm)
Robert M. G., s Edward W. & Elizabeth F., d 5-3-1919 ae 70y bPP; m Sadie ----- (both nm) (H)
Ch: Adis H. m 1902 Ernest J. STRINGHAM
Alice

WALKER
Anna G., dt Richard L. & Anna (Griffen), b Bkn. 8-14-1891; m Geo. P. HYDE (nm) (H)
recrq of parents 12-4-1895; name rem 9-14-1925
Augusta, dt Isaac & Gulielma, N. Y.; m 1848 Sylvanus F. JENKINS (H)
Avis M., dt Wm. M. & Mary N. BARNEY, b 7-6-1838; dis mo 7-7-1858; joined Episcopal Church (H)
Charles, s Richard L. & Anna (Griffen), b Bkn. 4-14-1888; m 12-13-1922 Hope ROCHFORD (nm), dt John (H)
name entered by comm. 11-5-1890
Edward (nm) & -----
Ch: Infant stillborn 5-25-1810
Elizabeth Ann, dt Thos. E. & Eliz.; m 4-16-1859 David TWEEDY (H)
cf Pur. with parents 11-1836
Evan T., s John J. & Rachel T., d 9-13-1882 ae 51y 4m 29d; rocf Phila. with parents 2-1847; relrq 5-2-1860 (H)
Florence Litchfield, dt Rich. Jr. & Mary T. E. (Litchfield), b Bkn. 10-31-1911; m Ernest W. WATERS (H)
Francis Thompson, s Joseph & Sarah, b 5-12-1833; dis 5-1856 (H)
Geo. Edmondson, s Thos. E. & Eliz., b 10-14-1837 in Balt; cf West Chester 11-1836 with parents; dis mo 9-1-1869 (H)
Henry, s Robert & Eliz. (dec), Scarboro, Eng.; m N. Y. 8-27-1861 at Jos. W. Hilyard's, Mary T. HILYARD, dt Joseph W. & Hannah T.
Ch: Arthur Edward
cf Pickering & Hull, Eng. 6-19-1861 for Henry; ct Pickering & Hull 1-7-1863 for both with ch named
Henry Edmund, s Rich. L. & Anna (Griffen), b Bkn. 3-15-1895; m Margaret H. PARTRIDGE (nm), dt Mason H. & Ella MILLER (H) divorced; name entered on rq of parents 12-4-1895
Isaac Henry, s Isaac & Gulielma, N. Y.; m at W. H. Macy's 12-10-1856 Cornelia T. MACY, dt Wm. H. & Eliza L., N. Y., d 5-15-1897 (H) (W. H. Macy not under care of N.Y. MM)
Jane recrq 4-1874; d 5-6-1883
John rocf Leeds, Eng. 8-21-1812 (clear); ct Leeds, 2-1-1815 (clear)
John m Emma C. SEED, dt Joseph & Sarah (Green), b Eng. 1852 d 3-29-1935 bPP
Ch: Cleveland b 9-1888 d 4-1-1900 bPP
all nm; parents of England
John J. d 3-22-1863; m Rachel T. ----- d 6-14-1872 (H)
Ch: Evan T. d 9-13-1882 ae 51y 4m 29d
cf Phila. 2-1847 for all; Evan relrq 5-2-1860
John Jackson rocf Pur. 5-12-1824 (clear); dis 10-1830 (O)
Joseph, s Joseph (dec) & Sarah, Leeds, Eng., b 3-26-1798 d 3-22-1866; m N. Y. 8-8-1832 Sarah THOMPSON, dt Francis (dec) & Mary, N. Y., b 3-12-1810 d 1-13-1842 (H)
Ch: Francis Thompson b 5-12-1833
Sarah b 10-10-1834 d 9-3-1837
Joseph b 1-23-1836
Theodore b 1-8-1838 d 10-2-1841
Charles b 2-11-1840 d 9-23-1841
Sarah T. b 1-7-1842
cf Knaresbro MM 7-13-1801 (clear); ct Knaresbro 5-1-1816; cf Brighouse 6-18-1824 (clear); dis 6-1830 (O)
Joseph Henry recrq 7-1872; ct Brighouse, Eng. 7-6-1873
Philip Thomas, s Thos. E. & Eliz., d 7-9-1854 at Wampoa, China; cf Pur. with parents 11-1836 (H)
Richard L., s Robt. I. & Hannah (both dec), b 8-2-1837; m at Wm. Underhill's, Croton Pt., 6-17-1863 Mary UNDERHILL, dt Wm. & Abbie, Cortland
cert of clear to Ama. 6-10-1863 (O); ct Ama. 3-1866 (O)
Richard L. (nm), s Robt. I. (dec) & Maria Louisa Bkn., b 2-2-1857 d 11-25-1923 bPP; m 2-5-1880 at Charles Griffin's, Anna T. V. GRIFFIN, dt Charles & Sarah A. (Valentine), Bkn., b 5-17-1854 N. Y.
Ch: Richard L. Jr. b 2-1-1882
Edith b 8-15-1883 d 8- 3-1893 bPP
Sara G. b 11- 5-1884
Robert I. b 8-13-1886
Charles S. b 4-14-1888
Harold L. b 10-23-1889
Anna G. b 8-14-1891
Louisa b 5-29-1893
Henry Edmund b 3-15-1895
Percy Williams b 9-11-1896

WALKER, Richard L. & Anna T. V., continued
6 elder ch's names entered by comm. 11-5-1890, remainder entered by MM 1895-1898
Richard L. Jr., s Rich. L. & Anna (Griffen), b Bkn. 2-1-1882; m Mary Ten Eyck LITCHFIELD (nm) (H)
Ch: Florence Litchfield b 10-31-1911
recrq of parents 7-11-1927
Robert I., s Richard L. & Anna (Griffen), b Bkn. 8-13-1886; m Gwendolyn GWYER (nm) (H)
name entered by comm. 11-5-1890
Robert J., s Thomas & Eliz. (dec), N. Y.; m Manhattanville 5-13-1819 Mary BARROW, dt John & Mary (dec), N. Y., d 3-1-1831 (or 2-25-1831, ae 35y) rem to PP
Ch: John B. b 1-25-1822 d 6-13-1845 at New Orleans
Elizabeth b 4-25-1824 d 12-8-1825
Infant stillborn 2-25-1826
Mary b 12-1826 d 6-18-1828
Thomas d 3-2-1826 ae 6d
cf Pur. 5-8-1817 for Robert (clear)
Robert J., West Farms, d 12-3-1845; m 2d N. Y. 4-10-1833 Hannah L. LAWRENCE, dt Robert R. (dec) & Hannah, d 6-12-1855
Ch: Robert J. b 1-24-1834
Richard L. b 8-2-1837
Robert J., s Robert J. & Hannah L., b 1-24-1834 d 8-6-1868; m 3-1856 Maria Louisa PLATT (mo)
Ch: Richard L. b 2-2-1857
Mary d 6-18-1828 ae 1y 6m
dis mo 4-1856
Sarah M., dt Charles & Sarah C. (Murphy), b E. Smithfield, Pa. 2-11-1844; m 1-1-1889 Dr. Orpheus Brainard BIRD (H)
cf Phila., Green St. 1-4-1902; ct Orange Grove, Pasadena 8-13-1910
Sarah T., dt Joseph & Sarah, b 1-7-1842 d 5-25-1876; m 5-7-1863 Mansfield YOUNG (mo) (H)
dis 12-2-1863
Thaddeus H. & Margaret E.
Ch: Sarah
Otis
cf Glens Falls 10-1884 with 2 ch named; ct Glens Falls 4-3-1885 for all
Thomas, s Robert, d 3-2-1826
Thomas, s Robert & Hannah, Merchant N. Y.; m Elizabeth ----- d 8-11-1800 bHS (H)
Ch: Robert J. b 3-1-1795
John Jackson b 10-25-1796
Thomas E. b 9-18-1798
Eliza J. b 7-16-1800 d 2-6-1843
cf Brighouse in Halifax 12-13-1793 for both
Thomas d 3-10-1842; m 2d N. Y. 1-3-1802 Elizabeth HOYLAND, dt William & Mary (both dec) ct Pur. 12-1-1802 with 4ch named first; cf Pur. 11-1836 for Thomas; Elizabeth rocf Birmingham, Eng. 6-13-1798 (clear)
The Walker, of Gildersome; the Hoylands of Sheffield, Yorks
Thomas E., s Thomas & Elizabeth, b 9-18-1798 d 4-11-1871; m Ann ----- d 11-13-1868 (H)
Ch: Philip Thomas
Thomas George d 2-26-1891
Elizabeth Ann
William Thomas b 8-9-1836 d 8-9-1836
George Edmondson b 10-14-1837
Lewen W. b 4-25-1839 d 2-1-1897
Harriet b 5-14-1843 d 8-14-1845

WALL
Abigail (nm) b Conn. d 7-29-1810 ae 74y 4m bHS
Alexander J. (name changed to Wall by Court 9-18-1917), s Lorenz Wohlager & Augusta (Ziemer), b N. Y. 10-25-1884; m 11-28-1906 Lillian B. HASHAGEN, dt Henry O. & Caroline (Steiger), b 1-5-1883 (H)
Ch: Alexander J. Jr. b 9-12-1912
all recrq 4-11-1932
Ann R., dt Humphrey & Edith, N. Y.; m 1835 John G. SEAMAN (H)
cf Chesterfield 6-1830
Isaac C., s Matthias & Sarah; m ----- (H)
Ch: Emma E. b Harlem d 5-28-1845 ae 6m bHS
cf Pur. 6-12-1806 with parents; dis 6-1838
James (nm) & -----
Ch: William b N. Y. d 10-5-1831 ae 1y 4m bHS
Matthias m Sarah ----- b West. Co. d 5-25-1833 ae 63y (H)
Ch: James B.
Isaac C.
William U. b 8-9-1808
Sarah Ann
cf Pur. 6-12-1806 with two ch, James & Isaac; dis 3-4-1818; all dis 1830-1839 (O)
Renee, dt Philip & Anna Frances (Delsomme), b 12-1-1900; m 1921 Joseph WEGER (H)
Sarah Ann, dt Matthias & Sarah, d 6-9-1844; m David KENNY (H)
William U., s Matthias & Sarah, b 8-9-1808; dis 2-1837 (H)
----- & ----- (nm)
Ch: Emily b N. Y. d 11-23-1834 ae 5m bHS
James b Hurlgate d 5-22-1836 ae 1m 14d bHS
William H. b N. Y. d 8-8-1841 ae 10m 2d bHS
William M. b Wards Is. d 8-18-1842 ae 24d bHS

WALLACE
Edward Lew, s John & Annie P. (Barnes), b 12-31-1890; cf Phila. with parents 11-10-1906; ct Makefield, N. J. 12-13-1913, not accepted; dropped 5-14-1934 (H)
John, s Allen & Achsah Ann (Dickinson), b Woodtown, N. J. 6-22-1850 d 6-19-1922; m Annie Pancoast BARNES, dt Joseph & Phebe Ann (McClintock), d 1-2-1908 (H)
Ch: Edward Lew b 12-31-1890
cf Phila. 11-10-1906 for all

WALLIS (or Wallin)
Edward (nm) & -----

WALLIS, Edward, continued
Ch: Infant stillborn 5-30-1811 bHS
" " 3-25-1812 bHS

WALN
Rebecca, w Jesse
Ch: Mary
Sarah
cf Hardwick, N. J. with 2 small ch, Mary & Sarah, 4-13-1780

WALSH
----- & ----- (nm)
Ch: Emily d 9-10-1841 ae 1y 10m 10d bHS

WALSHEID
----- (nm) m Dorothy Selma LINTON, dt Albert W. & Isabella (Goerke), b 7-28-1906

WALTER
Alfred, s Ellwood & Elizabeth H. (Bowne), b 10-2-1851 Westchester d 2-12-1907 ae 55y 4m 10d; m 1-6-1886 Regina Henrietta KIRCHOFF (H)
Anna, dt Ellwood & Deborah, Englewood, N. J., b 1-20-1841 d 3-21-1894; m 1870 Edwin W. COGGESHALL (H)
Elwood, s Thomas & Sarah, Phila., b 8-16-1803; m N. Y. 8-9-1827 Deborah COGGESHALL, dt Caleb & Eliz., N. Y., b 12-7-1804 d 6-26-1844 (H)
Ch: Elizabeth b 6-13-1829 d 5-4-1833
Thomas Jr. b 12-5-1830
Sarah " 10- 7-1836
Ellwood Jr. b 11-28-1838
Anna " 1-20-1841
cf West Chester 11-1836 for Elwood with Eliz. & Thos.; ct Phila. 5-1829 for Deborah; cf Phila.
Ellwood d 5-7-1877; m 2d 1-6-1848 at Sidney B. Bowne's, Elizabeth H. BOWNE, dt Sidney B. & Jemima H., Westchester, b 7-27-1819 d 1-23-1863 (H)
Ch: Agnes b 12-12-1848 d 1-3-1852
Alfred W. b 7-10-1851
Emilie b 1-11-1855 d 10-13-1875
Helen " 11-15-1861 d 6-30-1903 bPP
Ellwood m 3d Anna HAVILAND, dt Mary (Cooley) Haviland, b 10-8-1816 Fairfield, Conn. d 1-4-1905 ae 88y 2m 27d
cf N.P. for Anna 6-5-1867
Ellwood Jr., s Ellwood & Deborah, b 11-28-1838 in Spokane 1898 (H)
Henry, s Henry & Lena, b N. Y. 8-18-1894; recrq 6-1-1917; name erased 3-1928
Sarah, dt Ellwood & Deborah, Bkn., b 10-7-1836; m 1863 Thomas B. HALLOCK
Thomas (nm) b Pa. d 6-9-1842 ae 67y bHS (m)
Thomas, s Ellwood & Deborah (Coggeshall), b 12-5-1830; m Caroline E. ----- (nm) d 6-8-1906 ae 75y 7m 11d bPP (H)

WALTERS
Anthony d 6-9-1813 ae 62y bHS; m Ruth ----- b Ama. d 9-22-1827 ae 82y
Ch: Ruth
cf Ama. 6-11-1808 for Ruth (clear); ct Licking Creek, Ind. for Ruth & dt, Ruth, 4-11-1818 (both clear); cf Licking Creek not found
Caroline, dt Felix M. & Martha (Cock), b Glen Cove 8-12-1836; recrq of mother; ct Wby 1-13-1906 (H)
Daniel rocf Chap. 5-3-1796, a lad, apprentice; d 5-30-1801 bHS
Daniel D. (nm) b Yorktown d 11-16-1825 ae 49y bHS (m)
Felix M. (nm) b Va. d 9-9-1844 ae 43y bHS; m Martha T. COCK, dt Andrew & Mary (Titus)
Ch: Felix b N. Y. d 3-21-1831 ae 9m bHS
Catharine b N. Y. d 2-17-1834 ae 1y 8m bHS
Elizabeth b N. Y. d 1-8-1839 ae 4y 6m bHS
Mary b N. Y. d 1-11-1839 ae 4y 6m bHS
Caroline b 8-12-1836
Felix M., Elizabeth & Mary rem to PP
Joseph b Ama. d 7-9-1817 ae 28y bHS; m Ann ----- b Westchester Co. d 5-21-1817 ae 28y bHS
cf Ama. 3-12-1803 (clear)
Martha, w Felix M., dt Andrew COCK, d 4-3-1881 (H)
Ch: Caroline
Caroline recrq of mother 12-1844
Reuben & Ruth
Ch: (order uncertain)
Ruth Jr. d 6-22-1827
Edward
Stephen
Anthony Lockwood
Phebe
Daniel
Isaac
Lydia
Reuben rst 9-1827; Ruth & first named 4 ch rocf Lick Creek 10-20-1827; Phebe, Isaac & Daniel recrq of parents 4-1830 (0); ct Lick Creek (for all) 6-1830 (0); parents dis 1829 (H)
Stephen L. (nm) d 12-20-1864 ae 21y 21d bPP, rem to Paramus, N. J. 10-18-1884
William A., M.D. d 10-10-1866 rem from Greenwood to PP, rem to Paramus, N. J. 10-18-1884; m ----- (H)
Ch: (perhaps) William A. d 3-5-1870 ae 28y bPP, rem to Paramus, N.J. 10-18-1884
----- & ----- (nm)
Ch: Ann b Bedford, N. Y. d 1-27-1812 ae 2m 2d bHS
Daniel b N.Y. d 9-27-1824 ae 3y 6m bHS
John b Ind. d 8-16-1827 ae 1y 7m bHS

WALTON
Amos rocf Buckingham, Pa. 1827; ct Buckingham, Pa. 3-3-1830 (clear) (0); rel 7-5-1871 (H) absent over 5y

WALTON, continued
Elizabeth recrq 11-4-1914
Elizabeth R., dt John F. & Ann S., d 9-13-1921 ae 89y bPP; m Richard CROMWELL (H) (both nm)
Esther, w Thomas (H)
Ch: David G.
John
Lucy
Sarah Ann
Stacy P. d 2-8-1832
Isaac
Amos
cf Buckingham, Pa. 11-2-1818 with 5 ch; ct Phila. 8-1831; Esther, David & John dis 1830-1839 (O)
Hannah, dt Wm. E. & Ellen (Janney), b Genoa, Neb. 10-1-1884; m 1916 Henry L. MESSNER (H) cf Balt. with ch 3-9-1925
Isaac, s Thomas & Esther, d 4-14-1884; m Prudence ----- d 12-23-1881 (H)
Ch: William Marsh b 5-22-1828
Sarah Jane b 3-12-1830
Joseph James b 2-21-1832 d 3-22-1894
Isaac Marion b 7- 4-1837 d 1-14-1883
cf Fallowfield MM, Pa. 8-11-1826; Prudence rocf R. & P. 3-15-1827; Isaac dis 5-1830 (O)
J. Bernard, s Joseph T. & Dora E. (Brosius), b Ercildoun, Pa. 5-29-1885; m 8-17-1910 Louise HAVILAND, dt James S. & Elizabeth (Griffen), b 10-1-1875 Pur. (H)
Ch: Joseph Haviland b N. Rochelle 9-2-1911
Edward Haviland b N. Rochelle 1-3-1913
Bernard rocf Makefield, N. J. 8-14-1909; Louise rocf Pur. 12-10-1910; ct Swarth. for all 3-10-1917
James L., s Wm. & Susan M. (both dec), Phila.; m at Rebecca Collins' (not under care of N. Y. MM) N. Y. 11-28-1867 Mary Foster COLLINS, dt Isaac (dec) & Rebecca, d 3-12-1904, Phila. (wd)
cf WD MM 11-18-1863 for Mary
James M. rocf Phila. 9-2-1868; d 5-25-1874 (H)
Mary Abby, w Robert, rocf Swansea, Mass. 6-1874; mbrp relinquished 5-1880
Sarah Ann, dt Thomas & Esther, gct ND MM 4-4-1832 (minor
Sarah Jane, dt Isaac & Prudence, N. J., b N.Y. 3-12-1830; m 1849 John Howard WRIGHT (H)
William, s Edward Hicks & Anne M. (Townsend), b 11-10-1843; cf Phila. 1-3-1872; relrq 4-10-1909 (H)
William (nm) d 11-13-1915 ae 72y bPP (H)
William E. rocf Alexandria 9-1-1875; ct Balt. 12-6-1893 (H)
William Marsh, s Isaac & Prudence, b 5-22-1828; dis mo 6-1-1859 (H)

WANSBROUGH
John Jr. rocf Bristol, Eng. to Alton, Hants. 11-30-1819 (clear), endorsed by Alton to Friends in U.S. 5-11-1820; ct Hardshaw West 5-1-1822 (clear)

WANTON
Mary, dt Stephen (dec), rocf Portsmouth 10-30-1792 (clear); ct Newport 10-5-1796 (clear)

WANZER
Abraham, s John & Grace (dec), Sherman, Conn.; m N. Y. 11-8-1843 Phebe HATHAWAY, dt Benj. & Phebe (dec) HAVILAND, of Pur.
ct Oblong 9-4-1844 for Phebe H. with her 2 ch, Elizabeth & Benjamin Hathaway
Phebe, wd Benoni
Elizabeth B., dt Ebenezer L. & Esther (Irish), b Fairfield Co., Conn. 7-12-1831 d 2-27-1902; m 1855 Charles C. WAKELEY (H)
cf Scip. 9-1855
John Jay rocf Oblong 7-13-1835 (clear); mo before 10-1849; dis 1-1850
Margaret Holcomb (form Wanzer) dis mo 12-1853
Sarah d 10-7-1801 bHS

WARD
Alta, dt Barton B. & Minnie G.; m ----- THOMPSON; recrq of parents 2-4-1891
Anna b Westchester d 10-4-1811 ae 40y bHS
Anna Hazard, dt Jacob & Eliza BARKER; mo; joined R. C. Ch. before 6-1860; dis 8-1-1860 (H)
Barton B. d 3-24-1926; m Minnie G. ----- d rpd 4-1926
Ch: Henry Paul b 3-4-1889 d 11-30-1931
Norman b 10-4-1890
Alta
cf Kingston, Canada 4-1889 for Barton; Minnie recrq 10-2-1889; Henry P. recrq of parents 2-4-1891
George M. rocf Phila. 6-1-1887;d 1911 (H)
Hannah Ann rocf Phila. Cherry St. 5-1846; d 6-24-1868 (H)
Sarah (nm) b New Rochelle d 6-6-1825 ae 25y 9m bHS
----- & ----- (nm)
Ch: Maria d 4-6-1824 ae 11d bHS

WARDELL
Charles (nm) b Shrews. d 12-30-1815 ae 50 bHS (m)
Elizabeth b Shrews. d 11-12-1817 ae 90y bHS (wd)
Hannah b Shrews d 2-3-1826 ae 90y; w -----
Ch: Hannah M. d 5-24-1830 ae 50y bHS; left legacy of $200 to mtg
cf Shrews. 12-5-1814
Jane b Scotland d 8-26-1818 ae 27y
John (nm) d 7-20-1840 ae 77y 5m bHS
Raymond Wesley, s Levinus & Ella L. (Brown), b Bkn. 12-31-1886; m 10-20-1923 Constance JACKSON, dt Chas. Lincoln & Martha (Pogue), b Melrose Highlands, Mass. 3-14-1899 (H)
Ch: Anthony Wentworth b 1-11-1932
both recrq 7-12-1926
Rebecca (nm), w John N. (or Jos. N.), b Middle-

WARDELL, Rebecca, continued
town, N. J. d 3-11-1822 ae 60y bHS
William Henry rocf Lurgan, Ire. 7-1883; name erased 4-3-1929
----- & ----- (nm)
Ch: Lavinia d 9-6-1811 ae 11m 12d bHS

WARE
Henry, Jr., s Henry & Louisa F., Brookline, Mass.; m Bayport, L. I. 1-17-1931 Eliz. Bancker DAHL, dt Geo. W. & Annabel B. C., Bayport, L. I., b Bayport 6-23-1910 (H)
Hieskaell S. recrq 2-1854; d 3-23-1868 ae 42y bPP (H)
Richard (nm) d 1-15-1856 ae 78y bPP; m Hannah ----- d 11-26-1866 ae 78y bPP
Ch: Jane E. d 10-12-1900 ae 76y 1m bPP
Virginia, dt Wm. P. & Isabel (McKay), d 5-27-1931 ae 71y bPP; m William THOMPSON (H)

WARING
Adelaide L., dt Wm. F. & Frances L., b 5-29-1843; relrq 12-1881
Arthur B. b Bkn. 8-6-1904 (stepson of Arthur W. (or N.) Waring) recrq 9-5-1917 as Arthur W. Greene (name changed)
Arthur W. (or N.), s Thomas & Anna, b Md. 12-9-1880; m -----
Ch: (stepson) Arthur B. b Bkn. 8-6-1904
cf Germantown 1-1918; Arthur recrq 9-5-1917 as Arthur W. Greene; rpd 3-1928 having changed name to Arthur B. Waring
Frances, dt Wm. F. & Frances L., b 12-5-1847; m Robert L. CASE, Jr.; relrq 10-1880
Frances L., w William F., d 5-30-1884
Ch: Adelia L. b 5-29-1843
Amelia L. (in Stamford, Conn. 1912)
cf Pur. 10-12-1842
John Monroe L., s J. Van Vechten & Harriet (Kellers), b Bkn. 7-4-1906; ct Montclair 11-11-1932 (H)
Junius Van Vechten, s John Burger & Henrietta H. (Tufts) b 7-27-1863 Stamford, Conn.; m 6-19-1889 Harriet H. KELLERS, dt Bohl & Hattie Lavinia (Henry), b 3-21-1869 Jersey City (H)
Ch: Alethia Portia b 10-25-1890 d 3-6-1914
Meta Louisa Beatrice b 2-19-1898
John Monroe Livingston b 7-4-1906
parents recrq 5-7-1890
Lydia, dt Wm. & Sarah, N. Y.; m 1830 Wm. Henry WILLIS
Sarah Ann, dt Wm. & Ann, N. Y.; m 1822 George UNDERHILL
William, s Thaddeus & Deborah, N. Y.; m N. Y. 5-10-1809 Sarah UNDERHILL, dt Solomon & Lydia (dec), N. Y., d 9-15-1839 ae 56y 4m 7d bHS
Ch: Lydia b 4-15-1810
William F. b 12-9-1812
Samuel F. b 12-20-1814 d 8-26-1849
James Parsons d 7-7-1817 ae 3d
James Parsons b 2-26-1819 d 8-11-1830 bHS
Ch: Edward d 1-10-1822 ae 4m 9d
William recrq 1808; parents dis 1829 (H); William dis 7-1850
William F., s William & Sarah; m Frances L. FERRIS
Ch: Adelaide L. b 5-29-1843
Frances " 12- 5-1847
Amelia
cert of clear to Pur. 8-4-1841; William F. dis

WARNER
George (nm) & -----
Ch: Infant stillborn 4-7-1838 bHS
Infant stillborn 8-16-1839 bHS
Georgianna d 8-16-1846 ae 1y 3m bHS, rem to PP
George & Edith W. (H)
cf Bucks 1-3-1849 for George; Edith recrq 2-7-1849; ct Burl. 3-2-1870 for both
George m Nellie ----- d rpd 1-2-1929
both recrq 6-12-1901; George's name erased 1-2-1901

WARNOCK
David K., s James & Martha, d 9-8-1913 ae 29y 11m 25d bPP; m Mary ROBERTS (H)
both nm

WARREN
Grace Lower, dt Geo. W. & Mary A., Harrison, N. Y.; m 1926 Edward P. STURGE, of Eng. recrq 11-6-1912; ct Westminster & Longford, Eng. 9-1926
----- (nm) m Josephine J. JENKS, dt Wm. P. & Bertha C., b 12-30-1903 (m rpd 8-7-1929)

WASHBURN
Abel, s Elijah & Anna
Elijah m Hannah ----- d 9-28-1824
Ch: Eliza Ann
Abel
Tamar
Thomas W.
Daniel d 9-16-1842 ae 26y
Mary d 6-15-1823 ae 5y 5m
Elkanah
Richard d 12-3-1822
Robert " 12-3 -1822 ae 1m 22d
Rebecca " 12- 3-1822 ae 1m 22d
Elijah m 2d Anna -----
Elijah recrq 4-2-1817; Hannah recrq 3-5-1817; first 5 ch recrq of parents; eldest about 10; cf Chap. 5-11-1826 for Anna; all dis (0); ct Chap. 2-1839 for all (H)
Eliza Ann, dt Elijah & Hannah, recrq of parents 2-1818; dis 11-1829 (H)
Elkanah, dt Elijah & Annah, recrq of parents 2-1818; ct Chap. 11-1844 (H)
Joseph (nm) m Elizabeth ----- b Me. d 7-25-1833 ae 26y bHS
Ch: Frances H. d 2-29-1832 ae 3m bHS
Mary, dt Wm., m Richard WILLITS, Jericho

WASHBURN, continued
Sarah (late Wright) dis mo 6-3-1818
Tamar, dt Elijah & Annah; m before 5-6-1829
 Thomas WRIGHT (mo)
 dis mo 6-1829; dis mo 4-1829 (H)
Thomas W., s Elijah & Anna, recrq of parents 2-1818; dis mo 3-1835 (H); ref. to Pur., Pur. replies 6-1-1836 unknown; rpd in Mich but finally located at Round Hill & again ref. to Pur. (O); Pur. rpt dis him 1-3-1838 (H)
----- & ----- (nm)
Ch: Margarum b N. Y. d 12-30-1825 ae 6y 4m bHS

WATERBURY
Harriet A. recrq 5-5-1875; relrq 5-1885
Ruannah, dt Azariah & Mary, N. Y.; m 1845 Samuel I. SMITH (H)
 recrq 12-1840

WATERS
Daniel dis mo 2-6-1799
Ruth, w -----
Ch: Ruth Jr.
 cf Lick Creek, Ind. 10-20-1827
----- & ----- (nm)
Ch: Ann b N. Y. d 1-10-1829 ae 2h bHS

WATKINS
Ethel m 1928 Frank CRUTCHFIELD
 letter from Wodeville M. E. Ch. of Mt. Gilead, N. D. 3-1928
Robert J. (nm) d 8-6-1868 ae 35y bPP
Aldren, s Ernest W. & Eva M. (Auld), b Bkn. 5-10-1917; recrq 12-10-1934 (H)

WATSON
Emma (nm) m 1889 Oliver C. TITUS (H)
Jemima (nm) m 6-5-1888 Edward HAVILAND (H)
John rocf Dublin 3-14-1854; ct Belfast 5-1861
John Jay, s John & Mary Elizabeth (Lundy), b Schomberg, Ont. 6-17-1869; m 9-20-1893 Mary PHILLIPS, dt Daniel & Susan (Yonge), b Newmarket, Ont. 8-25-1869 (H)
 cf Yonge St., Ont. for J. Jay 5-9-1908; Mary P. recrq 5-9-1908
Joseph, Merchant, N. Y., rocf Alendale MM, Conwood, Eng. 8-22-1792 & 6-26-1793, the latter stating him clear; dis 1-3-1798
Mary rocf Phila. 4-25-1788 (clear)
Mary b N. J. d 6-2-1816 ae 88y (wd)
 (mother of Gilbert Evernghim, prob m ----- Watson 2d)
Merlin A., s Everett W. & Eva M. (Auld), b Bkn. 5-15-1913; m 6-8-1935 Marsia Anne PRICE (nm), dt Frank O. & Florence (H)

WATTON
Stacey P. b Pa. d 2-8-1832 ae 18y 11m (unm)
 (prob mbr in Pa.)

WAY
Abner P., s Jacob (dec) & Rachel (Pugh), Pa., b West Chester, Pa. 11-7-1876; m at 15th St. 4-11-1908 Helen FINK, dt Emil (dec) & Ada P., Phila., b Jersey City 8-11-1878 (H)
Ch: Robert Fink b 5-18-1912
 cf Birmingham, Pa. 11-10-1906 for Abner; Helen recrq 2-10-1912; ct Pur. 4-12-1935 for all
Charlotte M., dt Jacob H. & Rachel Ann (Pugh), b Nebraska City, Neb. 2-24-1867; rocf Birmingham, Pa. 11-5-1898; ct Birmingham, 11-13-1922 (H)
Esther rocf Wby 6-7-1786, she having rem with her h
Frances C. (nm), dt Geo. Pierce & Carline A. (Dobuest); m 1885 Franklin HAINES (H)
John, s John & Sarah (Dean), Newtown, b 6 Mo (Aug) 15, 1708 d 3-21-1795; m -----
Ch: Thomas d (unm)
 John " "
James, s John & Sarah, Newtown, b 6 Mo (Aug) [15, 1708
Jemima Dunham (form Way) dis mo 12-3-1800
John, Newtown, L. I., d 8 Mo (Oct) 3, 1723; m at Samuel Dean's, Jamaica 9 Mo. (Nov) 22, 1687; Sarah DEAN (or Dane), dt Samuel, Jericho, d 8 Mo (Oct) 13, 1747
Ch: John b 8 Mo (Oct) 15, 1688 d 1688
 Sarah b 2 Mo (Apr) 20, 1690 d 7 Mo 13, 1690
 Elizabeth b 8 Mo (Oct) 11, 1691
 John b 11 Mo (Jan.) 26, 1693/4
 Samuel b 7 Mo (Sep) 11, 1696
 Sarah b 8 Mo (Oct) 27, 1698
 Mary b 2 Mo (Apr) 14, 1701
 James d 10 Mo 25, 1706
 Joseph b 6 Mo (Aug) 2, 1703 d 10 Mo 1704
 James b 6 Mo (Aug) 15, 1708
 active mbr 1686-1701
John, Newtown; m Flushing 5 Mo (July) 1716
 Sarah BURLING
Ch: John b 8 Mo (Oct) 12, 1721
 Samuel b 9 Mo (Nov) 11, 1723
John about to rem with w to Pa., gc 1 Mo (Mar) 5, 1718/19
John, Newtown, took cert of clear to Wby 12-6-1759
John 3d, Newtown, b 4 Mo (June) 18, 1747; m
 Mary ----- b 9 Mo (Nov) 22, 1748
Ch: Jemima b 9-16-1769
 James " 4-21-1771 d 3-21-1795
 Mary " 5-31-1773
 Samuel Marsh b 5-14-1775
 John b 4-14-1777
 Judith b 5-24-1779
 Elizabeth b 7- 3-1783
 Charles Farrington b 6-14-1786
 Sarah b 9- 7-1789
John Way took cert of clear to Woodbridge 3-3-1768; Mary brought cf Woodbridge 2-15-1769
John Jr. con mo 9-1-1773
Judith Foulke (form Way) dis mo 6 Mo 1803
Mary, dt Samuel, Newtown; m 1744 Richard HALLETT

WAY, continued
Mary Thorn (form Way) dis mo 11-1-1797
Phebe rocf Wby with dt, Eliz. Lancaster, 6-5-1760; Eliz. gct Richland, Pa. 10-2-1765; Phebe gct Wrightstown, Pa. 12-7-1774
Samuel Jr., s Samuel, con mo 2-6-1744; cert of clear to Wby 11-6-1753; ct Wby 9-6-1759
Samuel d 10-20-1896
Samuel, Flushing, N. Y. rocf Wby 2-26-1786; dis mo 2-1-1797; "Hatter, late of Flushing"
Sarah, dt John & Sarah, Flushing; m 1716 Thomas FARRINGTON
----- & ----- (nm)
Ch: Mary D. d 7-3-1863 ae 30y bPP

WAYMAN
Helen Bentley recrq 6-4-1930
Suzanne (nm) m Levon Peter DONCHIAN

WEARE
Fred Lincoln (nm), s John & Ruth Jane; m 6-28-1893 Edith CARPENTER, dt Robt. H. & Amy T. (Griffen), b 2-23-1864 (H)

WEBB
Eliza, w Richard, rocf Grange, Ireland 12-19-1845; ct Grange, Ireland 10-6-1847, her h dec since their rem
Frances Maria rocf Grange, Ireland 4-18-1855; ct Balt.
Frank Thomas (nm), s Thos. Dutton & Mary H. J.; m 5-4-1876 Mary Albino PUSEY, dt Joseph M. & Elizabeth (Phillips), b Hockessin, Del. 9-18-1853 (H)
cf Wilmington 4-10-1909
Isaac rocf Lisburn, Ireland, held by comm a long time, but unknown 1-6-1836, cert ret.; Lisburn rq dealing for mo 9-6-1837; dis by Lisburn & N. Y. notifield 10-3-1838
Jacob rocf Richhill, Ireland 4-23-1801 (clear); ct Ama. 10-6-1802 (clear)
Job & Hannah
Ch: Thomas
Sarah
John
Isaac
cf Wby with their 4 ch 5-18-1791; ct Wby with their 3 ch 11-3-1791
Priscilla d 11-15-1882; m ----- JOHNSON
cf Dublin 8-16-1854
Richard dis by Grange MM, Ireland

WEBBER
Edith m 1913 Henry Griffen WILLETS (H)
Henry Headford rocf Bristol & Frenchay, Eng. 1-1871; ct Bristol 4-1880, ret to Bristol 7-1880; name erased 5-1886
----- m Ellean ----- d 11-30-1877 ae 31y bPP
Ch: Jeffrey d 10-24-1877 ae 2m bPP

WEBLUS
Antonia, dt John C. & Helen (Hartwig), b Hoboken 9-27-1886; m 1906 Julius SCHLICHT (H)
both recrq 8-13-1917

WEBSTER
Eden S. & Susan L.
Ch: Elizabeth
cf R. & P. 3-21-1838 with 1 ch named; Eden dis 8-1842; ct R. & P. 6-1849 for Susan & Elizabeth; dis 8-1842
Hugh dis mo 7-5-1781
James (nm) b Plainfield d 7-2-1824 ae 21y 10m 10d bHS (unm)
Mary Ann (nm) d 9-17-1860 ae 44y 6m bPP
Nelson P. (nm), s Rev. Calvary M. & Ann Catharine (Parker); m Elizabeth LILLEY, wd first of Louis R. La MONT; 2nd George W. Lillie; dt Lewis P. & Laura J. COOK, b Bay of Biscay 8-16-1864 (H)
Elizabeth gct Alexandria 5-14-1923
Rachel Elizabeth, dt Jesse & Ellen (Conrad), b Lancaster Co., Pa. 5-8-1877; cf Sadsbury 2-9-1901; ct Sadsbury 6-9-1906 (H)
Rebecca rocf R. & P. 6-17-1839; "mother of Solomon Jenner's w"
Sarah rem to Woodbridge 2 Mo (Apr) 2, 1746
Sarah Eliz., w David D., dt Stephen & Sarah HAVILAND, b 10-22-1842
Susanna Webster (form Webster) dis mo 6-5-1782
Susannah rocf R. & P. 11-15-1787
William, Elizabeth Town, N. J.; m Newtown 9 Mo (Nov) 13, 1745 Sarah HALLETT, Newtown, L. I.
William, Plainfield m Ann HALLETT (mo) dis mo 10-4-1781
William, Newtown, b 10-15-1757; m Susanna ----- b 4-5-1765
Ch: Elizabeth b 10- 4-1782
Ann " 5-14-1788
Mary " 4-11-1790
Sarah " 5- 1-1793
ct R. & P. 2-4-1794 with 4 minor ch & their apprentice lad, Aaron Shotwell
William dis by Plainfield MM; con mo 1-3-1787; took cert of clear to Plainfield 6-6-1787
William S. b Kingwood, N. J. d 8-17-1840 ae 35y 7m 17d bur Plainfield, N. J.; m Margaret -----
Ch: Infant stillborn 4-9-1840 bHS
Margaret m 2d Solomon JENNER; cf R. & P. 9-18-1839
----- & ----- (nm)
Ch: Edward b N. Y. d 10-9-1824 ae 2m bHS

WEEDEN
Holder C. & Abigail
Ch: George Anthony
Anna Anthony
cf Newport 5-27-1824; ct Providence 2-4-1829 (clear) with 2 small ch named; withdrew to Orthodox 1828
Joseph A. recrq 3-1884; d 9-26-1887

WEEKS
Abbie S., dt Joseph & Elizabeth (Underhill),

WEEKS, Abbie S., continued
b Lewisboro 10-6-1828 d 10-29-1921 ae 93y 22d; m 1849 Alvah WILLIAMSON (nm) (H)
Abraham rocf Chap. 6-1838; ct Chap. 5-1856
Adeline, dt James & Lydia H.; m John BRYANT (H) ret a mbr
Alexander B. d 3-8-1859; m Sarah Ann ----- (H)
Ch: Mary Catharine b 6-15-1846
Semantha " 7-20-1848
Henrietta " 4- 8-1853
Richard Henry " 10- 1-1855
cf Oswego 11-1843 for Alex.; cf Creek 1-1847 for Sarah; ct Adrian, Mich. 4-7-1869 for all
Anna b L. I. d 10-3-1823 ae 66y bHS (wd)
Ann b L. I. d 9-28-1848 ae 84y 14d bHS (wd)
Anna B., dt Silas B. & Emma (Willets), b Bkn. 12-31-1879; m 5-26-1925 John McDowell BUNN (H)
Benjamin (nm) b N. Y. d 6-11-1819 ae 21y bHS (unm)
Benjamin & Deborah (H)
Ch: Abraham
cf Chap. 4-1837; ct Chap. 2-1842
Benjamin K., s James & Lydia H., b 10-9-1839; dis mo 4-5-1865
Charity d 5-3-1803 ae 85y bHS
Charles Melville (nm), s Washington W. & Cynthia (E----), d 12-5-1912; m 6-27-1906 Alice H. CLOUGH, dt Dana B. & Lucinda E., b Lock Haven, Pa. 5-10-1879 (H)
Alice recrq 10-7-1899
Cornelius, s John & Ann, dis 4-1856 (H)
Dorothy gct Ama. 11-6-1811 (clear)
Edwin W., s Silas B. & Emma (Willets), b 6-10-1876; cf Wby with mother 5-6-1885; ct Wby 9-13-1920 (H)
Elizabeth, dt Thomas T. & Mary, b 10-4-1827; in Birmingham, Erie Co., Ohio 1858; rel 5-6-1869, absent 5y (H)
Hannah m Henry SUTTON (H)
cf Alexandria for Henry & ch 1-2-1861
Hannah, dt James, d 7-3-1920 ae 79y bPP; m John CROMWELL (H) (both nm)
Henry H., s Thos. T. & Mary (Hoag), b 3-10-1831 d 5-16-1912; m 10-14-1872 Louise J. SHAFFER (nm), dt Thos. & Amanda HAZARD (H) at Kipton, Ont. 1900
Hester (nm) b Greene Co. d 4-22-1833 ae 25y bHS
Isaac m Phebe ----- d 6-12-1863 ae 89y 9m 4d bPP (m Pur. 1803)
Ch: Charity b 3-30-1804
Jane " 1-11-1806
Jesse
Sarah " 3-25-1810
Phebe " 4- 2-1812
Samuel
Isaac rocf Pur. 7-9-1801 (clear); took cert of clear to Pur. 6-2-1803; Phebe rocf Pur. 8-11-1803; ct Scipio 5-7-1823 for all; cf Chap. 5-10-1816 for both with 6 ch named
James (nm) b N. Y. d 3-29-1827 ae 26y bHS (unm)
James d 8-29-1841; m Mary ----- d 7-12-1835 (H)
Ch: Edmund b 1-20-1808 d 3-18-1856
Jesse " 8- 5-1810
Melissa b 5-18-1812 d 2- 6-1844
Robert H. b 12-23-1813
Rebecca " 8- 1-1817
cf Chap. 3-13-1828; all dis 1830-1840 (0)
James, s Benjamin; m Lydia H. ----- d 9-27-1866
Ch: Mary H.
Abraham H.
Adaline b 10- 3-1826
Deborah b 11-24-1829 d 12- 7-1830
Benjamin K. b 10- 9-1839
Infant stillborn 7-23-1835
cf Ama. 10-1825 with first 2 ch; all dis 1829-1849 (0); ct Chap. 8-5-1868 for James
James Edward, s Jesse K. & Eliza, b 2-12-1830 d 11- 9-1899 bPP; m 4-23-1861 Emma Jane CARPENTER, dt Thos. & Sarah (Weeks), b New Castle 5-23-1839 d 2-21-1916 bPP (H)
Ch: Ada Louise b 2-26-1864
cf Chap. 11-1862 for Emma
Jane S., dt Jesse K. & Eliza, b 2-14-1814; m 1836 Aaron CARPENTER (H)
Jesse, s James & Mary, b 8-5-1810; rocf Chap. 3-13-1828 with parents; dis 4-7-1847 (H)
Jesse K. d 8-5-1857 ae 66y 11m bPP; m Eliza ----- d 6-4-1866 ae 79y 2m 12d bPP (H)
Ch: Jane S. b 2-14-1814
Daniel S. b 5-12-1818 d 7-28-1895
Moses H. b 10-29-1820 d 4- 8-1906
Phebe S. b 9-26-1827
James Edward b 2-12-1830
Sarah Louisa b 5-10-1833 d 12-16-1902 bPP
cf Chap. 1829 (0); all dis 1830-1849 (0); cf Chap. 10-1830 (H)
John d 2-26-1837; m Ann ----- d 4-8-1880
Ch: Mary
Samuel
Cornelius
cf Wby 5-16-1827 for all;all dis 1829-1849 (0)
Joshua rocf Chap. 1-14-1814 (clear); ct Chap. 12- 6-1815
Leonard K. rocf Chap. 5-1839; ct Chap. 10-1855 (H)
Lydia M., dt Thos. T. & Mary (Hoag), b New Castle, N. Y. 2-16-1822 d 1-18-1905; m 1846 Edgar WRIGHT (H)
cf Chap. with parents 11-18-1835; dis 5-5-1847; rst
Mary, wd George, Wby; m 1726 Roger HARRISON
Mary, dt James & Lydia (Hoag), b So. Salem, N. J. 12-23-1821 d 4-25-1909; m 1868 Benjamin GILMORE (H)
cf Ama. with parents 10-1825
Mary, dt John & Ann, d before 1900; m John DICKINSON (H)
cf Wby with parents 5-16-1827; ret a mbr
Mary, w -----
Ch: Mary Ella
cf Chap. 1-1866 for both; ct Chap. 3-2-

WEEKS, Mary, continued
1870 for both
Mary H., dt James & Lydia; m 6-1-1868 Benjamin GILMORE (H)
cf Ama. with parents 10-1825
Moses K., s Jesse K. & Eliza, b 10-29-1820; m a nm (H)
Nathaniel M., s Richard &Semantha, d 3-10-1874; m 1858 Sarah Elizabeth ALLEY, dt Sidney B. & Eliz. (Titus), b 8-21-1839 d 11-4-1903 (H)
Ch: Ida L. b 2-1873 d 3- 4-1874
Alice L. d 11- 2-1862 ae 2y 1m 14d
cf Farm. 10-28-1847, minor; cf Wby 3-1868 for Sarah
Peninah m ----- DEAL (H)
ret a mbr; cf Chap. 1-1835; ct Pur. 11-1837
Phebe d 6-12-1863 ae 89y 9m bPP
Phebe, dt Jesse & Sarah, N. Y.; m 1804 Job COLLINS
cf Chap. 7-9-1802
Phebe, N.P. rpd to women's mtg that she rq rst, which N.P. approved 2-5-1823; way not clear; joint comm. & involved dealing, apparently adverse 3-5-1823
Phebe Jane, dt Richard & Semantha, b Milan, N. Y. 11-21-1828 d 1-12-1908; m 10-21-1850 David KETCHAM (nm) (H)
cf Oswego with mother 1-1844
Phebe S., dt Jesse K. & Eliza, N. Y., b 9-26-1827; m 1859 William T. CARPENTER (H)
Rebecca, dt James & Mary, b 8-1-1817; m James MILLER (mo) (H)
cf Chap. 3-13-1828 with parents; dis 8-2-1848
Richard & Martha
Ch: Hannah
Elizabeth
Samuel b 4-22-1793
Martha b 10- 8-1795
cf Jericho 4-18-1793 with 2 dt (clear); ct Wby 5-4-1796, dt clear
Richard & Semantha (H)
Ch: Phebe Jane
Samuel
Nathaniel M.
cf Oswego 1-1844 for Semantha & Phebe Jane; Semantha m 2d Samuel FROST 9-9-1846; ct Creek 1-1847
Robert H., s James & Mary, b 12-23-1813; cf Chap. 3-13-1828 with parents; rel 7-5-1871, absent over 5y (H)
Robert S. rocf Farm. to Creek 10-28-1847 & cf Creek 2-16-1849; d 1-17-1886 (H)
in Toledo 1858
Samuel, s John & Ann, rocf Wby 5-16-1827 with parents; dis 9-1837 (H)
Samuel C., s Richard & Semantha, d 6-1-1874; m 9-24-1853 Anna B. BULL, dt Ebenezer & Jane (Pearsall), b Hamptonburgh, N. Y. 9-15-1828 d Hamptonburgh, N. Y. 5-26-1921 ae 93y (H)
cf Oswego 8-1853 for Samuel; cf Corn 3-1855 for Anna
Samuel M. rocf Farm. 5-1848; m Wby 10-1858; at Adrian later (H)
Sandford H., Jr., s Leonard K. & Ann H., b N.Y. 6-21-1844 d 9-17-1905; m 10-18-1865 Dorinda E. VAN TASSEL, dt Wright & Phebe, b Mt. Kisco 5-28-1850 d 9-19-1905 (H)
both recrq 3-7-1894
Sarah H., dt Thos. T. & Mary, b 5-14-1820; m ----- DARLY (H)
cf Chap. with parents 11-8-1825; rel 5-6-1869; absent 5y; in Erie Co., Ohio 1855
Silas B., s Benjamin & Susan M. (Burling), b Somers, N. Y. 5-3-1846 d 1-29-1907; m 5-13-1875 Emma WILLETS, dt Isaac U. & Mary (Cromwell), b Mineola, L. I. 7-10-1852 d 8-26-1912 at E. Willeston, L. I. (H)
Ch: Edwin Willets b 6-10-1876
Anna Bertha b 12-31-1879
Sarah Cromwell b 10- 3-1884
cf Ama. for Silas 5-6-1885; cf Wby for others 5-6-1885
Stephen rocf Wby 6-17-1795; ct Scipio 9-4-1822
Stephen d 3-12-1867 ae 78y bPP; m Hannah ----- d 8-11-1872 bPP (H)
cf Corn. 3-27-1823 for both; dis 1829-1832 (O); Stephen relrq 7-1843
Thomas F. & -----
Ch: Benjamin b Dutchess Co. d 3-10-1830 ae 6m bHS
Thomas T. m Mary ----- b Ulster Co. d 5-3-1833 ae 31y (H)
Ch: Sarah H. b 5-14-1820
Lydia " 2-16-1822
Sanford " 8- 9-1825 d 3- 2-1827
Elizabeth b 10- 4-1827
Benjamin K. b 8-29-1829 d 3-10-1830
Henry H. " 3-10-1831
cf Chap. 11- 8-1825; all dis 1830-1848 (O)
Thomas T. m 2d Freelove FOWLER (H)
Thomas dis 9-1836; Freelove dis 5-1836
Willet rocf Chap. 2-11-1830 (clear); dis 4-1831 (O); dis 11-1-1848 (H)
Wm. Burling, s Benj. & Susan M. (Burling), b Md. 7-2-1857 d 7-5-1934 bPP; m 6-7-1886 Marion ALLEN (nm), dt Martin D. & Adelaide L. (H)
Zeno (nm) b L. I. d 1-18-1819 ae 64y 24d bHS (m)
----- & ----- (nm)
Ch: Martha b New Castle d 7-14-1810 ae 4y 4m bHS
Jane Ann d 5-26-1814 ae 1y 8m bHS
Robert H. b N. Y. d 12-21-1821 ae 1y 6m bHS
John D. d 2-13-1827 ae 7m 2d bHS
Sanford b Westchester Co. d 3-2-1827 ae 1y 7m bHS
Theodore b N. Y. d 2-2-1837 ae 19d bHS
Allithena b N. Y. d 5-29-1841 ae 1y 4m bHS

WEGER
Joseph (nm), s Gottlieb & Mary (Bok); m 12-25-1921 Renee WALL, dt Philip & Anna Frances

WEGER, Joseph & Renee, continued
(Delsomme), b 12-1-1900 (H)
Renee recrq 1-11-1932

WEIKERT
Emma Johnson rocf Cincin. 12-1881; letter to Englewood Presby. Ch. 4-1922

WEIMER
Karl John m Ruby S. ROACH, dt Mary R.
Ch: Karl John Jr. b 5-19-1911; active 7-1925
Robert A. b 1-23-1918; active 3-4-1935
father recrq 2-2-1916; Ruby rec with her mother 11-7-1906

WEINWURM
Grace, s Maurice & Anna (Brandeis), b London 10-16-1907; cf London, Eng. 8-14-1933 (H)

WEISMAN
Harriet m ----- TAYLOR (nm)
letter from Oliver Pres. Ch., Bkn. 7-2-1902; letter to M. E. Ch., South Meriden, Conn. 7-1923

WELDING
Anna H., dt Watson J. & Sarah H.; m 1881 John ATKINSON
ct Phila. 5-1886
Watson J. d 3-2-1881; m Sarah H. ----- d 5-6-1866 ae about 40y bPP
Ch: William H.
Charles F. d 9-21-1875
Anna H.
cf WD MM 3-1853 with 3 ch named; Wm. H. unknown 1912
William H., s Watson J. & Sarah H., rocf WD MM 3-1853 with parents; name erased 4-1928

WELDON
Hannah G., dt Josiah & Phebe BARNES, b 8-22-1827 d 2-22-1891 (H)
ret a mbr

WELLS
Ernest rocf Northampton & Wellingboro, Eng. 7-10-1907
Gideon Hill (nm) d 3-26-1837 ae 71y 6m 1d bHS
Lamar G. rocf Chesterfield 11-2-1830; dis 2-1838

WELLSTOOD
James rq 4-7-1819, ret to him 8-2-1819

WELSH
Lewis E., s John S. & Lena (Schlager), b Hawley, Pa. 11-21-1888; m 10-7-1919 Therese Marie HOHOFF-HALLOCK, dt Ernest A. & Anna (Hallock), b N. Y. 7-3-1898 (H)
Ch: Ann b N. Y. 9-3-1922
John Hallock b 12-21-1924
Lewis E. recrq 6-12-1922; divorced 1929; the ch assigned to Lewis
Mary, dt Joseph B. & Emelia L. (Taylor), b E. Bethlehem, Pa. 1-26-1876; m 1902 John Paul J. WILLIAMS (H)
both recrq 5-13-1918

WEMMELL
A. Andrew (nm), s Andrew & Ann E.; m 11-25-1875 Sarah Rebecca JOHNSON, dt Rich. A. & Eliz. (Hampton), b Darlington, Pa. 2-27-1857 d 4-19-1935 (H)
cf Makefield, Pa. 12-1-1880 for Sarah

WENTWORTH
Mary (nm) m James McCONAUGHY (nm) (2d w)

WERNER
Edgar Schell (nm), s Philip P. & Mary M., Wash., D. C.; m 6-3-1896 Melle Stanleyetta TITUS, dt Jos. (dec) & Ruth Amelia, N. Y. (H)
Stanleyetta recrq 3-4-1885; the first woman admitted to the Bar in N.Y. State; relrq 8-12-1916
----- (nm) m Helen Edith YOTT; dt Malcolm C. & Edith M.
Helen recrq 7-11-1906

WEST
Caroline, dt Geo. W. & Mary (Chaffin), b Booneville, Mo. 6-8-1847; m 1884 Adrian VAN HELDEN (H)
recrq 6-13-1914; ct Swarthmore 11-11-1918
Col. West, form Governor of Carolina, left a legacy to Friends of London. Duplicate of his will sent to London by the mtg 1697 & recorded in Secretary's office in N. Y.
Eli rocf Balt. 3-1837; d 6-1-1881 ae 78y bPP
Elizabeth, dt Peter WOOD, d 12-12-1804 ae 52y bHS
Isaac rocf Collins 10-1837; rel 7-5-1871, absent over 5y
Lena m T. Homer COFFIN
recrq 3-6-1907; letter for both with 2 ch to First Presb. Ch., Portland, Ore. 7-1915
Sarah, dt Joseph & Mary; m 1848 Thomas DENNIE (H)
cf Balt. 5-5-1869
Susan P., dt Amos & Eliz. (Coates), b Balt. 10-1813 d 3-25-1905 ae 91y 5m; m 1848 Henry JACKSON
William A. (nm) m Josephine A. THORNE, dt Levi E. & Anna R., d 3-7-1929
cf Cincin. 1-1880 for Josephine with parents

WESTALL
George W., s John W. & Catharine S. (Wiebert), b Corn. 2-22-1872 d 6-12-1935; m 2-23-1898 Elizabeth COCKS (mbr Corn), dt Rowland & Mary M. (Torrey) (H)
George recrq 11-12-1917

WESTERVELT
Elenor (form Dickinson) dis mo
----- (nm) m Eleanor Jane DICKINSON (mo)
Ch: (prob) Theodore W. d 1-20-1840 ae ly 7m bHS
Edward H. b N. Y. d 2-3-1840 ae 3y 4m 3d bHS
cf Corn. for Eleanor 1-1829; dis mo 1834

WETHERALD
George rocf Tiperrary 8-1860; mbrp relinquished 12-1868 for mo
James & Mary Anne
cf Lisburn 12-12-1844; ct Pickering 9-1867

WHARTON
Dorcas (late Clark) dis mo before 7-3-1805
Mary, dt Wm. Jr. & Anna (Walter), b Phila. 11-8-1858; m 1885 Dr. Walter MENDELSON (H)
cf Green St., Phila. 9-1-1886; ct Germantown 1-10-1921
Samuel (nm) b Phila. d 8-25-1828 ae 18y bHS (unm)
----- & ----- (nm)
Ch: Mary Frances b N. Y. d 5-12-1842 ae 2y 6m bHS

WHEELER
Anna L. (nm) d 5-23-1874 ae 59y bPP (H)
Clark (nm), s Samuel (nm) d 5-24-1865 ae 52y 8m 10d bPP
Daniel d 6-15-1840 ae 69y 6m 16d bHS, rem to PP, rem from PP to -----
on a religious visit with cert of London YM (author)
Edna V. recrq 12-2-1903; d rpd 4-1928
Elias & Sarah
Ch: Daniel
Joseph
cf Ama. 4-16-1814 for both; ct Licking Creek, Ind. 11-4-1818 for Elias & his 2 minor ch named
Julia C. (nm), dt B. C. & Julia C.; m 1880 William Francis DAVENPORT (H)

WHERLEY
Abraham, N. Y., mbr 1676

WHESON
Thomas active contributor 1685-1686

WHIPPLE (see Whippo)
John dis mo 12-2-1762

WHIPPO
Deborah (nm) b L. I. d 2-8-1833 ae 79y bHS (wd)
John (nm) b L. I. d 1-14-1829 ae 81y 6m bHS
Laurence, s John, d 10-18-1802 ae 25
Maria, dt John & Deborah, N. Y.; m ----- ROBINS; m 2d 1820 Edmund KIRBY
Priscilla (nm) b N. Y. d 5-26-1842 ae 62y bHS (unm)

WHITAKER
Thomas A., s Thos. & Frances F. (both dec), Providence, R. I.; m at Mary Alley's (not under care of N. Y. MM) 5-24-1860 Louise ALLEY, dt Saul (dec) & Mary, N. Y. (H)

WHITALL
Anna M., dt Israel & Alice E.; m ----- FOSTER (mo)
cf Phila. 12-1854 with parents; dis mo 11-1856
Caroline, dt Israel F. & Alice, N. Y.; m 1857 Henry LAWRENCE
cf Phila. 12-1854 with parents; dis
Charles D. rocf WD MM 9-1870; mo before 3-1874, ret a mbr; ct Minneapolis 4-1880
Israel F. & Alice E.
Ch: Anna M.
Caroline
Alice B.
cf Phila. 12-1854 with 3 ch named; ct Gwynedd 1-1858 with Alice
Dr. Samuel rocf ND MM 8-1863; d 2-18-1882
Sarah R. d 12-22-1897; mo before 2-1872, ret a mbr; cf Woodbury 2-1884

WHITE
Aaron d 10-12-1798 bHS
Alice B., w Henry Alva, dt ----- PAIGE (m 9-7-1910)
cf Salem, Mass. 11-6-1907; ct High Point, N. C. 11-2-1910
Allen & -----
Ch: Peter b N. Y. d 11-20-1830 ae ly 6m bHS
cf Shrews. 8-1-1808; dis mo 12-2-1818
Amos d 11-17-1846 ae 69y bPP; m Ann ----- d 7-17-1843 ae 63y bPP (H)
Ch: Mary B.
Jane
Amos
Joseph
Sarah Ann b 9-10-1810
Elizabeth d 9-14-1847
Peter b 11-4-1815
Hannah b 6- 2-1818
cf Shrews. 11-5-1804 with 2 dt; all dis 1830-1839 (0)
Amos, s Amos & Ann, dis mo 4-1834
Ann, dt John & Elizabeth, b 5-30-1787; dis 10-1830 (0); d 2-3-1840
Anna, dt Robt. Cornell White & Hannah, rocf Shrews. with mother 2-4-1846; relrq 9-1855 (H)
Anna D., dt Francis & Susan RATHBONE, rocf Creek with mother 4-1861; ct Raysville, Ind. 4-1880
Anna J., dt Amos & Ann, dis 4-1834 (H)
Benjamin F., s John & Elizabeth, b 12-18-1782; ct Pur. 5-10-1798, placed with a Friend; cf Pur. (not found); missing, sailed in the Brig "Mary", for Antigua, 1803
Britton, Jr. & -----
Ch: Britton d 3-18-1804 ae ly 8m

WHITE, Britton, Jr., continued
cf Shrews. 5-4-1795, apprentice to Joseph Hopkins; ct ND MM 7-3-1799 (clear)
Charles E. (nm), s Chas. Farnum & Teresa (Deeds); m 6-30-1905 Alice GOODENOUGH, dt Thos. & Nancy S. (Kelley), b New Bedford, Mass. 5-28-1881 d 1-5-1933 (H)
Ch: Willis Farnum b 4-3-1921
Alice recrq 1-13-1930; Willis recrq of parents 3-10-1930
Clifford Burr, s Emmons & Sarah I. (Sleeper), b Holbrook, Mass. 12-9-1885; m 11-6-1909 Ruth Alice POWELL, dt Walter & Lucy G. ((Harned) b Bethpage 12-15-1886 (H)
Ch: Edmund Alden b S. I. 3-16-1913
Cynthia Burr b W. Collingswood, N. J. 4-17-1915
David Underhill b Atlantic City 8-7-1920
Clifford recrq 1-9-1909; Ruth rocf Jericho 2-8-1913
Cornelia, dt Geo. F. & Hannah T., b 5-24-1833; m 12-23-1862 Edwin MAYNARD (H)
Cornelia, dt Robt. Cornell & Hannah D. (Baker), d 3-11-1924 ae 65y bPP; m Walter Douglas DESPARD (H) (both nm)
Edna m Harry Noble WRIGHT
cf West Richmond, Ind. 11-3-1932 for both
Edward, O.B., m at Simon Cooper's 1 Mo (Mar) 1685/6 Mary COOPER, dt Simon & Mary, O.B. active contributor 1685
Edward H., s Geo. F. & Hannah T.; dis 6-1834 (H); dis mo 2-7-1838 (O)
Edward N. & -----
Ch: Charles B.
Edward Nelson, Jr.
ch recrq 4-3-1929; Roselle, N. J. 1928
Elizabeth rocf Pur. 2-13-1783; ct Pur. 8-3-1831 (clear)
Elizabeth rocf Shrews. 7-4-1814
Elizabeth, dt Geo. F. & Hannah T., b 3-11-1814; d at Bush Mills, near Giants Causeway Ireland 6-24-1875 (H)
Elizabeth, dt Patience, rocf Shrews. 6-2-1817 with mother; ct Pur. 8-1831
Elizabeth S. (nm) d 9-14-1848 ae 33y bPP
Esther gct Phila. 12-2-1756
George rocf Shrews. 12-4-1786, as apprentice or under care of John White; ct Shrews. 4-4-1792 (clear)
George, s John, rocf Pur. 8-9-1804, placed with a Friend
George F., s John & Elizabeth, N. Y., b 2-4-1789 d 10-9-1847; m N. Y. 4-9-1812 Hannah S. HAYDOCK, dt John W. & Elizabeth, N. Y., d 4-30-1867 ae 84y bPP (H)
Ch: Edmund b 3-16-1813
Elizabeth b 3-11-1814
Sarah H. b 10-5-1815 d 1-5-1859
Henry Kirk b 10-22-1818 d 12-26-1843
Edward H.
William H. d 6- 8-1844 ae 22y
Anna " 11- 5-1849 ae 22y
----- " 6-23-1832 ae 9m 8d
Ch: Cornelia b 5-24-1833
George dis 6-6-1820; rst 12-1832 (H); all dis 1830-1849 (O)
Hannah Mills (form White) mo; rocf Upper Springfield (clear); dis 1-2-1811
Hannah, dt Amos & Ann, b 6-2-1818 d 12-5-1869; m ----- STRATTON (mo) (H)
ret a mbr
Hannah rocf Oswego 2-1871; d 1-25-1883
Henry Beale, Mt. Mellick rpd him as mo
J. Corlies (nm) d 7-8-1872 ae 37y 6m 3d bPP (H)
Jane rocf Shrews. 1-1-1787 (clear); ct Shrews. 1-5-1791 (clear)
Jane, dt Patience, rocf Shrews. with mother 6-2-1817; ct Shrews. 1850
Jane rocf Flush. 5-1847; d 7-17-1866 (H)
Jennie E. recrq 6-1928
John & Elizabeth (mo 1778)
Ch: Benjamin F. b 12-18-1782
Ann b 5-30-1787 d 2-3-1840
George F. b 2- 4-1789
Sarah " 10-25-1790
Elizabeth
John rocf Shrews. 10-17-1771, rec 12-4-1771; dis mo 1-6-1779; con mo 4-4-1782
ct Pur. 4-6-1796 with the 4 above named, & Elizabeth b N. Y.; cf Pur. 6-12-1817 for Elizabeth with dt, Ann
John B., s John, rocf Pur. 2-13-1812, apprentice; d 8-30-1813
John F., s Joseph, d 6-17-1806 ae 61y bur Greenwood, rem to PP 4-24-1867; m Rachel C. ----- d 12-6-1881 ae 69y bur Greenwood, rem to PP 4-24-1867 (H)
cf Phila. Cherry St. 8-1852
John H. rocf Stanford 7-1836; ct Rochester 1-1848 (H)
Joseph, s Briton (or Brittain), rocf Shrews. 9-1-1806 (clear)
Joseph b Shrews. d 6-12-1817 ae 35y bHS (unm)
Joseph, s Amos & Ann, dis 4-1838
Joseph Baker (name changed from Abel Baker in childhood), s Robt. Cornell & Hannah (Baker); m 11-11-1897 Estelle PENDLETON (nm), dt Nathan & Lydia G., d 3-27-1927 ae 74y 1m 14d bPP (H)
Margaret Beale, Mount Mellick rpd her as mo
Marshall & -----
Ch: Henry Beale
Marshall
Thomas
Beale
Margaret Beale
on receipt of a letter from Wm. Wood, on behalf of N. Y., all dis by Mount Mellick, Ireland & N. Y. notified 9-21-1871
Mary Ann, w Philander, rocf Troy 5-1830; ct Troy 1-1838 (H)
Mary B., dt Amos & Ann, Bkn.; m 1833 Zephaniah BIRDSALL (H)
Mary B., dt Robert B. & Susan B. P. (Cook), b Shrews. 12-1-1869; m 1-27-1890 Charles W. BILLINGS (nm), s Stephen B. & Maria T. (H)

WHITE, Mary B., continued
cf Shrews. 4-4-1894
Oliver rocf So. 8th St., Richmond, Ind. 5-3-1905; ct So. 8th St., Richmond, Ind. 7-10-1907
Patience b N. J. d 1-18-1829 ae 72y 4m (wd)
Ch: Phebe
Jane
Peter
Elizabeth
cf Shrews. 6-2-1817 with ch; Peter & Jane dis 1828 (O); Patience & Phebe dis 1830 (H)
Peter rocf Shrews. 1-3-1774, rec 6-1-1775; ct Shrews. 12-6-1775
Peter rocf Shrews. 9-3-1804, apprentice to Samuel Falconer; had performed military service 11-2-1814; has obtained his discharge 12-7-1814; con his misconduct 3-1-1815
Phebe, dt Robert J. Cornell & Hannah G., gct Shrews. 7-2-1834, minor with brother, sister & mother
Rachel C., dt Robt. J. Cornell & Hannah G., N. Y.; m 1847 Joseph BAKER
ct Shrews. 7-2-1834, minor, with brother, sister & mother
Richard rocf Waterford, Ireland 4-25-1850, long mislaid & forwarded to Farm. 9-1856 where he now resides
Robert J., s Colvin & Phebe, N. Y., d 1-12-1856 ae 63y 1m 11d bPP; m N. Y. 4-9-1818 Hannah GIBBS, dt Abel (dec) & Eliz., N.Y., d 9-22-1872 ae 75y bPP (H)
Ch: Abel b 10-18-1819 d 8-30-1820
Robert b 12-10-1821
Phebe
Robert Cornell
Rachel b 1-10-1826
Anna
Robert recrq 10-6-1813; ct Warwickshire North 10-2-1822 with ch, Phebe; cf Warwichshire North 5-13-1824 with 2 ch; parents dis 1829 (O); ct Shrews. 7-1834 for ch (O); cf Shrews. 12-1833; cf Shrews. 2-4-1846 for Hannah G.; ct Shrews. 4-5-1865 for her; Robert dis 3-1832 (H); Robert offered resignation 11-1828, & was discontinued 1829 (O)
Robert Barnes, s Wm. C. & Mary, b 7-11-1837; ct Shrews. 3-2-1859 (H)
Robert Bowne rocf Shrews. 8-5-1805, apprentice to Robert Bowne
Robt. Brown dis 5-1-1816
Robert Cornell, s Robt. Jr. & Hannah G., N. Y., d 8-29-1884 ae 60y 9m 29d bPP; m at Dobel Baker's 11-4-1847 Hannah D. BAKER, dt Dobel & Mary C., N. Y., d 5-20-1914 ae 88y 4m 3d bPP (H)
Ch: Henry Haydock b 9-13-1848 d 1-11-1880 ae 31y 3m 28d bPP
Ch: Sarah Baker b 6-2-1851 d 5-31-1861 ae 9y 11m 29d bPP
Joseph Baker b 6-15-1854
Cornelia

ct Shrews. 7-2-1834 for Robert C., minor, with mother & sisters (O); cf Shrews. 9-1845 for Robt. C.; Robert dis 3-2-1859 (O) for non-attendance; Hannah relrq 2-1862 (O)
Sarah, dt Patience; m ----- SKELTON (mo)
cf Shrews. 2-2-1801 (clear); dis mo 8-4-1802
Sarah, dt John & Elizabeth, N. Y.; m ----- CORLIES; m 2d 1836 Charles MARRIOTT (H)
Sarah Ann, dt Amos & Ann, b 9-10-1810 d 11-13-1883 ae 67y (?); m ----- MATHEWS (mo) (H)
William rocf Flushing 12-3-1810, apprentice
William C., s Robert & Esther (dec), N. Y., b 9-8-1794 d 6-13-1880; m N. Y. 9-14-1820 Mary BARNES, dt Robert & Eliz. (dec), N.Y., b 3-1-1796 d 2-6-1877 (H)
Ch: Elizabeth B. b 7-20-1821 d 2-8-1877
Caroline b 8-24-1822 d 4-12-1830 bur in grave of Robt. Barnes, PP
Mary Anna b 8- 4-1826 d 9-14-1835 bur in grave of Robt. Barnes, PP
William C. Jr. b 6- 4-1834 d 4-27-1842 bur in grave of Robt. Barnes, PP
Robert Barnes b 7-11-1837
all dis 1829-1843 (O)

WHITEHEAD
Elisha & Rachel
Ch: Elizabeth b 1-31-1789; m 1806 ----- EVERS
Joseph b 8-12-1790 d 8-24-1809 ae 19
Samuel b 1-26-1793
Hannah b 8-22-1798
Jesse b 11-17-1800
William b 7- 4-1803
Mary b 8-16-1805
David b 10-10-1807
cf R. & P. 8-16-1797 with their ch, Eliz., Jos. & Samuel; ct Concord, Ohio 1-6-1813 with their 6 ch last named
Elizabeth, dt Elisha & Rachel; m ----- EVERS (mo)
dis mo 1806
John (nm) b Eng. d 4-13-1826 ae 46y bHS (m)

WHITEHOUSE
Catharine rocf Chap. 4-15-1785; ct Wby 5-1-1788 with John Whitehouse
John rocf Pur. 5-10-1786; ct Wby 5-1-1788 for John & Catharine Whitehouse

WHITFIELD
Jane m Elijah HARRIS
recrq 3-1870; ret a mbr; ct Cottonwood 6-1882
Rebecca d 2-7-1915; m ----- DUMARTHARAY (nm)

WHITFIELD, Rebecca, continued
recrq 2-4-1874
Selena Grace m John BYRNE
recrq 7-1872 as Grace
Susan d 5-5-1919; m ----- RAYNOR
cf Lurgan, Ireland 5-1870; ret a mbr

WHITING
Phebe Latham (form Whiting) rocf Pur. 5-9-1827 (clear); dis 1-1830 (O); dis 4-1837 (H)

WHITLEY
James H. (nm) (probably) m Elizabeth ----- d 1-26-1886 ae 86y bPP
Ch: ----- (dt) d 12-2-1863 ae 9d bPP
----- (s) d 9-1865 stillborn bPP
Martha, dt Jonathan & Philena BIRDSALL; name erased 4-1928; unknown 1912
----- & ----- (nm)
Ch: Edgar d 10-18-1888 ae 22y bPP

WHITLOCK
Lydia rocf Ferrisburgh 10-1872; ct Chap. 2-1877

WHITMAN
Isaac m Nancy ----- d 12-30-1853 ae 60y 3m 20d bPP (H)
Ch: Isaac b Nantucket d 10-3-1833 ae 2y 1m bHS

WHITNEY
George G. & Janet E.
Ch: William Gillett b 8-20-1920
cf Westminster & Longford Eng. 6-12-1918 for parents; ct Westtown, Pa. 3-1921 for all
James H. (nm) d about 1891 bPP
Nella, dt Chas. B. & Katie Gould (Robinson), b Chelsea, Mass. 1-10-1889; m 1915 Winthrop STEARNS
Sarah, dt Richard A. & Esther TITUS, rocf Oswego 9-1833; dis 12-1833 (H)
Sarah T. rocf Wby 3-4-1857; d 2-6-1889 (H)
William H. A. (nm) & -----
Ch: Infant d 3-12-1837 ae 1d bHS

WHITSON
Abigail P., dt John PLUMMER, rocf Jericho 7-1845; ct Wby 9-3-1862 (H)
Ann, dt Jos. & Hannah, N. Y.; m 1829 John HILYARD
dis 10-1829 (H)
Charity recrq 7-1836; d 10-15-1840 (H)
Daniel rocf Jericho 10-1829; d Flushing 5-26-1839 (H)
David (nm) & -----
Ch: Ludlow d 9-10-1832 ae 1y 21d bHS
Charles b Ulster Co. d 7-29-1841 ae 1y 4m 15d bHS
David, s Abraham, Flushing, rocf Flushing 6-1832; dis mo 3-6-1833 (O); ret a mbr (H); In Madison, Wis. 1878-1889
Esther Willets (form Whitson) dis 11-2-1831
Florence Edna, dt Henry & Phebe, b 4-30-1901 ae 24y 11m bPP; m Harry BROWN (H) (both nm)
Gilbert E., s Joseph & Hannah; m ----- (mo before 4-1835) (H)
Ch: (prob) Gilbert b Boston d 11-1-1840 ae 2y 4m bHS
referred to Salem, Mass. 5-6-1835 but unknown there; at Roxbury, Mass. a Mfg. of grate & fender fixtures; dis 4-4-1838 (O); dis 4-1835 (H)
Henry d 5-25-1878 ae 45y; m Phebe ----- d 2-12-1899 ae 58y 8m 20d bPP (H)
Jacob H. rocf Jericho 9-1836; ct Flushing 4-1854 (H)
John, s Joseph & Hannah, dis 2-1840 under Orthodox rule; d 1-23-1853 ae 37y bPP (H)
Joseph m Hannah ----- d 7-4-1858 ae 73y bPP (H)
Ch: Jacob S. b L. I. d 8-29-1831 ae 25y
Maria d 5-27-1863 ae 56y 2m 9d bPP
Ann
Thomas
Gilbert E.
John
Samuel S. d 1- 7-1844 ae 26y 3m 4d
Margaret " 8-15-1854 ae 34y 5m bPP
Susan H.
Edward (or Edmund) Hicks b 1-6-1825 d 3-31-1830
cf Wby 4-14-1824 (Joseph, the father, d 2-17-1833 ae 50y
Margaret (nm) d 8-15-1854 ae 34y 5m bPP
Mary E. (mbr Wby), dt Samuel & Phebe, Jr.; m 1900 Edgar J. TAYLOR (H)
Phebe, w Henry, dt Daniel & Ann Eliza MILLER, b 5-26-1840 d 2-12-1899 (m 4-22-1857); ret a mbr (H)
Sarah m Thomas UNDERHILL (H)
ct Wby with Thomas & ch 8-2-1826
Susan H., dt Joseph & Hannah; m 5-1-1860 Alex. H. CAMPBELL (mo) (H)
ret a mbr
Thomas, s Joseph & Hannah; mo; dis 6-1834; dis 4-4-1838 (O)
Thomas, Jr., Bethpage; m Wby 3 Mo (May) 9, 1716 Deborah FEAKS
----- & ----- (nm)
Ch: Thomas U. b N. Y. d 5-15-1840 ae 9m bHS

WHITTAKER
Harry H. recrq 7-1925

WHITTEN
Henry John rocf Dublin 9-1854, ret.; dis by Dublin 3-13-1855 & N. Y. asked to inform him

WICK
----- (nm) m Martha B. GOERKE, dt Rudolph & Paulina, b 10-8-1860; name erased 4-1928

WICKERSHAM
Amos Jr. rocf Phila. 9-24-1812; ct Radnor 8-3-1836 (clear) (O); ct Radnor 9-1836 (H)

WICKES
George F. d 3-1-1896; m M. Louisa ----- d 3-26-1905
both recrq 4-1886

WIDDIFIELD
Charles rocf Phila. Cherry St. 3-1844; d 9-17-1869 (H)
Samuel rocf Phila. Cherry St. 12-1845; d 2-21-1889 (H)

WIGAM
Isaac & -----
Ch: John S. b N. Y. d 3-6-1825 ae 3y 10m 6d bHS

WIGERT
Mary F., w Arthur, rocf Phila. 2-1867; ct WD MM 2-7-1894

WIGHAM
Elizabeth, dt Isaac & Mary S., b 3-18-1819; dis mo 1850
Isaac d 9-3-1832 ae 54y bHS; m Jericho 1818 Mary L. ----- d 5-25-1875
Ch: Elizabeth b 3-18-1819
John S. b 4-13-1821 d 3- 6-1825
Thomas b 3-,2-1826
Mary Caroline b 4-16-1828
cf Brighouse 9-16-1808 (clear); cert of clear to Jericho 5-6-1818; Mary S. rocf Jericho 12-17-1818; parents dis 1829 (H)
Thomas, s Isaac & Mary S., b 3-2-1826; dis non-attendance 7-1857

WILBACKS
Stephen gct Dartmouth, Mass. 12 Mo (Feb) 6, 1745/6

WILBER
Emma F. recrq 6-7-1911; d 1911
William rocf Easton 6-7-1824 (clear); dis 1-1831 (O); ct Easton

WILBOUR
Amy R. rocf R. I. 8-27-1874; d 8-26-1893
Israel (nm) b Wash. Co. d 1-2-1835 ae 26y bHS (unm)

WILBUR
Elizabeth, dt Allen E. & Jane (Lawton), b No. Easton 12-29-1850 d 11-29-1932; m 1869 Charles B. HOAG (nm) (H)
cf Easton 12-4-1897
Henry W., s Humphrey & Ann (Pierce), b Easton, N. Y. 5-15-1851 d Sara. Spg. 9-5-1914; m 10-21-1880 Eliza M. SOWLE, dt Jethro & Mary (Grinnell), b Little Compton, R. I. 9-7-1849 d 2-23-1922 (H)
Ch: William Pierce b 11-25-1885 d 6-21-1920
John Finch b 1-22-1887 d 8-10-1920
cf Easton 11-7-1896 for Henry; Eliza recrq 7-7-1900; ch's names entered by MM 3-5-1898; Ernest an eloquent preacher

WILCOMB
John (nm) d 9-26-1870 ae 77y bPP; m Hannah ----- (nm) d 1864 bPP
Ch: Charles K. d 5-6-1853 ae 20y 6m bPP

WILCOX
Maria, dt Sarah, rocf Albany 3-5-1851 with mother; dis 4-2-1862 for non-attendance & jas (H)
Sarah, w ----- (H)
Ch: Maria
cf Albany 3-5-1851 with dt; ct Easton for Sarah 4-5-1865
Sidney (late Randolph b N. J. d 12-19-1829 ae 30y 11m 20d bHS; dis mo 11-5-1823

WILDE
Charles, s John & Eleanor, rocf Plains 12-22-1829 with parents; ct Plains 6-5-1833 with parents; cf Plains 2-25-1834 with parents
Elizabeth, dt John & Eleanor, dis 1855
Harriet, dt John & Eleanor, dis 1-1854
Herbert, s John & Eleanor, dis 8-1842
Jennet (or Jane), dt John & Eleanor; m ----- MORELAND (mo)
dis mo 9-4-1839
John & Eleanor
Ch: Jennet (or Jane)
Herbert
Mary
William
Jonathan
Sarah Ann
Harriet
Charles b 9-16-1830
cf Plains 12-22-1829 with 7 ch named; ct Plains 6-5-1833 with 5 minor last named; cf Plains 2-25-1834 with 5 minor ch (last named); Elizabeth given as another ch in Reg.
Jonathan, s John & Eleanor, charged with enlisting in U.S. Army 9-1846 & mo; dis 10-1846, recorded 11-1846, although he had not actually enlisted; cf Plains 12-22-1829 with parents; ct Plains 6-5-1833 with parents; cf Plains 2-25-1834
Mary, dt John & Eleanor; m Emmor KNIGHT
Richard [Wildey], s Elizabeth, Flushing; m Flushing 8 Mo (Oct) 10, 1717 Patience TATUM, dt Samuel
Sarah Ann, dt John & Eleanor; m ----- NORTHRUP dis mo 6-1848; cf Plains 12-22-1829 with parents; ct Plains 6-5-1833 with parents; cf Plains 2-25-1834 with parents
William, s John & Eleanor, dis mo 12-1841; cf Plains 12-22-1829 with parents; ct Plains 6-5-1833 with parents; cf Plains 2-25-1834 with parents
----- [Wildey] m Elizabeth ----- wd, d 7 Mo (Sep) 13, 1748
Ch: Richard

WILEY
Phebe rocf Creek 8-1834; ct Clear Creek 6-7-1848 (H)
----- & ----- (nm)
Ch: William b N. Y. d 1-28-1843 ae 6m bHS

WILKENS
James De Voe, s J. G. H. & Hannah A., recrq 2-1925; d 12-5-1929
J. G. [Wilkins] (nm) m Hannah A. ----- d 9-1921
Ch: James De Voe
Hannah recrq 10-1876; James recrq 2-1925

WILLETS
Abraham [Willett] d 3-15-1799 bHS
Amelia, dt Samuel & Sarah H., N. Y.; m 1848 Edward MERRITT (H)
Amos, s Robert & Mary, d 10-17-1864; m Ann ---- d 10-17-1826
Ch: Daniel T.
Mary b 4- 1-1820
Amos m 2d Caroline ----- d 1-5-1859
cf Wby 4-17-1816 for Amos, Ann & Daniel; cf Flushing 6-1830 for Caroline
Amos m 3d at Willis Haviland's, Harts Village 12-20-1860 Phebe M. LAPHAM, dt Philip & Susanna HART, d 6-10-1880 (H)
cf N.P. 6-1861 for Phebe
Andrew, s Samuel & Hannah (dec), N. Y., d 5-27-1855; m N. Y. 5-11-1837 Sarah RUSHTON, dt James & Hannah (both dec), N. Y., d 4-25-1849 (H)
Ch: Samuel S. b 2-12-1838
James R. b 4-24-1841
Sarah rocf Brighouse, Eng. 7-20-1798 (clear)
Ann, dt John & Mary, Flushing; m 1738 John STEVENSON, of Newtown
Ann, dt Thomas, gct Little Egg Harbor 5-11-1809
Anna, dt Daniel T. & Eliz. T., N. Y., b 6-26-1839; m 1859 Thomas W. JENKINS (H)
Carrie S., dt Wm. U. & Clara H., b 1-1-1868; m Isaac S. Vanderbilt, Jr. (H)
Caroline F. rocf Flushing 3-5-1829
Charles rocf Wby 10-18-1815 (clear)
Charles Edwin, s Wm. J. & Annie Ann (Lapham), b 7-12-1840; cf Scip. 4-2-1856; name cancelled 4-9-1904 as long unknown
Clara Louise, dt Wm. U. & Clara (Hitt), b N.Y. 7-6-1878; m 1900 George Howard AMOS
her name entered by comm. 1-10-1879
Clara H. recrq 8-3-1892
Cornelia A., dt Jacob & Susan A., d 9-21-1894 ae 73y 8m 26d bPP; m Oliver GRIFFEN (H)
both nm
Cornelia W., dt Robert R. & Lydia; m 1874 John J. CARLE
recrq of parents 4-1857
Daniel rocf Wby 11-16-1803, he having ack. form mo
Daniel, s Edmond & Martha (Whitson), N. Hampstead, b Roslyn 3-21-1846; m at Henry Griffen's 10-6-1870 Hannah GRIFFEN, dt Henry & Martha (Valentine), Bkn. b 12-17-1850 Bkn. d 4-9-1910 (H)
Ch: Joseph J. b 10-22-1873 d 7-23-1874
Elizabeth b 8-15-1884
Henry Griffen b 12-17-1888
cf Wby 8-3-1870 for Daniel; ct Chesterfield, N. J. 4-12-1913 for Daniel
Daniel T., s Amos & Ann; m Elizabeth F. BOWNE d 1-15-1890 (mo before 6-9-1836) (H)
Ch: Edward B. b 6- 2-1837
Anna " 6-26-1839
Frederick " 8- 8-1841 d 1-24-1844
Eliza B. " 1- 4-1844
Daniel relrq 6-2-1869; dis m a Friend contrary to discipline 1-9-1839 (O); cf Flush. 10-1837 for Elizabeth
Deborah, wd, dt Samuel LAWRENCE, Flushing; m 1748 Samuel DOUGHTY
Deborah [Willett] (nm) b Schenectady d 5-30-1836 ae 19y 6m 25d bHS (unm)
Edmund & Martha (H)
Ch: Joseph b 10- 7-1830
Anna " 5-27-1833
Mary " 4-30-1836
Sarah Maria b 4- 7-1838
Martha H. " 5- 7-1841
Thomas W. " 8- 6-1843
Daniel " 3-21-1846
cf Wby 4-1826 for Edmund; cf Jericho 10-1830 for Martha
Edward, s Samuel & Hannah, b 2-25-1822 d Paris, France 10-13-1864 bPP; m at James R. Wood's (not under care of N.Y. MM) N. Y. 10-1-1857 Cornelia A. CROSSMAN, dt Alfred B. & Mary R HUNTINGTON, L. I., d 12-15-1908 ae 78y 11m 11d bPP (H)
Edward B., s Daniel T. & Eliz. F. (Bowne), N.Y. b 6-2-1837 N. Y. d 2-21-1916; m at Peter C. Barnum's, N. Y. (not under care of N.Y.MM) 4-16-1861 Sarah F. CARMAN (nm), dt Samuel R. (dec) & Sarah A., N. Y. (H)
Elbert S. rocf Flush. 11-1842; d 6-17-1852 (H)
Elizabeth, dt John & Mary, Flushing; m 1744 William BOWNE
Elizabeth, dt Samuel & Hannah (Carpenter), b N. Y. 11-4-1824; m 1848 Aaron G. HAVILAND (H)
Elizabeth (or Eliza B.), dt Daniel T. & Eliza, b 1-4-1844; m 6-20-1866 William T. LAWTON (H)
rel 5-5-1875
Elizabeth, dt Daniel & Hannah (Griffen), b 8-15-1884; relrq 2-12-1910 (H)
Elizabeth, dt John & Amelia, N. Y.; m 1893 Samuel W. LAMBERT (H)
Elizabeth F. (form Bowne) dis mo 6-7-1837
Elma C., dt Wm. U. & Clara H., b 4-2-1866; m 11-2-1887 Charles W. BAYLISS (nm) (H)
(Charles joined later)
Emma, dt Isaac U. & Mary (Cromwell), b Mineola, L. I. 7-10-1852 d 8-26-1912 at E. Williston, L. I.; m 1875 Silas B. WEEKS (H)
Esther (form Whitson) dis mo 11-2-1831
Esther, dt Samuel & Hannah, rocf Jer. 8-15-

WILLETS, Esther, continued
1823 with parents; ct Wby 4-3-1861 (H)
Frances, dt Caleb W. & Letitia BARNES; rocf Scip. with parents 1868; ct Chicago 3-1877
George d 9-7-1872; m Ann M. ----- d 3-17-1881 ae 72y bPP
cf Wby 4-13-1808; con mo & rst; ct Wby 6-7-1809
Grace Caroline, dt Jacob & Susan A., d 9-12-1925 ae 63y 7m 3d bPP; m Willet McCORD (H)
Hannah, dt Thomas & Dinah; m 1701 Samuel UNDERHILL
Hannah, dt Richard, rocf Wby 6-4-1783 with her father
Hannah, dt Richard & Eliz. LAWRENCE, d 5-25-1806 ae 70
Hannah, dt Samuel & Hannah, rocf Pur. 8-15-1823 with parents; ct Wby 4-3-1861 (H)
Hannah, dt Isaac & Amy, b 9-20-1836 d 12-4-1901; m Willet ROBBINS (H)
cf Jericho 9-4-1867
Helena, dt Abraham (dec), Flushing; m 1758 Joseph RODMAN
Henry & Phebe
Ch: Thomas
Anny
Phebe d 8-17-1803 ae 23
Martha
Richard
cf Little Egg Harbor 7-10-1794
Henry G., s Daniel & Hannah (Griffen), b 12-17-1888 d about 1920 or 1921; m 11-29-1913 Edith WEBBER (H)
Henry T. (or T. Henry), s Samuel & Hannah (both dec), m at Chas. M. Carpenter's, Bkn. 12-5-1867 Sophia UNDERHILL, dt Adonijah & Sarah U. (both dec), b 5-23-1830 d 6-28-1917 (H)
cf Jer. 8-1823 for Henry; ct Wby 4-3-1861 for Henry; ct Wby 7-1-1868 for Sophia
Harold Reginald, s Wm. U. & Clara (Hitt), b N. Y. 12-7-1886; m 12-11-1909 Florence Mary BALDWIN (nm) (H)
Howard, s John T. & Amelia, N. Y.; m at C. I. Macy's 1-20-1886 Mary Kingsland MACY, dt Josiah J. (dec) & Caroline L., N. Y., b 11-14-1860 (H)
Ida, dt Joseph & Esther (Griffen), b Bkn. 9-10-1856; m 6-1-1881 J. Sherwood COFFIN (nm), s And. G. & Eliz. S. (H)
ct Wby 11-5-1884
Jacob d 12-30-1871 ae 75y 1m 2d rem from Mamaroneck to PP; m Susan A. ----- b 1-19-1801 d 3-14-1885 ae 84y 1m 23d bPP (H)
Ch: Caroline
James
William U. b 6-29-1839
Cornelia A. d 9-21-1894 ae 73y 8m 26d bPP
cf Oswego 3-1845 with 3 ch; ct Chap. 10-1855 with 3 ch; cf Chap. 1-1859 with Wm.; ct Chap. 8-1863 for parents; cf Chap. 9-5-1877 for Susan A.
Jacob, grandson of Jacob, d 7-25-1860 ae 3m bPP
Jacob H., s Samuel & Sarah, b 9-1818; cf Flushing 3-1840 (H)
Jacob S. & Esther
Ch: Mary U.
Sarah Jane
cf Ama. 2-11-1831 with 1 ch named; ct Ama. with 2 ch 7-4-1832
James R., s Andrew & Sarah, b 4-24-1841; ct Wby 8-5-1863 (H)
Jane, dt Samuel & Hannah, rocf Jer. 8-15-1823, with parents; ct Wby 4-3-1861 (H)
John, s Col. Thomas, Flushing, d 11 Mo (Jan) 31, 1738/9; m Flushing 7 Mo (Sep) 14, 1714 Mary RODMAN, dt John & Mary
Ch: John b 4 Mo (June) 10, 1715
Thomas b 10 Mo (Dec) 10, 1716 d 12 Mo 8, 1727/8
Ann b 10 Mo (Dec) 19, 1718
Hannah b 12 Mo (Feb) 7, 1720/1
Jonathan b 8 Mo (Oct) 21, 1722
Samuel b 12 Mo (Feb) 15, 1723/4
Elizabeth b 10 Mo (Dec) 17, 1725
Mary b 6 Mo (Aug) 19, 1727
Helena b 4 Mo (June) 19, 1729
Thomas b 2 Mo (Apr) 4, 1731
Caroline b 12 Mo (Feb) 8, 1732/3 d 7 Mo 1751
Catharine b 6 Mo (Aug) 28, 1735 d 6 Mo 26, 1735 (dates of b & d apparently transposed)
Thomas, s John, d 2 Mo (Apr) 1, 1727
John T., s Robert R. & Lydia (Titus), N. Y., b 8-2-1835 N. Y. d 11-13-1912; m at S. Underhill's 11-2-1858 (not under care of N. Y. MM) Amelia UNDERHILL, dt Samuel & Hannah W., N. Y. (H)
Ch: Howard
Amelia mbr of Orthodox; ch not recorded in either mtg
Jonathan [Willett] with w rocf Wby 7-5-1758
Jonathan d 7 Mo (Sep) 1753; m Deborah -----
Ch: Obediah d 7 Mo (Sep) 1753
Anne " 7 Mo 1753
Elizabeth d 7 Mo 1753
Jonathan took ct Wrightstown, Pa. 9-4-1755 with w on their return from Pa. 8-3-1758; Jonathan & w, Deborah, gct Middleton 8-2-1759
Joseph, s Hope & Mary, Wby; m at Mary Willets', Jericho 11 Mo (Jan) 6, 1702/3 Deborah SIMONS, dt Solomon & Elizabeth, Wby
Joseph dis mo 5-1803
Joseph d 5-18-1855; m Phebe ----- d 1-8-1837 (H)
Ch: Rachel S. b 8-29-1817
William Jackson b 1-21-(or 1-20-) 1820
Latitia V. b 12-29-1821 d 10-19-1842
Jacob S. b 5-21-1825 d 3- 5-1847
Phebe Ann b 12-11-1826 d 3-18-1830
Charles b 2-15-1829 d 3-19-1830
Anna b 9-19-1831 d 10- 9-1831
cf Wby 3-19-1817 for both; all dis 1829-

WILLETS, Joseph & Phebe, continued
1842
Joseph m 2d 7-11-1838 N. Y. Jane F. FARRINGTON, dt Geo. & Elizabeth (both dec), N. Y., d 4-2-1856 (H)
cf Flushing 12-1830 for Jane
Joseph, s Edmond & Martha, Manhasset; m at John T. Griffen's, Williamsburgh, 10-5-1854 Esther GRIFFEN, dt Edmond (dec) & Abigail F., d 8-20-1871 (H)
Ch: Ida E. b 9-10-1856
Fannie A. b 10-12-1860
cf Wby 5-1852 for Joseph; ct Wby 1-7-1874 for father & ch
Joseph C., s Wm. J. & Annie Ann (Lapham), b 3-4-1846 d 8-31-1904; cf Scip. 4-2-1856 (H)
Mabel Maria, dt Robert R. & Tacie, b N. Y. 7-10-1884; m 1913 William Philip ABENDROTH (nm)
Maria, dt Robert R. & Lydia, b 4-7-1843 d 2-9-1903; recrq of mother 2-1849
Martha, dt Henry & Phebe, N. Y.; m 1802 John R. WILLIS
Martha rocf Wby & Jericho 11-20-1830 rem with h; dis
Martha E. T., dt Robt. R. & Tacie P., Harrison, b N. Y. 11-14-1885; m 1816 Hugo H. Lupinski, of Liberty, N. Y. (H)
Mary, dt Thomas, Jericho; m 1691 Thomas POWELL active mbr
Mary [Willett], dt Col. Thos., Flushing; m 1723 Samuel RODMAN
Mary dis mo before 11-2-1758
Mary gct Corn. 8-5-1807 (clear)
Mary, dt Joseph & Unity PANCOAST, d 7-29-1804 ae 29y 9m bHS
Mary, dt Samuel & Hannah, N. Y.; m 1824 Samuel P. UNDERHILL
Mary, dt Amos & Ann, N. Y., b N. Y. 4-1-1820; m 1840 Aaron WRIGHT (H)
Mary, dt Obadiah & Elizabeth; m Edmund KIRBY; m 2d by the Mayor 4-20-1857 John GIBBS (H)
Mary K. M., w Howard, dt Josiah Jr. & Caroline L. MACY, b 11-14-1860 d 5-12-1893 (m 1-20-1886) (H)
Howard, s John T. & Amelia; nm
Mary S. rocf Sandwich, Mass. 10-1870
Obediah, s Jonathan, d 7 Mo (Sep) 1753; sisters, Anne & Eliz. d same time
Priscilla rocf Jericho 12-18-1794 (clear)
Rachel, dt Thos. & Leah, Flushing; m 1794 Edmund PEARSALL
Rachel S., dt Joseph & Phebe, Bkn., b 8-29-1817; m 1840 Joshua W. BROWN (H)
Richard d 6-25 (or 26) 1785; m -----
Ch: Hannah
cf Wby 6-4-1783 for Richard & Hannah
Richard rocf Jericho 4-20-1797 (clear); ct Jericho 9-6-1804 (clear); cf Jericho 5-21-1812 (clear); ct Jericho 10-1-1828 (clear) (O); dis 6-1830 (H)
Robert, s Samuel & Sarah, b 12-1-1825; ct Flushing 6-1847
Robert R. d 1-22-1879; m Lydia ----- d 2-9-1903
Ch: John T. b 8- 2-1835
Elizabeth b 2-16-1838 d 4-13-1841
William Henry b 10-12-1840
Maria b 4- 7-1843
Robert R. b 6-15-1846
Cornelia P. b 1-14-1850
cf Wby & Jericho 4-15-1829 for both; Robert R. dis 5-1830 (O); Robert Hicksite; Lydia Orthodox; Maria & Cornelia mbr Orthodox
Robert R., s Robert R. & Lydia, b 6-15-1846 d 8-22-1903; m Tacie P. PARRY, dt Isaac C. & Sarah (Hicks), d 7-19-1934 (H)
Ch: Lydia b 6-24-1870 d 9-1-1870
Sarah Parry b 3-12-1872
Tacie P. b 11-22-1873 d 9-3-1894
Mabel M. b 7-10-1884
Martha E. T. b 11-14-1885
Cornelia b 8-10-1888 d 5-23-1900
Robert R. Jr. b 12-5-1890 d 3-30-1911
cf Horsham 6-1-1870 for Tacie
Samuel & Rebecca
Rebecca gc 8-1-1754
Samuel & Elizabeth
Elizabeth rocf Middletown, N. J. 12-1-1759; con mo 5-3-1753; ct Ephemane (or Esphemane) Pa.
Samuel, s Wait, rocf Jericho 5-21-1801
Samuel (nm) b Pa. d 1-18-1824 ae 50y bHS (m)
Samuel m Hannah ----- d 1832 (H)
Ch: John C. b 2-25-1819 d 1834
Edward b 2-25-1822
Elizabeth C. b 11-4-1824
cf Pur. 8-8-1816; ct Pur. 7-11-1827 with 3 ch named; ct Pur. 8-1835 with ch; flour merchant
Samuel d 6-23-1850; m Hannah ----- d 4-16-1837 (H)
Ch: Mary
Andrew
Jane
Esther
Henry
Hannah
cf Jericho 5-15-1823 with 6 of their ch as named; all dis 1830-1840 (O); ct Jericho 4-3-1861 for last 4 ch
Samuel b 6-15-1795 d 2-6-1883; m Wby 1816 Sarah H. ----- b 9-16-1794 d 1-12-1881 (H)
Ch: Jacob Hicks b 9-27- (or 9-30-) 1818
Robert b 12-1-1825
Amelia b 3- 2-1828 d 11-25-1848
Edward b 7-31-1832 d 10-13-1864
cert of clear to Wby 10-2-1816; Sarah H. rocf Wby 1-14-1818; cf Wby 7-13-1813 for Samuel; cf Wby 3-1818 for Sarah; all dis 1829-1839; hardware merchant
Samuel S., s Andrew & Sarah, b 2-12-1838; ct Wby 7-6-1859 (H)
Sarah, dt Stephen & Maria, N. Y.; m 1856 Richard S. COLLINS
Sarah, dt Edmund & Martha (Whitson), b Flush.

WILLETS, Sarah, continued
4-7-1838 d 10-30-1918; m 1879 Caleb W. SHEPHERD (H)
cf Wby 8-3-1887
Sarah E., dt Jacob, d 5-28-1884 ae 61y 17d bPP; m ----- LEAVITT (H) (both nm)
Sarah H., w Samuel, rocf Wby 1-14-1818
Sarah P., dt Robert R. & Tacey (Parry), N. Y., b N. Y. 3-12-1872 d 2-26-1909; m 1897 Jos. S. PARRY (H)
Stephen d 1-4-1862; m Maria ----- (H)
Ch: Sarah b 12-29-1827
Stephen T. b 1-1-1845
Stephen rocf Wby; Maria & Sarah marked Orthodox 1850; ct Pur. 6-5-1861 for Stephen & s
Stephen T., s Stephen & Maria, b L. I. 1845 d 4-10-1899; ct Pur. 6-5-1861 with father; cf Pur. 12-1-1869 (H)
Susan (nm) b Flush d 9-20-1826 ae 48y bHS
Susannah (late Murray) dis mo 11-4-1784
Thomas mo before 2-1-1759
Thomas & Mary
ct Shrews. 3-3-1763 for both; Shrews. declined 5-3-1764, so still mbr in N. Y.
Thomas & -----
Ch: Mary
Phebe
Rachel
cf Jericho 7-15-1790 with w, Leah, & 3 dt, Mary, Phebe & Rachel, all clear
Thomas m Mary PANCOAST (mo before 10-4-1797)
Ch: Joseph b 7-9-1798 d 12-1-1803 bHS
Ann b 12-14-1800
Mary rocf Burl. 1-6-1794 (clear); they con mo 2-7-1798
Thomas (nm) b Islip, L. I. d 1-30-1823 ae 63y bHS (m)
Thomas d 1-6-1800 bHS
Thomas dis m first cousin 4-5-1809; Egg Harbor MM notified
Thomas (nm) b L. I. d 7-12-1834 ae 38y bHS (unm)
Wait & Mary
Ch: Phebe
Sarah
cf Jericho 4-15-1802
Walter R. (nm), s Stephen T. & Mary S., Bkn.; m at Bkn 1-12-1904 Elizabeth W. ROBERTS, dt John H. & Sarah, Flatbush, b Camden, N.J. 7-19-1876
cf Chester, N. J. 10-7-1891 for Elizabeth; ct Po'keepsie 9-9-1929 (O)
William Henry, s Robert R. & Lydia, b 10-12-1840 N. Y. d 3-24-1903; m Martha T. TABER, dt Samuel T., d 1912 (H)
Martha T. recrq 7-5-1871; lived at Roslyn
William J., s Joseph & Phebe, d 6-13-1846; m Annie Ann F. ----- (H)
Ch: Charles Edwin b 7-12-1840
William Russell b 4-10-1842
Josephine Louisa b 12-4-1844 d 4-30-1845
Joseph Clarence b 3- 4-1846
cf Scip. 3-1840 for Annie Ann; ct Scip. 11-4-1846 with ch; Annie Ann m 2d Anson LAPHAM (H)
William R., s Wm. J. & Annie Ann, b 4-10-1842; rocf Scip. 4-2-1856; ct Scip. 10-5-1864 (H)
William U., s Jacob & Susan A., N. Y., b Po'keepsie 6-29-1839 d 7-12-1912 bPP; m at James E. Miller's, Bkn. 4-10-1861 Elma A. HOAG, dt David & Sarah H. (both dec), Bkn., d 2-2-1863 (H)
cf Chap. 1-1859 with parents
William U. m 2d 6-24-1865 Clara HITT, dt Hiram & Clarissa (Jessup), b 10-12-1846 Somers d 5-12-1931 bPP (H)
Ch: Elma C. b 4- 2-1866
Carrie S. b 1-1-1868
Annie J. b 1-18-1871 d 11-9-1901 bPP
Clara L. b 7- 6-1878
Harold Reginald b 12-7-1886
Clara recrq 8-3-1892; 4 ch's names entered by comm. 1-10-1879; Harold's name entered by comm. 4-3-1888
Zebulon (nm) b Jericho d 12-15-1827 ae 42y bHS; m -----
Ch: Henry b N. Y. d 1-1-1823 ae 1y 8m bHS
Charlotte b N. Y. d 8-3-1825 ae 2m 14d bHS
----- & ----- (nm)
Ch: ----- girl drowned 6-30-1809 ae 1y 10m bHS
Mary b N. Y. d 10-3-1840 ae 41y bHS (unm)

WILLIAMS
Arthur, s Hezekiah & Mary, rocf Coey. 2-1836 with parents; dis 11-1-1865 for serving in the Army (H)
Asher Ellwood (or Elwood), s Jacob R. & Jane M., b 7-3-1854 d 4-28-1892; m Frances E. HUNTER (nm) (H)
Ch: Daisy H. b 12-29-1881
Daisy's name entered by comm. 10-13-1885
Augusta S. d 7-14-1858 bur Morris, Otsego Co., rem to PP 6-12-1893 (H)
Caroline rocf Coey. 1-27-1836 (Eliza Williams same date) (H)
Charles, s Hezekiah & Mary G., rocf Coey. with parents 2-1836; cancelled 1-13-1906, long unknown (H)
Charles & Lilla F.
Ch: Walter H.
Marjorie F. b 11-29-1899
Charles recrq 8-2-1899; Lilla recrq 4-5-1899; Walter recrq 8-2-1899
Charles R., s Geo. R. & Anna R., b 6-8-1892; m Grace E. -----
Ch: Justin Cadwalader
Anne Nicholson b 12-16-1922
Gerard Rhodes b 2-25-1925
Charles rocf Salem, Mass. with parents 6-4-1913; ct Wby 12-1926 with last 2 ch
David, s Grace d 9-15-1875 ae 22d bPP (David a nm) (H)
Deborah Ann, w Charles T., rocf Ama. 2-1853; cancelled 1-13-1909, long unknown (H)
Eliza rocf Coey. 1-27-1836 (Caroline Williams

WILLIAMS, continued
same date)
Elizabeth rocf Pontefract, Eng. 9-16-1850; ct Devonshire House 5-1866; cert ret from Devonshire House 10-1866; ct Australia
Elizabeth rocf Troy 4-1855; ct Troy 1-1-1862 (H)
Elizabeth J. d 12-3-1882 ae 62y bPP; m Joseph S. COHU (H)
Elsie C., dt Samuel B. & Helen (Bogert), b Bkn. 1-24-1912; m 4-1-1932 Henry Franklin BROWN (nm) (H)
recrq of parents 2-10-1917
Emma, dt Isaac & Amy, b N. Y. 7-31-1850 d 2-22-1929 bPP; m Joseph Phelps WINGATE (both nm)
George rocf Troy 1-1831; dis mo 11-5-1856 (H)
George G. & Anna R.
Ch: Charles R. b 6-8-1892
Grace D. b 1-11-1895
Jonathan G. b 5-20-1897
cf Salem, Mass. for all 6-4-1913; ct Pasadena 11-1917 for parents & Grace
Hezekiah d 11-1-1849; m Mary ----- d 7-30-1847 ae 56y 11m (H)
Ch: Charles
Arthur
Caroline d 7-24-1877 ae 62y bPP
Eliza G. " 9- 7-1875 ae 58y 2m 2d bPP
cf Coey. 2-1836 for all
Hezekiah, s John & Jane (both dec); m at Daniel A. Galloway's 4-5-1849 Lydia MACY, wd Benjamin Macy, dt Silas & Deborah BUNKER (both dec) (H)
Lydia m 3d Nathaniel STARBUCK 4-3-1851; ct Troy for Lydia 9-3-1851
Horace E. (nm) d 1-23-1916 (Gr s of Hezekiah, s of Arthur or Charles) (H)
Jacob R., s Fredk. W. & Maria (Romêr), b Tarrytown 6-6-1826 d 2-8-1912 ae 86y; m Jane M. BETTS, dt Silas & Mary, d 1-25-1896 (H)
Ch: William D. b 12- 3-1849
Maria Louisa b 9-16-1852
Asher Ellwood b 7- 3-1854
Julia Matilda b 9-10-1856
cf Pur. 9-7-1864 for Jacob; Jane recrq 5-1869; ch recrq of father 10-1868
James M., s Riley W. & Mary T., b 1876; m 1-22-1913 Lucinda NOYES, (nm), dt Henry T. & Lucinda (Chamberlain) (H)
Ch: Henry Noyes b 9-24-1915
James & Henry recrq 1-13-1933
Jane, dt Hezekiah, d 12-15-1897 ae 87y 1m 21d; m William DISTURNELL (nm) (H)
cf Coey. 7-1836
Jennie M., dt Morris R. & Eleanor (Hanna), b N. Y. 1-19-1852 d 3-2-1923; m Lee WITTY (nm); m 2d 1899 Egbert O. STEVES (nm) (H)
recrq 5-8-1915 (H)
Jeremiah, N. Y. m Philadelphia MASTERS, dt George & Mary (1tm 2 Mo (Apr) 1, 1708) d 3 Mo (May) 6, 1715
Ch: Joseph b 3 Mo (May) 15, 1710
Hannah " 9 Mo (Nov) 8, 1711

Jeremiah m 2d Mary -----
Ch: Ann b 4 Mo (June) 17, 1719
Walter b 10 Mo (Dec) 17, 1720
Benjamin b 9 Mo (Nov) 4, 1722
Mary b 9 Mo (Nov) 26, 1724
Jeremiah 2d b 2 Mo (Apr) 18, 1726
John active mbr 1686
John rocf Shrews. 10-3-1796 (clear)
John Paul J., s Henry B. & Elizabeth P. (Wilson), b Camden, N. J., 11-9-1876; m 10-18-1902 Mary WELSH, dt Joseph B. & Emelie (Taylor), b E. Bethlehem, Pa. 1-26-1876 (H)
both recrq 5-13-1918
Jonathan G., s George G. & Anna (R----) b 5-20-1897; cf Salem, Mass. with parents 6-4-1913; ct Berkeley, Calif. 10-1920
Joseph rem to Merion, Pa. 1 Mo 20, 1737/8
Joseph rocf Phila. 3-1853; dis non-attendance 9-7-1859
Julia Matilda, dt Jacob R. & Jane Maria, Newark, N. J., b 9-10-1856 d 10-27-1924; m 7-17-1901 Lanphear H. SCOTT (nm), of Cadiz, O.
Julia recrq of father 10-1868
Justin Cadwalader, s Chas. R. & Anna K., rocf Salem, Mass. with parents 6-4-1913; ct Germantown 2-1922
Lydia, dt Silas & Deborah BUNKER, N. Y.; m Nathaniel STARBUCK 1851 (H)
Maria Louisa, dt Jacob R. & Jane M. (Betts), b 9-16-1852; m 5-8-1890 Charles C. PHILLIPS (nm) (H)
recrq of father 10-1868
Marjorie, dt Chas. & Lilla F., b 11-29-1899; m ----- REID
Martha, dt Thos. & Abigail THORNE, d 4-12-1840 bur out of city; cf Marl. 10-27-1813 with parents (H)
Mary, dt Jeremiah, rem cf Wby 4 Mo (June) 27, 1744; rem cert 7 Mo (July) 6, 1744
Mary Jane, w George N., rocf Flush. 5-1849; relrq 4-7-1875 (H)
Myrtle L. (nm), dt David & Laura; m 6-1-1916 Wm. Harold CARPENTER (H)
Wm. H. recrq of parents 10-6-1894
Nicholas, having mo some time since, Hudson MM refers it to N.Y. 11-4-1797; he having gone on a sea voyage, but since con mo 1-3-1798; cf Hudson 3-22-1798; ct R. I. MM 3-6-1799
Phebe gct Ama. 5-1837 (H)
Purdy recrq 2-1835; ct Ama. 11-2-1837 (H)
Richard Downing, s Edw. P. & Eleanor H. (Boulden) b Phila. 1-5-1874 d 9-9-1935 at Castleton, S.I.; m 6-1-1899 Ella Hansell LIPPINCOTT, dt Rich. Robt. & Ella (Hansell) b Rancocas, N. J. 10-11-1875 (H)
cf R. & P. for both 3-13-1933
Sallie B., dt Isaac & Mary H. (Borton), b Chestnut Hill, Pa. 7-10-1852 d 3-28-1912; m 1874 John H. ROBERTS (H)
cf Chester, N. J. 10-7-1891 with ch & h
Samuel Byron, Jr., s Sam'l B. & Amanda C., b Dayton, O. 5-26-1881; m 189 S. Oxford St.,

WILLIAMS, Samuel Byron & Helen, continued
Bkn. 5-18-1910, Helen BOGERT, dt Rudolphus R. & Elsie C., Bkn., b Bkn. 10-10-1876 (H)
Ch: Elsie Cromwell b 1-24-1912
David Gordon " 4-15-1925
Samuel recrq 2-10-1917; Elsie recrq of parents 2-10-1917
Sarah active mbr 1682
Sarah b Shrews. d 12-11-1822 ae 42y 9m bHS
Sarah A. rocf Pur. 3-4-1874; relrq 5-5-1880
Thankful (nm), b Stonington, Conn. d 1-3-1821 ae 50y 3m 3d bHS (wd)
Thomas d 3-29-1878 ae 84y 6m bPP; m Anna ----- (H) cf Troy 7-2-1851 for both
Thomas R. gct R. I. 9-1861; d in Phila.
Timothy D., s G. C., d 5-12-1906 ae 66y 10m 8d bPP (Timothy nm)
Tylee rocf Shrews. 7-3-1786, as apprentice to Thomas Pearsall; ct Shrews. 10-1-1788 (clear)
Wm. D., s Jacob R. & Jane M., Newark, N. J.; m at 15th St. 5-20-1874 Mary Elizabeth MARLOTT, dt Jacob & Rachel (dec) (H)
Ch: Rachel Tilton b 10-13-1875 d 4-10-1896
Rachel's name entered by comm.; ct R. & P. 11-6-1897 for William
----- & ----- (nm)
Ch: Henry b Berks Co. d 10-13-1827 ae 4y 2m 1d bHS
Maria b Howel, N. J. d 11-5-1827 ae 1y 7m 24d bHS
Arthur d 7-15-1874 ae 29y bPP
Walter " 4-19-1873 ae 17y bPP

WILLIAMSON
Alvah (nm), s Wm. & Sarah, d 3-7-1905 ae 75y 11m 4d bPP; m 6-12-1849 Abbie S. WEEKS, dt Joseph & Elizabeth (Underhill), b Lewisboro 10-6-1828 d 10-29-1921 ae 93y 22d bPP (H)
Ch: Joseph d 5-15-1896 ae 42y bPP
cf Ama. for Abbie 10-4-1882
Arthur M., s Chas. D. & Mary E., rocf Farm. with parents 2-1883; relrq 12-6-1893
Benjamin (nm), s Wm. & Sarah; m 1-23-1856 Caroline CARPENTER, dt James & Mary (Haviland), b N. Y. 3-22-1837 d 4-20-1910 (H)
cf Pur. for Caroline 9-1860; in Madison, Wis. 1879-1899
Charles D. & Mary Emma
Ch: Arthur M.
recrq 5-1872; ct Farm. 3-1879; cf Farm. 2-1883 with w & s; parents relrq 1-1884
Elizabeth (form Heaton), having mo, Marl. ref. to N. Y. 11-1849; dis mo 12-1849
George F. m Lydia H. ----- d 7-28-1885 ae 31y 18d bPP (H)
Ch: George F. Jr. d 3-22-1884 ae 6m bPP
Clara May d 3-22-1884 ae 5m 20d bPP
(all nm)
Harvey R. rocf Marl. 11-1879; relrq 11-1881
Jean Margaret (nm) m Walter Ernest ROBERTS (H)
John contributor 1680
Joseph m Mary Louise ----- d 10-18-1908 ae 50y bPP (both nm) (H)
Laurette, dt Frank H. & Anna (Nieweg), b Lincoln Univ., Pa. 12-25-1886; m 1913 Horace R. STUBBS (H)
recrq 1-8-1920
S. Heaton recrq 10-1-1913; ct Clintondale 7-1920
William R. (nm), s Wm. & Sarah; m 6-4-1861 Rachel H. WILLITS, dt Edmund S. & Esther (Whitson), b Wby 9-30-1840 (H)
cf Wby for Rachel 3-2-1862; ct First M. E. Church of Madison, Wis. 6-11-1917 for her

WILLIS
Alfred, s John P. & Martha, b 11-13-1803 d 3-30-1860; m N. Y. 7-8-1829 Mary F. MOTT, dt Wm. F. & Phebe, b 2-27-1809
Ch: John R. b 7-14-1830
Martha b 7-14-1833
Wm. Mott b 5-20-1836
Phebe M. b 9-12-1841
Alfred R. rocf Jericho 12-20-1827; dis 5-1833 (0); ct Jericho 10-1835 (H)
Ann (Anne or Anna), dt Wm. & Amy, Summerset Co., N. J.; m 1794 Benj. STRATTON, Jr.
Ann, w William, d 5-21-1821
Cornelia G., dt Grinnell (nm) & Mary B. H., b 8-28-1877; name entered by comm. 1882; relrq 5-7-1898 (H)
Edward, s John R. & Martha (dec), N. Y., b 2-6-1812; m N. Y. 1-8-1834 Ann Augusta COCK, dt Thos. & Eliz. F. (dec), N. Y.
Ch: Anna F. b 11-30-1834; relrq 2-3-1857
Thomas C. b 11-5-1837 d 6-26-1853
Emily relrq
parents dis 1842-1843
Eliza, dt William & James, N. Y.; m Dr. John Lindley FITZ RANDOLPH 1811
Esther, dt Henry & Mary, Wby; m 1695 Wm. ALBERTSON
Esther (nm) b L. I. d 1-1-1826 ae 67y bHS (wd)
Esther b L. I. d 9-14-1834 ae 68y bHS (wd)
George G. rocf WD MM 11-15-1826; dis 8-1830 (0)
George T. & Phebe (H)
Ch: Obadiah S.
Richard
John James b 5-19-1837
Ann Elizabeth b 7-18-1841
cf Corn. 7-1836 with 3 ch; ct Corn. 5-1843 with all
Grinnell (nm), s Nathaniel P. (dec) & Cornelia G., N. Y.; m at R. Haydock's 10-24-1874 Mary B. HAYDOCK, dt Robert & Hannah, N. Y., b 3-13-1849 N. Y. d 1-27-1911 (H)
Ch: Hannah Haydock b 12-31-1875
Cornelia Grinnell b 8-28-1877
Joseph Grinnell b 7-24-1877
ch's names entered by comm. 1882
Hannah H., dt Grinnell (nm) & Mary B. H., b 12-31-1875; name entered by comm. 1882; relrq 5-7-1898 (H)
Henry b Eng., came from London after 1667, Jericho & Hempstead, d 7 Mo (Sep) 11, 1714 ae 86; m Mary PEACE (or Pease) d 4 Mo (June)

WILLIS, Henry & Mary, continued
1747 ae 82y
Ch: Hester d 5 Mo (July) 23, 1677
other ch not in records
William b 10 Mo (Dec) 16, 1663
Mary
Sarah
Rachel
Henry d 10 Mo (Dec) 1675
active from 1677-1700; Mary active 1676-1701
Henry took a cert (prob of clear) 3 Mo (May) 25, 1700 to place not stated
Henry & Phebe
ct Little Egg Harbor 4-6-1808, having ret there
John R., s William & Jane, Merchant, N. Y., d 12-7-1844 ae about 65 (he fell through a skylight of a roof); m N. Y. 11-10-1802 Martha WILLETS, dt Henry & Phebe, N. Y., d 6-22-1832 ae 49y 2m 18d bHS
Ch: Alfred b 11-13-1803
William Henry b 6- 7-1809
Edmund (or Edward) b 2- 6-1812
Walter d 1805
Infant stillborn 5-29-1818
parents dis 1829 (H)
John R. m 2d N. Y. 11-11-1840 Elizabeth UNDERHILL, dt Joshua & Mary (both dec), d 7-9-1869 ae 75y bPP
John R., s Alfred & Mary F., b 7-14-1830; dis mo & non-attendance 6-1856
Jordan (nm) b L. I. d 7-30-1809 ae 20y 5m 13d bHS
Joseph Grinnell, s Grinnell & Mary B. (Haydock), b N. Y. 7-24-1877 d 6-21-1919; m 6-30-1906 Emily MAYER (nm) (H)
Joshua & -----
Ch: Jane Ann d 9-6-1804 ae 1m 15d bHS
Martha rocf Wby 7-27-1763; ct Wby 2-4-1773; sister of Mordecai
Martha b Wby d 8-30-1824 ae 92y bHS (wd)
Martha (nm), dt Esther, b Oyster Bay d 8-30-1824 ae 25y bHS (unm)
Martha, dt Alfred & Mary F., b 7-14-1833; m ----- WOOD (mo)
dis mo 7-1853
Mary, dt Henry, Wby, m 1678 N. Y. George MASTERS
Mary, ancient minister, d 12 Mo (Feb) 17, 1713/14
Mary, dt Robert, rocf Woodbridge 8-2-1760, apprentice to Margaret Bowne
Mary rocf Wby 9-1-1763
Mary Cornell (form Willis) dis 2m-1803
Mary, dt Daniel & Phebe, N. Y.; m ----- CHADWICK; m 2d 1818 David HARKNESS, of Peru
Mordecai & Marcy
cf Wby for Mordecai's w & his sister, Martha, 7-27-1773
Phebe M. (or W.), dt Alfred & Mary F., b 9-12-1841; relrq 10-1863

Rachel, dt Henry & Mary, Wby; m 1695 Nathaniel SEAMAN
Rebecca Prince (form Willis)dis 9-4-1800 (mo)
Richmond C. (or Richardson C.) dis 7-2-1823
Robert & -----
Ch: Samuel
Mary
these ch apprenticed to Friends of N. Y.; cf Woodbridge 12-4-1760; a worthy Friend accompanied Wm. Jones on religious visit 1779
Samuel, s Robert, rocf Woodbridge 8-2-1760 as apprentice to Margaret Bowne
Samuel & Mary
Mary, w Samuel, rocf Wby 7-27-1774; Mary gct Wby 11-6-1777
Sarah, dt Henry & Mary, Wby; m 1695 John TITUS
Sarah R. gct Hardshaw West, Eng. 8-6-1817 to live with her brother, Walter; cf Hardshaw West, Eng. 9-30-1818 (clear)
Sarah R., dt William & Jane; m Capt. Thomas LAVENDER; ret a mbr
Sarah W., dt Wm. Henry & Lydia, b 6-3-1831; dis 5-1856 for attending mtgs of another religious society
William, s Henry, Wby, b Eng. 10 Mo (Dec) 16, 1663; m at Edmund Titus' 6 Mo (Aug) 10, 1687 Mary TITUS, dt Edmund, Wby
Ch: William b 4 Mo (June) 14, 1688
Henry b 6 Mo (Aug) 19, 1690
John b 2 Mo (Apr) 15, 1693
Jacob b 9 Mo (Nov) 6, 1695
Silas b 6 Mo (Aug) 26, 1700 d 1 Mo 15, 1704/5
Samuel b 6 Mo (Aug) 30, 1704
Mary b 5 Mo (July) 1709
William active mbr 1689-1701
William & Sarah
Sarah rocf Wby 7-27-1763; Sarah ret. with h, William, to Wby 11-6-1766
William d 1-22-1839 ae 89y 7m bHS; m Jane ----- d 1-4-1817 ae 64y bHS
Ch: John b 12- 5-1779
Walter b 4-24-1784
Mary " 4- 9-1786
Sarah R. b 6-18-1788
Elizabeth b 2-17-1791
Richardson b 1-28-1795
Peggy b 5-31-1798 d 7-7-1802 bHS
cf Wby for Wm. 7-27-1763; ct Wby 1-6-1766; cf Wby with their 6 ch 6-17-1795
Wm. Henry, s John R. & Martha, N. Y., b 6-7-1809; m N. Y. 7-14-1830 Lydia WARING, dt William & Sarah, N. Y.
Ch: Sarah W. b 6- 3-1831
Anna " 9-10-1833 d 9- 7-1834 bHS
Frances " 7-16-1835 d 2-13-1840 bHS
Mary Augusta b 3-11-1838
Francis b 3-29-1840
William Henry
ct Oswego 1853 for all; ret from Oswego 6-1854 for all; ch dis 5-1856; ct Oswego

WILLIS, Wm. Henry & Lydia, continued
3-1866 for Lydia W.
Wm. Mott, s Alfred & Mary F., b 5-20-1836; mbrp relinquished by mo 9-1871
William Thomas & Maria T.
Ch: Annie
William A.
Lizzie T.
George Henry
cf Wby 11-1873 for all; ct Stanford 6-9-1875 for all
Zebulon S. dis mo 1-1-1812
----- & ----- (nm)
Ch: Oliver d 1-21-1835 ae 9m bHS
----- & ----- (nm)
Ch: Anna W. d 9-7-1867 ae 83y bPP
Edmund d 2-1868 ae 73y bPP

WILLISON
Margaret rocf R. & P. 6-15-1843

WILLITS
Abraham [Willitt] & -----
Ch: Charity d 5 Mo (July) 13, 1735
Adelaide, dt Wm. H, & Ella (Osborne), b 7-21-1878; m 12-4-1901 Robert Wentworth FLOYD (H)
Ann, N. Y. m 1798 Robert BARNES (mo)
Charity, Flushing, d 5 Mo (July) 1712
Charity, dt Benjamin, d 5 Mo (July) 13, 1735
Edmund rocf Wby 1-18-1826 (clear); dis 5-1830 (O)
Elizabeth, dt Hope & Mary, Wby; m 1701 Jarvis FARO
Hannah con mo 9-6-1769
Henry mbr & contributor 1682-1684
Henry & Phebe
cf Little Egg Harbor 7-9-1818 with w, Phebe, & gr dt, Ann P. Willits; ct Little Egg Harbor for Henry & Phebe, 5-3-1826
Hope, s Richard & Mary, Wby; m Mercy LANGDON
Ch: Joseph b 10 Mo (Dec) 13, 1677
Mary b 10 Mo (Dec) 9, 1679
Elizabeth b 12 Mo (Feb) 3, 1681/2
Richard b 1 Mo (Mar) 14, 1683/4
Esther b 2 Mo (Apr) 15, 1686
Timothy b 12 Mo (Feb) 25, 1687/8
Hope b 8 Mo (Oct) 21, 1689
Phebe b 11 Mo (Jan) 29, 1690/1
James
Hannah b 8 Mo (Oct) 3, 1696
Patience b 8 Mo (Oct) 3, 1696
Abigail b 8 Mo (Oct) 3, 1696
Jacob, s Richard (dec) & Mary, Jericho, d 2 Mo (Apr) 20, 1722; m Flushing 10 Mo (Dec) 25, 1717 Mary JACKSON, dt James, Flushing
Jacob brought cert of clear from Wby
James, s Fred'k E. & Anna W., Glen Cove; m at Stephen Valentine's 2-14-1906 Anna K. VALENTINE, dt Stephen & Annie L., Bkn., b Bkn. 3-26-1882 (H)
John, s John, Flushing; m Flushing 8 Mo. (Oct) 3, 1734 Deborah LAWRENCE, dt Samuel, Flushing
John [Willitt], Flushing, d 4-11-1774 (prob s John)
Martha, dt Richard & Abigail, O.B.; m 1715 Obadiah VALENTINE
Mary, Jericho, ancient wd, d 11 Mo (Jan) 17, 1713/4, ae about 84y
Mary, dt Richard; m 1687 Jericho John FRY
Mary, dt Hope & Mary, Wby; m 1701 Richard RIDGWAY
Mary, dt William, Jericho; m 1719 John RODMAN, Jr.
Mary (form Murray) dis mo 4-6-1796
Mary S., dt Edward S. & Esther (Whitson), b Wby 2-10-1832 d 1-10-1928 ae 96y; m 1865 Edmund SEAMAN (H)
cf Wby 3-7-1903
Rachel H., dt Edmund & Esther (Haviland), b Wby 9-30-1840; m 1861 Wm. R. WILLIAMSON (nm) (H)
cf Wby 3-2-1862; ct First M. E. Church of Madison, Wis. 6-11-1917
Richard b Eng., Jericho, O.B., m Mary WASHBURN dt Wm. & Jane (nm) d 4 Mo (June) 16, 1688
Ch: Thomas b 3 Mo (May) 1650
Hope " 7 Mo (Sep) 1652
John b 5 Mo (July) 1655
Richard b 10 Mo (Dec) 1660
Mary b 2 Mo (Apr) 1663
Jacob
Elizabeth d 2 Mo (Apr) 25, 1722
both active mbr from 1676
Richard, s Richard & Mary, Jericho, b 10 Mo (Dec) 1660 d 3 Mo (May) 14, 1703; m Flushing 1 Mo (Mar) 25, 1686 New Year's Day Abigail BOWNE, dt John, d 4 Mo (June) 16, 1688
Ch: Hannah b 11 Mo (Jan) 24, 1687
Richard m 2d at Thomas Powell's 3 Mo (May) 15, 1690 Abigail POWELL, dt Thomas
Ch: Abigail b 12 Mo (Feb) 28, 1690/1
Mary " 1 Mo (Mar) 16, 1792/3
Martha b 11 Mo (Jan) 24, 1694/5
Jacob b 4 Mo (June) 6, 1697
Phebe " 2 Mo (Apr) 14, 1699
Elizabeth b 4 Mo (June) 27, 1701
Richard rocf Wby 2-5-1868; ct Wby 11-2-1870 (H)
Samuel, s Richard, rocf Wby 5-26-1762 (clear); cf Wby 4-4-1764
Sarah T., dt Stephen & Maria; m 1856 Richard S. COLLINS
Stephen & Maria
Ch: Lydia b 1-15-1825 d 1827
Sarah T. b 12-29-1827
cf Pur. 10-13-1824; Stephen dis 5-1830; ct Pur. 12-1860 for Maria
Thomas active mbr 1691
Thomas, s Thomas & Dinah, Sanketange, L. I.; m at John Hallock's 10 Mo (Dec) 24, 1706 Catharine HALLOCK, dt John & Abigail, Brookhaven, L. I.
Thomas, Flushing, b 1 Mo (Mar) 4, 1738/9; m Leah ----- b 3 Mo (May) 22, 1744

WILLITS, Thomas & Leah, continued
Ch: Mary b 6-22-1768
Phebe " 2- 1-1770
Rachel b 4- 1-1773
Rebecca b 2- 1-1776
Joseph b 2- 1-1778
Sarah " 9- 5-1782
Zebulon b 5-15-1786
Wm. H., s Edward S. & Esther (Whitson), b Wby 11-11-1843 d 9-17-1909; m 10-3-1877 Ella OSBORN, dt Abner & Sarah, b 8-18-1850 d 4-20-1933 (H)
Ch: Adelaide O. b 7-21-1878
cf Wby for Wm. 2-5-1868; Ella recrq 6-5-1878; Wm. H. clerk of N. Y. YM

WILLOUGHBY
Robert C. (nm) b Columbia Co. d 1-12-1837 ae 25y bHS (unm)

WILLS
Anna D. (nm), dt Micajah R. & Martha M., Medford, N. J., b Medford, N. J. 1844 d 7-7-1927 bPP; m 1883 George D. HILYARD
Chalkley J. & Ann D.
Ch: Benjamin D. b 1- 3-1848 d 5- 8-1854
Anna T. " 12-21-1854
Edward D. " 8-21-1849
Charles T. " 12-13-1851
Elizabeth H. b 6-27-1853
George J.
cf Burl. 11-3-1845; cf Burl. 5-3-1847 for Ann D.; ct Chesterfield 3-1859 for all
Charles rocf Burl. 1849; ct Burl. 9-1861
Daniel J. d 7-8-1871 ae 35y bPP; m 1862 Elizabeth G. -----
Ch: Elizabeth G. (or Lizzie S.) b 1-28-1864
cert of clear to N.P. 11-5-1862; cf Burl. 6-1853 for Daniel; cf N.P. 12-1863 for Elizabeth; ct Providence 4-1873 for Eliz. & dt; cert changed to N.P. 6-1873
Elizabeth m 1864 George D. HILYARD
cf Burl. 3-10-1864

WILMOTT
Harold E. rocf Lewiston, Me. 4-5-1905; relrq 7-3-1912
Robert R. [Willmott] rocf Whitewater, Ind. 12-7-1910; name erased 4-1928

WILSEY
George W., s George & Marietta (Britt), d 6-5-1932 ae 75y bPP; m Ida ----- (H)
both nm
Marietta Bellows, dt Wm. & Marietta, d 1-13-1925 ae 70y bPP; m John C. HENRY (both nm) (H)

WILSON
Achsah d 6-14-1890 ae 60y bPP; in grave with Daniel Billings (H)
Catharine, dt Peter DOBSON, d 12-6-1804 ae 43y bHS
Cornelius A. (nm) m Caroline J. MATTHEWS, dt Jos. B. & Eliz. S. (Jones), b Balt. 9-19-1888 (H)
Caroline m 2d Glen H. NOYES; cf Balt. for Caroline 7-9-1898
Cyrus J., s John W. & Emily (H----), b Bkn. 4-5-1884; m 11-2-1910 Anna ROBERTS, dt John H. & Sallie (Borton), b Camden, N.J. 11-13-1885 (H)
Ch: John Cyrus b 10-1-1912
Robert Armitage b 8-25-1915
Richard Roberts b 10-19-1918
Anna Elizabeth b 7-11-1925
Cyrus J. recrq 6-9-1919; cf Camden for Anna, with parents 10-7-1891
Dorothy, N. Y., abt to rem to Crosswicke 5 Mo 2, 1730; ct Wrightstown, Pa. 9 Mo (Nov) 4, 1731 (clear); she had con mo 11 Mo (Jan) 6, 1725/6
Elizabeth, dt Jesse S. & Rebecca D., b 10-31-1861 d 1-1-1831; m 1899 Albert R. LAWTON (H) cf Goose Creek 12-11-1890 & rec here 9-2-1891
Florence, dt Jesse & Rebecca (Stratton), b Springfield, O. 10-18-1875; m 1897 John Herbert FLOURNOY (nm) (H)
Hanson Z., s Wm. & Mary (Taylor), b Sylmer, Md. 4-22-1874; cf Rising Sun, Md. 1-14-1911 (H)
Harold Lincoln (nm), s Richard S. & Ellen (Yerkes); m 5-12-1927 Elizabeth P. COLKET, dt J. Hamilton & Ethel (Paxson), b Balt. 12-12-1903 (H)
Henry B. (nm), s Thomas & Hannah M. R.; m 12-24-1901 Teresa L. MARTENS, dt Carl & Josephine (Weeks), b N. Y. 1-2-1880 (H)
Teresa recrq 1-11-1926
Hester M., w Edward DART (H)
Ira mo before 10-1838; Phila. WD refers it to N. Y. 10-17-1838; rpd adversely 3-6-1839
James (nm) b Bedford d 10-21-1811 ae 29y 1m 28d bHS (m)
James Clark rocf Hudson 3-25-1835 (clear); dis mo 4-1848
John [Willson] (nm) b Flush. d 3-31-1815 ae 61y 27d bHS (widower)
John C. & Olive M. (H)
Ch: Elmira d 6-4-1918 ae 47y 8m 5d bPP (unm)
all nm
Louisa, dt Ebenezer & Hepzibah, N. Y.; m 1827 Joseph D. EVERNGHIM
recrq 1825
Margaret [Willson] rocf R. & P. 1843; ct Farm. 11-6-1862
Maria rocf Lisburn, Ireland 2-2-1910
Martha R. (nm), dt Robert & Mary (Anderson); m 7-6-1895 George John BARTON (H)
Mary con mo 12-6-1759
Mary (nm) b N. Y. d 1-8-1811 ae 66y 8m bHS
Mary (late Knowles) dis mo before 3-7-1804
Mary (late Clark) dis mo before 1-6-1808
Susan R., dt Jos. D. Evernghim & Susan, dis 9-1844 (H)

WILSON, continued
Victor, s Samuel D. & Mary (Mendenhall), b Sylmar, Md. 3-12-1892; m 9-27-1924 Alice MERRITT, dt Jesse & Pauline (W----), b Bethpage (H)
cf Nottingham, Pa. 6-11-1923 for Victor; Alice mbr Jericho
----- & ----- (nm)
Ch: Catharine Maria d 8-20-1811 ae 4m bHS
Mary d 3-13-1820 ae 1y 2m 14d bHS
Eliza d 9-29-1821 ae 5y 5m 27d bHS
James b N. Y. d 4-13-1826 ae 1y 3m bHS

WINANS
Carrie B. (nm) m Francis W. COFFIN (H)

WINDER
Alfred, s Joseph & Rebecca H. (Engle), b Woodstown, N. J. 10-13-1834 d 6-11-1913 bPP; m 11-24-1866 Martha L. HAWKINS (nm), dt Chas. B. & Martha (L----) d 5-24-1924 ae 81y bPP
Ch: Bessie
Joseph M. d 7-12-1913 ae 40y bPP
cf Whitewater, Ind. 3-8-1913; his parents mbr Whitewater
Bessie, dt Alfred & Martha L., d 3-28-1925 ae 47y bPP; m ----- FITZPATRICK (H)

WINE
John d 5-31-1869 ae 79; m Jane L. ----- d Flushing 10-9-1865 (H)
cf Oswego 1-1855 for both; ct Flush. 8-1861 for both
----- & ----- (nm)
Ch: Thomas b N. Y. d 2-9-1824 ae 7m bHS
Charles b N. Y. d 8-27-1827 ae 1y 6m bHS

WING
Anna Maria m Francis MORGAN (H)
Ch: John
cf Roch. 7-1844 with s; dis 12-3-1846 (H)
Cynthia T. rocf Creek 11-1857; ct Creek 8-1861
Emma O., dt Jonas & Julia A. (Osborn), b Lansingburgh, N. Y. 8-2-1864; trans. from Albany 1-8-1816 (H)
Hannah S. rocf Sandwich, Mass. 4-1887; ct Sandwich, Mass. 12-4-1895
John D., s Anna Maria, rocf Roch. 7-1844 with mother; dis 10-3-1860 for non-attendance & jas (H)
Joseph (nm) d 11-15-1892 ae 70y bPP; m Margaret ----- d 12-28-1905 ae 59y 11m bPP
Ch: Joseph d 6-14-1860 ae 1y bPP
Irene " 11-14-1878 ae 1y 3m 3d bPP
Hannah J. d 9-22-1874 ae 1y 1m 15d bPP
Mary Alice d 1-19-1872 ae 10y 7m 10d bPP
all nm
Mary m John BENTLEY (mo)
dis mo 9-5-1832
Mary, dt Oliver H. & Rachel H. (Ketcher) (H)
Oliver rocf Stanford 9-19-1836; ct Stanford 5-1838
Oliver (nm) & -----
Ch: Joseph K. d 3-9-1852 ae 15y 10m bPP

William G. & Hannah
Ch: Mary Elizabeth
William George b 7-30-1861
cf Providence 2-1861 with 1 ch; ct New Bedford 8-1864 for all

WINGATE
Charles d 3-2-1903 ae 90y 1m 2d bPP; m Mary P. ROBINSON, d 10-18-1897 ae 86y 1m bPP (both nm)
Ella W., w Otto A. DRANDT, dt Charles & Mary (Robinson) Wingate, b Bkn. 9-12-1856 d 12-13-1928 bPP
General George W. (nm) b N. Y. 7-1-1840 d 3-22-1928 bPP; m Susan P. MANN, dt Buel H. & Louise D., b 1843 d 8-31-1915 bPP
Hannah W. (nm) d 1-6-1930 ae 82y bPP
Joseph Phelps (nm), d abt 1894 bPP; m Emma WILLIAMS (nm), dt Isaac & Amy, b N. Y. 7-31-1850 d 2-22-1929 bPP

WINSLOW
Grace Eliza rocf Brighouse, Eng. 5-1888; ct Lynn, Mass. 8-6-1902

WINTER
Harry W. (nm), s Geo. C. & Catharine; m 12-20-1887 Ella ROBBINS, dt Silas T. & Susan H. (Seaman), b Bkn. 2-13-1868 (H)
John rocf Shrews. 10-2-1754

WINTRINGHAM
Clement V., s Jere. & Eliz. V., b 5-5-1860; relrq 2-3-1892 (H)
David Lawton, s Jere. & Eliz., b 2-14-1810; dis 11-4-1846 (H)
Helen Eliz., dt Jere. & Eliz. V., Bkn., b 2-28-1863 d 1-1917; m 1891 Lucien B. SQUIER, Jr. (H)
Jeremiah, s Thos. & Ruth (both dec), Bkn., d 9-19-1891 ae 74y 6m 14d bPP; m at Stephen Valentine's 10-4-1855 Elizabeth V. VALENTINE dt Stephen & Ann T., N. Y., d 12-3-1889 ae 65y 4m 11d bPP (H)
Ch: Louise V. b 7-3-1856 d 11-13-1857 bPP
Valentine " 10- 8-1858 d 12- 7-1858 bPP
Clement V. b 5-5-1860
Helen E. b 2-28-1863
John rocf N. P. 10-14-1795, apprentice to Robert Bowne; dis mo 9-2-1802
Ruth L., dt Thos. & Ruth, N. Y.; m 1847 Henry CLEMENT, of Flushing (H)
Sidney, s Thos. & Ruth (Lawton), b N. Y. 2-24-1815 d 1-15-1908 ae 92y 10m 22d (unm) (H)
Thomas d 1834; m N. P. 1808 Ruth LAWTON, b R.I. d 3-7-1819 ae 40y bHS (H)
Ch: David Lawton b 2-14-1810
Hannah " 2-27-1812
Sidney d 7-27-1813 ae 5m 23d bHS
Sidney " 2-24-1815
Jeremiah " 3- 4-1817
Ruth L. " 2-28-1819
cf N. P. 8-15-1805 (clear); cert of clear to N.P. 1-6-1808; Ruth brought cert from N. P.

WINTRINGHAM, Thomas & Ruth, continued
11-17-1808; all dis 1829-1839 (O)

WISEMAN
Elizabeth, dt William & Anna (Giles), b Birmingham, Eng. 8-2-1849 d 10-31-1913 bPP; m Alfred DAYBILL
cf Warwickshire, Eng. 7-1887 for both with ch
Harriet, dt William & Annie (Giles), b Eng. 2-16-1853 d 6-6-1923 bPP; m Cyrus WOOLSTON (nm)
Harriet recrq 4-3-1901; "aunt of Fred & Wm. Daybill"

WISTAR
Casper, Phila.; m bet. 11-1- & 12-6-1764, Mary FRANKLIN
Ch: Thomas
Catharine
Sarah
Casper rocf Phila. (clear); Mary gct Phila. (not recorded); ct Birmingham, Pa. 1-5-1785 for Mary with 2 dt; ct same for Thomas; Caspar gct Concord 9-7-1797
Lydia, w Edward H. KENDALL, rocf WD MM 5-1879; relrq 12-6-1893
Thomas, s Casper & Mary, gct Birmingham, Pa. 1-5-1785
Virginia, dt Robert, rolf E. Presby. Ch., East Cleveland, O., 8-5-1931

WITTY
Lee (nm) m 10-5-1899 Jennie M. WILLIAMS, dt Morris R. & Eleanor (Hannah), b N. Y. 1-19-1852 (H)
Jennie M. m 2d Egbert O. STEVES

WOELFLER
Bertha, dt Ludwig & Clara, b N. Y. 6-16-1888; m 1912 Carl Victor BERTSCHE (H)
recrq 5-9-1927 with h & ch

WOLCOTT
Ann O. (nm) d 10-2-1877 ae 61y bPP (H)
Henrietta, dt Henry W. & Sybillah, Eatontown, N. J.; m 1852 Rowland JOHNSON, of Phila. (H)
Joseph (nm), s Joseph & Mary, d 4-3-1891 ae 75y bPP; m -----
Ch: Charles Henry d 5-22-1843 ae 1y 3m bHS
Mary d 7-30-1871; w ----- (H)
Ch: Henry L. b 4-5-1829 d 11-16-1906
cf Shrews. 3-1845 with s
Samuel P. rocf Shrews. 12-6-1824; d 1830
Sarah L., dt Jos. & Mary (Lewis), b Eatontown, N. J., 8-20-1813 d 8-12-1901; m 1831 James LAFETRA (H)

WONG
Dow recrq 6-12-1901; went to China for health before 1909; d 1911
Yow recrq 7-1-1903 (chinese)

WOOD
Aaron, s Thomas & Mary, dis 8-1829 (O);dis 12-1828 (H)
Abigail, dt Samuel & Mary POWELL, b Bethpage d 12-3-1809 (or 12-4-) ae 50y 8m 13d
Alfred rocf R. & P. 10-1864; ct Chesterfield 5-3-1865
Alice S., dt David S. & Lydia, rocf New Bedford, Mass. 11-1883 with parents; letter to St. Paul's Episc. Ch., Englewood, N.J. 2-23-1910
Anna, dt Samuel & Mary, b 3-21-1799 d 11-2-1888 ae 89y bPP; dis 8-1838
Ann Eliza, dt Joseph & Eliza Ann, d 12-26-1844; m Leander TOWNSEND (H)
ret a mbr
Arnold, s Wm. H. S. & Emma (Congdon), b N. Y. 9-23-1872; relrq 9-1920
Arthur King, s Stephen J. & Mariana, b 9-2-1875; rel 8-7-1901
Benjamin, Jr., s Wm. S. & Abigail; dis mo 2-1848
Blanche E. m 1847 Samuel T. VALENTINE (H)
Caleb gct Pur. 4-3-1811 (clear); cf Pur. 11-12-1818; d Bethpage, L. I. 9-1828
Caroline, dt John & Sarah, N. Y.; m 1849 Wm. BIRDSALL, Jr.
Charles recrq 7-7-1813; ct Corn. 2-2-1820
Charles, of Ama. d 1845; m -----
Ch: Samuel P. d 9-17-1817 ae 1y 5m bHS
Charles rocf Chap. 7-8-1841 (clear); dis 6-1843 (O)
Charles & Sarah S. (H)
Ch: Phebe
Elma
Ajah d 7-1855
Henry
cf N.P. 7-20-1843 for all; ct Shrews. 8-4-1852 with Phebe
Charles, s John & Martha, gct R. & P. 2-4-1846 (clear)
Charles, s Arnold & Mary B. (Spencer), b New Salem, N. Y. 9-11-1845 d 2-24-1928; m 12-2-1868 Catharine H. FLANSBURGH, dt John H. & Maria (Bradt) b New Salem 2-18-1847 (H)
both trans from Albany 1-8-1916
Clement, s Sterling Alex. & Ida May (Richardson), b Tuscaloosa, Ala. 9-1-1888; m 10-31-1914 Mildred CUMMER, dt Harry & Mildred (Swartz) b Buffalo, 10-14-1886 (H)
Ch: Janet b N. Y. 10-6-1917
John Thornton b 4-5-1929
parents recrq 9-10-1917; Mildred secured divorce; Clement cancelled 3-13-1933 for lack of interest; he m 2d time
Daniel (nm) & -----
Ch: William R. b N. Y. d 4-4-1827 ae 1y 5m bHS
David S. d Wellsby, Mass. 3-23-1913; m Lydia H. -----
Ch: Joseph R. b 7- 5-1872
Alice S.
cf New Bedford, Mass. 11-1883 with ch named; Lydia relrq 3-6-1918

WOOD, continued
Deborah recrq 1833; d 8-24-(or 26) 1863 ae 60y bPP
Edmund, s Thomas & Mary, dis 6-1834 (H); dis 1838 (O)
Edward H., s John & Martha, N. Y.; m N. Y. 12-14-1842 Phebe H. HULL, dt Wager & Eliza. C. N. Y., d 1-18-1879
Ch: Wager H. b 10-27-1843
Francis Howgill
Elizabeth Hull
Phebe rocf ND MM 7-1868 with her 2 ch last named; Edward dis 3-1845; rst; ct R. & P. 4-1848 for Phebe H. & Wager H.; ct R. & P. 1855 for Edward H.
Eleanor K., dt Stephen & Catharine M., N. Y.; m 1857 Edward MARIS, of Phila.
Eliza, dt Wm. S. & Abigail, dis 2-1838
Eliza J., dt Thomas & Mary; m ----- SEYMOUR (mo) dis mo 11-1830 (H) [----- WEST
Elizabeth, dt Peter, d 12-17-1804 ae 52y; m
Elizabeth C., dt John & Martha; m 1843 Henry R. POST
Elizabeth Hull, dt Edw. H. & Phebe H., rocf ND MM 7-1868 with mother; name erased
Elizabeth U., dt Wm. & Mary S., N. Y.; m 1869 David S. TABER
Elkanah m Anna ----- b L. I. d 4-22-1837 ae 54y 10m (m Jericho 1810) (H)
Ch: James R.
cert of clear to Jericho 1-3-1810; Anna rocf Jericho 6-21-1810; rem to Pur. 2-1-1811; cf Pur. 11-12-1818 with their s, James; all dis 1829-1839 (O); Elkanah gct Wby 4-1840
Elma, dt Charles & Sarah; m Hugh B. HOWARD (H); cf N.P. 9-1843 with parents; ct N.P. 9-1852
Ernest W., s Stephen, Jr. & Eleanor, b 3-21-1877; relrq 1-8-1902
Ezra rocf Oswego 9-18-1833 (clear); dis 4-1834 (O); d 8-20-1849
Francis, s Stephen & Catharine M., b 12-5-1839; m Mary Ann E. ----- d 4-20-1903
Ch: Mary Anna Esterbrook b 8-27-1870
Katharine Murray b 12-8-1874
cf Haddonfield 3-1869 for Mary Anna; Francis relrq 10-4-1905
Francis Howgill, s Edw. H. & Phebe H., rocf ND MM 7-1868; name erased
Francis Sydney rocf Balby, Eng. 2-3-1904; name erased 10-1928
Frederick R., s Wm. S. & Abigail; dis mo 5-1849
George d 3-18-1865 ae 63y; m Peru Elizabeth K. ----- d 9-24-1855
Ch: Henry T. b 8-22-1854
William K. b 9-17-1855
cf New Bedford 1848; cert of clear to Peru 3-2-1853; cf Peru 3-23-1854
George & Mary E.
Ch: Hannah Leggett [for all
parents recrq 3-1877; ct Pokeepsie 6-1879
George H. m Hazel OLER
Ch: Robert Walter
Frances Adelaide d rpd 1-1925
Ch: George H. Jr.
cf Indianapolis 10-1-1919 for all; ct Hartland 1-1925 for all living [1837
George S., s Samuel & Mary, b 8-28-1802; dis 4-
Gilbert Congdon, s Wm. H. S. & Emma (Congdon), b N. Y. 6-21-1865; relrq 2-6-1929
Grace R. (nm), dt Robert & Stella (Read); m 1893 Wm. Robert HAVILAND (H); Wm. R. relrq 6-14-1913
Harriet V. S., dt Wm. S. & Abigail; m ----- SEELY
cf Marl. with parents 1-21-1835; ct Haddonfield 2-5-1840, minor; cf Haddonfield 5-10-1841; dis mo 3-1849
Henry rocf Chap. 1831; d 1-16-1835 ae 79y bHS
Henry, s John & Martha, N. Y.; m N. Y. 9-9-1835 Anna B. HINSDALE, dt Henry & Mary, N. Y., d 8-20-1838 ae 22y 3m 11d bHS
Ch: Rebecca b 9-3-1836 d 1-27-1916 Germantown, Pa., bPP [town
Anna B. Jr. b 6-25-1838 d 9-3-1838 German-
cf Chap. 11-11-1830 (clear)
Henry M. 2d N. Y. 4-8-1840 Elizabeth T. KING, dt John & Mary R. (both dec), N. Y., d 6-6-1858 at Rahway, ae 47y bPP
Ch: John Henry b 4-27-1841
ct R. & P. 1842 for those living
Henry, s Charles & Sarah, rocf N.P. with parents 7-20-1843; rel 6-2-1875, absent over 5y; in Calif. 1849 (H)
Henry, s Stephen & Phebe, Croton Valley; m 2-19-1835 at Croton, Mary Jane UNDERHILL, dt Robert (dec) & Mary, Cortlandt
Ch: Stephen b 1837
Robert H. b 11-12-1841
Mary Augusta
cf Chap. 7-13-1837 for Henry; cf Ama. 7-14-1837 for Mary; ct Chap. with 3 ch 2-1846
Henry (nm) & -----
Ch: Infant stillborn 1-13-1836
Henry T., s George & Elizabeth K., b 8-22-1854; ct New Bedford 8-1860 with brother, Wm. K., infants of dec parents
Irene B. m 1912 Dudley DAVENPORT (H)
Isaac d 3-25-1868 ae 76y bHS; m Ann M. ----- b N. Y. d 12-23-1820 ae 22y bHS
Ch: Ann Augusta d 3-19-1820 ae 11m 15d bHS
dis mo 10-1818
Isaac m 2d Mary ----- d 7-2-1830 ae 28y bHS under Orthodox comm.
Jacob d 5-31-1818 ae 51y bHS; m Mary -----
Ch: Moses b 1-8-1794
Walter b 11-6-1795
cf Pur. 5-8-1794 for both, with s, Moses
Jacob m Wby 1801 Mary ----- d 1-25-1862 (H)
took cert of clear to Wby 3-4-1801; Mary rocf Wby 5-20-1801; Mary, wd, dis 3-1831 (O)
Dr. James R., s Elkanah & Anna, rocf Pur. 11-12-1818 with parents; d 5-4-1882 (Eminent Sur-

WOOD, Dr. James R., continued
geon (H)
John rocf Chap. 5-15-1812
John, s Samuel & Mary, N. Y., d 7-25-1850; m N. Y. 10-19-1816 Sarah MOTT, dt Samuel & Sarah, N. Y., d 4-16-1875
Ch: Mary H. b 7-12-1817 d 3-29-1824
Louisa M. 7-17-1818 d 12-28-1903 bHS
Anna Mott b 1-24-1822 d 11-11-1893
Margaret b 8-20-1823
Caroline b 11-9-1824
Edward b 1-25-1827 d 2-3-1894
Walter b 10-28-1828 d 1-7-1832 bHS
Sarah b 9-17-1832 d 3-19-1849
Emily d 10-13-1832 bHS
parents dis 1829 (H)
John d 5-12-1845; m Martha -----
Ch: Daniel dis 1826
Henry
Stephen
David d 6-19-1824 ae 11y 6m
John Jr.
Edward H. b 5-7-1822
Charles " 10-2-1824
Elizabeth C.
George
Mary
five ch, Daniel, Henry, Stephen, David & John, recrq of father 1-1-1817; Martha, with George & Mary, gct R. & P. 11-1845 (O) parents & Henry dis 1829 (H) (Flour merchant)
John Jr., s John & Martha; m Abigail S. GRIFFEN
Ch: Phebe Jane
Ann R. d 11-12-1824 ae 1y 1m
cf Creek for Abigail 7-18-1834; ct Creek 9-5-1838 for both with ch named
John rocf Pokeepsie 3-1889; d 3-2-1901
John Jay rocf Chap. 7-10-1845; dis 6-1847
Jonas & Mary
Ch: Mary
Jacob
Hannah
Jonas & Mary rocf Wby 6-1-1774; ct Wby with 3 ch 5-7-1778
Joseph b L. I. d 7-14-1835 ae 45y 4m; m Eliza Ann ----- b Westchester Co. d 10-8-1828 ae 32y (H)
Ch: Mary Elma
Ann Eliza
cf Pur. 7-12-1826 with 2 ch named; all dis 1830-1839 (O); Joseph dis 4-1835 (H)
Joseph R., s David S. & Lydia H., b 7-5-1872 d 6-21-1911 at Wellesley, Mass. bPP; m Phila. Elizabeth R. NICHOLSON
Ch: David Shove b 9-17-1896 d 11-4-1896 bPP
cf New Bedford with parents 11-1883; ct Phila. WD 2-2-1898 for both; cf WD MM 3-4-1896 for Elizabeth
Louisa K., dt Geo. D. & Harriet A. KIMBER
name erased 5-1886
Lydia, dt Samuel & Mary, b 8-18-1803 d 1-12-1887 ae 84y 5m bPP; dis 1-1842
Margaret, dt John & Sarah M., N. Y.; m 1848 Thomas W. BIRDSALL
Maria, dt Andrew & Phebe SOUTHERLAND; dis mo 2-1848
Marianna, dt Walter R. & Mary Anna, N. Y., b 1-29-1827; m 1855 Edward BROWN
Martha recrq 4-5-1820
Martha, dt Alfred & Mary F. WILLIS, dis mo 7-1853
Mary, dt Samuel & Mary, N. Y.; m 1823 Manning L. SEYMOUR
Mary Anna, dt Walter R. & Mary Anna, b 1-29-1827; m ----- BROWN (mo)
Mary Elma, dt Joseph & Eliza Ann; m ----- COLMAN (H)
dis 11-1836
Mary Jane, dt Wm. S. & Abigail; m ----- McANNALLY (mo)
dis mo 8-1846
Mary U., dt Wm. Henry S. & Emma (Congdon), b N. Y. 7-19-1881; m 1907 Merrill Edward GATES, Jr.
relrq 1-1-1919
Moses Q., s Jacob & Mary, b 1-8-1794; dis 10-1827
Morris (nm) & -----
Ch: Anna B. d 9-4-1838 ae 6 wks. bHS
Phebe, dt Samuel & Mary, N. Y.; m 1819 Isaac HATCH
Phebe E., dt Thomas & Mary, b 11-9-1825; dis 12-1844 (H)
Phianah m Cornell RHOADS (mo)
recrq 1833; ret a mbr
Raymond A., s Vincent A. & Grace (Ransome); m 12-16-1924 Elizabeth LAWTON, dt Albert R. & Emily W., b N. Y. 1-24-1895 d 4-1-1931 Po'keepsie
Ch: Raymond Albert b 3-26-1931
Raymond a mbr at Po'keepsie (O); Raymond Albert's name trans. to Pokeepsie MM as per Discipline 4-1-1931 (O)
Richard, s Samuel & Mary, b 1-9-1801; dis 4-1837
Samuel d 5-5-1844 ae 83y 9m 18d; m Mary ----- d 6-19-1855
Ch: Phebe
Sarah b 7-2-1785 d 4-22-1867 ae 82y
Silas
Samuel S. d 9-24-1861
John
Isaac
William b 5- 6-1797
Mary " 7- 7-1795
Anna " 3-21-1799
Richard " 1- 9-1801
Sidney
George S. b 8-28-1802
Lydia " 8-18-1803
Hannah " 12-15-1804 d 9-29-1805
cf Pur. 12-5-1803 with 11 ch; all dis 1829 (H) (Printer)
Samuel S., s Samuel & Mary, gct Balt. W. Dist. 8-5-1818 (clear); cf Balt. W. Dist. 9-5-

WOOD, Samuel S., continued
1828; d 9-24-1861 ae 72y bPP
Sarah Ann, dt Thomas & Mary; m ----- BARTON (mo) (H)
dis 11-1838
Sarah M., dt John & Margaret, b 8-20-1823
Silas & -----
Ch: Samuel b N. Y. d 7-24-1826 ae 4y bHS
Virginia b N. Y. d 8-29-1826 ae 1y 4m bHS
Wm. Pitts d 12-29-1835 ae 10m 11d bHS
Julia d 1-1-1834 ae 1y 28d bHS
had borne arms & performed military duty before 10-12-1814; dis 1-4-1815; living at Williamsburgh, Va.
Simeon, s Thomas & Mary, dis 10-1832 (H)
Simmons dis mo & jas 8-1842
Stephen, s John W. & Martha, N. Y., d 3-7-1884 ae 73y bPP; m N. Y. 10-8-1834 Catharine M. WING, dt John & Mary R. (dec), N. Y., b 3-18-1814 d 5-14-1898 bPP
Ch: Eleanor b 9-20-1835
Mary R. King b 11- 3-1837 d 10-31-1846
Francis b 12- 5-1839
Robert b 2-12-1843 d 7-25-1866
Stephen b 3-25-1845
John King b 3-18-1847 d 4-13-1906
Benjamin B. b 6-15-1850 d 4-1-1926
Anna C. b 7-24-1851 d 5-1855
Howard b 12-19-1855
Caroline b 9-11-1861 d 2-13-1878 bPP
Howard's d rpd 7-1920
Stephen, s Henry & Mary Jane, Chicago; m at Benj. D. Hicks' 1-18-1865 Anna H. TERRY, dt Chas. M. & Margaret (dec), N. Y. (H) (Benj. D. Hicks not under care of N.Y. MM)
Stephen Jr., s Stephen & Catharine M., b 3-25-1845; m Deer Creek, Md. 1868 Marianna M. MARIS
Ch: Herbert Stephen b 12-27-1870 d 2-27-1872 bPP, rem to Flush. Cem.
Frederick M. b 2-19-1873 d 4-13-1874 bPP, rem to Flush. Cem.
Arthur King b 9- 2-1875
Ernest W. b 3-21-1877
cert of clear to Deer Creek, Md. 2-1868; cf Deer Creek 4-1869 for Marianna M.; Stephen rel 7-5-1905; Marianna 5-6-1901
Thomas d 11-1836; m Mary ----- d 3-4-1861 (H)
Ch: Aaron
Jane
Simeon
Edmund
William H.
Eliza J.
Sarah Ann
Daniel M.
Phebe E. b 11-9-1825
cf Chap. 6-12-1818 with first 5 ch; all dis 1829-1849 (0)
Walter (nm) & -----
Ch: Walter b N. Y. d 8-21-1829 ae 5m bHS
Walter R., s Jacob & Mary (both dec), d 5-19-1830 ae abt 35y bHS; m N. Y. 5-9-1821 Mary Anna BUCKLEY, dt Thomas & Anna, N.Y., d 7-24-1873
Ch: Anna B. b 10-13-1823 d 11-12-1824
Thomas B. b 10-13-1825 d 3-6-1834 bHS
Mary Anna b 1-29-1827
Walter R. b 1829 d 1829
Walter R. b 5-28-1830
Walter R., s Walter R. & Mary Anna, b 5-28-1830; m ----- (mo)
Ch: Anna Buckley d 8-17-1860 ae 21d bPP, rem to Greenwood 1874
dis 4-14-1858
Willett rocf Pur. 8-10-1809 (clear); dis mo 6-3-1812
William, s William, Dartmouth, N. E.; m Flush. 3 Mo (May) 14, 1730 Keziah HEDGER, dt Joseph, Flushing
William, s Samuel & Mary, N. Y., d 4-9-1877; m N. Y. 11-11-1835 Mary S. UNDERHILL, dt Joshua & Mary (dec), N. Y., b 9-8-1805 d 4-10-1894
Ch: Frederick William b 9- 9-1837 d 9-25-1839 bHS
William Henry S. b 4-13-1840
Elizabeth U. b 4- 7-1842
Wm. Congdon, s Wm. Henry S. & Emma (Congdon), b N. Y. 7-22-1866; relrq 11-1927
William H., s Thomas & Mary, dis mo & jas 4-1838 (H); dis mo & jas 2-1841 (0)
Wm. Henry S., s William & Mary, b 4-13-1840; m Emma C. CONGDON, d 11-26-1896
Ch: William Congdon b 7-22-1866
Gilbert Congdon b 6-21-1869
Arnold b 9-23-1872
Philip Hopkins b 5-22-1876 d 5-10-1882
Mary Underhill b 7-19-1881
cert of clear to Providence 8-1865; cf Providence 7-1866 for Emma C.
Wm. Henry S. d 12-11-1907; m 2d 1-16-1907 Cornelia ELLIOTT, wd Wm. L., dt Abraham S. & Mary F. UNDERHILL, b 3-15-1846 d 5-9-1925
William K., s George & Elizabeth K., gct New Bedford 8-1-1860 with brother, Henry T., infant ch of dec parents
William L., s Wm. S. & Mary, dis mo 6-8-1859
William S. (or W.) m Abigail ----- d 9-19-1838 ae 49y 3d bHS.
Ch: Benjamin
Eliza L.
John S. d 5-16-1836 ae 13y 7m bHS
Frederick R.
Mary Jane
Harriet V. S.
William L.
cf Marl. 1-21-1835 with 7 ch named; ct Marl. 4-1-1874 for Wm. S.
William S. m 2d Mary ----- d 3-16-1869 (mo) ret a mbr
----- & ----- (nm)
Ch: Charles d 8-28-1814 ae 2m bHS
Julia d 1- 1-1834 ae 1y 28d bHS
Wm. Penn d 2- 8-1834 ae 1y 7m bHS

WOOD, continued
Ch: Robert d 7-29-1866 ae 23y bPP
Sarah d 4-22-1867 ae 82y bPP

WOODBRIDGE
Elsa, (nm) dt J. L. & E. T., d 12-29-1905 ae 14y 7m 17d bPP (H)

WOODNUT
Anna rocf Wby 10-6-1873; ct Flush 6-6-1877 (H)

WOODROW
Grace, dt Henry H. & Eliz. (Watson), b Easton, Pa. 5-22-1904; m 1932 Allen H. MAGILL recrq 12-11-1933; Allen mbr Solesbury, Pa.

WOODRUFF
Benjamin d 11-25-1821 bHS (unm) (listed in boy's column)
Charles S. & Maude G.
cf Po'keepsie 11-1924; ct Arch St., Phila. 7-2-1930

WOODSON
Josiah & -----
Ch: William Penn b 2-8-1834 ae 1y 7m bHS (not a mbr here)

WOODWARD
Cornelia, dt Thos. Jr. & Eliz. (Cromwell), b N. Y. 9-29-1855 d New Bedford, Mass. 11-11-1923 bPP; m George H. RHODES (nm)
Cornelia relrq 6-14-1876
Edgar H., s Henry E. & Marie H. (Kowlinski), b N. Y. 12-31-1879; m 6-19-1918 Bertha C. LEAVEY, dt Samuel & Rose (Uprumney), b N.Y. 7-14-1893 (H)
Ch: Edgar Hunt 2d b 4-3-1920
Bertha recrq 6-12-1933; Edgar recrq 1-8-1934; Edgar 2d recrq 12-10-1934
Elizabeth, w Thomas, d 10-4-1842
Ch: Elizabeth d 8- 2-1884
Mary D.
Benjamin d 1821
Martha
John D. d 8-1841 (lost on Steamboat "Erie" when she burned)
Thomas Jr.
cf Pur. 7-10-1817 with her 5 ch named, rem with h; Thomas Jr. recrq of mother 5-1827
Francis, s Thos. Jr. & Eliz. (Cromwell), b 12-2-1849; relrq 6-1882
Gilbert b L. I. d 12-17-1811 ae 33y bHS
Martha, dt Thomas & Eliz.; m John D. GRIFFEN
Mary rocf Phila. 4-25-1811; dis 8-7-1816
Mary b N. Y. d 8-21-1843 ae 79y (H)
Mary D., dt Thos. & Eliz., N. Y.; m 1834 Benj. B. HUSSEY
Morris & Elizabeth
Ch: Infant stillborn 2-7-1840 bHS
all nm
Nathaniel (nm) b Newtown, L. I. d 9-29-1812 ae 48y bHS (m)
Thomas (nm) & Elizabeth C.
Ch: Jane d 7-27-1818 ae 9m bHS
(prob) Infant stillborn 2-17-1840 bHS
" " " 2-23-1841 bHS
Thos. Jr., s Thos. & Eliz., N. Y., d 12-19-1885 ae 70y bPP; m N. Y. 6-12-1839 Elizabeth CROMWELL, dt Daniel & Eliz., N. Y., b N. Y. 12-8-1816 d 3-12-1903 ae 86y 3m 4d bPP
Ch: John D. b 10-10-1842 d 2-22-1842
Daniel C. b 5-28-1844 d 8- 8-1849
Thomas Jr. b 4- 2-1846
Anna C. b 3-30-1848 d 8-16-1851
Francis b 12- 2-1849
Floyd b 9-13-1852 d 3-28-1854
Cornelia b 9-29-1855
Lizzie b 12- 3-1857 d 12-16-1858
Thomas W., s Thos. Jr. & Elizabeth, b 4-2-1846 d 1-1918; m Emma SMITH d abt 1894 bPP
Ch: Francis b N. Y. d New Bedford, Mass. 11-19-1927 bPP (unm) (nm)

WOOLCOTT
Joseph (nm) & -----
Ch: Mary N. d 9-12-1839 ae 14d bHS
(prob) Joseph H. b N. Y. d 3-13-1841 ae 8m bHS

WOOLLEY
Elizabeth, dt John, Shrews.; m 1721 John FIELD
Elizabeth brought cert of clear (especially from John Herior (or Leaware) of Phila) from Shrews. 11 Mo (Jan) 2, 1720/1
Jacob B., s Jacob Jr. & Letitia (Kirby), b Shrews. 11-13-1840 d 11-19-1910; m 1-5-1865 Susan Louisa DUGAN (nm) (H)
Ch: a dt (nm)
recrq 2-6-1889
Joseph C. (nm) b N. J. d 7-12-1843 ae 29y bHS (m)
Margaret, dt Wardell & Mary U., b 8-16-1859; m 1891 Albert W. KISSAM (nm) (H)
Sidney (nm) & -----
Ch: Infant stillborn 1-30-1831 bHS
Wardell, s Robt. H. & Julia A. (Wardell), d 6-8-1899; m 9-30-1841 Mary V. TUNISON, dt Hardenburg & Sarah J. (King) b 6-29-1818 d 7-13-1906 (H)
Ch: Margaret b 8-16-1859
Wardell recrq 5-6-1868; Mary recrq 6-3-1868; Margaret recrq 2-7-1894
----- & ----- (nm)
Ch: Helen Justina b N. Y. d 3-27-1838 ae 2y 3m 4d bHS

WOOLSEY
Benjamin, s Jere. & Hannah, dis 3-1827
Charlotte dis jas 5-2-1821
Isaac m Hannah ----- b North Castle d 2-15-1809
Ch: a dt stillborn 2-15-1809
Isaac & Hannah mbr
Jeremiah b Marl. d 5-7-1848 ae 78y 8m 18d;

WOOLSEY, Jeremiah, continued
m Hannah SUTTON, dt Joshua & Martha, d 2-23-1809 ae 35y 8m
Ch: Benjamin
Susanna
Grennette
Gardner b 1-15-1803
Charlotte b 1-31-1805
cf Corn. 7-28-1803 with 3 small ch
Jeremiah m 2d Catharine ----- d 7-7-1849
Ch: Hannah d 10-21-1813 ae 1y 11m bHS (nm)
Peter " 11-28-1813 ae 6m bHS (nm)
Elizabeth d 1-27-1815 ae 1y 10m bHS (nm)
Jeremiah dis mo 6-6-1810; Catharine, his w, recrq 8-1-1821
Margaret b Westchester Co. d 7-17-1811 ae 78y bHS (wd)
Sarah, dt Jeremiah; m ----- OSTRANDER (mo)
cf Marl. 8-25-1809; dis mo 1-1-1812
Sarah dis 10-7-1818

WOOLSTON
Cyrus (nm), s Daniel, d 12-24-1927 bPP; m Harriet WISEMAN, dt William & Anne (Giles), b Eng. 2-16-1853 d 6-6-1923 bPP
Harriet recrq 4-3-1901

WOOTON
Amelia J. m Harold W. GAMMON
letter from Nostrand Ave. M. E. Ch., Bkn. 3-4-1903
Harriet R. [Wooten], dt Wilfrid E.; m ----- QUEST
Harriet recrq of father 3-4-1903; name erased 11-6-1929
Wilfred Edward [Wootton]
Ch: Harriet R.
recrq 2-1882; Harriet R. recrq of father 3-4-1903

WORTH
Anna, dt Benjamin & Phebe, rocf Nantucket 2-25-1802 (clear); ct Nantucket 3-7-1804 (clear)
Edward H. (not a mbr in N.Y.), s Wm. P. & Caroline H., Coatesville, Pa.; m at Harriet F. Merritt's 12-19-1906 Anna V. MERRITT, dt Richard P. (dec) & Harriet (Frost), Bkn., b Bkn. 10-1-1880 (H)
Ch: Margaret b Coatesville 11-13-1909
ct Wilmington 7-13-1925 for Anna & Margaret

WORTHINGTON
J. Kent, s Wm. C. & Susannah H., Darlington, Md. (both dec); m N. Y. 10-17-1878 Josephine G. HARLAN, dt Joseph G. & Anna (both dec), of Haverford, Pa., Josephine in N. Y.
cf Radnor 3-1860 for Josephine; ct WD MM 2-1880 for Josephine
Joshua H., Phila.; m N. Y. 11-23-1876 at Hannah W. Collins', Sarah COLLINS, N. Y.
ct Balt. 4-1878 for Sarah C.

WRAY
Alfred Busselle, s Jos. B. & Hannah B., b 9-3-1880; m Sarah DEAN
ct Union Springs 3-6-1912 for Alfred
Ann, dt Christopher & Elizabeth, d 5-1-1846 ae 30y bHS; m ----- BRADLEY (mo)
dis 7-10-1842
Anna M., dt Christopher & Sophia J., N. Y.; m 1890 Harry N. HOFFMAN
Christopher [Ray] d 1843; m Elizabeth ----- d 6-1854
Ch: Susan E. d 7-30-1824 ae 2m 2d
Henry
Mary
Edward
John
Hannah
Ann
Christopher (changed name to Wray)
Joseph d 2-28-1841 bHS ae 22y 2d
Martha
William b 11-2-1826 d 1827
cf Corn. 1826 with 9 ch named; all but Hannah & Christopher Jr. dis 1831-1849 (O); parents dis 1829 (H)
Christopher, s Chris. (dec) & Eliz., N. Y., d 10-23-1891; m N. Y. 12-9-1846 Sophia Jane BUSSELL, dt George & Eliz., N. Y., d 1-25-1894
Ch: Joseph Bowman b 4- 6-1850
Elizabeth Daw b 6- 2-1852 d 1- 3-1854
Edward Marshall b 2-20-1854
Alfred Bussell b 6-25-1857 d 3-23-1869
Samuel Daw b 2-24-1859
Infant stillborn 9-26-1861
Anna Maria b 10-29-1863
Sophia Jane rocf Bristol, Eng. with parents 6-13-1820
Edith Sophia, dt Joseph B. & Hannah B., N. Y.; m 1904 Clyde Cecil HOLLIDAY
Edward, s Christopher & Elizabeth, dis mo 10-2-1839; lives in Texas
Edward Marshall, s Chris. & Sophia J., b 2-20-1854; m 9-9-1880 Elizabeth L. WRAY, dt John & Elizabeth C., b 1-13-1852
Edward relrq 8-1880 (O); Elizabeth relrq 11-4-1899 (H)
Elizabeth L., dt John & Elizabeth C., b 1-31-1852; m 9-9-1880 Edward M. WRAY (mbr O)
relrq 11-4-1899 (H)
John, s Christopher & Eliz., b 10-18-1811 d 3-29-1885; m Elizabeth C. ----- d 6-27-1875 (H)
Ch: Mary H. b 8-10-1850
Elizabeth L. b 1-31-1852
William H. b 7-1-1854
Ann d 7-13-1858 ae 8m 7d bPP
cf Corn. 6-1826 for John; cf R. & P. 5-1850 for Eliz.; dis mo & non-attendance 6-1849
Joseph Bowman, s Chris. & Sophia, b 6-5-1850 d 1-27-1887; m Hannah B. ----- d 8-26-1900
Ch: Edith Sophie b 1-19-1878

WRAY, Joseph Bowman & Hannah B., continued
Ch: Alfred Bussell b 9- 3-1880
Josephine B. b 2-27-1885
cf Phila. ND 9-5-1877
Josephine B., dt Joseph B. & Hannah (B----), b 2-27-1885; m ----- FISHER
Mary H., dt John & Elizabeth C., b 8-10-1850; relrq 1-4-1896 (H)
Samuel Bussell, s Chris. & Sophia J., b 2-24-1859; m Phila. 4-11-1894 Helen B. MASTERS
Ch: Cecil Masters b 4-21-1896
Marjorie Rebecca b 7-28-1897
cf WD MM 5-6-1896 for Helen; lt Pilgrim Cong. Ch., Seattle, Wash. 4-1914 for all
William H., s John & Elizabeth, b Rahway 7-1-1854 d before 1921; m 5-18-1880 Ida ----- 2 Tudor Road, Upper Norwood, Eng. 1900 (H)

WRIGHT
Aaron, s Jonathan & Mary, d 12-15-1885; m at Amos Willets' 4-2-1840 (or 4-1-1840) Mary WILLETS, dt Amos & Ann (Titus) (dec), N.Y., b 4-1-1820 N. Y. d 4-18-1904
Ch: Infant stillborn 3-13-1841
Mary Ann b 3-14-1843
Amos Willets b 11-20-1844
Frederick W. b 8-12-1851
Jonathan b 2- 2-1860
Aaron rocf Springboro, O. 3-1840; ct Springboro 3-1864 for all; cf Springboro 12-7-1881 for parents
Achsah L., w ----- (H)
Ch: Edwin
cf Chesterfield 5-1839 with s; ct Chesterfield 5-1841 for both
Ann rocf Hudson 1-25-1848 with sisters, Hannah & Elizabeth; relrq 11-1858 (H)
Annie A., dt John Howard & Sarah Jane, N. Y., b 11-3-1857; m 11-13-1877 Joseph P. MASON (nm), of Worcester, Mass.; m 2d 10-6-1903 John B. DUMONT (H)
Anthony d 7 Mo (Sep) 8, 1680 (unm) prominent mbr; gave land for O.B. MH
Arthur rocf Westminster & Longford, Eng. 10-1881; name erased 10-1928
Barnabas, s John & Hannah; m -----
Ch: Charles
Hannah T. (or C.)
George Edward d 12-12-1873
cf Corn. 8-27-1846 with ch; ct Chap. for Barnabas 9-6-1854 with w, Hannah
Barnabas m 2d Chap. 8-13-1846 Hannah T. WEEKS, dt Benj. R. & Sarah (H)
Ch: Edgar
Carrie Louisa, dt J. Howard & Sarah Jane, b 12-29-1853; m 1873 Henry COOLIDGE (nm) (H)
Charles, s John, rocf Wby 9-30-1772
Charles mo, since his rem it is ref. to Pur. 9-2-1778; ct Pur. 10-7-1778; cf Pur. 8-12-1784
Charles gct Flushing 10-3-1810
Charles, s Barnabas, rocf Corn. 8-27-1846 with father; ct Chap. 6-2-1858 (H)
Charles A. m Edith Virginia THOMPSON, dt William, d 6-29-1909 ae 31y bPP (both nm) (H)
Chauncey (nm) m 10-6-1863 Rachel HANCE, dt Anselm B. & Ellen, d 6-26-1904 ae 69y bPP Rachel recrq of father 11-1842 (H)
Edgar, s Barnabas & Hannah, d 11-9-1894; m 1-7-1846 Lydia M. WEEKS, dt Thos. T. & Mary (Hoag), b New Castle 2-16-1822 d 1-18-1905 (H) both recrq 2-3-1886
Edgar S. m Anna Louisa PRINDLE b Charlotte, Vt. 10-30-1863 d Richmond Hill, N. Y. 7-14-1918 bPP
Edward A. d 9-15-1880 ae 78y bPP; m Mary N. ----- d 1-1857 ae 51y bPP (both nm)
Edward E., s Nathan & Emeline (Johnson), b Harrisville, O. 4-23-1859; m 8-30-1886 Ella REARDON (nm), dt Ralph & Mary J. (Curry) (H)
recrq 6-8-1912
Eliza, dt John W. & Eliza; m 1832 William R. SMITH
ct Farmington 12-1832
Eliza, dt William & Jane, b 12-4-1810; m ----- TOMPKINS (mo)
dis mo 1-1-1834 (O); dis mo 3-1834 (H)
Elizabeth rocf Hudson 1-25-1848 with sisters, Hannah & Ann; relrq 11-1858
Ella, dt William & Emily, b 12-27-1848; relrq 6-4-1879 (H)
Emily, dt William & Emily, b 6-25-1852; relrq 6-4-1879 (H)
Francis T., s William & Jane, b 7-29-1814; lost at sea abt 1842 (H)
George, s John W. & Eliza, rocf Lisburn, Ire., 10-13-1825, a youth; ct Phila. 10-3-1838 for George A. (clear)
Hannah (nm) b Pa. d 7-18-1818 ae 38y (wd)
Hannah m ----- GOULD
cf Hudson 1-25-1848 with sisters, Eliz. & Ann; relrq 3-1852 (H)
Hannah, O.B., drowned in Md. while on a religious visit
Hannah C. (or T.), dt Barnabas; m ----- HALSTEAD (H)
cf Corn. 8-27-1846 with father; ct Chap. 11-1863
Harry Noble m Edna WHITE
cf West Richmond, Ind. 11-3-1932 for both
Isaac, Flushing, b L. I. d 8-9-1832 ae 72y; m Sarah ----- d 1-28-1836 ae 73y bPP (H)
Ch: Mary b 4- 2-1785
William b 12- 6-1787
cf Wby 8-25-1784 for Isaac & Sarah; parents dis 1829 (O); parents rem to PP in one grave
Isaac M., s William & Jane, b 6-7-1812 d 11-9-1868; dis 1-1850 (H)
Joannah (nm) b West Chester d 3-14-1809 ae 35y 7m 8d
Job (nm) & Mary
Ch: Solomon

WRIGHT, Job & Mary, continued
Ch: John
Mary
cf Corn. 5-19-1800 for Mary & dt; cf Corn. 5-19-1800 for Solomon & John
John dis mo 3-3-1813
John (nm) & -----
Ch: William P. b Belfast Ire. d 5-22-1818 ae 2y 1m
John, s Wm. & Anna (dec), Belmont, Ohio; m N.Y. 7-9-1851 Sarah VALENTINE, dt Geo. & Mary (dec), Pickering, Canada
John & Sarah
Ch: Isaac
cf Ire. 1848; ct Whitewater, Ind. with 1 ch 1855; cf Cincin. 4-1863 for parents; ct Pickering 7-1867 for parents
John C. rocf Corn. 12-1-1847; dis 7-1850 (H)
John D., s Jordan & Rebecca, b 9-19-1799; m Mary B. ----- d N. Y. 11-30-1843
Ch: James Byrd b 12-16-1822 d 3-20-1879
Caroline b 5-29-1825 d 1-6-1864
John Howard b 8- 2-1828
cf Flush. 6-2-1825 with 1 ch named; all dis 1830-1848 (O)
John D. m 2d at Catharine F. Smith's 6-5-1845 Amelia FARRINGTON, dt Geo. & Eliz. (dec), N. Y., d 6-13-1863 (H)
cf Flush. 12-1830 for Amelia; cf Flush. 9-2-1846 for John & ch; ct Oswego 6-1-1853 for John & Amelia
John D. m 3d at John Shapter's, N. Y. 10-6-1864 Lydia E. UNDERHILL, dt Samuel & Eliza B. (dec), N. Y., b 8-15-1826 d 7-1-1898 (H)
Ch: Amelia Eliza b 8- 4-1865 d 1-10-1872
Albert Aiken b 9-25-1870 d 4-19-1894
cf Oswego 2-2-1876 for John
John Eldridge (nm), s Samuel L. & Sarah Helen; m 12-14-1924 Elizabeth A. HALLOCK, dt Henry B. & Anna B., b Bkn. 4-18-1874 (H)
John Howard, s John D. & Mary (Byrd), N. Y. (dec), b N. Y. 8-2-1828 d 11-19-1915; m at Isaac Walton's 1-4-1849 Sarah Jane WALTON, dt Isaac & Prudence, N. Y., b N. Y. 3-12-1830 d 4-8-1913 (H)
Ch: Mary B. b 5-13-1850
Carrie Louisa b 12-29-1853
Annie Augusta b 11- 3-1857
John Dunbar Jr. b 5- 3-1862 d 10-5-1917
John H. rocf Flush. with father 9-2-1846
John W. b Ire. d 9-7-1829 ae 56y; m Eliza -----
Ch: Richard
Eliza
John
William Penn
George rocf Lisburn 1825
dis by Lisburn MM, Ire., he rq rst; rpd favorable; cf Lisburn 12-4-1822 for John W.; cf Lisburn 7-17-1817 for Elizabeth & 4 first ch; ct Farm. 7-1840 for Eliza; parents dis 1829 (H); John W. dis
John Wm., s Reuben & Phila, b 3-30-1809; dis mo & non-attendance 1-1854

Jordan, s John & Phebe, Merchant, N. Y.; m Elizabeth ----
Ch: Jane b 3-14-1788
Susan " 4-16-1789
Charles b 3-12-1790
Eliza b 4-12-1793
Margery 5- 1-1794
Jordan m 2d N. Y. 3-14-1798 Rebecca DUNBAR, dt Daniel & Naomi, N. Y.
Ch: John D. b 7-19-1799
Daniel " 6-14-1801
Robert " 10-11-1803
cf Jericho 7-19-1792 with w, Elizabeth, & ch, Jane, Susannah & Charles
Joseph rocf Balby MM, Yorkshire 8-13-1807 (clear); endorsed to Balby 4-6-1808 (clear)
Justus (nm) d 12-6-1872 ae 83y, rem from Canada to PP 9-18-1886; m Betsey TUCKER (nm) d 12-6-1862 ae 73y 3m 13d bPP
Ch: David d 1-20-1886 ae 68y 4m 10d bPP
Leah (nm), dt Job & Mary A., d 3-7-1922 ae 76y 7m 9d ashes bPP; m 1889 Charles E. DAVENPORT (H)
Lydia, dt Peter; m 1684 Isaac HORNER
Lydia, dt Thomas T. & Mary WEEKS, b 2-16-1822 (w Edgar); cf Chap. with parents 11-8-1835; dis 5-5-1847 (H)
Lydia S., dt Joseph, d 4-24-1866 ae 50y 2m 7d bPP; m John G. STREET (nm) (H)
cf New Garden, Ohio 7-1847
Martha Jane rocf Carlow, Ire. 1-10-1851; ct Dublin 6-1857 (clear)
Mary, O.B. m 1663 Samuel ANDREWS
Mary rocf ND MM 10-27-1789; ct NS MM 1-4-1792 (clear)
Mary, w Job
Ch: Mary
cf Corn. 5-19-1800 with dt, Mary
Mary, dt Isaac & Sarah, N. Y.; m 1804 Francis THOMPSON
Mary rocf Ama. 1-12-1811 (clear); ct Ama. 4-3-1816
Mary, w Edward, dt. James & Hester NELSON, d 2-6-1857
Mary, wd, d
Mary B., dt John Howard & Sarah J., b 5-13-1850; m 1869 J. Edgar CORLIES (H)
Mary F. m Daniel (or Lewis) HOUSTON (H)
cf Jericho 6-1842; ct Flush. 7-1-1874
Mary N., w Edward, d 2-6-1857 (H); marked Orthodox 2-1850
Obadiah, s John, Wby, rocf Wby 9-28-1774 (clear)
Phebe J., dt Samuel & Jane, d 5-29-1894; m ----- BOND (nm) (H)
Rachel, dt Job & Rachel, O.B.; m 1715 Thomas STOKES
Reuben & Phila
Ch: Seaman H.
Sarah b 2-20-1802
Jane Maria b 11-28-1806
John William b 3-30-1809
Reuben Jr. b 3-18-1812
William

WRIGHT, Reuben & Phila, continued
Ch: Wilson
Seaman
cf Corn 3-24-1800 for parents; all dis 1829-1839 except Reuben & William, who had ct Scip. 7-1832 (O); ct Scip. 10-1831 for parents with Reuben & William (H)
Reuben, s Reuben & Phila, gct Scipio 7-4-1832, minor, with brother, William
Richard, s John W. & Eliza, rocf Lisburn, Ire. with mother 7-17-1817; ct Phila. 12-2-1840 (clear)
Samuel (nm) b Westchester Co. d 12-28-1812 ae 39y bHS (m)
Sarah (nm) b Queens Co. d 3-22-1824 ae 53y 22d bHS
Sarah Washburn (form Wright) dis mo 6-3-1818
Sarah, dt Wm. & Emily, b 2-3-1847 d 5-12-1908; m Frank L. EAMES (nm) 1874 (H)
Seaman, s Reuben & Phila; m ----- (H)
Ch: Infant d 4-25-1830 ae 3hr bHS
Twins stillborn 4-7-1831 bHS
dis 12-1838
Solomon (nm) d 4-5-1820 ae 38y 8m 17d bHS (unm)
Susanna dis mo before 11-7-1765
Thomas (nm) & Sarah A.
Ch: Eleanor d 9-16-1816 ae 4m
Sarah Ann b 11-12-1817 d 3-31-1821 ae 3y 5m bHS
Hannah " 6-24-1819
William
cf Balby MM, Eng. 6-14-1804 (clear); ct Hudson 12-7-1814 (clear); cf Hudson 10-24-1815 for both; ct Hudson 5-1-1822 with 2 infant ch, Hannah & William
Thomas gct Farm. 10-3-1838 (note at margin states cert not sent as he not a mbr)
Thomas L. d 1-15-1872 ae 42y 4m 24d bPP (H)
Wilbur Teed (nm), s Wm. H. & Arena (M----); m 11-14-1900 Florence MEAD, dt Geo. V. & Mary (Birdsall), b 4-28-1877 d 1-10-1923 (H)
Ch: Wilbur Teed, Jr. b 10-19-1901
George Mead b 3- 5-1907 d 7-10-1924
Wm. Harrison b 6-20-1908
Florence Birdsall b 12-17-1911
Florence's name entered by comm. 3-13-1883; ch recrq 6-12-1922
William m Easton 1809 Mary -----
cert of clear to Easton 9-6-1809; Mary rocf Easton 1-18-1810
William, s Isaac & Sarah, N. Y., b 12-6-1787 d 2-26-1830 ae 63y bPP; m Jane M. ----- d Troy, N. Y. 9-20-1824 (H)
Ch: Elizabeth (or Eliza) b 12-4-1810
Isaac M. b 6- 7-1812
Francis T. " 7-29-1814
Hannah M. " 5- 2-1820
cf Easton 1-18-1810 for Jane M.; all dis 1829-1839 (O)
William Jr. (nm) & -----
Ch: a s b N. Y. d 10-30-1830 ae 3y 8m bHS

William, s Thos. & Sarah A., Claverack, N. Y., d 7-25-1900; m at Thos. Carpenter's 11-11-1845 Emily CARPENTER, dt Thos. & Phebe, Bkn., d 4-7-1872 (H)
Ch: Sarah b 2- 3-1847
Ella " 12-27-1848
Emily b 6-25-1852
cf Hudson 7-2-1845 for William
William S., s Reuben & Phila, gct Scipio 7-4-1832, minor, with brother, Reuben
Wilson, s Reuben & Phila, marked Orthodox 2-1850
----- & ----- (nm)
Ch: Augustus d 8-11-1828 ae 8m bHS
James M. d 8-19-1831 ae 3m bHS
Sidney M. b Cayugu Co. d 12-18-1834 ae 5m 4d bHS
Phila Eliz. b N. Y. d 1-22-1838 ae 5d bHS
Maria S. d 8-16-1856 ae 20y 10m bPP
Ada B. " 4-12-1888 ae 13y bPP

WURTS
Lionel (nm), s Henry & Augusta, N. Y.; m at 15th St. 10-1-1904 Anna C. HUTCHINSON, dt John Wm. & E. Eliza, Hempstead, b N. Y. 11-11-1878 (H)
Ch: Richard b 9-18-1905
Anna Virginia b 3-24-1914
ch recrq of parents 5-12-1906 & 2-12-1916

WYATT
John gct Oblong 9-1-1779 (clear); cf Oblong 7-14-1783 (clear); ct Pur. 11-5-1783 (clear)

WYER (or Wyar)
Barzillai (nm) & Elizabeth
Ch: boy d 5-10-1809 stillborn
infant 3-23-1810 "

YARDLEY
Isaac (prob) m Harriet ----- b Pa. d 3-25-1834 ae 34y bHS
having mo, Falls, Pa. ref. it to N. Y. 12-9-1830; rpd adversely 4-6-1831
William W. rocf Phila. 1828; dis 1-1831 (O)

YARNELL
J. Howard d 3-20-1903; m M. Francis B. ----- d 7-25-1902
cf Chester, Pa. 9-1881 for J. H.; M. Francis recrq 1-1886

YARUS
Della Louise (nm), dt Westley F. & Edna L., East Orange; m 1923 Fareh MEGIRIAN

YEATES
Anna Smith, dt Samuel & Jane (Minard), b N. Y. 8-11-1838 (or 8-11-1837); m 1-1-1858 (or 12-31-1857) in Chicago Daniel GOODMAN (H)
long unknown; name rem 11-9-1925
Dinah [Yeats, Yates] m 1696 Daniel KIRKPATRICK
Elizabeth [Yates] rocf Weare 6-14-1821 (clear);

YEATES, continued
dis 1829 (H)
Francis [Yates] b 2 Mo (Apr) 27, 1710; m Hannah ----- b 5 Mo (July) 1712
Ch: Hannah b 6 Mo (Aug) 2, 1732
Ann " 2 Mo (Apr) 12, 1734
Sarah b 4 Mo (June) 18, 1736
John b 1 Mo (Mar) 23, 1746/7
Jane [Yates, Yeats], dt John, Flush.; m 1721 James PARSONS
Mary Abby, dt Samuel & Jane, b 1-16-1844; m 2-22-1886 Erastus FERRIS (nm) (H)
ret a mbr
Samuel m Jane ----- d 1864
Ch: Anna Smith b 8-11-1838
Phebe Jane
Mary Abbey b 1-16-1844
Jane recrq 4-1836; cf Phila. 11-23-1820; ct Norwich, Canada 8-4-1830 (0); ct Roch. 5-1831 (H); cf Roch. 7-1836
William [Yates] b Eng. d 9-6-1826 ae 67y bHS (unm)

YELLOTT
Bethiah, w George, b Eng. d 8-7-1838 ae 54y 4m 7d; recrq 4-3-1822; dis 11-1830 for non attendance (0) (wd) (H)
John J. (nm) m Caroline M. ----- (nm) d 1-19-1838 ae 32y 6m bPP
Ch: Worthington d 7-25-1838 ae 3y 3m 13d bHS, rem to PP
Bethia G. d 5-7-1863 ae 34y 3m 16d bPP
John Jr. (nm) d 10-25-1895 ae 88y 14d bPP; m 1839 Phebe T. UNDERHILL, dt Josiah J. & Hannah, b Hudson d 1-11-1848 ae 37y 9m 15d bPP
John G., s John Jr. & Phebe T., recrq of mother 1-1841; ct Corn. 10-1-1862 (H)
William (nm) & -----
Ch: Edward F. b N. Y. d 2-3-1833 ae 8m bHS

YEOMANS
Charles C. (nm) m 3-23-1853 Hannah Louisa UNDERHILL, dt Abraham C. & Eliz. B., b 3-2-1835 d 12-18-1924 (H)
at Seneca, Ill. 1858-1890
----- & ----- (nm)
Ch: Esther W. d 7-20-1878 ae 1y 11m bPP

YERKS
Affa rocf Chap. 1-1832; ct Ama. 4-5-1837; cf Ama. 2-2-1848; cf Chap. 12-10-1830 (0); dis 4-1831 (0); d 7-15-1873 (H)

YOTT
Helen Ethel, dt Malcolm C. & Lillian M.; m ----- WERNER (nm)
recrq 7-11-1906
Malcolm C. d rpd 1920; m Lillian M. -----
Ch: Eliot Ives
Helen Ethel
all recrq 7-11-1906

YOUDLE
Susannah d 1818

YOUNG
Abby Jane, dt Charles & Martha FIELD, b 5-24-1806 N. Y. d 8-6-1837 ae 31y 2m
Alexander d 7 Mo (Sep) 1712
Alexander b Ulster Co. d 6-18-1844 ae 77y 7m 16d; m Elizabeth ----- b N. Y. d 11-21-1838 ae 73y 11m (H)
Ch: Phebe
cf Plains 8-1828 (H); Phebe & mother dis 1831 (0); cf Plains 1830 for Elizabeth & Phebe (0)
Edward rocf Renss. 6-1843; ct Oswego 10-3-1849 (H)
Edward rocf Marl. 12-6-1848; ct Oswego 12-3-1851; cf Marl. 12-6-1848 (H)
Emily Grace, dt Geo. P. & Mary Amanda (Frick) b Easton, Pa. 1-5-1894; m 1917 Charles TEMPLE (H)
recrq 7-9-1917
George rocf Coey. 4-1856; ct Coey 8-1864 (H)
George H., s Robert W. & Rebecca, gct Cincin. 12-5-1832
Henry D. rocf Marl. 10-23-1833 (clear); dis mo 4-2-1842 (0)
Laurence & Sarah S. (H)
Ch: Charles Alexander b 5- 9-1829 d 7-21-1829
Ann Elizabeth b 1-26-1831 d 7- 7-1831
Anna b 6- 9-1832
Charles Wager b 2- 5-1834
Alexander b 1-19-1836
Henry H. b 11-17-1837
Elizabeth L. b 7-24-1841
cf Plains 1-1830 for Lawrence; cf Stanford 1-1829 for Sarah; ct Oswego 10-1849 for all; cf Stanford for Sarah 1834 (0); dis 1835 (0)
M. Alma, dt Geo. F. P. & Mary Amanda (Frick), b Quakertown, Pa. 6-16-1884; recrq 10-12-1912 (H)
Margaret, dt Geo. F. & Mary Amanda (Frick), b Easton, Pa. 2-12-1900; m Henry RAUB (H)
recrq 7-9-1917
Phebe B., dt Alex. & Eliz., N. Y.; m 1835 Henry C. HULL, of Catskill (H)
Robert W. & Rebecca
Ch: William L.
George H.
Joseph
Rachel d 3- 5-1826
Elizabeth
Robert Jr.
Hiram
Edward Cummings
cf Balt. W. Dist. 1-7-1825 with their 6 ch first named; ct ND MM 4-7-1830 with 7 ch as named; directed 7-7-1830 that this cert be ret. to recorder, as residence unknown; ct ND MM 12-5-1832 for Robert W. & 5 minor ch, Joseph & others as named; Rebecca dis 1-1830 (0); rst by Cincinnati MM 4-18-

YOUNG, Robert W. & Rebecca, continued
1830 & rpd to N. Y.; ct Phila. 4-1830 for all (H)
Sarah M., dt John S. & Sarah Marie, b 11-4-1849 d 12-27-1901; m 9-9-1869 Abram C. HARRIS (H)
recrq 3-7-1883
Sarah T., w Mansfield, dt Joseph & Sarah WALKER, d 5-25-1876 (H)
dis mo 12-2-1863
William L., s Robert W. & Rebecca, gct Cincinnati 1-5-1832
----- & ----- (nm)
Ch: Rachel b Balt. d 5-4-1826 ae 9y 9m bHS
Charles A. d 9-3-1837 ae 3m bHS

YUEN
Chang recrq 5-2-1906
H. recrq 4-2-1913

ZANE
Rachel, Wby, m 1723 Samuel PINE

ZILBOORG
Gregory, s Moses & Anna (Brannstein), b Kier, Russia 12-25-1890; m 12-14-1919 Ray ----- dt Nathaniel & Anne (H)
recrq 11-13-1922

ZUCKER
Mary, dt Richard & Mary E. (Bannan), b Lansdowne, Pa. 6-15-1910; m 1934 Bukk Griffith CARLETON (H)
both recrq 1-14-1935

Z----
Bessie m Paul D. DONCHIAN
rolf First Cong. Ch. of Pasadena 10-1925

Mary prc 4-6-1757

* * * * * * *

COPELAND
Ambrose, Flushing, m Deborah -----
Ch: Cowperthwaite
Ann Hankinson (form Copeland) dis mo 11-4-1779
David Josiah rocf Paoli, Ind. 10-1927; letter to First Bapt. Ch., Rich., Ky. 1935
George W. m Ada M. BEDELL, dt Caleb C. & Martha, d 2-2-1898 ae 35y 6m 14d cremated bPP (H)
Ch: Helen M. d 9-14-1893 ae 5y 8m bPP

CORBIN
Warren & Clara B.
both recrq 4-5-1933

CORLESS
Bernard b N. Y. 1-1-1898; recrq 12-4-1917; name erased 10-1928

CORLIES
Amelia C., dt John W. & Phebe; m 4-20-1873 Alfred HOPE DOEG
Amos rocf Shrews. 2-6-1804, apprentice with George Parker
Ann (nm) b N. J. d 9-23-1836 ae 54y 2m bHS (wd)
Annie W., dt John Edgar & Mary B. (Wright) b 8-22-1874 N. Y.; m 2-5-1895 Wm. C. DELANOY d 12-30-1899; m 2d bet. 1916 & 1921

* * * * * * *

Charles G. CORNELL (H)
Benjamin & Phebe
Ch: Elizabeth
George b 1-11-1804
Hetty " 2-25-1806 d 4-7-1813 ae 7y bHS
Sarah L. b 7-29-1808
Henry De Witt b 7-27-1810
Mary b 7-11-1812 d 4-18-1813 ae 11m bHS
Margaret N. b 2-12-1814
Joseph N. b 9-18-1815
Walter b 4-11-1817
Mary N. b 2-8-1819
cf R. & P. 2-22-1804 with their dt, Elizabeth; all dis 1829-1839 (O); ct Shrews. 8-1839 for parents

SHERPICK
Eugene A. (nm) & Eva
Ch: Eugene Arthur b Bkn. 2-2-1895 (or 1-2-1895)
Eva Ella
Eva recrq 7-11-1917; her s recrq of mother 6-1917
Eva Ella, dt Eugene A. & Eva; m ----- GREEN (nm) recrq 6-6-1934

FLEWELLIN
Sarah Jane, w Albert, dt Geo. & Mary HALLOCK (m 5-24-1866); relrq 7-7-1900 (H)

F L U S H I N G   M O N T H L Y   M E E T I N G

The original Monthly Meeting of Flushing, Newtown and New York became in time known as New York Monthly Meeting. It was so large in 1805 that the Preparative Meetings of Flushing and Newtown were set off as Flushing Monthly Meeting.

The Flushing Friends met, perhaps irregularly, from 1657 until John Bowne's house was built in 1661, after which they held a regular meeting there until 1694, when the meeting house was built. They had a burial ground in 1676. At Yearly Meeting, 1696 to 1716, the men met at the meeting house and the women at the Bowne house. The meeting house was built in 1693 of timbers, cut and hewn the preceding winter. It was the largest room in the town, and ample for the Yearly Meeting of 1696.

Stones were never over common on sandy Long Island but in building this house, besides the foundation under the walls, a space in the centre, three by five feet, was surrounded by a stone wall below the floor line, making a pit two feet deep, evidently intended for an open fireplace, where a fire could be burned before a meeting, with a roof opening probably arranged to release the smoke, until the fire was reduced to embers. There are however no ashes or other evidence of a fire there, the early Friends being sufficiently puritanical not to consider warmth a necessity.

By 1716 the house was too small for the Yearly Meeting. A large addition was made, and the west wall of the original house removed, to make the whole into one larger room, for worship, with sliding panels to partition it into two rooms for the business meetings of the men and women. This is the oldest house of worship in the state.

The Friends were early mindful of education, and John Bowne employed a school master for his children. Probably others did the same. With an increasing population in the town, the Friends saw the need of a school house, as shown by the following minute, 6 Mo (Aug) 5, 1703:

> "That a School Ma[r] being Judged Necessary for ye towne of flushing, it is thought fitt by this meeting yt Samuel Hoyt & ffrancis Doughty Do Seek out a Convenient piece of Ground, to purchase it, & build a School house,thereon, for ye use of friends, about Richard Griffin's lott, uppon the Cross-way, w[ch] is neere ye Center of Ye towne." The teacher offered to bring the school to mid week meeting in 1709.

The School Fund accounts 1792-1816 shownnames of several Friends not appearing elsewhere in our records.

The Friends in Newtown and Maspeth Kills were a part of the Gravesend Meeting in 1682. On 9 Mo (Nov) 24, 1684 a meeting for worship was allowed, to be held at Robert Field's house every Fourth day. In 1697 the meeting was settled to be every second First day. The Preparative Meeting was laid down in 1771, and the members attached to Flushing Preparative Meeting. Monthly Meeting, however, was held there at intervals until 1780, and occasional meetings were held there as late as 1840. The first meeting house was built in 1722, the second 1760, at what is now Maspeth, L. I. It is long gone, and the adjacent burial ground is neglected and overgrown with weeds.

The records of the Monthly Meeting are in good condition, but for a long period there was negligence in recording data. There are certificates issued for persons of whose membership no record is found, and deaths are recorded, with like lack of background. The records of the other Monthly Meetings in this volume may clear up some of these missing data.

John Bowne was the most notable member in early Flushing. Dr. John Rodman was also very prominent. Data regarding them and other Flushing Quakers before 1805 will be found under New York Monthly Meeting.

As the Orthodox branch in the Monthly Meeting existed only 1828-1829 there are but few references herein concerning them.

RECORDS

ALBERTSON
----- (nm) m Sarah WILLETS
dis mo 5-1-1806 after she had offered ack.

ANDERSON
James, Jr. m abt 4-10-1921 Esther DOUGHTY
Ch: Mary Jane
cf N. Y. 8-5-1829 for Esther & dt

ARCHER
Jane gct N. Y. 8-6-1843; cf Ama. 12-10-1824

BALDWIN
Ann recrq 10-3-1805; cf Wby 10-3-1811; d 4-13-1852
Jesse & Elizabeth
cf Wby 7-4-1805 for Jesse & Elizabeth; ct Wby for both 11-7-1805

BASSETT
Fannie d 1885

BELL
Abraham, Jr. b 8-27-1841; m Melissa R. -----
Ch: William b 5-24-1874; m Ella E. HOLLEY
cf New Garden, Pa. 5-9-1872 for Melissa R.
Annie L., dt Thomas C. & Eliza H., b 7-12-1847; m 1876 Frederick STORM
Brinton C. b 9-24-1874
Carrie J., dt Thomas C. & Eliza H., Flush., b 7-15-1849; m 1875 S. Clement SATTERTHWAIT of Aiken, S. C.
Mary gct West Nottingham, Eng. 1-7-1830
Robert dis mo 5-2-1833
Thomas C. d 12-9-1864; m Eliza H. -----
Ch: Abraham Jr. b 8-27-1841
Jane Hough b 5-19-1843 d 4-20-1859
Mary Christy b 3-1-1845 d 9-4-1854 [STORM
Ann Lawrence " 7-12-1847; m Frederick
Caroline Jackson b 7-15-1849; m S. Clement SATTERTHWAIT
cf N. Y. 11-4-1840 for Thomas C.
William, s Abraham & Melissa, b 5-24-1874 d 12-11-1931; m 9-5-1905 at 15th St., Bkn., N.Y. Ella E. HOLLEY, dt Samuel P. & Ann Eliza
Ch: William Lawrence b 6-30-1907

BERGEN
----- (nm) m Sarah BOWNE
dis mo 5-3-1832

BETTS
Anthony d 12-21-1814 ae abt 73y
Jane, Newtown, b 8-21-1752
Sarah, Newtown, b 3 Mo (May) 8, 1727; ct Jericho 5-5-1808

BIRDSALL
Avis rocf Pur. 12-9-1874 with Sarah Jane Birdsall
Sarah Jane rocf Pur. 12-9-1874 with Avis Birdsall

BOWNE
Agnes d 4-16-1834
Benjamin, s Willet & Hannah, b 2-9-1794; ct N. Y. 8-2-1810 as apprentice
Caroline rocf N. Y. 7-7-1825
Catharine d Aug. 1, 1848 ae 79y
Eliza, dt Samuel & Hannah; m 5-13-1813 Samuel UNDERHILL
Elizabeth, dt Philip & Eliza F., Flushing; m 1836 Daniel T. WILLETS
George F., s Philip & Eliza, b 5-4-1821; ct N. Y. 8-7-1845
Isaac W., s Wm. W. & Mary, b 8-2-1795; dis mo 9-3-1829
John & Hannah
Ch: Hannah d 9-1821
ct N. Y. 8-4-1825 for Hannah Bowne & dt, Abigail Bowne (appears to be this one)
John P., Flush. d 4-2-1804; m Anne ----- d 4-16-1834
Ch: Mary b 1- 7-1784
Anne " 9- 5-1785
Elizabeth b 8-30-1787
Catharine " 9-20-1789
Lindley M. rqct Jericho 12-4-1823, not likely to go there for the present; again rqct Jericho 7-7-1825 & comm. app. No further action found
Mary, dt John & Anne, b 1-7-1784; m 1-9-1806 Samuel PARSONS
Mary, dt William & Mary, b 2-17-1806; m ----- WRIGHT (mo)
dis mo 5-3-1827
Philip, s Willet & Hannah, Flush., b 8-5-1785 d 1-13-1859; m 7-8-1813 at Flush. Eliza F. FARRINGTON, dt George & Elizabeth (dec), d 1870
Ch: Elizabeth b 4-20-1814
William W. b 4-12-1817
George F. " 5- 4-1821
Mariah F. " 8-23-1824
Catharine S. b 9-26-1826
Edward Hicks b 1-27-1829 d 9- 2-1831
Philip Jr. " 5- 7-1832
ct N. Y. 6-5-1845 for Philip & fam
Samuel, s Willet & Hannah, b 1-1-1789 d 11-30-1854; ct Pur. 4-7-1825
Sarah m ----- BERGEN (mo)
dis mo 5-3-1832
Scott H., s Willet & Hannah, b 9-30-1796; ct N. Y. as apprentice 2-1-1816; cf N. Y. 4-7-1830; d 2-11-1864
Stephen C., s Wm. & Mary, b 4-23-1799; dis mo 4-3-1834
Thomas P. gct Crosswicks, N. J. as an apprentice 4-5-1810
Willet, Flush., b 6 Mo (Aug) 8, 1745 d 3-27-1832; m Hannah ----- b 3-26-1755
Ch: Philip b 8- 5-1785
James " 10-26-1787
Samuel " 1- 1-1789

BOWNE, Willet & Hannah, continued
Ch: John Willet b 10-1-1790 d 10-23-1869
Hannah H. b 7-23-1792 d 4-7-1870
Benjamin b 2- 9-1794
Scott " 9-30-1796 d 2-11-1864
William, s Willet & Deborah, Flush., b 3-15-1771 d 12-10-1824; m Mary ----- b 5-15-1773 d 12-31-1819 ae 47
Ch: Isaac Willett b 8- 2-1795
Stephen " 4-23-1799
Cornell " 1-25-1801 (or 10-25-1801) d 12-19-1864
Mary " 2-17-1806
Sarah " 4- 3-1808
Elizabeth " 4-20-1814
William W., s Philip & Eliza, b 4-12-1817; dis mo 3-6-1856; ct N. Y. 8-7-1845; cf N. Y. not found

BURLING
Abigail d 6-4-1842
Ann recrq 6-4-1829
Elizabeth b 1 Mo (Mar) 14, 1744 d 1-14-1828
Rebecca d 11-18-1812

BURNET
Henry, Flush., d 1-10-1814; m Mary -----
Ch: Anabella b 6----1784 d 9-29-1807
Jane " 7-17-1794
ct Balt. Eastern Dist. 1-5-1815 for Mary & dt, Jane

BYRD
Elizabeth R. d 6-10-1878
James d 5-27-1842; m Elizabeth ----- d 5-20-1842
Ch: Mary m John D. WRIGHT
Mary, dt James & Elizabeth; m 1-13-1820 John D. WRIGHT
Phebe (late Cock) mo before 6-9-1807 & then dis; rst 7-5-1821; d 6-29-1864 ae 79y (6-19-1864 ae 79 on Tombstone)
Thomas G. gct Ferrisburgh 1-5-1832 (clear); cf Monkton, Vt. 8-29-1811 as apprentice

CARHART
James & Elizabeth
cf Jericho 6-15-1815; ct Pur. 8-1-1816 for both; ct Jericho for both 6-7-1821

CARTER
Emily W. d 1-30-1869

CASE
Paul Edward, s Frank Edw. & Matilda M., Mt. Tremper, N. Y.; m 10-3-1931 at Flushing Eleanor Frost POWELL, dt Chas. U. & Harriet Van Nostrand Powell

CHAPMAN
Elizabeth d July 12, 1838 ae 88y

CLAPP
Silas & Sarah
Ch: Thomas b 1-7-1819

CLEMENT
Henry (or William) & Ruth
Ch: William B. b 2-3-1850 (or 2-5-1850) d 2-9-1855 ae 5y 4d
Henrietta b 2-18-1855
cf N. Y. 5-4-1848 for Henry & w
Stephen d 1822

COCK
Abraham, s Benjamin & Hannah, Flush., b 9-21-1780 d 8-20-1828; m 12-8-1808 at Flush Susan WRIGHT, dt Jordan & Elizabeth (dec) b 4-11-1789 d 4-2-1872
Ch: Alexander W. b 9-13-1809 d 10-9-1811
Elizabeth T. b 12-6-1810
Benjamin
Sarah " 4- 1-1815
Jordan W. " 3-28-1817
William Henry b 5- 1-1819
Charles W. " 2-10-1822
Abraham " 1824 d in infancy
Amy, dt Benjamin & Hannah; m 10-12-1815 Benjamin R. SEAMAN
Andrew, s William, b 2-26-1769 d 6-21-1832 N.Y.; m 12-31-1790 Mary TITUS, dt Henry & Martha b 12-30-1771 d 5-1-1803 N. Y. [other ch
Ch: Isaac b 11-15-1800 d 2-16-1807 drowned; 5
Andrew m 2nd 7-10-1806 Sarah Emma EMBREE, dt George & Abigail, Flush., b 3-1-1774 d 11-30-1863
Ch: Mary b 1-21-1808 d 12-26-1809
George b 6-26-1810 d 7-6-1810
Effingham b 9-26-1811
William E. b 5-17-1814; m Mary E. HICKS
George E. " 7- 3-1816
ct N. Y. 5-5-1825 for Andrew & fam
Benjamin d 1-26-1835
Elizabeth T., dt Abraham & Susan, b 12-6-1810; m Alfred Carmen SMITH (mo)
dis mo 9-6-1838
Hannah b 9-15-1756 d 1-5-1829
Sarah b 3-1-1774 d 11-30-1863
Sarah, dt Abraham & Susan, b 4-1-1815; m Manuel FETTER (mo before 8-2-1838)
Susan W. d 4-2-1872 ae 83y
William E., of N. Y., s Andrew (dec) & Sarah, Flush., b 5-17-1814 d 7-19-1868 (7-20-1868 on Tombstone); m 4-9-1856 at Silas Hicks', Flush., Mary E. HICKS, dt Silas & Sarah, Flush.
Ch: William E. Jr. b 3-22-1857
Robert E. " 4-28-1861
Mary Augusta " 2-27-1865

COLES
Jordan & Mary
cf N. Y. 9-5-1810 for Mary, having rem with her h

COLLEY
Jane m 1818 David TITUS
Jane Colley recrq 5-1-1817

CORLIES
Joseph W., Merchant, N. Y., s Briton (dec) & Sarah, Monmouth Co., N. J.; m 11-10-1825 at Flush. Lydia L. TITUS, dt Silas & Elizabeth, Queens Co.
ct N. Y. for Lydia 5-4-1826

CORNELL
Deborah, Flush., b 8 Mo (Oct) 26, 1736 d 1822
Silas & Sarah M.
Ch: James Mott b 10-13-1820
Richard Mott b 5-5-1822
cf Pur. 8-8-1816 for Silas, rec 10-3-1816 & cf N. Y. same date for Sarah M.; ct Farm. 4-3-1823 for Silas & fam

CORSA
Sarah, Newtown, b 10 Mo (Dec) 23, 1729 d 3-11-1812

CORSE
Barney, Flush. d 1878; m Mary E. -----
Mary E. rocf N. Y. 4-3-1861, has been settled there for a considerable time

COX
Benjamin, s Abraham [Cock] (dec) & Susan; m 7-4-1841 at Samuel Leggett's, Martha LEGGETT, dt Samuel & Eliza, Whitestone
Benjamin dis 8-4-1859
Charles W. (or Cock), s Abraham & Susan [Cock] b 2-10-1822; dis mo 1-2-1851 (Cock-Cox Gen. - Charles W. Cox m 5-30-1850 Mary C. HOLMES. His birth given 2-24-1822)

DENNIS
Wilmot rocf N. Y. 11-3-1813; ct Wby 9-6-1821

DICKINSON
John & Susan
Ch: Margaret
Ann
Eliza
Mary
Lydia
ct N. Y. 11-4-1813 for all, the dt clear; cf N. Y. 8-1-1810 for John & Susanna, with 4 ch, Margaret, Ann, Lydia & Mary

DOUGHTY
Benjamin, s William & Mary, b 12-28-1785 d 8-26-1801 ae 56y; m -----
Ch: Benjamin d 2-10-1839
ct Jericho 4-3-1823; cf Jericho 2-1-1827
Charles, Flush., b 12 Mo (Feb) 30, 1741/2 d 2-1-1816 ae 74y 2m; m Sarah ----- b 10 Mo (Dec) 26, 1738 d 1-19-1813
Ch: Margaret b 3-16-1772 d 9-15-1827 (unm)
Mary " 9-16-1773
Ch:Charles b 7-24-1777
Sarah " 10-22-1780 d 9-7-1851 (unm)
Charles (prob Charles, s Samuel) d 2-1-1816 ae abt 62y
Charles, s Samuel C., Flush., b 12-1-1760; dis long non-attendance 1-4-1821
George M., s Wm. & Mary, b 5-6-1793; dis mo 3-7-1833
Hannah d 5-16-1826 ae 97y
Moses M. [Doty] rocf Wby 9-7-1815; mo before 6-2-1825; referred to Chap.; dis 1-5-1826
William d 9-22-1826 (not clear, 72d yr. or 12th)
William, s Benjamin, Flush., b 11-17-1755 d 6-8-1814 ae 58y 20d; m Mary WILLIAMS b 8-22-1757 d 11-16-1824
Ch: Benjamin b 12-28-1785
Esther b 4- 6-1789
George Masters b 5- 6-1793
Peggy Ann " 10-25-1800 (Margaret Ann d 9-7-1828)

DOWNER
Ernest Page m 12-2-1928 at Forty Fort, Pa. by Rev. Ferris D. Cornell, Helen May HILLER

DUSENBURY
Abigail, dt Peter & Mary; m 1-9-1812 John WINE
Peter b 1 Mo (Mar) 1740 d 4-7-1827; m Mary ----
Ch: Abigail m John WINE
cf Marl. 11-27-1811 for Peter

EMBREE
Abigail d 2-12-1806 (prob. w of George)
Deborah L. b 5-18-1778 d 5-21-1821
Effingham d 12-3-1817 ae 58y 2m 9d; m Mary ----
Ch: Hannah
Effingham rq advice regarding placing his s out as apprentice 1-4-1810; Hannah recrq of parents 4-3-1817
George d 1-14-1799
Hannah, dt Effingham & Mary; m ----- WRIGHT (mo) dis mo 10-4-1827
Jane L., dt Effingham & Mary, d 10-9-1865; m 1826 John WINE
Jane L. Embree recrq 9-1-1825
John L. (name only on Tombstone)
Mary's ack for mo rec from N. Y. 1-4-1816; ct N. Y. 6-4-1829
Robert & Phebe S.
Ch: Carrie b 6-1-1853 d 1-3-1860
cf N. Y. 6-4-1842
Sarah, dt George & Abigail; m 7-10-1806 Andrew COCK

ENGLAND
Elizabeth m Thos. Clarke SMART, in England

FARRINGTON
Amelia gct N. Y. 11-4-1830 (clear) (H)
Ann, dt Walter & Mary, b 12-25-1793; m 4-11-1816 Thomas LEGGETT, Jr.
Caroline, dt George & Elizabeth; m 1828 Amos WILLETS

FARRINGTON, continued
Catharine, dt George & Elizabeth; m 11-10-1814 Elihu SMITH, of N. Y.
Edmund dis mo 2-2-1809
Eliza, dt George & Elizabeth; m 7-8-1813 Philip BOWNE
George b 7-20-1750 d 12-8-1825; m Elizabeth ----- d 4-25-1813 ae 51y 4m 17d
Ch: Charles d 9-30-1807
Catharine m Elihu SMITH
Jane
Amelia
Jane & Amelia recrq of Elizabeth, her h consenting 1-1-1807; George had cert of clear to Phila. 4-6-1817
George, having ack mo, N. Y. sent ct Flush. 12-5-1816, accepted
Jane gct N. Y. 11-4-1830 (clear) (H)
Jesse gct N. Y. 2-4-1813
Lydia d 2-7-1808
Maria gct N. Y. 11-4-1841; d 3-26-1857 ae 70y
Mary, dt John, Flush. b 12-12-1763 d 10-28-1805
Walter, Flush; m Mary ------ b 11-29-1752
Ch: Sarah b 10-20-1790
Anne b 12-25-1793; m Thos. LEGGETT

FETTER
Manuel m Sarah COCK, dt Abraham & Susan (mo) dis mo 8-2-1838; Manuel, from Carlisle, Pa. was adopted by Rev. Wm. Muhlenberg & educated in Flush.; Prof. at Chapel Hill, N. C., Cock-Cox Gen.

FICKET
Phebe M. con mo 9-2-1824; ct N. Y. 8-4-1825

FIELD
Elizabeth b 10 Mo (Dec) 7, 1750 d 4-12-1818 ae 67y 6m
Hannah b 10 Mo (Dec) 6, 1728 d 12-7-1813 ae 86y

FISH
Preserved & Mary
Mary recrq 4-2-1807; ct New Bedford for Mary 7-2-1807

FITCH
Joseph, of New Orleans, s Joseph & Mary, Flush., b 6-13-1811 d 10-27-1868; m 10-17-1855 Avis L. LEGGETT, dt Thos. H. & Frances V.
Ch: Joseph Jr. b 8-27-1857 d 10-27-1868

FORSTER
Thomas & Margaret
cf N. Y. 5-6-1857 for Margaret, rem to reside with her h

FOULKE
Judith b 5-24-1779 d 1860; cf N. Y. 10-4-1837
Maria rocf Middle MM, Warwickshire 8-7-1822; ct Oswego 7-3-1823; women's mtg made an endorsement on Alice Maria Fowler's cert

FRAME
Catharine D., dt Jesse & Mary, rocf N. Y. 10-5-1814 with parents; ct N. Y. 4-5-1832 with mother; d 6-27-1857 (or 6-28-1857) ae 56y
Charles, s Thos. L. & Ann P.; m 10-2-1861 at Sarah A. Willets', Caroline WILLETS, dt Jacob H. & Sarah A., b 9-30-1841
Eliza, dt Jesse & Mary, Flush.; m 1843 Gilbert H. PEARSALL
cf N. Y. 10-5-1814 for Eliza with parents
Jesse, Flush., d 7-12-1826; m Mary ----- d 2-2-1853 ae 77y
Ch: Eliza m Gilbert H. PEARSALL
Elizabeth b 5-18-1814
Benjamin b 12-13-1816 d 2-17-1836
William " 7-15-1819
cf N. Y. 10-5-1814 for Jesse & Mary with 5 ch, Catharine D., Joseph, Maria, Thomas & Eliza, having rem; ct N. Y. 4-5-1832 for Mary with dt, Catharine & Maria (clear) & Eliza, Benjamin & William, minors; cf N. Y. 1-1-1834 for Mary with Catharine C., Marie, Eliza, Benjamin & William
Joseph L. gct N. Y. 4-3-1825 as a minor
Maria, dt Jesse & Mary; m 1839 William L. TITUS
cf N. Y. 10-5-1814 for Maria with parents
William & Phebe
Ch: Catharine b 3-19-1858
Mary " 11-24-1861
ct Jericho for William 2-2-1854 (of clear)

FRANKLIN
Anthony, Flush., d 1854 ae 87y; m Lydia ----- d 1837 ae 64y
Ch: Joseph b 8-22-1795
Elizabeth b 2- 5-1798; m Wm. SMART
Richard L. b 1-31-1802
Anthony dis 6-5-1823; Lydia dis 5-1-1823
John m Elizabeth WRIGHT (mo before 6-6-1811) gct N. Y. 5-3-1810, now living there; John dis mo 10-3-1811; Elizabeth dis mo 8-1-1811 (John L. d 1863 ae 73y on Tombstone)
Joseph F., of Cincinnati, O., s Jos. L. (dec), late of Flush., & Mary; m 12-5-1854 at Thos. H. Leggett's, Miriam LEGGETT, dt Thos. H. & Frances V.
Joseph L. dis mo 8-1-1816
Richard L., s Anthony & Lydia, b 1-31-1802; dis mo 9-6-1827

FROST
John d 11-2-1869
Mary, wd of Penn, rocf Wby 12-2-1824; d 2-18-1826 in 84th yr.

GARDNER
Lydia rocf Wby 1-5-1819; ct N. Y. 11-6-1828

HALLETT
Gideon, Newtown, b 12-8-1773; rocf Plainfield 4-16-1806; ct N. Y. 8-3-1815; cf N. Y. 3-3-1824; d 1-16-1845
Priscilla A. m 1930 Ira R. HILLER

HALLOCK
Nicholas, s James & Elizabeth, of Marlboro; m 3-13-1806 at Flushing Elizabeth TITUS, dt Samuel & Abigail
Elizabeth recrq 10-3-1805

HAUGHTON
----- (nm) m Eliza LOWERRE, dt Thomas & Mary (mo) dis mo 3-6-1828; rst 5-1-1828; ct N. Y. 6-6-1833

HAUXHURST
James, Flush. & Sarah
Ch: Stephen b 1-16-1806
Penelope b 12-12-1808
Charles " 6- 2-1812
ct Corn. 5-6-1813 for Jesse & fam (not recorded)
Robert, Flush., b 9-27-1801

HICKS
Anna D. b 9-5-1826 d 7-3-1891
Charles, Flush., b 12 Mo (Feb) 17, 1746/7 d 6-9-1824
Hannah d 5-15-1798
Mary E., dt Silas & Sarah; m 1856 William E. COCK
Sarah T. d 11-21-1874 ae 84y 8m
Silas, s Benjamin (dec) & Mary, d 3-30-1861 (8-30-1861 on Tombstone); m 2-13-1817 at Flushing Sarah TITUS, dt Silas & Elizabeth
Ch: Joseph b 12-10-1834
Mary E. m Wm. E. COCK
Silas Jr.
ct N. Y. 9-4-1817 for Sarah T. Hicks; cf N. Y. 7-3-1833 for parents with 4 ch, William, Anna, Silas & Mary Elizabeth
Silas Jr. (apparently) s Silas & Sarah, gct N. Y. 8-2-1849

HILLER
Helen May m 1928 Ernest Page DOWNER
Ira R. m 4-21-1930 at St. Georges Ch., Flush. by Rev. Geo. F. Taylor, Priscilla A. HALLETT
Ch: Priscilla Alden b 2-11-1933
Louise Hemstreet m 1935 William POOLE
Martha B. m 1935 Jack F. LORRAINE
Mary Elizabeth, dt Charles E. & Helen May; m 1931 Harry Nathan LEIBY

HOLLEY
Ella E., dt Samuel P. & Ann Eliza; m 1905 William BELL

JACKSON
Elizabeth A. b 6-10-1817 d 9-17-1869 in 53rd yr.
Jarvis m Mary ----- d 9-8-1862
Mary ack. (prob. for mo) accepted 7-4-1822

KIMBER
Joshua & Rachel J.
Ch: Anna
George Dillwyn b 3-27-1824
William G. " 1-30-1826 d 3-8-1827
Lydia G. " 1-30-1828
cf Phila. 5-29-1823 for parents with dt, Anna

KING
Charles D. d 11-26-1826 in 28th yr.
Joseph, Flush. & Mary
Ch: Ann b 6----1801
Joseph Jr. b 8-20-1810
Thomas b 3-18-1789 d 2-23-1888

KIRBY
Edmund gct N. Y. 8-1-1839 with w

KISSAM
Margaret d Nov. 18, 1886

LAWRENCE
Charles D. recrq 12-4-1817; ct Scipio 5-4-1820
Charlotte d 10-22-1838
Deborah Ann d Apr. 28, 1886
Effingham W., s Elizabeth, gct N. Y. as apprentice, 2-1-1816 (although included in his mother's cert 1806, it was perhaps considered necessary to have his own as apprentice)
Esther P., dt Henry & Amy, Flush., b 4-25-1815; m 1845 William T. POST
Gilbert, s Leonard & Margaret, b 7-1776 d 9-23-1870; m 1-8-1818 at Flushing Esther PEARSALL, dt Thomas & Ann, b 3-21-1772 d 2-26-1847
cert of unity to accompany John Wines to Canada Mtg 11-6-1817; several returning cert 1818
Henry, s Joseph & Phebe, b 4-24-1767 d 9-11-1824; m 7-14-1814 at Flushing Amy PEARSALL, dt Thomas & Ann, dec, d 4-29-1843
Ch: Esther b 4-25-1815; m Wm. T. POST
Maria C. b 5-30-1817 d 9-14-1817
Henry recrq 4-7-1814
Joseph, Flush., d 11-10-1813 ae 72y 2m 18d; m Phebe ----- b 9 Mo (Nov) 14, 1740 d 9-17-1816 ae 76y 3d
Leonard d 12-13-1821; m Margaret ----- d 11-24-1821 ae 72y
Ch: Gilbert m Esther PEARSALL
Mary, dt Elizabeth; m ----- TALMAN (mo) mo before 8-4-1808 & then dis
Mary gct N. Y. 5-2-1833
Robert d 1847
William d May 9, 1893
Zipporah recrq 11-3-1814; d 12-24-1826 in 62nd yr.
----- m Elizabeth W. ----- d Nov. 24, 1852
Ch: Mary mo 1808
Anna
Effingham
Elizabeth W. & dt, Anna, rel from mbrp 10-7-1830; ct N. Y. 12-4-1806 for Elizabeth & dt, Mary (both clear) & Ann & Effingham,

LAWRENCE, ----- & Elizabeth W., continued
minors; cf N. Y. 9-2-1807 for same; ct N. Y. 5-2-1816 for Elizabeth W. & dt, Anna, both clear; cf N. Y. 9-1-1819 for Elizabeth W. & dt, Anna, both clear

LEAVITT
G. Howland m 10-10-1878 Amelia WILLETS
Ch: Sarah H. b 4-3-1880

LEGGETT
Anna F., dt Thos. Jr. & Patience H., Flushing; m 1858 Joseph T. MOORE
Avis m 1855 Joseph FITCH
Catharine T. rocf N. Y. 11-6-1850
Francis V. d 6-15-1877
Margaret d 1851
Martha, dt Samuel & Eliza; m 1841 Benjamin COX
Mary F. rocf N. Y. 11-6-1850
Miriam, dt Thos. H. & Frances V.; m 1854 Joseph F. FRANKLIN
Samuel b 10-4-1782 d 1-5-1847; m Eliza P. ----- d 4-17-1849
Ch: Charlotte F.
Martha P.
Samuel
cf N. Y. 4-1-1840 for parents with 3 ch as named
Samuel Jr., s Samuel & Eliza, dis mo 10-4-1849
Thomas Jr., s Thomas & Mary (dec), b 1-30-1793 d 1-8-1865 or 8-1-1865; m 4-11-1816 at Flushing Ann FARRINGTON, dt Walter & Mary
Ch: Anna F. m Jos. T. MOORE
ct N. Y. 6-5-1817 for Anna F.
Thomas Jr. m 2nd Patience H. -----
Ch: Sarah
Anna F.
Caroline H. b N. Y.
Susan H.
ct N. Y. 12-3-1846 for Thomas Jr., w Patience H., & 4 minor ch as named; Tombstone Caroline Leggett d 1853
Thomas H. d 6-29-1867; m Frances V. -----
Ch: Miriam m Jos. F. FRANKLIN
Frances d 1-24-1838
Pemberton " 2-3-1838
Nancy " 12-14-1839
Avis m Jos. FITCH
Thomas Jr.
cf N. Y. 4-5-1837 for parents with 7 ch, Avis, Chas. Pleasants, Miriam, Thos. H., Pemberton, Francis Pleasants & Nancy Emlen; ct N. Y. for Thos. H. & fam 8-5-1847; cf N. Y. 7-7-1852 for Thos. H. & w, Frances, & 4 ch, Avis, Charles P., Miriam & Thomas H. Jr.

LEIBY
Harry Nathan, s Jonathan & Sarah; m 6-9-1931 at Flushing, Mary Elizabeth HILLER, dt Charles E. & Helen May, Flushing

LORRAINE
Jack F. m 5-14-1935 at 280 Park Ave., N. Y. by Rev. Charles C. Cole, Martha B. HILLER

LOWERRE
Daniel, s Thomas & Mary, rocf Oswego with parents 12-20-1809; ct Wby 12-5-1816 as apprentice
Eliza (apparently Elizabeth, dt Thomas & Mary) m ----- HAUGHTON (mo)
dis mo 3-6-1828
Giles H. b 3---1803 d 3----1850 ae 47
John d 1831 ae 64y 6m
Lewis, s C. P. & A. B., d 1846 ae 1y 7m
Thomas b 2-12-1766 d 4-19-1824; m Mary -----
Ch: Elizabeth d 1844 ae 74y
Walter gct N. Y. 6-3-1813
Mary
Daniel
cf Oswego (Moores Mills) 12-20-1809 for parents with 4 ch named, Elizabeth clear
Walter, s Thomas & Mary, gct N. Y. as a minor 6-3-1813

LYON
Sener, Flush., b 2-21-1752 d 11-10-1826 in 74th yr.

MACKENZIE
Ida J. (nm) m 1875 Charles H. WRIGHT

MATLACK
Hannah b July 21, 1783 d July 25 1886; ct N. Y. 5-3-1827
Mary (perhaps mother of Timothy) rocf N. Y. 7-1-1819; d 4-6-1825
Timothy d 8-4-1845 ae 53y; m Mary -----
cf N. Y. 5-5-1819 (clear); cf N. Y. 5-5-1829 to reside with her h

MICKEL
Annie L. (nm) m 1875 Samuel WILLETS

MITCHELL
Elizabeth T. b 5-4-1760 d 9-29-1827
Henry d 1843 ae 86y
Phebe recrq 1-7-1819

MOLENEUX
Jesse, Flush. & Phebe
Ch: Henry b 10-16-1799
Mary " 10-16-1799
Royal " 9-27-1801
Samuel b 12-18-1802
Ann " 3-19-1805
Martha
ct Wby 4-5-1810 for parents & Henry, Sarah, Royal, Anne, Martha & Benjamin

MOORE
Joseph T., of N. Y., s Robert R. & Hadassah, Sandy Spring, Md.; m 9-8-1858 at Thomas Leggett Jr.'s Anna F. LEGGETT, dt Thomas

MOORE, Joseph T. & Anna F., continued
Jr. & Patience H., Flushing
Ch: Mary L. b 9-14-1859
Frederick Potts b 12-9-1865 (or 9-12-1865)
George H. b 11-15-1866
cf Phila. (Race St.) 4-21-1858 for Joseph T.
Lindley M. & Abigail L.
Ch: Mary H. b 9-13-1821 d 2-22-1822
Lindley Murray b 11-19-1822
Mary Hicks " 7-25-1825
Edward M.
Gilbert A.
Ann M.
ct Pur. 11-1-1827 for parents with 5 ch, Lindley & Mary being named last; cf N. Y. 9-6-1821 for parents with 3 ch, Edward M., Gilbert & Anna

MOTT
Henry & Jane
Ch: Esther
Eliza
Maria
ct N. Y. 8-3-1815, the dt clear
John W. gct N. Y. 8-2-1810 (clear)
Valentine & Elizabeth
Ch: Daniel W. (or D.)
cf N. Y. 8-5-1868 for Elizabeth & minor s, Daniel W.

NELSON
Deborah's ack accepted 5-4-1820; d 1-6-1828 ae abt 75y

NICOLL
Gloriana M., dt Samuel Benj. & Sarah (Payne), Shelter Island; m 1875 Robert WILLETS

PARSONS
James, s Samuel & Mary, b 5-17-1809; dis joining (O) Friends 2-3-1831
John Bowne d 12-15-1830
Samuel, s James & Mary, Flush.; m 1-9-1806 at Flushing Mary BOWNE, dt John & Anne
Ch: James b 5-17-1809
Robert B. b 2-14-1821
William B. b 11-10-1823
Anna " 12-17-1824 d 1825
ct N. Y. 2-7-1811 for Samuel & Mary & s, James; cf N. Y. 5-5-1813 for Samuel & Mary with 4 minor ch, James, Mary B., John Bowne & Samuel

PEARSALL
Amy, dt Thomas & Ann; m 7-14-1814 Henry LAWRENCE
Ann, dt Samuel & Margaret; m 4-9-1818 Seaman WILLETS
Edmund, Flush., d 8-10-1816 ae 48y 3m 13d; m Rachel -----
Ch: Thomas W.
Charles
Mary
Robert W. b 10-4-1808
cf N. Y. 11-4-1807 for Rachel, having rem with her h with 3 ch, Thomas, Charles & Mary; ct Jericho 6-5-1817 for Rachel & 3 ch, Charles, Mary & Robert
Esther, dt Thomas & Ann; m 1-8-1818 Gilbert LAWRENCE
Gilbert H., s Samuel & Margaret (both dec), b 1-6-1799 d 3-3-1879; m 10-10-1843 at Mary Frame's, Eliza FRAME, dt Jesse (dec) & Mary
Ch: Catharine b 8-10-1844
Samuel " 3- 3-1846 d 5-24-1850
Antoinette Graham b 11-17-1847
Richard b 1- 5-1850
Jacob, s Thomas & Ann, b 2-15-1767 d 9-30-1846
Mary d 12-9-1799
Samuel, s Thomas, Flush., b 2-5-1764 d 12-9-1841; m Margaret ----- b 3-8-1767 d 2-10-1833
Ch: Mary H. b 1-15-1790 d 9-30-1811
Anne " 8-29-1791; m Seaman WILLETS
Gilbert " 1- 6-1799
Sarah " 7-10-1800
Samuel " 8- 9-1802 d 8-12-1805
Margaret b 4-26-1810
Sarah b 4-23-1774; cf N. Y. 8-4-1825; d 8-13-1825
Sarah, dt Samuel & Margaret, b 7-10-1800; dis 7-5-1821
Thomas, Whitestone, b 8 Mo (Oct) 2, 1725 d 11-3-1807; m Ann ----- b 6 Mo (Aug) 31, 1733 d 3-23-1806 [67y 10m 10d
Ch: Sarah b 8 Mo (Oct) 18, 1746 d 4-28-1814 ae
Jacob " 2-15-1767
Esther b 3-18-1772
Thomas b 9-13-1744 d 1-27-1825; m Elizabeth ----- d 2-4-1813 ae abt 68y
Thomas W., s Edmund & Rachel, gct N. Y. 7-3-1817 (clear)

PELL
Mary rocf N. Y. 2-6-1811 (clear); d 10-11-1821

PENFIELD
Edmund d 1-4-1797

PERKINS
Benjamin D. & Mary S.
Ch: John Murray b 11-13-1827 d 10-27-1828
Lindley " 9----1829
cf Plainfield 7-19-1827 for Mary S. rem with her h; cf N. Y. for Benjamin D. 6-8-1827

PIERCE
Ezekiel (spelled Parce also) b 2-17-1752; m Mary ----- b 1 Mo (Mar) 18, 1746/7 d 9-23-1826 in 81st yr; Ezekiel [Parce] dis non-attendance 3-3-1808

PINKHAM
Abigail b 1-1792 d 10-1861
Libni, Flush., b 10-10-1771; m Sarah ----- b 10-12-1774

PINKHAM, Libni & Sarah, continued
Ch: Ann b 1- 4-1799
Zebulun
Daniel b 11- 2-1808
John d 11-1805
ct N.P. 5-7-1812 for parents with Ann, Zebulun & Daniel
Obed, a mbr of N. P., for some yrs resident here, mo before 5-4-1809; dis 7-6-1809 & N.P. informed

POOLE
William, of Wilmington, Del., s Gilpin & Louise Caroline (Fahnestock); m 9-11-1935 at Mattapoisett, Mass. (under care of New Bedford MM) Louise HILLER, Hemstreet, dt Chas. Eldridge & Helen May (Gordon), of Marion, Mass. Res. 1311 Clayton St., Wilmington, Del.

POST
Daniel, Flush. b 11-12-1768 d 12-11-1833; m Rosetta ----- d 11-19-1868 ae 89y 10m
Ch: Mary
William
Edward b 6-11-1808 d 11-6-1870
cf Wby 7-16-1806 for parents with ch, Mary & William, minors
Edward, s Daniel & Rosetta; m Elizabeth K. -----
cf Wby 7-16-1806 for Edward with parents; cf Wby 12-16-1868 for Elizabeth K.; cert of clear to Wby for Edward 7-5-1868
Mary T., dt Daniel & Rosetta; m 1822 Ellwood VALENTINE
cf Wby 7-16-1806 for Mary with parents
William T., s Daniel (dec) & Rosetta, d 9-28-1845; m 6-5-1845 at Robert Bell's at 7 P.M. Esther P. LAWRENCE, dt Henry & Amy (both dec) b 4-25-1815

POWELL
Chas. U. m Harriet VAN NOSTRAND
Ch: Eleanor Frost m Paul Edward CASE
Eleanor Frost, dt Chas. U. & Harriet; m 1931 Paul Edward CASE
Elizabeth rocf Wby 12-16-1812 (clear); ct Wby 1-5-1815
John, Flush., b 10 Mo (Dec) 27, 1740 d 8-31-1828; m Phebe ----- d 9-19-1825

PRINCE
Ann, Flush., b 12 Mo (Feb) 15, 1734/5 d 1-18-1806 (wd of William)

QUINBY
George W. rocf N. Y. 7-2-1851; d 3-24-1855 ae 32y

ROBERTS
Mary, Newtown, b 2 Mo (Apr) 13, 1725

ROE
----- (nm) m Ann UNDERHILL
dis mo before 2-6-1817

ROGERS
----- (nm) m Catharine WRIGHT, dt Jordan & Rebecca, b 3-5-1810
dis mo 4-3-1828

SATTERTHWAIT
S. Clement, dt Isaac H. & Caroline B., Aiken, S. C.; m 6-9-1875 at Eliza H. Bell's, Carrie J. BELL, dt Thos. C. (dec) & Eliza H., Bayside, L. I., b 7-15-1849
Ch: Bessie B. b 4-5-1876

SAVAGE
Charity rocf N. Y. 12-2-1812; ct N. Y. 10-6-1842; cf N. Y. 10-3-1821

SEAMAN
Benjamin R., s Willet & Mary (both dec), N. Y.; m 10-12-1815 at Flushing Amy COCK, dt Benjamin & Hannah, Flushing
ct N. Y. 11-7-1816 for Amy Seaman
Martha recrq 1-7-1819
Rebecca d 10-26-1827

SHOEMAKER
----- m Penelope ----- d 6-30-1809
Ch: Elizabeth
Penelope & dt, Elizabeth, rocf Corn. 7-2-1807, cert incomplete, sent back, corrected & rec again 3-3-1808

SMART
Benjamin, s Thos. & Elizabeth, b Warwickshire; rocf Middle MM, Warwickshire, 8-7-1822; ct Oswego (Moores Mills) 7-3-1823
Hannah, dt Thos. C. & Elizabeth, b Warwickshire; rocf Middle MM, Warwickshire, 8-7-1822; ct Oswego 7-3-1823
Thos. Clarke m Elizabeth ENGLAND
Ch: Joseph
William
Thomas Clarke Jr.
Benjamin
Mary
Lucy
Hannah
cf Middle MM, Warwickshire, 8-7-1822 for parents with s, Joseph (27 signatures; no Clarke or England); ct Oswego 7-3-1823; Thomas Clarke Jr., Benjamin, Mary & Lucy roc same date; William prob. b later
Thomas Clarke, Jr., s Thomas C. & Elizabeth, b Warwickshire; cf Middle MM, Warwickshire with others 8-7-1822; ct Oswego (Moores Mills) 7-3-1823 (clear)
William, s Thomas C. & Elizabeth, of Warwick, Eng.; m 12-14-1820 at Flushing, Elizabeth FRANKLIN, dt Anthony & Lydia, d 8-1-1868 ae 71y

SMART, William & Elizabeth, continued
Ch: Lucy Ann b 9-24-1821
Catharine b 5- 6-1826
Lydia Franklin b 3-16-1832 d 3- 4-1840
William Edward " 7- 3-1834
Frederick Robert b 10-11-1841
cf Middle MM, Warwickshire, for William 3-2-1820 (not recorded) (clear)

SMITH
Alfred Carman, s Carman & Catharine (nm); m 6-1838 Elizabeth T. COCK, dt Abraham & Susan, b 12-6-1810 d 4-22-1888 (mo) dis 9-6-1838
Elihu, s Abner & Zeruiah, N. Y.; m 11-10-1814 at Flushing, Catharine FARRINGTON, dt George & Elizabeth (dec)
Nathaniel d 5-20-1835 ae 77y; m Abigail ----- d 1-7-1843 ae 82y
cf N. Y. 2-3-1819 for both

STORM
Frederic, s George & Mary, b 7-12-1847; m 9-26-1876 at Eliza H. Bell's, Annie L. BELL, dt Thomas C. (dec) & Eliza H.
Ch: Frederick
Mary, dt Thos. C. & Elizabeth E., b Warwickshire; rocf Middle MM, Warwickshire 8-7-1822; ct Oswego 7-3-1823

STRONG
Lucy, dt Thos. C. & Elizabeth, b Warwickshire; rocf Middle MM, Warwickshire 8-7-1822; ct Oswego 7-3-1823

SUYDAM
Martha recrq 11-10-1827; d 6-8-1838

SWEEZY
Hannah rocf Jericho 7-19-1838

TABOR
Stephen rocf N. P. 7-11-1850; ct Wby 2-5-1857

TALMAN
----- m Mary LAWRENCE, dt Elizabeth (mo) mo before 8-4-1808 & then dis

TAYLOR
George W. rocf New Garden MM, Pa. 1-4-1827; ct New Garden 5-7-1829 (0)

THOMPSON
Joshua rq mbrp 3-4-1824, returned to him in 7th mo.

THURSTON
Joseph D. m Mary U. ----- d 10-27-1856 ae 28y 9m
Ch: Hetty Wharton b 10-23-1850
William Wharton b 4-25-1852
Anna U. b 4-23-1854 d 11-19-1856
cf N. Y. 5-3-1845 for Joseph D.; cert of clear to Spruce St., Phila. for Jos. D. 4-5-1849; ct Phila. Race St. for Joseph D. & two minor ch, John W. & Thos. C. Bell 11-1-1860
William d 5-24-1855 ae 88y 9m 14d; m Abigail ----- d 5-28-1851 ae 66y 18d

TITUS
David, s Samuel & Abigail (Robbins) b 12-28-1788 d 4-13-1838; m 6-11-1818 at Flush. Jane COLLEY, d 9-7-1864 ae 64y
Ch: Elizabeth b 6-27-1819
Mary " 2-16-1821 (unm)
Peter " 8-15-1824
Martha " 11- 3-1826 (unm)
Hannah " 8- 6-1831 d 9-25-1831
Henry " 9-28-1832
Edward P. " 3- 3-1835 (unm)
David Jr. " 1- 3-1838 (unm)
cf N. Y. 7-17-1811 for David (clear); cf Wby 9-5-1811; Jane recrq 5-1-1817
Elizabeth, dt Samuel & Abigail; m 3-13-1806 Nicholas HALLOCK
Elizabeth recrq 10-3-1805
Elizabeth, dt Silas & Elizabeth, b 1-8-1809; m ----- TOWNSEND (mo)
dis mo 1-5-1832
Jacob gct Wby 5-4-1809 (clear); cf Wby 4-16-1817 (clear); d 9-13-1828
Jerusha d 10-15-1805
John, Flush., b 2-13-1758; m Phebe ----- b 7-28-1761
Ch: Anne b 9- 8-1785
Thomas b 10-12-1788
Phebe " 2- 5-1795
Lydia L., dt Silas & Elizabeth; m 1825 Joseph W. CORLIES
Michael d Mar. 21, 1837 ae 65y
Michael d 8-6-1859 ae 41y 8m 8d
Peter, s David & Jane, b 8-15-1824; ct Wby 10-4-1849
Phebe L. d 1-26-1882 ae 76y
Richard, Flushing, & Sarah
Ch: Susan
Mary b 5-19-1813
Deborah b 3-11-1815
cf N. Y. 6-2-1813 for parents, with 2 dt, Susan & an infant; ct N. Y. 8-7-1817 for parents with 3 ch, Susannah, Mary & Deborah
Samuel, N. Hempstead, & Abigail
Ch: Elizabeth m Nicholas HALLOCK
Samuel C. prcf N. Y. 1-4-1855, not rec as no such Friend attends here
Sarah, dt Silas & Elizabeth; m 2-13-1817 Silas HICKS
Silas, Flush., d 5-20-1829; m Elizabeth ----- d 8-28-1856 ae 91y 5m
Ch: Sarah b 3-24-1790; m Silas HICKS
William b 12-21-1794
Lydia " 4-23-1797
Eliza " 11-25-1799
Mary " 11-28-1802 d 12-5-1811
Phebe " 9-21-1805

TITUS, Silas & Elizabeth, continued
Ch: Elizabeth b 1- 8-1809
Elizabeth d 4-10-1806 (probably same as Eliza)
William L., s Silas (dec) & Elizabeth, b 12-21-1794 d 11-26-1859; m 2-15-1839 at Flushing Maria F. FRAME, dt Jesse (dec) & Mary
Ch: William L. Jr. b 12-29-1839
Silas " 6-16-1842
Mary F. " 2-21-1844
ct N. Y. for William 2-2-1826; cf N. Y. 1-4-1832 for William (clear)
William L., s Wm. L. & Maria F., b 12-29-1839; dis mo 9-7-1865

TOMKINS
----- (nm) m Elizabeth WAY, dt John D. & Mary, b 7-3-1783 (mo)
dis mo 5-4-1809

TOWNSEND
Edward O. d 1-29-1864 ae 18y
----- (nm) m Elizabeth TITUS, dt Silas & Elizabeth, b 1-8-1809 (mo)
dis mo 1-5-1832

TREADWELL
Mary d 3-25-1861

UNDERHILL
Ann d 6-17-1799
Ann m 1817 ----- ROE (mo)
dis mo 2-6-1817
Anna, dt Samuel, Flush., b 5-13-1785; ct Pur. 10-4-1810 (clear)
Edmund, Flush., b 2-1-1754 d 9-14-1826 in 74th yr.
Isaac, Flush., b 5 Mo (July) 21, 1732 d 6-4-1817 ae 85y 11d; m Mary ----- b 5-9-1730 d 11-9-1806
John d 11-15-1823; m Elizabeth ----- d 5-21-1812
John Jr. dis mo 5-6-1819
Maria gct Hamburgh 9-2-1858; cf East Hamburgh 2-28-1867; recrq 3-1-1827
Mary d 2-8-1800
Samuel, s Solomon & Lydia (dec); m 5-13-1813 at Flushing Eliza BOWNE, dt Samuel (dec) & Hannah
Thomas dis mo 3-6-1806

VALENTINE
Ellwood, s David (dec) & Hannah, Mk.; m 12-12-1822 at Flushing Mary T. POST, dt Daniel & Rosetta, Flushing

WATSON
Mary d 6-23-1799

WAY
Burling, Newtown, d 12-13-1811
Charles F., s John D. & Mary, b 6-14-1786; dis 7-6-1809
Elizabeth, dt John D. & Mary, b 7-3-1783; m
----- TOMKINS (mo)
mo before 5-4-1809 & then dis
John D., Newtown, b 4 Mo (June) 18, 1747; m Mary ----- b 9 Mo (Nov) 22, 1748
Ch: Judith b 5-24-1779
Elizabeth b 7- 3-1783; mo 1809
Charles Farrington b 6-14-1786; dis 7-6-1809
Sarah b 9- 7-1789
Rebecca " 10-15-1820
ct Rahway & Plainfield 11-5-1812 for Mary & dt, Sarah
Jordan & Rebecca
Ch: Dunbar b 1-14-1818

WHITE
----- m Jane WRIGHT (mo)
mo before 4-3-1817 & dis
Catharine J. White b 9-14-1827 d 10-6-1872 Tombstone, prob dt of Jane; cf Wby 11-19-1823 for Jane White; Jane con mo 4-4-1822; Wby reports having rec Jane into mbrp 8-1-1822; John White d Mar. 8-1844; Tombstone, prob. this one

WHITSON
Abraham, s Samuel & Phebe, d 9-5-1857 ae 76y; m Mary ----- d 8-15-1865 (8-5-1865 ae 88y 5m on Tombstone)
Ch: Amy b 3- 3-1824; m Edward S. WILLETS
Sarah d 9-14-1819 ae 5y 5m 17d (unless this was error for Phebe, she must be dt of another Abraham)
Esther m Edward S. WILLETS
cf Jericho 9-4-1817 for parents with 7 ch, Phebe, David, Esther, Abraham, Underhill, Charles & Samuel
Abraham U. dis mo 8-2-1838
Amy, dt Abraham & Mary; m 1860 Edward S. WILLETS
Anna, dt Thomas & Mary; m 1871 Frederick WILLETS
Charles, s Abraham & Mary, d 9-5-1868; cert with parents from Jericho 9-4-1817
David mo before 1-20-1831; ret mbrp; cf Jericho with parents 9-4-1817; ct N. Y. 4-5-1832
Esther, dt Abraham & Mary, Newtown; m 1831 Edward G. WILLETS; cf Jericho with parents 9-4-1817
Jacob H. rocf N. Y. 4-5-1854
Phebe C., dt Thomas & Ann, Flushing; m 1845 James B. WRIGHT
Samuel, s Abraham & Mary; m Phebe J. -----
Ch: William E. b 12-3-1867
Abraham W. b 10-25-1877
Eugene d 1-7-1867 ae 1m 4d
Samuel with parents rocf Jericho 9-4-1817
Sarah P. d 5-16-1865 ae 51y 6m 5d
Thomas, Flushing, b 3-1796 d 9-1-1846 (Tombstone 9-4-1846); m Ann ----- b 8-1779 d 10-10-1869 in 91st yr.
Ch: Phebe C. m Jas. B. WRIGHT
Thomas

WHITSON, Thomas & Ann, continued
cf Jericho 7-21-1836 for Thomas & Ann with 2 ch, Thomas & Phebe
Thomas & Mary
Ch: Daniel b 2-26-1849
Thomas Jr. b 6-19-1863
Anna m Fred'k WILLETS
Milton S. d 8- 8-1874 ae 3y 9m (prob s of Thomas & Mary)
cert of clear to Jericho 4-6-1848

WILCOMB
John, of Wilcomb & King, Flushing, d 9-8-1864, ae 58y (prob another person); m Hannah -----
Ch: William
Sarah
Mary
Charles
Margaret
John
Anna Harris b 6-17-1843
John Wilcomb recrq 11mo-1841 d 1870; Hannah recrq 5-5-1831; 6 minor ch recrq of Hannah 8-3-1837

WILLETS
Abigail's name appears among deaths 1865-1868; no date
Amos, of N. Y., s Robert & Mary; m 5-8-1828 at Flushing, Caroline FARRINGTON, dt George & Eliz. (both dec)
ct N. Y. for Caroline 5-6-1830
Ann, dt Seaman & Ann, b 1-6-1828; m 1848 Robert WILLETS
Tombstone; Ann P. Willets d 1851
Benjamin F. dis mo 4-5-1827
Caroline, dt Jacob H. & Sarah A., b 9-30-1841; m 1861 Charles FRAME
Charles, s Joseph & Abigail, b 4-20-1814 d 2-4-1834
Daniel, s Jacob & Hannah, b 5-24-1753 d 4-4-1825; m 9-1782 Martha SEAMAN, dt Zebulon & Phebe, b 2-28-1756 d 4-29-1816
Ch: Seaman b 10-12-1794; m 1818 Ann PEARSALL
Daniel T., of N. Y., s Amos & Anne (both dec); m 6-9-1836 at Flush., Elizabeth T. BOWNE, dt Phillip & Eliza F., Flush.
Edward S., s Richard & Mary (dec) Wby; m 1-13-1831 at Flush. Esther WHITSON, dt Abraham & Mary, Newtown; ct Wby 1-5-1832 for Esther
Newtown, Amy WHITSON, dt Abraham (dec) & Mary, Newtown, b 3-3-1824
Frederick, s Jacob H. & Sarah A., Wby, b 1-24-1851; m 10-12-1871 at Thomas Whitson's, Anna WHITSON, dt Thomas & Mary, Flushing
Jacob H. d 7-12-1857 ae 40y; m Sarah A. -----
Ch: Caroline b 9-30-1841; m Charles FRAME
Emily " 9-20-1845
Edward " 6-28-1849
Frederick b 1-24-1851
Walter R. " 1- 1-1855
ct Wby 1-6-1870 for Sarah A. with 3 minor ch, Edward, Frederick & Walter; cf N. Y. 3-4-1840 for Jacob H.
John J. gct Pur. 8-2-1810; cf Jericho 3-18-1852; d 1-23-1878
Joseph, s Thomas & Leah; m Catharine -----
Catharine's 4 ch rec by her rq 1-5-1815; her h also being desirous
Martha d 4-29-1816 ae 60y 2m 1d
Mary P., dt Seaman & Ann, b 8-10-1821; m 1843 Jordan WRIGHT
Robert, s Samuel & Sarah H., Flush.; m 1-10-1848 at Ann P. Willets', Margaret Ann WILLETS, dt Seaman (dec) & Ann P., Flush.
Ch: Samuel b 2-10-1849 d 7-15-1877
Amelia b 1-26-1856
Robert m 2d 12-15-1875 at Matthias Nicoll's, N. Y. City, Gloriana M. NICOLL, dt Sam'l Benj. (dec) & Sarah (Payne), of Shelter Island; cf N. Y. 6-2-1847 for Robert
Samuel gct Pur. 11-6-1806 (clear)
Samuel, s Robert & Margaret Ann; m 9-29-1875 Annie L. MICKEL
Sarah, dt Thomas & Leah, b 9-5-1782; m ----- ALBERTSON (mo)
mo before 10-3-1805 & dis
Seaman, s Daniel & Martha, b 10-12-1791 d 8-24-1827; m 4-9-1818 at Flushing, Ann P. PEARSALL, dt Samuel & Margaret, d 10-5-1851
Ch: Thomas S. b 5- 9-1819
Mary " 8-10-1821; m Jordan WRIGHT
Samuel P. " 9-25-1825 d 2- 6-1827
Margaret Ann b 1- 6-1828; m Robt. WILLETS
Seaman recrq 11-6-1817
Sener b 4-26-1807 d 5-29-1848
Thomas, Flush., b 1 Mo (Mar), 4, 1738/9; m Leah ----- b 3 Mo (May) 22, 1744
Ch: Mary b 6-22-1768
Phebe " 2- 1-1770
Rachel " 4- 1-1773
Joseph " 2- 1-1778
Sarah " 9- 5-1782
Zebulon b 5-15-1786
Thomas dis mo 7-5-1832
Wait, Flushing, & Mary
Ch: Amy b 10-20-1805
ct Pur. 8-2-1810 for Wait (clear)

WILLETT
Elbert S. recrq 8-1-1816; ct N. Y. 8-4-1842

WILLIS
Thomas & -----
Ch: Mary
Phebe
ct Wby 5-1-1806 for Thomas, his w & 2 dt

WINES
Gilbert H., s John & Jane, b 6-29-1827; m Eliza T. ----- d Apr. 12, 1861 in 36th y
John [Wine], s James (dec) & Elizabeth, Flush., b 7-24-1789 d 5-30-1869 in 79th yr.; m 1-9-1812 at Flushing, Abigail DUSENBURY, dt Peter & Mary (dec), d 12-17-1814

WINES, John & Abigail [Wine], continued
Ch: Mary b 2- 8-1814 d 10-20-1814
John m 2d 4-13-1826 Jane L. EMBREE, dt Effingham (dec) & Mary, d 10-9-1865 in 69th yr.
Ch: Gilbert H. b 6-29-1827
Edward S. " 8-28-1828
Robert C. " 7-27-1832
John recrq 6-12-1810; cert of unity to Canadian mtg 1817, returning minutes from several mtg 1818; ct N. P. 1-4-1838 for John & Jane L. with 3 ch named; cf N. Y. for John & Jane, he a minister 8-7-1851

WOODNUT
Anna F. rocf N. Y. 6-6-1877

WRIGHT
Amelia d 6-11-1863 ae 64y
Caroline E. d 1-6-1864
Catharine, dt Jordan & Rebecca, b 3-5-1810; m ----- ROGERS (mo)
dis mo 4-3-1828
Charles rocf N. Y. 10-3-1810
Charles, s Jordan & Rebecca, b 1-14-1818; m -----; dis mo 9-4-1844; ct N. Y. as a minor 4-5-1838; cert ret as he not resident there
Charles H. d 10-12-1824; m 6-8-1875 Ida J. MACKENZIE
Ch: Mary Pearsall b 3-25-1876
Robert Willets b 12-30-1877
Daniel Dodge, s Stephen & Elizabeth, b 1-24-1809 d 4-29-1892; m 4-14-1840 Mary F. MOTT, dt Stephen & Sarah, b 8-13-1817 d 3-7-1880
Ch: Two
cf N. Y. for Mary F. to reside with h 7-1-1874; Daniel D. dis 7-6-1826 for long absence
Dunbar d 1-14-1817 ae 2d
Eliza b 4-12-1793 d 1-15-1831
Elizabeth m John FRANKLIN (mo)
both dis mo before 6-6-1811
James B., s John D. & Mary D. (dec), Flush., b 12-16-1822; m 3-6-1845 at Thomas Whitson's, Phebe C. WHITSON, dt Thomas & Ann, Flush.
Jane m 1817 ----- WHITE (mo)
ct Wby 11-19-1823 for Jane White
John D., s Jordan & Rebecca, b 9-19-1799 d 8-21-1879; m 1-13-1820 at Flushing, Mary B. BYRD, dt James & Elizabeth, d 11-23-1843 ae 46y
Ch: Rebecca d 3-7-1822 ae 1y 4m 22d
James Byrd b 12-16-1822 d 3-20-1879
ct N. Y. for John D. & fam 6-2-1825; cf N. Y. for John D. & fam 8-3-1843, ch not named; cert of clear to N. Y. for John D. 5-8-1845; ct N. Y. for John D. & 2 ch 5-7-1846
Jordan, Flushing, b 11-27-1780 d 11-12-1829; m Rebecca -----
Ch: Robert b 10-11-1803 d 8-1825
Alexander b 9- 2-1805 d 7-20-1807
Mary " 1- 1-1808
Catharine b 3- 5-1810
Caroline " 3- 5-1810 d 3-18-1822 ae 12y
Harriet T. b 11-18-1814 d 9-29-1826
Charles " 1-14-1818
Tombstone, Rebecca White & her s, Robert (no date)
Jordan d 6-12-1837 ae about 75y
Jordan, s Abraham & Susan COCK (Jordan Cock had name changed to Wright); m 6-12-1843 at Ann P. Willets', Mary P. WILLETS, dt Seaman (dec) & Ann P., b 8-10-1821
Ch: Thomas Searing b 4-22-1845
Charles Henry " 5-18-1848
Margaret Ann " 4-11-1858
Robert, s Jordan & Rebecca, b 10-11-1803 d 1825
ct N. Y. 7-7-1825; 9-1-1825, Robert, having d before his cert was forwarded, it is now returned to the mtg
Susan, dt Jordan & Elizabeth; m 12-8-1808 Abraham COCK
Thomas S., s Jordan & Mary, b 4-22-1845; m 7-11-1877 Martha CADNESS
Ch: John Jordan b 4-19-1878
----- (nm) m Mary BOWNE, dt Jordan & Rebecca, b 1-1-1808 (mo)
Mary dis mo 5-3-1827
----- (nm) m Hannah EMBREE, dt Effingham & Mary (mo)
dis mo 10-4-1827

GRAVESTONE RECORDS
FRIENDS BURIAL GROUND AT FLUSHING

BASSETT
Fannie d 1885

BOWNE
Catherine d 1 Aug. 1848 ae 79y
Cornell d 12 Mo 19, 1864 in 64th yr
Isaac W.

BYRD
James & Elizabeth d 1842
Phebe d 6 Mo 19, 1864 ae 79y 7m

CHAPMAN
Elizabeth d 12 July 1838 ae 88y

CLEMENT
Wm. B., s Henry & Ruth L., d 2 Mo 9, 1855 ae 5y 4d

COCK
Sarah b 3 Mo 1, 1774 d 11 Mo 30, 1863
Susan W. d 4 Mo 2, 1872 ae 83y
Wm. E. b 5 Mo 17, 1814 d 7 Mo 20, 1868

EMBREE
Carrie, dt Robt. & Phebe, b 6 Mo 1, 1853 d 1 Mo 3, 1860
Deborah L. b 5 Mo 18, 1778 d 5 Mo 21, 1821
John L.

FARRINGTON
Maria d 3 Mo 26, 1857 ae 70y

FITCH
Joseph b 13 June 1811 d 27 Oct. 1868

FRANKLIN
Anthony d 1854 ae 87y
John L. d 1863 ae 73y
Lydia d 1837 ae 64y

HICKS
Anna D. b 9 Mo 5, 1826 d 7 Mo 3, 1891
Sarah T. d 11 Mo 21, 1874 ae 84y 8m
Silas d 8 Mo 30, 1861

JACKSON
Elizabeth A. b 6 Mo 10, 1817 d 9 Mo 17, 1869

KING
Thomas b 3 Mo 18, 1789 d 2 Mo 23, 1888

KISSAM
Margaret d 18 Nov. 1886

LAWERENCE
Deborah Ann d 28 Apr. 1886
Elizabeth W. [Lawrence] d 24 Nov. 1852
Esther d 1847
Robert d 1847
Wm. d 9 May 1893

LEGGETT
Caroline 1853
Margaret 1851
Samuel d 1 Mo 5, 1847 ae 64y 3m 1d
Thomas b 1 Mo 30, 1793 d 8 Mo 1, 1865

LOWERRE
Elizabeth d 1844 ae 74y
Giles H. b 3 Mo 1803 d 3 Mo 1850 ae 47y
John d 1831 ae 64y 6m
Lewis, s C.P. & A.B., d 1846 ae 1y 7m

MATLOCK
Hannah b 21 July 1783 d 25 July 1886
Timothy d 8 Mo 4, 1845 ae 53y

MITCHELL
Henry d 1843 ae 86y

PEARSALL
Jacob d 1846

PINKHAM
Abigail b 1 Mo 1792 d 10 Mo 1861

SMART
Lydia F. d 1840 ae 8y

SMITH
Abigail d 1 Mo 7, 1843 ae 82y
Nathaniel d 5 Mo 20, 1835 ae 77y

THURSTON
Abigail E. d 5 Mo 28, 1851 ae 66y 18d
Wm. R. d 5 Mo 24, 1855 ae 88y 9m 14d

TITUS
Elizabeth d 8 Mo 22, 1856 ae 91y 5m
Michael d 21 Mar 1837 ae 65y
Michael d 8 Mo 6, 1859 ae 41y 8m 8d
Phebe L. d 1 Mo 26, 1882 ae 76y
Wm. L. b 12 Mo 21, 1794 d 11 Mo 26, 1859

TOWNSEND
Edward O. d 1 Mo 29, 1864 ae 18y

WHITE
Catherine J. b 9 Mo 14, 1827 d 10 Mo 6, 1872
Jane d 7 Mo 19, 1866 ae 79y
John d 8 March 1844

WHITSON
Ann b 8 Mo 26, 1779
Eugene, s Sam'l & Phebe J., d 1 Mo 7, 1867 ae 1m 4d
Mary d 8 Mo 5, 1865 ae 88y 5m
Sarah P. d 5 Mo 16, 1865 ae 51y 6m 5d
Thos. b 3 Mo 1776 d 9 Mo 4, 1846

WILLETS
Abigail

WILLETS, continued
Ann P. d 1851

WINES
Edward S.
Elizabeth T., w Gilbert H., d 12 Apr 1861 in 36th yr
Gilbert S.
Jane L. d 10 Mo 9, 1865 in 69th yr
John b 7 Mo 24, 1789 d 5 Mo 30, 1869

WRIGHT
Amelia d 6 Mo 11, 1863 ae 64y
Caroline E. d 1 Mo 6, 1864
D. D. d 1841
James B. b 12 Mo 16, 1822 d 3 Mo 20, 1879
John D. b 9 Mo 19, 1799 d 8 Mo 21, 1879
Jordan d 1837
Mary B. d 11 Mo 23, 1843 ae 46y
Rebecca & s, Robert

W E S T B U R Y   M O N T H L Y   M E E T I N G

Meetings for worship had already been held at Woodledge, now Westbury, and at the Farms, later called Lusum, and still later called Jericho, when the earliest Quaker minute in America was written, in 1671. These meetings still exist. Westbury Monthly Meeting may be considered as old as that of Flushing, but no minutes are extant before 1697. Its vital records were for many years recorded in the parchment bound book in which Isaac Horner, an Oyster Bay man, copied in 1685 the vital data of all Quakers on Long Island, and which was continued in use by Flushing (now New York) Monthly Meeting.

While the Quakers of New York City Meeting were largely in commercial business, those of Westbury were always almost universally agricultural. They and their wives rose "while it is yet dark", and tended their flocks and herds, cleared the land they had purchased by definite deeds from the Indians, paying whatsoever the latter asked. Much land so bought and so cleared is still owned and lived on by descendants.

By 1730 a book for their own vital records was begun, in which numerous earlier data were recorded, a few being definitely noted as copied from Flushing records.

Westbury Monthly Meeting included meetings established approximately in the following order:

Oyster Bay; Westbury; Jericho; Matinecock; Cow Neck (now Manhasset), and Bethpage; all of which are still part of the Monthly Meeting except Oyster Bay, which faded out, and Jericho and Bethpage, which were set off as a separate Monthly Meeting. It also had for short periods meetings at Rockaway, Hempstead, Huntington and Secatogue. Secatogue or Sequatague is the old name for Islip, in Suffolk County. A meeting house was mentioned there in 1771.

In the deplorable Separation which occurred in 1828, out of 340 members only 41 including children, were of the Orthodox body. These, with 7 adult and 2 children of Jericho MM called themselves Westbury and Jericho Monthly Meeting, which has ceased to exist. The vital data from their records is herein indicated by the letter O.

It should be noted that besides the Cock-Cocks-Cox Genealogy, 1914, which I have cited as "Cox Gen." there are other Genealogies of Long Island families, Frost, Seaman, Underhill, Jones, etc. and the Oyster Bay Town Records, 1653-1878, which will add to the data herein given. A comparison of dates in some of these genealogies, especially before 1752, will show numerous differences, owing to the number of a month being transposed to the name of a month, and very generally wrong in the genealogies. Besides these printed genealogies, the extensive and accurate data on 60 Long Island families, gathered from Bibles and other family records by the late George W. Cocks, of Glen Cove, now in my possession, cited herein as "Bibles", will probably in time be preserved in some metropolitan Library.

The term "priest" in the records, means an Evangelical or Episcopalian minister - never a Roman Catholic priest.

The dates from tombstones in Quaker burial grounds at Westbury, Matinecock and Manhasset taken by Frank Haviland and George W. Cocks, 1904, have been herein incorporated. In all our Quaker burial grounds many non-members were interred. Most of these were related to members.

RECORDS

ADAMS

Nancy, dt Jacob & Betsey, b 9-14-1833; m 1853 Benj. TITUS

ADEE

Henry, s Daniel & Jemima, Pleasant Valley, Dutchess Co.; m 10-30-1817 at Mk. Mary UNDERHILL, wd James, dt John, dec, & Sarah TITUS, b 10-22-1769; cf Oswego (clear); Mary m 3rd Jacob CONKLIN

ALBERTSON

A. Raymond, s J. Augustus & Mary W., Wby, b 4-22-1892; m 9-8-1914 at Lebanon, O., Harriet CADWALLADER, dt Francis W. & Mary L., Monrow, O., b 7-15-1897 Lebanon, O.

Ch: John Augustus b 8-29-1915
Raymond " 2- 5-1918
Robert Francis b 11-16-1926
Harriet & ch recrq 7-17-1927

Benjamin, s Derick & Sarah, b 3-16-1782 d 11-11-1841 ae 60; m Sarah WILLETS, dt Thomas & Leah (Seaman), b 9-5-1782 d 10-5-1870 ae 87 (d 10-5-1871 on Wby tombstone & Bible Records) (m 7----1806)

Ch: Richard b 11-28-1810
Hicks " 2-18-1816
Benjamin " 12-16-1823

Benjamin, s Benjamin & Sarah, b 12-16-1823; m Elizabeth JACKSON, dt Jacob & Phebe (Duryea) b 10-19-1828 d 11-22-1854 bur Wby (Bible)

Ch: Richard b 1852 d 2-13-1853 ae 1y 16d bur Wby
Mary " 1848

Benjamin m 2nd Martha JACKSON, dt Jacob & Phebe (Duryea), b 1827 d 12-1-1914 ae 87

Ch: Anna b 1859 d 3-2-1915

Caroline, dt Silas & Kezia, b 11-8-1816; m Alexander UNDERHILL

Daniel, s Derick & Rebecca, b 4-15-1739; m Adah THORNICRAFT, dt Derick & Temperance (mo about 1764)

Ethel Mary, dt Jno. Augustus & Mary W., b 2-16-1890; m 1913 Arthur Wood POST

Hicks, s Benjamin & Sarah, b 2-8-1806 d 8-12-1863 ae 47y 5m 23d; m 1828 Elizabeth C. WILLIS, b 3-27-1808 d 9-28-1889 (Wby Stone)

Ch: Emily b 1-9-1849 d 12-8-1849 (Wby Tombstone)
Sarah W. b 4-29-1842 (Wby Stone)

Ida, dt Silas W. & Caroline, b 6-12-1858; m Edwin C. WILLETS

J. Augustus,(nm), s Rich. (dec) & Phebe W., O.B. b 12-16-1856 d 12-17-1923; m 6-7-1888 at Cath. M. Willis', Mary P. WILLIS, dt Sam'l, dec, & Catharine M., N. Hemp, b 12-26-1866 d 3-11-1916

Ch: Ethel Mary b 2-16-1890
Raymond " 4-12-1892
Ethel & Raymond recrq of mother 9-19-1900

Martin J. D., s Townsend & Alletta P., b 1-28-1876 d 6-23-1938 at Phoenix, Ariz.

Richard, s William & Barbara, d 1753; m Sarah McCoun, dt Wm. & Sarah (Townsend), d 5-5-1818 ae 73y & abt 3m
Sarah Albertson dis mo 6-26-1765; rst 5-27-1778

Richard, s Benjamin & Sarah, b 11-28-1810 d 5-18-1879 ae 86; m Phebe W. PRIOR, dt John & Elizabeth, b 1-3-1824 d 6-8-1902 ae 78

Ch: John Augustus b 12-16-1850
Benjamin d 1-8-1872
Richard P. " 7-15-1860 ae 9m
John recrq 11-14-1906
(Wby Stones)

Sarah, dt Silas W. & Caroline L.; m 1897 J. Wheeler GLOVER

Sarah m 2nd William WOOLEY

Sarah H. m 1869 Daniel TUTTLE

Sarah W., dt Hicks & Elizabeth C., b 4-29-1842; m 1879 William K. MOTT

Silas, s Derick & Sarah, b 4-28-1784 d 1-2-1847 ae 63y; m 1813 Keziah WHITSON, dt Henry & Clemence, b 1788 d 8-21-1853 ae 66y 3m 1d

Ch: Sarah H. b 1- 8-1815
Caroline " 11- 8-1816
Phebe " 12-16-1818
Elizabeth b 9-15-1821 d 1-20-1823
Silas " 8-23-1825

Silas W., s Silas & Kezia, b 8-23-1825 d 12-23-1906; m Caroline LYON, dt Walter S., b 3-4-1828 d 1-9-1904

Ch: Sallie L. b 1-30-1854 d 3-2-1856
(Wby Stone)

William m 4-9-1891 Annie H. COLES, dt Wm. H. & Mariah A.
Annie recrq of parents 10----1874

Willmett, dt Derick & Dinah; m Thomas THORNICRAFT

----- m S. Louisa MOTT, dt Wm. K. & Sarah, b 6-12-1879
S. Louisa recrq 6-16-1912

ALLEN

Elizabeth, dt Henry & Mary, b 6 Mo. (Aug) 6, 1709; m 1742 William MOTT

Elizabeth Ann, dt Richard & Olive, d 8-2-1858 ae 1y 3m 10d

Freelove [Alling], dt Abraham & Mary; m Thomas UNDERHILL, s Abraham & Sarah, b abt 1706 (Underhill Gen.)

George b 4-7-1811 d 12-15-1886; m Margaret ----- b 10-27-1812 d 2-23-1898

Ch: Sarah m Aug. CORNING

John b Scotland 6-23-1791 d 12-18-1870 ae 79y 5m 28d; m Susan D. ----- b 2-12-1806 d 12-19-1890 ae 84y 10m 7d

Mary gct Shrewsbury 11 Mo (Jan) 27, 1724/5

Nehemiah (nm) & Mary

Mary rst 12-19-1798; ct N. Y. next mo.

Samuel (nm), Great Neck; m Pamelia ----- d 8----1817
Pamelia's ack referred from N. Y., accepted 5-16-1816

ALLEN, continued
Sarah m 1809 ----- SMITH (mo)
Sarah, dt George & Margaret, b 4-7-1811; m Augustus CORNING
Violetta [Alling], dt John & Violetta, b 1765; m William HAWXHURST (Bible)

ALLEY
Sarah Elizabeth, dt Sidney B. & Elizabeth; m 1858 Nathaniel M. WEEKS
Saul b 1778 d 10-19-1852; m Mary UNDERHILL, dt Israel & Mary, b 5-18-1791 d 2-11-1868 (m 12-13-1817 in N.Y.)
Ch: John
William S.
George B.
Louisa
Josephine d N. Y. 11-19-1841
Mary Anna
Lydia m Geo. GRISWOLD
Mary dis mo 2-18-1818 (Underhill Gen.)
Sidney B., s Enos & Rebecca (both dec), N.Y.C.; m 3-25-1835 at Wby Elizabeth C. TITUS, dt Rowland & Sarah, N. Hemp
Ch: Sarah Elizabeth m Nath. WEEKS
William b N. Y. 1850 d N. Y. 4-1868
Sidney B. m 2nd Lydia TITUS, dt Rowland & Sarah, b 8-23-1819
Ch: Lydia b Jericho
Lydia m 2nd Samuel HOSIER; Lydia & William gct N. Y. 1863

ALLISON
John, Cow Neck, signed epistle abt 1725; in arbitration with Joseph Lotham re Creek thatch 1727; of Orange Co. dis 7-25-1753, have not esteemed him a mbr for many years

ALMY
Catharine m Solomon TOWNSEND

ALSOP
Hannah, dt Richard & Sarah, b 12-18-1757; m 1777 Thomas CARPENTER
Hannah m 2d 1785 Job WEBB, of Pa.
Mary, dt Richard & Ann; m 1762 Joseph WOOD, Jr.
Richard Jr., s Richard & Hannah; m Ann BETTS
Ch: Mary m Joseph WOOD Jr.
Richard, Jr., s Thomas & Susannah, Newtown; m 4 Mo. (Apr) 3, 1747 Sarah MOTT, wd Richard, dt Thomas PEARSALL
Ch: Sarah b 11 Mo (Jan) 3, 1747/8
Phebe " 10 Mo (Dec) 2, 1749
John " 2-27-1753
Hannah b 2- 7-1755 d 9-18-1757
Hannah " 12-18-1757
Sarah's ack accepted 8 Mo (Oct) 13, 1748; Richard cf Flushing (clear); Sarah ct Flushing; cf Flushing for both 7-3-1754
Sarah, dt Richard & Sarah, b 11 Mo (Jan) 3, 1747/8; m 1767 William LOINES Jr.
Thomas, s Richard & Hannah; m Susannah BLACKWELL, dt Col. Robt. & Mary
mo before 7-26-1762; dis 12-29-1762

ANDERSON
Mary, dt Peter & Jane; m 1812 Wm. HAWXHURST

APPLEBY
Catharine b 9-17-1775; m 1796 Samuel MOTT
Deborah d 1854 in 59th yr. bur Manhasset
Epinetus d 1857 in 76th yr bur Manhaset
John d 1865 in 74th yr bur Manhasset
Sarah d 1827 in 74th yr bur Manhasset
Thomas d 1837 in 87th yr bur Manhasset

ARISON
Jane W. m George S. UNDERHILL

ATKINSON
Dorothy, dt Francis B. & Eleanor; m 1913 W. R. ROBINSON

BACH
Jacob b 11-15-1847 d 6-2-1903 (Wby Stone)
Philip b 1812 d 2-1-1857 ae 45; m Catharine ----- b 9-11-1812 d 2-26-1886
Ch: Theodore b 7-22-1854 d 1-5-1881
William & Elizabeth
Ch: Theodore d 12-2-1890 ae 7y

BAILEY
Martha [Baley], Buckram, d 9-6-1817

BAISLEY
Edward N. m 10-1-1817 Mary W. THORNE, dt Isaac & Emily
Howard N., s DeWitt C. E. & Evelyn O., Bkn.; m 10-1-1917 at Mary W. Thorne's, Bkn., Mary W. THORNE, dt Isaac C. & Emily B., both dec, b 10-18-1872

BAKER
Asa m Elizabeth DODGE, dt John & Mary, d 3-30-1866 ae 77y 7m
Elizabeth recrq
Martha, dt Richard & Deborah; m 1778 James HUBBS
Mary, dt Ann, wd; m 1784 Emery HEWLETT (mo)
Stephen m 1780 Sarah A. MOTT, dt Micajah & Rachel
Sarah dis mo 5-31-1780

BALDWIN
Benjamin & Elizabeth
mo, her ack accepted 6-18-1794; ct N. Y. for Elizabeth 10-15-1794
Catharine, dt Henry & Anna; m ----- STRONGITHAM
Gilbert d 6-5-1867 ae 37 (unidentified stone [Wby
Jesse, s Jesse & Mary, N. Hemp.; m 8-2-1804 at Wby Elizabeth VAN COTT, dt Peter, O.B.
Kitty d 11-9-1875 ae 83 (unidentified stone,Wby)
Rebecca, dt Henry & Anna, Wby, d 3-7-1848 ae nearly 60
Richard d 3-4-1863 ae 66(unidentified stone,Wby)

BANE
Nathan (nm), Goshen, Pa., s Mordecai, d 1748;

BANE, Nathan, continued
m 27 Dec 1735 in Christ Church, Phila., Mary COCK, dt Henry & Mary, b 8 Mo (Oct) 8, 1711
Mary ack 2 Mo (Apr) 18, 1743; ct Goshen 3 Mo (May) 25, 1743; Mary m 2d Francis MEECHAM (mo) & dis; rst by Goshen MM 9-8-1786 (Cox Gen.)

BANKS
Daniel G., s Nathan O., dec, & Cynthia, Granesville, Fairfax Co., Va., d Sea Cliff 8-13-1915 ae 84y; m 6-21-1855 at Rebecca Hauxhurst's, Maria HAUXHURST, dt Townsend, dec, & Rebecca, N. Hemp., b 6-16-1830 d Sea Cliff, N. Y. 1-13-1920 ae 89
Ch: Annie L. b 3-15-1856
Daniel N. b 4-6-1861 d 9-9-1863
Rebecca C. b 4- 6-1861 d 7-8-1862 ae 1y 3m 2d
Caroline M. b 12-2-1864 d 9-5-1931
Nathan " 4-13-1868
Ch b near Roslyn

BARBEY
Aline G. b 12-3-1851 d 12-31-1852 (Stone Man.)

BARKER
Ann, dt Samuel; m John TITUS
Julia Anna, dt David D. & Julia; m 1869 John Howard RUSHMORE
Robert m 1735 Phebe DICKINSON (wd)
cf R. I. (clear)

BARNARD
Ford B., s Verne Joshua & Caroline Theodosia, b 11-3-1893; m 9-3-1927 at White Plains, Margaret Shepard WITTER, dt Geo. Henry & Maud B., b Wellsville, N. Y. 10-14-1906
Margaret recrq 5-20-1928; Geo. Henry born Stannards, N. Y.; Maud Bingham b Higginsville, N. Y.
John T. m Mary SEAMAN, b 11-19-1815 d 7-1-1870 ae 56y 7m 12d
Ch: Thos. Upham b 5-16-1837 d 7-21-1849
Harrison " 1-11-1840 d 10-25-1842
Mary Emma " 10-4-1844 d 8-31-1845
(All from Wby Stones)

BARNED
Geo. R. & Ellen D.
Ch: Hester Wilcox b 1-13-1867 d Nov. 2, 1867 (Wby Stone)

BARRET
Samuel A., s Absalom & Deborah, Marlboro; m 4-28-1836 at Mk Mary J. UNDERHILL, dt Daniel (dec) & Phebe, O.B.
cf Marlboro (clear); Mary J. rocf Jericho 1830; ct Oswego MM 6-19-1872

BARROW
John Jr., s John & Mary (dec), N.Y.C.; m 11-22-1821 at Cow Neck, Elizabeth Moode PRIOR, dt Edmund & Mary, N. Hemp., b 8-30-1800 d 2-28-1885 ae 65y 5m bur Man.
cf N. Y. (clear)

BATES
Sarah ack mo 7-25-1787, accepted 9-26-1787

BATTY
Abigail ack mo 1-14-1752
Abigail [Battey], dt Daniel; m 1785 Adam MOTT

BEACH
Martha S., dt Jas. Harvey & Mary Emily, Norwood, Pa., b Pratt, Kans. 4-6-1904; m ----- NEITZKE
recrq 11-21-1926; ct Boston MM 12-21-1930; Jas. Harvey b Laurence, Kans.; Mary Emily b Norwalk, Conn.

BECK
Wally b Milwaukee 9-27-1890; m 1918 Austin Allan SCOTT

BEDELL
Benajah [Bedle], s Joseph & Hannah, d 10-23-1825 ae 80y & abt 2m
Elizabeth d 5-28-1883 ae 65y 9m 10d (Wby Stone)
Jehiel mo before 6-26-1782 & dis
Jehiel's ack referred to Ferrisburgh 5-20-1818, rpd accepted 11-18-1818
Mary ack mo before 1 Mo (Mar) 28, 1744
William [Bedle], nm & Mary
Ch: Mordecai b 4 Mo (Jan) 11, 1745/6
Rachel " 11 Mo (Jan) 18, 1750/1
Jehiel " 7-27-1755
Mary ack mo 1 Mo (Mar) 28, 1744/5

BELL
Chrissie m 1924 Wm. Lawrie SEAMAN
Katherine L., dt Arthur E. & Martha, b 4-10-1898; m 1927 James B. SMITH, Jr.

BENNETT
Phebe, dt William & Elizabeth; m abt 1761 Daniel WRIGHT
mo & dis

BERGEN
Maria m Stimonson POWELL

BERGER
Peter m Ursula ----- d 11-14-1877 ae 68y (Wby Stone)

BETTS
Ann m Richard ALSOP Jr.
Israel d 10-11-1855 ae 24y 2d (Wby Stone)
Jane (or Bates) m 1699 Richard OSBORNE

BEWLEY
Mungo's cert signed 4 Mo (June) 27, 1733

BINNEY
Sam C., s Sam'l & Kathryn (Scott), b 10-28-1905 Denver, Colo.
recrq 2-18-1934; Samuel M. b Urbana, Ill.; Kathryn Scott b Lincoln, Neb.

BIRDSALL
Benjamin, s Benj. & Mercy, Jerusalem; m 2 Mo (Apr) 10, 1729 Charity FARRINGTON, wd Benjamin HAVILAND
Ch: Mary m Anthony TRIPP
Isaac m Mary BURNS
Benjamin m 2d 12 Mo. (Feb) 21, 1734/5 at Wby, Elizabeth HOPKINS, dt Ichobad, dec, & Sarah, O.B.
Elizabeth ack mo 2 Mo (Apr) 28, 1747; cert issued for her, destination not stated; Benjamin b 1 Mo (Mar) 15, 1691/2 d 11-27-1754 (Bible)
Daniel, s Samuel & Mary, Mk, d 4-14-1758; m 1727 Joanah HAUXHURST, dt Samson & Hannah
Ch: Sarah m Henry TITUS
Amy
Mary Hannah
Daniel b 1735; m Hannah MANDEVILLE (Bible)
Elizabeth, dt Thomas & Rosannah; m Parmenus JACKSON
Elizabeth m 2nd James DOWNING
Elizabeth m 3d 1799 Amos WILLETS
Rosannah d 12-7-1813 ae 85y 11m 7d
Sarah, dt Daniel & Johannna; m 1749 Henry TITUS
Susan, dt Jas. & Elizabeth, b 10-31-1837; m 1859 Leonard F. COLES

BLACKBURN
Alexander M., s Alex. & Marg. H., b Oak Park, Ill. 2-12-1878; m Jean Gertrude JOUETT, dt Isaac W. & Annie B., b Cambridge, Mass. 8-18-1878
Alexander & Jean recrq 3-18-1923
Isabelle, dt Alex. & Margaret, b Chicago 3-9-1874; m S. Archibald SMITH

BLACKWELL
Susannah, dt Col. Robt. & Mary; m (probably) Thomas ALSOP

BLADE
John m Sarah DORLAND
mo before 11-16-1791 & dis next mo; rst 1-20-1796

BOGART
Ethelene, dt Dr. Jos. & Ethelene; m 1910 Samuel J. SEAMAN Jr. (1st w)
Jane, dt Dr. Jos. & Ethelene; m Samuel J. SEAMAN Jr. (2nd w)

BOHACK
Christian m Catharine SCHALK d 9-8-1861 ae 35

BOND
Abraham d 5-19-1883 ae 84y 10m; m Cornelia ----- d 3-28-1864 ae 65y 6m
Ch: Sarah d 1-15-1879 ae 50y 9m 11d
(Wby Stones)

BOOTH
Vincent Vergin Rave, s Vincent R. & Mariam V. R., Cambridge, Mass.; m 11-28-1936 at Bkn., Anne S. CHAPMAN, dt A. Wright & Grace S., Bkn.

BOWNE
Abigail, dt John & Hannah, b 12 Mo (Feb) 5, 1662; m 1686 Richard WILLITS
Catharine S. b 9-26-1826 d 3-7-1900 (Wby Stone)
Daniel gct Flushing 9 Mo (Nov) 26, 1746 (clear)
Edward S. m Sarah CARLE, dt John Jr. & Susan (Hicks), b 10-6-1836 d 6-29-1884
Elizabeth, dt John & Hannah, b 8 Mo (Oct) 8, 1658; m 1678 John PRIOR; m 2nd Samuel TITUS
Elizabeth F., dt Sidney B. & Jemima, b 4-20-1814; m 1836 Daniel T. WILLETS
Hannah, dt Thomas & Penelope THORN, b 1732; m abt 1752 Jacob BOWNE; m 2nd 1789 Wm. TITUS
Hannah, dt Jacob & Hannah, b 8-11-1761; m 1783 Townsend WILLIS (mo)
Herbert S., s Sidney B. & Martha W., b 4-11-1878; m 3-30-1910 Helen Isabel HEAKES, dt Jas. B. & Isabel N., b Toronto 10-13-1885
Ch: Janet Isabel b 9-25-1916
Harold Herbert b 12-22-1918
Helen recrq 9-17-1911
Jacob, s Thomas & Hannah, b 8 Mo (Oct) 6, 1724 d abt 1786; m abt 1752 Hannah THORN, dt Thomas & Penelope b 1732
Ch: Martha b 10-23-1753 d 1-13-1757
Thomas " 10-23-1755
Hannah " 8-11-1761
Daniel " 6- 2-1764
Jacob " 2- 9-1769
Hannah ack mo 2-22-1758; Jacob ack mo & bearing arms 6-9-1759; Hannah m 2d William TITUS (Bible)
Johanna Sr. signed epistle abt 1725
John, s Samuel & Mary, b 7 Mo (Sept) 11, 1698 d 4-14-1757; m 27 Jan. 1738 Dinah UNDERHILL b 7 Mo (Sept) 20, 1705 d 2-1-1770
Dinah gct Flushing 3 Mo (May) 31, 1738
Mary, dt Thomas & Hannah, b 5 Mo (July) 4, 1717; m 1736/7 Henry COCK (Cox Gen.)
Richard M., s Sidney & Jemima, rocf N. Y. 9 Mo 1849; d 6-5-1899 ae 82y
Robert, s Samuel & Mary, b 1700 d 6-1743; m 9 Mo (Nov) 6, 1724 Margaret LATHAM, dt Joseph & Jane, d 4-2-1773
Robert signed epistle abt 1725 (Bibles)
Sarah, dt Samuel & Sarah, b 1724; m 1753 William TITUS
Sidney B., s Rich. M. & Mary Margaret, d 7-27-1915 ae 65y; m Martha -----
Ch: Herbert S. b 4-11-1878

BOWNE, Sidney B. & Martha, continued
Martha rocf Jericho
Thomas, s Samuel & Mary, b 11 Mo (Jan) 29, 1694/5 d 3-28-1762; m 1 Mo (Mar) 7, 1715/16 Hannah UNDERHILL, dt John & Mary, b 1 Mo (Mar) 23, 1689/90 d 5-2-1761
Ch: Jacob b 8 Mo (Oct) 6, 1724
Mary " 5 Mo (July) 4, 1717
Thomas & Hannah signed an Epistle 1725

BOYD
Elizabeth, dt Benj. F. & Phebe, b 6-28-1814; m 1835 Silas DOWNING

BRAGG
Roger signed Epistle abt 1725; rem cert to Pa. or elsewhere 6 Mo (Aug) 30, 1727, did not go, had similar cert 7 Mo (Sept) 25, 1728; a third cert to Goshen, Pa. 12 Mo. 24, 1730/1; schoolmaster (clear); a fourth cert 12 Mo (Feb) 25, 1735/36 to Abington, refers to his return from Ireland

BRANSON
Ann, dt Wm. E. & Florence D., b 9-14-1910; m 1930 K. Fritz EILERS

BREWSTER
Isaac H. & -----
Ch: Isaac H. d 2-25-1876 ae 2y 6m 8d
Fanny May d 4-5-1872 ae 27y

BRIDGES
George & Sarah F.
Ch: Reta d 7-11-1875 ae 1y 2m 18d (Mk Stone)

BRIGGS
Joseph d 9-1-1878 (Wby Stone)

BROOKE
Abraham, N.Y.C., s Charles & Amy (both dec) Cow Neck, d 3-12-1852 ae 64; m 5-23-1816 at Cow Neck, Phebe HICKS, dt Benjamin (dec) & Mary, b 1793 d 10-20-1839 ae 39y 6m
Ch: Sarah H. d 3-19-1903 in 84th yr.
Lydia b 11-21-1834 d 11-27-1897
Charles A. b 2-13-1837 d 7-11-1889
Phebe H. d 4-14-1838 ae 5y 5m
Mary B. b 5-20-1819; m Jas. F. RANDOLPH
Abraham & fam rocf N. Y. 10-16-1833; cf N. Y. (clear); in d record, w called Sarah HAIGHT; tombstone Sarah W., w Abraham, d 10-20-1839 in 40th yr
Elizabeth [Brook], dt Abraham & Phebe; m 1846 Wm. M. ROBBINS
Mary B., dt Abraham & Phebe, b 5-20-1819; m 11-29-1843 James FITZ-RANDOLPH

BROWN
Pamela m Edward T. FROST
William d 5-21-1877 ae 63; m Lydia ----- d 2-14-1879 in 65th yr (Wby Stones)

BULL
Martha, dt Ebenezer & Jane; m Benjamin W. CRAFT

BULLOCK
William d 10-31-1898 (Wby Stone)

BULOW
Adolph S. m Maria Barbara ----- d 1-3-1877 ae 38 (Wby Stone)

BURKE
James Leighton m 8-7-1912 Helen Hicks EARLE, dt John D. & Caroline H. HICKS, b 9-5-1867
T. d 1851 (Wby Stone)

BURLEY
Ann, near Hemp., d 11-8-1805 ae 68y 2m 14d
Benjamin [Burleigh] m 1736 Hannah MOTT
Ch: Jane d 7-30-1825 ae over 80
Hannah d 2-11-1835 ae 88y 21d
Sarah, near Hemp., d 2-22-1819 ae abt 76y 11m

BURLING
Henrietta, dt Thomas & Elizabeth, b 12-17-1821; m Valentine H. HALLOCK
Mary F. m Charles F. TITUS

BURR
John, Northampton, N. J.; m 1712 Keziah WRIGHT
John brought cert from Burlington (clear); Kezia took cert there 7 Mo (Sept) 24, 1712
Joseph & Hannah (mo)
Hannah ack mo 9-18-1756

BURT
Anna, dt Charles & Anna, b 10-15-1792; m George HAUXHURST
Charles b Scotland

BURTIS
George W. (Man. Tombstone)
Jno. Henry, nm; m Lucretia MOTT, dt Adam & Mary J., d 5-28-1906 in 67th yr
Cornelia M. b 6-30-1835 d 10-2-1879 (Wby Stone)
Cornelia M. b 8-29-1874 d 6-25-1875 (Wby Stone)
M. Pauline b 4-3-1867 d 8-1-1884 (Wby Stone)
Sarah, dt Elias & Hannah; m Joseph HIGBIE

BUTLER
Keziah, dt John & Martha, b 13 Sept. 1738; m 1756 Nathaniel COLES

BYRNES
William, Fishkill, N. Y., s Daniel & Dinah, New Winsor, N. Y.; m 12-4-1794 at Wby, Sarah TOWNSEND, dt Thomas & Mary, N. Hemp.

CADWALLADER
Harriet, dt Francis W. & Mary L., b Lebanon, O., 7-15-1897; m 1914 A. Raymond ALBERTSON

CAMPBELL
Jehoiakim m Ann NELSON, dt Thomas & Catharine

CARHART
Helen bur Man.
John bur Man.
Rachel m James PRIOR
Sarah, dt Joshua & Phebe; m 1809 John ROBBINS

CARLE
Elizabeth, dt Gadron & Elizabeth (Davis), b Virginia City, Nevada, 11-24-1867; m Edward C. WILLIAMS
Jacob, s John & Phebe, O.B., d 8-10-1831; m 2-25-1801 at Wby, Phebe TITUS, dt Peter & Elizabeth, N. Hemp., b 1-14-1770 d 2-8-1850 ae 89y 25d
Ch: Ann d 3- 7-1877 ae 75y 1m 15d bur Wby
Mary m Rich. EVERITT
John b 12-18-1804; m Susan HICKS
Elizabeth b 3-8-1807 d 8-8-1808
Edward " 12-25-1808
(Wby Stones & Bible)
John [Carll], Wby; m 1772 Phebe HICKS, dt Benjamin & Phebe, d 8-20-1811 ae 57y & nearly 10m
Ch: Mary b 7-28-1781
Silas b 7-13-1786
Jacob
John d 3-28-1819 ae near 71
John m Cornelia WILLETS b 1-14-1850 d 7-28-1892
John Jr., s Jacob & Phebe (Titus), b 12-18-1804 d 10-28-1888; m Susan HICKS, b 11-9-1806 d 1-24-1872
Ch: Sarah b 10-6-1836 [George P. TITUS
Mary, dt John & Phebe, b 7-28-1781; m 1823
Sarah, dt John Jr. & Susan, b 10-6-1836; m Edward S. BOWNE
Silas, s John & Phebe, b 7-13-1786 d 1-16-1861 ae 74y 6m 3d; m Mary Elizabeth ----- d 4-26-1881 ae 94
Ch: (perhaps)
Silas J. d 9-21-1843 ae 2y 6m 19d
Edward " 6-24-1839
Phebe Ann d 3- 8-1846 ae 12y 2m 9d
Silas & Mary E. rocf N. Y. 4-1833
(bur Wby)

CARMAN
Abigail, dt Thomas & Susannah; m 1775 Jarvis COLES
James dis 12-31-1783 for neglect of mtg
Martha ack mo 9-27-1758
Mary P. d 1-26-1894 ae 70y 9m 18d (Wby Stone)
Ruth, dt Thomas; m Solomon POWELL

CARPENTER
Abel, s Benedict & Hannah, b 2-12-1757; form resident of Purchase, now resident here; dis bearing arms 6-26-1782
Ann, dt Joseph & Mary, b 7 Mo (Sept) 24, 1716; m 1737 Samuel UNDERHILL
Barbara, dt Richard E. & Florence, b 11-7-1907; m 1931 Dave WHYTE, Jr.
Isaac mo before 7 Mo (Sept) 26, 1744
Jacob mo before 4-25-1780, birthright mbr, but bore arms, took oaths & kept slaves; ack accepted 1-31-1781
James, s Jacob & Hannah, d 1-24-1820 ae 68y; m 8-3-1809 at Mk., Dinah COCK, dt William & Anne, b 9-23-1776 d 4-18-1812 (2nd w) (Cox Gen.)
John, s John & Anne; m 1713 Martha FEAK, dt John & Elizabeth (Bible)
John, s John & Martha, b 7 Mo (Sept) 12, 1714; m 1736/7 Charity WEEKS, dt Samuel & Anna (Bible)
John, s Joseph, b abt 1715 d 4-28-1790; m 1748 Sarah IRELAND, dt John & Sarah
Ch: Elisha
m cert not recorded; m bet. 7 Mo (Sept) 28, & 8 Mo (Oct) 26, 1748
Joseph, s Joseph & Anne, M.C., b 8 Mo. (Oct) 16, 1685 d 5-3-1776 ae 90y 6m 6d; m 29 Feb. 1709, Mary WILLETT, dt Andrew & Mary, b 21 Sept. 1691
Ch: Willit b 4 Mo (June) 8, 1714 d 11 Mo 13, 1732/3
Ann b 7 Mo (Sept) 24, 1716
Phebe " 6 Mo (Aug) 28, 1718
Joseph b 5 Mo (July) 15, 1720
Andrew " 10 Mo (Dec) 1, 1722
Thomas " 2 Mo (Apr) 15, 1726
Francis b 9 Mo (Nov) 8, 1728
James " 1 Mo (Mar) 5, 1730/1
Willit " 11 Mo (Jan), 5, 1735/6
Joseph called Mariner in s, Thomas' m cert
Joseph, Jr., s Jos. & Mary, b 5 Mo (July) 15, 1720; m Sarah -----
Sarah, wd Joseph, ack mo 3-30-1768
Mary, dt Jacob; m 1764 Jonas WOOD
Mary P. d 1803 (Unidentified Stone Wby)
Phebe, dt Joseph; m 1742 Daniel WILLITS
Richard E., s Benedict & Phebe, Bkn.; m 11-17-1864 at Phebe W. Titus', Mary TITUS, dt William, dec, & Phebe W. (0)
Richard E. m 10-24-1900 Florence Amelia HAUXHURST, dt Wm. E. & Marianna, b 1-18-1875
Ch: Richard Earle Jr. b 9- 3-1905
Barbara " 11- 7-1907
Ruth " 11- 7-1907
ch recrq of parents 5-18-1919
Richard E. Jr., s Rich. E. & Florence, b Mamaroneck 9-3-1905; m 5-10-1933 at Freeport by Rev. David Jacksheimer, Lutheran, Alice RATH, b Pittsburgh 11-23-1904
Ruth, dt Richard E. & Florence, b 11-7-1907; m 1931 Allan Stewart MATHER
Samuel, s Benedict & Hannah, b 6-10-1759
Form of Purchase, for some time resident here, dis 6-5-1782 for neglect of mtg, bearing arms
Thomas, s Thos. & Anne (Stocker) b 1757 d 1779; m 12-4-1777 at Mk, Hannah ALSOP, dt Richard & Sarah (Pearsall), b 1- 2-1757
Ch: Alsop b 11-18-1778
Hannah m 2nd 1785 Job WEBB
Thomas, s Thomas & Hannah, b 6 Mo (Aug) 25,

CARPENTER, Thomas, continued
1710; m 1736 Martha CLEMENS (sometimes called Clement)
Ch: Phebe b 5 Mo (July) 24, 1741
Signed Epistle abt 1725;ct Purchase for both 4 Mo (June) 30, 1742
William, s Joseph & Elizabeth; m abt 1711 Elizabeth PRIER, dt John & Elizabeth
Elizabeth ack mo 11 Mo (Jan) 15, 1715/16; both signed Epistle 1725
Sarah ack mo 12-22-1767
----- m Rebecca MOTT (mo)
dis 5-29-1782; Rebecca rst 9-29-1784

CARR
Hannah, nm, ack mo 12 Mo (Feb) 19, 1717/18
Hannah, dt Jeremiah & Hannah; m abt 1732 Jeremiah ROBBINS

CASHOW
Ellen, dt Helena; m Peter CRAFT

CHAMPION
John & Sarah
Ch: Mary m Jarvis MARTIN
Sarah gct Newton MM, West Jersey 6 Mo. (Aug) 25, 1708
Mary, dt John & Sarah; m 1698 Jarvis MARTIN

CHANDLEE (or Chandler)
Ruth, dt Webster & Emily J., b Montgomery Co., Pa. 1890; m 1915 Walter P. PAXSON

CHANDLER
David m Deborah ----- d 5-29-1898 ae 74
Ch: Alonzo D.
(Wby Stone)

CHAPMAN
A. Wright m 1-23-1909 at Felton, Del., Grace STEVENSON, dt M. Morris & Lydia W., b Felton, Del. 1875
Ch: Anne S. b Bkn 12-14-1910
Grace W. b Bkn. 2-9-1913
Grace recrq 7-17-1927; ch recrq of parents
Anne S., dt A. Wright & Grace S., b 12-14-1910; m 1936 Vincent Virgin Rave BOOTH
Grace W., dt A. Wright & Grace, b 7-9-1913; m 1936 Leon A. LAPHAM Jr.
Seth dis mo 5-19-1841

CHEESMAN
John L. b 3-31-1815 d 3-25-1891; m Phebe A. HAUXHURST, dt Nath. O. & Eliz.
Ch: (probably)
Alfred W. b 1-17-1853 d 7-27-1872
Mary E. " 2-18-1855 d 3-17-1858
Annie E. b 6-18-1869 d 11- 2-1871

CHEYNEY
Eugene Price, s George S. & Mary P., both dec, Westchester, Pa.; m 6-28-1926 at Glen Head, Ada U. TEMPLE, dt Richard & Mary K. UNDERHILL, both dec, b 10-30-1879 d 11-24-1938

CLAPP
John, N. Y., s John, dec, & Phebe, Greenwich, now N. Y.; m 12-27-1815 at Wby Phebe HICKS, dt Samuel & Phebe, dec, Wby
Ch: Samuel b 10-8-1816
cf N. Y. (clear)
Phebe, dt John; m 1739 Edward HALLOCK

CLARK
George, s Geo. P. (dec) & Samaria J., Emerson, O.; m 11-19-1891 at bride's parents, Amelia HICK, dt Stephen R. & Hannah U., Wby., b 1-13-1859 d 3-27-1934 ae 75
Ch: Tacy E. b 1-11-1893; m Jas. J. JACKSON Jr.
Stephen R. b 1-29-1894 d 7-30-1894 bur Wby
Tacy E., dt George & Amelia, b 1-11-1893; m 1920 James J. JACKSON Jr.

CLEMENT
Charles & Sarah [Clements] (mo)
Charles ack mo 3-29-1775; Sarah ack mo 2-22-1775
Jane, dt Joseph; m 1773 Jonathan DICKINSON
Jarvis mo before 9-24-1777 & dis; ack 4-27-1776 having signed an Association, so he would not have to go to war
Joseph & Jane
Ch: Mercy
Joseph & Jane ack mo 11 Mo (Jan) 30, 1716/17; Joseph ack bearing arms 6-19-1754
Joseph Jr. ack mo & bearing arms 8-28-1754; dis 8-30-1775
Martha [Clemens] m 1736 Thomas CARPENTER
Mary m Mordecai WILLIS
Mercy, dt Joseph & Jane; m 1751 ----- WILLIS
ack mo 4-24-1753
Sarah, dt Joseph; m 1756 William WILLIS

COCK
Alfred, s Daniel & Mary, nm, b 7-14-1811 d 3-14-1844; m 9-3-1834 by Marmaduk Earle, Phebe Ann TOWNSEND, b 1-17-1817 d 10-24-1889
Phebe m 2nd 1859 Jacob Smith UNDERHILL (Cox Gen.)
Amey, dt Henry & Mary, b 12 Mo (Feb) 9, 1708/9; ct Concord, Pa. 9 Mo (Nov) 25, 1730 (clear) (rem); m Rees JONES in Pa.
Ann, dt Samuel & Martha, b 10 Mo (Dec) 23, 1736; m 1756 James TITUS
Ann, dt Zoar; m John WHITEHEAD
Anna, dt Henry & Mary, b 7 Mo (Sept) 23, 1751; m 1790 Isaac COLES (2nd w)
Andrew, s William & Dinah; m Mary TITUS, dt Henry & Martha, b 12 Mo (Feb) 30, 1771/2
Ch: Rachel b 12-24-1794 d 12-7-1867 bur Wby
Augustus G., s Samuel & Fannie, d 8-23-1914 in 83d yr; m 12-12-1860 Elizabeth SEAMAN, wd Dr. William, dt Silas & Mary TITUS,b 4-4-1839 d 11-27-1921
Augustus recrq 11----1888
Benjamin, s Henry & Mary, b 10 Mo (Dec) 5, 1702 d Thornbury, Pa. 1783; m 8 Mo (Oct) 25, 1731 at Birmingham, Pa., Ann BRINTON,

COCK, Benjamin & Ann, continued
dt Joseph & Mary, Thornbury, Pa.
ct Concord, Pa. 12 Mo (Feb) 23, 1725/6
(Concord MM gives 7 ch) (Cox Gen.)
Benjamin, s John & Sarah, O.B., b 3-22-1754
d 2-22-1835 Flushing; m 12-2-1779 Hannah
PRIOR, dt Thomas & Martha, O.B., b 9-15-
1756 d 1-15-1828 (4 ch) (Cox Gen.)
Benjamin, s James & Dorothy, b Thornbury, Pa.
9-14-1780 d in O.B. Town 9-7-1848; m 12-
18-1808 Lanah FROST, dt Penn & Sarah
(Underhill), b 8-11-1782 d 1-14-1875 at
G.C. (mo)
Ch: Mary b 11- 4-1809; m Jos. U. VALENTINE
Hannah b 4-6-1812; m Joshua KIRK
Benjamin dis mo 1809
Benjamin F., s Samuel & Fanny, b 9-12-1829
d 9-30-1882 bur Mk; m 3-12-1859 Marianna
UNDERHILL, dt Jacob S. & Amy, b 1838
Marianna recrq 8-15-1888 (Cox Gen)
Clark, s Samuel & Martha, Buckram, b 8 Mo (Oct)
14, 1738 d 3-29-1822; m 3-20-1760 Eliza-
beth PEARCE, dt James & Elizabeth, d 11-8-
1835 ae 92y 6m 11d bur Mk.
Ch: Freelove b 9-26-1761
Samuel " 6-28-1765
Joshua " 5- 4-1767
Clark, s Samuel & Elizabeth, b 7-4-1790 d 8-5-
1866; m 6-27-1816 by Rev. Marmaduke Earle,
Catharine FEEKS, dt Robt. & Mary (Covert),
b 5-15-1793 d 8-28-1875 in 83d yr. (3 ch)
(Mk Stones & Cox Gen.)
Daniel, s John & Dorothy, b 8 Mo (Oct) 5, 1699
d 1771; m (1) (supposed) Levine (Kissan)
CARMAN
Daniel m 2d 2 Mo (Apr) 27, 1748 Sarah RUSHMORE,
dt Thomas & Sarah, d before 1765
Ch: Sarah b 1 Mo (Mar) 6, 1748/9; m Jacob COLES
Daniel m 3d Susannah YOUNGS, dt Richard &
Phebe (mo)
Daniel dis mo 11-26-1766
Daniel, nm, s James & Deborah, Mk., b 1 Mo
(Mar) 26, 1747 d 10-22-1804; m 12-20-1768
Roseannah TOWNSEND, dt Wm. & Elizabeth,
b 1751 d 4-10-1831 ae 80y 4d (8 ch)
Daniel, s Henry & Mary, Mk., b 1 Mo (Mar) 6,
1743 d 12-10-1823 ae 80y; m 1-14-1893 at
Aponquague, N. Y., Catharine SWEET, dt
Elnathan & Abiah, b 6-17-1757 d 11-20-1837
Ch: Hannah b 9- 2-1793; m David VALENTINE
Abram " 2- 1-1795 d 10-1836 (unm)
Peter " 11- 5-1796; m Ann FEEKS
(Cox Gen.)
Daniel F., s Ambrose & Phebe, b 11-11-1806
d 10-28-1850; m 2-19-1829 Jane MERRITT, dt
John & Sarah Ann, b 4-27-1810 d 3-26-1884
Ch: Jannette b 11-19-1840 d 10-17-1864 (unm)
bur Wby (3 other ch)
(Cox Gen.)
David, s Thomas & Mary, M.C., b 3-28-1765 d 1-
26-1854 bur Mk; m Lydia TITUS, dt Charles
& Margaret, b 2-11-1767 d 3-30-1847 ae 80y
1m 19d

Ch: Mary Ann b 3-12-1800 d 1-21-1856 (unm)
Margaret T. b 1-9-1798 d 3-30-1862 (unm)
Silas " 12-22-1790
(3 other ch)
(Mk Stones & Cox Gen.)
Deborah, dt Samuel & Elizabeth, b 11-2-1794;
m 1817 Caleb Covert
Dinah, dt William & Anne, b 9-23-1770; m 1809
James CARPENTER
Dorothy, dt Hezekiah & Rosannah; m 1761 James
COCK
Edward McD., s Isaac & Ann Elizabeth, b 3-14-
1830 d 7-31-1909 bur Mk; m 11-2-1853 Lo-
retta COCK, dt Samuel & Fanny, b 1-2-1826
d 8-11-1889 in 64th yr
(Mk Stones & Cox Gen.)
Elizabeth, dt John & Sarah; m 1765 Samuel
ROBBINS
Elizabeth, dt Daniel & Roseannah, b 12-7-1769;
m 1785 Samuel COCK
Elizabeth, dt Samuel & Jemima, b 6-27-1768;
m 1806 Thomas PEARSALL (mo)
Elizabeth, dt Isaac & Ann, b 2-23-1801; m 1817
James COCK
Esther, dt William & Dinah, b 2 Mo (Apr) 22,
1756; m 1773 Charles FROST
Eugenie P., dt Isaac & Emeliza, b 3-11-1852;
m 1888 Abraham C. UNDERHILL
Frances S., dt Geo. Wm. & Matilda K., b 7-8-
1859; m 1902 Isaac R. COLES
George dis mo 7-1795
George E., s Andrew, dec, & Sarah, N.Y.C.,
b 7-3-1816 d 8-24-1889; m 6-4-1840, Mary M.
HICKS, dt Benjamin & Elizabeth, N. Hemp.,
b 6-26-1819 d 10-12-1892
Ch: George Embree b 5- 1-1841; took name of
HICKS
Elizabeth M. b 4-30-1845; m Thos. STEWART
Benjamin E. " 1-14-1843; took name of
HICKS (unm)
Mary H. b 1- 8-1847 d 2-19-1858
Frederick E. b 1-12-1860 d 8-6-1864
All bur Man. (Cox Gen.)
Hannah, dt Henry & Mary, b 4 Mo (June) 15,
1745; m 1764 Jeremiah ROBBINS
Hannah, dt Daniel & Catharine, b 9-2-1793; m
1813 David VALENTINE
Hannah, dt Benjamin & Lanah, b 4-6-1812; m 1847
Joshua KIRK
Henry A., s James & Sarah, Mk, b 2 Mo (Apr) 1,
1678 d 3 Mo (May) 4, 1733; m 6 Mo (Aug)
28, 1699 at John Feke's, Mary FEKE, dt
John & Eliz. (Prior), b 2 Mo (Apr) 30,
1678 d 10 Mo (Dec) 30, 1715
(9 ch) Henry on Com 1705; Mary on com 1706;
signed rem cert 1707
Henry A. m 2nd 1717 Martha PEARSALL, dt Nathaniel & Martha, b 10 Mo (Dec) 10, 1681
(2 ch)
Henry, s Henry & Mary, O.B., b 6 Mo (Aug) 10,
1713 d 1802; m 12 Mo (Feb) 1736/7 at Mk,
Mary BOWNE, dt Thomas & Hannah, O.B., b
5 Mo (July) 4, 1717 d 8-21-1818

COCK, Henry & Mary, continued
Ch: Thomas b 11 Mo (Jan) 25, 1738/9
Sarah " 9 Mo (Nov) 4, 1741
Daniel " 1 Mo (Mar) 6, 1743/4
Hannah " 4 Mo (June) 15, 1745
Mary " 8 Mo (Oct) 11, 1747 d 8-21-1818 (unm)
Henry " 3 Mo (May) 15, 1749
Anne " 7 Mo (Sept) 23, 1751
Abraham b 4-11-1755
Henry & Mary ack giving s, Thomas, a dinner after his mo (ack 9-17-1764)

Henry, s John & Sarah, b 7 Mo (Sept) 10, 1735 d Orange Co. 5-24-1816; m 1-2-1760 at Wby Elizabeth ROBBINS, dt Jeremiah, b 11 Mo (Jan) 19, 1736/7
(9 ch)

Isaac, s William & Dinah, b 2-5-1760 d 2-6-1814 Flushing; m 10-6-1781 Elizabeth SEAMAN, dt Willet & Mary, b 12-6-1762
(5 ch) (Cox Gen.)

Isaac [Cocks], s Richard & Abigail, b 9-6-1811 d 2-21-1881; m 1-23-1838 Mary Elizabeth THORNE, dt Sam'l C. & Maria H., b 8-1-1818 (or 8-1-1819) d 11-9-1890
(7 ch) (Cox Gen.)

Isaac H., s William T. & Elizabeth H., Wby, b 8-31-1836 d 6-12-1810; m 6-16-1859 at Eliz. P. Willets', N. Hemp., Mary T. WILLETS, dt William & Elizabeth P., b 3-22-1837 d 12-28-1907
Ch: William W. b 7- 4-1861
Elizabeth H. b 7- 5-1865
Frederick H. b 3-6-1872; changed name to Frederick Cox HICKS
(Cox Gen.)

Isaac Hicks [Cocks], s Wm. W., dec, & Jessie W., Old Wby; m 6-25-1938 at Mk, Florence Eliz. WILLITS, dt James & Florence, G.C. (Isaac Hicks Cocks b 4-23-1912)

James, s James & Sarah, b 2 Mo (Apr) 4, 1674 d 3 Mo (May) 27, 1728; m 1698 Hannah FEEKS, b 8 Mo (Oct) 6, 1675 d 2 Mo (Apr) 28, 1750 ae 74y 6m 22d
(10 ch)

James, Immigrant Ancestor, & Sarah
Sarah on Com 1697-1706

James, s Josiah & Rebecca, b 4 Mo (June) 29, 1731 d Yorktown 7-30-1816; m 1-21-1756 (cert not recorded) Phebe THORN, dt Thomas & Penelope, b 3 Mo (May) 12, 1737 d 11-10-1796
(14 ch) (Cox Gen.)

James, s Benjamin, Thornbury, Pa., b 12 Mo (Feb) 6, 1732/3 d before 12-5-1781; m 6-25-1761 at Mk, Dorothy COCK, dt Hezekiah & Rosannah, O.B., b 4 Mo (June) 5, 1742
(5 ch)
Dorothy joined mtg 5-27-1761; cf Woodbridge (clear)

James, s James & Dorothy, b Thornbury, Pa., 3-24-1774 d Monkton, Vt. 1-22-1826; m 10-11-1801 Mary FEKE, dt Daniel & Elizabeth (Coles), b Mk 4-24-1780 d Monkton 4-4-1860
Ch: (9)
Coles Feke b 8-28-1802; changed name to Cook
James dis mo & rst
(Cox Gen.)

James, s Samuel, b 2-1-1792 d 3-25-1874 bur Mk; m 1817 Elizabeth COCK, dt Isaac & Ann (Underhill), b 2-23-1801 d 1-14-1881 ae 80 bur Mk
(Cox Gen.)

John, s James & Sarah, b 11 Mo (Jan) 22, 1666/7 d 1717; m 2d Dorothy HARCUT, dt Richard & Elizabeth, d 1739 (1st w unknown)
ack mo twice 4 Mo (June) 25, 1707
(Cox Gen.) (2 ch by 1st w; 5 ch by 2nd w)

John, s Henry & Mary, b 1 Mo (Mar) 22, 1705/6 d abt 1778; m abt 1729 Sarah CARPENTER, dt Wm. Jr. & Elizabeth
Ch: Mary b 7 Mo (Sept) 5, 1730
William b 10 Mo (Dec) 11, 1732
Henry " 7 Mo (Sept) 10, 1735
Rees " 11 Mo (Jan) 26, 1738/9
Elizabeth b 11 Mo (Jan) 9, 1740/1
Ann " 6 Mo (Aug) 23, 1743 d 11mo-1750
Elijah " 10 Mo (Dec) 18, 1745
Sarah " 1 Mo (Mar) 15, 1748/9 d 12 mo-1750/1
Unnamed stillborn 1-25-1752
Benjamin b 3-22-1754
Amy " 11-25-1756
ack mo rec 10 Mo 30-1730

Joseph, s Henry & Mary, b 2 Mo (Apr) 29, 1701 d abt 1733 (unm); ct Concord, Pa. 12 Mo (Feb) 23, 1725/6

Josiah, s James & Hannah, b 1 Mo (Mar) 27, 1709; m abt 1730 Rebecca FROST, dt William & Hannah, b 8 Mo (Oct) 28, 1714 (Josiah d [1766)
Ch: James b 6 Mo (Aug) 29, 1731
Deborah b 7 Mo (Sept) 21, 1734
Jacob " 9 Mo (Nov) 28, 1736
George " 4 Mo (June) 24, 1739
Isaac " 9 Mo (Nov) 6, 1741
Rhoda " 9 Mo (Nov) 8, 1741
(3 more b in Westchester Co.)
ct Purchase (Cox Gen.)

Joshua, s Samuel & Fanny (Cock), b 12-10-1842; m Elizabeth FLEET, dt Joseph & Susannah (Underhill), b 10-18-1854
Elizabeth ack mo to first cousin 1-18-1792

Joshua, s Samuel & Elizabeth, b 8-1-1778 d 7-20-1883; m Susan COCK, dt David & Lydia, b 7-6-1794 d 12-18-1870 in 77th yr.
(Wby Stone) (Cox Gen.)

Loretta, dt Samuel & Elizabeth, b 11-24-1786; m 1806 Isaac Covert

Loretta, dt Samuel & Fanny, b 1-2-1826; m 1853 [Edward McDERMOTT

Marie Louise [Cox], dt Daniel D. & Mary L.; m Ellwood V. TITUS

Mary, dt Henry & Mary, b 8 Mo (Oct) 8, 1711; m 1735 Nathan BANE; m 2d 1755 Francis MEECHAM (Cox Gen.)

COCK, continued
Mary, dt John & Sarah, Mk, b 7 Mo (Sept) 5, 1730; m 1752 Isaac UNDERHILL
Mary, dt Henry & Elizabeth, b 3-13-1761; m 1784 William TITUS
Mary, dt Samuel & Elizabeth, b 6-25-1763; m 1796 James THORN
Mary, dt Benjamin & Lanah, b 11-4-1809; m 1832 Joseph V. VALENTINE; m 2d Wm. M. WEEKS
Phebe T., dt David & Lydia, b 1-1-1808; m 1851 James WEEKS
Phiany, dt James, b abt 1730; joined Friends, bur later joined Baptists & dis 1-29-1772 (Cox Gen.)
Phiany, dt Daniel & Roseannah, b 4-23-1785; m 1804 Charles THORN
Rees, s John & Sarah, O.B., b 11 Mo (Jan) 26, 1738/9 d 1-9-1812 North Castle; m 3-3-1762 at Wby Hannah ROBBINS, dt Jeremiah, O. B., b 2 Mo (Apr) 19, 1739 d 1778
Ch: Phebe b 4-18-1763
Sarah " 11-28-1764
Deborah b 1-23-1767
Job " 5-22-1768
Israel " 1-19-1770
Amos " 4- 1-1772
Noah " 2-18-1774
Rees ack abt 1779 carting part of his hay for the Army on requisition
(Cox Gen.)
Richard, s John & Freelove, b 7-27-1787 d 4-6-1859; m 4-17-1823 Rebecca UNDERHILL, dt Israel & Mary, b 4-26-1801 d 7-22-1888
Ch: Infant d 1-4-1828
Amelia b 8-25-1835 d 8-15-1841
Rebecca dis 8-1826; changed to Cox per Stone; all bur Mk
(Cox Gen.)
Richard, s Samuel & Elizabeth, b 5-22-1766 d 10-25-1851 Bkn; m 1789 Abigail UNDERHILL, dt Daniel & Sarah, b 1-17-1771 d 1-15-1849 (12 ch) dis mo 3-1789
Robert, s James & Hannah, b abt 1718; m before 12 Mo (Feb) 27, 1739/40 -----
(3 ch)
mo & trained before 12 Mo (Feb) 27, 1739/40; ack accepted
Samuel, s James & Hannah, b 5 Mo (July) 20, 1702 d 7 Mo (Sept) 20, 1741; m probably by Elder Feke, Martha ALLING, dt Abraham & Mary
Ch: Hannah b 2 Mo (Apr) 4, 1731
Samuel " 6 Mo (Aug) 13, 1734
Ann " 12 Mo (Feb) 23, 1736/7
Clark " 8 Mo (Oct) 14, 1738
Penelope b 1 Mo (Mar) 27, 1741
Samuel Cock, who must be this one, had mo before 11 Mo (Jan) 26, 1725/6; his ack 1 Mo (Mar) 26, 1729 accepted (this item not in Cox Gen.)
Samuel, s Samuel & Martha, b 6 Mo (Aug) 13, 1735 d 6-14-1819; m 6-8-1757 Elizabeth TITUS, dt John & Sarah, d 1-13-1759 (Cox Gen.)
Samuel m 2nd Jemima POWELL, dt Wait & Mary, b 1 Mo (Mar) 31, 1736 d 8-30-1816
Ch: Mary b 6-25-1763
Richard b 5-22-1766
Elizabeth b 2-27-1768
Isaac " 5- 8-1775
Samuel ack obeying requisition to cart his hay for the army abt 1779
(Cox Gen.)
Samuel, s Clark & Elizabeth, b 6-28-1765 d 8-5-1855 ae 90; m 12-14-1785 Elizabeth COCK, dt Daniel & Roseannah, b 12-7-1769 d 3-30-1859 ae 90
Ch: Clark b 7- 4-1790
James " 6-21-1792
Samuel " 12-12-1800
Joshua " 8- 1-1788
William T. " 11-26-1803
bur Mk
(Cox Gen.)
Samuel, s Samuel & Elizabeth, b 12-12-1800 d 6-7-1882 ae 81; m 2-3-1821 by Rev. Marmaduke Earle, Fanny COCK, dt Isaac & Anne, b abt 1803 d 4-10-1859 ae 55
(5 ch)
Samuel m 2nd Jerusha S. KEYSER
(Mk Stones) (Cox Gen.)
Sarah, dt Daniel & Sarah, b 1 Mo (Mar) 6, 1748/9; m 1765 Jacob COLES
Sarah, dt James & Dorothy, b 4-27-1777; m 1801 Samuel HARLAND
Silas, s David & Lydia, b 12-22-1790 d 10-6-1868 ae 78; m 9-23-1813 Searington, L. I., Sarah SMITH, dt Timothy & Mary (Skidmore), b 1-5-1793 d 4-8-1882
Ch: Lydia b 3-11-1821 d 9-10-1845 (unm)
(2 other ch)
Susan, dt David & Lydia, b 7-6-1794; m Joshua COCK
Thomas, s Henry & Mary, b 11 Mo (Jan) 25, 1737/8 d 6-16-1812; m 10-6-1763 Mary SMITH, dt Thomas & Phebe, b 5 Mo (July) 13, 1748 d 3-28-1836 (mo)
(13 ch)
Thomas dis mo 6-26-1765
(Cox Gen.)
Townsend, s Daniel & Roseannah, b 12-4-1773 d 2-14-1868; m 11-14-1792 Margaret FARLEY, dt Capt. James & Zerviah, b 3-1-1775 d 3-8-1848 (3 ch)
(Mk Stones) (Cox Gen.)
Uriah, s Thomas, b 3-13-1772 d 10-28-1846 ae 74; m 1-28-1800 Mary THORN, dt Stephen & Elizabeth, b 6-25-1780 d 4-2-1860
Ch: Elizabeth C. b 4-10-1813 d 9-20-1853 (unm)
Jemima S. " 12-15-1802 d 11-28-1869 (unm)
Allen S. " 10-29-1806 d 9-19-1834 (unm)
(Wby Stones) (Cox Gen.)
William, s John & Sarah, b 10 Mo (Dec) 11, 1732 d after 1812; m abt 1755 Dinah HOPKINS dt Daniel & Amy
William ack mo before 7-30-1755 (3 ch)

COCK, William, continued
William m 2d abt 1764 Anne FEKE, dt Charley & Catharine, b 11 Mo (Jan) 17, 1741/2 d 4-20-1796
Ch: Dinah b 9-23-1770; m James CARPENTER 1809; d 4-18-1872
William mo 2d time dis 8-29-1764
William m 3d Clemence FEKE, sister of Anne (Cox Gen.)
William E., s Richard & Rebecca, b 4-13-1829 d 11-13-1909; m 10-20-1858 Ellen M. LAYTON, dt David & Sarah, b 5-30-1837 d 5-8-1892 ae 54y 11m 8d bur Mk
Ch: Albert L. b 8-6-1870 d 7-29-1881 bur Mk
His father changed name to Cox
(Cox Gen.)
William T., s Daniel & Roseannah, b 3-22-1780 d 6-1858 bur Mk; m Abigail THORN, wd Leonard, dt John & Sarah SOMARINDYCK
(2 ch)
(Cox Gen.)
William T., s Samuel & Elizabeth, b 11-26-1803 d 2-18-1885 bur Mk; m 10-1831 Elizabeth H. SEAMAN, dt Isaac & Sarah HICKS, b 10-6-1805 d 1-2-1865 bur Wby
Ch: Mary H. b 7-10-1832 d 12-3-1851 bur Wby
Isaac H. b 8-31-1836
Elizabeth ack mo 1-18-1832
(Elizabeth, wd Dr. Wm. Seaman)
(Cox Gen.)
William T. m 2d 11-14-1867 at or near New Rochelle, Hannah BURLING, dt Benj. & Hannah, b 1832 d 11-22-1908 (Mk Stone)
Ch: Wm. Burling b 1-10-1870 d N. Y. 5-21-1913
William T. recrq 4-1833
William Willets, s Isaac H. & Mary W., Wby., b 7-4-1861 d 5-24-1932; m 7-24-1901 at 15th St. MH, N. Y., Caroline R. HICKS, dt Willet & Sarah A., Locust Valley, b 5-25-1861 d 12-27-1901
William W. m 2d 4-29-1911 at 15th St. MH, N.Y., Jessie F. WRIGHT, dt Wm. B., dec, & Almeda, Flushing, d Wby 11-13-1938
Ch: Isaac Hicks b 4-23-1912
Wm. Burling b 3-20-1915

COFFIN
Henry d 3-18-1893 ae 75y 9d (Wby Stone)
I. Sherwood, N. Hemp., s Andrew G. & Elizabeth, dec, Bkn.; m 6-1-1881 at Martha Willets', Ida E. WILLETS, dt Joseph & Esther G., dec, Trenton, N. J.
Ida m Joseph WILLETS

COLES
Albert, s Joseph & Temperance, b 1732; m 3-24-1762 Anne DEAN, dt Thomas & Mary KIPP (mo)
Ch: Benjamin b 1763; m Hannah COCK
Anne ack mo 11-30-1763
(Anne, wd William Dean)
(Bible)
Amelia, dt Daniel & Anne; m 1764 Benjamin KIRK; m 2d 1782 William JONES
Amelia, dt Jacob & Sarah, b 5-7-1773; m 1793 Benjamin HICKS
Ann mo some years before 5 Mo 3, 1745
Ann, dt Jacob & Sarah (Cock), b 8-22-1768; m 1788 Wm. M. HEWLETT (mo)
Annie H., dt Wm. H. & Mariah O.; m 1891 William ALBERTSON
Daniel C., s Jacob & Sarah, b 5-24-1771 d 12-29-1827; m 10-12-1794 Eleanor KASHOW, dt Jacob & Lena, b 11-4-1777 d 12-7-1853 ae 76y 1m 3d bur Mk
(10 ch)
mo before 11-19-1794 & dis next mo
Divine Hewlett, s Thos. & Amelia (Hewlett), b 4-7-1819 d 1904; m Lydia A. DELAVAL (Mk Stones)
Elizabeth, dt Nathaniel & Hanna, b 12-24-1758; m 1779 Stephen THORN
Elizabeth, dt Samuel & Lavinia, b 6-28-1814; m Silas DOWNING
Elizabeth H., dt Thomas & Amelia; m 1865 Joseph VALENTINE
Franklin Albert, s Isaac & Mary W., both dec, b 8-24-1861; m 9-6-1906 at J. H. Reed's, Peekskill, Caroline Sarah REED, dt Jas. Harvey & Sarah Frances, Peekskill, d 12-24-1929 G. C.
Ch: Robert Reed b 9-21-1907
Caroline recrq 9-14-1910; Robert R. recrq 6-15-1913
Hannah, dt Samuel & Martha PRIOR; m 1731 Joseph COLES; m 2d 1789 Matthew PRIOR
Henry, s Isaac & Kezia, Cedar Swamp, b 4-17-1778 d 8-20-1850 ae 72y 4m 9d bur Mk; m 6-25-1818 at Mk, Martha FROST, dt Caleb & Sarah, b 9-12-1793 d 9-4-1875 bur Mk
Ch: Anna b 5-29-1819 d 11- 4-1821 bur Mk
Henry Whitson b 3-24-1821 d 9-29-1853 bur MK
Edward Frost b 3-29-1824 d 1-3-1899 bur Mk
Isaac C. b 1-15-1826 d 1-13-1875 bur Mk
Leonard b 11-21-1831
(Bibles)
Isaac, s Daniel & Anne, O.B., b 9 Mo (Nov) 6, 1748 d 12-5-1819; m 3-5-1777 at Beth., Keziah WHITSON, dt Henry & Hannah, O.B., b 2-17-1753 d 7-6-1788
Ch: Henry b 4-11-1778
Thomas b 4- 9-1782
(Bibles)
Isaac m 2d 8-26-1790 at Mk, Anna COCK, dt Henry & Mary, dec, O.B., b 7 Mo (Sept) 23, 1751 d 12-2-1829
Ch: Isaac b 9-30-1794 d 8-31-1795
(Cox Gen.)
Isaac, s Thomas & Amelia, Glen Cove, O.B., b 1-7-1817 d 11-2-1897 ae 80y 9m 26d; m 11-20-1845 at Henry T. Willits', Mary WILLITS, dt Richard & Mary, b 2-10-1822 d 6-13-1895
Ch: Thomas H. b 6-6-1851 d 8-9-1896 [ae 73y
Mary Amelia b 8-25-1854 d 2-2-1858
Isaac R. " 6-25-1858
Franklin Albert b 8-24-1861

COLES, Isaac & Mary, continued
Ch: Oscar L. b 1865
Isaac R., s Isaac & Mary, b 6-25-1858 d 6-23-1937; m 6-17-1902 Frances S. COCKS, dt Geo. & Matilda K., b 7-8-1859
(Bibles)
Jacob, s Daniel & Ann, Duck Pond, Glen Cove, b 3 Mar. 1743 d 6-3-1808; m 7-4-1765 at Mk, Sarah COCK, dt Daniel & Sarah, dec, b 1 Mo (Mar) 6, 1748/9 d 9-18-1788
Ch: Sarah b 9-18-1766
Anne " 8-23-1768
Daniel b 5-24-1771
(Cox Gen.) (Bible)
Jacob, O.B.; m 2d 2-27-1800 at Mk, Jane MUDGE, dt Coles & Dorothy, d 2-2-1818 in 66th yr

Jarvis, s Benjamin & Mary, b 5 Mo (July) 30, 1751 d 6-28-1828; m 6-1775 Abigail CARMAN, dt Thomas & Susannah, baptized St. George's Adult 1-23-1769 d 7-28-1832 of Cholera
(6 ch) (Bibles)
Joseph, nm, s Joseph & Temperance, b 2 Mo (Apr) 4, 1731; m abt 1750 Hannah COCK, dt Samuel & Martha
(10 ch)
Hannah ack mo 4-25-1753; Hannah m 2d Matthew PRIOR
(Cox Gen.)
Keziah, dt Thomas & Amelia; m 1838 Charles VALENTINE
Leonard F., s Henry & Martha, b 11-21-1831 d 10-13-1913; m 11-16-1859 Susan BIRDSALL, dt Jas. & Elizabeth, b 10-31-1837 d 10-2-1908 in 71st yr bur Mk
Ch: Elizabeth B. b 9-30-1861
Martha T. " 8- 1-1863
Henry " 6-25-1865
Elizabeth & Martha recrq 9-15-1876
Lorette m 1800 ----- KILSEY (mo)
Martha, dt Jacob & Sarah, b 8-5-1784; m 1801 Wm. M. HEWLETT (mo)
May Gertrude, dt Thos. H. & Sallie P.; m 1891 Stanley Justus DONALDSON
Nathaniel Coles b 28 Aug 1734 d 1-7-1814 in 80th yr; m June 17, 1756 at St. George's, Hannah BUTLER, dt John & Martha, b 13 Sept. 1738 d 1-17-1828 ae 90y 4m
(9 ch) (Bibles)
Penelope, dt Joseph & Elizabeth; m 1725 Thomas THORN
Samuel, nm, & Abigail P.
Abigail rocf N. Y. 1862
Sarah m 1727 Alexander YOUNGS
Sarah, dt Jacob & Sarah, b 9-18-1766; m 1785 Isaac TITUS
Sarah, dt Thomas & Amelia; m William WOOD
Sarah Amelia, dt Wm. H. & Mary A.; m George C. DRAEGERT
Solomon, s Jacob & Sarah (Cock), b 5-1-1778 d 10-31-1834; m 11-16-1808 Phebe TRAVIS, dt Samuel & Elizabeth (mo)
(7 ch)
Solomon dis mo 12 mo 1808
(Bibles)
Thomas, s Thomas & Penelope; m Hannah -----
Thomas ack mo 4-1-1754
Thomas, s Isaac & Keziah, b 4-9-1782 d 1-26-1859 bur Mk; m 11-15-1808 Amelia HEWLETT, dt Divine & Ann, b 9-28-1789 d 4-19-1878 bur Mk
Ch: Ann C. b 11-13-1809
Keziah " 8-23-1812
Sarah H. b 11-26-1814 d 11-30-1817
Isaac " 1- 7-1817
Divine H. b 4- 7-1819; dis 9----1860
Thomas " 5- 3-1822 d Wading River, N.Y. 6-30-1891
Sarah Amelia b 3-15-1825
Elizabeth H. b 11-16-1829
William H. b 12-28-1832
Thomas dis mo 6-1809; rst 6-17-1812
(Bibles)
Thomas H., s Thos. & Amelia (Hewlett), b 5-3-1822 d 6-30-1891; m 12-3-1844 (or 5) Anna Adelia HOPKINS, dt Anne, b 5-21-1826 d 6-7-1899
Ch: Little Tommy d 4-16-1865 ae 2y 8m 25d
Henry W. " 12-21-1879 ae 26y 4m 19d
(5 other ch)
(Mk Stones & Bibles)
Thomas H., s Isaac & Mary (Willits), b 6-6-1851 d 8-9-1896; m abt 1893 Sallie P. PANCOAST, d 5-6-1937
Ch: May Gertrude b 6-6-1894
William C., s Chas. & Mary (Crooker) b 1811 d 12-17-1885; m Ann VALENTINE, dt Samuel & Deborah, b 2-27-1814 d 5-20-1886
(7 ch) (Man. Stones)
William H., s Thomas & Amelia, b 12-28-1832 d 3-12-1900 bur Mk; m Maria A. NORTON, dt Anson & Almena, b Holland N. Y. 11-1-1835 d 8-5-1926 ae 89y 9m
Ch: Thomas A. d 8-7-1916 ae 59y 9m 13d
Sarah Amelia
Anna or Annie H.
William H. Jr. d 4-17-1885 ae 12 bur Mk
John Hewlett b 8-31-1877
ch recrq of parents 10-1874

COMBS
Daniel D. d 2-26-1847 (Wby Stone)
Elias m Deborah Ann ----- d 2-5-1852 ae 51y 6m 10d bur Wby
Mary d 8-23-1848 ae 46y 6m 24d (Wby Stone)

CONKLIN
Edward B., s Wm. & Ellen, b 1877 d 1900 (Wby Stone)
Jacob, s James W. & Deborah, Somers, N. Y., d 5-5-1886 ae 71; m 3-25-1840 at Wby, Elizabeth TITUS, dt John & Sarah P. (O)
Ch: (perhaps) Phebe d 1849 bur Wby
James m 2d Mary TITUS, dt John & Sarah, wd James UNDERHILL & of Henry ADEE

CONKLIN, continued
James & Anna H.
Ch: Henrietta d 11-28-1874 ae 3y 9d (Wby Stone)
Martha [Conckling] m 1796 ----- REMSEN

CONN
Richard D. b St. Bart, W. I. 5-6-1812 d 5-16-1858; m Phebe -----
Ch: Eunice Celeste b N. Y. 2-11-1852 d Bkn 10-23-1882
Sarah b 11-26-1841 d 2-28-1846
(Wby Stones)
Richard D. m 2d Grace K. -----
Ch: Richard b 7-10-1889 d 10-16-1889
(Wby Stones)

COOK
Hannah, dt Samuel & Martha; m 1731 Joseph COLES; m 2d 1789 Matthew PRIOR

COOLEY
Marjorie m John S. HICKS

COOKER
Mary, dt Simon & Martha, b 7 Mo (Sept) 17, 1696; m 1717/18 John LATHAM (mo)

COOPER
Dr. Simon, O.B., d 11 Mo (Jan) 11, 1690/1; m 20 Jan. 1663 Mary TUCKER, d 9 Mo (Nov) 2, 1710
Ch: Simon b 1 Mo (Mar) 4, 1672
(3 other ch)
Mtgs held at Mary's 1697 & later
(Bibles)
Simon, s Dr. Simon & Mary, O.B., b 1 Mo (Mar) 4, 1672; m Martha PRIAR, dt Matthew & Mary, b 8 Mo (Oct) 15, 1672
Ch: Mary b 7 Mo (Sept) 17, 1696
(3 other ch)
Martha knew nothing of her dt, Mary's, mo 1717/18

COPELAND
John m Lucretia ----- d 6-9-1856 ae 21 (Wby Stone)
Ch: Annie d 5-26-1860 ae 5m 9d (Wby Stone)

CORNELIUS
Anne, dt Jonathan & Sarah; m ----- POWELL; m 2d 1801 George WEEKS
John & Mary
mo before 10-29-1766; Mary ack mo 10-25-1769
Lott, s Samuel & Jemima (Mott); m 2-1-1838 Mary C. VALENTINE, dt David & Hannah, b 4-6-1816 d 1-14-1893
Mary, dt John & Mary; m 1789 Jesse MERRITT

CORNELL
Caleb, Manhasset; m 1743 Freelove -----
Ch: Catharine d 9----1867
Caleb gct Flushing 4 Mo (Apr) 29, 1743
(clear)
Hannah m 1728 Josiah QUINBY
Mary, dt Richard & Hannah, b 10 Mo (Dec) 17, 1703; m abt 1725 Edward SANDS
Richard, s John & Mary (Russell), b 1670 d 1755; m 1701 Hannah THORNE, dt John & Mary (Pearsall), b 1678 d 1756
(10 ch)
Richard signed Epistle abt 1725; ct Mamaroneck (Purchase MM) for both, having rem
----- m Phebe HAIGHT
cf Flushing for Phebe (late Haight) 8 Mo (Oct) 5, 1743

CORNING
Augustus m Sarah Allen -----
Ch: Allen d 4-23-1882 ae 8y 10m 17d (Wby Stone)

CORNWALL
Aspinwall m abt 1795 Priscilla MITCHELL, dt Robert & Mary (mo)
dis 12-16-1795
Jane Mitchell also m Aspinwall Cornwall
(Bibles)
John E. [Cornwell] d 7-5-1849 ae 47y 10m 11d; m Jerusha ----- d 4-11-1891 ae 86y 11m 6d
Ch: (perhaps) Phebe d 1860
(Wby Stones)
Willis [Cornwell] d 3-2-1848 ae 77; m Elizabeth ----- d 12-15-1848 ae 73
(Man. Stones)

CORTELYON
Adrienne m Samuel G. TITUS

COVERT
Caleb, s Adolph & Hannah, b 2-9-1788 d 12-15-1865; m 1-2-1817 by Marmaduke Earle, Deborah COCK, dt Samuel & Elizabeth, b 11-2-1794 d 2-28-1886 in 92d yr
(2 ch)
(bur Mk) (Bibles)
Isaac, s Adolph & Hannah (Frost), b 1-18-1780 d 7-12-1839 ae 59; m 12-1806 by Rev. Marmaduke Earle, Loretta COCK, dt Samuel & Elizabeth, b 11-24-1786 d 12-10-1880
Ch: Jacob F. b 9-13-1807
Elizabeth b 7-12-1812
(Mk Stone & Cox Gen.)
Phebe d 5-3-1883 ae 91 (Wby Stone)

CRAFT (See THORNICRAFT)
Ann, dt James & Hannah; m 1826 Richard M. REYNOLDS
Benjamin W., s Simon & Temperance, b 1831 d 1908; m Martha BULL, dt Ebenezer & Jane, b 10-6-1839 d 2-10-1922
Ch: John T. b 10-21-1863 d 10-11-1897
Frederick M. b 8-30-1868 d 1-24-1896
Jennie B. d 9-3-1865 ae 5m 7d
Edward E. " 10-26-1866
Martha rocf Cornwall 1861; bur Mk (Bibles)

CRAFT, continued
Edward E., s Benj. & Martha, b 10-26-1866 G.C.; m Evelyn T. WEEKS, dt Sam'l & Jane M., b 8-12-1877 G.C.
both recrq 11-17-1912
Fannie, dt Richard & Hannah; m 1822 ----- CROOKER (mo)
Freelove, dt Stephen & Hannah, b 4-2-1794; m 1822 Isaac R. VALENTINE
Isaac dis mo before 9-17-1823
Isaac Craft, s James & Hannah (Doty); m Rachel McBANE, perhaps this one, I find no other Isaac
(Bibles)
James, nm, s Thomas & Mary; m 12-29-1784 Hannah DOTY, dt Isaac & Hannah, d 1-10-1825 ae 64y 4m 12d (mo)
Ch: Phebe m Stephen FROST
Ann m Richardson REYNOLDS
Esther
Mary m Rufus REYNOLDS
Isaac m Rachel McBANE
Hannah dis mo 1st Mo 1785
(Bibles)
Oliver b 3-18-1790 d 4-27-1865; m Esther TITUS, dt Isaac & Jemima (Frost), b 2-27-1796 d 6-18-1869
bur Mk
(Cox Gen.)
Peter, s Derick & Temperance, b 8 Mar 1749/50 d 1-22-1831 ae 81y 8m 4d; m Helena CRAFT, dt Abraham & Sarah, b 3----1756 d 10-26-1834 ae 77y 7m 26d
Ch: Derick b 1774 or 1775; m Sarah COCK & Ann DOWNING
(Bibles)
Phebe, dt James & Hannah; m 1815 Stephen FROST
Stephen, s Joseph & Achsah THORNICRAFT, G.C., b 8-6-1765 d 10-26-1854 ae abt 89; m abt 1791 Hannah FROST, dt Thomas & Phebe, b 9-17-1766 d 8-22-1831 (mo)
Hannah ack mo 4-18-1792; Stephen m 2d Abigail BENNETT, wd Jas., dt James & Amy COLES
(Bibles) (mo before 10-16-1833; ret mbrp)
Richard, s Solomon & Frances, Mk; m Hannah FARRINGTON
Ch: Wilmot
Solomon
Fanny
Freelove b 6-12-1812
William
Ann
Coles
Edward
(Bibles)
Wright, nm, Ensign in Capt. Dan. Cock's Co. M.C. Militia 1776, s Thos. & Mary (Frost); m Judith WHITE, dt Simon & Phebe (Wright), b 6-23-1761 d 9-4-1856 (mo)
Ch: Oliver b 3-18-1790; m Esther TITUS
Simon m Temperance CRAFT
Judith, a Friend

CROMWELL
Charlotte, dt Jas. & Jane R., b 12-26-1879; recrq 4-15-1903
John, Newtown; m 1825 Phebe WHITSON, dt Henry & Clement (or Clemence), d 7-16-1860 ae 86y 11m 10d
cf Purchase 1830
Mary b 6-7-1818; m Isaac U. WILLETS
Oliver, s James & Charlotte (Hunt), Cornwall, b 4-8-1792 d 5-4-1843; m 12-22-1813 at Wby, Sarah TITUS, dt Joshua & Hannah, Wby, b 6-28-1794 d 11-7-1848
Ch: Mary b 6-7-1818
(9 other ch)
cf Cornwall (clear)

CROOKER
Isaac, s Jarvis & Mary (Townsend); m before 2-20-1822 Fannie CRAFT, dt Richard & Hannah (mo)
Ch: John T. m Phebe A. MOTT
dis mo 3-1822
(Bibles)
Jacob, s Samson & Eliz. (Titus) Cedar Swamp, b 8-13-1776 d 11-30-1850; m before 8-16-1797, Elizabeth WEEKS, dt Richard & Martha, b 1776 d 1828 (mo)
dis 9-1797
Jacob m 2d Phebe UNDERHILL, wd Daniel, dt Israel & Mary (Wright) Underhill, b 7-8-1780
Ch: John b 9-22-1830 d 10-18-1852 (unm)
Phebe d 8-1-1866; cf Jericho 1830
(Bibles)
Ruth, dt William & Esther, b 1778; m Francis TITUS
William, nm, s Wm. & Anne, Wheatley; m Esther TITUS, dt Timothy & Charity, b 1752 d 5-26-1838 ae 85
(Bibles)

DARNELL
Alice C., dt Warrington & Anna Mary, b N. Y. 1-3-1875; recrq 12-17-1911; ct Green St., Phila. 12-16-1917

DAVIS
Nancy B., dt Mathias & Frances; m James McDONALD

DAWSON
Helen D., dt Geo. W. & Ellen M., b 4-6-1893; m 1913 Henry M. RILEY

DEAN
Joseph, nm, m abt 1761 Mary WOOD, dt Joseph & Mary (mo)
Mary ack mo in young years from Bedford, N. Y. 10-3-1761

DELAPLAINE
Joseph Jr., N. Y.; m between 9-29- & 10-27-1779 (cert not recorded) Philadelphia SEAMAN, probably dt Obadiah & Maria, probably

DELAPLAINE, Joseph Jr. & Philadelphia, cont.
b 5-26-1759
cf N. Y. (clear)
Joshua m 1716 Easter ZANE

DELAVAL
Lydia A. m Divine Hewlett COLES

DELBON
Melisande, dt Ange & Argia D., b Elmhirst, L. I. 9-28-1914; m 1935 Wm. S. MUDGE

DeMILT
Obadiah, Cow Neck, & -----
Ch: Mary d 6----1833 ae 76y

DE MOTT
Charles Fowler, s Davis & Sarah Ann (Fowler), b 4-16-1854 d Hemp. 10-19-1934
recrq 9-15-1929

DENTON
James & Jane
James & Jane ack their s's mo & receiving the company in their house 11 Mo (Jan) 30, 1716/17
John, Herricks, & -----
Ch: Ruth declared m intentions with John EMBREE Jr 1716

DEYO
Eleanor b 2-22-1866; m 1892 Irving J. STRINGHAM

DICKINSON
Isaac J., s David & Susan, d 8-12-1878 ae 69; m Ruth A. ----- d 3-13-1875 ae 76
Ch: (prob) Sarah L. d 3-1-1871 ae 26
(Mk Stones & Bibles)
Jonathan, N.Y.C. m 7-1-1773 at Wby Jane CLEMENT, dt Joseph, Hemp.
Jonathan, s Jonathan, dec, & Alice, N. Y. C.; m 8-27-1856 at Wby, Anna W. SMITH, dt Samuel & Mary (O)
Joseph, s Joseph, b 1730 d abt 1760; m Sarah HALLOCK, dt William & Dinah
Ch: Henry
Isaac
Sarah, wd Joseph, dis 1-27-1762; Henry & Isaac went to Oblong & desired mbrp
(Bibles)
Joseph dis bearing arms 9-24-1755
Matthew Reid [Dickson], s Jas. & Pamelia (Rush) b Greenville, S. C. 6-20-1856; m Phebe UNDERHILL, dt Jacob & Amy (Kirk), b 5-5-1853
Ch: Marianna Rush b 4-29-1894
Marianna recrq of parents 4-21-1929
Mary rocf Flushing 9 Mo (Nov) 2, 1749
Nathaniel dis carting hay for army 2-27-1782
(See Purchase)
Phebe, wd Henry, dt Samuel & Anna WEEKS; m 1735 Robert BARKER
Townsend, s Zebulun & Rose, Cedar Swamp; m abt 1754 Anne UNDERHILL, dt Amos & Elizabeth
Anne ack her mo when very young 4-16-1760
Zebulun gct Flushing 6 Mo (Aug) 1747 (clear)

DODGE
Elizabeth, dt John & Mary; m Asa BAKER
Isaac H. d 9-18-1879; m Jane ----- d 4-7-1866 ae 77y 1m 23d
Jeremiah ack outgoing 11 Mo (Jan) 29, 1728/29
John, N. Hemp.; m 9-25-1811 at Wby, Abigail PLUMMER, wd Enoch
Com to see abt rights of ch
Joseph d 3-30-1835 ae 52; m Catharine C. ----- d 9-30-1852 ae 58
Joseph b 12-17-1824 d 1-6-1887 (Man. Stone)
Phebe, dt Benjamin & Phebe DOWNING; m Tristram DOWNING; m 2d 1820 Obadiah WILLETS
Tristram d 1760; m 11-28-1741 Phebe MOTT, wd Adam, dt Richard & Abigail WILLITS, b 2 Mo (Apr) 14, 1699 d 9-7-1782
(Bible)
Tristram, Cow Neck, s Joseph & Sarah, d 11-19-1816 ae 45y

DOLE
John & Mary
ct Newton MM, West Jersey for both 6 Mo (Aug) 25, 1708

DONALDSON
Stanley Justus m 2-9-1891 May Gertrude COLES (now Gertrude C. Donaldson), dt Thos. H. & Sallie P.

DONVIN
Phebe rpd mo, com to speak to her a second time 4 Mo (June) 29, 1748; rpd favorably

DORLAND
Sarah m 1791 ----- BLADE (mo)

DOUGHTY
Benjamin, s Charles, Rocky Hill; m 12 Mo (Feb) 2, 1737/8 at Cow Neck, Hannah WILLIAMS, dt Jeremiah
Charles [Doty], nm, s Samuel & Charity; m abt 1753 Elizabeth TITUS, dt James & Jane
Elizabeth ack mo 5-20-1753
Donald Morgan, s Wm. E. & Evelyn, Roslyn; m 6-28-1930 Lydia STRINGHAM, dt Irving Jr. & Eleanor, b 2-23-1909 (in father's cf N.Y.)
Resident Williston Pk
George d 10-22-1873 ae 80y 5m 16d; m Harriet ----- d 12-9-1871 ae 66y 8m 29d (Supposed w of George as stones adjacent in Wby)
George [Doty] d 1-22-1874 ae 84y 6m 4d; m Elizabeth ----- d 3-31-1873 ae 75 (supposed w as stones near by in Wby)
Hannah [Doty], dt Isaac & Hannah; m 1784 James CRAFT (mo)
Isaac [Doty], s Isaac & Elizabeth, b 1704 d 5-11-1777; m 1733 Hannah SEAMAN, dt Richard & Jane, b 1710 d 7-26-1753

DOUGHTY-DOTY, Isaac & Hannah, continued
Ch: Richard m Phebe WILLIAMS
Isaac
Samuel
Elizabeth
Hannah
Hannah ack mo 7 Mo (Sept) 1733 (Bibles)
Isaac m 2d 12-3-1755 at Wby Sarah TITUS, wd Edmund, dt John & Sarah TITUS, b 1708 d 8-30-1772 ae 64y 5m 12d
Ch: Daniel m John TOWNSEND
Elizabeth
Phebe
Mary m Wm. MOTT
(Bibles)
Isaac [Doty], s Isaac & Hannah; m Anne SEAMAN, dt David & Temperance
(3 ch)
(Bibles)
Isaac [Doty], s Richard & Phebe (Williams), b 3-26-1764; m 10-7-1782 Elizabeth WILLIAMS
Ch: Richard m Margaret TITUS
both dis mo 12-25-1782; Elizabeth rst 1-17-1810 & gct N. Y.
(Bibles)
Jane [Doty] d 10-1-1866 ae 76y bur Mk
John m 10 Mo (Dec) 1723 Hannah SLEIGH
Com rpd m accomplished 10 Mo (Dec) 25, 1723, cert not recorded
Keziah [Doty] m 1803 ----- STIVERS (mo)
Martha, dt Chas. & Eliz., b 1705; m Samuel HICKS; m 2d 1739 Nathaniel TOWNSEND
Mary, dt Isaac & Elizabeth, b 1710; m abt 1732 Hezekiah SEAMAN
Mary [Doty] m 1787 ----- TOWNSEND
Mary E. b 1836; m Nicholas HALLOCK
Philadelphia, dt Benj. & Hannah, b 1738/9; m 1762 Nicholas TOWNSEND
Richard [Doty], s Isaac & Hannah; m Phebe WILLIAMS, d 5-12-1777 (mo)
Ch: Thomas d 9-26-1778 in 25th yr
Phebe ack mo 3-9-1756; Richard ack mo 3-20-1759
Richard [Doty], s Isaac & Elizabeth, b 9-4-1783 d 12-28-1852; m Margaret TITUS, dt Charles & Margaret, b 7-8-1782 d 3-9-1859
(5 ch)
(Mk Stones)
Sarah, dt John; m Isaac DOUGHTY
William, s Benjamin & Hannah, Flushing; m 3-2-1785 at Wby, Mary WILLIAMS, dt John & Elizabeth, N. Hemp.

DOWNING
Amy, dt Benj. & Martha; m Amos WILLITS
Asa, s Silas; m 1803 Theodosia VALENTINE, dt Charles (cert not recorded, m bet. 1-19 & 2-16-1803)
Benjamin, s George & Phebe, b 7 Mo (Sept) 22, 1722 d 10-17-1805; m Phebe WILLIS, dt Henry & Phebe, b 1719 d 2-28-1766
Ch: Silas b 8 Mo (Oct) 11, 1747
Ch: Benjamin b 6-29-1753
Phebe ack mo 2 Mo (Apr) 16, 1751
(Bibles)
Benjamin m 2d Martha HOPKINS, d 8-13-1807 ae 77y 3m 15d
(11 ch)
(Bibles)
Cornelia, dt Silas & Elizabeth; m 1861 Elbert H. THORN
Elizabeth, dt Thos. & Rosannah BIRDSALL; m James DOWNING; m 2d 1799 Amos WILLETS
George, (prob) s George & Eliza, d 3-3-1873 ae 92y 4m 3d; m Mary C. ----- d ae 75y (Wby Stones) (Bibles)
Isaac d 12-13-1857; m Charity ----- d 5-10-1854 ae 75
Isaac, s Silas & Phebe, O.B., G. C., b 7-25-1779 d 1-30-1847 ae 67y 6m 5d; m 2-3-1803 at Mk, Theodosia VALENTINE, dt Charles & Mary, b 4-27-1776 d 1857
Ch: Phebe R. b 1-27-1805 d 1-28-1881
Silas " 12- 3-1806
Latitia W. b 2-23-1809
Benjamin b 8-22-1820 d 2-23-1825
(Bibles)
Letitia, dt Isaac & Theodosia, b 2-23-1809; m 1827 William WILLIS (mo)
Mary W. d 4-15-1878 ae 72 (Mk Stone)
Phebe ack mo 2 Mo (Apr) 24, 1751
Phebe, dt Benj. & Phebe; m Tristram DOWNING; m 2d 1820 Obadiah WILLETS
Samuel, s (perhaps) Benj. & Martha, d 9-2-1861 ae 82y 10m 25d (Wby Stone)
Some Samuel m Rachel CARMAN, wd Lax
(Bible)
Sarah R., dt Silas & Phebe; m 1815 Samuel WEEKS
Silas, s Benjamin & Phebe, Hemp., b 8 Mo (Oct) 11, 1747 d 4-16-1822; m 10-2-1777 at Mk, Phebe RUSHMORE, dt Isaac & Sarah, O.B., b 2-18-1758 d 4----1844 ae 86y
Ch: Isaac b 7-25-1779; m Theodosia VALENTINE
Stephen b 6- 1-1783
Sarah b 4-23-1793
Phebe b 9-17-1789
(Bibles)
Silas, s Moses & Phebe, Po'keepsie; m 3-22-1826 at Wby, Sarah HYATT, wd Alvan, dt John & Sarah TITUS (both dec), b 2-18-1782
cf Oswego (clear)
Silas, s Isaac & Theodosia, b 12-3-1806 d 8-23-1856 ae 49y 12m 20d; m 5-27-1835 Elizabeth BOYD, dt Benj. F. & Phebe, b 6-28-1814 d 10-10-1896
Ch: (3)
Cornelia m Elbert H. THORN
Silas F., s George & Mary; m Elizabeth F. COLES, dt Samuel & Lavinia (Mk Stones & Bibles)
Stephen, s Silas & Phebe, Wby, b 6-1-1783 d 1-30-1847; m 5-17-1804 Phebe WOOD, dt Jonas & Mary, b 2-20-1780
Ch: Alfred b 2-12-1805 d 3-8-1805

DOWNING, Stephen & Phebe, continued
Ch: Mary W. b 2- 1-1806 d 4-15-1878 ae 72y 3m 12d
Thomas R. b 3-15-1808
Isaac P. " 6-29-1810 d 4-8-1832
Sarah " 9-29-1812
Phebe " 10-25-1817 d 10-13-1821
(Bibles)

DOXEY
Samuel & Margaret
Ch: Emily d 5- 1-1865 ae 15y 5m 18d
Sarah " 9-19-1865 ae 1y 11m
(Man. Stones)

DRAEGERT
George m Sarah Amelia COLES, dt Wm. H. & Mary A.

DUNCAN
Robert gc 4 Mo (June) 26, 1723 (clear)

DURYEA
Phebe, dt George & Elizabeth, b 1803; m Jacob JACKSON
----- m Jane ----- d 4-18-1855 ae 28y 5m 2d
Ch: Robert d 8-14-1855 ae 4m 5d
(Wby Stones)

DUSENBURY
Benjamin m 1828 Sarah SEAMAN, b 1 Mo (Mar) 4, 1706/7
Benjamin ack misconduct 9-16-1755

DUTCHER
----- m Helen T. WILLETS, dt Edw. & Hannah, b 8-10-1871
Helen resigned 6-20-1894

EARLE
----- m Helen HICKS, dt John D. & Caroline H., b 9-5-1867
Helen m 2d 1912 Jas. L. BURKE

EATON
Helen, dt John W. & Mary A.; m 1828 Stanley G. FLITCRAFT

EILERS
K. Fritz, Sea Cliff; m 10-1-1930 Ann BRANSON, dt Wm. E. & Florence Dell (Doing), Wash., D. C., b 9-14-1910
cf Alexandria MM, Wash., D. C. for Ann 11-19-1933

ELDRED
Martha, dt Richard & Phebe; m Henry W. JACKSON
Richard d 7-14-1866 ae 91y 1m 25d; m Phebe WILLITS, dt Thomas & Leah, b 2-1-1770
Ch: (prob) Phebe
Martha m Henry W. JACKSON
(mo before 4-19-1815, dis next mo)
Richard m 2d Rebecca ----- d 2-12-1872 ae 76y 2m 25d
Ch: Rebecca Ann d ae 6y 5m
(Man. Stones & Bibles)

ELDRIDGE
Simeon L. d 1-31-1879 ae 40y 5m; m Sarah E. HAUXHURST

ELFRETH
Jeremiah, Phila.; m 1 Mo (Mar) 30, 1738, Rachel SEAMAN, dt Nathaniel & Rachel, Hemp.
Cert to be prepared for Rachel to Purchase

ELLISON
Amory, having mo, Purchase refers it to this MM 12-26-1785; women to return the matter to Purchase informing of the care taken 1-25-1786
----- m 1823 Mary HEALEY (mo)
Queensbury referred it to this MM 12-24-1824; dis 1-18-1826

ELLIOTT
Gilbert Alex. Boswell, s Arthur Boswell & Lilla Burbank, b Ipswich, Mass. 5-5-1885; m 10-10-1912 Dora Flournoy HOPKINS, dt Alex., Atlanta, & Dora Adams, Athens, Ga. b 10-29-1889, Atlanta
Ch: Veronica B.
Arthur B.
John Livingston B.
Jean Cecilia
cf Orange Grove, Calif. for Gilbert & fam 12-21-1924; Dora m 2d Willoughby SHARP
Veronica, dt Gilbert Alex. B. & Dora F.; m 1936 Landon Ketcham THORNE Jr.

EMBREE
John Jr. m Ruth DENTON, dt John, of Herricks
Sarah R. b 1-12-1798 d 1-9-1864 (Mk Stone)
Thomas rocf ----- 2 Mo (Apr) 23, 1717

EMORY
John Martin Groome, s George S., dec, & Hannah W., Wby; m 6-15-1929 at Wby, Esther Jackson HICKS, dt Henry & Caroline J., Wby, b 11-5-1902
Ch: David Lloyd b Wby 3-20-1930; recrq of parents 9-19-1937

EVERITT
Henry b 6-30-1809 d 7-20-1885; m Sarah Ann ---- b 4-26-1810 d 12-30-1899 (Wby Stones)
Richard d 12-13-1880 ae 82y 9m 16d; m Mary C. ----- d 10-21-1860 ae 57y 3m 2d (Wby Stone)
Ch: (perhaps)
Mary E. 1853
Mary d 1854
Phebe " 1854

EYRE
Elizabeth Ann, dt Col. Benj. & Mary m 1799 Jacob VALENTINE
Harriet, dt Col. Benj. & Mary; m 1800 Samuel

EYRE, Harriet, continued
ROBBINS

FANNING
Carrie L., dt David G. & Elizabeth; m 1898 Wm. W. SEAMAN

FARLEY
Margaret, dt James & Zerriah, b 3-1-1775; m 1792 Townsend COCK

FARO
Jarvis m 1700 Elizabeth WILLITS

FARRINGTON
Edward m 1732 Frances SMITH
Ezra mo before 7-18-1793 & dis next mo
Hannah m Richard CRAFT
Keziah, dt Thos. & Keziah; m Abraham UNDERHILL

FATHERLY
Robert E., s Wm. E. & Edna J.; m 10-19-1935 at Darien, Conn. Cong. Ch., Emeline WALKER, dt Claude & Harriette
Robert rocf N. Y. (20 St) 8-6-1930

FEKE
Anne, dt Charles & Catharine, b 11 Mo (Jan) 17, 1741/2; m William COCK (2nd w)
Clemence, dt Charles & Catharine; m William COCK (3rd w)
Deborah [Feake], dt John & Eliz. (Prior), b 5 Mo (July) 11, 1695; m 1716 Thomas WHITSON
Elizabeth [Feak], dt John & Eliz (Fones), b 4 Mo (June) 9, 1694; m 1710 Benj. FIELD
Hannah [Feeks], dt John & Elizabeth, b 8 Mo (Oct) 6, 1675; m 1698 James COCK
John [Feake], s Robert & Elizabeth (Fones), wd Henry WINTHROP, b 1638 or 1639 d 3 Mo (May) 1724; m 7 Mo (Sept) 15, 1673 Elizabeth PRIAR, dt Matthew & Mary, b 6 Mo (Aug) 1656 d 11 Mo (Jan) 25, 1701/2
Prominent in mtg 1697-1724
(Cox Gen.)
Martha [Feak], dt John & Elizabeth, b 8 Mo (Oct) 27, 1688; m 1713 John CARPENTER (Cox Gen)
Mary, dt John & Elizabeth, b 2 Mo (Apr) 30, 1678; m 1699 Henry COCK
Mary, dt Daniel & Elizabeth, b 4-24-1780; m 1801 James COCK
William [Feeks] on com 1697

FERRIS
Hannah, dt John & Mary (Jackson), b 5-3-1679; m 1705 William MOTT

FIELD
Benjamin, s Anthony & Susanna, d 1732; m 1691 Hannah BOWNE, dt John & Hannah, b 1665 d 1707
(8 ch)
(Bible)
Benjamin m 2d bet 12 Mo 22 & 1 Mo 29 1710, Elizabeth FEAK, dt John & Eliz (Fones), b 4 Mo (June) 9, 1674
(Bible)

FIRTH
John d 11-24-1885 ae 72y 3d; m Henrietta ----- d 6-17-1894 ae 77y 6m
J. E. & M. E.
Ch: Addie d 8-19-1872 ae 2m 25d
(Wby Stone)
Thomas d 4-17-1850 ae 63 (Wby Stone); m Elizabeth ----- d 10-10-1872 ae 83y 3m 6d (Wby Stone)
Ch: Sarah E. d 1-23-1850 ae 1y 3m 20d (Wby Stone)

FITZ RANDOLPH
James T. m Mary B. BROOKE, dt Abraham & Phebe, b 5-20-1819 d 3-19-1903 bur Man.

FLEET
Elizabeth, dt Joseph & Susannah, b 10-18-1854; m Joshua COCK

FLECKLES
Helen E., dt Leopold Victor & Mary (Fish), b 6-28-1903; m 1927 Howard W. HINTZ

FLITCRAFT
Stanley G., s Clement B. & Luella W., Chicago; m 8-11-1928 at Wby under care of MM at rq of Chicago MM of which Stanley is a mbr; Helen EATON, dt John W. & Mary A., Floral Pk

FORBES
Edward E., s John & Catharine S., b 7-10-1857 d 12-25-1929; m Elizabeth OLNEY, wd Lafayette, dt Edwin & Mary HOPKINS, d 6-18-1933
Edward recrq 9-1918

FOSTER
John d 5-17-1843 ae 68y 7m 28d; m Fanny ----- d 2-1-1874
(Wby Stones)
William C. m Susan M. ALDEN, d 12-23-1867 ae 33y 3m
Ch: (prob) George S. d 8-8-1859 ae 9m 14 d
" Erastes T. d 8-12-1865 ae 11m 14d
(Wby Stones)
William C. m 2d Sarah K. -----
Ch: Frank d 12-30-1871 ae 1m 11d
(Wby Stones)
----- m Amy I. ----- b 11-18-1816 d 2-6-1903 (perhaps mother of Wm. C.)

FOWLER
Duncan m Caroline Amanda ----- d 8-12-1854 ae 25y 5m 6d (Wby Stones)

FRANKLIN
Charles F., nm; m Annie T. UDALL, dt Richard &

FRANKLIN, Charles F. & Annie T., continued
Deborah, b 1861
Charles F. d Toledo, O. 1828; m 2d 7-30-1884 at Locust Valley, Annie T. UNDERHILL, dt Jacob S. & Phebe (Smith), b 4-26-1861
(5 ch) (Charles F. nm)
Henry, Merchant, N. Y., s Henry, dec, & Sarah, Greenwich; m 1-5-1763 at Wby Mary SEAMAN, dt Thomas, O.B.
cf Flushing on consent of Sarah Franklin (clear); Mary gct Flushing 10-26-1763
Mary gct Purchase 12 Mo (Feb) 22, 1726/7
Peter B., Bkn.; m Mary HICKS, dt Elias & Sarah, b 9-4-1839 d Toledo 6-27-1914
Mary rocf N. Y. 11-2-1870

FRASER
Alfred Valentine, s Alfred & Mary C., Bkn., b 2-14-1869 d 10-4-1931, N. Hemp; m 10-30-1897 at Thomas Mott's, Sandy Point, Martha W. MOTT, dt Thos. & Martha, b 4-5-1873
Ch: Thomas Mott b 9-16-1898
Martha " 1-19-1902
Martha W. recrq of parents; Alfred recrq 2-15-1914
Martha, dt Alfred V. & Martha W.; m 1925 Cola Godden PARKER
Thomas Mott, s Alfred & Martha, b 9-16-1898; m 10-28-1922 Margaret WINFIELD

FRITH
Anna, dt W. Oscar & Margaretta A., b 10-22-1901; m 1925 Herman VAN BLARCOM (See Firth)

FROST
Alice, dt Jacob & Sarah, b 3-26-1851; resigned 7-16-1873
Anna Elizabeth, dt Edw. L. & Hannah H., b 9-22-1835; m 1861 Henry C. WOODNUT
Caleb, nm, Cedar Swamp, s Joseph & Martha, b 18 June, 1749 d Oct. 27, 1830; m 11-5-1788 by Rev. Murdock at Greenwich, Sarah HALSTEAD, dt Philemon & Jane, b 12-6-1768 d 9-30-1830
(9 ch)
Catharine M., dt Charles & Martha, b 8-5-1842; m Levi MUNSON
Charles, s William & Jemima, O.B., b 2 Mo (Apr) 1750 d 3-9-1820; m 1773 Esther COCK, dt William & Dinah, b 2 Mo (Apr) 22, 1756
Ch: Jemima b 2-24-1774; m (1) Isaac TITUS (2) Stephen COCK (3) Edw. McDERMONT
(Cox Gen.)
Charles m 2d 2-10-1780 at Mk Mary RUSHMORE, dt Isaac (dec) & Sarah, O.B., b 2-11-1760 d 4-28-1837
Ch: (9)
William d 8-18-1869 (unm)
(Cox Gen.)
Charles, s Charles & Mary, Wheatly, b 1794 d 5-18-1882 ae 87; m 5-22-1821 Martha TITUS, dt Timothy & Margaret, b 7-25-1800 d 11-23-1889 ae 89y 4m 1d
Ch: Esther b 1-29-1822 d 3-23-1885
Jacob " 12-17-1823
Edward T. b 3-29-1827
Stephen " 6-19-1829
Timothy T. b 10-9-1831 d 10-7-1861
Maria b 11-24-1833 d 2-8-1835
William b 1838 d 3-10-1905 in 67th yr
Margaret b 5- 5-1840
Catharine M. b 8-5-1842
Sarah M. b 12-29-1845
(Wby Stones & Bibles)
Edward L., s Caleb & Sarah, Cedar Swamp, b 12-17-1795 d 3-31-1878; m 8-1-1827 at Richmond, Ind., Hannah H. HOLLOWELL, dt David & Hannah, Ind., d 8-5 (or 26) 1857 ae 49y 11m 1d
Ch: Marshall S. b 3-17-1830
Halstead H. b 6-7-1832
Anna Elizabeth b 9-22-1835
Henrietta b 10- 4-1842
Howard b 8- 1-1846 d 1868
Edward m (1) 1-30-1821 at Richmond, Ann H. SHUTES, who d with her ch
(Bibles)
Edward T., s Charles & Mary, b 3-29-1827; m Pamela BROWN
dis 1860 (Frost Gen.)
Elizabeth, dt Caleb & Sarah; m 1820 John PRIOR
Gideon, s Caleb & Sarah, Cedar Swamp, b 1-11-1798 d 2-25-1880 ae 82; m 4-24-1823 Mary U. WILLETS, dt William & Latitia, b 2-24-1803 d 12-15-1847 ae 44 bur Mk
Ch: Leonard b 4-10-1824 d 10-17-1870
ct Scipio 1-15-1823 (clear); cf N. Y. for all 3-12-1843; Gideon founded Friends' Academy, at Locust Valley
(Frost Gen.) (bur Mk)
Halstead H., s Edw. L. & Hannah H., b 6-7-1832; m 3-19-1861 Mary VERNON, dt James & Ann, b 4-30-1835 d 2-20-1864 (name only on Wby Stone)
(2 ch)
Halstead H. m 2d Mary STEARNS, dt Rev. Charles & Susan, b 6-6-1845
(2 ch)
(Bibles)
Hannah, dt Thomas & Phebe, b 9-17-1766; m abt 1791 Stephen CRAFT
Henrietta, dt Caleb & Sarah; m 1815 Abraham WILLETS
Henrietta, dt Edw. L. & Hannah, b 10-4-1842; m 1862 Jacob M. WEEKS; m 2d 1901 Ezekiel H. MILLER
(Bibles)
Henry T., s Jacob & Sarah, b 8-29-1849; m 12-14-1875 Mary W. RODMAN, dt Thos. H. & Mary A., b 7-12-1853 (Henry T. d 10-24-1883)
(3 ch)
Henry resigned 3-1877
Isaac, s Charles & Mary, Herricks, b 12-23-1807 d 1810; m 12-23-1807 Hannah WHITSON, dt Amos & Amy, b 4-24-1784 d 12-14-1858 bur Wby
Ch: Amy b 10-25-1808 d 7-27-1863

FROST, Isaac & Hannah, continued
Ch: Isaac d 8-1-1837
Amy rocf Jericho 9-1832
(Wby Stones & Bibles)
Jacob, s Jos. & Martha (Cock), b 4-2-1752 d 3-17-1837 ae 84; m Grace SCARLETT, dt Sir James, b 2-26-1772 d 9-16-1797
(Wby Stone & Frost Gen.)
Jacob, s Caleb & Sarah, Mk, b 2-17-1808 d 11-22-1862 bur Wby; m 6-14-1838 Sarah TITUS, dt Stephen W. & Hannah, b 1-1-1817 d 8-30-1898 bur Wby
Ch: Newbury H. b 9-24-1846
Henry T. " 8-29-1849
Alice " 9-26-1851
Louisa C. " 4-27-1853
Jacob L. " 9-17-1855 d 11-22-1862
Sarah resigned 7-16-1873; Jacob mo but ret mbrp
(Bibles)
Jacob, s Charles & Martha, b 12-17-1823; resigned 9th mo (yr not given)
Jemima, dt Charles & Esther, b 2-24-1774; m before 6-19-1795 Isaac TITUS; dis next mo; m 2d Stephen COCK; m 3d Edward McDERMOT
Joseph, nm; m abt 1763 Sarah ----- (mo)
Sarah dis mo 5-25-1763
Lanah, dt Penn. & Sarah, b 8-11-1782; m 1808 Benjamin COCK
Leonard, s Gideon & Mary, Los Angeles, b 4-10-1824 d 10-17-1870 bur Mk; m Lizzie J. MALONE
(Bibles)
Louisa C., dt Jacob & Sarah, b 4-27-1857; resigned 7-16-1873
Margaret, dt Charles & Martha; m 1861 Stephen NELSON
Marshall S., s Edw. L. & Hannah H., b 3-7-1830 d 4-21-1911; m 3-19-1851 by Mayor Kingsland, Cornelia VALENTINE, dt Townsend & Anne, d 11-16-1870 ae 39 bur Wby
Marshall S. m 2d 7-15-1873 by Rev. P. S. Grosvenor, Josephine L. PERRIN, dt Jathniel & Lucy W.
Ch: (6)
Ettie W. d 8-23-1876 ae 1y 10m 13d bur Wby
(Bibles)
Martha spoken to regarding mo, was glad of Friends' care 6 Mo (Aug) 30, 1738
Martha rpd mo before 5 Mo (July) 31, 1745
Martha, dt Caleb & Sarah, b 9-12-1793; m 1818 Henry COLES
Mary, dt Jacob & Sarah, b 8 Mo (Oct) 6, 1741; m 1762 Charles VALENTINE
Mary, dt Robert & Mary; m James MITCHELL
Newbury H., s Jacob & Sarah, b 9-24-1846 d 5-13-1900 ae 53 (unm); resigned 7-16-1873
(Wby Stone)
Penn, s Wright & Freelove, b 3 Mar. 1733 d 4-3-1824; m Sarah UNDERHILL
(9 ch)
ct N. Y. 5-20-1795 (clear) (Bibles)
Phebe, dt Charles & Mary; m 1810 Samuel TITUS
Rebecca, dt William & Hannah, b 8 Mo (Oct) 28, 1714; m 1730 Josiah COCK
Sarah, dt Charles & Mary; m 1815 Stephen MOTT
Sarah Ann d 4-30-1881 ae 84y 10m (Mk Stone)
Sarah M., dt Charles & Martha, b 12-29-1845; m Stephen T. VELSOR
Stephen, s Charles & Mary, Wheatly, b 6-19-1829; m 11-2-1815 at Mk, Phebe CRAFT, dt James & Hannah, O.B., d 8-30-1824 ae 91y 1m
Stephen rel 3-1870
William, nm, s William & Rebecca, b 1674 d 1728; m abt 1700 Hannah PRIOR, dt John & Elizabeth, b 10 Mo (Dec) 22, 1681 d 12-18-1771 (mo)
Hannah ack mo 6 Mo (Aug) 24, 1712
Wright, nm, s William & Rebecca; m abt 1712 Mary UNDERHILL, dt John & Mary (mo)
Mary ack mo when very young 6 Mo (Aug) 15, 1746
Wright, s Penn & Sarah, b 1760 d 12-1831 ae 71; m 3-24-1784 Mary WOOD, dt Jonas & Mary (Carpenter), b 1765 d 7-3-1841 (mo)
(4 ch)
dis 5m-1784; rst 3-17-1819
(Frost Gen.)
----- & Phebe
ack mo 6 Mo (Aug) 23, 1742

FRY
John ack neglect of mtg 1707
John Jr., Jericho, b 11 Mo (Jan) 15, 1687; m 1711 Mary URQUHART
Ch: Mary b 12 Mo (Feb) 16, 1712/13; m Sam. WILLIS
Mary ack mo 5 Mo (July) 30, 1712
Mary m 1707 Wm. GLADING; m 2d 1715 James SCRIVEN
Mary, dt John & Mary, b 12 Mo (Feb) 16, 1712/13; m 1728 Samuel WILLIS
William d 5 Mo (July) 28, 1717; m Tamison ----- d 6 Mo (Aug) 18, 1732 ae abt 80y
William joined Quakers in Bristol, England; prominent in mtg 1697; signed rem cert 1707, both "came out of England"

FULLERTON
John b 7-31-1830 d 3-4-1894 (Wby Stone)

GARDNER
Alfred A. & Katherine T. W.
Ch: Richard L. b 12- 6-1890 d 8-19-1891
Martha W. b 10-26-1899 d 3-8-1904
Alfred H. & Adelaide S.
Ch: Alfred H. b 5-15-1890 d 12-23-1893
John J., nm m Florence L. THORNE, dt Isaac C. & Emily B., b 5-2-1871
Noah, s Seth & Sarah, N.Y.C.; m 12-6-1786 Sarah WRIGHT, dt John & Phebe, O.B.
Ch: Phebe b 9-1-1789; m Daniel HOPKINS
cf N. Y. (clear); Sarah gct N. Y. 6-6-1787
Phebe, dt Noah & Sarah, b 9-1-1789; m Daniel HOPKINS

GERALD
Thomas J. m before 2-19-1834 Hannah TITUS, dt Henry & Phebe, b 4-28-1810 (mo)
Ch: (prob) Harriet d 8-31-1843 ae 4m 7d bur Mk
Hannah dis 1834

GERMOND
Seaman (or Simon), s James & Sarah, Dutchess Co.; m before 3-31-1784 Sarah TITUS, dt James & Anne (Cock) (mo)
(10 ch)
dis mo
(Bibles & Cox Gen.)

GIFFORD
Isaac R., s Wm., dec, & Freelove, Dartmouth, Mass.; m 12-15-1831 at Wby, Phebe T. RUSHMORE, dt Stephen & Phebe, b 6-10-1803 (O)

GILMORE
John d 7-27-1890 ae 27 (Wby Stone)
Sarah d 7-14-1903 ae 73 (Wby Stone)
Thomas H., s Thomas & Eliza, Bkn.; m 9-14-1871 at Wm. P. Titus', Maria TITUS, dt William P. & Ann H., d 5-9-1885 ae 39y 8d (O)

GLADING
Mary, dt William FRY; m 1707 William GLADING; m 2d 1715 James SCRIVEN
William m 1707 Mary FRY
Mary m 2d 1715 James SCRIVEN; William brought cert from Burlington, form of that town, 1707

GLOSSER
H. m Mary E. ----- b 11-27-1833 d 3-25-1865
Ch: Ida b 6-1-1863 d 8-10-1863
(Stones Wby)

GLOVER
J. Wheeler, nm; m 8-25-1897 Sarah ALBERTSON, dt Silas W. & Caroline
Sarah m 2d William WOOLLEY
Sarah recrq 5-15-1889
Sarah A., dt Silas W. & Caroline ALBERTSON; m 1897 J. Wheeler GLOVER; m 2d William WOOLEY

GOFF
Duett Mortimer, s Mortimer L. & Susan S., Man., b Bkn. 4----1857 d Man. 7-15-1919; m Fannie M. ----- d Flushing 12-28-1937
Ch: Clifton D. b 11-27-1888
Duett M. recrq 11-15-1914; Clifton recrq 9-27-1921; Fannie M. recrq 8-15-1915

GOLDEN
Cornelia A. m Edwin A. HOPKINS

GREEN
Rebecca dis mo 4-26-1775

GRIFFIN
Abraham m Eliza D. ----- d 6-23-1873 ae 31y 10m (Wby Stones)
Ezekiel, Flushing, s John; m 1727 Ann SMITH
Hannah, dt Henry; m Daniel WILLETS
Obadiah, s Bartholomew & Miriam, dec, Washington, Dutchess Co.; m 11-23-1820 at Cow Neck, Abigail KIRK, dt Richard, dec, & Ann, N. Hemp.
cf N.P. (clear)
William H. d 3-22-1898 in 33d yr (Wby Stone)

GRITMAN
Drusilla m ----- ROWLAND (or RULAND) (mo 1813)

GROFF
de Grove (or de Graef) m 1818 Rachel MOTT (mo) referred to Pilesgrove, N. J. 4-15-1818, which rpd adversely

HAIGHT
Nicholas, Flushing; m bet 3-31 and 4-28-1704 (cert not recorded), Patience TITUS, dt Edmund & Martha
Phebe m ----- CORNELL
cf Flushing 8 Mo (Oct) 5, 1743 for Phebe CORNELL

HAINES
Mary E., Scipio; m Richard SEARING

HAIRENGTON
John H. m Elizabeth ----- d 7-3-1868 ae 18y 7m 9d (Wby Stone)

HALLETT
Gideon d 1-16-1845 ae 71y 1m 8d (Wby Stone)
Mary d 9-18-1846 ae 73y 9m 2d (Wby Stone)
Phebe E. m Cornelius H. RHODES
Richard T. d 4-18-1847 ae 82y 7m 20d (Wby Stone)
Thomas d 2-27-1875 ae 77y 4m 26d (Wby Stone)
William P. d 9-13-1844 ae 45y 11m 20d (Wby Stone)

HALLOCK
Abigail m 1724/5 Thomas POWELL
Amy, dt John; m 1747 Jacob UNDERHILL
Clement m 1716 Isaac WILLITS
Clement m 1742 Caleb POWELL
David gct Pur. 3-29-1769
Edward, s John, Brookhaven, b 4 Mo (June) 8, 1717; m 11 Mo (Jan) 16, 1739/40 at Rye, Phebe CLAP, dt John, dec, Greenwich, b 11 Mo (Jan) 7, 1719/20
Ch: Hannah b 10 Mo (Dec) 4, 1740
Dorcas " 4 Mo (June) 21, 1744
Clement b 4 Mo (June) 21, 1746
Mary " 3 Mo (May) 30, 1748
Catharine b 3 Mo (May) 31, 1750
Phebe " 3-30-1752
Edward " 4-22-1754
Edward V., s Valentine H. & Henrietta (Burling) b 9-29-1850 d Floral Pk 3-2-1909
Elizabeth, dt William, dec, Brookhaven; m abt

HALLOCK, Elizabeth, continued
1765 ----- SMITH
Elizabeth ack mo 8-20-1765
Jesse gc 12 Mo (Feb) 26, 1745/6 (clear)
John, Brookhaven, d 5 Mo (July) 22, 1737; m Abigail ----- d 1 Mo (Mar) 23, 1737
Ch: Abigail d 7-1-1768 ae over 80
"Both very antient"
John Jr., s John & Abigail, Brookhaven, d 8-11-1765 ae near 86y; m Hannah ----- d 11-28-1752
Ch: Sarah b 6 Mo (Aug) 28, 1702
Abigail b 7 Mo (Sept) 10, 1705
Hannah " 1 Mo (Mar) 2, 1707/8
John " 3 Mo (May) 20, 1710
Catharine b 12 Mo (Feb) 15, 1712/13
Edward " 4 Mo (June) 1717
Phebe " 4 Mo (June) 12, 1720
Clement b 2 Mo (Apr) 17, 1723
Samuel b 11 Mo (Jan) 17, 1724/5
Amey " 6 Mo (Aug) 28, 1727
John gct Mamaroneck (Purchase) 9 Mo (Nov) 24, 1731 (clear)
Katharine m 1706 Henry WILLITS
Katharine, dt John & Abigail; m 1706 Thos. WILLITS
Katharine m 1732 Moses POWELL
Margaret m 1704 John POWELL; m 2d 1740 Richard WILLETS
Mary m 1713 Amos WILLITS
Nicholas, s Edward & Anna (Mott) (Sherman), Milton, N. Y., d Seattle, Wash. 8-5-1915 ae abt 85; m Mary E. DOUGHTY, b 1836 d 1897
Ch: Sherman N. b 8-4-1884 d 4-2-1892 (Stone adjacent to Mary's)
Peter m 1723 Abigail POWELL
Peter Jr. ack mo 2-1-1756
Phebe, dt John; m 1746 Abraham UNDERHILL
Richard, Setamket, ack mo 11-27-1765
Sarah m 1727 Caleb HUNT
Sarah, dt William & Dinah; m Joseph DICKINSON
Thomas rpd mo; referred to Oblong 5-30-1764; ack mo 3-22-1764; ct Oblong 11-28-1764
Valentine H. m Henrietta BURLING, dt Thomas & Elizabeth, b 12-17-1821 d 4-2-1901
----- m Hebe JOHNSON d 8-17-1872 ae 81 (Wby Stone)

HALLOWELL
William R. rocf New Garden, Chester Co., Pa., 6-12-1885; ct New Garden, Chester Co., Pa., 2-29-1891

HALSTEAD
Adelaide, dt Henry P.; m 1880 Stephen T. RUSHMORE
Sarah, dt Philemon & Jane, b 12-6-1768; m 1788 Caleb FROST

HAM (or Hane)
Rachel m 1766 Elisha POWELL

HANSEN
C. William, s Christian Wm. & Helen D., Denmark (they became citizens 1871), b 2-24-188-; m Lillian SMITH, dt Alexander & Josephine, b Osccola, Mich, 10-13-1883 Bkn. Both recrq 1-17-1932

HARLAN
Samuel, nm, s Joshua & Mary (Wiley), b 7-20-1775 d Wilmington, Del.; m before 9-16-1801 Sarah COCK, dt James & Dorothy, b Thornbury, Pa. 4-27-1777 d Wilmington 1-5-1831 (mo)
(5 ch)
mo before 9-16-1801; dis next mo
(Cox Gen.)

HARRISON
Arthur Dudley, s Arthur J. & Ethel, Port Washington; m 6-27-1931 at Mk MH, Elizabeth U. POWELL, dt G. Thomas & Grace A., O.B.

HATTON
Daisy Georgia, dt Dr. Jos. & Georgianna, b 1872; m 1900 Albert W. SEAMAN

HAVILAND
Isaac E. b 6-23-1803 d 12-29-1885 ae 82y; m Ruth ----- (prob w of Isaac, as stones adjacent) b 8-22-1801 d 11-29-1850
cf N.P. 1-1832
Richard F., s Wm., dec, & Anna, N.Y.C.; m 2-19-1846 at Rosanna Hicks', Matilda HICKS, dt Robert M., dec, & Rosannah, N. Hemp.
cf Chappaqua (clear)

HAWXHURST
Anna rocf N. Y. 1843; d 6-18-1860 ae 70y
Benjamin, s Samson, dec, & Hannah, O.B., b 6 Mo (Aug) 31, 1720; m 8 Mo (Oct) 1, 1746 at Wby, Hannah PEARSALL, dt Thomas & Sarah, Hemp., b 10 Mo (Dec) 17, 1721
Ch: Mary b 9 Mo (Nov) 22, 1747
Sarah b 6 Mo (Aug) 4, 1749
Martha b 2-5-1752
Hannah b 3-25-1754
Bertha, dt Wm. E. & Marianna, b 9-24-1881; m 1901 Chester J. TYSON
Caroline, dt Wm. E. & Marianna, b 4-23-1866; m 1892 Fred Farley SHARPLESS
Daniel, nm, s Samson & Hannah, b 10 Mo (Dec) 13, 1723 d 3-26-1770; m 12 Mo 1745/6 Sarah SEAMAN, dt Thomas & Phila., b 20 Mar 1722 d abt 1795 (mo)
(6 ch)
Sarah ack mo 1 Mo (Mar) 20, 1748/9
(Bibles)
Deborah d 8-22-1865 ae 72 (Mk Stone)
Elisha m Ann ----- d 7-12-1898 ae 82y 2m 11d (Wby Stone)
cf N. Y. 1857; ct N. Y.
Elizabeth, dt Ephraim C. & Charity, b 2-7-1835; m Oliver VAN COTT

HAWXHURST, continued
Ephraim C. (or G.), s William & Vileta, both dec, Wby, b 4-29-1793 d 11-12-1859 ae 68; m 9-22-1823 Julia LEFFERTS
Ephraim C. m 2d 11-27-1824 Mary Ann McKENNY
Ephraim C. m 3rd 3-26-1834 at Wby, Charity TITUS, dt Timothy & Margaret, b 12-24-1802 d 11-7-1877
Ch: Elizabeth b 2- 7-1835; m Oliver VAN COTT
Caroline b 7-17-1836 d 6-21-1860 bur Wby
Wm. Ephraim b 5-19-1838; m Marianna HICKS
Margaret T. b 7-4-1845 d 3-14-1816 (unm)
Ephraim recrq 4-1831
(Bibles)
Esther d 2-5-1858 in 70th yr
Florence Amelia, dt Wm. E. & Marianna, b 1-18-1875; m 1900 Richard E. CARPENTER, of Pur.
George, a Sea Captain, s Simon & Lydia, b 7-1-1785 d New Orleans 8-16-1819; m Anna BURT, dt Charles & Anna, b 10-15-1792 d 6-18-1860 ae 67
Ch: Elizabeth Anna b 6-5-1818 d 8-3-1881 (unm)
(Bibles)
George W., s Jacob & Mary; m Isabella R. -----
Ch: George Henry d 8-30-1868 ae 4m 21d
(Wby Stone)
Harold, s Wm. E. & Marianna, b 9-8-1878; m 2-12-1913 Hazel Blossom SUTTON
Henry Sr., s Richard & Eleanor, b 1802 d 1-25-1855; m Clarissa ----- b 9-11-1811 d 1-22-1879 ae 64y 4m 11d (Wby Stone & Bibles)
Israel d 8-29-1861 ae 86y 2m 14d; m Sarah ----- d 1-31-1850 ae 75y 8d
Ch: Richard S. d 4-19-1846 ae 37y 5m 29d
Jacob m Mary -----
Letitia O. d 4-15-1869 ae 70y 10m 29d
(Wby Stones)
Jacob, s Israel & Sarah, d 7-26-1864 ae 61y 6m 27d; m Mary -----
Ch: Mary Etta d 7-8-1831 ae 10m 20d
Elizabeth d 12-20-1831 ae 1m
Augustus d 7-10-1833 ae 1m
(Wby Stones & Bibles)
James O. m Julia E. ----- b 9-25-1808 d 9-29-1900 (Wby Stone)
Joana, dt Samson & Hannah; m 1727 Daniel BIRDSALL
Job, s Townsend & Rebecca, b 3-30-1823; m Maria LEEDS
(12 ch, besides 2 adopted, 7 d young)
ct Mt. Holly, N. J. 4-1845
(Bibles)
John, s Townsend & Rebecca, b 1-24-1817; mo before 1-20-1841, ret mbrp; ct Alexandria, Washington, D. C. 1846
Maria, dt Townsend & Rebecca, b 6-6-1830; m 1851 Daniel G. BANKS
Mary W., dt Wm. E. & Marianna, b 9-27-1862; m 1887 Edwin C. TYSON
Nathaniel O., s Jas. & Eliz., d 7-12-1880 ae 84y 4m; m Elizabeth WALTERS, d 3-29-1875 ae 79y 4d
Ch (6)
Elizabeth m Jas. L. WEEKS
Phebe A. m J. L. CHEESMAN
Phebe A., dt Nath. O. & Eliz.; m John L. CHEESMAN
Richard Sr., s Jacob & Mary, d 3-27-1858 ae 85y 2m 3d; m Eleanor HENDRICKSON, d 2-19-1864
(5 ch)
(Wby Stones & Bibles)
Samuel, s Townsend & Rebecca, b 4-10-1821 d 1881
Sarah E. m Simeon L. ELDRIDGE
Townsend, s Henry, dec, & Esther, Wby, Searingtown, Great Neck, d 12-28-1829; m 3-28-1816 at Cow Neck, Rebecca SEARING, dt Samuel & Phebe, Wby, Searington, Great Neck, d 1874
Ch: John b 1-24-1817
Anna " 5-27-1819 d 12-13-1858
Samuel b 4-10-1821
Job " 3-30-1823
Leonard b 7-14-1825
Esther b 2-13-1827 d 6-22-1847
Elizabeth b 6-16-1830 d 1-16-1922
Maria " 6-16-1830
Townsend m Jane ----- b 6- 4-1804 d 12-21-1897
(Wby Stone)
Wallace, s Wm. E. & Marianna, b 1-7-1869; m 6-23-1900 Ida HUNNINGHAUS
William, s Joseph & Sarah, Mk, b 1761 d 4-22-1831; m Violetta ALLEN (Alling), dt John & Violetta, b 1765 d 9-25-1819
Ch: (7)
Ephraim C.
(Bibles)
William, s Thos. & Sarah, Wby; m 3-26-1812 at Cow Neck, Mary ANDERSON, dt Peter & Jane, Wby
Wm. E., s Ephraim, dec, & Charity, Wby, b 5-19-1838 d 2-5-1908; m 10-17-1861 at Isaac HICKS', Marianna HICKS, dt Isaac & Mary, Wby, b 9-27-1842 d 8-13-1915
Ch: Mary W. b 9-27-1862
Caroline b 4-23-1866
Wallace " 1- 7-1869
Florence Amelia b 1-18-1875
Harold b 9- 8-1878
Bertha b 9-24-1881

HAWKES
Charles D. d 1-15-1896 ae 22 (O)

HAYDOCK
Emily d 2-8-1840 ae 24 bur Man.
Emily W. (Man. Stone)
Henry, s Henry & Hannah, both dec, N. Hemp., d 3-25-1826 ae abt 50; m 8-27-1801 at Cow Neck, Sarah HICKS, dt Benjamin & Mary, N. Hemp.
Ch: Henry b 9- 3-1802
Hannah b 3- 3-1804
Robert H. b 12-3-1805
William Moode b 3-13-1808 d 7-19-1863

HAYDOCK, Henry & Sarah, continued
Ch: Mary b 12-29-1809
Elizabeth b 4-29-1812
Jane " 1-29-1816
Sarah " 7-18-1820
Richard L. b 3-28-1823
(Stone for S. Haydock at Man.)
John, N. Y.; m bet. 7-28 & 8-25 1878 (cert not recorded) Elizabeth TITUS, dt William cf N. Y. (clear)
Mary, dt Henry & Hannah; m 1793 Edmund PRIOR
Robert H., s Henry & Sarah, b 12-3-1805 d 1-20-1873 bur Man; m Mary R. ----- d 9-27-1876 ae 66 bur Man. (Stone only)
Ch: Sarah m ----- PHILLIPS; d 10-29-1896 bur Man.
Walter W. b 12-12-1836 d 5-23-1894 bur Man.

HEAKES
Helen Isabel, dt Jas. R. & Isabel N., b 1885; m 1910 Herbert S. BOWNE

HEALEY
Rachel, dt Christopher & Alice; m 1819 Cornelius POWELL

HEGEMAN
Jacob m Anna COLES d 12-19-1877 ae 64y 1m 6d

HELLER
Jediah P., s Richard & Hannah, Newburgh (town of Carroll Co., Chataqua, N. Y.); m 10-7-1884 at Jos. Post's, Elizabeth POST, dt Joseph & Mary R., Wby

HELMKEMP
Elizabeth recrq 2-14-1844 (O)

HENDRICKSON
Eleanor m Richard HAWXHURST, Sr.
Sarah A. d 4-28-1869 ae 45y 2m 8d (Wby Stone)

HENNION
Andrew J. m Jane ----- d 1-24-1870 ae 51y 11m 16d (Wby Stone)

HEWLETT
Amelia, dt Divine & Ann, b 9-28-1789; m 1808 Thomas COLES
Divine, s John & Sarah (Townsend), b 2-5-1767 d 10-28-1846; m 5-25-1786 Ann COLES, dt Jacob & Sarah (Cock), b 2-22-1788 d 4-22-1855
Ch: (10)
Amelia b 9-28-1789; m Thos. COLES
Ann dis mo 7-1786
(Bibles)
Emery, s George & Hannah; m before 3-25-1784 Mary (called Molly) BAKER
Ch: (9)
mo before 3-25-1784 dis next mo
(Bibles)
George, nm, s Daniel & Sarah; m 1-12-1754 Elizabeth WILLIAMS, dt Thomas & Mary, b 1724 (mo)
Ch: George m Jane WILLIAMS
Anne b 1755; m Hewlett TOWNSEND
Mary " 1757; " Richard TOWNSEND
Elizabeth dis mo 4-30-1760
(Bibles)
James d 8-31-1870 ae 79y 5m; m Elizabeth ----- d 5-28-1874 ae 75y 3m 5d
both recrq 5-1839
Mary E., dt James, b 1819; m Wm. B. ROBBINS
Samuel, nm, s Lewis & Grace, Cow Neck, b 1712 d 1800; m 11-8-1775 Ruth WILLIS, dt William & Mary, b 1751 d 3-4-1837 ae 85y
Ch: (5)
(Bibles)
Townsend, nm, s John & Sarah, b 6-7-1758 d 8-6-1832 ae 74y 2m; m 2-1-1779 Margaret JONES, dt Wm. & Phebe, b 8-1-1754 d 3-21-1825 ae 70y 7m bur Mk
Ch: (7)
(Bibles)
Wm. Moyles, s Townsend & Margaret, b 12-17-1779 d 1-1-1864; m before 6-17-1801 Martha COLES, dt Jacob & Sarah (Cock), b 8-5-1784 d 8-17-1859 (mo)
Ch: (5)
Martha dis mo 9-1801

HICKS
Albertson W., s John S., dec, & Caroline, Roslyn, b 9-28-1889; m 2-12-1913 at Sam'l J. Seaman's, Ann Louise SEAMAN, dt Sam'l J. & Matilda W., b 10-19-1885
Ch: Maria b 3-17-1922
Elizabeth b 3-27-1925
Barbara b 9-20-1928
These 3 ch were adopted & made mbr 3-20-1932
Albertson Jr. d 1-31-1890 ae 36y 11m (Wby Stone)
Abraham, s Stephen & Mary, Wby, Rockaway, d 5-8-1827 ae 36y 4m; m 12-27-1815 at Wby, Rachel C. SEAMAN, dt Gideon & Elizabeth, dec, Wby, b 4-10-1789 d 8-13-1878 ae 89y 4m 3d bur Wby
Ch: William b 10- 7-1816 d 11----1833 ae 17y [8m
Elizabeth S. d 8-10-1820
Gideon S. b 10-19-1823 d 10-29-1823 ae 2y
Abraham b 6-14-1826 d 11-1-1854 ae 28y 4m 16d
Gideon S. d 12-4-1831 ae 8y 1m 15d
Alfred d 11-7-1898 ae 39 bur Wby
Amelia, dt Stephen R. & Hannah, b 1-13-1859; m 1891 George CLARK
Augustine m 1728 Jane LATHAM
Jane gct Flushing 10 Mo (Dec) 28, 1743
Benjamin, s Jacob & Hannah, Rockaway, b 1716; m 12 Mo (Feb) 2, 1736/7 at Wby, Phebe TITUS, dt Silas & Sarah, Wby, b 7 Mo (Sept) 27, 1717 d 1800
Ch: Silas b 4 Mo (June) 10, 1737
Benjamin b 3 Mo (May) 23, 1739
Samuel b 8 Mo (Oct) 30, 1741

HICKS, Benjamin & Phebe, continued
Ch: Sarah b 1744
Phebe
Phebe, wd, dis 8-26-1752
(Bibles)
Benjamin, nm, kept company with Phebe PEARSALL, supposing they could be m among Friends 1 Mo (Mar) 28, 1739
Benjamin, s Benj. & Phebe; m 1765 Elizabeth MOTT, dt Henry
Ch: Mott m Esther COCK
Benjamin b 3 Mo (May) 23, 1739; m 2d 2-3-1774 at Micajah Mott's, Mary MOTT, dt John & Ruth, d 10-15-1824 ae 72y
Ch: Elizabeth b 4-24-1775
Silas b 10-23-1777
Sarah b 3-22-1780
Mary b 9-30-1782 d 12-9-1861 ae 79y 2m 9d
Temperance b 4-25-1785
Benjamin b 6-14-1790
Phebe " 1-16-1793
Robert M. b 4-13-1799 d 10-15-1843
Benjamin, Rockaway, took ct Nine Partners some years ago & came back without one; dis mo 6-26-1765
Benjamin, s Silas, dec, & Rachel, O.B., b 2-23-1763; m 6-27-1793 at Mk, Amelia COLES, dt Jacob & Sarah, O.B., b 5-7-1773 d 7-8-1799
Ch: (2)
Jacob d 9-24-1818 ae 20y 23d
Benjamin d 4-9-1819 ae 56y 1m 18d; m 2d 3-25-1801 at Wby Rachel WILLETS, dt Joseph & Hannah, b 7-17-1772 d 3-21-1847 ae 74y
Ch: Hannah b 5-20-1810 d 8-26-1811
Hannah b 11- 2-1816 d 4-30-1817
Amelia d 8-17-1817
Benjamin, Great Neck, b 6-14-1790; m before 6-18-1817, Elizabeth W. MORRELL, d 5-14-1878 ae 83 (mo) Benjamin d 12-14-1883
Ch: Mary M. b 6-26-1819
Susan " 8-26-1821 d 7-19-1851 ae 29y 9m 21d
Sarah T. b 7-28-1823
Elizabeth b 1-21-1827 d 4- 1-1833
Caroline H. b 1-3-1829
Benjamin M. b 10-15-1835 d 12-31-1838
Phebe B. b 1- 6-1832 d 10-14-1923
Parents bur Man.; Benj. rst 7-18-1821; Elizabeth recrq 6-20-1821
Benjamin rocf N. Y. 11-1836; ct N. Y. 4-1861
Benjamin, s Jos. & Lydia, b 3-24-1832 d 2-22-1891 ae 59; m Martha T. ----- d 1-26-1896 ae 63
Ch: Joseph W. d 7-1-1886 ae 11y 4m
Mary d 12-18-1880 ae 6y 4m
rem cert to N. Y. 8-15-1888
All bur Wby
Benjamin d 1-11-1894 ae 40y 10m 10d (Wby Stone)
Benjamin D. d 9-17-1835 ae 38; m Elizabeth T. HICKS, dt Whitehead & Margaret, d 12-21-1889 ae 86 (Wby Stone)
Ch: Benjamin D. b 2-24-1836
Benjamin D., s Benj. D. & Elizabeth T., b 2-24-1836 d 9-19-1906; m Alice H. -----
They adopted Frederick Hicks COCK, s Isaac H. & Mary W. in his 21st yr.; he took name of Frederick C. Hicks
Benjamin E., s George E. (changed name from Cocks to Hicks) & Mary COCK, b 1-14-1843 d 4-12-1916 (unm)
cf N. Y. 10-14-1905
Caroline rocf N. Y. with James M. & Sarah H.; dropped 3-14-1900
Caroline H., dt Benj. & Elizabeth, b 1-3-1829; m Amos ROGERS, M.D.
Caroline R., dt Willet & Sarah; m 1901 William Willets COCKS
Catharine, dt Whitehead & Margaret; m James M. HICKS
Cordelia b 3-28-1857 d 2-4-1858 (unidentified Stone, Wby)
Dwight T. b 5-17-1861 d 3-5-1864 (unidentified Stone, Wby)
Edward, s Isaac & Mary F., N. Hemp., b 6-29-1840; m Oct. 25, 1866 at Lorenzo T. Jarvis', Emma E. JARVIS, dt Lorenzo T. & Abigail, Otsego, N. Y., b 10-22-1845 d 2-12-1928
Ch: Grace
Marietta
Henry
Emily
Emma recrq 8-20-1902; Edward resigned 6-19-1907; ch recrq 2-17-1895
Edward J. m 2-22-1866 Anna W. MOTT, dt Leonard & Hannah, b 11-20-1845 d 12-30-1881 bur Man.
Ch: Catharine b 10-29-1873 d 3-19-1874
Edwin Willis, s Henry & Caroline J., Wby, b 12-17-1906; m 4-17-1937 by Dr. Fred K. Stamm, at Clinton St. Community Ch., Bkn., & Dr. Alfred G. Walton, of Thompkins Ave. Cong. Ch., Eloise Wentworth LANE, dt Alfred L. & Amy W., dec, Bkn.
Elias, s John & Martha, Rockaway, b 1 Mo (Mar) 19, 1748 d 2-27-1830; m 1-2-1771 at Wby Jemima SEAMAN, dt Jonathan, Jericho
Ch: Phebe b 7-5-1779; m Joshua WILLETS
9 other ch; the eminent preacher (Bibles)
Elias, s Valentine & Abigail, b 5-10-1815 d 1-9-1853 ae 38; m 6-8-1836 Sarah HICKS, dt Robert & Mary, b 2-27-1818 d 11-27-1884 ae 66
Ch: James b 1837 d 1839
Mary b 1839; m Peter B. FRANKLIN
Elias Jr. b 1843 d 4-6-1860
Caroline b 1850
All bur Wby
(Bibles)
Elias W. b 12-29-1863 d 2-14-1864 (unidentified Stone, Wby)
Elizabeth m 1800 ---- WILLETS (mo)
Elizabeth, dt Isaac & Sarah; m 1822 Wm. F. SEAMAN
Elizabeth, dt Benjamin & Mary; m Cornell WILLIS
Elizabeth T. (or Y.) d 12-21-1889 ae 86y
cf N. Y. 1865
Emily, dt Edward & Emma E.; m 1905 Harold

HICKS, Emily, continued
Truesdell PATTERSON
Esther J., dt Henry & Caroline J., b 11-5-1902; m 1929 John Martin Groome EMORY
Frederick C., s Isaac H. & Mary W. COCKS, b 3-6-1872; m Georgina STRONG
Frederick C. m 2d Marie STEVENS
adopted in 21st yr by Benjamin D. & Alice A. Hicks, changed his name to Hicks
George d 8-30-1860 ae 1y 10m 1d (Wby Stone)
Gilbert, s Isaac & Mary, Wby, b 1-24-1838 d 8-10-1922 Wby; m 1-21-1874 at Wm. P. Willets' Amelia WILLETS, dt Wm. P. & Mary Jane, Roslyn, d 12-24-1874 ae 25y 2m 9d
Hannah, dt Jacob & Hannah; m 1741 David TITUS
Helen, dt John D. & Caroline H., b 9-5-1867; m ----- EARLE; m 2d 1912 Jas. Leighton BURKE
Henrietta d 11-30-1846 in 25th yr, bur Wby
Henrietta 1860 (Wby Stone)
Henry, s Edward & Emma; m 6-27-1900 Jericho; m Caroline V. JACKSON
Ch: Esther J. b 11- 5-1902
Edwin Willie b 12-17-1906
Wm. Preston b 11-30-1910
Caroline brought cf Jericho 3-22-1901
Howard E., s John S. & Carrie A., b 3-2-1896; m Virginia HICKS
Ida Willets, dt John S. & Caroline A., b 6-4-1892; m 1915 Frederick Willits SEAMAN
Isaac, s Samuel & Phebe, Wby; m 5-12-1790 Sarah DOUGHTY, dt John & Abigail d 8-2-1847 ae 80y (Isaac b 4-19-1767 d 1-10-1820 bur Wby)
Ch: (6)
Elizabeth b 10-6-1805
Mary b 9-20-1807 d 12-12-1820
These two called youngest in Register
Isaac, s John D. & Sarah, Wby, b 8-8-1815 (3-7-1815 in Register) d 3-13-1900 in 86th yr bur Wby; m 1836 Mary F. WILLIS, d 2-28-
Ch: Gilbert b 1-24-1838 [1898 ae 81 bur Wby
Edward b 6-29-1840
Marianna b 9-27-1842
William C. b 1-7-1845 d 11-5-1846
ct Jericho (clear); Mary rocf Jericho 3-1839
(Bibles)
Isaac H., s Joseph & Lydia, b 5-22-1848 d Roslyn 5-11-1925; m Ida LOWE
James M. b 1815 d 11-24-1880; m Catharine HICKS, dt Whitehead & Margaret, d 10-1-1848 in 20th yr bur Wby
cf N. Y. 1870 with Caroline & Sarah H.
(Bibles)
Jane d 10-14-1872 ae 73 (Wby Stone)
John m bet 6-27 & 7-25 1764 Phebe POWELL (cert not recorded)
John D., s Isaac & Sarah, N. Hemp., b 1791 d 10-10-1829 ae 38y 6m; m 1-29-1812 at Wby Sarah RUSHMORE, dt Stephen & Phebe, Wheatley, b 1790 d 10-3-1893 ae 103y
Ch: Lydia b 2-15-1813
Ch: Isaac b 3- 7-1815
Phebe b 7-16-1817 d 1-4-1821
Samuel b 6-26-1820 d 4-28-1898 ae 77
Stephen R. b 2-18-1823
Valentine b 2- 5-1826 d 1-11-1910
John D. b 11-13-1829 (Bibles)
John D., s John D. & Sarah, b 11-13-1829; m Alice HAVILAND
Ch: Albert d 1857
John D. b 11-13-1829; m 2d 10-13-1857 Caroline H. HAVILAND, dt Daniel & Hannah, b Chappaqua 4-4-1832
Ch: Albert 10-20-1858
Alice b 2-10-1866
Helen " 9- 5-1867
Henrietta b 12-20-1863 d 8-17-1866 ae 2y 7m 27d
Caroline b 3-31-1870 d 8-19-1870
ct N. Y. 2-1851; cf N. Y. for parents & Albert 8-5-1863
John S., s Joseph & Lydia, b 9-20-1852 d 9-12-1904; m Carrie A. ----- b 10-23-1860
Ch: Albertson W. b 9-28-1889
Rachel V. " 10-25-1890
Ida " 6- 4-1892
John Samuel " 1-29-1894
Howard Ellis " 3- 2-1896
Carrie recrq 5-15-1889
John S., s John S. & Carrie A., b 1-29-1894; m Marjorie COOLEY
Joseph, s Benjamin, dec, & Rachel, Wby, b 12-31-1805 d 4-3-1832; m 11-3-1830 at Wby Lydia HICKS, dt John D., dec, & Sarah R., Wby, b 2-15-1813 d 9-29-1895
Ch: Benjamin b 3-24-1832
Robert H. b 8-28-1834 d 4-15-1905
Jacob " 2-23-1837 d 10-22-1896
Silas b 11-21-1839 d 9- 4-1842
John S. b 9-20-1852
Walter b 9- 7-1845
Isaac H. b 5-22-1848
Sarah b 3-10-1851 d 2-26-1906
Samuel b 2-22-1854 d 9- 7-1855
Rachel " 3- 3-1857
Joseph m Deborah W. ----- d 11-29-1893 ae 86y 1m 13d (Wby Stone)
Joshua T., s Benj. & Martha T., b 12-11-1861 Roslyn d 9-11-1928; m 12-25-1892 Grace A. BENNETT, dt Benj. & Emma T. (Bennett)
Ch: Lydia Treasure b Roslyn 8-4-1901
Grace & Lydia recrq 10-15-1911; Joshua recrq of his father 2-1874; ct N. Y. 8-15-1888; cf N. Y. 8-20-1911
Laura d 1856 (unidentified stone, Wby)
Lydia, dt John D. & Sarah R., b 2-15-1813; m 1830 Joseph HICKS
Marianna, dt Isaac & Mary; m 1861 William E. HAWXHURST
Martha recrq 2-18-1874 d 1-26-1896 in 66th yr
Mary b 9-30-1782 d 12-9-1861
Mary rocf N. Y. 2-18-1874 d 12-18-1880
Mary, dt Elias & Sarah, b 9--4-1839; m Peter B. FRANKLIN

HICKS, continued
Mary (stone sunken) (unidentified stone, Wby)
Mary M., dt Benjamin & Elizabeth, b 6-26-1819; m 1840 George E. COCK
Mary Titus b 1840 d 1889 bur Wby
Matilda, dt Robert M. & Rosannah; m 1846 Richard Y. HICKS
Phebe, dt Benjamin & Phebe; m 1772 John CARLE
Phebe, dt Samuel & Phebe; m 1815 John CLAPP
Phebe, dt Benjamin & Mary, b 1793; m 1816 Abraham BROOKE
Phebe, dt Stephen R. & Hannah U., b 11-25-1855; m John W. POST
Rachel m 1785 Joseph WILLETS
Rachel d 1847 (unidentified stone, Wby)
Rachel V., dt John S. & Carrie, b 10-25-1890; m 1912 Rudolph Burnie WATSON
Ralph, s Gilbert & Lillian B. N., b Wby 6-12-1894; recrq 11-17-1912
Robert, s Isaac & Sarah (Doughty), b 3-15-1793 d 5-26-1849; m 5-19-1814 at Pur., Mary U. MOTT, dt Adam & Anne, b 2-28-1793 d 1-20-1862 (stone has 1863) bur Wby
Ch: James M. b 1815; m Cath. HICKS
Anna Mott b 1817 d 1817
Sarah m 1836 Elias HICKS
ct Pur 4-13-1814 (clear)
(Bibles)
Rosana, dt Wm. L. & Rosita S., b G.C. 4-30-1910; m 1938 Bela ROZSO
Samuel, s Benjamin & Phebe, Wby, b 30 Aug. 1741 d abt 11-20-1819 ae abt 78; m 6-26-1765 Phebe SEAMAN, dt Samuel & Martha
Ch: Isaac b 4-19-1767; m Sarah DOUGHTY
Elizabeth b 5-19-1771
Samuel m Sarah HAYDOCK
Valentine m Abigail HICKS
Phebe m John CLAPP
Samuel m 2d 1794 Amy SHOTWELL, dt Joseph, who was then wd Charles BROOKE
(Bibles)
Samuel m Amy ----- d 9-19-1815 ae abt 67y
Samuel, s John D. & Sarah, b 6-26-1826 d 4-28-1898; m Rachel W. WILLIS, d 5-7-1905 in 85th yr
Ch: Anna b 11- 8-1844 d 12- 9-1907 Wby
Charles b 8- 9-1847
ct Jericho (clear); Rachel rocf Jericho 1843
(Bibles)
Samuel d 1855 (unidentified stone, Wby)
Sarah, dt Benjamin & Mary, b 1780; m 1801 Henry HAYDOCK
Sarah, dt Benjamin & Amelia; m 1816 Samuel WILLETS
Sarah, dt Robert & Mary; m 1836 Elias HICKS
Sarah d 1847 (unidentified stone, Wby)
Sarah H. rocf N. Y. 1870 with James M. & Caroline; d 10-27-1884 ae abt 66
Sarah T., dt Benj. & Elizabeth W., b 7-28-1823; m Charles R. ROGERS
Silas, s Benjamin, dec, & Phebe, Rockaway, b 4 Mo (June) 10, 1737; m 2-3-1762 Wby Rachel SEAMAN, dt Samuel, Wby
Ch: Benjamin b 2-22-1763
Willit " 12-15-1765
William " 2-12-1768
Martha b 10-12-1772 d 5-31-1795
Silas d 1842 (unidentified stone, Wby)
Stephen R., s John D., dec, & Sarah R., Wby, b 2-18-1823 d 1-21-1892 bur Wby; m 9-17-1846 at Thomas Underhill's, Hannah UNDERHILL, dt Thomas & Sarah, O.B.
Ch: Thomas b 9- 4-1852 d 8-26-1886
Phebe " 11-25-1855
Amelia " 1-13-1859
Emily " 11-14-1860 d 1-22-1864
Mary P. b 11-29-1863 d 3-21-1930 (unm)
Julia " 12- 5-1867 " 9-13-1938 (unm)
ct N. Y. for Hannah U., Mary P. & Julia 1-19-1898; cf N. Y. 10-8-1923 for Mary P. & Julia; all bur Wby
Susan b 11-9-1806; m John CARLE Jr.
Temperance, dt Benjamin & Mary; m 1811 Henry MOTT
Thomas, s Jacob & Hannah, Rockaway, Hemp.; m 11 Mo (Jan) 14, 1730 at Wby, Temperance TITUS, dt Silas & Sarah, Wby, b 10 Mo (Dec) 14, 1707
Ch: (6)
Hannah b 10 Mo (Dec) 3, 1730
Thomas " 12 Mo (Feb) 6, 1732/3
Jacob " 4 Mo (June) 15, 1740
Silas " " " " "
Friends at Rockaway allowed a mtg at his house 3 Mo (May) 30, 1739 (Bibles)
Valentine, dt Smith & Phebe M., d 4-1-1856 ae 22y 9m 26d (Wby Stone)
Walter, s Joseph & Lydia, b 9-7-1845 d Roslyn 10-13-1917; m Mary JARVIS
Ch: Lillie b 2- 2-1875 d 3- 7-1888 (Wby Stone)
Whitehead, s Gilbert & Mary (Allen), Flushing, d 1-4-1834 ae 62 bur Wby; m 3-26-1795 at Wby, Peggy (Margaret) TITUS, dt Peter & Elizabeth (Mudge), b 3-22-1774 d 5-9-1836
Ch: (10)
Mary d 2-14-1836 ae 37 (unm)
cf N. Y. (clear); ct N. Y. for Peggy 9-16-1795
(Bibles)
Whitehead, s Stephen & Mary, b 1797; m 1826 Mary A. MERRITT, dt Jesse & Mary, b 1-2-1799 d 1887
ct Jericho 1-18-1826 (clear)
(Bibles)
Willet, s William & Ruth, Manhasset; m Sarah A. MOTT, b 7-31-1832 d G. C. 1-3-1913 ae 96
Ch: Caroline R. b 5-25-1861
Gertrude R. b 2-17-1878
Samuel M. b 7-30-1854 d 1-9-1870
Willet J. b 8-3-1871 d 3-7-1872
Sarah W. b 7-10-1865 d 5-5-1866
Thomas M. b 8-20-1863 d 1-3-1864
William C. b 11-25-1856 d 11-13-1861
Caroline recrq 5-15-1901; Gertrude recrq 1-16-1901 [only)
Ch: Robert A. d 12-25-1890 ae 22y 9m 10d (Stone

HICKS, continued
William, s Benj. & Rachel, b 11-17-1803 d 2-21-1888 ae 84y 4m 2d bur Wby; m Ruth T. JACKSON, dt Obadiah & Sarah, b 10----1811 d 5-10-1900 bur Wby
Ch: Willet m Sarah A. MOTT
(Bibles)
Wm. Leonard, s Edw. Jackson & Anna W. (Mott), b 12-26-1866 d 12-1-1934; m Rosita SCHEBLE, dt Adolphus Edw., M.D. & Gertrude S., d 12-1-1934
Ch: Rosana b 4-30-1910
Wm. Mott b 5-30-1912
Wm. Mott, s William L. & Rosita S., b 5-30-1912; m 2-6-1933 at Glen Cove, Harriet SWARTZ

HIGBIE
Elias B. mo before 5-18-1831 dis next mo
Joseph, s Henry & Rhoda, Wby, d 11-7-1841 ae 68y; m Sarah BURTIS, dt Elias & Hannah, d 4-2-1842 ae 64y

HILLER
Jediah P. b 3-15-1826 d 6-28-1899 (Wby Stone)

HINMAN
Sarah ack mo 11-17-1830

HINTZ
Howard W., s Wm. E. & Katharine (Kaseman) Bkn, b 6-10-1903 Bkn; m 6-22-1927 in Bkn, Helen E. FLECKLES, dt Leopoldt Victor (b France) & Mary (Fish) (b Phoenix, N.Y.) b 6-28-1903 Bkn
Ch: Mary Helen b Bkn 10- 6-1932
Anne Kathryne b Bkn 2-8-1934
cf Easton, N. Y. 3-20-1938 for all 4

HOLLEY
Maud E., dt Lemuel P. & Ann Eliza, b 8-26-1880; m William Edward WHITSON

HOLLOWELL
Hannah, dt David & Hannah; m Edward L. FROST

HOLMES
Phebe ack mo from Nine Partners 11-30-1763

HOOGLAND (properly Hoagland)
Maria, dt Elbert & Willemptje; m Samuel C. THORNE

HOOTON
-----, nm, m 1782 Rachel MOTT, dt Jacob & Kezia, b 5-11-1757 (mo)
dis mo 6-5-1782

HOPKINS
Anna Adelia, dt Anne, b 5-21-1826; m 1844 (or 1845) Thomas H. COLES
Coles, s Wm. & Elizabeth, b 10-26-1783 d 10-8-1835; m 3-15-1807 Anna MUDGE, dt Daniel & Martha, b 1-22-1784 d 3-13-1837
Ch: Mary W. b 3-29-1808; m Robt. TITUS
Louisa " 9-12-1811 d 8-31-1873
Daniel M. b 5-20-1814; m Mary A. LEWIS
William D. b 3-30-1825 d 5-10-1860 (unm)
Daniel, s Ichabod & Sarah; m Amy WEEKS, dt Joseph & Hannah, d 2-20-1775
Ch: (12)
Dinah m Wm. COCK
Temperance m Derick CRAFT
Daniel signed Epistle abt 1725
(Bibles)
Daniel, s William & Rachel, G. C., d 3-14-1836 ae bet. 75 & 80; m 2-25-1776 Susannah ELLISON, dt Timothy & Mary
Ch: Daniel m Phebe GARDNER
Rachel m Chas. VALENTINE
Daniel, s Daniel & Susannah, b 1795 d 10-10-1833; m Phebe GARDNER, dt Noah & Sarah, b 9-1-1789 d 10-10-1833
Ch: (7)
Edwin A. b 1809
Daniel L. d 2-8-1864 ae 22y 9m 21d (Wby Stone)
Daniel M., s Coles & Anne, b 5-20-1814 d 3-3-1851 ae 31 (or 3-9-1851); m 9-23-1839 Mary Ann LEWIS, dt Dan'l & Ann, b 1-22-1820 d 11-7-1900 ae 90y 9m 15 d (Wby Stone)
(4 ch)
(Bibles)
Dinah, dt Daniel & Amy; m abt 1755 William COCK (1st w)
Dora Flournoy, dt Alex. & Dora, b Atlanta, 10-29-1889; m 1912 Gilbert Alex Boswell ELLIOTT; m 2d Willoughby SHARP
Edwin A., s Daniel & Phebe, b 1809; m Cornelia A. GOLDEN
Edwin A. recrq 10-20-1875
Edwin A. m 2d Mary HOPPER, dt Isaac T. & Hannah A., d 11-26-1910 ae 84
Ch: Mary A. b 11-27-1861
Milton " 7- 5-1863
Elizabeth G. b 4-4-1865
Julia G. b 5-4-1868
(Bibles)
Elizabeth, dt Ichabod & Sarah; m 1735 Benjamin BIRDSALL
Elizabeth, dt Edwin & Mary H., b 4-4-1865 d 6-18-1933; m Lafayette OLNEY; m 2d Edw. E. FORBES
Julia G., dt Edwin A. & Mary H., b 5-4-1868; m Alton WILES
Mary A., dt Edwin & Mary, b 11-27-1861; m 6-21-1882 Albert W. SEAMAN
took ct Jericho 12-20-1882
Mary W., dt Coles & Anne, b 3-29-1808; m 1842 Robert TITUS
Milton, s Edwin A. & Mary H., b 7-5-1863 d 3-4-1913 ae 49; m Sue WEST
Rachel, dt Daniel & Susannah; m abt 1808 Charles VALENTINE
Sarah, dt Daniel & Amy, b 12 Mo (Feb) 2, 1719/20; m 1736 Michael MUDGE
Susan, dt George & Mary; m abt 1839 Willets UNDERHILL

HOPKINS, continued
Temperance, dt Daniel & Amy; m 1741 Derick THORNECRAFT

HOPPER
Mary, dt Isaac T. & Hannah A.; m Edwin A. HOPKINS

HOUSTON
Moses B. d 4-19-1881 ae 47y 22d (Wby Stone)

HOYLE
Benj. W., s Albertus L. & Mabel B. (b Flushing, O.) Barnsville, O.; m N.Y.C. 1-30-1925, Harriet LOVEJOY, dt Clinton & Pauline (Kimball), b Portland, Me. 10-3-1897
CH: Richard Wilson b 6-29-1928
Frances Clinton b 9-19-1931
Clinton b Bethel, Me.; Pauline b Portland, Me; Harriet recrq 8-17-1919; cf Arch St., Phila. for Benjamin 11-20-1927

HUBBS
Esther gct Jericho 10-19-1879, although her name was not on the Register
Jacob dis mo 9-16-1818
James, s Robert & Mercy, both dec, Jericho; m 3-4-1778 at Wby, Martha BAKER, dt Richard & Deborah, both dec, Cow Neck
Jeddiah m 7-10-1884 Elizabeth P. HILLER, wd Jedediah, dt Joseph & Mary POST, b 5-26-1835 d 8-25-1934
John R. m 1870 Esther ROBBINS, dt Wm. S. & Elizabeth, b 8-24-1851
Joseph, nm, m Mary ----- (mo)
mo before 7-14-1830 & dis next mo
Mary mo when very young, against advice of her mother; ack mo 12-26-1759
Robert, nm, Jericho; m Mercy ----- d 8-19-1765 ae abt 53y
Mercy ack mo 11-21-1759 (mo when very young)
----- m before 8-17-1836 Hannah C. ROBBINS (mo)
mo before 8-17-1836 & dis next mo

HULIE
Benjamin m 1748 Sarah MOTT (cert not recorded, m bet 8 Mo 26 & 9 Mo 30)

HUNNINGHAUS
Ida m 1900 Wallace HAWXHURST

HUNT
Caleb m 1727 Sarah HALLOCK

HUTCHINGS
Ann ack mo 1 Mo (Mar) 25, 1730
William, Cow Neck, dis 7-25-1753

HUTCHINSON
John rocf N. Y. 9-20-1843 (0)

HUTTON
Julia Adelaide b 7-18-1821 d 11-7-1866 (Wby Stone)

HYATT
Alvan, s Alvan & Latitia, dec, N.Y.C.; m 10-31-1810 at Wby, Sarah TITUS, dt John & Sarah. [N. Hemp.
Ch: Isaac
Sarah m 2d 1826 Silas DOWNING

IRELAND
Sarah m 1748 John CARPENTER
Thomas, nm & Phebe (mo)
Phebe had mo before & ack accepted, now dis 3-28-1770

JACKSON
Caroline A., dt Arthur C. & Edith W.; m 1932 Leon A. RUSHMORE, Jr.
Caroline V. m 1900 Henry HICKS
Charity d 9-19-1834 (0)
Charles, s Thomas & Mary; m 1781 Sarah WHITSON, dt Nathaniel & Mary, b 1-20-1757 (mo)
Sarah ack mo 12-26-1787 (7 ch)
(Bibles)
Daniel, s Thomas & Mary (Townsend), Jericho; m Jane TITUS, dt James & Jane (mo)
Jane ack mo 7-17-1756
David, s Thomas & Mary (Willis), Jericho; m 6-3-1778 at Beth, Esther WHITSON, dt Nathaniel & Mary, Beth
Ch: Jarvis m Mary WHITSON
Mary m Abrm. WHITSON
David ack misconduct 8-28-1777
(Bibles)
Elizabeth, dt Jacob & Phebe, b 10-19-1828; m 1848 Benjamin ALBERTSON
Florence m 1912 James WILLITS
Hannah, Jr., dt Geo. & Eliz.; m George S. POWELL
Henry W., s Jacob & Phebe; m Martha ELDRED, dt Richard & Phebe (Henry b 5-7-1833)
Ch: Townie d 3-27-1872 ae 3y 5m 16d bur Man.
Reba S. d 1-3-1873 ae 1y 5m 16d bur Man.
All from Stones & Bibles
Jacob, s Thomas & Elizabeth, b 4-23-1791 d 12-31-1867; m Phebe DURYEA, dt George & Elizabeth, b 1803 d 11-24-1889 (mo)
Ch: (8)
Henry W. b 5- 7-1833; m Martha ELDRED
Elizabeth b 10-19-1828; m Benj. ALBERTSON
rst on ack 7-19-1815
(Bibles)
Jas. J., s James J. & Josephine, Christiana, Pa.; m 10-16-1920 at Wby MH, Tacy E. CLARK, dt George & Amelia, E. Williston
Ch: Hannah Amelia b Chicago 4-29-1925
James J. III b Evanston, Ill. 1-25-1928
Maria L. d 8-24-1874 ae 32 (Wby Stone)
Martha, dt Jacob & Phebe, b 1827; m Benjamin ALBERTSON
Mary, dt Jas. & Rebecca, b 11 Mo (Jan) 20, 1696/7; m 1739 Nathaniel TOWNSEND
Mary, dt Thomas; m 1768 Williams SEAMAN, Jr.; m 2d 1787 Willets KIRBY

JACKSON, continued
Phebe m Samuel WHITSON
Ruth T., dt Obadiah & Sarah, b 10----1811; m William HICKS
Solomon S. & Esther
ct Jericho for Esther 10----1867
Thomas, s Samuel, dec, Jerusalem, b 10 Mo (Dec) 24, 1723 d 7 Mo (Sept) 10, 1750 ae 26y 6m 16d; m 9 Mo (Nov) 2, 1748 at Wby, Mary WILLIS, dt Samuel, O.B., b 3 Mo (May) 7, 1731
Ch: Mary b 5 Mo (July) 6, 1749; m W. SEAMAN
Mary m 2d Thos. JACKSON, s Thomas & Mary, Jericho (mo) Mary ack mo 4-13-1755
(Bibles)
Thomas, nm, s Thomas, Jericho; m abt 1751 Mary WILLIS, dt Samuel & Mary, b 3 Mo (May) 7, 1731 (mo 2nd mo)
Mary m (1) Thomas JACKSON, s Samuel & Abigail; she ack mo 4-13-1755
(Bibles)
William, s Wm. & Katharine, both dec, London Grove, Pa.; m 3-5-1788 at Wby, Hannah SEAMAN, dt Thomas & Hannah, dec, N. Hemp., b 8 Mo (Oct) 3, 1749

JACOBS
Mary gct Little Egg Harbor, N. J., 5 Mo (July) 31, 1728

JARVIS
Emma E., dt Lorenzo T. & Abigail; m 1866 Edward HICKS
Martin m 1698 Mary CHAMPION, dt John & Sarah
Mary m Walter HICKS

JEFFRIES
F. L. m Jessie ----- d 11-18-1900 ae 25 (Wby Stone)
Robert d 7-17-1896 ae 65; m Sarah J. -----
Ch: Addie d 9-25-1877 ae 15
Wright d 11- 3-1867 ae 3y 7m 14d
(Wby Stones)

JENNINGS
Harry N. d 3-5-1883 ae 69 (Wby Stone)

JOHNSON
Hebe d 8-17-1872 ae 81 (Wby Stone); m ----- HALLOCK
Joseph d 7-24-1875 in 79th yr (Wby Stone)
Martha d 8-24-1849 ae 2y 4m
Mary d 1-9-1858 ae 60 (Wby Stone)
William, nm, Wby; m Anna JOHNSON, dt Joseph & Phebe MARSHALL, Nantucket, d 12-9-1842 ae 82y (William d 11-24-1880 ae 80 bur Wby)
Ch: Mary d 1-9-1857 (Anna, wd William JOHNSON)

JONES
Margaret, dt Wm. & Phebe, b 8----1754; m 1779 Hewlett TOWNSEND
Marietta, dt Israel S., b 12-24-1840; m 1862 Abraham C. UNDERHILL

Samuel, s Wm. & Mary, dec, Jericho; m 3-24-1825 at Mk, Abigail WILLIS, dt Townsend & Hannah, Cedar Swamp
cf Jericho (clear)
William, s William & Phebe, b 1736 d abt 1821; m 7-25-1762 Mary TOWNSEND, dt Timothy & Sarah
Ch: Townsend m Phebe HEWLETT
Samuel m Elizabeth HEWLETT; m Abigail WILLIS (Bibles)
William m 2d 1-6-1782 at Mk, Amelia KIRK, wd Benjamin, dt Daniel COLES
(Bibles)

JOUETT
Jean Gertrude, dt Isaac W. & Annie B., b Cambridge, Mass., 8-18-1878; m Alexander BLACKBURN
both recrq 3-18-1923

KEEN
Francis, nm; m Martha ----- d 3-24-1773 (mo before 3 Mo (May) 26, 1742)
Martha ack mo 3 Mo (May) 29, 1743
Mary m 1762 Henry POWELL

KEESE
Elizabeth gct Flushing 11 Mo (Jan) 30, 1750/1
Elizabeth, dt William & Mary; m 1782 Gideon SEAMAN
Hannah m 1881 James W. WILLETS
Hannah, dt John & Amy A., b Pur.; m Thomas WILLETS
John, s John & Mary; m 1750 Elizabeth TITUS, b 8 Mo (Oct) 26, 1729 d 1811 (m cert not recorded, m bet 12 Mo 28 & 1 Mo (Mar) 28, 1750)
John d 12-29-1908; m Amy A. ----- d 4-7-1904 in 80th yr.
Ch: Hannah b Peru
Samuel b Peru 1793 d 11-1-1880 ae 87 bur Man.
cf Peru for parents & Hannah 1864; cf Peru for Samuel 1866
John & Johanna

KELSEY
Edward L. b 1-2-1857 d 12-5-1897; m Sarah P. -----
Ch: dt b 10-1-1892
(Wby Stone)
Jesse P. b 3-5-1830 d 1-31-1896 ae 66y 10m 26d (Wby Stone)

KENNEDY
Catharine b 8-19-1817; m Stephen SLEIGH

KETCHAM
David, s Israel & Ester, Jericho, b 1-20-1752; m 2-2-1780 at Wby, Jane SEAMAN, dt Williams, Jericho, b 11 Mo (Jan) 16, 1746/7
George, s Geo. D. & Mary L., d 4-7-1905 in 78th yr.; recrq 2-19-1902

KETCHAM, continued
George D. d 2-3-1866 (Man. Stone); m Mary -----
Ch: (prob)
Mary d 10-15-1828
Fugene A. d 5-7-1863
Gulielma b 3- 3-1835 d 12-7-1898
(Man. Stones)
Israel, Huntington, & Esther
Ch: David b 1-20-1752
Margaret, dt Geo. W. & Gulielma; m Richard H. ROBBINS
Phebe (Man. Stone)
Philetus b 9-21-1813 d 8-18-1857; m Catharine ----- b 12-29-1820
Ch: Eugene A. d 3-27-1850 ae 8y 6m
Frederick W. d 1-1-1853 ae 1y 1m 24d

KIEFFER
Reginald, s Geo. & Jennie (Fowler), Bkn., b 3-30-1903; recrq 2-15-1920

KILSEY
-----, nm, m before 8-20-1800 Lorrette ----- (mo)
dis 9-1800

KIPP
Anne, dt Thomas & Mary; m William DEAN; m 2d 1762 Albert COLES

KIRBY
Ann, dt Joseph & Anne; m 1823 Robert MOTT (mo)
Elizabeth m James MOTT
cf Jericho
Hannah, dt Jacob & Mary, b 5-16-1799; m 1821 Isaac KIRBY
Jacob, s William & Sarah, b 8 Mo (Oct) 23, 1731; m 1-31-1759 at Wby, Amy SEAMAN, dt Jacob & Mercy, d 6-16-1759
Joseph mo before 5-18-1803, dis next mo
Sarah to be spoken to regarding misconduct 5 Mo (July) 26, 1732
Willets, s William, Jericho, b 1738 d 5-1-1825 ae 87; m 11-14-1764 at Wby, Hannah TITUS, dt Edmund, dec, b 7 Mo (Sept) 12, 1743 d 10-3-1784 ae abt 41y
Ch: Jacob b 8-11-1765
Edmund b 7-29-1768
Sarah " 3-23-1772
Phebe " 4- 3-1778
(Bibles)
Willets m 2d 5-3-1787 at Wby, Mary SEAMAN, wd Williams, dt Thomas & Mary JACKSON, b 5 Mo (July) 6, 1749
William, s Richard; m -----
Ch: Mary b 1738 d 7-24-1781 ae 43y
----- [Kirbey] m Mary VALENTINE, dt Richard, dec (mo)
Mary dis 7-30-1777

KIRK
Abigail, dt Richard & Ann; m 1820 Obadiah GRIFFEN
Amelia, wd Benjamin, dt Daniel & Ann COLES; m 1764 Benjamin KIRK; m 2d 1782 William JONES
Amy, dt Daniel & Mary, b 9----1817; m 1835 Jacob S. UNDERHILL (mo)
Anna, dt Daniel & Mary T., b 2-4-1822; m 1847 Samuel Y. VALENTINE
Anne, dt Arthur & Temperance, b 8 Mo (Oct) 3, 1731; m 1753 Jacob SEAMAN
Benjamin, s Arthur, dec, & Temperance, O.B., d 1778; m 5-3-1764 at Mk, Amelia COLES, dt Daniel & Ann
Amelia m 2d 1782 William JONES
Benjamin C., s Joshua & Hannah, b 10-16-1847; m Florence TUCKER, b 11-4-1858 d 8-11-1879 ae 31y 9m 26d bur Mk
Ch: Daniel
William
Emma
Benjamin C. m 2d Gertrude Townsend TABER (Cox Gen.)
Daniel, s Richard & Anne, Hemp Harbor, M.C.; b 10-29-1784 d 9-29-1827 ae 42y 11m; m 11-3-1814 at Wby, Mary TITUS, dt Joshua & Hannah, b 9-14-1788 (or 10-30-1788) d 5-6-1871 ae 82y 7m 22d
Ch: Joshua b 1- 2-1816
Amy " 9----1817
Anne " 2- 4-1822
Hannah " 10- 6-1827
Mary Ann d 9-20-1821 ae 2y 1m 15d
(Bibles)
Hannah, dt Daniel & Mary, b 10-6-1826; m 1851 Sylvanus LYON
John D., Wby, & Sarah R.
Ch: Valentine b 2- 5-1826
Joshua, s Daniel & Mary, b 1-2-1816 d 7-7-1872 ae 56y 6m d; m 10-13-1843, Hannah COCK, dt Benjamin & Lanah, b 4-6-1812 d 11-3-1897 ae 85y 6m 7d
Ch: Benjamin C. b 10-16-1847
Richard, s William & Abigail, b 8 Mo (Oct) 1737 d 3----1818; m 11-1-1766 Anne DOWNING, dt George & Amey
Ch: Rosetta b 3-10-1776 d 7- 6-1791
Abigail " 10-28-1779
Amey " 2-22-1781 d 6-17-1787
Daniel " 10-30-1784 d 9-28-1827
Silas " 9-26-1787
James " 2-25-1791
George
William
John
Last 3 ch by G. W. Cocks, prob earlier ch
(Bibles)
Richard d 6-4-1855 ae in 52nd yr; m Mary A. ----- d 8-14-1861 ae 30y 4m 24d
Ch: Daniel
Anna V. d 10-21-1872 ae 17y 9m
(Mk Stones)
William, s John & Deborah; m 3 Mo (May) 12, 1731 Abigail VALENTINE, dt Richard (mo)
Ch: Jerusha m Thos. IRELAND

KIRK, William & Abigail, continued
Ch: Jemima m Jas. BAKER
Richard m Anne DOWNING
Abigail ack mo 5 Mo (July) 1733

KUSCH
John G. b Mar. 8, 1897 d 8-7-1897 (Wby Stone)

LAKE
Joseph, nm, & Sarah (mc abt 1763)
Sarah dis mo 3-30-1763

LANCASTER
Aaron gct Purchase 7-29-1767 (clear); rem cert to Pur. 10-28-1767

LANE
Eloise W., dt Alfred L. & Amy W.; m 1937 Edwin Willis HICKS

LANGDON
Hannah dis mo 4-26-1775

LANSING
Gulian, s Jos. Mc C., dec, & Isabella (Strong), N. Y.C.; m 9-16-1919 at Sam'l J. Seaman's, Elizabeth PILLING, dt Simeon O., dec, & Katharine, G. C.
Elizabeth recrq 8-19-1917; Elizabeth resigned 1926

LAPHAM
Edw. Morgan, s Arden B. & Mary, Chicago; m 2-22-1908 at Thos. W. Willets', Anna WILLETS, dt Thos. W. & Hannah, dec, Roslyn
Ch: Edwin M. Jr. b Manhasset 6-5-1909
Thomas W. " " 1-28-1911
Ann W. " " 4-11-1916
Edward recrq 1-20-1909
Edw. Morgan Jr., s Edw. M. & Anna, Port Washington, b Manhasset 6-5-1909; m 8-14-1931 at Manhasset, Ruth Isabelle POLLOCK, dt Jas. R. & Eugenia, Queens Co., b 11-19-1910 Bkn.
Ch: Peggy Ann b 2-10-1935 d 5-18-1935
Annie Willets b 8- 2-1936 d 9-26-1936
Phebe Greer b 8- 6-1935 (adopted)
James Pollock b 2-22-1937 (adopted)
Phebe & James recrq cf adopted parents 2-21-1937 & 3-20-1938
Thomas Willets, s Edw. M. & Anna, Port Washington, b Manhasset 1-28-1911; m 8-8-1936 at A. W. Chapman's, Grace W. CHAPMAN, dt A. Wright & Grace, Port Washington

LATHAM
Jane m 1728 Augustine HICKS
signed Epistle abt 1725
John, nm; m before 12 Mo (Feb) 1717/18 Mary COOPER, dt Mary (mo)
Joseph d 7 Mo (Sept) 6, 1748; m Jane ----- d 10 Mo (Dec) 21, 1745
signed Epistle abt 1725; dis 9-24-1755
Mary m 1735 Nathaniel PEARSALL
Mary, dt Wm. & Amy; b 1739; m 1759 Robert MITCHELL (mo)
Sarah, dt William, b 1731; m 1755 William MITCHELL (mo)
ack mo 5-8-1755
William, Cow Neck, dis 5 Mo (July) 26, 1738

LATTING
Daniel d 12-22-1833 ae 92 (Wby Stone)
Daniel d 8-17-1852 ae 53y 9m 28d; m Martha ----- b 6-9-1805 d 6-17-1858 (prob w)
Isaac d 5-25-1830 ae 95 (Wby Stone)

LAWRENCE
Phebe, dt Joseph & Phebe, b 3-29-1769; m 1795 Obadiah TOWNSEND
Willet Jr. d 3-28-1887 ae 81y 2m 24d (Wby Stone)

LAWRIE
Margaret J., dt Wm. W. & Francis; m 1893 Wm. H. SEAMAN

LAWTON
William T. m Eliza W. ----- b 1-4-1844 d 9-22-1877 (Wby Stone)

LAYTON
Ellen M., dt David & Sarah, b 5-30-1837; m 1858 Wm. E. COX

LEE
Henry S. d 6-4-1848 in 41st yr; m Amy S. ----- d 8-9-1857 ae 40
Ch: Abraham B. d 2-2-1861 in 20th yr
Caroline A. d 5-19-1860 ae 13y 3m
Henry H. d 5- 6-1855 in 17th yr
Mary B. " 9-10-1843 ae 6m 22d
Mary d 7- 6-1845 ae 10m 26d
(Man. Stones)

LEEK
Philip d 8-27-1847 bur Man.
Sarah B. d 6-9-1863 ae 20y 9m

LEEMING
Laura G. F., dt Geo. L. & Laura L. (Barrows), b Cheyenne, Wyoming 9-26-1888; m Robert Henry WILLETS

LEFFERTS
Julia m 1821 Ephraim HAWXHURST (Bibles)

LEGGETT
Augustus, nm, N.Y.C. & Eliza
ct N. Y. for Eliza 4-1851
Thomas, N. Y., s Thos., dec, & Mary; m 11-3-1808 at Mk, Mary UNDERHILL, dt Jacob & Catharine

LESTER
Eastman, s Geo. W. & Jennie (Degrauw), b Ros-

LESTER, Eastman, continued
lyn 9-1-1890 d 12-28-1926 Wby; m Violet MERRITT
Ch: John Merritt b Mineola 2-26-1922
Gerald Jr. b Mineola 5-26-1925
Eastman recrq 5-17-1925; John M. recrq of parents 5-17-1925
John ack misconduct 11 Mo (Jan) 25, 1731/32

LEVI
Edward m Abigail ----- d 12-27-1868 ae abt 50 (Wby Stone)

LEWIS
Ann (unidentified Stone, Wby)
Elias Jr., nm, d 4-16-1864 ae 82y 6m 23d; m Mary W. POST, dt James & Phebe W., b 5-2-1823 (or 6-26-1823) d 4-28-1851 ae 27y 11m 26d bur Wby
Elias Jr., s Elias & Ann, dec, N. Hemp, b 12-30-1820 d 2-3-1894; m 2-8-1853 at Thos. Underhill's, Mary UNDERHILL, dt Thos. & Sarah, O.B., b 11-17-1829
Elizabeth T. d 4-23-1891 ae 55y 11m 22d (unidentified Stone, Wby)
Henry d 10-19-1881 ae 75y 4m 13d (Wby Stone); m Martha ----- (blank stone near Henry's)
Ch: Edmund P. d 9-16-1861 ae 28y 3m 23d
Louisa J. m John H. WARTMAN
Isaac Buck, shipping merchant & asparagus grower, s Capt. Ezra & Eliza N.; m 1843 Catharine S. VALENTINE, dt David & Hannah, b 5-7-1818 d 5-2-1902
Ch: Mary Anna m Dan. S. VAIL
Catharine resigned 3-18-1896
Jerusha m Robert WEEKS; m 2d Richard POWELL
John m 1850 Ann Elizabeth VALENTINE, b 6-16-1828
Mary d 10- 6-1863 (Wby Stone)
Mary W. (unidentified Stone, Wby)
Nancy (unidentified Stone, Wby)

L'HOMMEDIEU
Kenneth Edw. m 11-29-1935 at Manhasset, Nancy ROBINSON, dt Ward Reid & Dorothy A., b Springfield, Ill., 7-18-1915 [Neck
Nancy recrq 9-18-1938 (Kenneth Edw. b Great

LOINES
Anna, dt John & Phebe, b 3-13-1797; m 1820 John SEARING
John, s Stephen, dec, Wby; m 6-8-1779 at Wby, Phebe SEAMAN, dt Thomas & Hannah, b 5-5-1755 (John b 8-31-1760 d 8-5-1823)
Ch: Stephen b 3-20-1780
Simeon " 2- 9-1783
Hannah " 1-22-1786
Thomas b 11- 2-1789 d 11-19-1792
Anne " 3-13-1797
Phebe, dt Stephen & Phebe; m 1791 Jacob VALENTINE
Sarah W. d 10-2-1895 ae 94
cf N. Y. 1844

Simeon, s John & Phebe, b 2-9-1783; m Martha -----
Ch: Abigail b 5-20-1810
Elizabeth b 3- 3-1812
Stephen, s William & Ann, b 7 Mo (Sept) 26, 1737; m before 12-26-1759 Phebe TITUS, dt William & Elizabeth, b 10 Mo (Dec) 18, 1735

Stephen mo before 2-25-1778 & dis, perhaps rst as a Stephen mo before 12-19-1798 & dis next mo; rst 2-14-1810
Stephen m 1810 Sybil -----
Ch: Mary b 5-19-1811 d 12- 7-1814 (or 8-7-1815 ae 4y 2m 19d)
Jonas b 9-23-1814
Stephen gct Jericho 5-16-1810 (clear);
Sibbil rocf Jericho 12-19-1816
Stephen mo & referred to Creek 1-18-1815; Creek rpd 4-19-1815 having rec him in mbrp
William b 9 Mo (Nov) 23, 1706; m Ann ----- b 10 Mo (Dec) 7, 1715
Ch: Mary b 12 Mo (Feb) 21, 1734/5
Stephen b 7 Mo (Sept) 26, 1737
William Jr. b 5 Mo (July) 25, 1746
William Jr., s William & Ann, Hemp., b 5 Mo (July) 25, 1746; m 5-7-1767 Sarah ALSOP, dt Richard & Sarah, O.B., b 11 Mo (Jan) 3, 1747/8
Ch: James b 4- 1-1768
Richard b 12-18-1769
Anne " 12-14-1773
Sarah " 5- 1-1781
William ack mo 7-25-1759; cf N. Y. 1843; d 3-15-1875 ae abt 76

LOSEE
Caroline d 10-16-1843 (Wby Stone)
Isaac d 2-19-1853 ae 89 (Wby Stone)
Maria d 10-15-1846 (Wby Stone)
Oliver d 2-19-1873 ae 72y 8m 27d; m Abigail ----- d 9-21-1887 ae 90y 10m 24d
Ch: (prob)
Emmeline d 10-27-1863
Elias " 4- 1-1846 ae 18y 17d
(Wby Stones)

LOTT
Cornelius, nm; m Mary VALENTINE, d 1-7-1893 ae 77

LOVELL
Patience, dt John & Patience; m Joseph WRIGHT

LOWE
Ida m Isaac H. HICKS

LOWELL
Charles P. m Annie L. VALENTINE
Ch: Charles Frances b 1-20-1899 d 1-20-1908 (Mk Stone)

LOWERRE (written Lowree)
Daniel dis mo 3-16-1824

LOWTHROP
Francis Cowlyn, s Francis C. & Anastacia B., dec, Trenton, N. J.; m 10-3-1888 at Jos. Willets', Fannie Amelia WILLETS, dt Jos. & Esther G., N. Hemp.
Fannie resigned 4-20-1913

LUMPKIN
Audrey, dt Harry & Maude R., b Denver, Colo., 6-6-1908; recrq 4-18-1926 (father b Fort Dodge, Iowa 10-28-1878; Maude Robinson b Newburyport, Mass. 7-1-1881)

LUNDY
Joseph, s Thomas & Joanna, dec, Hardwick, N.J.; m 1-15-1795 at Wby, Mary TITUS, dt Richard & Abigail, Wby
cf Hardwick (clear); Mary gct Hardwick 3-18-1795

LYON
Caroline, dt Walter S., b 3-4-1828; m Silas ALBERTSON
Sylvanus, N.Y.C.; m 1851 Hannah KIRK, dt Daniel & Mary, b 10-6-1826

McCLELLEN
John d 9-13-1890 ae 58 (Wby Stone); m Charlotte Emily -----
Ch: Phebe Emily d 7-10-1857 ae 3y (Wby Stone)

McCOUN
Charles, nm; m Pamelia P. UNDERHILL, b 4-1-1828
Pamelia rocf E. Hamburg 4-29-1886; Pamelia resigned 5-15-1889
Sarah, dt Wm. & Mary (Townsend); m Richard ALBERTSON

McDONALD
James m Nancy B. DAVIS, dt Mathias & Frances, d 12-26-1864 ae 60 (Wby Stone)

McKENNY
Mary Ann m 1824 Ephraim HAWXHURST (Bibles)

MABBET
Joseph & Hannah
Ch: Jonathan b 7 Mo (Sept) 10, 1720 d 6 Mo 7, 1744
Susannah b 1 Mo (Mar) 7, 1722/3
Sarah b 7 Mo (Sept) 24, 1724
Samuel b 8 Mo (Oct) 24, 1726
Mary b 3 Mo (May) 25, 1729
Joseph b 1 Mo (Mar) 8, 1731/2
Hannah b 4 Mo (June) 7, 1736
Joseph abt to go to England, asks ct Bristol, or where his lot may be cast; rpd 5 Mo (July) 29, 1730 as signed by Friends of the Neck (Manhasset). He apparently returned soon
Joseph [Mabbett], s Joseph & Hannah, b 11 Mo (Mar) 8, 1731/2; mo before 8-25-1762 & referred to Oblong; dis 6-26-1765; ack mo & bearing arms 4-26-1780
Samuel, s Joseph & Hannah, b 8 Mo (Oct) 24, 1726; went to N.P. & mo; that mtg asked to deal with him 6-26-1765
Sarah [Mabbett] ack mo 9-29-1756
Susanna [Mabbett], dt Joseph & Hannah, b 1 Mo (Mar) 17, 1722/3; m 1751 Francis NASH

MALONE
Lizzie J. m Leonard FROST

MANNING
Catharine m Edward S. TITUS

MARSH
Almira Lora, dt Chester S. & Sara S., b Clymer, N.Y. 10-21-1875; recrq 11-16-1913
Mary E. d ae 74y 7m 11d (Wby Stone)

MARSHALL
Annie, dt Joseph & Phebe, Nantucket; m Wm. JOHNSON

MARTIN
Josephine, dt John P. & Bertha J., b Concordville, Pa. 3-12-1906; m 1935 Robert METON

MATHER
Allan Stewart, s Wm., dec, & Margaret, Banff, Alberta; m 10-19-1931 at Wby, Ruth CARPENTER, dt Richard E. & Florence, b 11-7-1907 d Banff, Alberta, 5-27-1932

MATHEWS
Eunice ack mo 6-25-1777

MATZ
Frieda, dt Jno. Henry Falk & Augusta (Erickson), b G.C. 3-25-1897; m 1925 Charles P. VALENTINE

MAYHEW
Charles m Mary Ann ----- b 3-1-1814 d 4-6-1889 (Wby Stone)
Jonah W. & Ellen E.
Ch: Infant s d 5-6-1868 ae 3d (Wby Stone)

MELTON
Robert, s George A. & Caroline R., Bkn.; m East Williston, 6-15-1935 by Tallman C. Bookhout, Josephine MARTIN, dt John P. & Bertha J., b Concordville, Pa. 3-12-1906

MERRITT
Jane, dt John & Sarah Ann, b 4-27-1810; m 1829 Daniel F. COCK
Jesse, s Nathaniel & Anne; m 5-6-1789 at Beth, Mary CORNELIUS, dt John & Mary
John gct Pur 8-25-1784 (clear)
Letitia d 4-15-1884; m Wm. B. MOTT
Mary A., dt Jesse & Mary b 1-2-1799; m 1826 Whitehead HICKS
Phebe A., dt Benj. A. & Hannah E., b Pinelawn,

MERRITT, Phebe A., continued
L. I. 10-30-1880; m 1909 Grove G. THOMPSON
Violet m Eastman LESTER

MILLER
Ezekiel H., s Richard & Sarah A., b 9-11-1837 d 4-24-1910; m 7-20-1901 Henrietta WEEKS, dt Edward L. & Hannah FROST, b 10-4-1842 d 9-7-1929 (Bibles)
Farrand Rogers, s Wilhelm & Mary R., b Elizabeth, N. J., 3-12-1909; m 8-22-1930 Gwendolyn STEWART, nm
Ruth Rogers, dt Wilhelm & Mary R., b N.Y.C. 4-29-1903; m 1926 Dr. Leonard Ramsey THOMPSON
Wilhelm, s Albert & Olive T., b Duane, Va. 11-14-1909 d 3-16-1938 Los Angeles; m Mary ROGERS, dt Daniel & Ruth (Ferrand), b Adel, Iowa 4-22-1868
Ch: Ruth Rogers b N.Y.C. 4-29-1903
Ferrand Rogers b Eliz., N.J. 3-12-1909
All recrq 11-17-1912; mother & ch took cert to Orange Grove, Calif. 12-19-1920; Wilhelm changed his name to William Tyler Miller in 1919; he resigned 1-1918

MITCHELL
Elizabeth m 1812 Daniel ROBBINS
James, s Robert & Mary (Latham); m Mary FROST, dt Daniel & Sarah (Cock)(James d 9-18-1835 ae 75 bur Man)
Ch: (7)
Latham, s Robert & Hannah, d 1844; m Sarah T. ----- d 10-31-1813
Ch: Gordon d 11-30-1841 (infant s)
(Man. Stones)
Miriam b 3-2-1782 d 7-29-1867
Priscilla, dt Robert & -----; m abt 1795 Aspinwall CORNWALL
Robert, s Robert & Hannah, b 6 July 1732 d 7-12-1789; m 6-22-1759 Mary LATHAM, dt William & Amy, b 1739 d 10-4-1806 (mo)
Ch: Latham
James
Jane
Priscilla
Mary ack mo 3-25-1761; Jane & Priscilla both m Aspinwall CORNWALL
(Bibles)
William, s Robert & Hannah, Cow Neck; m 1755 Sarah LATHAM, dt William b 1731 d 12-17-1824 ae nearly 90y bur Man. (mo)
Ch: Charles m Eliz. THORNE
William (unm)
Sarah ack mo 5-8-1755
(Bibles)
----- m William P. WILLETS

MOLLER
Sidney R., Hemp., s Olaf & Caroline, Christiana, Norway, b Chicago 1880; recrq 4-20-1930

MOLLINEUX
Benjamin H. d 7-8-1887 ae 78y 7m 9d; m Mary ----- d 9-11-1875 ae 59y 5m (Wby Stones)
Henry m Martha ----- d 8-8-1884 ae 75y 8m 18d (Wby Stone)
J. d 3-9-1842 ae 66y (unidentified stone, Wby)
Jesse, Wby, m Phebe ----- d 8-24-1856 ae 83
Ch: Sarah d 11-3-1815 ae 16y 18d
Irwin W. d 3-28-1898 ae 12y 1m 22d
Johnnie " 8-20-1879 ae 1m
Libbie d 8-19-1877 ae 6m
(Wby Stones)
John J. d 3-30-1882 ae 51y 2m 27d; m Lydia L. ----- d 12-28-1870 ae 32y 5m 10d
Ch: Edgar d 3-10-1862 ae 5m 15d
Albert d 4-14-1855 ae 16y 8m
Martin d 4-14-1855 ae 16y 8m (unidentified stone Wby)
Phebe, dt Horsman, d 1-30-1850 ae 80y (Wby stone has 1-30-1851 ae 80)
R. d 2-23-1842 ae 11y (unidentified stone, Wby)
-----, nm, m Martha POST, d 8-7-1875 ae 75 (mo before 4-16-1834 & dis)

MOORE
Joseph d 8-15-1871 ae 81y 6m 3d; m Deborah ----- d 7-28-1865 ae 60 (Wby Stone) (perhaps w of Joseph, stone nearby his)
Samuel M. d 8-28-1863 ae 25y 15d (Wby Stone)

MOREE
Abigail dis mo 8-26-1778

MORGAN
Eleanor, dt Floyd S. & Eleanor, b Chicago, 7-16-1895; m 1917 Wm. Walter TIMMIS

MORRELL
Elizabeth b 1795; m Benjamin HICKS
Phebe b 1801 d 6-1-1886 (Wby Stone)
Rebecca, dt Philip; m Benjamin POST

MORRIS
Jacob d 12-22-1812 ae 20y (Wby Stone)

MOTT
Adam, s Adam & Phebe, Cow Neck, b 10 Mo (Dec), 10, 1734 d 12-18-1790; m 3-5-1755 Sarah WILLIS, dt Samuel & Mary, b 7 Mo (Sept) 14, 1736 d 1-10-1783 in 47th yr
Ch: Elizabeth b 7-19-1756 d 4-10-1782
Unnamed dt b 10-18-1758 d in 3 d
Lydia b 11-24-1759
Adam " 10-11-1762
Samuel b 9-29-1773
Adam m 2d 1-5-1785 Abigail BATFY, dt David, of Hemp., b 1733 d 2-10-1807
(Bibles)
Adam, s Adam & Sarah, b 10-11-1762 d 1-10-1839; m 5-19-1785 Ann MOTT, dt James & Mary, b 7-31-1768 d 8-5-1852
Ch: Mary b 4-14-1786 d 2-16-1792
James b 6-20-1788

MOTT, Adam & Ann, continued
Ch: Sarah b 4- 6-1791
Mary U. b 2-28-1793
Abigail b 8- 6-1795
Thomas U. b 2-19-1798 d 7-1-1801
Richard b 1804
ct Purchase 4-27-1785 (clear)
(Bibles)
Adam, s Henry & Temperance, N. Hemp., b 6-14-1813 d 5-20-1881; m 5-24-1837 at Wby, Mary J. POWELL, dt John W. & Sarah, dec, N. Hemp., b 1814 d 7-22-1877 (both bur Man.)
Ch: Lucretia b 6- 3-1838
Elizabeth B. b 12-2-1843 d 1843
Henry B. b 8-14-1849 d 12-10-1849
Adam m 2d Margaret TINUCANE
Ch: George b 6- 3-1880
(Bibles)
Amy, dt Jacob & Kezia, b 10-26-1765; m 1787 ----- WIGGINS (mo)
Amy Ann d 1846 ae 1y 9m (Unidentified stone, Wby)
Ann, dt James & Mary, b 7-31-1768; m 1785 Adam MOTT
Benjamin, s Henry & Temperance, b 12-9-1814 d 4-16-1891 ae 76y 4m; m 12-9-1842 Eliza A. SECOR, d 12-31-1900 ae 83
ct Purchase 9-14-1842 (clear)
(Man. Stones & Bibles)
Caroline, dt Thomas & Martha W.; m 1898 Francis THAYER
Catharine d 5-24-1878 in 37th yr bur Man.
Daniel, Cow Neck, s Stephen; m 5-4-1786 Amy SEARING, dt John & Mary, Searingtown, O.B., b 2-23-1768
Ch: Phebe b 6- 8-1787 d 7-6-1788
Stephen b 8- 6-1789
Mary " 8-30-1791
John " 8-27-1793
Jane " 10-17-1796
Joseph " 11- 9-1798
Isaac " 4- 2-1801
Abigail " 1-29-1803
Phebe " 5-12-1805
Edmund, s Richbell & Elizabeth, Cow Neck, b abt 1700 d 1744; m 2 Mo (Apr) 2, 1726 at Cow Neck, Katharine SANDS, dt John & Sybil, Cow Neck, b 1700
Ch: Richbell b 6 Mo (Aug) 3, 1728
Edmund b 8 Mo (Oct) 25, 1730
John b 8 Mo (Oct) 1, 1732 d 1-22-1781
Margaret d young
Edmund, father or s, dis 2-28-1759; had brought cf Westchester Co.
(Bibles)
Edward K., s Jacob & Hannah, b 7-1-1823 d 8-12-1878; m before 4-15-1846, Mary NORTON, dt George, b 10-13-1823 d 7-30-1886 (mo & retained)
(Bibles)
Elizabeth, dt Adam & Elizabeth, b 3 Mo (May), 31, 1734; m 1755 John WILLIS
Elizabeth, dt William; m 1773 David UNDERHILL
Hannah, dt William & Hannah; m 1731 Philip PELL
Hannah m 1736 Benjamin -----
Henry, (prob) s John & Sarah, Rockaway, d (will 1767-1768); m -----
Ch: (9)
Not a mbr but cloaked himself as one
Henry, s William & Elizabeth, Hemp., b 5-31-1757; m 1 (or 4) 1, 1783 at Wby, Jane WAY, dt Samuel & Esther, Hemp., b 5-8-1761
Henry, s Stephen & Mary, Cow Neck, b 7-17-1782 d 8-17-1851 ae 69y 6m bur Man.; m 8-29-1811 at Cow Neck, Temperance HICKS, dt Benj. & Mary, Great Neck, b 4-25-1785 d 10-23-1843 ae 57y
Ch: Adam b 6-14-1813
Benjamin b 12- 9-1814
Elizabeth b 7-3-1820
Jacob, a carpenter, s John, dec, & Rebecca, Beth Hemp.; m 11-6-1754 at Wby, Kezia SEAMAN, dt Nathaniel & Sarah
Ch: Jacob b 8- 1-1755
Rachel b 5-11-1757
Phebe b 3- 4-1760
Samuel b 4-16-1762
Amy b 11-26-1765
Jacob, s Jacob & Kezia, Merchant, N.Y.C., b 8-1-1755 d 1-8-1820; m before 1-28-1784, ----- (mo)
Ch: Catherine m ----- FERRIS
Gulielma M. m ----- CRADY
dis mo 2-25-1784
(Bibles)
Jacob T. d 1844 ae 2y (unidentified stone, Wby)
James, s Richard, dec, & Sarah (now Sarah ALSOP) O.B.; m 1-5-1765 at Mk, Mary UNDERHILL, dt Samuel & Ann, O.B.
James, s Richard & Phebe (Smith), Wby, d 4-17-1856 ae 88y 6d; m Amy POWELL, dt Solomon & Jerusha (Hinton)
Ch: Stephen m Sarah FROST
James m Eliz. KIRBY
Phebe d 4-4-1862 bur Man. (unm)
Amy d 8-31-1888 ae 86y 11m 24d bur Man.
Jerusha m Ellison CROMWELL
Ann m Godfrey HAINES
Richard (unm)
James, s James & Amy, b 1813 d 3-13-1889 ae 78; m Elizabeth KIRBY, dt Jacob & Mary (Seaman) b 6-20-1814 d 3-10-1900 ae 87
Ch: William K. b 12-30-1839
J. Cromwell b 5-3-1837
4 others d unm
cf Jericho
(Wby Stones & Bibles)
James Jr. ack mo 5 Mo (July) 26, 1749
Jane, dt Jos. & Miriam, S.J.; m abt 1710 Benjamin SEAMAN
Jehu, s John & Rebecca, b 9-26-1723 d 9-30-1782; m 1748 Ruth POWELL, dt Thomas & Abigail, b 3-3-1731 (cert not recorded, m between 8 Mo 26 & 9 Mo-(Nov) 30, 1748)
Ch: (7)
Mary b 11-30-1752; m Benj. HICKS

MOTT, Jehu & Ruth, continued
Ch: Joseph b 5-14-1769 d 3-15-1842 ae 70
ack 2-23-1762 bearing arms when very young
J. Cromwell, s James & Elizabeth, b 5-3-1837
d 7-12-1887 ae 50y 2m 9d; m Hannah M. -----
d 7-12-1890 ae 50y 11m 17d
(Wby Stones)
John, s John & Sarah; m abt 1712 Rebecca -----
Ch: (9)
Jacob m Kezia SEAMAN
ack mo 6 Mo (Aug) 25, 1714
(Bibles)
John, s James, Rockaway; m 1751 Mary TITUS
(cert not recorded, m between 7 Mo 25 &
8 Mo (Oct) 30)
John dis mo before 7-30-1783
Leonard, s Samuel & Catharine, Cow Neck, b 5-11-1799 d 9-27-1866 in 68th yr; m 10-30-1823 at Cow Neck, Hannah C. WILLIS, dt Cornell & Elizabeth, Cow Neck, b 8-23-1805 d 2-4-1884 ae 78y
Ch: Edward b 10-20-1824; dis [20
Samuel Cornell b 6-16-1830 d 9-25-1850 ae
Sarah A. b 7-31-1832
Mary Elizabeth b 6-18-1835 [Valley
Catharine A. b 7-7-1841 d 2-10-1916 Locust
Anna b 11-20-1845
Samuel C. b 3-17-1852 d 5-19-1884
All bur Man.
Lucretia, dt Adam & Mary J.; m John Henry BURTIS
Lydia, dt Adam & Sarah, b 11-24-1759; m 1780 Solomon UNDERHILL
Lydia, dt Stephen & Sarah, b 7-29-1821; m ----- PERRY; m 2d 1860 Wm. M. VALENTINE
Martha W. b 4-5-1873; m 1897 Alfred VALENTINE FRASER
Mary, dt James; m 1744 Jacob RUSHMORE
Mary gct Purchase 12 Mo (Feb) 27, 1750/1
Mary, dt John & Ruth; m 1774 Benjamin HICKS
Mary d 10-7-1875 ae 81y 2m 13d (unidentified stone, Wby)
Mary W. d 9-14-1881 in 65th yr bur Man.
Micajah m 1759 Rachel SEAMAN (cert not recorded, m between 11-28 & 12-26-1759)
Ch: Sarah
Oliver d 5-22-1883 ae 91y 4m 28d; m Martha ----- d 6-2-1872 ae 76y 6m 25d
(Wby Stones)
Phebe (prob) dt Jacob & Kezia, b (prob) 3-4-1766; m 1787 ----- VAN NOSTRAND
Rachel m ----- GROFF (mo 1818)
Rachel, dt Jacob & Kezia, b 5-11-1757; m 1782 ----- HOOTON
(dis mo 5-29-1782)
Rebecca mo before 2-27-1760
Rebecca, dt Micajah, m ----- CARPENTER (mo) dis mo 5-29-1782
Richard, s Adam & Elizabeth, N.Y.C., late Hemp. b 1710 d 8 Mo (Oct) 15, 1743; m 1 Mo (Mar) 26, 1741 at Wby Sarah PEARSALL, dt Thomas & Sarah, Hemp.
Ch: James b 8 Mo (Oct) 8, 1742
Sarah m 2d 1747 Richard ALSOP Jr.
Richard, s Samuel & Hannah (Wood), b 5 Mo (July) 1, 1738 d 9-2-1775; m Phebe SMITH, d 1815 ae 69y 6m 5d
Ch: (3)
Richbell, s Adam & Elizabeth (Mott), b abt 1710; m per m bond dtd 1 June 1736 Mary SEAMAN, dt Richard Jr. & Sarah (Frost) (mo)
Ch: Richbell (minor 1777)
Mary ack mo 6-8-1761
(Seaman gen.)
Robert, s James & Sarah b 1796 (drowned); m before 3-14-1823 Ann KIRBY, dt Joseph & Anna, d abt 1862 (mo)
Ch: (2)
Joseph K.
Phebe A. b 1827
Ann mo before 3-14-1823; dis next mo
(Bibles)
Samuel, s (possibly) of John & Rebecca, b 12 Jan. 1712 d 4-7-1780; m 9 Dec. 1734 in St. George's Ch., Hemp., Hannah WOOD b 3 Mar. 1712 d 7-29-1800
ack mo 6-25-1755
(Bibles)
Samuel, s (possibly) of Henry & Mary, b 1-30-1768 d 10-14-1842; m before 8-29-1787 Merribeth RICKETSON, b 8-17-1771 d 1-10-1843 (mo)
Ch: (7)
ack mo 12-26-1787
(Bibles)
Samuel W., s Adam & Sarah, b 9-29-1773 d 5-16-1864; m 9-11-1796 Catharine APPLEBY, dt Thomas & Sarah, b 9-17-1775 d 4-8-1862 (mo)
Ch: (5)
Leonard b 5-11-1799
Sarah " 9-19-1804
Silas " 4- 4-1807
Samuel dis mo 11m 1796; rst 10-15-1800
Thomas d 6-27-1860 ae 59y 1d, a merchant in N. Y.
(Bibles)
Sarah, wd Richard; m 1747 Richard ALSOP, Jr.
Sarah m 1748 Benjamin HULIE
Sarah, dt Samuel & Martha, b 27 Apr 1731; m abt 1750 Stephen TITUS
Sarah, dt Micajah & Rachel; m 1780 Stephen BAKER
Sarah A., dt Samuel & Catharine; m 1822 Benj. H. WILLIS
Sarah A., dt Leonard & Hannah, b 7-31-1832; m Willet HICKS
Stephen, s Adam, dec, & Phebe, Cow Neck, b 2 Mo (Apr) 1, 1736 d 11-11-1813; m 10-6-1762 at Wby, Amy WILLIS, dt Samuel & Mary, Jericho, b 3 Mo (May) 27, 1738 d 11-10-1822
Ch: Daniel b 10-10-1763
Phebe " 6- 1-1766 d 10-26-1776
Mary " 9-19-1768 d 3-15-1792
Jane " 2- 5-1771 d 5-23-1794
Abigail b 9-12-1773 d 2-14-1795

MOTT, Stephen & Amy, continued
Ch: Stephen b 11-29-1779 d 2-25-1781
Henry " 7-17-1782
Stephen, s James & Amy, Wby, Wheatley & Roslyn, d 9-23-1873 in 81st yr., Wheatley; m 6-21-1815 at Wby, Sarah FROST, dt Charles & Mary, d 1-20-1864 ae 71
Ch: Mary b 8-13-1817
Lydia b 7-29-1821
Valentine b 3- 1-1824
cf N. Y. 1838; both bur Wby
Smith (unidentified stone, Wby, sunken in ground)
Thomas, s Samuel & Catharine, Manhasset, d 6-27-1860 ae 59y 1d
Thomas, s Silas & Mary W., N. Hemp.; m 12-1-1869 at Edmund Willets', Martha WILLETS, dt Edmund & Martha, Manhasset, b 5-7-1841 d 2-15-1916
William Sr., s Adam & Elizabeth, Great Neck, b 20 Jan. 1674 d 6 Mo (Aug) 31, 1740; m 2 Mo (Apr) 12, 1705 Hannah FERRIS, dt John & Mary (Jackson), b 5-3-1679 d 6-24-1759
Ch: William b 6 Mo 6, 1709 d 3-23-1786
Hannah m Philip PELL
Elizabeth
Martha
William signed epistle abt 1725
(Bibles)
William, s William & Hannah, Great Neck, b 6 Mo (Aug) 6, 1709 d 3-23-1786; m 6 Mo (Aug) 18, 1742, Elizabeth ALLEN, dt Henry & Mary, b 2 Mo (Apr) 28, 1724 d 1780
Ch: William b 1 Mo (Mar) 8, 1742/3
Hannah b 6 Mo (Aug) 4, 1744 d 3 Mo 15, 1750
James b 8 Mo (Oct) 29, 1745
Elizabeth b 2 Mo (Apr) 5, 1747
John b 2 Mo (Apr) 17, 1749 d 3 Mo 7, 1750
Samuel b 12 Mo (Feb) 16, 1750/1
Hannah b 4- 4-1753
John b 6-24-1755
Henry b 5-31-1757
Richard b 8-20-1759
Joseph b 1-11-1762
Benjamin b 3-19-1765
William ack mo 11 Mo (Jan) 25, 1743/4
William, s James & Jane (Burling), Mamaroneck; m 12 Mo (Feb) 7, 1749/50 at Wby, Mary SEAMAN, dt Richard, dec, & Jane, Hemp.
William B., s (prob) Wm. B. & Mary; m Letitia MERRITT, d 4-15-1884
(Wby Stones, Wm.'s sunk below ground)
Bibles
Wm. Kirby, s James & Elizabeth K., b 12-30-1839; m Sarah ALBERTSON, dt Hicks & Elizabeth, b 4-29-1842 d 12-19-1916 (wd)
Ch: S. Louisa b 6-12-1879
Bennie H. d 10-11-1889 ae 19y 10m 13d (Wby Stone)
Sarah recrq 6-16-1912
----- & Jerusha
Jerusha ack mo
----- m Lydia TOWNSEND, dt Obadiah & Thomas, d 11-19-1879 ae 74 (Wby Stone)

MUDGE
Amy, dt Daniel & Martha, b 12-15-1790 d 3-3-1873 ae 82 (unm) (Wby Stone) (Bibles)
Elizabeth b 11-25-1816; m John T. VALENTINE
Elizabeth d 4-10-1860 ae 81y 8m
Elizabeth, dt Michael & Sarah; m Peter TITUS
Jacob, s Coles & Dorothy, Mk. & G. C., b 1757 d 1-2-1846 ae 88y; m Elizabeth BAKER
Jacob m 2d 8-1-1810 at Wby, Hannah TITUS, dt Samuel, dec, & Abigail, N. Hemp., b 2-10-1781 d 2-22-1866 ae 85y 8m
Ch: William b 8-17-1812; m Martha WILLETS
Elizabeth b 11-25-1816; m John T. VALENTINE
(Mk Stones & Bibles)
Jane, dt Coles & Dorothy; m 1800 Jacob COLES
Michael, s William & Ann (Coles), b 8 Mo (Oct) 3, 1713 d 12-28-1801; m 10 Mo (Dec) 25, 1736 Sarah HOPKINS, dt Daniel & Amy, b 12 Mo (Feb) 2, 1719/20 d 3-11-1815 ae 95y 3m 9d
Ch: (4)
Elizabeth m Peter TITUS
(Bibles)
Sterling W., s Wm. J. & Irene S., b G.C. 1-13-1892; m Alice G. ----- b Elmira, N. Y.
Ch: William S. b 10-12-1913
Wm. S. recrq 2-20-1938; Alice recrq 2-20-1938
William d 4-18-1825 ae near 87y
William, Glen Cove, b 8-17-1812 d 12-18-1890 ae 78y 4m 6d; m before 6-15-1842 Martha T. WILLITS, dt Richard & Mary T., b 1-16-1819 d 1-1-1872 ae 52y 11m 19d (mo)
Ch: William J. b 10- 4-1854
Henry W. " 9-14-1857 d 1-19-1898
William retained mbrp; parents bur Mk
William J. b 10- 4-1854 d 4-2-1926 G.C.; m Irene STRINGHAM, dt John & Annie E., b Crum Elbow, Dutchess Co. 10-9-1862
Ch: Sterling W. b G.C. 1-13-1892
Irene recrq 8-20-1911
William S., s Sterling W. & Alice G., b 10-12-1913; m Etra, N. Y. 5-18-1935 Melisande DELBON, dt Ange, of Marseiles, France, & Argia D., b Bolognia, Italy, b Elmhirst, L. I. 9-28-1914
Ch: Todd Wm. b 5-9-1938

MUNSON
Levi, nm, s Levi & Rachel (Crasto), nm, b 2-16-1839 d 6-29-1924; m Catharine FROST, b 8-5-1842 d 8-15-1905
Ch: (8)
Frances H. d 9-17-1868 ae 6m 28d
Kate " 5-26-1890 ae 17y 5m 23d
Mary b 4-13-1875 Wby
Francis S. b 3-9-1882
Mary admitted a mbr 12-14-1910
(Wby Stones)

NASH
Francis m 1751 (cert not recorded, m between 2 Mo 24 & 3 Mo (May) 29, Susanna MABBETT, dt Joseph & Hannah, b 1 Mo (Mar) 17, 1722/23
cf Flushing (clear); Susannah took cert there 1751; both rocf Flushing 2-28-1753

NEITZKE
Martha S., dt Jas. Harvey & Mary Emily BEACH, b Pratt, Kan. 4-6-1904; recrq 11-21-1926; ct Boston MM 12-21-1930

NELSON
Ann, dt Thomas & Catharine, b 10-17-1816; m Jehoiakiam CAMPBELL
Ezra b 12-6-1825 d 11-22-190- (figure lost from Wby Stone)
Thomas, Hemp. & Catharine
Ch: Henry E. d 8-21-1842 ae 19y
Ann b 10-17-1816; m J. CAMPBELL
Thomas, Hemp., d 7-28-1860 ae 74; m Lucy ----- d 4-26-1862 ae 67
Ch: Lydia d 4-18-1849 ae 17y
Phebe d 5-17-1849 ae 15y

NEWTON
Infant b 2-17-1885 d 2-19-1885 (unidentified stone Wby)
Infant b 1-28-1887 d 1-29-1887 (unidentified stone Wby)

NICHOLS
Jonathan m Elizabeth ----- d 6-14-1891 ae 49y 11m 15d (Wby Stone)
Thomas rocf Flushing 7 Mo (Sept) 28, 1715 (rem cert)
William d 7-15-1896 ae 28y 4m 15d

NOBLE
Evelyn b Syracuse, N. Y.; m Neil Campbell STEVENS

NORTON
Maria A., dt Anson & Almena, b 11-1-1835; m Wm. H. COLES
Mary, dt George, b 10-13-1823; m 1846 Edward K. MOTT

NOSTRAND
Jacob T. d 8-17-1854 ae 38y 2m; m Sarah Ann ----- d 3-21-1867 ae 49y 9m 19d (Mk Stone) (See Van Nostrand)

NUTT
Sarah, Cedar Seamp, d 6-25-1861 ae abt 72 yr bur Mk
cf N. Y. 1855

OAKLEY
Henry, nm, m 4-28-1779 Wby, Hannah SEAMAN, dt Giles & Letitia, b 1747
Hannah ack misconduct 1-26-1780
Nathaniel, s James, d Cow Neck 12-7-1811 ae 76

OGILSBY
Patrick & Rebecca
cert signed for him 12 Mo (Feb) 26, 1734/5; cert rec by women for Patrick & Rebecca [Oglesby] 8 Mo (Oct) 27, 1736, place not stated; cert for both to North Wales, Pa. 1 Mo (Mar) 28, 1739

OLNEY
Lafayette m Elizabeth HOPKINS, dt Edwin & Mary H.
Elizabeth m 2d Edw. E. FORBES

OSBORNE
Richard m 1698/9 Jane BATES (or BETTS)
ct Crosswicks, N. J. for both 3 Mo (May) 28, 1707

PAGE
Wilson M., s Pelatiah P. & Amelia, Somers, N. Y.; m 12-15-1859 at Townsend Rushmore's, Rachel W. RUSHMORE, dt Townsend & Amy, b 3-16-1830 d 2-7-1861 ae 31 bur Wby
cf N. Y. for Wilson M. 10-20-1858 (O)

PALMER
Elizabeth, dt Solomon & Sarah; m 1761 Richard TITUS (2nd w)

PANCOAST
Sallie m abt 1893 Thomas H. COLES

PARKER
Cola Godden, s Geo. S. & Ella M., N.Y.C.; m 11-14-1925 at A. V. Fraser's, Sands Point, Martha FRASER, dt Alfred V. & Martha W. M., N. Hemp.
Ch: Martha b 3-28-1927
Sumner " 3-24-1828
Valentine F. b 2-11-1932
Martha & Sumner recrq 11-16-1930; Valentine recrq 1-20-1935

PARRY
Tacie m Robert R. WILLETS

PARSONS
James, s James & Jane (both dec), N. Y. City; m 11-1-1780 at Wby Jane WILLIE, dt Samuel & Mary, Jericho, b 11 Mo (Jan) 7, 1740/1

PATTERSON
Harold Truesdell, s Capt. Alfred, dec, & Sarah F., Wby; m 7-26-1905 at Edw. Hicks', Emily HICKS, dt Edward & Emma E., Wby
Emily resigned 10-20-1912

PAXSON
Walter P., s Joshua & Anna (Cutler), b Montgomery Co., Pa. 1890; m 11-20-1915 at

PAXSON, Walter P., continued
Landsdown, Pa., Ruth CHANDLEE, dt Webster & Emily (Jackson), b Richmond, Ind. 1891
Ch: Margaret Chandlee b Pa. 1916
Miriam Louise b Pa. 1917
Richard Chandlee b Phila. Co. 1923

PEARCE (or PIERCE)
Elizabeth, dt James & Elizabeth; m 1760 at Chappaqua Clark COCK

PEARSALL
Ann, dt Henry, b 2 Mo (Apr) 4, 1722; m 1741 Silas WILLIS; m 2d 1754 Matthew PRIOR
Daniel mo before 4-13-1814 & dis next mo
Hannah, dt Thomas & Sarah; m 1746 Benjamin HAWXHURST
Henry, s Thomas & Mary, Beth. Hemp., b 1689/90 d 12 Mo (Feb) 10, 1749/50 ae 60; m 11 Mo (Jan) 15, 1717/18 at Wby Mary TITUS, dt John & Sarah, Hemp., b 4 Mo (June) 13, 1696
Ch: (5)
signed Epistle abt 1725; ct Egg Harbor, N. J. for both 2 Mo (Apr) 29, 1741; ch are grown and orderly (Bibles)
Henry, s Rowland & Anne, b 8 Mo (Oct) 25, 1751 d 2-28-1786; m 1-5-1780 at Wby, Abigail POST, dt John & Phebe, Hemp.
ack 10-27-1779 taking arms & going with Militia Captain and others in pursuit of robbers (Bibles)
Martha m 1717 Henry COCK
Mary, dt Thomas & Sarah; m 1754 Obediah SEAMAN
Nathaniel, s Henry & Anne, Hemp.; m 1674 Martha SEAMAN, dt John, d 7 Mo (Sept) 6, 1712
Ch: Nathaniel b 11 Mo (Jan) 27, 1676/7 d 11 Mo 30, 1694
Thomas b 4 Mo (June) 18, 1679
Martha " 10 Mo (Dec) 10, 1681
Hannah b 1 Mo (Mar) 22, 1683/4 d 4 Mo 20, 1689
Sarah b 5 Mo (July) 1, 1686
Elizabeth b 8 Mo (Oct) 28, 1688
Hannah b 12 Mo (Feb) 14, 1690/1 d 11 Mo 31, 1718/19
Phebe b 10 Mo (Dec) 20, 1693 d 1 Mo 14, 1702/3
Samuel b 12 Mo (Feb) 18, 1695/6 d 12 Mo 4, 1720/1
Nathaniel b 7 Mo (Sept) 11, 1699 d 4 Mo 17, 1701
Mary b 2 Mo (Apr) 30, 1703
Martha ack aiding dt to mo 1708; Thos. on comm. 1698
Nathaniel, s Thomas & Sarah, Hemp. Harbor; m 9 Mo (Nov) 13, 1735 at Cow Neck, Mary LATHAM, dt Joseph & Jane, Cow Neck (Nathaniel b 7 Mo (Sept) 2, 1712 d 2-23-1758)
Ch: Sarah b 5 Mo (July) 10, 1737
Joseph " 6 Mo (Aug) 10, 1740
Jane " 8 Mo (Oct) 1, 1742
Thomas " 9 Mo (Nov) 13, 1744
Ch: Mary b 1 Mo (Mar) 21, 1746/7
Hannah b 8 Mo (Oct) 5, 1749
Robert b 3-12-1752
Phebe spoken to re keeping company with Benjamin Hicks 1 Mo 28, 1739; she had expectation of being m among Friends, was occasion of keeping him company
Phebe gct Little Egg Harbor 7 Mo (Sept) 30, 1741
Rachel ack several missteps 3 Mo (May) 27, 1747
Rachel, dt Thomas & Ann, b 6 Mo (Aug) 31, 1745; m 1785 Samuel WILLIS
Rowland, s Henry, Beth.; m 8 Mo (Oct) 5, 1748 at Beth, Anne (or Anna) POWELL, dt Wait Jr.
Ch: Jane b 7 Mo (Sept) 16, 1749
Henry b 8 Mo (Oct) 25, 1751
Mary b 6-30-1755
Phebe b 3-22-1757
William b 9-12-1759
Amy " 10-21-1761
Silas " 4-17-1764
Thomas " 9-17-1766
Wait " 2-17-1770
Samuel, s Nath. & Martha, b 1695 d 1720; left legacy of £40 to Wby Mtg
Samuel C. & Eliza A.
both rocf Oswego 1838; both gct Oswego 1-1880
Sarah m 1707 Thomas TOWNSEND
Sarah m 1722 John TITUS
Sarah m 1741 Richard MOTT
some Sarah Pearsall signed Epistle abt 1725; Sarah m 2d 1747 Richard ALSOP, Jr.
Silas mo before 10-26-1785 & dis next mo
Thomas, s Nathaniel & Martha, Hemp. Harbor, b 4 Mo (June) 18, 1679 d 12-29-1759; m 9 Mo (Nov) 25, 1708 Sarah UNDERHILL, dt John & Mary, b Mk. 6 Mo (Aug) 17, 1687 d 9-30-1768
Ch: Infant stillborn 6 Mo 29, 1709
Thomas b 6 Mo (Aug) 18, 1710
Nathaniel b 7 Mo (Sept) 2, 1712
Sarah b 11 Mo (Jan) 6, 1714/15
Phebe b 1 Mo (Mar) 7, 1716/17
Martha b 5 Mo (July) 9, 1719 d 12 Mo 16, 1721/2
Hannah b 10 Mo (Dec) 17, 1721
Samuel b 9 Mo (Nov) 16, 1724
Mary b 5 Mo (July) 24, 1727
appointed clerk of MM 3 Mo (May) 26, 1736, former clerk being dead
Thomas, s Thomas & Sarah, b 6 Mo (Aug) 18, 1710; m Ann -----
Ch: Israel b 9 Mo (Nov) 27, 1733
Thomas b 6 Mo (Aug) 20, 1735
Nathaniel b 12 Mo (Feb) 22, 1737/8 d 8 Mo 26, 1757
Mary b 1 Mo (Mar) 29, 1742
Martha b 9 Mo (Nov) 23, 1743
Rachel b 6 Mo (Aug) 31, 1745; m Samuel WILLIS
Thomas ack m b J.P. 12 Mo (Feb) 22, 1748/9
Thomas, s Henry, ack misconduct 12 Mo (Feb)

PEARSALL, continued
22, 1748/9
Thomas, Beth.; m 1763 (cert not recorded m bet 4-27 & 5-25-1763) Ann WILLIAMS
Thomas, s Thomas & Ann, Beth, b 6 Mo (Aug) 20, 1735; m Rachel ----- d 9-26-1759
Thomas ack mo
Thomas, nm, s Rowland & Anna, b 9-17-1766 d 8-21-1848 in 82d yr bur Mk; m before 12-17-1806 Elizabeth COCK, dt Samuel & Jemima, b 2-27-1768 d 7-11-1859 in 92d yr (mo)
Ch: (2)
mo before 12-17-1806, dis next mo; Thomas rst 1814
Cox Gen.
Thomas, s Rowland & Anna, Mk, b 9-17-1766 d 8-16-1848 ae 81y 11m bur Mk; m Freelove -----
Thomas & -----
Ch: Mary d 1-20-1824 ae 82y 2m

PEASER
William R. d 1-3-1890 ae 63y 9m (Wby Stone)

PEASLEE (or PEASELY)
Jonathan, form of Bucks Co., Pa.; m 8 Mo (Oct) 7, 1731 at Cow Neck, Rachel PINE, wd Samuel of Hempstead Harbor.
cert from Bristol, Eng. & Buckingham, Pa. for Jonathan (clear); Rachel gct Purchase 12 Mo (Feb) 23, 1731/2

PELL
Benjamin, s Joshua & Phebe; m 2-25-1795 at Wby Mary TITUS, dt William & Sarah, dec, Wby
cf N. Y. (clear)
Philip, s Thomas & Ann, Pelham, N. Y.; m 3 Mo (May) 5, 1731 at Wby, Hannah MOTT, dt William
Ch: (probably 6)
cf Purchase for Philip (clear)

PERRIN
Josephine L., dt Jathniel & Lucy W.; m 1873 Marshall S. FROST

PERRY
Lydia, dt ----- MOTT; m 2d 1860 Wm. M. VALENTINE
cf N. Y. 1858

PETERS
James mo before 2-17-1808, dis next mo
Mary, dt Dr. Chas. & Mary; m 1736 Richard TITUS

PETTIT
Ferdinand G. d 8-9-1866 ae 50y 4m 25d (Wby Stone)
Mott d 7-1-1865 (Wby Stone 6-30-1865) ae 81y 5m 2d; m Mary ----- d 3-10-1869 ae 79y 10m 18d (Wby Stone)
Mott recrq 9-1838; Mary recrq

PHILLIPS
Sarah H., dt Robert H. & Mary HAYDOCK, d 10-29-1896 bur Man.

PILLING
Elizabeth, dt Simeon & Katharine; m 1919 Gulian LANSING
Katharine Valine, dt Chas. B. & Eliz. C. DES JARDINE, b Atteborough, Mass. 10-6-1865; m 1918 Samuel J. SEAMAN
Katharine m 1st Simeon Pilling
Simeon m Katharine V. DES JARDINS, dt Chas. B. & Eliz. C., b Attleborough, Mass. 10-6-1865
Ch: Elizabeth

PINE
Elizabeth, dt James; m 1742 Richard WILLIS
Rachel m 1731 Jonathan PEASLEE
Samuel m 1720 Rachel ZANE
Signed Epistle abt 1725

PINKHAM
Zebulun, Jerusalem; m Amy WILLETS, dt Jonah & Mary, d 7-31-1860 ae 58y 24d

PLATT
Kezia m 1749 Amos WILLETS
William & Charlotte
Ch: Zopha H. d 7-12-1856 ae 8m 4d (Wby Stone)

PLUMMER
Abigail m 1811 John DODGE (Abigail wd of Enoch)
Elizabeth, dt Enoch, rocf Jericho 7-18-1872; gct Jericho 8-15-1877

POLLOCK
Ruth Isabella, dt Jas. R. & Eugenia; m 1931 Edwin Morgan LAPHAM, Jr.

POST
Abigail, dt John & Phebe; m 1780 Henry PEARSALL
Arthur Wood, s John W. & Phebe H., Wby, b Wby 9-27-1886; m 10-29-1913 at J. Aug. Albertson's, Ethel Mary ALBERTSON, dt Jno. Augustus & Mary W., Wby, b 2-16-1890
Ch: Richard b 1-26-1915
Arthur Willis b 5-3-1918
Arthur recrq 4-18-1920; ch rec 3-21-1920
Benjamin, s Michael, Wby, d 5-20-1844 ae 75y; m Rebecca MORRELL (or Morril), dt Philip, d 3----1839 ae 70y
Benjamin mo before 10-16-1839, ret mbrp
Caroline, dt James & Phebe W., b 6-21-1826; m 1847 Daniel UNDERHILL
Catharine, dt James & Phebe W., b 1-19-1833; m 1883 Daniel UNDERHILL
Catharine M, dt Joseph & Mary, b 5-20-1837; m Samuel WILLIS
Charles, s James & Phebe, b 1818 d 6-6-1898 ae 80; m 1844 M. Amelia TOWNSEND, d 12-8-1882 ae 64
Ch: Emily m Wm. M. VALENTINE
(Bibles)

POST, continued
Daniel, s Henry & Mary, b 11-12-1768 d 1833; m before 12-17-1800 Rosetta TITUS, dt Samuel & Abigail, b 2-12-1779 d 1868 (mo)
Ch: Mary T. b 11-16-1801; m Ellwood VALENTINE
William b 9-13-1803; m Esther LAWRENCE
Edward b 6-11-1808; m Eliz. POST
mo before 12-17-1800; dis 2-18-1801; rst 1-16-1806
(Bibles)
Edmund, s Henry & Mary, N. Hemp., Wby, b 3-27-1762 d 6-6-1830; m 3-1-1788 at Wby Catharine WILLITS, dt Joseph & Hannah, dec, N. Hemp., Wby, d 11-7-1844 ae 78y 8m 23d
Ch: Edmund Jr.
Edmund Jr., s Edmund & Catharine, N. Hemp., Wby, d 7-1-1832 ae 39y 8m 26d; m 11-22-1815 at (prob) Mk. Mary R. RUSHMORE, dt Stephen & Phebe, d 5-17-1875 ae 80 bur Wby [(0)
Ch: Henry b 11-21-1816
Robert b 4-24-1821
Lydia b 8-26-1824 d 7-12-1893 ae 68 bur Wby
Stephen b 5-3-1830
Edmund
Edmund, s Edmund, dec, & Mary R., Wby, d 4-29-1875 ae 44; m 5-15-1873 at Mary R. Post's, Lydia TITUS, dt Henry, dec, & Jane C., Wby, d 4-21-1875 ae 39 (0)
Ch: Henry T. d 10-20-1875 ae 6m 15d
Mary R. d 7-26-1902 ae 28y 4m 23d
All bur Wby
Edward, s Daniel, dec, & Rosetta, Flushing, d 11-6-1870 bur Wby, ae 62y 4m 25d; m 5-21-1868 at Joseph Post's, Elizabeth POST, dt Joseph & Mary, b 5-26-1835 d 8-25-1934
Elizabeth m 2d Jedediah HILLER 7-10-1884
Elisha mo before 12-26-1737, dis next mo
Elizabeth ack mo 6-27-1753
Elizabeth, dt Joseph & Mary, b 5-26-1835; m 1868 Edward POST; m 2d 1884 Jedediah HILLER
Eliza Jane b 12-10-1831; m Alfred SPRAGUE
Hannah dis 6-24-1767
Henry, a weaver, s Richard & Mary, Hemp., b 1 Mo (Mar) 8, 1733/4; m 6-3-1761 at Wby Mary TITUS, dt Edmund, dec, & Sarah, O.B., b 7 Mo (Sept) 17, 1740 d 10-13-1823
Ch: Edmund b 3-27-1762
Samuel " 6-21-1765
Daniel " 11-12-1768
Lydia " 4- 1-1772 d 1-28-1773
Henry " 1-11-1774
Sarah
Isaac
James
Henry ack enlisting in the militia 5-21-1759
(Bibles)
Henry R. d 5-25-1904 ae 87y 6m 4d; m Elizabeth C. ----- d 4-23-1879 ae 60 (Wby Stones)(0)
Ch: Stephen R.
John W.
Martha W.
Edmund
Ch: Charles M. d 5-21-1867 ae 14y 6m
William
cf Rahway & Plainfield for all 9-16-1857
Isaac, s Edmund & Catharine; m 2-1-1821 Hannah KIRBY, dt Jacob & Mary, b 5-16-1799
Ch: Mary b 2-20-1823
Isaac gct Jericho 1-22-1821 (clear)
James, s Henry & Mary, Wby, b 1785 d 9-8-1870 ae 85y 8m 5d bur Wby; m 1811 Phebe W. WILLIS, dt Samuel & Rachel, d 3-13-1883 ae 95y 5m 29d bur Wby
Ch: Elizabeth d 6-26-1858 by lightning ae 45y 3m 12d
Sarah b 7-29-1816 (or 1815) d 4-25-1879 ae 63y 8m 26d
Charles b 5-30-1818; resigned 12-27-1879
Rachel b 9-25-1821 d Jericho 11-30-1908
Mary W. b 2- 5-1823 d 4-28-1851
Caroline b 6-24-1826
Esther L. b 10-17-1829
Catharine A. b 1-19-1833
ct Jericho 5-15-1811 (clear)
Jane, dt John & Sarah TITUS; m 1793 Samuel Post; m 2d 1802 Lewis VALENTINE
John, East Meadow in Hemp., ack mo 1 Mo (Mar) 26, 1740; d 12-10-1835 ae 88y 10m 13d
John W. m Phebe HICKS, dt Stephen R. & Hannah U., b 11-25-1852
Ch: Arthur Wood b 9-27-1886
Joseph mo before 10 Mo (Dec) 28, 1737
Joseph, s Edmund & Catharine, b 11-30-1803 d 1-17-1888 (or 1-1-1888) bur Wby; m 1828 Mary W. ROBBINS, dt Willet & Esther, b 11-25-1806 d 10-31-1892 ae 85y 10m 26d
Ch: Elizabeth R. b 5-26-1835
Catharine M. b 5-20-1837
ct Jericho 9-17-1828 (clear); Mary W. rocf Jericho 4-14-1830
(Bibles)
Jotham d 11-30-1870 ae 42y 7m 25d (unidentified Stone, Wby)
Lydia, dt Edmund & Catharine; m 1813 Isaac RUSHMORE
Martha m abt 1775 ----- SALTS
Martha m ----- MOLLINEUX
Mary, dt John & Phebe; m 1780 Wait WILLETS
Mary m 1787 ----- SAXTON (mo)
Mary, dt James & Phebe W., b 5-2-1823; m Elias LEWIS, Jr.
Mary, dt Joseph & Mary, b 5-26-1835; m Jedediah HILLER; m 2d 1884 Jediah HUBBS
Mary m Gilbert SEAMAN
Mary Jane, dt Samuel & Mary; m Henry T. WILLITS
Mary T., dt Daniel & Rosetta; m Elwood VALENTINE
Micah, s John & Phebe; m Elizabeth POWELL, dt Thos. & Abigail (mo)
Ch: (2)
ack mo 4-21-1761; ct Oblong for Micah 7-29-1761; cert for w 11-25-1761; Elizabeth, w Micah, rocf Oblong 8-29-1764
(Bibles)
Phebe ack mo 6 Mo (Aug) 25, 1742

POST, continued
Phebe, dt John & Phebe, b 1744; m 1804 John POWELL
Phebe, dt Samuel & Catharine; m 1813 Henry WILLIS
Phebe W. d 3-13-1883 ae 90y 4m 29d (unidentified stone, Wby)
Richard Jr., s Richard & Phebe; m 1732 Mary WILLIS, dt Henry & Phebe, b 2 Mo (Apr) 22, 1713 d 5 Mo (July) 13, 1744 (mo)
Ch: Henry b 8 Mo (Oct) 1, 1733
    Richard b 5 Mo (July) 17, 1735
    Mary b 12 Mo (Feb) 6, 1737/8
    Jotham b 7 Mo (Sept) 14, 1740
    Richard signed cert 1727; both ack mo 8 Mo (Oct) 29, 1735
Richard dis mo before 9-20-1797
Richard, s Arthur W. & Ethel, b 1-26-1915; m 6-12-1937 at the bride's, Jenkintown, Pa. by Rev. John Muyskins, Helen M. SHILCOCK, dt Clarence J. & Beulah F.
Samuel, s Henry & Mary, Wby, b 6-21-1765 d 9-30-1795; m 6-26-1793 at Wby, Jane TITUS, dt John & Sarah, Wby, b 9-4-1773
Ch: Samuel b 1795
    Jane m 2d 11-3-1802 Lewis VALENTINE (Bibles)
Samuel, s Isaac & Jane, Mk., d 12-21-1867 ae 74
Sarah, (prob) dt Henry & Mary; m 1791 ----- WILLITS (mo)
Sarah, dt Henry & Mary; m 1802 John TITUS, Jr.
Stephen dis by N.P. for neglect of mtg 12-16-1774
William F. d 8-18-1869 in 70th yr (Wby Stone)

POWELL
Abigail, dt Thomas & Abigail b 1688; m 1690 Richard WILLITS
Amy, dt John & Margaret, b 1718; m 1745/6 Daniel WILLETS
Anne, dt Wait Jr.; m 1748 Rowland PEARSALL
Anne, dt Jonathan & Sarah CORNELIUS; m 2d 1801 George WEEKS
Annie d 3-30-1882 ae 8y (unidentified stone, Wby)
Caleb, s Caleb & Sarah; m 8th or 9th Mo (Nov) 1742 (prob) Wby Clement HALLOCK, dt John & Hannah
    cert of m not recorded, 2d intention 8 Mo (Oct) 27, 1742; rm 9 Mo (Nov) 24, 1742 (Bibles)
Caleb dis mo 6-15-1808
Catharine, w -----, dt Obadiah & Deborah SEAMAN; m 2d 1821 Jacob WILLETS
Charity d 11-3-1874 ae 87y 9m 14d (Wby Stone)
Charles U., s Geo. S. & Hannah J., b 4-19-1893; m Grace AUSTIN, dt Edward B. & Lucy T., b Port Byron, N. Y. 8-28-1874
    Grace m 1st G. Thomas Powell
Clement, dt John & Margaret, b 12 Mo (Feb) 27, 1709/10; m 1731 David WHITSON
Cornelius, s Reuben, dec, & Ann, Wby, N. Hemp.; m 2-2-1819 at Wby, Rachel HEALEY, dt Christopher & Alice, dec
Ch: Reuben b 11-18-1821
    Christopher b 12-26-1832
    Elizabeth b 8-9-1824
Daniel, s Jonas & Anne, Beth.; m Mary POWELL, dt Caleb & Sarah
Ch: Jacob b 6 Mo (Aug) 2, 1737; drowned in South Bay 12-14-1758
    Deborah b 10 Mo (Dec) 10, 1739
    Margaret b 12 Mo (Feb) 11, 1743
    Jonas b 4 Mo (June) 24, 1745
    Daniel b 1 Mo (Mar) 22, 1749
    Rachel b 2-17-1753 d 9-9-1759
    Mary b 1-29-1755
Daniel Jr., s Daniel & Mary, b 1 Mo (Mar) 22, 1749; ack misconduct 3-2-1781
David d 4-5-1853 ae 5y 8m (unidentified stone, Wby)
Deborah m Richard UDALL
Elisha, s Thomas & Abigail, b 1737; m 1766 Rachel HAM (or Hane)
    dis in Nine Partners for mo 2-24-1768 (Bibles)
Elizabeth, dt Thos. & Abigail; m Micah POST
Elizabeth U., dt G. Thomas & Grace A.; m 1931 Arthur Dudley HARRISON
Esther, dt Richard & Phebe; m 1789 Charles WILLETS
Etta d 9-14-1876 ae 8y (unidentified stone, Wby)
G. Thomas, s Geo. S. & Hannah; m Grace AUSTIN, dt Edw. B. & Lucy T., b Port Byron, N. Y. 8-28-1874
Ch: Elizabeth U. b 12-7-1910
    Grace T. " 6- 4-1913
    Grace m 2d Charles U. POWELL
George S. d 1----1933 ae 90; m Hannah JACKSON, dt Geo. & Elizabeth (Underhill) d 5-16-1929
Ch: G. Thomas
    Frederick J. b 8-20-1884 d 8-6-1905 bur Mk.
    Charles U. b 4-19-1893
    Little Belle d 5-29-1883 ae 2y 5d bur Mk.
    both recrq 10-17-1888
Hannah, dt Thomas & Elizabeth, b 5 Mo (July) 28, 1691; m 1712 William WILLIS
Hannah, dt Thomas & Mary, b 1707; m 1739 Henry WHITSON
Hannah, dt John & Margaret, b 1725; m 1744/5 Jacob WILLETS
Hannah, dt Joshua & Phebe, b 10 Mo (Dec) 15, 1745; m 1766 Jacob WILLETS
Hannah dis mo 4-27-1774
Henry, s Richard & Freelove; m 1762 Mary KEEN (mo) (Henry b 1741)
    Henry dis mo 1-26-1763; Mary dis 5-25-1763
Isaac, s Thomas & Mary, b 1711; m 1734 Martha WHITMAN
Ch: (6)
    Isaac ack mo 2 Mo (Apr) 26, 1738; Isaac probably m 2d Anne COCK, wd James TITUS (Bibles)
Isaac Jr., s John & Martha, b 5 Mo (July) 11,

POWELL, Isaac Jr., continued
1744; m abt 1778 Margaret POWELL, dt Daniel & Mary, b 12 Mo (Feb) 11, 1743/4 (mo)
Ch: (5)
Isaac dis m his cousin 12-30-1778; Margaret dis (prob his w)
(Bibles)
Jackson d 4-14-1893 ae 88y 11m 5d; m Letty ----- d 2-14-1881 ae 69y 6m
Letty recrq
(Wby Stones)
Jane m 1742 Samuel WILLITS
John, s Thomas & Abigail, d 9 Mo (Nov) 29, 1738; m 10-27-1704 Margaret HALLOCK, dt John & Abigail, b 1682 d 1769
Ch: (9)
John signed rem cert 1707; Margaret signed Epistle abt 1725
John Jr., (prob) s John & Margaret, b 10 Mo (Dec) 27, 1740 d 8-31-1828; m abt 1766 Elizabeth UNDERHILL, dt Thos. & Sarah, b 4 Mo (June) 13, 1745
Ch: Sarah b 6-27-1769; m 10-30-1799 James HAWXHURST, s John & Penelope
5 other ch
ack mo 6-29-1768
(Underhill Gen.)
John Jr. m 2d 6-27-1804 at Wby, Phebe POST, dt John & Phebe, Hemp., d 9-19-1825
Ch: (3) (Underhill Gen.)
(Bibles)
Jonah, s Isaac & Martha; m Jane RYDER
dis 8-30-1775
(Bibles)
Jonas, s Daniel & Mary, b 4 Mo (June) 24, 1749; m 1778 (cert not recorded m bet. 11-25 & 12-30) Sibyl POWELL, dt Isaac & Martha
(Bibles)
Joshua, s Thomas & Mary, Beth.; m 10 Mo (Dec) 5, 1744 at Wby, Phebe POST, dt Richard & Mary, Wby
Ch: Hannah b 10 Mo (Dec) 15, 1745
Willete b 6 Mo (Aug) 11, 1747
Phebe b 9 Mo (Nov) 19, 1749; m Amos WILLETS
Amos b 4-27-1752
Joshua b 10-15-1754
Richard b 11-2-1757
Benjamin b 8-13-1760
Phebe m 2d Richard WILLITS
Joshua, s Joshua & Phebe, O.B. & Wby, b 10-15-1754 d 5-7-1817 ae 62y 7m; m 5-5-1784 at Wby Phebe WILLIS, dt John & Elizabeth, b 4-5-1761 d 12-29-1851
Ch: Edmund b 2-17-1785 d 11-1-1844 ae 59y 9m 14d
Elizabeth b 8-18-1786 d 10----1836 ae 50y 2m
Mary b 7-2-1788
John W. b 5-29-1790
Phebe b 12-12-1796 d 2-8-1835 ae 38y 1m 26d
(Bibles)

Margaret m abt 1778 Isaac POWELL Jr.
Martha, dt Isaac & Martha; m 1756 Thomas TITUS
Mary, dt Thomas & Mary, b 1677; m 1728 Samuel PRIOR
Mary, dt Wait & Mary; m 1749/50 Nathaniel WHITSON
Mary, dt Joshua & Mary; m 1810 Samuel TITUS
Mary Jr., dt John W. & Sarah; m 1837 Adam MOTT
Matilda, dt John W. & Sarah M.; m 1837 Stephen RUSHMORE
Mercy, dt Thomas & Elizabeth, b 1702; m 1726 Jacob SEAMAN
signed Epistle abt 1725
Moses, s Thomas & Mary, b 5-15-1702; m 1732 Katharine HALLOCK, dt John & Hannah
Ch: (14)
Phebe, dt Thomas & Mary, b 3 Mo (May) 16, 1697; m 1712 Henry WILLIS
Phebe m 1764 John HICKS
Phebe, dt Joshua & Phebe, b 9 Mo (Nov) 19, 1749; m 1774 Amos WILLETS
Rachel, dt Thomas & Elizabeth; m 1719/20 Thomas WILLITS
Richard, s Richard & Mary, b 10 Mo (Dec) 25, 1660 d 3 Mo (May) 14, 1703; m 1 Mo (Mar) 21, 1686 Abigail BOWNE, dt John & Hannah, b 12 Mo (Feb) 5, 1662/3 d 4 Mo (June) 16, 1688
Ch: Hannah b 11 Mo (Jan) 24, 1686/7; m Job CARR
(Bibles)
Richard m 2d 3 Mo (May) 15, 1689/90 Abigail POWELL, dt Thomas, b 4 Mo (June) 18, 1668 d 9-2-1757
Ch: Abigail b 12 Mo (Feb) 27, 1690; m John WILLIS
Mary b 1 Mo (Mar) 6, 1692/3; m Henry SCUDDER & Thomas WILLIAMS
Martha b 11 Mo (Jan) 29, 1694/5; m Obad. VALENTINE
Jacob b 4 Mo (June) 6, 1697; m Mary JACKSON
Phebe b 2 Mo (Apr) 13, 1699; m Adam MOTT & Tristram DODGE
Elizabeth b 4 Mo (June) 27, 1701
(Bibles)
Richard, s Thomas & Mary, b 4 Mo (June) 17, 1704; m 1739 Freelove WEEKS
Ch: (3)
ack mo 3 Mo (May) 30, 1739
Richard m 2d 1748 Jerusha WEEKS, dt ----- LEWIS
m cert not recorded, 2d intention 8 Mo (Oct) 26, 1748; rm 9 Mo (Nov) 30, 1748
Richard Jr., s Richard & Freelove; m 1769 (cert not recorded, m bet. 5-31- & 6-28) Phebe WHITSON, dt John 3d
Richard Jr., s Joshua & Phebe, b 11-2-1757; m Jemima PRATT (mo)
Jemima dis mo 4-27-1774; Richard ack 1-26-1780 going with Militia Captain & others in pursuit of a robber
(Bibles)
Richard d 10-1-1860 ae 92 (Wby Stone); m E. P. ----- d 1846 ae 72 (Wby Stone)
Richard d 5-16-1890 ae 82y 4m 10d; m (prob)

POWELL, Richard, continued
Mary ----- d 1-15-1903 ae 78
Ruth, dt Thomas & Abigail, b _731; m 1748 Jehu MOTT
Samuel, (prob) s Thos. & Abigail, b 1725; m 1748 Mary WOOD (mo)
ack mo 4-29-1752
(Bibles)
Samuel Jr. dis mo before 6-27-1787
Sarah m 1722 Nathaniel SEAMAN
Sarah, dt John; m 1767 Joseph WALTERS
Sarah, dt Reuben & Anna; m 1819 Azariah WATERBURY
Sarah A., dt John W. & Sarah M.; m 1839 Jacob H. WILLETS
Sibyl, dt Isaac & Martha; m 1778 Jonas POWELL
Silas dis mo before 5-31-1780
Solomon, s Thomas & Elizabeth; m Ruth CARMAN, dt Thomas
rpd mo 8 Mo (Oct) 28, 1730, comm to speak to him 1732
Stephen d 9-25-1863 ae abt 80; m Phebe ----- d 9-1-1877 ae abt 94 (prob w of Stephen as stones are adjacent in Wby)
Stephen D. d 6-28-1873 ae 11y 9m (unidentified stone, Wby)
Stimonson m Maria BERGEN b 3-3-1800 d 9-8-1876
Ch: Stephen B.
Phebe A.
Jacob S.
Stimonson, s Stephen & Phebe, both dec, N. Hemp. b Uniondale, L. I. 2-24-1814 d 12-17-1903; m 2d 9-19-1878 Mary D. WIGGINS, dt Abel B. & Deborah, O.B., b 8-10-1821 d 2-5-1914
Mary recrq
Thomas Sr., Immigrant, b 8----1641 d 12 Mo (Feb) 28, 1721/2 ae 80y 4m; m Abigail WOOD, dt Thomas
Ch: Abigail b 1668; m 1690 Rich. WILLITS
Thomas m 1691 Mary WILLITS
Elizabeth m 1691 Sam'l TITUS
John m 10 Mo 27, 1704 Margt HALLOCK
Jonas m Anne -----
Caleb m Sarah -----
Wait
Elisha m Rebecca -----
on comm. 1698; signed rem cert 1707
(Bible record)
Thomas Sr. m 2d 9 Mo (Nov) 2, 1690 Elizabeth TOWNSEND, wd Theophilus PHILLIPS (his 3rd w), dt John & Phebe
Ch: Hannah b 1691; m 1712 Wm. WILLIS
Phebe b 1693; m 1712 Henry WILLIS
Rachel m 1719 Thomas WILLITS
Mercy m 1726 Jacob SEAMAN
Solomon m 1730 Ruth CARMAN
Sarah m Nathaniel SEAMAN
Amy
Thomas 2d, s Thomas & Abigail, Beth., d 9 Mo (Nov) 17, 1731; m 9 Mo (Nov) 6, 1691 Mary WILLITS, dt Thomas & Dinah, d 10 Mo (Dec) 24, 1739
Ch: Thomas b 5 Mo (July) 3, 1693; m Abigail HALLOCK
Mary b 1694 d 1695
Abigail b 12 Mo (Feb) 13, 1695/6; m Peter HALLOCK
Mary b 3 Mo (May) 16, 1697; m Sam. PRIOR
Wait b 9 Mo (Nov) 29, 1698; m Mary MUDGE
Amos b 1700 d 1 Mo 14, 1749/50 (unm)
Moses b 4 Mo (June) 5, 1702; m Cath. HALLOCK
Richard b 4 Mo (June) 17, 1704; m Freelove WEEKS & Jerusha WEEKS
Elizabeth b 1705
Hannah b 7 Mo (Sept) 18, 1707; m Henry WHITSON
Joshua b 5 Mo (July) 18, 1709; m Phebe POST
Isaac b 1711; m Martha WHITMAN
Martha b 6 Mo (Aug) 29, 1713; m Francis KEEN
Deborah b 10 Mo (Dec) 28, 1715; m John WHITSON
Thomas signed rem cert 1707
(Bibles)
Thomas 3d, s Thomas & Mary, b 5 Mo (July) 3, 1693 d 3-1-1757; m 1724/5 Abigail HALLOCK, dt John & Hannah, b 7 Mo (Sept) 10, 1705
Ch: (11)
(Bibles)
Thomas, s Solomon & Ruth; m Sarah SANDS, dt Samuel & Mary
Ch: (7)
ack mo 10-25-1758
(Bibles)
Thomas, s Isaac & Martha, Beth., b 1752; m 6-1-1774 at Wby Martha TITUS, dt James & Anne, Wby
Ch: (7)
(Bibles)
Wait, s Thomas & Mary, b 9 Mo (Nov) 29, 1698 d 2 Mo (Apr) 15, 1750/51; m 1 Mo (Mar) 15, 1723/4 d 12-24-1759 in 58th yr Mary MUDGE, dt James & Jane
Ch: Jane b 2 Mo (Apr) 22, 1725
Mary b 11 Mo (Jan) 31, 1727/8
Anna b 7 Mo (Sept) 22, 1730
Wait b 4 Mo (June) 30, 1733
Jemima b 1 Mo (Mar) 31, 1736
Esther b 11 Mo (Jan) 23, 1738/39
Sarah b 8 Mo (Oct) 23, 1745
ack mo before 1 Mo (Mar) 25, 1724
Wait, s Wait & Mary, b 4 Mo (June) 30, 1733; m 1756 (cert not recorded m bet. 10-26 & 11-24-1756) Hannah WILLETS
Willet, s Joshua & Phebe, b 6 Mo (Aug) 11, 1747; m 7-12-1779 Catharine SEAMAN, dt Obadiah & Sarah
Catharine dis mo 2-27-1780; Catharine m 2d 8-23-1821 Jacob WILLETS
(Seaman Gen.)
William d 4-7-1895 ae 30 (unidentified stone, Wby)

PRATT

Jemima m 1781 Richard POWELL, Jr.

John d 6-5-1870 ae 83y 1m 27d; m Sarah H. ----- d 8-26-1870 ae 74y 9m 8d (Wby Stones)

John & Elmina

Ch: Mary d 1862 ae 3y (Wby Stone)

John C. d 8-31-1864 ae 39 (Wby Stone)

PRINZ

Alex. Henry, s Alex. Chas. & Louise (Lehr), b 9-6-1903 New Haven; m Ruth B. SMITH, dt Archibald & Isabelle (Blackburn), b Elizabeth, N. J. 7-4-1905

Ch: Mary Elizabeth b G. C. 12-27-1932
Ruth recrq 3-18-1925; Alexander H. recrq 4-19-1933; Mary E. made a mbr 3-18-1934

PRIOR

Edmund, s Joseph & Phebe, N.Y.C., b 9-4-1755; m 12-1-1779 at Wby, Phebe WILLIS, dt Samuel & Mary, Jericho, b 5-28-1756 d 9----1791 (Bibles)

Edmund m 2d 9-10-1793 Mary HAYDOCK, dt Henry & Hannah

Ch: Edmund H. b 11-27-1809
4 other ch
(Bibles)

Elizabeth, dt Matthew & Mary, b 6 Mo (Aug) 1656; m 1673 John FEAKE

Elizabeth [Prier], dt John & Elizabeth; m abt 1711 William PRIOR
signed Epistle abt 1725

Elizabeth, dt Thomas & Martha, b 3-13-1761; m 1781 John UNDERHILL

Elizabeth, dt John & Hannah (Bowne), wd John Prior; m Samuel TITUS

Elizabeth Moode, dt Edmund & Mary, b 8-30-1800; m 1821 John BARROW Jr.

Hannah, dt Thomas & Martha, b 9-15-1756; m 1779 Benjamin COCK

Hannah, dt Edmund & Mary; m 1819 Samuel RODMAN Jr.

Henrietta M., dt John & Elizabeth, b 12-12-1831; m Abram P. VANDENBURGH

Henry, s Matthew & Ann, b 9-18-1755; m Esther -----

Ch: Anna
dis mo before 6-19-1793, rst 5-20-1795; Esther dis 10-16-1793, rst 10-14-1795
Anna recrq of parents 3-14-1798
(Bibles)

Horace, s James & Theodosia, b 12-7-1802 d 5-5-1886; m before 3-18-1840 Julia A. SOUTHWICK b 12-10-1817 d 5-2-1896 (mo)

Ch: Thomas
mo & ret mbrp
(Wby Stones & Bibles)

James, s Matthew & Ann, O.B., b 4-23-1757 d 4-9-1837 ae 80y 5m; m before 1-28-1784 Theodosia ----- d 2-7-1835 ae 75y 2m (mo)

Ch: Samuel d 10- 7-1837 ae 34y 3m
Henry d 3-27-1864 ae 67y 4m
James d 7-21-1866 ae 75
James dis mo 3-31-1784; Dosha recrq 8-17-1791; James rst 1-31-1787

James, s James & Theodosia, b 1791 d 7-21-1866 ae 75; m 1814 Rachel CARHART, dt John, d 12-24-1871 ae 82

Ch: William Henry b 3-16-1830; m Mary RANSOM; d Rockville Centre, L. I. 8-4-1909
Elizabeth d 4-2-1843 ae nearly 24
Rachel rocf Nine Partners 1815
all bur Mk. (Bibles)

John, s Matthew & Mary, b 12 Mo (Feb) 1651/2 d 4 Mo (June) 2, 1698; m 9 Mo (Nov) 2, 1678 Elizabeth BOWNE, dt John & Hannah, b 8 Mo (Oct) 8, 1658 d 12 Mo (Feb) 14, 1721

Ch: John b 7 Mo (Sept) 16, 1679 d 9 Mo (Nov) 18, 1748
Hannah b 10 Mo (Dec) 22, 1681
Elizabeth b 8 Mo (Oct) 9, 1683
Mary b 11 Mo (Jan) 4, 1685
Sarah b 8 Mo (Oct) 19, 1688
Matthew b 1 Mo (Mar) 29, 1690/91
Samuel b 6 Mo (Aug) 27, 1693
Joseph b 8 Mo (Oct) 20, 1695

John, s James & Theodosia, O.B., b 1787 d 1860; m 9-28-1820 at Wby, Elizabeth H. (or M.) FROST, dt Caleb & Sarah, b 12-29-1799 d 1862

Ch: Phebe b 1-3-1824
5 other ch
(Bibles)

John Augustus d 3-4-1885 ae 59; m Elizabeth R. ----- d 12-11-1888 ae 55
cf Scipio 1871

Joseph, s Samuel & Mary, O.B.; m 2 Mo 7, 1753 at Wby Phebe TITUS, dt Edmund

Ch: Sarah b 11-10-1753
Edmund b 9-4-1755

Mary, dt Samuel & Mary; m 1764 John SEARING

Matthew, Immigrant, d before Aug. 1692; m Mary ----- d 5 Mo (July) 4, 1700

Ch: (See Flushing records)
Mary on comm. 1697

Matthew, s Matthew, dec, & Hannah, O.B., b 1 Mo (Mar) 6, 1729/30; m 12-4-1754 at Beth. Ann WILLIS, wd Silas, dt ----- PEARSALL, Hemp., b 2 Mo (Apr) 4, 1722

Ch: Henry b 9-18-1755
James b 4-23-1757
Matthew ack inadvertent criticisms 1-26-1763

Matthew m 2d 6-27-1789 at Matthew Prior's, Hannah COLES, wd Joseph, dt Samuel & Martha COCK, b 2 Mo (Apr) 4, 1731

Phebe m William WILLETS

Phebe W., dt John & Elizabeth, b 1-3-1824; m Richard ALBERTSON

Philemon H., M.D., s John & Elizabeth, d 12-17-1867 ae 46; m Sarah WHEELER Jr.

Ch: Georgianna b 1850; m Jas. T. SHIPMAN
Henry b 1848 d 1902; m 1901 Olive Florence
(Bibles) [-----

Samuel, s John & Elizabeth, O.B., b 7 Mo

PRIOR, Samuel, continued
(Sept) 15, 1692 d 4-24-1778 ae abt 85y; m 8 Mo (Oct) 16, 1728 at Wby Mary POWELL, dt Thomas & Mary, Beth. b 1677 d 5-21-1776 ae 79y
Ch: Samuel b 10 Mo (Dec) 2, 1729 d 3 Mo 6, 1732
Joseph b 11 Mo (Jan) 27, 1732/3 d 5-31-1779
Thomas b 1 Mo (Mar) 30, 1734
Mary b 3 Mo (May) 22, 1738
Thomas, s Samuel & Mary, O.B., b 1 Mo (Mar) 30, 1734 d 8-3-1783; m 11-13-1755 at Sequatauge Martha WILLETS, dt Amos, dec, & Rebecca, Islip
Ch: Hannah b 9-15-1757
Phebe b 3-21-1759
Elizabeth b 3-13-1761
Sarah b 3-17-1765
Samuel b 9-7-1770

PURCELL
Thomas m Martha ----- b 4-2-1812 d 2-28-1833 (supposed w as stones adjacent in Wby)

QUINBY
Josiah m 1728 Hannah CORNELL

RATH
Alice, Lutheran, b Pittsburgh 11-23-1904; m 1933 Richard E. CARPENTER Jr.

RAYNOR
Martha, dt Joseph & Phebe; m Sylvanus SMITH

REED
Caroline Sarah, dt Jas. H. & Sarah F.; m 1906 Franklin Albert COLES

REEDER
Mellora Augusta, dt David B. & Rhoda M., b Galena, Ark. 4-24-1900; recrq 12-19-1926

REMSEN
Daniel H., s Aris & Sarah (Higbie), d Bayville 4-26-1907 ae 83y 3m 26d
Martha mo before 2-17-1796, dis next mo; rst 1806

REYNOLDS
Richard M., s Justus & Elizabeth, both dec, N.Y.C.; m 5-4-1826 at Mk. Ann CRAFT, dt James & Hannah, dec
cf N. Y. (clear)

RHODES
Cornelius H. m Phebe E. HALLETT d 4-8-1885 ae 76y 2m 24d
(Wby Stones)

RICKMAN
William, Cow Neck, dis in the past, ack 2-16-1784

RIDGWAY
Ann gct Little Egg Harber, N. J. 5 Mo (July) 31, 1728
John m 1728 Phebe TITUS, dt John
Phebe gct Little Egg Harbor, N. J. 9 Mo (Nov) 27, 1728
Richard m 1700 Mary WILLITS

RILEY
Henry M., s Thos. W. & Harriet E. (Theale), b Baltimore 6-28-1886; m 9-15-1913 at Washington, Pa. Helen D. DAWSON, dt Geo. W. & Ellen M. (Hill), b near Beallville, Pa. 4-6-1893
Ch: Martha Ann b Balt. 5-21-1914
Henry D. " " 5-24-1915
Robert T. " " 6- 2-1920
all rec mbr 6-20-1937

RITTENAUER
Joseph M. d ae 51 (Man. Stone)

ROBBINS
Daniel, s Jere. & Hannah, Hemp. Harbor, d 12-30-1822 ae 50y; m 12-12-1812 Elizabeth MITCHELL
Ch: Jeremiah b 9- 8-1813
Daniel Jr. b 10- 4-1815
William b 11- 4-1817
John b 6-6-1820
ct N.P. 11-18-1817 (clear)
(Bibles)
Edward, s Willet & Esther, O.B., b 1813 d 1-13-1892; m 11- 2-1836 at Wby, Rachel W. TITUS, dt Rowland & Sarah, N. Hemp., b 10- 9-1817 d 10-18-1888
Ch: (9)
(Bibles)
Elizabeth, dt Jeremiah, b 11 Mo (Jan) 19, 1736/37; m 1760 Henry COCK
Elizabeth m abt 1777 ----- WILLIAMS
Emily, dt Wm. S. & Elizabeth, b 6-17-1847; m 1867 Henry RUSHMORE
Esther, dt Wm. S. & Elizabeth, b 8-24-1851; m 1870 John F. HUBBS
Hannah, dt Jere. & Hannah, b 2 Mo (Apr) 19, 1739; m 1762 Rees COCK
Hannah C. m 1836 ----- HUBBS (mo)
Jacob dis mo 1-29-1783
James d 12-29-1822 ae 32y (Man. Stone)
Jane dis mo 3-31-1779
Jeremiah, s Jere.; m Hannah CARR, dt Job & Hannah, b 5 Mo (July) 24, 1716 (mo)
Ch: Almy b 9 Mo (Nov) 15, 1733
Elizabeth b 11 Mo (Jan) 19, 1736/37
Hannah b 2 Mo (Apr) 19, 1739
Sarah b 7 Mo (Sept) 1, 1742
Samuel b 2 Mo (Apr) 26, 1745
Isaac b 1 Mo (Mar) 12, 1748
Stephen b 4 Mo (June) 26, 1750
Phebe b 9-17-1752
Abigail b 8-9-1755
Job b 4-16-1758

ROBBINS, Jeremiah & Hannah, continued
Ch: Mary
    Hannah ack mo 4-15-1757 (mo several yrs ago)
Jeremiah, s John & Jane (Seaman), b 4 Mo (Jun) 10, 1744; m 12-10-1764 Hannah COCK, dt Henry & Mary, b 4 Mo (Jun) 15, 1745 d 3-7-1802 (mo)
Ch: Mary b 4-14-1765
    Anne " 1- 3-1768
    Daniel b 9-2-1772
    John b 5-28-1780
    Jane b 10-3-1785 d 5-7-1786
    Hannah ack mo 4-27-1758
    (Cox Gen.)
John, s Jere.; m 3 Mo (May) 28, 1731 Jane SEAMAN, dt Benj. & Jane, b 10 Mo (Dec) 14, 1713
Ch: (8)
    (Bibles & Seaman Gen.)
John, s Jeremiah & Hannah, dec, Hemp. Harbor, b 5-28-1780 d 4-25-1834 bur Man.; m 8-3-1809 Sarah CARHART, dt Joshua & Phebe, O.B. d 11-19-1826 ae 38 bur Man.
Ch: William B. b 7- 5-1811 d 4-8-1869
    Hannah " "
    Edward b 9- 8-1816
    Walter " 10-26-1818
    Phebe Ann b 9-23-1821
    John Jr. b 4-15-1824
Josiah, s John, gct Abington, rem some years past, 3 Mo (May) 26, 1736
Mary, dt Stephen & Miriam, b 8-15-1771 d 1819; m 11-25-1790 Robert WILLITS d 1851
Mary, dt Jeremiah & Hannah; m 1791 Jonathan SWEET, of Dutchess Co.
Mary K., dt Wm. S. & Elizabeth; m 1860 Richard UNDERHILL
Mary W. m Joseph POST
Richard H., s Wm. B. & Mary E.; m Margaret J. KETCHAM, dt Geo. W. & Gulielma
Ch: Margaret d 9-10-1898 ae 1m 24d bur Wby
    Mary H.
    Gulielma
Samuel, s Jeremiah & Hannah, O.B., b 2 Mo (Apr) 26, 1745; m 3-17-1765 at Mk. Elizabeth COCK dt John & Sarah, O.B., b 11 Mo (Jan) 9, 1740/1
Ch: (7)
Samuel, s Stephen & Miriam, Wby, b 1-11-1777; m 1800 Harriet EYRE, dt Col. Benj. & Mary
Ch: Valentine b 9-11-1803
    Elliot b 12-13-1806; m Ann Eliza SMITH
    Forman C. b 1802; m Eliz. WHITEHEAD
    Samuel d in infancy
    Elizabeth Ann m Eleazar PORTER
Samuel m 2d Mary Isabel REYNAULT
Samuel m 3d Sallie SIMPSON
    (Bibles)
Samuel, s Wm. S. & Elizabeth, b 3-16-1859 d 5-13-1931; m Julia STARKINS
Sarah, dt Jeremiah & Hannah, b 7 Mo (Sept) 1, 1742; m 1765 John TITUS
Stephen, s Jere. & Hannah, b 12 Mo (Feb) 26, 1750 d 5-25-1813; m Miriam SEAMAN, dt Samuel & Martha (mo)
Ch: Mary m 1790 Robert WILLITS
    Willet b 1781; m 1805 Esther SEAMAN
    Stephen
    Samuel b 1-11-1777; m 1800 Harriet EYRE
    Miriam ack mo 1-31-1787
    (Bibles)
William B., s John & Sarah, b 1811 d 4-18-1869 ae 57y 9m 13d; m Mary E. HEWLETT, dt James, b 1819 d 11-30-1884 ae 65y 8m
Ch: Sarah Elizabeth d 4-27-1846 ae 2y 6m 1d
    Thos. Franklyn d 8-31-1855 ae 2y 5m 14d
    Edward d 9-26-1861 ae 12y 2m 6d
    Willie E. d 7-7-1884 ae 22y 4m 9d
    Rebecca T. d 2-3-1869 ae 12y 6m 5d
    All bur Wby
William M., s Daniel, dec, & Elizabeth, N.Y.C.; m 2-24-1846 at Abrm. Brooks', 181 Monroe St., N. Y., Elizabeth BROOKS, dt Abraham & Phebe, dec, N. Hemp.
    cf Chappaqua (clear)
William S., Cow Neck & Glenwood, b 1809; m 9-1833 Elizabeth WILLITS b 1814 d 10-21-1873
Ch: Willet b 5-30-1834 [William S. d 5-21-1879
    Forman " 2-28-1836
    Mary K. b 8-11-1838
    Jacob " 7-25-1845 d Bkn. 3-7-1936
    Emily " 6-17-1847
    Charles W. b 4-1-1849 d 4-13-1861
    Esther " 4-28 (or 24) 1851
    Samuel b 3-16-1859
    Parents rocf Jericho 9----1833
    (Bibles)

ROBINSON
Nancy, dt Ward R. & Dorothy A., b Springfield, Ill. 7-18-1915; m 1935 Kenneth Edw. L'HOMMEDIER
W. R., Man.; m 10-1-1913 Dorothy ATKINSON, dt Francis B. & Eleanor, Rensselaer, Ind.
    Dorothy recrq 1-17-1932

RODMAN
Mary W., dt Thos. H. & Mary A., b 7-12-1853; m 1875 Henry T. FROST
Samuel Jr., s Samuel & Elizabeth, New Bedford, Mass.; m 11-2-1819 at Cow Neck Hannah H. PRIOR, dt Edmund & Mary, N. Hemp.
    cf New Bedford (clear)

ROGERS
Amos W., M.D. m Caroline HICKS, dt Benj. & Elizabeth, b 1-3-1829 d 11-16-1902
    both bur Man.
Charles R. (or W.) b 9-3-1821 d 12-30-1879; m Sarah T. HICKS, dt Benj. & Eliz. W., b 7-28-1823 d 12-13-1878
    both bur Man.
Martha, dt Morris M. & Sarah (Willets), b 5-4-1819; m Isaac SHERWOOD
Mary, dt Daniel & Ruth F., b Adel, Iowa 4-22-1868; m Wilhelm MILLER

ROGERS, continued
Morris M., M.D., d 10-14-1860 ae 75; m Sarah W. ----- d 6-12-1871 ae 85

ROWLAND (or Ruland)
Drusilla (late GRITMAN) dis mo 12-15-1813

ROZSO
Bela, s Lazos & Marguerite, both dec, Kecskemet, Hungary; m 5-22-1938 at Wm. Mott Hicks', Rosana HICKS, dt Wm. L. & Rosita S., both dec, b G.C. 4-30-1910

RUSHMORE
Charles gct Jericho 3-16-1796 (clear)
Edmund P. b 4-12-1818 d 1-26-1890 (Wby Stone)
Esther L., dt Townsend & Amy, b 5-13-1825; m abt 1846 Robert W. TITUS (0)
Halstead d 1829; m G.C. 1923 Emily SMITH, dt Halsey M. & Sarah (Underhill), b Rye, N.Y.
Ch: Constance b Roslyn 5-11-1925
Emily & Constance recrq 3-20-1932
Henry, s Townsend & Amy, b 10-25-1838 d 4-21-1902 ae 63y 5m 27d; m 1867 Emily W. ROBBINS dt Wm. S. & Elizabeth, b 6-17-1847 d 3-17-1885 ae 37y 9m
Ch: Freddie d 8-21-1868 ae 5m 27d
both bur Wby
Isaac, s Thos. & Anneke, O.B., b 2 Mo (Apr) 18, 1733 d 8-17-1779; m 4-18-1757 Sarah TITUS, dt Edmund & Sarah, b 10 Mo (Dec) 27, 1735 d 6-19-1775 in 40th yr (mo)
Ch: Phebe b 2-18-1758; m Silas DOWNING
Mary " 2-11-1760; m Chas. FROST
Stephen b 5- 1-1763; m Phebe TOWNSEND
Jane " 4-12-1768; m Lewis VALENTINE
Edmond " 11-27-1771 d 6-17-1782
Sarah ack mo 11-19-1760; Isaac ack mo, enlisting, bearing arms, hiring a substitute 1-26-1763
(Bibles)
Isaac, s Stephen & Phebe, Wheatley & Wby, b 5-19-1788 d 7 Mo 3, 1875 (Wby Stone); m 3-24-1813 at Wby Lydia POST, dt Edmund & Catharine, N. Hemp., d 7-12-1841 ae 52y 5m 29d
Ch: Edmund b 2-20-1816 d 2- 3-1817
Stephen b 9- 8-1814 d 1-13-1890 Wby
Edmund b 4-12-1818 d 1-26-1890
Lydia Jr. d 1844 (Wby Stone)
Jacob, s Thomas & Anneke, O.B., b 1720 d 12-28-1754; m 1744 Mary MOTT, dt James, b 1720 d 5-5-1765 (m cert not recorded, 2d intention 2 Mo 25; rm 3 Mo (May) 30, 1744)
Ch: James b 1745; m Deborah WHITSON
both bur Beth.
(Bibles)
James, s Jacob & Mary, Huntington, b 1745; m 5-7-1766 at Beth. Deborah WHITSON, dt John & Deborah, Huntington
Ch: (5)
Deborah d 11-26-1857 ae 79 bur Wby
(Bibles)
Jane, dt Stephen & Phebe; m 1817 Valentine

WILLETS
John Howard, s Stephen & Matilda, N. Hemp., d 10-12-1891 bur Wby; m 9-23-1869 at David Barker's, Julia Anna BARKER, dt David O. & Julia, Bkn.
Leon A., s Stephen T. & Adelaide, Roslyn, b Roslyn 8-25-1883; m 1-2-1909 Mary S. SEAMAN dt Samuel J. & Matilda W., b Jericho 5-4-1881
Ch: Leon A. Jr. b Roslyn 6-2-1910
Robert Stephen b Roslyn 2-15-1914
Leon recrq 10-20-1912
Leon A. Jr., s Leon A. & Mary, Roslyn; m 2-6-1932 at School Lane MH, Germantown, Caroline A. JACKSON, dt Arthur C. & Edith W., Germantown, Pa., b 9-12-1909
Ch: Mary Lee b Roslyn 1-3-1934
Carly Jackson b Roslyn 11-28-1935
Caroline rocf Germantown 11-19-1933
Maria d 11-24-1894 ae 68 (unidentified Stone, Wby)
Mary, dt Isaac & Sarah, b 2-11-1760; m 1780 Charles FROST
Mary, dt Stephen & Phebe; m 1815 Edmund POST Jr.
P. J. d 1-13-1897 ae 63 (unidentified stone, Wby)
Phebe, dt Isaac; m 1777 Silas DOWNING
Phebe T., dt Stephen & Phebe, b 6-10-1803; m 1831 Isaac R. GIFFORD (0)
Rachel W., dt Townsend & Amy, b 3-16-1830; m 1859 Wilson M. PAGE (0)
Samuel, s Townsend & Amy, b 11-12-1836; m Gertrude -----
Ch: Willie d 6-6-1868 ae 4y 3m (Wby Stone)
Samuel W. d 4-23-1871 ae 84 (unidentified stone, Wby)
Sarah, dt Thomas & Sarah; m 1748 Daniel COCK
Sarah, dt Stephen & Phebe; m 1812 John D. HICKS
Silas, s Thomas, b 5 Mo (July) 20, 1727; m 1753 (cert not recorded, m bet. 2-28 & 3-28-1753) Phebe TITUS, dt Edmund, b 8 Mo (Oct) 7, 1732
Ch: Martha b 5-17-1754; m Richard WEEKS
(6 other ch)
(Bibles)
Stephen, s Isaac, dec, & Sarah, O.B., b 5-1-1763 d 11-10-1852 bur Wby; m 2-7-1787 at Wby Phebe TOWNSEND, dt Thomas, dec, N. Hemp., b 11-23-1768 d 1866 ae 98y bur Wby [(0)
Ch: Isaac b 5-19-1788
Sarah b 9-10-1790
Townsend b 8-25-1792
Mary b 7-17-1794
Jane b 8- 7-1796
Thomas b 3- 1-1799
Phebe b 6-10-1803
Stephen, s Isaac & Lydia, N. Hemp. & Wby, b 9-8-1814 d 1-13-1890; m 9-27-1837 at Wby Matilda POWELL, dt John W. & Sarah M., Wby
Ch: Isaac b 9-27-1841 d 1-30-1842
Lydia M. b 8-14-1843 d 1-11-1844 ae 5m 7d

RUSHMORE, Stephen & Matilda, continued
Ch: Edward b 5- 8-1845; resigned 6-7-1891
John Howard b 2-28-1847
Unnamed d 8-26-1850 ae 3d
" " 11-20-1858 ae 2d
Matilda rocf N. Y. 1836
Stephen T., s Thos. & Jane, b 9-7-1849; m 11-13-1880 Addelaide HALSTEAD, dt Henry P.
Ch: Leon b 8-20-1883; m Mary SEAMAN
Edna L. d 6- 1-1887 ae 1y 11m
Lillian T. d 5-18-1893 ae 1y 7m
(Wby Stones & Bibles)
Thomas d 3-17-1778; m 2d Elizabeth SEAMAN, dt Benj. & Martha, wd James WOODEN (mo) both dis mo 1753; Elizabeth rst 10-31-1759
Thomas, s Stephen & Phebe, b 3-1-1779 d 4-30-1878 ae 79; m Jane VALENTINE, dt Oliver, d 1-11-1896 ae 90
Ch: Elizabeth
Stephen
Townsend, s Stephen & Phebe, Wheatley, b 8-5-1792 d 2-3-1870 ae 77y 6m bur Wby; m 1-29-1824 Amy L. WILLIS, b 9-12-1797 d 1-26-1881 ae 83y bur Wby (O)
Ch: Esther b 5-13-1825
Mariah b 4-22-1827
Rachel " 3-16-1830
Isaac " 1-20-1832
Phebe
Samuel b 11-12-1836
Henry W. b 10-25-1838
William T. b 5-29-1841 d 3-11-1881 ae 39 bur Wby
(Bibles)

SALTS
Martha (form Post) dis mo 7-26-1775

SANDS
Edward, s John & Sybil, b 1691 d 1 Mo (Mar) 9, 1746; m abt 1725 Mary CORNELL, dt Richard & Hannah, b 10 Mo (Dec) 17, 1703 d 9-15-1762
Ch: (8)
Mary ack mo 3 Mo (May) 25, 1726
(Bibles)
Hewlett b 11-29-1820 d 4-8-1901 (Wby Stone)
Katharine, dt John & Sybil, b 1700; m 1726 Edmond MOTT

SATTERLY
Hannah, dt John HALLOCK Jr., ack mo 4 Mo (June) 25, 1735

SAVAGE
Thomas b Pattinton, Yorks, Eng., d Flushing 4-8-1821 ae 39y 6m

SAXTON
Mary (form Post) dis mo before 6-27-1787

SCARLETT
Grace, dt Sir James, b 2-26-1772; m Jacob FROST

SCHALK
Catharine m Christian BOHACK

SCHNEIDER
Edwin C., s Louis & Louise F. (Valenta), b N.Y. C. 6-11-1918; recrq 12-19-1937; Louis b Germany; Louisa b N. Y.

SCHOTTERBECK
Frederick d 4-26-1859 ae 55y 6m 24d (Wby Stone)

SCHUFF
Aaron G. d 10-24-1832 ae 35 (Wby Stone)

SCOTT
Austin Allan, Rockville Cen., b Wilmington, Del. 12-8-1890; m Milwaukee 6-1-1918 Wally BECK, b Milwaukee 9-27-1890
Ch: Austin Allan Jr. b Bkn 1-6-1920
David Williams b Rockville 11-10-1925
Austin rocf N. Y. 10-20-1929; Wally & ch recrq 9-15-1929

SCRIVEN
Alice signed Epistle abt 1725
James m 1715 Mary GLADING, dt William FRY signed Epistle abt 1725; ct Kingston, R. I. 1 Mo (Mar) 29, 1732

SCUDDER
Henry, nm, & Mary
Henry's wd, Mary, ack mo 5 Mo (July) 27, 1715; she m 2d 1717 Thomas WILLIAMS
Mary, dt Henry, b 15 Mar. 1715; m Peter TITUS Jr.

SEAMAN
Abigail, dt Samuel; m 1770 Richard WILLETS
Abram (or Abraham), s Nathaniel & Rachel, b 9 Mo (Nov) 10, 1706; m 8 Mo (Oct) 1, 1731 Deborah TOWNSEND, dt James & Audrey
Ch: (5)
(Seaman Gen.)
Adam, s Richard & Jane, b 5 Mo (July) 11, 1704 d 1763; m 16 Jan. 1729/30 Hannah PINE, dt James & Edith
rpd mo 8 Mo (Oct) 28, 1730
(Seaman Gen.)
Alanson, s Henry O. & Almy, b 9-23-1793; m 7-15-1818 Elizabeth UNDERHILL, dt Israel
Ch: (2)
Elizabeth dis mo 10----1818
(Bibles)
Albert W., s Edward H. & Martha A., Jericho, b 10-3-1851; m 6-21-1882 Mary A. HOPKINS, dt Edwin & Mary, b 11-27-1861 d 12----1898
Ch: (3 s)
Mary gct Jericho 12-20-1882
Albert W. m 2d 2-14-1900 Daisy Georgia HATTON,

SEAMAN, Albert W. & Daisy Georgia, continued
dt Dr. Joseph & Georgianna, of Ga., b 1872
(Seaman Gen.)
Ambrose, s Nathaniel & Sarah; m Margaret SEAMAN, dt Samuel & Isabella
dis 8-27-1760, having mo several yr past
(Seaman Gen.)
Amy, dt Jacob & Mercy; m 1759 Jacob KIRBY
Andries, nm, s Jordan & Mary, b 7-23-1780 d 9-8-1825; m 12----1804 Sarah UNDERHILL, dt Israel & Mary, b 1-7-1880 d 8-12-1864 (mo)
Ch: (3)
dis mo 2 Mo 1805
(Bibles)
Ann Louise, dt Samuel Jr. & Matilda W., b 10-19-1885; m 1913 Albertson W. HICKS
Anne, dt Thomas & Catharine, b 12 Mo (Feb) 25, 1746/7; m 1770 Fry WILLIS
Benjamin (sometimes called Simmons), s Capt. John, Jerusalem; m abt 1684 Martha TITUS, dt Edmund & Martha, b 1 Mo (Mar) 1663
Ch: Benjamin
7 other ch
Martha on comm. 1700; both signed rem cert 1707
Benjamin, s Benj. & Martha, Wby, b 1685 d 9 Mo (Nov) 4, 1729; m 1709 Jane MOTT, dt Jos. & Miriam, of Staten Island d 7 Mo (Sept) 15, 1729 ae 36y 8m (mo)
Ch: Elizabeth b 7 Mo (Sept) 3, 1710
Martha b 12 Mo (Feb) 17, 1711/12
Jane b 12 Mo (Feb) 14, 1713/14
Miriam b 3 Mo (May) 24, 1716 d 7 Mo 30 1729
Hannah b 3 Mo (May) 22, 1718 d 1 mo later
Benjamin b 12 Mo (Feb) 11, 1719/20
Ann b 2 Mo (Apr) 8, 1722; d 3 Mo 1722
Phebe b 5 Mo (July) 3, 1723 d 2 Mo 20, 1724
Mary b 7 Mo (Sept) 16, 1726 d 8 Mo 1727
Edmond
both ack mo 8 Mo (Oct) 26, 1709
Benjamin dis 7-7-1785 for mo & being on a ship of war for several yr
Catharine, dt Obadiah & Sarah; m 1779 Willet POWELL; m 2d 1821 Jacob WILLETS
Catharine, dt Isaac & Lucretia; m 1816 Charles UDALL
Deborah, dt Solomon & Eliz.; m 1702/3 Joseph WILLITS
Edmund, Wby, s Jacob & Hannah, Smiths Clove, Orange Co., b 2-26-1832 d 7-4-1888; m 10-19-1865 at Rachel Hicks', Mary S. WILLITS, dt Edward, dec, & Esther, Wby, b 2-20-1832 d 1-10-1928
Ch: William W. b 12-28-1867
Elizabeth b 12-30-1870
Hannah b 3-25-1878 d 4-3-1878
Edmund rocf Cornwall 9----1866; Mary gct N. Y. 9-17-1902
(Bibles)
Elizabeth, dt Benj. & Martha, b abt 1697; m Thomas RUSHMORE
Elizabeth, dt Benj. & Jane, b 7 Mo (Sept) 10, 1710; m 1730 Amos UNDERHILL
Elizabeth, dt Thomas & Hannah; m 1730 William TITUS
Elizabeth, dt Richard Jr.; m before 6 Mo (Aug) 29, 1744 ----- TOWNSEND
ack mo 12 Mo (Feb) 1, 1748/49
Elizabeth, dt Willet & Mary, b 12-6-1762; m 1781 Isaac COCK
Elizabeth, dt Edmund & Mary W., b 12-30-1807; ct N. Y. 9-17-1902
Esther, dt Nathaniel & Rachel, b 9 Mo (Nov) 8, 1701; m 1722/3 John WHITSON
Esther, dt Samuel, dis 1-4-1775
Fred'k Willits, s Sam'l J. & Matilda W., dec, G.C., b 6-17-1888; m 4-3-1915 at Rachel Hicks', Roslyn, Eda (Register changed from Ida to Eda) Willets HICKS, dt John S., dec, & Caroline A., Roslyn, b 6-4-1892
Ch: John Samuel b G.C. 7- 1-1916
Frederick " " 7-28-1918
Albertson " Roslyn 5-6-1922
Anna Matilda b Mineola Hosp. 10-17-1927
Gideon, s Thomas & Hannah, b 12 Mo (Feb) 5, 1744/45 d 5-27-1837; m 2-14-1782 Elizabeth KEESE, dt William & Mary (0)
Ch: Rachel b 4-10-1789; m Abm. HICKS
Mary " 5-10-1783; " Rich. WILLITS
(Bibles)
Gilbert, s Jacob & Mercy; m 6-20-1762 Mary POST (mo)
Ch: Amy m Walter FARRINGTON
dis mo 6-30-1762; Mary dis 6-29-1763, rst 2-28-1770
(Seaman Gen.)
Giles, s Richard & Jane, d 1782; m 1735 Latitia ONDERDONK, dt Henry & Mary (mo)
Ch: Jordan b 1743
Richard m Sarah SMITH
Giles b 1748
Giles mo before 7 Mo (Sept) 24, 1735, rst; cert of mbrp abt 1750; dis 8-27-1755; Latitia joined mtg 12-26-1759
(Bibles)
Giles, s Giles & Latitia, b 30 June 1748 d Nov. 28, 1827; m before 12-27-1786 Lydia MOTT (mo)
Ch: Letitia M. m Elisha CARPENTER
Giles dis 1-1787; ack for mo referred to Pur. 12-19-1788, ct Pur. 4-17-1799
(Bibles)
Hannah, dt Thomas; m abt 1740 Solomon SEAMAN
Hannah, dt Thos. & Hannah, b 8 Mo (Oct) 3, 1749; m 1788 William JACKSON, London Grove, Pa.
Hannah, dt Giles & Letitia, b 1747; m 1779 Henry OAKLEY
Hannah, dt Williams & Mary, b 7-24-1776; m Samuel WILLETS
Hezekiah, s Nathaniel & Rachel, b 3 Mo (May) 4, 1711; m abt 1732 Mary DOUGHTY, dt Isaac & Elizabeth, b 1710
Ch: (4)
ack mo 7 Mo (Sept) 27, 1732; ct Pur. 4 Mo (June) 28, 1738; cf Pur.; dis 6-24-1761 for

SEAMAN, Hezekiah & Mary, continued
oath & serving as Constable
(Seaman Gen.)
Jacob, s Nathaniel & Rachel, b 10 Aug 1703
d 4-29-1759; m 1726 Mercy POWELL, dt Thomas
& Elizabeth, b 1702 d 3-13-1759
Ch: (9)
(Seaman Gen.)
Jacob, s Jacob & Mercy, b 2 Mo (Apr) 20, 1732;
m 1753 (cert not recorded, m bet 1-31- &
2-28-1753); m Anne KIRK, dt Arthur, b 8 Mo [(Oct) 3, 1731
Ch: Benjamin b 11-11-1753
Jemima b 10-13-1755
Jacob d 10-17-1856 ae 58 (Wby Stone)
Jacob, s Elijah & Phebe, b 11-20-1809 d 10-31-1879; m Mary B. SEAMAN, dt Thomas & Sarah
Ch: Samuel
(Seaman Gen.)
Jane signed rem cert 1707
Jane, dt Benj. & Jane, b 10 Mo (Dec) 14, 1713;
m 1731 (3 Mo (May) 28) John ROBBINS
signed Epistle abt 1725
Jane, dt Williams, b 11 Mo (Jan) 16, 1746/7;
m 1780 David KETCHAM
Jane, dt Richard & Jane; m James TITUS
Jemima, dt Jonathan; m 1771 Elias HICKS
Jonathan m Elizabeth WILLIS, dt John & Abigail,
b 1 Mo (Mar) 4, 1718/9 d 4-30-1777
Kezia, dt Nathaniel & Sarah; m 1754 Jacob MOTT
Leah, dt Zebulun & Phebe, b 1744; m 1762 Thomas WILLETS
Margaret, dt Samuel & Isabella; m Ambrose SEAMAN
Martha, dt Benjamin & Jane, b 12 Mo (Feb) 17,
1711/12; m 1743 Williams SEAMAN
Martha, dt Samuel & Martha, b 2 Mo (Apr) 3,
1745; m Henry B. TITUS
Martha, dt Zebulun & Phebe, b 2-28-1755 (or
1756); m 1782 Daniel WILLETS
Mary, dt Thomas & Mary; m John SMITH, of Hemp.;
m 2d 1722/23 John TITUS Sr.
Mary, dt Richard & Jane, Hemp.; m 1749/50
William MOTT
Mary, dt Thomas & Philadelphia, b 7 Mo (Sept)
28, 1737; m 1763 Henry FRANKLIN
(Seaman Gen.)
Mary, w Williams, dt Thomas & Mary JACKSON,
b 5 Mo (July) 6, 1749; m 2d 1787 Willets KIRBY
Mary, dt Gideon & Elizabeth; m 1800 Richard WILLITS
Mary, dt Samuel Jr. & Matilda M., b Roslyn
8-25-1883; m 1909 Leon A. RUSHMORE
Mary, dt Richard Jr. & Sarah; m Richbell MOTT
Mary W., dt Samuel J. & Matilda W.; m 1909
Leon Aug. RUSHMORE
Miriam, dt Samuel & Martha, b 12 Mo 25, 1751;
m Stephen ROBBINS
Miriam dis 8-25-1773
Nathaniel, s Capt. John, d 10-9-1757; m 8 Mo
(Oct) 9, 1695 Rachel WILLIS, dt Henry &
Mary, b 1680 d 8-31-1759
Mtg at his house 1698; Nathaniel & Rachel
signed Epistle abt 1725; Rachel on comm.
1700; Rachel had cert of unity for N.E.
1736; lived in Hempstead
(Seaman Gen.)
Nathaniel 2d, s Nathaniel & Rachel, b 9 Mo
(Nov) 18, 1699 d 6-14-1774; m 12 Mo (Feb)
28, 1721/22 Sarah POWELL, dt Thomas & Elizabeth
Ch: (7)
(Seaman Gen.)
Nathaniel 3d, s Nathaniel & Sarah, b 1724 d 11-21-1816; m Aug. 20, 1749 Sarah SMITH, dt
Richard (mo)
Ch: Richard b 6-17-1753; m Eliz. LAWRENCE
Nathaniel ack mo 2-2-1754
(Seaman Gen. & Bibles)
Obediah, s Thomas & Philadelphia, O.B., b 17
Feb. 1729; m 11-6-1754 at Wby Mary PEARSALL
dt Thomas & Sarah, Hemp.
Ch: Walter b 9-22-1755
Phila. " 3-26-1759
James " 12-26-1761
Thomas " 8-18-1764
Richard b 8- 2-1767
Obediah, s Samuel, dis mo before 7-29-1767
Phebe m 1753 John WRIGHT [25, 1744)
Phebe ack mo 5-29-1754 (mo before 5 Mo (July)
Phebe, dt Samuel & Martha; m 1765 Samuel HICKS
Phebe, dt Thomas & Hannah, b 5-5-1755; m 1779
John LOINES
Philadelphia, dt Obadiah & Maria, b 3-26-1759;
m 1779 Joseph DELAPLAINE Jr.
Rachel m 1738 Joseph ELFEREY (or Elfree)
Rachel m 1759 Micajah MOTT
Rachel, dt Samuel; m 1762 Silas HICKS
Rachel, dt Thomas & Hannah, b 3-30-1752; m 1783
Jacob SMITH
Rachel, dt Gideon & Elizabeth; m 1815 Abraham HICKS
Richard, s John & Eliz., b 1673 d 7 Mo (Sept)
25, 1749; m 1693/94 Jane MOTT, dt Adam &
Mary, d 8-31-1759 ae abt 79y
Ch: (12)
signed rem cert 1707; signed Epistle abt
1725; mtg at his house 1700
(Bibles)
Richard Jr., s Richard & Jane, b 11 Mo (Jan)
31, 1694/95 d 1752; m 1716/17 Sarah (perhaps FROST) (mo)
Ch: Richard m Sarah SEARING
Mary m Richbell MOTT
Sarah m Joseph LAKE
Richard ack mo 11 Mo (Jan) 30, 1716/17
(Bibles)
Richard, s Richard & Sarah; m Sarah SEARING
Richard dis mo 8-26-1761
(Bibles)
Richard, s Giles & Latitia; m 12-25-1799 at
Wby Sarah SMITH, dt Edmund & Deborah
of Jericho (clear); Sarah gct Jericho 2-19-1800
Richard I., s Zebulun, near Lakeville, d 8-15-1846 ae 77y

SEAMAN, continued
Richard W., s Elijah & Phebe, b 11-10-1821 d 2-16-1890; m Harriet VREDENBURGH (Wby Stone)
Richard W. m 2d Emma JONES
(Seaman Gen.)
Robert, s John, dec, O.B.; m 5 Mo (July) 6, 1743 at Wby, Esther WILLIAMS, dt Thomas, dec, Hemp.
Ch: Williams b 2 Mo (Apr) 22, 1744 d 4-22-1779
Samuel, s Nath. & Rachel, b 2 Mo (Apr) 13, 1715 d 1780; m 1736 Martha VALENTINE, dt Obadiah & Martha, b 9 Mo (Nov) 18, 1717
Ch: Willet m Mary SEARING
(10 other ch)
Samuel, s Samuel & Martha, b 10-13-1754; m 3-4-1778 Kezia TITUS, dt Thomas & Mary, b 4-23-1757
Ch: (8)
(Bibles)
Samuel d 10-30-1851 ae 88y 6m 9d; m Charity TREDWELL, dt John, d 3-17-1846 ae 76y 3m 15 d
her d recorded in both branches
(Wby Stones)
Samuel J., s Elias H. & Phebe, b 10-9-1857; m Matilda WILLETS, dt William, b 12-28-1854 d 5-1-1896 ae 42y 4m 3d
Ch: Mary b 5- 4-1881
Samuel J. b 3- 3-1883
Anna Louise b 10-9-1885
Frederick b 6-17-1888
Louis V. b 3- 1-1892 d 12-17-1892
cf Jericho for all but Louis
Samuel Jackson m 2d 6-25-1913 at Sam'l J. Seaman's, Jane R. WILLETS, dt Wm. & Mary V., both dec, Glen Cove, d 8-19-1817 in 64th yr
Samuel Jackson m 3d 8-31-1918 at Chas. H. Williams', New Rochelle, Katharine Valerie PILLING, dt Chas. B. & Eliz. C. des JARDINS both dec, New Rochelle, b Attleborough, Mass. 10-6-1865
Katharine recrq 8-19-1917; ct R. & P. 8-19-1934 for both
Samuel J. Jr., s Samuel J. & Matilda, b 3-3-1883; m Roslyn 10-8-1910 Ethelene BOGART, dt Dr. Jos. H. & Ethelene (Townsend), d 2----1920; m (2) Jane BOGART, sister of 1st w
Ch: H. Bogart b 12-24-1911
(Seaman Gen.)
Samuel J. Jr. m 2d 9-10-1921 Jane BOGART, dt Dr. Jos. H. & Ethelene
(Seaman Gen.)
Sarah b 1 Mo (Mar) 4, 1706/7; m 1728 Benjamin DUSENBURY
Sarah, dt Thomas & Phila., b 20 Mar. 1723; m 1745 Daniel HAWXHURST
Solomon, s Benj. & Martha; m before 1 Mo (Mar) 26, 1740 Hannah SEAMAN, dt Thomas
Solomon ack mo
(Seaman Gen.)
Thomas, s Richard & Jane, Wheatley, b 10 Mo (Dec) 19, 1696; m 1722/23 at Wby Philadelphia TITUS, dt John & Sarah, b 9 Mo (Nov) 29, 1700/01
Ch: Sarah b 3 Mo (May) 20, 1724
Obediah b 2 Mo (Apr) 17, 1729
Phebe b 1 Mo (Mar) 7, 1733/34
Mary b 7 Mo (Sept) 28, 1737
Thomas signed rem cert 1707
Thomas, s Nathaniel & Rachel, b 11 Mo (Jan) 2, 1712/13 d 1-13-1804; m 12 Mo (Feb) 3, 1741/42 Hannah WILLETS, dt Thomas & Catharine, b 10 Mo (Dec) 6, 1711 d 7-23-1775
Ch: Simeon b 8 Mo (Oct) 31, 1743 d 2 Mo 9, 1751
Gideon b 12 Mo (Feb) 5, 1744/45
Anne b 12 Mo (Feb) 25, 1746/47
Hannah b 8 Mo (Oct) 3, 1749
Rachel b 3-30-1752
Phebe b 5- 5-1755
(Bibles)
Willets, s Samuel & Martha; m Mary SEARING, dt Dr. Valentine
dis mo 4-28-1762
Wm. Jr., s Robert; m 1768 (cert not recorded, m bet. 4-27 & 5-25) Mary JACKSON, dt Thomas dec
William, nm, m before 8-14-1833 Jane SMITH (mo)
dis mo 9-18-1833 (2d w)
(Seaman Gen. & Bibles)
Wm. F., s Valentine & Anne; m 1822 (cert not recorded, m bet 10-16 & 11-30) Elizabeth HICKS, dt Isaac & Sarah
cf N. Y. (clear)
Wm. H., s Elias H. & Phebe, b 2-12-1868; m 6-7-1893 at Jno. W. Seaman's, Bkn. Margaret J. LAURIE, dt Wm. W. & Francis, both dec
Ch: Wm. Laurie
Annie Laurie
Faith Frances b 1-14-1898 d 10-22-1898
cf Jericho 1-15-1896; Margaret L. gct Christian Science Church 5-17-1931
(Jericho record)
Wm. Laurie, s Wm. H. & Margaret J., b G.C. 7-6-1894 d on Mt. Koscuisko, Australia 8-14-1928; m 6-14-1924 Sydney, Australia, Chrissie (or Christiana) BELL, dt Earnest W. & Christiana
(Seaman Gen.)
Wm. W., s Edmund & Mary W., b 12-28-1867; m 10-8-1898 at Flushing Carrie Lane FANNING, dt David G. & Elizabeth
Williams, s John & Hanna, b 6 Mo (Aug) 23, 1708; m 1743 Martha SEAMAN, dt Benjamin & Jane, b 12 Mo (Feb) 17, 1711/12 d 4-4-1774 (burned in their house as it burned)
Ch: Edmund b 12 Mo (Feb) 28, 1743/4 d 1 Mo 30, 1744
Micah b 5 Mo (July) 19, 1745 d 4 Mo 29, 1746
Jane b 11 Mo (Jan) 16, 1746/7
John b 12 Mo (Feb) 27, 1747/8 d 6 Mo 29, 1748
Benjamin b 8 Mo (Oct) 27, 1749 d 7 Mo 10 1750
John b 5 Mo (July) 14, 1751 d 8-23-1756

SEAMAN, continued
Williams Jr., s Robert, d 1779; m 5-4-1768 at Wby, Mary JACKSON, dt Thomas, dec
Ch: David b 6-12-1770
Mary b 3-27-1774
Hannah b 7-24-1776
Esther b 4-30-1779 8d after her father's d
Wright, s Jacob, d 10-7-1867 ae 64; m -----
Ch: (3 dt)
(Seaman Gen.)
Zebulun, nm, s David, b 17 Mar. 1718 d 2-19-1784; m 17 Apr 1743 Phebe VALENTINE, dt Obadiah & Martha, b 9 Mo (Nov) 29, 1721 d Aug. 4, 1803
Ch: Leah b 1744; m Thomas WILLITS
Mary b 1745; m Jordan SEAMAN
Zebulun b 1747
John Wm. b 1749; m Jane JACKSON
Martha b 2-27-1755; m Daniel WILLETS
Leonard b 9-27-1762; m Mary TITUS & Leah SIMONSON
Phebe b 1771; m Samuel SEARING
Phebe ack mo 4-24-1754
(Bibles)

SEARING
Amy, dt John & Mary, b 2-23-1768; m 1786 Daniel MOTT
Cynthia d 3-9-1869 ae 81y 7m 14d (Wby Stone)
Esther d 2-3-1882 ae 83y 9m 14d (Man. Stone)
George E. d 11-11-1861 ae 58 (Wby Stone)
John, s John, dec, Hemp., d 5-20-1822 ae 48y & abt 5m; m 1-5-1764 at Mk. Mary PRIOR, dt Samuel & Mary, O.B.
Ch: Mary b 12-12-1764
John " 2-11-1766
Amey " 2-23-1768
Phebe
John Jr. m Oblong 1789 Mary -----
ct Oblong 9-30-1789 (clear); Mary rocf Oblong 1-27-1790
John S., s Samuel & Phebe, Jericho; m 3-29-1820 at Wby, Anna LOINES, dt John & Phebe, Wby, b 3-13-1797
Ch: Phebe b 3-2-1821
Mary, dt Dr. Valentine; m Willets SEAMAN
Mary U., dt John; m 1782 Samuel WOOD
Phebe, dt John & Mary; m 1795 Thomas WILLIS
Rebecca, dt Samuel & Phebe; m 1816 Townsend HAWXHURST
Richard, Searingtown; m Mary E. HAINES, d 11-24-1835 (Man. Stone has ae 23y)
Ch: Ann Maria b 2- 2-1830
Samuel Haines b 9-22-1832
Mary Esther b 7-27-1835 d 10-30-1921 at Westwood, N. J.
ct Scipio 1-14-1829 (clear); Mary E. rocf Scipio 8-19-1829
Ruth d 3-24-1879 ae 54y 6m (Wby Stone)
Samuel, Searingtown, b 8-5-1756 d 3-31-1838; m Phebe SEAMAN, dt Zebulun & Phebe, b 1771 d 3-19-1846 ae 78y 10m (O)
Zebulon d 11-13-1865 ae 77 (Man. Stone)

SEATON
Jane had cert prepared for her 4 Mo (June) 28, 1738 (prob of unity)

SECOR
Eliza Ann, dt Isaac & Ann; m 1842 Benjamin MOTT
Willets, M.C. & Hannah
Ch: Elizabeth C. d 10-1-1826 ae 6y 8m

SHARP
Willoughby m Dora F. ELLIOTT, wd Gilbert Alex. Boswell Elliott, dt Alex. & Dora HOPKINS, b 10-29-1889

SHARPLESS
Fred Farley, Houghton, Mich., s Alfred & Eliz. (Cope), Westchester, Pa.; m 6-23-1892 at Wm. E. Hawxhurst's, Caroline HAWXHURST, dt Wm. E. & Marianna, Wby
Ch: Paul b Wby 4-26-1901
Frederick & Paul recrq 10-20-1912
(Register gives Fred's b 1-23-1866, record 4-23-1866)
Paul, s Fred'k F. & Caroline, Landsdowne, Pa., b Wby 4-26-1901; m Swarthmore, Pa. 6-20-1930 Elizabeth S. STANFORD, dt Albert & Helen (Whipple)

SHAW
Richard, at the Rock, house burned; Rock Friends contributed toward the loss 1730

SHEPHERD
Caleb W., s Wm. R. & Eliza, Bkn.; m 10-8-1879 at Martha Willets', Sarah M. WILLETS (signed as Sarah W. Shepherd), dt Edmund & Martha

SHERWOOD
Isaac, s Isaac & Eliz. (McEachin), b 2-14-1821 d Manhasset 9-4-1909; m Martha ROGERS, dt Morris M. & Sarah (Willets) b 5-4-1819 d 1-13-1909
cf N. Y 1855; Martha recrq 3-17-1886
Morris m 5-24-1871 Sarah C. WILLETS, dt Isaac U. & Mary C., b 10-14-1844 d 3-16-1891 ae 42y 5m 2d bur Wby

SHILCOCK
Helen M., dt Clarence & Beulah F.; m 1937 Richard POST

SHOTWELL
Amy, dt Joseph & Annie; m Charles BROOKE; m 2d 1794 Samuel HICKS
Joseph F., s Joseph S. & Deborah, N.Y.C., b 1-28-1827 d 6-14-1869 bur Wby; m 9-22-1847 Annie TITUS, dt William & Phebe W., b 12-3-1827 d 5-26-1904 ae 75y 4m 23d (O)
Ch: Joseph S. b 8-4-1849 d 7-11-1851 (Wby Stone)
William
Walter

SHOTWELL, Joseph & Annie, continued
Ch: Amy
Walter F., s Jos. F. & Annie (Titus); m Phebe T. -----
Ch: Joseph W. d 4-26-1899 ae 1y 2m 26d (Wby Stone)

SIMONSON
Amie B. d 1852 ae 17y (Wby Stone)
John R., nm, m 5-14-1890 Julia THORNE, dt Isaac & Emily, b 5-16-1867 d Glen Head 1-19-1938
Townsend W. m Mary F. ----- d 6-1-1863 ae 58y 6m 20d (Mk. Stone)

SKIDMORE
William J. b 4-3-1833 d 8-3-1866 (Man. Stone)

SLEIGH
Arthur Hastings m Mary Jane VALENTINE, dt John T. & Eliz., b 4-23-1857
Hannah m 1723 John DOUGHTY
Stephen m Catharine KENNEDY b 8-19-1817 d 6-26-1893 bur Mk.

SMEDLEY
Elizabeth, dt Arthur C. & Golda (Brown), b Wilmington, Del. 7-22-1913; m 1938 Moyer WOOD

SMITH
Abigail recrq; d 2-3-1875 ae 76y 1m 9d
Ann m 1727 Ezekiel GRIFFEN
Anna W., dt Samuel & Mary; m 1856 Jonathan DICKINSON (O)
Benjamin b at the Mote, West Meath, Ireland, 3 Mo (May) 6, 1685 d 1-17-1775; m 1719/20 Hannah TITUS, dt Edmund & Martha, b 9 Mo (Nov) 1667
Hannah signed a rem cert 1707; cert of clear from Ireland, wanting, but account from a man who was his neighbor there, satisfied he is clear; resided in Flushing several yr
Charles Valentine m 6-6-1925 Dorothy J. WILLITS, dt Charles F. & Grace O.
Deborah, dt Samuel & Mary; m 1851 Clarkson TABER (O)
Edmund, s James & Sarah, d 6-14-1831 ae 99y 5m 8d; m Deborah ----- d 1-27-1819 ae 74y 10m
Elizabeth, near Merricks, dt William HALLOCK; mo before 8-20-1765; ack mo 12-25-1765; ct Oblong 1-29-1766; d 1-9-1---
Emily, dt Halstead M. & Sarah U., b Rye, N. Y.; m 1923 Halstead RUSHMORE
Frances m 1732 Edward FARRINGTON
Halsey M. m 5-25-1885 Sarah UNDERHILL, dt Richard & Mary K., b 5-17-1861 d G.C. 11-1-1922
Hannah ack mo 9-20-1797
Hannah, dt Jacob & Rachel; m 1804 Joseph WHITSON
Jacob, s John, N. Hemp., d 6-17-1818 ae 59y 17d m 3-5-1783 at Wby Rachel SEAMAN, dt Thomas & Hannah, dec, Hemp., b 3-30-1752
Ch: Hannah b 12-24-1783
Ann b 9- 8-1786
Phebe " 12- 6-1789
James B. Jr., s James B. & Angelia E. (Reynolds) b Eureka, N. Y. 4-28-1896; m 7-23-1927 Katherine L. BELL, dt Arthur E. & Martha (Hallock) b 4-10-1898
James B. rocf Greenfield & Neversink 1-18-1931; cf Milton, N. Y. same day for Katherine; Arthur E. b Belfast, Ireland; Martha b Milton, N. Y.
James L. m Charlotte S. ----- d 2-23-1863 ae 32y (Wby Stone)
Jane m 1833 William SEAMAN
Lillian, dt Alex. & Josephine, b 10-13-1883 Bkn.; m C. Wm. HANSEN
Martha (some Martha signed Epistle abt 1725); ack misconduct 5 Mo (July) 30, 1707
Martha (form Townsend) dis mo before 8-27-1783
Mary, dt Benjamin & Mary; m abt 1746 Richard TITUS
Mary, dt Thomas & Phebe, nm, b 5 Mo (July) 13, 1748; m 1763 Thomas COCK
Mary b 10-10-1798 (O)
Moses d 7-28-1852 ae 28y 3m 28d (Wby Stone)
Nathan & Latitia (mo)
Latitia ack mo 2-28-1759
Phebe m Richard MOTT
Phebe Jr., s Jacob & Rachel; m 1816 Joseph WILLETS
Richard, nm & -----
Ch: Sarah m Nath. SEAMAN
Ruth B., dt Archibald & Isabelle (Blackburn); m Alexander H. PRINZ
S. Archibald, s Samuel & Frances C., b Wilton, N. H. 11-27-1870; m Isabelle BLACKBURN, dt Alex. & Margaret E., Chicago, b Chicago 3-9-1874
Ch: Ruth Blackburn b Elizabeth, N. J. 7-4-1905 (other ch nm)
Archibald & Isabelle recrq 4-17-1921; Ruth recrq 3-18-1923
Samuel & Mary
Ch: Anna W.
Deborah
cf N. Y. for Mary & ch 1-7-1846
Sarah's ack sent from Oblong, rst & ct Oblong 11-26-1777
Sarah (form Allen) dis mo before 5-17-1809; rst 1813
Sylvanus, S.S. Plains; m Martha RAYNOR, d 10-13-1852 ae abt 73
Ch: Phebe b 9-9-1819
William recrq 1-13-1854 (O)

SOUTHWICK
Julia A. b 12-10-1817; m abt 1840 Horace PRIOR

SPENCER
William D. b 3-23-1830 d 12-13-1885

SPRAGUE
Alfred m Eliza Jane POST b 12-10-1831 d 7-24-1902 (Wby Stone)

SPRAGUE, continued
Jacob m Elizabeth WILLIAMS, d 2-12-1854 ae 80
Ch: Caroline d 11-26-1858
(Wby Stones)
Micah [SPRAGG] m 1742 Hannah WILLIS
Hannah ack misconduct
Newberry d 4-4-1870 ae 60y 1m 7d
Rowland d 8-27-1883 ae in 78th yr; m Elizabeth S. ----- (perhaps Rowland's w as stones are adjacent, or Newberry's w as stones are adjacent in Wby) d 1-12-1876 ae in 64th yr

STANFORD
Elizabeth S., dt Albert & Helen (Whipple); m 1930 Paul SHARPLESS

STARKINS
Abigail d 3-12-1847 (Man. Stone)

STEVENS
Marie m Frederick C. HICKS
Neil Campbell, s Fred'k W. & Mary W. (Olden), b E. Orange, N. J. 10-23-1889; m Evelyn NOBLE b Syracuse, N. Y.
Ch: John Campbell b Millbrook, N. Y. 3-6-1921
recrq 8-16-1925; John C. recrq of parents same day
James d 11-30-1856 ae 63 (Wby Stone)

STEWART
Gwendolyn, nm, m 1930 Farrand Rogers MILLER

STIVERS
Kezia (form Doty) dis mo before 10-20-1803; rst 7-20-1808
Martha, dt Kezia, recrq 3-17-1813

STOAKS (or Stokes)
Thomas, Waterford, N. J., m 1715 Rachel WRIGHT
ct Newton, N. J. 6 Mo (Aug) 31, 1715 for Rachel, "being in election to m Thomas Stoaks"

STRATTON
Ruth m abt 1786 Willet TITUS

STREETER
Daniel Denison, s Milford B. & Mariah (Wycoff) b 7-27-1885; m Gladys M. -----
Ch: Catherine b Bkn. 1-23-1917
Daniel Denison Jr. b Bkn. 2-8-1925
Samuel Schuyler b Bkn. 5-19-1926
Daniel recrq 10-20-1912; Catherine & Daniel recrq of parents 3-15-1925; ct N. Y. for all 7-21-1930

STRINGHAM
Irene, dt John & Annie E., b Crum Elbow 10-9-1862; m Wm. J. MUDGE
Irving J., s John & Annie E., b 12-18-1867; m N. Y. C. 2-29-1892 Eleanor DEYO b 2-22-1866
Ch: Marion b 5-17-1898
Ch: Lydia b 2-28-1909
cf N. Y. for all 4 11-17-1912
Lydia, dt Irving J. & Eleanor D., b 2-28-1909; m 1930 Donald Morgan DOUGHTY
Marion, dt Irving J. & Eleanor, b 5-17-1898; m 1923 Harold Van Alden WAIT

STRONG
Georgina m Frederick C. HICKS
Hannah, dt Selah & Hannah; m 1736 Richard WILLITS

STRONGITHAM
Catharine, dt Henry & Anna BALDWIN, d 3-20-1846 ae 46y

SUTTON
Hazel Blossom m 1913 Harold HAWXHURST
Joseph d 10-30-1827 ae 45y

SWARTZ
Harriet m 1933 Wm. Mott HICKS

SWEET
Jonathan, s Elnathan & Abiah, Dutchess Co.; m 9-15-1791 at Cow Neck, Mary ROBBINS, dt Jeremiah & Hannah, Queens Co.

SYLVEN
Judith d 11-3-1880 ae abt 88 (Wby Stone)

TABER
Clarkson, s Daniel & Rebecca, Varsalboro, Me.; m 4-17-1851 at Wby Deborah SMITH, dt Samuel & Mary, Jericho (O)
Martha, dt Samuel T.; m 1867 Wm. Henry WILLETS
Samuel C. rocf Nine Partners 1860; d 2-4-1871
Samuel T., s Thomas & Phebe, b 4-13-1824 d 2-4-1870; m Katherine H. ----- b 2-10-1824 d 11-16-1902
Ch: Martha m Wm. H. WILLETS
(Wby Stones)
Stephen rocf Flushing 1857; d 4-23-1886
Thomas, Roslyn, b 5-19-1785 d 3-21-1862 (Wby Stone); m Phebe TITUS b 11-1-1799 d 8-13-1824
Ch: Samuel T. b 4-13-1824
ct N.P. not noticed; cf Nine Partners 1855

TAPPEN
Isaac d 7-12-1862 ae 36 (Wby Stone)
John B. C. m 5-21-1885 Caroline A. TITUS, dt James & Caroline V., b 7-4-1857
Leonard d 12-31-1861 ae 73 (Wby Stone)
Mary Ann, dt Jeremiah & Mary, b 12-3-1814; m abt 1834 Charles TITUS
Philena d 10-8-1880 ae 86 (Wby Stone)
Willet U. d 4-25-1901 ae 83y 1m; m Phebe Ann ----- d 5-16-1891 ae 70y 24d (Wby Stones)

TAYLOR
Edgar Jefferson m 10-9-1900 Mary Esther WHITSON, dt Samuel & Phebe, d Westbrook, Conn.

TAYLOR, Edgar Jefferson & Mary Esther, continued
11-16-1917

TEMPLE
Ada U., dt Richard & Mary K. UNDERHILL; m 1902
Jacob Paxson Temple; m 2d 1926 Eugene Price
CHEYNEY
Ada's name rem from the Reg. as she is recorded in Concord, Pa.
Jacob Paxson, s Chas., dec, & Philena, Concord,
Pa.; m 5-10-1902 at Mary K. Underhill's,
Ada UNDERHILL, dt Richard, dec, & Mary K.,
Glen Cove, d 11-24-1938
Ch: Emily M. d 4-30-1914 in 11th yr
Richard U. b 2- 8-1806
Jacob P. b 1-24-1909 d 9-10-1918
Ada m 2d 6-28-1926 Eugene Price CHEYNEY
Richard U., s Jacob & Ada (Underhill), b 2-8-1906; m Downington, Pa. 6-9-1928 Edna WELLS
dt Sherman & Deborah (Fayre)
Richard's name rem from Reg. as he is recorded in Concord, Pa.

THAYER
Francis Kendall, s Geo. A., dec, & Jane J.,
N. Hemp.; m 11-23-1898 at Thos. Mott's,
Port Washington, Caroline MOTT, dt Thomas
& Martha W., N. Hemp.
George A. Jr., s Geo. A. & Jane (Jones), Bkn.,
b 5-26-1867 d 5-15-1937; m 6-14-1892 at
Isaac H. Cocks', Elizabeth H. COCKS, dt
Isaac H. & Mary W.
Ch: George A. 3d b 12-22-1893
Wm. Frederick b 6- 2-1899
Robert Warren b 11-14-1906
George recrq 2-15-1914; 3 ch recrq 3-16-1913
George A. 3d, s Geo. A. Jr. & Eliz. H. (Cocks),
b 12-22-1893; m Jean WALTER, dt B. Franklin
& Eleanor (Wallace), b Christiana, Pa. 12-31-1904
Ch: George A. b 5-28-1930
George A. recrq 3-16-1913; Jean recrq 9-16-1926

THIMM
Morley, s Curt & Eliz. (Vasse), b Bayside,
L. I. 11-2-1908; recrq 4-18-1926
Curt b Germany; Elizabeth b Paris; they
reside Roslyn

THOMAS
Abigail mo before 2 Mo (Apr) 30, 1729; ack mo
Albert d 12-17-1896 ae 63y 1d; m Sarah M. -----
d 4-29-1885 ae 41y 4m 29d
Agnes d 5-16-1876 ae 82y 6m
Alice Ann d ae 4m 11d (unidentified stone, Wby)
Charles & Sarah
Ch: Libbie d 1-11-1874 ae 17y 8m 2d (Wby Stone)
James m Mary C. ----- d 2-5-1901 ae 67y 6m 5d
Ch: Jennie G. d 3-15-1901 ae 44
Annie A. " 11-30-1884 ae 20y 3m 15d
(Wby Stones)
William d 10-23-1883 ae 77y 8m 9d; m Agnes A.
d 4-25-1891 ae 82y 6m 15d

THOMPSON
Grove G. m 7-31-1909 Phebe A. MERRITT, dt Benjamin A. & Hannah E. (White), b Pinelawn,
L. I. 10-30-1880
Ch: Hazel b Lynbrook, L. I. 3- 2-1912
Grove " " " 1-18-1915
Phebe A. & ch recrq 12-18-1927; ct N. Y.
10-19-1930 with ch; Phebe A. m 2d -----
SMITH; Benj. Merritt b Bethpage; Hannah E.
White b Stoney Brook, L. I.
Dr. Leonard Ramsay, nm, Los Angeles; m in Quaker manner 6-15-1926, Ruth Rogers MILLER, dt
Wilhelm & Mary (Rogers), b N.Y.C. 4-29-1903

THORNE
Anna C., dt Samuel & Maria H.; m 1861 Lewis
VALENTINE
Charles [Thorn], s Chas. & Ann (Kirby); m 1804
by Rev. Marmaduke Earle Phiany COCK, dt
Daniel & Roseannah (Townsend), b 4-23-1785
[d 1840
Ch: (4) (Cox Gen.)
Elbert H. [Thorn], s Samuel & Maria, b 4-19-1827 d 9-9-1904; m 1861 Cornelia DOWNING,
dt Silas & Elizabeth
Ch: Lizzie d 9- 2-1865 ae 3y 1m
Samuel b 2-19-1865 d 2-19-1872
(Mk. Stones & Bibles)
Florence L., dt Isaac C. & Emily B., b 5-2-1871; m John J. GARDNER
Hannah [Thorn], dt John & Mary, b 1678; m 1701
Richard CORNELL
Hannah, dt Thomas & Penelope, b 1732; m abt
1752 Jacob BOWNE; m 2d 1789 William TITUS
Isaac C., s Samuel C. & Maria, Mk., b 2-2-1830
d 1-3-1910 G.C.; m Emily JACKSON, dt Jacob
& Phebe (Duryea), b 9-5-1846 d Bkn. 3-8-1812 ae 72y 6m 3d
Ch: Emily C.
Julia J. b 5-16-1867 (Reg. gives Emily C.
now Julia T. Simonson)
Adison C. b 5-16-1869
Florence L. b 5- 2-1871
Mary W. b 10-18-1872
Lucy L. b 3- 2-1866 d 5-12-1866 bur Mk
Emily rocf Jericho 11-20-1867
James [Thorn], s Thomas & Phebe; m before 10-19-1796 Mary COCK, dt Samuel & Elizabeth,
b 6-25-1763 d 1828 (mo)
Ch: Samuel C. b 1-27-1798
Leonard b 10-11-1800
mo before 10-19-1796, dis next mo
(Cox Gen.)
John, s Benj., dec, & Frances, Milan, Dutchess
Co.; m 9-28-1820 at Mk. Mary WEEKS, dt
Richard & Martha, O.B., d 9-30-1878 ae 77y
1m 11d bur Mk.
Julia, dt Isaac & Emily, b 5-16-1867; m 1890
John R. SIMONSON
Landon Ketcham, N. Y. & Bay Shore; m abt 10-29-1936 (not under care of mtg) Veronica
ELLIOTT, dt Gilbert Alex. B. & Dora F.

THORNE, continued
Mary [Thorn], dt Stephen & Elizabeth, b 6-25-1780; m 1800 Uriah COCK
Mary Eliz., dt Sam'l C. & Maria H., b 8-1-1818; m 1838 Isaac COCKS
Mary W., dt Isaac C. & Emily B., b 10-18-1872; m 1917 Edward N. BAISLEY
Phebe, dt Thomas & Penelope, b 3 Mo (May) 12, 1737; m 1756 James COCK
Samuel C. [Thorn], s James & Mary, Mk, b 1-27-1798 d 2-18-1862 ae 64y 22d; m 10-25-1818 Maria HOOGLAND, dt Elbert & Willemptje, d 5-3-1879 ae 77y
Ch: Mary Elizabeth b 8- 1-1820; m Isaac COCK
Anna C. b 9- 8-1822; m Lewis VALENTINE
James b 8- 8-1824 d 1-24-1891 G.C.
Elbert H. b 4-19-1827
Isaac C. b 2- 7-1830
William H. b 11- 7-1831; ct N. Y.
Leonard b 12-19-1833 d 3-3-1878
Samuel C. recrq; Maria recrq
(Cox Gen.)
Stephen, s Daniel & Mary; m 8-22-1779 Elizabeth COLES, dt Nathaniel & Hannah, b 12-24-1758 d 8-27-1827 ae abt 70
Ch: 3 dt)
(Bibles)
Thomas [Thorn], s Jos. & Martha J. (Bowne), b 1704 d 1746/7; m 1725 Penelope COLES, dt Jos. & Elizabeth (Wright), b 1707(?) d 1739
Ch: Hannah b 1732
Phebe b 3 Mo (May) 12, 1737
(4 other ch)
(Bibles)
William [Thorn], s Isaac & Hannah, Dutchess Co.; m 10-31-1765 at Wby Jemima TITUS, dt Samuel, dec, Queens Co.
cf Nine Partners (clear); Jemima gct N.P. 1-29-1766
Unidentified Stones, Wby
Mary [Thorn] d 2-13-1887 ae 70
Daniel [Thorn] d 4----1845 ae 64

THORNICRAFT
Adah, dt Derick & Temperance; m abt 1764 Daniel ALBERTSON
Derick, s Thomas & Wilmot; m 1741 Temperance HOPKINS, dt Daniel & Amey
Ch: Adah m Daniel ALBERTSON
Peter b 1749; m Helen DOWNING
Derick & Temperance ack 10-22-1764 consenting to their dt's m, too near akin, at his house
(Bibles)
Francis ack mo before 11-27-1765
Thomas, s William & Hannah; m Willmett ALBERTSON, dt Derick & Dinah
Ch: Anne m Isaac DOTY Jr.
Benjamin m Elizabeth KIRBY
Derick m 1741 Temperance HOPKINS
signed Epistle abt 1725; appeared in the records until 1737
(Bibles)

TIMMIS
Wm. Walter, s Walter Stott & Mary G. (Opey), b Bkn. 4-4-1896; m 8-18-1917 at Aunt's, Pleasant Plains, S. I. Eleanor MORGAN, dt Floyd S. N. & Eleanor, b Chicago 7-16-1895
Ch: Wm. Walter Jr. b Wash., D.C. 9-30-1918
Eleanor Patracia b Phila. 5-16-1921
ch recrq 9-18-1927; Wm. Walter recrq 9-18-1927; Wm. Walter resigned 12----1936, joined Episcopal Church; Floyd S. N. b Summit, N. J. 8-26-1867; Eleanor b N.Y.C. 1-16-1872 d La Grange, Ill. 7-3-1899; Walter b Wolverhampton; Mary Garetta Opey b Griggstown, N. J.

TITUS
Abigail, dt William & Sarah; m 1778 Edmund WILLIS
Ann, dt Samuel & Phebe, b 9-5-1811; m 1831 Townsend VALENTINE (mo)
Anna, dt Henry & Phebe; m 1837 James WILLITS
Anna, dt Geo. P. & Mary T., b 7-22-1861; m Benjamin VAN NOSTRAND
Anna C., dt Robert & Mary W.; m James R. WILLETS
Anne, dt Daniel & Amy; m 1814 Amos WILLITS
Annie, dt William & Phebe W., b 12-3-1827; m 1847 Joseph F. SHOTWELL (0)
Annie 1860 (unidentified stone, Wby)
Annie d 7-11-1856 ae 16y 7m 11d (unidentified stone, Wby)
Benjamin, s Timothy & Margaret, b 6-11-1814 d 11-4-1883 ae 67; m 12-28-1853 Nancy ADAMS dt Jacob & Betsey, b 9-4-1833 d 11-4-1895
Ch: (8)
(Bibles)
Caroline A., dt James & Caroline V., b 7-4-1857; m 1885 John B. C. TAPPEN
Charity, dt Timothy & Margaret; m 1834 Ephraim C. HAWXHURST
Charles, (prob) s Francis & Ruth, b 2-1-1805; m before 10-15-1834 Mary Ann TAPPEN, dt Jeremiah & Mary, b 12-3-1814 (mo)
Ch: Caroline m Henry HARTT
Charles dis mo 12-7-1834
(Bibles)
Charles F., s Samuel B. & Phebe, b 7-2-1815 d 2-15-1899 ae 83y 7m 13d; m 4-12-1843 Mary F. BURLING, dt Benj. F. & Hannah, b 1-17-1815 d 5-19-1903 ae 88y 4m 2d
Ch: George B.
Hannah B.
cf N. Y. 1855 for all
bur Wby
(Bibles)
Daniel, s Henry & Sarah, Wby & Hemp., b 3-9-1762 d 10-22-1826; m 1-1-1783 at Beth. Amy WILLETS, dt Samuel & Jane, both dec, Hemp.
Ch: Henry b 4- 7-1784
Mary b 1-27-1786 d 7-30-1821
Sarah b 3-29-1788 d 10-21-1819 bur Wby
Anne " 8-19-1794
Phebe b 11-19-1796 d 10-15-1818

TITUS, Daniel & Amy, continued
Ch: William b 12-7-1799
Daniel, s Wm. & Phebe, b 6-1-1826 d 12-12-1896 bur Wby; m Annie -----
Ch: Annie d 1867 ae 9m 24d
(Wby Stones)
David, s Silas & Sarah, b 4 Mo (June) 20, 1719; m 6-26-1741 Hannah HICKS, dt Jacob & Hannah
Ch: (2)
(Bibles)
Edmund, s Robert & Hannah, Wby, b 1630 d 2 Mo (Apr) 7, 1715; m Martha WASHBORNE, dt William & Jane, d 2 Mo (Apr) 17, 1727 in 90th yr
Ch: Samuel b 6 Mo (Aug) 1658; m Eliz. POWELL
Phebe " 1 Mo (Mar) 1660; m (1) Samuel SCUDDER (2) Robt. FIELD
Martha b 1 Mo (Mar) 1663; m Benj. SEAMAN
Mary b 5 Mo (July) 1665; m Wm. WILLIS
Hannah b 9 Mo (Nov) 1667; m Benj. SMITH
Jane b 2 Mo (Apr) 1670; m James DENTON
John b 2 Mo (Apr) 29, 1672; m 1695 Sarah WILLIS
Peter b 6 Mo (Aug) 1674; m Martha JACKSON
Silas b 1676; m 1704 Sarah HAIGHT
Patience b 12 Mo (Feb) 4, 1678/9; m 1704 Nicholas HAIGHT
Temperance b 1 Mo (Mar) 1681 d 11 Mo 15, 1704
prominent in mtg 1692; signed rem cert 1707
(Bibles)
Edmund, s Silas & Sarah, b 8 Mo (Oct) 1, 1705 d 5-23-1754; m abt 1732 Sarah TITUS, dt John & Sarah, b 1 Mo (Mar) 2, 1708/9 d 1772
Ch: Phebe b 4 Mo (June) 29, 1733; m Jos. PRIOR
Sarah b 8 Mo (Oct) 27, 1735; m Isaac RUSHMORE
Martha b 1 Mo (Mar) 24, 1737/8 d 7-15-1769
Mary b 7 Mo (Sept) 17, 1740; m Henry POST
Hannah b 7 Mo (Sept) 12, 1743; m Willets KIRBY
Sarah m 2d Isaac DOTY
(Bibles)
Edward Francis b 1-7-1839 d 9-2-1892 (unidentified stone, Wby)
Edward S. m Catharine MANNING b 4-29-1849 d 10-15-1896
Eliza d 10-13-1895 ae 79 (unidentified stone, Wby)
Elizabeth, dt Samuel & Mary, b 8 Mo (Oct) 26, 1729; m 1750 John KEESE
Elizabeth, dt James & Jane; m 1753 Charles DOTY (mo)
Elizabeth, dt Samuel; m 1757 Samuel COCK
Elizabeth, dt William; m 1779 John HAYDOCK
Elizabeth, dt Richard; m 1786 Jordan WRIGHT
Elizabeth, dt John & Sarah P.; m 1840 Jacob CONKLIN (0)
Elizabeth, dt Henry & Phebe, b 9-23-1829; m Scudder V. WHITNEY
Elizabeth d 3-6-1859 ae 49y 3m 3d (unidentified stone, Wby)
Elizabeth, dt Peter; m Henry TOWNSEND (mo)
Elizabeth Ann recrq 5-15-1844 (0)
Elizabeth C., dt Rowland & Sarah; m 1835 Sidney B. ALLEY
Elizabeth P., dt Samuel & Mary P., b 10-14-1815; m 1835 William WILLETS
Ellwood V., s James & Caroline, b 1-18-1852; m Maria Louise COX, dt Daniel D. & Mary L.
Ch: Mary L. d 8- 9-1882 ae 8m 25d
Helen L. d 9-25-1905 ae 29y 19d
Caroline V. b 1-4-1849; m Percival EASTMAN
(Bibles)
Emily 1860 (unidentified stone, Wby)
Esther, dt Isaac & Jemima, b 2-27-1796; m Oliver CRAFT
Francis, s Isaac & Martha, d 9-28-1845 ae 76 yr
Francis, s Jacob & Martha, Wheatley; m Ruth CROOKER, dt William & Esther, b 1778 d 3-12-1850 (wd)
Ch: Martha d 3-10-1799 ae 15d
William C. b 8-23-1800
James b 10-29-1802; dis
Charles b 3- 1-1805
Samuel C. b 6-20-1807
Stephen R. b 12-16-1811
Edward b 6-29-1816 d 7-28-1827
George B., s Charles F. & Mary F., Wby, b 12-31-1843 d 2-2-1911; m 5-20-1869 at Isaac U. Willets', Marietta WILLETS, dt Isaac U. & Mary C., N. Hemp., b 10-14-1844 d Bkn. 1-9-1921
Ch: Alice W.b 5-18-1870
Mary W. b 11-19-1873
Georgiana b 2-16-1876
ct N.Y. for all 5-17-1876; cf N.Y. 9-14-1881 for Alice Mary & Georgiana
George P., s Peter & Elizabeth (Mudge), Wby & N. Hemp., b 6-30-1776 d 2-25-1842 ae 65y 7m 25d; m 1-29-1806 at Wby Mary CARLE, dt John & Phebe (Hicks), O.B., b 7-28-1781 d 9-13-1829 ae 48y 1m 15d
Ch: Phebe C. b 2-11-1807 d 1-11-1828 ae 20y 11m
Elizabeth b 12-3-1809 d 3-6-1859
Robert b 7-13-1813; m Mary W. HOPKINS
Silas b 2-12-1817 d 7-11-1882 (unm)
(Bibles & Wby Stones)
George P., s Robert & Mary W., b 1-15-1843 d 5-7-1918; m 10-17-1867 Mary TOWNSEND, dt Jos. L. & Hannah W., b 3-10-1838 d E. Williston 12-3-1909
Ch: Anna W. b 7-22-1868; m Benj. VAN NOSTRAND
William E. b 10-9-1871 d 4-11-1902
Robert b 1-14-1873 d 8-24-1873 ae 7m 10d
ch recrq of mother 4-15-1874
bur Wby
(Bibles)
Gilbert, s James & Jane; m 1753 Mary YOUNGS, dt Alexander & Sarah (Coles) (mo) Gilbert a nm
Mary ack mo 5-19-1753; Gilbert ack mo 6-27-1753
(Youngs Gen.)
Hannah, dt William; m 1755 Joseph WILLETS

TITUS, continued
Hannah, dt Edmund; m 1764 Willet KIRBY
Hannah, dt John; m 1785 Joshua TITUS
Hannah, dt Samuel & Abigail; m 1810 Jacob MUDGE
Hannah, dt Henry & Phebe, b 4-28-1810; m Thomas J. GERALD
Hannah 1849 (unidentified stone, Wby)
Hannah B., dt Charles F. & Mary F.; m 1870 Edward WILLETS
Henrietta, dt Silas & Mary; m Daniel D. WHITNEY
Henry, s John & Sarah, b 12 Mo (Feb) 1, 1722/23 d 11-4-1767 ae abt 44y 9m; m 9 Mo (Nov) 28, 1749 Sarah BIRDSALL, dt Daniel & Johannah
Ch: Sarah b 2- 2-1753
William b 9-28-1754
John b 11- 1-1757
Samuel b 1- 8-1760
Daniel b 3- 9-1762
Johanna b 11- 9-1765
(Bibles)
Henry, s Peter & Mary, York Ferry, b 9 Mo (Nov) 9, 1739 d 4-9-1829; m 1766 Martha SEAMAN, dt Samuel & Martha, b 2 Mo (Apr) 3, 1745 d 6-5-1816 (mo)
Ch: Mary b 12 Mo (Feb) 30 1771; m Andrew COCK
(4 other ch)
Mary ack mo 6-26-1771
(Bibles)
Henry, s Daniel & Amy, Duck Pond & N. Hemp., b 4-7-1784 d 11-1-1872 ae 88y 7m; m 11-6-1806 at Wby Phebe TITUS, dt Joshua & Hannah, N. Hemp., b 10-23-1786 d 7-11-1865 ae 78y 8m 18d
Ch: Jane b 9-23-1807 d 3- 7-1881
Hannah b 4-28-1810; m Thos. J. GERALD
Anna b 11- 1-1812; m Jas. WILLITS
Mary b 1-17-1815; m Silas TITUS
James b 2-12-1818; m Caroline VALENTINE
Sarah b 11- 6-1822; m D. WHITNEY
Elizabeth b 9-23-1829; m Scudder V. WHITNEY
Henry, s John Jr. & Sarah (Post), b 8-16-1805 d 1-15-1865 ae 59; m Jane C. ----- b 2-17-1812 d 10-30-1889 (0)
Ch: John J. b 12- 2-1837 d 8-30-1838
Sarah P. b 5- 7-1839
Isaac b 8-15-1842
Emma b 5- 8-1849 d 8-26-1849 bur Wby
Henrietta b 5-31-1852
(Wby Stones)
Henry rocf Flushing 1849 (some Henry d 12-26-1877)
I. T. d 1851 (unidentified stone, Wby)
Isaac, s Thomas, Hemp.; m 1-6-1785 at Mk. Sarah COLES, dt Jacob & Sarah, b 9-18-1766
Isaac b 9-23-1804 d 9-9-1887 (unidentified stone, Wby)
Israel, s (perhaps) James & Jane; m Betsey -----
Ch: Richard
Mary
Phebe
Sarah
Israel
rem to Rensselaerville 6-4-1817; dis 5-26-1762
(Bibles)
Jacob, s John & Sarah, b 5 Mo (July) 1, 1703 d 1777; m 9 Mo (Nov) 18, 1725 Margaret GERMAIN, dt Isaac (mo)
Ch: (8)
Jacob dis mo 9-19-1838
James, s Peter, d before 1750; m abt 1722 Jane SEAMAN, dt Richard & Jane, b 1701 d 4-29-1759 ae abt 58 (called wd of James)
Ch: Joshua
(6 other ch)
Jean signed Epistle abt 1725; James ack mo 1-30-1758 (this may be s, James)
James, s John & Sarah (Pearsall), b 5 Mo (July) 16, 1730; m 4-28-1756 (cert not recorded) Ann COCK, dt Samuel, dec, & Martha, b 10 Mo (Dec) 23, 1736
Ch: John b 11-2-1758
(4 other ch)
(Cox Gen.)
James d 1826 (unidentified stone, Wby)
James mo before 7-17-1833, ret mbrp
James, s Henry & Phebe, O.B., b 2-12-1818 d 9-15-1892 ae 74; m 11-16-1843 at Elwood Valentine's, Caroline VALENTINE, dt Elwood & Mary, O.B., b 10-31-1824 d 12-3-1876 ae 52y
Ch: Edward P. b 11-19-1845 d 2-15-1924 G.C.
Henry E. b 9-1-1850 (or 1-19-1850) d 8-15-1926, Plainfield
Elwood V. b 1-11-1853
Mary V. b 3-3-1855 d 3-21-1937, G.C.
Caroline R. b 7-4-1857; m Jno. B. C. TAPPEN
Emily N.
Jane, dt John & Sarah; m 1793 Samuel POST; m 2d 1802 Lewis VALENTINE
Jane, dt James & Jane; m Daniel JACKSON
Jemima m 1765 William THORN, of Dutchess Co.
Joanna (or Johanna), dt Henry & Sarah, b 11-9-1765; m 1784 James WILLETS
(Bibles)
John Sr., s Edmund & Martha, Wby, b 2 Mo (Apr) 29, 1672 d 1 Mo (Mar) 4, 1749/50; m 8 Mo (Oct) 9, 1695 at Henry Willis', Sarah WILLIS, dt Henry & Mary, b 5 Mo (July) 6, 1671 d 1 Mo (Mar) 1, 1729/30
Ch: Mary b 4 Mo (June) 13, 1696; m 1718 Henry PEARSALL
John b 5 Mo (July) 28, 1698; m 1721 Sarah PEARSALL
Philadelphia b 9 Mo (Nov) 29, 1700; m Thos. SEAMAN
Jacob b 5 Mo (July) 1, 1703; m Margaret GERMAIN
William b 7 Mo (Sept) 23, 1705; m 1730 Eliz. SEAMAN
Sarah b 1 Mo (Mar) 7, 1708/9; m (1) Edmund TITUS (2) Isaac DOTY
Phebe b 5 Mo (July) 6, 1710; m 1728 John RIDGWAY
John Sr. m 2d 1 Mo (Mar) 7,1732/3 at Wby Mary SMITH, wd John, of Hemp., dt Thomas & Mary

TITUS, John & Mary, continued
SEAMAN, Hemp.
Ch: Richard b 2 Mo (Apr) 29, 1725; m Mary SMITH
John Jr., s John & Sarah, b 5 Mo (July) 28, 1698 d 5-28-1757; m 1 Mo (Mar) 28, 1722 Sarah PEARSALL
Ch: Henry b 12 Mo (Feb) 1, 1722/23
Mary b 11 Mo (Jan) 23, 1724
James b 7 Mo (Sept) 16, 1730
Elizabeth b 2 Mo (Apr) 16, 1733
Sarah b 10 Mo (Dec) 23, 1737 d 5-1-1755
Jonathan b 11 Mo (Jan) 8, 1743/44
John cert of clear 9 Mo (Nov) 28, 1739
John, s Peter & Martha; m Ann BARKER, dt Samuel
Ch: Richard m 1770 Rebecca BURLING
accompanied Sam Titus to mo 3 Mo (May) 25, 1726
(Bibles)
John m Wrightstown, Pa. 1757 Phebe -----
ct Wrightstown, Pa. 4-27-1757 (clear); Phebe rocf Wrightstown 9-28-1757 as a minister; Phebe and brother-in-law, Richard Titus, gc of unity to Wrightstown 3-29-1758
John, s William, dec, & Elizabeth, Wby, b 12 Mo (Feb) 30, 1743/44 d 4-24-1816 ae 73y 8m; m 7-4-1765 at Mk. Sarah ROBBINS, dt Jeremiah & Hannah, O.B., b 7 Mo (Sept) 1, 1742 d 6-28-1825
Ch: John Jr. b 8-25-1779; m Sarah POST
Mary b 10-22-1769; m James UNDERHILL
Jane b 9- 4-1773; m Sam'l POST
Richard b 10-23-1771
Hannah b 1-28-1766; m Joshua TITUS
Sarah b 2-18-1782; m Alvin HYATT; Silas DOWNING
3 othersunm
John, s James & Ann (Cock), b 11-2-1758 d 3-9-1828 ae abt 67; m 1781 (cert not recorded, m bet 6-27 & 7-25)Phebe TITUS, dt Thomas & Martha, b 7-29-1761 d 1818 (Wby Stone)
(Cox Gen.)
John Jr., s John & Sarah, Wby, b 8-25-1779 d 6-19-1865 ae 85y 9m 24d bur Wby; m 3-24-1802 at Wby, Sarah POST, dt Henry & Mary, b 3-23-1779 d 1859 bur Wby (O)
Ch: Maria b 4-23-1803
Henry b 8-16-1805
Lydia b 3-24-1808; m Robert R. WILLETS
Robert P. b 9-26-1811 d 3-20-1848 bur Wby
William P. b 3-30-1818
Elizabeth " 3-30-1818
(Bibles)
John m Phila. ----- b 10-26-1826 d 4-3-1904 ae 25y 5m 8d (error in stone or copy)
John V. d 8-30-1861 ae 38 bur Wby; m Phebe W. UNDERHILL, dt Thos. & Sarah W.
ct N. Y. 6-18-1879 for Phebe W.
Jonathan, s John 2d, dec, Wby; m 1-7-1767 at Beth. Mary WHITSON, dt John, Huntington
Joshua, s James, Wby, b 9-25-1760; m 11-2-1785 Hannah TITUS, dt John & Sarah, Wby, b 1-28-1765 d 2-2-1849 ae 84y 2d
Ch: Phebe b 10-23-1786
Mary b 10-30-1788
Sarah b 6-28-1794
Joshua b 3-25-1797
Joshua Jr., s Joshua & Hannah, b 3-25-1797; mo before 3-15-1820
Joshua d 3-10-1866 ae 69y 11m; m Ann ----- d 8-22-1882 ae 81y 6m
(Wby Stones)
Kezia, dt Thomas & Mary, b 4-23-1757; m 1778 Samuel SEAMAN
(Bibles)
Lydia, dt Charles & Margaret, b 2-11-1767; m David COCK
Lydia, dt John & Sarah P., b 3-24-1808; m 1828 Robert R. WILLETS
Lydia, dt Rowland & Sarah, b 8-23-1819; m Sidney B. ALLEY; m 2d Samuel HOSIER
Lydia, dt Henry & Jane C.; m 1873 Edmund POST(O)
Margaret, dt Chas. & Margaret, b 7-8-1782; m Richard DOTY
Margaret d 11-15-1896 ae 80y 2m 12d
Maria, dt John & Sarah P.; m 1822 Stephen WILLITS
Maria, dt Wm. P. & Ann H.; m 1871 Thomas H. GILMORE (O)
Martha, dt Edmund & Martha, b 1 Mo (Mar) 1663; m abt 1684 Benjamin SEAMAN
Martha (some Martha Titus signed Epistle abt 1725) rpd mo 8 Mo (Oct) 27, 1736
Martha, dt James; m 1774 Thomas POWELL
Martha, dt Timothy & Margaret, b 9-22-1800 m 1821 Charles FROST
Martha m Jacob VALENTINE
Mary, dt John & Sarah, b 4 Mo (June) 13, 1696; m 1717 Henry PEARSALL
Mary ack mo 10 Mo (Dec) 28, 1737
Mary m 1751 John MOTT
Mary, dt Silas & Sarah, b 3 Mo (May) 8, 1725; m 1754 Thomas WALTON
Mary, dt Samuel & Mary, b 6 Mo (Aug) 7, 1732; m 1756 Samuel TITUS
Mary, dt Edmund & Sarah, b 7 Mo (Sept) 17, 1740; m 1761 Henry POST
Mary, dt John & Sarah; m 1788 James UNDERHILL; m 2d 1817 Henry (or Hobby) ADEE; m 3d Jacob CONKLIN
Mary, dt William & Sarah; m 1795 Benjamin PELL
Mary, dt Richard & Abigail; m 1795 Joseph LUNDY, of Hardwick, N. J.
Mary, dt Samuel & Abigail; m 1812 Richard WILLETS
Mary d 1821 (unidentified stone, Wby)
Mary, dt Henry & Phebe, b 1-17-1815; m 1838 Silas TITUS
Mary b 12-9----- d 10-23-1861 (unidentified stone, Wby)
Mary, dt Henry & Martha; m Andrew COCK
Mary T., dt Samuel & Abigail; m 1812 Richard WILLITS
Mary W., dt William & Phebe W.; m 1864 Richard E. CARPENTER (O)
Oliver b 1826 d 1903 bur Wby; m Elizabeth WILLETS, dt Isaac & Rachel, d 12-18-1907

TITUS, Oliver & Elizabeth, continued
ae 79
Ch: James (Wby Stone)
cf Jericho for Elizabeth 1849
Patience, dt Edmund & Martha; m 1704 Nicholas HAIGHT
Peggy, dt Peter & Mary; m 1795 Whitehead HICKS
Peter, s Edmund & Martha, b 6 Mo (Aug) 24, 1674 d 10-23-1753; m Martha JACKSON, dt John & Elizabeth, b 1678 d 12-10-1753
Ch: (6)
signed cert 1726
Peter Jr., s Peter & Martha, b 1709 d 9-8-1788 m Mary SCUDDER, dt Henry, b 15 Mar 1715 d 6-9-1794
Ch: (9)
Peter ack mo 8 Mo (Oct) 27, 1736
(Bibles)
Peter, s Richard & Mary, Hemp. & Wby, d 11-2-1832 ae 93y 6m 7d; m Elizabeth MUDGE, dt Michael & Sarah, d 9-29-1829 ae 87y & abt 6m
Phebe m 1728 John RIDGWAY
Phebe m 1736/7 Benjamin HICKS
Phebe, dt Edmund; m 1753 Joseph PRIOR
Phebe, dt Edmund; m 1753 Silas RUSHMORE
Phebe m 1759 John WAY
Phebe, dt William & Elizabeth, b 10 Mo (Dec) 18, 1735; m 1759 Stephen LOINES
Phebe, dt Peter, dis mo 1-25-1775
Phebe, dt Thomas & Martha; m 1781 John TITUS
Phebe, dt Peter & Elizabeth; m 1801 Jacob CARLE
Phebe, dt Joshua & Hannah; m 1806 Henry TITUS
Phebe b 11-1-1799; m Thomas TABER
Phebe, dt Rowland & Sarah; m George W. VALINTINE
Philadelphia m 1723 Thomas SEAMAN
Rachel W., dt Rowland & Sarah, b 10-9-1817; m 1836 Edward ROBBINS
Richard, s Peter & Martha, d 1784; m 8 Apr 1736 (mo) Mary PETERS, dt Dr. Charles & Mary
Ch: (4)
mo before 9 Mo (Nov) 26, 1739; did not look on himself as a Friend 10 Mo (Dec) 20, 1739
(Bibles)
Richard, s John Sr. & Mary, Hemp., b 2 Mo (Apr) 29, 1725; m abt 1746 Mary SMITH, dt Benjamin & Mary
Ch: Augustin b 2 Mo (Apr) 21, 1747
Phebe b 9 Mo (Nov) 6, 1749
James b 8-22-1752
Benjamin
Peter
Richard m 2d Elizabeth PALMER, dt Solomon & Sarah (m 12-12-1761)
Ch: Margery b 8-27-1762
Samuel b 9-12-1765
Elizabeth b 7-18-1767
Richard gct Purchase 11-25-1761 (clear); Elizabeth rocf Purchase 1-27-1767; Richard ack hiring a substitute in the Expedition against the French & taking oath
Richard, s Samuel, dec; m 4th day of the mo 1770 at Cow Neck, Abigail WEEKS, dt Samuel, dec, Hemp. Harbor
Richard ack 1-29-1763 having when very young hired a man in his stead to stop progress of the enemy in the province
Richard, s John & Sarah, b 10-23-1771 d 5-11-1850; m 11-1-1810 at Mk. Sarah UDALL, dt Thomas & Susanna, b 1765 d 6-25-1868 ae 81
Ch: Susan d 8-20-1811
Deborah m Joseph LEE
Sarah b 9-17-1817; m Henry GRIFFEN
Mary d unm
Caroline B. b 2-25-1828 d unm
Richard b 10-6-1820 d in infancy
(Bibles)
Richard gct Jericho 11-20-1839 (clear)
Richard W. d 12-3-1896 ae 85y 1m 18d (Wby Stone); m Mary P. ----- d 4-12-1881 ae 96y 2m 4d (Wby Stone)
cf Jericho 4----1863 for both; ct Jericho 1898 for Mary P.
Robert mo before 8-15-1838 & retained
Robert, s George P. & Mary (Carle), b 7-13-1813 d 4-6-1885 ae 71y 6m 23d; m 1-6-1842 Mary W. HOPKINS, dt Coles & Anne (Mudge), b 3-29-1808 d 1-11-1900 ae 91y 9m 12d
Ch: Anna H. b 1843; m 1867 James R. WILLETS
George P. b 1-15-1843; m 1862 Mary TOWNSEND
Robert dis mo
(Wby Stones & Bibles)
Robert P. rocf Little Falls, Md. 6----1862
Robert W., s William L. & Phebe (Willets), Wby, b 2-1-1824 d 1893 ae 49; m 9-25-1844 at Wby, Esther L. RUSHMORE, dt Townsend & Amy L., b 5-13-1825 (or 5-25-1825), d 8-4-1896
Ch: Emily b 2-14-1847 d 3-1-1860 [(0)
Walter b 12-24-1850 d unm
Annie W. b 10-1-1854 d 3-13-1860
Robert Franklin b 7-7-1861; m Phebe CARPENTER
(Wby Stones)
Rosetta, dt Samuel & Abigail, b 2-12-1779; m 1800 Daniel POST
Rosetta d 8-5-1847 ae 11m 18d (unidentified stone, Wby)
Rowland, s Jacob & Martha, Wheatley & Wby, b 9-11-1776 d 11-6-1861; m Sarah WEEKS, dt Richard & Martha, b 7-29-1779 d 3-25-1844 ae 64y
Ch: Phebe b 4-14-1801; m Geo. VALENTINE
Isaac D. b 9-23-1804 d 9-9-1887 (unm)
Silas b 12-29-1807; m Mary TITUS
Jacob b 10-28-1809; m Mary SMITH
Richard W. b 10-15-1811; m Mary PLUMMER
Robert b 1-24-1814; m Eliza CHAPMAN
Elizabeth b 12-6-1815; m Sidney ALLEY
Rachel b 10-9-1817; m Edward ROBBINS
Lydia b 6-23-1819; m Sidney ALLEY (2) Samuel HOSIER
Stephen W. b 2-28-1821 d 6-2-1825

TITUS, continued
Samuel, s Edmund & Martha, b 6 Mo (Aug) 1658 d 11 Mo (Jan) 1, 1732/33; m 9 Mo (Nov) 6, 1691 Elizabeth POWELL, dt Thomas & Abigail, d 9 Mo (Nov) 1704
Ch: Phebe b 8 Mo (Oct) 8, 1693; m 1716 John HAIGHT
Temperance b 1 Mo (Mar) 6, 1695/6 d 1704
Martha b 12 Mo (Feb) 23, 1698/9; m Epenetus WOOD
Samuel b 9 Mo (Nov) 23, 1704; m Mary JACKSON
Samuel m 2d Elizabeth BOWNE, dt John & Hannah, b 8 Mo (Oct) 8, 1658
Samuel signed rem cert 1707; Elizabeth m (1) 1678 John PRIOR
Samuel, s Samuel & Elizabeth, b 9 Mo (Nov) 23, 1704 d 2 Mo (Apr) 19, 1750; m 1725 Mary JACKSON, dt John & Elizabeth (mo)
Ch: Stephen b 12 Mo (Feb) 24, 1727/8
Elizabeth b 8 Mo (Oct) 16, 1729
Mary b 6 Mo (Aug) 7, 1732
Samuel b 9 Mo (Nov) 4, 1734
Richard b 11 Mo (Jan) 16, 1736/7
Phebe b 11 Mo (Jan) 15, 1739/40
Jemima b 1 Mo (Mar) 16, 1742
mo before 2 Mo (Apr) 27, 1726
Samuel, s Jacob & Mary, b 1734; m 12-31-1755 (cert not recorded) Mary TITUS, dt Samuel dec & Mary, b 6 Mo (Aug) 7, 1732
Ch: (6)
(Bibles)
Samuel, s Samuel & Ruth, b 8-22-1769 d 11-7-1818; m Mary TOWNSEND, dt Richard & Mary
Samuel m 2d Mary TOWNSEND, dt Samuel & Eliz., b 8-1-1786 d 6-9-1865
(Bibles)
Samuel, s Stephen, dec, & Phebe, Wby; m 2-21-1810 at Wby Mary POWELL, dt Joshua & Phebe, d 9-13-1884 ae 92y 2m 10d
Ch: Elizabeth b 1813 d 2- 9-1815 ae 2y 2m 14d
Elizabeth P. b 10-14-1815
Stephen b 3-27-1813
Samuel Jr. b 1821 d 7-18-1854 (Wby Stone)
cf Jericho (clear); Mary gct Jericho 10-19-1810
Samuel d 2-25-1894 ae 56 (unidentified stone, [Wby)
Samuel G., s Francis & Ruth, b 6-20-1807 d 7-26-1856; m ----- CORTELYON, b 11-28-1814 d 12-18-1884 (w's name Adrienne)
Ch: (2)
(Wby Stones & Bibles)
Samuel R., s Samuel & Abigail, both dec, Wby, d 11-8-1852; m 11-21-1810 at Wby, Phebe FROST, dt Charles & Mary, O.B., d 9-14-1854
Ch: Ann [(0)
Charles T. b 7- 2-1815
Jacob S. b 3-25-1817
Deborah C. b 3-26-1824 d 7-17-1826
Sarah, dt John & Sarah, b 1 Mo (Mar) 2, 1708/9; m (1) abt 1732 Edmund TITUS; m 2d 1755 Isaac DOTY
Sarah m 1735 William WALMSLEY
Sarah, dt Edmund & Sarah, b 8 Mo (Oct) 27, 1735; m abt 1757 Isaac RUSHMORE
Sarah, dt William & Sarah, b 10-1-1760; m 1784 Isaac WRIGHT
Sarah, dt James & Ann (Cock); m Simon GERMOND mo before 3-31-1784, dis next mo
Sarah, dt John & Sarah; m 1810 Alvan HYATT; m 2d 1826 Silas DOWNING
Sarah, dt Joshua & Hannah; m 1813 Oliver CROMWELL
Sarah d 1-21-1814 ae 85 (unidentified stone, Wby)
Sarah, dt Stephen W. & Hannah, b 1-1-1817; m 1838 Jacob FROST
Sarah, dt Henry & Phebe, b 6-11-1822 d 2-26-1889; m 7-5-1845 Daniel D. WHITNEY
Silas, s Edmund & Martha, b 8 Mo (Oct) 3, 1676 d 2 Mo (Apr) 30, 1750; m 8 Dec 1704 Sarah HAIGHT, dt Samuel & Sarah, b before 1686
Ch: Edmund b 8 Mo (Oct) 1, 1705
Temperance b 10 Mo (Dec) 14, 1707
Silas b 9 Mo (Nov) 14, 1709
Sarah b 8 Mo (Oct) 6, 1712
Hannah b 9 Mo (Nov) 29, 1715
Phebe b 7 Mo (Sept) 27, 1717
David b 4 Mo (June) 20, 1719
William b 8 Mo (Oct) 14, 1722
Mary b 3 Mo (May) 8, 1725
ct Flushing 9 Mo (Nov) 29, 1704
Silas, s Silas & Sarah, b 9 Mo (Nov) 14, 1709; m 1731 Sarah TOWNSEND, dt Thomas & Sarah, b 1713 (mo)
Ch: (3)
Silas signed Epistle abt 1725 (this was his father); cert signed for Silas 12 Mo (Feb) 26, 1734/5; ct Abington, Pa. for Sarah 6 Mo (Aug) 28, 1734
Silas dis mo 4-23-1789; rst 6-20-1792
Silas, s Rowland & Sarah, N. Hemp., b 1-29-1807 d 4-8-1842 ae 34y 4m; m 3-22-1838 at Mk, Mary TITUS, dt Henry & Phebe, O.B., b 6-17-1815 d 4-17-1891 ae 76y 3m
Ch: Elizabeth b 4-14-1839; m Aug. C. COCK
Henrietta b 5-30-1841; m Dan. D. WHITNEY
bur Mk
Silas C. d 7-10-1882 ae 65y 4m 29d
Stephen, s Samuel & Mary, b 12 Mo (Feb) 24, 1727/8 d 12-13-1761; m abt 1750 Sarah MOTT, dt Samuel & Martha, b 27 Apr. 1731 d 1-8-1764 (mo)
Ch: Stephen b 6-10-1753
(4 other ch)
ack mo 8-26-1752
(Bibles)
Stephen, s Stephen & Sarah, Wby, b 6-10-1753; m 11-7-1781 at Wby, Phebe WILLETS, dt Jacob, dec, & Hannah, Hemp., b 1763
Stephen ack 1-29-1777 having served as guard with other soldiers
Stephen d 3-28-1876 ae 83y 4m 21d (Wby Stone); m Elizabeth -----
Ch: Samuel d 8-12-1858 ae 54y 8m 4d (Wby Stone)

TITUS, continued
Stephen W., s Stephen & Phebe, Cedar Swamp; m 8-3-1815 at Mk, Hannah UNDERHILL, dt Israel & Mary, Cedar Swamp, b 9-7-1793 d 10-22-1847 ae 54y 1m 15d bur Mk [stone, Wby
cf Jericho (clear)
Susan d 11-25-1848 ae in 67th yr (unidentified
Thomas, s William, dec, & Elizabeth, Hemp., b 2 Mo (Apr) 1, 1738; m 2-4-1756 at Beth., Martha POWELL, dt Isaac & Martha, Beth.
Ch: Kezia b 4-23-1757
William b 3- 4-1759
Phebe b 7-29-1761
Isaac b 4-26-1764
Martha b 7-28-1778
(Bibles)
Thomas U. d 9-14-1861 ae 15 (unidentified stone, Wby)
Timothy, Wby & Wheatly, d cert recorded 1850; m Margaret -----
Ch: Martha b 7-25-1800
Charity b 12-24-1802
Mary b 12-9----- d 10-23-1861 ae 56y 10m 14d
Ruth b 12-14----- d 5-10-1856 ae 49y 4m 27d
Sarah b 1-29-----
Benjamin b 6-11-----
Margaret b 9-3-1816 d 11-15-1896 (Wby Stone)
Timothy Jr. dis mo 9-20-1837
Waller (or Walter) R. d 1872 ae 22 (unidentified stone, Wby)
Willet, s James & Ann (Cock); m before 10-23-1786 Ruth STRATTON (mo)
Ch: (7)
Willet dis mo before 10-23-1786
(Cox Gen.)
William, s John & Sarah, Wby, d 4 Mo (June) 18, 1750 ae abt 44; m 9 Mo (Nov) 18, 1730 at Wby, Elizabeth SEAMAN, dt Thomas & Hannah, Jerusalem, d 4 Mo (June) 18, 1750
Ch: Elizabeth b 7 Mo (Sept) 8, 1731
Hannah b 5 Mo (July) 26, 1733
Phebe b 10 Mo (Dec) 18, 1735
Thomas b 1 Mo (Mar) 20, 1738
John b 10 Mo (Dec) 30, 1743
(Seaman Gen.)
William, s Silas & Sarah, b 8 Mo (Oct) 14, 1722 d 1794; m 1753 Sarah BOWNE, dt Samuel & Sarah, b 1724 d 7-11-1787
Ch: Abigail b 9-21-1755
Elizabeth b 4- 3-1758
Sarah b 10-1-1760
Mary b 2- 3-17--
Silas b 6-14-1765
Mary " 1- 8-1769
William m 2d 6-12-1789 at Pur. Hannah BOWNE, wd Jacob, dt Thomas & Penelope THORN
ct Pur. 5-27-1789; Hannah rocf Pur. 8-26-1789
(Bibles)
William, s Thomas & Martha, O.B., b 3-4-1759; m 1-8-1784 at Mk, Mary COCK, dt Henry & Elizabeth, b 3-13-1761 d 7-14-1833 Quaker Hill
Ch: (4)
(Cox Gen.)
William, s Daniel & Amy, N. Hemp., b 12-7-1799; m 3-26-1823 at Wby, Phebe WILLETS, dt Robert & Mary, N. Hemp., b 4-23-1805 d 1886 bur Wby (0)
Ch: Robert W. b 2- 1-1824
Daniel b 6- 1-1826
Amy b 12-3-1827 d 1844
Edmund b 3-17-1831
William W. b 3-27-1835 d 1862
Samuel b 2-19-1838
Henry b 9-16-1840
Mary W. b 10- 7-1843
Amelia b 8-28-1851
William P., s John Jr. & Sarah, b 3-30-1818; m Ann H. ----- b 1-12-1822 (0)
Ch: Maria b 5- 1-1846
Edward b 2- 8-1848
Emma C. b 9-17-1851 d 12-17-1866 ae 15 bur Wby
John C. b 9- 5-1853
Elizabeth b 3----1856
William b 11-16-1861
Ann H. rocf Amawalk 3-13-1846
Zilpah d 1-19-1875 in 89th yr (Wby Stone)
----- m Emma ----- d 8-26-1849 (0)
Ch: Robert W. b 2- 1-1824
Esther L. b 5-13-1825

TOBIAS
Margaret, dt Jacob & Rebecca; m 1786 Refine WEEKS

TOWNSEND
Ann, dt Thomas, dis mo 3-25-1778
Catharine gct Concord or elsewhere in Pa. 8 Mo (Oct) 31, 1722 (lately rem)
Deborah m 1731 Abram SEAMAN
Elizabeth, dt John & Phebe, b abt 1665; m (1) Theophilus PHILLIPS 1685 (3rd w of Theophilus)
Dt. Hannah
Elizabeth
Mary
Elizabeth m 2d abt 1690 Thomas POWELL
Ethelanna dis mo before 9-15-1902
Frederick E. m Mary EMBREE, d 7-9-1890 ae 61y 5m 14d
Ch: (prob) Mary E. F. b 11-7-1853 d 5-20-1875
" Rebecca Gracey b 1-21-1861 d 12-31-1863
(Mk Stones)
Hannah, dt Thos. & Sarah; m 1728 Benjamin UNDERHILL
Hannah, dt Prior & Sarah, b 5-21-1755; m 1774 David VALENTINE
Henry, nm, s Henry & Eliphal; m Elizabeth TITUS, dt Peter (mo)
Elizabeth ack mo 2 Mo (Apr) 1, 1748/9
(Bibles)

TOWNSEND, continued
Jacob m Mary ----- b 6-7-1790 d 4-29-1863 (Wby Stone)
Jacob m Phebe ----- d 4-14-1774 ae 77y 6 or 7m
John B. m Sophia ----- d 4-8-1870 ae 72y 3m 8d (Wby Stone)
Joseph L., s Obadiah & Phebe, Wby, d 12-24-1854 ae 57y 2m 17d; m Hannah W. ----- b 1-22-1805 d 3-4-1900 in 96th yr
Ch: Thomas W. b 12-12-1833 d 4-9-1834
Henry b 8-15-1835
Mary b 3-10-1838; m Geo. P. TITUS
William E. b 7-21-1840 d 12-11-1919
Lydia M. b 11-30-1842 d 9-30-1924 Whitestone
Phebe Anna S. b 6-16-1849
Joseph L. b 8-31-1851; resigned 1-25-1904
Letitia, dt Sylvanus & Susannah; m 1763 Benjamin UNDERHILL (See Jacob Underhill)
M. Amelia m 1844 Charles POST
Martha rocf Flushing 9 Mo (Nov) 2, 1749
Martha m 1783 ----- SMITH (mo)
Mary ack mo 3-17-1757
Mary, dt Timothy & Sarah; m 1762 William JONES
Mary, dt Thomas & Mary; m 1801 Jacob WOOD
Mary, dt Samuel & Eliz., b 8-1-1786; m Samuel TOWNSEND (as 2d w)
Mary, dt Joseph L. & Hannah W., b 3-10-1838; m 1867 George P. TITUS
Mary (form Doty) dis mo before 3-28-1887
Mary, dt Richard & Mary; m Samuel TITUS
Mary P. m George P. TITUS
Nathaniel, s James & Audry, b 25 Feb 1698 d 5-22-1754; m Mary JACKSON, dt James & Rebecca, b 11 Mo (Jan) 20, 1696/7
Ch: (3)
cert of clear for Nathaniel 8 Mo (Oct) 31, 1739
(Bibles)
Nathaniel m 2d 1739 Martha HICKS, dt Chas. & Eliz. DOUGHTY, b 1705 d 7-19-1759
Ch: (4)
(Bibles)
Nicholas, s Henry, dec, & Eliz., b abt 1728 d 4-29-1810; m 1762 Philadelphia DOUGHTY, dt Benj. & Hannah, b 1738/9 d 10-25-1831
Ch: (3)
ct Flushing 10-27-1762 (clear); Philadelphia rocf Flushing 11-30-1763; ct Flushing for both 8-28-1765
(Bibles)
Obadiah, s Thomas & Mary, Wby, b 6-7-1770 d 5-6-1847 ae 76y 7m; m 11-11-1795 Phebe LAWRENCE, dt Joseph & Phebe, b 3-29-1769 d 8-21-1839 ae 70y 5m (mo)
Ch: Sally d 11- 7-1874 ae 75
Lydia m ----- MOTT
Thomas J. b 8-20-1802; m Elizabeth TITUS
Obadiah dis 2 Mo 1796; Obadiah rst 4-15-1812
(Bibles)
Pamelia, dt Thomas; m 1784 Richard UNDERHILL
Phebe m 1787 Stephen RUSHMORE
Phebe Ann m 1834 Alfred COCK; m 2d Jacob S. UNDERHILL (Phebe Ann b 1-17-1817)
Richard, s Timothy & Sarah; m 8----1775 (License Aug. 2, 1775) Deborah UNDERHILL, dt Abraham & Dinah, d 1776 (mo) Richard's 2nd w
Ch: Deborah b 9-18-1776; m Israel HOREFIELD
Deborah dis mo 1-31-1776
Roseannah, dt Wm. & Elizabeth; m 1768 Daniel COCK, nm
Sarah, dt Thomas & Sarah; m 1731 Silas TITUS (mo)
ack mo 5 Mo (July) 28, 1731; Sarah gct Abington, Pa. 6 Mo (Aug) 28, 1734
Sarah d 9-11-1833 ae 83y bur Mk
Sarah, dt Thomas & Mary; m 1794 William BYRNES
Solomon, s John & Phebe; m (prob in R. I.) Catharine ALMY
Ch: (6)
Solomon gct R. I. 2 Mo (Apr) 30, 1707
Thomas, s John, b 1680 d 1732; m 1707 Sarah PEARSALL, dt Nathaniel & Martha
Signed Epistle abt 1725; Sarah gct Concord, Pa. 4 Mo (June) 28, 1732
William, s George & Roseannah, b 13 Feb. 1716 d 5-5-1777; m before 9 Mo (Nov) 25, 1741 Elizabeth COCK, dt Henry & Mary, b 12-14-1715 d 11-30-1794 (mo)
Ch: James b 4 Mo (June) 26, 1742
Roseannah b 1751; m Daniel COCK
Elizabeth ack mo 1 Mo (Apr) 26, 1746
(Cox Gen.)
William m 1787 in N. Y. Elizabeth -----
Ch: Thomas
William gct N. Y. 2-28-1787 (clear); William dis 1-30-1788; Elizabeth's ack from N. Y. accepted 7-26-1788; Elizabeth & s, Thomas, gct Cornwall 4-23-1789; William ack favorably rpd to Cornwall 12-15-1790
William E. & Anna W.
Ch: Eliza b 10-12-1886; m ----- WILLETS
Zerviah, dt John & Esther; m Dr. Matthew PARRISH
Matthew gct Concord, Pa. 4 Mo (June) 24, 1724 (lately rem)

TRACY
Akeley d 5-12-1866 ae 66y (Wby Stone)
Capt. Jirah, s Daniel,of Colchester, Conn., d 4-28-1867 ae 78 (Mk Stone)

TRAVIS
Alfred M. m Sarah Maria ----- b 4-26-1830 d 4-6-1897 (Wby Stone)
Edmund D. d 4-26-1860; m Mary A. ----- d 3-10-1862 (supposed w as stone adjacent in Wby)
Phebe, dt Samuel & Elizabeth; m 1808 Solomon COLES

TREDWELL
Charity, dt John; m Samuel SEAMAN
Daniel T. & Margaret A.

TREDWELL, Daniel T. & Margaret A., continued
Ch: Margaret d 2-13-1876 ae 6d (Wby Stone)
Rachel (form Townsend) dis mo 7-31-1782

TUCKER
Mary m 1663 Simon COOPER

TURNER
Henry C. m Charlotte CHAPMAN
Ch: Marian Chapman d 8----1900 bur Wby

TURRELL
Franklin S. & Frances E.
Ch: Huldah C. d 8-10-1892 ae 3m 16d (Wby Stone)
Jesse M. d 10-14-1895 ae 42y 6m 22d (Wby Stone)
Jonathan m Lucy ----- d 4-8-1863 ae 74 (Wby Stone)
Stephen H. d 9-26-1888 ae 71y 4m 17d (Wby Stone)

TUTTLE
Daniel m 7-12-1869 Sarah H. ALBERTSON
Sarah H. b 1-25-1815 d 6-7-1898 (Wby Stone)

TYSON
Chester J. m 2-16-1901 Bertha HAWXHURST, dt Wm. E. & Marianna, b 9-24-1881
Edwin C., s Chas. J. & Mariah E., Adams Co., Pa.; m 6-9-1887 at Wm. E. Hawxhurst's, Mary W. HAWXHURST, dt Wm. E. & Marianna, Queens Co., b 9-27-1862

UDALL
Annie T., dt Richard & Deborah, b 1861; m Charles F. FRANKLIN
Charles, s Thomas & Susanna, dec, N.Y.C.; m 11-28-1816 at Mk, Catharine SEAMAN, dt Isaac & Lucretia, dec, Mk
cf N.Y. (clear); Catharine gct N. Y. 2-18-1818
James b 8-5-1807 d 4-4-1888 (Man. Stone)
Joseph, nm & Phebe (mo 1750)
Phebe ack mo 10-31-1753
Margaret A. b 5-17-1817 d 12-12-1889 (Man. Stone)
Richard d 5-25-1861 ae 80y 8m 28d; m Deborah POWELL d 3-21-1870 ae 88
Ch: Annie T. b 1861
Sarah, dt Thomas & Susanna, b 1765; m 1810 Richard TITUS
Thomas P. b 12-12-1838 d 4-12-1881

UNDERHILL
Abigail, dt Daniel & Sarah, b 1-17-1771; m 1789 Richard COCK
Abrah m, s Abraham & Hannah, b N. Castle 1723; m 1 Mo (Mar) 20, 1746 Phebe HALLOCK, dt John, d 5-29-1758 in Pur.
Ch: (4)
cf Pur. (clear)
Abraham m 2d Keziah FARRINGTON, dt Thos. & Keziah (mo)
Ch: (13)
ack mo 1-22-1754
(Underhill Gen.)
Abraham, nm, s Samuel & Hannah, b 12 Mo (Feb) 12, 1716; m abt 1754 Dinah WILLETS, dt Isaac & Clemence
Ch: Isaac
Israel
Deborah
both ack mo 1-21-1754 (too near kin)
(Bibles)
Abraham C., s Stephen C. & Sarah P., b 10-14-1839; m 5-6-1862 Marietta JONES, dt Israel S., b 12-24-1840 d 1-21-1873
Ch: (2)
Abraham C. m 2d 4-17-1888 Eugenie P. COCK, dt Isaac S. & Emeliza, b 3-11-1852
resigned 10----1896
(Underhill Gen.)
Ada, dt Richard & Mary K., b 10-30-1879; m 1902 Jacob Paxson TEMPLE; m 2d 1926 Eugene Price CHENEY
Adonijah, s Thomas, b 2 Mo (Apr) 9, 1743 d 10-21-1821; m 1769 (cert not recorded, m bet. 11-29 & 12-27) Phebe WILLETS, dt Daniel & Amy
Ch:(2)
Alexander m Caroline ALBERTSON, dt Silas & Kezia, b 11-8-1816 d 5-21-1854 ae 37y 6m 13d bur Wby
Ch: Caroline Jr. d 7-25----- ae 17m bur Wby
Amery signed Epistle abt 1725
Amos, s John & Elizabeth, b 1698; m 1730 Elizabeth SEAMAN, dt Benj. & Jane, b 7 Mo (Sept) 10, 1710
Ch: Solomon d 2-5-1827 ae abt 78y
(7 other ch)
(Underhill Gen.)
Andrew, s Samuel & Ann, Rye; m 11-3-1774 Deborah WILLETS, dt Richard & Hannah, Islip
cf Flushing (clear)
Anne, dt Amos & Elizabeth; m abt 1754 Townsend DICKINSON
Annie T., dt Jacob S. & Phebe Ann, b 4-26-1861; m Charles F. FRANKLIN
Benjamin, s David & Hannah; m 3 Mo (May) 29, 1728, Hannah TOWNSEND, dt Thomas & Sarah
Ch: Elizabeth
Thomas b 1735
John
Daniel d New Castle, N. Y. 10-11-1824 ae 73y 9m
Benjamin dis 3 Mo (May) 28, 1740; Hannah gct Purchase 2 Mo (Apr) 26, 1749
(Bibles)
Benjamin, s Amos & Eliz., b 9 Mo (Nov) 26, 1736; m 4-29-1763 Letitia TOWNSEND, dt Sylvanus & Susannah, b 10 Mo (Dec) 26, 1738 d 8-28-1804
Ch: (2)
mo & complied with military discipline before 12-26-1764, referred to N. Y., ack accepted; ct Flushing 5----1765 (Under. Gen)

UNDERHILL, continued
Catharine b 7-26-1797 d 9-20-1877 (Wby Stone)
Charles, s Israel & Mary, b 2-4-1783 d 1-27-1843; m 1810 Hannah POWELL (mo)
Ch: (2)
dis mo before 3-14-1810 (Underhill Gen.)
Daniel b 9 Mo (Nov) 3, 1672 d 12 Mo (Feb) 9, 1713/14 (unm)
on comm 1698
Daniel, s Adonijah; m 1810 (cert not recorded, m bet. 10-17- & 11-14) Phebe UNDERHILL, dt Israel, b 7-8-1780 d 8-1-1866
Ch: Elizabeth m Jacob WEEKS
Phebe m 2d Jacob CROOKER
Daniel, s Samuel J. & Mary, Mill Neck in O.B.; m 10-21-1847 at James Post's, Caroline POST, dt James & Phebe W., N. Hemp., b 6-21-1826
Ch: Stephen d 11-16-1835 ae 70y 2m 22d
cf Jericho (clear)
Daniel, s Samuel J. & Mary, both dec, Jericho; m 9-20-1883 at Jas. Post's, dec, Catharine POST, dt James & Phebe W., both dec, Wby, b 1-19-1833
David, s Amos, dec, Flushing; m 12-2-1773 Elizabeth MOTT, dt William, dec, Hemp.
Deborah, dt Abraham & Dinah; m abt 1775 Richard TOWNSEND
Dinah m 1738 John BOWNE
signed Epistle abt 1725
Dinah rpd mo to first cousin before 4 Mo (June) 29, 1748; comm to speak to her
Elizabeth, dt Thomas & Sarah, b 1742; m abt 1746 John POWELL Jr.
Elizabeth, dt Israel; m 1818 Alanson SEAMAN
George S., s Willets & Susan, b 1839 d 9-25-1910; m Jane W. ARISON
Ch: (8)
Hannah signed Epistle abt 1725
Hannah, dt Israel & Mary; m 1815 Stephen W. TITUS
Hannah, dt Thos. & Sarah; m 1846 Stephen R. HICKS
Henry W., s Thomas & Sarah W., gct E. Hamburgh, N. Y.
Isaac, s Amos & Elizabeth, Cedar Swamp, b 5 Mo (July) 21, 1732 d abt 1816; m 2 Mo 7, 1752 at Mk, Mary COCK, dt John & Sarah, O.B., b 7 Mo (Sept) 5, 1730 d Flushing before 1816
dis 9-24-1782 for carting hay for the army
Israel, s Abraham, O.B., d 8-9-1825 ae 78y 3m; m 8-6-1777 at Wby, Mary WRIGHT, dt John
Ch: Sarah m Andries SEAMAN
Jacob, s Abraham & Hannah, b 3 Mo (May) 25, 1730; m 8 Mo (Oct) 29, 1747 (cert not recorded) Amy HALLOCK, dt John & Hannah, b 4 Mo (June) 3, 1728 d 7-30-1808
Ch: (11)
cert of clear (MM not stated); Amy gct Pur. 1 Mo (Mar) 27, 1751
(Underhill Gen.)
Jacob, s Thomas & Sarah, b 7 Mo (Sept) 12, 1736 d 1-5-1818; m 5-21-1760 Catherine WILLETS, dt Amos & Mary, b 9 Mo (Nov) 29, 1739 d 2-9-1819 (mo) (Jacob a nm)
Ch: Richard b 11- 7-1761
James b 5-15-1764
Mary " 8- 7-1770
Catharine ack mo 6-30-1762
(Bibles)
Jacob, s Amos & Elizabeth, b 26 Nov 1736 d 1788; m 4-29-1763 by Presbyterian Minister in N. Y. Letitia TOWNSEND, dt Sylvanus & Susannah, b 26 Dec 1738 d Aug 28, ----
Ch: Townsend b 1765
Elizabeth
Benjamin ack mo 2-17-1765; Letitia m 2d 5-13-1789 John FRANKLIN
(Bibles)
Jacob S., s David C. & Phebe (Smith), b 8-14-1816 d 1-13-1886; m 10-23-1835 Amy KIRK, dt Daniel & Mary (Titus), b 9----1817 d 6-16-1854 ae 37y 3m
Ch: (7)
Amy ack mo & ret mbrp
(Bibles)
Jacob S. m 2d Phebe Ann TOWNSEND, dt Jackson S. & Jemima T., b 1-1-1817 d 10-24-1889 ae 72y 9m 7d
Ch: Anne T. b 4-26-1861
Jacob recrq 1860; Phebe m 1st 1834 Alfred COCK
James, s Jacob & Catharine, O.B., d 2-15-1816 ae 51y 9m; m 7-30-1788 at Wby Mary TITUS, dt John & Sarah, N. Hemp., b 10-22-1769
Mary m 2d Hobby ADEE; Mary m 3d Jacob CONKLIN
Jemima, dt Joseph & Anne; m Daniel VALENTINE
John, s Thomas, O.B.; m 3-8-1781 at Mk, Elizabeth PRIOR, dt Thomas & Martha, O.B., b 3-13-1761
Marianna, dt Jacob & Amy K.; m Benjamin T. COCK
Mary, dt John & Mary; m 1712 Wright FROST (mo)
ack mo 5 Mo (July) 30, 1712
Mary, dt Samuel & Ann; m 1765 James MOTT
Mary, dt Jacob & Catharine; m 1808 Thomas LEGGETT, of N. Y.
Mary, dt Israel & Mary, b 5-18-1791; m 1817 Saul ALLEY
Mary, dt John & Sarah TITUS; m 2d 1817 Henry ADEE
Mary, dt Thos. & Sarah; m 1853 Elias LEWIS Jr.
Mary J., dt Daniel & Phebe; m 1836 Samuel BARRET
Pamelia, dt Thomas & Sarah W., b 4-1-1828; m Charles McCOUN
Phebe, dt Jacob & Amy, b 5-5-1853; m Matthew Reid DICKSON
Phebe, dt Israel & Mary, b 7-8-1780; m 1810 Daniel UNDERHILL; m 2d Jacob CROOKER
Phebe W., dt Thomas & Sarah W.; m John V. TITUS
Rebecca, dt Israel & Mary, b 4-26-1801; m 1826 Richard COCK

UNDERHILL, continued
Richard, s Jacob, O.B.; m 3-3-1784 at Wby, Pamelia TOWNSEND, dt Thomas, dec, Hemp.
Ch: William d 2-14-1842 ae nearly 60y
Richard, s Thomas & Sarah W., Cedar Swamp, b 6-7-1835 d 3-3-1897 ae 61; m 5-24-1860 at Wm. S. Robbins', Mary K. ROBBINS, dt Wm. S. & Elizabeth, Glenwood, Queens Co., b 8-11-1838 d Glen Head 5-12-1912
Ch: Sarah b 5-17-1861
Charles b 1863 d 3-15-1876 ae 12y 4m
Annie b 1-30-1866
Elizabeth b 3-30-1868
Thomas b 10-14-1871
Mary b 8-17-1874
Emily b 6-28-1877
Ada b 10-30-1879
Richard Henry b 3-26-1839 d 7-6-1879
Samuel, s Samuel & Hannah, O.B., b 8 Mo 9, 1708; m 10 Mo (Dec) 8, 1737 at Mk, Ann CARPENTER, dt Joseph & Mary, O.B., b 7 Mo (Sept) 24, 1716
Ch: Joseph b 8 Mo (Oct) 1, 1738
Samuel b 5 Mo (July) 26, 1740
Robert b 10 Mo (Dec) 1, 1742
Mary b 1 Mo (Mar) 31, 1745
Andrew b 4 Mo (June) 17, 1749
James b 8 Mo (Oct) 29, 1751 d 11-18-1752
Thomas b 5-18-1755
Hannah b 3-10-1757 d 9-12-1760
Samuel signed Epistle abt 1725; rem to Mamaroneck 1769
Samuel, s Samuel & Ann, Mamaroneck; m 3-28-1771 at Islip, Ann WILLETS, dt Richard & Hannah, Islip
Samuel, Cedar Swamp, b 4-16-1801 d 9-20-1877; m Hannah W. ----- d 12-10-1888 ae 75y 7m 10d (Wby Stone)
Ch: Henry T. b 6-4-1813
ct Jericho 4-15-1812 (clear)
Sarah, dt John & Mary, b 6 Mo (Aug) 17, 1687; m 1708 Thomas PEARSALL
Sarah, dt Israel, b 1-7-1780; m 1804 Andries SEAMAN (mo)
Sarah, dt Richard & Mary K., b 5-17-1861; m 1885 Halsey M. SMITH
Sarah m Penn FROST (See N.Y.)
Stephen C., s Stephen & Jemima (Coles), Roslyn, b Roslyn 8-20-1801 d 7-19-1869; m 9-3-1823 Sarah P. PEACOCK, dt Wm. & Mary (Jessup), Greenwich, b Conn. 12-9-1799 d 4-22-1889, Mill Neck
Ch: Isabella B. d Bkn. 11-1-1902 in 68th yr
(6 other ch)
Stephen recrq 7----1820; Sarah recrq 11-1831
Solomon, s Amos & Elizabeth, both dec; m 5-4-1780 at Cow Neck, Lydia MOTT, dt Adam & Sarah, Cow Neck, b 11-24-1759 d 5-17-1791
Ch: Isaac b 10-14-1781
Sarah b 5- 8-1783
Elizabeth b 3-30-1786 d 6-28-1801
Samuel b 4-16-1788
Ch: Henry b 3-13-1790
Thomas, Cedar Swamp, b 3-15-1790 d 6-29-1872 ae 82; m 2-2-1820 Sarah WHITSON, dt Henry & Clement, d 11-8-1866 ae 71
Ch: Phebe W. b 4-11-1824; m Jno. TITUS
Hannah W. b 12-11-1825; m Stephen R. HICKS
Henry W. b 12-18-1822
Pamelia b 4-1-1828; m Chas. McCOUN
Mary b 11-17-1829; m Elias LEWIS Jr.
Richard b 7----1832 d 4-13-1833
Richard b 6- 7-1835; m Mary K. ROBBINS
Elizabeth b 1838 d 6-11-1839 ae 1y
Thomas rocf N. Y. 8-2-1826 with w & ch, Henry, Phebe & Hannah
(Underhill Gen.)
Willets, s Israel & Mary, b 1-3-1796 d 8-9-1870 in 75th yr; m Mary PRIOR, dt Samuel & Mary
Ch: Benjamin R. d 5-15-1871 ae 46y 10m 1d (unm)
(3 other ch)
dis mo before 12-17-1817
(Underhill Gen.)
Willets m 2d abt 1839 Susan HOPKINS, dt George & Mary
Ch: George S. b 1839
William's ack referred from N. Y. 4-17-1822; accepted 6-19-1822

URQUHART
Mary m 1711 John FRY Jr.

VALENTINE
Ann, dt Samuel & Deborah, b 2-27-1814; m William C. COLES
Ann E. d 1838 (Wby Stone)
Anne L. m Charles P. LOWELL
Caroline d 5-27-1865 ae 54y 13d (Wby Stone)
Caroline, dt Elwood & Mary, b 10-31-1824; m 1843 James TITUS
Catharine S., dt David & Hannah, b 5-7-1818; m 1843 Isaac Buck LEWIS
(Cox Gen.)
Charles, s Jacob & Martha, N.Y.C., b 4-15-1815 d 2-25-1887 ae 71y 10m 8d; m 5-17-1838 at Mk, Kezia W. COLES, dt Thomas & Amelia, O.B., d 8-29-1897 ae 85y 6d bur Mk
Charles, s Jacob & Mary, Mk, b 7 Mo (Sept) 30, 1742 d 3-22-1815; m 3-4-1762 Mary FROST, dt Jacob & Sarah, b 8 Mo (Oct) 6, 1746 d 6-13-1808
Ch: Daniel b 11-25-1784
Lewis b 4-2-1765 d 2-3-1846 bur Mk
Elizabeth d 12-15-1847 ae 74y 1m 15d bur Mk
(7 other ch)
(Bibles)
Charles m abt 1808 Rachel HOPKINS, dt Daniel & Susannah
rst 12-14-1808
(Bibles)
Charles Post b 4-4-1871 d G.C. 10-25-1928; m Annie Laurie SEAMAN, dt Wm. H. & Margaret L., d E. Orange, N. J. 3-15-1913 ae 42
Ch: Charles Lowell b 1-20-1899 d 1-18-1908

VALENTINE, Charles Post & Annie Laurie, cont.
Ch: Alan Chester b 2-23-1901
Charles recrq 1-20-1897
Charles Post m 2d 4-30-1925 Frieda Harriett MATZ, dt J. Henry Fredk & Augusta (Erickson), G.C., b G.C. 3-25-1897
Ch: Charles Post Jr. b 6-9-1927
Frieda recrq 5-20-1928; John H. F. Matz b Hamburg, Germany; Augusta Erickson b Hpenrade, Denmark
Cornelia, dt Townsend & Anne; m 1851 Marshall S. FROST
Daniel, s Charles & Mary (Frost), b 11-25-1784 (11-26-1785 in Underhill Gen.) d 7-21-1814 bur Mk; m Jemima U. UNDERHILL, dt Joseph & Anne (Rogers), d 9-20-1874 ae 83y 4m 12d (mo)
Ch: Joseph U. m Mary COCK
ack mo 5-20-1812
David, s Jacob & Mary, M.C., b 7 Mo (Sept) 27, 1745 d 4-18-1812 ae 66y 5m; m 9-27-1774 Hannah TOWNSEND, dt Prior & Sarah, b 5-21-1755 d 1837
Ch: Susan d 1-6-1862 ae 86y 5m 25d
Sarah d 6-26-1862 ae 85y 1m 21d
bur Mk
(Bibles)
David, s Charles & Mary, Mk, b 4-28-1783 d 11-28-1849 ae 66y 7m; m 6-29-1813 Hannah COCK, dt Daniel & Catharine, b 9-2-1793 d 2-18-1875 ae 81y 5m 16d
Ch: Henry C. b 3-26-1814; m Anna WILLETS
Mary C. b 4-5-1816; m Lot CORNELIUS
Catharine S. b 5-7-1818; m Isaac Buck LEWIS
Daniel b 10-22-1821 d Mk 1-24-1902 (unm)
Charles b 4-13-1823 d 4-9-1828
Ann Elizabeth b 6-16-1828; m John Henry LEWIS
Latitia b 8-17-1833 d 3-30-1858 ae 24y
Chas. Edward b 4-18-1840; m Mary A. RICKBACK
(Cox Gen.)
Deborah m 1736 Samuel WEEKS
Elizabeth, dt Charles & Mary, Mk, d 12-16-1846 ae 73y
Elizabeth, dt Daniel & Hannah, b 6-16-1828; m 1850 John LEWIS
Ellwood, s David & Hannah T., M.C., b 10-2-1796 d 11-1-1872 in 89th yr (G.W. Cock's has 12-25-1872); m 12-2-1822 Mary T. POST, dt Daniel & Rosetta, b 11-16-1801 d 12-7-1854 ae abt 53y
Ch: Caroline b 10-31-1824
Emily N. b 12-18-1832 d G.C. 5-4-1921
Susan b 7-3-1839 d 10-20-1918
ct Flushing 10-15-1822 (clear)
Ellwood d 12-26-1872 ae 76y; m Mary C. ----- (Wby Stones)
Ephraim d 2-13-1873 ae 69y; m Susan D. ----- d 4-3-1884 ae 68 (Wby Stones)
Ephraim C. d 5-20-1893 ae 45 (Wby Stone); m Helen A. -----
Ch: Oliver T. d 7-18-1885 ae 10m (Wby Stone)

George W., nm, Wby; m before 4-19-1837 Phebe TITUS, dt Rowland & Sarah, d 8-15-1856 (mo)
(George W. d 5-2-1870 ae 71)
Phebe ret mbrp
Hannah gct Woodbridge 10 Mo (Dec) 27, 1732; ack mo
Henry N. d 7-20-1893 ae 11m 26d (unidentified stone, Mk)
Isaac R., s Lewis & Jane, b 11-11-1792 d 6-20-1871 (Mk Stone); m 12-16-1822 Freelove CRAFT, dt Stephen & Hannah, b 4-2-1794 d 10-27-1868
Ch: Joseph C. b 9-24-1823; m Eliz. COLES
ack mo 6-18-1823; cf N. Y. 1839
(Bibles)
Jacob, s Charles & Mary, Huntington, b 1-29-1763; m 12-21-1791 at Wby Phebe LOINES, dt Stephen, dec, & Phebe, N. Hemp. (mo)
Ch: (2)
mo 12-1-1791; dis next mo
Jacob m 2d 1799 Elizabeth Ann EYRE, dt Col. Benj. G. & Mary
Ch: (9)
(Bibles)
Jacob d 9-3-1868 ae 77y 8m 20d; m Martha TITUS, d 3-6-1880 ae 89y 1m 8d
Ch: Charles b 4-15-1815
Mary
Lewis b 5- 1-1820 d 11-12-1821
Lewis b 12-20-1829
Jane R. b 1-23-1834 d 1-12-1882
ct N. Y. 5-18-1814 (clear); Martha rocf N. Y. 1814
all bur Mk
James m abt 1763 Phebe ----- (mo)
Phebe ack mo 8-31-1763
James I. M. d 12-10-1845 in 39th yr (unidentified stone, Mk)
Jane, dt Oliver; m Thos. RUSHMORE
Jane R. d 4-30-1831 ae 13y 4m 13d (unidentified stone, Wby)
John T., s Lewis & Jane, Glen Cove, d 8-15-1884 ae 78th yr bur Mk; m Elizabeth MUDGE b 11-25-1816 d 10-8-1875
Ch: Hannah E. b 4-17-1850 d 4-27-1857
Elwood b 9- 1-1852
Mary Jane b 4-23-1857
William M. b 4-7-1839
Joseph C. m 6-7-1865 Elizabeth H. COLES, dt Thomas & Amelia, b 11-10-1829 d 7-30-1900 at Wading River
Ch: (3)
Joseph U., s Daniel & Jemima, b 1810 d 4-17-1862 (4-7-1862 in Underhill Gen.); m 4-10-1832 Mary C. COCK, dt Benjamin & Lanah (Frost), b 11-4-1809 d 3-24-1877 ae 67y 4m 20d
Mary C. m 2d William M. WEEKS
Latitia, dt Charles & Mary; m 1789 William WILLETS
Leonard d 9-27-1875 ae 63y 2m 5d (unidentified stone, Mk)
Lewis, s Charles & Mary, O.B., b 4-2-1765

VALENTINE, Lewis continued
d 3-2-1846 ae 80y 10m 20d; m 1-7-1790 at Mk, Jane RUSHMORE, dt Isaac & Sarah, O.B.
Ch: Silas d 3-11-1831 ae 36y 5m
Lewis m 2d 11-3-1802 at Wby Jane POST, wd Samuel, dt John & Sarah TITUS, b 9-4-1773 d 9-25-1852 ae abt 79y
Ch: Jane b 1-22-1814 d 4-17-1886 in 73d yr
Townsend
John T.
George m Hannah WILLETS
Lewis, s Jacob & Martha, O.B., b 12-20-1829 d G.C. 9-12-1912; m 11-13-1861 at Sam'l C. Thorne's, Anna C. THORNE, dt Samuel C. & Maria H., O.B., d 2-8-1889 ae 67 bur Mk
Maria d 8-17-1866 ae 57y 9m 21d (unidentified stone, Mk)
Martha, dt Obadiah & Martha, b 9 Mo (Nov) 18, 1717; m 1736 Samuel SEAMAN
Ch: (11)
signed Epistle abt 1725
(Seaman Gen.)
Mary, dt Richard; m 1777 ----- KIRBEY
Mary b 4-6-1816; m 1838 Cornelius LOTT
Mary, dt Jacob & Martha; m 1846 William WILLETS
Mary d 2-14-1894 ae 86y (unidentified stone, Mk)
Mary Jane, dt John T. & Elizabeth, b 4-23-1857; m Arthur Hastings SLEIGH
Obadiah, s Richard, d 10-8-1767 ae near 77y 3m; m Martha -----
Ch: Martha b 11 Mo (Jan) 18, 1717
Mary b 2 Mo (Apr) 12, 1719
Phebe b 9 Mo (Nov) 29, 1721
Elizabeth b 2 Mo (Apr) 28, 1724
Esther b 1 Mo (Mar) 16, 1733/34
(4 other ch)
Obadiah signed cert 1726
Obadiah W., s Wm. & Phebe, d 7-17-1854 in 45th yr; m -----
Ch: Wm. Augustus d 11-6-1846 in 13th yr
(Wby Stones)
Oliver d 1858 (unidentified stone, Wby)
Oliver d 7-3-1863 ae 20y 9m 3d (unidentified stone, Mk)
Peggy, dt Wm. Jr., b 5-1-1758; gct N. P. 6-19-1795
Phebe, dt Obadiah & Martha, b 9 Mo (Nov) 29, 1721; m 1743 Zebulun SEAMAN (mo)
ack mo 4-24-1754
Phebe ack mo 7-20-1763
Phebe d 8-14-1856 ae 50y 4m (unidentified stone, Wby)
Richard, s Richard d (will 1705 but appears to have signed Epistle abt 1725) m 1686 Sarah HALSTEAD, dt Timothy & Sarah (Williams)
Ch: (7)
(Bibles)
Richard Jr., s Richard & Sarah; m 1755 Phebe ----- (mo)
Phebe ack mo 10-21-1755; Richard Jr. ack mo same day
Samuel T., s Stephen & Ann T., N.Y.C.; m 10-21-1847 at Mary T. Kirk's, Anna KIRK, dt Daniel, dec, & Mary T., O.B., b 2-4-1822 cf N. Y. (clear)
Sarah d 6-26-1862 ae 85y 1m 21d (unidentified stone, Mk)
Sarah T. d 5-4-1851 ae 11y 6m 23d (unidentified stone, Mk)
Silas T. d 8-20-1873 ae 30y 7m 15d (unidentified stone, Mk)
Theodosia, dt Charles & Mary; m 1803 Asa DOWNING
Townsend, s Lewis & Jane, b 7-30-1804 d 7-17-1866 ae 61y 11m 18d; m before 6-15-1831 Ann TITUS, dt Samuel R. & Phebe, b 9-5-1811 d 3-21-1886 ae 74y 6m 16d (mo)
Ch: Silas d 10-21-1906 ae 67y 4m 25d
(2 other ch)
both dis 9-14-1831
(Bibles)
Vandewater d 1-24-1894 ae 3y 6m 27d (unidentified stone, Wby)
William Jr. d 9-2-1859 ae 23y 10m 12d bur Wby; m -----
Ch: Peggy b 5- 1-1758
Rachel b 2-13-1755
Mary " 8-19-1757
William d 9-15-1899 ae 93y 28d; m Mary Ann ----- d 7-21-1883 ae 70y
(Wby Stones)
William d 11-24-1863 in 85th yr; m Phebe ----- d 4-24-1859 in 68th yr
Ch: Obadiah W.
Eugene d 3-24-1853 in 32d yr
Ann Eliza d 10-25-1865 ae 51y 12d (Ann Eliza NICHOLS, may have m a Nichols)
(Wby Stones)
William M. d 7-17-1884 ae 75y 5m 27d (Wby Stone); m Emily POST, dt Charles
Ch: Charles P.
(Bibles)
William M., s John T. & Eliz. (Mudge), b 4-7-1839 d 5-7-1919; m 1860 Lydia P. PERRY, dt ----- MOTT
Lydia rocf N. Y. 1858; Lydia gct Flushing 12-15-1886

VAN BLARCOM
Herman, s Herman L. & Ella M. (Dimock), b 2-18-1898 Portland, Me.; m 2-28-1925 Bkn Anna FRITH, dt W. Oscar & Margaretta A. (Mac Taggart), b 10-22-1901 Bkn.
both recrq 6-19-1935; Herman b Raymond, N.H.
Ella M. b Portland, Me.

VAN COTT
Cornelius, s Nicholas & Jane, d 11-12-1849 ae 83y 3m 28d
Elizabeth m 1804 Jesse BALDWIN
Oliver m Elizabeth HAWXHURST, dt Eph. & Charity, b 2-7-1835
Elizabeth gct Nine Partners 10-7-1860 as former w of Oliver

VANDENBURGH
Abram P., b 1-1-1825 d 3-1-1875; m Henrietta W. PRIOR, dt John & Elizabeth, b 12-12-1831 d 3-2-1884
(Bibles)

VANDEVOORT
G. M. & Catherine
Ch: Charles Augustus b 7-15-1850 d 9-6-1854
(Man Stone)

VANDEWATER
C. G. b 9-20-1813 d 11-22-1871; m Charlotte ----- d 11-6-1891 ae 72y
Ch: Peter d 6-9-1868 ae 29y 4m 7d
Oakley d 3-6-1863 ae 16y 6m 16d
Oscar d 1-22-1874 ae 25y
(Wby Stones)
David d 5-18-1866 ae 44y 3m 6d (Wby Stone)
James, s Peter & Naomi, d 7-6-1873 ae 56y; m Jessie ----- (supposed w as stones are adjacent in Wby) d 5-28-1874 ae 54
Peter d 12-21-1837 ae 55y 2m 7d; m (probably) Naomi C. ----- d 10-31-1830 ae 46y 7m 26d (Wby Stone)
Ch: (prob) James
Phebe d 6-13-1863 ae 70y 2m 20d (Wby Stone)
Robert d 10-30-1852 ae 74y (Wby Stone)

VAN KLEECK
Louis Ashley, s Geo. B. & Florence (Willey), Manhasset, b Castil, N. Y. 9-14-1887; m Grace VAN NOSTRAND, dt Albert & Phebe Eliza (Wooley), b Little Neck, L. I. 12-24-1894
Ch: Martha Louise b 4-22-1921
Albert Van Nostrand b Little Neck 1857; Phebe b Lakeville, L. I. 5-19-1869; Grace & Louis A. recrq 1931; George Baltus Van Kleeck b Mt. Morris, N. Y.; Florence Willey b Nunda, N. Y.

VAN NOSTRAND
Benjamin Treadwell, Bkn; m Anna TITUS, dt Geo. P. & Mary T., b 7-22-1861 d 5-19-1930 in 67th yr
Grace, dt Albert & Phebe E., b Little Neck 12-24-1894; m Louis Ashley VAN KLEECK
Phebe, (prob) dt Jacob & Kezia MOTT, b 3-4-1760; dis mo before 6-6-1787

VAN VELSON
Losee b 6-3-1813 d 8-1-1895; m Amy ----- (supposed w as stones are adjacent in Wby) b 11-4-1814 d 10-25-1896

VELSOR
Cornelius & Sarah
Ch: Arthur d 6-28-1867 ae 1y 8m 7d
(Wby Stones)
Francis Augustus d 2-7-1862 ae 19y 3m 27d (unidentified stone, Wby)
John d 4-5-1887 ae 82y 4m 25d; m Sarah ----- d 2-2-1888 ae 82y 9m 21d
Mary Lavinia d 11-6-1841 ae 1y 3m 27d (unidentified stone, Wby)
Stephen T. m 1861 Margaret FROST, dt Charles & Martha, b 5-5-1840 d 7-16-1864 ae 24y 2m 11d (Wby Stone)
Stephen T. m 2d Sarah M. FROST, dt Charles & Martha, b 12-29-1845
Ch: son d 1-17-1867 ae 10d
Sarah resigned 9-16-1896
Valentine b 7-13-1830 d 11-29-1898; m Ruth WILLITS
Ch: Libbie d 6-11-1865 ae 3y 17d
Infant
Ruth rocf Jericho 1861
(Wby Stones)

VERITY
Walter J. d 1-31-1867 ae 9y 6m 4d (Man Stone)

WAIT
Harold Van Alden, s Irving V. A. & Lillian (Best) b Schodack Landing, N. J. 2-14-1897; m 8-31-1923 Marion STRINGHAM, s Irving J. & Eleanor, b 5-17-1898
Ch: Elizabeth b 10-24-1925
Harold Van A. b 1-2-1927
Irving S. b 12- 2-1928
Harold & ch recrq 10-2-1928; Irving Wait b Johnstown, N. Y.; Lillian Best b Kinderhook, N. Y.

WAKEFIELD
Louise Ruth F., dt Robert; m 1938 Silas Burling WEEKS

WALDRON
Cornelius b 2-4-1804 d 2-29-1884; m Rhoda ----- b 4-1-1804 d 3-16-1892
Ch: Cornelius H. d 7-5-1816
John Jr. d 1-7-1858 ae 8y 11m 22d
(Wby Stones)

WALKER
Emeline, dt Dr. Claude & Harriette V.; m 1935 Robert E. FATHERLY

WALMSLEY
William, s Thomas & Mary, Bybury, Pa.; m 11 Mo (Jan) 7, 1735/6 at Wby, Sarah TITUS, dt Silas, Wby
Sarah gct Abington, Pa. 12 Mo (Feb) 25, 1735/6

WALTERS
Caroline P., dt Felix M. & Martha, b 8-12-1836 d 11-9-1908
Elizabeth m Nathaniel HAWXHURST
Felix M. m Martha ----- d 4-3-1881 ae 83y 3m 9d (Wby Stone)
Jean, dt B. Franklin & Eleanor, b Christiana, Pa. 12-31-1904; m George A. THAYER 3d
Joseph, Cortlandt Manor; m 10-1-1767 at Islip

WALTERS, Joseph, continued
Sarah POWELL, dt John, dec, Islip

WALTON
Thomas, s Jeremiah, dec, & Eliz., Moreland, Pa.; m 12 Mo 26, 1754 at Wby, Mary TITUS, dt Silas, dec, & Sarah, b 3 Mo (May) 8, 1725 (Thomas b 8 Mo (Oct) 20, 1721
cf Abington (clear)
(Bibles)

WANSER
Isaac d 11-5-1866; m Abbey ----- (supposed w as stones adjacent in Wby) d 10-18-1865

WARTMAN
John H. b 3-1-1832 d 2-26-1902; m Louisa J. ----- d 2-12-1861 ae 27y 10m 15d
John H. m 2d Mary E. ----- b 5-7-1839 d 1-4-1904

WATERBURY
Azariah, s John & Martha, both dec, Middlesex, Conn.; m 2-19-1819 at Wby, Sarah POWELL, dt Reuben, dec, & Anna, Wby

WATSON
Rudolph Burnie m 1-15-1912 Rachel V. HICKS, dt John S. & Carrie, b 10-25-1890

WAY
Jane, dt Samuel & Esther, b 5-8-1761; m 1783 Henry MOTT
John m 1759 (cert not recorded, m bet 11-28 & 12-26-1759) Phebe TITUS
cf Flushing (clear); Phebe gct Flushing 3-26-1760
Samuel Jr. m 1755 (cert not recorded) Esther VALENTINE, dt Obadiah, b 1 Mo (Mar) 16, 1733/34
Ch: Valentine b 5-30-1756
Jane b 5-8-1761
m between 11-26-1755 & 12-31-1755; Esther ack misconduct; Samuel rocf Flushing (clear)

WEEKS
Elizabeth m 1797 ----- CROOKER
Edwin W. m Beulah WOLFE, dt Levi B. & Lettie (Pearle), dec, b N. Granville, N. Y. 1-14-1885
Ch: Silas Burling b E. Williston 11- 1-1914
Janet Burling b " " 11- 9-1919
Evelyn, dt Sam'l & Jane M., b 8-12-1872 G.C.; m Edward E. CRAFT
Freelove m 1739 Richard POWELL
George, N. Hemp. m 10-21-1801 at Wby, Anne POWELL, wd, dt Jonathan & Sarah CORNELIUS
cf N.P. (clear) (George d 12-25-1815 ae abt 80y 5m
Hannah rst on act 2-17-1813
Isaac D., s Silas & Sarah, d 1-20-1892 ae in 66th yr
Jacob M., s Wm. M. & Margaret M.; m 11-12-1862 Henrietta W. FROST, dt Edward L. & Hannah, b 10-4-1842
Ch: (5)

Ch: (5)
Henrietta m 2d 7-20-1901 Ezekiel H. MILLER
James, s Richard & Martha, dec, O.B., b 6-29-1799 d 7-22-1876; m 11-20-1851 at Mk, Phebe T. COCKS, dt David & Lydia, dec, O.B., b 1-1-1808 d 8-5-1891 ae 85y 7m
bur Mk
(Cox Gen.)
James L. m Elizabeth HAWXHURST b 1-18-1822 d 6-6-1849 bur Wby
Jerusha, w Robert, dt ----- LEWIS; m 2d 1748 Richard POWELL
John m Ann (or Anna) CORNELIUS, dt Jonathan & Sarah, d 5-24-1826 ae abt 66y
Ch: Cornelius b 9-1-1824 (?)
Martha m Jacob B. WILLIS
Mary, dt Richard & Martha; m 1820 John THORNE
Mary rocf Chappaqua 10-8-1871; gct Chappaqua 7-15-1874
Mary Ella rocf Chappaqua 10-8-1871; ct Chappaqua 7-15-1874
Nathaniel M., s Richard, dec, & Samantha, d 3-10-1874 ae 43y; m 10-21-1858 at Isaac Titus', N. Hemp., Sarah Elizabeth ALLEY, dt Sidney B. & Eliz., both dec, d 11-4-1903 ae 64y 3m
Ch: Alice L. d 11-2-1861 in 3d yr
Ida d 3-1-1874 ae 1y 1m
ct Rome
(Wby Stones)
Phebe M. d 5-9-1864 ae 22y 16d (Wby Stone)
Refine, s Augustine & Elizabeth; m N.P. 10-19-1786 Margaret TOBIAS, dt Jacob & Rebecca
Ch: (7)
ct N.P. (clear); Margaret rocf N.P. 6-6-1787
(Bibles)
Richard m Martha ----- d 1-12-1835 ae 80y 7m 26d
Ch: Rachel b 11-30-1781 d 10-19-1820
Samuel d 8-26-1827 ae 34y 4m 4d
Samuel m 1736 Deborah VALENTINE
Samuel (sometimes written Wickes), s Richard & Martha, Cedar Swamp; m 9-28-1815 at Mk, Sarah R. DOWNING, dt Silas & Phebe, Cedar Swamp
Ch: Stephen d 11- 7-1821 ae 6m 12d
Samuel D. b 4-25-1821
Silas D. b 3-11-1823
Isaac b 11-18-1824
Samuel W. b 9- 5-1826
Samuel D., s Samuel & Sarah, b 4-25-1821; dis mo 4----1848
Silas, s Richard & Martha, Wby & Roslyn, d 3-8-1855; m Anna POWELL, dt Reuben & Anna, d 11-13-1836 ae 43y 8m 26d
Anna Weeks rst on ack 10-15-1828 (perhaps this one, but proof not found)
Silas m Emma WILLETS, dt Isaac & Mary, b 10-7-1852
Ch: Edwin W. b 6-10-1876
Anna B. b 12-31-1879
Sarah C. b 10-3-1884

WEEKS, Silas & Emma, continued
ct N. Y. 3-18-1885 for all; ch b Bkn
Silas Burling, s Edwin W. & Beulah, b E. Williston 11-1-1914; m 12-24-1938 Watertown, N.Y. by Rev. Middleton, Louise Ruth F. WAKEFIELD dt Robert
Silas D., s Samuel & Sarah, b 4-25-1821; m before 1-20-1847; ret mbrp
Willet, s John & Ann, d 1-17-1822; m 11-19-1779 Dorothy MUDGE, dt Coles & Dorothy
Ch: John b 11-28-1793; m Sarah FROST
Jane b 3-2-1792; m Jonathan UNDERHILL
(Bibles)

WEIR
George & Annie E.
Ch: Blanche b 2-5-1873 d 6-29-1896 (Wby Stone)

WELLS
Charlotte Elizabeth b Wading River, L. I. 8-17-1846; m 1864 Jas. Franklin YOUNG
Edna, dt Sherman & Deborah; m 1928 Richard Underhill TEMPLE

WHEELER
Sarah J. m Philemon PRIOR, M.D.

WHITE
Dave [Whyte] Jr., s Dave & Annie, Banff, Alberta; m 10-19-1931 at Wby, Barbara CARPENTER, dt Rich. E. & Florence, Wby
Ch: Barbara Jane b Wby 9-14-1933
Barbara J. recrq 10-15-1933
Estey R. d 8-15-1864 ae 56; m Anna C. ----- d 12-30-1880 ae 25y 9m 11d (Wby Stones)
Jane's ack referred from Flushing, accepted 6-19-1822
Judith, dt Simon & Phebe, b 6-23-1761; m Wright CRAFT

WHITEHEAD
John m Ann COCK, dt Zoar, d 6-22-1866 ae 75y bur Mk
(Cox Gen.)

WHITMAN
Martha m 1734 Isaac POWELL
Martha m 1751 John WHITSON

WHITNEY
Daniel D. m 1856 Sarah W. TITUS, dt Henry & Phebe, b 11-6-1822
Sarah W. gct N. Y. 3-19-1856
Daniel D. m 2d Henrietta TITUS, dt Silas & Mary, d Bkn. 12-26-1912 ae 71y 6m 27d
Scudder V. m Elizabeth TITUS, dt Henry & Phebe, b 9-23-1829 d Woodbury, L. I. 7-28-1912

WHITSON
Abram Underhill, s Sam'l & Phebe J., rocf Flushing with parents 10-5-1884; gct Flushing 1-18-1914
Anna, dt Thos. & Mary W.; m 1871 Frederick

WILLETS
Amos, s John & Deborah; m abt 1772 Amey WILLETS, dt Joseph & Hannah
Ch: Thomas b 6-26-1773
Rebecca b 2- 5-1780
Joseph b 6-13-1782
Hannah b 4-24-1784
Robert m Anna WHITSON
Deborah m David WILLETS
(Bibles)
Amy, dt Abrm. & Mary J., b 3-3-1824; m Edward S. WILLITS
David, s Thomas & Martha, b 7 Mo (Sept) 11, 1701; m 1731 Clement POWELL, dt John & Margaret, b 12 Mo (Feb) 27, 1709/10 d 5 Mo (July) 31, 1751
Ch: Ruth b 11 Mo (Jan) 23, 1732/33
Mary " 11 Mo (Jan) 5, 1736/37
Amey b 5 Mo (July) 18, 1739
Solomon b 2 Mo (Apr) 9, 1741
David b 7 Mo (Sept) 22, 1743
Clement b 5 Mo (July) 1, 1751
both ack mo 9 Mo (Nov) 26, 1735
Deborah, dt John & Deborah; m 1766 James RUSHMORE
Deborah, dt Amos & Amy; m 1818 David WILLETS
Esther, dt Nathaniel; m 1778 David JACKSON
Henry, s Thomas & Deborah (Feeks), Beth.; m 7 Mo (Sept) 5, 1739 at Beth., Hannah POWELL dt Thomas, dec, & Mary, Beth.
Ch: Mary b 7 Mo (Sept) 11, 1740
Hannah b 7 Mo (Sept) 5, 1742
Henry b 1 Mo (Mar) 15, 1745
Thomas b 6 Mo (Aug) 10, 1747
Kezia b 2-17-1753
John, s Thomas & Martha, Beth, b 19 Feb 1697 d 23 Dec. 1778; m 1722/23 Esther SEAMAN, dt Nathaniel & Rachel, b 9 Mo (Nov) 8, 1701 d 7-6-1759
Ch: Nathaniel m Mary POWELL
John m Martha WHITMAN
(Bibles)
John, s Thomas & Deborah, Huntington; m 8 Mo (Oct) 3, 1744 at Bethpage, Deborah POWELL, dt Thomas, dec, & Mary, Bethpage
Ch: Mary b 7 Mo (Sept) 26, 1745
Deborah b 2 Mo (Apr) 26, 1747
Elizabeth b 9 Mo (Nov) 1, 1749
Amos b 5 Mo (July) 3, 1751
John 3d, s John & Esther, b abt 1724; m 1747 Martha WHITMAN
Ch: (8)
mo before 2 Mo (Apr) 24, 1751; ack mo 4-29-1752
(Bibles)
Joseph, s Amos & Amey, Huntington; m 10-31-1804 at Wby, Hannah SMITH, dt Jacob & Rachel
Ch: Jacob S. b 10-21-1805
Mariah b 3-18-1807
Ann b 3-27-1809
Thomas b 5-15-1811
Gilbert E. b 7-19-1813

WHITSON, Joseph & Hannah, continued
Ch: Margaret b 11-21-1819
Susan b 7- 1-1822
cf Jericho (clear)
Keziah, dt Henry & Hannah; m 1777 Isaac COLES
Keziah, dt Henry & Clemence, b 1788; m 1813 Silas ALBERTSON
Martha m Edmund WILLETS
Mary, dt John; m 1767 Jonathan TITUS
Mary Esther, dt Samuel & Phebe; m 1900 Edgar Jefferson TAYLOR
Mary M., dt Jarvis P. & Abbie, b Beth 9-13-1839; recrq 5-19-1912
Nathaniel, s John & Esther, Beth; m 1 Mo (Mar) 7, 1749/50 at Beth, Mary POWELL, dt Wait & Mary, Beth
Ch: Jarvis b 12 Mo (Feb) 15, 1750/51
Esther b 1-4-1755
Sarah b 1-20-1757
Phebe, dt John; m 1769 Richard POWELL Jr.
Phebe, dt Henry & Clement; m John CROMWELL
Rebecca m 1717 Amos WILLITS
Samuel b 8-19-1816 d 6-10-1899 ae 82; m Phebe JACKSON b 11-23-1843 d 9-10-1886
Ch: Mary Esther m Edgar J. TAYLOR
Wm. Edward m Maud HOLLEY
Abram Underhill
cert for all from Flushing 10-15-1884
(Wby Stones)
Sarah, dt Nathaniel & Mary, b 1-20-1757; m 1781 Charles JACKSON (mo)
Sarah, dt Henry & Clement; m Thomas UNDERHILL
Solomon, s David, Bucks Co., Pa.; m 3-5-1766 at Wby, Phebe WILLIS, dt Silas, dec
Thomas, s Henry, b 20 Aug. 1652 d 8 Mo (Oct) 20, 1742; m Martha JONES, dt Thomas & Catharine
Ch: Thomas b 1689; m Deborah FEAKE
Martha
Ruth
John m 1722 Esther SEAMAN
Rebecca m 1729 Amos WILLITS
David m 1731 Clement POWELL
Henry m 1739 Hannah POWELL
Hannah d 1789
(Bible records)
Thomas, s Thomas & Martha; m 3 Mo (May) 9, 1716 Deborah FEAKE, dt John & Elizabeth, b 5 Mo (July) 11, 1695
Ch: Henry
John
Thomas
(4 other ch)
Thomas m 2d 1739 Elizabeth -----
Thomas ack mo 1 Mo (Mar) 22, 1746/7
Thomas, s Amos & Amy, Herricks, b 6-26-1773 d 7-11-1845 ae 75y
Thomas, Herricks; m Hannah WILLITS, dt Amos & Phebe, b 8-26-1775 d 10-28-1829 ae 54y 2m 2d
Wm. Edward, s Samuel & Phebe J.; m Maud E. HOLLEY, dt Lemuel P. & Ann Eliza, b 8-26-1880
Wm. E. rocf Flushing with parents 10-15-1884; Maud recrq 5-17-1905

WIGGINS
Benjamin m Ellen R. ----- d 1-25-1873 ae 34y 10m 24d (Wby Stone)
George Walter b 6-29-1839 d 2-1-1889; m Isabella Amanda ----- b 2-1-1848 d 8-6-1891 (Wby Stones)
Mary D., dt Abel B. & Deborah; m 1878 Stimusson POWELL
William S. d 6-2-1879 ae 70y 5m 9d; m Mary Ann ----- (prob w of William as stones adjacent in Wby) d 11-19-1874 ae 63y 9m 7d
----- m Amy MOTT, dt Jacob & Kezia, b 10-26-1765 (mo)
dis mo 12----1787

WILES
Alton m Julia G. HOPKINS, dt Edwin A. & Mary H., b 5-4-1868

WILLETS
Abbe ae 34y 2m 3d (Unidentified stone, Man)
Abigail [Willits], dt Richard, b 12 Mo (Feb) 27, 1690/91; m John WILLIS
Abraham, s Jonah & Mary, Wby & N. Hemp., b 11-7-1786; m 11-23-1815 at Mk, Henrietta FROST, dt Caleb & Sarah, Cedar Swamp
Ch: Elizabeth b 2-4-1821
Leonard b 10-23-1823
Amelia, dt Wm. P. & Mary Jane; m 1874 Gilbert HICKS
Amos, blacksmith, s Thomas & Dinah, d 1746; m 1713 Mary HALLOCK, dt John & Abigail
Ch: Samuel m Jane POWELL
(Bibles)
Amos m 2d 1717 Rebecca WHITSON, dt Thomas & Martha
Ch: Catharine b 1740; m Jacob UNDERHILL
Sarah m John WILLIS
Jacob b 2 Mo (Apr) 9, 1723; m Hannah POWELL
Amos m Kezia PLATT; Rebecca -----
Joseph b 1728; m Phebe WILLIAMS; Hannah TITUS
Jemima m Wm. JARVIS
Martha m Thos. PRIOR
Hannah b 1734; m Wait POWELL
Thomas b 1738; m Leah SEAMAN
Mary b 1740 d 6-8-1814 ae 74
Amos ack mo & bearing arms 6-10-1754 (he was the s)
Amos, s Amos & Rebecca; m 24 July, 1749 Kezia PLATT
Ch: (2)
ack mo 7-31-1754; dis joining Presbyterians 7-31-1765
(Bibles)
Amos, s Richard & Ruth, b 4-21-1754 d 12-21-1831; m 1774 (cert not recorded, m bet 5-25 & 6-29) Phebe POWELL, dt Joshua & Phebe, b 9 Mo (Nov) 17, 1749

WILLETS, Amos & Phebe, continued
Ch: Hannah b 8-26-1775
Joshua b 10-21-1780
Sarah
(Bibles)
Amos m 2d 12-21-1799 at Wby, Elizabeth DOWNING, wd James, dt Thomas & Rosannah BIRDSALL cf Jericho (clear); Elizabeth gct Jericho 3-19-1800
Amos [Willits], s Robert & Mary, Wby; m 2-23-1814 at Wby, Anne TITUS, dt Daniel & Amy, Wby
Ch: Daniel T. b 6-5-1815
Amos, Hemp. m Amy DOWNING, wd Amos, dt Benj. & Martha ----- d 1-4-1862
Amos dis mo 1-18-1826
Amy gct Pa. 2 Mo (Apr) 26, 1738 (clear)
Amy, dt Joseph & Hannah; m abt 1772 Amos WHITSON
Amy, dt Samuel & Jane; m 1783 Daniel TITUS
Amy [Willits] (form Williams) mo before 9-20-1826 & ret mbrp
Amy, dt Jonah & Mary; m Zebulun PINKHAM
Ann, dt Richard & Hannah; m 1771 Samuel UNDERHILL
Anna d 1826 (unidentified stone, Wby)
Anna, dt William & Mary, b Jericho 8-6-1848; m 1873 Frederick E. WILLITS
Anna, dt Thomas W. & Hannah; m 1908 Edw. Morgan LAPHAM
Catharine, dt Amos & Mary, b 9 Mo (Nov) 29, 1739; m 1760 Jacob UNDERHILL
Catharine [Willits], dt Joseph & Hannah; m 1788 Edmund POST
Catherine d 12-20-1846 ae 89
Charity ack mo 12-26-1787
Charles, s Thomas, Jericho; m 1-7-1789 at Beth., Esther POWELL, dt Richard, Beth.
Charles F. b 4-14-1861 d 3-16-1925; m Grace O. -----
Ch: Dorothy J. m Chas. V. SMITH
Grace O. & Dorothy recrq 8-19-1903
Charles H. b 5-2-1827 d 2-6-1896; m Mary E. ----- b 1-23-1832 d 4-10-1895
Ch: Infant s, Edgar
Cornelia b 1-14-1850; m John CARLE
Daniel, s Richard & Deborah, b 8 Mo (Oct) 14, 1718 d 2-6-1753; m 12 Mo (Feb) 3, 1742/3 Phebe CARPENTER, dt Joseph & Ann, b 28 Aug. 1718 d 11 Mo (Jan) 7, 1743/4
Ch: Jacob b 11 Mo (Jan) 7, 1743/4
(Bibles)
Daniel m 2d 1 Mo (Mar) 5, 1745/6 at Beth., Amy POWELL, dt John, dec, & Margaret, Beth., b 1718
Ch: Phebe b 12 Mo (Feb) 17, 1746/7; m Adonijah UNDERHILL
Charity
(Bibles)
Daniel, s Jacob & Hannah, b 5-24-1753 d 4-4-1825; m 11-9-1782 Martha SEAMAN, dt Zebulun & Phebe, b 2-28-1755 (or 1756) d 4-29-1816
Ch: (4)
dis mo; rst on ack & ct N. Y. 11-16-1803
(Bibles)
Daniel, s Edmund & Martha; m Hannah GRIFFEN, dt Henry
Ch: Joseph b 10-22-1873 d 7-23-1874 (Wby Stone)
(Pencil note in Register re Hannah not mbr here)
(Bibles)
Daniel ae 51y 8m 11d (Unidentified stone, Man.)
Daniel T., s Amos & Anne (Titus), b 6-1-1815 d 1-3-1878; m 6-9-1836 Elizabeth F. BOWNE, dt Sidney B. & Jemima (Hunt), b 4-20-1814 d 1-15-1890
(Wby Stones & Bibles)
David, s Isaac & Clemence, Islip; m (License) 29 May 1738, Deborah WILLETS, dt Richard & Deborah, d 3-29-1814 ae 95y 5m 7d
Ch: Jonah m Mary WILLITS
Charity d 12-26-1826 ae 84y 6m
ack mo 6 Mo (Aug) 25, 1742
(Bibles)
David, s Jonah & Mary, Wby, b 3-26-1785 d 3-16-1837; m Deborah WHITSON, dt Amos & Amy, b 12-28-1789 d 5-11-1866
Ch: Isaac U. b 12-7-1819; m Mary CROMWELL
William P. b 1-11-1823 d 8-18-1877
Jonah b 1-19-1825 d 1865
Amos b 1-29-1827 d 11-28-1828
Mary d 1-24-1833 ae 2y 11m 17d
ct Jericho 2-18-1818 (clear)
(Bibles)
Deborah, dt Jonah & Mary, b 4-5-1791; m Peter WILLITS
Deborah, dt Richard & Hannah; m 1774 Andrew UNDERHILL
Deborah ae 20y 4m 20d (unidentified stone, Man)
Dinah, dt Isaac & Clemence; m abt 1754 Abraham UNDERHILL
Dorothy, dt Charles F. & Grace O.; m 1925 Charles Valentine SMITH
Edmond m Annie C. ----- b 2-27-1807 d 3-10-1883 (Wby Stone)
Edmund, Manhasset, b 4-6-1800 d 3-10-1875; m Martha WHITSON, dt Thomas & Anne, d 9-10-1873 ae 76y 6m 13d
Ch: Joseph b 10----1830
Anna b 5-27-1833
Mary
Sarah Maria
Martha H. m Thos. MOTT
Thomas W. b 8-6-1843
Daniel m Hannah GRIFFEN
Edmund R. b 2-7-1852
Edmund rocf N. Y. 1846
(Bibles)
Edward, s Jacob H., dec, & Sarah A., Wby, b 6-25-1849 d Wby 11-19-1909; m 9-15-1870 at Chas. F. Titus', Hannah B. TITUS, dt Charles F. & Mary F., N. Hemp., b 3-6-1850 d Wby 10-11-1928
Ch: Helen T. b 8-10-1871; m ----- DUTCHER
Samuel b 1-20-1874

WILLETS, continued
Edward & Hannah T.
cf Flushing 1870
Edward ae 6y 10m 16d (unidentified stone, Man.)
Edward S. [Willits], s Richard & Mary, Wby, b 9-22-1803 d 12-11-1869; m Esther WHITSON, dt Abraham & Mary, b 3-8-1808 d 10-13-1857 ae 49y 7m 5d
Ch: Mary S. b 2-20-1832; m Edmund SEAMAN
William b 2-21-1835 d 7-20-1835
Abraham b 5-24-1836 d 8-1-1861
Richard b 3-26-1838
Rachel H. b 9-1-1839 d 9-25-1839
Rachel H. b 9-30-1840; m Wm. R. WILLIAMSON
William H. b 11-11-1843
ct Flushing 12-15-1830 (clear)
Edward S. m 2d Amy WHITSON, dt Abrm. & Mary (Jackson), b Beth. 3-3-1824 d Wby 6-18-1921 ae 97
Ch: Caroline b 8-17-1861 d Forest Hills 11-29-1927
Amy rocf Flushing 5----1861
Edwin C., s Isaac U. & Mary, b 6-25-1858 d Fla. 12-2-1925; m Ida ALBERTSON, dt Silas W. & Caroline, b 12-14-1858 d 10-17-1936
Eliza (form Townsend), dt Wm. E. & Eliza, b 10-12-18-- d 3-10-1900
Elizabeth [Willits] m 1700 Jarvis FARO
Elizabeth, dt Joseph, dis mo 4-29-1778
Elizabeth (form Hicks) dis mo before 11-19-1800
Elizabeth, dt Isaac & Rachel; m Oliver TITUS
Elizabeth [Willits] m Wm. S. ROBBINS
Emma, dt Isaac & Mary, b 10-7-1852; m Silas WEEKS
Eugene K. b 5-1-1875 d 12-6-1882 (Man. Stone)
Fannie Amelia, dt Jos. & Esther G.; m 1888 Francis Cowlyn LOWTHROP
Florence Elizabeth [Willits], dt Jas. & Florence; m 1938 Isaac Hicks COCKS
Frederick, s Jas. R. & Cath., b 1-25-1851 d 6-12-1895; m 10----1871 Anna WHITSON, dt Thos. & Mary (Willets) d Flushing 10-29-1924
Ch: Mary b 12-10-1873; resigned 5-15-1901
Clara b 5-27-1877 d 8-8-1877
cf Flushing 1-6-1870; resigned
Frederick E. b 9-13-1846 d 2-8-1923; m 9-25-1873 Anna WILLETS, dt William & Mary, Jericho, b Jericho 8-6-1848 d 8-9-1924
Ch: Everet F. b Mk 8-14-1874 d G.C. 8-20-1902
Martha V. b Mk 2-2-1876 d 8-23-1882
Elizabeth E. b Mk 6-27-1877 d 4-30-1903 (or 6-30-1903) Venice, Italy
James b G.C. 10-14-1880
George, s Jacob & Hannah, Cow Neck, b abt 1768 d 1844 ae 79th yr (?)
dis mo before 6-19-1793; rst 2-17-1808
George ae 79y 5m 8d (unidentified stone, Man.)
Hannah, dt Richard, rpd mo 1710
Hannah, dt Thomas & Catharine, b 10 Mo (Dec) 6, 1711; m 1741/42 Thomas SEAMAN
Hannah m 1756 Wait POWELL
Helen T., dt Edward & Hannah, b 8-10-1871; m ----- DUTCHER; resigned 6-20-1894
Henry ae 39y 3m 8d (unidentified stone, Man.)
Henry T., s Richard & Mary T., b 11-12-1815 d 3-17-1876 ae 60; m Mary Jane POST, dt Samuel & Mary U., b 11-27-1825 d G.C. 11-13-1906 ae 80y 11m 17d
Ch: William Henry b 4-3-1854 d G.C. 11- 2-1910
Charles F. b 4-14-1861
Samuel P. b 2-31-1866 d 3-13-1866 ae 11m
Mary J. rocf Rochester 1852; all bur Mk.
Henry T. d 4-3-1888 ae 75y; m Sophia U. -----
Ch: Esther d 3-31-1888 ae 79y
Jane P. d 10-18-1864 ae 58y
Sophia gct Jericho 10-18-1905; Henry rocf N. Y. 5----1861 with ch; Sophia rocf N.Y. 10-14-1868
Ida E., dt Joseph & Esther G.; m 1881 I. Sherwood COFFIN
Isaac, s Thomas & Dinah, d 6 Mo (Aug) 29, 1736; m 1716 Clemence HALLOCK, dt John & Abigail, d 7 Mo (Sept) 14, 1736
Ch: Katharine d 6 Mo (Aug) 29, 1736
Zebulun d 7 Mo (Sept) 1, 1736
David
(2 other ch)
Isaac U., s David & Deborah, lived at Herricks, b 12-7-1819 d 10-10-1899 bur Wby; m 12-29-1843 Mary CROMWELL, dt Oliver & Sarah (Titus), b 6-7-1818
Ch: Marietta (or Henrietta) b 10-14-1844; m Geo. B. TITUS
Sarah C. b 10-14-1848; m Morris SHERWOOD
Emma b 10- 7-1852; m Silas WEEKS
Isaac b 9-12-1855 d 7- 8-1859
Edwin C. b 6-25-1858; m Ida ALBERTSON
ct Cornwall 12-20-1843 (clear); Mary rocf Cornwall 2----1845
(Bibles)
Jacob [Willits], s Amos & Rebecca, Islip, b 2 Mo (Apr) 19, 1723 d 6-17-1780; m 11 Mo (Jan) 1744/5 at Beth., Hannah POWELL, dt John & Margaret, Beth., b 6 Mo (Aug) 17, 1725 d 1-17-1816
Ch: John b 9 Mo (Nov) 3, 1745
Job b 7 Mo (Sept) 10, 1748; m Deborah UDALL
Jacob b 11 Mo (Jan) 20, 1750/51
Daniel b 5-24-1753
Henry b 10-13-1755; drowned 7-24-1784
James b 5- 1-1758
Thomas b 9-12-1760
Phebe b 1- 1-1763
George b 6-14-1765
Samuel b 5-10-1763
Jacob, s Daniel, dec, & Phebe, Islip, b 1743; m 1-1-1766 at Beth., Hannah POWELL, dt Joshua & Phebe, O.B., b 10 Mo (Dec) 15, 1745
Ch: Daniel b 4- 9-1767
George b abt 1768
Joshua b 1769
Richard
Phebe

WILLETS, Jacob & Hannah, continued
Ch: Amos
Rebecca b 1778
Jacob, s Richard, Jericho; m 12-2-1767 at Wby, Martha WILLIAMS, dt John, Hemp.
Jacob Jr., s Jacob & Hannah, Sequatange, b 11 Mo (Jan) 20, 1750/51; ack 1-28-1778 carting prisoners for the privateers
Jacob, s Daniel & Phebe, both dec, O.B. & Great Neck; m 8-23-1821 at Mk., Katharine POWELL, wd Willet, dt Obadiah & Deborah, dec, SEAMAN, d 12-20-1846 ae 89y 6m
cf Jericho (clear)
(Bibles)
Jacob H., s Samuel & Sarah H., Flushing, b 9-17-1818 d 7-12-1857; m 8-21-1839 at Wby, Sarah A. POWELL, dt John W. & Sarah M., N. Hemp., b 9-1-1816 d 7-13-1836 (?)
both bur Wby
James, s Jacob, dec, & Hannah, Wby, b 5-1-1758; m 3-3-1784 at Wby, Joanna TITUS, dt Henry, dec, & Sarah, b 11-9-1765
Ch: (9)
(Bibles)
James, s Richard & Mary, Mk. in O.B., b 10-6-1813 d 5-1-1882 ae 68y 8m 21d; m 11-23-1837 at Mk., Anna TITUS, dt Henry & Phebe, Mk. in O.B., b 11-1-1812 d 5-11-1882 ae 69y 6m 10d
Ch: Thomas Everett b 9- 8-1838 d 5-6-1845
Henry T. b 9-21-1840 d 10-27-1840 ae 1m 6d
Frederick E. b 9-13-1846
James, s Frederick E. & Anna W., b G.C. 10-14-1880; m in N.Y. MM Annie K. VALENTINE, dt Stephen & Annie L., b 3-26-1882 d G.C. 12-24-1909
Ch: James Jr. b G.C. 5-30-1907
Annie rocf N.Y. 4-14-1906
James m 2d 4-24-1912 Florence JACKSON
Ch: Frederick E. b 2-26-1914
Florence Elizabeth b 8-13-1916; m Isaac H. COCKS
James R., s Andrew, d 6-6-1904 ae 63y 1m 13d; m 6-6-1876 Anna C. TITUS, dt Robert & Mary W.
cf N. Y. 9-1863
James W., s Edmund & Martha, b 8-6-1843 d Roslyn 1-24-1912; m Hannah KEESE d 3-8-1881 ae 34y
Ch: Edmund b 3-28-1872 d 9-26-1904
Eliza K. b 11-24-1873
Annie C. b 1-24-1876 d 4- 2-1891
Anna L. b 8-15-1878; m Edw. M. LAPHAM
Hannah K. b 1-11-1881 d 2-6-1883
Jane R., dt Wm. & Mary V.; m 1913 Samuel J. SEAMAN
Jesse [Willits] b 2 Mo (Apr) 19, 1714; m -----
Ch: Richard b 4-25-1753
Martha b 9-16-1755
Jesse ack mo 2-27-1754
Job, s Jacob & Hannah, b 7 Mo (Sept) 10, 1748 d 11-4-1820 ae 72y 4m; m before 1-28-1784 Deborah UDALL (mo)
dis mo
John dis mo 3-27-1776
John b 3-31-1841; m (perhaps) Jane H. WILLETS b 8-2-1844 d 5-25-1891 (Man. Stones)
Jonah, s David & Deborah, Wby, b 1762 d 1-1-1837 ae 75y; m 1-7-1784 Mary WILLITS, dt Samuel & Jane, d 5-21-1821 ae 60y & near 7m
Ch: David b 3-26-1785
Abraham b 11- 7-1786
Samuel b 1-21-1789 d 5-23-1820
Deborah b 4- 5-1791
Isaac b 8- 1-1798 d 2-19-1856 ae 57y 6m 18d
Amy b 7- 7-1802
Jonathan m Martha Amanda ----- d 1-5-1860
Ch: Wm. Edgar d 11-15-1853 ae 3y 8m I5d
(Wby Stones)
Joseph [Willits], s Hope & Nancy, b 10 Mo (Dec) 13, 1677; m 11 Mo (Jan) 6, 1702/3 Deborah SEAMAN, dt Sclomon & Elizabeth
Joseph, s Amos, dec, Islip; m 1752 Phebe WILLIAMS, dt Thos., dec, & Mary, Hemp. (as this Joseph m 1756, this proposed m may not have been completed; m int. 9-27-1752; no mention in following months in men or women's minutes; no cert recorded)
Joseph, s Amos, dec, Islip, b 5 Mo (July) 27, 1728 d 5-14-1799; m 5-7-1755 at Wby, Hannah TITUS, dt William, Wby, b 5 Mo (July) 26, 1733 d 11- 5-1776 ae 43y
Ch: Phebe b 5-12-1756 d 9- 1-1760
Amey b 7-14-1758
Elizabeth b 1-16-1761
William b 8-25-1763
Catharine b 2-14-1766
Robert b 7- 1-1768
Rachel b 7-17-1772
Joseph b 11- 3-1775 d 12-10-1777
Joseph m 2d 1-5-1785 at Wby Rachel HICKS, b 4 Mo (June) 19, 1742 d 7-20-1797
Joseph, s William & Latitia, N.Y.C.; m 10-30-1816 at Wby, Phebe SMITH Jr., s Jacob & Rachel, Wby
Joseph, s Edmund & Martha, b 10-7-1830 d Trenton, N. J. 12-14-1913; m Ida COFFIN
Ch: Fannie m F. C. LOWTHROP
cf N. Y. for all three 1-7-1874; Ida gct N. Y. 4-16-1884
Joseph m Esther G. ----- b 8-22-1834 d 8-20-1871 (Wby Stones)
Joseph ae 5y 9m 20d (unidentified stone, Man.)
Joshua m before 10-15-1828 Phebe HICKS, dt Elias & Jemima, b 7-5-1779 (mo)
dis mo 12-17-1828
(Bibles)
Katherine [Willits] dealt with 2-27-1760 for keeping company with one too near akin
Lorraine [Willits], dt Benj. Arnold & Alice A. (Mapson), b Jersey City, N. J. 4-4-1879; recrq 3-19-1933; Benj. A. b Macedon, N.Y.; Alice A. Mapson b DeRuyter, N.Y.
Louisa A. ae 1y 5m (unidentified stone, Man.)

WILLETS, continued
Marietta, dt Isaac U. & Mary C.; m 1869 George B. TITUS
Martha, dt Amos; m 1755 Thomas PRIOR
Martha, dt Edward & Martha; m 1869 Thomas MOTT
Martha m William MUDGE
Mary m 1700 Richard RIDGEWAY
Mary, dt Jacob & Hannah, b 1763; m 1781 Stephen TITUS
Mary, dt Samuel & Jane; m abt 1784 Jonah WILLETS
Mary d 1819 (unidentified stone, Wby)
Mary, dt William & Latitia, b 2-24-1803; m 1823 Gideon FROST
Mary [Willits], dt Richard & Mary, b 2-10-1822; m 1845 Isaac COLES
Mary ae 79y 11m (unidentified stone, Man.)
Mary S., dt Edward & Esther; m 1865 Edmund SEAMAN
Mary T., dt William & Elizabeth P., b 3-22-1837; m 1859 Isaac H. COCKS
Obadiah, s Richard & Abigail, dec, Jericho; m 8-2-1820 at Wby, Phebe DODGE, wd Tristram, dt Benj. & Martha DOWNING
cf Jericho (clear)
Peter m Deborah WILLETS, dt Jonah & Mary, b 4-5-1791 d 2-21-1846 ae 54y 10m 16d
Phebe, dt Richard & Abigail, b 2 Mo (Apr) 13, 1699/1700; m 1731 Adam MOTT; m 2d 1741 Tristram DODGE
signed Epistle abt 1725; rqc for religious visit to England with Susannah Morris, of Pa., 8 Mo (Oct) 9, 1728; deferred till 16th to see if her mother consents; no further mention
Phebe, dt Rachel; m 1769 Adonijah UNDERHILL
Phebe b 6-2-1770; m 1815 Richard ELDRED
Phebe, dt Robert & Mary; m 1823 William TITUS
Phebe J. ae 3y 8m 12d (unidentified stone, Man.)
Rachel, dt Joseph & Hannah; m 1801 Benjamin HICKS
Rebecca [Willits] b 6 Mo (Aug) 24, 1709 d 5-14-1778 in 70th yr
Richard [Willits], Immigrant ancestor, Jericho, d 1667; m Mary WASHBORN, dt William & Jane, b 1629 d 12 Mo (Feb) 17, 1713/14 ae near 85 y
Ch: Hope b 7 Mo (Sept) 1652; m Mercy LANGDON
John b 5 Mo (July) 1655
Thomas b 3 Mo (May) 1660; m Dinah TOWNSEND
Richard b 12 Mo (Feb) 1660/61; m (1) Abigail BOWNE; m (2) Abigail POWELL
Mary b 2 Mo (Apr) 1663; m John FRY
mtg held at her house 1697-1709; signed rem cert 1707
Richard, s Richard & Mary, b 10 Mo (Dec) 25, 1660 (copied into the record by Samuel Willis, recorder & clerk, 1771; this must be error; his father's Bible record appears to give it 12th Mo 1660/61); d 1703; m 1 Mo (Mar) 25, 1686/7 Abigail BOWNE, dt John & Hannah, b 12 Mo (Feb) 5, 1662 d 4 Mo (June) 16, 1688
Ch: Hannah b 11 Mo (Jan) 24, 1686/7
Richard m 2d 1690 Abigail POWELL, dt Thomas & Abigail, b 1688 d 1757
Ch: Abigail b 12 Mo (Feb) 27, 1690/91
Mary b 1 Mo (Mar) 16, 1692 (or 1692/93)
Martha b 11 Mo (Jan) 24, 1694/5
Jacob b 4 Mo (June) 6, 1697
Phebe b 2 Mo (Apr) 13, 1699
Elizabeth b 4 Mo (June) 27, 1701
mtg at Abigail's 1703,1704
Richard, s Thomas & Dinah, Islip; m 7 Mo (Sept) 16, 1706 Deborah UNDERHILL, dt John & Mary, wd Robert COLES Jr., b 2 Mo (Apr) 11, 1682
Ch: Sarah b 4 Mo (June) 24, 1707; m Wm. KIRBY
Thomas b 1710 d 2 Mo (Apr) 4, 1750
Richard b 2 Mo (Apr) 11, 1712; m Hannah STRONG
Jacob b 1716 d 1716
Daniel b 8 Mo (Oct) 14, 1718; m Phebe CARPENTER; Amy POWELL
Deborah b 1720; m David WILLITS
Phebe b 10 Mo (Dec) 12, 1722
Richard d 4 Mo (June) 13, 1753; m 2d abt 7 Mo (Sept) 1, 1740 (cert not recorded; rpd accomplished 7 Mo 24) Margaret POWELL, wd John, dt John & Abigail HALLOCK, d 4-24-1769 ae 87y
Ch: Samuel d 11-23-1768 ae 28y 10m
Richard [Willits], s Richard & Deborah, Sequatague, b 2 Mo (Apr) 11, 1712; m 25 Aug. 1736 Hannah STRONG, dt Selah & Hannah
Richard ack mo 2 Mo (Apr) 26, 1738; mtg at his house 1742
(Bibles)
Richard, s Jacob, dec, Jericho; m 7-7-1743 at Beth., Ruth WILLITS, dt Amos
Ch: Jacob b 8 Mo (Oct) 8, 1744
Mary b 6 Mo (Aug) 27, 1746 d 5 Mo 9, 1750
Richard b 6 Mo (Aug) 20, 1748
James b 2 Mo (Apr) 21, 1751 d 4-6-1752
Amos b 4-21-1753
Thomas b 4-7-1757 d 11-22-1758
Sarah b 10-23-1759
Richard, s Richard, Jericho; m abt 1770 (cert not recorded, m bet. 12-27-1769 & 1-31-1770) Abigail SEAMAN, dt Samuel, Wby
Richard, O.B. m 1-4-1786 at Beth. Phebe POWELL, wd Joshua, dt Richard POST
Richard, s Richard & Abigail (Robbins), Mk, b 5-28-1774 d 12-11-1840 ae 66y 6m 13d; m 4-30-1800 at Wby, Mary SEAMAN, dt Gideon & Elizabeth, b 5-10-1783 d 12-30-1808
Ch: Edward S. b 9-22-1803; m Esther WHITSON
Gideon b 10-10-1801 d 5-12-1803
cf Jericho (clear)
(Bibles)
Richard m 2d Mary T. TITUS, dt Samuel & Abigail, d 11-1-1869 ae 86y 8m
Ch: James b 10- 6-1813; m Anna TITUS
Henry T. b 11-12-1815; m Mary J. POST
Martha b 1-16-1819; m Wm. MUDGE
Mary b 2-10-1822; m Isaac COLES

WILLETS, continued
Richard, s Richard & Abigail, dec, N. Hemp.; m 12-24-1812 at Mk, Mary TITUS, dt Samuel & Abigail, both dec, Cedar Swamp
Richard [Willits], s Edw. S. & Esther, b 3-26-1838 d 9-7-1912
ct N. Y.; cf N. Y. 11-2-1870
Robert, s Joseph & Hannah, b 7-1-1768 d 5-22-1851 ae 82y 10m 21d; m Jericho 11-25-1790 Mary ROBBINS, dt Stephen & Amelia, b 8-15-1771 d 1-16-1849 ae 76y (?)
Ch: Amos b 9-14-1792 d 10-17-1864 bur Wby
Samuel b 6-15-1795
Stephen b 12-3-1797
Edmund b 4-6-1800
Robert R. b 11-20-1802
Phebe b 4-23-1805
William W. b 11-1-1808
ct Jericho 10-20-1790 (clear); Mary rocf Jericho 10-19-1791
(Bibles)
Robert Henry, s Wm. & S. Phebe (Taber), b Wby 6-24-1881; m Laura G. F. LEEMING, dt Geo. L. & Laura L. (Barrows), b Cheyenne, Wyoming 9-26-1888 (Laura adopted by her stepfather, Seth C. C. FINNEY, of Carver, Mass.)
Ch: Robert Tabor b N.Y.C. 2-25-1919
Seth Barrows b N.Y.C. 2-18-1921
all recrq 2-15-1925
Robert R., s Robert & Mary, N.Y.C., b 11-20-1802 d 1-22-1879 Wby; m 3-26-1828 at Wby Lydia TITUS, dt John & Sarah P., b 3-24-1808 d 2-9-1903
Ch: Elizabeth b 2-16-1838 d 4-13-1841
(Wby Stones)
Robert R., s Robert R. & Lydia; m Tacie P. PARRY
Ch: Tacie P. b 11-22-1873 d 9-3-1894
Cornelia b 8-10-1888 d 5-23-1900
(Wby Stones)
Roy b 4-13-1891 d 10-7-1895 (unidentified stone Wby)
Ruth [Willits], dt Amos; m 1743 Richard WILLITS
Ruth [Willits] m Valentine VELSOR
Samuel [Willits], s Amos, Secotaque & Islip; m 8 Mo (Oct) 6, 1742 at Bethpage, Jane POWELL, dt Wait & Mary, Beth., b 2 Mo (Apr) 22, 1725 d 5-11-1776
Samuel, s Jacob & Hannah, b 1-1-1763; m Hannah SEAMAN, dt Williams & Mary, b 7-24-1776
Ch: Jane P. d 10-18-1864 ae 58
(Seaman Gen.)
Samuel, s Robert & Mary, N.Y.C., b 6-15-1795 d 2-6-1883; m 10-30-1816 at Wby, Sarah HICKS, dt Benjamin & Amelia, dec, Wby, b 9-17-1794 d 1-12-1881
cf N. Y. (clear)
Samuel, s Andrew, b 2-12-1838 d 6-21-1886 ae 48y 4m 9d bur Wby
cf N. Y. 9----1859
Samuel, s Edw. & Hannah, b 1-20-1874 d 11-24-1929; m -----
Sarah m 1785 John WILLIS
Sarah [Willits], dt Henry & Mary POST, dis mo before 12-14-1791
Sarah A. rocf Flushing 1-6-1870; d 7-13-1896 ae 79y 10m 12d
Sarah C., dt Isaac U. & Mary C., b 10-14-1844; m 1871 Morris SHERWOOD
Sarah M., dt Edmund & Martha; m 1879 Caleb W. SHEPHERD
Stephen b 12-3-1797 d 1-4-1862; m Maria ----- b 4-23-1823 d 2-25-1885
Ch: Lydia b 8-15-1825 d 5-15-1827 (Wby Stone)
Stephen [Willits], s Robert & Mary, N. Hemp.; m 11-7-1822 at Wby, Maria TITUS, dt John & Sarah P., N. Hemp.
Stephen T. b 1-1-1845 d 4-10-1899; m -----
Ch: (prob) Mary E. d 3-22-1874 ae 1y 11m 12d
" Stephen E. d 7-14-1870 ae 6m 17d
Thomas [Willits], s Thomas & Dinah, b 1683; m 1706 Katharine HALLOCK, dt John & Abigail, d 1718
Ch: Clement b 9 Mo (Nov) 15, 1709 d 6-5-1772
Thomas rem to Pa., cert to be prepared 2 Mo (Apr) 26, 1737
Thomas m 2d 1719/20 Rachel POWELL, dt Thos. & Elizabeth
ct North Wales, Pa. 6 Mo (Aug) 25, 1736 for Rachel
Thomas, s Amos, dec, Islip, d 1818; m 3-3-1762 at Wby, Leah SEAMAN, dt Zebulun, O.B., b 1 Mo (Mar) 11, 1744 d 1-9-1813
Ch: Mary
Phebe
Rachel
Rebecca
Joseph
Sarah
Zebulun
Charles
(Bibles)
Thomas W., s Edmund & Martha, N. Hemp.; m 9-15-1870 at John Keese's, Hannah KEESE, dt John & Johanna, dec, N. Hemp., b 11-18-1846 d 3-8-1881 bur Wby
Ch: Martha b 1-10-1881 d 2-4-1883
Hannah K. b 2-4-1880 d 1-10-1891
Valentine, s Wm. & Latitia, dec, Cow Neck; m 11-6-1817 at Wby, Jane RUSHMORE, dt Stephen & Phebe, b 3-20-1807 d 8-27-1895
Ch: Latitia b 11-20-1818
Phebe b 5-10-1824
Mary (not in Quaker record)
Sarah " " " "
(Bibles)
Wait m 1780 Wby (cert not recorded, m between 11-29 & 12-27) Mary POST, dt John & Phebe
ack 11-24-1779 going with Militia Captain and others in pursuit of robbers
(Bibles)
Walter R. rocf Flushing 1-6-1870; dis 6-17-1891
William, s Joseph & Hannah, dec, N. Hemp., b 8-25-1763; m 1-8-1789 at Mk, Latitia VALENTINE, dt Charles & Mary, O.B. d 10-18-1803

WILLETS, William & Latitia, continued
Ch: Joseph b 8-31-1790 (or 1791)
Charles b 3-1-1793
Valentine b 10-2-1795
Jacob S. b 3-9-1800
Mary b 2-24-1803
William m 2d 11-27-1805 at Wby, Amy BEDEL, dt Benajah & Phebe, Wby
Ch: Hannah b 9-22-1808
George b 9-17-1810
Benjamin b 4-13-1813
William b 5- 9-1815
Stephen b 11-18-1818
William, Wby, & Ann
Ch: Thomas A. b 12-12-1832 d 9-21-1833
William, s Robert & Mary, Wby, b 11-1-1808 d 4-21-1844; m 4-29-1835 Elizabeth P. TITUS, dt Samuel & Mary P., Wby, b 10-14-1815 d 12-29-1884 ae 69y 2m 15d
Ch: Mary T. b 3-22-1837; m Isaac H. COCKS
Anna b 12-1-1839 d 7-11-1856
William b 11-29-1843 d 10-15-1914
(Wby Stones)
William, s Isaac & Amy, O.B.; m 10-15-1846 at Jacob Valentine's, Glen Cove, Mary VALENTINE, dt Jacob & Martha, O.B.
ct Jericho (clear); Martha gct Jericho 1847
William [Willits] m Phebe PRIOR d 4-12-1884 ae 84
William H., s Edw. S. & Esther, b 11-11-1843; ct N. Y.
William Henry, s Robert R. & Lydia, N.Y.C., b 10-12-1840 d 3-24-1903; m 9-12-1867 at Sam. T. Taber's, Martha TABER, dt Samuel T.
William P., s David & Deborah, b 1-16-1823 d 8-18-1877 ae 54y 7m 2d; m ----- MITCHELL
(Wby Stones & Bibles)

WILLIAMS
Amy m 1826 ----- WILLITS
Ann m 1763 Thomas PEARSALL
Benjamin d 1-20-1852 ae 29y 9m (Wby Stone)
Daniel W. b 4-11-1815 d 7-23-1889; m -----
Ch: (prob) Daniel b 5-8-1865 d 6-1-1883 bur Wby
Edward C. m Elizabeth CARLE, dt Gadron & Elizabeth (Davis), b Virginia City, Nevada 11-24-1867 d 12-4-1937 at Rockville Centre & bur Tangore Cem., Olive Bridge, N. Y.
Elizabeth, wd Edward, recrq 7-21-1930
Elizabeth dealt with 2 Mo (Apr) 20, 1745 for mo to first cousin; ret mbrp
Elizabeth, dt Thomas & Mary, b 1724; m 1754 George HEWLETT (mo)
Elizabeth (form Robbins) dis mo 6-25-1777
Elizabeth m 1782 Isaac DOTY (mo)
Elizabeth b 8-30-1812 ; ack mo 2 Mo (Apr) 29, 1747; d 2-18-1891 (Wby Stone)
Elizabeth m Jacob SPRAGUE
Esther, dt Thomas; m 1743 Robert SEAMAN
Hannah, dt Jeremiah; m 1737/8 Benjamin DOUGHTY
Isaac U. m Mary C. ----- b 4-17-1786 d 8-8-1854 bur Wby
Ch: Isaac d 7-8-1859 ae 3y 9m 26d bur Wby
Jeremiah & -----
Ch: Ann b 4 Mo (Apr) 17, 1719
Walter b 10 Mo (Dec) 17, 1720
Benjamin b 9 Mo (Nov) 4, 1722
Mary b 9 Mo (Nov) 26, 1724
Lidiah b 12 Mo (Feb) 6, 1729/30
ct R. I. 7 Mo (Sept) 24, 1716 (clear); signed cert 1726
John, s Robert
Martha, dt John; m 1767 Jacob WILLITS
Mary, dt John & Elizabeth; m 1785 William DOUGHTY
Morris R. d 2-21-1884 ae 70; m Effalina ----- d 11-9-1842 ae 23y 5m 7d
Ch: Morris d 1-19-1851 ae 10y 7m
Morris R. m 2d Ellen Hannah ----- d 1-16-1904 ae 86y 8d
(Wby Stones)
Phebe, dt Thos. & Mary; m 1752 Joseph WILLITS
Richard m Elizabeth ----- d 2-4-1859 ae 63y 7m
(Wby Stones)
Samuel m Charlotte ----- d 11-20-1845 ae 33y 5m 27d
Thomas m 1717 Mary SCUDDER, wd Henry
Ch: Phebe m Jos. WILLITS
Mary signed Epistle abt 1725
Washington d 3-24-1850 ae 29y (Man. Stone)

WILLIAMSON
Wm. R. m 6-4-1861 Rachel H. WILLITS, dt Edw. S. & Esther, b 9-30-1840
ct N. Y. for Rachel

WILLIS
Abigail, dt Townsend & Hannah; m 1825 Samuel JONES
Amy, dt Samuel & Mary; m 1762 Stephen MOTT
Amy, dt Samuel & Rachel; m 1824 Townsend RUSHMORE
Ann d 10----1866 near 80y (unidentified stone, Wby)
Annie b 6-18-1859 (not identified) (0)
Benjamin H., s Cornwell & Elizabeth, Cow Neck; m 10-31-1822 at Cow Neck, Sarah A. MOTT, dt Samuel & Catharine
Ch: Samuel C. b 9-8-1823
Epenetus b 9-1-1825
James C. b 4-25-1828 d 6-4-1832
Benjamin H. m 2d before 2-20-1833 (mo); ack mo 6-19-1833
(Bibles)
Charles b 4-21-1820 d 10-28-1894; m Hannah WILLIS, wd Charles, d 1833 ae 54y
Charles & Abigail
Ch: Rebecca A. d 4-15-1866 ae 19
C. Fremont b Mar. 31, 1857 d 10-8-1886
Sarah Leah d 3-13-1860 ae 17
(Wby Stones)
Charles C. d 5-5-1885 ae 82y (unidentified stone, Wby)
Cornell, s John & Margaret, Cow Neck, d 3-3-

WILLIS, Cornell, continued
1849 ae 76y; m Elizabeth HICKS, dt Benjamin & Mary, b 4-24-1775 d 12-15-1845 ae 73y 2m (?)
David ack mo & being clerk of Militia Co. 6 Mo 25, 1742
Edmund, s Samuel & Mary, Jericho; m 6-9-1778 at Wby, Abigail TITUS, dt William & Sarah, Wby
Ch: William b 1-6-1780
Elizabeth, dt John & Abigail, b 1 Mo (Mar) 4, 1718/19; m Jonathan SEAMAN
Elizabeth ack mo 6-14-1809
Elizabeth C. b 3-27-1808; m 1828 Hicks ALBERTSON
Epinetus A. b 9-12-1825 d 8-2-1886 (unidentified stone, Man.)
Fry, s Samuel & Mary, Jericho, b 4-9-1744; m 8-1-1770 at Wby, Anne SEAMAN, dt Thomas & Catharine, Wby, b 12 Mo (Feb) 25, 1746/7 d 8-2-1828
Ch: Thomas b 11-30-1771
Isaac " " " "
Hannah m 1742 Micah SPRAGUE
Hannah rst 10-20-1824
Hannah C., dt Cornwell & Elizabeth; m 1823 Leonard MOTT
Henry (Immigrant & one of the earliest Quakers in England), s Henry, of Devises, Wilts, b 9 Mo (Nov) 24, 1628 d 7 Mo (Sept) 11, 1714 ae 86y less a few days; m Mary PEACE (or Pease) b 6 Mo (Aug) 12, 1632 d 4 Mo (June) 23, 1714 ae 82y
Ch: Mary m 1678 Geo. MASTERS
Elizabeth m Robert ZANE
William b 10 Mo (Dec) 16, 1663; m 1687 Mary TITUS
Henry b 1666 d 1675
John b 1668; m Esther BRINTON
Sarah b 5 Mo (July) 6, 1671; m 1695 John TITUS
Rachel m 1695 Nathaniel SEAMAN
Esther b 5 Mo (July) 23, 1677; m 1695 William ALBERTSON
(Bible records)
Henry m 1706 Katharine HALLOCK
Henry signed cert 1726
Henry, s William & Mary, b 6 Mo (Aug) 19, 1690 d 10 Mo (Dec) 12, 1744; m 1712 Phebe POWELL dt Thomas, b 10 Mo (Dec) 16, 1693 d 15 Nov. 1751
Ch: Mary b 2 Mo (Feb) 22, 1713; m Richard POST
Silas b 1 Mo (Mar) 4, 1715/16; m 1740/41 Ann PEARSALL
Phebe b 1 Mo (Mar) 1, 1718/19; m Benj. DOWNING
Phebe signed Epistle abt 1725; Phebe m 2d Henry WILLIS
(Bibles)
Henry, s Samuel & Rachel, O.B. b 1786 d 5-3-1865; m 3-24-1813 at Wby, Phebe POST, dt Samuel & Catharine, Wby, d 1-26-1845 (0)
Ch: Samuel b 1-7-1815; m Catharine POST
Edmund P. m (2) Sarah KIRBY
Isaac m Mary H. SEAMAN
cf Jericho (clear); Phebe gct Jericho 2-16-1814
(Bibles)
Jacob Jr. rpd mo before 1 Mo (Mar) 25, 1747 while under dealing for enlisting in militia
Jacob B. m Martha WEEKS d 1881
Jane, dt Samuel & Mary, b 11 Mo (Jan) 7, 1740/41; m 1780 James PARSONS
Jane ack mo 6-25-1788
John, Jericho, m Abigail WILLITS, dt Richard, b 12 Mo (Feb) 27, 1690/91 d 5-29-1777 (mo)
Ch: Phebe b 1 Mo (Mar) 24, 1714/15
Richard b 10 Mo (Dec) 30, 1716
Elizabeth b 1 Mo (Mar) 4, 1718/19
William b 3 Mo (May) 23, 1720
John b 4 Mo (June) 5, 1726
Stephen b 8 Mo (Oct) 13, 1736
ack mo 11 Mo (Jan) 30, 1716/17; John signed Epistle abt 1725
John dealt with 7-29-1752 for mo & bearing arms
John, s Samuel, Jericho, b 2 Mo (Apr) 8, 1734 d 3-4-1789; m 3 Mo 5, 1755 at Wby, Elizabeth MOTT, dt Adam, dec, & Elizabeth, Cow Neck, b 5 Mo (July) 31, 1733 d 9-13-1783
Ch: Adam b 7-13-1757 d 3-9-1758
Samuel b 3-7-1759
Phebe b 4-5-1761
John m 4-6-1785 at Wby Sarah WILLETS
Leonard S. b 12-25-1844 d 11-11-1902 bur Wby
Maria recrq 10-15-1856 (0)
Martha R. d 8-4-1881 in 86th yr (unidentified stone, Mk.)
Mary signed rem cert 1707; signed Epistle abt 1725
Mary, dt Samuel & Mary, b 3 Mo (May) 7, 1731; m 1748 Thomas JACKSON, s Samuel; m 2d Thomas JACKSON, s Thomas
Mary, dt Joseph, dec, ack mo 6-27-1753
Mary D. d 5-4-1898 ae 71y 9m 10d (unidentified stone, Wby)
Mary F. m 1836 Isaac HICKS
Mary P. (or W.), dt Samuel & Catharine M.; m 1888 J. Augustus ALBERTSON
Mordecai, s Wm. & Hannah, b 10 Mo (Dec) 14, 1725; m 1751 Mercy CLEMENT, dt Joseph & Jane (mo)
Ch: Sarah
(6 other ch)
Mordecai dis 2-27-1754; Mary ack mo 4-25-1753
(Bibles)
Phebe, dt John & Abigail, b 1 Mo (Mar) 24, 1715; m 1740 John POST
(spoken to 4 Mo (June) 27, 1739 for keeping company with nm)
Phebe, dt Silas; m 1766 Solomon WHITSON
Phebe, dt Samuel & Mary; m 1779 Joseph PRIOR
Phebe, dt John & Elizabeth, b 4-5-1761; m 1784 Joshua POWELL
Phebe, dt Henry & Phebe; m Benjamin DOWNING
Phebe m James POST

WILLIS, continued
Phebe E. d 2-13-1887 ae 28y (unidentified stone, Wby)
Phebe P. d 1846 (unidentified stone, Wby)
Rachel m 1695 Nathaniel SEAMAN
Rachel m Samuel HICKS
Richard, s John & Abigail, Wby, b 10 Mo (Dec) 30, 1716 d 1782 to 1784 in Dutchess Co.; m 1742 Elizabeth PINE, dt James
Ch: James
mo before 6 Mo (Aug) 25, 1742
(Bibles)
Ruth, dt William & Mary, b 9 Mo (Nov) 7, 1751 m 1775 Samuel HEWLETT
Samuel, s William, Jericho, b 6 Mo (Aug) 30, 1704 d 12-24-1782 ae 78y; m 8 Mo (Oct) 2, 1728 Mary FRY, dt John & Mary, b 12 Mo (Feb) 16, 1712/13 d 1800
Ch: Mary b 3 Mo (May) 7, 1731
John b 2 Mo (Apr) 8, 1734
Sarah b 7 Mo (Sept) 14, 1736
Amy b 3 Mo (May) 27, 1738
Jane b 11 Mo (Jan) 7, 1740/41
Fry b 4 Mo (June) 9, 1744
Kezia b 4 Mo (June) 7, 1747 d 3-15-1781
Henry b 9 Mo (Nov) 13, 1749 d 9-28-1780
Edmund b 9-29-1752 N.S.
Phebe b 5-28-1756
Samuel signed Epistle 1725; ack 2-27-1754 enlisting in Cadet Company & m by J.P.
Mary ack mo long since 5-30-1753
Samuel Jr. (called Jr to distinquish him from his grand uncle), s Wm. & Hannah, b 12 Mo (Feb) 27, 1721/2; m before 11 Mo (Jan) 28, 1746/47 Mary WRIGHT, dt Joseph & Ann (mo) ack mo & bearing arms 5-29-1754
(Bibles)
Samuel, s John & Elizabeth, b 3-2-1759 d 6-28-1838; m 2-2-1785 at Beth., Rachel PEARSALL, dt Thomas & Ann, b 6 Mo (Aug) 31, 1745 d 5-31-1855
Ch: (4)
(some Samuel Willis Jr. dis 7-12-1765 for neglect of mtg)
(Bibles)
Samuel, s Henry & Phebe (Post), Jericho, b 1-17-1815 d 6-4-1870 ae 55y 5m 7d bur Wby; m Catharine M. POST, dt Joseph & Mary, b 5-20-1837 d Wby 4-3-1921 in 84th yr
Ch: Mary W. b 12-26-1866; m Aug. ALBERTSON
Phebe P. b 6-29-1869
Catharine gct Jericho 8----1866; cf Jericho 5-18-1871
(Bibles)
Sarah, dt Mordecai & Mary; dis mo before 8-25-1784
Silas, s Henry, b 1 Mo (Mar) 4, 1715/16; m 1 Mo (Mar) 4, 1741/42 Ann PEARSALL, dt Henry, b 2 Mo (Apr) 4, 1722
Ch: Jordan b 2 Mo (Apr) 15, 1742
unnamed dt b 11 Mo (Jan) 8, 1744 d 27th of same
Phebe b 3 Mo (May) 25, 1745
Ann m 2d 1754 Matthew PRIOR
Thomas, s Fry & Anne, Jericho; m 10-9-1795 at Cow Neck, Phebe SEARING, dt John & Mary, N. Hemp.
Townsend, s Wm. & Mary, b 6-23-1757; m 1783 Hannah BOWNE, dt Jacob & Hannah, b 8-11-1761
Ch: (7)
Hannah dis mo 5-28-1783; rst 9-14-1796
(Bibles)
William, s Henry & Mary, b England 10 Mo (Dec) 16, 1663 d 3 Mo (May) 7, 1736/7 ae 72y 5m; m 1687 Mary TITUS, dt Edmund & Martha, b 6 Mo (Aug) 1665 d 10 Mo (Dec) 31, 1747
Ch: William b 4 Mo (June) 14, 1688; m Hannah POWELL
Henry b 6 Mo (Aug) 19, 1690; m Phebe POWELL
John b 2 Mo (Apr) 15, 1693; m Abigail WILLITS
Jacob b 1695 d 1750
Silas b 1700 d 1704
Samuel b 6 Mo (Aug) 30, 1704; m Mary FRY
Mary b 5 Mo 23, 1709 d 7 Mo 25, 1709
William on comm. 1698
(Bibles)
William, s William & Mary, b 4 Mo (June) 14, 1688 d 3 Mo (May) 6, 1750; m 1712 Hannah POWELL, dt Thomas & Elizabeth, b 5 Mo (July) 28, 1691 d 3 Mo (May) 6, 1750
Ch: Mary b 4 Mo (June) 11, 1713; m Wm. BEDELL
Hannah b 12 Mo (Feb) 27, 1714/15; m Michael SPRAGUE
Elizabeth b 8 Mo (Oct) 8, 1716; m Rich. POST
Rachel b 7 Mo 5, 1718 d 7 Mo (Sept) 12, 1738
Jacob b 5 Mo (July) 5, 1720; m Eliz. (Denton) DUSENBURY
Samuel b 12 Mo (Feb) 27, 1721/22; m Mary WRIGHT
Amy b 1724 d 1729
Mordecai b 10 Mo (Dec) 14, 1725; m Mary CLEMENT
Silas b 7 Mo 5, 1727 d 1 Mo (Mar) 14, 1749/50
Martha b 7 Mo (Sept) 29, 1729
William b 12 Mo (Feb) 5, 1731/32; m Sarah CLEMENT
Joseph b 5 Mo (July) 15, 1734
William, s John & Abigail, b 3 Mo (May) 23, 1721 d 1-9-1779; m Mary TOWNSEND, dt Ruemourn & Mary, b 10 Mo (Dec) 5, 1729 d 9-7-1781
Ch: Ruth b 9 Mo (Nov) 7, 1751
Abigail b 11-18-1755
Townsend b 6-23-1757
Mary b 6-5-1760
Esther b 9-21-1762
Sarah b 6-30-1754 d 1787
ack mo & bearing arms 8-28-1754
(Bibles)
William, s William, dec, Wby; m 2-4-1756 at Wby, Sarah CLEMENT, dt Joseph, dec, Wby
William, s Townsend & Hannah, d 1855; m before

WILLIS, William, continued
2-19-1827 Latitia DOWNING, dt Isaac & Theodosia, b 2-23-1809 d 7-18-1897
Ch: (4)
William Alfred b 5-11-1834 d 3-22-1900 (unidentified stone, Wby)
William Daniel b 9-25-1861 (not identified)

WILSON
Levis d 11-12-1881 ae 6m

WINFIELD
Margaret m 1922 Thos. Mott FRASER

WITTER
Margaret Shephard, dt Geo. Henry & Maud (Bingham); m 1927 Ford B. BARNARD

WITTY
Lee b 4-18-1847 d 9-27-1892; m -----
Dt: (perhaps) Ella Maude d 6-14-1876 ae 5y 3m 5d
(Wby Stones)

WOLFE
Beulah, dt Levi B. & Lettie (Pearle), b N. Granville, N. Y. 1-14-1885; m Edwin W. WEEKS

WOOD
Elkanah b 1-16-1783 d 8-8-1870 in 88th yr; m Harriet ----- d 8-31-1871 in 75th yr
Harriet recrq 1861; cf N. Y. 1840
(Wby Stones)
Charles A. b 8-27-1852 d 11-28-1888 (unidentified stone, Wby)
Hannah b 3 Mar 1712 d 7-29-1900; m 1734 Samuel MOTT
Jacob, s Jonas & Mary; m 3-25-1801 at Wby Mary TOWNSEND, dt Thomas & Mary, b 3-20-1776 d 1-25-1862 bur Wby
Jeremiah, Huntington, dis neglect of mtg, 1-30-1782
Jonas, s Joseph, O.B.; m 6-7-1764 at Mk., Mary CARPENTER, dt Jacob, O.B.
Ch: Jonas m Mary TOWNSEND
Joseph d 3-29-1774; m Mary ----- d 10-5-1758
Ch: Abigail d 2-18-1773
Mary
signed cert 1726
Joseph Jr., O.B.; m 6-3-1762 at Mk., Mary ALSOP dt Richard & Ann, O.B., d 1-16-1764
Joseph dis 7-26-1769
Martha ack mo 12 Mo (Feb) 24, 1734/35
Mary, dt Joseph & Mary; m abt 1761 Joseph DEAN (mo)
Mary, dt Jonas & Mary, b 1765; m 1784 Wright FROST (mo)
Moyer, s Albert G. & Louise, b Vancouver, B.C. 1-29-1913; m 9-3-1938 at Cornwall, N.Y. Elizabeth SMEDLEY, dt Arthur C. & Golda (Brown), b Wilmington, Del. 7-22-1913
cf Cornwall for both 12-18-1938; Albert Wood b N.Y.C.; Louise Moyer, Walkertown, Ontario, Canada; Arthur C. Smedley b West Chester, Pa.; Golda Brown Cornwall, N.Y.
Samuel, s Samuel, dec, Hemp.; m 8-8-1782 at Cow Neck, Mary U. SEARING, dt John
Samuel b 2-18-1804 d 3-7-1881; m Ruth ----- b 8-15-1804 d 2-4-1885
Ch: Esther P. d 3-26-1873 ae 47y 3m
(Wby Stones)
Samuel b 4-4-1823 d 6-29-1864 (Wby Stone)
Sarah M. d 11-12-1900 ae 59y 1m 18d (unidentified stone, Wby)
William m Sarah Amelia COLES, dt Thomas & Amelia, d 1865

WOODNUT
Anna F. rocf Flushing 6-5-1879; resigned
Henry C. m Anne Elizabeth FROST
Anne E. gct N. Y. 7-16-1873; resigned

WOODRUFF
Anna F. b 9-22-1835 d 10-24-1895
Ch: (prob) Henrietta W. b 5-18-1869 d 2-25-1900
" Margaret O. b 6-9-1872 d 9-20-1900
(Wby stones)

WOOLEY
William m Sarah A. GLOVER, dt Silas W. & Caroline ALBERTSON

WRIGHT
Aaron b 9-30-1810 d 12-15-1885; m Mary W. ----- b 4-1-1820 d 4-18-1904
Ch: Katharine
(Wby Stones)
Daniel, s Daniel & Sarah, Mk., d abt 1819; m abt 1761 Phebe BENNETT, dt William & Elizabeth (mo)
Phebe dis mo 8-26-1761 "several yr ago" (Bibles)
Fred'k Willets, s Aaron & Mary W., b 1851 d Cockeyville, Md. 12-15-1915
cf Springboro Ex. Mtg, Ohio 4-23-1903
Hannah gct Burlington 5 Mo (July) 26, 1704 (clear)
Horace, Wby, m Mary ----- d 4-12-1856 ae 89y 10m 7d
Isaac, s John, O.B.; m 4-7-1784 at Wby, Sarah TITUS, dt William & Sarah, Wby, b 10-1-1760
Jessie F., dt Wm. B. & Almeda; m 1911 William Willets COCKS
John, s Joseph, dec, O.B.; m 2 Mo 7, 1753 at Wby (cert not recorded) Phebe SEAMAN, dt Thomas, Wheatley
Jordan, s John, O.B.; m 4-5-1786 at Wby, Elizabeth TITUS, dt Richard
Joseph, s Joseph & Ann, d 1769; m Patience LOVELL, dt John & Patience
Ch: (4)
ct Abington, Pa. 5 Mo (July) 29, 1741 "who was apprentice to Patrick Ogleby & went to live with him in your parts"

WRIGHT, continued
Keziah m 1712 John BURR
ct Burlington 7 Mo (Sept) 24, 1712
Mary, dt John; m 1777 Israel UNDERHILL
Mary, dt Joseph & Ann; m Samuel WILLIS
Phebe rpd mo before 3-25-1752
Rachel m 1715 Thomas STOKES
ct Newton, N. J.
Sarah, dt John & Phebe; m 1786 Noah GARDNER

YOUNG
Alexander [Youngs], s Alexander & Hannah (Rose), d New Castle, N. Y. 1758; m 1-29-1727 Sarah COLES, dt John & Sarah
Ch: Mary m Gilbert TITUS
(10 other ch)
Alexander & w & several ch gct Pur. 5-29-1754
(Youngs Gen.)
Mary, dt Alexander; m 1753 Gilbert TITUS (mo)
Jas. Franklin, s Benj. P. & Jane (Corwin) Manhasset, b Baiting Hollow, Suffolk Co. 10-7-1842; m 11-11-1864 Charlotte Elizabeth WELLS, dt Barnabas H. & Eliza A. (Reeves) b Wading River, L. I. 8-17-1846
Ch: (7)
James F. recrq 6-19-1901
(Youngs Gen.)
Elizabeth D. b 8-5-1810 d 4-30-1862 (Mk. Stone)

ZANE
Easter m 1716 Joshua DELAPLAINE
Rachel m 1720 Samuel PINE

* * * * * * *

* * * * * * *

MOTT
Adam, s Adam & Elizabeth, Cow Neck, b 1672 d 10 Mo (Dec) 10, 1738; m 11 Mo 5, 1731/32 at Wby, Phebe WILLITS, dt Richard & Abigail, b 2 Mo (Apr) 14, 1699 d 9-7-1782
Ch: Elizabeth b 3 Mo (May) 31, 1733
Adam b 10 Mo (Dec) 10, 1734
Stephen b 2 Mo (Apr) 1, 1736
Adam signed Epistle abt 1725; Phebe m 2d 11-28-1741 Tristram DODGE (Bibles)

WEBB
Job, s John, Pa.; m 6-15-1785 Hannah CARPENTER, wd, dt Richard ALSOP

POST
John, s Richard & Phebe; m 1740 Phebe WILLIS, dt John & Abigail, b 1 Mo (Mar) 24, 1715
Ch: (5)
Phebe spoken to 4 Mo (June) 27, 1739 for keeping company with nm
(Bibles)

WEEKS
Abigail, dt Samuel; m 1770 Richard TITUS
Charity m 1736/37 John CARPENTER

J E R I C H O M O N T H L Y M E E T I N G

The early history of this Monthly Meeting and its subordinate meetings is given in the preface of Westbury Monthly Meeting; from which the meeting of Jericho and Bethpage, still existing, were set off in 1789, as a separate Monthly Meeting. It also had a meeting at Half Hollow Hills in southern Huntington, from 1791-1802, and a meeting at Jerusalem, in Hempstead, allowed in 1813 at Samuel Seaman's, in 1819 at Zebulun Seaman's, and in 1827 in a meeting house. This meeting was maintained for many years.

The data from tombstones in the Quaker burial grounds at Jericho and Jerusalem, by Frank Haviland, 1904, and of Bethpage in 1894 by Miss Emma Toedteberg, Librarian of the Long Island Historical Society, have been included in this record. The Bethpage Quaker cemetery has been in use since 1740 or earlier. A Powell burial ground established after 1800, adjoins and also a public cemetery established 1859. Miss Toedteberg gave no clue, but apparently put all in one list. I have therefore included all. While the percentage of Quakers in these outer grounds may be small, those therein interred were largely related to those in the Quaker ground.

In the unfortunate Separation of 1828, out of 199 members in this Monthly Meeting, only 12, including children, were of the Orthodox body. These have been identified by the letter "O".

RECORDS

ACKERSON
Phebe, dt Henry & Phebe; m 1798 Jesse MOLLINEUX

ALBERTSON
Ella, dt Richard & Phebe, b 4-10-1863; m 1887 Eugene F. ROBBINS; (2) Jacob W. JACKSON
Emma, dt Richard & Phebe W.; m 1872 Samuel J. UNDERHILL
Phebe H., dt Benjamin & Sarah; m John C. MERRITT
Silas, s Richard, dec, & Sarah, N. Hemp.; m 11-24-1813 at Beth., Keziah WHITSON, dt Henry & Clementine, b 1788
Kezia gct Wby 9-15-1814

ALDRICH
Esek rocf Uxbridge in New England 2-18-1796, an apprentice; ct Uxbridge 5-15-1800 (clear)
Royal, O.B., s Stephen & Mary, Northbridge, Mass., d 3-28-1839 ae 69y (Jericho stone d 3-28-1859 ae 70); m 5-3-1792 at Jericho, Martha HICKS, dt Elias & Jemima, Jericho, d 9-11-1862 ae 90y 11m (Jericho Stone)
Ruth, dt Stephen & Mary; m 1812 Asa ALDRICH
cf Uxbridge, N. E. 2-18-1795; ct Uxbridge 4-18-1799 (clear); Ruth rocf Farmington 12-15-1808

ALLEN
Ann (form Pearsall) dis mo 11-17-1769
Susan (form Hawxhurst) dis mo 11-16-1826

ALLEY
Enos, N.Y.C., s Samuel & Deborah, Lynn, Mass.; m 2-22-1804 at Beth., Rebecca WHITSON, dt Amos & Amy, Suffolk Co., b 1780 d 9-1-1829 ae 48 (d Herricks)
Ch: Sidney B.
Sidney B. recrq of mother 9-18-1823; Rebecca gct N. Y. 10-18-1804; Rebecca rocf N. Y. 2-16-1815
Robert W. recrq 3-15-1821; ct N. Y. 3-21-1822 (minor)
Sidney B., s Enos & Rebecca, gct Wby 9-20-1832

AMATT
George, s James & Mary, d 6-25-1893 ae 45

ARNOLD
Ephraim (apparently here as apprentice, but not found); he returned to his parents at Hartford 3-21-1811

AVERILL
Sidney & Elmina L.
Ch: Julia M. (or Gulia)
Willis P.
cf Wby for both 9-18-1845; ct Rahway & Plainfield 12-17-1846

BAKER
Martha, dt Richard & Deborah, d 10-21-1831 ae 80y bur Wby; m ----- HUBBS

BALDWIN
Jesse & Elizabeth
Ch: Mary dis
Sarah [clear]
Esther
cf N. Y. for parents & 3 ch 12-17-1814; ct N. Y. 4-14-1825 with 2 dt
Mary, dt Jesse & Elizabeth; dis 3-17-1825 for joining the Methodists

BATTY
Abigail, dt John & Mary; m ----- DODGE

BAUCKER
Sally Ann m J. W. ROBBINS (Jericho Stones)

BAUSCH
Robert m Pauline FREDERICK d 11-5-1888 ae 54 (Beth. Stones)

BEDELL
Abby (perhaps w Isaac) d 11-15-1878 ae 79y 10m 15d (Beth. Stones)
Charles m Almira J. ----- b 3-17-1850 d 1-24-1883
Ch: Henry d 8-20-1869 ae 5m (Beth. Stones)
Charles H. m Rachel W. ----- d 11-8-1872 ae 22y 3m 26d
Ch: Amanda d 12-7-1870 ae 1y 10m 20d (Beth. Stones)
Elbert m Phebe M. ----- d 5-25-1868 ae 23y 6m 16d (Beth. Stones)
Henry d 2-22-1873 ae 52y 6m 5d; m -----
Ch: Isaac d 1-31-1888 ae 24y 11m (Beth. Stones)
Isaac b 8-29-1794 d 2-10-1868
Jane, dt Joseph & Martha; dis mo 4-171837
Joseph [Beadle in the record], s Isaac & Rhoda, Beth., d 8-29-1842 ae 63y; m Martha MOTT, dt Benj. & Rachel, d 4-19-1857 ae 74y
Ch: Sarah
Jane
Rachel
Elizabeth b 6-27-1819
3 ch recrq of parents 3-19-1818; Joseph recrq 2-15-1816; Martha recrq 2-15-1816
Rachel m ----- NOSTRAND (mo)
dis mo 9-16-1790
Samuel rq mbrp 1806, after several mo rq returned to him
Sarah m 1823 ----- POWELL (mo)

BETTS
Elizabeth [Bates] d 3-2-1888 ae 57y (Jericho Stone); adjoining are stones to "Sister" d 11-41886 ae 58; "Mother" d 5-24-1881 ae 86
Mary, dt Anthony, d Jericho 5-21-1813; m ----- HUBBS
Sarah rocf Flushing 7-21-1808

BIRDSALL
James F., s Henry & Jerusha, dec, N.Y.C.; m 9-24-1829 at Jerusalem, Avis C. SEAMAN, dt Elijah & Phebe, Hemp.
cert for James (clear); ct N. Y. for Avis 12-16-1830

BISHOP
Samuel, s Samuel, dec, & Ann, Stamford, Conn., d Charlotte Precinct; m 1-18-1794 at Jericho Phebe MOTT, dt John & Mary
Samuel rocf Pur. (clear)

BOWNE
Sidney B., s Richard M. & Mary M., G.C.; m 11-1-1871 at Mary V. Willets', Martha V. WILLETS, dt Wm. & Mary V., Jericho, b 12-28-1850
Martha gct Wby

BRACKETT
Abbie, dt Charles & Abbie, b 10-8-1857; m Alvate(?) MOSHER

BREWSTER
Elizabeth Mott d 2-11-1895 ae 88y (Jericho Stone)
Isaac, Brookhaven; m Sarah ELLISON, dt Thomas, d 9-6-1813 Setucket
Sarah recrq 6-17-1813

BRIDGES
Bessie, dt George & Sarah F.; m 1895 James H. SEAMAN

BROWN
Aaron H. b 12-20-1817 d 3-23-1879 (Beth. Stone)
Archibald F. (Beth. Stone)
James M. & Patience I.
Ch: Richard R. b 1-31-1850 d 7-19-1856 (Beth. Stones)
Phebe, wd, b 11-26-1768; m Thomas WILLIS (as 2nd w)

BRUSH
Elizabeth m 1799 ---- VAN COT (mo)

BUNKER
Alexander C., s Timothy W. & Eunice C., dec, b Hudson, N.Y. 11-9-1816 d 4-27-1907; m Mary P. SEAMAN, dt Arden & Elizabeth (Merritt), b Jerusalem 2-27-1820 d 8-19-1906 (m 10-17-1839 at Beth)
cf Hudson (clear); cf Hudson 7-18-1843; cf N.Y. for both 1875; ct Hudson for Mary P. 2-20-1846

BUNTING
Jane E., dt Wilmot & Elizabeth; m Noah JACKSON

BURLING
Mary b 1737; m James PARSONS

CARHART
Hendrick W., s James & Eliz., recrq of parents 9-19-1793; ct N. Y. 5-15-1800, a youth (clear)
James, Jericho, d 3-1-1829 ae 84; m Elizabeth DURYEA, dt Daniel, d 9-12-1841 Jericho
Ch: Hendrick Wright
James & Elizabeth gct N. Y. 6-15-1815; James & Elizabeth rocf Flushing 6-20-1821; James recrq 12-15-1796; Elizabeth recrq 9-20-1792; Hendrick W. recrq of parents 9-19-1793

CARLL
Albert G. d 10-10-1872
Joel B. d 2-16-1851
John Sidney d 2-15-1856 ae 30
Katharine A. d 1-17-1895
Sally B. d 2----1837
Selah S. d 1-15-1857
Thos. J. d 6-9-1845
(above stones, except Katharine A., adjacent at Jericho)

CARPENTER
Esther G., dt Ferris & Julia, b 9-7-1829; m 1853 Stephen ROBBINS
Robert R., s Wright & Hannah, N.Y.C.; m 12-15-1853 at Richard S. Powell's, Hannah W. POWELL, dt Richard S. & Sarah T., O.B.
Samuel, s Geo. & Amy, both dec, Pleasant Valley, N. Y.; m 11-26-1835 at Jericho, Phebe KIRBY dt Willets & Hannah, O.B.
cert of clear; Phebe K. gct Oswego 6-15-1837

CARY
William, s Ebenezer & Mary, both dec, Half Moon, N. Y.; m 11-17-1826 at Jericho, Kezia JACKSON, dt Charles & Sarah, both dec, O.B.
cert for Wm. (clear); Kezia recrq 8-21-1900; Kezia gct Saratoga 7-19-1827

CHICHESTER
Mary m 1796 ----- OGDEN (mo)

CLARK
John D. b 11-9-1821 d 2-22-1892 ae 70y 3m 13d (Beth. Stones)

CLEMENT
Charles & Sarah
Ch; Henry
Charles & fam gct N.P. 9-20-1794
Henry, s Charles, rqct Pur. (apprentice) 8-19-1790; not used, returned to mtg 3-17-1791

COIT
Sarah m W. A. GRIFFIN

COLES
Amelia, dt Daniel & Ann; m William JONES
Kezia, dt Thomas & Pamelia; m Charles VALENTINE

COLES, continued
Mary, dt Charles & Sarah; m 1741 Jacob VALENTINE

COLLINS
Job rocf Little Egg Harbor 12-20-1798; ct N.Y. 7-17-1800 (clear); cf N.Y. 6-16-1803; ct Chappaqua 9-20-1804 (clear)

COLYER
Jacob d 5-23-1865 ae 61y 6m 15d; m Elizabeth ----- d 2-19-1894 ae 83y 4m 9d
Ch: (prob)
Clarence S. d 10-17-1876 ae 20y 6m 17d
George F. d 11-4-1874 ae 21y 9d
Caroline E. d 12-12-1864 ae 19y 5m 27d
(Beth. Stones)

COMBS
Elias H., Beth., d 2-31-1876 ae 46y
John, Beth., d 10-23-1872 ae 78y

CONKLIN
Martha, dt Stephen & Phebe; m Rhyneer REMSEN; m (2) 1821 Daniel DOWNING

CONROW
Sarah rocf Little Egg Harbor 4-18-1791

COOPER
Joseph gct Wby 5-22-1802 (clear); cf Wby 4-16-1807; ct Wby 5-15-1823

CORNELIUS
John d 4-10-1814 Beth.; m (prob) Mary ----- d 3-21-1826 ae 86y at Beth
prospect of rem to N. Y. with his fam 1795; left at liberty 2-19-1795
Mary, dt John & Mary; m ----- MERRITT

CORNELL
Phebe gct N. Y. 1792

CORSA
Bennington & Minnie
Ch: Frankie W. d 9-15-1886 ae 3m 21d
(Beth. Stones)
Isaac V. m Sarah ----- d 2-25-1884 ae 58y 7m 28d
Ch: George W. d 1-8-1888 ae 22y 9m 5d
(Beth. Stones)

CROMWELL
John, s John & Anna, dec, Harrison; m 11-18-1825 at Jericho, Phebe WHITSON, dt Henry & Clement, O.B.
Phebe gct Pur. 6-15-1826

CROOKER
Jacob & Phebe
Phebe gct Wby 3-18-1830 (rem & settled with her h)

CROSSMAN (or Clossman)
Mary, dt (prob) Jacob & Esther RUSHMORE; dis mo 3-19-1824

DARBY
John, O.B. m 6-25-1794 at Beth., Kezia POWELL, dt Samuel & Mary, O.B.
Ch: Anne
John & fam gct N. Y. 5-17-1798

DARLING
Kezia recrq 11-21-1816; dis separating from Friends 5-20-1830
Sarah rpd mo; Nantucket MM sends her ack for mo & asks care 8-15-1799; rpd favorably 4-17-1800; cf Nantucket 7-16-1801

DAVIS
Edgar m Phebe SMITH d 3-3-1887 ae 46y 4m 24d (Jericho Stone)

DENNIS
Wilmet recrq 6-16-1791; ct Wby 6-18-1801 (clear)

DICKEY
Mary E. d 12-14-1901 ae 14y 8m 14d

DINGEE
Esther, dt Arthur; m 1794 Jacob RUSHMORE

DODGE
Abigail, dt John & Mary BATTY, d 9-29-1843 (Beth. Stone)
Elizabeth, dt John & Hannah; m 1850 John PLUMMER
John, Beth., d 8-12-1851 ae 68y

DOUGHTY
Benjamin gct Flushing 1-18-1827 (clear)
Phebe [Doty] gct N. Y. 4-18-1791

DOWNING
Coe rocf Wby 5-15-1800, minor; dis mo 2-20-1812
Daniel, s Ananias & Deborah, Wolver Hollow, d 4-6-1849 Brookville; m 5-3-1821 at Jericho, Martha REMSEN, wd Rhyneer, dt Stephen & Phebe CONKLIN, d 3-27-1857 ae 90y at Cedar Swamp
Daniel recrq 6-15-1820; Martha Remsen roc 11-20-1806
Elizabeth recrq 9-17-1795
Elizabeth, dt Henry & Margaret, gct Wby 5-16-1805 at father's rq, she was a minor
Henry Jr., s Henry & Jemima, b 10-14-1760 d 8-1-1840; m Margaret ----- d 1805 or earlier
Ch: Jemima
Elizabeth
Anne
Daniel
James
Henry recrq 6-16-1791; Margaret recrq 1797; ch recrq of parents 6-21-1798; Henry & fam

DOWNING, Henry & Margaret, continued
gct Oswego 5-16-1805 (w not named) & ch as follows
Henry (clear)
Jemima (clear)
Anna (clear)
Daniel
James
George
Henry m 2d Ruth ----- b 7-22-1772 d 6-23-1847
Ch: Susan
Jacob, s Ananias & Deborah, Jericho; m 1775 Elizabeth SMITH
Ch: Deborah
(7 other ch)
Jacob & Elizabeth & dt, Deborah, gct Creek 1-20-1803; Jacob recrq 7-16-1795
Margaret recrq 5-16-1822
Margaret (form Vanderbilt) d 4-15-1849 N.Y.; recrq 8-17-1797
Phebe, dt Benjamin & Martha, b 12-1-1782; m 1820 Obadiah WILLITS
Richard Jr. m Sarah T. POWELL, dt Walter & Lucy, b 5-4-1883
Sarah T. recrq 1-17-1895

DOXEY
William F. m Mary G. ----- d 7-17-1873 ae 17y 2m 19d (Beth. Stone)

DUMPSON
Mary Ann d 7-22-1891 ae 83y (Jericho Stone)

DURYEA
Daniel P. m 12-20-1883 Cornelia ROBBINS, dt Edward & Rachel W., b 10-1-1854 Syossit
Cornelia resigned 1915
Elizabeth, dt Daniel; (prob) m James CARHART
Jane b 11-16-1810; m Andrew POWELL
Jemima (form Rogers) recrq 1797; dis mo 10-16-1800
John Jr. b 10-5-1817 d 7-24-1901; m Caroline S. ----- b 7-10-1815 d 5-20-1898
Ch: Henry Sands d 1-20-1849 ae 3m 18d
Mary "Emer" d 12-2-1852 ae 3y 28d
Ethalinda d 4-5-1855 ae 3y 4m 16d
(Jericho Stones)
Mary Ella, dt Edgar H. & Mary J.; m Seaman POST
Phebe m Jacob JACKSON

EASTMAN
Gerard Lester, s Geo. W. & Jennie D., Roslyn; m 7-8-1916 at John C. Merritt's, Violet A. MERRITT, dt John C. & Eliz. (Hicks), Farmingdale, b 2-17-1889
Violet rocf Wby 2-15-1914; Violet gct Wby 3-10-1939

ELLISON
Eliza, dt Benjamin & Charlotte, Jericho, d 11-18-1849; recrq 6-20-1822
Sarah, dt Thomas, d Setauket 9-6-1813; m Isaac BREWSTER

EMIGH
Adam, s Philip & Margaret, Clove D. Co.; m 4-20-1838 at (prob) Jericho, Ann M. SEAMAN, dt Arden & Eliz., Hemp., d 5-26-1864 ae 46y
Ch: Margaret b 3-10-1850 Jerusalem
Elizabeth b 3-29-1844 Jerusalem
cf N.P. (clear); Adam rocf N.P. 3-20-1845; Adam rel from mbrp 7-15-1852; Ann M. gct N.P. 7-17-1838
Elizabeth S., dt Adam & Ann, b 3-29-1844; m 1861 Luther B. LEE
Margaret E., dt Adam & Ann M., b 3-10-1850; m 1869 George W. LEE

FEIGE
Maria A. E. b 10-18-1857 d 4-1-1859 (Beth. Stone)

FITZGERALD
Daniel rocf Pur. 11-20-1794; dis 5-21-1802
Sarah rocf Pur. 2-16-1792; ct Pur. 8-21-1800 (clear)

FLEET
Jesse, dt Parret & Abigail, Jerusalem, recrq 11-17-1791; left at liberty to rem 2-19-1795; d 4-18-1822 ae 83y

FRAME
William, s Jesse & Mary, both dec, Flushing; m 7-16-1854 at Isaac Willets', Phebe WILLETS, dt Isaac & Amy, O.B.

FROST
Amy, dt Isaac & Hannah, gct Wby 8-16-1832 (clear)
Hannah gct Wby 8-16-1832 (clear)
Isaac, s Charles & Mary, O.B., d 1810; m 12-23-1807 at Beth., Hannah WHITSON, dt Amos & Amy, Huntington, b 4-24-1784 d 12-14-1858
Ch: Amy
Isaac
cf Wby 12-17-1807 (clear); Hannah rocf Wby 9-17-1812; Hannah gct Wby 3-16-1809; Isaac gct Wby 12-19-1833 (clear)
(Frost Gen.)

GALLOWAY
Charlotte, dt Wm. & Eliza; m Samuel S. UNDERHILL

GARDNER
Lydia gct Wby 3-18-1813 (clear)

GARNER
Charlotte T., dt Wm. & Caroline, b 6-24-1859 at Beth.; recrq 7-19-1888
William, s John & Sarah, dec, Jerusalem; m 10-19-1852 at Arden Seaman's, Caroline Elizabeth SEAMAN, dt Arden & Elizabeth, Jerusalem, b 2-20-1829 d 5-13-1903
Ch: Annie E. b 7-25-1862 d 2-12-1934

GARNER, William & Caroline Elizabeth, continued
Ch: William b 8-27-1868
Charlotte T. b 6-24-1859 d Beth 1-11-1920
ch recrq of parents
William, s William & Caroline, b 8-27-1868 d 2-24-1922; m Eliza -----

GIBBS
Mary R. b 2-26-1812 d 3-18-1886 (Jericho Stone)

GILES
Maria m 1836 Isaac HAWXHURST

GODDARD
Gladys rocf MM of S. Division of Wales, Penarth Glamorgonshire 6-18-1939

GRANT
Charles R. d 8-5-1869 ae 56y 10m 15d (Beth. Stone)

GREEN
Elizabeth (form Vanderbilt) recrq 2-17-1825; d 5-30-1847

GRIFFIN
W. A. m Sarah M. COIT, d 9-1-1867 ae 58y 1m 15d

HALLOCK
A. A. & C. D.
Ch: Alfred H. b 5-4-1878 d 2-15-1883 (Beth. Stones)
David S., s Nicholas & Elizabeth, dec, Utica; m 8-21-1845 at John Ketcham's, Martha S. KETCHAM, dt John & Rebecca, Jericho, d 7-11-1846 ae 20
cf Verona MM (clear)
Edward, s James, dec, & Eliza., Milton, Ulster Co.; m 6-28-1821 at Jericho, Anna U. SHERMAN, dt Isaac & Margaret, Jericho
Anna gct Marlborough 7-18-1822
Martha T. m David KETCHAM

HALLOWELL
Jeffries, s Nathan, dec, & Lydia, Aurora, N.Y.; m 10-19-1838 at Jericho, Sarah L. KIRBY, dt Jacob & Mary, Jericho
cf Scipio (clear); Sarah L. gct Rochester 4-16-1840
Thomas C., s Nathan & Lydia, Gananuoqua, Canada; m 4-17-1845 at John Ketchem's, Phebe KETCHAM, dt John & Rebecca, O.B., b 9-12-1817 Jericho

HALSTEAD
David Jr. rocf Pur. as apprentice 10-20-1796; ct Pur. 9-20-1798 (clear)

HARNED
Jacob recrq 1-20-1791; d 1-10-1822
Lucy m Walter POWELL
Mary, dt Benjamin NICOLS, d 4-11-1831 ae 70 recrq 10-17-1816

HARRIS
Mrs. Sarah b Windsor, Nova Scotia 3-16-1823 d 8-7-1880 (Jericho Stone)

HATTON
Daisy Georgia, dt Joseph & Georgianna, b 1872; m 1900 Albert William SEAMAN

HAVILAND
Florence m James H. SEAMAN
James C., s Wm. & Anna, N.Y.C.; m 5-1-1823 at Jericho, Phebe SEAMAN, dt David & Sarah, Jericho
Ch: Maria d 4-17-1837 ae 12 Jericho
Edwin b 10- 6-1833 d young Jericho
Henry
Anna
William S.
Edwin
Sarah b 11-23-1835 Jericho
Lydia b 4-28-1838 Jericho

Phebe gct N. Y. 1-15-1824; cf N. Y. for parents & 5 ch (Maria & later ones) 5-21-1835; ct N. Y. for parents & 5 ch 5-16-1844
William Jr., s Wm. & Anna, N.Y.C.; m 10-31-1839 at Jericho, Esther SEAMAN, dt David & Sarah, Jericho
cf N. Y. (clear); Esther gct N. Y. 12-17-1840

HAWXHURST
Elisha recrq 9-21-1843; ct N. Y. 9-21-1848
Isaac, s Israel & Sarah; m before 3-12-1836 Maria GILES (mo)
ct N. Y. 9-20-1832 (minor); cf N. Y.; dis 4-14-1836
Israel, s Jacob & Mary, b 1775 d 8-29-1861 ae 86y; m Sarah STRATTON, d 1-31-1850 ae 75y 8m
Ch: Sarah b 7-24-1802; m J. Searing CARPENTER
Jacob b 1803; m Catharine -----
Letitia m Samuel BETTS
Susan m John ALLEN
Mary m John T. BARNARD
Isaac m Maria GILES
Rachel m Samuel SEARING
Eliza d ae 18y
Phebe Ann m Richard CONN
Richard d 4-19-1846 ae 37y 5m 29d
ct N. Y. 9-20-1832 for Israel; recrq 5-20-1813; six ch recrq of Israel 5-19-1815; ct N.Y. 5-19-1825 with 5 ch, Susan being clear; obstruction appearing, cert ret; ct N.Y. with s, Isaac, 9-20-1832; cert ret because of obstruction
James m Elizabeth OAKLEY
Ch: James O.
cf Wby for James 7-16-1812; James O. recrq of father 1-21-1813
James O., s James & Eliz.; m 1818 or 1819 (mo) ------

HAWXHURST, James O., continued
recrq of father 1-21-1813; dis mo 3-18-1819; rst
James O. m 2d 1828 Julia E. ----- b 9-25-1808 d 9-29-1900 (mo)
Ch: Phebe C. b 5- 1-1844
Caroline b 5- 8-1847
Nathaniel
ack mo 1-15-1829
(Bibles)
Mary, dt Israel, gct N. Y. 10-21-1830 (clear)
Nathaniel P., s James & Julia, Beth., recrq 4-20-1843; d 7-12-1880 ae 84
Rachel, dt Israel, gct N.Y. 10-21-1830 (clear)
Richard dis joining a military company 4-15-1830
Susan m 1826 ----- ALLEN
Wm. C. (or G.), s Nath. O. & Elizabeth, d 7-24-1882 ae 62y 3m 22d; m Sarah Ann -----
Ch: Ann d 7- 3-1862 ae 1m 2d
Sarah d 6-26-1862 ae 27d
Nathaniel d 3-11-1864 ae 3m 13d
Martha Jane d 3-26-1870 ae 4y 5m 13d
Infant s d 3-23-1863 ae 14d
Phebe d 9-17-1864 ae 9m 20d
William H. d 2-29-1848 ae 5m 18d
Sylvester d 8-25-1852 ae 1m 1d
Geo. Washington d 7-14-1871 ae 1m 2d
Charles P. d 1-24-1861 ae 3m 15d
(Beth. Stones)

HAYDOCK
Henry b 9-2-1802 d 7-29-1884 (Jericho Stone)

HEALY
Rachel rocf Coeymans 12-17-1818, forwarded to Wby where she now resides

HECK
Amos Robert, s Carl August & Anna Caroline, recrq 4-21-1929

HENDRICKSON
Charles m Julia A. ----- d 2-14-1891 ae 58y 4m 17d
Ch: Samuel J. d 11-11-1890 ae 22y 2m
(Beth. Stones)
Jesse m 1822 or 1823 Anna TOWNSEND, dt George & Phebe (mo)
Anna dis 4-17-1823

HEUSER
Augustus & Mary
Ch: Martha b 6-26-1893 d 7-16-1893
(Beth. Stone)
Katharina, of Hier ruht in Frieden, Geb. KRAFFT 13 Feb. 1829, Gesb 27 Sept. 1890 (Beth. Stone)

HEWLETT
Hannah, dt John & Sarah, b 2-4-1762; m 1779 John JONES

HICKS
Abigail, dt Elias & Jemima; m 1804 Valentine HICKS
Benjamin gct Wby 5-16-1793 (clear); ct Wby 6-19-1794
Caroline, dt Valentine & Abigail; m 1831 William SEAMAN
Elias, the eminent preacher, s John & Martha, Jericho, b 3 Mo (May) 19, 1748 d 2-27-1830 ae 84y 1m 3d; m 1-2-1771 Wby, Jemima SEAMAN, dt Jonathan & Eliz., d 3-17-1829 ae 78y
Ch: Elizabeth d 7-5-1871 ae 79y 9m bur Jericho
(10 other ch)
Elias placed his dt in N.P. School 9-17-1807
Elias, s Valentine & Abigail, b 5-10-1815; ct N. Y. 5-16-1833
Elizabeth S., dt Wm. S. & Letitia, b 7-31-1854; m 1883 John C. MERRITT
Harriet, dt Smith & Phebe, b 8-3-1845; m Peter McGREGOR
Henry, s Edmund & Emma E. (Jarvis), Wby; m 6-27-1900 at Solomon S. Jackson's, Caroline U. JACKSON, dt Solomon S. & Esther L. (Post) Jericho, b 2-25-1872
Isaac, s John D. & Sarah, N. Hemp.; m 3-24-1836 Mary F. WILLIS, dt John & Mary W., O.B.
Mary F. gct Wby 1-17-1839
James d 4-6-1856 ae 63y; m Hannah ----- b 12-16-1802 d 12-6-1896 ae 93y 11m 20d
Martha, dt Elias & Jemima; m 1792 Royal ALDRICH
Martha W. d 1-18-1879 ae 36y (Wby Stone)
Mary d 1-1-1886 ae 36y (Jericho Stone)
Mary Ann, dt Jesse & Mary MERRITT; m 1867 Robert SEAMAN
Phebe, wd John, rocf Wby 8-19-1790
Phebe, dt Elias & Jemima; m 1799 Joshua WILLETS
Phebe, dt Valentine & Abigail; m 1826 Adonijah UNDERHILL
Phebe Amelia, dt Smith & Phebe, b 1-12-1842; m Sidney VAN NOSTRAND
Samuel, s John D., dec, & Sarah R., Wby; m 9-17-1841 at John Willis' in O.B., Rachel WILLIS, dt John & Mary W., Jericho
cf Wby (clear); ct Wby for Rachel 3-16-1843
Sarah Cornelia, dt Smith & Phebe, b 1-12-1842; m 1858 Henry JAMES
Sarah R., dt Elias & Jemima, b 10-9-1793; m 1814 Robert SEAMAN
Smith, dt Valentine & Mary, Beth. & Jericho, d 2-14-1876 ae 72y; m Phebe M. -----
Ch: Sarah Cornelia S. b 1-12-1842
Phebe Amelia W. " " "
Harriet L. b 8-3-1845
Smith recrq 7-16-1840
Valentine, Merchant, N.Y.C., s Samuel & Phebe, dec, Wby, b 2-4-1784 d 3-5-1850 ae 67y 10m bur Jericho; m 2-23-1804 at Jericho Abigail HICKS, dt Elias & Jemima, b 3-3-1782 d 2-26-1850 ae 67y bur Jericho
Ch: Phebe
Mary S. d 8-17-1826 ae 20y

HICKS, Valentine & Abigail, continued
Ch: Caroline
Infant
Elizabeth B. b 8-1-1812 d 11-29-1820
Elias b 5-10-1815
ct N. Y. for Abigail 9-20-1804; cf N. Y. 7-16-1812 for parents & 4 small ch
Whitehead, s Stephen, dec, & Mary, Wby; m 2-1-1826 at Beth., Mary Ann MERRITT, dt Jesse & Mary, Beth., b 2-1-1799 Beth. d 5-27-1887
Ch: Merritt b 3- 3-1827 d 9-20-1849 Jerusalem
William S. b 7-7-1829
Mary Ann m 2d 1867 Robert SEAMAN
William gct N. Y. 4-18-1791 (clear)
William S., s Whitehead & Mary Ann, b 7-7-1829 Jerusalem; m 10-6-1853 Letitia SEAMAN, dt Benjamin & Jemima, b 10-6-1833
Ch: Elizabeth b 7-31-1854; m Jno. C. MERRITT
(6 other ch)

HILL
James Christian, s Eugene & Julia, Richmond Co., Va.; m 9-10-1938 at Albert Lewis', Ruth Mary LEWIS, dt Albert & Ruth, b 4-22-1917
Ruth recrq 8-20-1938

HORTON
Freelove dis 7-17-1817
Joseph d 4-20-1841 ae 85y; m (prob) Jane PROBASCO, dt Abraham & Charity, d 5-4-1837 ae 77
Joseph recrq 8-16-1792; Jane recrq 10-20-1796

HUBBS
Arden d 7-22-1878 ae 66y 2m; m before 7-21-1836 ----- (mo)
dis mo 8-18-1836
Elias, s Valentine, gct N.Y. 5-16-1833
Hiram mo abt 1843; dis 11-16-1843
Jacob gct Wby 4-18-1816 (clear)
James, Jericho, d 12-30-1828 ae 79y
John d 3-28-1889 ae 69y 3m 1d (unidentified stone, Jericho)
John R. b 2-23-1839 d 12-25-1900 ae 61y 10m 2d; m Esther P. ROBBINS, dt William & Elizabeth, d 6-21-1931
Esther rocf N. Y.
Joseph dis mo 6-17-1830
Joshua d 12-8-1886 ae 85y 1d (Beth. Stone); m Elizabeth W. ----- (prob w as stones are adjacent) d 4-12-1890 ae 84y 10m 2d (Beth. Stone) (mo)
dis mo 3-18-1824
Margery d 5-20-1872 in 86th yr (unidentified stone, Wby)
Martha, dt Richard & Deborah BAKER, Wby, d 10-21-1831 ae 80y
Mary b 3-5-1808 d 12-3-1887 (unidentified stone, Jericho)
Mary, dt Selah & Hannah; m 1851 Jonah POWELL
Mercy d 3-7-1868 in 90th yr (unidentified stone, Jericho)

Phebe Ann, dt Thomas & Mary, gct N. Y. 4-20-1837; d 8-15-1879 ae 77y (Jericho stone gives 8-15-1875 ae 77y 9m)
Platt, Beth.
Richard d 5-11-1864 in 80th yr (unidentified stone, Jericho)
Richard C. d 7-7-1894 ae 88y 1m 11d; m 1818 Hannah C. ROBBINS, d 11-1-1884 ae 71y 3m 27d (mo)
Richard C. dis mo 5-21-1818; dis mo 8-18-1836
(Jericho Stones)
Samuel dis 5-20-1802
Sarah E., dt Richard C. & Hannah C.; m 1871 Walter ROBBINS
Selah, Beth., d 10-5-1869; m Hannah ----- d 3-11-1865 ae 87y Beth.
Ch: Joshua
Jemima
Mary m Jonah POWELL
Platt
Arden
Hyman b 9-23-1815
Hannah recrq 10-20-1808; Selah recrq 8-19-1813; ch recrq of parents 2-17-1814
Selah Platt ack mo 3-17-1831
Thomas, Jericho; m Mary BETTS, dt Anthony, d 5-21-1813
Ch: Jane d 12----1838 ae 39 Jericho
Phebe Ann d 8-15-1879 ae 77y (Jericho stone 8-15-1875 ae 77y 9m)
Richard
Thomas recrq 7-21-1807; Mary recrq 5-21-1807; ch recrq of mother 4-14-1808; ct N.Y. for Mary B. 3-18-1841
Thomas B. & Jefferson 1843 (unidentified stone, Jericho)
Thomas Jefferson 1844 (unidentified stone, Jericho)
Thomas Franklin 1851 (unidentified stone, Jericho)

HUNT
Abraham R. d 11-18-1887 ae 72y; m Mary B. ----- (prob w as stones adjacent at Jericho) d 2----1888 ae 77y

JACKSON
Ancel T. & Abigail
Ch: George A.
Gertrude
Ancel d 8-4-1890 ae 6y 6m 4d
Lillie d 6-30-1887 ae 11y 2m 11d
ch recrq 9-18-1921
2 ch recrq 9-18-1921
Annie T., dt Ancel T. & Abbie; m 1894 M. Franklin JACKSON
Caroline U., dt Solomon S. & Esther L., b 2-5-1872; m 1900 Henry HICKS
Charles, nm, s Thomas & Mary; m 3-28-1781 Sarah WHITSON, b 1-20-1757 d 8-3-1825 ae 68y
Ch: Kezia m Dr. Wm. CAREY
Esther m Sam'l SHERMAN

JACKSON, Charles & Sarah, continued
Ch: Phebe
Solomon m Mary BROWER
3 ch recrq of parents 1-19-1797
(Bibles)
Elizabeth, dt Obadiah & Almy, b 5-6-1762; m 1782 Thomas JACKSON
Emily B., dt Jacob & Phebe; m 1865 Isaac THORNE
Esther m 1818 ----- SHERMAN (mo)
Florence, dt Ella A.; m 1912 James WILLITS
Grace Anna, dt Solomon & Annie; m 1889 Henry C. WOODNUT Jr
Harold A. (took name from step-father, Jacob W. Jackson), s Jacob W. & Ella A., Bkn., b 11-25-1893; m 8-20-1917 at Morton M. Curry's, Douglaston, L.I., Carolyn Louise WINDOES, dt Morton M. & Bertha CURRY
Jacob, s Thomas & Elizabeth, Locust Grove, b 4-23-1791 d 12-31-1867 ae 77y (Jericho Stone) m Phebe DURYEA, dt George & Elizabeth, b 1803 d 11-24-1889 ae 87y (Jericho Stone)
Ch: Martha B. b 9-6-1826; m John JACKSON; Benj. ALBERTSON
Elizabeth b 10-19-1828; m Benj. ALBERTSON
Townsend b 3-27-1831; m Martha WILLETS
Henry W. b 5-7-1833; m Martha ELDRED
James K. b 9-5-1835; m Julia TAYLOR
Sidney W. b 5-27-1838; m Caroline ROBBINS; Mary Jane HUBBS
Emma b 9-5-1840; m Isaac C. THORNE
Mary S. m Townsend WILLIS
Jacob recrq 2-19-1807; ct Wby 3-19-1812 (clear); probably dis mo there; Phebe recrq 2-19-1835; Jacob recrq 3-19-1835
Jacob W., s Townsend & Martha; m Ella ALBERTSON (Ella m (1) Eugene S. ROBBINS, whose mbrp was cancelled 10-21-1897) dt Richard & Phebe, b 4-10-1863
Ch: (by Ella's first h; all took name of Jackson)
Stephen b 4-25-1888
Florence b 12-1-1889
Harold b 11-25-1893
James K., s Jacob & Phebe, b 9-5-1835 d 10-11-1879 ae 44y; m Julia C. TAYLOR
Ch: Lonnie d 4-2-1874 ae 10y 3m (Jericho Stone)
Jarvis m before 6-21-1804 Mary WHITSON, dt Henry & Clementine (mo)
Mary dis mo 7-19-1804; referred to Flushing which rpd 7-18-1822 having rst & rec her
Jemima, dt Solomon & Mary, d 6-4-1875 ae 70y
Jeremiah B. recrq 9-21-1848
John, s John & Keziah, Jericho, d 1-1-1821 ae 88y; m -----
Ch: Mary
John recrq 1-20-1791; Mary recrq 3-17-1791; John dis 4-15-1830
Josephine, dt Solomon & Annie, b 6-28-1859; m 1888 George M. PRINCE
Julia m ----- PUTNAM
(perhaps wd James K.)
Kezia, dt Charles & Sarah; m 1826 William CARY
Lillian Irene, dt Townsend & Mary, b 11-3-1890 d 1-3-1904 (Jericho Stone)
Margaret, Jericho, dt Zebulun & Clement WRIGHT, d 3-3-1828 ae 87y
Mary, dt John & Margaret; m 1794 Daniel UNDERHILL
Mary, dt David & Esther; m 1804 Abraham WHITSON
Matthew Franklin, s Sidney W. & Caroline R., dec, Jericho, d 11-3-1895 ae 25y; m 10-10-1894 at Ancel T. Jackson's, Annie T. JACKSON, dt Ancel T. & Abbie
Ch: Marion Frances
Annie T. recrq 10-20-1910; Marion F. recrq of parents 11-17-1910
Noah, s Parmenus & Charity; m Mary Jane JENKINS
Ch: Edgar d 4-10-1864 ae 28y
Mary d 8-19-1857 ae 20 (unm)
(Bibles)
Noah m 2d Jane E. BUNTING, dt Wilmot & Elizabeth
Jane recrq; Jane gct N. Y. 11-18-1886
(Bibles)
Obadiah, s John & Margaret, Jericho, d 9-14-1825 ae 51y; m 3-22-1804 at Jericho, Rachel UNDERHILL, dt Adonijah & Phebe, Jericho
Ch: John b 6-12-1813
Elizabeth d 6-2-1827 ae 18
Ruth, dt Samuel & Mary, Jerusalem, recrq 4-19-1792; d 2-17-1824 ae 84y
Samuel, s Thomas & Mary, Jerusalem, d 3-1-1833 ae 85y; m 7-15-1773 in Hemp., Deborah SEAMAN, dt Solomon & Elizabeth, d 9-6-1827 ae 78y
Ch: Solomon m Mary BROWER
James
Deborah recrq 4-18-1793
(Bibles & Seaman Gen.)
Sidney W., s Jacob & Phebe, Syosset, b Syosset 5-27-1838 d 8-10-1910; m 9-24-1865 at Matthew Robbins', Jericho, Caroline ROBBINS dt Matthew F. & Hannah S., d 5-6-1881 ae 39
Ch: Matthew Franklin b 2-16-1870 d 11-3-1895 at Jericho
Sidney W. m 2d Mary Jane HUBBS, dt Richard C. & Hannah, d 3-3-1932
Mary J. recrq 4-20-1893
Solomon S., s Solomon & Mary, Jericho, b 12-6-1817 Jerusalem d 3-23-1905 ae 88y; m Annie TITUS
Ch: Josephine b 6-28-1859; m Geo. M. PRINCE
Grace Anna b 5-13-1864; m H. C. WOODNUT Jr.
ch recrq of parents
Solomon S. m 2d 3-14-1867 at Jericho (cert not recorded) Esther L. POST, dt Jarvis & Phebe W., b 10-17-1829 d 1-27-1928 ae 98y 3m 10d
Ch: Caroline U. b 2-5-1872; m Henry HICKS
Esther rocf Wby
Stephen F. (took surname of step-father), s Eugene & Ella A. ROBBINS, b 4-25-1888; m 1919 Josephine -----
Thomas, s Samuel & Mary, Jerusalem, b 12-24-1754 d 11-25-1842 ae 88y; m 2-26-1782 Elizabeth JACKSON, dt Obadiah & Almy, b 5-6-1762 d 9-8-1828

JACKSON, Thomas & Elizabeth, continued
Ch: (5)
Thomas recrq 8-15-1833
(Bibles)
Townsend, s Samuel & Mary, d 10-21-1830; m 10-17-1770 at Hemp., Mary SEAMAN, dt Thomas & Martha
Some Townsend recrq 11-20-1806
(Seaman Gen.)
Townsend m 2d 2-7-1778 at Hemp., Polly SEAMAN, dt Jecaniah & Jane
(perhaps this one recrq 5-20-1830; this appears to be a 2nd m but no evidence)
Townsend, s Jacob & Phebe, East Woods, b 3-27-1831 d 3-3-1896 ae 65y; m 3-11-1857 Martha WILLETS, dt Jacob & Abigail, b 12-17-1836 d 4-6-1920
Ch: Jacob W. m Ella (Albertson) ROBBINS
William d 2-15-1866 ae 59y 9m; m Sally (probably w as stones adjacent) ----- d 8-15-1885 ae 78y
William dis 4-14-1825

JAGGAR
William Jr., Bkn., s David & Maria, Richmond Co., d 9-4-1890 ae 48; m June 17, 1851 at John KETCHAM's, Margaret S. KETCHAM, dt John & Rebecca, Jericho, d 1-7-1870 ae 48y Jericho

JAMES
Henry P. m 12-30-1858 Sarah Cornelia HICKS, dt Smith & Phebe, b 1-12-1842 Beth
Mary E. recrq 12-15-1910; d 10-7-1935

JARVIS
David m Sophia ----- d 9-28-1874 ae 81y 11d
(Beth Stone)
John d 4-14-1893 ae 82y 7m 8d; m Jane ----- d 7-2-1881 ae 68y 2m 2d
(Beth Stones)
Jonathan, s Robert & Sarah, Sweet Hollow, d 4-7-1835 ae 66y; m Deborah WHITSON, dt John & Mary, d 12-17-1857 ae 81 at Beth.
Deborah recrq 11-20-1817; Jonathan recrq 11-18-1830
Whitson m Susannah MOTT d 10-12-1886 ae 76y
(Beth Stones)

JENNINGS
Rebecca recrq 3-19-1801

JOHNSON
George W. d 4-19-1889; m 10-11-1867 Harriet VANDEWATER, dt Geo. & Margaret, d 4-3-1889 ae 78y (Beth. Stone)
George recrq

JONES
Abigail, dt Townsend & Hannah (Willis); m 1838 Robert SEAMAN
David, s William & Phebe; m 2-4-1768 in Hemp., Elizabeth SEAMAN, dt Thomas & Martha
Elizabeth m 2d 1770 Townsend JONES
Elizabeth d 12-8-1816
Hallet, s William & Phebe, Cold Spring, rocf Wby 4-16-1795; d 2-29-1836 ae 76y
John, s William & Phebe, Cold Spring, b 11-31-1755 d 8-21-1819 or 8-29-1819; m 5-2-1779 Hannah HEWLETT, b 2-4-1762 d 12-9-1850
Ch: Mary P. (or S.) b 6-4-1790
John recrq 2-19-1807
(Bibles)
Mary, dt John & Hannah, Cold Spring, b 6-4-1790 d 11-10-1858 ae 68y; recrq 9-18-1817; ct N.Y. 7-17-1823 (clear); cf N.Y. 12-16-1830 (unm)
Richard, s William & Phebe; m Ruth MOTT, dt John & Abigail, b 2-11-1775 d 8----1834 Oswego
Ch: Phebe
Abigail
Gideon
Lydia
James
William
Esther
(3 other ch)
cf N.P. with Phebe 2-28-1800; ct Oswego 6-15-1809
(Bibles)
Samuel, s Wm. & Mary, Locust Grove, b 3-9-1765 d 5-19-1836 ae 71y bur Jericho; m Abigail WILLIS, dt Townsend & Hannah, d 1-9-1866 ae 73y
cf Flushing for both 6-20-1793; ct Wby 2-17-1825 (clear); Abigail rocf Wby 1-19-1826; Abigail m 2d Robert SEAMAN
Townsend, s William & Phebe; m 10-17-1770 Elizabeth SEAMAN, wd David, dt Thomas & Martha
Ch: William
Elizabeth recrq 8-21-1823
William, s Wm. & Phebe, b 1736 d 6-13-1819; m 7-25-1762 Mary TOWNSEND, dt Timothy & Sarah; Mary recrq 3-15-1832
Ch: Townsend m Phebe HEWLETT
Samuel m Eliz. HEWLETT; Abigail WILLIS
William m 2d Amelia COLES, dt Daniel & Ann
(Bibles)
William D., s David & Elizabeth, Jerusalem; m Almy SEAMAN, dt Benjamin & Jane, d 4-5-1843 ae 56y
William D. recrq 9-18-1823
(Seaman Gen.)

JUNG
Elizabeth Hier Ruht in Gott Geb. Graf 8 Oct 1809 Gestorben 4 Nov 1880
(Beth. Stone)

KEIL
Charles G. m Julia Francis ----- b 8-24-1852 d 12-31-1890
Ch: Charles (this may be the father)
Francis
(Beth. Stones)

KENNEDY
James & Mary
Ch: Arthur d 1-4-1886 ae 1y 6m 22d
(Beth. Stone)

KETCHAM
Alanson drowned 9-11-1866 ae 46y; m Ruth H. POWELL, dt George & Sarah, d 4-5-1863 ae 38y 6m 28d
(Beth. Stone)
David, s Israel & Esther, Jericho, b 1753 d 1-29-1845; m 2-2-1780 Jane SEAMAN, dt Williams & Martha, b 11 Mo (Jan) 16, 1746/7 d 7-10-1833 ae 86y
Ch: Martha d 1-29-1837 ae 51y
John m Rebecca SHERMAN
David m Martha HALLOCK
(Seaman Gen.)
David (sometimes called Jr), s David & Jane, Jericho; m 12-22-1814 at Jericho, Phebe WILLITS, dt Jacob & Martha, Jericho, d 5-27-1816 Jericho
David d 1-29-1845 ae 92y; m 2nd Martha T. HALLOCK
Ch: Edward
John T. b 1-12-1838
David gct Marl. 6-16-1836; cf Marl. 6-15-1837 for both with ch, Edward; ct Oswego 4-18-1836 with Edward & John
Ebenezer d 6-5-1874 ae 29y 7m 23d; m Sarah E. ----- d 9-14-1871 ae 24y 10m 10d
Ch: Susie m Eugene VELSOR
Edward d 7-4-1880 ae 61y 9m 7d; m Melissa ----- b 2-22-1823 d 10-27-1889 ae 66y 8m 5d
(Beth. Stones)
Hannah Ann m Thomas U. POWELL
Ida A. d 7-26-1880 ae 15y 8m 11d (unidentified stone, Beth.)
Isaac S., s John & Rebecca, b 11-2-1823 Jericho d 10----1891 ae 67y 11m 14d; m 9-18-1867 at Milton, N. Y., Sarah MANN (2nd w) dt John & Phebe (Hallock), b 2-22-1832 Littleton, N. J. d 2-23-1906
Ch: Phebe H. b 1-13-1872; m H. McALLISTER Jr.
Rebecca Sherman d 10-25-1870 ae 1y 5m 17d
Sarah rocf Plainfield, N. J. but the record of her b in Hardwick & Randolph MM lost; she was rec without cert; Isaac resigned 10-20-1887
Israel, Huntington, d 1-8-1818 ae nearly 95y; m Esther SKIDMORE, dt Joseph, d 2-6-1815 ae 90y Huntington
Ch: David m Jane SEAMAN
on comm. as early as 1791; mtg approved in his house at Huntington 7-19-1804
John, s David & Jane, Jericho, d 8-28-1865 ae 83y Jericho; m 10-31-1816 at Jericho Rebecca SHERMAN, dt Isaac & Margaret, both dec, d 3-9-1881 ae 88y
Ch: Phebe b 9-12-1817
William b 5-24-1819
Margaret b 8-17-1821
Isaac S. b 11-2-1823
Ch: Martha S. b 7-4-1826; m David S. HALLOCK
Jane S. b 1-3-1829 d 1-5-1846 ae 17y
James S. b 1-24-1831 d 9-1-1860 ae 29
Townsend S. (probably their ch) d 2-19-1862 ae 11y 3m 7d
Joshua d 5-10-1867 ae 71y 9m 24d; m Keziah TERRY d 7-29-1876 ae 78y 2m 22d
(Beth. Stones)
Latitia (form Oakley) dis mo 10-17-1805; rst 3-15-1821
Margaret E. d 9-1-1878 ae 25 (unidentified stone, Jericho)
Margaret S., dt John & Rebecca; m 1851 William JAGGAR
Martha S., dt John & Rebecca; m 1845 David HALLOCK
Martin d 9-13-1868 ae 31y 10m 38d; m Almira -----
Ch: Adelaide d 4-19-1861 ae 1y 6m
Mary A. F. d 3-13-1865 ae 49y (unidentified stone, Jericho)
Mary Elizabeth b 7-13-1845 d 2-14-1881 ae 35y 7m 1d (Beth. Stone)
Nathaniel d 9----1883 ae 76y; (prob) m Charity ----- d 5----1877 ae 57y
(Beth. Stone)
Peter V. d 3-16-1882 ae 28y 4m 8d; m Emma -----
Ch: Edna b 1-16-1882 d 11-1-1882
(Beth. Stones)
Phebe, dt John & Rebecca; m 1845 Thomas HALLOWELL
Phebe H., dt Isaac S. & Sarah M., b 1-13-1872; m 1896 Henry McALLISTER Jr.
Philip b 6-24-1800 d 2-5-1863; m Ruth ----- d 6-19-1864 ae 40y 6m 2d
Susie, dt Ebenezer & Sarah; m Eugene VELSOR
Sybil P. d 1-2-1881 ae 71y 10m 24d (Beth. Stone)
Terry & Ruth
Ch: William A. d 4-5-1865 ae 19y 5m 11d (Beth Stone)
William, s John & Rebecca, b 5-24-1819 d 9-15-1879 ae 60y

KING
James (See James Ring)

KIRBY
Amy m 1828 ----- POST (mo)
Edmund, s Jacob & Mary, Jericho; m 10-21-1831 at Jericho Mary R. WILLITS, dt Obadiah & Elizabeth, dec
ct Flushing for both 4-17-1834
Elizabeth, dt Jacob & Mary, b 6-21-1814; m before 1-28-1836 ----- MOTT (mo)
Hannah, dt Jacob & Mary; m 1821 Isaac POST
Jacob, s Willets & Hannah, Jericho, b 8-11-1765 d 12-3-1859 (or 3-12-1859) ae 94y; m 6-24-1790 at Jericho Mary SEAMAN, dt Wm. S. & Mary, both dec, b 3-27-1774 d 9-21-1854
Ch: Mary W. b 7-30-1791; m Jno. WILLIS
William b 3-17-1795 d 9-19-1797
Hannah b 5-16-1799; m Isaac POST

KIRBY, Jacob & Mary, continued
Ch: Amy b 12-20-1803; m Isaac POST
Willets
Edmond b 2-8-1808; m Mary A. WILLETS
Elizabeth b 6-21-1814; m James MOTT
Sarah b 1-16-1818
Mary W., dt Jacob & Mary; m 1812 John WILLIS
Phebe, dt Willets & Hannah; m 1835 Samuel CARPENTER
Sarah, dt Willet & Hannah, b 3----1772; m 1791 David SEAMAN
Sarah L., dt Jacob & Mary; m 1838 Jeffries HALLOWELL
Willet, s William & Sarah, Jericho, d 5-1-1825 ae 87y; m Hannah -----
Ch: Jacob d 12-3-1859 ae 9y
Sarah b 3----1772
Willet, s Jacob & Mary, Jericho, d 12-3-1882 ae 76 bur Jericho; m before 3-16-1837 Matilda ----- d 2-9-1894 ae 86y 3m 18d bur Jericho (mo)
Willet ret mbrp; Matilda recrq

KISSAM
Emeline, dt Oscar; m 1909 Edward W. UNDERHILL

LATTING
Ethelinda, dt Joseph & Mary; m 1756 William FROST; m 2d Jacob VALENTINE (Frost Gen.)
George & Emily
Ch: Joseph H. d 9-30-1868 ae 1y 3m 14d (Beth. Stones)
Henry m Julia ----- d 10-27-1893 ae 60y 7m 3d
Ch: Deborah Jane d 8-29-1861 ae 2y 11m 24d
Charles G. d 12-25-1869 ae 19y 6m 22d
Susannah d 8-27-1868 ae 27y 7m 20d
(Beth. Stones)
Wm. H. d 11-7-1871 ae 29y 3m 28d; m Ella T. ----- d 4-15-1871 ae 26y 10m 19d
Ch: Amy d 4-1-1870 ae 2m
Attell d 12-14-1874 ae 7y 11m
(Beth. Stones)

LAURIE
Annie, dt Wm. W. & Frances F.; m 1895 Charles P. VALENTINE
Margaret J., dt Wm. W. & Frances F.; m 1893 William H. SEAMAN
William W., s Patrick & Mary, b 8-20-1825 d 1-21-1893 (Jericho Stone); m 3-29-1866 Frances F. SEAMAN, dt David & Ann Maria, b 4-12-1838 d 2-19-1893 (Jericho Stone)
Ch: Margaret J. b 11-14-1869; m Wm. H. SEAMAN
Annie b 2-20-1871; m Chas. P. VALENTINE
(1 other dt)
(Seaman Gen.)

LAWRENCE
Abraham B. b 9-28-1814 d 7-22-1886; m Martha ----- b 11-1-1813 d 6-8-1889
(Beth. Stones)
Jarvis W. m Antoinette ----- d 9-26-1888 ae 35y 11m 14d (Beth. Stones)

LAYTON
Albert & Sarah A.
Ch: Baby d 10-22-1881 ae 2y 8m 29d
Davie d 8-8-1875 ae 5y 1m 8d
(Beth. Stones)
Elbert m Harriet ----- d 12-3-1877 ae 55y 10m 25d
Ch: Henrietta d 8-20-1849 ae 6m 11d
(Beth. Stones)
Willet & Hannah
Ch: Maria d 11-8-1850 ae 1y 1m 1d
(Beth. Stones)

LEE
George W. m 10-25-1869 at Jerusalem Margaret C. EMIGH, dt Adam & Ann, b Jerusalem 3-10-1850
Luther B., s Frederick & Eugenia, Jerusalem; m 12-2-1861 at Andrew Seaman's, Jerusalem, Elizabeth S. EMIGH, dt Adam & Ann, b Jerusalem 3-29-1844

LEFFERTS
Samuel & Anna
Anna recrq 4-20-1815; Anna gct N. Y. 8-19-1819

LEWIS
Edward m Margaret LONGSTREET
Ch: Robert W.
Noedore (?)
all recrq 4-17-1938
Ruth Mary, dt Albert & Ruth, b 4-22-1917; m 1938 James Christian HILL

LOINES
Anne rec in mbrp at Creek 1-18-1816
James, s William & Sarah, N.Y.C.; m 1-27-1791 at Jericho Phebe WRIGHT, dt John & Phebe, O.B.
cf N. Y. (clear); Phebe rocf N. Y. 12-15-1791
Simeon, s John & Phebe, Wby; m 10-29-1807 at Jericho, Martha WILLITS, dt Richard & Abigail, dec, Jericho
Martha gct Wby 1-19-1809
Stephen, s John & Phebe, Wby; m 5-23-1810 at Beth., Sybil POWELL, dt Jonah & Sybil
Ch: John
Jonas
cf Wby (clear); Sybil gct Wby 11-15-1810; Sybil gct N. Y. with two ch 1----1828

LONGSTREET
Margaret m Edward LEWIS

LYONS
Bessie, dt George & Elizabeth, b 11-8-1898 d 12-27-1901 (Jericho Stone)

McALLISTER
Henry Jr., s Henry & Eliz. (Croper) (or Cooper) Colo. Springs; m 6-24-1896 at Sarah M.

McALLISTER, Henry Jr., continued
Ketcham's, Phebe H. KETCHAM, dt Isaac S., dec, & Sarah (Mann), Jericho, b 1-13-1872 Jericho

McGONIGAL
Nancy d 2-12-1904 ae 76y (Jericho Stone)

McGREGOR
Peter m Harriet HICKS, dt Smith & Phebe, b 8-3-1845 Beth; her name "discontinued"

McVEIGH
----- & -----
Ch: Josie d 4-11-1882 ae 16y 11m
Frankie d 4-10-1869 ae 11m 21d
Hattie b 10-15-1876 d 4-4-1887
(Beth. Stones)

MANN
Sarah, dt John & Phebe, b 2-22-1832; m 1867 Isaac S. KETCHAM

MARBLE
John B. d 10-5-1889 ae 41y 4m 5d (Beth. Stone)

MARSHALL
John Jr. m Cora ROBBINS, dt Walter & Sarah E., b 7-12-1880
Cora resigned 1909

MAXSON
John m Catharine W. ----- d 3-9-1886 ae 61y 1m 23d

MERRITT
Ann, dt John, gct N. Y. 11-17-1796; she returned before it was rec; ct N. Y. 7-19-1798, she being young
Benjamin A., s John C. & Phebe, b Beth. 1-18-1841 d 3-23-1902; m Hannah WHITE
Elizabeth, dt Jesse & Mary; m 1817 Arden SEAMAN
Elizabeth, dt Jesse & Mary, gct Wby 10-19-1838
James & Sarah
both gct N. Y. 6-19-1794
Jesse, s Nathaniel & Anna, Beth., b 2-20-1767 d 3-30-1843 ae 75y; m 1789 at Beth. Mary CORNELIUS, dt John & Mary (Powell), b 1-31-1767 d 11-9-1840 ae 73y
Ch: John C. b 7-3-1796
Elizabeth
Mary Ann
left at liberty to rem to N. Y. with fam 2-19-1795, but did not go; ch, John & Elizabeth in N.P. School with minute to be furnished them 9-18-1806; two more placed there 3-21-1811
Jesse, s John C. & Phebe, Beth., b 9-20-1839 d 4-20-1903; m Pauline WILLIS, dt Charles & Abigail (m 10-17-1888 at Manorville)
Ch: Jesse b 9-4-1889
Phebe A. b 11-2-1891
Marjory Mae b 12-9-1892
Pauline W. recrq 5-16-1895
Jesse, s Jesse & Pauline, b 9-4-1889; m 4-3-1918 at 535 - 2nd St., Bkn., Mabel WITTE
Ch: Jane b 2-13-1920
Jessica b 1-2-1824
Mabel recrq 8-16-1925
John (prob) m Phebe WEEKS
John & Phebe & their sister, Dorothy WEEKS, young, & under their tuition, gct N. Y. 4-18-1793
John C., s Jesse & Mary, Beth., b 7-3-1796 Beth. d 2-26-1891 (Beth. Stone); m before 6-18-1835 Phebe H. ALBERTSON, dt Benj. & Sarah, b 7-13-1806 d 6-14-1883 ae 76y (mo)
Ch: Mary C. b 2-28-1836 d 10-14-1850
Jesse b 9-20-1839
Benjamin A. b 1-18-1841
John b 5-1-1844 (8-1-1844 in Register)
ret mbrp 8-20-1835
John C. Jr., s John C. & Phebe H., Beth., b Beth. 8-1-1844 d 11-29-1920; m 10-13-1883 at Jerusalem, Elizabeth S. HICKS, dt Wm. S. & Letitia, b 7-31-1854
Ch: John W. b 1-25-1887
Violet A. b 2-17-1889
Elizabeth recrq 8-16-1925
John W., s John C. & Elizabeth S., b 1-25-1887 d 8-8-1930; m 6-26-1911 Ellen QUINLAN
Ch: Evelyn Helen b 9-2-1912
Anna b 1-2-1915
Marjorie Mae, dt Jesse & Pauline W., b 12-9-1892; m 1915 Valentine WILLIS
Mary Ann, dt Jesse & Mary; m 1826 Whitehead HICKS; m 2d 1867 Robert SEAMAN
Phebe Alice, dt Jesse & Pauline W.; m 1924 C. Victor WILSON
Violet A., dt John C. & Elizabeth H.; m 1916 Gerard Lester EASTMAN

MITCHELL
Myron Colyer, s Wm. H. & Mary L., Seacliff; m 10-5-1929 at bride's parents, Alice J. UNDERHILL, dt Samuel S. Jr. & Carrie Jr., Jericho b 10-25-1901
recrq 9-18-1921

MOLLINEUX
Jesse, Jericho, s Horsman & Sarah, Westchester Co.; m 11-22-1798 at Jericho Phebe ACKERSON, dt Henry & Phebe, dec, N.Y.C.
Ch: Henry
Sarah
Jesse rocf Pur. 12-17-1795; Phebe recrq 8----1795; ct Pur. 3-16-1797 (clear); cf Pur. 2-15-1798; ct N.Y. with fam 5-21-1801

MONROE
David S. d 12-4-1873 ae 65y (Beth. Stone)

MOORE
Alfred H., s Alfred & Charlotte, Lagrange Co.;

MOORE, Alfred H., continued
m 7-24-1868 at Jacob Willets', Phebe P. WILLETS, dt Jacob & Abbie, O.B.
Lydia, dt Alfred & Charlotte; m 1850 Daniel WILLETS

MOSHER
Alvate(?) m Abbie BRACKETT, dt Charles & Abbie, b 10-8-1857 Indian Valley, Calif. d 11-5-1931 at Weeks' Mills, Me.
Abbie recrq 5-16-1926

MOTT
Andrew V. b 2-17-1799 d 10-19-1884 (Jericho Stone)
Benjamin, s Samuel & Hannah, Beth., d 3-25-1833 ae 81y; m Rachel WHITSON, dt John & Martha, d 3-25-1835 ae 77y
Ch: Elizabeth d 3-13-1867 ae 73y
Benjamin recrq 10-20-1808
Charity d 2-6-1861 ae 66y 11m 6d (perhaps mother of Jacob who d 1856, as stones appear to be adjacent)
Charity Ann b 10-21-1856 d 5-15-1866 (unidentified stone, Beth.)
Charles b 11-19-1823 d 6-19-1884; m Mary Jane ----- (Beth. Stones)
Elizabeth recrq 7-16-1818
Elizabeth, dt Jacob & Mary KIRBY, b 6-21-1814; mo before 1-28-1836 & ret mbrp; ct Wby 7-19-1737
Grace recrq 12-15-1910
Hannah, dt Benjamin & Rachel, Beth., recrq 2-19-1824; d 5-15-1825 ae 48y
Jackson m Mary Ann ----- d 4-1-1875 ae 45y 3m 2d (Beth. Stones)
Jacob d 2-11-1856 ae 25y 6d (See Charity) (Beth. Stone)
Jarvis d 4-22-1884 ae 61y 1d; m Susan ----- d 7-23-1873 ae 44y 11m 12d
Ch: Mary Ann d ae 2y 3m
(Beth. Stones)
Martha, dt Benjamin & Rachel; m Joseph BEDELL
Phebe, dt John & Mary; m 1794 Samuel BISHOP
Phebe, Beth., d 11-22-1880 ae 96y
Rachel, dt Benj. & Rachel; m ----- POWELL
Rachel recrq 10-20-1808
Ruth b 2-18-1823 d 8-28-1888 (Beth. Stone)
Samuel & Emily
Ch: Ann Maria d 1-2-1856 ae 4y 1m 3d
Anna M. d 7-4-1860 ae 2y 3m 14d
(Beth. Stones)
Stephen & Sarah
Ch: Mary F.
Lydia P.
Valentine
cf Wby for all 12-10-1830
Susannah d 1-5-1858 ae 76y 10m (Beth. Stone)
Susannah m Whitson JARVIS
Valentine gct N. Y. 9-16-1851 (clear); ct N. Y. 3-18-1852
Whitson d 5-17-1860 ae 82y 5m (Beth. Stone)

MURPHY
William d 10-5-1881 ae 44; m Martha -----
Ch: Georgie d 9-10-1878
Jamie d 9-10-1878
William Henry d 3-12-1862 ae 1y 11m 23d
(Beth. Stones)

NEALE
Joseph d 9-12-1875 ae 71y 9m 12d (Beth. Stone)

NEWMAN
Silas recrq 5-19-1791; complained of for non-attendance 1808; care deferred 5-19-1808; cert sent to N. Y. 8-18-1814; unwilling to rec it, returned 4-20-1815

NICOLS
Mary, dt Benjamin, Smithtown; m ----- HARNED
Mary d 4-11-1831 ae 70y (perhaps Jacob Harned)

NOSTRAND
Fannie recrq 5-21-1835
Hewlett m Sarah P. ----- d 2-18-1933
Sarah P. recrq 5-20-1897
Jemima's ack rec 4-15-1830
John R. d 9-1-1884 ae 79y 2m 9d; m Ann SMITH d 1-31-1893 ae 89y (Beth. Stones)
Rachel (form Bedell) dis mo 9-16-1790
Susannah recrq 4-17-1817

OAKES
Stella H. recrq 10-15-1922

OAKLEY
Elizabeth m James HAWXHURST
Henry, Half Way Hollow Hill; m 4-28-1779 Hannah SEAMAN, dt Giles & Latitia, b 1747 d 9-10-1826 ae 81y (b 1745?)
(Seaman Gen.)
Latitia m 1805 ----- KETCHAM (mo)
Mary m 1802 ----- SNEDEKER
Nathaniel, Beth., recrq 9-16-1790; ct Wby 3-15-1798

OGDEN
Gilbert recrq 12-18-1794; ct N.Y. 5-21-1795
Mary (form Chichester) recrq 6-21-1792; dis mo 5-19-1796

PARSONS
James m Mary BURLING b 1737
Ch: John b 1767
James b 1772
Samuel b 1774
(Bibles)
James, Jericho, b 4 Mo (June) 17, 1736; m 2d 1780 Jane WILLIS, dt Samuel & Mary, b 11 Mo (Jan) 7, 1741/42 d 11-7-1825 ae 84y

PEARSALL
Amy, dt Thomas & Ann, rocf N. Y. 3-17-1790 (clear)
Ann m 1796 ----- ALLEN (mo)

PEARSALL, continued
Charles W. gct N. Y. 10-15-1818 (apprentice)
Elizabeth m 1793 ----- PERKINS (mo)
Hannah, dt John & Mary; m 1794 Jacob POWELL
John, Huntington, & Mary
Ch: John m 1794 Hannah POWELL
John & s, John, with their fam, rqct Little Egg Harbor 1799, deferred 1-15-1801; John & Mary gct Coeymans 6-18-1807
John, s John & Mary, Huntington; m 1-22-1794 at Beth., Hannah POWELL, dt Samuel & Mary, O.B.
Ch: Samuel
Andries
Mary
Elijah
Kezia
ct Little Egg Harbor with 2 ch 12-18-1800; cf Little Egg Harbor for parents & 4 ch 9-20-1804; John & Hannah & 5 ch gct Coeymans 6-18-1807
Phebe, dt Rowland & Anne; m 1791 John THOMPSON
Rachel, dt Thomas & Ann, b 6 Mo (Aug) 31, 1745; m 1785 Samuel WILLIS
Robert, s Thomas, Flushing, rocf N. Y. 2-21-1793; ct N.Y. 12-19-1793, returned to his father after apprenticeship
Rowland, prospect of rem to N.Y. with fam 1795
Thomas gct N.Y. 8-19-1802
Wait & Hannah (mo)
Ch: Amy
Rowland
Ann
Henry
Jane
Elizabeth
dis mo 3-21-1793; Hannah recrq 6-16-1796; ch recrq of parents 3-16-1797; Wait gct Wby 4-17-1806 (with fam)
William & Elizabeth
Ch: Samuel
Amy
Richard
ct N.Y. 7-19-1792
----- & Rachel
Ch: Mary
Robert
cf Flushing with 4 ch 7-17-1817; ct N.Y. with Mary & Robert 8-19-1819

PERKINS
Elizabeth (form Pearsall) dis mo 6-20-1793

PERRY
Lydia P. gct N.Y. 3-18-1852 (settled there with her h)

PETERS
Clayton Ames m 12-21-1891 in Pa. Mary K. McCREARY, dt Thos. Amos & Sarah Ann, b 2-23-1863 Adams Co., Pa.
Ch: Marion b 3-30-1900; m John M. WOOD
Mary recrq 9-17-1922
Marion, dt Clayton A. & Mary K., b 3-30-1900; m 1923 John M. WOOD
Elizabeth, dt Daniel & Hannah TRAVERS, d 8-19-1838

PILKINGTON
Sarah d 12-31-1887 ae 69y (Beth. Stone)

PINKHAM
Libni, s Ebenezer & Eliz., Washington Co.; m 5-4-1797 at Jericho Sarah POWELL, dt Zebulon & Anne, dec
Libni, who had come from N.P. several years ago under a minute of N.P. desiring rem to Flushing; N.P. is notified of his good life & conversation, so he had cf N.P.; Sarah recrq 6-20-1793; Sarah gct N.Y. 4-19-1798

PLUMMER
David N. & Sarah
Ch: Albert d 6-19-1880 ae 40y 7m 27d (Beth. Stones)
Elizabeth d 11-22-1867 ae 72y 11m 14d (Beth. Stone)
John, s Enoch & Abigail, Wby, b 2-20-1784 d 4-17-1865 ae 81y 2m (Beth. Stone); m 1-31-1816 at Beth., Martha POWELL, dt Jonas & Sybil, b 11-14-1779 d 4-10-1843 ae 64y 5m Beth.
Ch: Mary b 11- 6-1816 d 11- 9-1816
Mary P. b 1-28-1818
Abigail b 8-15-1819
John Jr b 12-29-1822
cf Wby (clear); John rocf Wby 5-16-1816 (rem cert)
John m 2d 9-19-1850 Elizabeth DODGE, dt John & Hannah, dec, d 2-17-1886 ae 88y
John J., s John & Martha, b 12-29-1822 d 11-22-1902
Mary P., dt John & Martha, b 1-28-1818; m 1839 Richard W. TITUS

POOLE
Charles D. b 8-29-1825 d 8-20-1873 (Jericho Stone)
John b 1-31-1850 d 2-1-1898 ae 48y (Jericho Stone)

POST
Alanson m Martha ----- d 10-3-1886 ae 60y 4m 5d (Beth. Stone)
Albert S. d 4-9-1859 ae 12y 8m 6d (Beth. Stone)
Amy (form Kirby) dis mo 12-18-1828; ack mo 4-16-1829 & Scipio informed
Benjamin recrq 1-16-1794; dis mo 1-18-1798; referred to Coeymans; ct Coeymans 12-20-1804
Caroline, dt James & Phebe, b 6-25-1826; m 1847 Daniel UNDERHILL
Catharine M., dt Joseph & Mary W.; m 1865 Samuel WILLIS
Edmund & Catharine
Ch: Lydia

POST, Edmund & Catharine, continued
Ch: Phebe
Edmund
ct Wby with fam 5-19-1796
Elisha, s Michael & Eliz., d 2-21-1845 ae 79y; m Sarah ----- d 12-15-1890 ae 62y 11m 15d (Beth Stone)
Ch: Mary E. d 5-8-1856 ae 11m 13d
Elisha recrq 7-21-1844
Elizabeth d 1-23-1812 in 85th yr
Esther L., dt James & Phebe W., b 10-17-1829; m 1867 Solomon JACKSON
Evie d 6-24-1897 ae 6y 6m 2d (unidentified stone, Beth.)
George d 9-18-1857 ae 54y (Beth. Stone)
Isaac, s Edmund & Catharine, Wby; m 2-1-1821 at Jericho, Hannah KIRBY, dt Jacob & Mary, O.B.
Hannah gct Wby 11-15-1821
James, s Henry & Mary, Wby; m 5-23-1811 at Jericho, Phebe WILLIS, dt Samuel & Rachel, Jericho
Phebe gct Wby 2-20-1812
Jane rocf Wby 12-17-1829
Joseph, s Edmund & Catharine, Wby; m 9-25-1828 at Jericho, Mary W. ROBBINS, dt Willet & Esther, Jericho
cert of clear; Mary W. gct Wby 3-18-1830
Mary, dt John & Phebe, b 11-11-1756; m Wait WILLITS
Mary rocf Saratoga 6-17-1802; ct Coeymans 7-16-1807
Micah, s John & Phebe; m 1761 Elizabeth POWELL, dt Thomas & Abigail
Ch: Susannah m Dan'l NOSTRAND
Amy m Caleb SAXTON
(Bibles)
Micah m 2nd before 7-17-1794 ----- (mo)
dis mo & bearing arms 11-20-1794
Phebe, dt Edmund & Catharine; m 1813 Henry WILLIS
Ruth m 1797 Isaac POWELL Jr.
Seaman d 3-11-1873 ae 84y 5m; m Hannah ----- d 5-14-1859 ae 65y
Ch: George d 1-1-1872 ae 39y 3m
Seaman m 2d Mary Ella DURYEA, dt Edgar H. & Mary J., d 6-5-1876 ae 23y 6m 15d (Beth. Stones)
Smith, Beth., d 10-16-1876 ae 82y 24d; m Elizabeth (SMITH in record) d 3-7-1863 ae 58y 10m 16d (Beth. Stone)
Susannah, dt Micah & Elizabeth; m Daniel NOSTRAND

POTTER
Asa, s Abel & Anna, dec, Scipio; m 11-26-1812 at Jericho, Ruth ALDRICH, dt Stephen & Mary, dec
cf Scipio (clear); Ruth gct Scipio 2-18-1813

POWELL
Abraham, s Robert & Mary, Beth.; m 8-5-1835
Eliza SEAMAN, dt Noah & Martha
Eliza rpd mo but ret mbrp; Eliza gct N.Y. 7-20-1837
Alice d 11-26-1857 ae 82y 6m 17d (Beth. Stone)
Amy, dt John & Margaret, b 1718; m 1745 Daniel WILLETS
Andrew, s Henry & Ruth; m Jane DURYEA b 11-16-1810 d 10-18-1882 (Beth. Stone)
Ansel b 4-10-1813 d 3-25-1862 ae 48y 11m 5d; m Harriet -----
Ch: William K. d 1-23-1872 ae 17y 6m 13d
Josephine b 6-17-1849 d 9-26-1897
Benjamin, s Joshua & Phebe, b 8-13-1760; m before 2-16-1791 Elsie SMITH (mo)
dis 2-16-1792
Caroline, dt Richard S. & Sarah T.; m 1857 James H. REED
Catharine recrq 6-15-1797; ct Wby 7-16-1812
Charles d 7-19-1870 ae 44y 11m 17d (Beth. Stone has 7-19-1860 ae 44y 5m 25d); m Mary E. ----- d 4-5-1874 ae 40y 6m 1d
Ch: Deborah Jane d 2-1-1864 ae 1y 3m 13d
Mary Emma d 2-18-1864 ae 3y 23d
Louisa d 9-26-1869 ae 5m 6d
(Beth. Stones)
Charles H. d 9-18-1859 ae 19y 7m 27d (unidentified stone, Beth.)
Charles L. d 7-18-1871 ae 86y 6m 17d (Beth. Stone)
Charles S. & Antoinette
Ch: Phebe d 2-4-1866 ae 2y 3m 17d
Charles W. d 2-20-1890 ae 40y 9m 5d; m Emily -----
Ch: Jennie d 7-3-1892 ae 2m 29d
(Beth. Stone)
Emmeline, dt James & Phebe, recrq; d 1-3-1903
Esther, dt Richard & Phebe; m ----- WILLETS
Esther d 9-6-1825 ae 53y
George m Sarah BEDELL d 12-9-1865 ae 77y 1m 27d (Beth. Stone); (mo)
Sarah dis 3-20-1823
George F. & Elsie
Ch: E. Georgiana d 1-29-1888 ae 4y 7m
(Beth. Stone)
Green m Sarah ----- d 12-9-1865 ae 77y 1m 17d (wd of the late Green Powell) (Beth. Stone)
Hannah, dt Samuel & Mary; m 1794 John PEARSALL
Hannah W., dt Richard S. & Sarah T.; m 1853 Robert R. CARPENTER
Hannah W. d 5-11-1863 ae 9y 7m 4d (Beth. Stone)
Harriet d 11-8-1859 ae 8m (unidentified stone, Wby)
Henry, (prob) s Richard & Phebe; m 12-19-1805 Ruth WOOD (Henry b 1782)
Ch: Andrew m Jane DURYEA
Esther m Jesse BRYANT
Eliza m Wait POWELL
dis 6-16-1803
Isaac Jr, s Thomas & Martha; m 11-18-1797 Ruth POST (mo)
dis 12----1797
Isaac d 4-13-1864 ae 40y 5m 17d (Beth. Stone)
Jacob, s Samuel & Mary, O.B.; m 1-22-1794 at

POWELL, Jacob, continued
Beth., Hannah PEARSALL, dt John & Mary, Huntington
Ch: Israel
Samuel
Abigail
John
Jacob & fam gct N.Y. 3-21-1805
James dis 6-21-1804
James, s John & Ruth d 9-19-1844 ae 37y 3m 16d; m Amelia ----- d 9-22-1875 ae 61y 11m 22d (Beth. Stones)
John, s Richard & Phebe, Beth., d 1-6-1851 ae 68y; m -----
Ch: (perhaps) John Jr. b 10-31-1843 d 12-9-1886 (Beth. Stone)
dis 2-18-1802; rst 9-19-1816
John Jr. b 2-20-1850 d 5-8-1891
Jonah & Rachel
Ch: Rachel m Smith STYMUS
Jonah, s Thomas & Martha, O.B. & Beth., d 1-7-1867 ae 65y 5m 19d; m 1-18-1851 at Selah Hubbs', Mary HUBBS, dt Selah & Hannah, d 10-21-1876 ae 70y 6m
Jonah recrq 4-20-1843
(Beth. Stones)
Jonas, s Daniel & Mary, Beth., d 5-21-1815 ae 69y; m Sybil POWELL, dt Isaac & Martha
Ch: Mary d 5-20-1854 ae 10y
Sybil m 1810 Step. LOINES
Joshua d 1-25-1857 ae 49y 4m 8d; m Fannie -----
Ch: Adaline d 4-20-1857 ae 6y 7m 14d
(Beth. Stones)
Kezia, dt Samuel & Mary; m 1794 John DARBY
Lessie d 6-27-1887 (unidentified stone, Beth.)
Libbie W. d 8-1-1875 (unidentified stone, Beth.)
Martha, dt Jonas & Sybil; m 1816 John PLUMMER
Mary Alice d 5-24-1892 ae 28d (unidentified stone, Beth.)
Phebe, dt Richard S. & Sarah; m 1852 Harrison YOUNG
Phebe d 9-1-1863 ae 78y (Beth. Stone)
Phebe d 6-24-1882 ae 50y 11m 6d (Beth. Stone)
Phebe Emma d 8-1-1864 ae 19y 6d (unidentified stone, Beth.)
Prudence, Beth.
Rachel, dt Benjamin & Rachel MOTT, d 8-10-1848; dis mo 8-21-1800
Rachel, dt Jonah & Rachel; m Smith STYMUS
Richard, s Joshua & Phebe, Beth., b 11-2-1757 d 6-26-1842 ae 84y; m 1781 Jemima PRATT, dt Jonathan, d 3-9-1836 ae near 80y
Jemima recrq 11-18-1790
(Bibles)
Richard Jr. (called Richard 3d), (prob) s Thomas & Sarah; m Martha JACKSON
dis by Wby, now rst 12-15-1790; dis 8-18-1796; ack accepted 10-16-1796; dis 4-20-1809
Richard P. recrq 8-15-1844
Richard S., s Benj. & Alice, Beth., d 8-11-1862 ae 66y 3m 20d (Beth. Stone); m Sarah UNDERHILL, b 4-1-1803 Beth. d 11-16-1888 ae 85y 7m 16d (Beth. Stone)
Ch: Alice b 12-28-1829 d 7-1-1912
Hannah b 11-22-1834
Walter b 1-21-1837
Caroline b 2-15-1839
Pamelia C. b 2-15-1841 d 1914
Thomas U.
Phebe m Harrison YOUNG
Richard recrq 9-21-1815; ct Pur. 12-21-1826 (clear)
Ruth, Beth., recrq 12-18-1806; d 9-13-1816 ae 55y
Ruth Alice, dt Walter & Lucy G., b 12-15-1886; m 1909 Clifford Burr WHITE
Samuel, s Thomas & Sarah; gct Coeymans 7-17-1806 (clear)
Sarah, dt Willets & Ruth, Beth., d 12-10-1865 ae 78y
Sarah, dt Zebulon & Ann; m 1797 Libni PINKHAM
Sybil, dt Jonah & Sibbel; m 1810 Stephen LOINES
Sybil, dt Isaac & Martha; m Jonas POWELL
Thomas, s Isaac & Martha, b 1752; m 6-1-1774 Martha TITUS, dt James & Anne, d 11-23-1813 (Beth. Stone)
Ch: Isaac m Ruth POST
John m Freelove VALENTINE
Anne
Jonah m Abigail STILLWELL
Phineas
Sarah
Jarvis
(Bibles)
Thomas U., s Richard S. & Sarah (Underhill), b 1832 d 6-6-1902; m Hannah Ann KETCHAM
Wait b 1-30-1805 d 2-20-1872 ae 67y 15d (Beth. Stone)
Walter b 11-6-1792 d 1-30-1853; m Maria ----- b 10-3-1797 d 5-30-1879
(Beth. Stone)
Walter, s Richard S. & Sarah T., Beth., b 1-21-1837 d 7-23-1908; m Lucy G. HARNED d 7-29-1930
Ch: Sarah T. b 5-4-1883
Ruth Alice b 12-15-1886
ch recrq of parents 2----1895; Lucy recrq 10-17-1895
Wellington, s Charles S. & Antoinette, b Farmingdale 2-16-1862 d 8-21-1933; m 8-16-1888 at Babylon, Addie L. PURDY
Wellington recrq 11-20-1927
Whitson & Phebe A.
Ch: Jarvis W. b 2-8-1856 d 1-12-1879 ae 22y 11m 4d
Phebe b 3-4-1858 d 7-23-1782
Artie b 7-3-1872 d 2-23-1877
Willets & Catharine
Catharine gct Wby 8-20-1812
Willet d 2-19-1860 ae 21y 10m 5d (Beth. Stone)
Willets b 8-15-1820 d 7-23-1863; m Mary Jane ----- b 3-14-1823 d 5-8-1891
Ch: Willie d 1-19-1864 ae 6m
Jamie d 1-12-1864 ae 4y 7m 2d
(Beth. Stones)

PRATT
Jemima, dt Jonathan; m 1781 Richard POWELL

PRINCE
George M. m 10-4-1888 Josephine JACKSON, dt Solomon S. & Annie, b 6-28-1859 d 3-31-1890 bur Jericho

PRIOR
John, Jericho & Elizabeth
Ch: Philomon F.
Phebe W. b 1-3-1824
John Augustus
John & Elizabeth rocf Wby 2-15-1821; ct N. Y. for John & Elizabeth with 3 ch 7-20-1826

PROBASCO
Jane, dt Abraham & Charity; m (prob) Joseph HORTON

PURDY
Addie L. m 1888 Wellington POWELL

PUTNAM
Julia (form Jackson) d 6-4-1895 ae 55y (Jericho Stone)

QUINLAN
Ellen m 1911 John W. MERRITT

REED
James H. m 11-17-1857 Caroline POWELL, dt Richard S. & Sarah T., d 7-14-1865 ae 26y 5m (Beth. Stone)

REMSEN
Rhyneer m Martha CONKLIN, dt Stephen & Phebe
Martha roc 11-20-1806; Martha m 2d 1821 Daniel DOWNING

RING
James (or King) rocf New Castle, Eng. to Nova Scotia, but as he rem thence, & no MM there, cert accepted here 8-16-1792; James, having rem, ct N.P. 8-15-1793 (clear)

ROBBINS
Anna W., dt Samuel & Phebe, d 10-16-1868 ae 30y 4m 12d (Beth. Stone)
Annie H., dt Walter & Sarah E., b 4-17-1877; m Thomas H. RUSHMORE
Benjamin gct Wby 4-16-1795; cf Wby 4-19-1798
Caroline, dt Matthew F. & Hannah S.; m 1865 Sidney U. JACKSON
Carrie J., dt Walter & Sarah E., b 7-6-1873; m 1894 Wm. G. UNDERHILL
Charles W. d 4-13-1861 ae 12y 13d (Jericho Stone)
Cora S., dt Walter & Sarah E., b 7-12-1880; m John MARSHALL Jr
Cornelia, dt Edward & Rachel W., b 10-1-1854; m 1883 Daniel DURYEA
Edward, s Willet & Esther, Jericho, b 8----1813 d 1-13-1892 ae 79y; m 1836 at Pur. Rachel W. (or T.) TITUS, d 10-18-1888 ae 71y
Ch: Silas T. b 9-13-1837 Jericho
William H. b 8-26-1841 Jericho d 1-20-1917
Rowland b 6-26-1843 Jericho d 1-17-1814
Esther b 2-8-1839 Jericho d 8-31-1839
Edwin b 12-14-1846 Woodbury d 3-19-1904
Augustus W. b 5-25-1840 Woodbury d 7-17-1840
Franklin M. b 9-19-1850 Woodbury d N.Y. 5-23-1882
Sarah T. b 12-15-1852 Woodbury d 2-27-1862
Cornelia b 10-1-1854 Woodbury
Phebe T. b 9-28-1856 Woodbury d 10-6-1874
Willet S. b 7----1863 Woodbury d 7----1863
ct Wby 9-15-1836 (clear)
Edward G., s John & Sarah, b 9-3-1816 d 7-17-1847 ae 30y 11m 20d; m Martha C. WHITSON d 5-12-1844 ae 27y 9d
(Beth. Stones & Bibles)
Elizabeth, dt Jacob & Abigail, b 8-20-1788; m 1807 Obadiah WILLITS
Elizabeth, dt Samuel & Phebe; m Willet P. WHITSON
Esther P., dt William & Elizabeth; m John P. HUBBS
Eugene F., s Stephen & Esther, b 9-7-1859; m 4-13-1887 at Glen Head, L.I., Ella ALBERTSON, dt Richard & Phebe, b 4-10-1863
Ch: (See Jackson)
Eugene dropped from mbrp 10-21-1892; Ella m 2d Jacob W. JACKSON & ch took that name
J. W. m Sally Ann BAUCKER b 12-9-1845 d 6-6-1904
(Jericho Stone)
Julia, dt Stephen & Esther G., b 12-17-1861; m 1888 George SCHRYVER
Mary, dt Stephen & Miriam; m 1790 Robert WILLETS
Mary, dt Willet & Esther; m 1828 Joseph POST
Mary, dt Stephen & Esther G., b 12-17-1861; m 1884 Jacob SMITH
Matthew F., s Willet & Esther, b 4-30-1815 d 5-22-1893 ae 78y bur Jericho; m 9-28-1837 at Jericho, Hannah SEAMAN, dt Robert & Sarah, b 4-14-1817 d 7-12-1900 ae 83y bur Jericho
Ch: Caroline b 12-13-1841
Walter b 2-18-1849
Scudder, Beth., recrq 1-20-1791; dis attending M.E. Mtg 9-18-1806; rst 7-20-1820; dis 3-18-1830 for separating from Friends
Stephen, s Jeremiah & Hannah (Carr), b 12 Mo (Feb) 26, 1750/51 d 5-25-1813; m Miriam SEAMAN, dt Samuel & Martha, d 1826 ae 74y
Ch: Willet b 12-11-1781; m Esther SEAMAN
Mary
dis mo before 1-21-1813; Willet & Mary recrq of Miriam 3-16-1797
(Bibles)
Stephen, s Willet & Esther, Jericho, b 7-5-1821 d 4-4-1883 ae 61y bur Jericho; m 8-1-1853 Esther G. CARPENTER, dt Ferris &

ROBBINS, Stephen & Esther G., continued
Julia, b 9-7-1829 d 3-8-1901
Ch: Eugene F. b 9-7-1859
Mary b 12-17-1861
Julia b 12-17-1861
Valentine, s Samuel & Harriet, d 5-6-1873 ae 69y 6m (Jericho Stone)
Walter, s Matthew F. & Hannah S., Jericho, b 2-18-1849 d 1-7-1886 ae 36y; m 10-11-1871 at Rich. C. Hubbs, Sarah E. HUBBS, dt Richard C. & Hannah C., b 8-14-1846 Jericho d 1-30-1933
Ch: Carrie J. b 7-6-1873
Annie H. b 4-17-1877
Cora S. b 7-12-1880
Sarah E. recrq
Willet, Merchant, N.Y.C., s Stephen & Miriam, Jericho, b 12-11-1781 d 4-11-1861 ae 79y; m 12-26-1805 at Jericho Esther SEAMAN, dt Williams, dec, & Mary, d 11-30-1863 ae 84y 8m
Ch: Mary
Wm. J.
Edward
Matthew F.
Willet S. b 4-8-1818 d 3-12-1856 (Stone 8-4-1819 d 3-12-1855)
Stephen b 7-5-1821
Willet gct N.Y. 5-21-1801; Esther gct N.Y. 7-17-1806; parents & 4 ch rocf N.Y.
Willet, s Wm. S. & Elizabeth, N.Y.C.; m 11-23-1864 at Amy Willets', Hannah WILLETS, dt Isaac, dec, & Amy, Jericho, d 12-4-1901 ae 63y
ct N.Y. 4-20-1843
William S., s Willet & Esther, Jericho, b 1809 d 5-21-1879 ae 70y; m 3-28-1833 at Jericho Elizabeth WILLETS, dt Obadiah & Eliz., dec, b 1814 d 10-21-1873 ae 59y
ct Wby with w 7-18-1833
(Jericho Stones & Bibles)

ROGERS
Jemima m 1800 ----- DURYEA (mo)
recrq 1-19-1797
Sarah (form Willis) dis mo 4-14-1814; rst 4-23-1818; ct N.Y. 4-14-1842

RUSHMORE
Anna, dt James & Deborah; m 1810 Elkanah WOOD
Charles, s Benj. & Jemima, Cedar Swamp; m 6-2-1796 at Jericho Elizabeth WILLETS, dt Jacob & Martha, Jericho, d 3-18-1836 ae 64y at Jericho
Elizabeth rocf Wby 8-17-1797
Jacob, s James & Deborah, Half Way Hollow Hills, Huntington, d 7-21-1824 ae 56; m 7-31-1794 at Half Way Hollow Hills, Esther DINGEE, dt Arthur, d 12-23-1818
Ch: Mary
Mary placed in N.P. School 3-18-1819; Esther recrq 8-15-1793
James, Half Way Hollow Hills, b 2 Mo (Apr) 26, 1747 d 5-9-1823 ae 78y; m 1766 Deborah WHITSON, dt John & Deborah, b 2 Mo (Apr) 26, 1747
Ch: Anna m Elkanah WOOD
Jacob m Esther DINGEE
(3 other ch)
Deborah gct N.Y. 3-16-1837
(Bibles)
John gct Wby 5-20-1802 (clear)
Mary, (prob) dt Jacob & Esther; m 1824 ----- CROSSMAN (mo)
Thomas H. m in Jericho Annie H. ROBBINS, dt Walter & Sarah E., b 4-17-1877 d 6-5-1928
Townsend, s Stephen & Phebe, Wheatley; m 1-29-1824 at Jericho, Amy WILLIS, dt Samuel & Rachel, Jericho
Amy gct Wby 4-14-1825

RUSHTON
Sarah m Andrew WILLETS

ST PIER
Father d 3-3-1892
Mother d 1-27-1892

SANDS
Mary gct N.Y. 10-16-1794
Samuel Jr., Jericho, recrq 1-16-1812; gct Wby 11-17-1814 (clear)

SCHEIBLE
Elizabeth Geboren 4 May 1776 Gestorben 5 Aug 1877 (Beth. Stone)

SCHEUER
Charles P. d 1-3-1891; m Elizabeth -----
Ch: Margaret E. d 4-1-1887 in 14th yr
of Co. B. 1st Reg. N.Y. Cavalry
(Beth. Stone)

SCHRYVER
George m Julia ROBBINS, dt Stephen & Esther G., b 12-17-1861 d 12-24-1932 (m 4-18-1888 in Brooklyn)

SCOTT
Jennie d 4-18-1895 ae 23y (Jericho Stone)

SEAMAN
Albert William, s Edward H. & Martha A., both dec, b 10-3-1851; m Mary Atmore HOPKINS, dt Edwin & Mary, d 12-29-1898 (m 6-21-1881)
cf N.Y. for Mary
Albert William m 2d 2-14-1900 at Joseph Hatton's, 508 - 3d St., Bkn., Daisy Georgia HATTON, dt Dr. Joseph & Georgianna, b 1872
Albert William known as William & as Albert W. in Quaker record; Joseph & w were from Grovetown, Columbia Co., Georgia (Seaman Gen.)
Andries, s Jordan & Mary, b 7-23-1780 (or 1781) d 9-8-1825 ae 45y; m 12----1804 Sarah

SEAMAN, Andries, continued
UNDERHILL, dt Israel, b 1-7-1780 d 8-12-1864 ae 84y
Ch: Mary b 11----1806; m Townsend BAILEY
Lydia b 3-8-1812; m Jonathan G. FLEET
(Jericho Stones & Seaman Gen.)
Almy, dt Benjamin & Jane; m 1806 William D. JONES
Ann M., dt Arden & Eliz.; m 1838 Adam EMIGH
Anna, Jerusalem, recrq 8-16-1821; d 12-16-1855 ae 90y
Arden, s Zebulon & Mary, Jerusalem, d 4-2-1875 ae 80y; m 3-26-1817 at Beth., Elizabeth MERRITT, dt Jesse & Mary, d 2-3-1875 ae 82y
Ch: Ann b 2-19-1818
Mary b 2-27-1820; m Alex C. BUNKER
Edward b 3-8-1822
Caroline E. b 2-20-1829; m Wm. GARNER
Arden recrq 2-18-1813
Avis C., dt Elijah & Phebe; m 1829 James F. BIRDSALL
Benjamin recrq 4-17-1794; rpd mou, referred to Coeymans, he being resident there 4-19-1804
Caroline E., dt Arden & Elizabeth, b 2-20-1829; m 1852 William GARNER
Charlotte, dt Zeb. & Mary, b 10-31-1805; recrq 5-19-1815; d 2-20-1891 (unm) (Seaman Gen.)
David, s Williams & Mary, Jericho, b 6-12-1770 d 10-2-1843 ae 73y; m 11-24-1791 at Jericho, Sarah KIRBY, dt Willet & Hannah, b 3----1772 d 11-16-1844 ae 72y
Ch: Robert b 10-31-1792; m Sarah R. HICKS
Hannah b 6-11-1794 d 9-22-1795
Dr. William b 7-21-1796; m Caroline HICKS
Phebe b 7-26-1798; m Jas. C. HAVILAND
Lydia b 2-7-1802
Esther b 4-12-1809; m Wm. HAVILAND
(Seaman Gen.)
David b 8-10-1808 d 5-2-1881 (Jericho Stone)
Deborah, dt Solomon & Eliz.; m 1773 Samuel JACKSON
Edward H., s Ardon & Elizabeth, b 3-8-1822 d 2-12-1891; m 1-18-1848 Martha A. SEAMAN, dt Benjamin & Jemima, b 2-27-1829 d 2-9-1899
Ch: (2)
(Seaman Gen.)
Elias H., s Robert & Sarah R., dec, O.B. & Jericho, b Jericho 5-2-1826 d 10-25-1904 (1-24-1904 Jericho Stone); m 2-15-1855 at Samuel Underhill's, Jericho, Phebe UNDERHILL, dt Samuel & Mary, b 10-16-1830 d 12-23-1903
Ch: Samuel J. b 10- 9-1857
Anna b 11-13-1861
Sarah R. b 9-25-1860 d 1-15-1861
Robert b 9-28-1864
William H. b 3-12-1868
Mary D. b 5-4-1856 d 9-4-1856
James H. b 11-18-1871
Elias H. gct N.Y. 5-20-1852
Elijah, s Samuel & Mary, b 3-26-1772; m 1803 Phebe WILLETS, dt Jacob (mo)
Ch: Avis b 6-1-1806; m Jas. F. BIRDSALL
Jacob W. b 11-20-1809; m Mary B. SEAMAN
Hannah W.
Ch: John
Phebe dis mo 7-21-1803; rst 10-19-1809; 2 ch recrq of Phebe 4-15-1813; 2 ch recrq of Phebe 5-18-1820
(Seaman Gen.)
Eliza, dt Noah & Martha (Totten); m 1835 Abraham POWELL (mo)
Elizabeth, dt Thomas & Martha; m 1768 David JAMES; m 2d 1770 Townsend JONES
Elizabeth, dt Robert & Sarah; m 1839 Edward WILLIS
Elizabeth, dt Arden & Eliz.; m 1852 William GARNER
Esther, dt Williams & Mary; m 1805 Willet ROBBINS
Esther, dt David & Sarah; m 1839 William HAVILAND Jr
Gideon dis mo 4-19-1827
Hannah, dt Giles & Letitia, b 1747; m 1779 Henry OAKLEY
Hannah, dt William & Mary, b 7-24-1776; m 1794 Samuel WILLETS
Hannah, dt Robert & Sarah, b 4-14-1817; m 1837 Matthew ROBBINS
Henry, d 11-21-1887 ae 69y; m Martha -----
Ch: Elias H. d 4-22-1876 ae 20y 7m 13d
(Beth. Stones)
Jackson, (prob) s Stephen & Lucretia; m Jemima -----
Jemima rocf Wby 11-20-1817
Jacob, s Jacob & Mercy, both dec, Huntington; m 4-30-1795 at Half Way Hollow Hills, Susannah UDALL, dt Jacob & Mary VALENTINE, dec
Ch: Sarah
Charles
Sarah's 2 ch by form h recrq of mother, with full approval of Jacob 2-15-1798 (See Udall for her ch); Jacob & Sarah & ch, Sarah & Charles, gct Wby 7-16-1801
Jacob, s Thomas & Martha, Jerusalem, rocf N.Y. 3-21-1793; d 9-15-1823 ae 61y
Jacob V., s Noah & Elizabeth, b 1842 d 11-28-1877 (Seaman Gen. 11-28-1878) ae 35y; m 11-1-1863 Ruth E. SMITH, dt Edwin & Susan
Ch: (3)
(Seaman Gen.)
Jacob W., s Elijah & Phebe (Willets), b 11-20-1809 d 10-31-1879; m Mary B. SEAMAN, dt Thomas & Sarah
Ch: Samuel
Jacob recrq 7-19-1821; Jacob m his first cousin before 3-18-1841, ret mbrp; Elijah & Thomas brothers
(Seaman Gen.)
James H., s Elias H. & Phebe, Jericho, b 11-18-1871; m 10-16-1895 at Joshua Cock's, Locust Valley, Bessie BRIDGES, dt George & Sarah F., d 6-2-1902 ae 26y 10m 2d bur Jericho
James H. m 2d Florence HAVILAND
appears to have rem to Glens Falls but still a mbr in Jericho
Jane, dt Williams & Martha, b 11 Mo (Jan) 16,

SEAMAN, Jane, continued
1746/47; m 1780 David KETCHAM
Jemima, dt Jonathan & Eliz.; m 1771 Elias HICKS
Jemima, dt Samuel & Mary, Jerusalem, d 9-30-1836 ae 70y
John G., s Zebulun & Mary, b 11-20-1802; m 11-10-1835 Ann R. WALL
Ch: Henry William b 11-1-1836; m Marianna CLARK
recrq 10----1821; ct N.Y. 3-19-1829
(Seaman Gen.)
John H. d 9-8-1882 ae 49y 4m 8d (Jericho Stone)
John M. b 6-10-1825 d 4-4-1897; m Elizabeth ----- d 2-4-1898 ae 68y
Ch: Charles C. d 10-20-1865 ae 16y
(Jericho Stones)
Latitia, dt Benjamin & Jemima, b 10-6-1833; m 1853 William S. HICKS
Letitia recrq 10-17-1793
Lydia, dt David & Sarah, b 2-7-1802; gct N.Y. 6-20-1844; d 1864 (unm)
Margaret, dt Noah & Martha; m George VANDEWATER
Martha, dt Noah, recrq 9-17-1804; d Beth. 12-12-1876
Martha A., dt Benjamin & Jemima, b 2-27-1829; m 1848 Edward H. SEAMAN
Mary, dt William S. & Mary, b 3-27-1774; m 1790 Jacob KIRBY
Mary, dt Thomas & Martha, Jerusalem; m 1794 Zebulun SEAMAN
Mary recrq 11-18-1813
Mary, Jerusalem, d 10-16-1819
Mary, dt Samuel & Mary, Jerusalem, d 9-23-1849 ae 62y 6m
Mary L., dt Zebulon & Mary; m 1818 Isaac WIGHAM
Mary P., dt Arden & Elizabeth, b 2-27-1820; m 1839 Alexander C. BUNKER
Miriam, dt Samuel; m ----- ROBBINS
Miriam d 1826 ae 74y
Noah recrq 5-17-1804
Noah, s Jacob & Latitia, b 2-12-1821 d 2-27-1881 ae 60y 15d; m 2-15-1842 Elizabeth POST b 8-25-1822 d 4-6-1888 (8-13-1888 in Seaman Gen.) ae 65y 7m 12d
Ch: Nellie d 6-17-1866 ae 1y 4d (Beth. Stone)
Oliver d 8-3-1873 ae 70y 11m 1d; m Hannah ----- d 5-13-1887 ae 84y 1m 3d (Jericho Stones)
Olte, s Charles & Hannah, d 12-23-1869 ae 1y 11m 23d (Jericho Stone)
Phebe, dt Thos. & Philadelphia; m 1753 John WRIGHT
Phebe, dt David & Sarah; m 1823 James C. HAVILAND
Richard, s Giles & Latitia, Jericho, d 2-22-1834; m Sarah SMITH, dt Edmond & Deborah, d 11-9-1833 ae 64y
ct Wby 11-21-1799 (clear); Sarah rocf Wby 2-28-1800
(Seaman Gen.)
Robert, s David & Sarah, b Jericho 10-3-1792 d 10-31-1870 ae 78y bur Jericho; m 11-30-1814 Sarah R. HICKS, dt Elias & Jemima, b 10-9-1793 d 11-19-1835 ae 42y (Jericho Stone)
Ch: Phebe d young
Hannah b 4-14-1817; m M. Franklin ROBERTS
Willet b 10-27-1818 d 10-20-1821 ae 3y
Elizabeth b 6-10-1820
Elias H. b 5-2-1826
Mary H. b 6-4-1828; m Isaac WILLIS
Willet H. b 5-14-1832
(Seaman Gen.)
Robert m 2d 12-27-1838 at Jericho Abigail JONES, wd Samuel, dt Townsend & Hannah (Willis, b 1793 d 1-9-1866 ae 73y at Cedar Swamp, bur Jericho
Robert m 3d 4-18-1867 at Wm. S. Hicks', Mary Ann HICKS, dt Jesse & Mary MERRITT, both dec, b 2-1-1799 (Mary Ann wd of Whitehead)
Robert, s Elias H. & Phebe, Jericho, b 9-28-1864; m 9-12-1894 at Lydia M. Willets', Hannah WILLETS, dt Daniel, dec, & Lydia M., Jericho, b 5-11-1858 d 3-2-1896 ae 38y bur Jericho
Ch: Phebe U. b 3-2-1896
Samuel, s Samuel & Anna, d 2-19-1828 ae 90y; m Mary -----
cf Wby for Samuel & Mary (perhaps this Mary) 4-17-1806 (See Wby)
Samuel rpd mo before 4-14-1841; case dismissed 11-18-1841; ct N.Y. 1-18-1844
Samuel J., s Elias H. & Phebe, Jericho, b 10-19-1857; m 9-10-1879 at Mary V. Willets, Matilda WILLETS, dt William, dec, & Mary V., Jericho, b 12-27-1854
Ch: Mary W. b 6-4-1881
Samuel J. b 3-3-1883
Anna Louisa b 10-19-1885
Frederick W. b 6-17-1888
ct Wby 7-16-1891 for all
Willet H., s Robert & Sarah, b 5-14-1832 d 4-22 (or 21) 1902 ae 69y bur Jericho; m 6-1-1864 Mary WING, dt Daniel & Achsah (Nye), b 12-23-1839 d 10-12-1923
Willet H. killed by railroad
(Seaman Gen.)
William, s David & Sarah; m 6-23-1831 at Jericho, Caroline HICKS, dt Valentine & Abigail
William gct N.Y. 3-20-1828; cf N.Y. (clear)
Caroline gct N.Y. 10-18-1832
William H., s Elias H. & Phebe, Jericho, b 2-12-1868; m 6-2-1893 at John W. Seaman's, Bkn, Margaret J. LAURIE, dt Wm. W. & Frances, both dec, Jericho
Ch: Wm. Laurie b 7-26-1894 G.C.
Faith Frances d 10-22-1898 ae 9m
Margaret recrq 4-20-1893; ct Wby for all 12-19-1895
Zebulun, s Jordan & Mary, Jerusalem, b 1-31-1771 d 9-7-1838 ae 67y; m 12-14-1794 Mary SEAMAN, dt Thomas & Martha, d 9-19-1861
Ch: Charlotte B. b 10-20-1805 d 2-20-1891
Charlotte recrq; Zebulun recrq 4-14-1814
(Seaman Gen.)

SEARING
John S. recrq 3-19-1818; ct Wby 2-17-1820 (clear); ct Wby 7-20-1820
Phebe, dt John & Mary, b 1-6-1773; m 1795 Thomas WILLIS

SECOR
Willet, Huntington, m Hannah RENONDS, dt Justus & Eliz., d 10-29-1829 ae 39y
Ch: Obadiah W. d 10-3-1828 ae 3y
Sarah Ann
Gilbert W. b 4-18-1827
Hannah K. b 10-26-1829
parents & 2 ch rocf N.Y. (ch, Sarah Ann & Obadiah) 6-15-1826; ct N.Y. with ch 4-17-1834

SELLECK (Silleck)
Nathaniel, Beth., recrq 1-17-1793; ct Cornwell 5-21-1795

SHERMAN
Anna, dt Israel & Margaret; m 1821 Edward HALLOCK
Esther (form Jackson) dis mo 3-19-1818
Isaac & Margaret
Ch: Margaret m Jos. L. TOWNSEND
Rebecca
James
Anna
ct N.Y. 3-17-1791 (clear); Margaret rocf N.Y. 7-21-1791; Rebecca sent to N.P. School 5-19-1808; James placed in N.P. School 12-15-1808; Anna & Margaret placed there 4-16-1812
James, s Isaac & Margaret, placed as apprentice at Marlborough; ct Marl. 2-21-1811
Margaret, dt Isaac & Margaret; m 1825 Joseph L. TOWNSEND
Rebecca, dt Isaac & Margaret; m 1816 John KETCHAM
Samuel (perhaps) s Isaac & Martha, Jericho; recrq 3-18-1802; dis mo 12-19-1805

SKIDMORE
Esther, dt Joseph; m Israel KETCHAM

SMITH
Burt A. d 1-23-1884 ae 4y (Beth. Stone)
Elizabeth m 1775 Jacob DOWNING
Elsie m 1791 Benjamin POWELL
Ephraim, s Sylvanus & Jane, d 1-25-1876 ae 62y 9m 11d (Beth. Stone)
Hannah m 1804 Joseph WHITSON
Herman H. & Phebe A.
Ch: Merritt L.
cf N.Y. for all 7-18-1837
Jacob, Centre Island; m 11-18-1884 Mary ROBBINS, dt Stephen & Esther G., d 8-24-1885 ae 23y
Kitty, dt Henry; m Daniel WILLETS
Lorana recrq 2-19-1824; dis separating from Friends 5-20-1830
Morley Lyford, s Jno. L. & Emma (Parks) Hicksville; m 7-30-1932 at bride's parents, Phebe Ella UNDERHILL, dt Sam'l S. & Carrie J., b 8-2-1906
recrq 9-18-1921
Nathaniel m Phebe ----- d 3-3-1879 ae 76y 1m 4d (Beth. Stone)
Nelson b 6-14-1826 d 8-20-1874; m (prob) Marie ----- b Brake, Germany 2-20-1825 d 3-22-1880
(Stones appear to be adjacent in Beth.)
Phebe D. m Edgar DAVIS
Ruhama, dt Azariah & Phebe WATERBURY, d 12-9-1866 ae 63y
Samuel, Catskill, s Jacob & Deborah, N.Y.C., d 11-3-1872 ae 77y 8m Jericho; m 8-30-1821 Mary WILLIS, dt Thomas & Phebe, d 3-3-1888 ae 84y 3m
Samuel J., s Sylvanus & Jane, Beth., recrq 3-21-1839; ct N.Y. 9-18-1845; (perhaps same) cf N.Y. with s, William 2-17-1848; ct N.Y. for William 12-18-1851; Samuel gct N.Y. 12-18-1851; d 5-11-1867 ae 70y
Sarah, dt Edmond & Deborah; m Richard SEAMAN
Sarah d 11-9-1833 ae 64y
Waite recrq 1-21-1836; d 6-14-1899

SNEDEKER
Deborah recrq 1-17-1793
Mary (form Oakley) dis mo 6-17-1802

STILLWELL
William & Mary
recrq 6-15-1797; ct N.Y. 4-19-1798

STRATTON
Sarah m Israel HAWXHURST

STRICKLAND
Simeon rocf Wby 6-19-1806; rqct N.Y. 5-21-1807; deferred

STYMUS
Smith m Rachel POWELL, dt Jonah & Rachel, d 10-30-1862 ae 26y 6m 15d
Ch: Jonah P. d 9-7-1854 ae 2m 25d
Sarah H. d 7-23-1862 ae 2m 24d
(Beth. Stones)

SULLIVAN
Amos G., s Jacob & Margaret Ann, b 8-25-1846 at Wakefield, Md. d 12-9-1930; m 6-5-1872 in Balto. Md. Mary Victoria ----- d 8-15-1919
Jacob recrq 10-16-1927

SUYDAM
Jacobus, Jericho, recrq 3-19-1801
Phebe gct N.Y. 2-21-1822 (clear)
Rebecca recrq 4-16-1801 (perhaps w Jacobus)

SWEZEY
Hannah, Beth., recrq 9-17-1835; ct Flushing

SWEZEY, Hannah, continued
7-19-1838; d 9-29-1865 ae 86y

TALBOT
Thomas & Julia
Ch: Annie S. d 7-20-1878 ae 9m 6d
(Beth. Stones)

TAPPEN
Lydia m Richard R. WILLITS

TATE
Hannah b 5----1768; m Richard WILLIS

TAYLOR
Francis J. m Ann ----- d 12-30-1880 in 60th yr
Ch: James Newton d 12-18-1862 ae 14y 6m
George Edwin d 12-6-1862 ae 7y 10m 7d
Francis J. m 2d Sarah ----- d 6-3-1886 ae in 62nd yr (Beth. Stones)
J. W. & Libbie
Ch: Grace b 4-19-1888 d 7-17-1888 (Beth. Stones)
Julia C. m James K. JACKSON

THOMPSON
Grove G. rocf N. Y. 7-18-1937
Hazel E. rocf N. Y. 7-18-1836
John, O.B. m 8-24-1791 at Beth., Phebe PEARSALL dt Rowland & Anne, O.B.
John & Phebe gct N.Y. 4-18-1793

THORNE
Isaac, s Samuel C., dec, & Maria; m 10-25-1865 Emily B. (or Emma) JACKSON, dt Jacob & Phebe, b 9-5-1840

TITUS
Abigail, dt William & Sarah, b 9-1-1755; m 1778 Edmund WILLIS
Annie m Solomon JACKSON
Daniel & Amy
Ch: Henry
Mary
Sarah
Anna
Phebe
ct Wby with 5 ch 3-15-1798; cf Pur. with 4 ch 5-19-1796
Elizabeth, dt Samuel & Mary P., gct Wby 1-18-1848
Hannah, dt Stephen & Phebe, b 1786; m 1812 Samuel UNDERHILL
Henry recrq 4-16-1812; ct Hudson for Henry W. 8-19-1824
James d 2-3-1852 ae 77y 2m 8d
Jonathan, s John & Sarah, Wby, b 11 Mo (Jan) 8, 1743/4 d 12-22-1824 ae 81y; m 1-7-1767 Mary WHITSON, dt John & Deborah, b 7 Mo (Sept) 26, 1748 d 11-22-1823 Jericho (Bibles)
Martha, dt James & Anne; m 1774 Thomas POWELL
Mary Powell rocf Wby 9-20-1898; d 7-20-1902 (or 1912)
Obadiah m 1825 Mary TOWNSEND, dt George & Phebe (mo)
Mary dis mo 1-19-1826
Phebe, dt Jacob & Hannah WILLITS; m 1781 Stephen TITUS; m 2d 1798 George TOWNSEND
Rachel W. m Edward ROBBINS
Richard W., s Howland & Sarah, N. Hemp.; m 11-27-1839 at Beth., Mary P. PLUMMER, dt John & Martha
Ch: John Jr. b 9-24-1840 d 7-19-1846 (Beth. Stone)
ct N.Y. for Mary P. 7-15-1841
Samuel & Mary P.
Ch: Elizabeth
ct Wby 1-18-1810 (clear); cf Wby for Mary P. 10-18-1810; ct Wby 7-16-1812 with ch
Stephen, s Stephen & Sarah, b 6-10-1757; m 11-7-1781 Phebe WILLETS, dt Jacob & Hannah, b 1763
Ch: Hannah b 1786; m Sam'l UNDERHILL
Samuel b 3-27-1788; m Mary POWELL
Henry W. b 1790 d 1829 (unm)
Stephen W. b 1792; m Hannah UNDERHILL
2 d young
Phebe m 2d 10-25-1798 George TOWNSEND; cf N.P. for Phebe with Henry & Stephen 9-21-1797
(Bibles)
Stephen W., s Stephen & Phebe, b 11-7-1792 d 3-28-1876; m 1815, Wby, Hannah UNDERHILL, dt Israel & Mary, b 9-7-1793 d 10-22-1847
Ch: Sarah
(1 other ch)
ct Wby 5-15-1815 (clear); cf Wby for Hannah 5-16-1816; ct N.Y. for parents & ch 10-15-1818
(Underhill Gen.)

TOWNSEND
Anna, dt George & Phebe, b 12-6-1799; m 1822 or 1823 Jesse HENDRICKSON (mo)
George, s George & Rosannah, dec, Norwich, O.B.; m 10-25-1798 at Jericho, Phebe TITUS, wd Stephen, dt Jacob, dec, & Hannah WILLIS
Ch: Anna b 12-6-1799; m Jesse HENDRICKSON
Mary b 3-3-1802; m Obad. TITUS
George b 4-10-1805; m Sarah TRACY
George recrq 4-15-1790
(Bibles)
George, s George & Phebe, b 4-10-1805 d Illinois 1-1-1864; m 3-26-1846 Sarah TRACY
Ch: Sarah
George
dis 8-21-1828
(Bibles)
Joseph Lawrence, s Obadiah & Phebe, W. Hemp., b 10-7-1797 d 12-24-1854; m 9-22-1825 at Jericho, Margaret SHERMAN, dt Isaac & Margaret, both dec, b 1799 d 7-4-1826 ae 27y (Bibles)
Joseph L. m 2d 11-3-1831 at Jerusalem Hannah W. WHITSON, dt Thomas & Ann
cf Wby (clear); ct Wby for Hannah W. 3-21-

TOWNSEND, Joseph L. & Hannah W., continued
1833
Martha, dt James & Mary; m 1794 Edmund WILLIS
Mary recrq 5-19-1796
Mary, dt Timothy & Sarah; m 1762 William JONES
Mary, dt George & Phebe, b 3-3-1802; m 1825 Obadiah TITUS (mo)
Richard, s George & Rosannah, d 12-23-1813, Norwich; m 11-30-1775 Abigail WILLIS, dt Wm. & Mary (Townsend), b 11-18-1755 d 3-29-1836
Ch: Rosannah b 1779 d 3-20-1836 (unm)
cf Wby for parents & Rosannah, 7-17-1794 (Bibles)

TRAVERS
Elizabeth, dt Daniel & Hannah, Norwich; m ----- PETERS

TREDWELL
James recrq 7-21-1791; ct N.P. 10-15-1795

TURNER
John E. & Phebe E.
Ch: Lucie d 11-24-1886 ae 2m 10d
Willie d 9-8-1881 ae 5m 1d

TYLER
Susan Abernethy b Madrid, St. Laurence Co., N.Y. d 3-19-1891 (Beth. Stone)

UDALL
Deborah, dt Joseph & Phebe; m 1763 Job WILLITS
Thomas b 9 Mo (Nov) 22, 1748 d 1789; m 3-27-1776 Susanna VALENTINE, dt Jacob & Mary
Ch: Richard m Deborah POWELL
Sarah m Richard TITUS
Charles m Cath. SEAMAN
Susanna recrq 7-15-----; 2 ch recrq of Susanna 2-15-1798; Susanna m 2d 1801 Jacob SEAMAN

UDELL
Phebe dis 1-17-1799

UNDERHILL
Adonijah, s Thos. & Sarah, b 2 Mo (Apr) 9, 1743 d 10-21-1821; m 1745 Phebe WILLETS, dt Daniel & Amy (Powell), d 6-16-1819
Ch: Daniel m 1794 Mary JACKSON
Rachel m 1804 Obadiah JACKSON
parents gct N.Y. 10-18-1827
(Underhill Gen.)
Adonijah J., s Daniel & Mary, N.Y.C., b 8-16-1800 d 6-27-1854; m 5-25-1826 at Jericho, Phebe HICKS, dt Valentine & Abigail, Jericho, b 12-24-1804 d 6-23-1852
ct N.Y. for Adonijah Jr. 1-16-1817; cf N.Y. 1-23-1821; ct N.Y. for both 10-18-1827
Alice J., dt Samuel S. & Carry J.; m 1929 Myron Colyer MITCHELL
Amy, dt Daniel & Mary, b 2-17-1795; m 1818 Isaac WILLETS
Anna, dt Samuel & Anne; m 1810 William WILLIS
Clementine, dt Abrm. & Keziah; m 1772 Henry WHITSON
Daniel, s Adonijah & Phebe, Jericho; m 2-27-1794 at Jericho, Mary JACKSON, dt John & Charity (Tredwell), Jerusalem
Ch: Amy m Isaac WILLETS
Samuel
Adonijah
(Underhill Gen.)
Daniel m 2d 11-1-1810 at Mk, Phebe UNDERHILL, dt Israel & Mary (Wright), b 4-3-1787 d 8-1-1866
Ch: Jackson b 12-6-1811
Mary J.
Elizabeth J. m Joseph WEEKS
Mary recrq of Phebe 1-23-1821; ct Wby (clear); cf Wby for Phebe 5-20-1812 (Underhill Gen.)
Daniel dis 12-16-1813
Daniel, s Sam'l Jr. & Mary, Jericho, b 6-24-1826 d 2-10-1899; m 10-21-1847 at Wby, Caroline POST, dt James & Phebe, N. Hemp., b 6-25-1826 d 1-12-1882 ae 56y Jericho
Ch: James b 10-16-1851 d 1-16-1859 ae 7y 3m
Samuel Jr. b 11-14-1848
ct Wby (clear); cf Wby for Caroline (Underhill Gen.)
Daniel m 2d 9-20-1883 Catharine POST, dt James & Phebe W., b 1-19-1833 Wby d 1-13-1922
cf Wby for Catharine
Daniel, s Samuel J. & Emma A., b 11-19-1874; m 6-16-1938 Bertha COER
Edward W., s Stephen J. & Henrietta, b Jericho 10-31-1877 d Syosset 11-25-1927; m 10-20-1909 at Huntington by Rev. James F. Aitkins Emeline S. KISSAM, dt Oscar
Hannah, dt Israel & Mary, b 9-7-1793; m 1815 Stephen W. UNDERHILL
Hannah W. dis mo 6-16-1836
Hannah W., dt Stephen Jr. & Henrietta, b 2-8-1880; m 1913 James Arthur MALCOLM
Helen, dt Samuel J. & Emma A.; m 1815 L. Hollingsworth WOOD
Henry F., s Daniel & Hannah, O.B. & Cove, d 3-6-1842
Henry T., s Stephen & Henrietta, b 7-26-1884; m 10-13-1904 at East Norwich, Dorothy VERNON, dt Andrew, d 10-25-1918 at Syosset ae 32y 2m
Ch: Winifred
Dorothy recrq 9-15-1910; Winifred recrq of parents 10-20-1910
Henry W., s Samuel J. & Emma, b 4-7-1882 d 2-3-1926; m 2-14-1912 Harrisburg, Pa., Helen WOLLOWER
Ch: Henry Willets Jr. b 4-7-1913
Catharine J. b 12-11-1914 d 4-11-1926
Samuel J. b 8-26-1917
Isaac rocf Wby 9-15-1808; dis mo 8-17-1809
Jackson (prob) s Daniel & Pheby, b 10-6-1812; dis 3-16-1837

UNDERHILL, continued
Jacob d 8-25-1889 ae 82y 9m 15d (Beth. Stone)
Jordan W., s Samuel & Hannah, O.B. & Cove, b 3-4-1817 d 8-24-1854 ae 37y; m 12-3-1844 (m by a magistrate before 1-16-1845) Hannah WILLITS (Willis in record of Hannah), dt Obadiah & Phebe, b 5-30-1821 Jericho d 8-29-1879 ae 58y 2m 29d
Ch: Henry T. b 2-10-1846 d 1-19-1911
Samuel S. b 3-5-1848
Amelia b 10-19-1853 d 2-24-1854
Stephen J.
Phebe, Jericho, d 6-18-1819
Phebe, dt Israel & Mary, b 4-3-1787; m 1810 Daniel UNDERHILL
Phebe, dt Richard & Pamela, Jericho, b 4-25-1794; m 1835 William WILLITS b 10-10-1780 d 12-1-1853
Phebe d 4-30-1852 ae 58y
Phebe, dt Samuel & Mary; m 1855 Elias SEAMAN
Phebe Ella, dt Sam'l S. & Annie J.; m 1932 Morley Lyford SMITH
Rachel, dt Adonijah & Margaret; m 1804 Obadiah JACKSON
Samuel, s Israel & Mary, Cedar Swamp, d 2-10-1845 ae 71; m 4-30-1812 at Jericho Hannah TITUS, dt Stephen, dec, & Phebe, Washington D. C., d 12-3-1849 ae 63y
Ch: Stephen T. d 8-19-1834 ae 20y
Hannah rocf N.P. 4-17-1800; Hannah gct Wby 12-17-1812
(Underhill Gen.)
Samuel J., s Daniel & Mary, Jericho, b 7-31-1797 d 10-7-1868 ae 72y; m 12-2-1824 Mary WILLETS, dt Samuel & Hannah, b 6-5-1801 d 2-10-1878 ae 76y
Ch: Daniel b 6-24-1826; m Caroline POST
Phebe b 10-16-1830; m Elias H. SEAMAN
ct N.Y. 12-18-1823; cf N.Y. for Mary 7-21-1825 (Mary's name Willis in d record; Willets in Gen.); some Samuel, a lad, gct Wby 5-19-1803
(Underhill Gen.)
Samuel J., s Daniel & Caroline, Jericho, b 11-14-1848 Jericho d 6-30-1910; m 10-30-1872 at Richard Albertson's, Emma ALBERTSON, dt Richard & Phebe W., N. Hemp., b Mineola 2-28-1853 d 10-17-1937
Ch: Daniel b 11-19-1874 Jericho
Henry W. b 4-7-1882 Jericho
Helen b 12-30-1887 Jericho
Richard d 5-18-1880 ae 7y (Jericho Stone)
Emma recrq 5-17-1894
Samuel S., s Jordan & Hannah W., b 3-5-1848 d 2-16-1911; m 3-17-1870 Charlotte B. GALLOWAY, dt William & Eliza, Canandaiqua
Ch: Jessie d 5-23-1889 ae 7y 14d
(5 other ch)
Sarah, dt Israel, b 1-7-1780; m 1804 Andries SEAMAN
Sarah T., dt Richard & Pamelia, b 4-1-1803 Beth.; m Richard S. POWELL
Stephen J., s Jordan & Hannah W., Jericho, b 8-2-1853 d 8-22-1922 Syosset; m 2-1-1877 at Edward Willis', Syosset, Henrietta WILLIS, dt Edward & Elizabeth, b 8-12-1854 d 9-7-(or 9) 1936
Ch: Edward W. b 10-31-1877
Hannah W. b 2-6-1880 (Helen W. in Gen.)
Henry T. b 7-26-1884
Arthur S. b 3-4-1894
(Seaman Gen.)
Thomas, s Richard & Pamelia, N.Y.C., b 3-15-1790 d 6-29-1870; m 2-2-1820 at Beth., Sarah WHITSON, dt Henry & Clementine, Cedar Swamp
Ch: Pamelia T. b 1-4-1828; m Chas. T. McCOUN
Mary J. b 11-17-1829; m Elias LEWIS
parents & 3 ch rocf N.Y. 8-2-1826 (rem cert); Sarah gct N.Y. 11-16-1820
(Underhill Gen.)
Virginia Jones, dt Arthur S. & Virginia J., recrq 3-20-1938
William G., s Sam'l S. & Charlotte B., Jericho, b 1870; m 10-17-1894 at Sarah E. Robbins', Carrie J. ROBBINS, dt Walter, dec, & Sarah E., Jericho, b 7-6-1873 d 4-26-1913
Ch: (3)

VALENTINE
Charles, s Jacob & Martha, d 3-23-1887 (2-3-1887 in Register) ae 72y; m Kezia COLES, dt Thomas & Pamelia
Ch: Jacob L. b 4-16-1857
cf N.Y. for all
Charles P., s Wm. M. & Emily T., G.C.; m 11-12-1895 at Wm. H. Seaman's, Annie LAURIE, dt Wm. W. & Frances F., Jericho
Annie recrq 4-20-1893; ct Wby 12-19-1895
Jacob, (prob) s David & Charity, b 10-22-1718; m 1-5-1741 Mary COLES, dt Charles & Sarah
Ch: Charles b 7-30-1742; m Mary FROST
David b 7-27-1745; m Hannah TOWNSEND
Susannah b 9-20-1748; m Thos. UDALL
Valentine m 2d Ethelinda LATTING, wd Wm. FROST; Jacob gct Wby 5-17-1792
(Bibles)
Jacob L., s Charles & Kezia, Beth., b 4-16-1857; m Nettie M. VALENTINE
Jacob recrq 4-18-1791; ct Wby 11-20-1791; rem cert to Wby
Sarah, dt Richard & Phebe, Beth., rocf Wby 6-15-1797; d 8-12-1836 ae 84y (unm)
Susannah, dt Jacob & Mary, b 9 Mo (Nov) 22, 1748; m 1776 Thomas UDELL; m 2d 1795 Jacob SEAMAN

VAN COTT
Alanson & Florence
Ch: Gussie d 1-2-1890 ae 4y 2m 27d
Elford d 1-2-1890 ae 2y 9m 2d
(Beth. Stones)
Elizabeth rocf N.P. 8-21-1800; ct Wby 3-19-1801 (clear)
Elizabeth (form Brush) dis mo 4-18-1799; rst 6-18-1812, as she lived in N.Y. that MM

VAN COTT, Elizabeth, continued
notified

VANDERBILT
Elizabeth m ----- GREEN
Margaret m ----- DOWNING

VANDEWATER
George, s John & Phebe, d 5-19-1862 ae 83y 3m 9d m Margaret SEAMAN, dt Noah & Martha, d 2-4-1864 ae 76y 3m 17d (Beth. Stone)
George recrq 10-16-1845
Harriet, dt Geo. & Margaret; m 1867 George JOHNSON
John Jr. & Susan Jr.
Ch: Clarence W. d 6-28-1880 ae 3y 9m 28d (Beth. Stone)
Silas T. d 6-3-1889 ae 73y 2m 30d (Beth. Stone)

VAN NOSTRAND
Daniel, Beth, d 4-30-1852 ae 96y; m Susannah POST, dt Micah & Eliz., d 9-12-1843 ae 86y (Bibles)
Daniel, Beth, d 11-14-1867 ae 96y
J. Sidney m Phebe Amelia HICKS, dt Smith & Phebe, b 1-12-1842 (1-2-1842 on another page of Register) Beth d 4-12-1926
Richard b 12-28-1843 d 12-10-1887 (Beth Stone)

VAN SISE
Charles, of Co. G. 67th Reg. N.Y.S. Volunteers, d 9-13-1868 (Beth Stone)

VELSOR
Eugene m Susie KITCHAM, dt Ebenezer & Sarah, d 2-22-1888 ae 21y 2m 1d
Valentine m 6-8-1859 Ruth W. WILLITS, dt Jacob & Abigail

VERITY
Abigail recrq 3-19-1835
Samuel recrq 4-16-1829; d Jerusalem 1-18-1879 ae 94y

VERNON
Dorothy m 1904 Henry UNDERHILL

WALLOWER
Helen m 1912 Henry W. UNDERHILL

WARNER
Walter L. d 1-17-1892 ae 33y 10m 8d (Beth Stone)

WATERBURY
Ruhama, dt Azariah & Phebe, Beth; m ---- SMITH
Ruhama d 12-9-1866 ae 63y

WEEKS
Dorothy, young & under tuition of John & Phebe MERRITT, called their "sister"; ct N.Y. with them 4-18-1793
Elizabeth recrq 7-19-1792
Hannah recrq 11-15-1792
Jemima recrq 4-17-1800
Rachel b 8-14-1804 d 1-13-1858 (Beth Stone)
Richard recrq 12-20-1792; ct Flushing for Richard & fam 4-18-1793

WHITE
Clifford Burr, s Emmons & Sarah I., Richmond Co., N. Y.; m 11-6-1909 at Lucy Gertrude Powell's, Ruth Alice POWELL, dt Walter, dec, & Lucy G. (Harned) Farmingdale, b 12-15-1886
Ruth gct N.Y. 12-15-1912
Hannah m Benjamin A. MERRITT

WHITEHOUSE
John, Beth, d 4----1821 ae nearly 80y

WHITSON
Abraham, s Henry & Clemmy, O.B.; m 2-1-1804 at Beth, Mary JACKSON, dt David & Esther, O.B.
Ch: Phebe
David
Abraham
Underhill
Charles
Sarah b 3-13-1814
Samuel b 8-19-1816
ct Flushing with 7 minor ch 7-17-1817; ch b Beth
(Bibles)
Amos, s John & Deborah, Beth, b 5-5-1757 d 2-27-1830 ae 73y; m Amy WILLETS, dt Joseph, d 1-23-1812 in 54th yr
Ch: Thomas b 6-26-1773; m Hannah WILLETS
Rebecca b 2-5-1780; m Enos ALLEY
Joseph b 6-13-1782; m Hannah SMITH
Hannah b 4-24-1784; m Isaac FROST
Robert m Ann WHITSON
Deborah m David WILLETS
(Bibles)
Ann, dt Thomas & Ann; m 1831 William WILLITS
Ann d 10-23-1846 ae 14y 10m 8d
Daniel gct N.Y. 7-16-1829
Deborah, dt John & Deborah, b 2 Mo (Apr) 26, 1747; m 1766 James RUSHMORE
Deborah, dt Amos & Amy; m 1818 David WILLETS
Deborah, dt John & Mary; m (prob) Jonathan JARVIS
Eliphalet d 1-15-1856 ae 18y 8m 5d (Beth Stone)
Elizabeth, dt John & Deborah, d 12-25-1827 ae 75y
Hannah, dt Amos & Amy; m 1807 Isaac FROST
Hannah m 1814 ----- WILLIS (mo)
Hannah, Beth, d 10-14-1823 ae 81y
Hannah W., dt Thomas & Ann; m 1831 Joseph TOWNSEND
Henry m Phebe ----- d 3-5-1870 ae 80y 2m 6d
Henry d 8-4-1891 ae 75y 9m 9d Beth
Henry, s Henry & Hannah, b 1 Mo (Mar) 15, 1745 m 8-14-1772 Clementine UNDERHILL, dt Abrm.

WHITSON, Henry & Clementine, continued
& Kezia
Ch: Mary m Jarvis JACKSON
Abraham m Mary JACKSON
Thomas b 3-4-1776; m Ann WILLETS
Hannah m Chas. WILLETS
Phebe m John CROMWELL
Henry b 1786; m Sarah COLYER
Keziah b 1788; m Silas ALBERTSON
Sarah b 1795; m Thos. UNDERHILL
(Bibles)
Henry, s Henry & Clemence, b 1786 d 12-11-1857 ae 72y 2m 8d; m 1811 Sarah COLYER, d 2-16-1864
Ch: Charles G. d 3-9-1832 ae 12y 6m
ct N.Y. 7-21-1836 to reside with his brother
James d 8-25-1877 ae 70y 5m (Beth Stone)
Jarvis d 12-20-1848 ae 37y 8m 3d (Beth Stone)
Jarvis d 8-1-1852 ae 28y 7m; m Sarah I. ----- d 11-30-1865 ae 41y 11m 3d (Beth Stones)
John, s Thomas & Deborah, d 5-14-1815; m 8 Mo (Oct) 3, 1744 Deborah POWELL, dt Thomas & Mary
Ch: Deborah b 2 Mo (Apr) 26, 1747; m James RUSHMORE
Mary b 7 Mo (Sept) 26, 1748; m Jonathan TITUS
Amos b 5-5-1757; m Amy WILLETS
Elizabeth b 1 Mo (Mar) 9, 1749/50
(Bibles)
Jonah R. & Helen F.
Ch: Jennie B. d 12-12-1885 ae 17y
(Beth Stone)
Joseph, s Amos & Deborah, Norwich, b 6-13-1782; m 10-31-1804 Hannah SMITH
Ch: Maria
Ann
Thomas
Gilbert
John b 11-3-1815
Samuel b 10-3-1817
Joseph gct Wby 7-17-1800 (apprentice); cf Wby 9-15-1803; ct Wby 9-19-1805; cf Wby 12-15-1814 with 4 ch; ct Wby with 6 ch 9-19-1819
(Bibles)
Keziah, dt Henry & Clemmy; m 1813 Silas ALBERTSON
Martha, dt Thomas & Ann; m 1829 Edmund WILLETS
Mary, dt John & Deborah, b 7 Mo (Sept) 26, 1748; m 1767 Jonathan TITUS (Mary d 11-22-1823 Jerusalem)
Mary, dt Henry & Clementine; m 1804 Jarvis SEAMAN (mo)
Mary, Beth, d 5-22-1815 ae 87y
Phebe, dt Henry & Clementine; m 1825 John CROMWELL
Rachel, dt John & Martha; m Benjamin MOTT
Rebecca, dt Amos & Amy; m 1804 Enos ALLEY
Robert dis mo 11-16-1809
Sarah, dt Nathaniel & Mary, b 1-20-1757; m 1781 Charles JACKSON (Sarah d 8-3-1825 ae 68y)
Sarah, dt Henry & Clement; m 1820 Thomas UNDERHILL
Sarah Ann d 2-26-1852 ae 34y 10m 22d (unidentified stone, Beth)
Thomas, s Amos & Amy, Huntington, b 1773; m 5-25-1797 at Jericho, Hannah WILLITS, dt Amos & Phebe, O.B.
Thomas & w & fam gct Wby 4-17-1800; cf Wby for them 6-17-1802; Thomas & Hannah gct Wby 6-20-1811
Thomas, s Henry & Clemence, South O.B., b 3-4-1776; m 3-21-1804 at Beth, Ann WILLETS, dt Jacob & Hannah, Islip, b 8-26-1779
Ch: Hannah W. b 1-22-1805
Martha b 2-27-1807
Daniel b 4-19-1810
Jacob b 4-18-1813 d 9-21-1813 ae 5m
Thomas b 4-19-1821; m Mary WILLETS
Ann b 9-13-1814
Jacob H. b 1-8-1818
Phebe b 1-3-1824
ct Flushing for Thomas, Ann & ch, Thomas & Phebe, 7-21-1835
Thomas, s Thomas, dec, & Ann, Flushing, b 4-19-1821; m 4-20-1848 at Isaac WILLETS', Mary WILLETS, dt Isaac & Amy, O.B.
cf Flushing (clear); Mary gct Flushing 1-18-1848
Willet b 4-1-1780 d 10-5-1847; m Amy ----- b 10-2-1784 d 1-13-1852
Ch: Elizabeth d 5-9-1852 ae 42y 3m 18d
Ruth d 9-30-1871 ae 54y 2m 12d
Ann d 10-23-1846 ae 14y 10m 8d
(these stones appear to be in one group, hence probably related as shown)
Willet P., s (perhaps) Willet, d 12-2-1883 ae 64y; m Elizabeth ROBBINS, dt Samuel & Phebe, d 8-26-1859 ae 34y 2m 22d
Ch: Franklin B. d 6-15-1876 ae 23y 1d
Elizabeth d 8-25-1858 ae 2m 9d
(Beth Stones)

WIDDOWS
Peter rocf Carlow, Ireland, endorsed by Wexford MM 11-20-1794; ct ND MM 7-21-1796

WIGGINS
Henry m Julia E. ----- d 2-18-1873 ae 2y 10m 4d (Beth Stone)

WIGHAM
Isaac, s Thomas & Dorothy, dec, N.Y.C.; m 6-3-1818 at Beth, Mary L. SEAMAN, dt Zebulon & Mary, Jerusalem
Mary recrq 2-15-1816; Mary L. gct N.Y. 12-17-1818

WILLETS
Abigail [Willits], dt Obadiah & Eliz., b 3-11-1809; m Jacob WILLETS
Albert [Willits], s Richard R., recrq 7-20-1911; d 11-29-1921
Amos [Willits] gct Flushing with fam 1-15-1795
Amos [Willits] & Elizabeth

WILLETS, Amos & Elizabeth [Willits], continued
ct Wby 11-21-1799 (clear); Elizabeth rocf
Wby 3-20-1800
Amos [Willits] gct Wby 11-21-1822 (clear)
Andrew d 5-27-1855 ae 51y; m Sarah RUSHTON d 4-25-1849 ae 41y (Jericho Stones)
Ann, dt Jacob & Hannah; m 1804 Thomas WHITSON
Anna, dt Wm. & Mary V.; m 1872 Frederick E. WILLETS
Anna W., dt William & Martha, b 8-6-1848; m 1872 Frederick E. WILLITS
Catharine gct Wby 11-21-1839
Charles, s Thos. & Leah, Jericho, d 5-22-1828 ae 63y
Charles D. [Willits], s Obadiah & Phebe, b 5-16-1826 d 4-5-1924; m Sarah M. WOOD, d 12-29-1866 ae 36y 4m 17d
Ch: Franklin F. d 8-17-1867 ae 3y 6m 5d
Daniel d 10-16-1849 ae 82y 6m (Beth Stone); m 1745 Amy POWELL, dt John & Margaret, b 1718 d 9-30-1815 ae 97y
Ch: Amy b 1746; m Adonijah UNDERHILL
(Bibles)
Daniel, s Jacob & Hannah, b 4-4-1767 d 10-16-1849 ae 82y 6m; m Kitty SMITH, dt Henry
Ch: Hannah m Richard UDALL
Jacob
(Bibles)
Daniel dis mo 7-20-1815
Daniel, s Isaac & Amy, Jericho, b 10-26-1824 d 7-28-1884 ae 59y bur Jericho; m 9-18-1850 in Oswego MM, Lydia MOORE, dt Alfred & Charlotte, b 12-27-1830 d 10-4-1904
Ch: Amy b 9-20-1852 d 8-16-1937
Charlotte M. b 12-31-1854 d 10-9-1921
Hannah b 5-11-1858
Mary b 5-14-1861
Minnie d 5-22-1864 ae 3y 8d (Jericho Stone)
ct Oswego (clear); Lydia rocf Oswego MM
David, s Jonah & Mary, N. Hemp.; m 2-25-1818 at Beth, Deborah WHITSON, dt Amos & Amy, dec, Huntington
Deborah gct Wby 4-15-1819
Edmund, s Robert & Mary, N.Y.C.; m 10-29-1829 at Jerusalem, Martha WHITSON, dt Thomas & Ann, O.B.
Ch: (8)
cf N.Y. (clear); Martha gct N.Y. 9-16-1830
Elizabeth, dt Jacob & Martha; m 1796 Charles RUSHMORE
Elizabeth, Jericho, d 8-14-1817
Elizabeth, dt Obadiah & Eliz.; m 1833 William ROBBINS
Esther, dt Richard & Phebe POWELL, d 9-6-1825 ae 53y
Frederick E. [Willits], s James & Annie E., G.C.; m 9-25-1872 at Mary V. Willets', Anna WILLETS, dt William, dec, & Mary V., Jericho, b 8-6-1848
Ch: James
Anna gct Wby
Hannah [Willits], dt Amos & Phebe; m 1797 Thomas WHITSON
Hannah [Willits], dt Obadiah & Eliz., b 1821; m 1820 Jordan UNDERHILL
Hannah, dt Isaac & Amy; m 1864 Willet ROBBINS
Hannah, dt Daniel & Lydia, b 5-11-1858; m 1894 Robert SEAMAN
Henry T., s Samuel & Hannah, Manhasset, b 10-6-1812 d 4-3-1888 ae 75; m 5-12-1867 Sophia UNDERHILL, dt Adonijah & Sarah, b 5-23-1830 d 6-28-1917 bur in Prospect Park
Isaac, s Samuel & Hannah, Jericho, d 2-11-1855 ae 60 bur Jericho; m 11-26-1818 in Jericho Amy UNDERHILL, dt Daniel & Mary, dec, b 2-17-1795 d 2-24-1884 bur Jericho
Ch: John b 10-3-1819
William S. b 8-21-1822; m Mary VALENTINE
Daniel b 10-26-1824
Mary b 12-25-1826; m Thos. WHITSON
Elizabeth b 4-28-1829
Phebe b 2-2-1832
Hannah b 9-20-1836
Jacob [Willits], Beth, gct Wby 5-19-1821 (clear)
Jacob [Willits], s Obadiah & Sarah, b 2-18-1824
Jacob, s Daniel & Phebe, N. Hemp., d 7-15-1836 ae abt 92y; m 1831 Abigail ----- (mo)
Ch: Richard
Jacob mo before 10-20-1831; transgression passed by on ack; Abigail's transgression passed by
Jacob b 7-24-1813 d 6-20-1843 (unidentified stone, Beth)
Jacob [Willits, s Jacob & Martha, Jericho, b 6-14-1784 d 5-1-1875; m Abigail WILLITS, dt Obadiah & Eliz., b 3-11-1809 d 8-15-1885 ae 75y both bur Jericho
Ch: William S. b 9-25-1832; m Frances HEWLETT
Elizabeth b 9-29-1835
Martha b 12-17-1836; m Townsend JACKSON
Caroline b 2-23-1841 d 1-16-1924
Mary R. b 10-14-1848 d 1-11-1927
Ruth
Phebe
(Bibles)
Jacob R. [Willits], s Richard & Ruth, Jericho, d 9-20-1823 ae 79y; m (perhaps) Abigail -----
Ch: Elizabeth d 12-31-1854 ae 19
James [Willits], s Frederick E. & Anna W., G.C.; m 4-24-1912 at Ella A. Jackson's, Florence JACKSON, dt Ella A., Bkn. (2nd w)
Jane R., dt William & Mary, b 10-31-1852; ct Wby 7-15-1891
Job [Willits], s Jacob & Hannah, b 7 Mo (Sept) 10, 1748 d 11-14-1820; m 1763 Deborah UDALL dt Joseph & Phebe
Ch: (6)
frequently on comm; minute to R.I. YM 4-19-1791
(Bibles)
Job & Charity
Job & Charity gct Wby 6-19-1806
John Jr. gct Flushing 3-18-1852
Jonah, s Deborah; m Mary -----
Ch: David

WILLETS, Jonah & Mary, continued
Ch: Abraham
Samuel
Deborah
Isaac
Amy
ct Wby for all, including aged Deborah, 5-19-1803
Joshua, s Jacob & Hannah, Islip, b 1769 d 1-22-1865 ae 94y 11m 4d (Beth Stone); m 9-26-1799 at Jericho, Phebe HICKS, dt Elias & Jemima, b 7-5-1779
Ch: Elias d 6-20-1819
Joshua gct Wby 11-21-1822 (clear)
(Bibles)
Martha [Willits], dt Richard & Abigail; m 1807 Simeon LOINES
Martha [Willits], Jericho, d 3-9-1832
Martha [Willits], dt Jacob & Abigail; m 1857 Townsend JACKSON
Martha V., dt Wm. & Mary V.; m 1871 Sidney B. BOWNE
Mary, dt Jacob & Martha, Jericho, d 10-16-1822
Mary [Willits], dt Obadiah & Eliz.; m 1831 Edmund KIRBY
Mary, dt Isaac & Amy; m 1848 Thomas WHITSON
Matilda, dt Wm. & Mary V.; m 1879 Samuel J. SEAMAN
Obadiah [Willits], s Richard & Abigail, Jericho, b 2-28-1772 d 9-9-1842; m 1807 Elizabeth ROBBINS, dt Jacob & Abigail, b 8-20-1788 d 11-4-1815 (mo)
Ch: Abigail b 3-11-1809; m Jacob WILLETS
(3 other ch)
Obadiah dis 7-16-1807 for mo; rst 7-24-1817
Obadiah m 2d 8-20-1820 Phebe DOWNING, dt Benjamin & Martha, b 12-1-1782 d 9-26-1826
Ch: Hannah b 6----1821; m Jordan UNDERHILL
Charles D. b 5-16-1826
Jacob b 2-18-1824 d 6-9-1919 Santa Anna, Calif.
(Bibles)
Obadiah m 3d before 3-19-1840 Martha WILLETS, dt Jacob & Martha, b 7-19-1774 d 10-10-1842 (mo)
Obadiah's 4 minor ch (by 1st w) Richard, Abigail, Mary & Elizabeth recrq of father 2-15-1821
ct Wby 6-15-1820 (clear); Obadiah ret mbrp 1840
(Bibles)
Phebe, dt Daniel & Amy; m 1745 Adonijah UNDERHILL
Phebe, dt Jacob & Hannah, b 1763; m 1781 Stephen TITUS
Phebe, dt Jacob & Hannah; m ----- TITUS; m 2d 1798 George TOWNSEND
Phebe m 1803 Elijah SEAMAN (mo)
Phebe [Willits], dt Jacob & Martha; m 1814 David KETCHAM
Phebe (form Downing) d 7-25-1826 ae 43y
Phebe, dt Isaac & Amy; m 1854 William FRAME
Phebe P., dt Jacob & Abbie; m 1868 Alfred H. MOORE
Priscilla gct N.Y. 12-18-1794 (clear)
Richard [Willits] Jr. gct Wby 3-20-1800 (clear); rem cert to Wby 6-17-1802
Richard [Willits], s Jacob, gct N.Y. 4-20-1797 (clear); ct N.Y. 5-21-1812 (clear); d 9-18-1858 ae 85y 9m 11d (Beth Stone)
Richard R. [Willits], s Obadiah & Eliz., b 2-26-1808 d 11-30-1859; m Lydia TAPPEN, d 9-14-1863 ae 51y 6m 2d (Jericho Stone)
Robert [Willits], s Joseph & Hannah, dec, N. Hemp.; m 11-25-1790 at Jericho, Mary ROBBINS, dt Stephen & Miriam, O.B.
Robert rocf Uxbridge, Eng. (clear); Mary gct Wby 7-21-1791
Ruth W. [Willits], dt Jacob & Abigail; m 1859 Valentine VELSOR
Samuel [Willits], s Wait, gct N.Y. 5-21-1801 (apprentice)
Samuel, s Jacob & Hannah, b 1763 d 6-8-1850; m 2-27-1794 at Jericho Hannah SEAMAN, dt William & Mary (Jackson), b 7-24-1776
Ch: Isaac b 12-16-1794; m Amy UNDERHILL
Robert b 1-21-1797 d 8-4-1797
William b 8-12-1798; m Phebe PRIOR
Mary b 5-6-1801; m Sam'l J. UNDERHILL
Andrew b 1804; m Sarah RUSHTON
Jane P. b 1806 d 10-18-1864 ae 58y
Esther d 3-31-1888 ae 79y (unm)
Henry b 10-6-1812; m Sophia UNDERHILL
Hannah b 1-21-1818 d 12-22-1896
Samuel rocf N.P. to Wby & endorsed to Jericho 6-16-1791; ct N.Y. with 6 minor ch 5-15-1823
Thomas [Willits] rocf Wby 11-20-1791; dis mo 11-21-1793
Wait [Willits], s Samuel & Jane, b 2-3-1754 d 6-24-1818; m Mary POST, dt John & Phebe, b 11-11-1756 d 12-31-1846
Ch: Samuel b 8-18-1781; m Hannah CARPENTER
John m Eliz. HORTON
Henry m Nancy TOMPKINS
Sarah d 12-3-1878 (unm)
Phebe b 1-28-1783 d 2-21-1835 (unm)
Amy m Eleazer THEALL
Mary b 7-18-1796 d 10-2-1828
Jane
Samuel apprentice in N.Y. 5-21-1801; Wait & fam (ch, Phebe, Sarah, John, Mary & Henry) gct N.Y. 4-15-1802
(Bibles)
William [Willits], s Robert & Mary, Wby; m 11-3-1831 at Jerusalem, Ann WHITSON, dt Thomas & Ann, O.B., d 1-21-1833 ae 18y
William, s Isaac & Amy, Jericho, b 8-21-1822 d 8-30-1864 ae 42 bur Jericho; m 10-14-1846 at G.C., Mary VALENTINE, dt Jacob & Martha, b 12-23-1823 G.C. d 12-24-1891 ae 68y bur Jericho
Ch: Anna W. b 8-6-1848; m Fred'k E. WILLITS
Martha V. b 12-28-1850; m Sidney B. BOWNE
Jane R. b 10-31-1852
Matilda b 12-27-1854; m Sam'l J. SEAMAN

WILLETS, William & Mary, continued
cert of clear Wby; cf N.Y. for Mary
(Bibles)
William S., s (prob) Jacob & Abigail; m Frances HEWLETT, b 3-3-1835 d 3-7-1890
(Jericho stone Fannie Hewlett)
Williams [Willits], s Jacob & Martha, b 10-1-1780 d 12-31-1853 ae 74y (Jericho Stone); m 1835 Phebe UNDERHILL, dt Richard & Pamela, b 4-25-1794 d 5-1-1852
Ch: Elizabeth b 9-29-1835 d 7-5-1855
ct Pur 10-15-1835 (clear); Phebe gct Pur 9-15-1836; Wm. dis 10-20-1828
(Jericho stones & Bibles)

WILLIAMS
John, s John & Jane, Beth, d 1-25-1855 ae 71y

WILLIS
Abigail, dt Wm. & Mary, b 11-18-1755; m 1775 Richard TOWNSEND
Abigail, dt Townsend & Hannah; m (1) Samuel JONES (2) Robert SEAMAN
Alfred R., s Richard & Hannah, b 1-6-1809 d 3-27-1875 (Jericho Stones); m before 2-17-1842 Letitia Ann ----- d 4-25-1886 ae 66y 11d (Jericho Stones) (mo)
ct N.Y 12-20-1827 (apprentice); dis mo 4-14-1842
Amy, dt Samuel & Rachel; m 1824 Townsend RUSHMORE
Edmund, s Samuel & Mary (Fry), b 9-29-1752 d 5-16-1813; m 6-29-1778 Abigail TITUS, dt Wm. & Sarah, b 9-1-1755 d 2----1793 (or 3-17-1793)
Ch: William b 1-6-1780; m Anna UNDERHILL
(Bibles)
Edmund m 2d 10-30-1794 at Jericho Martha TOWNSEND, dt James, dec, & Mary, Jericho
Martha recrq 11-21-1793; Martha gct N.Y. 9-16-1830
Edmund P., s Henry & Phebe, b 12-16-1817 d 3-14-1882 ae 60y Rochester, N.Y.; m -----
Edmund P. m 2d Sarah KIRBY, (prob) dt Jacob & Mary, b 1-16-1818
ct Rochester 12-16-1841
(Bibles)
Edward, s John & Mary, Jericho, b Syosset 5-15-1814 d 5-20-1904; m 10-18-1839 at Robert Seaman's, Elizabeth H. SEAMAN, dt Robert & Sarah, dec, Jericho, b 6-10-1826 d 2-8-1885 ae 64y 7m 28d Syosset
Ch: Sarah R. b 12-26-1840 d 2-15-1922 Locust Grove
Caroline H. b 5-21-1845 d 9-4-1847 Jericho
Mary S. b 4-24-1850 d 3-15-1862 Jericho
Caroline H. b 4-24-1850 d 4-25-1862 (4-20-1862 per stone) Jericho
Henrietta b 8-12-1854 Locust Grove
Fry, s Samuel & Mary (Fry) b 4 Mo (June) 9, 1744 d 3-22-1820; m 8-1-1770 Anne SEAMAN, dt Thomas & Hannah (Willets), b 12 Mo (Feb) 25, 1746/47 d 8-2-1828
Ch: Thomas b 11-30-1771; m Phebe SEARING
Isaac b 11-30-1771 d 1-31-1793 ae 21y 2m
(Bibles)
George T. m before 7-17-1828 Maria Phebe ----- b 5-25-1808 d 8-31-1855 (Jericho Stone) (mo)
ack accepted 8-21-1829; ct Cornwall 10-15-1829
Henrietta, dt Edward & Elizabeth; m 1877 Stephen UNDERHILL
Henry, s Samuel & Rachel, Jericho, b 1786 d 3-5-1865 ae 79y; m 1813 Phebe POST, dt Edmund & Catharine, d 1-31-1846 ae 56y
Ch: Samuel b 1-17-1815; m Cath. POST
Catharine b 7-14-1822 d 3-15-1882 ae 60y
Isaac b 7-22-1825; m Rochester, Mary H. SEAMAN
Edmond P. b 12-16-1817; m (1) ----- (2) Sarah KIRBY
ct Wby 2-18-1813 (clear)
(Bibles)
Henry, s Isaac & Mary H., b 5-17-1866 Jericho; m Jane -----
Isaac, s Henry & Phebe, d 10-4-1904; m 6----1865 Mary H. SEAMAN, dt Robert & Sarah, b 6-4-1828 d 7----1903
Ch: Henry b 5-17-1866 Jericho
Robert S. b 11-5-1868 d Rochester 8-25-1923
(Bibles)
Jane, dt Samuel & Mary; m 1780 James PARSONS
Jane d 11-7-1825 ae 84y
John, s Samuel & Rachel, O.B., d 10-5-1864 ae 74y; m 12-24-1812 at Jericho Mary W. KIRBY, dt Jacob & Mary, Jericho, d 6-28-1873 ae 86y 10m 3d
Ch: Edward b 5-15-1814
Mary F. b 1-14-1817
Rachel b 7-21-1820
Lucretia M. b 1-22-1837 d 9-17-1838 Locust Grove
bur Jericho
John P. dis mo 7-18-1822
Mary, dt Thomas & Phebe; m 1821 Samuel SMITH
Mary F., dt John & Mary W.; m 1836 Isaac HICKS
Mary H. b 8-17-1805 d 1-5-1888 ae 84y 2m 19d
Mary H. dis 11-19-1835
Pauline m 1888 Jesse MERRITT
Phebe, dt Jacob & Hannah; m 1781 Stephen TITUS; m 2d 1798 George TOWNSEND
Phebe, dt Samuel & Rachel; m 1811 James POST
Precilla recrq 7-19-1792
Rachel, dt John & Mary W.; m 1841 Samuel HICKS
Richard C., s Stephen & Sarah, Jericho, b 4----1774 d 11-22-1848 ae 74y bur Jericho; m Hannah TATE b 5----1768 d 4-12-1850 bur Jericho
Ch: Alfred R. b 4----1809
Richard b 11-14-1811 d young
ch, George, John, Alfred, Sarah & Mary
recrq of parents 8-19-1813; Richard recrq 12-20-1804; Hannah recrq 7-18-1811
(Bibles)
Richard J. dis complying with military require-

WILLIS, Richard J., continued
ments 12-9-1839
Samuel, s John & Eliz. (Mott), b 3-7-1759
d 6-28-1838 ae 70y; m 1785 Rachel PEARSALL,
dt Thomas & Ann (Valentine), d 5-31-1855
Ch: Henry b 5- 2-1786
Phebe b 10-14-1787
John b 1-2-1790
Amey b 9-12-1797
(Bibles)
Samuel & Hannah
parents & ch gct N.Y. 5-15-1823
Samuel, s Henry & Phebe, dec, Syosset; m 12-5-1865 at Joseph Post's, Catharine M. POST,
dt Joseph & Mary W., Wby
Ch: Mary W. b 12-26-1866 Jericho
Phebe b 6-29-1869 Jericho
Sarah, near Jericho, recrq 2-19-1807; d 1-9-1827 ae 82y
Sarah m 1814 ----- ROGERS (mo)
Sarah S. dis 11-19-1835
Thomas, s Fry & Anne (Seaman), Jericho, b 11-30-1771 d 9-11-1864 ae 92y 10m; m 1795
Phebe SEARING, dt John & Mary, b 1-6-1773
d 6-20-1804
Ch: Mary b 10-10-1798; m Samuel SMITH
Silas b 7-7-1802 d 9-13-1820
Isaac b 1-2-1804 d 6-4-1813
Thomas m 2d Phebe BROWN, wd, b 11-26-1768 (m 1807)
Ch: Anne b 2-23-1813 d young
ct Wby 9-17-1795 (clear); Phebe rocf Wby
5-19-1796; ct Marlborough 11-19-1807 (clear)
Phebe rocf Marlborough 5-19-1808; Mary
placed in N.P. School 1812; Thomas & Phebe
dis 11-19-1828 for separating from Friends
(Bibles)
Valentine m 4-17-1915 Marjorie Mae MERRITT, dt
Jesse & Pauline W., b 12-9-1892 d 12-18-1928
Ch: Mary Esther b 5-23-1916
Virginia Alice b 3-28-1918
Thomas Hallett b 11-17-1928
2 ch recrq of parents 7-16-1922; Thos. H.
recrq of parents 1929
William, s Edmund & Abigail, Jericho, b 1-6-1780 d 8-2-1851 ae 75y 6m; m 12-19-1810
Annie UNDERHILL, dt Samuel & Anne,
d 7-20-1853 ae 40y bur Jericho
Ch: Edmond b 4-8-1812
Samuel d young
William dis separating from Friends 12-17-1829; Anna rocf Pur 2-21-1811
(Bibles)

WILSON
C. Victor, s Samuel D. & Mary M., Bkn; m 9-27-1924 at Pauline W. Merritt's, Phebe Alice
MERRITT, dt Jesse, dec, & Pauline W.
Ch: Paul Victor b 9-3-1926
C. Victor rocf N.Y. 9-8-1936

WINDOES
Carolyn Louise, dt Morton M. & Bertha CURRY;
m ----- WINDOES; m 2d 1917 Harold A. JACKSON

WING
Mary, dt Daniel & Achsah, b 12-23-1839; m 1864
Willet H. SEAMAN

WITTE
Mabel m 1918 Jesse MERRITT

WOOD
Abel recrq 10-16-1794; d 8-26-1820
Charles & Hannah Z.
Ch: Hannah P. d 10-2-1859 ae 4y 3m 2d
Elkanah, s Caleb & Abigail, dec, N.Y.C.; m 2-22-1810 at Jericho, Anna RUSHMORE, dt James &
Deborah, dec
cf N.Y. (clear); Anna gct N.Y. 6-21-1810
Israel d 8-30-1854 ae 37y 9m 27d (Beth Stone)
John & Theodosia
Ch: Martha (clear)
Deademi (minor)
Theodosia recrq 7-21-1803; ct Cincinnati
for John & fam 3-20-1817
John M. m 6-30-1923 at Bkn, Marion PETERS, dt
Clayton & Mary, b 3-30-1900
Ch: John M. Jr. b 9-12-1924
Clayton Peters b 1-17-1930
Marion & ch recrq 5-21-1939
L. Hollingsworth, s James & Emily H., Bedford,
N.Y.; m 10-28-1915 at Jericho, Helen UNDERHILL, dt Samuel J. & Emma A., Jericho,
b 12-30-1887 d 1-30-1924
L. Hollingsworth m 2d at Swarthmore, Pa. Martha
SPEAKMAN
Leander & -----
Ch: Charles F. d 8-4-1872 ae 2y 4m
(Beth Stones)
Martha recrq 3-19-1807
Ruth m 1805 Henry POWELL
Sarah d 8-9-1877 ae 60y 3m 18d (perhaps w Israel)
Sarah m Charles D. WILLITS

WOODNUT
Henry C. Jr., s Henry C. & Anna, d 12-23-1908;
m 10-3-1889 Jericho Grace Anna JACKSON, dt
Solomon S. & Annie, b 5-13-1864 Jericho
Ch: Catharine A.
Josephine J.
Henry recrq 8-20-1898; ch recrq of parents

WRIGHT
Elizabeth d ae 80y 8m 18d (Jericho Stone)
Jane b 7-26-1807 d 12-25-1879 (Jericho Stone)
John, s Joseph & Temperance, Cedar Swamp; m 2-7-1753 Wby, Phebe SEAMAN, dt Thos. & Philadelphia, b 1 Mo (Mar) 7, 1733 d 4-18-1828
ae 95y
John d 3-17-1859 ae 77y (Jericho Stone); m
(perhaps) Hannah WRIGHT d 3-6-1849 ae 67y
(stones adjacent)
Jordan & Elizabeth

WRIGHT, Jordan & Elizabeth, continued
Ch: Jane
Susannah
Charles
ct N.Y. for all 7-19-1792
Margaret, dt Zebulun & Clement; m ----- JACKSON
Margaret d 3-3-1828 ae 87y
Mary F. gct N.Y. 4-14-1842
Phebe, dt John & Phebe; m 1791 James LOINES
Sarah, Jericho, recrq 9-18-1806; d 10-30-1816
William d 4-15-1891 ae 73y 4d (Jericho Stone)

YOUNG
Frank C. & Phebe C.
Ch: Ernest H. d ae 7m 20d
(Beth Stones)
Harrison, s John & Sarah, both dec, Bedford, N.Y.; m 10-19-1852 at Beth, Phebe POWELL, dt Richard S. & Sarah, d 6-3-1920

ZEBLEY
Jacob S. m Sarah S. WILLIS, b 2-14-1803 d 4-15-1875

GRAVESTONE RECORDS
FRIENDS BURIAL GROUND AT
JERUSALEM MEETING HOUSE

BAKER
Tredwell d July 24, 1867 ae 59y 6m 22d

BALDWIN
Mary Ann d July 31, 1910 ae 71y 5m 22d
Selah d Sept. 22, 1920 ae 86y

BRITTON
Florence E. ae 3m

BUNTING
Elizabeth d Aug. 14, 1833 ae 59y

CLOCK
Albert V. d Oct. 15, 1843 ae 3y 8m
Asa M. d Feb. 22, 1862 ae 20y 2m (d near Alexandria)
Elizabeth S., w Jesse M., b Jan. 29, 1819 d Apr. 13, 1891
Jesse A. d Jan. 13, 1853 ae 4y 3m
Jesse M. d June 10, 1894 ae 77y 5m 18d
Jetlie Pierce d June 23, 1861 ae 4y 11m

CORNELIUS
Antoinette b Aug. 17, 1843 d Aug. 7, 1921
Henry d June 12, 1855 ae 75y
Jane d Sept. 28, ---- ae 90y
Mary J., w Samuel
Samuel ae 78y

Elizabeth B. b 1806 d 1894
Henry S. b 1830 d 1857

EMEIGH
Ann M., dt Arden & Elizabeth SEAMAN, b 2 Mo 19, 1818 d 5 Mo 26, 1861

FARRELL
Libbie, w William, dt Tredwell & Hannah BAKER, d Nov. 10, 1872 ae 18y
Libbie A. d Apr. 16, 1875 ae 3y 4m 16d

HICKS
Mary Ann, w Whitehead, b Feb. 1, 1799 d May 27, 1887
Mary M. b Feb. 22, 1832 d Nov. 6, 1897
Merritt b Mar. 3, 1827 d Sept. 20, 1849
Whitehead b Sept. 20, 1797 d March 1, 1858

HOFF
David b Apr. 14, 1844 d Feb. 20, 1915
Edgar b 1841 d 1922
Fanny ae 82y 3m 3d
Frankie b Sept. 8, 1872 d Nov. 6, 1872
Henry b Sept. 22, 1809 d Jan. 12, 1881
Mary A., w Henry, b May 9, 1822 d July 21, 1900
Nelson d Feb. 16, 1832 ae 47y
William Watson d Sept. 16, 1838 ae 7y 7m

HORTON
----- J. b May 27, 1870 d Dec. 3, 1871

HOWARD
Gracie b Apr. 2, 1885 d Aug. 1885 ae 3m 12d
I Howard d Jan. 1, 1879 ae 3y 10m 21d
Susie b Sept. 23, 1886 d Aug. 2, 1887 ae 10m 23d
W. H. d July 4, 1879 ae 2y 2m 3d

JACKSON
Ann, w Sol. S., d April 25, 1863
Lieut. H. P., Adjt. 5th N. Y. H. H.
Jane Elizabeth, w of the late Noah, dt Wm. & Elizabeth BUNTING, b Feb. 19, 1812 d May 28, 1896
Jeremiah B. d 6 Mo 4, 1875 ae 70y
Jerusha, w Jeremiah B., d Jan. 3, 1861 ae 54y 11m 16d
Mary S., w Robert B., b June 28, 1835 d Aug 30, 1889
Robert B. b Sept. 13, 1932 d Sept. 11, 1905

JONES
Adelia b July 25, 1845 d Nov. 15, 1845
Almy b Feb. 5, 1787 d Apr. 6, 1843 ae 56y 2m 1d
David b May 23, 1807 d Jan. 28, 1831 ae 23y 8m 5d
Elbert b Apr. 5, 1816 d Aug. 16, 1846 ae 30y 4m 11d
Eleanor, dt Israel & Elizabeth, ae 6m
Elizabeth b Nov. 19, 1719 d Mar. 26, 1801 ae 81y 4m 7d
Elizabeth, w Israel S., b Sept. 15, 1814 d Jan. 11, 1887
Ellen A., dt Wm. H. & Alma, b Apr. 7, 1867 d Aug. 18, 1867 ae 4m 11d
Israel S. b Aug. 20, 1812 d Jan. 29, 1893
Martha A. b July 1849
Mary J., w Elbert, b July 3, 1829 d Sept 14, 1849 ae 29y 1m 14d (?)
Townsend b March 16, 1818 d Oct. 21, 1884
Wm. D. b Apr. 5, 1771 d Sept. 2, 1845 ae 74y 4m 27d

JAGGER
Mary E. (Seaman) d Nov. 5, 1917 ae 86y

KNIFFIN
Mary, dt J. M. & Elizabeth CLOCK, d Oct. 20, 1880 ae 36y 2m

LAURIE
Mary, infant dt Wm. & Fannie

LIVINGSTON
Harry b 1860 d 1923

LOINES
Sarah W. b Aug. 18, 1801 d Oct. 2, 1895

POST
Ann B., w John B., d Feb. 15, 1847 ae 38y 1m 3d

POST, continued
Asa J. b Dec. 23, 1844 d Aug. 16, 1895
Mary A., w Asa, b Apr. 16, 1848 d May 6, 1919
Mary Louisa d Nov. 20, 1872 ae 20y
Mary M. b Jan. 13, 1822 d Jan. 2, 1901
Samuel C. d Nov. 26, 1872 ae 53y 1m 7d

POWELL
Ann b March 5, 1799 d Jan. 22, 1872
Coles C. d Sept. 28, 1906 ae 63y
Elizabeth b July 9, 1808 d Jan. 18, 1885
John T. d Aug. 26, 1877 ae 54y
Susan d Jan. 11, 1908 ae 80y
William d Oct. 18, 1908 ae 82y

SEAMAN
Albert d May 2, 1886 ae 4m 4d
Alfred d Oct. 13, 1901 ae 95y 1m 1d
Ann d July 10, 1849 ae 11y 8m 12d
Ann Maria (Bunting) Seaman, w David Sands, d Jan. 22, 1864 ae 55y
Ardon b 9 Mo 5, 1795 d 4 Mo 2, 1875
Armenia d July 14, 1896 ae 59y
Benjamin b 1798 d 1848
Charles P. d Feb. 16, 1913 ae 73y
Charlotte B. b 10 Mo 31, 1805 d 2 Mo 20, 1891
Daniel d Sept. 29, 1879 ae 2y 1m 16d
David Sands d Jan. 10, 1880 ae 81y
Edward H. b 3 Mo 22, 1822 d 2 Mo 12, 1881
Elizabeth b 10 Mo 20, 1893 d 2 Mo 3, 1875
Elizabeth H., dt Benjamin & Jemima, d Apr. 18, 1858
Ellen A., dt David Sands & Ann Maria, d ae 24y
Esther, w John J., b Feb. 14, 1826 d July 31, 1894
Gilbert, Co. G. 139 Regt. N. Y. Volunteers, d Oct. 5, 1901 ae 63y
Jacob d Feb. 22, 1868 ae 81y
James d March 16, 1891 ae 59y
Jemima, dt Alfred & Martha, d March 2, 1861 ae 9y 1m 6d
John J. b Dec. 4, 1776 d Oct. 25, 1824
John R. d Dec. 11, 1883 ae 1y 11m 2d
Martha, w Alfred, d Oct. 6, 1881 ae 50y 5m 2d
Martha Althouse, wd Edwin H., b March 1, 1828 d Feb. 9, 1899
Mary, w Zebulun, b 8 Mo 11, 1774 d 9 Mo 19, 1861
Mary, w Daniel, d Sept. 1, 1861 ae 89y 10m 11d
Mary Attmore, w Albert W., b Nov. 27, 1861 d Sept. 28, 1898
Mary E., dt Edwin H. & Martha A., b 12 Mo 3, 1848 d 8 Mo 19, 1876

Phebe, w J. J., d Nov. 29, 1855 ae 32y 6m 14d
Sarah Jane, dt David Sands & Ann Maria, d Apr. 11, ----
Susan d May 5, 1886 ae 39y 2m 23d
William B. d July 15, 1905 ae 79y
Zebulun b 1 Mo 30, 1771 d 9 Mo 7, 1838

SEELIG
George W. b 1901 d 1915

SMITH
Angeline, w Richard, d Oct. 5, 1884 ae 24y 7m 9d
Howard E., s Richard & Angeline, d Oct. 4, 1884 ae 1y 11m 10d [ae 11y 3m
John G., s George G. & Alma J., d Dec. 26, 1877

SOUTHARD
Emeline R., w John H., d June 3, 1880 ae 21y
Lucilla b June 23, 1862 d Aug. 21, 1865
Mary E. b May 27, 1841 d March 24, 1910
Sarah E., dt John H. & Emeline R., d Sept. 19, 1880 ae 3m 23d

STEIN
Mary A. b March 20, 1809 d Dec. 19, 1878

TITUS
Dewitt C. d June 24, 1859 ae 32y 2m
Martha, w Ancil, d Aug. 8, 1859 in the 65th yr

TOTTEN
Richard b 1810 d 1887

VALENTINE
Charlotte B., w Daniel, b May 18, 1836 d Jan. 5, 1866
Sidney b Dec. 3, 1864 d Feb. 18, 1866

VAN SISE
Elbert b July 31, 1837 d Aug. 1, 1917
Maria A. (Smith), w Elbert, b Aug. 3, 1848 d Dec. 25, 1907

VAN WYCK
Richard P. b 1880 d 1902

VERITY
Alonzo b Oct. 6, 1872 d May 11, 1938
Ann Maria b May 22, 1817 d Oct. 20, 1884
Edward b 1846 d 1928
Hannah, w Stephen H., d ae 42y
Jacob J. b Jan. 7, 1812 d May 14, 1901
Mary E. d Oct. 29, 1856 ae 14y
Samuel, s Stephen & Hannah, d Sept. 8, 1883 ae 25y 10m
Sarah M. b Aug. 2, 1847 d Apr. 29, 1919
Smith b Oct. 15, 1845 d Apr. 20, 1920
Stephen H. d Sept. 22, 1901 ae 80y 7d

WANZER
Daniel B. b March 17, 1855 d Feb. 10, 1933

WEEKS
Julia, w Luke B., d Sept. 19, 1819 ae 80y 25d
Luke B., s Jesse & Sarah, d March 11, 1860 ae 42y 4m 6d

WILLIAMS
John b Nov. 9, 1829 d Dec. 2, 1904
Mary b Nov. 21, 1835 d June 6, 1911
Maryette, dt John & Mary, d May 10, 1862 ae 3y 8 8m

WILLITTS
Maria Louisa, w of the late Abraham, dt David & Anna W. SEAMAN, b March 15, 1854 d 1895

WILSON
Charles d 1872 ae 32y (Co. H. 119 Regt. N. Y. Volunteers)

Charles Henry, s Samuel & Ruth, d Apr. 7, 1869 ae 9y 2d
Eliza, w Willet, d Oct. 10, 1911 ae 82y 5m 27d
Sarah M., dt Willet & Eliza, d March 21, 1881 ae 22y 10m 23d
Willet d July 3, 1894 ae 61y 10m 6d

Page numbers without parenthesis refer to family groups. Numbers in parenthesis refer to individuals mentioned in places other than their own family groups.